Operations Now

REVIEWERS, *Third Edition*

Bahram Alidaee,University of Mississippi
J. Brian Atwater,Utah State University
Cem Canel,University of North Carolina–Wilmington
Alan R. Cannon,University of Texas at Arlington
Chiang-Nan Chao,Arizona State University
Ming-Ling Chuang,Western Connecticut State University
Henry L. Crouch,Pittsburg State University
Eduardo C. Davila,Arizona State University
Renatto DeMatta,University of Iowa
James T. Donovan,Duquesne University
Kurt Engemann,Iona College
Charles M. Ermer,Howard University
Farzaneh Fazel-Sarjui,Illinois State University
Lynn A. Fish,Canisius College
Eugene Fliedner,Oakland University
Richard M. Franza,Kennesaw State University
Dean Frear,Wilkes University
Phillip C. Fry,Boise State University
Thomas F. Gattiker,Boise State University
Damodar Golhar,Western Michigan University
Justin Goodson,University of Missouri–Columbia
Zhimin Huang,Adelphi University
Michael S. Hutkin,Roanoke College
Thomas Arnold Janke,Webster University
Jayanth Jayaram,University of South Carolina
Seong-Jong Joo,Central Washington University
Yunus Kathawala,Eastern Illinois University
George Kenyon,Lamar University
Joseph N. Khamalah,Indiana University Purdue University–Fort Wayne
Elias T. Kirche,Florida Gulf Coast University
Beate Klingenberg,Marist College
John F. Kros,East Carolina University
Kenneth D. Lawrence,New Jersey Institute of Technology
Anita Lee-Post,University of Kentucky
Christian N. Madu,Pace University
Renato de Matta,University of Iowa
John S. Mays,SUNY Oswego
Jacquelynne W. McLellan,Frostburg State University
Laura Meade,Texas Christian University
Ajay K. Mishra,SUNY Binghamton
Michael L. Monahan,Frostburg State University
Elizabeth R. Perry,SUNY Binghamton
Richard E. Peschke,Minnesota State University–Moorhead
Jan Pitera,Broome Community College
Ranga Ramasesh,Texas Christian University
Stephen Alexander Raper,University of Missouri–Rolla
Gary J. Salegna,Illinois State University
Steven B. Saperstein,University of North Florida
Herb Schiller,Stony Brook University

Raj Selladurai,Indiana University
Sridhar Seshadri,New York University
Jadranka Skorin-Kapov,SUNY Stony Brook
Donald G. Sluti,University of Nebraska at Kearney
Manuel J. Tejeda,Barry University
Rajen K. Tibrewala,New York Institute of Technology
Oya Tukel,Cleveland State University
Hugo L. Vandersypen,University of Michigan–Dearborn
Timothy Vaughan,University of Wisconsin–Eau Claire
Robert J. Vokurka,Texas A&M University-Corpus Christi
Gustavo Jose Vulcano,New York University
Ray D. Walters,Fayetteville Technical Community College
John Wang,Montclair State University
Theresa Wells,University of Wisconsin–Eau Claire
Susan C. White,George Washington University
Nesa L. Wu,Eastern Michigan University

FOCUS GROUP ATTENDEES, *Third Edition*

Bahram Alidaee,University of Mississippi
Jerry Allison,University of Central Oklahoma
J. Brian Atwater,Utah State University
Leslie Bobb,CUNY Baruch
Ajay Das,CUNY Baruch
James Donovan,Duquesne University
Arthur Duhaime,Nichols College
John Howard,University of South Alabama
Thomas Janke,Webster University
Vijay Kannan,Utah State University
John Kros,East Carolina University
Shrikant Panwalker,Purdue
Leonard Presby,William Paterson University
Kaushik Sengupta,Hofstra University
Donald G. Sluti,University of Nebraska at Kearney
Young Son,CUNY Baruch
Donna Stewart,University of Wisconsin–Stout
Daniel Wright,Villanova University

REVIEWERS, *Second Edition*

Ajay K. Aggarwal, Millsaps College
John Aje, University of Maryland–University College
Suad Alwan, Chicago State University
Jayanta Bandyopadhyay, Central Michigan University
Kathleen Barnes, University of Wisconsin–Superior
Victor Berardi, Kent State University
Daniel Castle, University of Oregon / Oregon State University
Rex Cutshall, Indiana University
Ajay Das, Indiana University
Dinish Dave, Appalachian State University
Ray Eldridge, Freed-Hardeman University

Ross Fink, Bradley University
Phillip C. Fry, Boise State University
Mike Godfrey, University of Wisconsin–Oshkosh
Bob Grenier, Augustana College
Jeff Hefel, St. Mary's University
Craig Hill, Georgia State University
David Ho, Columbus State University
Johnny Ho, Columbus State University
Zhimin Huang, Adelphi University
Erik P. Jack, University of Alabama–Birmingham
Vijay Kannan, Utah State University
Ibrahim Kurtulus, Virginia Commonwealth University
Thomas W. Lloyd, Sam Houston State University
Henry Maddux, Sam Houston State University
Lisa Maillart, Case Western Reserve University
Tomislav Mandakovic, Florida International University
Laura Meade, Texas Christian University
Mary J. Meixell, George Mason University
Scott Metlen, University of Idaho
Ajay Mishra, SUNY Binghamton
Hilary Moyes, University of Pittsburgh
Britt M. Shirley, University of Tampa
Charles Smith, Virginia Commonwealth University
Harm-Jan Steenhuis, Eastern Washington University
Willbann Terpening, Gonzaga University
B. J. Tolia, Chicago State University
Oya Tukel, Cleveland State University
Joel Wisner, University of Nevada–Las Vegas
Jinfeng Yue, Middle Tennessee State University
Zhiwei Zhu, University of Louisiana at Lafayette

FOCUS GROUP ATTENDEES, *Second Edition*

Nazim Ahmed, Ball State University
Suad Alwan, Chicago State University
Mark Cotteleer, Marquette University
Bangalore Lingaraj, Indiana University–Purdue University Fort Wayne
Ajay Mishra, SUNY Binghamton
John Orr, McKendree College
Kumar Palaniswami, Central Michigan University
Frank Pianki, Anderson University
Behrooz Saghafi, Chicago State University
Raj Selladauri, Indiana University Northwest
Larry Taube, University of North Carolina–Greensboro

REVIEWERS, *First Edition*

Scott Dellana, East Carolina State University
Joe Felan, University of Arkansas–Little Rock

Gene Fliedner, Oakland University
Barb Flynn, Wake Forest University
Stella Hua, Oregon State University
Ken Klassen, California State University–Northridge
Brad Meyer, Drake University
John Nichols, Loyola University–Chicago
Chwen Sheu, Kansas State University
Victor Sower, Sam Houston State University
Tom Wilder, California State University–Chico
Keith Willoughby, Bucknell University

FOCUS GROUP ATTENDEES, *First Edition*

Vijay Agrawal, University of Missouri at Kansas City
Henry Aigbedo, Oakland University
Nael Aly, California State University–Turlock
Bob Ash, Indiana University at New Albany
Mehmet Barut, Wichita State University
Donald A. Carpenter, University of Nebraska at Kearney
Christopher Craighead, University of North Carolina at Charlotte
Gene Fliedner, Oakland University
Lawrence Frenendall, Clemson University
Paul Hong, University of Toledo
Zhimin Huang, Adelphi University
Nancy Hyer, Vanderbilt University
Alan Khade, California State University–Turlock
Daniel Krause, Arizona State University
Rhonda Lummus, Iowa State University
Mary J. Meixell, George Mason University
Michael Mancuso, Purdue University
Charles Petersen, Northern Illinois University
Frank Pianki, Anderson University
William Pinney, Alcorn State University
Madeline (Mellie) Pullman, Colorado State University
Richard Reid, University of New Mexico
Edie Schmidt, Purdue University
Britt M. Shirley, University of Tampa
Marilyn Smith, Winthrop University
Gilvan Souza, University of Maryland at College Park
Bharatendu Srivastava, Marquette University
Rajesh Srivastava, Florida Gulf Coast University
Bill Talon, Northern Illinois University
Vincente Vargas, Emory University
T. J. Wharton, Oakland University
Joel Wisner, University of Nevada–Las Vegas

Operations Now

SUPPLY CHAIN PROFITABILITY AND PERFORMANCE

BYRON J. FINCH

Miami University

THIRD EDITION

McGraw-Hill
Irwin

Boston   Burr Ridge, IL   Dubuque, IA   Madison, WI   New York   San Francisco   St. Louis
Bangkok   Bogotá   Caracas   Kuala Lumpur   Lisbon   London   Madrid   Mexico City
Milan   Montreal   New Delhi   Santiago   Seoul   Singapore   Sydney   Taipei   Toronto

McGraw-Hill
Irwin

OPERATIONS NOW: SUPPLY CHAIN PROFITABILITY AND PERFORMANCE
Published by McGraw-Hill/Irwin, a business unit of The McGraw-Hill Companies, Inc., 1221
Avenue of the Americas, New York, NY, 10020. Copyright © 2008 by The McGraw-Hill
Companies, Inc. All rights reserved. No part of this publication may be reproduced or distributed
in any form or by any means, or stored in a database or retrieval system, without the prior written
consent of The McGraw-Hill Companies, Inc., including, but not limited to, in any network or
other electronic storage or transmission, or broadcast for distance learning.

Some ancillaries, including electronic and print components, may not be available to customers
outside the United States.

This book is printed on acid-free paper.

1 2 3 4 5 6 7 8 9 0 CCI/CCI 0 9 8 7 6

ISBN   978-0-07-312449-0
MHID 0-07-312449-4

Editorial director: *Stewart Mattson*
Executive editor: *Scott Isenberg*
Developmental editor: *Cynthia Douglas*
Marketing manager: *Sankha Basu*
Senior media producer: *Victor Chiu*
Project manager: *Kristin Bradley*
Manager, New book production: *Heather D. Burbridge*
Senior designer: *Artemio Ortiz Jr.*
Senior photo research coordinator: Jeremy Cheshareck
Photo researcher: *Julie Tesser*
Media project manager: *Matthew Perry*
Cover design: *Dave Seidler*
Typeface: *10.5/12 Goudy*
Compositor: *Laserwords Private Limited, Chennai, India*
Printer: *Courier Kendallville*

Library of Congress Cataloging-in-Publication Data

Finch, Byron J.
    Operations now : supply chain profitability and performance / Byron J.
Finch.—3rd ed.
        p. cm.—(The McGraw-Hill Irwin series operations management)
    Includes index.
    ISBN-13: 978-0-07-312449-0 (alk. paper)
    ISBN-10: 0-07-312449-4 (alk. paper)
    1. Production management. I. Title.
TS155.F556 2008
658.5—dc22

                                                                    2006031075

www.mhhe.com

With love to my wife, Kim,
my son, Matt, and my daughter, Meredith.

— *Byron J. Finch*

Guided Tour

A Context and Structure to Reflect Today's Reality

Byron Finch's Resource/Profit Model provides the *critical context* and *organizing structure* often lacking in operations management coverage. Unlike some business disciplines such as marketing, accounting, and finance, the field of operations management is not universally recognized by students as being critical, despite its position at the core of all service and manufacturing businesses. This lack of familiarity with the subject can lead to a perceived lack of relevance, prompting students to ask: "Why do we need this?" That's a great question and one that, if not answered and reinforced throughout the course, can destroy the course's impact.

Putting Operations Management in a Context All Business Students Can Appreciate: The Bottom Line

The Resource/Profit Model

The Resource/Profit Model is used as an organizational model and framework throughout the text. It is discussed in Chapter 1 and appears on all part openers, emphasizing the conceptual structure of the book.

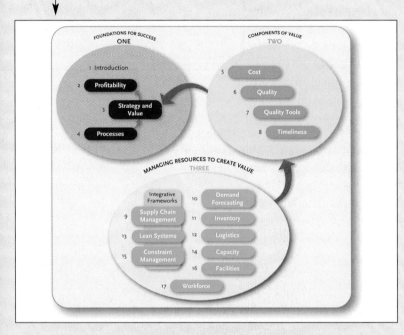

"Utilizing the Resource/Profit Model as a framework for the entire book is a great idea because it highlights the importance of adding value, in particular the effective and efficient utilization of resources to develop, produce and deliver value-adding and profit-maximizing products and services that satisfy consumer needs and wants."

—Renatto DeMatto, University of Iowa

Supply Chain Profitability and Performance

The Resource/Profit Model addresses the true core of operations relevance— *its direct link to enterprise profitability.* Profitability forms the foundation of long-term business success. No business exsists in a vacuum. *Operations Now* examines the critical links between the successful management of operations and supply chain resources and how it directly affects the creation of value for a firm's customers, and therefore the firm's profitability. Value creation precedes profitability, and is maintained through strategic decisions. Value is viewed by the customer as a desired balance between the components of processes, costs, quality, and timeliness. Value components are achieved through effective management of resources, including inventory, capacity, facilities, and workforce. Broader decision-making frameworks, such as supply chain management, lean systems, and constraint management, assist managers in effectively managing those resources. All exist to enhance profitability. Rather than address specific decision-making techniques within the contexts of such topics as inventory or resource scheduling, the Resource/Profit Model places operations management into its *real* context—the business and its success.

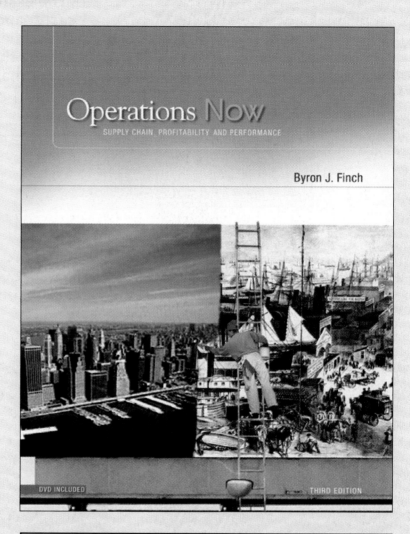

Operations Now
SUPPLY CHAIN PROFITABILITY AND PERFORMANCE
Byron J. Finch
DVD INCLUDED
THIRD EDITION

> **"No Operations textbook I know of covers supply chain as well as the Finch text."**
>
> —Laura Meade,
> Texas Christian University

> **"The thing I like most is the way the book is set up. Beginning with the "Foundations of Success" and the "Components of Value" is very unique and does a great job of motivating the subject of Operations Management for the students."**
>
> —Richard M. Franza,
> Kennesaw State University

Guided Tour

Getting Business Students Motivated about Operations Management

To get motivated about any subject, students need to see how it relates to them, or how it will relate to them in the future. *Operations Now* is the most approachable text on the market, with a wide variety of examples—and kinds of examples—of operations topics put into a context that all business students can understand.

As you'll see on the following pages, *Operations Now* offers students a multitude of aides and hands-on learning tools that will help them not only understand the material, but understand why the information is important to them.

> "The examples, interactive cases, and other exercises are all excellent, and I think would engage the student much better than my current text.
>
> —J. Brian Atwater,
> Utah State University

Each chapter opens with a vignette illustrating how one of the main points of the chapter affects a real company. By putting the chapter's information into a context they will recognize, students can see that operations management is about more than just factories.

AN ENGINE FOR THE NEW ECONOMY

Hundreds of businesses come and go every year. Some are barely noticed. Still others make such an impact that they actually seem to drive the economy. FedEx is one of those companies.

Fred Smith has transportation in his genes. While taking a course at Yale University, Smith wrote a paper on difficulties he expected businesses of the future to have because they would not be able to maintain inventories of computer parts for repairs and replacement. He proposed a logistics system that could transport those items door-to-door overnight. His idea wasn't looked on with favor, because at that time the air cargo industry was a sideline for airlines to use the empty space in the planes' bellies, but he never forgot it. After flying over 200 missions in Vietnam, Fred Smith returned and took over Arkansas Aviation in 1969. He founded Federal Express in 1971.

Smith's idea of using a hub-and-spoke system for deliveries was modeled after the way banks handle canceled checks. His initial desire, to set up the Federal Express headquarters in Little Rock, was turned down. Airport officials in Memphis were optimistic, however, and offered him the use of some empty National Guard hangars. The rest is history. Those hangars in Memphis turned into a $28 billion business, with over 250,000 employees, a fleet of more than 1,300 planes, 90,000 vehicles, and deliveries to 220 countries.

In today's economy, rapid and dependable movement of goods allows the economy to function as it does. "Speed" is the most important attribute for business logistics needs. Reduced time results in faster turnaround for customers and a quicker return on financial investments. Dependability of delivery enables businesses to reduce levels of inventory because they can be certain goods will arrive when promised.

FedEx's impact on the New Economy continued when in 1994 it decided to give customers the ability to track their own shipments online. In the late 1990s, FedEx took another step by seeking state-of-the-art solutions for improving its services. By 2000 it had initiated Global Inventory Visibility System (GIVS®), which allows customers to view inventory anywhere. The growth of FedEx's capabilities enabled it to double its volume time and time again, until it reached 6 million packages per day in 2006.

With continued investments in information technology (IT), new shipping hubs, sorting technology, and ground and air transportation, FedEx not only contributes to the New Economy but can provide the engine that makes it work. It has developed these capabilities by effectively utilizing a unique set of resources, some of which include:

- Data centers that process more than 20 million transactions per day.
- Terminals at over 100,000 customer sites, proprietary software used by 650,000 customers.
- The largest digital network of any company in the world.
- An IT staff of more than 5,500 people.
- Its own staff of meteorologists.

As the New Economy drives companies to move faster and with greater flexibility, FedEx will very likely be leading the logistics field to make it happen.

Source: http://www.fedex.com; "FedEx Keeps Delivering," *BusinessWeek*, April 26, 2002; Face Time with Fred Smith, *Fast Company*, June 2001, p. 64; *The Global Impacts of FedEx in the New Economy*, SRI International, http://www.sri.com, March 25, 2004; "The FedEx Edge," *Fortune*, April 3, 2006.

Keyword: "Real-World"

An abundance of real-world examples are used throughout the text to illustrate key points in the chapters. Three categories of boxed inserts (OM Advantage, Targeting Technology, and Going Global) give students current, real information about how what they're studying applies to the world outside the classroom.

om ADVANTAGE — PayPal: The Worst Idea of the Year?

PayPal, the largest Internet payment network, allows money to be sent by e-mail. It has dominated the auction company Ebay as a safe and convenient way to transfer money from buyer to seller. It has a customer base of 10 million and has grown rapidly. It expects $3 billion in transactions per year. Surprisingly, PayPal didn't start out with that concept in mind at all. Originally, PayPal started in 1998 as a specialized service for owners of Palm computers who needed to transmit funds to each other using the device's infrared port. In its early days, however, to actually use the feature the two Palm users had to be so close they could have easily handed checks to each other. One trade publication voted the idea the worst of the year. PayPal also provided a means for non-PayPal users to transfer money, and it was this capability that began to become popular. The Palm-only service was dumped and PayPal began to grow. PayPal is expanding its position to be the online means of transferring money for all types of online business transactions, including traditional bills like phone and utility bills. PayPal has 40 million account members worldwide in 38 countries.

PayPal's success lies in the fact that it doesn't try to reinvent everything. It recognizes what needs to be reinvented and does that quickly. The rest PayPal leaves alone. PayPal has been particularly attractive to small merchants, which can be charged as much as 5 percent by credit card companies. PayPal charges only 2.9 percent plus 30 cents per transaction.

Source: "Fix It and They Will Come," *Wall Street Journal*, February 12, 2001, p. R4; www.paypal.com, March 23, 2004; "These Guys Will Make You Pay," *Fast Company*, November 2001, online edition.

"OM Advantage" boxes call attention to and discuss real businesses that exemplify (for better or worse) the topic at hand.

TARGETING technology — The Value of Precision

Differentiating capabilities often result from the application of technologies not originally designed for business use. One technology having a profound impact on customer service in logistics and transportation businesses is global positioning systems, or GPS technology, which was originally intended for military application. GPS technology incorporates the use of 28 satellites to enable anyone with a GPS device to pinpoint a position on earth with extreme accuracy, often within 1 foot.

The ability to track exact location and movement has many implications for customer service. For businesses that must be able to tell customers exactly *when* a delivery will arrive, knowing exactly *where* that shipment is at any given moment is critical. GPS technology yields that information, and more. Con-Way NOW is an example of the important role GPS can play. Con-Way NOW is a small division (350 trucks) of the huge transportation company CNF, which manages 41,000 trucks, tractors, and trailers. Con-Way NOW operates on the principle of "time-definite delivery." If a delivery is more than two hours late, it's half price. If it's four or more hours late, it's free. That promise holds for deliveries of a few miles or thousands of miles.

GPS satellites orbit approximately 11,000 miles above the earth. The satellites are supported by the U.S. military, and GPS access is free to anyone. Applications range from attaching GPS devices to products for theft prevention, to attaching GPS collars to cattle, to systems that warn when delivery vehicles are approaching.

Commercial applications, like those of Con-Way NOW, are booming, but consumer use is also about to explode. By 2005 all cell phones will have GPS technology so they can be located in emergencies.

Source: Charles Fishman, "The Sky's the Limit," *Fast Company*, July 2003, p. 90; http://www.trimble.com, May 3, 2004; "High-Tech Help for Lost Souls," *BusinessWeek*, December 8, 2004.

"Targeting Technology" boxes explore how today's companies use today's technologies to improve their operations.

GOING global — Reducing Inventory Carrying Costs with RFID

Radio-frequency identification (RFID) is viewed as a silver bullet for some activities in supply chain management, but it also has direct implications for in-house inventory management. Metro AG, a German retailer, has extended the use of RFID beyond Wal-Mart. Metro is Germany's largest retailer, owning almost 2,400 stores in Germany and 27 other countries. 2003 revenues were up almost 25 percent from the previous year.

While Wal-Mart instructed its suppliers to utilize RFID at the pallet level by 2005, Procter & Gamble, Kraft, and Gillette were already putting RFID tags on goods they supplied to Metro in 2004. Metro expects to track inventory in and out of warehouses and stores with the technology. Expectations are to reduce inventory carrying costs by up to 20 percent by cutting loss and theft, increasing levels of stock on shelves, and reducing staffing needs.

Source: K. J. Delaney, "Inventory Tool to Launch in German; Wireless System Is Seen as Successor to Bar Codes; Metro AG Leads Wal-Mart," *Wall Street Journal*, January 12, 2004, p. B5.

Globalization is a hot topic in business today; "Going Global" boxes explore how global trends and concerns affect operations management, as well as how firms deal with the challenges and opportunities offered by a global economy.

Guided Tour

PROBLEMS

Solutions to odd-numbered problems are located on the text's Online Center (http://mhhe.com/opsnow3e).

1. Big Screen Theater has set procedures for opening the movie house in preparation for customers. Management expects opening the theater to take no longer than 30 minutes for the two people involved (the assistant manager and the director of concessions). Activities required for opening are as follows:

   - The first activity for the assistant manager is to check for messages detailing any large groups that will be attending the theater. Checking the messages takes the assistant manager about 5 minutes.
   - The assistant manager must then walk through the theater and verify that it is clean, an activity that takes approximately 10 minutes.
   - The assistant manager then prepares the movie projector, readying the first movie of the day, which takes the assistant manager up to the time when customers arrive.
   - The theater operates using a computer system to print out tickets, and the first duty of the director of concessions is to start the computer system and properly input the correct data. Preparing the computer takes around 10 minutes.
   - The director of concessions must then prepare the needed food, candy, and drinks for the incoming crowd, an activity that takes another 10 minutes. The director of concessions must also measure the food quantities to be consistent with the expected attendance, keeping in mind any messages passed on from the assistant manager.
   - Finally, the director of concessions must prepare the cash register, an activity that will last until the first customer is seen.

   Construct a Gantt chart that presents the needed activities in opening the theater.

2. Bob, Kelly, and Joe work for HC Consulting, which specializes in identifying problems with clients' customer service operations. Even though they work as a team, each performs a distinct function. Bob is always the first to interact with the clients, asking questions from appropriate employees. Kelly and Joe perform the next task,

Pumping Up Problem-Solving Skills

In addition to nearly 300 end-of-chapter problems, *Operations Now*, third edition, adds two more levels of problems to ensure student mastery. Solved Problems walk the student through the problem before they move on to the traditional problems. Advanced Problems, contributed by knowledgeable, classroom-tested instructors, give students even more challenging tests of their skills. All problems are framed in business contexts to remind students of *why* they're working the problems.

SOLVED PROBLEMS

Constructing X-bar Charts

Sammy's Sammiches is reputed to have the best sandwiches in town. Sammy makes sure his sandwiches have enough meat, but needs to monitor the amount of meat on a sandwich in order to control costs. He wants 5 ounces of meat on a sandwich. He doesn't want his employees to weigh each portion of meat, however, because he thinks that if customers see that happening, it will it look like he is scrimping on the sandwich. Instead, he trains his employees to be able to judge approximately what a 5-ounce portion of meat is. Sammy is concerned that lately, his employees have gotten careless and are adding too much meat to the sandwiches. Each day last week, during the lunch hour, Sammy discretely took 6 portions of meat from sandwiches that were being assembled. He weighed each portions and those data are presented below:

	Monday	Tuesday	Wednesday	Thursday	Friday	Saturday
Sample 1	5.1	4.8	4.9	4.8	5.2	4.8
Sample 2	5.0	5.1	5.2	5.0	5.0	5.3
Sample 3	4.8	4.9	4.7	4.6	5.3	5.0
Sample 4	5.3	5.0	5.2	5.4	4.8	5.3
Sample 5	4.7	5.5	5.2	5.2	5.2	5.1
Sample 6	5.4	5.3	5.1	5.0	4.8	5.1

Construct an X-bar chart. Calculate the sample means and $\bar{\bar{X}}$, and using the range values and Exhibit 7.15, determine the upper and lower control limits. Interpret the chart using the criteria from Exhibits 7.19 and 7.20.

Solution

Step	Objective	Explanation
1.	Compute the sample means.	For each sample of 6 weights, compute the average. The sample means are shown below.
2.	Compute $\bar{\bar{X}}$.	Compute $\bar{X}$ by computing the mean of the sample means. The grand mean is 5.06.
3.	Calculate the ranges and $\bar{R}$.	The ranges are calculated as the largest minus the smallest in each sample. Compute the mean of the ranges ($\bar{R}$).
4.	Compute the upper and lower control limits.	Using Exhibit 7.15 with a sample size of 6, the A_2 value is .48. Using Equations 7.5 and 7.6: $(\text{UCL}) = \bar{\bar{X}} + A_2\bar{R}$ $= 5.06 + (.483 \times .6167)$ $= 5.06 + .2968$ $= 5.3568$

ADVANCED PROBLEMS

1. Ray plans to start a catering service, and is considering two different business models. Under Option A (the highest level of vertical integration), Ray will purchase raw materials and ingredients, cook his own food, and provide delivery and catering service.

   Under Option B, Ray will purchase frozen entrees and other dishes from a local restaurant supply house. This eliminates the need to do his own cooking, and also avoids a large investment in restaurant-grade kitchen equipment and facility.

   Ray's revenue per dinner served will average about $20.00 per plate. If he does his own cooking, his monthly fixed costs will be $1,200, and his variable cost will be about $7.00 per plate. Under Option B, his monthly fixed cost will be only $200, but his variable cost increases to about $12.00 per plate.

   a. Find the breakeven volume (number of plates per month) for each alternative. Which alternative has the larger breakeven volume? Is this consistent with your intuition? Explain why or why not.

   b. At this point Ray faces uncertainty regarding the monthly demand volume his business will realize. Under Option A, what is Ray's profit (loss) if demand volume is 20 percent greater (less than) the Option A breakeven point? Under Option B, what is Ray's profit (loss) if demand volume is 20 percent greater (less than) the Option B breakeven point?

   c. Which option appears to generate greater *profit sensitivity* to variability around its' respective breakeven point? Why?

2. Morgan Manufacturing builds complex pumps for the chemical industry. They cast the aluminum components, machine them to specifications, and assemble the pumps. A check valve on the pump is made out of plastic, which they purchase for $31 each. Morgan's Plant Manager, Sean, feels that the plant can produce the parts at the same quality for a variable price of $18 to $26, depending on the process that they use. One process that they are looking at (process A) will cost $10,000 in fixed costs for the machinery, and has a variable cost of $26 per check valve. Another process (process B) costs $50,000 with a variable cost of $18. Tom, the Operations

Skill-Building Tools

Additional skill-builders appear within the chapters. More than 50 examples demonstrating quantitative concepts are included in the third edition of *Operations Now*. Each text example has a cross-referenced Excel Tutorial, which shows how to work the problem using Excel, on the Student DVD and Online Learning Center.

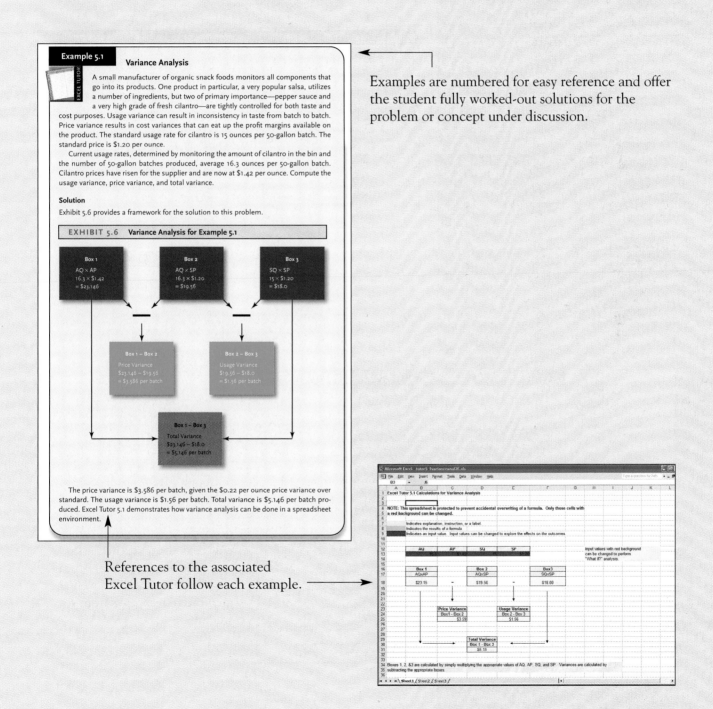

Examples are numbered for easy reference and offer the student fully worked-out solutions for the problem or concept under discussion.

References to the associated Excel Tutor follow each example.

Guided Tour

One of the best ways to get students interested in operations management is to show them practical applications of operations concepts and give them the tools for exploring and analyzing real-world problems. *Operations Now* includes three types of end-of-chapter cases to do just that.

Application Cases provide an opportunity for the student to examine a real-world business situation. Each case requires the student to extract the relevant information, analyze it, and make recommendations to address the problems the business is experiencing.

APPLICATION CASE 2.2

Office Outlet Stock Reduction

Office Outlet, a small chain of office supply stores carries the standard variety of office-oriented products, including paper, printer cartridges and supplies, pens and pencils, shipping materials, etc. Mark Ellison, owner of the seven-store chain, would like to reduce inventory levels by requiring suppliers to deliver more frequently. Mark has chosen one particularly fast-moving product as a prototype for his plan. That product, standard copy paper in $8\frac{1}{2} \times 11$, is currently delivered to the stores every two weeks. Order size varies somewhat but averages 560 boxes (10 reams to a box) to each store. Mark's cost is $23.00 per box.

1. Evaluate Mark's current delivery policy. What is his average level of inventory at a single store? What are the costs associated with carrying that much inventory?

2. If Mark can negotiate deliveries every two days (assuming five-day weeks, he would go from one delivery to five in the two-week period), what happens to his average inventory level per store? Across the entire chain?

3. Across the entire chain, how much money would the change free up for Mark to use elsewhere?

4. What other types of benefits would Mark obtain from increasing the order frequency?

5. What costs might Mark incur from reducing the delivery quantity? How could he address these issues?

VIDEO CASE 2.1

Profitability by Continuing to Meet Customer Needs: Louisville Slugger

Based on Video 2 on the Student DVD

In some markets technological change can make an existing product obsolete instantly. In others, the process takes longer. In the baseball bat market, aluminum bats experienced increased popularity in the 1970s and 1980s, and by the 1990s they dominated all but professional baseball.

Hillerich & Bradsby, manufacturer of Louisville Slugger bats, shifted its focus from dominating the wooden bat market to aluminum when it purchased a factory from Alcoa.

1. Why do you think Louisville Slugger purchased the Alcoa factory rather than continue letting Alcoa make its bats? In hindsight, was this a good decision? Why, after deciding to build a new plant, did Louisville Slugger stay in California?

2. Product variety adds to costs and cuts into the profitability for any manufacturer. For Louisville Slugger, what costs do you think are added because of product variety? How do the different Louisville Slugger bats vary from one another? What value is added by the different types of product variety?

The acceptance of aluminum bats has not been universal. Years of controversy surrounded aluminum bat safety. The primary concern was that the baseball came off aluminum bats so fast that pitchers were at higher risk of being hit by the ball. Others felt that the aluminum bats destroyed the offensive/defensive balance of the game. This concern was supported by high scores. As an example, the final score at the 1998 NCAA Division I baseball championship game was 21–17.

In 1998 the NCAA Executive Committee approved new ball-speed standards. The new standards mandate that bats used by college players be narrower and heavier and that baseballs not be able to come off a bat faster than 93 mph. The move was basically to make aluminum bats perform more like wooden bats.

3. What would be the impact of the new rules on Louisville Slugger's costs and profitability? What capabilities would enable them to easily transition to these new standards?

Operations Now's **Video Cases** take advantage of the latest technology by tying the textbook into the full-length videos presented on the Student DVD. Each Video Case sets up the video, putting it in the chapter's context, then asks engaging questions that often require quantitative as well as qualitative responses from the student.

Cases, Cases, Cases

The third edition's **Interactive Cases** combine the author's innovative Interactive Models—praised for their ability to demonstrate complex quantitative concepts to students—with a business-context scenario and questions that build students' analytical skills. Each case offers a real-world scenario—from overbooking to waiting-line management—that can be analyzed and solved using the appropriate Interactive Model.

> **"I think the Interactive Cases really bring a lot to the book in terms of engaging and motivating students. They are the biggest strength of this text for me."**
>
> —Theresa Wells
> (need to get permission)

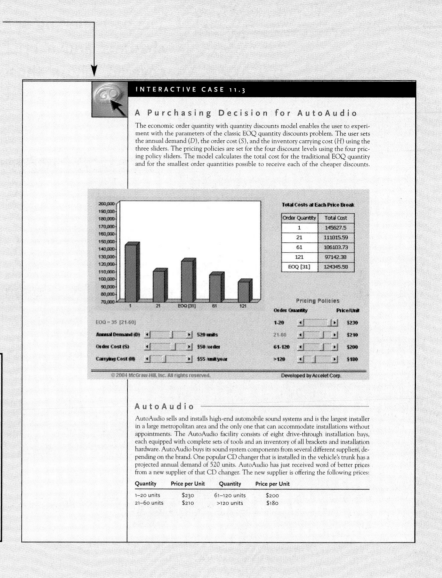

INTERACTIVE CASE 11.3

A Purchasing Decision for AutoAudio

The economic order quantity with quantity discounts model enables the user to experiment with the parameters of the classic EOQ quantity discounts problem. The user sets the annual demand (D), the order cost (S), and the inventory carrying cost (H) using the three sliders. The pricing policies are set for the four discount levels using the four pricing policy sliders. The model calculates the total cost for the traditional EOQ quantity and for the smallest order quantities possible to receive each of the cheaper discounts.

Total Costs at Each Price Break

Order Quantity	Total Cost
1	145627.5
21	111015.59
61	106103.73
121	97142.38
EOQ [31]	124345.58

EOQ = 35 [21-60]

Pricing Policies

Order Quantity	Price/Unit
1-20	$230
21-60	$210
61-120	$200
>120	$180

Annual Demand (D) — 520 units
Order Cost (S) — $50 /order
Carrying Cost (H) — $55 /unit/year

Developed by Accelet Corp.

AutoAudio

AutoAudio sells and installs high-end automobile sound systems and is the largest installer in a large metropolitan area and the only one that can accommodate installations without appointments. The AutoAudio facility consists of eight drive-through installation bays, each equipped with complete sets of tools and an inventory of all brackets and installation hardware. AutoAudio buys its sound system components from several different suppliers, depending on the brand. One popular CD changer that is installed in the vehicle's trunk has a projected annual demand of 520 units. AutoAudio has just received word of better prices from a new supplier of that CD changer. The new supplier is offering the following prices:

Quantity	Price per Unit	Quantity	Price per Unit
1–20 units	$230	61–120 units	$200
21–60 units	$210	>120 units	$180

> **"I love the Interactive Models. They allow me to explain complex concepts using graphical, interactive approaches. . . . The coverage of Kanban systems aided by an interactive model is where I see the future of OM pedagogy in the introductory course."**
>
> —Ajay Mishra,
> State University of New York, Binghamton

Guided Tour

The part-opening spread presents an outline of the chapters and a brief introduction to the material covered within those chapters, again setting the material in terms of the overall profitability of a firm.

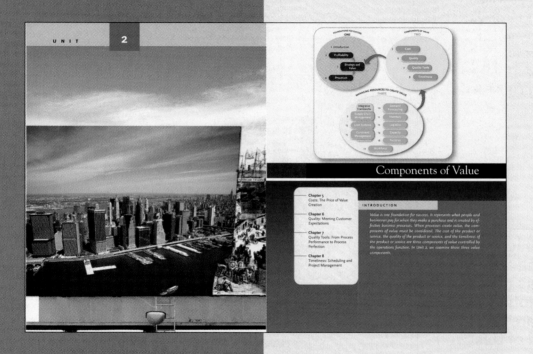

Each chapter opens with a vignette that shows how operations management affects a real company.

The chapter-opening spread provides the student with a detailed overview of the material being presented in the chapter, in the form of a Chapter Outline and Learning Objectives.

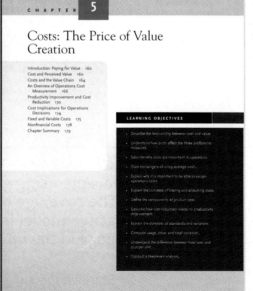

Cost and Profitability

Costs incurred by a business affect the prices the business must charge, which have an immediate impact on the customer's perception of value. But why should a company care about costs if its prices are in line with those of competitors? The answer is that cost savings that are not passed on to the customer go directly to profitability. Let's review how this happens. Recall from Chapter 2 that net income is the numerator for all profitability measures:

(5.1)   Profit Margin = Net Income/Sales

(5.2)   Return on Assets = Net Income/Total Assets

(5.3)   Return on Equity = Net Income/Total Equity

Also recall that the net income calculation starts with net sales. Net sales is the direct result of customers' perceived value. The cost of goods sold, depreciation, and interest paid are subtracted to provide the taxable income. Subtracting the taxes gives us net income:

(5.4)   Net Income = Net Sales − Cost of Goods Sold
− Selling and Administrative Costs − Depreciation
− Interest Paid − Taxes

Dollar General's net sales for fiscal year 2005 were $8.58 billion.

"Callbacks" bring the student back to the firm discussed in the chapter-opening vignette, offering facts about the company that tie in to the specific topic at hand.

Appraisal Costs

Appraisal costs are linked to inspection and testing processes and to the auditing of quality-related systems. Inspection and testing activities ensure that products and services meet predetermined specifications. System auditing activities ensure that the systems designed to maintain quality do what is necessary to achieve specifications and not deviate from their intended objectives.

Inspection activities, used primarily in manufacturing, examine products and compare their characteristics to characteristics specified by customers. Inspections can occur at any point, from the incoming raw materials, through all production stages, to the finished product. In services, when inspections are possible, they typically precede the customer's involvement. Inspections are used to ensure that the facilities a customer will encounter will be acceptable. The hotel and lodging industry, for example, inspects to ensure that

appraisal costs
Costs associated with product inspection, testing, and auditing of quality-related systems.

Definitions of key terms used in the text are presented in the margin. Each chapter's key terms are indexed in the end-of-chapter material, and the text offers a full Glossary as well.

Crash tests on automobiles, performed by the Insurance Institute for Highway Safety, as well as tests by the manufacturers themselves, provide evaluations of passenger injury potential for different models of autos as well as damage costs. Results identify areas for improvement in design. Effectiveness of process control charts depends not only on the interpretation of the data used, but also on the accuracy of the data being collected. Precision measurements require consistent techniques and employee skills in using and reading measuring instruments.

Full-color photographs with detailed captions illustrate chapter concepts, bringing the topics being discussed to life. Colorful and easy-to-understand exhibits present material graphically.

Taking Things Step-by-Step

Whenever possible, processes that can be broken down into simple steps are presented in the "Step-by-Step" format shown here.

EXHIBIT 6.15	House of Quality

HOWs Correlation Matrix: Relationships among HOWs

HOWs: Potential ways to achieve the WHATs in technical terms

WHATs: Customer Needs

Relationships between HOWs and WHATs

Importance Ranking

Competitive Evaluation

Performance Goals

Competitive Evaluation

Importance

Step-by-Step: The Project Scheduling Process

The process followed in project scheduling can be organized into the following sequence:

1. Determine the activities that need to be accomplished to complete the project.
2. Determine the precedence relationships and estimated completion times for each activity.
3. Construct a network diagram for the project.
4. Determine the critical path by identifying the path that takes the longest.
5. Determine the early start schedule and late start schedules by calculating ES, EF, LS, and LF for each activity. Add this information to the network diagram, using the conventional notation.

Guided Tour

at the business level, will improve. The ability to predict possible scenarios and actually test the performance of current practices under those conditions will enhance businesses' capabilities, particularly in matching supply with demand.

CHAPTER SUMMARY

Because of increasing global competition, supply chain management has expanded to become a framework to allow businesses to go beyond decisions that offer short-term value enhancement to providing long-term enhancement to the entire supply chain. Just as businesses have gone through the realization that what is best for one function may not be the best for the business, they have come to realize that what is best for one business may not be the best for the supply chain. And ultimately, because the customer receives the value added by the entire chain, that's what matters most.

This chapter provided an overview of supply chain management as a perspective that guides decision making by broadening the scope of decision impact. Like TQM, JIT, and constraint management, it provides a framework for managers to judge their actions, leading to improved value for the customer and improved profitability for themselves.

KEY TERMS

bullwhip effect, 374
collaborative planning, forecasting, and
    replenishment (CPFR), 381
perfect order, 393
retailer-supplier partnerships (RSPs), 379

risk pooling, 392
supply-chain network optimization, 379
third-party logistics providers
    (3PLs), 385
vendor managed inventory (VMI), 379

KEY FORMULAE

Percentage of perfect orders

$$\text{Percentage of Perfect Orders} = 100\% \times \frac{\text{Total Orders} - \text{Defective Orders}}{\text{Total Orders}} \quad (9.1)$$

SOLVED PROBLEMS

Perfect Order Calculation

Andrew's Equestrian Products is an online retailer of horseback riding the past six months, the order processing department has gather data product and service quality. They have summarized it below.

Total number of orders filled	11,210
Order entry errors	221
Warehouse "pick" errors	149
Defective products	176
Damaged goods in shipment	58
Missing products	82
Billing/invoicing errors	91

Compute the percentage of perfect orders.

Each chapter concludes with a Chapter Summary that recaps the chapter's salient points, followed by the index of that chapter's Key Terms, a review of any formulas presented in the text, and one or more Solved Problems.

Review questions test knowledge of concepts—they reinforce the reading, and are a great way for the students to study for quizzes and tests, or can be assigned as homework.

REVIEW QUESTIONS

1. What is the overall objective of lean systems?
2. What are the different types of waste lean thinking strives to eliminate? Give examples of each.
3. Describe the techniques that have broad implications for waste elimination.
4. Which techniques focus on inventory reduction?
5. Why is matching the demand rate and the production rate at the root of inventory reduction?
6. How does a kanban system work? How does management control the levels of inventory in that system?
7. How does inventory reduction improve quality?
8. How does the standardization of product components reduce inventory waste?
9. What is meant by small-batch production? How does it reduce inventory?
10. Why are reduced changeover times important to maintain small-batch production?
11. How do frequent deliveries of inventory support the goal of matching the production rate to the rate of demand?
12. How does the electronic transfer of information support inventory reduction efforts?
13. What are the characteristics of supplier relationships in a lean environment?
14. Describe the importance of employee involvement. Why is employee involvement important to a lean business?
15. Identify the techniques that assist in eliminating the waste of capacity.
16. How does leanness improve the productivity of facilities? What specific facility layout approaches aid in this effort?
17. Describe how lean methods enhance competitive priorities.

Discussion and Exploration questions are useful for student review or for spurring classroom discussions. They are designed to require critical thinking and reasoning in situations that often lack a "right" answer.

DISCUSSION AND EXPLORATION

1. Identify ways leanness has been implemented in the service sector. How has this affected you as a customer?
2. Reduction of inventory has been criticized for resulting in plant shutdowns during crisis situations. Should lean production be eliminated? If not, how should it be modified?
3. What would be the results of the inventory waste elimination efforts of a lean effort if quality levels weren't high?
4. How does lean production enhance product value for customers?
5. How can services benefit from waste reduction?

End-of-Chapter Pedagogy

Two levels of end-of-chapter problems (with McGraw-Hill's Homework Manager® and McGraw-Hill's Homework Manager Plus™) test the students' understanding of the quantitative material presented in the chapter. They require that the student perform calculations or analyses using the equations and other tools presented in the chapter. Again, these will be helpful for individual or group practice, in-class demonstration, or assignments. Advanced Problems give students an extra challenge. McGraw-Hill's Homework Manager allows the instructor to assign these problems as self-grading homework, quizzes, or even tests, using the innovative online system.

---

d. Adding a class.

e. Purchasing a book on Amazon.com.

PROBLEMS HM

Solutions to odd-numbered problems are located on the text's Online Center (http://mhhe.com/opsnow3e).

1. Using the house of quality as a model, identify WHATs and HOWs for one of the following businesses:
   - a tanning salon
   - an ice cream shop
   - a taco stand
   - an in-home computer repair service
   - a while-you-wait oil change service

2. Design a poka-yoke device for a process you frequently use. What mistakes does it prevent?

3. Identify an online retailer you have used. Develop a process map of the checkout process. How could the process be improved?

4. Identify a service you frequent (a sandwich shop, a doctor's office, a college administrative office, etc.). Create a service blueprint for the service. Be sure to include potential fail points and the line of visibility.

5. Develop a process map for correctly jump-starting a car with a dead battery. Why is the sequence of the steps important?

6. Develop a process map for changing a car tire. Begin with accessing the spare. How does your process map compare to the instructions provided in the user's manual? Would this process map be a beneficial addition to the manual?

7. Create a written set of instructions for copying a CD on a computer. Create a process map for the same process. Which is easier to follow?

8. Create a service blueprint for your college's class registration process. Examine the completed blueprint. Examine the fail points. Do they often result in service failure? Have any resulted in service failure for you? What could be done to reduce the likelihood of service failure at these points?

9. For the blueprint you developed in question 8, perform an analysis of the processes used. Identify non-value-adding steps and develop a plan for eliminating them. Evaluate the sequence of steps in the processes. Could they be done better? How?

10. Create a service blueprint for the checkout process of a retail store you frequent. Identify the line of visibility and fail points. How critical is the business's placement of the line of visibility to its strategic objectives? Have they placed it correctly? Which of the fail points, in your opinion, result in the most frequent service failure? How critical are these failures to the business's strategy? What is the typical reaction of the customer to these failures?

ENDNOTES

1. P. Hines and N. Rich, "The Seven Value Stream Mapping Tools," *International Journal of Operations and Production Management*, Vol. 17, No. 1, 1997, pp. 46–64.

2. C. H. Fine, *Clockspeed: Winning Industry Control in the Age of Temporary Advantage* (Reading, MA: Perseus Books, 1998), pp. 71–76.

3. John Grout's Poka-Yoke Page, www.campbell.berry.edu/faculty/jgrout/pokayoke.shtml. Examples used with permission.

ADVANCED PROBLEMS

1. Otto's Part, a chain of automotive parts stores, is having a problem with the central distributor. Otto's has 6 stores, and receives parts from the distributor every day. For replenishment, the distributor is fairly accurate, with only 15 percent of the orders having some kind of problem. This may be a substitution, where the part ordered is substituted with a like part that may be a different brand, backorders, where nothing arrives, or wrong, where the wrong part is shipped. The biggest problem that Otto's has is with customer-ordered parts, where a customer comes into the store and orders a part that is not a stock item. Before placing the order, Otto's always checks for availability. Otto's tries to get the part within two days, but half of the time it takes longer than that. The third problem is that the parts that are custom ordered and received on time do not match the order. This happens to 1 out of 10 custom orders. Each store places an average of 30 orders a day, 10 custom orders and the rest replenishment orders. What is the percent of perfect orders for Otto's per day?

2. Fred Smart, a shipping agent for Williams Electric, is reviewing delivery performance in order to direct process improvement efforts. At present, Mr. Smart has collected the following information.

On Time Delivery	Complete	Accurate Invoice	Number Damaged in Transit	Total Number of Orders
88.00%	90.00%	93.00%	5	74

a. While these numbers appear to present a good testament to the performance of the shipping department, Fred wishes to develop an overall measure for his department's performance. To that end, he has asked you to calculate the percent perfect orders that Williams is currently shipping to its customers.

b. Based on this new metric, Fred is determined to improve the department. For several months he has worked diligently with manufacturing, shipping dock workers, and contract shippers to improve Williams's overall performance. What is the new percent perfect order that Williams has been able to achieve based on the following data?

On Time	Complete	Accurate Invoice	Damaged in Transit	Number of Orders
93.00%	96.50%	95.00%	2	68

What is the percent improvement in perfect orders that Williams has been able to achieve?

ENDNOTES

1. R. B. Handfield and E. L. Nichols, *Introduction to Supply Chain Management* (Upper Saddle River, NJ: Prentice Hall, 1999), p. 2.

2. M. R. Leenders and D. L. Blenkhorn, *Reverse Marketing* (New York: Free Press, 1988), p. 8.

3. Ibid, p. 11.

4. Adapted from D. Simchi-Levi, P. Kaminksy, and E. Simchi-Levi, *Designing and Managing the Supply Chain* (New York: McGraw-Hill, 2000), pp. 8–10.

Guided Tour

The *Operations Now* Student DVD takes full advantage of the DVD format to present 16 full-length videos, as well as other text-specific resources, including:

- **Full-Length Videos to Accompany Chapter Video Cases:** 16 full-length videos that form the basis of the Video Cases found in selected chapters.

- **Interactive Models to Accompany Chapter Interactive Cases:** 24 fully interactive Java models that form the basis of the Interactive Cases found in selected chapters.

- **Excel Tutorials:** More than 50 annotated Excel templates, corresponding to examples given in the text.

- **Self-Assessment Chapter Quizzes:** Test your knowledge of chapter content.

- **Web Links:** Easy access to even more resources found on the text's Online Learning Center and the Operations Management Center.

The DVD opens to the DVD Video menu, from which you can navigate to all the other resources.

Using the chapter menu bar at the top of the screen as a navigation tool, click the chapter you're interested in to see the menu of associated resources. You can move from chapter to chapter with a single click.

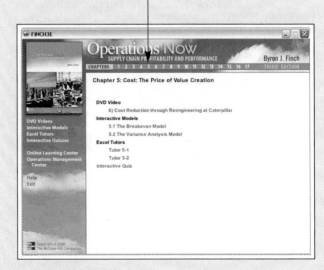

The Student DVD

If you'd rather view a complete list of a certain category of assets, you can select a specific resource group from the list on the list.

Select "Interactive Models" to view all the Java applets.

Choose an Interactive Model from within the full list.

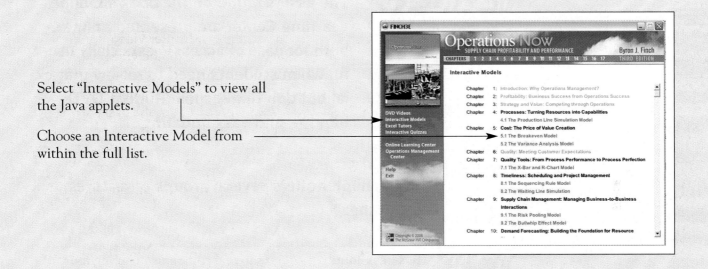

The model will open in a new window.

"The supporting DVD and the interactive exercises are great additions! Students can get up to speed quicker on basic concepts—especially within EXCEL without having to deal with all the computational attentions to detail. For an introductory/required course, this is ideal."

—Laura Meade,
Texas Christian University

Guided Tour

Operations Now's approach has always been to present material and assets in the format in which they are best suited. The assets found on the book's Online Learning Center are presented online both for ease of access—especially useful when students need to review material but don't have their Student DVD handy—and easy updating.

Each chapter offers several groups of features, including:

Business Tours	Links to real companies offering tours of their facilities.
OM on Site	Links to resources illustrating how real companies apply the concepts discussed in the chapter.
Readings	Links to online articles relevant to operations management.
Resources	Links to sites with reference material about topics discussed in the chapter.
Excel Tutors	Annotated Excel templates, corresponding to examples appearing in the text.
Interactive Case Models	Fully interactive Java models that form the basis of the Interactive Cases found in selected chapters.
Reel Operations Video Clips	Real Player video clips illustrating operations concepts, framed by brief descriptions that put the material in context.
Additional Advanced Problems	Even more of the new Advanced Problems found in the text.
Self-Assessment Quizzes	Test your knowledge of chapter content.
PowerPoint Presentations	Chapter-by-chapter study aid.
Glossary	Glossary of key terms found in each chapter.

Byron J. Finch

Byron J. Finch is a Professor of Operations Management in the Richard T. Farmer School of Business Administration at Miami University, Oxford, Ohio. He earned his BS and MS degrees from Iowa State University and received his doctorate from the William Terry College of Business Administration at the University of Georgia in 1986. He began teaching and research responsibilities in 1987 at Miami University, where he has taught operations management and supply chain management courses at the undergraduate and graduate levels.

Dr. Finch's research interests have evolved from the topic of manufacturing planning and control systems early in his career, to spreadsheet models to his most recent research endeavors involving the use of Internet-based conversations as information to improve quality and quality expectations in the anonymous environments of online auction. As the U.S. economy has shifted toward services, Dr. Finch's research interests have become more inclusive of services as well, particularly online services. Research projects that Dr. Finch has been involved with have resulted in numerous publications in such outlets as the *Journal of Operations Management, International Journal of Production Research, Quality Management Journal, Academy of Management Journal, Production and Inventory Management Journal,* and *International Journal of Quality and Reliability Management.* Dr. Finch is also the author and co-author of *The Management Guide to Internet Resources* (1997), *Operations Management: Competing in a Changing Environment* (1995), *Spreadsheet Applications for Production and Operations Management* (1990), and *Planning and Control System Design: Principles and Cases for Process Manufacturers* (1987). In addition to the traditional print publications, Dr. Finch has been the managing editor for the Operations Management Center Web site (http://www.mhhe.com/pom/) since 1998. Dr. Finch serves on the Editorial Boards of the *Journal of Operations Management* and the *Quality Management Journal.*

Dr. Finch has been actively involved in teaching innovation since beginning his academic career in 1986. He received the Southern Business Administration Innovative Teaching Award in 1987, the NCR Computer Innovation Award in 1990, and the Richard T. Farmer School of Business Teaching Award in 1996. Dr. Finch was nominated for the Miami University Associated Student Government Teaching Award in 2002 and 2005.

Dr. Finch has held various offices in the Midwest Decision Sciences Institute, including president. He has also been involved in the Decision Sciences Institute at the national level, including a term as a regionally elected vice president. Dr. Finch is also a member of the Production and Operations Management Society (POMS).

CONTENTS

CHAPTER FOUR: PROCESSES: TURNING RESOURCES INTO CAPABILITIES   118

UNIT TWO: Components of Value   156

CHAPTER FIVE: COSTS: THE PRICE OF VALUE CREATION   158

UNIT THREE: Managing Resources to Create Value **366**

CHAPTER NINE: SUPPLY CHAIN MANAGEMENT: MANAGING BUSINESS-TO-BUSINESS INTERACTIONS 368

CHAPTER TEN: DEMAND FORECASTING: BUILDING THE FOUNDATION FOR RESOURCE PLANNING 406

CHAPTER ELEVEN: INVENTORY: MANAGING TO MEET DEMAND   478

CHAPTER TWELVE: LOGISTICS: POSITIONING GOODS IN THE SUPPLY CHAIN   534

CHAPTER THIRTEEN: LEAN SYSTEMS: ELIMINATING WASTE THROUGHOUT THE SUPPLY CHAIN   572

CHAPTER FOURTEEN: CAPACITY: MATCHING PRODUCTIVE RESOURCES TO DEMAND 608

CHAPTER FIFTEEN: CONSTRAINT MANAGEMENT: SIMPLIFYING COMPLEX SYSTEMS 658

CHAPTER SIXTEEN: FACILITIES: MAKING LOCATION AND LAYOUT DECISIONS 686

CHAPTER SEVENTEEN: WORKFORCE: OPTIMIZING HUMAN CAPITAL 738

OPERATIONS NOW IS
OPERATIONS TODAY

A colleague of mine once made what I found to be a most pertinent observation about our discipline. He noted that operations is arguably the function most critical to the success of any organization, yet it is almost always the least visible function within it. A major goal of the Third Edition of *Operations Now* is to raise the visibility of operations and supply chain management so that their importance to the overall enterprise is understood and acknowledged by all business students—not just students of operations and supply chain management. Two other goals remain from previous editions: One is to challenge the misperception that operations and supply chains are somehow isolated from other functional areas of the business. To gain a true understanding of operations and supply chain management, it is important to understand how intricately these functions intersect with other functional areas of a business and how their effectiveness depends on the extent to which their goals are aligned with the strategic goals of the organization they serve. The final goal of the book is to demonstrate how good operations and supply chain practices are vital to the success and profitability of any organization.

Heightened visibility of operations and supply chains, strategic alignment of the operations function with other functions of the organization and with its supply chain, and competitiveness appropriate to the contemporary business landscape: conveying these concepts is the goal of the Third Edition of *Operations Now*—a goal that I've tried to suggest with the image that appears on the cover of the book. As the advertising billboard suggests, *Operations Now* is as much my attempt to promote the importance of operations and supply chain management as it is to explain them. To be a good manager, one must understand all the functional areas of an organization, regardless of the specialized function one may perform. What is depicted on the billboard—the image of an old, preindustrialized city being painted over with and replaced by the image of a contemporary, high-tech metropolis—also acts as a metaphor for the evolution of operations and supply chain management. *Operations Now* is operations today, and these days operations is about organization integration, performance, and profitability—profitability not only with regard to the operation itself but also throughout the organization and the entire supply chain.

In the years since I began studying and teaching operations management, dramatic changes have occurred in the business environment. These changes have informed the operations management course as well as the expectations of the students who take it.

The discipline itself has changed in at least three fundamental ways.

- The focus is no longer limited to manufacturing concerns but, reflecting the direction in which our economy is moving, has broadened to include services as well.

- Today it is necessary to regard the operations function within its larger, organizational context. No discussion of operations is complete without addressing other functional areas of business. Regardless of the vantage point from which one begins the study of operations management, sooner or later one observes the operations function interacting with other business functions—intersecting with marketing here, nudging up against finance there. In short, it is no longer possible to view operations as less critical than, or in isolation from, other key functional areas of business: high-performance operations depend on their close coordination with all functional areas of the organization.

- Finally, the body of knowledge constituting "operations management" has expanded considerably in recent years. Such topics as project management, e-business and e-commerce, lean manufacturing, and enterprise resource planning have found their way into a management curriculum that has begun to deemphasize the traditional departmental silos. Particularly representative of this fundamental change is the emergence—some would say "reemergence"—of supply chain management as a critical factor in the success and competitiveness of any organization. In fact, because of such factors as specialization, outsourcing, globalization, and dramatic advances in information technology, the lines between "operations management" and "supply chain management" have blurred so considerably in recent years that many practitioners could plausibly make the claim that the terms are now interchangeable. At the very least, it is no longer possible to discuss operations management without extending that discussion to include supply chains.

CHANGES IN HOW STUDENTS LEARN DICTATE HOW OPERATIONS MUST BE TAUGHT

Beyond the changes in our discipline, an even more fundamental change has occurred in our students. As primary beneficiaries of rapid advances in information technology, students today have easier and quicker access to more information than any previous generation. Such access has made them arguably more sophisticated than their counterparts of a decade earlier, but having access to such an abundance of information often leads to overload.

These are some of the fundamental issues by which I have been challenged through all three editions of this book. How can I create a table of contents that accurately reflects the state of operations management today? How can I package this information in a way that will be both appealing and digestible to today's students—not just to operations management majors, but to all business students? Finally, how can I exploit new technology to produce better, more relevant instruction and learning materials?

OPERATIONS NOW: SUPPLY CHAIN PROFITABILITY AND PERFORMANCE

Operations Now: Supply Chain Profitability and Performance is my attempt to confront these issues. The "Now" indicates an effort to address both the changing content in the field of operations management as well as the latest methods available to help improve the quality of the instruction we deliver. A new subtitle to the Third Edition, *Supply Chain Profitability and Performance*, is intended to reflect the increase in the coverage and integration of supply chain concepts now found in the book. As with previous editions, every attempt has been made to ensure that the DVD and Web site accompanying *Operations Now: Supply Chain Profitability and Performance* create seamless extensions of the text rather than assets that were belatedly included after the fact.

From its conception in the First Edition, the Web site was intended to house only those assets that were best utilized in a virtual environment—assets that could not be used, or used far less effectively, in print. This design principle remains in place with the Third Edition. It is certainly possible to use the textbook independently of the DVD and Web site, though using the three together provides an infinitely richer and more rewarding learning experience for students.

PROFITABILITY AS THE FOCUS OF OPERATIONS MANAGEMENT

At the core of every business is the need to create products and services of value and sell them at a price that is greater than the cost of creating them. Operations management is the management of the processes used to create that value and the resources needed to make those processes possible.

Business profitability—measured by profit margin, return on assets, and return on equity—depends on a firm's ability to generate sales of the products and services it creates and manage the associated costs, so that a margin of profit is attained. Operations managers are expected both to control the costs of resources that are required to create processes and to manage the processes needed to create value. Because customers ultimately establish the value of a product or service according to the quantities in which they purchase it, operations management has a significant impact on the profitability of a business, its ability to compete, and its ultimate success.

MOTIVATING TODAY'S STUDENTS

Because it dictates the financial productivity of a firm's assets, operations management is at the core of business success; yet operations is often viewed by business students as an inessential part of their business education. This misperception makes the course difficult to teach. More important, it can result in students entering the workforce insufficiently acquainted with operations management and the pivotal role it plays in the success of virtually every organization. *Operations Now* addresses this challenge by changing the context in which operations management is presented. *Operations Now* places operations decisions and concepts into their real-world context—the financial performance of the firm—through the use of a unique organizational model: the Resource/Profit Model.

WHAT'S NEW? CONTINUOUS IMPROVEMENT IN *OPERATIONS NOW*

Advances made in product and service quality evolve from pressures that force businesses to differentiate themselves from their competitors. New products and services often start with the idea of "building a better mousetrap." A different perspective on solving an old problem—combined with the availability of new technologies—is often all that is needed to form the impetus for a product or service that is truly different.

It is precisely this series of events that resulted in the first edition of this text, and the same motivation has driven improvements made to the Second and Third Editions of the book. *Operations Now* continues to differentiate itself from other operations management texts through content, organization, and pedagogy.

The Resource/Profit Model

Users of previous editions will recognize the Resource/Profit Model. This model formed the organizational and conceptual model upon which the First and Second Editions were based; this framework continues, with some adjustments with the Third Edition.

The model places the content of the text within the context of financial performance and provides students with an intuitive organizational framework within which the operations and supply chain functions can be regarded. The model's financial foundation enables *Operations Now* to present operations and supply chain management concepts and tools in a way that will interest all students whose futures will include increasing business profitability. It suggests a correlation between the soundness and efficiency of the operations and supply chain functions and the profitability of the firm that it serves.

As noted, the Resource/Profit Model has been modestly reorganized for this edition to heighten the importance of supply chain management by positioning it not simply as one integrating framework but as an extension of the operations core.

An Optimal Balance of Textbook, Web Site, and DVD Assets

Operations Now continues to deliver its content across print and virtual environments. With the Third Edition, an optimal distribution of these assets has been achieved across these media, offering greater flexibility to instructors and a wider variety of learning opportunities for students. Courses can be conducted with equal success using either "print-only" or cross-media options.

An Organization Reflecting the Current State of the Discipline

The Table of Contents has been reorganized in response to reviewer recommendations and in order to better reflect the realities of the changing business landscape. The key change in this edition is an increased emphasis on supply chain management and the integration of supply chain concepts throughout the text.

Unit One, "Foundations for Success," remains a strong introduction to the field of operations Management, exploring the concepts of Profitability, Strategy and Value, and Processes. Unit Two, "Components of Value," focuses on topics essential to businesses of all kinds in their quest for customer value: Costs, Quality, and Timeliness. In Unit Three, "Managing Resources to Create Value," specific approaches to resource management are discussed. As well as the chapters found in this unit in the Second Edition, like Resource Planning, Inventory, Lean Systems, Capacity, Constraint Management, Facilities, and Workforce, there is a substantially revised Supply Chain Management chapter and an entirely new chapter on Logistics.

A Substantially Greater Number and Variety of Problems with More Emphasis on Quantitative Techniques

The Second Edition increased the number of end-of-chapter problems by 50 percent over the First Edition. The Third Edition has increased the quantitative material even more. First, there are now Solved Problems at the end of all appropriate chapters—a feature that is new to this edition. Second, *Operations Now* boasts not only a greater number of problems than ever before but a greater variety of problems as well. Included with the Third Edition is a new category of problems, labeled "Advanced Problems." These problems, contributed by active instructors, serve as a bridge between the simple problem sets found in earlier editions of the book and the Interactive Cases that were a hallmark of the Second Edition and which have been retained and updated in the Third Edition. Presenting students with Solved Problems for reference and then Advanced Problems as an intermediate step between the basic problems and the cases enables students to progress through the material at a more graduated pace. With more study aids at their disposal and progressively more challenging opportunities to practice the concepts in the text, students are likely to retain more of what they learn.

New, Revised, and Updated Chapters

The scope of the revision of Operations Now is considerable. Among the changes incorporated into the Third Edition are:

- An entirely new chapter (Chapter 12), "Logistics: Positioning Goods in the Supply Chain," which covers the fundamentals of logistics and transportation.
- Significant revisions of Chapter 3, "Strategy and Value"; Chapter 4, "Processes"; Chapter 7, "Quality Tools"; and Chapter 9, "Supply Chain Management."

Below is a comprehensive list of the key changes and updates for all the chapters of the Third Edition of *Operations Now*:

Chapter	Major Changes and Additions
Chapter 1 Introduction	■ Updated box inserts. ■ Enhanced discussion linking operations and supply chain management. ■ Reorganized introduction to the text.
Chapter 2 Profitability: Business Success from Operations Success	■ Updated box inserts. ■ Enhanced coverage of the links between OM and SCM and profitability measures. ■ Added references to not-for-profit organizations. ■ Solved Problems and Advanced Problems. ■ Application Case.
Chapter 3 Strategy and Value: Competing through Operations	■ Updated box inserts. ■ Enhanced coverage of strategic supply chain issues. ■ Expanded mission coverage. ■ Enhanced coverage of "core competencies." ■ New section on supply chain strategies. ■ New section on environmental scanning. ■ Application Case.
Chapter 4 Processes: Turning Resources into Capabilities	■ Updated box inserts. ■ Enhanced linkages between process decisions and strategy for manufacturing and service. ■ Enhanced linkages between process decisions and profitability. ■ Expanded coverage of design for logistics (DFL) and new coverage of design for environment (DFE). ■ Coverage of process-oriented, product-oriented, and cellular layouts moved from Chapter 3. ■ New sections on developing new products and services. ■ Enhanced coverage on process improvement tools. (mapping, service blueprinting, etc.). ■ Solved Problems and Advanced Problems. ■ Application Case.
Chapter 5 Costs: The Price of Value Creation	■ Updated box inserts. ■ Enhanced linkages to OM decisions. ■ Solved Problems and Advanced Problems. ■ Application Case.
Chapter 6 Quality: Meeting Customer Expectations	■ Updated box inserts. ■ Enhanced linkages to SCM. ■ Updated Baldrige coverage. ■ Application Case.
Chapter 7 Quality Tools: From Process Performance to Process Perfection	■ Updated box inserts. ■ Major revision and expansion of SPC coverage. ■ Enhanced coverage of X-bar and R-charts, with new chart construction examples. ■ New coverage, with chart-construction examples, for P- and C-charts.

Chapter	Major Changes and Additions
	■ Revised six sigma coverage. ■ Expanded Taguchi methods coverage. ■ Solved Problems and Advanced Problems. ■ Application Case.
Chapter 8 Timeliness: Scheduling and Project Management	■ Updated box inserts. ■ Increased description of the relationship between queue length and resource utilization. ■ Solved Problems and Advanced Problems. ■ Application Case.
Chapter 9 Supply Chain Management: Managing Business-to-Business Interactions	■ Updated box inserts. ■ Increased linkages to strategy and competitive advantage. ■ New section on purchasing. ■ Expanded coverage of perfect order measure and calculation problem/example. ■ Solved Problems and Advanced Problems. ■ Application Case.
Chapter 10 Demand Forecasting: Building the Foundation for Resource Planning	■ Updated box inserts. ■ Expanded SCM integration, CPFR. ■ Expanded discussion of the importance of graphing prior to any forecasting effort. ■ Expanded accuracy measures to include MAPE and tracking signals. ■ Solved Problems and Advanced Problems. ■ Application Case.
Chapter 11 Inventory: Managing to Meet Demand	■ Updated box inserts. ■ Replaced periodic review model with target level model. ■ Replaced advanced MRP example with smaller example. ■ Solved Problems and Advanced Problems. ■ Application Case.
Chapter 12 Logistics: Positioning Goods in the Supply Chain	This chapter focuses on logistics and transportation. Level 1 topic headings for this chapter are: ■ Introduction to Logistics ■ Logistics Network Configuration ■ Outsourcing Logistics Services ■ Reverse Logistics ■ Transportation ■ Transportation Management Systems ■ Warehousing ■ Supply Chain Security ■ Information Technology ■ Measuring and Monitoring Logistics Costs Logistics-specific content from the Second Edition chapter on SCM was also moved into this chapter.

Chapter	Major Changes and Additions
Chapter 13 Lean Systems: Eliminating Waste throughout the Supply Chain	■ Updated box inserts. ■ Enhanced coverage of the linkage between lean and competitive advantage/strategy. ■ Solved Problems and Advanced Problems. ■ Application Case.
Chapter 14 Capacity: Matching Productive Resources to Demand	■ Updated box inserts. ■ Enhanced linkages between capacity and SCM. ■ Solved Problems and Advanced Problems. ■ Application Case.
Chapter 15 Constraint Management: Simplifying Complex Systems	■ Updated box inserts. ■ Solved Problems and Advanced Problems. ■ Application Case.
Chapter 16 Facilities: Making Location and Layout Decisions	■ Updated box inserts. ■ Expanded coverage of location decisions in the supply chain (warehouses, distribution centers, etc.). ■ Discussion of infrastructural issues in decisions. ■ Expanded coverage of outsourcing. ■ Solved Problems and Advanced Problems. ■ Application Case.
Chapter 17 Workforce: Optimizing Human Capital	■ Updated box inserts. ■ Enhanced coverage of globalization issues. ■ Solved Problems and Advanced Problems. ■ Application Case.

New Pedagogy

- **Solved problems.** The Second Edition had an example of each problem introduced. Each example also corresponds to an Excel Tutor that shows how that example can be solved in a spreadsheet. The Third Edition maintains those example problems and the Excel Tutor and adds a section of solved problems at the end of the chapter. There is a solved problem for each type of problem in the chapter. The solved problems are explained in a step-by-step fashion.

- **Advanced Problems.** The Second Edition increased the number of end-of-chapter problems by more than 50 percent. The Third Edition, in addition to adding solved problems above and beyond the previously existing examples, adds Advanced Problems for each chapter. Advanced Problems are more integrative, require more effort in terms of extracting and identifying relevant information, and give students a chance to extend their problem-solving skills.

- **Application Cases.** The Second Edition had Video Cases, Interactive Cases, and Exploratory Cases at the end of chapters. Exploratory Cases required investigation and searching online. We have eliminated the Exploratory Cases and replaced them with more traditional Application Cases. The new application cases provide an integrated or more complex scenario for the student to study, analyze, and provide recommendations for.

- **Callbacks.** We have kept the Second Edition's chapter-opening vignettes, which provide a real-world example of the chapter's main subject and explain how it affects a real company. We have further integrated these real-world examples into the chapter by using "Callbacks," which appear in the margins to show how the topic at hand affects the company from the vignette, further reinforcing the day-to-day importance of operations in every company's functions.

- **Chapter names.** We have added subtitles to all chapter names to better describe chapter content.
- **Solutions to odd-numbered problems.** In the First and Second Editions, we did not provide students with end-of-chapter problem solutions. Instructors had all solutions on their CD. In the Third Edition, we will provide solutions to all odd-numbered end-of-chapter problems on the student Web site. We will continue to provide all solutions on the instructor's CD.

Updated and Improved McGraw-Hill's *Homework Manager* ® Option

McGraw-Hill's Homework Manager, which serves as a study aid for students and homework resource for instructors, is available to the student at a modest additional cost. It offers students online practice in solving problems and instructors the capabilities and convenience of automatic, online grading. McGraw-Hill's Homework Manager also provides instructors with the opportunity to assign problems from the book that are algorithmically generated.

Making the Most of the Media Available

Used in conjunction with the integrated Web site and DVD, *Operations Now* creates a new standard for the delivery of operations management content and pedagogy. It moves beyond the traditional framework by exploiting technologies to provide a wealth of content and support that is accessible through the DVD and at its Online Learning Center at http://www.mhhe.com/opsnow3e. To maximize their effectiveness, each of the three delivery channels is used for what it presents best.

Text

The text delivers a basic narrative covering the fundamental concepts of operations management, with both traditional end-of-chapter material and innovative pedagogy, including Video, Interactive, and Application Cases. The first two of these cases are designed to be used in conjunction with videos and Java-based, interactive models and simulations found on the Student DVD and Online Learning Center.

Student DVD

The DVD delivers static multimedia content, including:

- Sixteen full-length videos that accompany the Video Cases presented in the text.
- Excel Tutor spreadsheets.
- Interactive Models.
- Self-Assessment Quizzes.

Online Learning Center

The text's dedicated Web site delivers dynamic content such as:

- PowerPoint presentations.
- Supplemental readings.
- Business tours.
- Other activities that depend on the most up-to-date resources maintained online by businesses.

- McGraw-Hill's *Homework Manager*®, a new technology designed to add an almost endless variety to automatically graded end-of-chapter problems.

Giving Students a Competitive Advantage

By using *Operations Now: Supply Chain Profitability and Performance*, students will learn that a fundamental prerequisite to the success of any business is its ability to combine resources to create value. It will become clear to those students that in order to compete effectively, the value created must exceed that of competitors. The ownership of the resources is necessary, but is not alone sufficient to ensure that enhanced levels of value are created. The firm must creatively combine resources into value-creating processes. Those resources come from across the business, not from within any single functional silo.

When all these variables interact and intersect in a coordinated fashion, the outcome, like the music emanating from a good symphony orchestra, is high performance that leads to profitability.

Acknowledgments

Any book succeeds because of the combined efforts of a number of people who contribute in a variety of ways, and I owe all of those people my thanks. First of all, thanks to my family, Kim, Matt, and Meredith, for their support and tolerance of my work on this project—particularly during the summer—and occasional need to be away from home.

As in any large project, one person cannot contribute all of the content. I would like to thank Mark Cotteleer of Marquette University for his enthusiastic support and for the PowerPoint presentations he created to accompany the text; Joe Felan of the University of Arkansas, Little Rock, for his work on the Instructor's Manual; and Yunus Kathawala of Eastern Illinois University for his accuracy check. In addition, many reviewers have contributed to the revision of this book at its various stages of completion, and many of my peers attended focus groups held to target various aspects of the book to the user. I would like to thank them for the contributions they made through their participation. I would also like to thank Tim Vaughan of the University of Wisconsin–Eau Claire, Kevin Watson of the University of New Orleans, Tom Wilder of California State University–Chico, and Victor Sower of Sam Houston State University for their contribution of the Advanced Problems that were used to enhance the end-of-chapter materials for the Third Edition.

I would like to express sincere thanks to the editorial staff and project team at McGraw-Hill/Irwin for their commitment to this project. At the top of that list is Cynthia Douglas, who had to live with this project day in and day out for the two years of its initial development, and for a full year in its revision. Cynthia, in her role as developmental editor, worked tirelessly on the details of this project, kept me on track, and made sure all of the behind-the-scenes due dates were met. Also at the top of the list from a support standpoint is Scott Isenberg. As sponsoring editor and good friend, Scott was willing to take a chance on a project that was very different from the norm, and supported it from its inception. His support has continued in the revision.

Thanks to Stewart Mattson, editorial director, for his support of this project and to marketing manager Sankha Rasu and marketing coordinators Angela Cimarolli and Dean Karampelas. A special thanks to Kristin Bradley, project manager, who kept the project on schedule and saw it through to its ultimate publication. Thank you to Matthew Perry for coordinating the supplements. I would like to thank Artemio Ortiz for his work on the design, Julie Tesser for photo research, and Clair James for copy editing.

Operations Now

UNIT 1

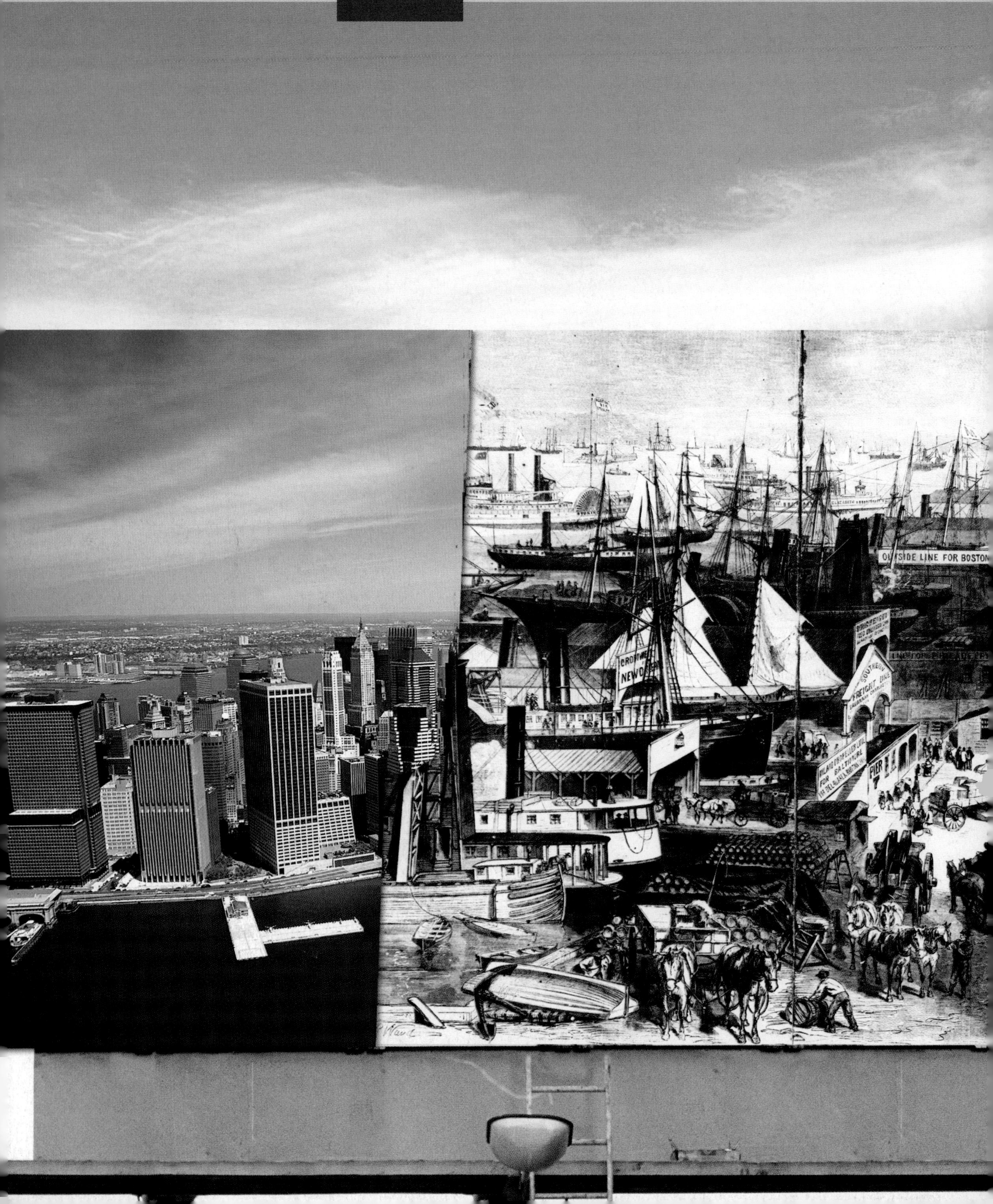

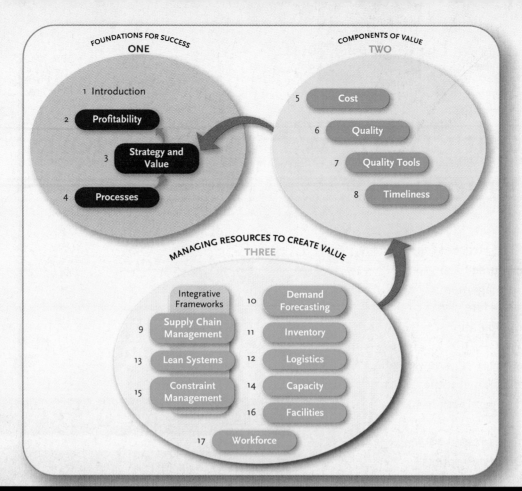

Foundations for Success

INTRODUCTION

Operations management is best described when it is placed in the context in which it exists—the business. As we'll soon understand, operations management is necessary for the financial success of the business. To see how operations decisions affect financial performance, several foundation components that form the context of operations must be understood. These components are at the heart of the business itself.

Introduction: Why Operations Management?

LEARNING OBJECTIVES

- Describe the relationships among value, profitability, cost, processes, and capabilities.

- Describe the components of value.

- Differentiate between the resources that create value.

- Describe the changes in the business environment and the impact they have.

- Describe the external forces that can affect the business.

- Explain the differences between service and product outputs.

- Explain why B2B and B2C customers may define value differently.

- Describe how operations concepts will affect you in your field.

AN ENGINE FOR THE NEW ECONOMY

Hundreds of businesses come and go every year. Some are barely noticed. Still others make such an impact that they actually seem to drive the economy. FedEx is one of those companies.

Fred Smith has transportation in his genes. While taking a course at Yale University, Smith wrote a paper on difficulties he expected businesses of the future to have because they would not be able to maintain inventories of computer parts for repairs and replacement. He proposed a logistics system that could transport those items door-to-door overnight. His idea wasn't looked on with favor, because at that time the air cargo industry was a sideline for airlines to use the empty space in the planes' bellies, but he never forgot it. After flying over 200 missions in Vietnam, Fred Smith returned and took over Arkansas Aviation in 1969. He founded Federal Express in 1971.

Smith's idea of using a hub-and-spoke system for deliveries was modeled after the way banks handle canceled checks. His initial desire, to set up the Federal Express headquarters in Little Rock, was turned down. Airport officials in Memphis were optimistic, however, and offered him the use of some empty National Guard hangars. The rest is history. Those hangars in Memphis turned into a $28 billion business, with over 250,000 employees, a fleet of more than 1,300 planes, 90,000 vehicles, and deliveries to 220 countries.

In today's economy, rapid and dependable movement of goods allows the economy to function as it does. "Speed" is the most important attribute for business logistics needs. Reduced time results in faster turnaround for customers and a quicker return on financial investments. Dependability of delivery enables businesses to reduce levels of inventory because they can be certain goods will arrive when promised.

FedEx's impact on the New Economy continued when in 1994 it decided to give customers the ability to track their own shipments online. In the late 1990s, FedEx took another step by seeking state-of-the-art solutions for improving its services. By 2000 it had initiated Global Inventory Visibility System (GIVS®), which allows customers to view inventory anywhere. The growth of FedEx's capabilities enabled it to double its volume time and time again, until it reached 6 million packages per day in 2006.

With continued investments in information technology (IT), new shipping hubs, sorting technology, and ground and air transportation, FedEx not only contributes to the New Economy but can provide the engine that makes it work. It has developed these capabilities by effectively utilizing a unique set of resources, some of which include:

- Data centers that process more than 20 million transactions per day.
- Terminals at over 100,000 customer sites, proprietary software used by 650,000 customers.
- The largest digital network of any company in the world.
- An IT staff of more than 5,500 people.
- Its own staff of meteorologists.

As the New Economy drives companies to move faster and with greater flexibility, FedEx will very likely be leading the logistics field to make it happen.

Source: http://www.fedex.com; "FedEx Keeps Delivering," *BusinessWeek*, April 26, 2002; Face Time with Fred Smith, *Fast Company*, June 2001, p. 64; *The Global Impacts of FedEx in the New Economy*, SRI International, http://www.sri.com, March 25, 2004; "The FedEx Edge," *Fortune*, April 3, 2006.

Operations management is the management of the resources a business uses to create value. Value creation from resources lies at the heart of all businesses—those that make consumer products, products for other businesses, or consumer or commercial services. Without resources management, value is never formed, products and services are never sold, there is no profit, and the business fails.

Operations: The Heart of the Business

What is operations management? Why is operations management a critical topic of business study? Operations management is the management of resources used to create salable products and services. It consists of those tasks necessary to turn business inputs into more valuable outputs. The inputs consist of the traditional business resources—employees, equipment, inventory, and facilities—combined with some not-so-traditional assets—knowledge, skills, customer relationships, and reputation. For an increasing number of firms, the resources include such things as Internet server speed and capacity, the technical acumen of staff, and bandwidth. The salable outputs are products, services, information, and experiences. The challenge of operations management is to manage these resources effectively to generate a positive financial return.

For decades, operations management has been described as a business function, analogous to accounting, marketing, and finance. To be fair, there's nothing inherently wrong with that statement. Many businesses have taken on a very different look in recent years. Business functions look different, too. Responsibilities have changed, decisions have changed, and the role of traditional business functions has changed. In many firms it has become difficult to distinguish between some of these functions. Despite the fact that marketing, engineering, and operations tasks are still accomplished, their role as distinct and independent functions has changed. Managers in all functions must interact and coordinate their decision-making processes.

While it is generally agreed upon that operations management consists of managing resources that create value, some of those resources extend to beyond the walls of a business. They include resources used to transport products from a supplier on to a customer, or to store products somewhere in between. The management of the interactions between businesses has come to be known by many businesses as supply chain management (SCM). It is difficult, if not impossible, to draw a line between what is supply chain management and what is operations management. Fortunately, it doesn't really need to be drawn. Supply chain activities are so dependent on operations activities and operations activities are so dependent on supply chain activities that they can't be realistically separated.✦

Many companies bring experts together into cross-functional teams rather than have them continue to function behind the barriers that have traditionally separated business functions. The teams change as each project is accomplished and as new ones arise. All team members must be cognizant, from a broad business perspective, of what has to be done and why. The isolated departments that once existed, sometimes referred to as "functional silos," have seen their walls disappear. The business where people interact only with their own kind—accountants, human resource managers, or information systems staff—is no longer effective.

Differentiate Yourself

Put more simply, and from the perspective students must have for their future: Businesses want to hire bright people, trainable people, who can ultimately make decisions that are best for the business. They don't want employees who cannot grasp the big picture or

Overlapping Functions in Enterprise Decision Making	EXHIBIT 1.1

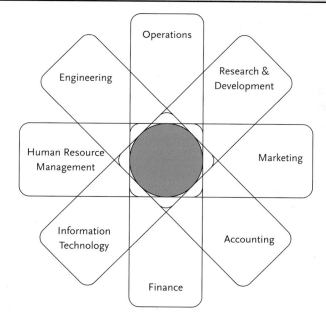

who cling to a belief that what looks best for marketing or finance is obviously the best decision for the entire business. The present and future manager must have functional expertise with an enterprise perspective.

If a student imagines herself as a marketing brand manager for a consumer products firm, a president of a bank, or a consultant, and assumes she will be working with people whose expertise and background are the same as hers, she should think again. She is placing constraints on her career potential. She'll work with systems experts. She'll work with engineers. She'll work with people whose expertise lies in areas that haven't even been thought of yet. She needs to understand what they do and why they do it. She needs to understand how her business converts resources and capabilities into a healthy profit. She needs to understand operations management.

Good managers are effective at solving problems in complex systems. They must understand cause and effect. A physician's role is an appropriate analogy. A physician who specializes in a particular aspect of human health, whether it be an endocrinologist, an orthopedist, a dermatologist, or a gastroenterologist, has to have an understanding of the entire body. If she doesn't, she won't be able to identify symptoms elsewhere that point to problems within her own area of specialty or the potential problems that can result from problems within her area of focus. She can't make the best decision for the endocrine system, the best decision for the skeletal system, the best decision for the skin, or the best decision for the gastric system. She has to make the best decision for the person.

Business functions do not act independently. The overlapping rectangles in Exhibit 1.1 illustrate how information sharing and decision making involve many functions and personnel with diverse expertise. A business is a system. No functional department can make a decision that doesn't affect the rest of the firm. The important decisions of the firm—those that have critical implications for its success—occur at the interface. The decision makers recognize the implications because they understand the business.

Operations Management: How We Got Here

To understand the environment of operations management today, it helps to have a bit of an understanding of where it's been. In the late 1700s and early 1800s Europe, and eventually the United States, was involved in the Industrial Revolution. During the Industrial Revolution, products were produced by individuals who had highly developed skills working with iron and wood. This type of production, known as **craft production**, was capable of producing high-quality products, but since products were produced individually, no two were exactly alike.

Since products were not exactly alike, repairs and replacement parts had to be custom produced. Producing products individually did not take advantage of the scale economies of producing in higher volumes. The concept of interchangeable parts was first introduced in the late 1700s, and the production of some products shifted from one-at-a-time to more efficient and economical volumes.

Managing work in a more sophisticated way was not introduced until the early 1900s, when Frederick W. Taylor promoted an approach that came to be known as scientific management. Scientific management embraces the idea that the best way for performing a task could be determined, and once determined, all workers should perform the task in that way. Others extended Taylor's theory.

Taylor's views radically changed manufacturing in the United States. High-volume production and standardized work methods evolved into the **mass production** that characterized U.S. manufacturing until well after World War II. As efforts to increase wartime production of goods reached a peak, various quantitative tools were developed to optimize production. These tools, which include linear programming, simulation, and other modeling approaches, began to see common usage for decision making.

Following World War II, several experts in process quality assisted Japan in its reconstruction efforts. These experts included Walter Shewhart and W. Edwards Deming. The work of Shewhart and Deming transformed the quality of Japanese products to the point where by the early 1980s Japanese auto imports were far superior to those manufactured in the United States. The quality deficiency of U.S. products relative to those of Japan triggered an increasing emphasis on quality in the United States. This quality revolution shifted to include other aspects of Japanese production known as just-in-time (JIT). The high-quality, low-inventory production systems have remained popular in U.S. manufacturing as proven ways of increasing value and reducing costs.

By the 1980s the U.S. economy had become more service oriented as manufacturing began to shift out of the United States toward countries with lower labor costs. Increasingly, through the 1980s and 1990s, services became a greater part of the U.S. economy.

craft production
Production of goods by highly skilled and specialized artisans.

mass production
High-volume production of standardized products.

EXHIBIT 1.2	Contrasting Corporate Characteristics: 20th and 21st Century	
Corporate Characteristic	20th Century (Old Economy)	21st Century (New Economy)
Organization structure	Pyramid hierarchy	Network
Focus	Internal	Customer
Management style	Structured, rigid	Flexible
Market reach	Regional/national	Global
Productive resources	Physical assets	Information/knowledge
Production mode	Mass production	Mass customization
Production structure	Self-sufficiency	Network alliances
Inventories	Months of supply	Hours of supply
Production cycle time	Weeks/months	Days
Timeliness of information	Weekly	Real time
Product life cycle	Years	Months
Desired quality level	Affordable best	Perfection

Used with permission from SRI International.

By the late 1990s the Internet was realizing its potential to change the way businesses communicate with each other and with customers. As technologies for information sharing improved, businesses began to recognize the effects that individual decisions had on their suppliers and customers, and so was born the concept of supply chain management.

Today business embraces mass production in services and manufacturing, but technology is making inroads into the "holy grail"—mass customization. Products and services designed and delivered to meet an individual's needs, quickly and at low cost, constitute the latest attainable goal. Corporate characteristics have changed substantially in the last century. These differences define the New Economy and are contrasted in Exhibit 1.2.

The Future of Operations Management

Service-oriented businesses, whether they are banks, retail stores, insurance companies, or hairdressers, have long recognized the customer as an integral part of the firm's formula for success. The firm's location, design, and layout, as well as the training of employees, have always had a customer focus. Manufacturers, on the other hand, have been able to isolate themselves from the consumer with barriers of distributors, wholesalers, and retailers. Now, however, even such hard-core manufacturers as auto producers have recognized that service-related issues are as important as—if not more important than—the product they sell.

All businesses received a wake-up call when personal computer (PC) manufacturers began to sell customized PCs directly to the public. That business model was immediately copied. Toyota, Ford, and General Motors are rapidly approaching the day when the customer will have the ability to configure a car over the Internet and climb behind the wheel in days, not weeks.[1] Internet speed forces a company to place the customer at the center of everything and design itself for customer satisfaction rather than mass production. Today's definition of customer satisfaction extends beyond product quality to incorporate speed, flexibility, and other service-related issues.

It's true that the Internet has not removed all the stumbling blocks to good customer service. We all still occasionally encounter products of poor quality. We encounter poor quality service, such as slow responses and long delays, much too frequently. Is this Internet speed? No, but it's a great opportunity for a competitor wanting to increase market share.

United Parcel Service (UPS) has experienced the dramatic change in consumer expectations for customer service. In December 1995 it experienced its first month with 100,000 online tracking requests. In December 1996 it experienced its first month with 1 million online tracking requests. In December 1997 it experienced its first *week* with 1 million online tracking requests. In December 1998 it experienced its first *day* with 1 million online tracking requests. In December 1999 it experienced its first day with 2.5 million online tracking requests. In December 2000 it experienced its first day with 5 million online tracking requests. In five years the demand for that service grew by a factor of 1,500.[2] WOW

It used to be easy to distinguish between manufacturers and services. Manufacturers made things you could get your hands around. Services fulfilled needs, but their outputs were intangible. Apple's iPod and music download business has so intertwined the selling of products (MP3 players, accessories, songs, TV shows, and movies) and services (iTunes software and updates, iTunes music store, song reviews, podcasts, and playlists) that it will forever blur the lines between products and services.

Today all successful firms must deliver services. Companies *know* this. They even provide the mechanisms—customer service hotlines and Web sites with "Contact Us!" buttons. Automakers like Ford, GM, and Toyota thrive on the services they bundle with cars. Computer makers provide on-site repairs. These mechanisms can be effective, but for the business that doesn't take them seriously, they can also be dangerous. Expectations increase because customers think the businesses mean what they say. Unfortunately, many companies don't know how to follow through on their implied promises. They raise the customers' hopes and then dash them.

Today's managers must be committed to continuous learning to remain current and aware of advancements made in their area of expertise and in other areas of the business. As the cross-functional and global characteristics of business become more important, an enterprise perspective, enhanced by ongoing educational efforts, is critical.

Many traditional manufacturing firms, including automobile manufacturers, computer manufacturers, and other consumer product manufacturers, no longer manufacture at all; they'll merely assemble components provided by a deep network of suppliers. Some don't even assemble, but invest their expertise in product development and look outside the company for manufacturing capability. In fact, the notion of vertical integration is beginning to take on a new look. In the past, manufacturers were likely to buy up suppliers in order to have better control over quality and costs. They were disconnected from the consumer by distributors and independent retailers.

The pendulum has now swung the other way. Manufacturers are outsourcing more of their needs and at the same time becoming more directly linked to the customer through services. Even Japanese manufacturers, despite decades of close-knit supplier networks, have begun to outsource manufacturing processes to contract manufacturers.[3] These changes are made possible by advancements in technology that enable firms to maintain accurate and almost instantaneous communication between customers and suppliers.

Computers quickly process information over the Internet, but how can the actual physical systems move goods and services so fast? In the current business environment, speed is critical. How can an order for a customized automobile be completed in five days when many of us can't get a response from an e-mail in 48 hours? How are many businesses able to react that quickly and why can't they all? How can machines produce products so swiftly? How can products be moved that rapidly? The answers are that the processes must not only accomplish their objectives quickly but also be designed for almost split-second response to change. Suppliers must provide instantaneous replenishment, and production processes must be totally flexible. Services must meet customer needs immediately. They must know in advance what individual customers want.

An Economy Based on Knowledge

The world economy itself is changing drastically, and businesses must exist within that changing environment. We often hear reference to a "knowledge-based" economy: What does that mean? And, more to the point, "So what?" In a knowledge-based economy, innovations substitute knowledge for other capital. Some creative person comes up with a great idea, and suddenly some other product or service is obsolete. Someone gets rich, and someone else is looking for a new job. But more important, we, as a society, gain knowledge. Knowledge breeds more knowledge. Just imagine the ideas and wealth that have been dependent on the development of the first Web browser created by graduate students at the University of Illinois. The World Wide Web wasn't their idea. Their creative input was in developing a different way *to use it*. The creativity that sparks innovation is often the ability to recognize another use or potential for someone else's idea.

Knowledge expands at an even faster rate when more people talk to each other and share ideas. This principle has expanded to create a global business network—enhanced even more by close relationships between companies that trade with each other to the point that they invest in each other, help develop each other's new products and services, and help each other solve problems. These strategic alliances have created a new business environment.

Rapid change, driven by technology and expanding global markets, has changed the way we make business decisions, the way we value assets, and the way we calculate costs. The traditional understanding of value and how customers perceive it has been turned inside out. For a while, even the way people thought about profit changed. Market share was the only important measure. Profit didn't matter. Just ask shareholders of "pavingstones.com" or "petfoodinbulk.com." No one should be surprised that consumers would not pay $13 plus $7 shipping for a $15 bag of dog food. That was then. This is now. Profitability matters.

A New Business Environment

Businesses today range from a traditional manufacturer of corrugated paper containers (cardboard boxes to you and me), such as General Packaging Corporation, to one running an online auction of banner space on Web pages, like WebmasterBids. Imagine selling, through a virtual auction, a virtual commodity (Web page advertising space) that may even be purchased by companies wishing to advertise their virtual services. Boxes are traditional products that have been around for years and will be needed for years to come. Both have value. Imagine selling either of those "products" anywhere in the world and purchasing materials, information, and employee talent from anywhere in the world as well.

Virtual products and services that are now commonplace could barely be imagined 10 years ago. An online auction of *anything* would have seemed unlikely. An auction of advertising banner space on Web sites would have seemed ridiculous. Will online auctions

---

om_ADVANTAGE_   PayPal: The Worst Idea of the Year?

PayPal, the largest Internet payment network, allows money to be sent by e-mail. It has dominated the auction company Ebay as a safe and convenient way to transfer money from buyer to seller. It has a customer base of 10 million and has grown rapidly. It expects $3 billion in transactions per year. Surprisingly, PayPal didn't start out with that concept in mind at all. Originally, PayPal started in 1998 as a specialized service for owners of Palm computers who needed to transmit funds to each other using the device's infrared port. In its early days, however, to actually use the feature the two Palm users had to be so close they could have easily handed checks to each other. One trade publication voted the idea the worst of the year. PayPal also provided a means for non-PayPal users to transfer money, and it was this capability that began to become popular. The Palm-only service was

dumped and PayPal began to grow. PayPal is expanding its position to be the online means of transferring money for all types of online business transactions, including traditional bills like phone and utility bills. PayPal has 40 million account members worldwide in 38 countries.

PayPal's success lies in the fact that it doesn't try to reinvent everything. It recognizes what needs to be reinvented and does that quickly. The rest PayPal leaves alone. PayPal has been particularly attractive to small merchants, which can be charged as much as 5 percent by credit card companies. PayPal charges only 2.9 percent plus 30 cents per transaction.

Source: "Fix It and They Will Come," *Wall Street Journal*, February 12, 2001, p. R4; www.paypal.com, March 23, 2004; "These Guys Will Make You Pay," *Fast Company*, November 2001, online edition.

exist in 10 years? That's hard to say. You can bet, however, that we'll still be using cardboard boxes.

In addition to the added pressures and capabilities resulting from technological progress, many other pressures exert forces on business. Pressures vary in different industries, but globalization of businesses is a prominent issue for many. As businesses increasingly expand to international markets, increase their use of product and service suppliers from around the world, and form alliances and relationships with businesses from other countries, the U.S. business landscape disappears. "Market share" as defined by the percentage of the U.S. market a company has is meaningless.

The vast range of products and services makes it impossible to come up with a general model that perfectly represents operations in all businesses. A model is important, however, to understand operations and its role in businesses. An effective model helps relate operations activities to business goals. Such a model is critical if operations concepts are to be integrated into the firm's success, and not treated as independent entities. The Resource/Profit Model, shown in Exhibit 1.3, provides a framework for placing operations management in the larger business context.

EXHIBIT 1.3	Resource/Profit Model

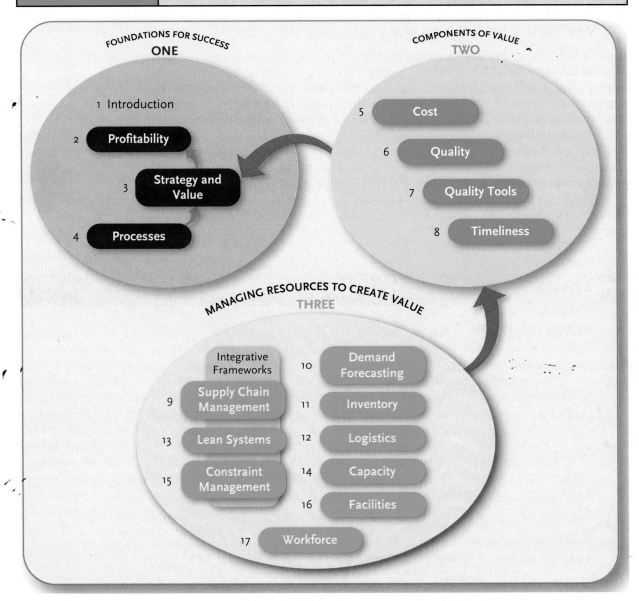

The elements in the model are parallel to the chapters in this text. The purpose of the model is to identify how topics relate; it doesn't limit the sequence of coverage of chapters to the order in the model.

Operations Management in the Business

Foundations for Success

The Resource/Profit Model begins, quite logically, with the overriding objective of the business—profitability—and proceeds with two of its most critical prerequisites—strategy and processes. These concepts are presented in Exhibit 1.3 as "foundations for success" because they form the foundation for decision making throughout the business. It is no coincidence that there are parallels between finance classes and the coverage of profitability, as it relates to operations management, in this book. This connection is critical because finance exists in the environment of operations management decisions. Operations management, on the other hand, exists within an environment of financial decision making. It is also no coincidence that the coverage of strategy will link closely to concepts in marketing. Strategy is a plan for creating value and is an important operations management responsibility. Determining what customers value, however, is at the root of marketing responsibility.

Profitability = why?

Every business organizes resources into processes and uses these processes to create goods and/or services to sell. Ideally, the sale results in a positive financial return on the investments that were utilized to create the goods and services. **Profitability** is the primary objective of any business. It is the answer to the question "Why?" when asked about the existence of any business.

The goal of a business is profitability, not profit. When most people say "profit," they really mean "net income," but net income doesn't provide enough information to measure a business's success. It's simply the measure of an output. If a business's net income was $100,000, it's impossible to know whether it was successful. Profitability measures compare outputs to inputs to determine how productive the investment is. A successful business strives for long-term profitability. That requires staying power, growing market share, and, most of all, treating customers well.

Businesses have other objectives, including employment and development of individuals and contributing to society as a whole, but none can be accomplished without profitability. Financial return, short and long term, at a rate that is greater than other alternatives must be at the forefront or all other objectives will fail when the company folds. Operations management is at the heart of that cycle, managing the productive resources to provide profitability.

> **profitability**
> A measure of the productivity of money invested in a business, typically a ratio of net income to some input such as net sales or total assets.

Strategy = How?

The goal of any investor is to find an investment that will create **value** for the owner. Resources are company assets that are expected to provide a financial benefit to the owner. If the answer to the "Why?" question of a business's existence is profitability, then the answer to the "How?" question is value. You bought the shoes you're wearing because you thought they were a better value than other alternatives. You prefer one restaurant to another because of how you define value. The difference between the perceived benefits and the perceived costs establish the customer perception of value.

Customers are willing to pay for value, and therein lies the potential for the business's owners to benefit from their investment. The difference between the amount customers are willing to pay for something and the cost of creating it provides the opportunity for profitability.

Changes in pricing approaches have dramatically changed the way customers must determine value. As businesses gather more data about customers' purchasing habits,

> **value**
> The amount a customer is willing to pay for a product or service, sometimes thought of as benefits divided by cost.

they are setting different prices for different individuals. This has been a standard practice for airlines, hotels, and car rental companies. In mortgage lending, different interest rates are applied for different risks. This is actually advantageous for some, because they would pay an even higher rate elsewhere. Grocery stores have followed, offering reduced prices automatically for customers who normally buy certain products only during promotions or with coupons.

A business must identify how it will continue to add value to its inputs in ways that customers will desire. What type of customer will the business seek to attract? What will customers want? What will competitors do to meet customer wants? What must a business do to compete against them? A business must determine how it can create value as its environment changes and as customer desires change. The business must plan its **strategy**, which sets the direction for the future. The strategy is the way of offering value to a specific set of customers and is the means by which the company positions itself for future profitability. By establishing goals for the future, and creating the mechanisms to reach them, the business is able to adapt to changing customer expectations and changing environmental pressures.

The **capabilities** the company has formulated are the answer to the customer's questions "What exactly can you do for me?" and "What is it that I'm paying for?" The answer to those questions can be, simply, "This company can sell you a collar for your dog cheaper than anyone else." Or it can be "This company can offer you a selection of 50 different dog collars on our Web site. Our Web site is easy to navigate and quick to download. Purchasing products on the site is simple, secure, and quick. We can deliver your collar in 48 hours at a price lower than anyone else." Are the capabilities that enable a company to make such claims valuable? Certainly. Are they important parts of its strategy? Definitely.

Processes

Capabilities are the direct outcome of processes. Processes are made up of activities. Activities are specifically designed to contribute to a product or service in a way that will be valuable to a customer. The grouping of simple activities into processes, and the grouping of processes in a way that creates capabilities, is at the core of creating value. One might argue that—unlike capabilities—processes are not viewed by customers as important. This argument may be true for product-oriented processes, because customers aren't as concerned about how a product is produced. However, customers care very much about the **processes** they must interact with to purchase that product. They care about service-oriented processes, such as those they interact with to get assistance when they need it. Customers care deeply about those business processes that affect them directly.

Processes and capabilities are a responsibility of operations management. They range from being extremely simple to extremely complex. For some businesses, the need for consistency mandates that processes be standardized and accurately documented. For others, the need for customization requires processes to be flexible in order to satisfy each

strategy
The means by which a company positions itself for future profitability.

capabilities
The abilities a business has that result from its processes. Capabilities create value.

FedEx can deliver pallets of freight weighing from 151 pounds to 2,200 pounds to any U.S. location in one to three business days.

processes
Organized tasks accomplished by grouping resources together.

TARGETING technology — Eliminating Customer Risk-Taking at Borders

We've all considered purchasing a CD when we're not entirely sure we'll like it. Maybe we've heard a song or two but hate to shell out $18 for one that will never be played. Some stores have dealt with that problem by offering to open any CD that a customer wishes to listen to. This satisfies the customer but creates logistical issues for the store trying to deal with all of those opened CDs. Technological advancements have enabled Borders to eliminate that dilemma for its customers in a much more elegant way. In the past, Borders had

listening carrels and a selection of several CDs to choose from. Using new technology, a customer can scan the bar code of any CD, which remains unopened, and the entire contents of the CD can be played. With this capability, risk is eliminated for the customer through unlimited preview options that are available. For Borders, CDs need not be opened for a customer to listen to them, but customers are able to sample everything offered.

Unique products or services depend on the business's ability to create capabilities that are distinctive. Entrepreneurs have responded to Bangkok, Thailand's air pollution problem with oxygen bars. In this bar, named "O2O," curious Thais and foreign tourists pay 90 baht (US$1.80) for 20 minutes of oxygen. The ability to add oxygen to other services a business offers requires an investment in sophisticated equipment, facilities in a high-traffic location, current and interesting reading material for a broad range of interests, and personalized music selection.

customer's special needs. Processes range tremendously, from the method that McDonald's uses to ensure that a small paper bag is full of french fries, to the steps taken when KPMG audits a Fortune 500 firm's books, to how a credit card account number is transferred securely online by L.L. Bean. Most firms utilize a variety of processes that create capabilities of interest to customers. Often these capabilities set one firm apart from another. If the customer wants what the business capability provides, the processes have created value. For someone trying to make money in the stock market, investment decisions ultimately determine the return on the dollars invested. Make a good decision—get a good return. Make a poor decision—get a poor return. For product- and service-oriented businesses, processes act in a manner similar to that of a stock fund manager. Processes define how resources are used. If resources are used well, the return will be good. Processes play two critical roles in defining the financial return of a resource investment. First, the lower the cost (as long as value remains the same), the greater the difference between cost and market value. Second, the process is a major factor in the customer's perceived value. The more value added by the process, the greater the difference between market value and cost (as long as cost remains the same). Processes define the way resources are used through design, implementation, and use.

Components of Value

The capabilities made possible through the effective development and management of processes create the services and products customers value. That value is the result of the interactions among three components of value—**cost**, **quality**, and **timeliness**—influenced by operations decisions and shown in Exhibit 1.3.

Cost

When a customer orders a pizza, he is thinking about the taste of the pizza. When the manager of the pizza restaurant orders flour, she is concerned about the flour, but other aspects of the business transaction also affect the value of the dough. The first is the cost

cost
The expenses associated with ownership.

quality
Meeting customer expectations.

timeliness
The speed at which a business completes tasks and the degree to which it completes tasks on schedule and as promised.

associated with obtaining the product or service. Cost can be defined as the amount of scarce resources consumed to achieve a specified objective. The cost of owning a new car, for example, is not just the price one has to pay to drive it off the dealer's lot. The total cost of owning it includes all costs associated with it over a specified period of time. If the customer wishes to own the car for six years, for example, the cost includes expenditures over that time period. Certainly, the price paid is part of the total cost, but so is the interest on the loan, the price of insurance, the cost of maintenance and repair, and the value depreciation on the car over the six years.

Costs can have very different meanings to different customers. In the previous example, the customer was assumed to be a consumer. A business customer might have a very different view of cost. A Toyota dealer, for example, would view the cost of purchasing a car as more of a financial investment. The total costs would include the cost of the space it would take on the lot, work that would need to be done on the car to get it ready to sell, administrative costs associated with ownership transfer, advertisement costs, and opportunity cost of the dollars invested in it that could be used for something else.

Processes cost money to operate. Resources cost money to maintain. The costs of employee time, materials consumed, and electricity are passed on to the customer and contribute to her costs as well. Cost is a critical component of value and an important criterion for many operations decisions.

Quality

The quality of the product or service is another component of its value. For virtually any product or service, different levels of quality exist. Why? Because customers view quality very differently. What's high quality for one customer is not important for another. Higher levels of quality don't always translate into higher levels of value. Remember, value is in the eye of the beholder. Quality has very different meanings when products are compared to services. As mentioned earlier, outcomes dominate the customer's perception of value *and* quality when products are considered. For consumers, quality is often judged by how well the product met the customer's expectations. Did the product last as long as it should have? In other words, was it durable? Was it reliable? Did it do what it was designed to do? However, as soon as services are examined, the concept of quality becomes broader and more difficult to define. Were the employees friendly? Was the service quick? Did I have to wait in line long? The answers to each of these questions can be different for different customers. No matter what the customer's definition, however, the perception of quality will be a major determinant of value.

Timeliness

The third component of value consists of the timeliness associated with the product's or service's creation, delivery, and availability. Something *now* is generally perceived as more valuable than the same thing *later*. Timeliness is often less critical for consumers than it is for business customers, but enhances value for both. Timeliness is often lumped together with quality when services are evaluated. When products are evaluated, particularly those purchased by a business, the product quality is certainly important, but issues of timeliness can be equally or even more important. For a business, time has a critical role in determining financial return on any investment. Achieving timeliness goals involves scheduling activities and processes so that process times can be minimized or due date promises can be met.

Managing Resources Used to Create Value

Resources provide the direct inputs that either are converted into salable goods and services or enable that conversion to happen. As presented in Exhibit 1.3, among the most important resource management topics are inventory, logistics, capacity, facilities, and workforce. They provide critical inputs to creating the products and services customers seek. Operations, although critical in the creation of value, can't claim responsibility for all value added. There are other important resources as well, such as intangibles like patents that result from the creativity of engineers and research and development specialists. Employee knowledge and skills—instilled in the workforce through training and development—and the creativity that emerges with the help of the business culture are also important. The communication networks that provide management with the data needed to make timely and appropriate decisions are also essential to the success of the business. This large pool of resources is tapped to provide capabilities that can differentiate a business from its competition.

The effective management of inventory, logistics, capacity, facilities, and workforce requires an understanding of the decision-making processes associated with those resources. As businesses have integrated business functions, however, that is not enough. In the last two decades, several **integrative management frameworks** have changed the way resource decisions are made. Supply chain management (SCM), the most recent integrative framework, recognizes that resource decisions within one business affect outcomes of customers and suppliers. SCM extends the realm of decision making beyond the business's walls and considers effects up and down the supply chain. **Lean systems** have evolved from the just-in-time (JIT) movement of the 1980s and focus on waste reduction in all its forms, but particularly emphasizing leanness in inventory and capacity. **Constraint management** takes a system view of how one limiting resource can reduce system productivity in a manner similar to the weakest link in a chain. Constraint management focuses on capacity-related resources, but has implications for inventory and workforce as well.

Integrative management frameworks provide a set of principles that eliminate the need to evaluate day-to-day decisions on the basis of profitability. They are, in a sense, an intermediate standard on which to evaluate decisions. A good analogy would be the way different basketball, football, and hockey teams identify a particular offensive or defensive *system* to run. The system provides guidance for players' actions, no matter what the opposing team does. Each system comes with a general objective and a specific set of rules of behavior that, if implemented effectively, should result in the team being able to compete. Different systems emphasize a different approach to utilizing resources (player talent or capabilities). One system might be used if a team is extremely fast but not very tall. Another system might be more effective if the team has two very tall players but no outside shooters. Integrative management frameworks are similar in that each has a general objective, each comes with a set of techniques or tools, and each focuses on specific resources.

The rise of integrative management frameworks has been interesting to observe. In virtually every case, they have been born out of the need to adapt to changing external forces. Each has become very popular, creating a frenzy to learn and adopt the system, as well as charge countless billable hours for consulting firms. Each has been labeled a "new philosophy of management." Some have gained an almost cultlike following. And then each has declined in popularity—not because managers no longer believe in their value, but because they have been absorbed into mainstream management practice. They become such a part of good management practices that they are no longer viewed as a distinctive way of doing things.

Supply Chain Management

Supply chain management focuses on the relationships among customers and suppliers, recognizing that the effects of decisions aren't limited to the business that made them but extend to suppliers and customers as well. Ultimately, the entire supply chain creates the value a customer perceives and receives. Optimizing that value and minimizing its costs require a decision-making perspective that includes the entire supply chain.

The integrative management frameworks tie together the foundations for success, the components of value, and the resources used to create value in a consistent set of decision-making priorities. Managers familiar with the objectives and the techniques inherent in each framework are provided with a systematic approach to decision making that will be consistent with global performance measures. Each provides a means of making day-to-day decisions consistent with the firm's profitability goals.

integrative management framework
A management approach or "philosophy" that guides day-to-day decisions in a way that is consistent with a firm's profitability goals. Examples include lean systems, constraint management, and supply chain management.

lean systems
A productive system that functions with little waste or excess, usually with low inventory levels.

constraint management
A framework for managing the constraints of a system in a way that maximizes the system's accomplishment of its goals.

Demand Forecasting

Simply owning inventory, capacity, and facilities, and paying a workforce does not result in the production of goods and services or the creation of value. These resources must be brought together into processes that provide the firm with capabilities. The firm's level of success or failure will be determined not by what resources the company owns, but by how it uses them. Resources aren't free, so the business must possess them in the appropriate quantity and at the appropriate time. If a company has invested in too many resources, those resources won't contribute to value. If the firm has too few resources, it can't meet demand. If the resources arrive too early, they aren't used. If they arrive too late, customer needs aren't met. Effective resource planning depends on an accurate forecast of demand. The demand forecast gives managers the basis upon which to order more inventory, identify more transportation or storage facilities, add to capacity, expand facilities, or increase the workforce.

Lean Systems

Lean systems' primary focus is on the elimination of waste in producing goods and services. It is frequently used to eliminate waste related to inventory, processes, and the workforce, and it is also used when inventory reduction is desired. Just-in-time (JIT) management has been implemented in the United States since about 1980 after being practiced in Japan since the 1960s. Efforts to maintain lean systems utilize a variety of techniques and approaches to minimize inventory and increase flexibility of capacity.

Constraint Management

Constraint management, also known as the theory of constraints, first attained visibility around 1987. It focuses on the role constraints play in an organization and how best to manage those constraints. Its goal is to increase the productivity of the system as a whole by focusing on its constraints and recognizing that optimizing specific parts of the system will not optimize the entire system. The role a constraint plays is often misunderstood. Its impact is so critical to system productivity that a better understanding can affect such wide-ranging issues as investment decisions, product and service pricing, and inventory levels.

Inventory

inventory
Materials used in the production of products and services. Examples include raw materials inventory, work-in-process inventory, and finished goods inventory.

A retailer performs what appears to be a simple function—selling products to consumers. It's easy to assume that the products, or **inventory**, would be one of its most important resources. The retailer must have it when the customer needs it, or sales are lost. To produce the product being sold, a manufacturer needs raw materials, which are used to create component parts, which in turn are assembled into finished products and sold to the retailer. All forms of materials make up a category of resources known as inventory, which serves many critical functions. It buffers one work center from direct dependency on another. It allows customers to be satisfied immediately. It enables retailers to offer their customers many choices. It is an asset on the balance sheet, but it is widely recognized by managers as a liability as well. Despite all of its benefits, surplus inventory has been blamed for many business failures. A resource that, when in either short supply or excess, can destroy a business must be managed with extreme care.

Logistics

logistics
The flow and storage of goods, services, and related information from production to consumption.

Logistics consists of managing the flow and storage of goods and services. It adds value by ensuring that the products and services are *where* they need to be. It contributes to timeliness because the movement of goods is often more time consuming than their production. It is intertwined with inventory management because effective inventory management extends beyond simply managing inventory within the business. The increasing dependency on outsourcing requires effective management of inventory *between* businesses as well. Logistics is a critical component of supply chain management because of increased competition, globalization, and technological advancements, and to increase the value offered to consumers. Effective logistics management reduces costs and increases value.

Capacity

Capacity can be summed up as the level of productive output of an organization in a specified period of time. Productive output results from a variety of resources, but in most cases it is dominated by the availability of labor and/or equipment. H&R Block's ability to meet its demand is dictated by the number of skilled employees who can complete the IRS forms. Bank of America's ability to keep up with demand at a drive-up service is determined by the number of drive-up bays and tellers. A Target store's ability to keep pace with customers making their purchases is determined by the number of cash registers and operators.

One similarity should stand out in each of the above examples. Capacity is almost always expressed as an average. Why? Because the time required per unit can vary. In some cases that variability is a function of what's required. One person's income taxes are more complex than another's. Drive-up banking customers have different needs. In other cases, the employee or equipment varies in its ability to complete the required tasks. One particular accountant is faster in the morning and slower in the late afternoon. Ultimately, the management of capacity is to match output to demand. Excess capacity results in a financial return on those resources that is lower than that desired. A shortage of capacity results in an inability to meet demand.

capacity
The level of productive output of an organization in a specified period of time.

Facilities

The land and the building that houses a business can be the least important decision for management, as in the case of where to place a Web server, or it can be the most important decision, as when a retailer is determining store location. In addition to facility location, **facility** decisions also include how the facility should be arranged, or its layout. The facility layout often determines the business's ability to meet customer expectations. It dictates such outcomes as the ability to customize products and services, the ability to produce in high volumes, and the type of skills needed from employees. In many businesses, the layout determines the ease with which employees can interact with each other and with customers.

Every business has to be somewhere. The location decision makes that determination. Within that facility, every thing and every person also has to be somewhere. Where they are matters. The layout dictates possible processes and capabilities, as well as the costs, the quality, and the timeliness.

facilities
The buildings and structures that house various aspects of a business.

Workforce

Most managers will claim that the **workforce** is their business's most critical resource. Inventory can be purchased, capacity can be purchased, facilities can be purchased, but good, talented, skilled employees are not easy to come by. They are developed, over a long period of time and at great expense. They are also the only resource that can leave the business for a better offer elsewhere.

Employees' skills, talents, experiences, attitudes, and backgrounds range tremendously. The diversity adds to the potential capabilities of the firm and also adds to the skills necessary at the managerial level. Great potential isn't free. The diversity of ideas, the creativity, and the ability to recognize potential value can come only from the widest possible set of experiences. The result of this diversity is truly any business's most valuable resource, but it is also one of the most difficult to manage.

workforce
The employees required to produce a product or service.

Environmental Forces

A business is an open system. No business that has an impact on external entities (customers, demand, and so on) can function without itself being influenced by external forces. The forces that exist within a particular business's environment often depend on competitive and regulatory forces within the industry, but there are also many environmental forces that cross industry boundaries.

Globalization

The first and probably the strongest environmental force that product- and service-oriented firms must cope with is the increased competition and emerging markets resulting from

FedEx started its Asian Pacific Operations in 1984 and now employs more than 9,700 people in more than 30 APAC countries and territories.

the globalization of most businesses. This phenomenon has resulted in increased competitive pressures in a firm's home country and increased opportunities in foreign markets. This trend will have a negative impact on firms unable to mobilize and seek new markets, but firms wishing to expand their markets will perceive this as a wide-open field in which they can excel. However, it's important to remember that along with expansion into emerging markets comes risk associated with political unrest, unknown competitive forces in those markets, unexpected expectation for products and services, and uncertainties associated with transportation, supplies, labor, and financial exchange rates.

The globalization of business has substantial effects on operations. Moving into global markets with products and services creates new definitions of value. As value changes, so does the creation of value, and so do requirements for processes and capabilities as well as cost, quality, and timeliness. It creates new objectives, but it also creates new challenges. Geographic distances translate into time differences, creating an entirely new set of challenges for managing all resources.

In addition to moving into global markets with products and services, businesses also move readily into global markets for purchasing products and services they need. Extending the supply base into global markets creates a new set of advantages and management challenges as well. Time necessary to obtain inputs increases. Infrastructures must be built. Employees must be trained. Along with these challenges come advantages. New ideas are generated. New skills and talents are identified. Extending the supplier base sometimes involves extending the location of facilities into foreign countries to take advantage of resources, talents, and markets. All of these decisions affect the way resources are obtained, utilized, and brought together in the value-creation process. They provide great potential, but they require managers to recognize the diversity of cultures and the talent, creativity, and views those cultures bring as well.

The Internet and Other Technologies

The second environmental force being felt by most businesses is coming from the increased levels of communication and competition brought about by technologies. One of these technologies, the Internet, has created a business environment that makes geography a

om ADVANTAGE   A Different Type of Environmental Pressure

Few changes in consumer behavior have had the industry impact of the low-carbohydrate, high-protein diet trend. As eating preferences of millions of people have shifted away from sugars, soft drinks, bread, and other high-carbohydrate staples, restaurants and food producers have had to adapt or be left with dwindling demand.

For some food producers, particularly producers of high-carbohydrate products like bread, demand has dropped off. Other businesses have been able to adapt. Restaurants jumping on the bandwagon range from Burger King and Hardee's bunless hamburgers to menu items at Chili's, T.G.I. Friday's, Ruby Tuesday, and many more.

To counter the slump in demand for some producers, the shift in eating habits has created some opportunities as well. Low-carb muffins, low-carb bread, and low-carb cereal

are common in special low-carb sections of some grocery stores. "Pizza in a bucket" has all the toppings, but no crust. Soft drinks and snack foods have been the victims of decreasing demand. Beer producers have felt the pinch and Michelob's Ultra Brew uses an extended mashing process to reduce carbohydrates to 2.6 grams (regular Michelob has 13.3 grams). A new artificial sweetener, Splenda (made by Johnson & Johnson), has had increasing demands since 2003. The diet has had indirect effects on product demands as well. High-protein foods have little fiber, so laxative demand has increased.

Source: "Health," Fortune, March 31, 2004; "PepsiCo: Getting into Niches," BusinessWeek Online, April 5, 2004; "Mania over Atkins Diet Growing Still," Washington Daily News, March 31, 2004.

nonissue for many firms. Businesses that were successful simply because of their location must develop other capabilities to maintain a competitive advantage.

The Internet has also placed a tremendous amount of pressure on businesses that act primarily as intermediaries between the producer and consumer. Manufacturers can deal directly with consumers, and do so at low cost. Intermediaries are finding it difficult to add enough value to warrant their markup. This phenomenon is not limited to product-oriented firms. Banks, investment houses, insurance companies, and numerous types of retailers must compete against firms that exist solely online, with no expenses tied to brick and mortar facilities.

Other technologies create environmental pressures as well. Geographic information systems (GIS), for example, have merged database technology and mapping technology to create new capabilities in location planning. Global positioning system (GPS) technology has enhanced our abilities to locate shipments precisely. Radio frequency identification (RFID) has the potential to enable businesses to track inventory through the supply chain and evaluate and count the contents of containers and trucks without opening them. These technologies and others enhance the information manager's capabilities, but can enhance the capabilities of competitors as well.

Disruptive technologies, as they have become known, wreak havoc and create opportunities. Napster, for example, turned the recording industry upside down. That same technology has enhanced collaboration efforts for many businesses. General Motors uses E-vis. IBM uses E-workplace. As more disruptive technologies emerge, managers adapt or watch as their competition takes advantage of new capabilities. Not surprisingly, the product that is the newest disrupter may, in a year or so, be the target of new disrupters.

FedEx Ground scans each package 14 to 16 times as it moves through delivery points.

FedEx's annual technology budget is $1 billion.

disruptive technology
A new technology that displaces an existing technology.

The Natural Environment

Changes in the natural environment constitute a third force exerting pressures on businesses. Air and water pollution are still a vital concern, even though the "point-source" origin of these pollutants is no longer the most significant source. Automobiles and homes have become the most significant threat to the health of our air and water. Greenhouse gas levels have raised global warming concerns. Household consumption levels threaten to overflow landfills, endanger drinking water supplies, and fuel a demand for agricultural products that may cause deforestation half a world away. Businesses now assess

Environmental impact from businesses is probably impossible to eliminate completely, but progressive businesses have begun to include their potential impact and its costs in their decision making.

om *ADVANTAGE*   Kinko's—Grace under Pressure

As pressures from globalization, disruptive technologies, and environmental concerns stretch some companies to their limits of flexibility, Kinko's continues to adapt. Purchased by FedEx in February of 2003, Kinko's expects to continue under its current mission and core values. Kinko's, by any definition, is a huge consumer of resources. The power to keep a store running is equivalent to that used by 23 homes. The firm estimates that it uses 32 million sheets of paper per day, 60,000 tons per year (that's 10.5 square miles of forest).

Kinko's has nine core value statements, ranging from acceptance of responsibility for its actions to customer service excellence and teamwork, but one in particular stands out as evidence of its concern for the environment:

Community and environment: We strive to help and improve the communities where we work and live. We are concerned about the environment and promote the use of recyclable products and renewable energy.

Kinko's has restricted stores so that only its busiest remain open 24 hours per day. Even though costs are higher, in 2003 it purchased 10 percent of its energy from geothermal, solar, and wind sources.

Source: http://www.kinkos.com, March 26, 2004; "Can This Copy Shop Go Green," *Fast Company,* March 2004, p. 33.

The FedEx Envelope is made of 100-percent recycled material. FedEx Paks are made of 25 percent recycled Tyvek and can be returned to the manufacturer for recycling.

environmental impact as part of their decision-making processes. They have begun to accept the fact that sustainable use patterns must be developed for many of our resources, including process inputs as far-ranging as timber, fossil fuels, and fish.

Minimizing environmental impact has numerous implications for a business. Sometimes it increases processing costs in the short term. Sometimes it means that what appears to be a prime location from one perspective really isn't acceptable. Sometimes it opens new markets for "greener" products and actually gives the firm a competitive advantage over firms that haven't addressed these issues.

Regional Pressures

In addition to global forces, regional pressures also influence business decisions. Included among these pressures are population growth and land development in rural areas. In some parts of the country there are concerns about maintaining the levels of undisturbed forests or wildlife habitat. In other parts of the country, such as the Midwest, there are concerns about the loss of farmland and the family farm. In the West, there are concerns about water use and water rights. In large cities there are health worries related to the number of smog days. Clearly, businesses have begun to recognize their role in a larger natural system and are learning how to minimize the negative impact on that system. The importance of these issues for future decisions can only be expected to increase.

Business Outputs: Products and Services

In today's economy, it is impossible to completely separate service-producing industries (traditionally known as "services") from product-producing businesses (traditionally known as "manufacturers"). Successful firms have recognized that potential customers do not compartmentalize value that way. Customers look at the total package, which includes aspects of both services and products. Failure to recognize this greatly reduces a firm's ability to compete. Studies by the American Society for Quality (ASQ) confirm this perspective. Since 1994, despite significant improvement in product quality, overall customer satisfaction has continued to drop, leaving no doubt that the service aspects of doing business are not meeting expectations. From a competitive standpoint, it means that providing a high-quality product is necessary, but not sufficient, to effectively compete.[4]

Despite the integrated nature of business outputs and the difficulty in defining a business as a service or a manufacturer, it is important to understand that business outputs *can* be defined distinctly as either a service or a product. Even though these components are perceived by the customer as one entity, they are often produced separately.

Products

Products are *things*. They're tangible. They can be seen, they can be touched, they can be counted, they can be measured, and they can be stored for later use. They are produced by manufacturers. The fact that products are tangible has many management implications, most of them advantageous to managers.

Because a product is tangible, its quality can be measured in a relatively straightforward manner before a customer has a chance to examine it. The function of the product can be measured and actually tested to make sure it works properly, allowing management to avoid exposing customers to poor quality. Electronic products are tested upon completion. Automobiles are examined for defects. Clothing is inspected for flaws in the fabric. The defective product is separated from the good products and is either fixed or destroyed.

A completed product can be stored in finished-goods inventory until needed, or it can be shipped anywhere in the world for use. Some products are stored for only a short time before being consumed (some food, pharmaceuticals, stylish clothing, and newspapers, for example), but others have an extremely long shelf life (furniture, books, and toys, for example). When products can be stored for later use, their actual rate of production does not have to match the rate of demand in the short term. Matching output rate to a fluctuating demand is difficult, particularly when materials have to be ordered in advance and employees have to be hired and trained in advance. The ability to store products is important to production management.

When a product is purchased, the customer typically has no idea of the conditions associated with its production. She doesn't care if processes are noisy, if they smell bad, or if the machines are dirty. It's the outcome of those processes that matters. The finished product is evaluated in terms of quality, but the process used to create it isn't. As consumers become more aware of production, however, they have also become more concerned. Consumers were shocked, for example, when they found out that certain clothing items they wore were being manufactured by children and in unacceptable conditions. In some cases, the companies that purchased the goods weren't even aware of the conditions in which they were manufactured. Issues such as employee exploitation and impact on environment have begun to interest consumers. Attributes such as the friendliness of the employee or the ambiance of the factory, however, make no difference.

Services

Services are intangible. They can't be touched or counted or examined the way a product can. They can't be stored for later use. Services are tasks that are done for the customer or done to the customer. They can't be examined or tested for quality before the customer gets them. In fact, they are often produced in a process that the customer is actually a part of. Sometimes it is the customer that is actually processed. The intangibility and customer involvement create a situation that can be quite difficult to manage. In a service, the customer *does* care about the production process because he spends time in it. The process can be as important as the outcome. The process utilized to entertain a customer at a theme park matters a great deal. The process a retailer uses to sell products defines the quality of service a customer perceives. The process a financial consultant uses to plan investments for a client matters because she is a player in that process.

A close match between the output rate and the demand rate is critical for services because people aren't willing to wait for a process to catch up with them. Access to an online retailer, for example, must be immediate or the customer will click on an alternative. A seat on an airplane must be available when a customer wants it or he'll simply buy a ticket on a competing airline. If either business has idle server capacity or empty seats at a particular time, it can't store that capacity for later use.

Unfortunately for managers of services, service quality cannot be determined until after the fact. For customers, this means that they're exposed to poor quality service more often than they're exposed to poor quality products. Unlike manufacturing managers, who can "scrap" or "rework" defective products, service managers must attempt a "recovery" when customers are exposed to quality failures. When a restaurant finds out that a customer is dissatisfied, management attempts the recovery by providing complimentary drinks or a gift certificate for free meals at a later date.

Customers place higher expectations on the employees in services because they are often face to face with them. When the customer watches a service production process and is involved in it, expectations for "special treatment" are common. A rule of thumb is that the greater the customer contact, the greater the expectation for customization, and the more difficult it is to maintain efficient processes. Banking by ATM, phone, and online removes customers from direct contact with bank personnel. For students, online registration has improved the efficiency of that process by removing direct student contact. The need to meet varied expectations and customize the service can make the management of a service more difficult and customer expectations harder to meet. Many services have removed service processes from customer access to increase productivity. Exhibit 1.4 summarizes the characteristics of products and services.

As can be seen in Exhibit 1.5, business outputs often blend product and service components. For example, you might order a product directly from a manufacturer, but along with that product comes a lot of services. Dell Computer Corporation provides an excellent example of a manufacturer that has blended products and services. A customer buys a computer directly from Dell and receives services as well. One is fast delivery. The second is on-site support. The customer can also buy additional services, such as extended support. Dell's success, particularly in quantity purchases for businesses and schools, is not dependent solely on the quality of its products but can also be traced directly to its reputation for after-the-sale support.

For many traditional product-oriented companies, managers are finding that good service not only helps sell products but can also be profitable. Auto companies dramatically increased incentives to buyers in 2001 in response to declining sales during the economic downturn, resulting in record sales. They expected a sharp decline in 2002 and hoped to balance that decline by improved used car sales, which actually have higher margins than new cars. The economic slowdown resulted in customers keeping cars longer. Those older cars needed more service. At large dealer chains, repairs and service part sales made up 10 to 12 percent of revenues but created up to 35 percent of the net profits.[5]

EXHIBIT 1.4	Summary of Product and Service Output Differences	
	Products	**Services**
	Products are tangible.	Services are intangible.
	Products are easy to measure.	Services are difficult to measure.
	Products can be stored for later use.	Services can't be stored for later use.
	Products can be checked for conformance to quality prior to customer receiving them.	Services can't be checked for conformance to quality prior to customer receiving them.
	Production processes for products are relatively unimportant to customers.	Production processes for services are very important to customers.
	Producers of defective products can repair or scrap the defects.	Producers of defective services must attempt to recover to retain the customer.

Continuum of Service and Product Producers		EXHIBIT 1.5
Produces Services Only	**Produces a Balance of Products and Services**	**Produces Products with Very Few or No Services**
Examples:	*Examples:*	*Examples:*
Advertising firm	Retailer	Furniture manufacturer
Brokerage firm	Computer manufacturer	Paint manufacturer
Bank	Automobile manufacturer	Grocery product manufacturer
Prison	Restaurant	Steel mill
Tanning salon	Car rental agency	
Hair stylist	Landscaping firm	
	Printing shop	

Service management tends to follow manufacturing management in adopting new management approaches. Productivity and quality improvement efforts initiated in manufacturing often move to the service sector. In the past decade it has become increasingly common for manufacturers to outsource labor-intensive aspects of production to countries with cheaper labor. That has been made possible by the ease of transporting products, compared to the difficulty in transporting services. Services have begun to follow suit. Labor markets in the United States have increased the incentive for U.S. services to seek labor from outside the country.

An excellent example of this trend is the **maquiladoras**. Maquiladoras have traditionally been known as foreign-owned manufacturing (usually assembly) plants in Mexico. A company establishes a plant in Mexico, usually just across the border from the United States. Since the plant is company-owned, the company could import the components into Mexico duty-free and then export finished products back to the United States. Maquiladoras have been very popular as a means of lowering labor expenses in a variety of manufacturing industries, including automotive, electronics, and garment manufacturing. They have also been controversial in that some companies' primary motivation to manufacture in Mexico has been to avoid Environmental Protection Agency (EPA)

maquiladoras
Foreign-owned (typically U.S.-owned) manufacturing plants in Mexico.

For many businesses, classification as a "service" or a "manufacturer" is difficult. For KFC, which is typically classified as a service, the product is also very important to the customer. A customer could just as easily be dissatisfied about the meal as the service offered along with it.

requirements. The use of maquiladoras extended into the service sector and by early 2000, approximately 50,000 Mexican workers were employed by service maquiladoras. Outsourcing of services has since moved to India and the Philippines, and even to China. Providing back-office support services such as call center management and other services for retailers, financial services, telecom, and software companies is commonplace.[6]

Different Types of Customers

The impact customers have on a business is enormous. After all, they determine the value of what the business produces. Unfortunately, what's valuable to one is worthless to another. For a successful business, knowing which is which is critical. One important way to categorize customers is by their use of the product or service being sold.

Businesses buy material goods for their own consumption, and also as components used in the products or services they sell. The materials they consume, such as cleaning compounds, lubricants, or machine repair parts, are known as maintenance, repair, and operating (MRO) inventory. Component parts, such as memory chips for a computer manufacturer, also become part of the company's inventory. A business also purchases services. It might contract with a firm to provide security, hire a consulting firm to design an information system, or hire a transportation company to deliver its products. Business-to-business transactions have become such a major part of the economy that they have taken on an acronym—B2B. Business-to-consumer transactions have been tagged B2C.

Consumers buy products and services that they utilize in their day-to-day activities. Businesses have very different uses for what they buy than a consumer would have. Consequently, they define the value of products and services differently than consumers would. In some cases, a firm might produce a product or service for a business as well as for a consumer. Despite the fact that the product or service might be the same for each type of customer, the business customer and the consumer would still define value differently. Exhibit 1.6 shows a comparison of companies that produce different types of outputs and serve different types of customer.

EXHIBIT 1.6	Business Output/Customer Matrix			
		Business Output		
		Predominantly Services	**Products and Services**	**Predominantly Products**
Customer Type	**Consumers (B2C)**	*Examples:* Mayo Clinic Disney World Time Warner Cable	*Examples:* General Motors Dominos Pizza Amazon	*Examples:* Coca-Cola Panasonic Mattel Kraft Longaberger
	Consumers and Businesses (B2C and B2B)	*Examples:* Staples UPS Verizon Wireless CitiBank Ebay	*Examples:* Dell Computers Hewlett-Packard General Electric	*Examples:* Herman-Miller SanDisk Linksys
	Businesses (B2B)	*Examples:* TQL Logistics iX Web Hosting Accenture Covisint	*Examples:* Ariba PeopleSoft Cintas Flextronics	*Examples:* Delphi Xerox Opticon

Operations, Other Business Functions, and You

A business environment characterized by speed and flexibility cannot afford to be constrained by the boundaries imposed by traditional departmental barriers. Business decisions must be made quickly and made from an enterprise perspective, considering implications for all aspects of the business. For this very reason, companies increasingly use cross-functional teams on tasks such as new product and service development, systems implementation, and process improvement. These companies have become more organized around their products and services, and less organized around the functional areas within their organizations. For many firms, responsibilities are dispersed among a variety of staff. It is not at all uncommon for someone with financial expertise to be involved in what have traditionally been marketing issues or for someone with marketing expertise to be involved in quality management.

As businesses continue to break down functional barriers, functional experts will continue to take on broadened responsibilities that relate to business processes, rather than department functions. For business functions like operations, marketing, finance, accounting, and information systems, departmental affiliations will continue to become less meaningful than the needs of the organization. The functional responsibilities and tasks must still be accomplished, because they are part of an important business process. That process, however, will be the focal point instead of the department. As these trends continue we will see all business functions take on new shapes and new roles in the business.

Value derives from processes. A process is an accretion of resources. The resources necessary to create a value-adding process often come from different parts of the business. Amazon.com provides an excellent example of how differentiating capabilities emerge from bringing together very different resources. Amazon's ability to provide a book (or other product) at a very low price and do it very quickly sets it apart from competitors. There is no need to go elsewhere, because if the book exists, Amazon can get it. An examination of all the processes required to take the order, process the credit card information, and deliver the book to the customer shows that resources from many different parts of the company have to come into play: marketing and information technology experts develop the customer interface; financial, accounting, and computer experts develop the mechanisms necessary to handle the credit card transactions online; purchasing and contract experts develop relationships with suppliers; logistics and operations experts design and maintain the outgoing flow of products. Amazon could be broken into a series of small processes, but they must all interact with each other. Without any single piece, the differentiating capability doesn't exist.

The interaction among processes makes it particularly important for all managers to have a basic knowledge of all business functions. As transaction speeds increase, and as companies interact more directly with customers, the need to see across boundaries and recognize potentially valuable resources will increase. An employee who can recognize resources in other areas of the business that can be combined with resources of his own to form new processes has mastered one of the most difficult and valuable aspects of new product and service development. Without the knowledge of how all functions interact in the business, ideas will be limited to very narrow applications of resources. There is little remaining "low-hanging fruit" in the area of new products and services. The lack of an enterprise perspective limits the firm's potential for success, and it limits the career potential of its employees as well. A business student's differentiating capability, which separates her from her classmates in the eyes of a recruiter, will not be her major. Even when she compares her preparation to that of any other business major, the difference is only 10 to 15 percent of the courses taken. The differentiating capability is something special: Any ability a student has that enables her to perceive the business from a broader perspective will set her apart.

CHAPTER SUMMARY

This chapter introduced operations management as a critical component of the successful management of a business. Operations management is the management of productive resources that are used to create salable products or services. It is that sale of products and services that provides an opportunity for profitability.

The Resource/Profit Model was introduced as an organizing framework of operations concepts. The model provides three primary elements. The first, foundations for success, consists of value, strategy and value, and processes. The second, components of value, consists of cost, quality, and timeliness. The third, managing resources used to create value, consists of demand forecasting, followed by inventory, logistics, capacity, facilities, and workforce. These resource management topics are enhanced by three integrative frameworks: supply chain management, lean systems, and constraint management.

An overview of the Resource/Profit Model shows that profitability results from the creation of value and a strategy for maintaining a link to the customers who define it. The creation of value at a level that exceeds the cost of creating it provides the potential for profitability. Operations management has responded to and will continue to respond to four dominant environmental forces: competition resulting from the globalization of business, increasing levels of communication and competition brought about by the Internet and other disruptive technologies, the impact of the natural environment, and regional pressures that have varying impacts on business decisions.

Two business outputs—products and services—are critical to the management of operations resources. Effective operations management must acknowledge the differences and similarities of those environments. Two different types of customer—B2B and B2C—must be recognized because of the differences in their expectations and needs.

Last, but certainly not last in importance, the importance of operations familiarity—and familiarity with all aspects of the enterprise—is discussed as an important way for the business student to differentiate himself or herself from other students. It is an employee's ability to make the best decisions for the business, after all, that is most highly prized.

KEY TERMS

capabilities, 14	logistics, 18
capacity, 19	maquiladoras, 25
constraint management, 17	mass production, 8
cost, 15	processes, 14
craft production, 8	profitability, 13
disruptive technology, 21	quality, 15
facilities, 19	strategy, 14
integrative management framework, 17	timeliness, 15
inventory, 18	value, 13
lean systems, 17	workforce, 19

REVIEW QUESTIONS

1. Why is it important for students with any business major to have a basic understanding of all aspects of a business?

2. What does operations management mean?

3. Describe the Resource/Profit Model. What are the foundations for success? What are the components of value? What resources are managed to create value?

4. What is the relationship between value created and profitability?

5. How does cost affect the amount of profitability that results from value?

6. Why do resources alone not create value for a business?

7. Who ultimately defines the value of a product or service?

8. What are "differentiating capabilities"?

9. Provide an example of how inventory, capacity, facilities, and workforce can each contribute to value.

10. What are integrative management frameworks? What do they provide for managers?

11. How do products and services differ?

12. What is the management impact of the intangibility of services?

13. Why are most manufacturers also typically service providers?

14. What do B2B and B2C mean? Why is the difference important?

DISCUSSION AND EXPLORATION

1. How has the speed of transactions made possible by the Internet had a positive impact on your life? What are some of the ways the impact has been negative?

2. Identify a product or service that you frequently purchase. Identify all of its value components. Which are the most important? Which are you are most frequently dissatisfied with?

3. Examine a process on your campus that you are familiar with. What steps in it do not add value? What are the costs, for the customer, associated with these steps? What are the costs for the university? In what ways would the process be improved if the non-value-adding steps were removed?

4. Identify and describe a business you are familiar with that has had to adapt to increasing levels of competition. Where has the competition come from? How has the business changed in response? Have its changes been successful?

5. Identify and describe a business you are familiar with that has had to adapt to increasing competition from an Internet-based business. How has it changed? Has it been successful?

6. How do most students prioritize cost, quality, and timeliness for services? For products?

7. Consider a recent significant purchase you made. Beyond the price, what other costs were associated with that purchase? Did they affect your purchase decision?

8. What changes have you observed in products and services that indicate pressures on business to have less impact on the natural environment? Have these changes had an impact on your purchase decisions?

9. Describe a business whose major focus is difficult to classify as either a product or a service. What makes it difficult to categorize? Which parts of the business would be the most difficult to manage—producing the services or producing the products? Why?

10. Identify a product or service that would likely be purchased by both consumers and businesses. How might the B2B and the B2C customers differ in terms of how each defines value? What components of value would be the most important for each?

11. Exhibit 1.6 provides examples of businesses that fit into the business output/customer matrix. Identify two businesses with which you are not familiar that provide products and/or services to businesses. Explain what each does.

ENDNOTES

1. "Customers Move into the Driver's Seat," *BusinessWeek*, October 4, 1999, pp. 103–106.
2. "People Who Need People," *Wall Street Journal*, February 12, 2001, p. R20.
3. "Why Some Sony Gear Is Made in Japan—By Another Company," *Wall Street Journal*, June 14, 2001, pp. A1, A10.
4. Deloitte Research, *Making Customer Loyalty Real* (New York: Deloitte & Touche, 1999).
5. "Can Car Dealers Keep the Profits Rolling?" *BusinessWeek*, January 14, 2002, p. 37.
6. "Outsourcing: Make Way for China," *BusinessWeek*, August 4, 2003.

LEARNING ACTIVITIES   www.mhhe.com/opsnow3e

Visit the Online Learning Center (www.mhhe.com/opsnow3e) for additional resources. Content varies by chapter, and includes

- Business Tours
- OM on Site
- Readings
- Resources
- Excel Tutors
- Interactive Case Models
- Reel Operations Video Clips
- Additional Advanced Problems
- Self-Assessment Quizzes
- Glossary

SELECTED REFERENCES

Hammer, M., and Stanton, S. "Deep Change: How Operational Innovation Can Transform Your Company,"*Harvard Business Review*, April 1, 2004, Vol. 82, No. 4.

Hayes, R. H., Pisano, G. P., Upton, D. M., and Wheelwright, S. C. *Operations, Strategy, and Technology: Pursuing the Competitive Edge*. Hoboken, N.J.: John Wiley & Sons, 2004.

Ready, D. A. "Leading at the Enterprise Level," *Sloan Management Review*, Spring 2004, Vol. 45, No. 33.

Sawhney, M., Balasubramanian, S., and Krishnan, V. "Creating Growth with Services," *Sloan Management Review*, Winter 2004, Vol. 45, No. 2.

VIDEO CASE 1.1

Operations Management at St. Alexius Medical Center

Based on Video 1 on the Student DVD

St. Alexius Medical Center has eight Centers of Excellence, one of which is their Pediatrics Center. Like all businesses, the St. Alexius Pediatrics Center must bring inventory, capacity, facilities, and workforce resources together to create value in ways that patients feel is superior to alternative pediatrics treatment centers. St. Alexius has designed a new Pediatrics Center facility to meet this challenge.

1. In their study of other hospitals that was done prior to the Operations Plan, what did they find out about customer expectations? How does this link to St. Alexius's creation of value?

2. In the new design, what are the considerations being made to better manage inventory and suppliers, capacity, the facilities, and the workforce?

3. Are the value components of cost, quality, and timeliness important for the St. Alexius Pediatrics Center? How would patients (and their parents) define the components of value? How will the new facility enhance these components?

4. Like other businesses, changes are often driven by technological advances. What technologies are driving changes at St. Alexius?

5. Examine the St. Alexius Medical Center Web site at www.stalexius.org. Read the "About St. Alexius" information and describe how, in general, St. Alexius characterizes itself.

CHAPTER 2

Profitability: Business Success from Operations Success

LEARNING OBJECTIVES

- Understand and describe the concepts of value and profitability.

- Understand and describe the effects operations management has on profitability measures.

- Describe economic value added (EVA).

- Calculate the average level of inventory from a delivery pattern.

- Understand productivity measures for resources.

- Calculate utilization and efficiency.

- Explain the importance of customer relationships.

- Distinguish between local and global productivity measures.

- Identify conflicts between productivity measures.

- Describe how to improve productivity measures.

- Set up and complete a decision tree analysis.

- Describe the balanced scorecard approach.

PROFITABILITY IN THE DISCOUNT AIRLINE INDUSTRY

As the major "legacy" airlines have struggled for profitability since September 11, 2001, discount airlines such as Southwest and JetBlue in the United States, Ryanair in Ireland, and EasyJet in the United Kingdom have taken market share and recorded profits. The concept of a discount airline is a bit of a misnomer, though, because quite often the legacy airline fares are as cheap as those of the discount airlines. Profitability, however, is a different matter. The discount airlines are more profitable, but how can that be?

Discount airlines are more profitable because they use resources more effectively. By resources, we don't mean people. Labor costs are no cheaper for the discount airlines. They use their planes more effectively. How do they do this? There are several ways. First, rather than fly their planes seven or eight hours a day, they have their planes in the air nine or ten hours a day. That's an increase of 25 percent, which translates into a 25 percent increase in the return on assets for those planes. They're in the air more, which means the airline needs fewer of them to achieve the same return.

Beyond simply flying the planes more, the discount airlines are structured to fly what are called "point-to-point" (pt-pt) routes. This contrasts with the more typical hub-and-spoke structure used by the larger airlines. Pt-pt routes provide several advantages. First of all, the shortest distance between two points is a straight line. Travelers flying a hub-and-spoke airline rarely fly one leg. They fly to the hub and then on to their final destination, usually nothing like a straight line. The pt-pt routes mean that passengers usually fly a single leg. This eliminates costly baggage transfers and all of the resources necessary to accomplish that function. It also helps keep planes in the air more of the time by avoiding larger airports.

In addition to planes being in the air a greater percentage of the time, while they're in the air, more of their seats are full. The percentage of the seats that are full, known as the "load factor," means that there are more paying customers on each flight.

These approaches have been so successful that the large airlines have gone beyond noticing it and have decided to copy it.

On many flights seats have more legroom, and may have their own video monitors for satellite TV, MP3s, and multiplayer interactive games. On United's Ted, passengers can also purchase food and access TV monitors. The airlines try to promote an image that is more fun and personal and provide a sense of individualized service, reminiscent of other discount airlines.

When a business is having a difficult time maintaining profitability, it doesn't take much to be pushed over the edge. For Delta and Northwest, the increase in fuel costs that followed Hurricane Katrina in 2005 was the final straw. Delta filed for Chapter 11 protection on September 14, 2005. Northwest filed only a few minutes after Delta.

Source: Scott Kirsner, "Song's Startup Flight Plan," *Fast Company*, June 2003; *Air Transport World*, April 2004, Vol. 41, No. 4; "JetBlue Skies Ahead," *CIO Magazine*, July 2002; National Public Radio, Morning Edition, March 30, 2004; http://www.flysong.com, March 31, 2004; http://www.flyted.com, March 31, 2004; http://news.delta.com/article_display.cfm?article_id = 9861, accessed 12/12/05; http://money.cnn. com/2005/09/14/news/fortune500/northwest/index.htm, accessed 12/12/05.

No matter which functional area of business one chooses to specialize in, the profitability of the business is the overriding measure of performance. It is the end that justifies the money invested in all of the firm's resources. While the "whats" and "hows" of business drive many decisions, profitability is the "why," and without it, nothing else matters.

The Link between Value and Investment Results

There may be many reasons for the existence of a business, but none are as fundamental as profitability. Without it, no other objectives can be achieved, because the business will die. The primary objective of this chapter is to put operations into the context in which it exists: that of using resources to generate value, which can be sold at a profit. The chapter defines profitability measures as they relate to operations management and by sampling resource productivity measures that link directly to profitability.

It is no coincidence that the content of this chapter will be familiar to students of finance. Although not often emphasized in finance texts, operations management is the context of many financial decisions because it provides the means to accomplish the financial goals of the firm. Operations management is not a set of independent decision-making tools. It has links to all other business functions because of its position at the heart of the business—the creation of value.

The owner of any investment expects a financial return. It doesn't matter if the investment is a share of stock, a rental property, or a restaurant. The money is tied up; if it wasn't, it could be invested somewhere else. The same holds for any part of that business. For example, when a restaurant owner invests in a new computer system, a financial return is expected, because the money could have been invested in a new stove, new dishes, or any number of other functional assets. A business invests in resources—inventory, equipment, facilities, and staff—and expects a financial return that is acceptable.

opportunity cost

But what is acceptable? Simply earning a financial return on the investment isn't enough. The investor must gauge the potential return of the investment compared to what could be earned on alternative investments. Just as mutual fund managers utilize various measures to assess investment productivity for stocks or bonds, operations managers use various measures to monitor and assess investment productivity for their resources.

Like any other financial investments, operations resources are associated with varying degrees of uncertainty. Higher potential gains are often accompanied by higher potential losses. For operations resources, a key source of uncertainty is **net present value (NPV),** which cannot be known before the fact.

> **net present value (NPV)**
> The difference between the market value of a product or service and the cost of creating it.

The NPV is the sum of the discounted cash flows received or disbursed over the life of the investment. The cash flows are discounted to take into account the time value of the money received and spent. It is the difference between the ultimate worth to the customer (as determined by the customer's perception of value) and the cost of adding that value. If there were no uncertainty concerning cash to be disbursed and no uncertainty concerning cash to be received, the business would be a classic example of a "sure thing." But there is no sure thing. Businesses do not typically go bankrupt because they erred in their calculation of the NPV. They go bankrupt because their estimate of future cash disbursals and/or receipts was wrong. Operations generates many of the costs through the creation of products and services. Through the creation of the products and services, operations also generates the receipts. An example provides some possible reasons why this happens.

A small retail sporting goods chain has six stores. The owner is considering expanding into the snow ski and snowboarding market. In addition to the floor space and fixtures

om ADVANTAGE   Profitability at Lowe's

While cost cutting and driving down the denominator of profitability measures works in some cases, it's hard to argue with a strategy that increases sales. Lowe's, long in a fierce competition with Home Depot, is showing how more knowledge of the customer can increase sales. Market research convinced Lowe's management that 80 percent of home improvement decisions were initiated by women. In response, Lowe's committed to making their stores neater and brighter and began carrying more designer brands. Lowe's profits rose 28 percent in 2003, and sales rose 18 percent. An investment in 100 shares of Lowe's stock in 1961 for $12.21 per share would have grown to 48,000 shares by 2004 because of stock splits and dividends. In 2001 that investment would have grown to nearly $3.5 million.

Lowe's continued its success as it responded to customer wants and needs. In the final quarter of 2005, Lowe's earnings jumped by 37 percent, compared to 23 percent for Home Depot. Some credit Lowe's success to the advantage

of being Number 2, as opposed to Number 1. The number 2 competitor in the market has an advantage in terms of being able to react and respond to number 1. Number 1 is always the target.

Source: www.lowes.com; "How Lowe's Hammers Home Depot," *BusinessWeek*, April 5, 2004; "Second-Mover Advantage," *Fortune*, March 20, 2006, pp. 20–21.

required for the stock, expanding into that market requires significant investment in equipment for mounting bindings and for tuning skis (waxing, sharpening edges, repairing, and so on). Personnel must be trained to correctly fit, mount, adjust, and tune equipment, and that will be expensive and ongoing. The upside, however, is that sales of the equipment are expected to be good, and sales of related clothing and accessories should also increase as new customers come into the store. There are alternative uses for the money, however. The two oldest stores could use a general upgrading in appearance and fixtures. The entire chain is running on a seven-year-old inventory system that does not take advantage of point-of-sale (POS) data collection. The owner doesn't have the cash reserves or credit line to do everything. How can the owner decide what to do?

When making these types of decisions, the owner must estimate the value each alternative will have and estimate what the cash flows will be. Value, as perceived by the customer, will determine what the financial return will be. What will sales of ski-related products be, over time? What additional sales will be generated by remodeling the two oldest stores? What additional sales will be generated by better item availability, more accurate and timely orders, and reduced stockouts made possible by POS data collection? These questions are not too different from those a broker might consider when trying to decide between recommending General Electric and Procter & Gamble stock to clients, but these questions are answered by operations managers. The question is, What is the expected return, over time, and what is the value of that return in present dollars?

Certainly the sporting goods store alternatives have been simplified. For example, in addition to adding to customer perception of value, some alternatives might result in a reduction of costs for operations. A remodeled store might need fewer repairs and less maintenance. A better inventory management system might actually reduce inventory levels, reducing inventory carrying costs.

Manufacturers of products must perform similar analyses when trying to decide if a particular product improvement should be made. For example, should a miniature global positioning system (GPS) be added as standard equipment in a sport utility vehicle so that drivers will know exactly where they are? Or would customers see equal value in a compass that merely told them which way their car was pointing? The expected return, as dictated by customers' perception of added value, must be compared to the cost. The cost will be the result of the materials and processes used to include the GPS. Is the return positive and, if so, is the return on the investment better than the alternatives?

Investments in operations require that money be spent to purchase, maintain, and power a particular resource and train workers to use it. Maybe the resource is a machine, maybe it's additional facilities or remodeled facilities, maybe it's a skill obtained through training. Many current and future expenditures contribute to the total cost for that investment. In most situations, the business is capable of determining what the costs will be in advance. They typically have more difficulty predicting what *value* the customer will put on a product or service prior to its design and production. Market research provides some information, but forecasting for a new product or service is always a very subjective process. For that matter, forecasting for *anything* is fraught with error. For a product that has been around a while and has an established market, that uncertainty is somewhat reduced, but even then, the value can decline as competing products become more popular.

Managers cannot escape the customer's perception of value as being the most critical component of success for any operations investment *and* one of the most difficult to predict. That's the business's uncertainty. Notice that care has been taken here to use the word "uncertainty" rather than "risk." Risk is measurable uncertainty. Businesses have the ability to measure some uncertainties, but the uncertainty associated with customer perception of value is very difficult to accurately determine.

Usually an investment decision in an operations resource is more complicated than the sporting goods store example. A business cannot assume, for example, that whether it makes a particular choice or not, its competitors will maintain the status quo. Looking back at the retail sporting goods example, it should be acknowledged that the store's competitors have options as well. If the owner of the sporting goods chain decides not to enter the snow ski market, and neither does the competitor, the owner can reasonably assume that the customer base will remain constant. But what happens if he doesn't enter the ski market and his biggest competitor does? Will he lose customers? What if he decides not to remodel the oldest store and his competitor opens a brand new store nearby? What if he doesn't invest in a new inventory system, but his competitor does and is therefore able to promise 48-hour availability on any item currently not in stock in the store?

The estimation of the customer's perception of value must recognize that customers also make comparative judgments. The value of a product or service is always related to

About 75 percent of airlines' revenues comes from passengers, 15 percent from cargo, and the other 10 percent from other related services.

Decisions to expand retail services into specialty areas are challenging for managers. Risks are high because of the costs and uncertain outcomes involved. In this small ski shop located within a large sporting goods store, managers must make sure sales personnel are trained in providing advice and in fitting equipment.

om *ADVANTAGE*   Profitability Requires Adaptation

Many industries must cope with short product life cycles, fast rates of technological change, and thin profit margins. Disk drive manufacturers face all three of these challenges and more. As competition has pushed them, they have increased the capacity of storage devices to the point that they've exceeded the needs of the typical PC user. Disk drives have reached "commodity" status, so costs have been cut, prices have been cut, and profit margins are slim. R&D costs, however, remain high. Now, in order to stay profitable, the manufacturers are faced with finding demand for the high-capacity drives they have created.

The need to find new markets for high-capacity storage devices has caused manufacturers to look to the future. They have had to wait for a new technology to generate the need for more storage space. What started with Napster and has evolved into the iPod has created a surge in consumer desire to store MP3s. New consumer devices, from digital TVs, to MP3 players, to personal digital assistants (PDAs), offer potential future applications for high-capacity storage devices.

With high R&D costs, profitability rests on increasing sales volumes. One of the biggest potential applications is TV. Building digital video storage capacity directly into a TV set is not as easy as it might appear. The added complexity causes a TV to more closely resemble a PC.

As the technology for small hard drives expands, the demand for them may drop as flash memory technology moves forward. Flash memory offers faster access times than a mini hard drive and is more shock resistant but is currently more expensive to produce. As flash memory volumes increase, costs can be expected to drop.

Looking to the future for profitability enhancement forces a disk drive manufacturer to be anticipating what new features or characteristics might be needed. Reducing the noise made by the disk drive has been one priority. The result has been millions of dollars spent on acoustic improvement. The other issue for disk drive manufacturers that hope to utilize their designs in consumer products is to make them robust enough to handle the shocks they must be able to withstand as PDAs are dropped in briefcases or carried around in pockets. It is in this area that they lose advantage to flash drives. Disk drive manufacturers are also struggling to create devices that run cooler, eliminating the heat generation of disk drives.

For disk drive manufacturers, profitability requires investing in the appropriate R&D while patiently hoping and waiting for someone else to develop a technology that will depend on their type of data storage, while at the same time hoping that the new technology will be more appropriate for hard drives than for flash memory.

Source: "Disk-Drive Makers Have Reached a Profitability Wall—and They're Looking for Ways around It," *Wall Street Journal*, October 15, 2001, p. R21; Cool Tech Zone http://www.cooltechzone.com/index.php?option = content&task = view&id=1787&Itemid=0&limit=1&limitstart=1, accessed December 12, 2005.

---

the alternatives available to customers. If the alternatives change, the value of all competing products changes as well. The decision isn't simply a matter of deciding between making the investment and not making it. It is much more complex, as shown in Exhibit 2.1, which provides some alternative scenarios for the sporting goods store.

Management must try to predict not only how customers will value what the business does, but also how that value will be affected by what competitors decide to do. And they must recognize that competitors are making those same analyses. In even the simplest of scenarios, many predictions are required. Realistically, the decision requires an analysis of even more outcomes because predicting a competitor's actions would include more than one possible act. The difficulty is compounded when more than one competitor is involved.

After a positive investment decision is made, the resource is purchased and put to use. The purchase of the resource doesn't guarantee the expected return on the investment; the return is dependent on how the resource will be used in processes. Just like giving money to a stockbroker, there are no guarantees. The return depends on how the broker uses the money. Thus one important role of managers is to ensure that the value created by processes is at least equal to the initial NPV estimate, thereby providing the necessary return on the investment.

NPV : ROI

Northwest tried to pass airport fees on to its passengers in 2005, but reversed its move when its competitors did not do the same. Airport fees cost Northwest $80 to $100 million each year.

EXHIBIT 2.1	Realistic Cost/Benefit Decision

	Invest in Ski Shop Capabilities		Don't Invest in Ski Shop Capabilities	
	Costs	**Benefits**	**Costs**	**Benefits**
Competitor Moves into Ski Market Also	Risks of failure Costs of equipment Costs of training	Can compete in ski market Opportunity to gain profits from new market	Competitor moves into more favorable competitive position Change in market share and profits	No expenditures on ski shop capabilities
	Costs	**Benefits**	**Costs**	**Benefits**
Competitor Keeps Status Quo	Risks of failure Costs of equipment Costs of training	Great potential for gains of market share Enhanced profit as only suppllier	None	None

Profitability Measures

To earn a profit is the goal of a business enterprise. Even for a not-for-profit organization, covering expenses is critical, and generating enough revenue to make this happen is necessary for the continued viability of the endeavor. Although the goal of earning a profit certainly simplifies the objectives of a business nicely, it falls short as a measure of performance to provide direction for day-to-day decisions.

First, it is difficult to predict the impact daily operations decisions have on profit. There is too much separation between daily decisions and a measure like profit. Managerial accounting has evolved into a system designed to provide that link.

Second, profit alone isn't a measure of investment success. Any measure of investment success must measure the **productivity** of the resources involved. For example, suppose I tell you I have made $500 on an investment. Is that good? You don't know because you don't know how much money was invested. Suppose I tell you I made the $500 on a $1,000 investment. Is that good? You still don't know because without knowing how long it took to gain that $500, you can't evaluate the performance of the investment.

Financial productivity is frequently referred to in terms of profit. The term *profit* is often misused, however. When people say "profit," they often actually mean "net income." Net income provides an absolute measure but lacks the input comparison necessary for a measure of productivity. It doesn't really tell us anything about the productivity of resources. Profitability measures, on the other hand, are measures of the productivity of money. They relate outputs (net income) to inputs. The three most common measures of profitability are **profit margin**, **return on assets**, and **return on equity**. Each compares net income to a particular input and each is a critical measure of the success of operations. Equations 2.1, 2.2, and 2.3 are the formulas for these profitability measures:

productivity
A measure of how well inputs are used by a business, typically the ratio of an output to the input of interest.

profit margin
Profit generated per dollar of sales.

return on assets (ROA)
Profit per dollar of assets.

return on equity (ROE)
Profit per dollar of equity.

$$(2.1) \qquad \text{Profit Margin} = \text{Income/Sales}$$

$$(2.2) \qquad \text{Return on Assets} = \text{Net Income/Total Assets}$$

$$(2.3) \qquad \text{Return on Equity} = \text{Net Income/Total Equity}$$

Before examining each in detail, let's take a closer look at net income, which is used in all three. To determine net income, we start out with net sales, subtract the cost of goods sold, selling and administrative costs, and depreciation, and then subtract interest paid to provide taxable income. Subtracting the taxes gives us net income, as seen in Equation 2.4.

(2.4)

$$\text{Net Income} = \text{Net Sales} - \text{Cost of Goods Sold} \\ - \text{Selling and Administrative Costs} \\ - \text{Depreciation} - \text{Interest Paid} - \text{Taxes}$$

Net income is often expressed on a per-share basis for shares outstanding to give us earnings per share (EPS). As an output measure, it shouldn't be surprising that net income provides a critical measure of success. It is, in fact, *the bottom line*. Without being compared to inputs, however, it doesn't provide us with a sense of how productive our assets were. Now that we have a conceptual understanding of net income, let's examine each of the profitability measures.

Profit Margin

Profit margin tells us how much profit is generated per dollar of sales. It measures the productivity of our entire business. A high profit margin, which is desirable, can result from low expenses relative to sales or high sales relative to expenses. Operations decisions have a significant effect on profit margin by influencing both the numerator and denominator. High levels of sales result from products and services valued highly by customers. The value is created by processes. Processes are at the root of many costs, and they are also key to adding the value that leads to sales. Low costs result from processes that make good use of inventory, capacity, facilities, and workforce. Effective processes can provide a double impact on net income by increasing net sales through value enhancement *while at the same time* decreasing costs of goods sold by using resources productively.

The most immediate way to reduce processing costs relative to sales is by eliminating process steps that do not add value. This action is a significant part of process improvement efforts. By using this approach, costs are reduced but value isn't. Reduction of non-value-adding steps can provide a nice boost to profit margin by increasing net income, but focusing only on cost reduction as a way to increase profit margin can be a mistake. Costs have an absolute minimum—zero. For most firms, the minimum is really a lot more than zero, and trying to squeeze out that extra dollar can take a tremendous amount of effort and may not provide much benefit. And it might result in an actual reduction in value. In addition, the same amount of effort devoted to increasing value and net sales may have a greater impact on the bottom line. The key to increasing sales relative to processing costs is to effectively design and manage processes to create products or services for which the customer is willing to pay more. To do that you must know what the customer wants, produce it, deliver it, and then service it in a way that delights the customer.

Delta, under bankruptcy protection, lost more than $500 million in January and February 2006.

Increasing fuel costs resulted in a fourth quarter 2005 loss of $42 million for JetBlue.

---

om ADVANTAGE   Profitability from Competitors

Generating profitability from investments in research and development has always been a challenge for industries associated with short-life-cycle products. Many find that they can't sell enough volume fast enough to fund the development of future products. Many electronics manufacturers are discovering a way around this dilemma. By selling or licensing their technological achievements to competitors, who then sell them to consumers under their own brands, volume increases, and investments begin to pay off. Motorola sells the entire electronic interior of its most advanced cell phone to 13 other manufacturers. The increased volume allows it to cut prices more quickly and compete better. Philips (Royal Philips Electronics of the Netherlands) supplies circuitry for a full one-third of the world's DVD recorders. Xoceco, a Chinese manufacturer on the other end of this phenomenon, manufactures flat-screen TVs from standardized parts it purchases from other manufacturers.

Source: "Big Picture: Off-the-Shelf Parts Create New Order in TVs, Electronics," *Wall Street Journal,* December 16, 2003, p. A.1; Xoceco Web site: http://www. xm.gov.cn/eng/major/ma011.html, April 8, 2004; http://www.philips.com/.

Financial investment in productive assets, such as those at Disney World, can be staggering. Assets that must provide a financial return include not only those directly related to the visitors' experiences and visible to everyone, but also the supporting facilities and equipment that make the customers' experience enjoyable.

Return on Assets

The second profitability measure, return on assets (ROA), is an indication of profit per dollar of assets. It is the broadest measure of asset productivity. ROA is to operations as an overall GPA is to a student. It measures how well assets are used to generate income. Return on assets is extremely relevant to operations because operations controls an extremely valuable set of assets. While ROA is a critical measure, it does not provide specific direction for improvement, just as a student's overall GPA doesn't provide information useful for directing improvement efforts. If the ROA is lower than desired, a red flag is raised, but management still has to identify those assets not being used to their fullest. More narrowly defined measures of asset productivity are needed to provide more direction and are more useful as an evaluative tool of asset productivity. To carry the GPA analogy further, a student needs to examine grades in individual courses to begin to direct improvement efforts. Then she must look at her grades on exams or homework within those courses to determine where the improvement efforts should be directed.

Return on Equity

Return on equity (ROE) quantifies how well stockholders did during a year by providing a measure of the productivity of *their* investment. ROE is important because providing a good investment for stockholders is important. It is the stockholders' gauge of the effectiveness of *their* investment, which, in turn, becomes *their* evaluation of how well the firm's management utilized its assets. For operations, ROE is not typically used as a performance measure because ROA and profit margin provide more transparent indicators of asset productivity. Ultimately, however, the performance of the operations resources dictates net income, given a fixed amount of equity. Increasing value and reducing costs, once again, increases net income, and increases ROE.

All three profitability measures are important for the business and important for operations. Once again, notice that all have net income in the numerator. Net income is the overriding indicator of the firm's output.

While not-for-profit organizations don't focus on the productivity of their investment using the typical profitability measures examined here, they are often concerned about the amount of money spent on providing their programs or services compared to the amount of money spent on management and administrative expenses. This is also a measure of productivity. The output is the dollars that actually go toward their objective, while the input is the dollar cost of the "overhead" necessary to make that happen. Improved productivity increases the numerator or decreases the denominator in the ratio.

Economic Value Added

A fourth profitability measure that is gaining popularity is **economic value added (EVA)**, also called economic profit (EP). EVA (trademarked by Stern, Stewart Corp.) is the after-tax operating profit minus the annual cost of capital:

$$(2.5) \quad EVA = \frac{\text{Net Operating}}{\text{Profit after Taxes}} - \left(\frac{\text{Average Cost}}{\text{of Capital}} \times \frac{\text{Total Capital}}{\text{Employed}} \right)$$

A positive EVA indicates that the company is creating wealth from its capital. A negative EVA means that it is actually destroying wealth—it ends up worse than it started. Some financial experts recommend that the only way to prevent more fiascoes like Enron is to throw out the traditional earnings per share calculation because it doesn't measure what really matters and encourages managers to do dumb things and replace it with a true measure of economic profit—EVA. The current failure to deduct the cost of equity creates a distortion of earnings that misleads investors.

For most companies, the difficulties associated with using EVA are that the average cost of capital is a *weighted* average. To calculate the weighted average cost of capital, companies consider capital obtained from different sources, including capital obtained from borrowing and capital obtained from issuing stock.

Once the cost of capital is determined, the actual EVA value is easy to determine. Let's look at a simple example. Suppose you decided to start a small business to help you earn money in your spare time. You are able to borrow $3,000 at 8 percent interest. Your EVA will be your net operating profit after taxes, minus the $240 cost of capital (8 percent of $3,000). If your after-tax profit is less than $240, you have not successfully added economic value. The amount of after-tax profit above $240 is your EVA.

EVA is very relevant to operations for the same reasons other profitability measures are relevant to operations. Operations generates many of the costs associated with the after-tax profit. In addition, through value creation, operations generates net income. In addition to the impact on value and costs, financing operations resources creates a demand for capital that has an impact on capital costs.

EVA differs from the other three profitability measures in that it is not a ratio of net income to a business input, but it is an absolute measure of dollars. Examples of industries that use EVA to help guide decisions are mining, pulp and paper, and high-volume manufacturers. All are extremely capital-intensive. For many of them, capital costs include about everything that goes into their businesses: buildings, equipment, inventory, property, and so on. When a company earns greater than a certain after-tax threshold on capital, a positive EVA results. The importance of operations in generating that return should be obvious, given the fact that operations decisions dictate how those buildings, equipment, inventory, and property are used. As EVA is improved, shareholder value is created.

EVA has been used by a variety of firms. Stern Stewart[1] provides the results of a study comparing 66 clients who use EVA to their competitors, and over a five-year span the EVA companies' shares had increased an average of 49 percent above those of competitors. As an example of the breadth of companies using EVA, the study included:

Eli Lilly	Johnson Outdoors
Coca Cola	Bausch & Lomb
Best Buy	Herman Miller

economic value added (EVA)
A productivity measure that indicates whether or not a business is creating wealth from its capital. It is equal to the after-tax operating profit minus the annual cost of capital.

Hershey Foods   Quaker Oats
Spring   Toys R Us
Tupperware   Whirlpool

Employees can improve EVA directly in three different ways. First, they can improve profitability without increasing the investment required. The most frequent use of this method is reducing the costs associated with production processes. Second, they can recommend investments to grow the business; investing in certain technologies, for example, could improve efficiency and therefore improve EVA. And third, they can reduce investments that don't enhance earnings. Reducing inventory is an example of this method. Notice that these efforts would result in positive impact on the other profitability measures as well. All three of these EVA improvement approaches require operations decisions. These direct links between EVA and decisions have resulted in performance incentive plans being directly tied to EVA outcomes.

Profitability from Operations Resources

Processes are derived from grouping resources together. These processes create value. Profitability is generated by selling that value. Without the effective use of resources, value isn't created, and the potential for profitability is lost. Clearly, operations resources are critical to a firm's profitability. Operating resources are often broken into the four broad categories of inventory, capacity, facilities, and workforce.

Measures of how well resources are used are generally thought of as productivity measures, but viewing them as local profitability measures can be enlightening. They provide important insights into how various operations resources contribute to the firm's profitability. Literally hundreds of performance measures are used to evaluate the productivity of these resources. The following sections demonstrate how such measures can be used and how they link to profitability through a common example for each resource group.

Inventory

Inventory consists of products and the components of products sold. Some items, like an inventory of retail items, are sold in the same form they were in when purchased. Others, like the raw material inventory of a manufacturer, are changed substantially before being sold. For services and manufacturers, no other resource group has come under as much scrutiny as inventory in the last 15 years. As Toyota's just-in-time (JIT) or "lean" manufacturing approaches were introduced in the early 1980s, U.S. manufacturers quickly came to realize that excess inventory was a huge drain on the productivity of assets. Many services, including retailers and financial services, followed the manufacturers' lead. They streamlined processes and slashed inventory. They didn't call it JIT, however; they called it "reengineering" and "continuous replenishment." A quick examination of inventory levels during those times reveals levels that look extremely high by today's standards. Before examining the inventory reduction phenomenon, let's look, for a moment, at an example of the use of inventory as an investment.

Best Buy's inventory exists to satisfy demand. If demand for a specific CD player, for example, is 100 units per month, evenly dispersed through the month, Best Buy must receive 100 units per month from its supplier. They might receive 100 units on the first day of the month, or 25 units every Monday (assuming four weeks per month), or 5 units every weekday (assuming five days per week). As long as delivery costs are the same, from the standpoint of meeting a steady demand, it wouldn't matter *when* these units are delivered. From the standpoint of getting a financial return on that investment in inventory, however, it makes a huge difference. Let's suppose they buy each CD player for $200 and sell it for $249. What are the financial implications of different delivery patterns?

Inventory investment varies among different types of businesses, and even among different types of retailers. A retailer of fine wines, for example, would probably have greater investment in inventory than a typical liquor store. Individual bottles could cost hundreds of dollars. A lack of customers would result in slow turnover, and a low return on that inventory investment. A key to success would be obtaining sales volumes necessary to move the inventory. That would require high levels of customer traffic and customers interested in purchasing expensive wines.

If Best Buy were to take delivery and pay for all 100 units on the first day of the month, they have invested $20,000 in inventory at the beginning of the month. If demand is even through the month, the investment drops to zero by the end of the month. The average investment in inventory would be $10,000:

(2.6) $$\text{Average Inventory} = \frac{100 + 0}{2} = 50$$

(2.7) $$\text{Average Inventory Investment} = 50 \times \$200 = \$10,000$$

For that $10,000 investment, which was held, in effect, for the entire month, earnings would be $4,900 (100 units sold and $49 contribution margin on each). That's a 49 percent return (4,900/10,000) in one month. Obviously, when all of the expenses of running the store are included, things won't look as good, but it's still a good return.

What would happen if, instead of one monthly delivery, they took a daily delivery of 5 units every weekday and paid for them immediately? Exhibit 2.2 provides a graphical comparison of these two scenarios. With daily delivery, inventory would start out at 5 units and drop to zero at the end of the day. The average level of inventory would be 2.5 units, or $500:

(2.8) $$\text{Average Inventory} = \frac{5 + 0}{2} = 2.5$$

(2.9) $$\text{Average Inventory Investment} = 2.5 \times \$200 = \$500$$

At the end of the month they would have sold the 100 units and made $4,900 on an average daily investment of $500. That's a 980 percent return in a month, or 20 times what the return was with monthly deliveries. Add to these numbers the fact that the average investment in inventory is $500 instead of $10,000, which yields $9,500 to invest somewhere else. Besides that they don't need as much space to store inventory, *and* the risk of inventory becoming damaged during storage is decreased.

EXHIBIT 2.2	Daily Orders versus Monthly Orders to Meet 100 Unit/Month Demand

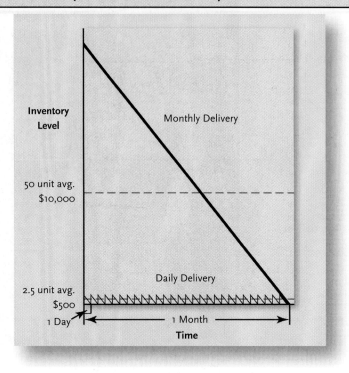

This simplified example demonstrates how powerful inventory productivity's effect on the return on investment can be. For services and manufacturers that turn over millions of dollars in inventory annually, it's no wonder that effective inventory management is a critical responsibility of operations management. Example 2.1 demonstrates how to calculate average inventory levels for different delivery patterns.

inventory turnover
A measure of inventory productivity computed by dividing sales by the average value of inventory.

The most frequently used measure of inventory productivity is known as **inventory turnover,** or "inventory turns." Inventory turnover compares annual sales generated by the inventory (cost of goods sold) to the average level of inventory. The intent is to show how many times the inventory "turns over" as a result of sales. The more frequently it turns over, the greater its productivity.

Inventory turns vary widely from industry to industry and from one business to another. The U.S. average for manufacturing today is around 8 inventory turns.[2] CVS stores averaged 5.2 turns for 2003, while Walgreens had 5.8 turns in 2002.[3] Dell, a manufacturer, had more than 100 turns in 2005.[4] Amazon had 19 turns for 2003.[5] Wal-Mart met its 2002 goal of 6.9, and is targeting 10 for its long-term objective.[6]

In Example 2.1, assuming a 52-week year, we can compare the inventory turns for monthly delivery to the turns for daily delivery. For the monthly delivery pattern, the annual cost of goods sold was $240,000. For the electronics retailer the average level of inventory for the CD player was $10,000 initially. Inventory turnover was 24. For the daily delivery pattern, cost of goods sold was still $240,000, but the average level of inventory was $500, yielding an inventory turn value of 480. To provide a point of reference, in the early 1980s, prior to lean manufacturing approaches, many manufacturers experienced inventory turns of less than 5.

Capacity

Capacity is the capability of workers, machines, plants, servers, or organizations to produce output in a specific period of time. Capacity, particularly that associated with equipment utilized in the production of a service or product, is expensive. Maximizing

Example 2.1

EXCEL TUTOR

Average Inventory Calculations from a Delivery Pattern

A distributor of novelty items has asked a manufacturer of incense sticks to begin daily deliveries instead of weekly. The manufacturer currently delivers 800 cases each Monday. Cases are valued at $265. What is the average level of incense inventory in units before the change? In dollars? What will the average level of inventory be after the change?

Solution

The average level of inventory for a period is the average of the beginning and ending period levels. In this example, the average level of inventory with weekly shipments is

(2.10)
$$\frac{800 + 0}{2} = 400 \text{ cases}$$

(2.11)
$$400 \text{ cases} \times \$265 \text{ per case} = \$106,000$$

For the daily delivery pattern, assuming 20 days/month, the average level of inventory would be

(2.12)
$$\frac{160 + 0}{2} = 80 \text{ cases}$$

(2.13)
$$0 \text{ cases} \times \$265 \text{ per case} = \$21,200$$

Excel Tutor 2.1 demonstrates how this problem can be solved in a spreadsheet.

---

the return on equipment investments is a high priority for any manager. Ineffective measurement of the productivity of equipment has long resulted in disagreement and poor decision making for many businesses. The logical approach to justifying the large cost of equipment has been to look at it from a "cost per unit" point of view. Basically, the question was: Could the purchase of a bigger (faster) machine reduce the per-unit cost of what it makes? To justify a large piece of equipment, its cost must be spread among a large number of units. That seems quite logical on the surface. This led to a measure of machine productivity known as **machine utilization.** Utilization is computed as another ratio of output over input:

(2.14)
$$\text{Utilization} = \frac{\text{Actual Running Time}}{\text{Time Available}}$$

In this case the output is the amount of time the machine was actually running divided by the total time the machine could have been running, which is the input. For example, a machine running for seven hours of an eight-hour shift would have a utilization of 87.5 percent. Increasing that utilization to 100 percent will result in more units being produced and a corresponding reduction in the cost per unit. Example 2.2 provides an example of the utilization calculation.

Producing more units will spread the fixed costs associated with a resource over more units, but it won't necessarily result in an increase in net income, particularly if the production rate exceeds the demand rate in the marketplace. Producing at a rate greater than the demand rate actually results in a reduction in net income because costs are increasing, but sales revenues aren't. This is a narrow or resource-specific productivity measure that is out of sync with broader measures of productivity. Logic and intuition dictate that producing more products than demand will consume is probably a pretty dumb idea. All productivity measures, if used incorrectly, can cause problems that lead to bad decisions. Utilization can be an important measure of resource productivity when used appropriately, for example, on a resource that needs to run 100 percent of the time in order to meet demand.

machine utilization
A productivity measure for machines that is equal to actual running time divided by time available.

"Load factor" is the term used in the airline industry for the percentage of seats filled. For some airlines, the breakeven load factor (the percentage of seats that must be filled to cover the airline's operating expenses) has risen above 100 percent.

Example 2.2

Utilization Calculation

A newly purchased welding robot has been monitored for the past week to provide information to be used for scheduling. The observations are noted in Exhibit 2.3. What was the total utilization of the robot? What impact on utilization did each category of downtime have?

EXHIBIT 2.3 Utilization Calculations for Example 2.2

Reason for Downtime	Minutes	Utilization Impact (%)
Operator/monitor not present	107	4.46
Preventive maintenance	149	6.21
Breakdown	40	1.67
Adjustments and programming	160	6.67
Material quality problems	46	1.92
Total downtime	502	20.92
Total uptime	1,898	
Total time available:	2,400	
Total utilization:	79.08%	

Solution

Total utilization can be calculated by dividing the minutes of total uptime by the total time available. The utilization impact of each category of downtime is determined by dividing the minutes of downtime for each category by the total available minutes. The results of these calculations are presented in Exhibit 2.3. Spreadsheet calculations to obtain utilization values are presented in Excel Tutor 2.2.

efficiency
The ratio of actual output to standard output.

Another often used, but misunderstood, capacity-related measure is **efficiency**. People typically use the term to describe how well something works or how effective it is. Efficiency is actually a productivity measure that is calculated using the following formula:

(2.15)
$$\text{Efficiency} = \frac{\text{Actual Output}}{\text{Standard Output}}$$

In other words, it compares what actually happened to what should have happened.

This productivity measure also creates a ratio of outputs to inputs. It's not as direct a comparison as some, however. The outputs are obviously the actual machine output. The input, however, is a standard that represents the resource's proven or documented potential. The machine should be able to operate at the standard rate. If the standard was 1,000 units per hour, for example, that is the expectation of the machine under normal circumstances. Employees are also measured by their efficiency when there is a standard of performance in place. Unlike utilization, efficiency can actually be greater than 100 percent in cases where a resource is performing better than the standard.

Efficiency calculations are quite straightforward, as demonstrated in Example 2.3.

Facilities

Facilities consist of the buildings used to house all aspects of a business. The measurement of facility productivity is very specific to what the facilities are used for, and it often varies a great deal from company to company. Facilities are expensive, they are frequently a long-term investment, and they are used for a variety of important purposes.

Example 2.3

Efficiency Calculation

EXCEL TUTOR

A bank's check-clearing operation uses automated machines to read and sort checks. A newly purchased machine has been monitored for two months in order to develop a standard. The standard developed was 5,400 checks per hour. Hourly counts of checks in a recent eight-hour study are reported in Exhibit 2.4.

Calculate the efficiency of the bank's check-reading machine.

EXHIBIT 2.4	Check Reading Data for Example 2.3
Hour	**Quantity Read**
1	5,756
2	5,235
3	5,540
4	4,886
5	5,267
6	4,656
7	5,346
8	5,104
Total read	41,790
Standard:	43,200
Efficiency:	96.74%

Solution

Efficiency is calculated by dividing the total number of checks read by the number that should have been read during that period of time. Over an eight-hour period, 43,200 checks should have been read according to the standard. Only 41,790 were actually read, resulting in an efficiency of 96.74 percent.

Excel Tutor 2.3 provides an example of how efficiency calculations are made in a spreadsheet.

The size of an investment in a particular facility is often closely related to the cost of the land on which it is located. Land costs and building costs mean that facility cost is almost always associated with the facility's size. To determine how well such an investment generates a financial return, output measures (sales revenues, customers served, and so on) must be compared to the input measure most closely tied to the initial investment. An input measure frequently used is the size of the facility in square feet.

For retailers, a commonly used measure of facility productivity is sales revenues per square foot. Not only can this measure be used to compare stores to each other, but standards can be generated based on the return desired from that facility investment. These standards can be used for evaluation purposes or to make expansion decisions. Performance of other stores can be used as a basis for determining whether the costs of a particular new facility can be justified, given likely sales volumes.

Workforce

The workforce consists of all of the employees of the company. Employees are often described as being a company's most important asset. Employees are also commonly accepted as the source of a manager's greatest problems. Certainly they are expensive, and they are getting more and more difficult to attract as labor markets become tighter in some industries. Hiring, training, and managing employees has always been expensive. One can argue that many businesses, particularly manufacturers, have moved toward increasing levels of automation to eliminate the need for as many employees. Many would gladly trade all of the costs associated with employees for a sizable up-front cost of a numerically controlled machine or robot. Automated machines and robots do not, however, provide the flexibility and critical thinking of a human worker. The increasing importance of response and flexibility has resulted in some businesses eliminating automated equipment in favor of hiring more workers.

In some manufacturing industries, the percentage of total product costs resulting from direct labor is less than 10 percent. The service activities of those manufacturers, however, including sales, delivery, and after-sale service, as well as internal business services such as information systems, human resources, facility management, and equipment maintenance, are still very labor-intensive.

In the service sector, where the labor market can often be tight, good service can be difficult to find. A tight labor market often means tight competition for the most qualified workers and high levels of employee turnover. When poor service quality is received, it is often perceived as the result of employees' actions or inactions. Sometimes low-quality service is the employee's fault, but it may well be caused by systems and processes that don't take advantage of the employee's strengths and weaknesses. Those processes are the management's responsibility. Employees, like other productive resources, are utilized in those processes, and like other resources, an employee can be part of an ineffective process that does not add value.

Employees, whether they are white or blue collar, are increasingly finding themselves the subject of productivity measures that compare outputs, like sales dollars and units produced, to inputs, like hours, weeks, customers, and calls. A quick examination shows a very close relationship between a ratio such as the dollars generated by an individual per week and the number of phone calls made, and a broader profitability measure like ROA. Ratios of outputs to inputs for individuals can create productivity measures that are like local profitability measures for individual salespersons. Productivity measures for employees, particularly white-collar employees, vary tremendously across industries. It is important to ensure that assets, including human assets, are as productive as possible. Productivity measures aid in decision making for those assets. Despite the fact that broader measures indicate business success, it is at the level of the individual asset that many decisions are made.

om ADVANTAGE   Productivity Measures Explain Class Size

A particularly relevant example of a measure of an employee's productivity is one typically used at universities, student credit hours generated per full-time equivalent faculty (FTE). One student taking a 3-credit-hour course generates 3 student credit hours. Thus, a 3-hour course with 40 students would generate 120 credit hours. Credit hours is an important output measure because it determines tuition revenues, state subsidy revenues, and so on. FTE is important as an input measure because it defines the equivalent of one full-time faculty member. Faculty frequently have fractional appointments, so it allows two half-time faculty, for example, to be counted as one FTE. University administrators make comparative analyses of departments across campus by looking at the average student credit hours generated per FTE for each department. This measure helps explain why class sizes for freshman and sophomore courses are often larger than those taught for juniors and seniors. The large classes provide a way to keep the average class size up when departments want to have small class sizes for their advanced courses. Granted, in the university setting, profitability of the firm isn't the objective, but a financial return of operational resources is still critical. Salaries and utility bills must be paid, and buildings must be maintained. Operational dollars come from tuitions and, in the case of state schools, state subsidy. Both are driven by student credit hours generated.

Value added by a good employee or value lost by a lousy one contributes directly to net income in a number of ways. Obviously, a customer's decision to return to a business can be greatly influenced by interactions with employees, so as a crucial part of the process for most services, employees add or detract value. Like any resource in any process, employees must add value to contribute to profitability. Besides adding value through direct interaction with customers in service environments and with products for manufacturers, employees add value in other ways, such as through creative decision making and problem solving that reduces costs or improves processes.

Two important considerations when designing productivity measures are to use appropriate output measures and appropriate input measures. The output measures should be consistent with the employee's objectives. They should provide a measure of the most important job outcomes. The input measures should represent resources consumed that are important and that the employee can control.

Productivity measures for employees are often a challenge to create and interpret, and they can be quite deceiving. This phenomenon can best be understood through the use of an example. Example 2.4 provides the calculations for several relevant productivity measures and also demonstrates how it can be difficult to determine which are the most important.

Example 2.4

Calculating Productivity Measures

Exhibit 2.5 presents productivity measures for a three-person sales force. A cursory examination of the data in Exhibit 2.5 shows that performance measures are variable and that different salespeople perform differently, depending on the measure. Use the performance measures provided in Exhibit 2.5 to create productivity measures for the three salespeople. Compare their productivity.

EXHIBIT 2.5   Monthly Performance Data for Sales Force

	Jeannie	Al	Carla
Sales dollars	$26,000	$31,000	$37,000
Clients visited	95	109	67
Clients in region	130	127	198
Miles traveled	3,900	3,150	2,070
Salary (monthly)	$5,800	$4,200	$7,300

Solution

Exhibit 2.6 provides several productivity measures for the sales force.

EXHIBIT 2.6   Possible Productivity Measures for Sales Force

	Jeannie	Al	Carla
Sales dollars per mile	$6.67	$9.84	$17.87
Sales dollars per visit	$273.68	$284.40	$552.24
Sales dollars per client	$200.00	$244.09	$186.87
Percent of clients visited	73%	86%	34%
Sales dollars generated per dollar of salary	$4.48	$7.38	$5.07
Clients visited per day	4.75	5.45	3.35

(Continues)

Example 2.4   *(Continued)*

One measure of the productivity of the salesperson's activity with clients could be represented by the sales dollars per visit, showing Carla to be the most productive. Sales dollars per client in their region, however, provides a very different result, with Al being highest and Carla being the lowest. Carla appears to make the most of her visits, as measured by sales dollars per mile traveled and sales dollars per visit. One could conclude that Carla doesn't waste visits and visits only clients with a high likelihood of ordering. One might also conclude that she isn't very effective at reaching all of her region's potential clients. Al, on the other hand, seems to be the best at visiting clients, which may be important for maintaining relationships and getting future sales. Al also had the highest number of clients visited per day. The productivity of the salary paid to the sales staff seems to be highest with Al and lowest with Jeannie.

Excel Tutor 2.4 demonstrates how these productivity measures can be derived using a spreadsheet.

The link between resource productivity and profitability can often be pronounced when competing businesses are compared. Exhibit 2.7 provides a comparison of Toyota and General Motors based on data available in 2005. Resource usage and resource costs contribute dramatically to the profitability of these two competitors.

EXHIBIT 2.7	Comparison of GM and Toyota	
	Toyota	**General Motors**
2004 U.S. sales	2,060,049	4,655,459
U.S. market share	26.8%	13%
2004 North American production	5.2 million	1.44 million
Production time per vehicle	34.3 hours	27.9 hours
Average plan capacity utilization	85%	107% (using overtime)
Profitability per vehicle	$1,488	−$2,331
Average hourly salary	$27 per hour	$31.35 per hour
Health care costs per vehicle	$1,525	$201
Workforce	White collar: 17,000	White collar: 36,000
	Production: 21,000	Production: 21,000
	Retirees: 1,600	Retirees: 1,600

Source: National Public Radio, www.npr.org/news/specials/gmvstoyota/gm_toyota_comparison.html, accessed December 12, 2005.

Local versus Global Optimization

The gradual trend for businesses to pay more attention to broad profitability measures by widening management's perspective and eliminating functional boundaries has implications for resource-specific performance measures. Global measures—profit margin, ROA, ROE—are very important, but since they are acceptable only when resources are used effectively, measures of resource effectiveness are needed as well. The challenge arises when these resource-specific "local" measures are in conflict with broader "global" measures. This can lead to situations where management makes decisions to improve resource-specific measures only to find that the decisions actually harm global measures. How does this happen?

Earlier in this chapter, in the discussion of profitability, the issue of productivity measures being out of sync or even in direct conflict with each other was mentioned. This phenomenon also appears when local and global productivity measures are compared. It may seem logical to assume that optimizing or maximizing all of the local or "resource-specific" measures of performance will also optimize global measures. If all of the resources are at the highest level of productivity, the system must also be at its highest level of productivity, right? Wrong. For example, if utilization of all work centers in a factory were maximized, would ROA be maximized as a result? Probably not. Products do not require exactly equal time on all equipment. If equipment utilizations were maximized, there might be too much inventory of some items.

It doesn't take long to discover that there are many examples of conflict between local and global productivity measures. Optimization of global measures, like the company's profitability, generally requires coordination and balance that precludes optimization of all local measures.

Inventory turns have long been the dominant measure for identifying inventory productivity. The lower the level of inventory, the higher the turns. A manufacturer that fulfills orders from a finished goods warehouse might initiate an inventory reduction effort by simply making substantial across-the-board cuts in inventory. A retailer could accomplish the reduction by decreasing the quantity ordered and increasing the frequency of orders to suppliers. A manufacturer would have to decrease the production quantity ordered while increasing the frequency of production orders to the factory. Initially, given a substantial amount of excess inventory, there would probably be no detrimental effect. As inventory is reduced, however, another measure—service level—will be affected. This measure isn't typically thought of as a measure of productivity, but it is. The **service level** of a particular inventory is the number of orders satisfied from the inventory divided by the total number of orders. In other words, it is the percentage of demand satisfied from stock.

Whenever demand occurs that cannot be met directly from inventory, a **stockout** results. The relationship between product demand, order delivery frequency, order quantity, and customer service is an interesting one. Obviously, if demand were 10 units per day and 10 units per day were received from the supplier, demand would be met. However, demand is not always even. A demand pattern that averaged 10 units per day would have days of higher and lower demand. That uncertain aspect of demand creates the possibility of stockouts, even though, on average, supply and demand are equal. Additional inventory, known as **safety stock,** is used to help cope with demand uncertainty. Once a certain point in an inventory reduction effort is reached, the low inventory can start to have a negative impact on service level because of the variability of demand. The problem can be magnified when an unforeseen problem arises. A supplier strike, for example, could quickly result in stockouts if there were initially low levels of finished products.

The conflict between measures of performance arises quite often. Businesses are complex systems. It's not possible to change the way any one resource is being used

service level
The percent of orders satisfied from existing inventory.

stockout
An instance when demand cannot be satisfied by existing inventory.

safety stock
Additional inventory used to help meet demand uncertainty.

without having an impact somewhere else. Quite often that impact is far-reaching and unexpected.

Measurement Improvement

Most productivity measures can be thought of as local profitability measures. Most are ratios of an output measure to an input measure. Obviously, increasing the numerator or decreasing the denominator can improve such a measure. A balanced approach to productivity improvement, and one that is more likely to be successful, focuses on the numerator and denominator in a measure *and* targets more than one measure. The focus on more than one measure reduces the likelihood that one measure is improved at the expense of another.

An attempt to increase the numerator of a productivity measure is an attempt to increase a measure of output. As long as that output level is in sync with product or service demand, and is not increased at the detriment of other measures, this approach can be effective. An examination of what is required to increase the ROA provides a good example of why one must give attention to *both* the numerator and denominator. Recall that ROA is net income divided by total assets. On paper, increasing net income can be accomplished in a number of ways, including increasing net sales, reducing the cost of goods sold, reducing interest paid, or reducing taxes. The most direct approach would be to increase net sales, which could be accomplished by increasing the volume of goods sold, or by increasing the selling price, or both. Increasing the selling price is a somewhat risky approach, however, because its impact on the volume of goods sold is difficult to predict, and the increase could actually result in a reduction in net sales.

---

om ADVANTAGE Adobe: Turning a Popular Product into a Profitable Product

In 1992, Adobe Systems demonstrated software that enables a document created on one computer to be opened, edited, and saved on another computer, even with different applications and operating systems. Despite the fact that this was three years before the introduction of the World Wide Web, it was lauded as the most significant technology at Comdex, an annual technology show. The concept of document sharing was new, it was viewed positively, but its importance was not really known.

In the years since its introduction, 320 million copies of the Adobe Acrobat Reader have been distributed. The Reader, however, is free. Since 1993, fewer than 6 million copies of the full program have been sold. Adobe products have a tradition of dominating their market segments. They are driven by the pledge to allow users to publish content wherever the user wants, whether it's a printer, Web page, cell phone, handheld device, PC, or Internet appliance.

But in the early and mid-1990s, the concept of electronically sharing documents wasn't on anyone's radar screen. Over time, the number of Acrobat Reader users grew. By the end of 1997, some 11.7 million had been distributed. By the end of 1998 that figure had jumped to 57.4 million. During that time, however, the sale of the full program still represented less than 7 percent of Adobe's $894 million in revenues.

Increasing the sales of the complete program was critical to Acrobat's success, but Adobe was not successful at doing it. Finally, by building alliances with system integrators that are specific to certain industries (government, pharmaceutical companies, banks, and so on), Adobe began to educate potential users about the software's capabilities. The effect of that education was dramatic.

R&D efforts in fast-paced technology-driven organizations may create products and services that are ahead of their time. Patience and educating customers may be required to bring about profitability.

Source: "Adobe Had a Popular Product—Making It Profitable Took Some Work," *Wall Street Journal*, October 15, 2001, pp. R18–R19; www.adobe.com/aboutadobe/main.html, accessed March 16, 2006.

The other approach to increasing ROA is to decrease the value of assets required. In other words, the output stays the same, but ROA improves because the denominator (input) is reduced. This approach to productivity improvement is often thought of as "cost cutting" and is quite common. When applying this approach to more local measures of productivity, such as the productivity of a particular department or the productivity of equipment, a change in productivity may be demonstrated more quickly than would be the case if one were trying to increase the output measure. Unfortunately, a productivity-improvement effort based solely on cost cutting often leads to undesirable side effects. Keep in mind that there is an absolute limit to how much the inputs can be reduced. After all, they can't go below zero. As they are reduced, other measures—particularly those related to customer service or service quality—can be harmed. ✳

Quite often, cost-focused efforts to improve productivity are aimed at getting short-term results. For example, one can lay off workers quickly, and the results will appear on financial reports almost as quickly. Such efforts frequently end up as a tradeoff between short-term performance and long-term performance. The short-term benefits of reduced labor expense can later be outweighed by the costs associated with retraining new, inexperienced workers or by poor-quality service.

stop here.
NO.

Decision Tree Analysis

The nature of many operations management decisions often requires that decision-making tools consider the financial implications of alternatives. In this chapter we examine one robust, general-purpose tool that often finds its way into operations management decision-making processes. This tool, known as decision tree analysis, compares the expected financial performance alternatives and can be used in the context of many different resource decisions.

Decision tree analysis is a useful technique for organizing some decisions by identifying expected revenues associated with each alternative. Decision outcomes that depend on demand are often structured using decision tree analysis because demand is uncertain. Such decisions include those involving location, facility expansion, capital equipment investments, and the like. Decision trees are applicable to a wide variety of decisions where the outcomes of the choices are uncertain. They approach the calculation of expected revenues by multiplying the revenue expected for each alternative by the likelihood of its happening. This logic, combined with a "tree" structure for decision sequences and chance occurrences, forms the basis for decision tree analysis.

Step-by-Step: The Decision Tree Analysis Process

1. Start by drawing a small square, with a line coming out to the right for each possible decision alternative. Make sure there is plenty of space between the lines and label each line for the alternative it represents.

2. At the right end of each line, indicate the type of results that are possible. If the result of a particular alternative is uncertain, attach a small circle to the end of the line. If the result of an alternative is another decision, attach a small square to the end of the line. Squares always represent decisions; circles always represent uncertain outcomes.

3. From the circles, draw lines going to the right for the possible outcomes. Label each and include the probability of the outcome occurring. The probabilities of the outcomes emanating from a circle must sum to 1.0. From the squares, draw lines to the right representing each of the decision choices. Label all lines so you know what

they mean. Leave the right ends of lines blank if there are no more alternatives or decisions.

4. Repeat this process until you have drawn a (horizontal) tree that represents all of the possible decisions and all of the possible outcomes.

5. Assign a revenue or dollar value to each possible outcome. Outcomes are at the right end of each line.

6. For each decision, compute the expected benefit by multiplying each expected outcome by its associated probability, and then summing the values for that decision.

7. The branch with the highest expected benefit is the best choice.

Exhibit 2.8 illustrates a generic decision tree for a decision involving designing a new product or improving an existing one.

Decision trees are helpful in decision making because:

- They provide a very structured framework for a decision, so that all alternatives can be understood.
- They enable the decision maker to quantify uncertainty.
- They allow the decision maker to mix facts and predictions.
- They provide the best outcome, given the information available.

Example 2.5 provides an example of decision tree analysis in a location decision.

EXHIBIT 2.8	**Decision Tree for New Product Design Decision**

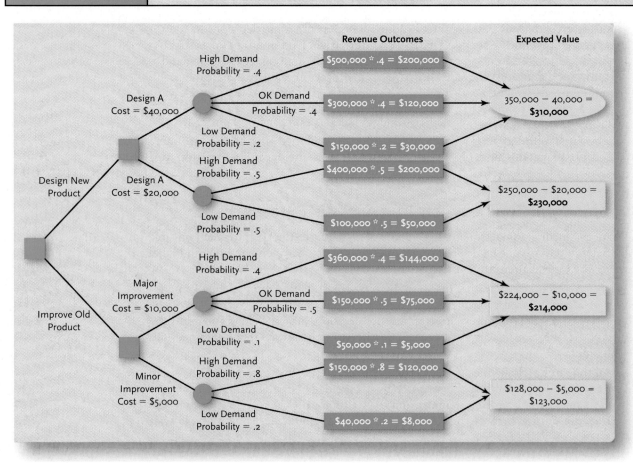

Example 2.5

Decision Tree Analysis

The owner of The Gourmet Guy, a local gourmet food store, is confronted with a decision. The store opened nine years ago and has enjoyed steady growth. The store is adjacent to a large condominium complex that is expected to begin major expansion within the next year. Unfortunately, the expansion also means that Guy will lose his lease on the current facility and be forced to relocate. Guy identified two alternatives for relocation. Site 1 will cost $66,000 to purchase and an additional $14,000 to remodel with appropriate fixtures. It can handle the existing level of demand as is, but if demand were to increase, it would require an addition that would cost $55,000. Site 2 is large enough to handle any foreseeable demand increase. It can be purchased for $135,000, with no remodeling needed.

Guy wants to apply decision tree analysis to assist in making the decision. He assumes the following:

1. The initial cost of Site 1 is $80,000 (purchase plus remodeling costs). If demand expands above the current level, which he estimates to have a probability of 0.75 given the condominium complex expansion, and he doesn't expand on Site 1, he expects the revenues to remain at their current level of $90,000 per year. If demand expands and Site 1 is expanded also, he expects an additional $65,000 per year. The expansion would cost $55,000. If demand doesn't increase, which has a 0.25 probability of happening, and he does expand, his revenues would remain at $90,000 per year.

2. Site 2 will cost $135,000. With a high demand (probability of 0.75), Guy expects revenues of $170,000 per year. With a low demand (probability of 0.25), he expects annual revenues of $80,000 per year.

Solution

Exhibit 2.9 provides the decision tree for The Gourmet Guy store location problem. Each branching point represents either a decision (represented by a box) or a chance occurrence (represented by a circle). In this example, there are two decision points and two chance occurrences. To solve the decision tree, work from right to left.

EXHIBIT 2.9   Decision Tree

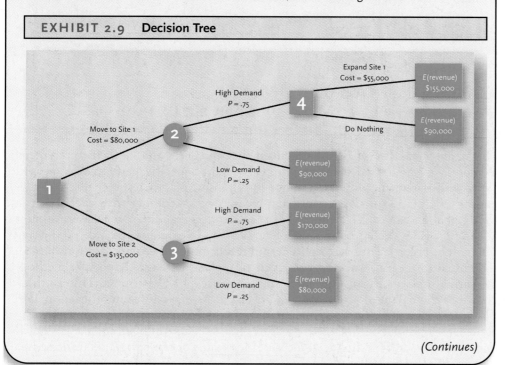

(Continues)

Example 2.5   *(Continued)*

The first step in solving the tree is to determine the best decision at decision point 4, by determining the financial return for each of the two alternatives. The revenue generated by expanding Site 1 is

$$\$155,000 - \$55,000 = \$100,000$$

The revenue generated by doing nothing is $90,000. Since expansion has a higher expected value, it would be chosen and the do-nothing alternative would be pruned from the decision tree.

The next step is to determine the expected values for moving to Site 1 and Site 2. The expected values of chance occurrences are determined by summing the products of the probabilities and the expected values branching from each decision point. The expected revenues of moving to Site 1 would be calculated as follows:

$$(0.75 \times \$100,000) + (0.25 \times \$90,000) = \$97,500$$

Subtracting the cost of Site 1:

$$\$97,500 - \$80,000 = \$17,500$$

To calculate the expected value of moving to Site 2, the same process is used:

$$(0.75 \times 170,000) + (0.25 \times \$80,000) = \$147,500$$

Subtracting the initial cost of Site 2 provides the expected value of moving to Site 2:

$$\$147,500 \times \$135,000 = \$12,500$$

Moving to Site 1 has a higher expected value.

Excel Tutor 2.5 uses Excel to solve this problem.

A Broader Approach to Productivity Measurement: The Balanced Scorecard

This chapter has discussed global performance measures and local, resource-specific measures. It has looked at a sampling of resource-specific performance measures, along with a frequently used technique for choosing among resource alternatives. It has also identified the dangers of local measures that conflict with each other and with global measures. We've seen that the use of several different measures simultaneously provides the best and most objective way to examine resource productivity. The potential for measures to conflict and result in poor business decisions has been recognized in recent years and has given rise to an increasingly popular method of measuring and evaluating the global performance of the business. This method is known as the **balanced scorecard.** The balanced scorecard was introduced in 1992.[7] The method argued that the performance of a business cannot be captured with financial measures alone, and other measures that are more difficult to quantify are also important. In addition, financial measures look only at the past, and businesses need to look into the future.

balanced scorecard
A performance measurement system that combines financial and nonfinancial measures of business performance.

Consistent with recommendations to use several performance measures simultaneously, the balanced scorecard approach is based on four perspectives:

- Financial objectives
- Customer outcomes
- Internal business processes
- Learning and growth

The Balanced Scorecard Institute provides an excellent overview of these perspectives, summarized below.[8]

Financial Objectives

The balanced scorecard does not eliminate the use of financial measures. On the contrary, it fully recognizes the importance of financial measures and their need to be accurate and current. The balanced scorecard merely recognizes that financial measures alone are not enough to help a firm guide its actions and strategic decisions.

Financial measures used in the balanced scorecard are not necessarily the same traditional financial measures used in other reporting frameworks. Companies that have embraced a lean systems approach, for example, may use financial measures for internal use that are very different from those used in traditional financial reporting. Not-for-profit and government organizations have been attracted to the balanced scorecard because the financial measures can be tailored to the organization's objectives. In addition, the importance of customer outcomes, which are the most important measures for not-for-profits, can be emphasized.

Customer Outcomes

The importance of the customer is widely recognized. However, the link between providing what the customer wants has never been strong when evaluating business performance. The balanced scorecard recognizes that customer satisfaction is absolutely necessary. Poor performance in satisfying the customer may not result in immediate failure, but does not speak well for the future viability of the firm. The balanced scorecard utilizes metrics that focus on the processes customers interact with.

Internal Business Processes

Internal business processes ultimately determine business outcomes. They define value and quality for the customer and dictate how well resources are used. Metrics that focus on

---

TARGETING technology | **Balanced Scorecard Software Support**

As new approaches become mainstream, parts of them can be automated to make data collection and other associated tasks easier. The increasing popularity of the balanced scorecard is no exception. Software producers have responded with a variety of products designed to aid in tying business operations to the balanced scorecard. Balanced scorecard software is so plentiful that the Centre for Business Performance at Cranfield School of Management and Gartner, Inc., recently released an extensive evaluation of 31 balanced scorecard software vendors. Balanced scorecard software solutions ease the burden of collecting data, converting it to usable information, and translating that into metrics which are then used to help align tactical and strategic decisions. The financial and nonfinancial performance metrics can be tracked and used to guide improvements.

Source: www.infoedge.com; www.qpr.com; www.peakanalytics.com; www.bma.com.

internal processes must capture how well the processes contribute and must be developed by people who understand those processes very well. The balanced scorecard recognizes two types of internal processes. Mission-oriented processes are those that contribute directly to product and service value and are more likely to be unique to the business. Support processes are more repetitive and generic and are more likely to be similar to those used in other organizations.

Internal business process improvement is at the heart of business improvement. In the case of for-profit organizations, enhanced processes translate into improved quality and resource use, which affect customer outcome measures as well as financial measures. For not-for-profit organizations, improved processes contribute to customer outcomes and reduce costs, so that more resources can be devoted to increasing customers served.

The Learning and Growth Perspective

Learning and growth include issues that are associated predominantly with the workforce. Training and education, the use of coaches and mentors, communication systems within the organization, knowledge management, self-improvement, as well as the organizational culture are all part of this perspective. Metrics are used to guide investments in these tools.

Exhibit 2.10 illustrates these four perspectives.

Rather than merely looking at past performance, the balanced scorecard approach examines past performance and future plans so that efforts can be aligned with needed improvement. The balanced scorecard approach, combined with productivity and performance measures that provide useful information, help a firm keep up with changing markets and changing environments.

EXHIBIT 2.10	Four Perspectives of the Balanced Scorecard

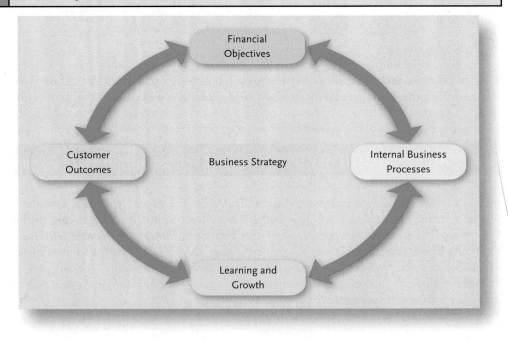

Source: The Balanced Scorecard Institute, http://www.balancedscorecard.org, April 1, 2004.

The Balanced Scorecard and Business Strategy

The balanced scorecard is not just a performance measurements system that goes beyond financial measures. It also creates a mechanism by which the organization's strategy can be more tightly linked to the day-to-day activities and decisions of employees. Stragegy maps can help develop that link. A strategy map consists of the corporate objectives for each of the four balanced scorecard perspectives. By developing objectives for each area at the corporate level, employees can more directly identify performance that links to corporate strategy. The link to strategy also helps in the selection of appropriate nonfinancial measures. By identifying the nonfinancial drivers of business success at the corporate level, and mapping them to the balanced scorecard, the measures and priorities are consistent.[9,10]

CHAPTER SUMMARY

In this chapter, three traditional profitability measures were reviewed: profit margin, return on assets, and return on equity. Profit margin provides a measure of productivity of the entire business. Return on assets provides a measure of the productivity of all of its assets. Return on equity provides a measure of productivity of the investment the company's owners have made. Although each measure may appear to be separate from day-to-day activities, management's challenge is to understand the linkage between their actions and these measures. Each profitability measure is tightly linked to a firm's ability to create value and sell it for an amount greater than its cost.

A common theme of all operations-oriented decisions is the direct impact on net income. By managing resources effectively, managers can reduce costs associated with the production of goods and services by making processes more effective. A reduction in costs translates directly into an increase in net income. Net income can also be increased by enhancing product or service value, which enables the business to increase sales. Both approaches require effective operations decision making regarding productive processes.

This chapter introduces each of the four resources presented in the Resource/Profit Model: inventory, capacity, facilities, and workforce. Links to profitability are created for each resource through a cursory examination of common productivity measures. Calculations for several common resource-specific productivity measures, including inventory turns, utilization, and efficiency, are presented. A common approach to decision making under uncertainty, known as decision tree analysis, was also described.

The balanced scorecard, a relatively global performance measurement approach that addresses quantitative and qualitative measures of performance, was introduced.

KEY TERMS

balanced scorecard, 56
economic value added (EVA), 41
efficiency, 46
inventory turnover, 44
machine utilization, 45
net present value (NPV), 34
productivity, 38

profit margin, 38
return on assets (ROA), 38
return on equity (ROE), 38
safety stock, 51
service level, 51
stockout, 51

SOLVED PROBLEMS

Quantitative problems in Chapter 2 provide several examples of resource productivity measures. A solved example, with explanation for each step, is provided below.

Calculating Average Inventory from a Delivery Pattern

Randal's Department Store receives weekly deliveries of shoes. One particular style is delivered in quantities of 14 pairs for each size. The store owner is considering reducing delivery frequency to once every two weeks, increasing the delivery quantity to 28 pairs. Assuming that all shoes are sold during the week, what is the average level of inventory for each size under the current delivery pattern? What will be the average level of inventory if the delivery frequency is changed to a delivery every two weeks?

Average Inventory Calculation:

Step	Objective	Explanation
1	Identify the beginning and ending inventory levels under the current system.	Under the current delivery system, the inventory is increased to 14 units and drops to zero.
2	Compute the average of the beginning and ending quantities.	$\dfrac{14 + 0}{2} = 7$
3	Identify the beginning and ending inventory levels under the new system.	Under the new delivery system, the inventory is increased to 28 units and drops to zero.
4	Compute the average of the beginning and ending quantities.	$\dfrac{28 + 0}{2} = 14$

Solution

The average level of inventory under the current delivery pattern is 7 units. Changing the delivery pattern to one delivery every two weeks will yield an average inventory level of 14 units.

Calculating Machine Utilization

Lighthouse Graphics produces custom graphic designs for signs, banners, T-shirts, hats, and virtually anything else anyone might want. They utilize silkscreening and embroidery technologies. Lighthouse recently purchased a new Shintoya embroidery machine. The new machine has 15 needles, can run at 1,200 stitches per minute, and is expected to greatly increase Lighthouse's embroidery capacity. Its memory can hold up to 200 digitized designs. During its first two weeks of operation, Lighthouse production supervisors maintained a detailed log of its use. The content summary of that log is presented below.

Total time Lighthouse Graphics was open	5,800
Changeover time	325
Maintenance time	179
Employee break time	500
Breakdown time	156
Embroidery machine run time	4,640

Compute the utilization of the new embroidery machine.

Utilization Calculation

Step	Objective	Explanation
1	Determine the total time available.	Total time available = 5,800 minutes
2	Determine the time the machine was actually operating.	Actual run time = 4,640 minutes
3	Calculate utilization.	Run time/time available = 4,640/5,800 = .80

Solution

The new embroidery machine has a utilization of 80 percent during its first two weeks of operation.

Calculating Efficiency

The Shintoya embroidery machine recently purchased by Lighthouse Graphics is expected to run at a rate of 1,200 stitches per minute. During the 4,640 minutes the machine ran during its first two weeks of operation, it completed two large hat orders. The first order was a design that had 2,884 stitches per unit. There were 510 units in that order. The second order was a design that had 3,876 stitches per unit. That order was for 425 hats.

Determine the efficiency of the new embroidery machine for its first two weeks of operation.

Efficiency Calculation

Step	Objective	Explanation
1	Determine the standard output.	4,640 minutes × 1,200 stitches/minute = 5,568,000 stitches
2	Determine the actual output.	(510 × 2,884) + (425 × 3,876) = 3,118,140 stitches
3	Calculate efficiency.	3,118,140/5,568,000 = .560011 (round to .5600)

Solution

The new embroidery machine had an efficiency of 56.00 percent during its first two weeks of operation.

Decision Tree Analysis

Belinda Lords is faced with a decision regarding her pastry shop. She opened the shop four years ago and has been quite successful. Her location has led to her success, but she has lost her lease on her current site and must move. Belinda has identified two possible sites. She is not willing to lease and have to move again. Site A will require an initial cost of $70,000. It may not be large enough to handle growth in demand, but could be expanded at a cost of $75,000 if demand were to grow. Site B is large enough to handle any future demand. It will cost $130,000. Construct a decision tree based on the following information:

1. The initial cost of Site A is $70,000. If demand is high, which Belinda thinks has a .6 probability of happening, and Site A is not expanded, her annual revenue is expected to be $80,000. If demand is high and Site A is expanded, she expects revenue to be $160,000 per year. If demand is low (.4 probability) Belinda expects annual revenues of $85,000.

2. Site B will cost $130,000 initially. With a high demand (.6 probability) she expects revenues of $185,000 per year. With a low demand (.4 probability) she expects revenues of $75,000.

Calculation of Best Alternative

Step	Objective	Explanation
1	Construct the decision tree following steps 1–5 in step-by-step decision tree analysis.	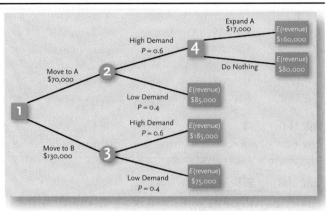

2	Compute expected benefit for second decision.	Start at second decision (node 4). Revenue for expanding A: $160,000 − $75,000 = $85,000 Revenue for doing nothing: $80,000 "Do Nothing" branch is eliminated.
3	Compute expected benefit for decision regarding moving to A or B.	Sum products of the demand probabilities and the expected revenues for each demand: Move to Site A: (.6 × $85,000) + (.4 × $80,000) = $83,000 Subtract the cost of Site A: $83,000 − $70,000 = $13,000 is expected benefit for Site A. Move to Site B: (.6 × $185,000) + (.4 × $75,000) = $141,000 Subtract the cost of Site B: $141,000 − $130,000 = $11,000 is expected benefit for Site B.

Solution

Moving to Site A has a higher expected benefit.

REVIEW QUESTIONS

1. Who determines value?
2. How are value and costs related to profitability?
3. Why is net present value (NPV) often so difficult to determine accurately?
4. Describe the three global measures of profitability.
5. What are two general ways profit margin can be improved?
6. What are the two general ways return on assets (ROA) can be improved?
7. Why would ROA be important to the owner of a business?

8. Why is economic value added (EVA) becoming so popular? What are its unique characteristics?

9. How can employees of a company improve EVA?

10. Describe common productivity measures for inventory, capacity, facilities, and workforce. How do these measures link to profitability measures?

11. What is meant by "local" versus "global" optimization? Which is more important? Why are local and global measures sometimes in conflict?

12. What is the objective of decision tree analysis? What are its potential weaknesses?

13. Describe the balanced scorecard approach to performance measurement. What are its advantages over traditional financial measures?

DISCUSSION AND EXPLORATION

1. Describe a business you are familiar with whose product or service value was reduced, not by what it did, but by what a competitor did. How could the business you chose have reacted to maintain the value of its product or service?

2. Identify a business you are familiar with. What could be done to increase the value of its product or service? Trace the effects of those changes to determine how they would change profit margin and ROA. Include specific effects on the components of net income.

3. Some people have said that inventory should actually be considered to be similar to a loan that the company takes out, rather than an asset. Why might someone promote such a view?

4. Identify local performance measures you are familiar with that are not in sync with global performance objectives. What do you think was the motivation for the development of these local measures? Why do they remain in existence? What behaviors do they motivate?

5. Many people have criticized the use of academic grades as the sole criterion for evaluating a student's performance in college, just as others have insisted that financial performance measures can't be the sole measure of a business's performance. Design a balanced scorecard approach for evaluating college students.

PROBLEMS

Solutions to odd-numbered problems are located on the text's Online Center (http://mhhe.com/opsnow3e).

1. A local pharmacy manages its inventories to meet customer demand and also to prevent particular drugs from violating their shelf-life limits. Currently, the major supplier delivers orders every Friday. One particularly common medicine is delivered in a 1,000-tablet pack. If the head pharmacist takes delivery on Wednesdays and Fridays, 500 tablets with each delivery, what happens to the average level of inventory?

2. As a fund-raiser, the theatre club gets to run the concession stand at three baseball games this spring. In order to offer something different, they plan to grill hamburgers and hot dogs outside and bring them into the concession stand to sell. Celia, the chair of the fund-raising committee, is concerned about having the dogs and burgers sit too long in the concession stand, and then not looking very good to customers. She has decided that, on average, there should be eight dogs and six burgers on hand in the concession stand. In what quantities should the burgers and dogs be delivered to the concession stand?

3. PetToys, a national pet supply warehouse store, takes delivery of all products at its central warehouse in St. Louis. It then ships products to its store on a weekly basis, based on individual store purchases. One particular product, the Doggie Jolt Training Collar, is shipped every other month from a manufacturer in China. The PetToys warehouse, on average, ships 800 collars per month to its retailers. At a value of $80 per unit, how much can PetToys reduce its inventory investment by changing to a monthly delivery pattern from China?

4. Ron's Music Supply currently sells 18 units of a particular CD player per week, on average. The inventory manager takes monthly delivery of 72 units. The CD players cost Ron's Music Supply $100 each.

   a. What is the average investment in the inventory of the CD player?

   b. Ron needs to free up $2,700 to help pay for a new promotional campaign. Can he accomplish this by increasing the delivery frequency of the CD player? How?

5. TiteRite manufactures a variety of plastic containers that are sold nationally at discount stores. The molding process used to produce the popular container is accomplished by a machine that also produces three other products. Currently, the machine produces three-day production runs of each product, changing molds after each run. Management has inquired about the possibility of investing in quick-change molds that would make the changeover easier and make it possible to reduce the production runs to one day in length. Current batch size and product values are presented as follows:

Product	Batch Size	Product Value ($)
Product 1	1,800	1.32
Product 2	2,400	1.69
Product 3	2,000	1.74
Product 4	2,600	1.86

How much money could be spent on changeover improvement if it was limited to the money made available by an inventory reduction resulting from one-day production runs?

6. Ward's Sporting Collectibles has an eclectic supply of antique sports memorabilia, from antique fishing gear to baseball, football, and basketball memorabilia. Mark Ward, the business owner, buys items from 12 "pickers" he has contracted with around the country. Pickers search for items, buy them, and send $100,000 worth of products to him four times per year, on the first of January, April, July, and October. Considering these four peaks in his inventory level, Mark estimates his average inventory level to be $600,000, peaking at about $1.2 million at delivery time. Customers have complained that his inventory doesn't change much. Mark would like to reduce his inventory and increase the turnover in his shop by having pickers deliver more products, but deliver monthly. He wants deliveries of $50,000 per month from each of the 12 pickers. What would his average inventory level drop to?

7. Spotted Cow Dairy collected the following downtime data on its bottle-filling machine:

Categories of Downtime	Minutes
Breakdowns	70
Changeover time	189
Restocking	221
Worker break and lunch	300
Total time available	2,400

What was the utilization of the filling machine?

8. Warville Carpets, a producer of customer carpet for commercial uses, often finds it-self producing smaller quantities of carpet than might be desired by a high-volume producer. Smaller quantities result in shorter production runs for a particular setup. More setups cut into production time of the tufting machine because while the machine is being set up for a new run, it isn't producing carpet. Warville operates 2 shifts per day, 5 days per week, for a total of 80 hours each week. A typical setup takes 20 minutes. Setup data for the past two weeks are as follows:

Day	Setups
Monday	3
Tuesday	2
Wednesday	3
Thursday	4
Friday	2
Monday	1
Tuesday	2
Wednesday	3
Thursday	2
Friday	2

What was the utilization of the tufting machine over the past two weeks?

How much tufting time could be gained each week, on average, if setup times could be reduced on average by 20 percent?

9. End-of-the-Road Air is a small charter air service in Canada specializing in flying clients to remote lodges in the north woods. Flights of up to 180 miles are provided to customers who schedule a pickup for a later date. Due to the long days in the northern summers, the service owners have determined that flights are actually possible for 14 hours each day. Plane maintenance is required, however, and takes one full day each week and two hours per day on each of the remaining six days. What is the plane utilization per week given the maintenance requirements?

Bad weather wreaks havoc for small-plane pilots. Based on three previous seasons' records, End-of-the-Road management expects its planes to be grounded 15 days out of the 120-day season due to bad weather. If that happens, what will the utilization be? What utilization improvement would occur if six of the bad weather days were used as the weekly maintenance day for each plane?

10. J-I-T taxes completes federal and state income tax forms for individuals and businesses. Files are completed by a consulting staff and submitted to Owen Clark, who runs an accuracy checking program and then submits the file electronically to the IRS. This process, no matter what the characteristics of the return, takes exactly two and a half minutes. Because files submitted by the consultants are not spaced out evenly throughout the day and week, there are times when Owen gets quite a backlog of files to process. He has argued for more help and another computer, but J-I-T managers don't think capacity is that stressed. Use the following data to determine the utilization on Owen and his computer. Owen works seven and a half hours per day (he gets 30 minutes off for lunch), 5 days per week. The following data are fairly typical for a week:

Day	Files to Process
Monday	70
Tuesday	150
Wednesday	130
Thursday	120
Friday	160

What is the utilization of Owen's computer?

11. The faculty in the Management Department office have complained about having to wait in line for the copying machine. The department chair, always tight with his money, has resisted buying an additional one. His data show that for the week studied, the machine was used the following amount:

Day	Time in Use (minutes)
Monday	420
Tuesday	180
Wednesday	244
Thursday	171
Friday	143
Total	1,158

The department chair claims that since there are 10,080 minutes in a week, the utilization is just over 10 percent, making it unnecessary to purchase an additional machine.

a. What is wrong with that argument?

b. What do you think the appropriate utilization is?

12. The standards for each of three scanning robots used in the shipping department of a major online retailer are presented below:

Scanner 1	3,600 pieces per hour
Scanner 2	3,000 pieces per hour
Scanner 3	2,150 pieces per hour

Actual output of the three scanners averages:

Scanner 1	3,200 pieces per hour
Scanner 2	2,650 pieces per hour
Scanner 3	2,400 pieces per hour

a. What is the standard output for the entire scanning department?

b. What is the efficiency of each machine?

c. What is the department efficiency?

13. The standard for manual entry of check information for those checks rejected by an automatic check reader is 265 checks per hour. The actual output of three check readers follows:

Reader	Output
1	218
2	269
3	253

a. Compute the efficiency of each reader.

b. What is the efficiency of the group?

14. A local one-hour film developing lab recently purchased a new automated developer. The machine was described by the supplier as being able to develop and print 720 prints per hour, with a trained operator. After 30 days of operation, management collected the following data for one 40-hour week:

Total hours available	40.0
Hours down for maintenance	3.5
Hours down for chemical refill	0.5
Hours down for cleaning	0.8
Hours down for paper jam	0.2
Total hours downtime	5.0

The following data were collected on 35 full hours of operation:

Hour	Output	Hour	Output
1	723	19	735
2	694	20	740
3	790	21	701
4	719	22	729
5	702	23	717
6	753	24	687
7	698	25	729
8	707	26	691
9	709	27	724
10	697	28	710
11	680	29	701
12	739	30	679
13	702	31	725
14	715	32	686
15	736	33	726
16	684	34	716
17	687	35	733
18	684		

a. Calculate the utilization and efficiency of the new machine.

b. To increase output, management plans on scheduling the machine for 50 hours next week. What would the expected output be, based on past efficiency and utilization?

15. The student government at a small university is in charge of all logistics for an upcoming concert. The band coming in has included, as a part of their contract, a clause that mandates every entrant to the coliseum must pass through a metal detector. Because 11,000 tickets were sold, an opening act was scheduled as a means of spreading out the arrival period. Concert planners expect that the arrival of the 11,000 attendees will be spread out over one and one-half hours. Metal detectors are rented from a security firm. They are delivered, set up, and calibrated on site, at a cost of $1,300 each. That includes the cost of two operators for each. The security firm claims that each metal detector can process 11 people per minute. However, recalibration and adjustment result in an average utilization of 91 percent.

a. How many metal detectors will be needed to process all concert attendees in time?

b. The opening act costs $8,500. Without the opening act, the arrival period is projected to be 45 minutes. Would it be cheaper to cancel the opening act and rent enough metal detectors for a 45-minute arrival period? Justify your answer.

16. A small law firm with two partners and four associates has begun to evaluate the productivity of the four associates. The following data were assembled:

Associate	Clients Served in Current Year	Total Hours Billed This Year	New Clients Served This Year	Experience at This Firm (years)
Sam	37	1,910	28	6
Sarah	42	2,430	24	5
Nick	56	1,870	33	3
Julie	32	2,200	12	2

a. What productivity measures would be useful for these associates?

b. From a strict "profitability" standpoint, which measure would be most appropriate?

c. What measure might indicate the associate that can provide the greatest growth for the firm?

d. What measure might indicate the best productivity, given the person's experience level?

17. The following table provides production, price, and sales data for two models of CD player:[11]

Year	Product	Units Produced	Price ($)	Sales ($)
2001	Z40	12,000	60.00	720,000.00
2001	Z60	12,000	120.00	1,440,000.00
2002	Z40	6,000	150.00	900,000.00
2002	Z60	18,000	120.00	2,160,000.00

a. Identify different ways of comparing the productivity of 2002 to that of 2001.

b. What happens to production? What happens to sales revenue?

c. What is your assessment of the changes in productivity if 2001 prices are used for the evaluation of 2002?

d. Overall, do you think productivity has increased from 2001 to 2002?

18. A brokerage firm provides newly hired associates a list of contacts that they are required to call on in hopes of building their client base. The first contact is by mail with a personal letter. The second call is by telephone, with the objective of setting up a face-to-face meeting to discuss investments. The following table shows data collected over the past year for five new associates:

Broker	Number of Contacts Given	Mailings	Phone Calls Made	Meetings Scheduled	Meetings Completed	Meetings Resulting in Investments	Total Investments ($)
Armstrong	450	450	450	43	42	28	724,000.00
Frederickson	450	450	450	64	52	16	380,000.00
Davis	450	450	450	85	55	12	520,000.00
Foster	450	450	450	70	61	32	643,000.00
Kinney	450	450	450	30	26	19	256,000.00

a. Who was best able to convert a phone call into an agreement to meet face-to-face?

b. Who was best able to convert a commitment to meet into an actual meeting?

c. When meeting, which broker seems best able to turn the client into an investor?

d. Who is the most productive of the brokers? Why did you select the measure you used?

19. A manufacturer of paper has three paper machines of various ages. The oldest was installed in 1961, the second oldest was installed in 1983, and the newest was installed in 1998. The following production statistics have been collected over the past six months of operation:

Machine	Total Production (hours)	Total Paper Produced (tons)	High-Grade Paper Produced (tons)	Low-Grade Paper Produced (tons)	Labor Required (hours)	Maintenance Required (hours)
1961	3,000	39,000	4,000	35,000	6,000	760
1983	2,500	28,000	28,000	0	6,000	510
1998	4,000	33,000	14,000	19,000	4,000	420

a. Which machine is most productive, per hour of operation?

b. Which machine is most productive, per hour of labor?

c. If high-grade paper generates twice the profit of low-grade paper, which machine is most productive per hour of labor?

d. What other productivity measures might be useful in looking for improvements in paper machine productivity?

20. Tri-State Bank would like to install a new ATM machine. There are two possible locations for the machine. Location 1 will cost $15,000. There are three possible revenue outcomes: a 45 percent probability of $45,000, a 35 percent probability of $85,000, and a 20 percent probability of $160,000. Location 2 will cost $20,000 with a 30 percent probability of $80,000 in revenue and a 70 percent probability of revenues of $110,000. Use a decision tree to decide which location the bank should use for its ATM.

21. University Pharmacy would like your assistance in solving the decision tree below. Which is the best alternative?

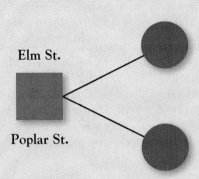

Elm St.

20% probability of $60,000 revenue
25% probability of $130,000 revenue
25% probability of $125,000 revenue
30% probability of $90,000 revenue

Poplar St.

30% probability of $30,000 revenue
45% probability of $110,000 revenue
25% probability of $170,000 revenue

22. Brit Swanson, owner of Brit's Car Wash, has decided to expand his thriving business by adding a new location. Three sites are available in locations he deems to be suitable. Brit has evaluated the potential of each site as follows:

Site A
Cost: $320,000
High revenue potential: $160,000 per year for 4 years, probability 0.7
Low revenue potential: $84,000 per year for 4 years, probability 0.3

Site B
Cost: $320,000
High revenue potential: $210,000 per year for 4 years, probability 0.4
Low revenue potential: $95,000 per year for 4 years, probability 0.6

Site C
Cost $75,000
High revenue potential: $100,000 per year for 4 years, probability 0.3
Low revenue potential: $50,000 per year for 4 years, probability 0.7

Using a decision tree, identify the site that should be chosen by evaluating the expected return over the 4-year period. Ignore the time value of money.

23. Mona Thompson owns a burrito stand that she started while she was a college student. It has gained a very loyal clientele and she has been quite successful. She is currently at a crossroads with regard to the business. She must decide whether to expand, relocate, or just remodel her existing restaurant. Business development in her area will determine the growth of her business at this location. Another location, to which she could move, has similar growth issues, but is a higher-traffic location. At present, there are plans for a new office complex to be built one block from her restaurant. Whether all the space in that new complex will be occupied, however, is not certain. Mona views the growth potential as being 60 percent likely that high

growth will occur, and 40 percent likely that there will be slow growth. Using a decision tree, evaluate her three alternatives.

Expand
Initial Cost: $80,000
High growth revenue expectation: $60,000 per year for 4 years; 60 percent probability
Low growth revenue expectation: $25,000 per year for 4 years; 40 percent probability

Relocate
Initial Cost: $270,000
High growth revenue expectation: $85,000 per year for 4 years; 60 percent probability
Low growth revenue expectation: $35,000 per year for 4 years; 40 percent probability

Remodel
Initial cost: $25,000
High growth revenue expectation: $8,000 per year for 4 years; 60 percent probability
Low growth revenue expectation: $4,000 per year for 4 years; 40 percent probability

24. Mary O. LeMew, owner of Mary-O's Hockey Supply, is being evicted for refusing to pay her rent after her landlord refused to fix a leak in her basement. Mary has two options. Site A is a small shop near an ice arena. It can be bought cheaply but will need to be expanded if growth reaches Mary's expectations. Site B is more expensive, but is large enough to accommodate future demand. Mary plans to go back to Montreal in 4 years, so she is interested in choosing the site with the best 4-year return. Use a decision tree to select the best site. Ignore the time value of money.

Site A
Initial cost: $60,000
Expansion cost: $110,000
High demand (probability = 0.7): $120,000 per year expanded; $80,000 per year not expanded
Low demand (probability = 0.3): $70,000 per year

Site B
Initial cost: $135,000
High demand (probability = 0.7): $155,000
Low demand (probability = 0.3): $110,000

25. QuikCopy, a local copy shop, is considering whether to purchase a new high-speed copier, to refurbish the one they own, or to do nothing. If they buy a new one, they have two alternatives. Model #1 costs $80,000, but can meet a higher demand. Model #2 costs $60,000, but can't meet as high a demand. If they refurbish their existing copier, a major overhaul will cost $25,000, while a minor overhaul will cost only $10,000. A third alternative is to do nothing. Management wants to evaluate the alternatives over a three-year horizon. Use a decision tree analysis to identify the best alternatives over three years. Do not consider the time value of money in your analysis. Expected 3-year revenues, and the probabilities associated with those expectations, follow:

Outcome	Probability	Revenue
New Model #1		
High	0.6	$52,000
Medium	0.2	$36,000
Low	0.2	$16,000
New Model #2		
High	0.7	$38,000
Medium	0.2	$20,000
Low	0.1	$ 7,000

Outcome	Probability	Revenue
Major Overhaul		
High	0.6	$34,000
Medium	0.2	$20,000
Low	0.2	$ 5,000
Minor Overhaul		
High	0.4	$24,000
Medium	0.3	$10,000
Low	0.3	$ 6,000
Do Nothing		
High	0.4	$12,000
Medium	0.4	$ 8,000
Low	0.2	$ 4,000

26. Collegiate T's is considering the purchase of a new embroidery machine that will embroider logos and lettering on jerseys, tote bags, and hats. They currently have a machine that is not totally automatic, but it could be converted to run automatically. C.J. Twombley, the owner, has projected high, medium, and low revenue projections based on each possible alternative. If C.J. opts for the new automated machine, they have a choice between a $70,000 and a $50,000 model. If C.J. opts to convert the existing machine, one conversion would be $33,000 and the other would be $10,000. C.J. could also do nothing. C.J. wants to select the best alternative based on two years of benefits. Probabilities and 2-year revenue expectations follow:

Outcome	Probability	Revenue
Automatic Model #1		
High	0.5	$60,000
Medium	0.3	$30,000
Low	0.2	$ 15,000
Automatic Model #2		
High	0.6	$45,000
Medium	0.3	$28,000
Low	0.1	$10,000
High-Cost Overhaul		
High	0.5	$36,000
Medium	0.2	$24,000
Low	0.3	$ 8,000
Low-Cost Overhaul		
High	0.4	$24,000
Medium	0.3	$10,000
Low	0.3	$ 6,000
Do Nothing		
High	0.4	$12,000
Medium	0.4	$ 8,000
Low	0.2	$ 4,000

How low does the high-cost conversion price need to drop in order to make that the best alternative?

ADVANCED PROBLEMS

1. I have to fly out of town in three weeks. I can buy a ticket in week 1 (now), week 2 (next week), or week 3. Any ticket I buy is non-refundable. The current price of the ticket is $500. If I wait until week 2, there is a 25% chance the price of the ticket will have risen to $750, and a 75% chance the price remains at $500.

   If the week 2 price is still $500, there is a 30% chance of getting a last minute "Super Saver" fare in week 3. The Super Saver fare is $100. If the Super Saver fare is not available, the week 3 price is $500 with probability 0.8, and $750 with probability 0.2.

   If the week 2 price has risen to $750, there is only a 5% chance of getting the $100 Super Saver fare in week 3. If the Super Saver fare is not available, the week 3 price is $750 with probability 0.8, and $1,000 with probability 0.2.

   Draw a decision tree to find the alternative that minimizes the expected cost of the ticket. Also identify the possible outcomes under the optimal policy.

2. Fleck Engineering produces motor mounts for a machine manufacturer. The mounts are comprised of three different sub-assemblies, each manufactured on a Bridgeport Mill.

   Set-up time on a mill is one hour and 15 minutes; however, Fleck has three Bridgeports, so they do not have to break down the set-up each day.

   Daily demand for the motor mounts is 100 units.

   Product structure for the mounts:

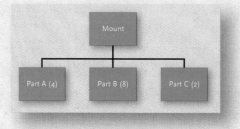

   a. Charlie runs work center A. His standard output is 500 units and he produces 400 units. What is the efficiency?

   b. Joe runs work center B. His standard output is 1,000 units and he produces 1,200 units. What is the efficiency?

   c. Sally runs work center C. Her standard output is 180 units and she produces 180 units. What is the efficiency?

   d. What is the average efficiency? What is the plant efficiency?

ENDNOTES

1. The Comparative Stock Market Performance of Stern Stewart Clients, http://www .sternstewart.com/evaabout/evaworks.php, April 5, 2004.

2. "Lean Manufacturers Recognized for Excellence," *PR Newswire*, March 22, 2004.

3. P. Grimaldi, "CVS Posts Healthy Rise in Fourth-Quarter Income," *Providence Journal*, February 13, 2004.

4. "Catch Me If You Can" (interview with Michael Dell), AlwaysOn.com, January 16, 2004, www.alwayson-network.com/comments.php?id=2466_0_3_0_C.

5. Jeff Zeiler, "The Need for Speed," *Operations and Fulfillment*, April 1, 2004.

6. "Retailing's Backstage Crew," *Business and Industry*, December 8, 2003.

7. R. S. Kaplan and D. P. Norton, "The Balanced Scorecard—Measures That Drive Performance," *Harvard Business Review*, January–February 1992, pp. 71–79.

8. The Balanced Scorecard Institute, http://www.balancedscorecard.org, April 1, 2004.

9. D. P. Norton and R. S. Kaplan, "Having Trouble with Your Strategy? Then Map It," *Harvard Business Review On Point Article*, www.economista.4t.com/finanzas/estrategias/mapit.pdf, accessed December 14, 2005.

10. C. D. Ittner and D. F. Larcker, "Coming Up Short on Nonfinancial Performance," *Harvard Business Review On Point Article*, November 2003. www.motivationmanagement.com/images/NonFinanPerfMeasure.pdf.

11. W. B. Chew, "No-Nonsense Guide to Measuring Productivity," *Harvard Business Review*, January–February 1988, pp. 110–118.

LEARNING ACTIVITIES

- Business Tours
- OM on Site
- Readings
- Resources
- Excel Tutors

- Interactive Case Models
- Reel Operations Video Clips
- Additional Advanced Problems
- Self-Assessment Quizzes
- Glossary

SELECTED RESOURCES

Hansen, D. R., and Mowen, M. M. *Cost Management*. Cincinnati: South-Western College Publishing, 1997.

Kaplan, R. S., and Norton, D. P. "Putting the Balanced Scorecard to Work," *Harvard Business Review*, September–October 1993.

Ross, S. A., Westerfield, R.W., and Jordan, B. D. *Essentials of Corporate Finance*. New York: Irwin McGraw-Hill, 1999.

Profitability by Continuing to Meet Customer Needs: Louisville Slugger

Based on Video 2 on the Student DVD

In some markets technological change can make an existing product obsolete instantly. In others, the process takes longer. In the baseball bat market, aluminum bats experienced increased popularity in the 1970s and 1980s, and by the 1990s they dominated all but professional baseball.

Hillerich & Bradsby, manufacturer of Louisville Slugger bats, shifted its focus from dominating the wooden bat market to aluminum when it purchased a factory from Alcoa.

1. Why do you think Louisville Slugger purchased the Alcoa factory rather than continue letting Alcoa make its bats? In hindsight, was this a good decision? Why, after deciding to build a new plant, did Louisville Slugger stay in California?

2. Product variety adds to costs and cuts into the profitability for any manufacturer. For Louisville Slugger, what costs do you think are added because of product variety? How do the different Louisville Slugger bats vary from one another? What value is added by the different types of product variety?

The acceptance of aluminum bats has not been universal. Years of controversy surrounded aluminum bat safety. The primary concern was that the baseball came off aluminum bats so fast that pitchers were at higher risk of being hit by the ball. Others felt that the aluminum bats destroyed the offensive/defensive balance of the game. This concern was supported by high scores. As an example, the final score at the 1998 NCAA Division I baseball championship game was 21–17.

In 1998 the NCAA Executive Committee approved new ball-speed standards. The new standards mandate that bats used by college players be narrower and heavier and that baseballs not be able to come off a bat faster than 93 mph. The move was basically to make aluminum bats perform more like wooden bats.

3. What would be the impact of the new rules on Louisville Slugger's costs and profitability? What capabilities would enable them to easily transition to these new standards?

Saddle Peak Ski Resort

Saddle Peak is a small "regional" ski resort in southwest Montana. It provides "no-frills" skiing for skiers who want a variety of "black diamond" and "double black diamond" slopes. Its skiers are local. Out-of-state skiers often ski Saddle Peak as the first or last day of a Big Sky vacation, or just drive up from Big Sky for a day of something different. While Saddle Peak never intends to compete head-to-head with Big Sky, it must provide a reason for skiers to select it for a day or two instead of skiing at that larger resort. It will always position itself as a place for hard-core skiers, rather than people who want to ski a little as part of a larger fashion/dining/shopping experience. Skiers at Saddle Peak are as likely to be wearing cowboy hats and Carhartt jackets as they are to be wearing the latest in ski fashion.

Saddle Peak has gradually increased lift capacity by converting its double and triple chair lifts to quads. The four converted quads currently allow skiers access to the entire eastern face of Saddle Mountain. Lift #1 takes skiers to the southern end of the face. The bottom ends of lifts #2 and #3 start at each end of the lodge but unload only about 30 yards apart at the top center of the face. Lift #4 is the longest, going to the north end of the face and providing access to skiers who want to ski the center or take the "Meadow Run," which provides nearly a mile of intermediate level skiing.

Sandy Teague, Saddle Peak's operations manager, was asked by its owners to evaluate the construction of a new lift that would begin at the top of lifts #2 and #3 and extend to the absolute crest of Saddle Peak. Skiers unloading from this new lift would be able to ski down through the face or cross a small bowl and join up with the Meadow Run. After a short period of thinking about the suggestion, Sandy responded, "What about capacity? With two quad lifts feeding the new one, which will also be a quad, there is a potential of it not having enough capacity to handle demand created by the people from lifts #2 and #3. It might make more sense to put the new lift at the top of Lift #4."

Sandy has collected the following information for lifts #2, #3, and #4. One hundred percent utilization would mean that every chair contained four skiers.

Lift	Average Utilization				
	8:00–10:00	10:00–12:00	12:00–2:00	2:00–4:00	4:00–6:00
Lift #2	52%	74%	76%	72%	54%
Lift #3	48%	66%	60%	56%	44%
Lift #4	70%	95%	92%	84%	72%

1. If Saddle Peak's new lift is a quad, with the same capacity as lifts #2 and #3, can you describe what is likely to happen if it is placed at the top of #2 and #3?

2. What information does Sandy need to get a better idea of whether the new lift could handle the demand coming from #2 and #3? How could she get that information?

3. What is the average utilization of lift #4? If the new lift is placed at the top of #4, should management consider a triple instead of a quad? Is "average utilization" useful in determining what is likely to happen?

4. Should management design the lift capacity to meet "peak" demands? Average demands? Or somewhere in between?

APPLICATION CASE 2.2

Office Outlet Stock Reduction

Office Outlet, a small chain of office supply stores, carries the standard variety of office-oriented products, including paper, printer cartridges and supplies, pens and pencils, shipping materials, etc. Mark Ellison, owner of the seven-store chain, would like to reduce inventory levels by requiring suppliers to deliver more frequently. Mark has chosen one particularly fast-moving product as a prototype for his plan. That product, standard copy paper in $8\frac{1}{2} \times 11$, is currently delivered to the stores every two weeks. Order size varies somewhat but averages 560 boxes (10 reams to a box) to each store. Mark's cost is $23.00 per box.

1. Evaluate Mark's current delivery policy. What is his average level of inventory at a single store? What are the costs associated with carrying that much inventory?

2. If Mark can negotiate deliveries every two days (assuming five-day weeks, he would go from one delivery to five in the two-week period), what happens to his average inventory level per store? Across the entire chain?

3. Across the entire chain, how much money would the change free up for Mark to use elsewhere?

4. What other types of benefits would Mark obtain from increasing the order frequency?

5. What costs might Mark incur from reducing the delivery quantity? How could he address these issues?

CHAPTER 3

Strategy and Value: Competing through Operations

LEARNING OBJECTIVES

- Describe the concepts of business-to-business (B2B) and business-to-consumer (B2C) interactions.

- Define the concept of a supply chain.

- Describe the value attributes common to B2B and B2C customers.

- Describe the role of the strategies that form the strategy hierarchy.

- Describe the role and importance of supply chain strategy.

- Describe Porter's three strategies.

- Define order winners, order losers, and order qualifiers and relate them to value.

- List and describe examples of strategic structural and infrastructural decisions.

- List and describe the competitive priorities of operations.

- Summarize the effects each strategic decision category has on operations' competitive priorities.

- Distinguish between capabilities and processes.

- Compare the strengths and weaknesses of process-oriented, product-oriented, and cellular layouts.

- Describe the continuum of choices related to production volume and the alternatives available for linking to customer demand.

- Describe what is meant by a capability chain.

A NEW MARKET AND DELIVERY CHANNEL FOR MUSIC

What started as a teenager's lark with Napster is turning seemingly untouchable retailers like Tower Records and Musicland into dinosaurs. For decades, music listeners were forced to buy record albums, then 8-tracks, then cassettes, and then CDs, with 12 or 14 tracks, when they really only wanted to own a couple of the songs. Recording companies could produce what customers wanted, but they didn't deliver it in a way that met customer desires. Today, as customers browse at music retailers, many leave empty-handed. The alternative of buying one digitized song for under a dollar, and placing it on their MP3 player, has finally created a match between customer desires and the products and services offered by the recording industry.

In reaction to this change in customer behavior, some music stores are adapting, others (Tower Records, Wherehouse, etc.) have filed for Chapter 11, and others have simply disappeared. New technology has totally changed the cost structure of a business that was heavy in inventory and distribution infrastructure. Trans World Entertainment had $378 million in inventory and $155 million in plants and equipment at the end of fiscal year 2003. It now competes with online retailers who have no inventory, no distribution system investment, and who can sell individual songs. Meanwhile, more businesses have entered the online music sales market—even Wal-Mart sells music online.

Record retailers and recording companies are merging in hope of creating viable businesses in these changing markets. Five music companies have 83 percent of the U.S. market, 78 percent in Europe, and 75 percent globally. Some record retailers are creating their own music downloading service.

Changing customer expectations hasn't been the only pressure on music retailers and the recording industry. Piracy has played a role in the downturn in record profits, but the key factor is that the music industry and retailers have refused to provide customers what they want for decades. As evidence of how technology has finally enabled consumers to get true value for their money, iTunes sold 70 million songs in its first year. iTunes' capabilities range from merely selling songs online to linking the purchase directly to the customer's music management software and MP3 player. Just as customer expectations drive product and service design, leading-edge companies like Apple create products and services that set the expectations of customers. The capabilities of the iPod Nano, for example, which include its small size, 1.5-inch color screen, and 14-hour battery were described simply as "impossible."

The ability to match capabilities to customer values is a prerequisite for business success. In the recording industry, customers had long wanted better value, but had no alternatives. Online music sales has found a market segment long neglected and has created an opportunity for new firms to replace those who can't keep up. The traditional retailers will need to adapt or fold. Those selling music online must recognize that another unforeseen technology could render them just as obsolete if they don't continue to offer their customers value.

The capability to sell online music, a service, has become so intertwined with Apple's iPod products that products and service have become almost indistinguishable. By June of 2005, Apple had sold 22 million iPods. That would not have happened without the iTunes interface. The iTunes interface, which allows for easy purchases of downloads, has resulted in 10 million iTunes accounts, each averaging over 60 song downloads, and 1.8 million downloaded songs per day.

The impact of the iPod and iTunes technologies has also opened up opportunities for alliances with many other companies. Apple, Motorola, and Cingular, for example, have joined to provide the Motorola Rokr phone, with has the equivalent of an iPod Mini inside the Motorola phone, with an iTunes client made available through Cingular.

Source: P. Keegan, *Business 2.0*, March 2004; "Come Together," *The Economist*, November 13, 2003; "How to Pay the Piper," *The Economist*, May 1, 2003; http://www.apple.com/itunes/download/, April 29, 2004; Apple Special Event, www.apple.com/quicktime/qtv/specialevent05/.

*P*rofitability comes from the difference between the value perceived by customers and the cost of creating it. What customers will value, however, is not always obvious or constant. The plan for creating value now and in the future is a strategy. The creation of a strategy at corporate, business, and functional levels provides a framework for achieving the business's goals. That strategy dictates how the company will meet customers' value expectations.

Introduction

The previous chapter established the fact that value creation is the key to successful investment in operating resources. Value for the customer is the result of what the business can do—its capabilities. Capabilities are the result of processes. A business's strategy is its plan for creating value for its target customers. It is the difference between the customer's perception of value and the cost of creating it that provides the opportunity for profitability. This chapter investigates the concepts of value and strategy, and processes used to link them.

Value

The introductory chapter examined the components of the resource/profit model as well as two dominant outputs for businesses—products and services—and two primary customers—consumers (B2C) and businesses (B2B). Products and services move from business to business and ultimately to a consumer. Different types of customers have different perceptions of value. The perceptions differ between business customers and consumer customers, but also from one business customer to another, and one consumer to another. For businesses, the differences are often due to the business's relationship with other businesses. These relationships are examined in the following section, which introduces the concept of supply chains.

Supply Chains

To acquire a "big-picture" understanding of the role customers must play in business decisions, it is necessary to look at the entire network of producers and customers for both products and services. The creation of product value begins with **basic producers**, which mine minerals or harvest trees and other agricultural products. It then shifts to **converters**, which refine those natural resources. Next, **fabricators** take over to transform these inputs into usable product components. Finally, **assemblers** put them all together. A very simplistic view of this process is presented in Exhibit 3.1. The path ends with the sale of a consumer product or service. This entire network is known as a **supply chain**. Supply chains consist of both products and services, and they can be dominated by either. For example, automotive supply chains are dominated by the products used in manufacturing automobiles, but they contain many services as well, including transportation, distribution, and warehousing services. Financial services can play an important role as well, as do services provided by dealerships. Examination of a banking supply chain shows that it is dominated by service providers but also uses some products. Most supply chains, like most companies, are involved with products and services, making it difficult to distinguish between value added by products and value added by services. All product-oriented supply chains require support services. All service-oriented supply chains consume products.

Whether the supply chain is oriented toward a product or a service is often simply a matter of perspective. A service-oriented business, for example, will have that perspective when examining its supply chain. Likewise, if a company supplies products to the

---

basic producer
A manufacturer that extracts raw materials from natural resources.

converter
The second stage of product value creation, which refines natural resource inputs.

fabricator
The third stage of product value creation, which takes inputs from converters and transforms them into components used by assemblers.

assembler
The final step of the four stages of product value creation, which puts together the outputs of fabricators.

supply chain
The path of value creation, from basic producer through consumer, including all transportation and logistics services that connect them.

Generic Supply Chain Model	EXHIBIT 3.1

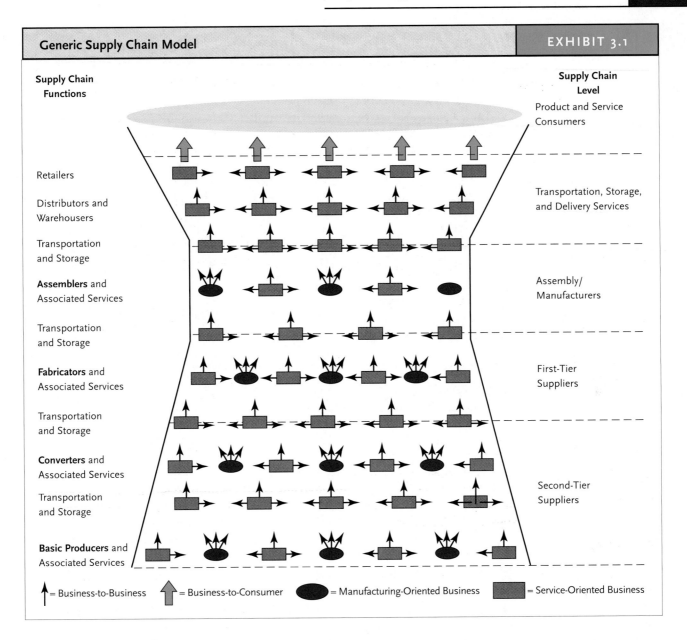

Supply Chain Functions

Supply Chain Level

- Retailers
- Distributors and Warehousers
- Transportation and Storage
- **Assemblers** and Associated Services
- Transportation and Storage
- **Fabricators** and Associated Services
- Transportation and Storage
- **Converters** and Associated Services
- Transportation and Storage
- **Basic Producers** and Associated Services

- Product and Service Consumers
- Transportation, Storage, and Delivery Services
- Assembly/ Manufacturers
- First-Tier Suppliers
- Second-Tier Suppliers

↑ = Business-to-Business   ⬆ = Business-to-Consumer   ⬭ = Manufacturing-Oriented Business   ▭ = Service-Oriented Business

supply chain, it will view it from a product perspective. A retailer will view the supply chain differently from a basic producer, even though they may be at opposite ends of the same supply chain. A supply chain "encompasses all activities associated with the flow and transformation of goods from the raw material stage (extraction), through to the end user, as well as the associated information flows. Material and information flow both up and down the supply chain."[1]

Exhibit 3.1 shows how products start out at the basic producer level and move, ultimately, to the consumer with the aid of various services that contribute to value creation. It should not be a surprise that services can provide a significant portion of the value added in product-oriented supply chains and products can provide a significant contribution to value in service-oriented supply chains. Transportation and timely delivery, for example, add value to products in many ways. In addition, many manufacturers outsource different services related to their business, including such necessities as employee selection and training, uniform services, database management, Web site development and maintenance, marketing, advertising, and even new-product development. All add value.

om ADVANTAGE   At Starbucks, Suppliers Bring More Than Beans

When we think about suppliers, it is often assumed that we're talking about businesses that ship inventory for use by manufacturers and services. We know, though, that increasingly, businesses are outsourcing services as well. Suppliers can provide human resource expertise, product design services, and a host of other business needs. Starbucks's suppliers bring to mind companies that provide coffee and other edibles, packaging, paper products, and so on. Starbucks also has a supplier that may seem a bit unusual. Hear Music supplies music to enhance the atmosphere at all Starbucks stores.

Hear Music is dedicated to finding great music beyond the Top 40. The company looks for new and old albums and brings them together for Starbucks. Initially Hear Music was a catalog retailer, then it opened stores in Berkeley, Palo Alto, Santa Monica, Chicago, and Seattle. Hear Music joined Starbucks in 1999 to add an identifiable type of music to its coffeehouses worldwide.

Starbucks's playlist has become popular enough to warrant publishing it on its Web site. The music component of the Starbucks experience has expanded in importance to its customers. In early 2004, Starbucks announced an alliance with Hewlett-Packard to deploy CD burning services to selected Starbucks stores. Through wi-fi access in stores, customers could customize their own CDs from the large digital collection available through Hear Music.

As this capability expanded, a growing number of Starbucks stores added the Hear Music media bar, a virtual record store that allows customers to assemble albums where they get coffee. Two new Starbucks Hear Music Coffeehouses (Santa Monica and South Beach) allow customers to burn personalized CDs and explore themed music recommendations throughout the store using listening stations.

Source: http://www.starbucks.com/, April 13, 2004; "Local Starbucks Kicks Off In-Store CD Burning," *Los Angeles Business*, Bizjournals.com, March 15, 2004; In Our Stores, http://www.starbucks.com/hearmusic/inourstores.asp? category_name = In + Our + Stores

Traditionally, supply chains were considered to be vertical arrangements of buyers and suppliers that started at the basic producer level, progressed through the converter, fabricator, and assembler stages, and ultimately ended at the consumer. For many businesses, the goal was to integrate vertically until they controlled the entire chain. In the last 15 to 20 years, however, significant changes have taken place. First, a more global economy has resulted in a tremendous increase in competition. This has led to outsourcing of components and products to reduce costs and add focus to what a firm does. Second, firms have also increased the amount of business services they outsource. Businesses formerly provided various nonmaterial needs for themselves. If they needed additional staff, for example, they'd advertise, interview, hire, and train them. If they needed engineering work done, they'd hire engineers. If they needed products distributed to customers, they'd buy trucks and build warehouses. Today firms are much more likely to outsource material and service needs, resulting in a supply chain that involves many different businesses and many more relationships.

Outsourcing

By the end of 2006, 30 percent of new cars will have iPod connectivity as an option.

In many industries, the supply chain viewed from a particular company's perspective might show a vertical structure; when all of the players in the market are included, however, a web of relationships would be a more appropriate description. It is possible for two companies to be head-to-head competitors while at the same time being suppliers for each other. They might also be strategic business partners in another market. They might share suppliers and share customers as well. Firms no longer have an overall goal of owning the entire supply chain. In fact, many firms have divested themselves of major components of that chain in order to remain more responsive to market changes and focus on the processes they do best. The Internet has made outsourcing service and product needs easier because of the networks of business-to-business (B2B) contacts that can be found there. Businesses now frequently compete as providers of manufacturing capabilities, expertise in human resources, engineering, product design, information technology, purchasing, and other capabilities.

Despite the trend toward outsourcing as a way to enhance value while at the same time remaining focused on core capabilities, some firms resist outsourcing to maintain tight control of all of their processes. In some cases this is viewed as enhancing quality because the company can maintain tighter control, while in other situations, the business's expertise is so narrow that finding capable suppliers is impossible.

To fully understand value, it is important to understand the various types of customers that exist in today's supply chains. Customers have different priorities and different needs. A company defines its supply chain by its own interactions. If it supplies products directly to a retailer, it sees that part of the supply chain. A business is most concerned with its immediate suppliers and immediate customers.

Determining Value

Value means different things to different people. In the simplest possible context, the value of a product or service is the amount of money a particular customer is willing to pay for it. The seller is interested in increasing the difference between the customer's perception of value and production cost to maximize profitability. It is important to know how and why a customer ended up with a certain dollar figure in mind. Exactly what is it that a particular customer sees as valuable? To understand this, it is necessary to understand what value means to different types of customers.

Consumer customers have a different frame of reference from business customers because they use the product or service to fulfill different needs. But they do not evaluate services separately from the products that the services accompany. From the standpoint of the producer that must manage the creation of products and services, however, it may make sense to separate issues related to the production of services from issues related to the production of products. There are significant differences in the management of processes used to create them. Customers, however, whether they are consumers or other businesses, buy the "total package." For the purpose of identifying components of value, this chapter will distinguish between different types of customers and their differing views on value but will not distinguish between value for products and value for services. Customers typically don't make that distinction.

Consumers evaluate the alternatives when faced with a potential purchasing decision. Most people do this many times a day. Usually it happens so quickly that it doesn't even register as being a conscious thought.

Value truly is in the eyes of the beholder. The books, movies, and products surrounding the Harry Potter phenomenon demonstrate how even producers can be mistaken about who will find value in a product. While there was really no question that young children would be attracted to the Harry Potter movie, adults also added to the long lines and formed a surprisingly large segment of the demand.

Music subscription and download revenues grew by 397 percent in 2004 and 154 percent in 2005. A 45 percent growth rate is projected for 2006. 2005 revenues were projected to be $1.378 billion.

Whereas a consumer judges value based on specific product or service benefits, a business seeking to purchase a service or product considers a very different set of potential benefits. A business's goal is to create value for its customers in such a way as to also end up with value added that is greater than its cost. It is seeking a service or a product to add value to what it sells and to enhance profitability. It might be seeking consulting services to improve business processes, an information system to improve the ability to make quick decisions, components of one of the products it produces, or it might just seek mops to clean the cafeteria floor. Its decision-making process is a little more complex than the consumer's, but the ultimate objective is the same. It wants to ensure that it makes the best choice, given present and future alternatives. It must include not only the various purchase alternatives, however, but also the alternative of producing the product or service itself.

A business's decision to buy, rather than produce, results from thinking that it can get a better return on its investment. There are various reasons why buying a product or service may provide a better return than producing it in-house. First, the costs of gearing up to produce a product or service may be prohibitive and more expensive than outsourcing, particularly if a supplier can take better advantage of economies of scale. The argument is frequently made that a company should be able to do something cheaper than an outside firm because it doesn't need to make a profit on it. That's actually not true. In a sense, the company *does* need to make a profit on it. A company needs to get a financial return on any investment it makes—investments in services it performs for itself *and* investments in components it produces itself to go into its own products. Frequently, the financial return obtained from in-house production of a product or service is less than that obtained had the company outsourced it and invested the difference in a part of its business that could use the funds in a more productive manner. Consumers do the same thing when they purchase services rather than perform them for themselves. They could select their own investments. They could change the oil in their cars. They could sew their own clothes. They could even cut their own hair. But they've decided, in most cases *very wisely*, to outsource.

Back in chapter 1, a distinction was made between components of value and value attributes. The components of value controlled by operations include cost, quality, and timeliness, and are used to create the specific product and service attributes customers want. In that discussion, an analogy of a car was used to differentiate between the car's components (engine, transmission, seats, etc.) and the attributes of a car (comfort, mileage, style, etc.) that a customer might want. The following sections explore the attributes of service and products that different tyes of customers may find important.

Value Attributes for Consumer Customers

Several researchers have attempted to categorize consumer customers by the way they shop. One theory that has been particularly popular, originated by Stone,[2] dates back to 1954. Stone's list of classifications has been modified in the past,[3] and it is modified again in Exhibit 3.2, because decisions and alternatives are different than they were in 1954.

EXHIBIT 3.2	Value Attributes for Consumer Customers	
	Value Attribute	**Consumer Concern**
	Cost	What does it cost for the total time of ownership?
	Quality	Does it meet my needs?
	Convenience	How easy is it to get?
	Timeliness	How quickly can I get it?
	Personalization	Will the business treat me as special?
	Ethical issues	Is the business acting responsibly, according to my values?
	Style/fashion	Is the product the most current style?
	Technology	Does purchasing the product or service require that I have technological skills?

om ADVANTAGE   Two Airlines in a Battle to "Out Perk" Each Other

Many airlines are trying drastically to cut costs and eliminate services in order to compete with low-cost competitors on the basis of price. As an example of how different customers have different priorities, however, one segment of the industry is in a race to add expensive features in order to attract more fliers.

Business travelers on intercontinental flights appear to be unconcerned about price (a round-trip business class ticket between New York and London purchased one week in advance costs about $9,000) and are demanding greater amenities for their time in the air as well as in the airport. Two airlines—Virgin Atlantic and British Airways—have responded with head-to-head competition to offer the most attractive service package.

In 2003 Virgin invested nearly $200 million to provide a "bed seat" in its business class. It claims that the investment has paid for itself. Other improvements include on-the-ground dinner service so that sleep time on the plane is not interrupted and lounges that enable fliers to freshen up immediately upon landing. Virgin has been a long-time advocate of over-the-top services. Virgin's seat is more private than British Airway's and has a larger table and a larger TV screen; Virgin advertises "the biggest fully-flat bed in business class." Its "Upper Class" goes beyond limo pickup and drive-through checking to include clubhouse access in the airport (complete with fine dining and golf driving ranges), in-flight beauty therapy, laptop power, and in-flight meals freshly prepared to order.

While British Airways and Virgin remain popular with executives willing to pay for these amenities, some claim that their market share is also due to the fact that other airlines do not have access to Heathrow airport.

Source: D. Michaels, "Scrambling to Pile on Perks," *Wall Street Journal*, October 28, 2005, pp. B1, B2; www.virgin-atlantic.com/en/gb/whatsonboard/upperclass/index.jsp, accessed November 5, 2005.

It is not accurate to identify certain consumers as always being driven by certain attributes related to product or service value, but a relatively short list of product and service attributes represents the basis on which most people calculate the value of the products or services they buy. Some of the attributes are more often associated with products, some more often associated with services, and some are equally applicable to both. Every consumer purchase, in the consumer's own mind, is based on value. It doesn't make sense to say that some consumers are more value-conscious than others. All are value-conscious; they just value different things.

Value Attributes for Business Customers

In typical B2B relationships, business customers are seeking one thing from the supplier: the potential to increase the value they can pass on to their customers. Archer Daniels Midland (ADM), a large producer of food products, animal feed products, and industrial products made from agricultural products, sums up the definition of value in a B2B relationship in a very succinct "value promise":

Value is defined by the customer, the ultimate judge. At ADM, our focus on value creation is directed and measured continuously by the customer's need to improve its own products, quality and costs.[4]

The B2B customer determines the value of what it purchases based on its potential to improve the value of what it sells. A consumer service company should not expect that all of the value being transferred to the consumer would come from its suppliers. Some will, but the company must add value as well. The same holds for a consumer products producer. If suppliers contribute all of the value, and the consumer products producer contributes none, it will not be in business long, because it adds costs but not value. When a business's role in the supply chain is examined, customers quickly discover that without adding value, there really isn't one. Customers figure out that buying directly from that company's suppliers is a better value. The "middleman" that performs no

In order for a business to maintain reliable deliveries of products, the correct item must get to the customer at the promised time. Completing the production of the product on time doesn't guarantee success. Packaging, labeling, and sorting thousands of products per day, and shipping them to their destination in a timely manner, depend on equipment, technology, and processes designed to handle high volume with accuracy.

value-adding function, merely linking customers to suppliers, is becoming extinct. This phenomenon of eliminating intermediaries in supply chains has been coined by some as "disintermediation," a big word for a simple principle: If a company offers nothing of value, it can't survive.

What do businesses want, in terms of value attributes, from a supplier of goods or services? Some value attributes desired by businesses are identical to those of consumers but are important for very different reasons. Businesses view five criteria as being extremely important when deciding whether to order from a particular supplier: cost, quality, dependability of delivery, response time, and flexibility, as depicted in Exhibit 3.3. Depending on the product or service, and on the customer, the value attributes will be priority-ranked differently from one situation to another. They are so important, however, that they provide a framework for firms trying to identify a strategic focus. They are often referred to as the five competitive priorities for operations strategy. They are discussed in detail in a later section.

A Common Set of Value Attributes

Exhibit 3.4 combines the product and service value attributes presented in Exhibits 3.2 and 3.3. It distinguishes those value attributes that tend to be much more important for a particular type of customer from those that tend to be less important. Keep in

EXHIBIT 3.3	Value Attributes for Business Customers	
	Attribute	**Business Concern**
	Cost	What does it cost for the total time of ownership?
	Quality	Does it meet our specifications?
	Dependability of delivery	Does the firm meet its delivery promises?
	Flexibility	Can they adapt to special needs?
	Response time	How quickly can they get it to us?

| Primary and Secondary Value Attributes for Consumer and Business Customers | | | EXHIBIT 3.4 |

Value Attribute	Importance for Consumer Customers	Importance for Business Customers
Cost	Primary	Primary
Quality	Primary	Primary
Response time	Primary	Primary
Dependability of delivery	Secondary	Primary
Convenience	Primary	Secondary
Style/fashion	Primary	Secondary
Ethical issues	Secondary	Secondary
Technology	Secondary	Secondary
Flexibility	Secondary	Primary
Personalization	Primary	Secondary

mind, however, that these are generalizations and there are certainly exceptions to these classifications.

Merging the value attributes for consumer customers and business customers creates a relatively short list. They play an important role in the customer's calculation of value and, as a result, in the customer's purchase decisions.

If every alternative product or service possesses the same value attribute, that attribute is no longer an important part of the purchase decision process. The value attributes that make the difference in a purchasing decision are those that differentiate the product or service from the competition. Thus businesses in the same competitive market try to differentiate themselves on the basis of the value attributes they provide. Businesses routinely seek to attract customers that place a high priority on certain attributes. Some value attributes are very dominant and almost universal, whereas others tend to be less significant. It is important to recognize, however, that for a specific individual consumer or business customer, any one of the attributes could be perceived as critical. These attributes are changing as lifestyles change, new products and services replace old ones, and businesses create new ways to deliver products and services.

Value is passed to the consumer from many places. If the supply chain is examined from the consumer all the way upstream to its starting point, value is added by the network of service and product suppliers and is ultimately brought together by the consumer product or consumer service producer. The value that has been added along the way will be sold to the consumer. The value transfer model in Exhibit 3.5 illustrates how value is transferred from supplier to producer to consumer in a small segment of a supply chain.

The importance of the transfer of value through the supply chain is evidenced by the effort companies are willing to expend to develop and maintain good relationships with quality suppliers. Supplier capabilities, after all, determine a significant portion of the value the consumer sees. The management of these relationships is known as **supply chain management**. It is the effective combination of value from suppliers and value added to enhance it that offers great potential for profitability. No company can be best at everything. Recognizing when a particular part of the value-adding process should be outsourced to a quality product or service supplier is itself an important capability.

The process of alignment between what the customer wants and what a business provides, in the long term, is known as the business strategy.

The world's largest music retailer is Wal-Mart.

supply chain management
The management of supplier customer relationships.

EXHIBIT 3.5	Value Transfer Model

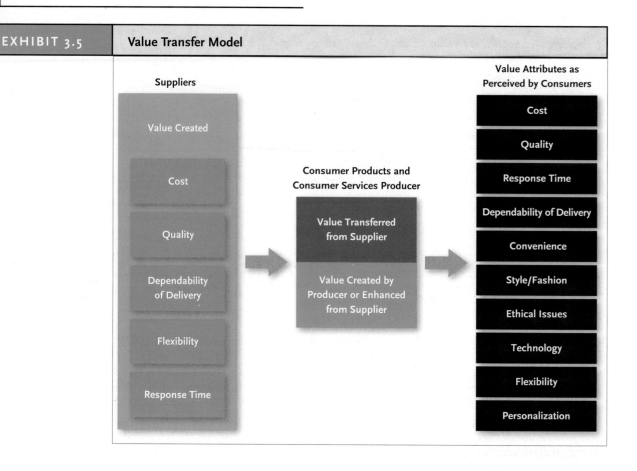

Strategy: A Plan for Creating Value

Simply stated, a strategy is a plan for creating value. The result of an effective strategy is that customers perceive a value that is greater than that offered by competitors, and the firm has made long-term decisions to enable that to continue at an acceptable cost.

Operations and supply chain decisions are such an integral part of any company's competitive success that many long-term resource decisions are strategic in nature. Recall from Chapter 1 that a business must continue to create value for its customers. This must occur even as the customer desires change and even as the business environment changes. Since most operations and supply chain decisions have implications for value, a plan for maintaining long-term consistency between the value attributes created and those desired by customers is necessary. Some decisions are day-to-day in nature, but many others are long term. A long-term decision made today may involve such a long-term commitment of capital or resources that it can't be "remade" in six months. The business commitments that result from these decisions are ongoing and they dictate the firm's ability to succeed in the future.

A strategy is implemented throughout the organization to help guide the decisions of the organization's functional units. Included among these functional units are marketing, finance, human resource management, information technology, and, of course, operations.

Within operations, a strategy is used to guide decisions in a variety of areas that will affect the value attributes sought by customers. The value attributes desired establish strategic priorities to guide day-to-day decisions and have the potential to increase profitability through value enhancement. Beyond that, however, and of key importance, is that in the development of the strategy, decisions affecting long-term use of resources are made. These decisions establish the competitive future of the firm.

The term *strategy* is widely used, but it is also widely misunderstood. A company's strategy is not necessarily what the company publicly says it is. A strategy is the pattern of decisions an organization adopts in order to link resource decisions to goals.[5] The actual pattern of decisions might not be consistent with the business's stated goals. For a business to decide on a particular strategy, it must identify a pattern it wishes to follow in decision making. This often involves the development of business goals. Some of the most important goals relate to how the business wants customers to perceive the value it offers for sale. For example, Avery may strive to be the most reliable supplier of printing supplies. UPS might desire to be the premier low-cost provider of delivery services. Manugistics might seek to be the most advanced developer of logistical computer support systems. If the business has a strategy for meeting its goals, more alternatives are available for making resource-oriented decisions, and those resource investments are more likely to provide the desired outcome.

The Strategic Hierarchy

The concept of a functional strategy, such as an operations strategy or marketing strategy, makes more sense when put into the context of the other levels of strategic management. Exhibit 3.6 shows the hierarchical nature of strategic management and the relative positions of the **mission statement, corporate strategy, business strategy,** and **functional strategies.**

Mission Statement

A short statement of what a business does, what its values are, who its market is, and why is known as a **mission statement**. A mission statement is important because of what it communicates to the public and to potential customers. Through its statement of values, it establishes codes of behavior for employees and tells the world what it views as most important. By defining in broad terms what the business is about, the mission statement sets boundaries for the business strategy. Ben & Jerry's[6] provides an example of a mission statement that addresses all of these issues:

> *Ben & Jerry's is founded on and dedicated to a sustainable corporate concept of linked prosperity. Our mission consists of 3 interrelated parts:*
>
> ### *Product Mission*
> *To make, distribute & sell the finest quality all natural ice cream & euphoric concoctions with a continued commitment to incorporating wholesome, natural ingredients and promoting business practices that respect the Earth and the Environment.*
>
> ### *Economic Mission*
> *To operate the Company on a sustainable financial basis of profitable growth, increasing value for our stakeholders & expanding opportunities for development and career growth for our employees.*
>
> ### *Social Mission*
> *To operate the company in a way that actively recognizes the central role that business plays in society by initiating innovative ways to improve the quality of life locally, nationally & internationally.*

Corporate Strategy

The corporate strategy defines the businesses the corporation will engage in and how resources will be expended in these businesses. Corporate strategies tend to be stated in broad terms because of the diversified nature of many corporations. It would be difficult, for example, to develop specific and directive language in a corporate strategy for a company like General Electric. GE's involvement in such businesses as consumer appliances, locomotives, jet engines, automotive controls, medical equipment, financial services, and broadcasting and entertainment makes it virtually impossible to provide more than general direction at the corporate level. Business strategies for GE, however, are another matter. They are focused, specific, and leave no doubt as to what the business wants to accomplish. The success of GE's businesses leads to corporate success.

---

mission statement
A short statement of what a business does, what its values are, who its market is, and why.

corporate strategy
Defines the businesses that a corporation will engage in and how resources will be expended.

business strategy
Defines the range of activities for a business, setting priorities so that it accomplishes the overall corporate strategy.

functional strategy
A strategy that establishes the link between functional decision making and business strategy.

EXHIBIT 3.6	Strategic Hierarchy

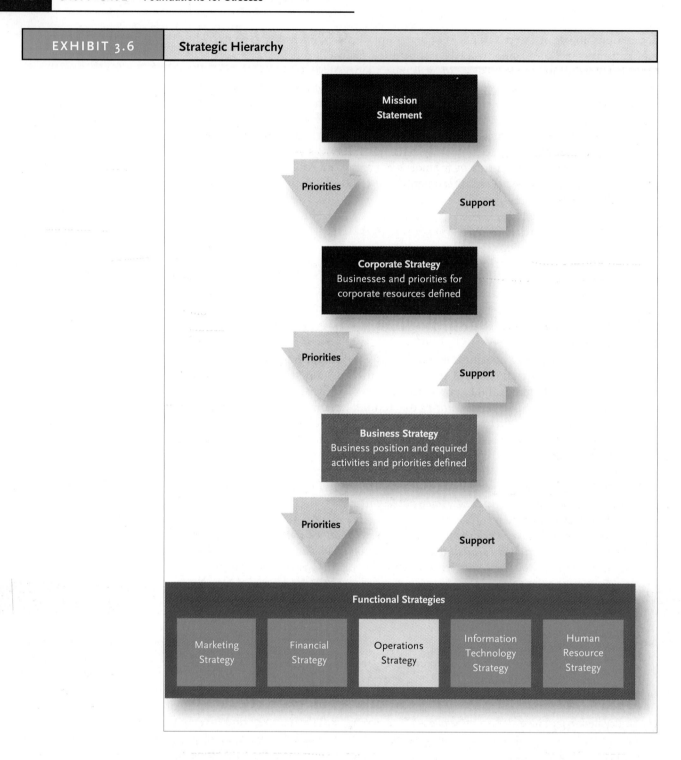

Business Strategy

A business strategy defines the range of activities for a business, setting priorities so that its position in the market can accomplish the corporate strategy. There are numerous effective ways of examining business strategies. One of the most popular ways to define strategies is using Michael Porter's three strategy categories: cost leader, differentiation, and focus.[7]

Cost leadership is obtained by keeping costs lower than those of the competition. This is made possible through efficient operations, good management or processes, removal of waste, and so forth. Cost leadership can lead to a business being able to price its

cost leader strategy
A strategy that seeks to produce goods and services at lower costs than competitors.

goods or services lower than competitors, but doesn't necessarily have to lead to that. The low costs may enable the business to do other things that make it more competitive as well.

A **differentiation strategy** is intended to create products or services that are different enough from those of competitors to be more attractive to potential customers or to result in customers being willing to pay more for them. Differentiators for services might relate directly to such value attributes as convenience, personalization, flexibility, and so on. Differentiators for products might include quality, durability, or services that are included.

A **focus strategy** is designed to focus products and services at a small segment of the market. Rather than seek a small portion of the broad market, the focus strategy seeks a large proportion of a smaller market segment.

Porter's three strategies can be described as plans for creating value. Each seeks to identify a set of customers who will be attracted to it through their own value definition. The success or failure of a business strategy is judged by the ability of the business to attract the customers it targeted.

When Porter's three strategies are examined closely, each can be seen as a way to distinguish one's products or services from the competition. Remember, different people have different perceptions of value. Specific strategies seek to attract customers who prioritize value in a particular way. A business's strategy determines how it will be profitable by identifying a certain target set of customers. For example, does it want to attract the customers whose highest priority is response time? Or does it seek the customers who value the latest fashions above all other attributes? Or can it place several issues of interest to customers at the top of its priority list? Does it seek to be a technological leader? Or does it shun technology in hopes of attracting technology-averse customers?

The business strategy seeks to identify the general basis on which the business will compete. This requires a thorough understanding of the available customers and what they want. It requires an understanding of the capabilities needed to create what those customers want, as well as an understanding of the types of processes needed to create them. In addition, it must project this into an uncertain business future.

In today's rapidly changing business environment, the ability to adapt quickly is a critical success factor. The firm that can react quickly to a changing environment has a distinctive advantage, but being able to react quickly makes long-term decision making even more critical. Decisions such as the business location, large purchases of specific

> **differentiation strategy** ✳
> A strategy that seeks to create products and services that are different from those of competitors.
>
> **focus strategy**
> A strategy that targets a small segment of the market with products or services.

---

om ADVANTAGE   The Competition Continues for Under Armour

Anyone, students included, who envisions a future of inventing that great product or "killer app" needs to realize that large companies don't take kindly to little guys with disruptive technology. Kevin Plank, founder and president of Under Armour, knows firsthand. Plank, a former college football player, developed a shirt to wear under pads. The polyester shirt fits snug, feels good, and wicks away sweat faster than other fabrics. This idea started an entire new category of sporting goods: performance apparel. To build his market, Plank maintained close ties to his customers. He talked to players, responded to their needs, and kept a low profile.

Under Armour is tiny compared to Nike, Reebok, Adidas, and others who missed the initial opportunity. They've noticed, however, and have responded with Dri-Fit, Hydro-move, and ClimaLite. For Under Armour, the challenge is to move from niche product to major market. Plank's plan was to build a women's line of performance apparel.

The first attempt was interrupted when Plank pulled the line at the last minute. The products just weren't good enough. The next attempt included more females in product development and resulted, within a year, of having the second- and third-best fitting sports bras. Unlike Nike, which pays thousands of athletes to wear products, Under Armour pays a few pros and looks for other endorsements. In a few short years the tight-fitting T-shirt has expanded into caps, beanies, jackets, wraps, bags, luggage, headbands, outdoor clothing, gloves, and even tactical camo clothing. Under Armour's first day of public trading was November 18, 2005. Shares opened at $13.10 and closed at $25.30.

Source: "Protect This House," *Fast Company*, August 2005; www.underarmour .com, October 2005, accessed November 7, 2005; "Briefly . . . ," *USA Today*, November 21, 2005, p. B1.

types of equipment, and workforce recruitment and training require large investments and, when changed, require additional investments. Imagine completing construction of a new store only to find that you should have built it three blocks closer to a new highway. Sometimes you simply can't reverse a decision and do it over.

Core Competencies

As competition becomes increasingly complex, product and service life cycles become shorter, and businesses struggle to increase value for customers, focus is often difficult. Many businesses gain strategic advantage by focusing on the few things that they do better than anything else. The capabilities that form the business's strengths are known as **core competencies**.

core competencies
Those capabilities that form a firm's strengths.

Recognizing core competencies is important for strategic planning and for adapting to environmental change for several reasons. First and foremost, a business's strengths become important to its customers. The core competencies form the most critical set of capabilities because these capabilities are not only performed well, but are very likely performed at low cost and provide a means by which the business can differentiate itself from competitors. Any business must guard its core competencies closely. In any strategic decision, it must consider any impact the decision may have on its ability to perform its core competencies.

Operations Strategy

For an operations strategy to be effective, the strategy must prioritize value attributes, identify which value attributes have long-term implications for operations resource (inventory, capacity, facilities, workforce) decisions, and determine what the implications are. The implementation of an operations strategy requires that decisions regarding those resources must be made. That is the execution of the plan and will require investing in resources, managing those resources, and following policies to guide day-to-day decisions.

Effective operations strategy can have a huge financial impact. Some strategic decisions involve large investments—purchases of big-ticket items—that would require a number of years to pay off, such as a new branch for a bank or a robotic machine for a manufacturer. Generally, longer-term decisions involve the largest financial investments. If the priorities of the business must change in a very short time—thus eliminating the need for the new branch or robot—the investment won't be paid off by the revenues it generates. Net income and profit margin suffer because the costs associated with the asset continue. Return on assets suffers because the asset generates no return. Return on equity suffers because the business owners receive a proportionately lower return on their investment. The business may try to sell the asset, but the likelihood that it will get back its initial investment is low. Effective operations strategy can substantially boost all measures of profitability because it guides the purchase of resources.

The competitive power of effective operations strategy has been recognized since the 1980s, when Japanese auto manufacturers began to dominate the U.S. auto market through more effective management of operations resources.

In many cases, the resource decisions that contribute to the firm's competitive position are long term in nature. The ability to effectively make such decisions requires that the business possess a sense of what it wants to accomplish, long term, with those resources. The easiest way to determine this is by establishing goals regarding the value attributes important to the customers the firm wishes to attract. For example, Best Buy might be the cheapest source of the top consumer electronics brands. Another electronics retailer might cater to the audiophile and carry a small inventory of top-end equipment. The selected strategy has implications that include the operations resources of inventory, capacity, facilities, and workforce.

Supply Chain Strategy

Any business or functional strategy defines how value will be created and how it will be matched to customers. The organization's ability to effectively accomplish that match defines its position in the market. Its ability to differentiate itself from competitors gives

om ADVANTAGE   A Focused Strategy in the Women's Clothing Industry

A focused strategy often evolves from learning about the market and about capabilities and finding a small match that no one else has. There are so many players in the retail clothing market, and so many that compete very effectively as cost leaders, that a focused strategy is one road to success. Many companies have attempted and failed, but one in particular, Coldwater Creek, found a narrow place in the market that has led to success selling women's clothing.

Coldwater Creek started in 1984 as a home business run out of a garage. In less than 20 years, it has grown to a company with 1,600 employees and a 20-acre home office campus in Idaho. It also has an East Coast Operations Center in West Virginia. Coldwater Creek sells primarily through its catalog and Web site but also has retail store locations in larger cities. For five consecutive years, Coldwater Creek has been among the 500 fastest-growing companies in the United States. Its emphasis on customer service has resulted in it being ranked at the top in mail-order customer satisfaction. In 1999 Coldwater Creek filled 3.5 million customer orders. By the end of 1999, more than 8 million customers had purchased products; 2.2 million of those had made purchases within the previous 12 months. Customer loyalty remains high, and the customer retention rate was at an all-time high in 1999.

High levels of service alone can provide Coldwater Creek with a different reputation than some mail order firms, but its focused strategy goes beyond that. This focused strategy is important enough that the company made sure investors are aware of it. The 2003 Annual Report provides an example of a true focus:

[Our] customer profile is a professional woman, 30–60 years of age, who puts in a long workweek before going home to care for her family. She is educated, has more discretionary income than free time, and favors the ease of catalog shopping and e-commerce. On those occasions when she has the time, she uses our retail stores as a place to get away from it all—while she shops.

Coldwater Creek does not sell clothing for kids. Not for teens. Not clothing for those under 30. It doesn't sell cheap clothing. It sells clothing for busy women who have money. And the strategy works. In 2000 the company was awarded the Number 1 spot for customer service via e-mail and live chat interactions on the Internet by Customer Relationship Management Grand Prix Awards. In 2001 it was named the nation's best provider of customer service on the telephone, Internet, and e-mail. In 2002, Coldwater Creek's Web site was named Number 1 in customer loyalty and "stickiness" by Nielsen/NetRatings. By the end of 2002, Coldwater Creek had 43 retail stores. By the end of 2004, it had 114 stores in 35 states, with 60 more scheduled for opening in 2005.

Source: http://www.coldwatercreek.com, June 7, 2001; *Coldwater Creek 1999 Annual Report; Coldwater Creek 2000 Annual Report; Coldwater Creek 2004 Annual Report;* Company News on Call, "Coldwater Creek Named #1 for Customer Service Centers in U.S," http://www.prnewswire.com/cgi-bin/stories.pl?ACCT= 105&STORY=/www/story/, June 19, 2001; Company Backgrounds, April 27, 2004, http://www.coldwatercreek.com/asp/HRbackground.asp.

customers a reason to select it over alternatives. We know that a business's ability to differentiate through internal processes and capabilities disappears as soon as a competitor is able to accomplish the same thing. The ability to differentiate products or services through what appear to be completely internal operations-oriented processes can often be enhanced through the behavior of suppliers and its customers. What a supplier does affects what a customer can do. What a customer demands affects how a supplier does it. Multiple firms, coordinating what they do and integrating their processes, find that their individual performance on internal processes improves. The value created for the ultimate customer is enhanced. This is why supply chain management has come to be important. Once businesses recognize that value is enhanced through coordination and integration of supply chain members, businesses have available another entire level of potential competitive differentiation.[8] The fact that supply chain management affects the firm's ability to differentiate competitively makes it an important strategic weapon.

Supply chain management enhances value, with its components of cost, quality (both service and product), and timeliness, not only through internal processes within the realm of operations, but also by processes that are shared between businesses. The value and costs associated with products and services are added throughout their supply chains. The effective management of those supply chains plays an important competitive role. In addition to the value and costs resulting from the operations strategies of all supply chain players, the decisions related to supply chain relationships and between-company processes also have a substantial impact on competitiveness. The competitiveness and success of any supply chain member is determined, to a great extent, by how well the supply chain competes against other supply chains in the same market.

Like operations management decisions, many supply chain decisions are also long-term in nature. Supply chain strategy addresses the various factors that affect supply chain design. Much like the operations decisions such as process or product design, supply chain design decisions are also not easily reversed. They require large investments and need to be made with an accurate forecast of future industry and market trends in mind. Many decisions that are strategic in nature for operations are also strategic decisions for the supply chain. An example of such a decision would be the "make or buy" decision: To what extent will the business supply its own product or service inputs? To what extent will it purchase from others?

Supply chain management pioneer Hau L. Lee has recognized three important qualities supply chains must have in order to provide companies with sustainable competitive advantage.[9]

- **Agility:** Great supply chains are able to react to sudden changes in demand or supply.
- **Adaptability:** Great supply chains adapt as markets and business strategies within the market evolve.
- **Alignment:** The interests of the individual firms with great supply chains are aligned so that when their performance is maximized, the performance of the supply chain is maximized as well.

Examples of supply chain design decisions that are particularly strategic in nature include:

Supply chain management goals: Is the goal of supply chain management to enhance value? Enhance speed? Or reduce costs?

Sourcing decisions: What type of relationship should be established with suppliers? Which products or services should be purchased through long-term relationships? Which products or services should be through one-time transactions? Which products or services should be purchased through auctions? To what extent will alliances with business partners be used in the supply chain?

Logistics network decisions: Where should warehouses be located? Should product inventory be stored centrally, regionally, or locally? Should warehouses be used as storage points or transfer points? Should warehouses be owned or leased?

Supply chain services outsourcing: Should transportation resources (trucks, rail cars, etc.) be owned? Leased? Should transportation and logistics services be done in-house or should they be outsourced? If they should be outsourced, should they all be outsourced to one multifunctional provider? Or should they be outsourced separately?

Globalization: To what extent should the supply chain be extended globally? Should the market end of the supply chain be extended internationally? Should the supply base be extended internationally?

Technology: To what extent is technology integrated in the supply chain? Are such technologies as global positioning systems (GPS) or radio frequency identification (RFID) appropriate? Will they reduce costs or add value? How, and to what extent, do supply chain members share information? What information will be shared with business partners? Which partners will have access?

Security: What efforts should be taken to secure transportation used in the supply chain? Are these efforts extended internationally? How are warehouses secured?

These supply chain decisions and many others have competitive impacts on a business. Many will be discussed in greater detail in later chapters.

om ADVANTAGE   Security: One of the Most Strategic Supply Chain Decisions

Few supply chain decisions have a potential impact as big as that of security. Since 9/11, security risks and prevention have been considered for hundreds of different contexts. The security of the food supply has received significant attention for two reasons. First, a contamination of the food supply would have staggering ramifications. Second, with so many small producers, the food supply chain is very difficult to secure. Imagine securing 2.1 million farms, 900,000 restaurants, 115,000 food processing plants, 34,000 super markets, and all of the transportation that occurs between them.

Take a simple example like milk. Milk supplies originate with thousands of small farms, any number of which are relatively unsecure. An introduction of a contaminant to the milk supply would take several days to identify, and by then it would have affected tens of thousands of people.

Securing the supply chain requires prevention, detection, and, potentially, decontamination. The Bioterrorism Act of 2002 requires that food companies keep records that can be checked by government officials, but, beyond requirements for keeping those records, few regulations exist.

Complicating the issue is the fact that most food products are "commodities." Commodity products compete on the basis of price. Competing on the basis of price creates thin margins and little room for a company to invest in security measures.

Source: M. Boyle, "A Recipe for Disaster," *Fortune*, November 14, 2006, pp. 59–60.

Coping with Change

Environmental forces must also be recognized as important influences on strategy. One of these environmental forces is constant change in competitors' actions that affect the value of products and services. Another is changes in technology that affect potential capabilities. Changes in business ownership also often result in changes in business strategy, because new owners often have different goals.

om ADVANTAGE   McDonald's Strategy Shift Increases Profitability and Demand for Suppliers

In the first quarter of 2003, McDonald's experienced its first-ever financial loss. Competitors that served higher quality food were taking its customers. Its strategy of catering to children and young males with inexpensive food was no longer working well. McDonald's change in focus resulted in more expensive items, such as its California Cobb salad with grilled chicken and a chicken club sandwich. The salads utilize a blend of 16 different lettuces. Along with these entrees came prices higher than McDonald's had ever had.

Despite its knowledge of the price-sensitivity of many McDonald's customers, executives took the risk. The average checkout total increased 5 percent to over $5. The $15.4 billion revenue in 2002 increased to $20.5 billion in 2005. Net income grew from $893.5 million to $2.6 billion in that same three-year period. McDonald's stock has gone from $12.12 in March 2003 to $36.06 in February 2006. Fast-food competitors like Hardee's and Burger King continue to focus on young males as their key customers. For McDonald's, white meat chicken and salads have accounted for more than half of the sales growth since 2003.

McDonald's also developed more expensive items for its breakfast menu, which accounts for up to 25 percent of sales at many franchises. The portability of its bacon, eggs, and hash browns made them more popular, but executives couldn't figure out how to make pancakes portable. The McGriddle, which uses pancakes as the bread in a sandwich, was priced at $2.60, higher than any other breakfast item. In the year following their introduction, McGriddles accounted for about 40 percent of McDonald's same-store sales growth, according to a restaurant industry analyst.

McDonald's strategic shift has had significant impact on its supply chain. Taylor Farms, its major lettuce supplier, provides about 800,000 pounds of specialty lettuce mix and 900,000 pounds of iceberg lettuce each month. Taylor Farms has had to expand its factories twice in recent years. Taylor Farms is supplied by lettuce grower Stan Pura, who has also been forced to expand by renting more land and adding mechanical harvesting equipment.

McDonald's now faces a conflict. Adding menu items and item complexity increases preparation time, which increases customer wait time. Customers expect to move through the drive-through quickly, but a long menu and long preparation times makes that unlikely.

Source: S. Gray, "McDonald's Menu Upgrade Boosts Meal Prices and Results," *Wall Street Journal*, February 18–19, 2006, A1, A7.

om ADVANTAGE   Changing Strategy to Match a Changing Environment

Many services depend on traffic for their customers. Customers, however, come from different sources. Some hotels, for example, may implement a strategy that seeks to attract business customers. Others may locate to attract tourists. Other service businesses in the hospitality and food service industries must make similar decisions. As U.S. business and leisure travel declined following the September 11, 2001, terrorist attacks on New York and Washington, D.C., businesses whose strategy was to seek out those customers had to change their focus.

By October 2001, business travel had dropped 80 percent from one year earlier and leisure travel had fallen off by 25 percent. Many restaurants, particularly high-end, expensive ones, depended on visiting business travelers and tourists for their demand. Restaurants in big cities were hit especially hard, while suburban and neighborhood restaurants were affected less. Expensive restaurants in cities like New York, Los Angeles, Washington, D.C., Boston, and San Francisco were directly hurt by the travel crunch. In some cities, however, New Orleans in particular, locals supported even the most expensive restaurants.

Reductions in demand can be a motivating factor for changes in business approaches. Many restaurants tried extra hard to provide better service during this period. Many needed to replace traveler customers with locals if they were to survive, meaning that they needed to attract more return customers. For many restaurants, a completely different approach to attracting customers was necessary. Changes in the market required changes in strategy for many affected by this disaster.

Source: "Across America, Restaurants Adjust to a Stay-Put Nation," *New York Times on the Web*, October 24, 2001.

Changes in political climate, both domestic and foreign, change cost structures and market access. International businesses, however, face much greater changes and larger risks. Any change can create havoc for the unexpecting company. Companies seeking international markets must adapt their strategies to fit the expectations of new customers.

Successful businesses have learned to adapt to changing conditions. Competition has increased and technology has increased the rate of new product and service development, which has, in turn, reduced the life span of existing products and services. Businesses must constantly scan for new threats to existing business and new opportunities for future businesses. This constant vigilance is known as **environmental scanning**. Environmental scanning is the first step toward adapting to those changing conditions.

Environmental scanning provides early identification of trends that can affect how businesses will or could compete. A close watch on these trends can increase awareness of many things that could affect competitiveness, including:

environmental scanning
Examining the environment for potential effects on strategic decisions.

- Changes in technology that could enhance our products or services, improve information flows, or speed up delivery times.

- Changes in customer expectations driven by changing demographics, by product or service capabilities of our customers, or by new offerings of ours.

- Changes in competitor's product or service offerings that will change how our products and services are viewed in the marketplace.

- Changes in global politics that will open up new markets or sources or that could make doing business more challenging or more costly, forcing us to shift our practices.

- Changes in the regulatory environment that would cause us to modify processes or practices in order to be compliant.

- Changes in costs of such inputs as fuel, raw materials, or transportation.

Retailers as wide ranging as Abercrombie, Eddie Bauer, Target, and CVS must all be aware of potential changes in their environment. A slight change can disrupt the current demand mix and result in missed sales. Services, whether they be financial, insurance, healthcare, or Internet auction houses, must get advanced warning on competitors' intentions. This is often gained through competitive intelligence efforts. Manufacturers must be aware of demand changes at the retail level that indicate potential shifts. Companies that outsource overseas or that have markets overseas must pay particularly close attention to those countries.

Globalization

In 2004, U.S. corporations' profits earned in the United States rose by 7 percent. Their profits earned outside of the United States rose by 26 percent. The share of profit that comes from foreign receipts is currently about 30 percent and is expected to continue to rise. Earnings from abroad are growing significantly faster than U.S. earnings. Clearly, global sales are a great opportunity for U.S. businesses to expand their markets. However, as U.S. businesses expand their markets overseas, they must also face greater competition for those markets.[10]

Expansion into the global economy goes beyond simply selling products abroad. It may involve purchasing inputs (raw materials, labor, etc.) abroad, building facilities abroad, or completely reconfiguring product or service designs to fit the needs of different cultures.

Many companies seek to diversify risks by expanding to international markets. However, as the global economy becomes more integrated, that diversification doesn't help, because the economies of individual countries are not independent. Instead, all tend to follow the rise and fall of global economic conditions.

Even within the United States, changing demographics have resulted in companies changing their strategies to meet the needs of different customers. For the company whose strategy includes flexibility and agility, however, changing demographics may create opportunities. Can a firm make strategically sound long-term decisions in an environment that appears to be in a constant state of flux? Many decisions depend on forecasts of what is likely to happen but will be made with maintaining flexibility as an objective. For example, without a clear picture of future demand, a business might design a new facility at the minimum acceptable size while retaining the capability for expansion in the future if necessary.

Tying Strategy to Decision Making

Grouping strategic decisions into categories of structural and infrastructural decisions is a useful way to examine them. Exhibit 3.7 lists strategic decisions and examples grouped in this way.

A quick overview of the examples listed in Exhibit 3.7 provides evidence that many of the decisions are not independent of each other. For example, the degree to which *process technology* is used in production of a service or product has implications for the skill level of *human resources*. The *capacity* of the service or manufacturing facility dictates the degree of *integration* and the emphasis placed on developing *business partners*. The degree to which the business outsources has implications for *quality management systems*. Just as operations affect other business functions, strategic decisions made within operations affect other decision areas of operations.

Strategic Decisions and Competitive Priorities

The relationships between strategic decisions and value attributes are presented in Exhibit 3.8. In reality, a connecting line drawn from almost every decision box to every value attribute in Exhibit 3.8 could be justified. These relationships enable a business to position itself to successfully compete in the future. Structural decisions relate to such tangibles as buildings, equipment, the way equipment and personnel are organized in processes, and how the business links to other businesses. For the most part, they relate to "bricks and mortar"–type issues. Infrastructural decisions, on the other hand, relate to systems used to enhance the utilization of the structural resources and to control those resources so the business achieves high levels of productivity.

EXHIBIT 3.7	Strategic Decisions in Operations

	Decision Categories	Examples
Structural Decisions	Capacity	High-volume vs. low-volume equipment
		Timing of additional capacity
		Flexibility of capacity
		Overbooking/yield management
	Facilities	Location
		Size
		Design
		Number
		Line of visibility
	Process technology	Type of equipment technology
		Customer involvement
		Layout
		Automation
		Internet presence
	Vertical integration/ supplier relationships	Linkages and business partnerships
		Integration versus outsource
Infrastructural Decisions	Human resources	Skill level
		Part time vs. full time
		Salary position in labor market
		Security
	Quality	Prevention vs. detection
		Control systems
		Specifications
		Involvement with suppliers
	Production planning/ inventory controls	Supplier decisions
		Inventory management systems
		Vendor and outsourcing policies
	New product or service development	Sequential versus parallel activities
		Makeup of new product or service development teams
		Supplier involvement
	Performance measurement and reward systems	Focus: individual vs. group incentives
		Types of performance measure
		Types of reward (bonus, stock options, etc.)
	Organization/systems	Organization structure
		Line and staff relationships

Source: Adapted from R. H. Hayes and S. C. Wheelwright, *Restoring Our Competitive Edge: Competing through Manufacturing* (New York: Wiley, 1984), p. 31; and R. H. Hayes, S. C. Wheelwright, and K. B. Clark, *Dynamic Manufacturing* (New York: Free Press, 1988), p. 351.

Ten strategic decision categories and ten value attributes create a lot of relationships, but they aren't all equally important for a specific company. For example:

- A bank having mostly business accounts would utilize the relationship between process technology decisions and response time.
- A clothing store specializing in fraternity and sorority logo clothing would take advantage of a strong relationship between facilities decisions and convenience.

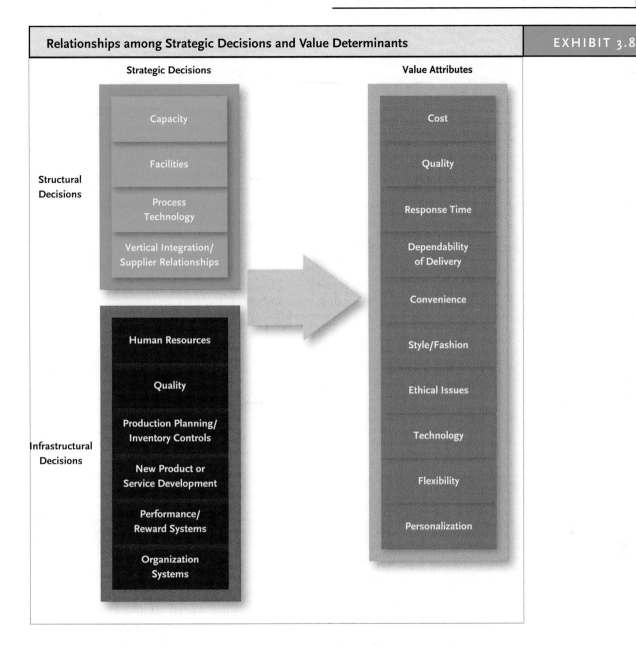

Relationships among Strategic Decisions and Value Determinants   EXHIBIT 3.8

- A contract manufacturer who assembled a variety of products for customers would take advantage of a strong relationship between vertical integration/supplier relationships and dependability of delivery.

- An information technology consulting firm with lots of ongoing projects and project teams would focus on the relationship between organization systems and flexibility.

The complexity of the network of relationships between decisions and their effects on value increases the likelihood that a decision will have an outcome that is not anticipated. This is sometimes referred to as the *law of unintended consequences*. The need to prioritize those value attributes that are more strategic in nature has led to an operations focus on a short list—**competitive priorities**—of cost, quality, dependability of delivery, flexibility, and response time. It is no coincidence that the competitive priorities of operations precisely match the B2B value attributes. These five attributes provide the means through which the operations function and members of the supply chain add value and enhance competetiveness.

competitive priorities
Key value attributes that are highly influenced by operations management: cost, quality, dependability of delivery, flexibility, and response time.

Competitive Effects of Structural Decisions

Capacity Decisions

Capacity decisions determine output capabilities. Capacity is generally defined in terms of an output measure per unit of time, or an output rate. Customers per hour, claims per hour, units per day—all are examples of measures of capacity. Since capacity determines rate of output, competitive priorities most closely tied to capacity decisions are those that are related to output rate and volume. Capacity decisions can affect all five competitive priorities.

design capacity
The capacity a facility is designed to accommodate on an ongoing basis.

The term *capacity* has many contexts, but an important one is **design capacity**, the capacity a facility is designed to accommodate on an ongoing basis. Design capacity may refer to a factory, a restaurant, a hotel, an airport, or any other productive system. Cost is affected by design capacity through its impact on cost per unit. For any facility, whether it be a factory or a service business, cost per unit is at its lowest when the production or service rate matches the design capacity.

Quality is also affected by the match between design capacity and demand. For manufacturers, output rates lower than design capacity do not typically result in lower levels of quality directly, but they can result in increases in inventory produced, which can negatively affect quality. For restaurants, bars, and other activity-oriented services, attempts to meet demands that exceed design capacity can cause long lines and poor service.

protective capacity
A layer of capacity above that which is absolutely required to meet known demand, providing the firm with the ability to handle occasional problems and enabling them to handle special requests.

Dependability of delivery has been increasing in importance for both consumers and business customers. In services and product-oriented businesses, when capacity is tight, any unexpected disruption can result in a missed due date. Protection from these disruptions can be achieved by incorporating **protective capacity.** Protective capacity is a layer of capacity above that which is absolutely required to meet known demand. It provides firms the ability to handle occasional problems that come up and also gives them the ability to handle a special request.

Flexibility is determined by the relationship between design capacity and the capacity required to meet demand at any given time. Flexibility can translate into new customers, stronger relationships with existing customers, and greater long-term profitability.

om ADVANTAGE   Making Room for Airbus

Facility-related decisions are often some of the most strategically important decisions a firm faces. Location and size decisions have tremendous cost implications and also play a key role in setting limits on the capacity of the business and the volume of customers or products it can process. Forecasts of demand are often included in the information used to make facility decisions, but forecasts of potential changes in the market, changes in customers, or even changes in technology are also important.

As facilities go, few are as costly or complex as airports. Airports process planes, customers, crews, and luggage. They serve as maintenance and repair centers for the planes, which belong to another business, so that places the airport in the position of having both business-to-business and business-to-consumer interactions. While the insides of many airports have been upgraded to the point that many resemble shopping malls, the facility components that accommodate aircraft have gone unchanged for decades.

Many airports are now facing the challenge of accommodating the Airbus A380. The A380 is 8 feet longer and has a tail that is 16 feet taller and a wingspan 50 feet greater than

the Boeing 747-400. While the 747-400 weighs a maximum of 875,000 pounds at takeoff, the 380 weights in at 1,230,000 pounds. It seats a maximum of 853 people, as opposed to 524 for the 747-400. Changes necessary to accommodate the 380 include such things as reinforcing and widening runways, speeding up luggage handling, increasing the space between terminals and gates and the size of taxiways and lounge areas, and expanding catering access.

The U.S. city expected to have the most 380 traffic by 2023 is Los Angeles. By 2010 it is expected to serve over 20 380s per day with over 15,000 passengers. The 380 will be in use in 2006. Currently, however, LAX lags behind other cities, such as London, Tokyo, and Hong Kong, in preparing to welcome the 380. Airbus managers have stated that carriers may need to switch to San Francisco if LAX is not ready. LAX will need to relocate runways and build new ones to accommodate the 380. This process will disrupt airline traffic of other planes for months.

Source: A. Pasztor, "Accommodating the 380," *Wall Street Journal*, November 29, 2005, pp. B1–B2.

Response time is of interest to consumers as well as business customers. Capacity has a direct impact on response time because idle capacity can respond immediately to demand. Busy capacity cannot. For services, the relationship between capacity and rate of demand often results in the presence or absence of a waiting line. For many customers, the length of a wait in a line is one criterion in evaluating service quality.

Facility Decisions

Facility decisions can also affect all five competitive priorities. The impact facility decisions have on cost can be traced to the facility's share of the overhead costs. It has an impact on other costs as well. Location decisions affect the initial cost of building or acquiring the facility, and taxes, utility rates, transportation costs, and labor rates.

Facility decisions also affect quality. Facility design and location have a direct impact on the quality of a service that requires the customer to actually come to the service. Customers want an environment compatible with their expectations. For some services, that environment is an integral part of the total package they're paying for.

While most customers who purchase products don't care about the "ambiance" of the factory in which they were made, facility location affects the type of skilled labor force available.

For B2B and B2C interactions, reliability depends on dependability of delivery at the promised time. Inventories are often held at low levels, so missing a delivery by only a day can create problems for a production schedule. Location decisions affect the reliability of delivery, if only because short transportation distances offer less opportunity for disruptions.

Long-term facility decisions have an important impact on flexibility. In some cases, a business flourishes, and expansion soon becomes necessary. Initial facility decisions can play a big part in the ease of an expansion to an existing facility. Demand changes over time, delivery methods change over time, so the successful business needs to stay abreast of changing needs.

Quick response time, particularly in a B2B relationship, is characterized by rapid response to requests and can depend on reliable transportation and a nearby location. Close proximity to customers has become more important as supplier relationships have become longer term and expectations have risen to daily—or even more frequent—deliveries of goods.

Wal-Mart's move from its smaller stores to super centers has created numerous empty buildings like this one. Lack of flexibility in store capacity prevents most stores from expanding; they build completely new facilities instead. Empty buildings are difficult to find a use for.

In most facility decisions, the outside appearance of the facility isn't as critical as such issues as the location or the interior design. As can be seen here, however, the external appearance of the Longeberger Basket Company Headquarters building in Dresden, Ohio, is quite unique.

Process Technology Decisions

Process technology decisions determine how technology will actually be used in the business. All competitive priorities may be affected by these decisions.

Cost reduction is a frequent objective of technology in the production of products and services. These cost reductions can be passed on to the customer or can be held to increase

TARGETING technology   The Value of Precision

Differentiating capabilities often result from the application of technologies not originally designed for business use. One technology having a profound impact on customer service in logistics and transportation businesses is global positioning systems, or GPS technology, which was originally intended for military application. GPS technology incorporates the use of 28 satellites to enable anyone with a GPS device to pinpoint a position on earth with extreme accuracy, often within 1 foot.

The ability to track exact location and movement has many implications for customer service. For businesses that must be able to tell customers exactly *when* a delivery will arrive, knowing exactly *where* that shipment is at any given moment is critical. GPS technology yields that information, and more. Con-Way NOW is an example of the important role GPS can play. Con-Way NOW is a small division (350 trucks) of the huge transportation company CNF, which manages 41,000 trucks, tractors, and trailers. Con-Way

NOW operates on the principle of "time-definite delivery." If a delivery is more than two hours late, it's half price. If it's four or more hours late, it's free. That promise holds for deliveries of a few miles or thousands of miles.

GPS satellites orbit approximately 11,000 miles above the earth. The satellites are supported by the U.S. military, and GPS access is free to anyone. Applications range from attaching GPS devices to products for theft prevention, to attaching GPS collars to cattle, to systems that warn when delivery vehicles are approaching.

Commercial applications, like those of Con-Way NOW, are booming, but consumer use is also about to explode. By 2005 all cell phones will have GPS technology so they can be located in emergencies.

Source: Charles Fishman, "The Sky's the Limit," *Fast Company*, July 2003, p. 90; http://www.trimble.com, May 3, 2004; "High-Tech Help for Lost Souls," *BusinessWeek*, December 8, 2004.

net income. Costs reduced by appropriate technological innovation include labor costs, cost of waste, costs of carrying too much inventory, and utility costs.

Technology can also be used to improve the quality of goods and services. Processes that are controlled so that variability is reduced are inherently better quality. In many manufacturing processes, quality tolerances would be impossible to maintain without automated processes and controls. In many services, processes can be automated to increase processing speed and provide quicker service.

Dependability of delivery can be affected by process technology decisions because making processes less variable makes them more consistent. For services, process technology also tends to make processing each customer more consistent and timely by reducing the time for interaction and reducing the likelihood that the customer would want special treatment.

Internet-based technology can result in virtually seamless communication links between business partners. The result is an ability to respond more quickly and with greater flexibility in a business environment that continues to increase its amount of outsourcing.

For many situations, technology results in shorter response time. This is particularly true with new product or service introductions. The process of designing the new product or service and then bringing it through production can take a long time, reducing the advantage gained by being first to the market. Technological enhancements to the design and engineering process enable product design and process design to be performed concurrently. Production processing times are often reduced when automated. Better communication with suppliers, also made possible through technological linkages, enables more and earlier involvement on their part as well.

Vertical Integration and Supplier Relationship Decisions

Strategies related to vertical integration, supplier relationships, and outsourcing also have implications for all five competitive priorities.

There used to be a strong incentive to vertically integrate, rather than depend on suppliers or subcontractors for inputs to productive systems. At that time, if you wanted it done right, you did it yourself. Doing something in-house was generally viewed as cheaper, and most businesses wanted to be able to control their own supplies of inputs. An increase in focus on core competencies has changed all that. Core competencies are those things a firm does really well. Sticking to what it does well keeps a business focused on those capabilities that distinguish it from others.

CD shipments to retailers totaled 705 million in 2005, down from 767 million in 2004.

Outsourcing can be a wise choice because it may take advantage of another business's core competencies. It can reduce costs, increasing value contributed to the supply chain. Businesses exist in a complex environment of contingent workforces, contract manufacturers, business partners, and long-term suppliers. A great deal of the value added to products and services results from outsourcing. The end result is better products, better services, and greater efficiencies within supply chains.

Outsourcing decisions can also improve quality. Processes controlled by suppliers and subcontractors have as much impact on quality as the processes owned by the company itself. Quality that is enhanced or reduced will become a part of the finished product or service, no matter where in the supply chain it was produced.

The processes completed by suppliers take time. All time-consuming portions of value-adding processes affect dependability of delivery. Dependability within the supply chain may be reduced as outsourcing increases because of transportation between the supplier and the producer. Good buyer–supplier relationships are the difference between an effective supply chain and a disjointed network of uncommitted suppliers.

The successful business must react to change. Flexibility is necessary to meet the needs of business customers, who themselves must reduce response time and increase adaptability. For some firms, a decision to outsource increases flexibility. The best long-term strategy for producing components that require frequent process change may be to not produce them at all. Outsourcing may increase component costs, but it will eliminate the uncertainty associated with investing in equipment that may become obsolete.

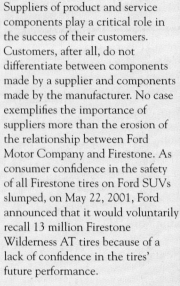

Suppliers of product and service components play a critical role in the success of their customers. Customers, after all, do not differentiate between components made by a supplier and components made by the manufacturer. No case exemplifies the importance of suppliers more than the erosion of the relationship between Ford Motor Company and Firestone. As consumer confidence in the safety of all Firestone tires on Ford SUVs slumped, on May 22, 2001, Ford announced that it would voluntarily recall 13 million Firestone Wilderness AT tires because of a lack of confidence in the tires' future performance.

Response time can be affected negatively as the amount of outsourcing increases, but strategic placement of inventory can reduce the effect. Transportation of materials always takes time, adding to the cash-to-cash cycle, but can be managed through effective supply chain management. If inventory is placed well, it might not add to the waiting time of customers, however. Location of suppliers can make a big difference in the transportation time required. In many industries, suppliers locate as close to their major customers as possible to minimize that impact. Exhibit 3.9 summarizes the competitive effects of structural decisions.

Summary of Competitive Effects of Structural Decisions					EXHIBIT 3.9
Strategic Structural Decision Categories	**Competitive Priorities**				
	Cost	**Quality**	**Dependability of Delivery**	**Flexibility**	**Response Time**
Strategic Capacity Decisions	Cost per unit and match between design capacity and load.	Demand and design capacity dictate queues, quality of customer interaction.	Protective capacity to cope with disruptions.	Protective capacity for quick response.	Idle capacity provides lack of queues, quick response.
Strategic Facility Decisions	Reduced purchase, lease, and upkeep costs.	Service "ambiance," work environment.	Delivery times resulting from location; effective layout improves processes.	Ease of facility expansion and change.	Location dictates delivery response time.
Strategic Process Technology Decisions	Reduced labor costs, inventory costs, utility costs.	Improved process control, reduced variability.	Reduced variability of completion times.	Improved communication along supply chain.	Reduced time for product design and production processes.
Strategic Vertical Integration/ Supplier Relationship Decisions	Focus on core competencies improves productivity.	Long-term relationships enhance quality.	Transportation from suppliers can reduce reliability.	Capabilities of large suppliers can affect flexibility.	Response time can be lengthened by adding suppliers.

Competitive Effects of Infrastructural Decisions

Human Resource Decisions

Strategic human resource decisions involve the skill and experience level required of employees, training commitments, staff development, contingent or temporary staffing issues, and, in general, how the organization views its investment in personnel. These decisions have implications for cost, quality, and flexibility.

Cost is influenced by strategic human resource decisions because of the labor component of the firm's cost structure. Labor costs, which are present in most business environments, are often more important for services. For many manufacturers, labor costs have been reduced through advances in automation. Overhead costs, however, have often increased as a result of an increased need for nondirect labor such as administrative personnel, technicians, and managers.

Quality is influenced by labor decisions in manufacturing and services. Manufacturing jobs are increasingly technical, requiring more expertise. Service-oriented firms struggle to find employees who can succeed when customer contact and expectations are high. Employee turnover leads to an overall lowering of the experience of the workforce, reducing employee effectiveness. Firms with variable demand may attempt to maintain flexibility by hiring temporary employees. This approach has many benefits, including reduced cost of salary and benefits, as well as an opportunity to "try out" an employee prior to hiring on a permanent basis. Using temporary employees also has some negative effects, however. Temporary employees typically haven't had as much experience, which can result in lower levels of quality.

Quality Decisions

Strategic quality decisions include those related to the design of systems used to maintain quality. Decisions regarding quality systems affect other competitive priorities as well, however. Because quality means doing what the customer wants, all customers are going to consider quality as important, and many will lump other competitive priorities into what they perceive as issues of quality.

Much of what the customer perceives as quality is determined by day-to-day decisions. The systems that specify those day-to-day decisions, however, are the result of more strategic decisions regarding the role quality will play competitively. An example of a quality system would be a business's efforts to become quality certified through a global certification body or to seek a national or state quality award.

Strategic quality decisions affect cost in several ways. First, efforts devoted to maintaining high-quality inputs to products and services require closer relationships with suppliers and better inputs to their systems. Better relationships result in lower quality-related costs. Processes with higher-quality goals may require more investment in process technology, more sophisticated equipment, or more highly trained employees, however. These may cause short-term cost increases, but over time costs decrease and value is enhanced as well. Higher levels of quality result in less waste, less scrap for manufacturers, and less labor required to fix what should have been done correctly the first time.

Quality systems also include the use of tools to reduce the variability in processes, which can improve delivery dependability. In addition, when processes are not functioning well, the length of time required can be even more difficult to predict. Problems with defects can occur at the worst possible time, delaying order completion.

Flexibility is also enhanced by the effective use of quality management systems. Better control over processes facilitates the understanding of the capabilities of those processes. Better knowledge of process capabilities makes it easier to respond to special requests.

Strategic quality decisions can influence response time by eliminating potential delays resulting from quality problems. Delays can also result from quality problems in services. Airlines, for example, frequently experience delays resulting from equipment maintenance problems. Poor-quality inputs, coming from a supplier that didn't meet specifications, can result in delays as well, because excess time is required when employees must identify and sort poor-quality inputs.

Production Planning/Inventory Control Decisions

Strategic production planning and inventory control decisions include the design, development, and role of systems used to manage production planning and scheduling, equipment use, capacity, and inventories. Production planning and control systems have been used predominantly in manufacturing; however, new technologies have resulted in an influx of capacity-related planning systems being used in services as well. Inventory management systems have been used in both manufacturing and services. Integrated systems, such as enterprise resource planning (ERP) systems, have become increasingly common. Competitive priority implications for these systems vary from one application to another but can affect all five competitive priorities.

Strategic production planning and inventory control decisions affect costs in different ways. Production planning and control systems contribute to the productivity of resources by making it possible to accurately match the supply of capacity and inventory to demand. Inventory, for example, can be reduced if order quantities and timing of orders are more accurate, and expensive equipment can be utilized more effectively if schedules are accurate. An appropriate match of demand and supply creates an environment where processes can run at their optimal rates.

Production planning and control systems enhance dependability of delivery by providing a means to improve the prediction of how long processes will take. With ineffective systems, schedules used to determine completion time are not accurate reflections of reality and accurate order promise dates are impossible.

For some firms, particularly manufacturers of products that must be customized, technologies have enhanced flexibility. Some sophisticated manufacturing systems allow design changes to a machined product to be made on a computer using a computer-aided design (CAD) system. The digital information is then transferred directly to the machining centers, and the product is automatically machined to match the design changes.

The ability to effectively plan and schedule demands on capacity and inventory can greatly improve response time. For many businesses, scheduling products and services through a complex series of steps can be a daunting process. Numerous systems have been developed—many that are industry-specific—to aid in this task.

New Product or Service Development Decisions

Strategic decisions related to new product or service development address such topics as market research, the product or service development process itself, and how the firm views itself in terms of new products or services. Is it an innovator or market leader? Or does it take on a more conservative follower role? These decisions have implications for cost, quality, flexibility, and response time.

New product and service design processes dictate the product or service attributes that will provide the value customers seek. Matching the product and service design to the business's capabilities keeps costs in check.

New product or service development processes contribute to quality because they link product and service design with customer expectations. Without that link to customer needs, creating a product or service that actually met the needs of the customer would be a random event. For products and services, the production process must ensure that quality levels are maintained.

Product and service design decisions have a long-term impact on flexibility. Robust designs enable the business to adapt in the future. Products that incorporate modular design schemes make it easier to integrate innovations when needed. Effective designs also make it easier to deal with different or changing suppliers of component parts. Flexibility can also be designed right into the processes that create services. Designing a process with a minimum of steps in a fixed sequence, for example, makes the process much more flexible.

As technology quickens the pace of innovation, product life cycles have been compressed. A product life cycle is the amount of time from a product's introduction through

The fourth quarter of 2005 marked the first quarter in which sales of digital music players made up a majority of Apple's overall sales.

om ADVANTAGE   A New Concept for Convenience Stores

Differentiation in a mature industry often requires an "outside of the box" approach. Convenience stores, notoriously difficult to run profitably, have long been a target for new and more profitable business models. In a typical convenience store, labor costs are high because of the need for a minimum of two or three employees on site at all times. Margins are low, and theft is rampant. Smart-Mart, opening its first store in Memphis, is the first fully automated drive-through convenience store. Each store offers up to 1,500 items, selected via a touch screen. After the items are selected, the customer pays with cash or credit, and the products are automatically delivered via a conveyor belt. Customers needing assistance can videoconference live with a SmartMart staffer at the headquarters call center.

SmartMart developer, Mike Rivalto, claims a 62 percent reduction in overhead makes the store much more productive than manned stores. Labor costs are the highest fixed expense in convenience stores and typically account for 6 to 7 percent of total sales. The pilot store in Memphis quickly became profitable after its May 2003 opening.

Source: "The Latest Evolution in Convenience Stores?" National Association of Convenience Stores Online, June 5, 2003, http://www.nacsonline.com/NACS/News/Daily_News_Archives/June2003/nd0605035.htm; J. Robertson, "The Really Convenient Store," *Business 2.0*, March 2004; http://www.smartmartinc.com/tour.htm, May 3, 2004.

declining demand. In this context, response time means responding to the market, not to an individual customer. These cycles are often short, so being first to market with a new product or service—or an innovation spun from an old one—is important. The time it takes for a product or service to get from the idea stage to market is inversely related to sales volume.

Performance/Reward System Decisions

Strategic decisions related to performance and reward systems determine how good performance might be rewarded and how bad performance might be punished. The effects tend to be indirect but quite broad and far-reaching. Cost and quality are affected substantially by reward systems.

Costs are affected because, in many cases, rewards are monetary. The issue isn't necessarily that the monetary rewards are given out, but it does raise the question of whether there is a return on that investment. Do the rewards result in higher retention of employees and greater levels of productivity? If so, the costs are justified by their effects. If not, the costs merely increase the cost of those employees.

The impact of the reward system on quality depends on the link between rewards and employee performance. Employees react to their work environment. The service–profit chain provides a model of how employee satisfaction leads to high quality in the service sector.[11] Satisfied employees are not as likely to leave to work for someone else, thus the rates of employee retention are higher. The higher retention rates result in the business having more experienced employees, and employees with greater levels of experience are able to provide higher levels of quality. These higher levels of quality result in improved customer satisfaction, higher levels of customer loyalty, and greater profit.

Organization System Decisions

The design and structure of the organization itself dictates the chain of command, the flow of decisions, the span of responsibility of managers, and how major decisions are made. This issue is most significant for two time-related competitive priorities: flexibility and response time.

Flexibility is valueless without speed. Customers who want something special or unique want to get a commitment for it within a reasonable length of time. Requests that must be passed through levels of management and then get signed off for approval take time that could be used producing what the customer wants. The customer wants a "yes" or a "no." Any delay in that response is time the customer could be using to locate someone else to do the work.

Organization systems influence decisions by identifying the authorities within the organization that make those decisions. Is decision-making authority given to front-line employees? Or must they seek approval from higher levels of management to make everyday decisions? The degree of autonomy given to lower-level employees plays a major role in the firm's response time. Decisions that must be passed up to higher levels of management add waiting time to the customer's experience. Autonomy can result in quick decisions and a customer that has greater confidence in the contact personnel. Exhibit 3.10 summarizes the effect competitive priorities can have on strategic decisions.

Strategic Decisions and Competitive Priorities

The previous sections provided a broad overview of the links between strategic decision categories and competitive priorities of operations. Competitive priorities themselves, however, are not independent. Each has implications for others. Response time is related to flexibility. Flexibility can be related to cost. Quality can be related to dependability of delivery. And the list goes on and on. Some priorities can conflict with others. For example, increasing flexibility may increase costs. Reducing response time may increase costs. Improving dependability of delivery may reduce flexibility. It is not uncommon to have to make tradeoffs between these priorities. Typical tradeoffs result in giving up one advantage for the sake of gaining another. Progress has been made, however, to eliminate

Strategic Structural Decision Categories	Competitive Priorities				
	Cost	Quality	Dependability of Delivery	Flexibility	Response Time
Strategic Human Resource Decisions	Direct and indirect labor costs.	Level of expertise, turnover, contingent worker use.		Training and skill enhancement lead to adaptability.	
Strategic Quality Decisions	Better supplier relationships, better processes, less waste.	Quality systems enhance ability to meet customer expectations.	Reduced process variability enhances stability and predictability.	Enhanced knowledge of capabilities and limitations of processes.	Elimination of quality-related delays.
Strategic Production Planning/ Inventory Control Decisions	Improved use of resources, enhanced productivity, inventory reduction.	Improved match of capacity and demand: better service.	Better schedules, more accurate delivery promises.	Enhanced communica-tion with equipment, quicker response.	Enhanced utilization increases avail-able capacity.
Strategic New Product or Service Decisions	Design compati-bility with current capabilities.	Link between new product or service design and customer.		Design with future modifica-tions in mind.	Time to market dictated by new product/service design process.
Strategic Performance/ Reward System Decisions	Effectiveness of monetary rewards in enhancing worker productivity.	Increased em-ployee retention leads to more experienced employees.			
Strategic Organization System Decisions				Quick reaction to special needs built into organization structure.	Decision making at lower levels reduces delays.

Summary of Competitive Effects of Infrastructural Decisions   **EXHIBIT 3.10**

some of the common tradeoffs. A classic example is the tradeoff associated with produc-ing high volumes (for low costs) and the ability to customize. Historically, high-volume production eliminated the ability to customize. This has typically meant that customiza-tion couldn't be done at low cost. Technological advances and enhancements in product design, however, have made **mass customization** possible. Decision categories aren't in-dependent either. Structural decisions affect infrastructural decisions. Capacity decisions affect facility decisions. Facility decisions affect process technology decisions. Facility de-cisions affect organization system decisions. And they *all*, ultimately, will influence prof-itability measures.

A model of the relationships among and between all strategic decisions and competi-tive priorities very quickly resembles a plate of spaghetti. Identifying and discussing every

mass customization
The ability to customize in high volumes.

one is overwhelming. The fact that the relationships are highly intertwined, combined with the fact that they all affect profitability, means that:

- Managers must first establish priorities and then make decisions that are consistent with those priorities.
- Managers must have a view and understanding of the enterprise as a whole. The interactions between and among strategic decisions and competitive priorities are numerous and complex, and ignore departmental boundaries. Without an enterprise perspective, the law of unintended consequences will run rampant because the ability to anticipate the effect one change has on other aspects of the business will be missing.

Capabilities

Value is rarely just lying around to be picked up by a savvy entrepreneur. If it were that easy to come by, no one would be willing to pay for it. Value must be created. Someone gets an idea for a product or service, but that's the easy part. The tough part is coming up with ways to produce that product or service so that it will not only satisfy the high-priority value attributes of the targeted customers, but also accomplish that goal at a cost that leaves room for profit. This is the challenge of designing and managing the processes and capabilities of the firm.

Capabilities versus Processes

The differences between capabilities and processes are subtle, but it is important to understand them, because any attempt to improve value must be focused on the correct target. In general, capabilities define what a business can do. For example, FedEx can deliver products quickly. Suburban Rails designs and constructs skateboard parks. A company might be able to provide excellent financial or tax advice. These are all capabilities. The capabilities are the firm's ability to create an outcome that customers value. Processes provide an organizing structure for resources so that they can create these capabilities.

It is important to recognize the difference between capabilities and processes because matching customer needs and identifying problems depend on it. Perhaps the capability matches the customer needs but the process doesn't create it effectively or the capability is wrong even though the process is effective. Customers buy the capability from the producer because they don't have it themselves.

Let's use as an example a simple idea for a business, then backtrack through all of the necessary requirements. Suppose a local entrepreneur wants to fill a void in the town's food service market with a very quick pizza delivery service. She wants to guarantee pizza delivery within 20 minutes of a phone order. That is her differentiating strategy, and it has serious implications for the way her business must operate. From a value attribute perspective, she's electing to compete on the basis of *response time* and *convenience*. She hopes that a delivery that is faster than everyone else will differentiate her business enough from competitors to gain substantial market share.

If the issue of "quick response time" is examined further and broken down into its components for the pizza business, we can identify three capabilities that are prerequisites to accomplishing our strategic objectives. These prerequisites are presented in Exhibit 3.11. The capabilities of fast preparation, fast baking, and fast delivery have significant impact on the process components of each. The sum must be less than 20 minutes. The component that will be the most difficult to control will probably be the delivery time, since the owner can't control traffic. As evident in Exhibit 3.11, each of these capabilities entails some commitments that are long term in nature and that have implications for the initial design of the business. These commitments relate directly to several of the strategic decision areas discussed earlier. Those that are particularly important in this case would be capacity (such as pizza preparation capacity, oven capacity, deliverer capacity), facilities (such as location, pizza prep area design), process technology

Strategic Objectives versus Capabilities versus Process Requirements

EXHIBIT 3.11

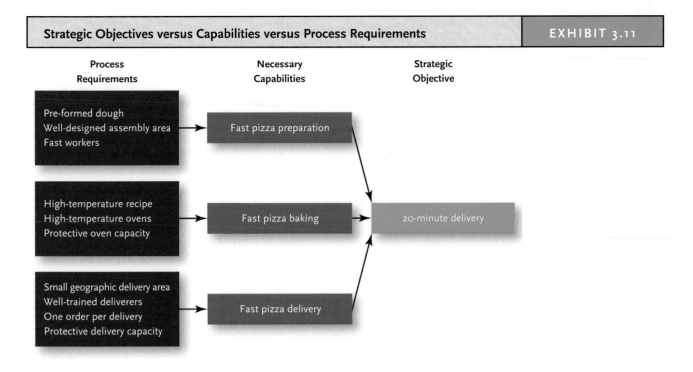

omADVANTAGE   Business Method Patents: Good or Bad?

Business method patents have been hotly debated since an appeals court validated them in 1998. During their first year of availability, 2,821 were issued. The next year 7,800 were issued. In fiscal year 2000, the U.S. Patent and Trademark Office issued only 899. The Patent Office now requires a "second pair of eyes" to see business method patent applications and has also begun to send out examiners to corporations to find out about the processes. This is an attempt to identify which ones are obvious and routine and therefore not eligible for patents. These steps have resulted in patent applications being returned with questions.

The debate has two distinct sides. The efforts to tighten up the issuance of business method patents are criticized by those who favor looser business patent approval processes. They claim that a patent is a patent, and these new examination procedures applied only to business method applications are, in effect, changing the law. On the other side of the argument are those who claim that many business method patents are issued for methods that are simply computerizing obvious tasks that were previously done with pencil and paper. Amazon's One Click Ordering (U.S. Patent No. 5,960,411) has been a target. Barnes & Noble, for example, appealed a court decision so it could continue to use its Express Lane feature. Other well-known business process patents include Priceline's Reverse Auction Patent (U.S. No. 5,794,207), DoubleClick's Banner Ad Patent (U.S. No. 5,948,061), and Open Market's Electronic Shopping Cart Patent (U.S. No. 5,715,314). The result of the scrutiny is that in the final quarter of 2000, only 36 percent of the business method patent applications were approved, compared to an approval rate on all patent applications of 72 percent for 2000.

Clearly a business method is different from a new-product design. Many suggestions have been put forth for changing the business method patent to make it distinct. For example, a patent is good for 17 years. There have been suggestions for business method patents to be for much shorter periods of time. The average patent approval process takes 26 months. For a business method, particularly one that is technology related, a 26-month delay could make the method obsolete before the company got the protection it sought.

Source: "Fewer Patents on Methods Get Clearance," *Wall Street Journal,* March 21, 2001, pp. A3, A6; "Raising the Bar on Business Patents," *BusinessWeek.com,* April 21, 2001; "In Business This Week: Patent Pounding at Amazon," *BusinessWeek .com,* February 26, 2001; R. Weisman, "Five Patents That Changed E-Business," *ECommerce Times,* November 11, 2002, www.ecommercetimes.com; "What Is a 'Business-Method Patent'?" http://www.gigalaw.com/articles/2001-all/ kirsch-2001-05-all.html, September 31, 2005.

(such as oven temperature, pizza dough recipe), and human resources (such as worker speed and training). These resources will perform well-defined tasks that make up the pizza preparation, baking, and delivery processes.

Most businesses, including this one, have more than one strategic objective. In addition to quick delivery, the pizza business might also have an objective relative to price and quality. Fast deliveries aren't worth much if the pizza is priced too high or if it tastes like cardboard. Capabilities related to these objectives are also important, as are the process requirements necessary to actually possess those capabilities. They might include specific ingredients, suppliers, reward systems, and so on. As evident in Exhibit 3.11, each capability can be broken down into its process requirements.

For some firms, the process is so critical to their success that they actually patent the process to prevent others from using it. This is particularly true when there is no way to effectively keep the process secret. But even with those breakthrough processes, other product and service attributes are necessary. The following section takes a closer look at the phenomenon of differentiation.

Order Qualifiers and Order Winners

Customers have many expectations of the services and products they purchase. One way to look at a customer's purchasing decision is by identifying **order qualifiers** and **order winners**. In addition to comparing the overall value of alternatives, other characteristics must be present just to get a product placed on the list of alternatives to consider. These

order winner
A product or service characteristic that is most important to a particular customer and results in the customer ordering.

order qualifier
Product or service characteristics that are necessary, but not sufficient to result in winning the order.

---

om ADVANTAGE   Minimills Make Money, Not Steel

The U.S. steel industry has seen rough times for the past decade, with 19 mills (25 percent of the entire U.S. capacity) filing for bankruptcy since 1998. Integrated mills, which produce virgin metal from iron ore, have suffered the most. Minimills, however, utilize a high percentage of scrap in their production and typically operate at lower cost levels. Even many minimills are having difficulty maintaining levels of profitability, but those that can control raw material costs, labor costs, and electricity costs succeed.

One company in particular, Steel Dynamics, has notably successful. Its operating profit is $55 per ton produced, $12 more than its largest competitor. Its profits increased 36 percent from 1999 to 2000, with only a 12 percent increase in sales. Steel Dynamics's initial decision to focus on high-margin products meant that it would produce higher quality steel and thinner steel. It endeavored to be the low-cost producer of automotive-quality steel, with 33 percent of its output going to automotive uses (door panels, frames, and chassis). Steel Dynamics has negotiated competitive contracts for scrap steel as well as power. After completing its mill in 1996, by 2003 Steel Dynamics was producing 2.2 million tons per year, with sales of nearly $1 billion.

Much of Steel Dynamics's success can be traced to the efficiency of its manufacturing processes. Scrap is turned into new steel in about two hours. After 55 minutes in a furnace, bringing the temperature of the scrap to 3,000 degrees, ladles of molten steel are tested by technicians and alloys are added. Ladles are then emptied and the molten steel flows into molds of a continuous caster. It exits the mold with an outside surface that is solid. Breaking the cooled surface at this point can result in molten steel all over equipment. The resulting cleanup costs about $10,000. A continuous ribbon of steel gradually moves through the mold and slabs are cut to length. After being processed through a second furnace, steel slabs move to rolling processes to flatten the steel to sheets as thin as 0.011 inch. Cold-rolled steel like that of Steel Dynamics is priced at $100–$150 per ton more than hot-rolled steel. Steel Dynamics also has the capability to produce steel rails up to four times longer than any American competitor.

Steel Dynamics's processes are complex and critical. Behind the company's success lies a hard-working and motivated workforce. Various incentives are in place to ensure that employees do everything possible to maintain the processes. When production objectives are met, employees receive a weekly bonus of $10 per hour above the $10 per hour base. In addition, meeting other objectives can add another $2. Annual profit-sharing awards also contribute to employee compensation. They averaged $6,700 in 2000. For Steel Dynamics, the capability of being the low-cost producer of high-quality steel is clearly the result of combining two resource groups: very efficient processes supported by an extremely motivated workforce.

Source: "America's Elite Factories," *Fortune*, September 3, 2001, pp. 206A–206L; www.steeldynamic.com; Jed Graham, "Diversity Can Temper Industry's Downturns," *Investor's Business Daily*, May 3, 2004, p. A11.

product or service attributes are called as order qualifiers.[12] Order qualifiers may vary from one customer to another, just as the prioritization of value attributes varies from one customer to another. Order qualifiers are necessary but not sufficient to win a customer.

Once an alternative meets the order qualifiers necessary for further consideration, order winners come into play. Order winners are those attributes that make the difference for a particular customer. In our pizza delivery example, the owner seeks customers who will view the short delivery time as an order winner. If she fails to meet the order qualifiers, however, her business will no longer be considered, and fast delivery won't matter.

The role of order qualifiers and order winners can change as markets mature. Price is often an important order winner in mature markets. Unfortunately for the producer, competing on the basis of price can often have detrimental effects on the bottom line. However, when all competitors are essentially equal on such quality measures as dependability of delivery and response time, price may be the only remaining value attribute that differentiates the rivals.

For many products, service-oriented attributes have become order winners. Desktop computers are a good example. For the most part, a computer is a computer, virtually indistinguishable once issues like memory, hard disk size, processor speed, and accessories included are resolved. However, if something else of value is added, like after-the-sale on-site service, the computer is different. In today's economy, services have become a viable order winner for many products. It is not uncommon for order winners to gradually turn into order qualifiers as competitors and the markets embrace them, however. In our pizza example, for instance, if competitors adapted, so that most were able to deliver in 20 minutes, quick delivery could become an order qualifier for many customers. Our entrepreneur would need a new differentiating capability for an order winner.

Domino's Pizza would undoubtedly be a strong competitor of our example business. It has been a major competitor in the pizza delivery business for decades because it continues to differentiate itself, even as the market changes. Over the years, Domino's has adapted to various order winners. Initially, it focused on short delivery times. As that became an order qualifier, it found other ways to differentiate the products and service.

Capability Chains

This chapter introduced the concept of supply chains. The network of producers and suppliers, from the consumer all the way back to the original raw materials, makes up that chain, and everyone in that chain needs to add value. Integrating service and product design with process design ensures that all members of the chain are adding their capabilities to the finished product or service. Charles Fine describes this as the **capability chain**.[13] Fine argues in his book *Clockspeed* that three critical principles related to capabilities must be observed. First, no capability lasts forever. Capabilities will and must change. Second, no capability exists alone, without interacting with and depending on other capabilities. And third, competitive advantage can be obtained by the concurrent design of capabilities along with products and processes. Without the concurrent design of capabilities, products, and processes, new products are likely to be difficult or impossible to produce. Investments in processes and capabilities that cannot produce a product—or investment in developing a product that cannot be produced by existing processes—turn out, ultimately, to be investments that provide no financial return.

capability chain
The capabilities added by all members of a supply chain.

| CHAPTER SUMMARY |

The prerequisite to profitability that stands out more than any other is value. Value is what the customer pays for and value creation is the most important contribution of operations management.

The first part of this chapter examined how two different types of customer, consumers and businesses, view value. Businesses seek products and services that can enhance value for *their* customers, whereas consumers seek those that meet their own needs. Value is transferred through products and services, from supplier to customer to consumer, within large networks of businesses called supply chains.

Those product and service characteristics consumer and business customers seek are value attributes. Value attributes for consumer customers are cost, quality, convenience, timeliness, personalization, ethics, style/fashion, and technology. Value attributes for business customers are cost, quality, dependability of delivery, timeliness, and flexibility.

A firm's competitiveness rests on its ability to match functional strategies—and the day-to-day decisions they guide—to business strategies so that they can successfully compete. For operations decisions, this means recognizing the value attributes important to customers as well as the competitive priorities of cost, quality, dependability of delivery, flexibility, and response time and making strategic decisions that enhance competitive priorities. For supply chain decisions, enhancing competitiveness involves make-or-buy decisions, determining whether supply chain management is designed for cost reduction or value enhancement, sourcing decisions, logistics network decisions, supply chain services outsourcing decisions, supply chain security decisions, and decisions regarding technology. Any strategic decision that affects the operations of a supply chain member affects the supply chain itself.

In the second part of this chapter, the relationships among value attributes, competitive priorities, and strategic decision categories were examined. Understanding these relationships is a responsibility of managers. The resources controlled by operations require a tremendous investment for both services and manufacturers. The return on these investments comes only through customer purchases, which result from that match between the value created and the value customers want.

The relationships among competitive priorities and operations resources are so numerous and complex that understanding all of them is a daunting task. Failure to consider them, however, can result in unexpected consequences of decisions. The large number of relationships makes prioritization critical as a means of focusing management attention on the most important issues.

The final section of this chapter examined capabilities. Capabilities provide value to customers by enabling a business to do things a customer can't. Processes are used by businesses to create those capabilities. Differentiating capabilities are used by a firm to distinguish itself from competitors by offering customers something that is different.

KEY TERMS

assembler, 78
basic producer, 78
business strategy, 87
capability chain, 111
competitive priorities, 97
converter, 78
core competencies, 90
corporate strategy, 87
cost leader strategy, 88
design capacity, 98
differentiation strategy, 89

environmental scanning, 94
fabricator, 78
focus strategy, 89
functional strategy, 87
mission statement, 87
mass customization, 107
order qualifier, 110
order winner, 110
protective capacity, 98
supply chain, 78
supply chain management, 85

REVIEW QUESTIONS

1. What are some reasons why firms outsource?
2. What is a supply chain?
3. For a profitable business, how must the value added and the cost to add it relate?
4. Traditionally, why did businesses resist outsourcing?
5. Describe the analysis a consumer uses when faced with a potential purchase.
6. How does a business's purchasing decision differ from that of a consumer?
7. Describe each of the value attributes for consumer products and services.
8. Why have response time and dependability of delivery gained so much importance in dictating value for B2B transactions?
9. What are the five competitive priorities for operations strategy? Why is it difficult to optimize all five?
10. What is the purpose of a mission statement?
11. Define and compare corporate, business, and functional strategies.
12. How are business strategies related to customers' value attributes?
13. Why is it important for a company to identify strategic priorities?
14. What are Porter's three strategies? How do they affect operations decisions?
15. For each of the strategic structural and infrastructural decision categories, describe the relationships to competitive priorities.
16. What is meant by an order winner? What are order qualifiers?
17. What is a capability chain?

DISCUSSION AND EXPLORATION

1. What are some reasons a manufacturer might outsource a product when it could manufacture it?
2. What are the most common value attributes for college students?
3. Describe purchasing decisions students make that require a tradeoff between quality and convenience. How valuable is convenience for students?
4. What businesses do students frequent that seek to add value through flexibility?
5. How will the value attributes that are most important to you change when you graduate? What will cause this change?
6. Provide an example of a product or service you purchased because of the price but later concluded that it was not a good value.
7. What is the fallacy associated with the belief that companies should always be able to do something themselves cheaper than they could outsource it?
8. Select a business that is familiar to you. Identify decisions it must make within each of the structural and infrastructural decision categories. How important are those decisions? What impact does each have on the firm's potential for success?
9. From your own work experience, provide an example of how performance/reward system decisions have affected the strategic success of a business. Have they encouraged you to perform in a manner consistent with the business's goals? Why or why not?
10. Identify, in several businesses you frequent, the competitive priorities that appear to be most important. Rank them based on their importance.

11. How do you think organization system decisions have changed as a result of Internet technologies? Which businesses depend heavily on this technology? Could they exist without it?

12. For businesses you frequent, what are the most important value attributes offered? Do all of the businesses you frequent emphasize the same value attributes? Are the attributes you prioritize the highest offered by all businesses you frequent?

13. From work experience you have had, identify situations where increased customer contact reduced efficiency. What tradeoff was being made that resulted in management not eliminating the customer interaction?

14. Select a successful business you often frequent. What are its capabilities? Describe its processes. Which processes are most critical to its capabilities?

15. Capabilities that lead to market dominance often result from combining processes that originate in different parts of a business. Describe a business you are familiar with that has created a unique set of capabilities in this way.

16. What are the order qualifiers for your choice of where to eat lunch? What are the order winners for this place?

17. What capabilities are made possible when a service is designed with high volume in mind? What capabilities might a competitor try to develop as a way of differentiating itself from that service?

ENDNOTES

1. R. B. Handfield and E. L. Nichols, *Introduction to Supply Chain Management* (Upper Saddle River, NJ: Prentice-Hall, 1999), p. 2.

2. G. P. Stone, "City Shoppers and Urban Identification: Observations on the Social Psychology of City Life," *American Journal of Sociology*, July 1954, pp. 36–43.

3. J. A. Fitzsimmons and M. J. Fitzsimmons, *Service Management* (New York: Irwin/McGraw-Hill, 1997), p. 247.

4. Archer Daniels Midland Company, *2000 Annual Report*, p. 7.

5. S. C. Wheelwright, "Manufacturing Strategy: Defining the Missing Link," *Strategic Management Journal* 5 (January–March 1984), pp. 77–91.

6. www.benjerry.com/our_company/our_mission/index.cfm, accessed November 4, 2005.

7. M. E. Porter, *Competitive Advantage* (New York: Free Press, 1985).

8. C. C. Defee and T. P. Stankl, "Applying the Strategy-Structure-Performance Paradigm to the Supply Chain Environment," *International Journal of Logistics Management*, Vol. 16, No. 1, 2005.

9. H. L. Lee, "The Triple-A Supply Chain," *Harvard Business Review*, October 2004.

10. "U.S.: Why Profits Are Defying Gravity," *BusinessWeek*, April 18, 2005, online edition, www.businessweek.com/magazine/content/05_16/b3929033_mz010.htm.

11. J. L. Heskett, T. O. Jones, G. W. Loveman, W. E. Sasser Jr., and L. A. Schlessinger, "Putting the Service–Profit Chain to Work," *Harvard Business Review*, March–April 1994, pp. 164–174; J. A. Fitzsimmons and M. J. Fitzsimmons, *Service Management*, 3rd ed. (New York: Irwin/McGraw-Hill, 2000), pp. 216–218.

12. T. Hill, *Manufacturing Strategy* (Homewood, IL: Irwin, 1989), pp. 36–46.

13. C. H. Fine, *Clockspeed: Winning Industry Control in the Age of Temporary Advantage* (Reading, MA: Perseus Books, 1998), pp. 71–76.

LEARNING ACTIVITIES   www.mhhe.com/opsnow3e

Visit the Online Learning Center (www.mhhe.com/opsnow3e) for additional resources. Content varies by chapter, and includes

- Business Tours
- OM on Site
- Readings
- Resources
- Excel Tutors

- Interactive Case Models
- Reel Operations Video Clips
- Additional Advanced Problems
- Self-Assessment Quizzes
- Glossary

SELECTED RESOURCES

Eisenhardt, K. M., and Sull, D. "Strategy as Simple Rules," *Harvard Business Review*, January 1, 2001.

Fine, Charles H. *Clockspeed: Winning Industry Control in the Age of Temporary Advantage.* Reading, MA: Perseus Books, 1998.

Fitzsimmons, J. A., and Fitzsimmons, M. J. *Service Management.* Boston: Irwin/McGraw-Hill, 2004.

Handfield, R. B., and Nichols, E. L. *Introduction to Supply Chain Management.* Upper Saddle River, NJ: Prentice-Hall Inc., 1999.

Hill, Terry. *Manufacturing Strategy.* Burr Ridge, IL: McGraw-Hill/Irwin, 2000.

Kaplan, R. S., and Norton, D. P. "Having Trouble with Your Strategy? Then Map It," *Harvard Business Review*, September 1, 2000.

Mankins, M. C., and Steele, R. "Turning Great Strategy into Great Performance," *Harvard Business Review*, July–August 2005.

Porter, M. *Competitive Advantage.* New York: The Free Press, 1985.

Porter, M. E. "What Is Strategy?" *Harvard Business Review*, November 1, 1996.

Porter, M. E. "Strategy and the Internet," *Harvard Business Review*, March 1, 2001.

Sawhney, M., Balusubramanian, S., and Krishnan, V. V. "Creating Growth with Services," *MIT Sloan Management Review*, Winter 2004.

Stalk, G., and Lachenauer, R. "Hardball," *Harvard Business Review*, April 2004.

VIDEO CASE 3.1

Hotel Monaco: Matching Value Creation to Market Desires

Based on Video 3 on the Student DVD

Hotel Monaco Chicago provides a unique set of services to meet its target market. Located in downtown Chicago, Hotel Monaco is recognized as a boutique hotel. It provides a unique atmosphere and a unique set of services.

1. Describe the characteristics of Hotel Monaco. What is its target market? How does Hotel Monaco Chicago differentiate itself in that market?

2. How does Hotel Monaco's small size support its strategy? Could a larger hotel do the same thing?

3. What has Hotel Monaco Chicago done to meet business travelers' needs? How does Hotel Monaco differentiate its treatment of weekend travelers from its treatment of business travelers?

4. Given any business's desire to minimize non-value-adding activities, which of the activities of Hotel Monaco would you evaluate for possibly not adding value?

5. How does customer feedback fit into Hotel Monaco's strategic success?

APPLICATION CASE 3.1

The One-Year Brewery

Larry Willis had looked forward to this day for what seemed like a decade. He was finally opening the doors to his new business, "Home Brew." Larry had been an enthusiastic beer maker for over twenty years. All of his friends enjoyed his flavorful beers and had encouraged him. Finally, in July 2004, he saw an opportunity. A building that was just the right size was vacant, and the owners had been unable to rent it. It had been vacant for six months. Larry signed a one-year lease that he felt was a good deal and went to work.

Larry knew the location was a risk. In a small college town, he was out of the major traffic paths, but he wasn't interested in the student crowd, anyway. His prices would be too high. He was trying to attract connoisseurs of unique beers.

Larry purchased used equipment whenever he could. He needed at least three brewing vats, which were the largest equipment investments. Larry borrowed from friends and relatives and put all of his own money into his project. He did the renovation work himself and did all of the plumbing required to get the brewing equipment working. After five months of work, he was ready to open. Timing was perfect—just prior to the holidays. During the first two weeks of being open, business was brisk. On almost every evening, small groups of adults came in and tasted his beers. Most were very complimentary. A Web site that reviewed beers gave three of his brews high praise. Larry was sure he could grow the business.

After the holidays, Larry wasn't surprised to see business subside a bit. The decline, continued, however, until demand was almost nonexistent. Only Larry's friends came in. After months of very few customers, Larry closed his business on the 1-year anniversary of signing his lease.

After the closing, the local newspaper reported on the demise of Home Brew. In the article, the Web site reviewer was quoted, "I'm not surprised that Home Brew couldn't survive. During the few times I went in, the beer was great, but the TV above the bar was so loud I couldn't hear anything. A small group of guys sitting at the bar were arguing, there were only five or six tables where people could sit, and the only food available was popcorn. It just wasn't an attractive place to sit and enjoy a good beer."

Randy Norman, a local restaurant owner is considering buying the building and the brewing equipment and employing Larry as the "brewmeister." Randy's thinking is that Larry knows how to make good beer, but really knows nothing else about successfully managing it.

Questions

1. From a strategic perspective, why do you think the business failed under Larry's leadership?

2. What value attributes would be of interest for the potential customers of Home Brew? Which ones, beyond "the product," would be most important in this situation? In this setting, how would those value attributes be created?

3. What implications do those value attributes have for structural and infrastructural decisions?

4. Describe the "experience" a customer would need to have in order to continue to frequent Home Brew.

5. What would your recommendation to Randy Newman be regarding the potential for successfully running the business?

APPLICATION CASE 3.2

Beyond Cheap, Fast Pizza

Alice, Amy, and Bill are three friends and business school graduates of a small midwestern university. They have complained for four years about the pizza in their town. Alice, more than the others, has been very critical. Sure, there are five or six delivery places, including the chains you'd expect, and there are several eat-in pizza restaurants, but they all compete on the basis of price or delivery speed or both. When friends from Chicago come to visit and want to be taken to the best pizza place in town, Alice, Amy, and Bill are all embarrassed. There just isn't a great pizza. In addition to being the loudest complainer, Alice also has access to her family's money. The three graduates have decided to pool their resources (50-25-25) and open a gourmet pizza restaurant to be called Alice's Restaurant. Rather than providing the most food volume for a dollar, their objective is to provide a variety of gourmet pizzas in a setting that would be attractive for a date or for parents when in town on weekends.

1. Develop a mission statement for Alice's Restaurant.

2. Describe the competitive advantages that Alice's Restaurant must have.

3. Given the value attributes consumers are most interested in, which will be most important to Alice's Restaurant?

4. Describe the structural and infrastructural decisions that will be critical to the success of Alice's Restaurant.

CHAPTER 4

Processes: Turning Resources into Capabilities

LEARNING OBJECTIVES

- Describe the function and importance of concurrent engineering for product and service design.

- Describe the service system design matrix and understand the relationships between sales opportunities, customer contact, and process efficiency.

- Describe the strengths and weaknesses of process-oriented, product-oriented, and cellular layouts.

- Describe the quality function deployment (QFD) process.

- Describe the component matrices in the house of quality.

- Use the house of quality to structure quality function deployment.

- Differentiate between lean production, value stream mapping, Six Sigma, business process analysis, reengineering, and poka-yoke.

- Construct a process flow chart.

- Construct a service blueprint.

KIOSKS—FINALLY SHOWING PROMISE

Tracking manufacturing trends over the years shows a definite trend to replace humans with machines. The service sector has, to a great extent, been unable to trade variable labor costs for the fixed costs associated with automated equipment. This is due to several factors, including the need for flexibility in dealing face-to-face with customers and the resistance many customers have to technology. Enter the kiosk.

Self-service kiosks have been gradually infiltrating the service sector, starting with the ATM machine in 1985. In 2002 there were 342,000 ATMs and 527,000 bank tellers in the United States. More recently, we have seen the arrival of self-service check-in kiosks in airports. Alaska Airlines was the first implementation in 1996. Kiosks are now being used by many airlines, including Continental, Delta, Northwest, AirTran, America West, and Spirit. In December 2003, 70.3 percent of Northwest Airlines passengers checked in using kiosks or online. That's an increase from 20 percent only two years earlier. Continental never expected kiosk check-ins to go above 20 percent, but reached 66 percent in 2003.

Kiosks are being used for department of motor vehicles (DMV) transactions in Nevada. Some universities offer students access to official transcripts through kiosks. Now kiosks are making headway in fast-food restaurants. Next, we should expect to see self-service kiosks in hotel lobbies for check-in and at rental car agencies. Eighty-five self-service kiosks have been installed in 48 franchised McDonald's restaurants, with no investment from McDonald's. A corporate-owned store in St Charles, Illinois, is also a test site for kiosks. Automating frontline customer contact comes with some risks. One danger is that the lack of face-to-face contact will leave the customer unconnected to the business. Another is the risk of the kiosk not being able to meet special needs of a customer. But it also comes with benefits. Kiosks are very reliable. They don't call in sick and they don't enter data incorrectly. A kiosk takes up far less space than workers, and in many applications (airports and McDonald's included), space is at a premium. And maybe most surprisingly, customers really like them. They speed up tedious processes and reduce the time waiting in line.

At the forefront of the kiosk phenomenon is Kinetics, the leading supplier of kiosks for airlines and the supplier for McDonald's. Kinetics estimates that at an investment of $6,000 to $10,000, one kiosk replaces 2.5 ticketing agents.

Back at McDonalds, contrary to speculation, kiosks actually increase sales. Kiosk purchases average $1 more than face-to-face purchases. McDonald's managers credit that to the kiosk's ability to prompt customers for more purchases by showing pictures of products they might want to buy. Despite the failure of many kiosk implementations, the success with airlines and with McDonald's paints a bright future. McDonald's, Burger King, Wendy's, Taco Bell, and Subway have a total of 48,000 restaurants in the United States. With two kiosks in each restaurant Kinetics sees a huge demand increase over the mere 1,341 machines it sold in 2003.

Source: Charles Fishman, "The Toll of a Machine," *Fast Company,* May 2004; *Kiosk Industry News,* Kiosk.com, "America West Announces Purchase of 40 Additional Kinetics Kiosks," www.kioskcom.com/articles.php, June 7, 2002; *Kiosk Industry News,* Kiosk.com, "DMV Electronic Kiosks Coming to Town," www.kioskcom.com/articles.php, May 6, 2004; *Kiosk Industry News,* Kiosk.com, "Official Transcript Kiosks Make Campus Comeback," www.kioskcom.com/articles.php, May 6, 2004; "Airline Kiosks" Trace Center, College of Engineering, University of Wisconsin–Madison. April 17, 2001; "McDonald's Expands Its Test of Self-Serve Kiosks," *Digital Transactions,* www.digitaltransactions.net/newsstory.cfm?newsid=189, March 4, 2004; www.kineticsUSA.com, May 11, 2004.

Chapter 4 investigates processes, the means by which businesses convert their investment in resources to value for which customers pay. Processes define how resources are organized and used. The way a business uses its resources defines the costs incurred as well as the value created. With profitability as a goal, a business must ensure that the processes create what customers desire at a cost that enables the firm to profit.

Introduction: Organizing Resources to Create Value

In the previous chapter, we made a clear distinction between capabilities and processes. Capabilities are what customers want from a product or service they purchase. If capabilities are the WHAT, processes can be viewed as the HOW. Businesses invest in resources so that they can create and sell capabilities, but those resources will not create capabilities on their own. They are organized into processes, which create the products and services the business attempts to sell. If the customers perceive them as having value, the business actually does sell them. If the selling price is greater than the cost to create them, a potential exists for profitability. At the end of the day, producing products and services that are valued by customers but that cannot generate a profit, is no better than not producing them at all.

In this chapter we focus on processes and their role in the creation of products and services. An overriding objective of all processes will be to maximize value added while minimizing the cost to add it. Taking a very simple view, we know that as we add features and amenities to products and services, we can reach a point where the added perceived value to the customer becomes very small. Basic product and service features—"order qualifiers," using terminology from Chapter 3—are essential, however. Adding above and beyond those order qualifiers is important for some customers, but not necessarily for others. Costs are added for everyone, however. Exhibit 4.1 provides one view of the relationship between adding product and service features and value.

From a simplistic view, it appears that profitability would be maximized if the product and service features were added to the point where the value to customers and the cost of adding the features are the greatest distance apart. If it weren't for the fact that different customers value different things, that would be true. One way to look at the relationship presented in Exhibit 4.1 is to view the "value to customers" as being dictated by the design of the product or service and the "cost of adding" as being dictated by the design of the process.

NCR, makers of Fastlane self-checkout systems, claim waiting line reductions of up to 40 percent.

Which Comes First—Product Design or Process Design?

The design of products or services and the processes that produce them cannot be completely independent. Obviously, the design of a product will determine to a great extent the types of processes used to create it. The same logic holds for services. This perspective has guided process design for decades. Traditionally, products were designed and then handed over to process engineers, who designed the processes to produce them.

More recently, however, there has been a desire to design products using a broader view that takes into account the fact that product design can make processes simpler and less costly. Research has shown that a significant portion of a product's life-cycle costs are determined during its design. As existing products are modified and enhanced, the processes that were used to produce them are already in place. This modification of existing products takes place at a faster rate as product life cycles become shorter. Product

| Additional Product and Service Features | EXHIBIT 4.1 |

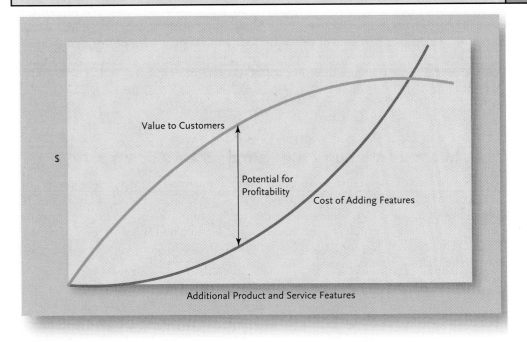

Additional Product and Service Features

life cycles are often so short that purchasing new equipment for processes specific to one product would not be economical.

The Importance of Process Decisions and Process Choice

Process decisions cannot easily be categorized. They range from the very strategic to the very tactical. Examples of very strategic process decisions would include:

- Golden Corral's decision to be an all-you-can-eat buffet.
- Indiana University's decision to offer courses online.
- First Financial Bank's decision to provide online banking.
- Dell's decision to allow customers to design their own computer configuration.
- Hyundai's decision to offer a 100,000-mile warranty.
- Domino's Pizza's decision to compete on delivery speed.
- Amazon's decision to offer next day delivery.

These decisions all affect processes and all require long-term resource investments. They relate directly to the firm's ability to compete.

Process decisions are also made at a very detailed level. These decisions might not affect competitiveness directly, but will have an impact on costs and productivity, and for services may directly affect how long customers have to wait. Examples of more micro-oriented or tactical process decisions include:

- Golden Corral's physical arrangement of its dessert counter.
- Indiana University's process for allowing students to view their grades online.
- The steps required in First Financial Bank's car loan approval process.
- The process used by Dell employees to retrieve computer components from inventory.
- Hyundai's process for adding interior trim components to automobiles.

Subway sandwich shops plan to use kiosks in three ways: inside the store, at the drive-up window, and at remote locations to order sandwiches for delivery.

- Domino's Pizza's process for spreading grated cheese on pizzas.
- Amazon's one-click order.

Strategic process decisions, because of the financial investment required, must be made carefully. In many ways, they will be a function of the competitive priorities dictated by the business strategy. Decisions related to more tactical process issues may determine how successfully those competitive priorities are actually implemented. The following section addresses some important strategic process alternatives for manufacturers and services.

Strategic Process Decisions for Manufacturing and Service

product-oriented layout

A layout that provides the necessary resources in a fixed sequence that matches the sequence of the steps required to produce the product or service.

The decision as to how facilities will be arranged, known as the layout decision, is critical to enhancing or limiting the business's range of capabilities. For most businesses, the general layout decision is a strategic decision that has implications for the type of equipment the business will purchase, the design of the facility, and the skill level of the employees. This decision has long-term cost implications, so it should not be taken lightly or with the attitude that if it doesn't succeed, it can be changed.

General Layout Alternatives

process-oriented layout

A layout that is organized by the function of each resource, allowing steps to be done in any sequence.

General facility layout decisions are often made in response to the firm's specific strategic objectives. Like many decisions, there are numerous alternatives involving general layout, but examining the two opposing ends of the continuum provides a good starting point. The two layout extremes are product-oriented layout and process-oriented layout. In brief, a **product-oriented layout** provides the necessary resources in a fixed sequence that matches the sequence of the steps required to produce the product or service. The **process-oriented layout** provides a layout that is organized by the function of each resource, allowing steps to be done in any sequence. Let's take a closer look at each alternative.

---

om ADVANTAGE IKEA: A Product Design Model

IKEA, the Swedish home furnishings retailer, is known for its functional product designs and low prices. IKEA opened its first U.S. store in Philadelphia in 1985 and has been expanding while other home furnishing stores haven't. Its annual 20 percent growth rate and locations in 31 countries resulted in 2002 worldwide sales of $10 billion.

The strategic goals of IKEA, producing functional designs at very low prices, have implications for product and process design. This retailer's products must conform to several critical performance criteria. First, the designs have to meet a consumer need. Second, it must be possible to produce the product cheaply enough to make it very affordable. Third, the product must be able to fit into a flat package for low-cost distribution in its unassembled state. Fourth, since it is sold unassembled, it must be easy to assemble. All

of these criteria must be addressed during the product design, but the price tag is designed first.

Cost savings generated by lower manufacturing and distribution costs have enabled IKEA to maintain its market advantage. The simplicity of product design enables IKEA to produce assembly instructions with no words, just illustrations. That, in turn, eliminates translation problems on instructions and contributes to another of IKEA's goals, which is to produce only products that can be sold in exactly the same form in any of its stores worldwide.

Source: www.ikea-usa.com/ms/en_US/about_ikea/splash.html, May 9, 2004; "IKEA Has Georgia on Its Mind," *National Real Estate Investor*, October 1, 2003; "Case 3/Principle Three: Simple and Intuitive Use. Worldwide Distribution Requires Simplicity in Product Assembly," *The Center for Universal Design*; "Ikea Mania," *Discovery Times* Television, April 5, 2004.

Product-oriented layouts are designed to be efficient producers of goods and services when there is little or no variation from one item to the next. This kind of layout lets the business take advantage of repetitive tasks to gain efficiency, processing speed, and low cost per unit. Production speed is enhanced by breaking bigger tasks into smaller ones and assigning them to more workstations. If high volumes are likely, and low cost per unit is important, a product-oriented layout is a good alternative. Product-oriented layouts are common in high-volume manufacturing of standardized products such as automobiles, boats, electronics, food, or other products produced in a uniform manner with little or no customization. They are common in high-volume standardized services where high volumes of customers must be processed and all customers will have the same processing needs: driver's license offices, health clinics, university registration offices, and so on.

Conceptually, a product-oriented layout can be viewed as a linear series of processing steps, as illustrated in Exhibit 4.2, which shows a hypothetical manufacturer laid out in a product-oriented fashion. Each product goes through the steps in the same sequence.

Despite its benefits, the product-oriented layout has several disadvantages. First is its lack of flexibility. Customization is virtually impossible in such a layout. Each unit being processed undergoes essentially the same processing steps. Although the layout does provide low cost per unit and high volume capability, the repetitive nature of the jobs associated with the layout can result in problems. Employees often complete the same task over and over, which can lead to boredom, job dissatisfaction, and potential quality problems. Greater volume is obtained by increasing the number of workstations or by reducing the amount of time at each workstation. That translates into chopping the work tasks into smaller and smaller pieces, making the contribution of each workstation a smaller proportion of the total production, which makes the work even more repetitive and less likely to seem meaningful. As in most decisions, trade-offs must be made when considering the product-oriented layout alternative. The trade-offs can be viewed from the perspective of the value attributes supported by this layout and those that would actually be reduced by it.

The process-oriented layout, sometimes called the functional layout, provides advantages that the product-oriented layout lacks. Its key advantages are flexibility and customization. In a process-oriented layout, resources are arranged by function. In a process-oriented layout, each functional department has a range of capabilities limited only by the extent of the department's resources. Flexibility and the ability to customize products or services are accomplished by being able to route products or customers through the functional departments in any sequence desired. Service examples include hospitals, government administrative offices, large legal firms, and banks. Manufacturers that use this

Conceptual View of a Product-Oriented Layout	EXHIBIT 4.2

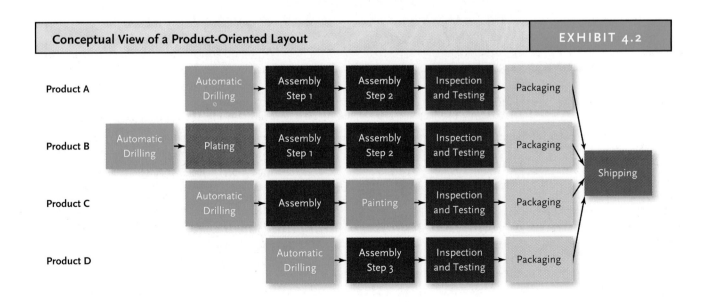

approach customize products and include such industries as custom machining businesses, custom furniture manufacturing, and custom electronics and chip manufacturers.

Exhibit 4.3 provides a conceptual view of a process-oriented layout for the same manufacturer presented in Exhibit 4.2. Obviously, even though similar products might be made, capabilities would be quite different. As compared to product-oriented layouts, weaknesses associated with process-oriented layouts include a higher cost per unit and less consistency from unit to unit or customer to customer. The high cost per unit results from lower efficiencies, inability to take advantage of economies of scale, and costs of moving materials between departments. The nature of this layout requires judgments to be made by employees, as customizing is done in each functional department. As would be expected, better judgment comes only with employees who are more highly skilled, and such employees are generally more expensive to employ than their unskilled counterparts.

Another weakness of this layout is transportation time and cost of moving customers from one department to another. A related drawback is that customers or products arriving at or moving into a department may have to wait. Time spent waiting can become problematic, particularly for services. Customers place a high level of importance on the brevity of waiting time when evaluating a business's quality.

Many businesses find that either a pure product- or process-oriented layout doesn't exactly fit their processing needs. They need a compromise. Some of their customers may need standard services or products that must be produced in high volume and at low cost to meet demand; others may require versatility and customization. In some situations, a new product or service may be produced in a process that requires great flexibility. However, as the business's managers learn more about the market, they find that much of their demand can be satisfied with a few alternatives, and that only a small portion of the market requires customization. In many cases a portion of the processes can be designed utilizing a process-oriented layout while the remainder uses a product-oriented one.

The more difficult scenario is when a firm must be able to integrate flexibility and customization with the low cost per unit and efficient production of high volumes of output.

| EXHIBIT 4.3 | Conceptual View of a Process-Oriented Layout |

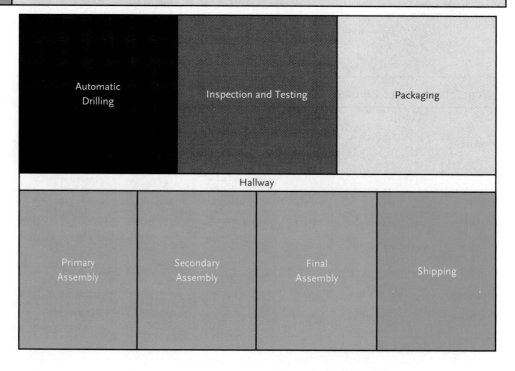

This need, particularly in manufacturing settings, has led to the evolution of a **cellular layout**. In a cellular layout, products whose processes require similar resources are grouped into product families. One cell is designed for each product family. Each cell contains all the resources or workcenters necessary to produce products in that family and some of the cells have resources that are duplicated in other cells. Exhibit 4.4 provides a conceptual view of a cellular layout.

There are several advantages to the cellular layout. First, it has flexibility, although perhaps not as much as a process-oriented layout. Movement from department to department is minimized since all needed resources are present in the cell, so costs associated with that movement and transportation disappear. Within a particular cell, there is similarity among the processes of the product family group members, resulting in fewer machine setups and increased productivity.

Process Type, Volume, and Flexibility

In addition to the general layout decision, the way products or customers will flow through processes must be considered when determining initial process design. Process flows are dictated by several factors, including volume of demand, changes required on equipment to meet varying needs, and the nature of what is being produced.

When making early decisions and commitments regarding productive processes, the expected volume is one aspect that must be considered. Different volumes will place different requirements on the system and will result in different management approaches. Exhibit 4.5 is a continuum identifying different production volume. The product/process matrix presented in Exhibit 4.6 shows how volume, flexibility, and product variety relate to different process types. These processes enable the firm to implement its chosen strategy.

Examining the low-volume extreme first, we see processes that produce only one unique unit. Unique, one-of-a-kind, products or customers are known as **projects.** Projects are generally large in size (building a bridge, installing a software system, implementing a

cellular layout
A layout in which products whose processes require similar resources are grouped into product families. Each cell contains all the resources necessary to produce products in that family.

project
A set of activities aimed at meeting a goal, with a defined beginning and end.

Conceptual View of a Cellular Layout	EXHIBIT 4.4

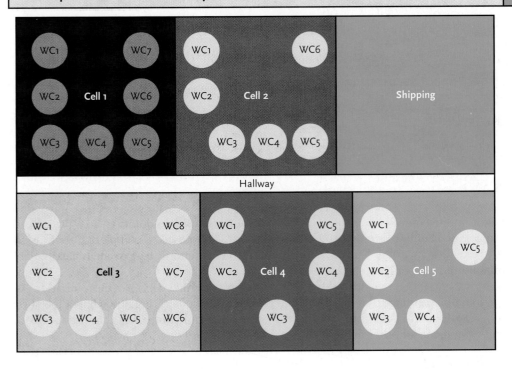

EXHIBIT 4.5	Continuum of Production Volumes for Product and Service Producers

Low Volume				High Volume
Project	Job Shop	Batch Production	Assembly Lines	Continuous Processing

EXHIBIT 4.6	Product/Process Matrix

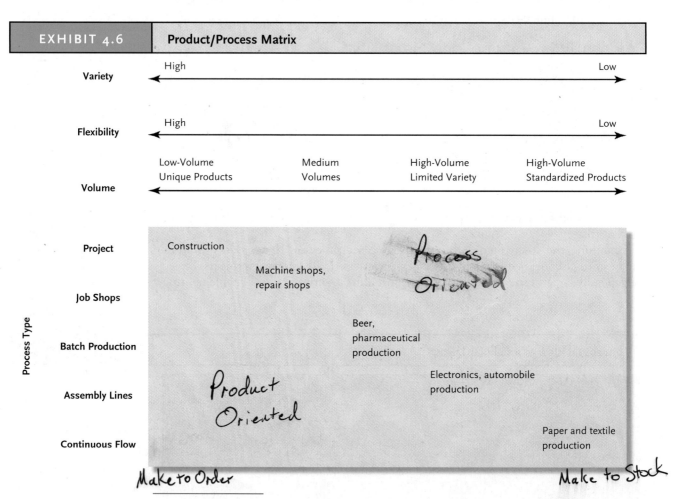

Source: Adapted from R. H. Hayes and S. C. Wheelwright, *Restoring Our Competitive Edge: Competing through Manufacturing* (New York: Wiley, 1984), p. 209.

job shop

A manufacturer, typically a process-oriented layout, that is able to produce custom tools and equipment for others because of its flexibility.

major improvement effort, and so on) and reasonably long in duration. In a project, resources are generally brought to the task at hand, as opposed to completing that task at the resources' location. Resources utilized in projects tend to be extremely flexible and may also be used only temporarily.

Moving to a little higher volume but maintaining a high degree of customization, we have an environment that exists predominantly in manufacturing, known as a **job shop**. Job shops provide flexibility to customers and dominate companies that produce tools and equipment for other manufacturers.

In the middle of the scale, at a slightly higher volume but still maintaining limited product variety, is **batch production.** Batch production addresses not only the volume, but also how the resources and processes deal with the volumes. Batch production means that a group of identical products or customers is processed through one step in the process and then the entire group moves to the next step, and the next, until it is completed. The equipment can then be adjusted or modified, if necessary, to process the subsequent batch. In general, batch processing is used because of a need for some flexibility on the part of the equipment. Rather than processing one unit, changing the equipment to process the next unit, and so on, a more productive use of the equipment is to process a number of units between each equipment change. The time required to change equipment or gear up for processing a different type of product or customer is known as **changeover** or **setup time.** The longer or more difficult the changeover, the greater the motivation to produce in larger batches to spread the cost of the changeover over more units.

At even higher volumes are traditional **assembly lines.** Assembly lines consist of narrowly defined processes, made up of equipment with little flexibility. In typical assembly line arrangements, however, there may be some ability to make adjustments on equipment to produce modified versions of similar products.

The high-volume extreme on the continuum is known as **continuous** or **repetitive processing.** In a continuous environment, any equipment or workstation is dedicated to one thing. High levels of efficiency can be obtained through economies of scale. An opportunity exists for automation in this environment for two reasons. First, the tasks are repetitive, and it is relatively easy to automate repetitive tasks. Second, volume is sufficient to provide a financial return on the investment in automated equipment. Automated equipment is expensive, and the investment in that equipment needs to be spread across a large volume to keep the per-unit impact on cost down. A continuous environment generally utilizes a product-oriented layout because of its compatibility with higher-volume production. There is a strong link between the volume desired from a process and the general layout decisions.

Demand Linkages

In addition to general layout and volume decisions, another broad decision that has implications for capabilities is the link to demand. This issue has little impact on services, since they can't store capacity in the form of inventory, but it has a major impact on manufacturers.

Manufacturers produce to meet demand in two fundamentally different ways. First, they can produce when they receive an order. This is known as **make-to-order** (MTO) processing. The term implies that the product is customized in some way, but this isn't necessarily the case. Standardized products can be made to order also. The advantage of MTO is that finished-goods inventories are kept to a minimum. The disadvantage of this choice is that the customer must wait for the products to be made. This lengthens the response time. The opposite alternative is **make-to-stock** (MTS). In an MTS environment, products are produced to be warehoused and customers purchase products out of that warehouse. The advantage is that customers get an immediate response to their order. The disadvantage of this alternative is that the product offerings are limited to those listed in the catalog.

A compromise system is known as **assemble-to-order.** In this environment, products are manufactured up to a point and then stored. Customer orders dictate the final configuration. It provides a quicker response than MTO and provides a greater ability to customize than MTS.

The Service System Design Matrix

The service system design matrix, presented in Exhibit 4.7, illustrates the relationships among several key factors that dominate service processes.

---

batch production
A type of production in which identical products or customers are processed through one step, and then the entire batch goes on to the next step.

changeover time
The time required to change equipment from producing one product or service to another.

setup time
The time required to change equipment from producing one product or service to another.

assembly line
A narrowly defined manufacturing assembly process made up of equipment with little flexibility in a product-oriented layout.

continuous processing
In a continuous processing environment, this is any equipment or workstation that is dedicated to one product or service, yielding high levels of efficiency.

repetitive processing
Processing on a continuous basis.

make-to-order
Producing a product when an order is received.

make-to-stock
Producing a product before an order is received and storing the product.

assemble-to-order
Producing major components of a product prior to receiving an order and assembling the product to meet a specific order.

| EXHIBIT 4.7 | Service System Design Matrix |

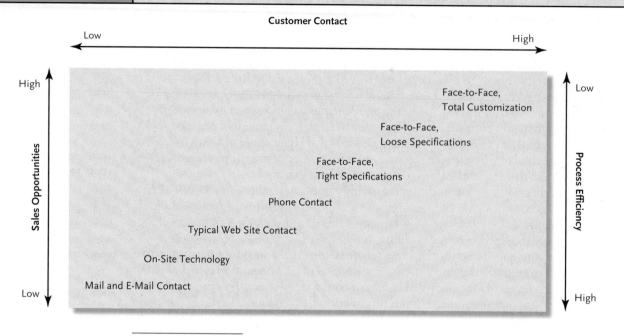

Customer Contact

Low ←→ High

Sales Opportunities: High ←→ Low
Process Efficiency: Low ←→ High

Face-to-Face, Total Customization

Face-to-Face, Loose Specifications

Face-to-Face, Tight Specifications

Phone Contact

Typical Web Site Contact

On-Site Technology

Mail and E-Mail Contact

Source: Adapted from R. B. Chase and N. J. Aquilano, *Production and Operations Management*, 6th ed. (Homewood, IL: Irwin, 1992), p. 123.

American Airlines can process a kiosk customer at check-in in 58 seconds.

For a service provider, customer contact has two significant effects—one positive and one negative. First, the more customer contact, the greater the opportunity for service providers to make additional sales to the customer. Think about your interactions with service providers ranging from automobile sales and electronics sales all the way to fast food. Would you like undercoating? Would you like an extended warranty? Would you like fries with that? Second, as customer contact increases, efficiency and productivity of the service process decline. Services must trade off their desires for efficient production processes with opportunities for sales similar to the way manufacturers must trade off flexibility and product variety for costs. The service system design matrix provides guidance for making service delivery decisions in ways that balance the desire for sales opportunities and the need for process efficiency. Starting at the lowest contact delivery system (mail or e-mail contact) and progressing all the way to three forms of face-to-face contact, efficiency decreases as sales opportunities increase. Face-to-face delivery offers

Sales staff can spend a tremendous amount of time with a potential customer, only to have them leave without making a purchase. Salespeople know, however, that for many purchases that face-to-face contact is critical. If the face-to-face time is reduced, the salesperson could interact with more people, but as that time is reduced, the sales opportunity (up-selling, cross-selling, etc.) disappears.

om ADVANTAGE   Turning a Process into an Experience

After a search for great ice cream failed, Donald and Susan Sutherland opened the first Cold Stone Creamery in Tempe, Arizona. Rather than produce ice cream "to stock," Cold Stone Creamery produced ice cream fresh each day. Every customer's ice cream was customized to order by blending "mix-ins" on a 16-degree Fahrenheit frozen slab of granite (the cold stone). The first franchise store opened in Tucson in 1995.

Cold Stone Creamery's unique mix of individualized ice cream creations, great locations, and lots of interaction between employees and customers creates an overall service experience that customers wait in line for. For Cold Stone Creamery, the process isn't something customers must endure in order to finally get what they want. The process is a critical part of the experience, and it is part of what the customer pays for. It's so enjoyable that it often draws spectators.

Cold Stone Creamery starts with about a dozen basic flavors of ice cream and another 15 or 20 that are available seasonally. Added to that are "mix-ins" that range from various candies (Kit-Kats, Oreos, M&Ms, etc.), nuts (pecans, walnuts, almonds, etc.), fruit (bananas, raspberries, pineapple, etc.), and other things like peanut butter, marshmallows, fudge, or cookie dough. The result is an enormous set of alternatives that, when combined with the experience, is fast

becoming the favorite ice cream for many, as premium and super-premium brands continue to increase their ice cream market share.

Source: www.coldstonecreamery.com, accessed March 18, 2006; "What's Your X-factor?" *Inc.com*, September 2005.

alternatives from tightly controlled "tight specification" interaction to wide open "total customization."

The strategic decisions identified in the service system design matrix can be directly related to the competitive priorities of cost, quality, dependability of delivery, flexibility, and response time. For example, customer contact may enhance quality for those who expect that contact, but as process efficiency suffers as a result, response time may be negatively affected. A service expecting to compete on cost will need to process high volumes of customers through a very efficient process, reducing the allowable customer contact. Specifications, which determine the degree to which an employee can make decisions, can affect flexibility and the ability to respond to changing conditions or customer expectations. These decisions affect information systems, employee training, employee selection criteria, facility location and layout, and many other decisions related to long-term resource investments. Their impact on processes that create value will extend all the way to the firm's profitability.

Determining New Process Requirements

Prior to the initial design of any process, the potential implications of what is actually being processed must be considered. In services, for example, are people being processed? If so, is something being done *to* them or is it being done *for* them? Is something that represents a person, like an application or an insurance claim, being processed or is something being done to property, like a home, a car, or money? A business that processes people has to consider whether people will like the process, since it will be a part of their total experience. Processing "things" for people tends to be more like manufacturing. The customer contact and opportunity for sales, as pointed out in the service system design matrix presented in Exhibit 4.7, must also be considered when making service process decisions.

Does the process go to the customers or do the customers come to the process? Response time, flexibility, and convenience are closely tied to location. For many services, the "on-site" alternative provides a way to differentiate competitively. Performing services in people's homes has serious implications for issues related to increased scrutiny of employee performance, honesty, cleanliness, and so on. More time is spent in transit, thus reducing productive capacity and increasing costs per customer. Equipment portability, transportation, communication costs, central facility location, and other costs associated with mobility also are affected.

If products or components of products are being processed, what are their characteristics? Some products can be processed in discrete units: clothing, electronics, furniture, and so on. Other products became discrete units only after packaging and are nondiscrete during actual production: many food items such as soft drinks, flour, and cereals, as well as textiles, paint, fuels, and most other liquids and powders. All of these characteristics create specific requirements for process design, packaging, staffing, storage facilities, and delivery systems.

Processes Affect Profitability

New-product and service design, and the corresponding process design, has become increasingly important as product and service life cycles have become shorter, as customers have become more demanding, and as global levels of competition have increased. To a great extent the success of new products and services hinges on the success of the processes designed to make them happen.

Customized clothing requires measurements. Here, a woman is scanned by Levi Straus's Intellifit process. Intellifit takes about 200 measurements using radio waves. Radio waves "see" through clothing, but provide privacy and accuracy for the customer.

If products and services do not meet customer expectations, the customer will not purchase them. In recent years there has been concern about the outsourcing of service and manufacturing jobs. Many manufacturers have outsourced components and finished products to reduce costs. Many services have outsourced technical support to call centers in Asia. Some, however, saw customers defect because the customer service process was not meeting customer expectations. Dell and CitiBank moved their technical support centers back to the United States. Failure to meet customer expectations can decrease net income, resulting in reduced profit margin, reduced return on assets, and reduced return on equity for the business owners. If processes are not used effectively, the investment in the processing equipment and facilities will not provide an acceptable return. ROA drops because the denominator (total assets) is large relative to the income generated. If ineffective use of processes results in increased costs (overtime labor, wasted material and supplies, and so on), net income drops, once again reducing all profitability measures. The financial implications for poor process design can be instantaneous and potentially devastating for the firm.

All of these issues affect profitability, but the most serious of them is the inability of a process to create value. No value means no customers, no sales, no income, and ultimately no business. Products and services will meet customer expectations only if customer expectations are known, understood, *and* designed into them. These facts point to an obvious need to link new-product and service design to customer expectations and the design of processes. The following sections examine the challenging tasks associated with new-product and new service design.

Developing New Products and Services

Designing new products and services is a critical capability, particularly as life cycles for products and services become shorter. New products and services must be developed to take the place of those becoming obsolete. Although both products and services must conform to customer expectations and must be producible and profitable, there is one key difference between them. Processes designed for use in service creation, if they will involve the customer, must add to the experience of the customer. Unlike processes in manufacturing, they cannot have efficiency as a top priority.

For both service and product design, the design of processes cannot be completely separated out or handed off to engineers. The outcome, although maybe most important to the customer, and the process used to create it must be designed together. A common approach used to facilitate product and process design is known as quality function deployment (QFD).

Quality Function Deployment

Quality function deployment (QFD) is a widely used approach for accomplishing product and process design tasks. Its history dates back to 1972 when it was first used by Mitsubishi. Its early U.S. users included Hewlett-Packard and Ford. QFD translates customer needs into product and service designs that guide the corresponding process requirements. This is accomplished through a four-phase procedure presented conceptually in Exhibit 4.8. The QFD process moves through the four phases with the aid of a set of intertwined matrices known as the **house of quality.** Exhibit 4.9 shows a generic house of quality. In the following discussion of the four phases of QFD, a more defined house of quality is developed as an example to better define this process.

Phase 1: Product Planning
The product planning phase of QFD consists of two major tasks. The first is to determine customer wants and needs. This process is often referred to as obtaining the "voice of the customer" (VOC) and is accomplished through customer interviews, customer complaints, and so on. VOC data are usually sorted into categories so that needs can be structured. Actual phrases used by customers often are listed in a table. Each need is linked to

quality function deployment (QFD)
A widely used approach that translates customer needs into product and service designs that guide the corresponding process requirements.

house of quality
A set of matrices used to guide the quality function deployment process.

EXHIBIT 4.8	QFD Conceptual Model

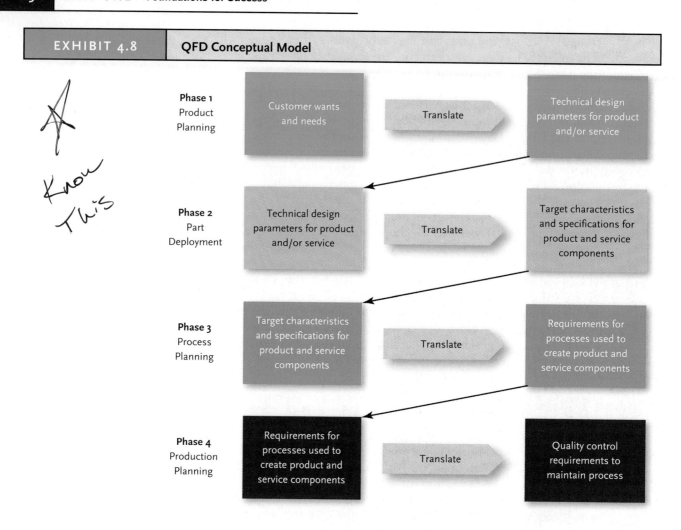

customer demographics and specific details like how the product or service would be used and where and when it would be needed. For example, suppose we were designing an emergency help kit to be kept in a car. We would want to place the customers' needs in a context of how the kit would be used (indicating the items needed in it), when it would be used (daylight, darkness, summer, winter), where it would be used (on the road), and so on.

The second task associated with Phase 1 of the QFD process is to translate the customer needs into a description of the product or service that is in technical language by using **substitute quality characteristics.** Substitute quality characteristics are aspects of the product or service controlled by the development team. Customer needs are stated in terms of functions. The translation of customer needs encompasses the translation of functions the customer expects into characteristics or capabilities of the product or service design. Included in defining customer wants in technical terms is creating target values for some of the technical characteristics. A customer need such as "I want a car with quick acceleration" or "I want my pizza delivered hot" or "I shouldn't have to wait in line too long" must be translated so that it is defined precisely. Should the acceleration be 0 to 60 miles per hour in four seconds or six seconds? Should the pizza be 100 degrees Fahrenheit or 120 degrees? Is "too long" 2 minutes or is it 10 minutes? If you can't measure it, you can't control it.

Phase 2: Part Deployment

The second phase of the QFD procedure is called part deployment. Customer needs that have been translated into technical design parameters create the HOWs and WHATs in the house of quality. Sticking with the pizza delivery example, suppose the customer needs presented in Exhibit 4.10 have been elicited through interviews. In Exhibit 4.11, the customer needs have been translated into technical parameters.

substitute quality characteristics
In quality function deployment, these are terms used to translate the customer needs into a description of the product or service that is in technical language.

| Generic House of Quality | EXHIBIT 4.9 |

HOWs Correlation Matrix:
Relationships among HOWs

HOWs: Potential ways to
achieve the WHATs in technical terms

WHATs:
Customer Needs

Relationships between HOWs and WHATs

Importance Ranking

Competitive
Evaluation

Performance Goals

Competitive Evaluation

Importance

| Customer Wants and Needs for Pizza Delivery | EXHIBIT 4.10 |

Pizza arrives quickly.

Pizza arrives hot.

Pizza toppings are of sufficient quantity.

Pizza tastes good.

Pizza is consistent with pizza ordered.

| Technical Parameters for Pizza Delivery | EXHIBIT 4.11 |

Customer Wants and Needs	Technical Parameters
Pizza arrives quickly.	Pizza arrives in 20 minutes or less from time of order.
Pizza arrives hot.	Pizza arrives with a temperature of 130°F.
Pizza toppings are of sufficient quantity.	Amount of each topping is consistent with pizza assembly guidelines specified for each topping and each size of pizza.
Pizza tastes good.	Exact recipe is followed for dough, sauce, and toppings.
Pizza is consistent with pizza ordered.	No orders are lost, misread, or misunderstood.

EXHIBIT 4.12	WHATs and HOWs in House of Quality

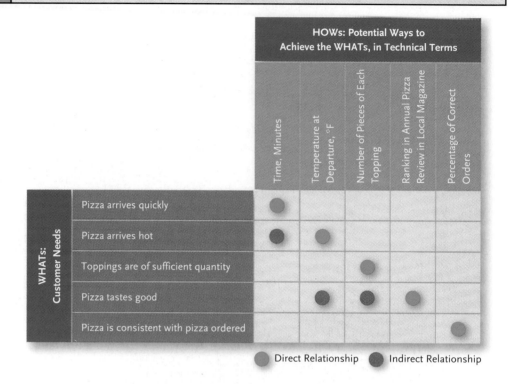

Technical design parameters quickly move beyond the "function" level to the component and "subfunction" level. The more specific a technical description of a product or service, the more precise the design of the product or service. Exhibit 4.12 shows how the customer needs (WHATs) and technical design parameters (HOWs) are placed in the house of quality.

Notice also in Exhibit 4.12 that the relationships between WHATs and HOWs are provided in the central matrix. Direct relationships are designated with a red circle, and

TARGETING technology   Moving beyond Two-Dimensional Printing

While consumers may think of technological advances that have a direct impact on their lives, the most influential technologies often enable businesses to improve processes. In many cases, they enable the businesses to shorten the duration of those processes. One seemingly obscure technology—3D printing—is having just such an effect for some businesses.

3D printing produces three-dimensional wax models rather than images on paper. It is changing the process of product design and is being applied to such products as Graco baby strollers and New Balance shoes. 3D printing is becoming commonplace in many industries, including automotive, aerospace, electronics, consumer products, entertainment, and medical products.

Models are used at various stages of a product's design for such things as ergonomic testing, mock-up with manufactured parts, presentations, casting, and even with focus groups. The ability to see what a product looks like much earlier in the design process makes changes easier and less costly to make and, most importantly, gets products to the market faster.

The Penske Racing NASCAR team uses the technology for producing models of car parts and body designs. Their ThermoJet printer, made by 3D Systems, cost $49,000 and makes small models for about $160. ZZ Corp. offers less expensive printers for under $30,000. Some 3D printers even produce models in full color.

Source: S. Kersner, "5 Technologies That Will Change the World," *Fast Company*, September 2003; Z Corporation, "Applications," www.zcorp.com/home.asp, May 10, 2004; 3D Systems, "Application Solutions," www.3dsystems.com/, May 10, 2004.

| House of Quality with HOW Relationships and Performance Goals | EXHIBIT 4.13 |

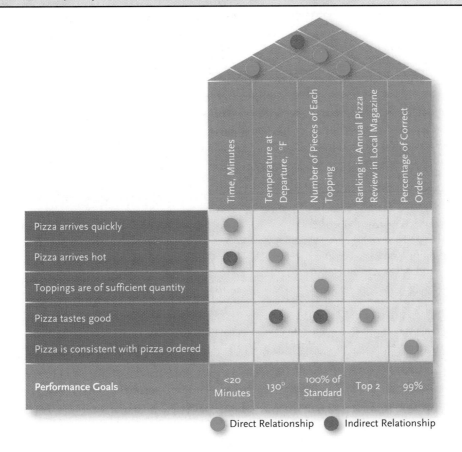

	Time, Minutes	Temperature at Departure, °F	Number of Pieces of Each Topping	Ranking in Annual Pizza Review in Local Magazine	Percentage of Correct Orders
Pizza arrives quickly	●				
Pizza arrives hot	●	●			
Toppings are of sufficient quantity			●		
Pizza tastes good		●	●	●	
Pizza is consistent with pizza ordered					●
Performance Goals	<20 Minutes	130°	100% of Standard	Top 2	99%

● Direct Relationship   ● Indirect Relationship

indirect relationships are designated with a green circle. Exhibit 4.13 shows the "roof" added, containing the relationships among the actual HOWs. The performance goals for the HOWS are provided in the row immediately below the central matrix.

Note in Exhibit 4.13 the designated relationships between measures: time and temperature, number of toppings and ranking, and so on. Also note that the performance goals are all quantitative and measurable.

Phase 3: Process Planning

In Phase 3, process planning, performance goals or targets are translated into process requirements. In our example, a desired temperature for the pizza would have implications for several processes, including the processes of baking the pizza, boxing the finished pizza, storing the boxed pizzas until delivery, and keeping the boxed pizzas warm on the way to the customer. Specific decisions related to the exact configuration of the general layout would also need to be made during this phase. Within the constraints of the general layout decision, many details need to be determined. A discussion of detailed layout decisions is presented in Chapter 15.

In these first three phases of QFD, customer needs are translated into technical definitions of product and service requirements, performance measures and targets for those technical requirements, and processes to make the requirements a reality. These three QFD phases provide a tight link between process design and what the customer needs. Customer needs define value, so the necessary link between value and process design is created. Linking value and process design in this manner ties operating resources (investments) to net income through value. This is a critical link in the firm's ability to attract and keep customers *and* to make money.

om ADVANTAGE Cost Savings from Product Design Alliances

As gas prices reached new highs in 2005, Toyota's hybrid Prius began to move from a cult classic to the mainstream. Toyota projected sales of one million by 2010, which would mean Prius sales would account for greater than 10 percent of Toyota's total sales.

The hybrid vehicle uses both a gasoline engine and an electric motor, greatly increasing fuel efficiency. In any new technology, competition arises as to which implementation is better. This is also the case with hybrid vehicles. Hybrid systems can be configured in different ways. In some systems, batteries power electric motors that drive each of the four wheels. In other systems the gasoline engine powers the rear wheels and the electric motors power only the front wheels.

Toyota has hoped, since it was the first real player in the field, to set the standard and then it could sell that technology to other auto producers. As hybrid popularity has increased, however, other automakers would also like to own the standard. General Motors has teamed up with DaimlerChrysler and BMW in an alliance to develop a system that is simpler, and cheaper, than Toyota's. Volkswagen has joined with Porsche for the same purpose. The development of new automotive drive systems is expensive. All of the automakers realize that those costs need to be spread over a large number of vehicles in order to provide a sufficient return on the investment. By joining forces with each other, the automakers insure that the fixed costs associated with the research and development will be recouped through sales of a greater number of vehicles.

Source: "As Hybrid Cars Gain Traction, Industry Battles Over Designs," *Wall Street Journal*, p. 1, October 19, 2005; "Hybrid Vehicles Provide the Best of Both Worlds," October 19, 2005, www.gm.com/company/gmability/adv_tech/300_hybrids/index.html.

In the previous chapter, we saw how the large number of relationships among strategic decision categories and value attributes makes it important for managers to prioritize. The same situation exists in this case, when managers are faced with many different customer needs. Some, obviously, are more important than others. The house of quality, as shown in Exhibit 4.14, aids in the prioritization process by ranking the HOWs on their importance. In addition, business performance is compared to that of competitors to help identify particular issues that need management attention.

The two additional columns added to the house of quality in Exhibit 4.14 bring a competitive assessment process into QFD by comparing performance to that of three competitors. Note the importance ranking of the five WHATs, as well as how the business performs relative to the competitors. It ranks first on "Pizza arrives quickly" and "pizza arrives hot." It ranks relatively low, however, on taste.

It is important to recognize that aspects of Phases 1, 2, and 3 are undertaken simultaneously in order to accommodate product, service, and process needs. No single aspect can have absolute priority over another. Even though product planning and part deployment are begun prior to process planning, the involvement of product engineering, process engineering, and suppliers in the development process ensures that what is designed can actually be produced.

Phase 4: Production Planning

The production planning phase of QFD consists of translating the process requirements into a system that will be able to control processes and maintain target goals. (Quality control systems are covered in depth in Chapters 6 and 7.) This phase provides the link between the control system and customer needs. In the pizza example, Phase 4 would include the development of systems to monitor and control the WHATs and ensure that performance goals are met.

QFD has been implemented quite successfully in the United States. Most efforts, however, have been devoted to Phases 1 and 2. The effects of QFD not only have resulted in products and services that better meet customer needs, but also have reduced cycle times for product and service development. As product and service life cycles have become shorter, the need to respond with new designs has escalated, and design

| Completed House of Quality | EXHIBIT 4.14 |

	Time, Minutes	Temperature at Departure, °F	Number of Pieces of Each Topping	Ranking in Annual Pizza Review in Local Magazine	Percentage of Correct Orders	Importance Ranking	Competitive Evaluation			
							First			Last
Pizza arrives quickly	●					1	X			
Pizza arrives hot	●	●				2	X			
Toppings are of sufficient quantity			●			4		X		
Pizza tastes good		●	●	●		3			X	
Pizza is consistent with pizza ordered					●	5		X		
Performance Goals	<20 Minutes	130°	100% of Standard	Top 2	99%					

● Direct Relationship   ● Indirect Relationship

enhancements are begun virtually as soon as the development of a product or service is completed. The QFD process shortens that cycle time.

The house of quality provides several benefits. It provides the link between marketing and product or service design. It helps product or service improvement teams establish priorities. It helps managers identify strategic opportunities by providing a better view of the competitive position of the firm.

New Product and New Service Concept Development

Prior to obtaining the voice of the customer regarding a new product or new service, a basic idea has to exist. We can't just hand a potential customer a blank sheet of paper and ask her, "What new product would you like?" The challenge of developing a new product, whether it is a new hybrid Ford car or a new version of the iPod, requires a multifunctional approach that includes identifying a potential product to produce (marketing), determining whether an actual market exists for the concept (marketing), designing the actual product (marketing, operations, engineering, supplier representatives), and determining whether the product can actually be produced profitably (engineering, operations, finance). It requires a blend of unfettered creativity and structured, objective analysis. The product design process is often difficult to separate from a product improvement process. A new service development effort would include these steps as well, but, as mentioned earlier, we must devote even more attention to the processes used.

While the most common approach to new product design is to identify a need and follow with a coordinated product and process design, sometimes it happens in reverse. A classic example is DuPont's Tyvek. Tyvek's discovery was an unexpected event in 1955 when a DuPont researcher noticed white polyethylene fluff coming from a process in an experimental lab. In 1959 a pilot program was established for trial applications of the material. Commercial production of Tyvek didn't start, however, until 1967.

Tyvek is formed by using continuous fine fibers of 100 percent high-density polyethylene that are randomly distributed and nondirectional. In other words, unlike cloth, these fibers are in random directions, forming a web. The fibers are first spun, then laid as a web, then bonded together by heat and pressure. By varying processing speed and the bonding conditions, DuPont can engineer the finished sheet to meet different market needs, such as soft- or hard-structure Tyvek. Soft structure Tyvek is used for textile applications. Hard structure Tyvek is used instead of paper. Both applications have very high tear resistance and light weight.

Tyvek has been used in many applications. One of the most common uses is in construction, where it is used as a "wrap" to decrease air and water infiltration and reduce heating and cooling costs. It stops air and water flow through cavities, but also allows moisture vapor to escape. Tyvek is also used for limited-use protective clothing used for hazardous environments. Tyvek is resistant to chemicals

and provides a barrier against such hazards as lead dust, asbestos, and radiation-contaminated particles.

One of the more visible uses of Tyvek is for packaging. Tyvek is the material of choice for sterile medical packaging because of its puncture resistance, bacterial penetration resistance, and ability to withstand sterilization methods. For more mundane applications, Tyvek envelopes are the strongest available, resistant to punctures, tears, and moisture. Their light weight reduces mailing costs. Federal Express has been using Tyvek for envelopes for over 25 years, and in 1983 the U.S. Postal Service also started using Tyvek large envelopes.

Source: "What Is Tyvek?" www.tyvek.com/whatistyvek.htm, accessed March 16, 2006.

Three product design approaches that consider process implications during product design are design for manufacture and assembly (DFMA), design for logistics (DFL), and design for environment (DFE).

design for manufacture and assembly (DFMA)
The practice of designing products with the capabilities of manufacturing processes in mind.

Design for manufacture and assembly requires that product design engineers consult with process engineers in a collaborative effort to ensure the product is designed so that it can be produced easily and at low cost. Product designs are evaluated from the standpoint not only of meeting customer needs, but also of the process required to actually produce them.

Design for manufacture and assembly is often supported by cross-functional product design teams that include product and process engineers as well as representatives from suppliers. DFMA software aids in the development of products that can be manufactured economically or assembled with other components.

design for logistics (DFL)
Including logistics and transportation concerns in the product design process, usually involving effective packaging.

Design for logistics takes a similar perspective, but focuses on a product design that considers costs associated with transportation. You've probably purchased products that were not preassembled and thought they were sold that way to reduce labor costs. More likely, they were sold unassembled to enable them to be packaged in a smaller, denser container. Products like bookcases, bicycles, and the like, which have great bulk relative to their weight, can be transported much more cheaply unassembled. It is cheaper to transport them this way because the package is more dense. Transportation costs per unit are much more expensive if a truck fills up because of volume (known as "cubing out") before it reaches its weight limit. Transportation costs for some products, particularly those manufactured overseas, can be such a dominant component of the total costs that product design can be driven by logistical concerns. When products are to be assembled by the customer, however, that fact must also play a role in the product design. The product must be designed so that a typical customer will actually be able to assemble it.

Design for environment brings still another perspective to the product design process. DFE requires the inclusion of environmental concerns in the product design. It consists of paying attention to manufacturing processes (use of low impact processes, energy conservation, etc.) and packaging issues (reuse, low waste, etc.) and to the disposal, refurbishing, or recycling of the product itself. Included in DFE designs is ease of serviceability so that the product can easily be refurbished rather than be disposed of.

Concurrent engineering is the ultimate in integrating process design and new product or service design. In this approach, development team members are responsible for each of the necessary tasks, but they work together throughout the development process. The traditional approach to product development is a set of sequential steps wherein each is started only after the previous one is completed. The result is a very long development time and frequent lapses in communication between functions that should communicate, like product and process engineering. In concurrent engineering, many of the steps are performed in tandem. This not only reduces the cycle time, but also enables

design for environment (DFE)
The inclusion of environmental concerns in the product design.

concurrent engineering
Performing product and service development engineering functions in tandem to reduce time and improve communication.

---

om ADVANTAGE   DFE Can Be Compatible with Good Overall Product Design

Managers sometimes think that they must compromise aspects of product design when implementing design for environment (DFE) practices. Steelcase has proven this theory wrong with their Think Chair. The Think Chair combines a design that actually has a memory and a system of tension-sensitive flexors that molds the seat and back to an individual's profile.

The chair is built almost entirely from recycled aluminum and plastic and 99 percent of its weight is recyclable. Forty four percent of its weight consists of already recycled materials. Disassembly and separation for recycling takes about five minutes. Steelcase worked with McDonough Braungart Design Chemistry (MBDC) to select materials considered safe to the environment. It is the first product to receive Cradle to Cradle (C2C) product certification from MBCD. That certification evaluates a product for human and environmental health impacts throughout its life and its potential for being truly recycled or safely composted. Certification of a finished product requires the evaluation of energy-use quantity and quality, water-use quantity, water-effluent quality, and workplace ethics associated with manufacturing. The Institute for Product Development in Denmark conducted a complete Life Cycle Assessment of the chair, evaluating its lifelong impact on the environment, including such impacts as global warming, smog, resource depletion, and waste.

Steelcase's partnership with MBDC has extended their commitment to reducing environmental impacts. The Steelcase Environmental Partnership is a corporate-wide environmental program that helps customers to resell, refurbish, donate, or recycle all Steelcase office products. Steelcase also helps customers extend the useful life of their furniture by refurbishing the furniture. Steelcase plans additional analysis of the top ten materials used in all of its products to eliminate waste and develop products and processes that are healthy for humans and the environment. This will require the company to use new processes to develop products that can be perpetually recovered and reused.

Source: Matthew Maier, Bridget Finn, Elizabeth Esfahani, *Business 2.0*, "What Works," January 24, 2005, www.business2.com/b2/web/articles/0,17863,1019658,00.html, accessed December 7, 2005; Steelcase, www.steelcase.com/na/products.aspx?f=15391, accessed December 7, 2005; MBDC, www.mbdc.com/features/feature_Think.htm, accessed December 7, 2005.

EXHIBIT 4.15	Comparison of Traditional New-Product Development and Concurrent Engineering

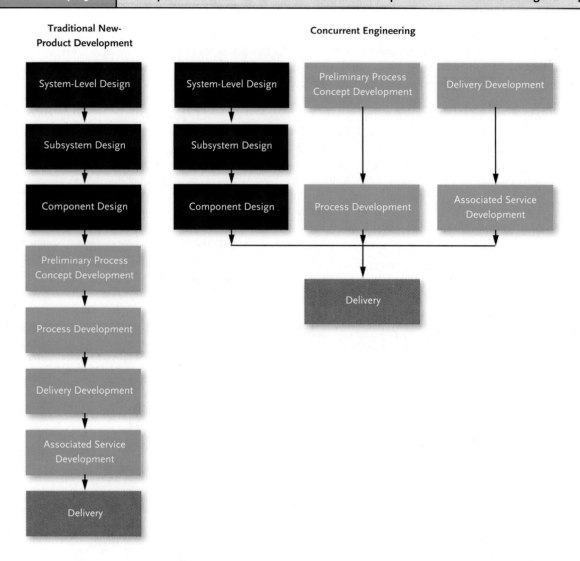

Source: Adapted from L. Cohen, *Quality Function Deployment* (Reading, MA: Addison-Wesley, 1995), pp. 33–36.

communication and coordination between various aspects of the product and service development process. The ability to design the product/service and processes simultaneously results in a design that is more consistent with process expertise and technology. The result is higher levels of quality and reduced costs. Exhibit 4.15 compares both approaches to the new product development process for a hypothetical product.

Process Improvement

In addition to QFD, which can be used to improve products and services as well as to develop new ones, there are other approaches used to assist in the improvement of processes. Some tend to focus on cost reduction, while others focus on efficiency and effectiveness, and still others focus on reduction of lead times or the improvement of quality.

It is difficult to separate process improvement tools from quality improvement tools, simply because many quality problems originate with processes. The following approaches, however, play important roles in process improvement. All pay close attention to identification of process steps that do not add value, and their removal from the system.

Tools

Process Maps

Process maps come in a variety of forms, from the traditional process flow charts to "before" and "after" maps of entire value chains. Process mapping is regarded by many as the most fundamental of all process design and process improvement tools. A process map provides a visual model of how process inputs, process activities, and process outputs are linked. The map itself is useful because it can provide information that is difficult to document in words. The process of building the map, however, can be even more beneficial. It forces people to examine the process closely and gain a thorough understanding of it. This process alone can lead to improvement.

A variety of mapping standards and symbols exist for different environments. Some popular mapping symbols are shown in Exhibit 4.16.

Exhibit 4.17 provides a process map for patient processing at a doctor's office. Notice the way decision branches enable alternatives to be documented. In this particular process, a focus on customer service would concentrate on reducing delays. Notice that in this case, as in many service processes, delays are a direct result of resources (exam room, doctor, etc.) not being immediately available.

Process maps
A diagram of the steps in a process.

Common Process Mapping Symbols	EXHIBIT 4.16

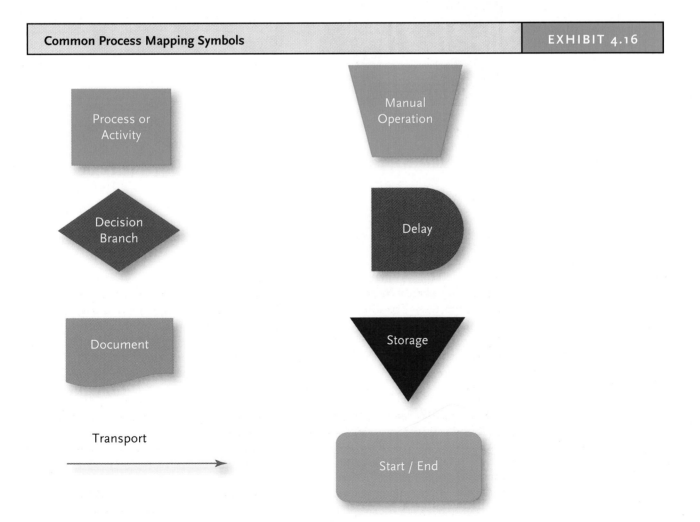

Process or Activity

Manual Operation

Decision Branch

Delay

Document

Storage

Transport

Start / End

EXHIBIT 4.17	Process Map of Patient Processing at Doctor's Office

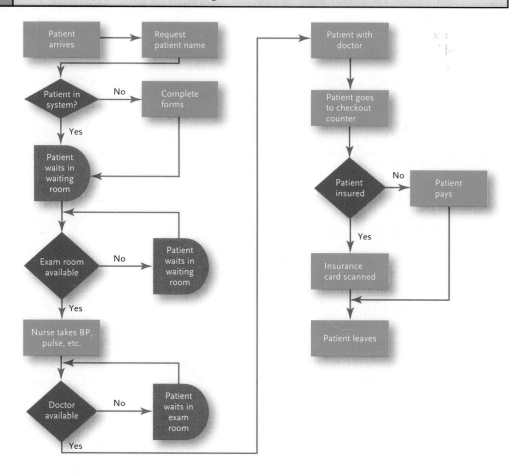

Value Stream Mapping

Value stream mapping (VSM) is sometimes considered a tool for accomplishing lean systems. It expands the narrow focus of many process improvement techniques to examine the entire value stream for wastes. The value stream is the part of the supply chain that actually adds value to the products or services being produced. Mapping the value stream is an approach to documenting the flows of goods and services that add value. A value stream map identifies the physical flow of goods and the information flows that are necessary to connect processes. The value stream mapping process is summarized by Hines and Rich[1] and utilizes seven tools: process activity mapping, supply chain response matrix, production variety funnel, quality filter mapping, demand amplification mapping, decision point analysis, and physical structure mapping. Value stream mapping is particularly useful for identifying where time can be reduced. VSM is covered extensively in Chapter 13.

Manual key entry error rates average about one error for every 300 characters entered.

service blueprint
A type of process map used for services that identifies decision points, failure points, and the line of visibility.

Service Blueprinting

Service blueprinting is an approach to creating a diagrammed model of a service to enhance management's ability to analyze its strengths and weaknesses.[2] Blueprinting is a modification of process mapping that has been used to model processes and provide a mechanism for evaluating processes prior to implementation. Traditional process mapping involves the development of a written model of a process, showing all activities and decisions along with their relationships and sequence. Additional key components specific to service blueprints include failure points, customer wait points, and employee decisions. Failure points are places in the process that can result in the failure of the service. Such points are critical to identify because each provides an opportunity to create a control mechanism such as a poka-yoke. Points in the process that require customers to wait are also critical because wait time is a non-value-adding activity that affects perceived quality, response time, and convenience. A service blueprint shows the line of visibility (the division between "up-front" and "back-office" activities) so that its position relative to various events can be evaluated. A primary advantage of service blueprinting is that these key points can be identified and addressed before the development of a new service or a change in an existing one. Exhibit 4.18 is a simple service blueprint of our proposed high-speed pizza delivery business.

In Exhibit 4.18, the line of visibility separates from the customer all processes except order taking and actual delivery. Failure points are at key process steps such as the entry of the actual order (it could be entered incorrectly), the assembly of the pizza (incorrect ingredients could be added or ingredients could be omitted), the driver pickup (wrong pizza could be picked up by driver), and delivery to the customer (driver could get lost or go to the wrong address). Poka-yokes could be developed to minimize the probability that any of these errors would take place. Quite often an "as-is" service blueprint is developed to model the existing system. After an analysis, a "should-be" blueprint is developed to provide a guide for improving the system.

Analysis of service blueprints starts out like the analysis of a process—to identify non-value-adding process steps and eliminate them. Any processing step that doesn't contribute to value is attacked, but a focus on customer wait points is an obvious starting

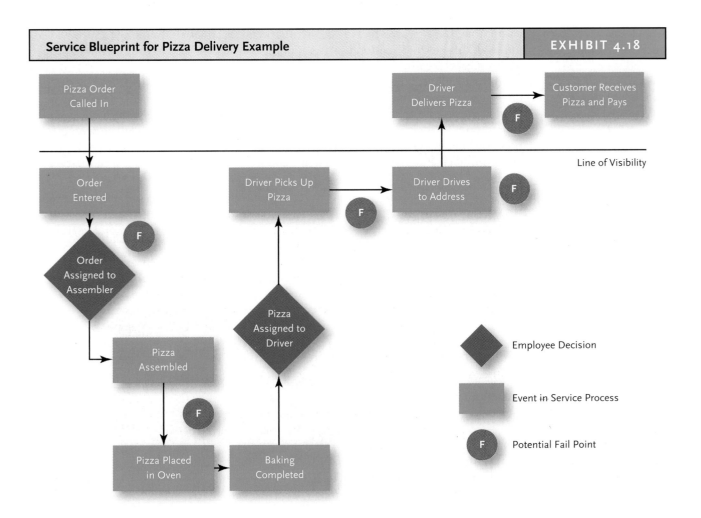

Service Blueprint for Pizza Delivery Example   EXHIBIT 4.18

The line of visibility, although not always totally blocking customer visibility, creates a line of demarcation between processes that involve the customer and those that do not. Here, as in many businesses, the line of visibility is created by a counter. Processes that take place behind that counter can utilize special equipment that enhances productivity, requires special training, or may be dangerous for customers.

place. Failure points are examined closely for improvement and ways to minimize the potential for failure. The relationship between process steps and the line of visibility is also examined, looking for potential ways to improve productivity (by moving processes behind the line of visibility) or to increase customer contact (by doing the reverse).

Business Process Analysis

business process analysis (BPA)
A productivity improvement approach that focuses on large processes and the transitions between different departments.

Business process analysis (BPA) is used to optimize large processes in ways that increase their ability to meet customer needs. BPA is particularly useful when a business is trying to improve large processes that cross functional boundaries. Exhibit 4.19 provides a model of this type of situation by diagramming the process used to initiate new contracts with a consulting firm.

In the example, a new contract initiates with sales and is then reviewed by the purchasing and procurement department for material and staffing needs. The contract is then reviewed by the legal department and finally by finance from a profitability standpoint. It then goes back to the customer. BPA focuses on all aspects of the process, paying particular attention to the transitions between departments, which are often neglected, allowing customer needs to fall through the cracks. In focusing on

EXHIBIT 4.19	Business Process Analysis Example

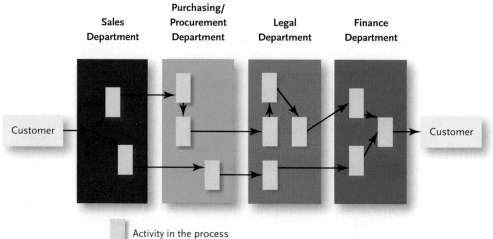

the process and how it performs, instead of individuals and how they perform, BPA attempts to identify and eliminate non-value-adding activities. Non-value-adding activities add cost but not value and reduce ROA, ROE, and profit margin.

In complex business processes crossing departmental or functional boundaries, the interface between departments is particularly critical and difficult to manage. If you think back to problems you've had with bureaucracies, departmental interfaces are frequently the source. Problems you've had with your university administration, for example, probably occurred at the interface between two departments. If you've ever been dropped from a class for nonpayment of fees when you'd actually paid them, you could probably track the problem down to a mixup between the bursar's office and the registrar.

Reengineering

Reengineering designs processes starting from a clean slate rather than incrementally improving the processes, as is done in BPA. In reengineering, everything is redesigned, including forms processing and information processing. Reengineering is not limited to those processes that directly involve a product or customer, however. It includes all business processes. In fact, more often than not, reengineering focuses on behind-the-scenes activities. Reengineering is equally applicable to service- or product-oriented businesses. The general objective is to create leaner processes and lower costs, but quite often the result is that processes are more robust and meet customer needs better. Common outcomes of reengineering programs include reduced lead times, costs, and staff (downsizing), and an overall reduction to process inputs. Reengineering has been particularly effective in service-oriented markets such as insurance and financial services.

A change in customer needs may require a completely new type of process, triggering a reengineering effort. Reengineering frequently is needed when an order winner becomes an order qualifier, and a new order winner must be developed.

Since reengineering efforts focus on processes, the generic procedure follows a typical problem-solving approach, with a focus on process effectiveness. Reengineering efforts are frequently accomplished by project teams whose first responsibility is to identify potential areas for process improvement. The team then follows a rigorous, step-by-step procedure like the one in Exhibit 4.20.

reengineering
Starting from a clean slate to improve a process.

---

om ADVANTAGE   Process Improvement for Enhanced Profitability

Insurance companies have long been leaders of the reengineering trend. Changing service processes can reduce costs, but often more importantly it can drastically affect the customer's experience. Progressive Insurance, the third largest U.S. auto insurer, with 11 million customers, has been successful in serving insurance needs of high-risk drivers, but feared competition from larger firms in the early 1990s. It reacted by completely redesigning its claims processing approach.

Traditional claims processing for insurance companies can take several days. Progressive customers have access to a claims representative 24 hours a day. Adjusters work from mobile vans rather than offices and can now respond much more quickly. This change in a fairly fundamental process provides many benefits. Customers are less likely to be dissatisfied with the claims process. Shortened cycle times for claims processing reduce the costs associated with car rentals. Cost savings from reducing the average car rental by only one day are an average of $28 per claim for over 10,000 claims per day. This focused approach to process improvement adds value (and revenues) while, at the same time, reducing costs.

Source: M. Hammer, "Deep Change: How Operational Innovation Can Transform Your Company," *Harvard Business Review*, April 2004; "Company Facts," www.progressive.com/progressive/company_info.asp, May 10, 2004.

EXHIBIT 4.20	Project Team Reengineering Procedure
	Step 1. **Process selection:** Identify potential areas for improvement based on need and likelihood of success.
	Step 2. **Description of current process:** Using process flow diagram techniques, describe, precisely, the current process.
	Step 3. **Process improvement:** Identify new ways to accomplish the process goals.
	Step 4. **Process verification:** Identify problems with the proposed changes and ensure that they can be eliminated.
	Step 5. **Implementation and monitoring:** Make the changes and monitor the results for effectiveness.

poka-yoke
A device that makes it impossible or nearly impossible to do something incorrectly.

Poka-Yoke and Mistake-Proofing

How many times have you realized, after leaving the drive-up window, that your fast-food order was wrong? A popular approach to minimizing mistakes made in production processes is to create barriers to doing tasks any way but the correct way. These mechanisms, known in Japan as **poka-yokes,** can take a variety of forms. In some cases a product component's design can prevent it from being assembled any way but correctly. In other situations, various mechanisms are used to help reduce the likelihood of errors. Such "fail-safe" systems are common in everyday life. Cars won't start unless the transmission is in Park. Lawnmowers have a "dead-man" switch that requires that the operator hold the handle, or the mower shuts off. McDonald's uses a specially designed tool to ensure that each order of fries has the right quantity. Urinals in some European airports have the small image of a fly etched into the center of the porcelain. Other examples of poka-yokes are shown below.[3]

- Computer diskettes can only be inserted the right way.
- The gas filler pipe in your car allows only unleaded fuel nozzles to be inserted.
- Space heaters shut off automatically if tipped over.
- Washer and dryer switches shut off the device when the door is opened.
- Some automatic coffee pots have a valve that shuts off the flow of coffee when the pot is removed.
- Some wheelchairs automatically lock when someone is sitting on them.
- Riding lawnmowers have a switch in the seat that shuts the mower off if the rider is not sitting.
- Automatic garage door openers have an electric sensor that prevents the door from being closed on a person or pet.
- Treadmills have a clip that attaches to the runner and shuts the machine off if the runner falls.
- At some restaurants the trash can opening is too small to allow trays to be accidentally discarded.

In the production of goods and services, poka-yokes include tools that can be used the correct way only, checklists to follow, or alarms that sound when something is done incorrectly. A mechanism is incorporated into the system to force correct procedures. Poka-yoke designs have gained popularity as a way to eliminate mistakes, increase quality, and reduce costs.

Process Technology

Technology has been incorporated into processes for hundreds of years to improve quality and increase productivity. In today's product-oriented processes technology takes the same roles plus more.

Technology has enhanced the product design process through the use of computer-aided design (CAD) and computer-aided manufacturing (CAM) which enables designers to create and produce products more effectively. Computer-integrated manufacturing (CIM) enables manufacturers to link the design or products and processes. Numerically controlled (NC) machines provide the capability to transfer designs directly to the machines that produce the product. The use of automation and robotics to perform repetitive or dangerous production activities has increased productivity and lowered costs for many high-volume producers.

Technologies have also enhanced the productivity of traditional business processes like billing, order entry, and communications. The reduction of paper transactions has reduced costs and time associated with these necessary functions.

Although not often thought of in the context of processes, the movement of goods through the supply chain has also benefited from technology. Global positioning systems (GPS) enable companies to track exactly where products are and how fast they are moving. Radio-frequency identification technology (RFID) allows businesses to scan the containers, pallets, and even individual products to track their movement in and out of warehouses, and actually make inventory counts, from a distance. These technologies will be examined in detail in Chapter 12.

Services have also benefited from technological advancement. The Internet has moved many service processes behind the line of visibility, improving productivity, but has also made many services more convenient to customers.

While the increased use of technology has had a positive impact on business productivity in general, there is no guarantee that every technological enhancement will provide a net benefit. Businesses need to be careful and assess the costs and benefits prior to an investment in technology. They must also recognize that with increased dependence on technology comes an increase in the requirements and expectations of employees. This can affect employee recruitment, training, and labor costs.

Broad Frameworks

Lean Systems

Lean systems have evolved from just-in-time systems that were originally used in Japan and transplanted to the United States in the 1980s. Lean systems focus on waste reduction in all of its forms. The waste attacked manifests itself in the form of excess inventory, overproduction, waiting, transportation, errors in processing, poor quality, and wasted labor—all resulting in inflated costs. "Leanness" can be thought of as the goal for all process improvement efforts. It's what processes should be. Lean systems have traditionally focused heavily on inventory reduction despite the fact that process improvement is an important part of any real waste reduction effort. Lean systems are examined in detail later in this text. It is so important to effective operations management that it is the focus of the entire Chapter 13.

Six Sigma

Six Sigma has evolved from having a very specific meaning in quality management (3.4 defects per million) to being used to define a much broader philosophy of continuous improvement. The Six Sigma approach to continuous improvement is very structured and consists of five steps: define, measure, analyze, improve, control (DMAIC). It uses a structured organizational architecture of personnel with varying levels of training, expertise, and responsibilities, including executive champions, deployment champions, project champions, master black belts, black belts, and green belts. Top management support is also an integral part of the Six Sigma system. Six Sigma is very metrics-intensive, which results in a need for extensive training, but also yields substantial returns in the depth and detail of analysis. Six Sigma is such a dominant force in quality management that it is covered in extensive detail in Chapter 7.

CHAPTER SUMMARY

This chapter examined processes. Capabilities provide value to customers by enabling a business to do things a customer can't. Processes are used by businesses to create those capabilities. One can look at the relationship from an input–output perspective, with resources being the inputs and capabilities the outputs of processes. Linking processes and capabilities to customer needs enhances value. Improving the productivity of processes reduces costs. The productivity of processes depends substantially on the costs associated with them.

In addition to the discussion of processes and capabilities, this chapter introduced two frameworks for strategic process decisions. The first, the product/process matrix, examined interactions and trade-offs made when deciding on such important process issues as volume, flexibility, degree of customization, and cost per unit. The product/process matrix has implications for manufacturing and service environments. This chapter also examined the service system design matrix, which clarifies the trade-offs services must make with regard to the degree of customer contact, sales opportunities, and process efficiency.

This chapter introduced quality function deployment, a popular framework to link processes to customer needs. Methods to improve existing processes beyond the QFD product and service design process include the process improvement approaches of process mapping, value stream mapping, service mapping, lean systems, Six Sigma, business process analysis, reengineering, and poka-yoke.

KEY TERMS

assemble-to-order, 127
assembly line, 127
batch production, 127
business process analysis (BPA), 144
cellular layout, 125
changeover time, 127
concurrent engineering, 139
continuous processing, 127
design for environment (DFG), 139
design for logistics, 138
design for manufacture and assembly
  (DFMA), 138
house of quality, 131
job shop, 125

make-to-order, 127
make-to-stock, 127
poka-yoke, 146
process maps, 141
process-oriented layout, 122
product-oriented layout, 122
project, 125
quality function deployment (QFD), 131
reengineering, 145
repetitive processing, 127
service blueprint, 142
setup time, 127
substitute quality characteristics, 132

REVIEW QUESTIONS

1. Why are customers usually more concerned about service processes than about manufacturing processes?

2. Why must the design of new products and services be integrated with the design of processes?

3. How do design for manufacture and assembly (DFMA), design for logistics (DFL), and design for environment (DFE) result in better value for customers?

4. Describe a product-oriented layout. What are its strengths and weaknesses?

5. Describe a process-oriented layout. What are its strengths and weaknesses?

6. What capabilities can be achieved from combining process- and product-oriented layouts into a cellular layout?

7. Describe the relationships examined by the product/process matrix.

8. With regard to flexibility, variety, and volume, compare projects, job shops, batch production, assembly lines, and continuous flow.

9. Describe the relationships in the service system design matrix.

10. What are the four phases of quality function deployment (QFD)? What role does each play in the process of matching product or service design to customers' needs?

11. What is meant by the "voice of the customer"?

12. In the house of quality, how are the relationships between WHATs and HOWs defined?

13. In the house of quality, how can competitive issues be included?

14. Why are process maps considered so fundamentally important to process improvement?

15. How do process maps, value stream maps, and service blueprints differ?

16. What is meant by lean systems? How do lean systems enhance value for the customer?

17. What is a poka-yoke?

18. Describe the components of a service blueprint. Why is each component important?

19. Compare and contrast business process analysis and reengineering.

DISCUSSION AND EXPLORATION

1. Select a successful restaurant you frequent. What are its capabilities? Describe its processes. Which processes are most critical to its capabilities?

2. Capabilities that lead to market dominance often result from combining processes that originate in different parts of a business. Describe a small business you are familiar with that has created a unique set of capabilities in this way.

3. Identify a university service you frequent (cafeteria, bursar's office, advising office, etc.). What would be the implications of moving the line of visibility *away* from the customer (involving the customer in activities that are currently behind the line of visibility)? Discuss implications for cost, productivity, sales, and quality of service.

4. Using the same service as in question 3, what would be the implications of moving activities the customer is currently exposed to behind the line of visibility? Again, discuss implications for cost, productivity, sales, and quality of service.

5. Identify two retailers that compete against each other but choose very different levels for involving the customer in their processes. What are the advantages and disadvantages of each approach? Evaluate each from the standpoint of value attributes as perceived by the customer. Which do you prefer?

6. Identify a product you use and are familiar with (for example, a running shoe, an mp3 player, a cell phone). Identify the WHATs that you consider to be important. Identify the HOWs by defining quantitative performance measures for each WHAT.

7. Of all of the products you own, what is your favorite? Why does this product stand above others?

8. Identify the last time a product or service failed to meet your expectations. In that experience, which of the four QFD steps failed?

9. Select one of the following processes and develop a process map.

   a. Studying for an exam.

   b. Cooking a meal.

   c. Getting from home to class.

    d. Adding a class.

    e. Purchasing a book on Amazon.com.

PROBLEMS   HM

Solutions to odd-numbered problems are located on the text's Online Center (http://mhhe.com/opsnow3e).

1. Using the house of quality as a model, identify WHATs and HOWs for one of the following businesses:

    a tanning salon
    an ice cream shop
    a taco stand
    an in-home computer repair service
    a while-you-wait oil change service

2. Design a poka-yoke device for a process you frequently use. What mistakes does it prevent?

3. Identify an online retailer you have used. Develop a process map of the checkout process. How could the process be improved?

4. Identify a service you frequent (a sandwich shop, a doctor's office, a college administrative office, etc.). Create a service blueprint for the service. Be sure to include potential fail points and the line of visibility.

5. Develop a process map for correctly jump-starting a car with a dead battery. Why is the sequence of the steps important?

6. Develop a process map for changing a car tire. Begin with accessing the spare. How does your process map compare to the instructions provided in the user's manual? Would this process map be a beneficial addition to the manual?

7. Create a written set of instructions for copying a CD on a computer. Create a process map for the same process. Which is easier to follow?

8. Create a service blueprint for your college's class registration process. Examine the completed blueprint. Examine the fail points. Do they often result in service failure? Have any resulted in service failure for you? What could be done to reduce the likelihood of service failure at these points?

9. For the blueprint you developed in question 8, perform an analysis of the processes used. Identify non-value-adding steps and develop a plan for eliminating them. Evaluate the sequence of steps in the processes. Could they be done better? How?

10. Create a service blueprint for the checkout process of a retail store you frequent. Identify the line of visibility and fail points. How critical is the business's placement of the line of visibility to its strategic objectives? Have they placed it correctly? Which of the fail points, in your opinion, result in the most frequent service failure? How critical are these failures to the business's strategy? What is the typical reaction of the customer to these failures?

ENDNOTES

1. P. Hines and N. Rich, "The Seven Value Stream Mapping Tools," *International Journal of Operations and Production Management*, Vol. 17, No. 1, 1997, pp. 46–64.

2. C. H. Fine, *Clockspeed: Winning Industry Control in the Age of Temporary Advantage* (Reading, MA: Perseus Books, 1998), pp. 71–76.

3. John Grout's Poka-Yoke Page, www.campbell.berry.edu/faculty/jgrout/pokayoke.shtml. Examples used with permission.

LEARNING ACTIVITIES

Visit the Online Learning Center (www.mhhe.com/opsnow3e) for additional resources. Content varies by chapter, and includes

- Business Tours
- OM on Site
- Readings
- Resources
- Excel Tutors

- Interactive Case Models
- Reel Operations Video Clips
- Additional Advanced Problems
- Self-Assessment Quizzes
- Glossary

SELECTED RESOURCES

Cohen, L. *Quality Function Deployment*, Reading, MA: Addison-Wesley Publishing Company, 1995.

Fine, Charles H. *Clockspeed: Winning Industry Control in the Age of Temporary Advantage*, Reading, MA: Perseus Books, 1998.

Hammer, M. "Reengineering Work: Don't Automate, Obliterate," *Harvard Business Review*, July 1, 1990.

Hammer, M. "Deep Change; How Operational Innovation Can Transform Your Company," *Harvard Business Review*, April 2004.

Hauser, John R., and Clausing, Don. "The House of Quality," *Harvard Business Review*, May 1, 1988.

Sullivan, L. P. "Quality Function Deployment," *Quality Progress*, June 1986.

Swank, C. K. "The Lean Service Machine," *Harvard Business Review*, October 2003.

VIDEO CASE 4.1

Process Improvement at Gortrac

Based on Videos 4 and 5 on the Student DVD

Gortrac is a producer of tracks for holding wiring and cable in industrial applications. Like many companies, they faced a downturn in demand, which, when coupled with high costs and inefficiencies, resulted in a serious downturn in profitability. To turn the business around, Gortrac went through a planning phase and then an implementation phase. Their goal was to triple business in a five-year period.

1. For Gortrac, why was the use of cross-functional teams so important? What did those teams do?

2. What is meant by the phrase "exposing the rocks"? Why was that an important part of Gortrac's transformation?

3. Why was flow charting the processes so important for Gortrac?

4. After changes were made, what was the purpose of the daily production meetings held by Gortrac?

5. How has lean processing made the jobs of Gortrac workers easier?

INTERACTIVE CASE 4.1

Process Improvement for CaseWorks Systems

This interactive case utilizes the Production Line Interactive Model on the student DVD. The Production Line Interactive Model provides an environment designed for exploring processes and the roles that variability and disruptions can play in those processes. In the Production Line Interactive Model, the user can specify the input rate and the production rate for each of five work centers in a small production line. The user can also specify the level of variability for each work center as well as the frequency of breakdowns. The user has four controls of the simulation itself. The first control is the start button. Starting the simulation causes the work centers to begin processing. The second control is for the clock speed. Speeding up the clock simply means that the simulation runs faster. The pause button allows the user to temporarily suspend the simulation. The stop button ends the simulation. A screen view of the Production Line Simulator is presented on the next page.

CaseWorks Systems

CaseWorks Systems is a contract assembler of automotive parts. They specialize in short assembly processes of high-volume components. One particular assembly line consists of five machines, each with an operator. These five machines (WC1, WC2, WC3, WC4, and WC5) perform a variety of operations that are standard to many of the components assembled by CaseWorks Systems. The variety of components that use the line, however, results in processing times that vary from job to job and, in some cases, processing times that are difficult to control. Changes in processing times, as well as variability in the system, have made it difficult for managers to predict process outputs and have them quite confused. For some components, output is high and products move smoothly through the production line. For others, however, inventory builds up in the system and output is low, inconsistent, and difficult to predict.

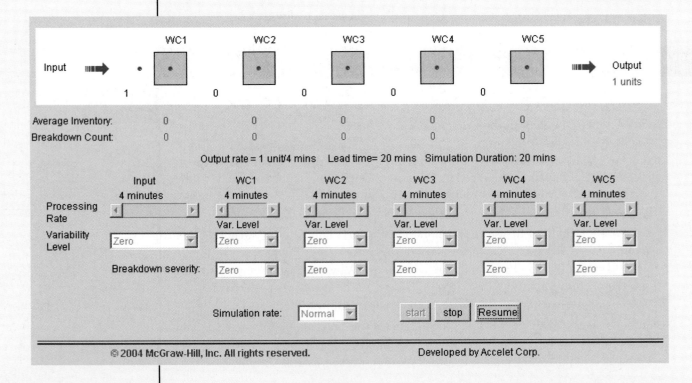

1. Set the input rate and processing time for all WCs at four minutes per unit with zero variability. Run the simulation for 100 simulator minutes.

   a. How many units were completed?

   b. Why weren't 25 units completed?

2. Set WC3 to a six-minute processing time. Leave the variability at zero for all WCs. Run the simulation for 100 simulator minutes.

   a. How many units were completed this time?

   b. What happens in front of WC3?

   c. Repeat the 100-minute simulation with WC3 processing at six minutes per unit, but reduce the input rate to one unit every six minutes. Now what happens?

3. Set the processing time of all WCs and the input rate to six minutes, with zero variability. Run the simulation for 100 simulator minutes.

   a. How many units were completed?

   b. What factors determine the number of units completed by the system in a set amount of time?

4. Set the input rate and processing time for all WCs back to four minutes per unit, with zero variability. Run the simulation for 100 simulator minutes.

   a. How many units were completed?

5. Reduce the processing time of any one of the five WCs to three minutes. Run the simulation for 100 simulator minutes.

   a. How many units were completed?

6. Reduce the processing time of an additional WC to three minutes. Run the simulation for 100 simulator minutes.

   a. How many units were completed?

   b. Why did a reduction in time not result in an improvement in system output?

   c. What does this tell you about investing in equipment to improve the speed of operations in service and manufacturing systems?

7. Set all processing times and the input rate to the initial four-minute value with zero variability. Run the simulation for 100 simulator minutes.

   a. Examine the use of resources during this time. Does inventory build up anywhere? Where?

   b. Are any of the work centers idle (white) during this time?

8. Leave the input rate and processing times at four minutes, but increase the variability of WC3 to the extreme level. Run the simulation for another 100 simulator minutes in five separate runs, recording the number of units produced for each simulation run.

   a. What is the average weekly output?

   b. Observe the simulation runs. Does inventory build up anywhere? If so, where does it build up? Explain why this happens.

   c. After the initial start-up phase, are any of the WCs ever idle? If so, which ones? Explain your observations.

   d. What implications does process time variability have for the productivity of resources?

9. Leave the input rate and processing times at four minutes, but increase the variability of all WCs and the input rate to the extreme level. Run the simulation five separate times for 100 simulator minutes each time. Record the results.

   a. What is the average weekly output? How does this outcome differ from the previous five simulation runs?

b. Does inventory build up anywhere? If so, where does it build up? Explain why this happens.

c. After the initial start-up phase, are any of the WCs ever idle? If so, which ones? Explain the results.

d. The average processing time for each WC is the same in the last two experiments. What is happening to make system output different? What implications does this have for the productivity of resources in a process?

APPLICATION CASE 4.1

Building a Better Backpack

Deb Richards and Steve Collins are junior business majors who have received a $5,000 grant from their school's entrepreneurial "incubator" fund to help them start a small business this summer. Their proposal was to develop a superior student backpack and sell it through bookstores. They have examined the top-selling backpacks (Jansport, Eddie Bauer, North Face, etc.) and have consulted with a contract sewing shop that can get material and components. Deb and Steve want to use the house of quality framework to make sure the final product meets customer expectations. They have identified several general areas in which to collect customer preferences but recognize that there may be others that they have overlooked. They have identified the following WHATs to help them begin the first house of quality matrix:

Size

Weight

Comfort

Durability

Pockets

1. By examining other backpacks and through experimentation, identify the HOWs for the five WHATs listed above. Be as specific as possible. For example, pockets includes the number, size and shape, location, etc. Identify the performance goals for each HOW.

2. Identify WHATs that are important but not included on the list Deb and Steve created. How could you determine the level of importance of these product attributes? Identify the HOWs for the new WHATs. What would be the performance goals?

3. Identification of the WHATs and HOWs completes Phase 1 of the QFD process. Use that information to develop component specifications (QFD Phase 2) for fabric, zippers, web strapping, shoulder strap padding, and plastic fasteners.

4. Assuming that zippers, straps, plastic fasteners, and padding will be outsourced by the contract manufacturer and that the assembly of all fabric and other components will be done in-house, identify the processing steps and sequence of those steps for your backpack. You may need to closely examine a competing backpack to get a sense of the assembly process.

APPLICATION CASE 4.2

Reducing Hangups at GOL

Georgia Outdoor Liquidators is a small retailer of surplus, overstock, and returned recreational merchandise. GOL sells through a catalog and Web site. Dan Terriat, the entrepreneur who started the company in 1996, would like to get out of the mail order side completely and focus entirely on Internet sales. Dan's primary reason for wanting to eliminate the phone-in orders is the labor cost associated with staffing phones. At this point in time, however, phone-in orders make up 38 percent of sales, and catalog buyers don't seem as price sensitive. Dan thinks that eBay is a major competitor for online sales, and catalog users tend to not compare GOL prices to those on eBay. In a recent conversation with Gretchen Beck, the chief operations officer, Dan recently remarked, "If I'm unable to eliminate telephone orders, let's at least evaluate the phone order process and make it as efficient as possible."

Despite having lots of projects "on her plate," Gretchen decided to start by putting together an accurate description of the current telephone order process. She asked the two most senior customer service specialists (CSS) to write down the steps of the process. Three days later Gretchen received the following:

1. First, we ask the caller, "How can I help you?" The caller then tells us whether he wishes to place an order, needs help with an existing order, or something else.

2. If the call is for something other than an order, we forward it to Steve in customer service.

3. If it's an order, the first thing we find out is the person's name and phone number. We enter that into the system. If the person has ordered before, all other information (except credit card info) is in the system. If the person hasn't ordered before, we enter the name, address, and phone number into the system.

4. The next thing we do is take the actual order from the customer.

5. When the order has been taken, we quickly review the items to make sure we've accurately entered them into the system.

6. The next thing we do is ask the customer if they would like to hear information about the daily sales item. If they are interested, we describe it to them. If they would like to purchase it, we add it to their order.

7. The next thing we do is ask the person what shipping method they would prefer (standard, 2nd day, or overnight).

8. If the person is from Georgia, we indicate that in the system and it adds sales tax to the order.

9. We then tell the person the total cost of the items, the shipping cost, and the grand total.

10. The last thing we do is ask the customer how they wish to pay for it. They give us their credit card number, expiration date, and security code, and we enter that into the system.

11. Our system automatically calls in to authorize the credit card and that takes a minute or so typically. As soon as that is approved, we thank the person and the process is over. If the credit card authorization fails, the first thing we do is re-submit it, just in case it was a system problem. If that fails, we tell the customer and they either give us information for another credit card, to re-try the authorization, or cancel the sale.

Questions

1. Map the process used by GOL to take phone orders. Use the symbols provided in Exhibit 4.16.

2. What aspects of the process would you pay closest attention to if you were trying to reduce labor costs?

3. What aspects of the process would you try to change if your focus was on improving customer service?

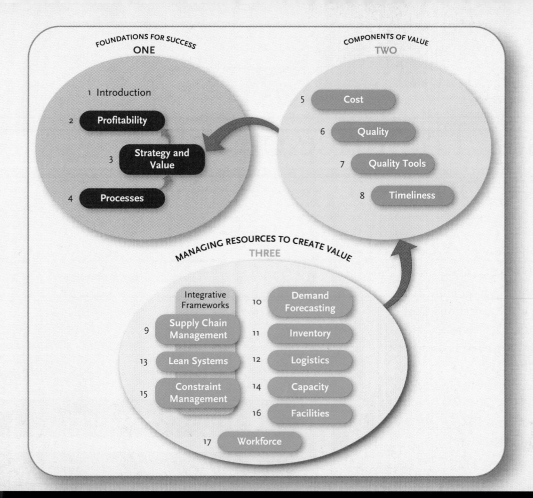

FOUNDATIONS FOR SUCCESS
ONE

COMPONENTS OF VALUE
TWO

1 Introduction

2 Profitability

3 Strategy and Value

4 Processes

5 Cost

6 Quality

7 Quality Tools

8 Timeliness

MANAGING RESOURCES TO CREATE VALUE
THREE

Integrative Frameworks

9 Supply Chain Management

13 Lean Systems

15 Constraint Management

10 Demand Forecasting

11 Inventory

12 Logistics

14 Capacity

16 Facilities

17 Workforce

Components of Value

INTRODUCTION

Value is one foundation for success. It represents what people and businesses pay for when they make a purchase and is created by effective business processes. When processes create value, the components of value must be considered. The cost of the product or service, the quality of the product or service, and the timeliness of the product or service are three components of value controlled by the operations function. In Unit 2, we examine those three value components.

Costs: The Price of Value Creation

LEARNING OBJECTIVES

- Describe the relationship between cost and value.

- Understand how costs affect the three profitability measures.

- Describe why costs are important in operations.

- State the dangers of using average costs.

- Explain why it is important to be able to assign operations costs.

- Explain the concepts of tracing and allocating costs.

- Define the components of product cost.

- Describe how cost reduction relates to productivity improvement.

- Explain the concepts of standards and variances.

- Compute usage, price, and total variances.

- Understand the difference between total cost and cost per unit.

- Conduct a breakeven analysis.

FINDING A NICHE IN A COST-FOCUSED MARKET

It would be difficult to come up with an industry whose margins are tighter than those of retailing. Tight margins translate into a situation where a small amount of cost cutting can have a large impact on profitability. With competitors like Wal-Mart, competing on the basis of price becomes even more difficult because Wal-Mart is extremely tough to beat on that basis. There are a few retailers, however, who have been able to find a niche and compete successfully.

Dollar General employs about 64,000 people in more than 8,000 stores operated in 34 states. Its 2005 sales reached $8.58 billion. Growing at a rapid rate, Dollar General opened 730 additional stores in 2005. The Dollar General strategy has been to place stores primarily in small towns and focus on a broad range of household items such as paper products, cleaning supplies, health and beauty aids, foods/snacks, housewares, toys, and basic apparel. Dollar General has begun a new extension to its market by opening up Dollar General Market stores, which will carry an expanded assortment of perishable items.

A similar example is Family Dollar. Family Dollar is also growing rapidly. In the last ten years, it has added more than 4,000 new stores to the chain. It, too, focuses on basic merchandise for the family and home, and prefers being the neighborhood discount store in low to middle income neighborhoods. A no-frills, self-service environment, and close attention to costs allow it to keep prices low. Its sales first exceeded $5 billion in 2005.

Family Dollar has stores in 44 states, and stores range in size from 7,500 to 9,500 square feet. The size makes it possible for Family Dollar to open new stores in rural areas and small towns, as well as urban neighborhoods. The stores are located in shopping centers or as freestanding buildings. During 2005, the Company opened 500 new stores and closed 68 stores to bring the number of stores in operation to 5,898. It operates eight distribution centers and planned to open 400 new stores during 2006.

Retail stores that compete on the basic of price must keep costs low. The cost of leasing the facility and the cost of employees is of particular importance. Those that succeed are finding that they can compete with Wal-Mart by providing a smaller store close to their customers.

Source: www.dollargeneral.com/, March 16, 2006; R. J. Bowman, "Discount Retailer Doesn't Skimp on Supply-Chain Investments," Supply ChainBrain.com, May 2004; www.supplychainbrain.com/archives/05.04. casestudy.htm?adcode=5, May 16, 2004; "Dollar General Unlocks Solution," *Chain Store Age*, December 2003, Vol. 79, No. 12; www.familydollar .com, August 24, 2006.

Cost is the first of three components of value. It is important because it represents what a customer must give up to purchase a product or service and what a business must give up to pay for what it consumes in value-adding processes. For the business, the higher the costs, the lower the profitability. Some type of cost forms the "input" for virtually all productivity measures, so productivity improvement is often a cost reduction effort. Many of the efforts emanating from operations and supply chain decisions are driven by costs.

Introduction: Paying for Value

Cost is shown in the resource/profit model as the first component of value. Whereas increasing quality or timeliness *adds* to value, increasing cost obviously *detracts* from it. Cost is often thought of as the realm of accountants, but it drives many decisions in operations and must be examined from that perspective. Not only are operations decisions often based on costs, but operations processes create many of the costs associated with products and services.

This chapter examines the concept of cost, its role in determining value and profitability, how it is measured, and how it is managed. By this point in your coursework, you have probably had one or two accounting courses. The intent of this chapter is to link operations and accounting by establishing the context for many accounting practices. This context is important for all managers because the origin of many costs is in the way resources are managed. Reducing or controlling these costs can only come from understanding the link between resource use and the costs created by that use.

This chapter structures the examination of cost and operations around four objectives. First, it presents an overview of different types of costs as they relate to operations. Second, because of the effect of cost on value, it examines the role costs play in supply chains. Third, it provides an overview of cost measurement and the operations implications of assigning, tracing, and allocating costs. Finally, because not all costs are financial, the concept of nonfinancial costs is introduced and examined as a critical component of effective decision making.

Chapter 3 presented the value attributes for business and consumer customers reviewed in Exhibit 5.1. The value attributes of quality, response time, dependability of delivery, convenience, ethical issues, flexibility, and personalization are often thought to enhance value. Style and fashion are occasionally viewed negatively, as is technology. Cost is almost always viewed as the overriding negative factor.

For the customer, cost is more than merely price. It includes all of the resource outlays over the life of the product or service. Cost is the currency by which the benefits of all of the other value attributes are measured. The link between costs and operations comes directly through the costs added in production processes. Cost's wide-ranging impact has many implications for a firm's profitability.

Dollar General is committed to "everyday low prices" and does not have sales or promotions.

EXHIBIT 5.1	Critical Value Attributes
	Cost
	Quality
	Response time
	Dependability of delivery
	Convenience
	Style/fashion
	Ethical issues
	Technology
	Flexibility
	Personalization

Cost and Perceived Value

For any customers, whether business or consumer, cost is a key factor in the purchasing decision. Even though a customer's cost of ownership consists of more than just the purchase price, purchase price is usually a very important component of the total cost of ownership.

Purchase price is so dominant in purchasing decisions that, all other attributes being nearly equal, it frequently sways the final decision. Just think about retailers trying to increase sales or reduce inventory at the end of the season. Do they offer quicker delivery? No. Do they offer a special or more congenial salespersons? No. Instead, they reduce price. Businesses selling to other business customers pay close attention to cost because all of *their* costs are translated into what they must in turn charge customers. For example, a clothing manufacturer closely monitors the costs of fabric because those costs are passed on to the retailers that purchase the finished products. High fabric costs either cut into the profit margin or are passed on, potentially hurting sales. The business is transparent in that all of the costs incurred are eventually either passed on to the customer or deducted from net income.

For consumers, the perceived value must be greater than the cost or they wouldn't spend the money to make the purchase. For business customers, potential for adding value to their product or service must be greater than the cost, or they will not be able to recoup the costs when they sell the product or service.

What Is a "Cost"?

Cost is a scarce resource given up in order to obtain a current or future benefit. Cost is often measured in monetary terms but does not have to be. Instead of money, cost could be in the form of some other scarce resource, such as time or customer loyalty. With the exception of a brief overview of nonmonetary costs at the end of this chapter, most of the discussion in this chapter is limited to monetary costs. This does not imply that nonmonetary costs are not important. On the contrary, they can be extremely important. In many cases, bad decisions are made because nonmonetary costs are overlooked.

Cost and Profitability

Costs incurred by a business affect the prices the business must charge, which have an immediate impact on the customer's perception of value. But why should a company care about costs if its prices are in line with those of competitors? The answer is that cost savings that are not passed on to the customer go directly to profitability. Let's review how this happens. Recall from Chapter 2 that net income is the numerator for all profitability measures:

(5.1)   Profit Margin = Net Income/Sales

(5.2)   Return on Assets = Net Income/Total Assets

(5.3)   Return on Equity = Net Income/Total Equity

Also recall that the net income calculation starts with net sales. Net sales is the direct result of customers' perceived value. The cost of goods sold, depreciation, and interest paid are subtracted to provide the taxable income. Subtracting the taxes gives us net income:

(5.4)   Net Income = Net Sales – Cost of Goods Sold
                            – Selling and Administrative Costs – Depreciation
                            – Interest Paid – Taxes

Costs have two direct effects on net income. They influence the selling price, which, to a great extent, dictates value. Value creates demand, which translates into net sales. Costs also dictate the cost of goods sold, which is used in the calculation of net income. Thus, the greater the cost, the greater the price, the less the perceived value by customers, the less the net sales, and, ultimately, the less the net income. *Also*, the greater the costs, the greater the costs of goods sold, and the less the net income. No wonder many firms seem to be on a never-ending cost-cutting binge.

The concepts of price and cost are often misunderstood. From the buyer's perspective, they are occasionally the same thing, but usually they are different. *Price*, or, more precisely,

Dollar General's net sales for fiscal year 2005 were $8.58 billion.

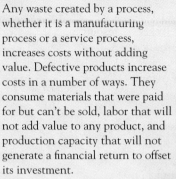

Any waste created by a process, whether it is a manufacturing process or a service process, increases costs without adding value. Defective products increase costs in a number of ways. They consume materials that were paid for but can't be sold, labor that will not add value to any product, and production capacity that will not generate a financial return to offset its investment.

sales price, is the amount of money a seller agrees to accept in return for something, like a product or service. That price might be the total cost of the product or service, but usually there are other costs as well. Shipping costs, for example, would add to the buyer's cost. Future repairs and maintenance would also need to be considered. There's a reason, for example, why reliability history is important when customers shop for a new car: Lack of reliability translates directly into higher cost of ownership. Consumers who have become accustomed to ordering online have rapidly come to recognize that price isn't as important as cost, since shipping and handling costs can be significant. Many Internet retailers have been criticized for providing customers with the sales price early in the purchasing decision but withholding other important cost information, like shipping and handling charges, until very late in the checkout process. This has been a major factor in customers abandoning their "shopping carts" at the online checkout. Even in the Internet auction environment of eBay, negative feedback for sellers frequently focuses on shipping costs.

For a business, sales price must be greater than the cost or there is no margin for profit. A business customer who purchased a piece of equipment would need to install it. There would also be costs associated with that installation and there would be maintenance costs associated with keeping the equipment running. Those costs would include labor costs, costs of downtime on the equipment, and costs for repair parts.

Types of Costs

There are many different types of cost. Some important ones are defined below.

- **Expected costs:** forecasted payments for future resources.
- **Actual costs:** the past payments for currently owned resources.

expected costs
Forecasted payments for future resources.

actual costs
Past payments for currently owned resources.

- **Out-of-pocket costs:** cash payments made for resources.
- **Product costs:** costs of the resources used to make products.
- **Period costs:** costs of resources used in nonproduction elements of the business.
- **Total costs:** the costs of all resources obtained in a particular period.

out-of-pocket costs
Cash payments made for resources.

product costs
Costs of resources used to make products.

period costs
Costs of resources used in nonproduction elements of a business.

total costs
The costs of all resources obtained in a particular period.

Average Costs

In many cases, the cost used to make an operations decision is an average cost. Average costs can be useful, but they can also be dangerous. Average costs provide an excellent way to compare current costs with historical costs, a frequently used measure of improvement. They can be helpful when a business is making comparisons with competitors, or when a comparison of costs versus sales prices is necessary. Caution should be used, however, because average costs can be misleading, particularly when a firm is trying to assign average costs to periods of time. Average costs typically do not represent all of the costs associated with a product during a specific period of time. For example, during a particular period of time, a business might not have enough demand to fully utilize equipment and labor. Restaurant capacity typifies this danger. Suppose that on Monday through Thursday a restaurant had very little business, and waiters were idle most of the time. On Fridays and Saturdays, however, it didn't have enough wait staff, provided very slow service, and even turned significant numbers of customers away. When management compares average daily and weekly labor costs to those of other restaurants in the chain, they find that the average is not lower than that of other restaurants, and therefore conclude that there is no need to add staff. In reality, the restaurant is short of capacity on weekends and has extra on weekdays. It's like standing with one foot in a bucket of ice and one foot in a fire: On the average, your feet are comfortable.

om ADVANTAGE   Cost versus Price: Surcharges, "Taxes," and User Fees

The Internet has made it relatively easy for consumers to seek out the lowest prices available. That doesn't necessarily mean they've found the lowest cost, however. A number of different industries are countering the consumers' money-saving efforts by adding on extra charges to the products or services they offer. Hotels commonly add surcharges for utilities, which they call an "environmental" surcharge because that name gets a better reaction from customers than just calling it a price increase. Businesses commonly tack on surcharges to cover renovations and recycling fees. Most drycleaners add a 5 percent "tax." Auto dealerships add as much as $500 in charges called "documentation fees."

It has become more common for businesses to directly charge customers for costs that used to be considered just a cost of doing business. Preparation of documents to transfer auto ownership, for example, was one of the costs a dealership bore. Travel agencies now charge service fees for airline tickets. Accessing an 800 number for Internet

access used to be a $.75 local call charge in a hotel. Today, many hotels are charging for that call or selling access to a network for at least $10 per day. Some hotels add on as much as $6 per night in "resort" charges to cover the access to the pool and spa, newspapers, and housekeeping. Others add health-club fees and mandatory valet parking. Some automatically charge for a newspaper unless the customer says they don't want one. Several airlines are considering charging for that soft drink. Banks have gradually increased surcharges for ATM use to the point that it has attracted congressional attention.

Source: "The Little Extras That Count (Up)," *Wall Street Journal*, July 12, 2001, pp. B1, B4; Senate Committee on Banking, Housing and Urban Affairs, Hearing on Automated Teller Machine Fees and Surcharges, June 11, 1997, http://banking.senate.gov/97_06hrg/061197/witness/mccool.htm, accessed December 20, 2005; NYC Insider, www.theinsider.com/nyc/save/HotelSurcharges.htm, accessed December 20, 2005.

Another negative aspect of using average costs is that they can lull a business into ignoring details of a situation. A comparison of average sales price to average cost, for example, might indicate that prices are sufficiently above costs. On an individual-product basis, however, some products might be priced extremely high and others priced too low relative to their costs. Even though there is an average product or service cost, for most businesses, an average product or average service doesn't exist.

Costs and the Value Chain

One way to gain an understanding of costs is in the context of a value chain. A *value chain* is a model of an organization that links all of its processes together, from the initial task of obtaining resources to the final task of delivering a product or service to the customer. A value chain is essentially all of the parts of the supply chain that add value. The value chain approach is extremely relevant to linking costs and operations, because many of the cost-adding components of the value chain fall under the realm of operations decisions.

Exhibit 5.2 provides a generic value chain. Here each link is expected to add value to the product or service being produced. Research and development provides the knowledge behind new products and services. Design utilizes that knowledge to create new product and service designs for production. Inbound logistics provides production with the necessary material inputs to processes. Operations actually produces the products or services. Marketing educates potential customers so that they will buy the product or service. Distribution handles the outbound side—making sure products and services get to the customers who've purchased them. Customer service provides after-the-sale service to customers.

All of the value of the product or service is added in the value chain. All of the costs, however, are not necessarily incurred along the value chain. Costs are also added by administrative support services: accounting, legal services, computer services, personnel functions, and so on. The value chain is a critical concept when cost implications for operations management are examined. First, the value chain illustrates which aspects of a business add value and which do not, a critical comparison in keeping attention focused on value-adding activities and keeping costs below the customers' perception of the

Thirty-three percent of Dollar General's merchandise is priced at $1 or less.

Many steps, adding value and adding costs, occur between harvesting cotton and placing a denim shirt in a Gap shopping bag. Included in that value chain are all of the activities associated with textile and apparel manufacturing, but also included are activities that depend on the skills and abilities of store managers and store employees, all the way to the friendly "May I help you?" that greets a customer entering the store.

| Value Chain | EXHIBIT 5.2 |

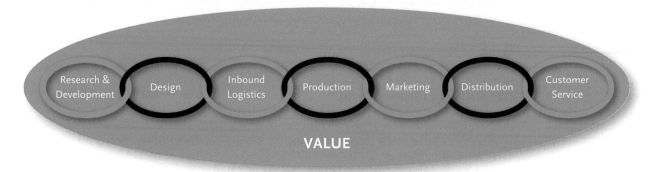

value. Second, with a thorough understanding of the value chain, the detailed analyses of processes—discussed in the previous chapter—can be conducted. Finally, the value chain concept provides a stepping-stone to the concept of an activity. An **activity** is a basic unit of work. Each component of the value chain is made up of processes, which are in turn made up of activities. Activities play a very important role in linking costs to the products and services responsible for them. As illustrated in Exhibit 5.3 the processes controlled by operations can all be broken into activities. In fact, they must be broken into activities in order to link them to product and service costs.

Recall the discussion of the supply chain in Chapter 3. The supply chain links value chains together and provides an integrative way to view how value and costs are added by the various elements of that chain. Just as value added anywhere in the chain can ultimately enhance the product or service, costs are also carried through the chain. Any focus on cost reduction must pay attention to the entire chain. Much of the motivation

activity
A basic unit of work.

↓
processes
↓
value chain

| Adding Activities in Value Creation | EXHIBIT 5.3 |

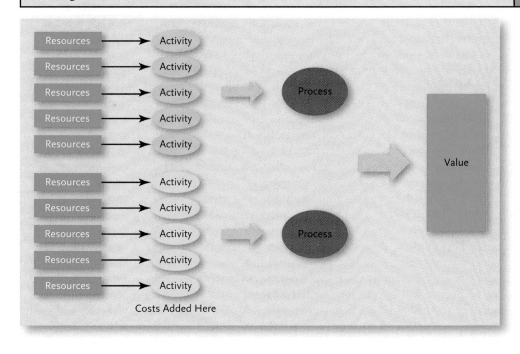

behind increased supply chain management (SCM) effort can be traced to cost reduction. The more businesses depend on suppliers for their inputs, the more they must absorb the costs of those suppliers. Increasing the coordination between customer and supplier can reduce costs dramatically. This will be discussed in detail in Chapter 9.

An Overview of Operations Cost Measurement

Assigning Operations Costs

One of the uncertainties associated with investing in operating resources is that knowing a priori what that value will be is difficult. Given the uncertainty surrounding the prediction of the value of the product or service, knowing what the cost of the product or service is and minimizing the uncertainty of the cost component are essential. Accurately assigning costs to products and services is important to potential profitability. Management accounting systems utilize cost objects as a basis for assigning costs. The costs identified by that system form the basis for many operations decisions.

cost object
An item for which costs are measured and assigned.

A **cost object** is an item for which costs are measured and assigned. A cost object can be a customer, product, service, department, or activity. Cost objects are typically those entities management would want to know the cost of. For example, if the cost of operating a branch bank in the mall were important, that facility would be the cost object. If the cost of processing loans were important, the loan-processing department would be the cost object. If the cost of maintaining ATMs were important, the ATMs would be the cost object. Labor, equipment, inventory, and other resources are common cost objects. Activities can also be important cost objects for operations because many of the costs associated with the production of goods and services are the result of process activities. For example, a manufacturer might be interested in the cost of packaging products, so packaging would be a cost object. An architecture firm might be interested in the cost of on-site consultation, so that would be a cost object.

The accurate assignment of costs to cost objects is important to good operations decision making. Without an accurate cost assessment, decisions that have financial implications can have no validity. As the saying goes, "Garbage in, garbage out." Operations decisions are often made by analyzing alternatives and selecting the one that has the highest net present value (NPV). Cost is such an integral part of NPV that if the costs associated with the alternatives are not predicted accurately, or if costs associated with existing cost objects are not assigned accurately, the expected value will be wrong, and the wrong decision could be made.

For example, the costs of a product are frequently reduced by increasing the productivity of processes. This, in fact, is a primary task of operations managers. Suppose a particular manufacturing process were used on four different products. If the estimate of the cost of that process associated with one of those products was very high, management could be motivated to reduce the cost of that particular product by improving that process. If, in reality, the costs associated with that product were small, the improvement of that process would not reduce the cost associated with the product. The result could be dollars spent on improving a process that didn't need it, which would in effect be an investment with no hope of a financial return.

Obtaining accurate costs is not just an issue of making sure the costs are accurate in terms of dollars; it is also important to assign costs to the correct cost object. Most businesses have a fairly accurate idea of what their total costs are, because they've spent the money. Their biggest difficulty comes when a business attempts to assign the costs of products or services accurately so it can obtain a reasonable idea of what a particular product or service actually costs and focus improvement efforts accordingly. The firm can never expect to know precisely, with 100 percent accuracy, what it costs to produce a product or service, however. Some costs associated with the product or service can be determined with precision, but other costs are difficult to assign accurately.

om ADVANTAGE   Online Contacts Reduce Costs

The UAL Corporation's United Airlines had a rough start using the Internet to reduce costs with a Web site that required special software to access, was difficult to read, and downplayed the UAL brand. After recognizing how important the Web site would be, however, UAL turned it into a site that is widely recognized as one of the best in the industry. A successful Web site is critical because online ticket purchases reduce the number of calls handled by employees, reducing labor costs. UAL expects that 20 percent of its revenues will be generated through its Web site by 2003.

The Internal Revenue Service provides another example of the power of a Web site to reduce costs. IRS forms are requested by the millions. Responding to mailed-in requests requires form pullers, envelope stuffers, and label addressors. Mailed-in requests cost an average of $3 each. Online forms, which utilize Adobe's Acrobat software, look as good as the mailed forms. During tax season, more than 100 million forms are downloaded at a cost of a fraction of a cent each. The need for employees to handle hard copy forms has dropped dramatically, reducing the staffing as well. In addition to cost savings from reduced mailings, the Web site also offers information and assistance, which reduces the need for IRS personnel to answer phones.

Source: "Fix It and They Will Come," *Wall Street Journal*, February 12, 2001, p. R4.

Tracing Direct Operations Costs

From accounting we know that the ease or difficulty associated with assigning costs to cost objects is known as **cost traceability.** Direct costs are relatively easy to trace, whereas indirect costs cannot be traced at all. A particular cost, however, might be a direct cost in one situation but an indirect cost in another, depending on the cost object. For example, maintenance required on a specific piece of equipment would be a direct cost when the cost object is that piece of equipment. When the cost object is one of several products produced on that piece of equipment, however, maintenance cost is an indirect cost because it cannot be traced to a particular product.

The actual assignment of costs to a cost object is accomplished by using some measure of resources consumed by that cost object. Assigning costs to cost objects can be done with direct tracing or with driver tracing. In direct tracing, the costs are physically associated with the cost object, like the maintenance costs for the machine mentioned in the example. Assigning them is simply a matter of observation. Driver tracing, on the other hand, is used when a direct observation cannot be used. A cost driver must be used to provide the link between a cost and the cost object.

Two types of drivers can be used to assign costs to cost objects. Both are important to operations. **Resource drivers** measure demands placed on resources by activities and are used to assign the costs of those resources to activities. For example, if the activity of interest was "maintaining the lawn" for a bank, resources consumed would include labor, water, fuel, equipment, and fertilizer. Some of the resources could be measured precisely. Labor and fuel, for example, would be directly measured by observation. Water, on the other hand, would be difficult to measure specifically for grounds use, because it isn't metered separately. One way to assign water costs to grounds would be to use a driver such as "labor expended watering grounds." A relationship between watering labor and water consumption could be created. It could be as simple as determining how much water flows through the sprinkler in a minute as measured by a bucket. If it was determined that it took three minutes to fill a five-gallon bucket with water, the relationship between time and cost of water could be created. Water is consumed at the rate of 100 gallons per hour. Since the groundsperson is watering the lawn, one hour of groundsperson labor on the lawn relates directly to 100 gallons of water consumed. The cost of 100 gallons of water is directly related to a labor hour. A direct relationship is created between the particular cost of interest (water) and another resource (labor) that is easy to measure.

cost traceability
The ease with which costs can be assigned to cost objects.

resource driver
A tool used to measure demands placed on resources by activities and to assign the costs of those resources to activities.

The production of any product, even one as small and inexpensive as a golf ball, creates direct material, direct labor, and overhead costs. For a high-volume, low-cost item production processes are likely to be automated, resulting in higher overhead costs when compared to labor costs. Expensive automated equipment must produce (and the businesses must sell) high volumes to spread the high overhead costs over a large number of products.

activity drivers

Used to measure the demands that cost objects place on activities and to assign the cost of associated activities to cost objects. See *cost object*.

Resource drivers are particularly useful to operations decisions because the resources are often controlled by operations.

Activity drivers measure the demands that cost objects place on activities. They are used to assign the cost of associated activities to cost objects. An activity driver might be the number of computer technician hours worked, for example. This driver could be used to assign the cost of computer programming to a cost object such as the loan-processing department. If the loan-processing department required 300 hours of computer programming that cost $28 per hour during one month, then $8,400 ($28 × 300 hours) of the total costs of computer programming would be assigned to the loan-processing department. This model for tracing costs provides the basis for activity-based costing (ABC). ABC links costs to cost objects by first assigning costs to activities and then assigning

TARGETING technology   Gaining Accuracy in Cost and Price Numbers

For consumers, for many products, price equals cost. Setting that price has always been difficult for businesses. One challenge has been to actually know what the cost of the product was so that a price could be set to provide a desired level of profit. The other challenge has been difficulty in predicting how customers will respond to a particular price. If it is increased, will demand disappear?

One company that has been developing technologies to address both of these issues is Acorn Systems. Acorn produces a variety of technology solutions to improve business decision making, but two particularly popular solutions are their Activity Based Costing software and their Profit Analytics software.

The Activity Based Costing software can assign costs to any cost object to provide a more accurate view of costs and profitability for individual products. This enables companies to negotiate better, to focus better on productivity improvement, and to improve the design of compensation systems.

The Profit Analytics solution helps companies identify which products are profitable and which aren't. It also provides guidance for setting prices to maximize profits using logic similar to that used by airlines to set variable ticket pricing.

Source: N. Heintz, "The Price Is Right," *Inc.com*, July 2003; S. Schulist, "Using ABC to Manage and Improve at CONCO Foods," *Journal of Corporate Accounting & Finance*, Vol. 15, Issue 3, March/April 2004, pp. 29–35; www.acornsys.com/solutions/solutionlines/activitybasedcosting.html, July 1, 2004; www.acornsys.com/solutions/solutionlines/profitananalytics.html, July 1, 2004.

Cost Assignment Alternatives
EXHIBIT 5.4

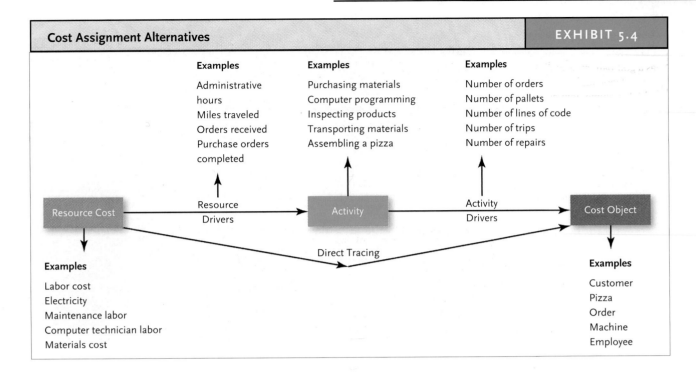

them to cost objects. Linking activities and costs can result in cost reductions because costs can be better controlled. Activity drivers are critical to operations because they are often part of processes used to create products and services.

Exhibit 5.4 provides a conceptual view of three alternatives to linking costs of resources to cost objects. Costs can be assigned directly through direct tracing, through resource drivers, and through activity drivers.

Allocating Indirect Operations Costs

Indirect costs cannot be traced precisely to cost objects, because no direct relationship exists; thus they must be *allocated* to cost objects. An example of a cost that must be allocated is the cost of electricity for a large computer system firm. Certainly each system design project would consume its share of the total amount of electricity used in a month, but if a particular project is the cost object, there would be no way to directly link electricity consumption to that project. Without that link, there'd be no way to determine what the total cost of that project was. It must be allocated in some way. One way might be to allocate electricity to projects proportionate to the number of days of project duration. Allocation of costs to cost objects, such as projects, products, or customers, is not accurate and is subject to substantial bias inherent in the assumptions used. Links between indirect costs and various cost objects may be required for external reporting, but they contribute very little to the precise needs of decision making.

Components of Product Cost

Cost management systems identify product costs for external financial reporting. Product costs are divided into two categories: production costs and nonproduction costs. **Production costs** are those costs associated with the actual production of goods or services. They are often the focus of operations-driven productivity improvement efforts. **Nonproduction costs** are the costs associated with selling and administration.

Production costs, in turn, are broken down into direct materials, direct labor, and overhead. **Direct materials** are materials that can be traced directly to the good or

Dollar General stores average only 6,800 square feet, making shopping simple and hassle free. Wal-Mart super stores are often more than 200,000 square feet.

production costs
Costs associated with the actual production of goods or services.

nonproduction costs
The costs of selling and administration.

direct materials
Materials that can be traced directly to the good or service being produced.

The assignment of costs to cost objects is not just a challenge for manufacturers. Services also need to understand the implications costs have for decisions. In a shopping mall, for example, individual shops must grasp the relationships between their facility, their staff, sales, and costs. The mall management must also be able to determine costs associated with maintenance, traffic, food courts, etc., and appropriately pass those costs on to lessees.

direct labor
Labor that can be traced directly to the good or service being produced.

overhead
All nondirect costs that exist after direct labor and direct materials have been identified.

In 2006 Dollar General plans to open at least 800 more stores, focusing on site selection and reducing rent as a percentage of sales.

service being produced. The component parts of a product, for example, are direct materials. Buns at your favorite fast-food restaurant are direct materials. Those little bottles of shampoo and conditioner, bars of soap, and toilet paper are direct materials for a hotel. Peanuts provided on an airline and those little envelopes banks use to put currency in when you cash a check are other examples of direct materials in services. Materials that actually become a part of the product or are consumed during the service are considered direct materials. **Direct labor** can also be traced directly to the products or services being produced. The amount used can easily be calculated by observing the production processes. All other nondirect costs are thrown into the category of **overhead.** Examples of overhead are the costs of employing maintenance workers, supervisors, and security staff. Some supplies consumed during production of a good or service can be included in overhead. Cleaning chemicals, for example, are overhead for a hotel. Machine lubricants are an example of overhead for a manufacturer.

The operations decisions categories of inventory, capacity, facilities, and workforce are clearly significant when viewed from a product cost perspective. Direct materials, for example, are the costs of purchasing inventory. Direct labor is the cost of paying the workforce that works on the product or service. Overhead consists of the costs associated with the facility, equipment, and workforce that are not directly involved in production. Operations controls most of the costs of the product or service.

Productivity Improvement and Cost Reduction

Measuring and managing costs, as they relate to operations resources, is an important component of decision making. As resource management is examined in detail in subsequent chapters, it will become apparent that the purpose of many of the decision models is to minimize costs. As discussed in the previous chapter, such process improvement approaches as lean systems, reengineering, and value stream mapping have a primary objective of reducing costs through eliminating non-value-adding activities.

For the operations resource categories of inventory, capacity, facilities, and workforce, managing costs is often synonymous with managing productivity. As has been mentioned previously, productivity measures are generally some measure of output divided by some measure of input, and the key input is cost. For employees, productivity can be expressed as a measure of work accomplished per labor hour. For inventory, it is expressed as a measure of sales per dollar of inventory value. For equipment, it is some measure of equipment output divided by machine time. For the facility, it is a measure of facility output (sales, customers served, and so on) divided by a measure of facility investment, such as square feet. In many of these cases the denominators will look very similar to the cost objects discussed earlier in this chapter, because they are resources management is interested in.

Reduction of inputs can take the form of eliminating waste, eliminating steps that don't add value, eliminating workers, and a host of other simplification and time-saving improvements.

Effort to improve any aspect of business processes invariably results in cost reduction. For many of these efforts, action is initiated by a desire to reduce the difference between the desired and actual cost or consumption rate (a standard). This difference is known as **variance.** Operations decisions are frequently motivated by the desire to decrease a variance. The following discussion introduces the use of variances to guide cost management efforts.

variance
The difference between desired cost or consumption rate and the actual cost or consumption rate.

Putting Cost Information to Work for Operations: Standards and Variances

A **standard** is a measure that should be achieved. It provides a goal and gives operations consistency in processes, costs, and output levels. It is simply a desired measure that provides managers with a basis for comparison to determine if performance is what it should be. In Chapter 2, efficiency was defined as being the actual output divided by the standard output. Calculating efficiency is a popular use for standards. Standards that are commonly used in operations include quantity usage standards (output or usage per unit of time) and price standards (price per unit). Not surprisingly, just as output rates do not always meet quantity standards, resulting in less than 100 percent efficiency, actual prices do not always meet price standards.

standard
A measure that should be achieved.

Variance Analysis

Cost systems aid operations decision making. They are used to develop standard product and service costs to aid in operations planning and control functions and also help in determining product and service costs. To assist in the planning and control of operations resource usage, a process known as **variance analysis** is used to compare what should happen to what actually is happening regarding inventory and capacity consumption. The resulting information provides a valuable input to operations so that costs are maintained and the appropriate levels of inventory and capacity can be planned for.

variance analysis
A process used to compare actual consumption of inventory and capacity to ideal consumption levels.

Variance analysis drives many operations actions because it facilitates the control of various contributors to cost. Exhibit 5.5 illustrates how the difference between the actual quantity at the actual price minus the actual quantity at the standard price provides the price variance. Similarly, the actual quantity at the standard price minus the standard quantity at the standard price yields the usage variance. The actual quantity at the actual price minus the standard quantity at the standard price provides the total variance. Direct materials costs can be monitored and controlled from two perspectives: the quantity consumed and the price of each item. If the quantity consumed or the price strays from the standard, the costs go up or down. An unfavorable price variance occurs when box 1 minus box 2 is greater than 0: The price is greater than it should be. An unfavorable usage variance occurs when box 2 minus box 3 is greater

| EXHIBIT 5.5 | Variance Analysis |

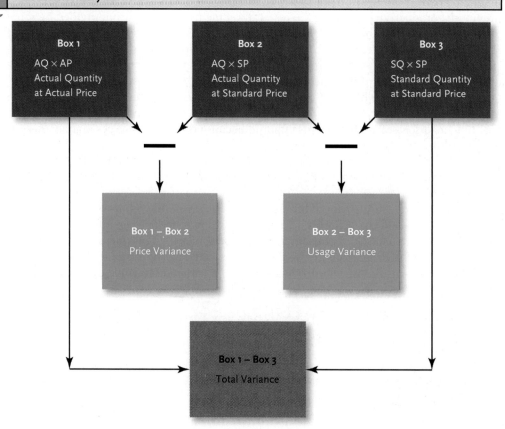

than 0: Too much material is being consumed. Variance analysis is used to help isolate costs that are not what they should be. Many operations control functions are guided by variance analysis.

Step-by-Step: The Variance Analysis Process

1. The actual quantity at the actual price minus actual quantity at the standard price is the price variance.

2. The actual quantity at the standard price minus the standard quantity at the standard price is the usage variance.

3. The actual quantity at the actual price minus the standard quantity at the standard price is the total variance.

Variance analysis can be used with a variety of resources. Almost any type of resource, including inventory, equipment capacity, facilities, and labor, can be analyzed using variance analysis. For example, labor variances are used to monitor the number of hours required (usage) and the hourly pay rate. Efficiency variances can be used to compare hours actually used and those that should have been used. Using variance analysis, specific variances can be isolated, giving management the ability to monitor resource usage and costs—critical tasks for effectively managing operations. Unfavorable variances often provide the catalyst for productivity improvement efforts.

Example 5.1

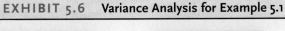

Variance Analysis

A small manufacturer of organic snack foods monitors all components that go into its products. One product in particular, a very popular salsa, utilizes a number of ingredients, but two of primary importance—pepper sauce and a very high grade of fresh cilantro—are tightly controlled for both taste and cost purposes. Usage variance can result in inconsistency in taste from batch to batch. Price variance results in cost variances that can eat up the profit margins available on the product. The standard usage rate for cilantro is 15 ounces per 50-gallon batch. The standard price is $1.20 per ounce.

Current usage rates, determined by monitoring the amount of cilantro in the bin and the number of 50-gallon batches produced, average 16.3 ounces per 50-gallon batch. Cilantro prices have risen for the supplier and are now at $1.42 per ounce. Compute the usage variance, price variance, and total variance.

Solution

Exhibit 5.6 provides a framework for the solution to this problem.

EXHIBIT 5.6   Variance Analysis for Example 5.1

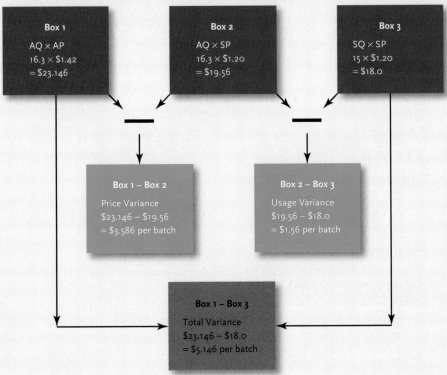

The price variance is $3.586 per batch, given the $0.22 per ounce price variance over standard. The usage variance is $1.56 per batch. Total variance is $5.146 per batch produced. Excel Tutor 5.1 demonstrates how variance analysis can be done in a spreadsheet environment.

Many businesses find that some very profitable offerings subsidize others, but the nonprofitable aspects of the business can't be discarded because of customer expectations. Hotels have long had this problem with the minibars in rooms. Minibars have a history of not being profitable, and being quite costly in terms of the initial investment and the labor required to keep them stocked.

Quite often products taken from the minibar were not billed to the room, or products taken from the minibar were replaced by similar products purchased cheaply elsewhere. Several hotels, including Hyatt and Marriott, are replacing old technology minibars with new "smart" equipment that has sensors. The sensors can tell if an item has been removed for more than 30 seconds, and if it has, it is automatically billed to the room. Surveys completed on smart minibars have shown that the profits generated by their products ranged from $1.45 to $5.78 per day.

Bartech Solutions, producer of the e-fridge, installed the world's first wireless minibar network at the Willard InterContinental Hotel in Washington, D.C. Their other products are designed to reduce labor and resource consumption. Other "smart" features being developed by Bartech include smart lighting. When the guest checks in, a microprocessor at the top of the e-fridge switches on a welcome light the moment it is notified by the hotel's property management system. If in-room lights are controlled by a relay, the Bartech e-fridge can monitor it, switch some lamps on at check-in, and switch them off at checkout. The e-fridge also can control the hotel thermostat at check-in and checkout. A stand-alone in-room safe can also be online via a connection to the Bartech e-fridge. At checkout time, the desk clerk can check the status of the safe and notify the guest if it is still locked.

Source: "Checking Out Your Hotel Minibar? If It's an E-Fridge, Select Quickly," *Wall Street Journal*, September 11, 2002; www.my-bartech.com/english/index1.htm, July 1, 2004.

Cost Implications for Operations Decisions

Total Cost versus Cost Per Unit

cost per unit
Total cost for producing the units of interest divided by the number of units produced.

Total costs were defined earlier in this chapter as the costs of all resources obtained in a particular period. Total costs are critical and have a direct impact on profitability via net income. A generic and frequently used measure of the productivity of resources is known as **cost per unit.** To determine cost per unit, a particular product or service becomes the cost object. Cost per unit is determined by dividing the total cost for producing the units of interest by the number of units produced.

Cost per unit is at the root of many productivity measures, including equipment utilization. It is really the "average" cost per unit. Like many uses of average costs, cost per unit can be misleading. Any average can be reduced by increasing the number of units (the denominator). Here, it is done by increasing the number of units produced.

The misuse of the cost per unit measure often results from an inherent assumption that reducing cost per unit is the same as reducing the cost of goods sold, and it will automatically increase profitability. It isn't and it won't. There is no reason to expect that total costs will be reduced simply because cost per unit for a particular product is lower.

If total costs are reduced, a reduction in cost per unit will follow if the number of units produced remains the same. If demand increases and an increase in units produced increases the denominator, the cost per unit may decrease. Managers can play deceitful games with cost per unit. It isn't that managers are dishonest or criminal in nature, it's just that they wish to maximize the performance measures that form the basis for their evaluation. These games not only are misleading about improvements to costs, but can lead to decisions that actually increase total costs while decreasing cost per unit.

Cost Trade-offs

Many business decisions require a trade-off of one cost for another. Quite often, the trade-off amounts to short-term costs being traded for long-term costs. This is not necessarily bad, but it frequently happens because the long-term costs aren't recognized or are given low priority. The long-term costs appear to be lower than they really are. The decision to place short-term costs above long-term costs may actually be consciously made. These decisions sometimes result from the short tenure of managers. A fast-track manager will be evaluated on this year's performance, not the financial performance five years down the road. They can also be motivated by the short-term perspective of investors. Many cost trade-offs also trade nonfinancial costs for financial ones.

Fixed and Variable Costs ———————————

Breakeven Analysis

Because of the nature of operations, managers are bombarded with questions that start with the two words "Should we?" Should we bring that new service online? Should we bring that new product into production? Should we expand? Should we upgrade our information system? Should we purchase that new piece of equipment? Should we build a new facility in another city? Often implicit in the question "Should we?" is a more detailed question: "Of these alternatives, which is the best investment?" Which is the best new product to produce? Which expansion design is the best? Which piece of equipment is the most desirable? Alternatives are often examined from a perspective of different costs associated with different alternatives. These questions are asked when managers consider the purchase of a variety of resources. Resources aren't free, after all, and there are always choices. Two types of cost are usually involved. **Fixed costs** are unrelated to the volume of output and include such costs as facility construction or other start-up costs. **Variable costs** are directly related to volume of output and include such costs as material costs and transportation costs. Labor costs are often considered to be variable costs, but in reality they usually aren't. Direct labor is generally paid by the week or month, no matter what the employee output, even though salaries are described as "hourly." In some cases, expected revenues are also different for the different alternatives. The analysis of decision alternatives in such situations is known as **breakeven analysis.** When fixed costs are high relative to variable costs, large volumes are needed to spread out that large fixed cost over a large number of units. However, when variable costs are high relative to the fixed costs, the alternative is more advantageous for small volumes. Conceptually, breakeven analysis seeks to identify the volumes that support different combinations of fixed versus variable costs.

Breakeven analysis is a relatively straightforward approach to comparing the total cost curves for each alternative. The total cost curves are assumed to be linear and can be created by using the basic formula for a line:

(5.5)
$$y = a + bn$$

where y is the total cost for producing n units or serving n customers, a is the Y intercept (and equals the fixed cost), and b is the slope of the line forming the total cost curve (and equals the variable cost per unit). The problem can be solved graphically by identifying the intersections of the cost curves and interpreting their meaning, or by identifying the intersections algebraically by setting the equations for the cost curves equal to each other and solving for n.

fixed costs
Costs that are not affected by volume.

variable costs
Costs that increase or decrease as units produced increase or decrease.

breakeven analysis
An analytical process that compares the fixed and variable costs of alternatives in order to identify the best alternative for a given volume of output.

Step-by-Step: The Breakeven Analysis Process

1. Graph the total cost curves for each alternative, using the fixed cost as the Y intercept and the variable cost per unit as the slope and coefficient of n.
2. From the graph, identify the line segments that define the low-cost alternatives.

3. Determine the intersections of the relevant cost curves by setting the appropriate pairs equal to each other and algebraically solving for *n*. Those values for *n* are used to define the ranges of *n* where each alternative is the low-cost alternative.

An example of breakeven analysis used in a software selection scenario is described in Example 5.2.

Example 5.2

Breakeven Analysis

EXCEL TUTOR

The ability to identify, understand, analyze, and track customer wants and needs has become extremely important to businesses. This has extended to the ability to access this information immediately as a customer calls to place an order. It is actually possible, for example, to know what a customer is likely to want prior to his asking for it. Technological advancements in data analysis and data mining techniques have made this possible, and customer relationship management (CRM) software combined with call-center technologies has made this practice commonplace for large mail-order retailers.

Like many software-related markets, a large share of the market for such technology is held by a very small set of companies, but there are also some "small players" with good products. There are also companies willing to collect and analyze the data on a contract basis, creating the potential to outsource this function entirely. It should not be a surprise that performing this function in-house using the largest and best-known software, as compared to outsourcing, is a trade-off. Management must weigh a large fixed cost with small variable costs against a small fixed cost but significant costs per unit down the road.

The management of a mail-order retailer has identified three alternatives for CRM software purchase. The market leader is Market Probe. It is very expensive, but well known and popular. WEEZL is a small upstart in the business. Prophecy is a subcontractor and a well-known provider of these types of services. Exhibit 5.7 compares the cost information of these alternatives.

EXHIBIT 5.7   CRM Software Choice Alternatives

Company	Description	Total Installation Costs ($)	Variable Costs ($ per customer)
Market Probe	Market upstart	360,000	0.38
Prophecy	Market leader	480,000	0.07
WEEZL	Contractor of services	224,000	0.97

Installation costs include software licensing, server and other hardware upgrades, and initial staffing expense associated with the CRM software installation (consultant fees included). Variable costs per customer include such costs as ongoing staffing time for data entry, data maintenance, and analysis, as well as the per-customer fees assessed by the subcontractor. Complete a breakeven analysis for the CRM software alternatives.

Solution

Exhibit 5.8 graphically analyzes the total costs given different numbers of customers and shows that at lower numbers of customers (below roughly 225,000 customers) WEEZL is the low-cost alternative. At very high numbers of customers (above about 380,000),

(Continues)

Example 5.2

(Continued)

Prophecy is the low-cost alternative. Between 220,000 and 375,000, Market Probe is the low-cost alternative.

EXHIBIT 5.8   Call Management Software Cost Comparison

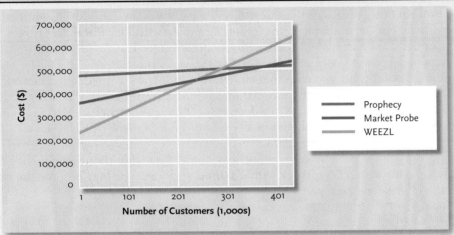

A more precise result can be obtained by identifying the intersections of the three lines as follows:

$$360,000 + 0.38n = 224,000 + 0.97n$$
$$136,000 + 0.38n = 0.97n$$
$$136,000 = 0.59n$$
$$230,508 = n$$

$$480,000 + 0.07n = 360,000 + .38n$$
$$120,000 + 0.07n = 0.38n$$
$$120,000 = 0.31n$$
$$387,097 = n$$

For a company with fewer than 230,508 customers, WEEZL is the low-cost alternative. For more than 387,097 customers, Prophecy is the low-cost alternative. For a company that falls in the middle, Market Probe is the low-cost alternative. The intersection of WEEZL and Prophecy is not needed because it does not form an endpoint of a line segment that is part of the solution.

An example of how breakeven analysis can be accomplished in a spreadsheet can be found at Excel Tutor 5.2.

At the functional level, for almost any department in a business, these types of decision are commonplace. Keep in mind, however, that the decisions are still dependent on uncertain data. In Example 5.2, for instance, we are not certain of the number of eventual customers, so we must make an educated estimate. Like any financial manager, the decision maker must consider not only the size and timing of cash to be received from an investment in an operating resource, but also the likelihood of receiving it. Uncertainty is a constant.

Nonfinancial Costs

As mentioned early in this chapter, not all costs are monetary and many involve resources that are difficult to measure quantitatively. The fact that businesses invest in hopes of obtaining these resources, however, means that they must be considered costs when given up. Unfortunately, since the resources are difficult to quantify, the costs are open to interpretation, and they are not required in external financial reports, they often receive little priority in trade-offs. Many nonfinancial costs will be familiar to you and correspond to value attributes or competitive priorities such as quality, flexibility, or response time. In other situations they are the very capabilities the company depends on to compete. Someone unfamiliar with the importance of a particular capability may be willing to sacrifice it for an apparent decrease in monetary costs. Lack of an enterprise view strikes again.

Time and flexibility are two costs that often lose to monetary cost reduction in a trade-off because placing a value on them is extremely difficult. They are of incredible strategic importance, however. Decisions to reduce costs often result in an increase in response time or a decrease in flexibility. Let's briefly examine an example for each case.

Outsourcing has become a popular way to reduce costs. However, outsourcing can increase transportation time to get components, thereby slowing the response time for customers. As a result, a competitor with a shorter response time may become the new supplier of choice for a customer with quick response time needs.

Reducing costs by eliminating excess capacity is also a quick way to improve the appearance of periodic performance numbers. Eliminating labor through layoffs, or even by eliminating equipment, reduces total costs and costs per unit but can have devastating effects on a firm's ability to quickly react to the unique need of a customer. Protective capacity provides flexibility, and a customer who can't get the response needed is motivated to try out the competition.

Quality is also frequently sacrificed in trade-off decisions. Pressures to improve end-of-period performance figures motivate managers to ship goods known to be defective. Substitution of cheaper and lower-quality raw materials and components for products and services is a way to reduce direct material costs. We've all experienced poor-quality service that results from too few staff at peak demand times. Often, managers attempt to quantify nonfinancial costs by estimating their impact.

Virtually any value attribute can be at risk during a cost-reduction push. Value attributes are important to customers because they cost the customer money. They're targets for cost cutting for the same reason. Activities that add the most value are often the most expensive. Businesses have begun to recognize that many nonmonetary costs are actually closely linked to future performance, although the impact on quantitative measures is merely delayed. An approach to ensure that performance measures are not improved at the expense of others, known as the balanced scorecard (BSC), was introduced in Chapter 2.

The BSC translates a business's vision and strategy into a set of performance measures distributed among perspectives beyond the purely financial. It links objectives, initiatives, *and* performance measures to the firm's strategy by integrating financial measures with nonfinancial performance indicators. Clearly, when looking at a firm's strategy, there are objectives that aren't stated in financial terms. BSC translates these objectives into a framework that provides an enterprise view of an organization's overall performance. In addition to a financial perspective, other key performance indicators relate directly to a customer perspective, internal business processes, and organizational growth, learning, and innovation. Balanced scorecards have become an increasingly popular way to ensure that a balance exists among performance indicators.

Exhibit 5.9 summarizes 10 benefits of the balanced scorecard approach.

Dollar General estimated losses from hurricane Katrina to be approximately $23 million from damaged inventory, fixtures, leasehold improvements, and business interruption.

| Balanced Scorecard Benefits | EXHIBIT 5.9 |

1. For government agencies, the BSC fulfills a legal requirement. The Government Performance and Results Act of 1993 requires a strategic plan and a method of measuring the performance of strategic initiatives for government agencies.

2. The BSC allows an organization to align strategic activities to the strategic plan. It supports deployment and implementation of the strategy on a continuous basis by providing feedback needed to guide efforts.

3. Visibility provided by a measurement system supports better and faster financial decisions and control of processes.

4. That visibility also provides accountability and incentives based on real data.

5. Measurements of process efficiency provide an objective, rational basis for selecting areas to improve first.

6. It allows managers to identify best practices and standardize their use elsewhere.

7. The measurements used make it possible to benchmark process performance against outside organizations.

8. The process cost data collected for past projects helps managers learn how to estimate costs more accurately for future projects.

9. It improves profitability by reducing process costs and improving productivity while at the same time improving mission effectiveness.

10. It raises the quality score of the organization as measured for the Malcolm Baldrige National Quality Award, increasing the probability of long-term success.

Source: Adapted from *The Balanced Scorecard Institute*, "Top Ten Reasons for a Performance Measurement System," www.balancedscorecard.org/, April 27, 2000.

CHAPTER SUMMARY

This chapter presented the concept of cost as the first component of value. Cost, although often thought of as the domain of accountants, drives so many critical decisions that all managers must understand its impact on the business, particularly the operational aspects of the business. Understanding costs and using cost data in decision making is critical to making decisions that are financially sound *and* serve the best interests of the business owners.

This chapter examined the types of cost that are relevant to operations, including a very widely used cost: average cost. Cost data, particularly average cost data, can be misused and can be misleading. The role costs play in the value chain was also examined in this chapter.

Cost measurement is critical to operations because the results drive many decisions. Cost objects form an important basis for assigning costs to resources and activities, both important to operations managers. Tracing direct costs and allocating indirect costs are cost measurement tasks that affect many operations decisions. Productivity measures often include a cost as the denominator, motivating most productivity improvement efforts to focus on cost reduction. For productivity improvement and cost reduction efforts, variance analysis is often used to help isolate the causes of costs being higher than they should be.

When using cost measures for making decisions, caution should always be exercised. Average costs, particularly average cost per unit, can be misleading and result in behaviors not beneficial to the company. Likewise, an enterprise view should be fostered by using performance measures beyond those that have a purely financial perspective. A popular nonfinancial performance measurement tool is the balanced scorecard.

The next chapter examines one of those perspectives that must also play a role in decision making because it is such a critical component of value—quality.

KEY TERMS

activity, 165
activity drivers, 168
actual costs, 162
breakeven analysis, 175
cost object, 166
cost per unit, 174
cost traceability, 167
direct labor, 170
direct materials, 169
expected costs, 162
fixed costs, 175
nonproduction costs, 169

out-of-pocket costs, 162
overhead, 170
period costs, 163
product costs, 162
production costs, 169
resource driver, 167
standard, 171
total costs, 163
variable costs, 175
variance, 171
variance analysis, 171

KEY FORMULAE

(5.1) $\text{Profit Margin} = \text{Net Income}/\text{Sales}$

(5.2) $\text{Return on Assets} = \text{Net Income}/\text{Total Assets}$

(5.3) $\text{Return on Equity} = \text{Net Income}/\text{Total Equity}$

(5.4) $\text{Net Income} = \text{Net Sales} - \text{Cost of Goods Sold}$
$- \text{Selling and Administrative Costs} - \text{Depreciation}$
$- \text{Interest Paid} - \text{Taxes}$

(5.5) Total Cost Curve for Breakeven Analysis, $y = a + bn$

SOLVED PROBLEMS

Variance Analysis

Mane Mills is a producer of animal feed blends. It blends various components to arrive at horse feed that contains the desired amount of protein, starch, fiber, and so on. Accuracy is important because high levels of protein cause some horses to be hard to handle. The desired proportions of nutrients are obtained by blending such things as alfalfa, barley, corn, molasses, and beat pulp. Depending on the season and other market factors, costs of some components change. Mane Mills pays particular attention to grains, because of their high cost. In one particular feed blend, pelleted alfalfa is used as one ingredient. Two hundred pounds of high quality alfalfa pellets are used for each one-ton batch of feed. The pellets cost $7.50 per 50-lb bag. This year, due to a shortage of alfalfa, Mane Mills has had to switch to a lower grade of alfalfa pellet. It costs $7.00 per 50-lb bag, but each ton of feed requires 270 pounds of the pellets. Compute the price, usage, and total variances.

Solution

Step	Objective	Explanation
1.	Identify the actual quantity, actual price, standard quantity, and standard price.	Actual quantity = 270 pounds Actual price = $ .14 per pound Standard quantity = 200 pounds Standard price = $.15 per pound
2.	Compute price variance.	$(AQ \times AP) - (AQ \times SP) =$ $37.80 - 40.5 = -2.70$
3	Compute usage variance.	$(AQ \times SP) - (SQ \times SP) = 40.5 - 30 = 10.5$
4.	Compute total variance.	$(AQ \times AP) - (SQ \times SP) = 37.80 - 30 = 7.80$
5.	Explanation.	With the new pellets, each ton of feed is costing an additional $7.80.

Breakeven Analysis

Maggie Floyd has been charged with evaluating three possible alternatives for new tanning beds for her boss's tanning salon. The beds vary substantially in purchase price, but also vary in the projected cost per customer because of different life expectancy for the lights and different labor requirements for cleaning. The fixed and variable costs for the three alternatives are:

Alternative	Purchase Price	Cost per user
1	$11,000	$.14 per user
2	$9,200	$.88 per user
3	$7,800	$1.68 per user

Solution

Step	Objective	Explanation
1.	Graph the three alternatives.	The graph, shown below, shows that the intersections of Alternative 2 and Alternative 3 are at the lowest volume and the intersection of Alternative 1 and Alternative 2 are at a higher volume. The intersection of Alternative 1 and Alternative 3 is not of concern.
2.	Determine the intersection points.	Alternative 2 intersection with Alternative 3: $9,200 + .88x = 7,800 + 1.68x$ $1,400 + .88x = 1.68x$ $1,400 = .8x$ $x = 1,750$ Alternative 1 intersection with Alternative 2: $11,000 + .14x = 9,200 + .88x$ $1,800 + .14x = .88x$ $1,800 = .74x$ $x = 2,432.4$
3.	Determine volume ranges for each alternative.	For volumes at or below 1,750, Alternative 3 is the lowest cost. For volumes between 1,750 and 2,432, Alternative 2 is the lowest cost. For volumes greater than 2,432, Alternative 1 is the lowest cost.

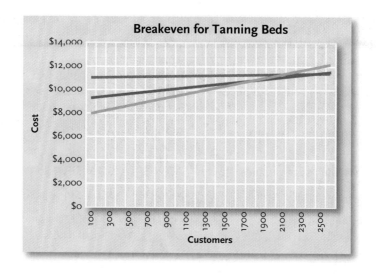

1. Define "cost."
2. Describe the difference between price and cost.
3. Why is price often considered to be the sole component of cost?
4. What role does cost play in profitability?
5. Describe two ways that increasing costs can reduce profitability.
6. Describe the following costs:
   a. Expected costs
   b. Actual costs
   c. Out-of-pocket costs
   d. Period costs
   e. Product costs
   f. Total costs
7. Why can the use of average costs be dangerous?
8. What is a cost object?
9. What does cost traceability mean? How does it relate to direct and indirect costs?
10. What is driver tracing?
11. What are resource drivers and activity drivers?
12. Describe the process of allocating indirect costs.
13. What are the components of production costs?
14. What is variance analysis? How can it be used to help manage the costs of resources?
15. Why is cost per unit sometimes misleading?
16. What are some common nonfinancial costs that should be considered when business decisions are made?

DISCUSSION AND EXPLORATION

1. What are the total costs of ownership for an automobile? Are those costs the same for students and nonstudents? How do those costs differ from one automobile to another? How important are those costs when considering an automobile purchase? Should parking costs be included as part of the costs of ownership?

2. Identify the major categories of cost for a university. Create alternative plans for calculating the cost per student. How does the plan change if the cost object becomes a "student graduated"? If the cost object is a "chemistry major graduated," would the cost per unit be different from that of a business student graduated? Why? If the costs per student are different, should tuition be different?

3. Labor costs are often a concern for services and manufacturers. Employee salaries are the most frequently discussed labor costs, but there are others. Quite often, salaries are not increased, because of the impact increases would have on labor costs. Some might argue that higher salaries would reduce total labor costs in the long term. How could this be true? Be sure to consider nonfinancial costs.

4. Much of the effort to improve cost measurement, including activity-based costing, focuses on providing more accurate ways to allocate costs to individual products. Why is it important to be able to know what a specific product costs? Which types of cost will be the most difficult to deal with?

5. Nonfinancial costs are often the most difficult to include in decision-making processes. What nonfinancial costs are most often part of financial decisions you must make? In jobs you have had, have you observed decisions made that ignored nonfinancial costs? Describe them.

PROBLEMS HM

Solutions to odd-numbered problems are located on the text's Online Center (http://mhhe.com/opsnow3e).

1. Mayflower Department Store offers a gift-wrapping service for its customers. Ribbon is the most expensive component of gift wrapping and must be controlled for both the cost of the service and the amount used. The current cost for ribbon is $0.48 per inch. The current usage of ribbon is 10 inches per package. The standard usage is 11 inches per package, with a standard price of $0.55. What are the price, usage, and total variances for the ribbon?

2. Dee's Cookies sells chocolate chip cookies on campus. Of course, chocolate chips are the most important ingredient for taste and cost. The standard usage of chips is 11 chips per cookie. The standard price for a bag of chocolate chips is $2.05. Dee has found that students like more than the standard amount of chocolate chips in the cookies. She therefore started to make her cookies with 15 chips. The store she buys the chocolate chips from has a sale on the chips, selling them for $1.89 per bag. There are 400 chips in a bag. Calculate the price variance, usage variance, and total variance.

3. Bill Howe is a project supervisor for Regal Homes, a builder of new houses. As the project supervisor, Bill must keep a careful eye on the number of worker-hours put into the construction of a new house. The standard number of worker-hours to complete a house is 1,075 and the standard hourly wage is $20.00. The current house has taken only 1,010 worker-hours and the workers are under contract for $20.00 per hour. What are the price, usage, and total variances for this house?

4. Stan operates a copy shop. The copy machines cost $0.05 per copy to operate, excluding the paper. Stan normally pays $2.90 per 500-sheet ream of paper, although he currently is buying paper from a wholesaler for only $2.50 per ream. When his

copiers are running well, paper jams are infrequent, resulting in an average usage of 1.07 sheets of paper to make one copy. The weather has been quite humid lately, causing his copiers to jam more frequently. It currently takes 1.27 sheets of paper to make one copy. Calculate the current price variance, usage variance, and total variance. What would the variance be if Stan began to use a more expensive brand of paper, costing $3.20 per ream, which eliminated paper jams?

5. Jordan's Machine Shop is examining four alternatives for the location of a new small factory. Each alternative has a standing building that can be purchased. Ralph Jordan, the business owner, has calculated the variable costs per unit based on the differences in prevailing wages and utility costs among the alternatives. The fixed and variable costs are shown below:

Site	Fixed Cost	Variable Cost per Unit
A	$345,000	$10.15
B	$323,000	$12.50
C	$310,000	$17.70
D	$395,000	$15.40

Identify the precise ranges of volumes for each site that could be the low-cost alternative.

6. PreCast manufactures various concrete products, including end stops for parking spaces, feed bunkers for cattle, and guard rails for highway construction. Because of the transportation costs associated with heavy concrete products, expanding the market means adding another facility. PreCast management has identified four possible sites for an additional facility in a new geographic region. Given the projected costs shown below, graph the total cost curves and identify the ranges of volumes for the sites with the lowest total costs.

Site	Fixed Cost	Variable Cost per Unit
A	$222,000	$8.60
B	$246,000	$10.00
C	$230,000	$7.26
D	$255,000	$5.02

7. Stevens Fabrication, a small manufacturing firm, has just won a long-term contract for the manufacture of motor mounting plates for refrigerators. The contract is with a high-volume appliance manufacturer. For its test run of parts, Stevens produced the parts with a process that was predominantly manual, using existing equipment. An automated stamping press would significantly lower the cost per unit by eliminating most of the labor, but such a press is expensive. After a cost analysis of the current process and an investigation of the purchase and setup of a new press, Stevens projects the following fixed and variable costs:

Alternative	Fixed Cost ($)	Variable Cost per Unit ($)
Automated	27,000	0.16
Manual	2,000	1.85

How much production volume is necessary to make the automated stamping press economically attractive?

8. A&F Tax service wishes to store data electronically, rather than in hard copy format. The owner has collected cost information on three different approaches to scanning and storing documents. All involve leased equipment with all hardware and software maintenance provided. Annual cost information for the alternatives is presented below:

Alternative	Fixed Cost ($)	Variable Cost ($)
1	1,000	0.02
2	800	0.08
3	500	0.25

Identify the breakeven points for the three alternatives. If A&F expects to scan 1,500 documents in the upcoming year, which alternative should be selected?

9. Junktractorparts.com provides a clearinghouse for antique tractor collectors to locate parts for their tractors. The site offers information on tractor restoration, links to new-part suppliers, and discussion groups. Its owner wishes to begin collecting statistics on Web site traffic. Several online services exist with essentially the same services. They track hits per page, unique visitors, new visitors, return visitors, referring search engines, duration of visit, path taken, entry page, domain, and other useful information. As would be expected, the services offer different cost structures. Three alternatives that are in the ballpark of the Junktractorparts.com budget are presented below:

Alternative	Monthly Fee up to 10,000 Hits ($)	Cost per Hit for Those above 10,000 ($)
HitCount.com	35	0.001
QuickStat	25	0.0035
TrafficCounter	50	unlimited hits

With a prediction of 20,000 hits for the next month, which service will be the low-cost provider? The owner has tracked the growth of Internet traffic and expects it to increase at a rate of an additional 1,000 hits per month. Each of the providers offers a $10 discount on the installation fee to customers signing a one-year contract. With next month's forecasted traffic at 20,000 hits, should a contract be signed? Explain your answer.

10. Elizabeth Wise is a very talented but unknown author. For years she has tried to get a book published, but no major publishing house has been willing to publish her product. She took advantage of Amazon.com's willingness to stock and sell any book and has begun to sell her books without the aid of a publisher. She is about to run out of the small quantity she had produced, however. Because publishers have never been willing to give her the chance she thought she deserved, she has decided not to use one, even though the sales volumes are creeping up. She is determined to produce her books herself through the use of an independent printer. Elizabeth's desktop publishing capabilities have resulted in a very nice looking product, but one with no cover or binding. She wants to make as much money as possible, so she will have an income while working on her next book, but she also recognizes the need for a quality printing and binding job. Elizabeth wishes to publish her book in paperback and has found four printers that can do the work she needs to have done. The fixed and variable costs associated with the four printers are presented below:

Printer Alternative	Fixed Cost ($)	Cost per Unit ($)
1	3,000	4.00
2	7,000	3.75
3	8,000	2.70
4	11,000	0.80

At the current demand rate, Elizabeth predicts sales of 4,000 units in the next six months. Her book sells for $7.95. Which printer should she select? What will be her profit for the next six months if she sells 4,000 units?

11. Tom Owens, the owner of Mr. T's Custom-Printed Shirts, is investigating the purchase of new silk screening equipment. Silk screening machines are expensive, but the better machines reduce the amount of labor required for production. They also produce shirts at a faster rate. Tom wishes to reduce labor costs and improve his response time to customers. In general, the more automated the machine, the more expensive it is, but the costs per unit drop because both labor costs and the time to complete an order drop as well. Material use is the same for each machine. The fixed and variable costs associated with each machine are presented below:

Alternative	Fixed Cost ($)	Variable Cost ($)
R&I Screener	10,500	6.24
Thomson Controls	24,000	4.20
Swede	39,000	3.10

Tom projects a demand of 26,000 shirts for next year alone. Which machine would be his best alternative?

ADVANCED PROBLEMS

1. Ray plans to start a catering service, and is considering two different business models. Under Option A (the highest level of vertical integration), Ray will purchase raw materials and ingredients, cook his own food, and provide delivery and catering service.

   Under Option B, Ray will purchase frozen entrees and other dishes from a local restaurant supply house. This eliminates the need to do his own cooking, and also avoids a large investment in restaurant-grade kitchen equipment and facility.

   Ray's revenue per dinner served will average about $20.00 per plate. If he does his own cooking, his monthly fixed costs will be $1,200, and his variable cost will be about $7.00 per plate. Under Option B, his monthly fixed cost will be only $200, but his variable cost increases to about $12.00 per plate.

   a. Find the breakeven volume (number of plates per month) for each alternative. Which alternative has the larger breakeven volume? Is this consistent with your intuition? Explain why or why not.

   b. At this point Ray faces uncertainty regarding the monthly demand volume his business will realize. Under Option A, what is Ray's profit (loss) if demand volume is 20 percent greater (less than) the Option A breakeven point? Under Option B, what is Ray's profit (loss) if demand volume is 20 percent greater (less than) the Option B breakeven point?

   c. Which option appears to generate greater *profit sensitivity* to variability around its' respective breakeven point? Why?

2. Morgan Manufacturing builds complex pumps for the chemical industry. They cast the aluminum components, machine them to specifications, and assemble the pumps. A check valve on the pump is made out of plastic, which they purchase for $31 each. Morgan's Plant Manager, Sean, feels that the plant can produce the parts at the same quality for a variable price of $18 to $26, depending on the process that they use. One process that they are looking at (process A) will cost $10,000 in fixed costs for the machinery, and has a variable cost of $26 per check valve. Another process (process B) costs $50,000 with a variable cost of $18. Tom, the Operations

Manager for Morgan's, has asked Sean how accurate the estimates are. "The fixed costs are based on machinery costs and set-up, so they are good. The variable costs are estimates, and I used the high end just to be safe. I really think that the variable costs will be $14 or $22, depending on the set-up."

a. Assuming that the higher variable costs are used, at what volume would you use Process A, Process B, or stay with outsourcing?

b. How does it change if the lower variable costs are used?

3. Sierra National manufactures garden gazebos for the garden and spa markets. The gazebos are made of California second growth redwood, a tree that is planted for harvest. The standard price for Redwood is $2,380/TBdF (Thousand Board Feet), or $2.38 per board foot. Each gazebo requires 250 BdF and takes 10 hours to produce at a labor rate of $18/hr. Riki Lee, the purchasing agent for Sierra National, has just been informed that the price of Redwood has gone up to $2,850/TBdF. She is concerned that the higher price will hurt profits, and wants to take a closer look at all costs. She found out that due to high orders the plant has been working overtime at an overtime rate of $27/hr. Each gazebo is only taking $9^{1}/_{2}$ hours to produce, meaning each gazebo now has one and a half hours of overtime costs associated with it. She also discovered that the gazebos actually use 230 BdF of redwood. Determine the total price variance, usage variance, and total variance for the gazebos.

LEARNING ACTIVITIES   www.mhhe.com/opsnow3e

Visit the Online Learning Center (www.mhhe.com/opsnow3e) for additional resources. Content varies by chapter, and includes

- Business Tours
- OM on Site
- Readings
- Resources
- Excel Tutors

- Interactive Case Models
- Reel Operations Video Clips
- Additional Advanced Problems
- Self-Assessment Quizzes
- Glossary

SELECTED RESOURCES

Hansen, Don R., and Mowen, Maryanne M. *Cost Management*. Cincinnati: South-Western Publishing, 1997.

Ross, S. A., Westerfield, R. W., and Jordan, B. D. *Essentials of Corporate Finance*. New York: Irwin/McGraw-Hill, 1999.

VIDEO CASE 5.1

Cost Reduction through Reengineering at Caterpillar

Based on Video 6 on the Student DVD

Reengineering is a clean-slate approach to improving systems, with particular attention paid to the interactions between functional departments. For Caterpillar's diesel engine manufacturing process, one of the most time-consuming and costly activities was the creation of engine drawings for customers. Customers needed timely access to drawings so that they could ensure fit with vehicles. Caterpillar undertook a substantial reengineering effort to completely overhaul that process with a goal of time reduction and cost reduction, while at the same time meeting customer needs.

1. What are the criteria used by Caterpillar to identify potential processes for reengineering?

2. Describe the five steps of Caterpillar's reengineering process. For each one, what is the contribution to cost reduction?

3. How can reengineering address the potential conflict between meeting customer needs and reducing costs?

INTERACTIVE CASE 5.1

Hollow Logs Furniture Tries to Control Costs

The Variance Analysis Model provides a visual mechanism for understanding the relationships among standards, usage, price variance, usage variance, and total variance. In this model, the user can modify actual price, standard price, actual usage, and standard usage by dragging the top edges of four bars. When these inputs are changed, the affected variances are highlighted and the new variance values are provided.

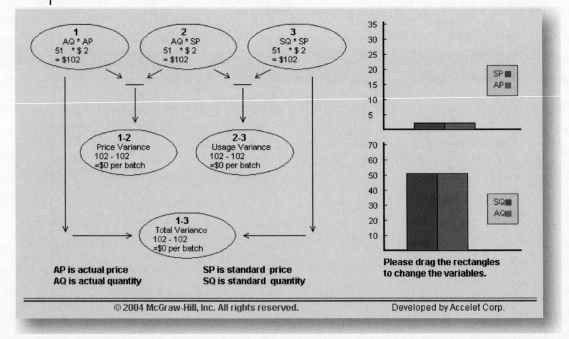

Hollow Logs

Hollow Logs, a premium quality furniture producer, started as a producer of custom home entertainment centers to fit unique room designs. After several years of customization, Alex Collins, the owner and head designer, developed a modular design that standardized much of their production but still provided a significant amount of product flexibility. Despite its ability to customize, Hollow Logs' sales are dominated by one particular design, known as the Video Center. The Video Center Shelf System, constructed of red oak, constitutes 58 percent of Hollow Logs' sales. As Alex has standardized components of his home entertainment centers, Hollow Logs has become more mechanized and labor costs per unit have dropped. Material costs, however, have remained high. High material costs are primarily a result of Hollow Logs' commitment to use real wood in their products. All of its home entertainment centers are solid wood, with the exception of the unit backs, which are oak veneered plywood, and the drawer bottoms, which are high-density fiberboard.

Like most natural resources, wood quality varies from piece to piece and batch to batch. Hollow Logs uses only clear oak (no knots) in their products. The presence of knots in boards results in the boards being cut to shorter lengths, wasting wood. The more knots, the less "yield" Alex gets from the wood he purchases. Alex purchases red oak from a hardwood supplier and has paid $2.00 per board foot for over three years. (A board foot is 12 inches by 12 inches by 1 inch thick.) Alex purchases 1 in. × 8 in. × 10 ft. boards (6.66 board feet per board) for $13.32. The Video Center Shelf System actually requires 43 board feet of red oak to construct, but waste from knots and defects results in the actual average consumption of 51 board feet of red oak per shelf. Alex considers $2.00 per board foot and 51 board feet per unit as his standard price and standard quantity for the Video Center Shelf System.

Alex's wood supplier has traditionally purchased standing timber within a 100-mile radius of his mill in southern Indiana. As the larger trees have been harvested, however, the remaining trees are smaller and have more knots. These trees are expected to increase Alex's usage rates from 51 board feet to 64 board feet per unit for next year and the foreseeable future. Recognizing the impending increases in costs, Alex has begun to explore other alternatives for his wood supply.

1. The start-up default values for the Variance Analysis Interactive Model are presented below:

   SP = $2   SQ = 51 board feet
   AP = $2   AQ = 51 board feet

   a. What is the current materials cost per unit?

   b. What will happen to the materials cost per unit if Alex's usage quantity increases from 51 to 64 board feet per unit?

   c. What is the usage variance that results from that change?

2. Alex's supplier has offered to transport red oak from northern Kentucky to increase the quality of the wood he ships. This wood is expected to reduce usage to 45 board feet per unit, but will cost $3 per board foot because of the increased transportation costs.

   a. What will be the materials cost per unit if Alex uses this wood?

   b. What will be the price, usage, and total variances if the higher quality wood is used?

   c. To what level will Alex need to reduce his actual quantity to make using the higher quality oak more economical than using the poor quality oak?

INTERACTIVE CASE 5.2

Identifying the Most Economical Spray Facility for SportsExchange

The Breakeven Model presents an interactive environment for a three-alternative decision scenario. The user can change fixed and variable costs of each alternative's cost curve by dragging the colored dots on the left and right of the line to see the impact on the output graph. The user can also drag the n line to investigate the three costs for any value of n. As the lines are dragged, all related volumes change.

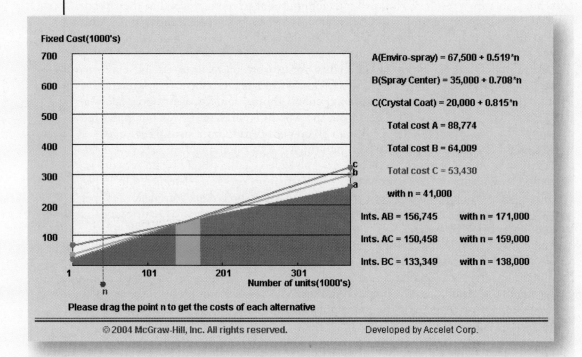

Fixed Cost(1000's)

$A(\text{Enviro-spray}) = 67{,}500 + 0.519 \cdot n$

$B(\text{Spray Center}) = 35{,}000 + 0.708 \cdot n$

$C(\text{Crystal Coat}) = 20{,}000 + 0.815 \cdot n$

Total cost A = 88,774

Total cost B = 64,009

Total cost C = 53,430

with n = 41,000

Ints. AB = 156,745   with n = 171,000

Ints. AC = 150,458   with n = 159,000

Ints. BC = 133,349   with n = 138,000

Number of units(1000's)

Please drag the point n to get the costs of each alternative

SportsExchange

SportsExchange is a regional refurbisher of sporting goods equipment. It specializes in upgrading football equipment it receives from high schools and colleges. The equipment is brought in during the late winter and returned during the summer. Processes used by SportsExchange include sewing pants and jerseys, replacing pads, repairing and painting helmets, and replacing laces, snaps, and elastic in pants. The most expensive process for SportsExchange is painting helmets. Regulations that control worker safety and environmental emissions mandate a paint room that manages fumes effectively. In order to continue in its lucrative business, SportsExchange is required to invest in a new state-of-the-art painting facility. Maria Hinson, the SportsExchange owner, has identified three manufacturers of turnkey spray booths. The fixed and variable costs associated with each of the three alternatives are presented below:

Alternative	Fixed Cost	Variable Cost
A: Enviro-Spray	$67,500	$.519 per unit
B: Spray Center	$35,000	$.708 per unit
C: Crystal Coat	$20,000	$.815 per unit

1. With the fixed and variable costs set to the values shown above, drag the n line to the volume of production desired.

   a. Maria Hinson has predicted that SportsExchange will need to refinish 156,000 helmets. What is the total cost, for each of the alternatives, of producing 156,000 units?

   b. If the fixed cost of Alternative C (Crystal Coat) is reduced to $15,000, what happens to the cost of producing 156,000 units on that alternative? What happens to the relative attractiveness of Alternative B (Spray Center) if Crystal Coat's fixed costs are reduced to $15,000?

   c. Assuming that the fixed costs for Enviro-Spray, Spray Center, and Crystal Coat are as originally stated ($67,500; $35,000; and $20,000), what must the fixed cost of Enviro-Spray be reduced to in order for it to be the low-cost alternative with a demand of 156,000 units?

2. Reset the fixed and variable costs to their start-up default values.

   a. Maria believes her forecast of 156,000 units demand for next year should be accurate to within 20 percent. What are the implications of a 20 percent error in either direction?

   b. If the company wishes to negotiate to lower the cost per unit for Crystal Coat, what must it come down to in order to be the low-cost alternative for producing 260,000 units?

3. Set the values to the default settings by downloading a fresh page. Record the equations and the intersection points for all three alternatives.

   a. Crystal Coat has a new design that has lowered fixed costs to $15,000, but variable costs are increased to $.903 per unit. How does this change the relationships among the three alternatives? How does this change the impact of Maria's demand forecast accuracy?

   b. Using the costs associated with Crystal Coat's new design, what must the variable costs for Enviro-Spray drop to for it to be the low-cost alternative at 156,000 units?

4. The fixed costs are often quite easy to determine, but variable costs can be difficult to predict. A small error in projecting the variable cost can make what seemed to be a correct alternative choice into the wrong one. We have seen the potential impact of inaccuracy in Maria's demand forecast, but it is also important to understand the effect of inaccuracy in predicting variable costs. Set the fixed and variable costs to their start-up defaults.

   a. Spray Center is the low-cost alternative at Maria's expected production level, but the range of volumes where Spray Center is the low-cost alternative is actually quite narrow. At a fixed cost of $35,000 and variable costs just under 71 cents per unit, Spray Center appears to be a "no-brainer" for the best choice if demand is expected to be 156,000 units. However, a closer look at variable costs may give different results. What happens if the variable costs for Spray Center go up $.02 to $.728? Do you think being off by $.02 on a variable cost of approximately $.71 is likely to happen?

   b. A shift in the variable costs of Spray Center can cause it to disappear as a low-cost alternative. Reset the variable costs of Spray Center back to $.708. Being wrong on the variable cost predictions for other alternatives can also affect the fate of Spray Center. Once again, with the fixed and variable costs set at their start-up defaults, take a close look at the range of low-cost demand for the Spray Center alternative. We have seen what can happen to this range when the Spray Center variable costs are inaccurate. Let's examine the impact of inaccuracies in predicting the variable costs for the other two alternatives. Suppose the variable cost for

Enviro-Spray was inaccurate, and instead of $.519 per unit, it was actually $.505 per unit, less than 2 cents lower. What happens to Spray Center as an alternative?

c. Set the fixed and variable costs back to the start-up defaults. How sensitive is Spray Center to inaccuracies in predicting variable costs for Crystal Coat? How low must Crystal Coat variable costs be to exclude Spray Center as an alternative?

APPLICATION CASE 5.1

Those Lazy Restaurant Workers

Stephanie Ochoa has been hired as a productivity improvement consultant by Ainsley's Seafood, a chain of 26 restaurants on the Gulf Coast. Ainsley's managers, who have mostly been promoted up from kitchen duties, have been confronted by the owners about their labor costs. The biggest complaint among the owners is that labor costs related to waitstaff, bussing, kitchen, and dishwashers are higher than they should be. The owners have looked at work schedules and compared them to meals served, and believe that the restaurants, on average, are overstaffing by about 20 percent.

As a first step in her analysis, Stephanie interviewed the managers of five of the restaurants. She questioned them about their customers, their busy periods, how long customers waited to be seated, and how long they waited to be served. She also asked questions about the scheduling desires of the staff, in particular, how many hours per week they worked, the proportion of full time to part time, and how long they wanted their shifts to be. Some of the key issues she discovered are summarized below.

- Customers consider a wait of over 45 minutes to be seated to be too long.
- Customers want to be served within 30 minutes of being seated.
- The busiest times during the week are 6:00–9:00.
- The busiest times on weekends are 5:00–10:00.
- Waitstaff and bus staff typically work part time. They expect shifts at least 4 hours long.
- Kitchen and dishwash staff work 8-hour shifts and work full time.

Stephanie gathered sufficient data to confirm that the data the owners were using was correct. The average hours worked seemed substantially higher than the hours needed to meet the needs, given the number of meals served. When confronted by that information, the managers complained that because of the variability in demand during the early and late part of the evenings, those numbers are deceiving. They maintain that in order to effectively meet the expectations of their customers, they must staff the way they do.

Quality: Meeting Customer Expectations

LEARNING OBJECTIVES

- State the contributions Shewhart, Deming, Juran, and Crosby made to quality management.

- Describe why customer loyalty is so important for profitability.

- Explain the importance of internal and external customers and the role each plays in TQM.

- Describe the three principles of TQM.

- Explain how the PDCA cycle is used to obtain continuous improvement.

- Describe the seven steps of the quality improvement story.

- Describe industry-focused and process-focused benchmarking.

- Describe how Six Sigma is used to enhance quality.

- Explain how certification programs can provide structure for quality improvement.

- State the criteria used for the Malcolm Baldrige National Quality Award.

1. Why would the variability of demand, particularly early and late in the evening, result in a need for higher levels of labor but low utilization for that labor?

2. If average labor hours are reduced, what nonquantitative costs might the restaurants experience?

3. How would you recommend Stephanie proceed with her analysis? What data should she collect?

QUALITY—COMBINING CULTURE AND PROCEDURE

Few businesses have the reputation for quality that Marriott has developed. Marriott operates over 2,600 units in 68 countries under brand names that include JW Marriott, The Ritz-Carlton, Renaissance, Residence Inn, Courtyard, TownePlace Suites, Fairfield Inn, SpringHill Suites, and Ramada International, with 80 hotels in Asia and 30 in China. Marriott has plans for 10 to 15 more per year in Asia. Marriott's reputation for putting customers first comes not from hype but from real customer satisfaction statistics. That performance to customer expectations doesn't just happen. It is the result of many components of a system designed for that end. The customer is at the forefront for all of Marriott's systems. Marriott has merged a set of beliefs that have guided a pride-based culture, rules and procedures that make sure activities are performed correctly every time, and technologies that enable it to know in advance what a particular customer expects.

In an industry with high employee turnover rates, one prerequisite to providing customers with good service is having high-quality employees. Marriott develops employee loyalty by taking good care of them. Managers strive to hire the right employees so that they learn faster and advance. They recognize good performance, and they promote from within. Managers are role models who spend time on the floor and demonstrate the importance of continuously focusing on the customer. In 1998 Marriott invested in Siebel software to begin to collect information on its customers. Customer preferences gathered by different departments and different hotels are available through the Customer Loyalty Anticipation Satisfaction System. When a customer asks about a particular type of restaurant, that information is stored for later use by another staffer.

Ritz-Carlton, a Marriott brand renowned for its service, has led J.D. Power's guest satisfaction ranking and has won the Malcolm Baldrige National Quality Award twice. It even has a leadership center where anyone can study the brand's approach to customer service. Ritz-Carlton's process to quality starts with employee interviews designed to identify employees who will become top performers. Selection is critical when any staff member can spend up to $2,000 to resolve a guest's problem *without* management approval. New employees get about $5,000 in training that includes a 2-day indoctrination into the company values and a 21-day course on job responsibilities. That training is reinforced for the duration of the employee's career. Every day, at all of the Ritz-Carlton hotels, employees take part in a 15-minute discussion of one of the basic core values.

Marriott has shown the world how the combination of attention to people and culture, along with attention to processes and detail, can generate the type of quality that continues to attract new customers and generate the level of loyalty that translates into profitability.

Source: "The Marriott Management Philosophy," http://marriott.com/Multimedia/PDF/Marriott_Management_Philosophy.pdf; "How Marriott Never Forgets a Guest," *BusinessWeek*, February 21, 2000; D. McDonald, "Roll Out the Blue Carpet: How Ritz-Carlton Can Teach You to Serve Your Customers Better," *Business 2.0*, May 2004; J. A. Byrne, "How to Lead Now," *Fast Company*, Issue 73, August 2003, p. 62; "Marriott Plans New Asian Hotels," *Wall Street Journal*, April 1, 2004, p. 1.

Quality is the second of three critical value components. The commitment to producing quality in services and products changes processes from just producing to producing things customers want. The development of the methods and techniques to manage quality and a culture of employees who want to produce quality is at the heart of any successful business.

Introduction: Product and Service Quality Defined

The concept of quality means different things to different people. Most people would agree that quality is an important characteristic of a product or service, but if you ask 10 people how a particular product or service stacks up in terms of quality, you may get 10 different responses. On the other hand, if you ask a manager to define quality, the response will probably be specific, describing the products or services the manager deals with every day and stressing how important quality is to profitability.

Despite its importance, quality can be understood only after agreement on its definition. A concept with as many potentially different interpretations as quality needs a precise definition if it is to be measured, controlled, managed, specified to suppliers, *and* evaluated by customers. Quality is defined as conformance to customer specifications and expectations. Recall that quality was described as a critical value component in B2B and B2C interactions. Quality is defined by the customer, but the two different types of customer may define it very differently.

The nature of today's products and services makes it difficult for companies to understand the expectations of all customers, let alone live up to them. Service quality expectations have increased the complexity of expectations that once were limited to products. Purchasing a product without at least some expectations of service is a rare experience today. Services that are purchased without associated goods are also unusual. The management of quality for a service creates challenges that are quite different from those associated with purchases of products. This can best be understood through an examination of the dimensions of product and service quality. Garvin and later Pisek summarized product quality through eight dimensions: performance, features, reliability, durability, serviceability, aesthetics, response, and reputation. They are briefly described in Exhibit 6.1. A contrasting set of dimensions for service quality consists of reliability, responsiveness, assurance, empathy, and tangibles.[2] Exhibit 6.2 provides brief descriptions of these dimensions.

Note that the product quality dimensions that are associated with services seem to be lumped into the categories of reliability and response. Likewise, the product-oriented dimensions of service quality are lumped into the category of "tangibles." Exhibit 6.3 provides an integrated view of product and service dimensions of quality. Businesses must meet those customer expectations in order to be competitive. The importance of both service and product quality attributes is undeniable when one recognizes the issues that make a particular supply chain more competitive than its competitors. Product quality is of little importance if delivery requirements aren't satisfied. Likewise, on-time or fast delivery means little if the product doesn't meet expectations.

Quality dimensions specific to products include performance, features, durability, and serviceability. The **performance** dimension of quality results from specific characteristics and capabilities of the product or service. Performance for a product may include the actual functions the product is able to perform. Performance for a service refers to the ability to respond accurately to customer needs. **Features** are additional capabilities that can be added to a product or service. Additional capabilities that go beyond the basic functional

performance
A dimension of quality that results from specific characteristics and capabilities of the product or service.

feature
A dimension of quality that consists of additional capabilities of products or services that can be added.

Dimensions of Product Quality	EXHIBIT 6.1

Performance:	What are the desirable characteristics of the product?
Features:	What additional characteristics of the product are possible?
Reliability:	Is the business dependable? Does it accomplish what it promises?
Durability:	How long will the product last?
Serviceability:	Can the product be easily and inexpensively repaired?
Aesthetics:	Does the product satisfy subjective requirements, like appearance and style?
Response:	Is the interaction between the customer and the product provider pleasant and appropriate?
Reputation:	What does information on past performance say about the company?

Source: Adapted from D. A. Garvin, "What Does Product Quality Really Mean? *Sloan Management Review* 26 (Fall 1984), pp. 29–30; and P. E. Pisek, "Defining Quality at the Marketing/Development Interface," *Quality Progress* 20 (June 1987), pp. 28–36.

Dimensions of Service Quality	EXHIBIT 6.2

Reliability:	Does the business keep its promises?
Responsiveness:	Does it promptly respond to the needs of its customers?
Assurance:	Can the employees generate customer trust and confidence?
Empathy:	Are employees approachable and sensitive to individual customers?
Tangibles:	Do the physical facilities, equipment, and written materials show care and attention?

Source: Adapted from J. A. Fitzsimmons and M. J. Fitzsimmons, *Service Management* (New York, McGraw-Hill, 2001), p. 45.

Dimensions of Service and Product Quality Combined	EXHIBIT 6.3

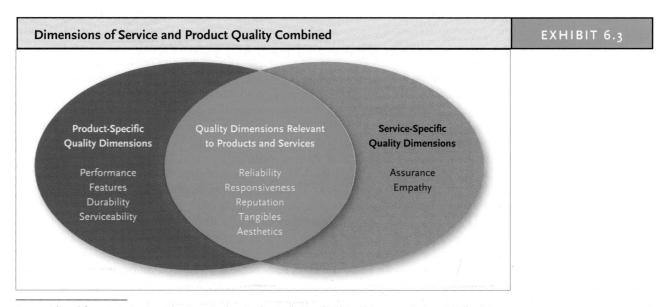

Source: Adapted from D. A. Garvin, "What Does Product Quality Really Mean?" *Sloan Management Review* 26 (Fall 1984), pp. 29–30; P. E. Pisek, "Defining Quality at the Marketing/Development Interface," *Quality Progress* 20 (June 1987), pp. 28–36; and J. A. Fitzsimmons and M. J. Fitzsimmons, *Service Management* (New York: McGraw-Hill, 2001), p. 45.

durability
How long a product will last.

serviceability
A dimension of quality that consists of the amount of effort required to repair a product.

assurance
A dimension of quality that relates to the level of trust or confidence generated by employees.

empathy
A dimension of quality that results from the approachability and sensitivity of employees.

reliability
A dimension of quality resulting from a company's consistency of performance.

responsiveness
A dimension of quality resulting from the company's ability to respond quickly.

reputation
A dimension of quality resulting from a company's performance history.

tangibles
A dimension of service quality that includes the physical items that are included in the service.

aesthetics
A dimension of quality that includes looks, sound, and smells.

In 2005 Marriott's quality and the customer's desire for it resulted in 18 percent more revenue per room than its competitors.

level, or additional services that add to the basic service, are considered features. The **durability** dimension describes how long a product will last under different conditions. **Serviceability** is a measure of effort required to repair a product.

Service-specific quality dimensions include assurance and empathy. **Assurance** relates to the level of trust and confidence generated by employees that customers interact with. **Empathy** is the approachability and sensitivity employees demonstrate.

Quality dimensions that are shared between products and services include reliability, responsiveness, reputation, tangibles, and aesthetics. The **reliability** dimension addresses the consistency of the performance. **Responsiveness** addresses the company's ability to respond promptly. **Reputation** summarizes the business's performance history. **Tangibles** are the physical facilities, equipment, and written material the customer comes in contact with. The **aesthetic** dimension covers aspects like the look, sound, or smell of a product, or the way it feels. Aesthetics go beyond the functional characteristics of a product and include subjective, ancillary characteristics.

Quality and Value

The components of value (cost, quality, and timeliness) are all necessary parts of the value equation. Without them, value cannot be created and sold. The components of value do not necessarily play equivalent roles, however. Recall that value is a function of costs and benefits. The "benefit" side of the value equation consists of processes and capabilities and the resulting quality and timeliness. A product or service with "bad" quality means that the product or service doesn't meet the customer's expectations. It is difficult to imagine how purchasing something that falls short of your expectations could ever be considered to be a good value, but most of us have done it. We are sometimes seduced by the "good deal" only to be disappointed later on. What actually happens is that we confuse price with cost. We see a low price and think "Hey, low cost!" Unfortunately, it turns out that the cost isn't low at all. As the saying goes, if you buy the best, you only cry once, but if you don't buy the best, you cry over and over again. This axiom makes it seem like those purchase decisions should be simple—always buy the best. In reality, most customers can't always buy "the best," and that's where the judgment of value comes into play.

Lack of quality means that the product or service doesn't meet customer expectations, but the presence of quality doesn't necessarily mean a good value. Outrageous costs or delays in availability may overshadow the quality component. Quality is a necessary component of value, but it is not sufficient. Quality is so important to value that many customers try to learn about product quality before making a purchase.

Quality and Profitability

Previous chapters examined the role value plays in a firm's profitability. Recall from the discussion of cost in Chapter 5 that cost has a double influence on profitability because it affects net income in two ways. First, a cost reduction results in a reduced cost of goods sold, which, by itself, results in an increase in net income. A reduction in cost also provides an opportunity to reduce the selling price, resulting in an increase in value for the customer and increasing demand and net sales.

Quality can also have a double effect on profitability. The most direct impact is through its relationship with value. As quality goes up, all else being equal, value goes up. If quality rises beyond the wants and needs of the customer, the customer may not recognize it as valuable and may not be willing to pay for it, however. A price increase necessary to cover the cost of added quality features may reduce value. The key is to focus on the customer by letting the customer define quality. In this way, a financial return on the quality added is ensured. The increase in net income that results from enhanced value can come in several forms, including increased demand, increased customer loyalty, increased market share, and the resulting increased sales. Increased value also provides an opportunity to increase the selling price, also increasing net sales.

Quality has another, less obvious impact on net income through its link to product and service production costs. Many quality improvements create reductions in costs through a variety of means. Among these are reductions in scrap, warranty claims, labor, recalls, repairs, rework, and inventory. These costs are worthy of a more in-depth examination.

Recall from the previous chapter that production costs are those associated with the actual production of goods and services. They consist of direct materials, direct labor, and overhead. Products and services are typically of poor quality because the processes used to create them were ineffective or tasks were improperly performed. Production costs increase as a result of several influences. Labor and materials consumed in those processes are wasted because the product can't be sold or the service doesn't meet the needs of the customers so they don't pay for it. Overhead costs associated with poor-quality products and services also often increase.

A defective product may lead to a number of possible cost scenarios. The defect might be discovered before the product is sold. In that case, the product might be fixed, or it might be thrown away or "scrapped." In the first case, additional labor and materials will be required to fix it. The product is eventually sold, but at higher cost. In the second case, the labor and materials consumed are discarded and provide no opportunity for a financial return. The worst case, from a total-cost perspective, is that the defective product is sold and the customer discovers the defect and expects a refund or exchange. In addition to all of the financial costs associated with that situation, customer loyalty decreases or is

om ADVANTAGE   Quality, Productivity, and Inventory Reduction: Inseparable Goals

Despite two decades of catch-up efforts by Ford, GM, and Daimler-Chrysler, Toyota still has the upper hand on auto industry quality and productivity. Much of Toyota's success can be credited to common sense and tremendous scrutiny of its own processes. That scrutiny has been transported from Japan to the American parts suppliers as well.

Toyota engineer Hajime Oba provides a classic example in a visit to a Kalamazoo, Michigan, supplier of dashboard vents. Summit, the supplier of the vents, had recently invested $280,000 in robots and paint ovens to bake the vents. The process of painting the vents took 90 minutes. The slow process actually reduced quality and productivity because it slowed the conveyor feeding the oven, and the parts gathered dust waiting to get into the oven. Hajime Oba demonstrated that the paint could be dried in under three minutes merely by using a hair dryer. The paint system was replaced with $150 spray guns and light bulbs for drying the paint. The result was improvements in quality and productivity along with a drastic reduction in inventory. Components parts inventory fell from 14 days' worth to four hours. Finished-goods inventory fell from 30 days' worth to eight hours.

Toyota's attention to quality has not gone unnoticed. J.D. Power and Associates' rankings of four- to five-year-old vehicles has placed Toyota highest for six consecutive years. Toyota consistently lands on *Consumer Reports'* lists of top vehicles. Toyota expects that as the auto market cools in the United States, consumers will be more interested in quality and durability. This presents a challenge to Toyota, because as the

company strives to increase its U.S. capacity by 60 percent, it must increasingly depend on U.S. suppliers of parts. U.S. suppliers are not as committed to the lean manufacturing principles as Toyota is. This approach to manufacturing strives to produce vehicles with one-third the defects, using half the factory space, half the capital, and half the engineering time, doubling the productivity of most resources.

The table below shows how, despite improvements made in the last two decades, U.S. automakers are significantly behind Japanese manufacturers. In 2000, reliability of new U.S. autos was approximately at the level the Japanese manufacturers had reached in 1985.

Year	Asian Automobile Manufacturers Problems per 100 Vehicles	American Automobile Manufacturers Problems per 100 Vehicles
2003	11	18
2000	11	23
1980	34	105

In 2003, Toyota led with just 10 problems per 100 vehicles, followed by Honda and Hyundai—each with 11 problems per 100 vehicles.

Source: "Why Toyota Wins Such High Marks on Quality Surveys," *Wall Street Journal,* March 15, 2001, pp. A1, A11; "Japanese Autos Lead in Quality; Gap Is Closing," *Wall Street Journal,* March 15, 2001, p. A4; "Cruising for Quality," *BusinessWeek,* September 3, 2001, pp. 74–75; car-data.com, *Automotive News,* March 10, 2003.

lost and that customer tells potential customers of the negative experience. Nissan, for example, saw quality drop in early 2004 as surveys identified problems in its new vehicles. Its drop from 6th place to 11th place in the J.D. Power and Associates rankings as a result of 147 problems per 100 vehicles was expected to be followed by an increase in warranty costs.[3] No matter what the specifics, defective products always increase costs.

The defective product always comes back, and the business incurs the costs associated with discarding it. What makes this scenario even worse, however, is when the business involves the customer in its poor performance. It has done the worst possible thing: given the customer a reason to try a competitor.

The repercussions of a defective service are very different from those of a defective product. Unlike product quality, service quality is difficult to measure before the customer receives it. Thus, in every case of defective service, the customer is directly involved. Customer exposure to defective service can have a variety of outcomes. In the best case, employees discover the impending error and fix it before the customer encounters it. If the customer is involved, however, the outcome can range from a mild problem to a total disaster. We've all had experiences at a retailer when we couldn't find any employees to help us or at a restaurant that served us the wrong meal (and by the time the correct one was brought, everyone we were with had already finished eating). These experiences are best dealt with through a process of prevention rather than correction after the fact.

Most of our experiences as consumers of product quality are positive, because defective products are typically not allowed to get to the customer. We have a variety of products to select from, but most manufacturers are managing product quality well. Service quality, on the other hand, is often poor. High levels of turnover, inexperienced employees, employees who lack the skills to interact effectively with customers, and managers who are unskilled at managing service quality all contribute to the problem.

In 2005 *Fortune* magazine named Marriott as one of "America's Most Admired Companies" for the seventh straight time.

Quality Management: A Critical Change for U.S. Business

Quality management can be traced back to the post–World War II reconstruction of Japan. Japan's economy was completely devastated by the war, and Japanese leaders recognized the necessity to produce exports in order to survive. Business leaders from the United States, including some quality experts, were invited to Japan by government leaders to teach quality practices. Japanese manufacturers embraced these quality practices to the extent that Japanese goods, previously known for their poor quality, became accepted among the best in the world. Despite the fact that the experts who taught the Japanese manufacturers how to produce quality products were from the United States, most manufacturers in the United States did not embrace quality concepts until they began to lose market share to Japanese products in the late 1970s and early 1980s. In some cases, entire industries were lost to Japanese competitors because U.S. products were of such inferior quality. As markets began to disappear, U.S. manufacturers began to pay attention to their own experts.

The early development of quality management in the United States can best be examined by looking at these experts and their philosophies. Although many people have contributed to its development, its proliferation can be traced to four individuals: Walter A. Shewhart, W. Edwards Deming, Joseph M. Juran, and Philip B. Crosby.

Walter A. Shewhart

Walter Shewhart was a Bell Labs statistician during the 1920s and 1930s. His primary contribution to product and service quality was the recognition that variability existed in all manufacturing processes and that statistical tools could help explain that variability. Shewhart developed the use of statistical process control charts, which provide an opportunity to control the variability of processes. Despite the fact that Shewhart developed much of the foundation for quality control, his impact is often viewed as less than that of the other people involved in quality management. This is primarily because he was not a "crusader" for quality like the others, and because he died in 1967, before the concept of quality management had become popular in the United States.

W. Edwards Deming

W. Edwards Deming, a statistician who had studied the work of Shewhart, was one of the principal trainers of Japanese manufacturers in the 1950s. Deming extended the techniques and tools developed by Shewhart to a set of principles (14 points) to guide management in the development of business systems. He felt that unless upper management was committed to quality and systems were developed to support it, the quality tools and techniques used at the process level would be ineffective. Deming stressed that significant quality improvement only comes from changing the organization, and that responsibility rests with upper management. Deming's principles are summarized in Exhibit 6.4.

Despite the fact that he was a statistician, Deming's 14 points place greater importance on the managerial aspects of quality than on statistics. Deming's 14 points still provide an important guiding framework for quality improvement. Dr. Deming died in 1993.

Joseph M. Juran

Joseph Juran and W. Edwards Deming were contemporaries. Deming was born in 1900, Juran in 1904. Juran was an employee of Bell Telephone and was involved in helping Japanese leaders restructure their businesses. Juran also argued that quality was achieved through organization and management systems, not through techniques. Like Deming, he believed that most quality problems could be traced to ineffective management.

Deming's 14 Points Principles of Quality Management	EXHIBIT 6.4

1. Create and publish to all employees a statement of the aims and purposes of the company or organization.
2. Adopt a philosophy of preventing poor quality products and service.
3. Understand the role inspection plays in quality management and eliminate its need by utilizing control and improving product and service design.
4. Develop relationships with suppliers that provide quality products. Do not base supplier selection on price alone.
5. Implement a system of continuous improvement of processes.
6. Provide employee training that teaches the skills required for continuous improvement.
7. Develop leadership.
8. Drive out fear by creating a culture of innovation and trust.
9. Develop an enterprise perspective on the aims and purposes of the organization by utilizing the efforts of teams that break down departmental barriers.
10. Eliminate slogans and themes that encourage results without training employees correctly.
11. Eliminate numerical quotas.
12. Improve employee pride by eliminating barriers to good workmanship.
13. Encourage education and improvement for everyone.
14. Take action at the top level of management to accomplish the transformation.

Source: W. E. Deming, *Out of the Crisis* (Cambridge, MA: MIT Press, 1986).

Juran created a framework for the management of quality that consisted of three elements: quality planning, quality control, and quality improvement. Quality planning provides employees with the direction needed to produce quality products. Quality control evaluates the performance by comparing actual results to goals and correcting variances. Quality improvement identifies quality problems, their causes, and solutions.

 ## Philip B. Crosby — BOOK CALLED "QUALITY IS FREE"

The contributions of Philip Crosby are dominated by his influence on the education and attitudes of top management, not the development of techniques, as was the case with the previous three quality "gurus." Crosby's career started in 1952. He worked for various manufacturing firms, culminating at ITT as corporate vice president of quality. In 1979 he started his new firm, Philip Crosby Associates, following the wide acclaim of his book *Quality Is Free*. Crosby's quality philosophy is built around four "absolutes," briefly presented in Exhibit 6.5.

Crosby's approach is also summarized in a set of 14 points, presented in Exhibit 6.6. It emphasizes a "zero-defect" program that is initiated with a celebration and emphasizes motivation, education, and recognition.

Proaction versus Reaction in Quality Management

When the objective of quality management is simplified to the extreme, it can change from "producing high-quality goods and services" to "making sure the customer gets only high-quality goods and services." There is a huge difference between these two objectives. The extra step involved in the second, which might appear to be reasonable, actually does a lot of damage. Prevention of poor quality yields a substantial reduction in costs. Merely stopping poor quality from getting to the customer, however, doesn't reduce costs nearly as much.

Costs associated with quality management are much more extensive than one might imagine. One approach to managing quality, known as "cost of quality," is discussed in the following section.

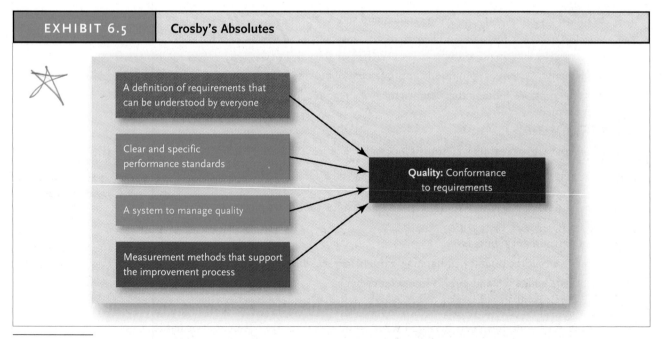

EXHIBIT 6.5	Crosby's Absolutes

- A definition of requirements that can be understood by everyone
- Clear and specific performance standards
- A system to manage quality
- Measurement methods that support the improvement process

Quality: Conformance to requirements

Source: J. MacDonald and J. Piggott, *Global Quality: The New Management Culture* (San Diego: Pfeiffer, 1993), p. 99.

Crosby's 14 Points	EXHIBIT 6.6

1. Management commitment to make it clear where management stands on quality.

2. Quality improvement teams to run the quality improvement programs.

3. Quality measurement to provide a display of current and potential nonconformance problems in a manner that permits objective evaluation and action.

4. Utilize the Cost of Quality framework to define the ingredients of the cost of quality and explain its use as a management tool.

5. Quality awareness to raise the personal concern felt by all employees.

6. Corrective action to provide a systematic method of resolving forever the problems that are identified.

7. Zero-defects (ZD) planning to examine the activities that must be conducted in preparation for the zero-defects program.

8. Supervisor training to define the type of training that supervisors need in order to carry out their part of the program.

9. ZD day to create an event that will let all employees realize that there has been a change.

10. Goal setting to turn pledges and commitments into action.

11. Error-cause removal to give the individual employee a method of communicating to management the situations that make it difficult to improve.

12. Recognition to appreciate those who participate.

13. Quality councils to bring together the professional-quality people for communication on a regular basis.

14. Do it over again to emphasize that the quality improvement program never ends.

Source: Adapted from P. B. Crosby, *Quality Is Free* (New York: McGraw-Hill, 1979).

Cost of Quality

Studies in the late 1970s and early 1980s provided proof that the costs of quality were significant. Costs associated with producing poor-quality goods and services—things like scrap, waste, rework, inspection, warranty costs, and recalls—can make up between 15 and 20 percent of the total costs of goods sold. Some studies showed that efforts to fix things that had originally been done wrong accounted for 20 to 30 percent of operating budgets. The **cost of quality (COQ)** concept was originally developed for manufacturing, but it has also been applied to services. COQ is defined as all of the costs associated with maintaining the quality of goods and services. It includes the general categories of external failure costs, internal failure costs, appraisal costs, and prevention costs. Let's examine external and internal failure costs first.

cost of quality (COQ)
All of the costs associated with maintaining the quality of goods and services.

External Failure Costs

External failure costs occur when a customer is exposed to poor quality. A quality problem that becomes an external failure is almost always more expensive than it would have been had it been dealt with internally, for several reasons. First, the fact that a product has made it all the way to the customer means that more costs have been expended on the product. Transportation and stocking costs, for example, that would not have been spent had the failure been identified internally, have now been added to the failure. In addition, sales staff time has been invested with no financial return. These quantifiable costs, though important and potentially sufficient to eliminate a profit, may not be the

external failure cost
Cost incurred when a customer is exposed to poor quality.

External failures are the most expensive result of poor quality. Exposing any customer to poor quality reduces the value and increases costs of ownership. Exposing a B2B customer to an external failure can cost that company in terms of productivity, as in this copying machine breakdown, or reduce its ability to provide *its* customers with quality products or services.

most critical. The most serious costs associated with an external failure may be the long-term costs of losing a customer.

In contrast to product failures, external failures in services that involve personal experience or that require a significant investment in time can be difficult to recover from. These failures can result in dissatisfied customers, the potential loss of customers, and negative "word of mouth." In the past, managers of services routinely predicted that a customer who had a bad experience would tell 10 others about it. Today, however, with the prevalence of Internet newsgroups, chat rooms, and the potential for anyone to publicize frustrations on a Web site, word of mouth can be even more devastating. Web sites like McSpotlight.org, walmartwatch.com, google-watch.org, and others provide forums for voicing dissatisfaction. Just as "buzz" can cause demand for a hot product to skyrocket, negative buzz can cause demand to nosedive. Large businesses spend millions of dollars each year in what is known as "issues management," dealinsg with untrue rumors being spread about their products or services, or countering negative publicity posted on the Internet. Many businesses, as a means of acquiring more information about customer wants and needs, monitor Internet newsgroups, chat rooms, and mailing lists, to gain from this information.

When an external failure does occur, however, a business still has an opportunity to salvage the situation and resolve it in a way that causes the customer to want to return. The way a business deals with an external failure is known as **recovery.** Recovery practices are addressed more specifically in the next chapter.

recovery
The way a business deals with an external failure when trying to satisfy the customer despite the failure.

Internal Failure Costs

Internal failure costs are costs associated with correcting a defect before the customer comes into contact with a product or service. For a manufacturing environment, where internal failures are most common, internal failure costs include the cost of scrapping the item (either discarding it or selling it for its scrap value), reworking the item so that it is no longer defective, selling the item at a reduced price as a second, or "blem," and all associated administrative costs. The costs may also include reductions in employee productivity and higher employee turnover. In some service industries, internal failure costs are comparable to those in manufacturing. Services that process documents, for example, are exposed to the possibility of defects that can be discovered internally. Restaurants can detect problems with food before it is served. Retailers can identify a defective item and remove it from the shelves. Internal failures affect consumers, however, through increased costs.

In many services quality problems are impossible to identify prior to the customer being exposed to them simply because the customer is involved in the production process itself. For example, if a customer walks out of a shop with a bad haircut, there really is no way the hairstylist could have known that it was going to be a bad haircut before it happened. The shop owner, however, should know that stylist experience and training reduce the likelihood of a bad haircut. The same holds for bank transactions, such as loan applications. Services that are experience-based, like expensive restaurants, bars and clubs, theme parks, and theaters, have great difficulty managing quality and customer satisfaction because of this very fact. Bad quality, from the consumer's perspective, cannot be identified until after the consumer experiences it.

Customer expectations for products tend to vary less noticeably. Customer reactions to service quality tend to be variable because expectations depend on individual tastes, mood, and the personalities (both customer and employee) that interact during the service encounter, whereas employee personalities or communication skills are rarely a factor in the customer's evaluation of a product's quality.

Appraisal Costs

Appraisal costs are linked to inspection and testing processes and to the auditing of quality-related systems. Inspection and testing activities ensure that products and services meet predetermined specifications. System auditing activities ensure that the systems designed to maintain quality do what is necessary to achieve specifications and not deviate from their intended objectives.

Inspection activities, used primarily in manufacturing, examine products and compare their characteristics to characteristics specified by customers. Inspections can occur at any point, from the incoming raw materials, through all production stages, to the finished product. In services, when inspections are possible, they typically precede the customer's involvement. Inspections are used to ensure that the facilities a customer will encounter will be acceptable. The hotel and lodging industry, for example, inspects to ensure that

appraisal costs
Costs associated with product inspection, testing, and auditing of quality-related systems.

Crash tests on automobiles, performed by the Insurance Institute for Highway Safety, as well as tests by the manufacturers themselves, provide evaluations of passenger injury potential for different models of autos as well as damage costs. Results identify areas for improvement in design. Effectiveness of process control charts depends not only on the interpretation of the data used, but also on the accuracy of the data being collected. Precision measurements require consistent techniques and employee skills in using and reading measuring instruments.

The elimination of variability in processes is at the root of all quality improvement. The microchip industry is striving to cut defect rates while being forced to cut costs *and* simultaneously increase output. Time-to-market is critical in an industry with life cycles so short that within four or five months price drops by 50 percent and the product line is obsolete in two years.

One of the first steps toward the elimination of variability is the standardization of processes. Not only must the process be done exactly the same as it is repeated, but it must be accomplished in exactly the same manner *wherever* it is done. Intel has adopted "copy exactly" as its mantra to ensure that chipmaking processes are completely standardized.

In any of its 13 factories, Intel produces chips exactly the same way and on exactly the same equipment. Employee activities and tasks are defined and performed in exactly the same way and are accomplished in exactly the same sequence. Intel essentially created one perfect plant, and then copied it. Without knowing for sure what mattered and what didn't, they were forced to copy to the smallest detail.

Some critics contend that the Intel approach is harmful and stifles innovation. Since no allowance is made for a process being slightly different than others, there is no possibility for improvement.

Source: S. F. Brown, "Building for the Next Chip Boom," *Fortune*, Vol. 146, Issue 3, August 11, 2002; E. Pfeiffer, "Chip off the Old Block," *Business 2.0*, July 2003.

the customer's accommodations are of expected quality. When products accompany the service, as in restaurants, retailing, or health care, inspections provide one last opportunity to ensure that the customer is not exposed to bad-quality products. In other services, however, there can be no inspection prior to the customer's service encounter. Legal counseling or other services with high levels of customer interaction are good examples of businesses that cannot take advantage of inspection.

testing
A specific type of inspection used when a visual inspection cannot reveal whether products meet specifications.

Testing is a specific type of inspection that is used when a visual inspection cannot reveal whether or not products meet specifications. Testing is frequently used with electronic and mechanical products that can be connected quickly to testing equipment in order to check out all system components. Products that are expensive or have high failure costs are often exposed to a barrage of tests prior to shipment. Testing of a service is often impossible, but testing of equipment used in some services is a means of ensuring that the equipment is up to the tasks required.

System auditing costs occur when in-depth analysis and improvement efforts are performed on quality management systems. A frequent cause of poor quality is the failure of systems that are intended to maintain quality. Recall the discussion of the quality function deployment (QFD) process from Chapter 4 in which the last step is the development of systems to maintain the process so that it continues to produce quality components. This is a critical part of the quality management effort. These systems must be periodically audited to make sure they continue to operate effectively and to identify ways they can be improved.

Prevention Costs

prevention costs
Costs associated with efforts to prevent errors or defects from happening.

Prevention costs are those associated with efforts to prevent errors or defects from happening. They include costs of employee training, process improvement and control activity, and quality planning activity. In services, prevention costs are often a much greater portion of the total cost of quality because of the customer interaction, the higher penalty for a customer being exposed to poor quality, and the inability of management to detect most quality problems before they get to the customer.

Prevention costs are obviously the most proactive of the firm's investments in quality management. If prevention were totally successful, appraisal costs, internal failure costs, and external failure costs would disappear. It is hard to imagine total prevention of all quality problems, but that is the goal for many companies. One frequently overlooked

| Cost of Quality from Prevention to External Failure | EXHIBIT 6.7 |

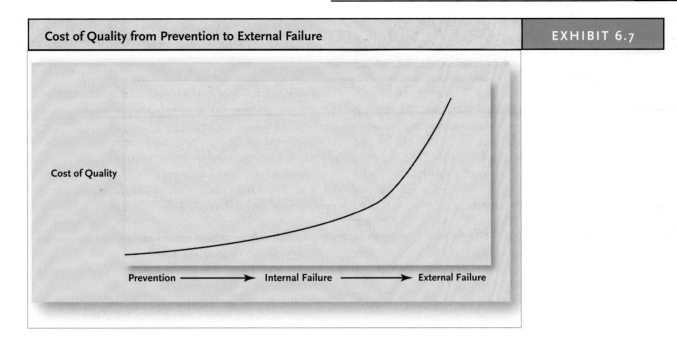

benefit of prevention is that even though the costs of total prevention might appear to be too great compared to the costs of appraisal and external and internal failure, prevention would eliminate many nonfinancial costs as well, including reduced market share, dissatisfied customers that switch to a competitor (known as defectors), and long-term impact on profitability. Exhibit 6.7 illustrates how quality costs increase as problems move externally.

It should not be a surprise that as companies expand prevention efforts, the total costs decline, resulting in an increase in profitability. In general, costs associated with poor quality increase the further along a product is in its process and as the poor quality gets closer to the customer. The earlier a defect is discovered, the lower its cost.

Quality and Customer Loyalty

We speak of value often: how value attributes are defined by the customer, how customers define it differently, and how they define it in terms of product and service characteristics that are most important to them. The product and service characteristics originate with inventory, capacity, facilities, and workforce. Customers may decide to buy products or services from us, but that doesn't mean they are excited about returning. In fact, next time they'll go through the same evaluation process to determine what to buy and maybe they'll buy from us, but maybe not. They're not loyal customers.

We don't want them to proceed with that evaluation. Instead, we want them to automatically return to us. That requires loyalty. How can a business get that level of commitment from its customers? Simply meeting customer expectations is not sufficient.

We all develop loyalties to some businesses. For example, I'm very loyal to my car mechanic. Why would I be loyal when sometimes I have to wait two weeks to get my car worked on? Because he does more than meet expectations. He has never let me down on a repair. He has never "not fixed" something. In fact, on several different occasions he concluded that nothing needed fixing and charged me nothing for the diagnosis. Plus, I like him. If I didn't like him, I wouldn't be loyal to him. I'm also loyal to some retailers. Those that get my loyalty have gone beyond providing good service. I can get their products from a dozen different places, maybe even at lower cost. I'm loyal to them because they give me advice and because it is fun to do business with them. They make money from me and I enjoy doing business with them, so it is a good relationship. We both benefit and that's what makes it successful.

om ADVANTAGE   Ski Resorts: Improving Customer Relationships When 85 Percent Never Return

Customer loyalty is important for all businesses, but particularly for the ski resort industry, which is engaged in a battle to improve customer relationships. The industry has been plagued with a lack of growth since 1978—about 50 million visitors per year, despite improved skis that are easier to control and the growth in snowboarding, which accounts for about 25 percent of those visits. (Without snowboarding there might well have been a substantial decline.) In fact, 85 percent of first-time skiers never return. No other business would tolerate such a low return rate. Some experts believe that the amount of planning, packing, traveling, and lifting of heavy ski gear makes a trip to a ski resort not only expensive, but too much work. The operations of ski resorts require vacationers to get up early and stand in lines for equipment rentals, lessons, lift tickets, lifts, and meals.

Intrawest Corp., owner of ski resorts at Stratton Mountain (Vermont), Whistler (British Columbia), Tremblant (Quebec), and Copper Mountain (Colorado), and others, hopes to improve profitability by boosting resort attendance. After studying a typical family preparing to visit an Intrawest resort and following them with a video camera while there, the company learned that their vacation was hectic and hard work. Results of the study included recommendations to provide pet-sitting services based on the family's inability to find a place for its dog to stay. In addition, the firm decided to offer large seasonal storage lockers, to eliminate much of the packing and transportation of equipment, and more child-oriented accommodations. One of the most significant findings was a need to make the experience more social, including communal dining, which had existed at many ski resorts, and a "village-centered" model.

The village-centered business model has proven to be successful for Intrawest. After its adoption, reservations grew at a 76 percent rate during the year from March 31, 2000, to March 31, 2001. Sales of property at resort sites grew as well. In the 90 days preceding July 1, 2001, Intrawest sold $233 million in property. Some 70 percent of the units offered for sale were sold. Prices per square foot were up 11 percent over the previous year.

Intrawest's "village" model has also been effective at attracting customers. With 10 mountains under its management, Intrawest has grown its clientele to over 8 million skiers per year. Its expansion into other leisure adventure activities includes 36 championship golf courses, exclusive beachside properties, and worldwide adventure travel.

Source: "In Pursuit of Hassle-Free Slopes," *Wall Street Journal*, March 16, 2001, pp. B1, B4; "Intrawest Reports an 18% Increase in Nine-Month Income from Continuing Operations," http://biz.yahoo.com/prnews/010710/va293.html, May 14, 2001; "Intrawest Sells Record US$233 Million in Real Estate in Past 90 Days" http://biz.yahoo.com/prnews/010710/va293.html, July 10, 2001; Intrawest Corp., www.intrawest.com/about-us/corporate-overview/index.htm, accessed February 16, 2006.

Customer Loyalty and Profitability

New-customer acquisition, which is the first phase of obtaining customers, is usually assigned to marketing. This is an expensive way to gain customers, because targeting can never be completely accurate. Businesses invariably invest in potential customers that never materialize. The value attributes used to persuade customers are limited, and price is often the most important. For services, the customer cannot be certain about any other value attributes before the service occurs. The customer must base the purchase decision on price along with a prediction, resting on other information, of what the experience will be. That information typically comes from a company spokesperson. Depending on the industry, costs of acquiring a new customer can range from 2 to 10 times as expensive as the cost of retaining a current one.

Customer retention efforts involve more people and more business functions than customer acquisition, and they create more opportunities to convince the customer to stay. Customer experience is the basis for retention efforts. The returning customer knows what the value attributes are if the company has delivered them in the past. As the customer becomes more loyal, retention costs decline.

The impact of customer retention on costs and revenues associated with that particular customer are obvious, but the cost of new-customer acquisition is reduced as well. Why? Because loyal customers become advocates and take on the role of company spokespersons. As the process repeats, new-customer acquisitions increase, but the cost of each new customer is reduced because of the effect of customer advocates. As information sources, customer advocates more reliably predict what the experience will be than would information obtained from a traditional company spokesperson. The advocate actually is a company spokesperson, but a more credible one, because of his or her perceived objectivity. The voice of company advocates is sometimes referred to as "buzz." Companies love to generate buzz, because it's believed to be more effective than advertisement and it costs much less.

The value of customer loyalty is quite convincing when industry-specific data are examined. A study commissioned for *Fortune* magazine showed that a 5 percent increase in loyalty in certain industries resulted in an average gain in life-time profits per customer of 73 percent.

If the retained customer has the potential to add profitability to the firm, certainly the lost customer can do the opposite. The lost customer creates a need to acquire another. The very disgruntled defector can create as much negative word of mouth as the advocate can create buzz.

Total Quality Management

One of the most popular approaches to establishing a culture committed to quality is total quality management (TQM). The framework provided by TQM provides goods and services that satisfy customers by meeting their expectations, but it also affects other components of value. How does this happen?

Product or service quality is an end to be measured and achieved, but TQM is a process. Some consider it to be a management philosophy; others consider it to be a business culture. Either way, TQM helps managers create a setting that embraces customer expectations as the most important consideration.

The TQM framework is based on three principles.[4] The first is **customer focus,** which means precisely what it says. The customer determines what quality is. The customer focus principle goes beyond our traditional view of the customer, however, by distinguishing between internal and external customers.

Every action in a business has a customer. A memo is generated for someone, and that person is an **internal customer.** Raw material inventory retrieved from a warehouse is retrieved for someone, and that person is an internal customer. Sick leave records are kept accurately for someone to access and use, and that person is an internal customer. If the quality needs of internal customers are not met, the firm cannot expect to meet the needs of external customers either. **External customers** are the consumers the business typically thinks of as "customers"—those who buy products and services. The external customer is the ultimate recipient of quality. Poor internal quality eventually makes its way to external customers.

Like other capabilities that add value, capabilities that contribute to internal and external value are often outsourced to provide the best possible outcomes.

The second principle is **continuous process improvement.** Improvement of service- and product-oriented production processes focuses on the elimination of variability. Variability is enemy number one of quality. If there is one overriding principle of obtaining outcomes that meet customer expectations, the elimination of variability would be it. TQM extends that objective even further, however, to make it never-ending. Reduction of variability is always desirable. If reduction is achieved, more reduction would be even better. Meeting customer expectations requires that the outcomes of processes be the same every time. Outcomes must also be predictable. To be predictable, they must be consistent, but a variable process is unpredictable. To eliminate variability, a variety of techniques are used to bring processes and work methods under control.

The third principle is **total involvement,** which is a culture that embraces the customer's view of quality in all aspects of the business. This requires a commitment at all levels of the firm, from the very top to the very bottom. All employees must have the knowledge, capabilities, and authority to improve processes. This extends upstream in

Before Marriott recruiters visit a college campus for interviews, they must complete the company's recruiter certification program.

customer focus
The first principle of total quality management, which dictates that the customer determines what quality is.

internal customer
An entity of a business that receives an output of some other part of the same business.

external customer
Consumers and businesses that buy products and services.

continuous process improvement
Ongoing improvement efforts for service-oriented and product-oriented production processes that focus on the elimination of variability.

total involvement
A commitment at all levels of the firm, from the very top to the very bottom.

EXHIBIT 6.8 | Resource Contributions to TQM

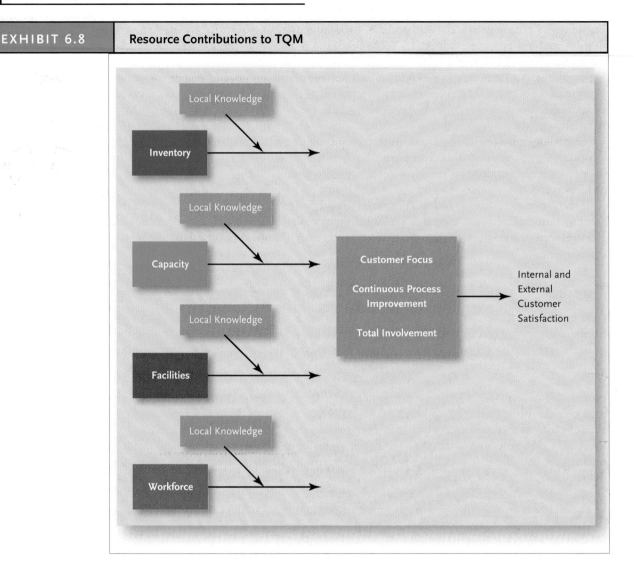

the supply chain to include suppliers and contractors as well. The "local knowledge" that exists among employees provides an excellent resource when tapped. The resultant improvements extend to all corners of the business.

As shown in Exhibit 6.8, in a TQM environment the business utilizes resources (inventory, capacity, facilities, and workforce) with the customer's needs as the top priority. The resources are managed within a priority system that emphasizes doing things right the first time.

An Enterprise View of Quality

TQM is an enterprise view of quality management that radiates from the top down; it doesn't just reside within the functional units. The complexities of quality management are demonstrated by the many different dimensions of quality presented earlier in Exhibit 6.3.

For the customer, the quality dimensions combine to form an overall impression that results in satisfaction or dissatisfaction. Each is important to varying degrees, depending on the nature of the product or service. For the business lacking a unifying structure, they may be viewed independently by different functions, but the customer doesn't view them independently. The dimensions of quality combine to provide an overall level of satisfaction with quality, which contributes to the overall perception of value. We know,

om ADVANTAGE TQM Results

Nelson Nameplates is a Los Angeles manufacturer of a variety of products, including nameplates and membrane switches that are used on electronic controls. Nelson was started in 1946 and has gone through a history of market and technology changes. It began its TQM effort in 1990 in response to management's desire to take a more proactive stance toward quality.

Traditionally, Nelson employees were reluctant to point out quality problems. Involvement with Philip Crosby Associates II, Inc., has resulted in numerous improvements in performance, including:

- Tripled revenue in 10 years.
- Fourfold drop in employee turnover.
- Threefold reduction in product returns.

- Improved quality at suppliers through Nelson's involvement.
- Achieved literacy in English for 100 employees (out of 300) who hadn't been English-literate through education.

A major component of Nelson's improvement process is the "error-cause removal" (ECR), in which employees identify causes of quality problems. More than 500 ECRs have been identified; more than 400 have been resolved.

During the 10-year effort, cost of quality dropped from 30 percent to 18 percent of sales.

Source: www.nelsonusa.com/about/index.htm, February 6, 2002; www.philipcrosby.com/main.htm, February 6, 2002.

however, that quality is not the only component of value. Since the customer doesn't view the quality dimensions independently, decisions that dictate them can't be made independently either. They are related and intertwined, despite the fact that each may be more closely linked to one particular business function than others. Ultimately, the customer makes a decision based on the *total* perceived value of the interaction.

Without TQM and without recognition of the internal customer, the desire to provide the best product or service quality to the external customer may fall short and lead to a less than optimal situation. Each business function can have a different perspective of what quality means. For example, marketing may place a very high priority on product and service features and options. Engineering may place a higher priority on conformance to specifications. Shipping may place the highest priority on meeting the promised delivery date. Each may be willing to sacrifice another criterion to improve its favorite. Their concept of the internal customer steps in. The recognition that tasks and processes serve other aspects of the business, and are of critical importance, provides a unifying framework that improves the total value package. The internal customer perspective results in improvements in all business processes, even those that do not directly serve the customer. As shown in Exhibit 6.9, these process improvements reduce costs. These improvements would not take place without the recognition of the importance of the internal customer.

The impact of quality on profitability is simple—as quality is enhanced, value is enhanced, increasing net sales. The impact of TQM is greater, however, because it includes internal customers. The recognition of internal customers implicit in TQM creates a closer relationship between quality and the other components of value. The result is a greater impact on value than could be had by merely improving quality solely for the external customer.

The TQM Process

This ongoing process of TQM requires more than the principles of customer focus, process improvement, and total involvement. A number of supportive approaches are used to adhere to these principles, including:

- Top management commitment.
- Employee involvement.

| EXHIBIT 6.9 | The Impact of Internal and External Customer Focus on Profitability |

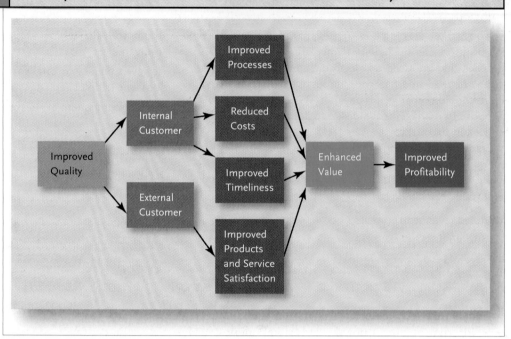

- Employee training and development.
- Reward and recognition.
- Measurement.
- A framework for using quality tools.

Exhibit 6.10 shows how the three principles of TQM are supported by these approaches.
Top management commitment has often been cited as a missing component in failed
TQM implementations. Without top management commitment, other priorities take

| EXHIBIT 6.10 | Supportive Approaches to Three Principles of Quality |

Top Management Commitment

Employee Involvement

Training and Development

Reward and Recognition

Measurement

Customer Focus

Continuous Process Improvement

Total Involvement

precedence. The TQM effort dies quickly as employees notice that management doesn't give it top priority. It doesn't take long for employees to abandon the principles when it is obvious to them that top management doesn't follow them. Employee involvement improves processes that affect internal and external customers. Local knowledge is valuable in improving these processes. Process and quality improvement teams are universal in TQM environments. To support employee involvement, training and development are crucial. The processes and analyses to solve quality problems are not simplistic. Most employees need training and practice in using these techniques. The expectation that employees are involved in the TQM process must be included in the company's reward and recognition systems.

The continuous improvement effort driven by TQM is not a haphazard "let's change things and see what happens" type of environment. Improvement can come only from the recognition of problems, and problems can be recognized and verified only from objective data. Obtaining the data requires a well-developed measurement system. Accurate measurement is a prerequisite to making decisions related to improvement. Without accurate measurement, problems can't be identified and solutions can't be generated and tested to see if they actually worked.

Not surprisingly, instituting a cycle of continuous improvement of processes and a continuous effort to find and eliminate problems affecting internal and external customers is not easy. It requires an organizing structure such as those examined in the following section.

Obtaining Continuous Improvement

The Plan, Do, Check, Act Cycle

The most frequently used framework for guiding improvement is Shewhart's Plan, Do, Check, Act (PDCA) cycle, presented in Exhibit 6.11. The PDCA cycle creates a structure for the continuous improvement process that reinforces the use of data in making decisions.

In 2006, Marriott projects that its owners and franchisees will invest over $5 billion in property improvements.

The first stage of the PDCA cycle, Plan, is probably the most difficult. Three important tasks are completed in the Plan stage. The first task is problem identification and validation. This is potentially the most important of all improvement tasks, because if it is not done correctly, there will be no improvement *and* a tremendous amount of time will have been wasted. Problem identification should be an obvious first step, but it must include validation. Problem validation means confirmation that the problem is a concern and does, in fact, exist.

The second task within the Plan stage is to gain a thorough understanding of the current situation. An understanding of the problem, how it affects other aspects of the business, and how it is affected by other aspects of the business establishes direction for the improvement process.

Shewhart's PDCA Cycle	EXHIBIT 6.11

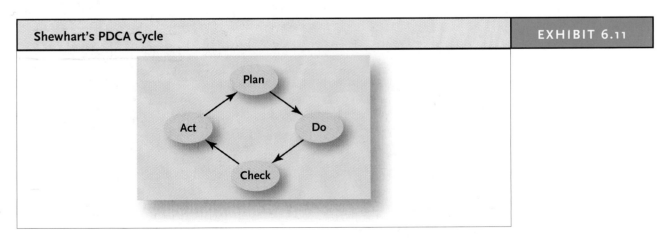

The third task associated with the Plan stage is the analysis of causes. Identifying root causes for any problem is always challenging. Since apparent causes are often symptoms of deeper causes, the challenge is to "peel the onion," so that the root cause is what is ultimately attacked. Figuring out what the problem is, understanding it, and identifying the cause summarizes the work to be done in the Plan stage. No wonder it is the most difficult to accomplish.

The Do stage is pretty straightforward when compared to its predecessor. The Do stage requires that the corrective action or proposed solution to the problem be implemented. That's it. If it's a process improvement, the change is made. If it's the elimination of the cause of some other problem, the action is taken to eliminate the cause.

The Check stage is also straightforward. After the Do stage is complete and a change has been made, the role of the Check stage is to see if that change has had the desired result. Did the change actually improve the process? Did it eliminate the cause of the problem? Is the problem gone? Like the problem identification and validation task, checking the results requires data and measurements.

The Act stage is where the improvement becomes enterprisewide. If the Check stage verified that the change had the desired impact, the first step in the Act stage is to standardize the change throughout the business. Thus, if a process change resulted in an improvement, that change should become part of the standard operating procedures for similar processes throughout the organization. If the action eliminated a problem, that action should become a standard operating procedure everywhere else as well. The second step in the Act stage is to bring the effort to its conclusion and then go back to the Plan stage to identify a new focus. Depending on the organization, concluding the cycle may require that a report be created or a presentation to management be made.

The Quality Improvement Story

Defining the PDCA cycle in terms of the seven steps just described has created an improvement process that is virtually universal with TQM-oriented firms. The seven steps have become known as the Quality Improvement (QI) story.[5] Exhibit 6.12 shows the QI story as it relates to the PDCA cycle.

EXHIBIT 6.12	PDCA Cycle and QI Story

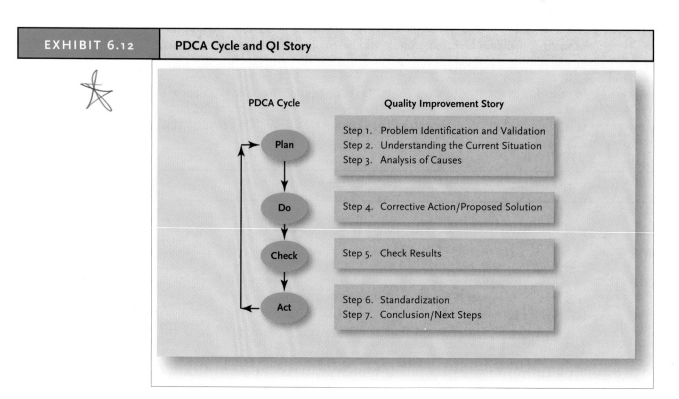

om ADVANTAGE   Standardizing Election Processes

The TQM focus on systems, standards, and elimination of variability provides interesting insights on the 2000 U.S. presidential election, which resulted in chaos from misinterpreted ballots, miscounted ballots, malfunctioning machines, and resulting uncertainty. Who better to examine what went wrong than the American Society for Quality (ASQ)? An examination of the areas for improvement reveals several obvious conditions causing quality problems.

First, and probably one of the most important characteristics, is the lack of standardized systems. For example, there are between 4,000 and 5,000 separate jurisdictions, with some jurisdictions having more than 100 precincts. Although strict procedures are in place, they vary from one jurisdiction to the next.

Second, the equipment and technology used in about one-third of the precincts is up to 40 years old. Punchcard equipment that is worn, in ill repair, and inconsistent in function provides opportunity for variability and poor quality. In addition to the lack of standardized processes and old equipment, standards and procedures related to ballot counting vary among precincts.

ASQ recommends five steps for improving the process:

1. Define what constitutes quality in the voting process.

2. Seek relevant and reliable data.

3. Examine all processes systematically.

4. Standardize election processes wherever possible.

5. Develop the will to improve continuously and to apply needed resources to the task.

Source: American Society for Quality, "Election Reform," www.asq.org/news/election/fix.html, March 7, 2002. Used by permission.

The popularity of the QI story, particularly with employee quality and productivity improvement teams, has established it as the standard process used throughout many TQM environments. Employees, however, must be able to accomplish its seven steps in order for it to be effective. The seven steps in the QI story are accomplished with the help of a variety of tools that enhance the ability to present and understand data. These tools are described in detail in Chapter 7.

Six Sigma

As companies developed the means to reduce variability to be almost nonexistent, the phrase "Six Sigma" became common to refer to very tight control over processes. Taken literally, it means that the company had reduced variability to the point that six standard deviations of variability on each side of the mean were inside of the customer's specifications. This will be addressed in greater detail in the following chapter, but suffice it to say that this results in only 3.4 defects per million opportunities, or put another way, defect-free 99.99966 percent of the time. Six Sigma has come to mean more than just the number of defects. It also refers to a methodology used to obtain that level of control and an overall philosophy for managing the business, which can be described as an evolutionary step for TQM. The "metrics" aspect of Six Sigma, as well as methodologies associated with it, will be discussed in Chapter 7. The philosophy and organizational structure will be discussed in the following sections.

Six Sigma, promoted early in its history by Motorola and General Electric, has come to be defined as the implementation of a measurement-based strategy that focuses on process improvement and variation reduction. Six Sigma does not set up a distinct quality management "silo" in the organization, as has often been the case with other quality improvement approaches. Six Sigma places quality responsibilities and training throughout the organization.

Six Sigma Methodologies

Two dominant processes are used to structure Six Sigma improvement projects. The first—define, measure, analyze, improve, and control (DMAIC)—is used to structure the improvement efforts for existing processes that are not performing as well as desired. The second—define, measure, analyze, design, verify (DMADV)—is used to guide the development of new products and services so that they meet Six Sigma quality levels. An overview of each of these processes is provided in Exhibit 6.13.

Six Sigma improves the quality of existing products and processes by applying the DMAIC process in improvement projects. The ability to successfully complete those projects depends on the skill and training provided to the employees as a part of the Six Sigma structure, described in the next section. New products and processes are designed using the DMADV process, which designs Six Sigma–level quality into those products and processes.

Product quality starts at the design stage. For how many years have traditional paint cans frustrated users because of the difficulty of holding, pouring, and reclosing? Dutch Boy attacked these problems head on with a product design that meets customer needs.

Implicit in Six Sigma is an ongoing effort to eliminate variability. General Electric, arguably as committed to Six Sigma as any other company, puts this issue quite succinctly when it states, "Customers feel the variance, not the mean."[7] GE identifies three key elements of quality: the customer, the process, and the employee. GE focuses on delighting

EXHIBIT 6.13	DMAIC and DMADV Processes
DMAIC	
Define	Define project objectives, internal and external customers.
Measure	Measure current level of performance.
Analyze	Determine causes of current problems.
Improve	Identify how the process can be improved to eliminate the problems.
Control	Develop mechanisms for controlling the improved process.
DMADV	
Define	Define project objectives, internal and external customers.
Measure	Measure current level of performance.
Analyze	Analyze the processes necessary to meet the customer expectations.
Design	Design the new product or service.
Verify	Determine whether the new design is effective.

Six Sigma Hierarchy		EXHIBIT 6.14
Title	**Role**	
Executive Leader	High-level executive supporter of Six Sigma.	
Champion	Provider of resources for Six Sigma projects. Oversees master black belts. Selects projects.	
Master Black Belt	Resource for black belts. Expertise in mathematical tools. Helps select projects.	
Black Belt	Six Sigma involvement full time. Leads Six Sigma processes.	
Green Belt	Project leader. Supports black belt in the DMAIC process.	

the customer, because it is the customer that defines exactly what quality is for every attribute that influences their perception. GE believes in examining the process from the customer's perspective, or "outside-in." This perspective enables GE to add value and improvement that meet customer needs. All GE employees are trained in Six Sigma strategy, tools, and techniques.

Six Sigma Training and Hierarchy

GE starts its employee training program with basic Six Sigma awareness. That is followed by training in the tools necessary to participate in Six Sigma teams and assist with Six Sigma projects. In-depth training that includes the use of statistical tools, change processes, and flow technology tools follows the hierarchy of green belt, black belt, and master black belt.

Six Sigma project responsibilities are structured by its hierarchy for training and assignment of responsibilities. That hierarchy consists of executives, champions, master black belts, black belts, and green belts. An overview of the role of each position is shown in Exhibit 6.14. Advanced training includes the use of statistical tools for new product and process design.

The Six Sigma hierarchy provides a structure that allows participants to advance in training and expertise, which allows them to increase their responsibilities in Six Sigma projects and their role in the organization's Six Sigma program.

Benchmarking

Improvement efforts are often better received and more successful if there is a goal or objective to strive for. This is true for quality improvement efforts as well as business process improvements that would benefit only internal customers. One way to identify goals is to identify "best practices" through a process known as **benchmarking.** Two different types of benchmark are commonly used. The first type, **industry-focused benchmarking,** seeks to identify the best practices among competitors. One of the more difficult aspects of benchmarking is identifying processes to benchmark. Numerous benchmarking services have evolved to aid companies seeking benchmarking information.

The house of quality, introduced in Chapter 4 as a part of the quality function deployment process, is often used to link product and service design to customer needs and requires industry-focused benchmarks in two places. It is reproduced from Chapter 4 here as Exhibit 6.15. Near the bottom of the house is a space for "Competitive Evaluation." This requires that target relationships for measures be compared to those of the competition. On the right side is the "Competitive Evaluation of WHAT/HOW Relationships." Both of these competitive evaluations rely on best-practice data about competitors obtained through benchmarking.

benchmarking
Identification of best practices of other companies.

industry-focused benchmarking
The identification of the best practices among competitors.

EXHIBIT 6.15   House of Quality

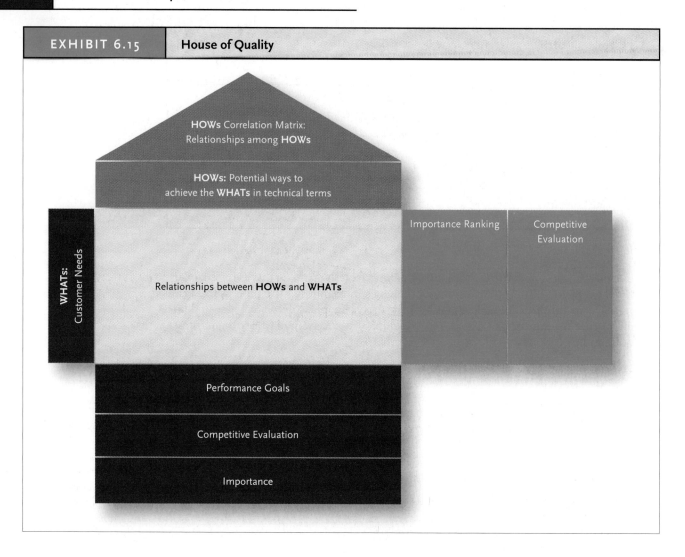

HOWs Correlation Matrix:
Relationships among HOWs

HOWs: Potential ways to
achieve the WHATs in technical terms

WHATs:
Customer Needs

Importance Ranking

Competitive
Evaluation

Relationships between HOWs and WHATs

Performance Goals

Competitive Evaluation

Importance

EXHIBIT 6.16   Industry-Focused Benchmarking Organizations

Airlines	Financial services	Not-for-profit
Airports	Government	Oil and gas
Aerospace	Health care	Petrochemical
Automotive	Higher education	Pharmaceutical
Banking	Hospitality	Retail
Broadcasting	Insurance	Retention
Cable and satellite television	Internet	Software
Computer hardware	ISP	Sports
manufacturing	Magazine	Telecommunications
Defense	Manufacturing	Transportation
Electric utility	Natural gas	Water utility
Energy	Newspapers	Wireless

The Internet has made it much easier to identify benchmarks through a variety of industry-focused organizations to show how pervasive this practice has become; Exhibit 6.16 lists industry-focused benchmarking organizations available on the Internet.

Process-Focused Benchmarking Organizations		EXHIBIT 6.17
Agile manufacturing B2B B2C Call center management Customer satisfaction Customer service Distribution and logistics Facilities and real estate Global operations	Inventory management Lean manufacturing Procurement and supply chain management Process management Product development Relationship management Six sigma	

The second type of benchmarking, known as **process-focused benchmarking,** is used when a business wants to identify a best practice for a process that is not industry specific. Many business processes are generic. For example, the way phone centers are managed for mail order retailers is similar no matter what the product. The operation of warehouses is similar from one industry to the next. Process-focused benchmarking provides a way for companies to identify best practices that are world class, even if no competitor has a good system in place. It is usually easier to get access to benchmarking partners for process-focused benchmarking, because there is no competitive advantage to be lost by sharing that information. Many of the processes closely related to operations management are selected for process-focused benchmarking because of their impact on quality. Many organizations offering members access to best practices for specific business processes have been formed. Exhibit 6.17 lists operations-related processes that are now such popular benchmarking targets that they have organizations devoted specifically to them.

process-focused benchmarking Benchmarking that focuses on similar processes of other companies, but those companies need not be competitors or even in the same industry.

The Kano Model

The **Kano model** is based on the work of a Japanese consultant, Noriaki Kano.[8] It proposes that there are actually three important levels of quality characteristics for customers. The first level is considered to be a "must-be." In other words, the characteristic

Kano model A business model that proposes that there are actually three important levels of quality characteristics for customers: must-be, one-dimensional, and delighters.

---

om ADVANTAGE Benchmarking Extends beyond For-Profit Business

Benchmarking, whether it be industry-focused or process-focused, is an attempt to learn from those who do it better, and apply it. It doesn't, however, have to be applied in a competitive, for-profit setting. The Greater Chicago Food Depository has used benchmarking to improve the efficiency of the processes it uses so that poor Chicagoans receive the maximum benefits possible.

The Greater Chicago Food Depository supplies food to more than 300,000 people through 600 different agencies. In 2002–2003 it processed more than 42 million pounds of food—over 87,000 meals per day. Daily consumption can be over 3,000 pounds of dairy products, over 50,000 pounds of produce, and over 18,000 pounds of meat. What better benchmarking model for improving the logistics associated with these volumes than Wal-Mart. Instead of just filling the warehouse with whatever was available, the food depository now has alliances with a consistent set of suppliers for staples

like bread, pasta, and peanut butter. Manufacturers like Kraft Foods, Con-Agra, Sara Lee, and Quaker Oats and retailers like Dominick's Finer Foods and Jewel-Osco, as well as restaurants, provide food. All food is sorted, packaged, and made available to shelters, kitchens, and pantries. The warehouse is efficient and well organized, and pallets are packed in advance for pickup.

Financial analysis shows the program to be extremely efficient—one of the most efficient charities in the country. For every dollar donated, the depository distributes enough food for four meals. Ninety-three percent of its expenses go directly to support food programs.

Source: C. Lake, "The Wal-Mart of Food Banks," *Fast Company*, September 2003, p. 42; www.chicagosfoodbank.org/factsheets/03_FactSheet.pdf, May 20, 2004.

has to be present for the product to be considered on the list as a possible alternative to purchase. The customer expects to find these characteristics and so is not particularly impressed when they are present. They are generally taken for granted. When these characteristics are not present, however, the customer will be very dissatisfied. An example is the availability of ATM access for a bank. It's expected, but not enough to win new customers.

The second level of characteristics covers "one-dimensional" characteristics. They are the characteristics that the customer looks for. The more products and services possess these characteristics and the better the performance on these characteristics, the more impressed the customer is. These are most frequently the characteristics that will separate a product or service from a competitor's. Examples are the friendliness of a bank's staff and the attractiveness of its lobby.

The third level of characteristics is known as exciting characteristics, or "delighters." They are a pleasant surprise to the customer. The customer doesn't expect them or look for them because he or she is unaware that they exist. These characteristics almost always set a product or service apart from its competition. Delighting characteristics do not remain delighters for long, however. They soon become expected, and competitors copy them if possible. An example of this type of characteristic is the rear seat system on the Honda Odyssey van, which allows the seat to disappear completely into the floor. Most customers were very surprised at this feature when it first came out. Over time, however, it has become expected, and competitors have been forced to provide something comparable. The Kano model offers a framework for moving customers beyond the point of being satisfied to being delighted with the quality.

Quality Improvement Frameworks: Awards and Certification

The challenge of building a stronger focus on product or service quality is a daunting one for any business. Issues are varied and complex. Unexpected consequences of decisions are common. In order to provide guidance and a tested method for improving quality, many companies have used the structured processes of applying for a quality award or quality certification. The most commonly sought certification is the ISO 9000 series, originally developed by the International Standards Organization. The most famous quality award is the Malcolm Baldrige National Quality Award. Each is discussed in detail in the following sections. The goal in each case is not the end result, but the gains made by going through the required processes.

The ISO 9000 Quality Certification Program

For many companies, particularly those that interact globally, quality certification has become a mandatory way of doing business. The most popular certification program is ISO 9000. As originally designed by the International Standards Organization, ISO 9000 was a series of five universal standards for quality assurance systems. It has been widely accepted and respected around the world and has been adopted by over 90 countries as the national standard. The ISO 9000 standards do not specify a level of product or service quality. Instead, they specify a set of quality assurance systems that must be in place. By requiring quality systems, they ensure that the certified company has the infrastructure, knowledge, and capability to produce quality products and services. The standards are identical for all companies, no matter what size or industry. The standards have been popular because customers can be confident that their suppliers have quality assurance systems in place. When the company gets certified, new markets open up. For U.S. companies doing business internationally, ISO 9000 certification is virtually required.

The ISO 9000 standards are developed and monitored by the International Standards Organization. The National Institute for Standards and Technology is the U.S. representative on that organization. The U.S. version of the ISO 9000 standards was developed by the American National Standards Institute (ANSI). The original five components of the ISO 9000 series of standards are presented in Exhibit 6.18.

ISO certification has become a hallmark in many industries. Although it doesn't guarantee product quality for automotive parts suppliers, it provides proof that quality systems are in place. Here, DaimlerChrysler advertises its ISO certification.

Original ISO 9000 Standards	EXHIBIT 6.18

ISO 9000:	Quality management and quality assurance standards.
	Part 1: Guidelines for selection and use.
	Part 2: Generic guidelines for the application of ISO 9000, ISO 9002, and ISO 9003.
	Part 3: Guidelines for the application of ISO 9001 to the development, supply, and maintenance of software.
	Part 4: Guide to dependability program management.
ISO 9001:	Quality system-model for quality assurance in design, development, production, installation, and servicing.
ISO 9002:	Quality system-model for quality assurance in production, installation, and servicing.
ISO 9003:	Quality system-model for quality assurance in final inspection and test.
ISO 9004:	Development of quality management systems.

The ISO 9000 standards received a major overhaul in 2000, resulting in the discontinuation of ISO 9002 and ISO 9003. In addition, ISO 9001 was replaced with one standard: ISO 9000 2000. The very complex 20-section set of requirements was reorganized into a more logical five sections. The original ISO 9000 standards had been criticized because they did not mandate continuous improvement or any level of actual product or service quality. Both criticisms were valid. The new ISO 9000 2000 standards are much more customer-oriented and address customer satisfaction in greater detail. In addition, the new standards mandate communication with customers and measurement of customer satisfaction. The ISO 9000 2000 standard also emphasizes continuous improvement. While the old standards implicitly expected organizations to make improvements, the new standard makes that requirement explicit. The standard now requires evaluation of the effectiveness of the quality management system and systematic improvement of that system. New requirements and modifications to old ones have definitely changed the tone of the standards. Terminology was changed as well, to make the standards more understandable. Exhibit 6.19 summarizes the requirements that were modified or changed. The nature of these changes shows the new emphases of the standards.

EXHIBIT 6.19	Summary of Changed and Modified Criteria in ISO 9000 2000

Communicate with customers.

Evaluate the effectiveness of quality management system.

Evaluate the effectiveness of training.

Evaluate the suitability of quality management system.

Identify customer requirements.

Identify quality management system improvements.

Improve quality management system.

Meet customer requirements.

Meet regulatory requirements.

Meet statutory requirements.

Monitor and measure customer satisfaction.

Monitor and measure processes.

Provide quality infrastructure.

Provide a quality work environment.

Support internal communication.

In both 2005 and 2006 Marriott was recognized as the U.S. Environmental Protection Agency Energy Star "Partner of the Year" for reducing electric energy consumption and greenhouse gas emissions by 64,000 tons annually.

Just as the ISO 9000 series requires quality management systems, its counterpart ISO 14000 requires environmental management systems. The requirements of ISO 14000 guide organizations in formulating policies that take into account environmental impact legislation. Just as ISO 9000 doesn't specify quality performance criteria, ISO 14000 doesn't specify environmental performance. It applies to the environmental aspects that business can control.

The Malcolm Baldrige National Quality Award

The Malcolm Baldrige National Quality Improvement Act was signed into law in 1987. Its award, managed by the U.S. Department of Commerce, is intended to increase the awareness of quality as an important component of competitiveness, to share information about successes, and to promote understanding of the requirements for quality. It accomplishes these objectives by publicizing and increasing public awareness of successes achieved by the winners of the award. No more than two awards can be given annually in each of five categories. The categories originally were manufacturing companies and their subsidiaries, service companies and their subsidiaries, and small businesses. In 1998 categories for educational and health care organizations were added.

The Baldrige program and award framework comprise an excellent structure for developing a quality-driven organization. This has become a popular means of improving quality, even for organizations not intending to apply for the award. The Baldrige award embraces the following values:[9]

- Visionary leadership
- Customer-driven excellence
- Organizational and personal learning
- Valuing employees and partners
- Agility
- Focus on the future
- Managing for innovation

- Management by fact
- Focus on results and value creation
- Systems perspective
- Public responsibility and citizenship

These values are translated into seven categories of award criteria:

- Leadership
- Strategic planning
- Customer and market focus
- Information and analysis
- Human resource focus
- Process management
- Business results

The model used to illustrate how these categories fit together is presented in Exhibit 6.20.

| Malcolm Baldrige National Quality Award | EXHIBIT 6.20 |

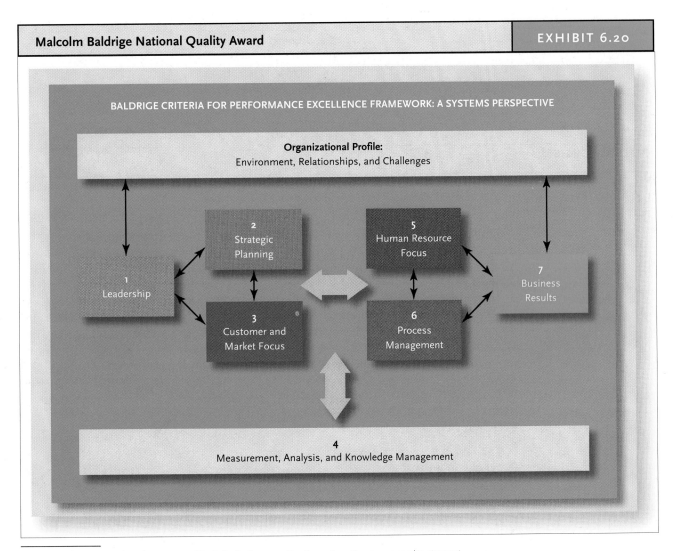

Source: "Baldrige National Quality Program Criteria for Performance Excellence," 2006, p. 5, www.quality.nist.gov/.

	EXHIBIT 6.21	Baldrige Award Criteria and Scoring Summary	

Criterion	Total Points	Item	Item Point Value
Leadership	120	Senior leadership	70
		Governance and social responsibility	50
Strategic planning	85	Strategy development	40
		Strategy deployment	45
Customer and market focus	85	Customer and market knowledge	40
		Customer relationships and satisfaction	45
Information and analysis	90	Measurement, analysis, and review of organizational performance	50
		Information and knowledge management	40
Human resource focus	85	Work systems	25
		Employee learning and motivation	25
		Employee well-being and satisfaction	25
Process management	85	Value creation processes	45
		Support processes and operational planning	40
Business results	450	Product and service outcomes	100
		Customer-focused results	70
		Financial and market results	70
		Human resource results	70
		Organizational effectiveness results	70
		Leadership and social responsibility outcomes	70
TOTAL POINTS	**1,000**		

Exhibit 6.21 provides an overview of the way the award criteria are scored. Each item is scored based on points for the approach and deployment of the item and points for the actual results. The maximum total score is 1,000. Exhibit 6.22 lists recent award winners.

In addition to the Baldrige National Quality Award, most states have implemented quality award programs that encourage businesses to seek quality reputations. There are also numerous industry-specific quality awards. One prestigious award, the Quality Cup, is a national award that focuses on the accomplishments of teams. The Quality Cup is awarded to up to three teams per year in each of the following categories:

- Education
- Government
- Health care
- Manufacturing industry
- Service industry
- Small businesses (fewer than 500 employees)

Baldrige Award Winners				EXHIBIT 6.22

Year	Manufacturing	Service	Small Business	Health Care	Education
1997	3M Dental Products Division Solectron Corporation	Merrill Lynch Credit Corporation Xerox Business Services			
1998	Boeing Airlift and Tanker Programs Solar Turbines Incorporated		Texas Nameplate Company, Inc.		
1999	STMicroelectronics, Inc.—Region Americas	BI Ritz-Carlton Hotel Company, L.L.C.	Sunny Fresh Food		
2000	Dana Corporation— Spicer Driveshaft Division KARLEE Company, Inc.	Operations Management International, Inc.	Los Alamos National Bank		
2001	Clarke American Checks, Inc.		Pal's Sudden Service		Pearl River School District University of Wisconsin–Stout Chugach School District
2002	Motorola Commercial, Government & Industrial Solutions Sector		Branch-Smith Printing Division	SSM Health Care	
2003	Medrad, Inc.	Caterpillar Financial Services Corporation U.S. Boeing Aerospace Support	Stoner, Inc.	Baptist Hospital, Inc. Saint Luke's Hospital of Kansas City	Community Consolidated School District 15
2004	The Bama Companies, Inc.		Texas Nameplate Company, Inc.	Robert Wood Johnson University Hospital Hamilton	Kenneth W. Monfort College of Business
2005	Sunny Fresh Foods, Inc.	DynMcDermott Petroleum Operations	Park Place Lexus	Richland College Jenks Public Schools	Bronson Methodist Hospital

CHAPTER SUMMARY

The quality of products and services has come to dominate the competitive efforts of businesses. This chapter has provided an overview of several approaches to managing quality. Included in that discussion were two broad frameworks—total quality management and Six Sigma—as well as other approaches. TQM and Six Sigma focus on continuous improvement and their reliance on quality tools and performance measurement to create a culture of quality-mindedness. That culture, when it permeates the business, creates a focus on internal *and* external quality and provides benefits beyond those obtained from simply producing high-quality outputs. It creates enhancements to processes and capabilities, costs, and timeliness as well. As we know, process quality improvement, when combined with product and service quality, enhances the entire value package. This increase in value translates into improved levels of profitability and overall improvements in financial measures for the business.

KEY TERMS

aesthetics, 198
appraisal costs, 205
assurance, 198
benchmarking, 217
continuous process improvement, 209
cost of quality (COQ), 203
customer focus, 209
durability, 198
empathy, 198
external customer, 209
external failure cost, 203
feature, 196
industry-focused benchmarking, 217

internal customer, 209
Kano model, 219
performance, 196
prevention costs, 206
process-focused benchmarking, 217
recovery, 204
reliability, 198
reputation, 198
responsiveness, 198
serviceability, 198
tangibles, 198
testing, 206
total involvement, 209

REVIEW QUESTIONS

1. Describe the impact of the four major contributors to TQM.
2. Why is recognizing internal customers so critical to TQM?
3. Explain the importance of eliminating variability in a TQM environment.
4. What role does total involvement play in creating a culture supportive of TQM?
5. Describe the following dimensions of quality:
   a. Performance
   b. Reliability
   c. Serviceability
   d. Responsiveness
   e. Features
   f. Durability
   g. Aesthetics
   h. Reputation
6. What is the role of an advocate for a company?
7. How does TQM enhance the value components of cost and timeliness?

8. Describe the PDCA cycle. How does it relate to the Quality Improvement story?

9. Why is a step-by-step process like the QI story important in accomplishing objectives?

10. Describe the two processes used to structure Six Sigma projects.

11. What are the two different types of benchmarking? How are they used?

12. What role have quality certification programs had in improving quality?

13. What is ISO 9000? Why would a company be interested in getting ISO 9000–certified?

14. Why do award programs like the Malcolm Baldrige Quality Award get criticized?

15. Why must TQM be a commitment that crosses departmental boundaries?

16. Describe the criteria of the Baldrige Award.

DISCUSSION AND EXPLORATION

1. From your work experiences, identify instances where you or your colleagues ignored an internal customer and it resulted in poor quality for the external customer.

2. Describe a business for which you consider yourself an advocate. Why are you an advocate for the business? What does it do that has resulted in it gaining your loyalty? What behaviors would cause you to abandon your loyalty?

3. Identify a recent incident in which you received poor-quality service. Describe what happened. What would have prevented the poor-quality service? What would have been the costs associated with preventing it?

4. How does the increasing emphasis on effective supply chain management change the focus on quality management? How does the concept of a "quality culture" change as one changes the perspective from a company's culture to the culture of the entire supply chain?

5. Suppose, after you graduate, you accept a managerial position for a large bank. The Director of Operations asks you to prepare a presentation to convince branch presidents that a proactive (preventive) approach to quality will be better in the long run than reacting to poor quality after it happens. Branch presidents have expressed concerns about prevention costs. What would you say to them?

6. When interviewing potential employees, Marriott has been said to ask the candidates how often they wash their hands. Why might they ask this question? What other questions might they ask to identify potential employees who will support their emphasis on quality service?

7. Identify a service or process on campus that you feel isn't as quality-oriented as it should be. Use Six Sigma's DMAIC process to develop a strategy for improving it.

8. Can company culture alone, with no knowledge of methods or techniques, succeed in improving product and service quality? Explain your answer.

ENDNOTES

1. D. A. Garvin, "What Does Product Quality Really Mean? *Sloan Management Review* 26 (Fall 1984), pp. 25–34; P. E. Pisek, "Defining Quality at the Marketing/ Development Interface," *Quality Progress* 20 (June 1987), pp. 28–36.

2. V. Parasuraman, V. A. Zeithaml, and L. L. Berry, "A Conceptual Model of Service Quality and Its Implications for Future Research," *Journal of Marketing* 49 (Fall 1985), p. 48.

3. "Nissan: The Squeaks Get Louder," *BusinessWeek Online*, May 17, 2004.

4. Adapted from A. R. Tenner and I. J. De Toro, *Total Quality Management* (Reading, MA: Addison-Wesley, 1992).

5. GOAL/QPC, *Total Quality Control in Japan*, Research Report no. 89-10-10 (Metheun, MA: Author, 1989).

6. Isixsigma, www.isixsigma.com/sixsigma/six_sigma.asp, May 19, 2004.

7. General Electric Comp., www.ge.com/sixsigma/sixsigstrategy.html, accessed February 21, 2006.

8. L. Cohen, *Quality Function Deployment* (Reading, MA: Addison-Wesley, 1995), pp. 36–40.

9. Business Criteria for Performance Excellence, www.quality.nist.gov/Criteria.htm, March 20, 2002.

LEARNING ACTIVITIES

www.mhhe.com/opsnow3e

Visit the Online Learning Center (www.mhhe.com/opsnow3e) for additional resources. Content varies by chapter, and includes

- Business Tours
- OM on Site
- Readings
- Resources
- Excel Tutors
- Interactive Case Models
- Reel Operations Video Clips
- Additional Advanced Problems
- Self-Assessment Quizzes
- Glossary

SELECTED REFERENCES

Aguayo, R. *Dr. Deming: The American Who Taught the Japanese about Quality.* New York: Simon & Schuster, 1991.

Crosby, P. *Quality Is Free.* New York: McGraw-Hill, 1979.

Juran, J. M. *Juran on Planning for Quality.* New York: Free Press, 1988.

Pande, P. S., Neuman, R. P., and Cavanagh, R. R. *The Six Sigma Way: How GE, Motorola, and Other Top Companies Are Honing Their Performance,* New York: McGraw-Hill, 2000.

Phillips-Donaldson, D. "Quality Gurus: One Hundred Years of Juran." *Quality Progress,* May 2004.

Tenner, A. R., and DeToro, I. J. *Total Quality Management.* Reading, MA: Addison-Wesley, 1992.

Manufacturing Quality at Honda

Based on Video 7 on the Student DVD

Honda was the first Japanese auto manufacturer to produce cars in the United States. At that time there was much skepticism as to whether U.S. workers could adapt to the Japanese emphasis on high quality. Honda has succeeded in the United States, and other Japanese auto manufacturers have followed.

1. At Honda, why is it so important to plan ahead, as much as five years, for quality of vehicle models? How is the design process related to quality management?
2. What is the role of the PDCA cycle at Honda? Describe what Honda does at each of the four steps in the process.
3. Why does Honda produce new and old models simultaneously? How does that practice fit into the PDCA cycle?
4. What is "quality fatigue"? How does Honda address it in its plant?

A Day in the Life of Quality at Honda

Based on Video 8 on the Student DVD

Systems as complex as automobiles require constant vigilance to identify problems and develop ways to prevent them from reoccurring. Honda's highly trained employees and lack of inventory contribute to the rapid detection of quality issues.

1. What role do Honda's QAC meetings have in the PDCA cycle? Why is it important for one shift to communicate with another?
2. Honda prides itself on a proactive approach to dealing with quality. Describe the issue with the trunk seal. How was Honda's handling of that issue proactive? What did they do that was reactive?
3. What data was going to be collected by the sorter of the trunk seals? How might that data be used to proactively deal with the problem?

Dealing with an Angry Customer

The following three letters provide the documentation for circumstances surrounding an angry customer. The first letter was sent by the customer to the CEO of a large car dealership. The second is a short memo from the CEO to the service manager. The third letter is the service manager's response back to the CEO.

Letter 1

Tom Hartwell
3738 Stoney Rd.
Riley, OH

Chief Executive
Quality Motors
Cincinnati, OH

Dear Sir:

I realize that this letter is long and you may be tempted to trash it now, but I would encourage you to read about how one of your customers was treated in your business.

My wife and I own one of your cars with 65k miles on it. The car has had a chronic problem with the accelerator sticking at about 1900 RPMs when decelerating at a stop sign. This was serviced by the dealer on Kemper Rd, but after a week or so, the problem was back. We decided to bring the car to Quality Motors to see if they were any better at servicing. This is what happened.

I made an appointment for Tuesday, November 15. I was to drop the car off Monday evening. Since I had a doctor's appointment, my wife and I arranged to meet at your dealership at 5:00. Unfortunately, my wife arrived about 10 minutes before I did. She was told that I had no such appointment and sent away. It seems that Cindy Rice, with whom the appointment was made, was not there and no one considered looking at her appointment book. When I arrived 10 minutes later, I was told that my wife and 2 children (ages 3 and 4) had been sent away. After waiting approximately 20 minutes, my wife called from the Kemper Road dealer. She had driven across town to that dealership to see if there had been a misunderstanding between us. She then drove back across town, in 5:00 traffic, to pick me up at your shop.

We left the car with several instructions. It was to be tuned up, the high RPM problem fixed, the dome light fixed, and a brake light replaced. I received a call the next day informing me that, in addition to a regular tune-up, the car needed new spark plugs, new spark plug wires, a new distributor cap, and a new coil before the RPM problem could be diagnosed by the computer. I was told by Cindy Rice that the coil was "worn." Although I was somewhat skeptical, I agreed to the replacements. Later that day I was informed that the throttle body needed to be replaced and the entire dome light assembly would have to be replaced. I pressed on both issues and was assured that the dome light could not be repaired because it came in one unit and the contacts were bad. The dome light assembly was not in stock and would have to be ordered. I also pressed Cindy Rice about the throttle body. She would not guarantee that replacement would solve the problem, so I refused to have it fixed. Imagine being asked to pay $660 for a product with no guarantee that it would work and no recourse if it wouldn't. For a bill of $330 the car was tuned up (including replacement of the parts mentioned above) and the tail light was replaced. Two of the problems (sticking accelerator and dome light) that were to be fixed weren't.

Several days later (Nov. 26) I received a call from a company that checks the satisfaction of your service customers. I described my dissatisfaction. Wayne Merrit, your service manager, called me the following week. I described my story to him and he was sympathetic. He checked the accuracy of my story and got back to me. He was anxious to have me back in to get the remaining repairs done. He checked and found that his top technician was involved in the work, so he was confident in the diagnosis. He guaranteed that replacing the throttle body would fix the problem. In fact he said that if it didn't, they would remove the new throttle body and put the old one back in. He also said they would order the dome light assembly and replace it at the same time. He offered a 10% discount and, after my insistence, agreed to eliminate the labor charge, which on this job was quite small anyway.

I agreed to bring it back, but after a day to think it over, called and left him a message that I would not be back. Given the likely mark-up on parts, I was convinced that your dealership was still going to make a hefty profit at my expense, and given the service I had received, I didn't think you deserved any.

I checked my records and found that the spark plugs and spark plug wires had been replaced by BP Procare about 1 year prior to Quality Motors replacing them again. It seemed very unlikely that they needed to be replaced. The plugs and wires Procare had replaced had lasted over 50,000 miles. Your shop insisted on replacing them at less than 15,000 miles. After finding this out, I was very glad I had not brought the car back to get the dome light and throttle body replaced.

I still had a dome light that didn't work and a throttle body that needed to be replaced, so I took it to a small independent shop specializing in foreign car repairs. The owner was anxious to look at the throttle body because, in his long experience, he had never had to replace one. He disassembled the throttle body (something I don't think your technicians ever did), cleaned it, and lubricated it. It now works fine. He has told me that if it begins acting up again, bring it back and he will replace a spring. He also checked on the dome light. By this time I was not surprised to learn that there was absolutely nothing wrong with the dome light assembly. It did not need to be replaced. A wire leading to the driver's side door switch was loose. He tightened that connection. The dome light works fine. The RPM problem has been solved. Total bill for both repairs: $18.38.

Not knowing how you or your business desires to operate, let me tell you how it *appears* to operate. I can only speculate as to why service personnel would recommend replacement of parts that do not need to be replaced. There are only two likely reasons. Either they are encouraged to, or they don't know any better. If they aren't being dishonest, your service people must not know how to diagnose problems with automobiles. No other options exist. Your service personnel don't appear to be able to solve a problem as simple as a loose wire on a switch.

At the worst, your staff tried to install (and possibly did install) parts that weren't needed to increase part sales. At best they just didn't know what they were doing. The dome light and throttle body fiascoes can be explained in no other way but either incompetence or dishonesty. When I questioned your "service guarantee," which is displayed in your shop, all I got was an apology. Nothing else. Your service guarantee, in effect, was this: "We guarantee our service. If it is not satisfactory, we will apologize."

I will never take business to your establishment again. I will not recommend anyone take business there either. Not only will I not frequent your establishment, but in addition, because I have not been able, in two tries, to find a dealer that is competent and provides good service when repairing your cars, I will not buy another.

Sincerely,

Tom Hartwell

Letter 2

Memo to: Wayne Merrit, Service Manager

From: Ross

RE: Angry Customer

Wayne, I received the attached letter yesterday. Please give me the background information.

Letter 3

Memo to: Ross Carlson

From: Wayne Merrit

RE: Angry customer

The customer has been in contact with me over the past several weeks. I called him when I was informed of his dissatisfaction. In fact, he called me and told me the results of his service at the independent repair shop. I asked him if he wanted a refund and he said that that would not result in him doing business with us and that it was our decision. He also told me that he was sending you a letter.

There really isn't much more background. What the customer says concerning the work we did is true. The problems at the dropoff time did happen, according to our service team leaders. Cindy had an emergency at home and had to leave. No one thought about examining her appointment book. We blew it.

My best technician did the diagnostics on his car. He admits that he did not check the door switch because he was in a hurry and assumed that it was the assembly because that is a common problem. Regarding the throttle body problem, our policies restrict us to using original equipment replacement parts. We do not have access to a replacement spring to repair a throttle body. We have no choice but to replace the entire unit. My technicians have no doubt that a replacement spring could fix it, but policies prevent them from finding such a spring and using it. Should we advise our customers to go elsewhere if they have that problem?

In response to the customer's complaints about replacing unneeded parts, that is difficult to judge. The problem with "repairing" rather than replacing is that the repairs often aren't permanent and the part must eventually be replaced anyway. As you know, however, over 80 percent of our parts sales are through our own service department. Part replacements are important to us. The markup on parts is significantly more than the markup on labor. Our satisfaction surveys show that our customers are very satisfied with the quality of our service, however.

In response to the customer's complaints, we refunded $126 for the distributor cap, wires, and rotor and for the associated labor as a goodwill gesture.

1. Quality Motors may, or may not, have some quality problems. With only one data point (this angry customer), it would be dangerous to draw conclusions. What are the possible areas of Quality Motors' operation that may have quality problems?

2. For each of those potential quality problems:
    a. Identify the type of data needed to confirm the existence of a quality problem.
    b. Describe how that data could be obtained.
    c. Describe what would be looked for in that data to provide the evidence necessary to either confirm that a problem exists or confirm that it doesn't.

Quality Tools: From Process Performance to Process Perfection

LEARNING OBJECTIVES

- Explain the function of the general-purpose quality analysis tools.

- Explain how each quality tool aids in the QI story and DMAIC processes.

- Explain how statistical process control charts can help prevent defects from occurring.

- Calculate control limits for X-bar charts, R-charts, P-charts, and C-charts.

- Construct and interpret X-bar charts, R-charts, P-charts, and C-charts.

- Describe and make computations for process capability using C_p and C_{pk} capability indices.

- Describe how acceptance sampling works and the role of the operating characteristics curve.

- Explain how Six Sigma quality relates to process capability.

- Describe how moment-of-truth analysis can be used to improve service quality.

- Describe Taguchi's quality loss function and its implications for the cost of variability from the target performance level.

- Explain how customer relationship management systems have changed the way businesses satisfy customers.

- Describe how "recovery" applies to quality failures.

THE NUMBERS DON'T LIE

Arguments about automobile quality are often anecdotal, citing experiences with one or two vehicles. While quality is often driven by perception, real data can tell a powerful story. One way to determine the comparative quality of automobiles is to inspect them for problems before they leave the dealership to see how many problems they have before customers even get them. Consumer reporting agencies often publish data on those types of defects. Getting information about external failures is a little more difficult. One approach, although the information gathered isn't model specific, is to compare money paid out by auto manufacturers for warranty claims.

In 2003, GM, Ford, and DaimlerChrysler held roughly two-thirds of the U.S. auto market. An estimated 4.757 million units were sold by GM, 3.485 million units by Ford, and 2.35 million units by DaimlerChrysler. Toyota estimated 1.87 million units in the United States and Honda estimated 1.3 million. All others were predicted to be 2.9 million units. GM's numbers include Saab sales, while Ford numbers include Jaguar, Volvo, and Land Rover.

In 2003, U.S. automakers spent $7.9 billion for warranty claims worldwide. About $5.9 billion of that was spent for claims in the United States. On a "per vehicle" basis, U.S. automakers averaged $560 in warranty claims, with GM spending about $537 per vehicle, Ford spending about $541 per vehicle, and Daimler-Chrysler AG spending about $628 per vehicle. In contrast, Japanese automakers spent an average of $226 per vehicle, with Toyota/Lexus averaging $223 and Honda/Acura averaging $216.

Another measure to look at is recalls. In 2003, approximately 8 percent of all automobiles on the road in the United States were subjects of a recall. That's 1 in 12 cars. Obviously, the cost of the recalls goes directly to the auto manufacturers, and recalls extend past warranty periods. A comparison of the share of recalls to market share provides a perspective on relative quality. Ford's share of all recalled vehicles exceeded its market share in 7 of 10 years from 1993 to 2003. DaimlerChrysler AG recalls exceeded its market share for 4 of 5 years from 1998 to 2003. GM was responsible for 38 percent of all vehicles recalled in 2003, despite the fact that it had only 28 percent of the market. Toyota's share of all recalled vehicles has never exceeded its market share.

Recent studies show gaps between perception of quality and the reality when it comes to the U.S. market and U.S. automakers. For some models, Mercury, for example, actual quality was far better than the perception of quality. For others, the situation was reversed. For Land Rover, actual quality was far worse than the perception. Cars that had a quality image that was better than the actual level of quality included Dodge, Saturn, Pontiac, Audi, Mitsubishi, Mercedes, and Volkswagen. Cars whose actual quality was better than the perception included Buick, Infiniti, Lincoln, Chrysler, Acura, Subaru, and Cadillac. Perceptions of quality are important. It is perception that matters most when a car is being sold. The under-appreciation of the value of a car forces prices down and incentives (rebates) up.

Source: "Auto Warranties," *Warranty Week*, www.warrantyweek.com/archive/ww2004127.html, January 27, 2004; "High Warranty Costs Haunt U.S. Auto Manufacturers," 6 Sigma Quality in Manufacturing, Society of Manufacturing Engineers, www.sme.org, May 26, 2004; S. Power and K. Lundegaard, "One in Twelve Cars Recalled Last Year; Despite Improvements in Safety and Design, Number of Defects Found Is on the Rise," *Wall Street Journal*, March 4, 2004, p. D.1.

Quality is defined as conformance to customer expectations. In order to manage and improve quality, the degree to which a particular attribute conforms or fails to conform must be verified. The only way that can happen is through actual measurement, collection of data, and analysis. Without the analysis tools to aid in this process, quality improvement is just wishful thinking.

Introduction: The Importance of Data in Improving Quality

In Chapter 6, quality was addressed as it relates to value, costs, and customer satisfaction. Several approaches to improving quality were examined, including the broad organizing frameworks of total quality management (TQM) and Six Sigma. In order for any quality improvement effort to be successful, improvement efforts must be based on actual problems that are known to exist because real data confirms their existence. Not only must the existence of the actual problem be confirmed, but any improvement must also be confirmed using objective measures of performance.

Quite often, measurements of specific service or product quality characteristics, in their raw form, do not provide enough information to indicate whether or not a quality problem exists. It is data, but not information. Analysis of the data turns it into a form management can understand and use in guiding the improvement effort. The cultural side of quality improvement is extremely important. No real quality focus exists without it. However, the data collection and analysis part of quality management is equally important. Without it, no serious quality improvement effort can succeed. An organization would have developed a set of enthusiastic employees, dedicated to the improvement of quality but unable to accomplish it. That leads to frustration and failure. Without the technical expertise, "quality improvement" is just wishful thinking.

Quality Analysis and the Improvement Process

TQM and Six Sigma offer two structured frameworks for guiding quality improvement. For TQM, the quality improvement (QI) story is a commonly used series of steps to operationalize the plan-do-check-act (PDCA) cycle. Six Sigma uses define-measure-analyze-improve-control (DMAIC) for quality improvement projects and define-measure-analyze-design-verify (DMADV) for new product and service design. As you can see from Exhibit 7.1, the QI story and DMAIC are not that different. The QI story breaks the "improve" step from DMAIC into two steps, determining what the corrective action is and making sure it actually works. In the last step, the QI story also directs the process to be started over again. Other than those two minor differences, the functionality of the two processes is similar.

The DMAIC and QI story provide a structure for what needs to happen and the sequence in which events should happen, but neither process defines how these activities are to be accomplished. For example, how should the area for improvement be selected? How should measures of performance for the status quo be determined? How can causes be identified? The answers to these questions can be determined through the use of a broad set of analysis tools.

Tools used to aid in quality management efforts range from the very simple to the very complex. This chapter examines a few fundamental tools that are general-purpose in nature and almost universal in acceptance. They by no means represent the entire scope of analysis tools.

According to J.D. Power, 52 percent of new-car buyers say long-term quality is one of the most important factors in their choice.

Comparison of DMAIC and QI Story Processes		EXHIBIT 7.1
The DMAIC Process for Six Sigma	**The QI Story for TQM**	
Define: Define project objectives, internal and external customers.	Problem identification and validation.	
Measure: Measure current level of performance.	Understand current situation.	
Analyze: Determine causes of current problems.	Analysis of causes.	
Improve: Identify how the process can be improved to eliminate the problems.	Corrective action/proposed solution. Check results.	
Control: Develop mechanisms for controlling the improved process.	Standardization. Conclusion/next steps.	

General-Purpose Quality Analysis Tools

Process Maps

Process maps, process flow charts, or process flow diagrams, form the basis for documenting a process. They were discussed in Chapter 4 from the perspective of improving process productivity but also have great utility in quality improvement. The ability to represent a process visually, in a way that emphasizes relationships between various activities in the process, can contribute substantially to better understanding of the process and its weaknesses. Looking at an entire production process and understanding all the relationships among resources can be difficult. A diagram, however, can be studied and analyzed to identify logical relationships and sequences. Exhibit 7.2 is a basic process map of a purchasing process for an Internet retailer.

Chapter 4 introduced a modification of the process map known as a service blueprint. A service blueprint models the entire service process from the customer's perspective, including activities "behind the scenes" (behind the line of visibility) as well as those that result in interaction with the customer. After potential service failures, as well as customer waits and transportation activities, are identified, management can focus improvement efforts, employee education, and special attention on these problems. For different uses of flow diagrams, different symbols are used.

Flow charts can be used at several points in the DMAIC and QI story processes. In both processes, they provide an excellent way to view the current process as it is and to evaluate it from a logical perspective. They also aid in making it easier to understand the sequential relationship among activities. This aids in identifying causes of problems because causes must precede effects. For services, service blueprints aid in prioritizing problems for attention because of the fail points and wait points identified in those flow charts.

Run Charts

A **run chart** is a plot of a variable on the y axis versus time on the x axis. Run charts are useful as an aid to understanding the current situation and also help in the analysis of causes. Run charts are helpful in understanding the relationship between changes in a variable measure over time. A measure of the problem plotted against time often leads to the cause of a problem. Identifying that the effect is related to time—that is to say, a pattern of change in the effect is linked to changes in time of day, day of the week, and so on—is often a major step toward identifying the cause. Once the time element of the problem is identified, other things that are time-related can be examined as potential

run chart
A plot of a variable of interest on the y axis and time on the x axis.

| EXHIBIT 7.2 | Process Map |

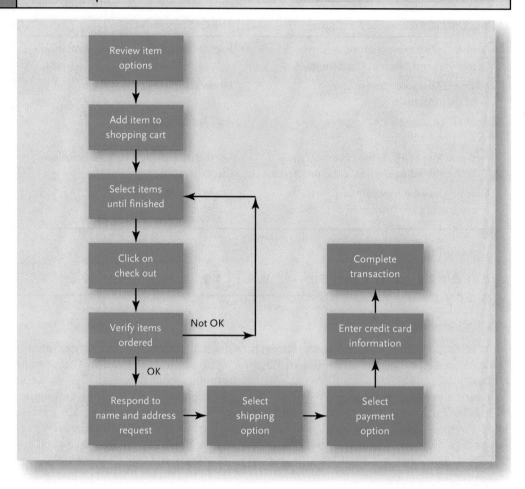

causes. For example, a hotel that noticed an increase in the number of customer complaints each week might want to see if the complaints were related to time. Complaints could be examined by day or by time of day. If the increase resulted from a large number of customers arriving every Monday, that information would lead the hotel to one set of possible causes, but if the increase came every morning, it would lead them to a different set of possible causes.

Other time-related variables that could cause quality problems include temperature, traffic level, specific employees on duty, and demand patterns. Exhibit 7.3 is a sample run chart for a paper company that had problems with $8\frac{1}{2}$-by-11-inch peel-off adhesive paper curling after being cut from large rolls. After seeing the relationship between curl and certain days of June and July, the managers were then able to link the curl problem to days with high temperature and humidity. The rolled paper had been wrapped in plastic when manufactured, and unwrapping it and exposing it to high humidity resulted in the label taking on moisture faster than the peel-off backing, causing it to curl. Ultimately, this link between humidity and curl led to the installation of an air-conditioning system in the plant.

Cause and Effect Diagrams

cause and effect diagram
A tool used to aid in the identification of root causes of quality problems.

The **cause and effect diagram** shown in Exhibit 7.4 is used to help identify the cause of a problem. It provides structure for evaluating possible causes and narrowing the field down to the most likely cause. Their most common use is for the analysis of possible

Run Chart   EXHIBIT 7.3

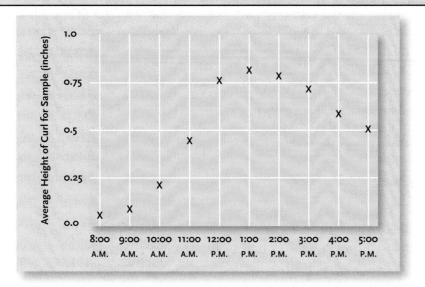

Cause and Effect Diagram   EXHIBIT 7.4

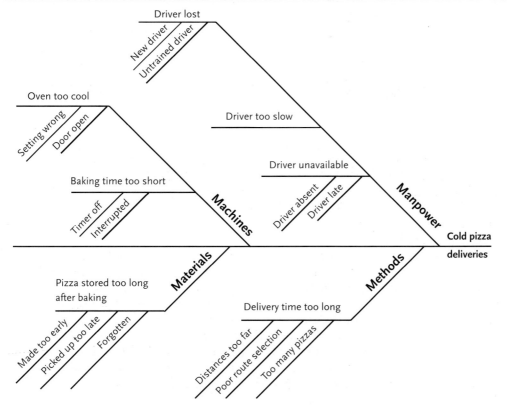

causes. Creating the diagram typically starts with the identification of potential causes and gradually, through a process of elimination, moves to the root cause.

Sometimes referred to as a "fishbone diagram" because of its appearance, cause and effect diagrams are great tools to use with a group of individuals who first examine all possible causes of a problem and then work their way to a root cause that all agree on. Cause and effect diagrams are often divided into four parts—manpower, machines, materials, and methods—to ensure all possible sources of problems are considered. The example in Exhibit 7.4 provides a sample cause and effect diagram for a pizza delivery company that was getting complaints about pizza being delivered cold. The pizza company determined that the root cause of the cold pizza was slow delivery time during high-traffic periods. Its solution was to reduce the number of orders that each driver would take during high-traffic times from four to two.

Pareto Charts

Pareto charts are simple bar graphs used to categorize data and help establish priorities for action. Often, data that are collected are difficult to interpret until they are organized. Pareto analysis is the process of identifying the most important category to give a focus to improvement efforts. Pareto charts provide a tool to display organized data in a variety of ways. A typical example of a large volume of data of little use without organization would be the calls a consumer products company receives through the 800 number printed on its products. Generally, the most valuable information companies can get through such a practice is complaints from customers. Before taking action to reduce complaints, however, a company must try to determine what initiated the complaints. A Pareto chart can be used to break the complaints down by category and prioritize by the category that has the highest frequency of complaints. Pareto charts help in the early stages of quality improvement by aiding in the decision of what the efforts should focus on.

Exhibit 7.5 is a Pareto chart representation of customer complaints for a shampoo manufacturer. The most frequent complaint was related to the difficulty in rinsing the shampoo out of the customer's hair. The company took action by experimenting with formulations that were less reactive to varying degrees of water hardness. Example 7.1 provides a demonstration of **Pareto analysis.** Pareto analysis is intended to separate the relatively few important problems from the many unimportant ones.

Pareto chart
A bar graph used to categorize data and help establish priorities.

Lexus, Jaguar, and BMW topped J.D. Power's 2005 Initial Quality Study, with the fewest problems out of 100 vehicles (81, 88, and 95 problems).

Pareto analysis
A process used to separate the relatively few important problems from the many unimportant ones.

EXHIBIT 7.5	Pareto Chart

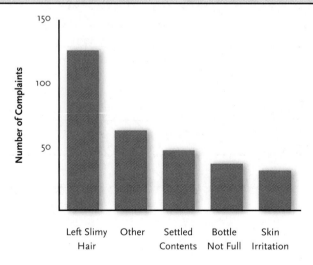

Complaint Category

Example 7.1

Pareto Analysis

The SleepCheap Hotel chain maintains 12 hotels that provide suites to business travelers. During the past three months, housekeeping staff have placed a complaint survey in each room. Each complaint was categorized in two ways. The first set of categories dealt with satisfaction with specific physical areas of the room. The second dealt with types of problems the customers had with different aspects of the room. The data collected are presented in Exhibit 7.6. Complete a Pareto analysis on the data.

EXHIBIT 7.6   SleepCheap Hotel Survey Data

Area	Complaint Frequency		Problem Type	Complaint Frequency
Shower	46		Dirty	105
Toilet	23		Not working	45
Vanity	63		Missing amenities	32
Desk	12		Not prepared	26
Bed	9		**Total**	**208**
Dresser	3			
Floor	38			
TV	14			
Total	**208**			

In order to begin work on improving the quality levels, management performed a Pareto analysis.

Solution

After being sorted by category, the percentage of the total number of complaints is calculated. The results for both sets of categories are shown in Exhibit 7.7.

EXHIBIT 7.7   Percentages for Each Category of Complaint in Example 7.1

Area	Complaint Frequency	Percentage	Problem Type	Complaint Frequency	Percentage
Shower	46	22.1%	Dirty	105	50.5%
Toilet	23	11.1	Not working	45	21.6
Vanity	63	30.3	Missing amenities	32	15.4
Desk	12	5.8	Not prepared	26	12.5
Bed	9	4.3	**Total**	**208**	
Dresser	3	1.4			
Floor	38	18.3			
TV	14	6.7			
Total	**208**				

(Continues)

Example 7.1   *(Continued)*

The next step is to sequence the categories by their frequency and construct a bar graph. This is presented in Exhibits 7.8 and 7.9.

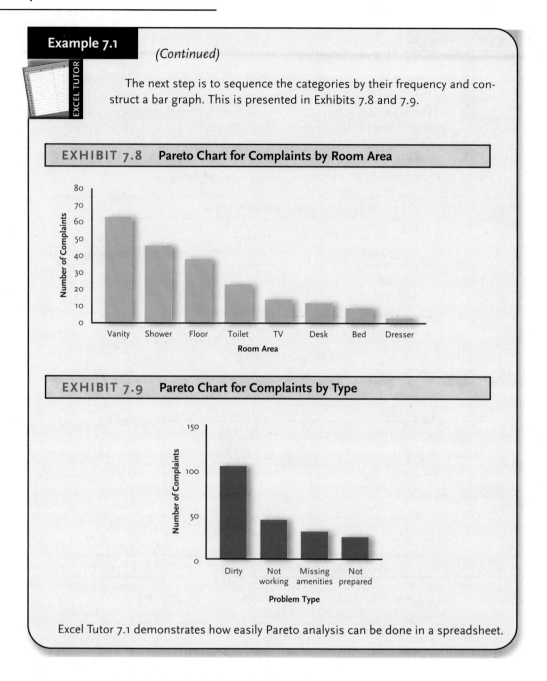

EXHIBIT 7.8   Pareto Chart for Complaints by Room Area

EXHIBIT 7.9   Pareto Chart for Complaints by Type

Excel Tutor 7.1 demonstrates how easily Pareto analysis can be done in a spreadsheet.

Histograms

histogram

A bar graph that plots a measurement on the *y* axis and the frequency of the occurrence of the measurement on the *x* axis.

A **histogram** is another bar graph, but it is configured differently than a Pareto chart. Exhibit 7.10 provides a histogram for the telephone wait time being experienced during one hour at a video game technical support center.

In a histogram, the *x* axis is used for a particular measurement and the *y* axis is used for the frequency of the occurrence of that particular measurement. Histograms are frequently used to get a rough idea of the distribution of variables. This is particularly important in many quality management situations that arise because of too much process variability. The histogram provides a visual means of presenting and understanding that variability.

The histogram's contribution of the distribution of the data can aid the quality improvement process in several ways. For example, the distribution of data can be very helpful in understanding the current situation, particularly the variability of the output

Histogram	EXHIBIT 7.10

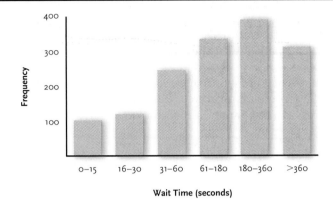

of a process of interest. If the variable of interest is plotted in the histogram, another histogram might be used after the improvement has been implemented in order to see if it has changed the output of the process, sort of a "before" and "after" view of the data.

Land Rover, Mazda, and Suzuki were at the bottom of J.D. Power's 2005 Initial Quality Study, with 149, 149, and 151 problems per 100 vehicles.

Check Sheets

The **check sheet,** as shown in Exhibit 7.11, is a simple, useful way to organize and tally data. Check sheets are frequently used for collecting and recording data that might later be used in another one of the quality tools. For example, customer complaints that might eventually undergo a Pareto analysis might be tallied on a check sheet. Check sheets can take a variety of forms, but they typically have blank cells for check marks or hash marks for categories of items being counted.

check sheet
A quality analysis tool used to tally occurrences of interest.

Check Sheet	EXHIBIT 7.11

	Issue 1	Issue 2	Issue 3	Issue 4	Issue 5
Item A	✓				
Item B		✓		✓	
Item C			✓		✓
Item D		✓			
Item E	✓	✓	✓		
Item F	✓				

Scatter Diagrams

scatter diagram
A chart that seeks to identify relationships between variables by plotting one variable on the *x* axis and another on the *y* axis.

The **scatter diagram** utilizes one variable on the *x* axis and another variable on the *y* axis to provide a visual means of identifying a correlation or a relationship between the two variables. Exhibit 7.12 is a scatter diagram plotting the number of admission tickets sold at the entry to a theme park against the number of complaints about waiting in line too long at the most popular ride.

Although the existence of a positive correlation is not sufficient to conclude that a cause and effect relationship exists, correlation is a prerequisite to cause and effect. Identifying relationships between variables is an important first step toward identifying the cause of a particular problem.

Controlling Process Variability

common cause variability
Variability in process outcomes that results from the inherent random fluctuation of the process.

A primary challenge of managing service or manufacturing quality is ensuring that processes are consistent, which means that variability from one instance to another must be minimized. Variability in processes, which causes variability in outputs, has two sources. The first source of process variability is known as **common cause variability**. Common cause variability comes from random fluctuation inherent to every process. It cannot be controlled in the processes and is unavoidable. The only way common cause variability can be reduced is to change the process. The second source of process variability is **assignable cause variability.** Assignable cause variability is sometimes called "special cause variability" because it is avoidable and is not an inherent part of the process. Assignable cause variability comes from something in the process being wrong and its affecting the process enough to actually change its parameters. In summary, common cause variability is expected and normal, while assignable cause variability is not normal and indicates that there is a problem.

assignable cause variability
Variability in process outcomes that results from special causes that are not part of the inherent random fluctuation of the process and indicate that something in the process has changed.

Imagine your performance on the weekly quizzes you take in a particular class. Ten weeks into the term, you know you don't get the same score on each quiz. Sometimes your score is higher, and other times it is lower, but the scores are "similar." Suppose your average at the end of the tenth week was a 93 with your highest score at 94 and your lowest at 87. The variability in your quiz scores was common cause variability. Suppose on the eleventh quiz you received a 68. You would probably be very surprised. A score that deviates that much from your previous performance indicates that an assignable cause exists. Either your preparation was very different or the quiz was very different from the previous ten.

EXHIBIT 7.12	Scatter Diagram

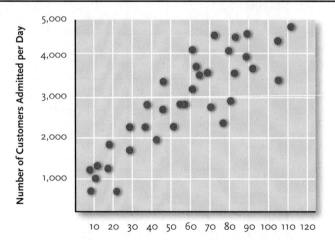

Number of Waiting Time Complaints per Day

For managers, the prevention of poor quality in service or manufacturing processes requires determining which variability has a common cause and which variability is the result of an assignable cause. Understanding these types of process variability and using quality tools known as process control charts makes this possible.

Statistical Process Control Charts

A **statistical process control chart** is a specific type of run chart used to plot measurements or test outcomes against time and distinguish between common cause variability and variability that has an assignable cause. The variability of a process determines whether it will be able to consistently meet customer expectations. Process variability creates some randomness in process outcomes. That variability can be described by its mean and standard deviation. As long as a process mean stays at the same point and the variability doesn't change, the process has not changed and is said to be "in control." If, however, the process begins to create outcomes that provide evidence that the amount of variability or the mean has changed, the process is said to be "out of control."

Data for process control charts are gathered from random samples of process outputs (critical dimensions of products, times of processes, and so on). By plotting the collected data and comparing the plotted data to the known standard deviations of the process, judgment can be made as to whether the process has changed or not.

Process control charts are used to monitor a variety of process types, always with the goal of distinguishing between common cause variability and assignable cause variability.

Process control charts are best understood as a part of **statistical process control (SPC)**, which is the context in which they are most often used. Control charts are such an integral part of the broader set of quality prevention procedures that the following section is devoted to that topic.

The eight tools just described constitute a foundation for identifying and solving problems related to quality. They can be used in many different ways, are often used independently of each other, and can also be used in conjunction with each other in a structured problem-solving process like DMAIC or the QI story.

Statistical process control provides a preventive approach to managing quality by monitoring processes in a way that identifies potential problems before defects are even created. Fundamental to SPC are several different control charts. Some are used when the aspect of interest is a variable, that is, a measure indicating a weight, dimension, strength, or other factor. Other control charts are used when a product attribute is of interest. Unlike variables, which potentially have an infinite number of possible outcomes, attributes have only two possible outcomes, such as pass or fail, fit or nonfit, on or off, and good or bad.

statistical process control chart
A specific type of run chart used to plot measurements or test outcomes against time and distinguish between variability caused by random fluctuation and variability that has an assignable cause. See *run chart*.

statistical process control (SPC)
A preventive approach to managing quality by monitoring processes in a way that identifies potential problems before defects are even created.

Mean or "X-Bar" Charts

A detailed examination of a particular type of statistical process control chart provides an excellent introduction to control chart concepts. A commonly used process control chart is known as the mean or **"X-bar" chart**. The X-bar chart is used to monitor the sample means of a variable that results from a particular process. A detailed examination of X-bar charts provides an overview of how all process control charts function. The values plotted on an X-bar chart are means of samples, as shown below:

X-bar chart
A process control chart that is used to monitor the sample means of variables that result from a process.

(7.1)
$$\overline{X_1} = \frac{x_1 + x_2 + x_3 + x_4 + \cdots + x_n}{n}$$

where n is the number of units in the sample, $\overline{X}$ is the mean of that sample, and x represents each measure in the sample. The center line on the control chart, representing X-double bar, is the mean of the sample means, as shown below:

(7.2)
$$\overline{\overline{X_1}} = \frac{\overline{X_1} + \overline{X_2} + \overline{X_3} + \overline{X_4} + \cdots + \overline{X_k}}{k}$$

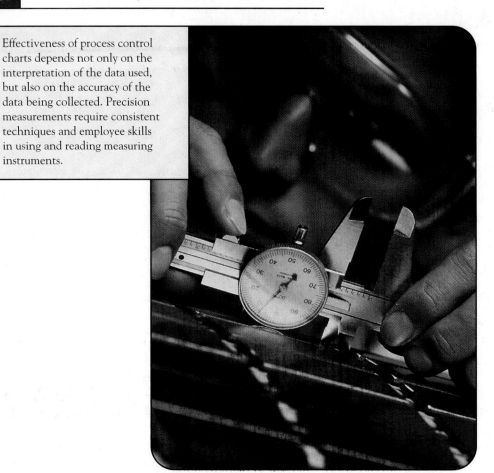

Effectiveness of process control charts depends not only on the interpretation of the data used, but also on the accuracy of the data being collected. Precision measurements require consistent techniques and employee skills in using and reading measuring instruments.

where $\overline{X}$ is the sample mean and k is the number of samples of size n. The process used for gathering data to be plotted on an X-bar chart is illustrated in Exhibit 7.13.

As an example of an X-bar chart application, let's examine its use to monitor the process of filling 12-ounce (355-milliliter) soft drink cans. Our process standard deviation is known to be 2 ml, and the mean of our sample means is 355 ml. Each data point plotted on the X-bar chart is the mean drink volume from a sample of 20 filled soft drink cans. The relationships between the entire population of cans filled since the last sample, the current sample of 20 cans, and the X-bar chart are illustrated in Exhibit 7.13.

EXHIBIT 7.13	Process Control Chart Data Gathering Process

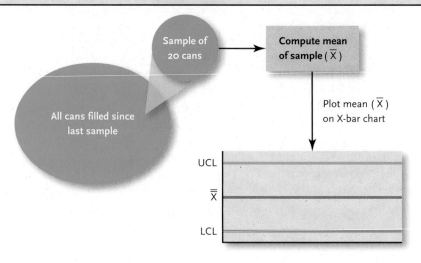

In Exhibit 7.13, the mean of the sample means ($\overline{\overline{X}}$) is shown in the simplified X-bar chart. We need to determine our upper **control limit** (UCL) and lower control limit (LCL). If the process standard deviation is known, the upper and lower control limits are calculated as:

(7.3) $$\text{Upper control limit (UCL)} = \overline{\overline{X}} + z\sigma_{\overline{x}}$$

(7.4) $$\text{Lower control limit (UCL)} = \overline{\overline{X}} - z\sigma_{\overline{x}}$$

Where

$\overline{\overline{X}}$ = the mean of the sample means

z = the number of normal standard deviations, given the desired confidence (for 95.44 percent confidence, use $z = 2$; for 99.74 percent confidence, use $z = 3$)

$\sigma_{\overline{x}}$ = the standard deviation of the distribution of sample means, calculated as $\sigma/\sqrt{n}$

σ = the process or population standard deviation

n = the sample size

By convention, $z = 3$, or 3-sigma, control limits have become accepted as the standard in most quality management applications. In our example, the upper and lower control limits would be calculated as:

$$
\begin{aligned}
\text{UCL} &= \overline{\overline{X}} + z\sigma_{\overline{x}} \\
&= \overline{\overline{X}} + z(\sigma/\sqrt{n}) \\
&= 355 + 3(2/4.47) \\
&= 355 + 1.34 \\
&= 356.34
\end{aligned}
$$

$$
\begin{aligned}
\text{LCL} &= \overline{\overline{X}} - z\sigma_{\overline{x}} \\
&= \overline{\overline{X}} - z(\sigma/\sqrt{n}) \\
&= 355 - 3(2/4.47) \\
&= 355 - 1.34 \\
&= 353.66
\end{aligned}
$$

Exhibit 7.14 provides the results of these calculations.

In our example the process standard deviation was known to be 2 ml. It was converted to the standard deviation of the sample means. In a typical application, the standard deviation of the process is not known, so control limits must be based on another measure of variability that is available. The average of the range values of the samples, instead of

Process Control Chart for Soft Drink Can	EXHIBIT 7.14

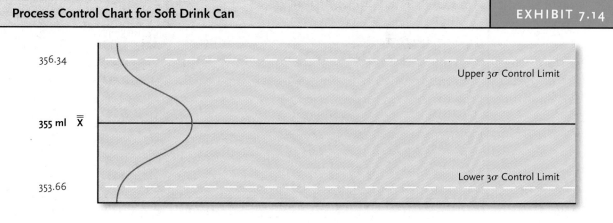

356.34 — Upper 3σ Control Limit

355 ml $\overline{\overline{X}}$

353.66 — Lower 3σ Control Limit

the actual process standard deviation, is used. The range is the difference between the largest and smallest measures in the sample. The use of range values as a measure of the variability requires access to a table of factors specifically developed for that purpose. A table that includes those factors is provided in Exhibit 7.15. Using range values, the upper and lower control limits are calculated as:

(7.5)

$$\text{Upper control limit (UCL)} = \bar{\bar{X}} + A_2\bar{R}$$

(7.6)

$$\text{Lower control limit (LCL)} = \bar{\bar{X}} - A_2\bar{R}$$

Where

$\bar{\bar{X}}$ = the mean of the sample means
A_2 = the value from Exhibit 7.15
$\bar{R}$ = the average range from the samples

Exhibit 7.15 provides the A_2 factors for use in Equations 7.5 and 7.6. The sample size column and the A_2 column are used for X-bar charts. The other two columns (D_3 and D_4) are used with R-charts, which are discussed in a later section.

Suppose that in our previous example, we did not know the process standard deviation, but had collected range data on our 20-can samples and our average range ($\bar{R}$) was 3.2 ml. We could calculate our upper and lower control limits using equations 7.5 and 7.6 and Exhibit 7.15. In Exhibit 7.15, since our sample size was 20, we would use the A_2 factor of .18. Those calculations would be made as follows:

$$\text{UCL} = \bar{\bar{X}} + A_2\bar{R}$$
$$= 355 + .18(3.2)$$
$$= 355.576$$

$$\text{LCL} = \bar{\bar{X}} - A_2\bar{R}$$
$$= 355 - .18(3.2)$$
$$= 354.424$$

EXHIBIT 7.15	Factors for 3-Sigma Control Limits for X̄-Charts and R-Charts		
Sample Size	**X̄-Chart Factor**	**R-Chart Factors**	
N	**A_2**	**D_3**	**D_4**
2	1.88	0	3.27
3	1.02	0	2.57
4	0.73	0	2.28
5	0.58	0	2.11
6	0.48	0	2.00
7	0.42	0.08	1.92
8	0.37	0.14	1.86
9	0.34	0.18	1.82
10	0.31	0.22	1.78
11	0.29	0.26	1.74
12	0.27	0.28	1.72
13	0.25	0.31	1.69
14	0.24	0.33	1.67
15	0.22	0.35	1.65
20	0.18	0.41	1.59
25	0.15	0.46	1.54

Example 7.2

EXCEL TUTOR

X-Bar Chart Construction

Exhibit 7.16 contains the measures obtained for the width of a mounting bracket used in securing the hard drive in a desktop computer.

EXHIBIT 7.16   Sample Measures

Item No.	Sample Time								
	8:00	8:30	9:00	9:30	10:00	10:30	11:00	11:30	12:00
1	2.34	2.33	2.30	2.33	2.32	2.30	2.33	2.32	2.35
2	2.29	2.30	2.30	2.29	2.33	2.29	2.30	2.34	2.31
3	2.31	2.32	2.29	2.31	2.31	2.35	2.34	2.29	2.29
4	2.32	2.34	2.30	2.31	2.32	2.30	2.34	2.31	2.32
5	2.30	2.31	2.30	2.31	2.32	2.33	2.31	2.31	2.31
6	2.30	2.32	2.34	2.32	2.32	2.31	2.32	2.31	2.32

The process standard deviation is not known. Determine the upper and lower control limits for this data and construct an X-bar chart.

Solution

The UCL and LCL can be determined using equations 7.5 and 7.6 and the A_2 factors provided in Exhibit 7.15. The mean of the sample means ($\bar{\bar{X}}$) is required, as is the mean range ($\bar{R}$). Exhibit 7.17 provides the sample means and ranges, as well as $\bar{\bar{X}}$ and $\bar{R}$.

EXHIBIT 7.17   Sample Measures with Sample Means, Ranges, Grand Mean, and Mean Range

Item No.	Sample Time								
	8:00	8:30	9:00	9:30	10:00	10:30	11:00	11:30	12:00
1	2.34	2.33	2.30	2.33	2.32	2.30	2.33	2.32	2.35
2	2.29	2.30	2.30	2.29	2.33	2.29	2.30	2.34	2.31
3	2.31	2.32	2.29	2.31	2.31	2.35	2.34	2.29	2.29
4	2.32	2.34	2.30	2.31	2.32	2.30	2.34	2.31	2.32
5	2.30	2.31	2.30	2.31	2.32	2.33	2.31	2.31	2.31
6	2.30	2.32	2.34	2.32	2.32	2.31	2.32	2.31	2.32
$\bar{X}$ values	2.310	2.320	2.305	2.312	2.320	2.313	2.323	2.313	2.317
R values	0.05	0.04	0.05	0.04	0.02	0.06	0.04	0.05	0.06
$\bar{\bar{X}}$	2.315								
$\bar{R}$	0.0456								

Using Equations 7.5 and 7.6, the upper and lower control limits are calculated as:

$$UCL = \bar{\bar{X}} + A_2\bar{R}$$
$$= 2.315 + .483(.0456)$$
$$= 2.315 + .0220$$
$$= 2.337$$

(Continues)

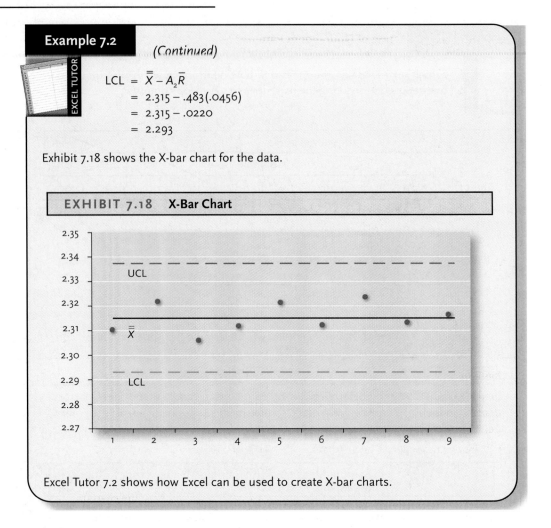

Example 7.2   *(Continued)*

$$LCL = \overline{\overline{X}} - A_2 \overline{R}$$
$$= 2.315 - .483(.0456)$$
$$= 2.315 - .0220$$
$$= 2.293$$

Exhibit 7.18 shows the X-bar chart for the data.

EXHIBIT 7.18   X-Bar Chart

Excel Tutor 7.2 shows how Excel can be used to create X-bar charts.

Control charts are maintained on an ongoing basis so that workstation operators can ensure that a process is not changing (i.e., moving out of control). Data points that are outside the control limits, as well as other nonrandom patterns of data points, indicate that the process has changed. Any pattern that shows a lack of randomness means that the variability is due to assignable causes.

Assignable cause variability is obvious when sample means or mean ranges go beyond the 3σ control limits. That's because the probability of those events happening due simply to random fluctuation are very small. There are other patterns of data that can also indicate variability from an assignable cause. To identify these patterns, the area between the upper and lower control limits are broken evenly into zones, as shown in Exhibit 7.19. Zone C consists of the area around the center line (grand mean) from $+1\sigma$ to -1σ. Zone B consists of the area between $+1\sigma$ and $+2\sigma$ and between -1σ and -2σ. Zone A consists of the area between $+2\sigma$ and $+3\sigma$ and between -2σ and -3σ. The rules presented in Exhibit 7.20 are based on statistical reasoning. For example, the probability that a particular $\bar{x}$ will be above the center line is .5. The probability that two in a row will be above the center line is .25(.5 × .5). The probability that nine in a row will be above the center line is $.5^9$ or .00195. That probability is about the same as the probability that a sample mean will fall outside of the 3σ limits due to common cause variability.

The chart provided in Exhibit 7.19 is used to identify certain nonrandom patterns, which provide additional evidence of a process being out of control. Those patterns are provided in Exhibit 7.20.

Variability with an assignable cause, even though the cause might not be found, is evidence that the process is out of control. Variability that has an assignable cause can be

Zones for Identification of Nonrandom Patterns   EXHIBIT 7.19

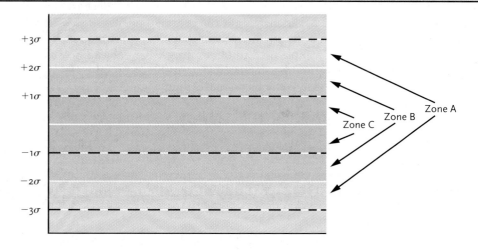

Nonrandom Patterns on Control Charts   EXHIBIT 7.20

Pattern	Possible Meaning
Individual points above the Upper Control Limit or below the Lower Control Limit.	The process average has changed.
9 points in a row, all above the mean or all below the mean.	The process average has changed (assuming a symmetrical distribution around the mean, which may not be the case for R charts or attribute charts).
6 points in a row, all increasing or all decreasing.	There is a drift in the process average.
14 points in a row alternating up and down.	Two alternating causes are producing different results (alternating parts from two different suppliers, for example).
4 out of 5 points in a row in Zone B or beyond.	Potential process shift.
15 points in a row in Zone 3, above and below the center line.	Smaller variability than should be expected.
8 points in a row in Zone B, A, or beyond, on either side of the center line, without points in Zone C.	Different samples are affected by different factors, resulting in a bimodal distribution of means.

Source: Adapted from "Quality Control Charts," www.statsoft.com/textbook/stquacon.html, accessed February 28, 2006.

analyzed, and the problem's cause can be corrected. This can all occur prior to the creation of any defective products when control charts are correctly used, providing that the process is compatible. If not, the process will produce defective items as a part of its common cause variability.

Like many business tasks that are labor-intensive or require extreme precision, process control tasks are sometimes performed automatically. In many industries they can be performed by equipment specifically designed to measure process outputs with high accuracy and create statistical process control charts.

R-Chart

A process control chart used to monitor sample ranges.

R-Charts

X-bar charts are always used in conjunction with a range chart (**R-chart**) because the means that are plotted on the X-bar chart show the central tendency of the sample group of measurements but do not indicate anything about that group's distribution. The R-chart plots the range for the same sample used to obtain the X-bar value. The range R for a sample is obtained by subtracting the smallest value in the group from the largest. The centerline on the R-chart, R-bar, is the mean of the sample ranges:

$$\bar{\bar{R}} = \frac{R_1 + R_2 + R_3 + R_4 + \cdots + R_k}{k}$$

---

om ADVANTAGE   Quality and Consistency Are Key for Wilson Tennis Balls

Wilson U.S. Open Tournament Select tennis balls have been the official ball of the U.S. Open since 1979. Despite the evolution in rackets, from wood and metal to carbon, there has been virtually no change in the ball. As service speed exceeds 140 miles per hour, the impact on the ball has changed tremendously, making durability, as well as consistent bounce, more important. The ball is available for four playing conditions: the US Open Extra Duty, the US Open Regular Duty, the US Open High Altitude, and the US Open Grass Court.

The U.S. Open uses more than 70,000 of these tennis balls (6 tons!). Wilson has to be extremely concerned about ball quality, because with the players' names or their sponsors' names on their shoes and rackets, only the balls and umpires will be blamed when things go wrong. Every ball must meet specifications of the International Tennis Federation and United States Tennis Association for size, weight, hardness, and rebound. A sample of eight dozen balls are submitted for tournament approval a year before the start of the tournament.

The hardness test for the ball is based on how it compresses when subjected to the squeezing of a machine known as the Stevens Machine. The Stevens Machine subjects the ball to an 18-pound load. Standard balls are allowed to deform between 0.220 and 0.290 inch. Balls used in the U.S. Open are allowed only 0.005 inch variability, from 0.240 to 0.245. A professional player can feel the difference between balls on opposite ends of the range of hardness.

Natural products are always variable. With two natural products (natural rubber and wool felt), it is particularly difficult to get consistency across the 100 million tennis balls produced by Wilson each year. The most difficult part of the production process is actually getting two flat pieces of felt to smoothly fit over a round surface. The two pieces, known as "dogbones," are assembled manually by a ball-coverer. For the ball-coverers, the squarer the dogbone shapes, the more likely the cover is going to wrinkle.

The composition of the cover requires a constant trade-off between durability and "fluffing." Durability is good. Fluffing is bad. Making the ball last longer can often make the covering fluffier. There needs to be enough hair on the ball so that the racket face will grab it, but not enough to create drag as it flies through the air. Balls that fluff up too much are known as "Don King balls" or "troll balls." Players actually sort through balls looking for those with the amount of fluff they like. For first serves, many players like a "skinny" ball, where the fluff is still down. They tend to go through the air faster and come off the court more quickly. Players like scuffed-up balls for the second serve so they can put more English on it to make sure it drops in.

Obviously, the air pressure in the ball is critical. Ten percent of the balls are actually tested by plunging a 12-gauge veterinarian's needle into the ball to make sure the ball has 12 pounds of air in it. The canning machines used by Wilson are actually from the food industry, but rather than create a vacuum as they would for food, they create a positive pressure of 13 pounds to make sure the ball maintains its pressure on the store shelf.

Source: "Under Pressure to Withstand an Unforgivable Beating," *The New York Times on the Web*, www.nytimes.com/2001/08/30/garden/30NOTE.html, August 30, 2001; Wilson, US Open Official Ball, www.wilsonsports.com/ corporate/ index.asp?content_id=1100, August 30, 2001.

The upper control limit and lower control limit for the R-chart are calculated as:

(7.8)
$$UCL = D_4\overline{R}$$

(7.9)
$$LCL = D_3\overline{R}$$

(p.248)

Exhibit 7.15 provides the D_3 and D_4 values for calculating 3σ control limits. Example 7.3 demonstrates the construction of an R-chart for variable data.

Example 7.3

R-Chart Construction

EXCEL TUTOR

Northeast Bottling Company is a regional contractor for a number of beverage companies. It recently acquired a new contract for a 1-liter bottle of Frantic, a new energy drink designed for 8- to 12-year-olds. Northeast is required to maintain control over a consistent volume of product in each 1-liter container. The company wishes to create the R-chart for the data below. For the first day of operation, machine operators took 20 samples, with 5 bottles in each sample. From that data, they calculated X-bars, the grand mean, and the mean range, as shown in Exhibit 7.21.

EXHIBIT 7.21   Bottling Data for Example 7.3

Sample Number	Sample X Values 1	2	3	4	5	X-Bar	UCL	LCL	Range
1	996	989	998	998	1,001	996.4	1,005.078	994.9224	12
2	1,004	1,007	1,001	1,004	1,002	1,003.6	1,005.078	994.9224	6
3	1,002	1,003	1,005	1,003	1,005	1,003.6	1,005.078	994.9224	3
4	995	996	995	999	1,001	997.2	1,005.078	994.9224	6
5	1,003	998	1,006	1,002	999	1,001.6	1,005.078	994.9224	8
6	999	997	1,006	1,003	998	1,000.6	1,005.078	994.9224	9
7	1,003	1,007	1,000	993	998	1,000.2	1,005.078	994.9224	14
8	1,002	1,003	999	1,003	998	1,001.0	1,005.078	994.9224	5
9	1,002	1,003	1,001	996	1,003	1,001.0	1,005.078	994.9224	7
10	997	997	988	1,001	999	996.4	1,005.078	994.9224	13
11	999	999	1,011	998	1,002	1,001.8	1,005.078	994.9224	13
12	1,005	1,003	995	1,000	998	1,000.2	1,005.078	994.9224	10
13	1,001	994	993	1,001	1,001	998.0	1,005.078	994.9224	8
14	999	1,002	999	1,002	1,002	1,000.8	1,005.078	994.9224	3
15	998	998	991	999	1,001	997.4	1,005.078	994.9224	10
16	1,002	997	1,011	998	996	1,000.8	1,005.078	994.9224	15
17	998	995	1,001	1,006	999	999.8	1,005.078	994.9224	11
18	996	1,006	997	1,003	998	1,000.0	1,005.078	994.9224	10
19	1,003	998	1,001	997	997	999.2	1,005.078	994.9224	6
20	1,002	1,001	1,003	996	1,000	1,000.4	1,005.078	994.9224	7

$$\overline{\overline{X}} = 1,000 \qquad\qquad \overline{R} = 8.8$$

(Continues)

Example 7.3 *(Continued)*

EXCEL TUTOR

Solution

The R-chart control limits are calculated by using Equations 7.8 and 7.9, as well as the table from Exhibit 7.15. The calculations are

$$UCL = D_4\overline{R}$$
$$= 2.114 \, (8.8)$$
$$= 18.6032$$

$$LCL = D_3\overline{R}$$
$$= 0 \, (8.8)$$
$$= 0$$

The R-chart is presented in Exhibit 7.22.
Excel Tutor 7.3 demonstrates how R-charts can be constructed in a spreadsheet.

EXHIBIT 7.22   R-Chart for Example 7.3

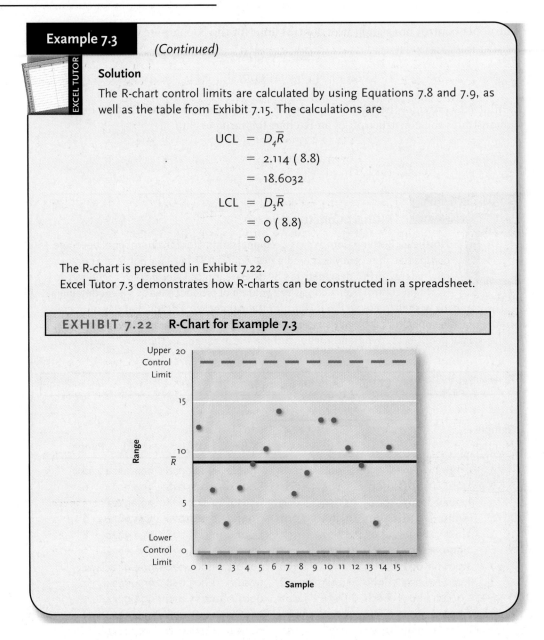

Even though a range value may occur below the lower control limit, which would indicate the sample variability has been dramatically reduced and may appear to be a good thing, it must still be treated as assignable cause variability and examined. It might actually be caused by someone who has found a way to perform the process better, in which case it would be useful to understand how it was changed, but it might result in detrimental effects elsewhere in the process.

Process Capability

The ability of a service or manufacturing process to consistently meet customer expectations is at the root of quality management. Put into the context of process variability, it means that common cause variability cannot result in an outcome that the customer would consider a defect. If it did, the service or manufacturer would be creating defects that were, in effect, unpreventable. The ability to contain all common cause variability inside of the customer specifications means that the 3σ control limits must be contained within the customer's specification limits. This characteristic of service or manufacturing processes is known as **process capability** and is typically measured using a **capability index**. One such capability index is the C_p index. The C_p index is the ratio of the spread of the customer's acceptability (upper customer specification limit minus lower customer specification limit) divided by the spread of the process (six standard deviations). The formula for computing C_p is:

(7.10)
$$C_p = \frac{\text{Upper Customer Specification Limit} - \text{Lower Customer Specification Limit}}{6\sigma}$$

A C_p index equal to 1 is minimally acceptable and means that the 3σ control limits are exactly the same as the upper and lower customer specification limits. A C_p index that is greater than 1 means that the 3σ control limits are within the customer specification limits. The greater the C_p index is, the farther inside the customer specification limits the 3σ control limits are. If the C_p index is equal to 1, the control limits and customer specification limits are equal. Because there is a .0026 probability that common cause variability will produce an outcome outside of the 3σ limits, there is also a .0026 probability of producing a defect (an outcome outside the customer specification limits). Thus, the larger the C_p index, the less likely the process is to produce a defect as a result of common cause variability. Example 7.4 demonstrates the calculation of the C_p capability index.

Process control requires precise measurement of the variables of interest. Without that measurement precision, the outputs are not accurate enough to provide meaningful direction. For many industries, measurement equipment is produced by companies with the expertise necessary to obtain these high necessary levels of precision.

process capability
The ability of a process to consistently meet customer expectations, demonstrated by the control limits being within the customer specifications.

capability index
A measure of process capability.

Example 7.4

EXCEL TUTOR

C_p **Capability Index Calculation**

Precision Machining is a subcontractor for manufacturers in the aerospace and defense industries. It was recently approached by Nuclear Triggers 'R' Us (NTRU) to machine some small parts. To determine if it had the capability to meet NTRU quality requirements, Precision Machining was asked to machine a sample batch of 100 parts. The most critical operation was that of surface grinding, which required very high tolerances. NTRU specified the thickness as 0.375 inch. Precision Machining finished the 100 parts and returned them to NTRU. NTRU technicians measured the parts and found that, indeed, the average thickness was 0.375 inch. What NTRU *did not tell* Precision Machining, however, was that the parts needed to be 0.375 inch but could not vary more than ±0.002 inch. NTRU's measurements showed that the standard deviation of the Precision Machining parts was 0.0024 inch. Can Precision Machining be counted on to provide parts that meet NTRU needs?

Solution

NTRU's upper customer specification is 0.375 + 0.002 = 0.377. Its lower customer specification is 0.375 − .002 = 0.373. Using Equation 7.10, the capability index is calculated as

$$C_p = \frac{0.377 - 0.373}{6(0.0024)}$$

$$= 0.27778$$

Because the capability index is less than 1, NTRU must conclude that Precision Machining is not capable of meeting its quality specifications.

Excel Tutor 7.4 shows how a spreadsheet can be used to aid in calculating the C_p capability index.

The C_p capability index calculated in Equation 7.10 and in Example 7.4 assumes that the process is centered—in other words, that the mean of the process output is at the target for the variable of interest, which is centered between the customer's specification limits. There are times when it is actually desirable not to center a process within the customer's specification limits. For example, in some manufacturing processes tools will wear and cause a process to "drift." A cutting edge might wear and cause a dimension to gradually increase over time. A drill bit might wear and cause the depth of a hole to change over time. In these situations, as long as the manufacturer understands the direction of the process drift, it may make sense to start the process closer to one of the customer's specification limits and let the process drift toward the other. The manufacturer is able to reduce costs associated with tool repair or replacement by obtaining longer useful life from them. Machine utilization is also increased because tools don't need to be changed as frequently.

For processes that aren't centered, the C_p capability index cannot be used. Instead, the C_{pk} capability index is used. Like the C_p index, the C_{pk} index measures how the process fits into the limits established by the customer. As the mean of a process shifts, the tails of the distribution of the process get closer to the upper or lower customer specification, depending on the direction of the shift. As this shift occurs, the direction of the shift and the nearness to the customer specification limit establish limits on the process capability. C_{pk} expresses the relationship between the process and the customer's specifications by identifying the distance between the tails of the process and the specification limit in the direction of the shift.

Exhibit 7.23 shows a process that was initially centered but shifted downward. Notice how the tail of the process has moved closer to the lower customer specification limit, although it is still a long way from that limit. As the process shifts, however, the likelihood of defects caused by violating the lower customer specification limit increases. The C_{pk} is calculated by computing the difference between the process mean and each of the customer specification limits. The result is divided by 3σ, to compute a ratio. The smallest of the two values is the one of interest, since it compares the distance between the process mean and the customer specification in the direction the process is shifting. The formula for computing the C_{pk} is

$$C_{pk} = \min\left[\frac{\text{Process Mean} - \text{LCS}}{3\sigma}, \frac{\text{UCS} - \text{Process Mean}}{3\sigma}\right]^t$$

EXHIBIT 7.23	Process Shifted Downward from Center

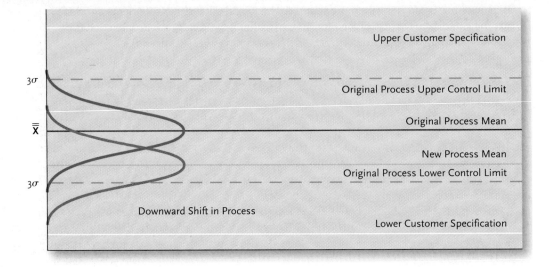

Example 7.5

EXCEL TUTOR

C_{pk} Calculation

Since getting the NTRU contract, Precision Machining was able to dramatically tighten its surface grinding operation and reached a standard deviation of 0.0003 inch. The customer specified 0.375 ± 0.002 inch for the part, giving customer specification limits of 0.373 to 0.377 inch. The operator of the surface grinder decided that it was to his advantage not to center the process within the upper and lower customer specification limits. He figured out that in order to maximize the use of the grinding tools, he should start with the process below center, giving it more room to shift, and less frequent tool changes. As the grinding wheel wore, the process mean would drift upward. By starting out low, the operator got longer life out of each wheel and spent less time changing wheels. He had to closely monitor the drift, however, to make sure that he maintained an acceptable C_{pk}. On one Friday afternoon, he collected data that showed the process mean had shifted to 0.376. Is the C_{pk} acceptable? Or does he need to change grinding wheels?

Solution

Using Equation 7.11, C_{pk} is calculated as:

$$C_{pk} = \min\left[\frac{\text{Process Mean} - \text{LCS}}{3\sigma}, \frac{\text{UCS} - \text{Process Mean}}{3\sigma}\right]$$

$$C_{pk} = \min\left[\frac{0.376 - 0.373}{0.0009}, \frac{0.377 - 0.376}{0.0009}\right]$$

$$= \min[3.333, 1.111]$$

$$= 1.111$$

The process has drifted upward, but since the C_{pk} is greater than 1, it is still acceptable. Excel Tutor 7.5 shows how a spreadsheet can aid in calculating the C_{pk} index.

where LCS = lower customer specification and UCS = upper customer specification. As the process shifts, the distance between the distribution tail and the customer specification limit gets smaller, until the 3σ limit goes beyond the customer specification, at which time the process is out of control because it will produce defects as a part of its common cause variability. A C_{pk} of 1 or greater is typically considered to be representative of a "capable" process. The larger the C_{pk}, the lower the likelihood of a defect being produced as a result of a common cause variability. Example 7.5 demonstrates the calculation of C_{pk}.

Process Control Charts for Attributes

Some characteristics of quality are not variables like weight, dimension, volume, and so on. Many dimensions of quality can be defined by one of only two possible conditions—OK or not OK. For example, color is either correct or incorrect. A label applied to a product is either straight or not straight. These quality characteristics are known as **attributes**. Attributes are monitored for the same reasons as variables—to ensure that the processes creating them are under control, but attributes are typically counted, rather than measured. Attribute control charts function in the same way as those used for variables. Three sigma control limits are established, based on the variability of the process, and those limits enable managers to discriminate between common cause variability and assignable cause variability in the "counts" of the attributes of interest. Two common attribute charts are the percent defective chart (P-chart) and the nonconformities per unit chart (C-chart).

attributes
A product or service characteristic that can be classified as either conforming or not conforming specifications.

P-Charts

P-chart

Used to monitor the proportion or percentage of items defective in a given sample.

P-charts are used to monitor the proportion or percentage of items defective in a given sample. Inexpensive items produced at very high volumes provide a typical application for the use of P-charts. It is often known that under such production conditions a very small proportion will be defective, but the proportion that is defective must be monitored with control charts to verify that the process is in control. The P-chart construction follows the same general guidelines as the X-bar and R-charts. The center line, which is the average percentage defective, is established, and then upper and lower control limits can be placed to enable the user to discriminate between common cause and assignable cause variability in the percentage defective. The centerline, $\bar{p}$, is the long-run mean percentage defective. The standard deviation of the distribution of percentage defectives (σ_p) is calculated as

(7.12)
$$\sigma_p = \sqrt{\bar{p}(1 - \bar{p})/n}$$

Where

n = the sample size
$\bar{p}$ = the long-run average and central line on the chart

And the upper and lower control limits are

(7.13)
$$\text{UCL} = \bar{p} + z\sigma_p$$

(7.14)
$$\text{LCL} = \bar{p} - z\sigma_p$$

Where z is the number of normal standard deviations given the desired confidence (for 95.44% confidence use $z = 2$; for 99.74% confidence use $z = 3$).

It is possible for the LCL calculation to result in a negative number, in a manner similar to the R-chart. If this occurs, the LCL is set at zero, since there cannot be a negative proportion defective.

The P-chart is used in a manner similar to the X-bar chart. Samples are taken periodically and the number of nonconforming services or items is counted. The number of nonconformers is divided by the sample size to determine the percentage defective, and that value is plotted. If the value falls outside of the control limits or meets any other criterion for nonrandom behavior, as listed in Exhibit 7.20, the variability is considered to have an assignable cause. Like the R-chart, even though the percentage defective may be outside the lower control limit, and appear to be an improvement, it must still be examined.

Example 7.6

EXCEL TUTOR

P-Chart Construction

Allied Insurance monitors claims approval time for automobile claims. At Allied, an approval time of 48 hours or less is considered to be OK. An approval time of longer than 48 hours is considered to be too long. Nathan Moody, the quality assurance director, samples 150 completed claims per week, calculates the time between claim submission and approval for each, and records the percentage that failed to meet the 48-hour objective. Nathan uses a P-chart to monitor the process. Over time, Nathan's data

(Continues)

Example 7.6

EXCEL TUTOR

(Continued)

have shown that the mean percentage of approvals that are too long is 7 percent. Over the past 12 weeks, Nathan has collected the following data from his samples:

Sample	Proportion >48 hours	Sample	Proportion >48 hours
1	0.08	11	0.05
2	0.06	12	0.06
3	0.08	13	0.07
4	0.08	14	0.09
5	0.05	15	0.08
6	0.05	16	0.06
7	0.06	17	0.08
8	0.08	18	0.07
9	0.07	19	0.07
10	0.05	20	0.06

Calculate σ_p and the upper and lower control limits for Nathan's data. Construct the P-chart and determine if the process is in control by using the guidelines provided in Exhibits 7.19 and 7.20.

Solution

The long-run mean percentage defective, $\bar{p}$, equals .06. The standard deviation of the distribution of percentage defectives (σ_p) is calculated (from Equation 7.12) as

$$\sigma_p = \sqrt{\bar{p}\,(1 - \bar{p})/n}$$

Where

$n = 20$ and $\bar{p} = .06$. In this case,

$$\sigma_p = \sqrt{.06\,(1 - .06\,)/150}$$

$$= .053104$$

From Equations 7.13 and 7.14, the UCL and LCL are calculated as

$$UCL = \bar{p} + z\sigma_p$$

$$= .06 + 3(.053104)$$

$$= .219311$$

$$LCL = \bar{p} - z\sigma_p$$

$$= .06 - 3(.053104)$$

$$= .09931$$

The P-chart is presented in Exhibit 7.24. Based on the nonrandom patterns from Exhibits 7.19 and 7.20, the process is in control.

(Continues)

Example 7.6 *(Continued)*

EXCEL TUTOR

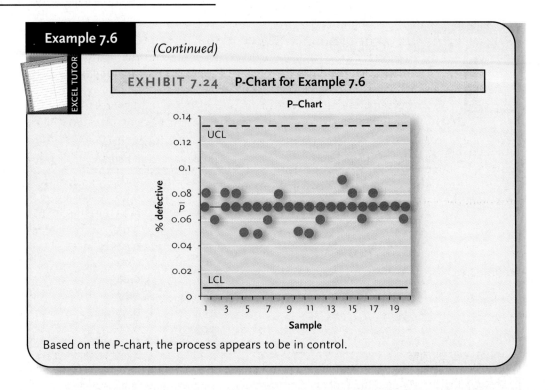

EXHIBIT 7.24 P-Chart for Example 7.6

Based on the P-chart, the process appears to be in control.

om *ADVANTAGE* Dead Pixels Haunt Monitor Makers

You might think that when you purchase something new, it should come out of the box in perfect condition. This is not the case, however, if you have just purchased a computer monitor. The thin film transistor (TFT) technology used in liquid crystal display (LCD) monitors contains many TFTs. As a transistor is activated, it produces a red, blue, or green color. The TFT LCD technology is not perfect and frequently produces monitors with pixels that are dead or "fixed." They remain light or dark, rather than changing as they are supposed to. Defective pixels can be seen on a monitor and typically show up as either dark dots or bright dots on the screen. Depending on the location and number of defective pixels, they can be quite annoying to the user. All monitor manufacturers have to deal with the dead pixel problem, but policies on monitor replacement vary from one manufacturer to another.

IBM publishes a large table that has the criteria for replacement of each of its monitors. On the IBM Thinkpad, for example, a 14.1-inch XGA monitor (1024 × 768 resolution) must have eight bright pixels or eight dark pixels, or a combination of light and dark pixels that totals to nine, before the LCD will be deemed faulty and be replaced. The criterion for the UXGA (1600 × 1200 resolution) 15-inch monitor is 11 bright pixels, 13 dark pixels, or a total of 16 bright and dark pixels before the monitor is considered faulty. Dell, on the other hand, has a more straightforward policy that covers all of its monitors. If you identify more than 6 fixed pixels on the screen, or if there are three or more together in a cluster, Dell considers the monitor faulty. Other manufacturers are more lenient. Nintendo's policy leaves it up to the judgment of the user:

With a small number of Nintendo DS screens, one or two dots on the screen may appear to be "stuck" on a particular color, such as white or red. This effect is caused when a particular pixel (the dots that make up the screen) is not working properly. . . .

We suggest you use your system for a few weeks to determine whether this interferes with your enjoyment of game play. If, after using your system for awhile, you feel that this tiny dot is too distracting, the Nintendo DS does carry a one-year warranty. We are happy to inspect and, if necessary, fix your system at no charge within the warranty period."

In order to help address the LCD monitor quality issue, ISO Standard 13406-2 introduced rules regarding a number of aspects of LCD screen quality. Included in the standard are such issues as display luminance, contrast, reflections, colors, and pixel faults. ISO13406-2 has four levels of LCD monitor quality. Most computer manufacturers consider their monitors as Class 2, which allows some pixel faults. ISO 13406-2 also identifies pixel defect types. Type 1 defects are always lit pixels. Type 2 defects are of always unlit pixels. Type 3 are subpixel faults. Under the ISO standard, a Class 2 monitor can have two pixel faults of Type 1 or 2 per million pixels and four pixel faults of Type 3 per million pixels.

www-307.ibm.com/pc/support/site.wss/document.do?Indocid=MIGR-4U953; http://support.dell.com; www.viewsoniceurope.com/data/63/l13406e2.pdf, accessed February 29, 2006.

C-Charts

C-charts are used most often for monitoring the counts of noncomformities per unit. The unit may refer to a product, a page, a square foot, a day, a month, or any other unit of inspection. A C-chart could be used for monitoring the number of typos per book chapter, for example, or the number of automobile crashes per month.

C-charts are used in a manner similar to the other process control charts. A sample is first extracted from the items being monitored and the number of noncomformities (c) is counted for each item. The next step is to compute the mean "c-bar" ($\bar{c}$) of the number of noncomformities for the units in the sample. As long as the events or occurrences are independent of each other and occur at a fairly constant rate overall, counts such as these have a Poisson distribution. Because the mean and variance of the Poisson distribution are equal, the variance (σ^2) is equal to $\bar{c}$:

C-chart
A process control chart used to monitor counts of nonconformities per unit.

(7.15)
$$\sigma^2 = \bar{c}$$

(7.16)
$$\sigma = \sqrt{\bar{c}}$$

and the upper and lower control limits are computed as:

(7.17)
$$\text{UCL} = \bar{c} + 3(\sigma)$$

(7.18)
$$\text{LCL} = \bar{c} - 3(\sigma)$$

Example 7.7   Constructing C-Charts

The Carroll County sheriff's office has been monitoring traffic accidents on a particularly troublesome 10-mile section of Highway 30. Over the past 6 years, there has been an average of 10 accidents per month on that stretch of road. Accident data for the 12 months of 2005 are presented below:

Month	Accidents
January	11
February	7
March	10
April	9
May	10
June	13
July	9
August	9
September	12
October	13
November	6
December	11

Construct a C-chart and determine whether the accidents are in control.

Solution

From Equations 7.15 and 7.16 we calculate σ as:

$$\bar{c} = 10$$
$$\sigma^2 = \bar{c}$$
$$\sigma = \sqrt{\bar{c}}$$
$$\sigma = 3.162$$

(Continues)

Example 1.7

Using Equations 7.17 and 7.18, the upper and lower control limits are computed as:

$$UCL = \bar{c} + 3(\sqrt{\bar{c}})$$
$$= 10 + 3(3.162)$$
$$= 19.487$$
$$LCL = \bar{c} - 3(\sqrt{\bar{c}})$$
$$= 10 - 3(3.162)$$
$$= .513$$

The C-chart is presented in Exhibit 7.25. Based on the chart and the criteria from Exhibits 7.19 and 7.20, it appears that the accidents are in control.

EXHIBIT 7.25   C-Chart for Example 7.7

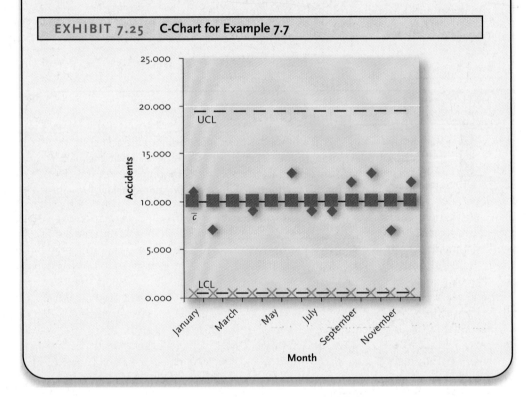

Acceptance Sampling

Acceptance sampling is used to identify suspect products or components of products without examining all of them. A sample group is extracted from a large quantity of products or components of interest, known as a "lot," and the entire lot is judged either good or bad based on the quality level of the sample group. Obviously, an inspection process of this type does not prevent poor quality from being produced; it merely identifies the quality after the fact. Moreover, since the decision is based on a sample, the wrong conclusions can be drawn. Sampling is always subject to the risks of sampling error, because there is always a possibility that the sample is not totally representative of the lot it comes from. It is possible to conclude from a sample that the lot is of poor quality when in fact it is good, or that the lot is good quality when in fact it is bad.

Acceptance sampling isn't as popular as it used to be, because it presumes that a given level of defects is acceptable. In addition, to reduce the potential of drawing

Characteristics of sampling processes differ as much as the products for which they are used. Here, wooden barrels of wine are sampled as a part of the aging process. While some aspects of the quality measurement are objective, such as measuring alcohol content and acidity, others are subjectively measured by expert tasters.

wrong conclusions, samples must be large. Despite these problems, it is still used when the products or components of interest are produced in very high quantities, when the quality of the components or products is somewhat inconsequential, and when a supplier of incoming products or components is being monitored closely. The following discussion provides an overview of the acceptance sampling process.

Acceptance sampling for any purpose requires a sampling plan. The basis of the sampling plan is the sample size n and the largest number of defects that can be present in an acceptable sample, referred to as c. The risks inherent in acceptance sampling that arise because the sample doesn't represent the lot must be addressed in the sampling plan because they determine the level of confidence one can have in the results. To address these risks, the plan must define acceptable and unacceptable levels of quality for the lot.

The **acceptable quality level (AQL)** identifies the quality level required for lots that will be sampled. A lot is considered to be good if the actual level of quality is at the AQL or better. The AQL is typically specified by the producer and must be agreeable to the customer. The **lot tolerance percent defective (LTPD)** is the level of quality in the lot that would be unacceptable to the customer. A lot known to be at or below the LTPD would be rejected by the customer. The LTPD is typically specified by the customer and must be agreed to by the producer.

The risks inherent in a plan can be specified in terms of the AQL and LTPD. The producer is most concerned with the risk of rejecting a good lot, which would happen if a sample indicated that a lot was defective when in reality it was at or above the AQL. The probability of this happening is known as **producer's risk,** which is the probability of rejecting a good lot, indicated by α. The customer is most concerned about the sample indicating that the lot was good, when in reality it contained the LTPD level of defective products. This is known as **consumer's risk** and is designated as β.

The values for n and c are derived from the values of α, β, the AQL, and the LTPD. A trial-and-error process can be used, as can the binomial or Poisson distribution, but most businesses use standard reference tables such as the MIL STD 105D (Military Standard 105D). The result of a completed sampling plan is a graph that demonstrates how well the plan discriminates between good and bad quality by showing the probability of accepting a lot of LTPD quality (a bad lot) and the probability of rejecting a lot of AQL quality (a good lot). Such a graph is known as an **operating characteristics (OC) curve.** Exhibit 7.26 shows an OC curve for a plan that has an AQL of 0.04 and an LTPD at 0.20.

acceptable quality level (AQL)
In acceptance sampling, it identifies the quality level required in order for lots to be considered to be good. See *acceptance sampling.*

lot tolerance percent defective (LTPD)
In acceptance sampling, the level of quality in the lot that would be unacceptable to the customer. See *acceptance sampling.*

producer's risk
In acceptance sampling, this is the probability of rejecting a good lot, indicated by α.

consumer's risk
In acceptance sampling, the probability of accepting a bad lot, designated as β.

operating characteristics (OC) curve
Used in the development of acceptance sampling plans, this is a graph that demonstrates how well the plan discriminates between good and bad quality by showing the probability of accepting a lot of LTPD quality (a bad lot) and the probability of rejecting a lot of AQL quality (a good lot).

EXHIBIT 7.26	Operating Characteristics Curve

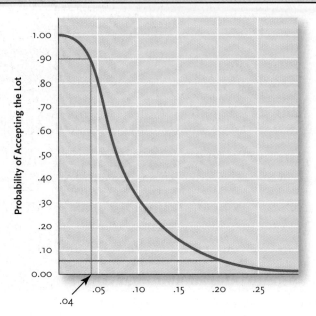

Actual Percent Defective in the Lot

Notice that the probability of accepting the lot with 4 percent defective is 0.90. The probability of accepting lots with greater numbers of defects is lower than 0.90, but it is still going to happen. The probability of accepting the lot when the quality level is at the LTPD of 0.20 is 0.05. The steeper the graph between the AQL and the LTPD, the more discriminating the plan. This steepness is obtained by manipulating n and c.

A Closer Look at Six Sigma Quality

As described in Chapter 6, Six Sigma (6σ) is an approach used to improve the control of production processes so that the likelihood of producing a defect is greatly reduced. As was discussed in the sections on statistical process control and process capability, the ability of a manufacturer to avoid production of defects depends on how the specifications for an item produced compare to the capabilities of the processes used to produce it.

As you know, there is some variability in all production processes. As a process becomes more tightly controlled, however, the variability is held to a narrower and narrower range. The variability of the process is measured by the standard deviation (σ). Traditional views of process capability hold that when the customer specifications for a product or component are compared to the process capabilities, the 3σ upper and lower control limits must be inside customer specifications ($C_p > 1$). To understand how this extends to 6σ, it helps to look at an example.

Suppose a manufactured automotive component was specified to be 0.60 inch long. It was also specified that the upper and lower customer specifications on that part were ±0.08 inch. In other words, parts from 0.52 to 0.68 inch were acceptable. The component was stamped out of sheet steel in a process that, like all processes, has a small amount of variability. When parts were measured, it was found that the average size, indeed, was 0.60 inch and the process standard deviation was 0.02. Exhibit 7.27 provides a comparison of the customer specifications and process capabilities. In Exhibit 7.27 it is evident that the process is capable.

| Process Capability for Three Sigma Quality | EXHIBIT 7.27 |

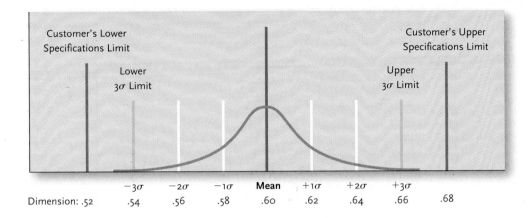

The proportion of the total amount of variability that will be within 3 standard deviations above and below the mean is 99.74 percent. For every 10,000 units, however, an average of 26 will be outside the 3σ limits, just because of common cause variability. If the 3σ limits were just inside the customer specifications, there is a small chance (no greater than 0.26 percent) of producing a "defect," or an outcome outside the customer specifications, as a result of common cause variability. That brings us to Six Sigma.

Six Sigma quality literally means that 6σ limits are used instead of 3σ limits. If 6σ standard deviations above and below the process mean must be inside the customer specifications, the process has to be much "tighter," and the likelihood of common cause variability extending beyond customer specifications becomes minuscule. The odds of random fluctuation creating a result that is 6 standard deviations from the mean is 2 in 1 billion. In other words, rather than being 0.9974 (99.74 percent) confident in products being within specifications, as we would be using 3σ limits, 6σ limits give us 0.999999998 (99.9999998 percent) confidence. In most manufacturing applications, the process is not centered, however, and is allowed to shift from 1 standard deviation above to 1 standard deviation below the mean. One advantage to reducing the process variability is the increase in the amount the process is allowed to shift. A noncentered process results in a reduction in confidence, to 3.4 defects per million, which is the commonly accepted quality level for Six Sigma.

Suppose we reduced variability in our process until the standard deviation was 0.01 rather than 0.02. That leaves 6 standard deviations above and below the mean inside the customer's specifications. Exhibit 7.28 shows how the tighter process looks with 6σ limits in place.

One might justifiably ask, "Why would anyone need this kind of accuracy?" There are two possible reasons. The first reason is that a company's ability to demonstrate that level of quality is an extremely important confidence-builder for customers. They know that any supplier able to meet 6σ quality levels has tremendous control of its processes and the discipline necessary to achieve a very difficult standard.

The second reason a company might use Six Sigma is that in some environments, the Six Sigma quality level is actually necessary to provide completed products of acceptable quality. Two notable companies that have committed to the Six Sigma level of quality are Motorola and General Electric. Both companies produce complex products that must also meet high quality standards, such as electronic components for communication equipment, medical equipment, and aviation equipment. Complex products often contain a large number of components that are interdependent. If a single component of the product fails, the entire product fails.

EXHIBIT 7.28	Process Capability for Six Sigma Quality

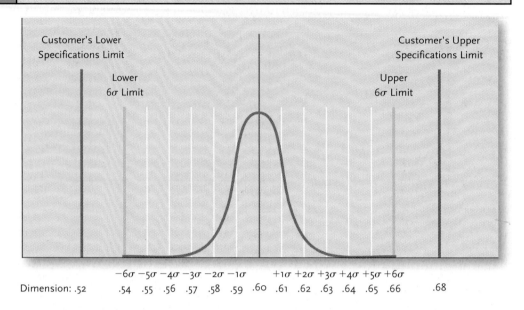

Suppose the small stamped part we discussed in our previous example is a component of such a product, and the product contains 125 components, each of which could cause a product failure. With 3σ limits in place, we know that there is a 99.74 percent likelihood of each component being good. With 99.74 percent confidence for each component, and 125 components, there is only a 72.22 percent (0.9974 raised to the 125th power) probability that all 125 components would be sound and that the product would work. A 72.22 percent confidence in a product being usable would not be sufficient for most producers. A much higher confidence in component quality is required to bring about an acceptable level of quality for the finished product.

om ADVANTAGE   What Does Six Sigma Really Mean?

Six Sigma has become synonymous with extremely high levels of reliability. With 6 standard deviations inside the customer specifications, the likelihood of a defect occurring due to random variation is less than two in one billion. With Three Sigma quality, there are nearly three defects in a thousand. It's hard to conceptualize the proportion of two in one billion, so here are some examples of Six Sigma in more visible contexts, compared to the accuracy associated with Three Sigma.

■ A book typed with a 3σ level of accuracy would average approximately 1.5 misspelled words per page. With 6σ accuracy there would be only one misspelled word in all of the books contained in a small library.

■ If the errors associated with 3σ were the months in a century, there would be $3\frac{1}{2}$ months. Six Sigma would be equal to 6 seconds out of a century.

■ If the error associated with 3σ was equal to a coast-to-coast trip across the United States, 6σ would be four steps.

Why would such a high level of quality be needed? Several examples drive the point home. With only Three Sigma quality, the following disasters would happen:

■ There would be 20,000 wrong prescriptions written per year.

■ More than 15,000 newborn babies would be accidentally dropped by doctors and nurses each year.

■ There would be nearly 500 wrong surgeries performed on patients *per week* in the United States.

■ The U.S. Postal Service would lose 2,000 articles of mail each hour.

■ Your drinking water would be unsafe for an hour each month, but you wouldn't know which hour.

Source: "Six Sigma: Motorola's Quest for Zero Defects," *APICS—The Performance Advantage*, July 1991, pp. 36–40; "Quality Control: U.S. Felt Earns a Business Practice Black Belt," *Midrange Enterprise*, April 2001, pp. 27–28.

This scenario actually opens up an opportunity to introduce another approach to obtaining high levels of quality in complex products. The greater the number of components, the higher the level of confidence necessary for each component in order to maintain an acceptable level of finished product quality. An alternative to increasing the confidence in components by reducing process variability would be to design the product with fewer components, which would also raise system reliability. Japanese auto manufacturers have utilized this approach extensively.

Between 1998 and 2004, Hyundai improved quality by 62 percent double the rate of industry improvement.

Taguchi Method

The tools presented in this chapter have focused on the needs of quality improvement approaches like TQM and Six Sigma. For the most part, they enhance managers' ability to detect and eliminate quality problems. Another approach to improving quality is to focus on the design of products and services. If products are designed appropriately, they should be robust enough to perform over a range of conditions that may exist during manufacture and use. This concept is known as **robust design** and is at the heart of the Taguchi Method. While quality is often defined as "meeting customer specifications" or "satisfying the customer," the Taguchi Method ties quality directly to cost. In this context, cost is not limited to production cost, but includes costs to the customer and to the economy. These economic costs include costs associated with rework and scrap, but also waste of resources, warranty costs, customer dissatisfaction, waste of time because of product failures, loss of market share, and so on. While traditional viewpoints maintain that as long as the parameter is within the customer's specifications, even though it deviates from the target value, it is not a defect and would not result in any economic loss. Taguchi's view is quite different. Taguchi describes this loss with the quadratic loss function presented in Exhibit 7.29. Rather than suggesting that as deviation from the target increases, customer dissatisfaction increases, the loss function is based on the square of the deviation from the target, which suggests that customers get increasingly dissatisfied and societal costs increase more as the deviation from the target value increases.

Taguchi's loss function shows how important it is to maintain performance at the target value. Maintaining performance at that value, according to the Taguchi Method, requires reducing the product design's sensitivity to sources of variability, rather than simply trying to control that variability. Developing designs that are insensitive requires that parameters in the design be tested by the designer, through experimentation. Those parameters that have the greatest influence on the performance must be identified. Given the potentially high number of design parameters that can make a difference, much of the

robust design
The design of products and services so that they perform over a wide range of conditions.

Sustainability

| **Taguchi's Quality Loss Function** | **EXHIBIT 7.29** |

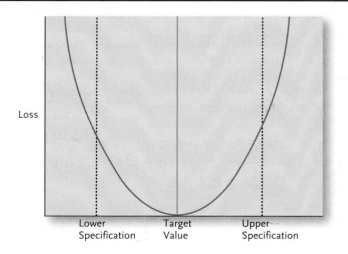

Loss

Lower Specification   Target Value   Upper Specification

Taguchi Method depends on the use of experiments to test the design parameters. The complexity and number of experiments required can be formidable. The Taguchi Method includes an approach to the design of these experiments that reduces the complexity of the experimentation process, improving the design and reducing the time required to reach the optimal design.

Moment-of-Truth Analysis

Certain instances in a customer's interaction with a business define the customer's perception of quality. These instances have a substantial impact and become ingrained in the customer's mind. If a service business can identify these critical instances and separate them from all other activities of the service, it can bring about a focus on issues that matter most to the customer. These instances, first identified by Jan Carlzon, CEO of Scandinavian Airlines System, are known as moments of truth, and the study of them is known as **moment-of-truth analysis.**[1,2] Moments of truth occur whenever a customer comes in contact with an organization and judges the quality of service being provided.

Close examination of how customers react to moments of truth provides valuable clues as to how to deal with customer interactions within the organization. Customers react in three different ways to moments of truth. Certain aspects of that interaction will be considered to be experience enhancers, some will be viewed as meeting standard expectations, and some will be perceived as experience detractors. **Experience enhancers** make the customer feel good about the interaction. They make the interaction better. A **standard expectation** is just that—the customer expects it and usually gets it. While enhancers are typically unexpected and viewed as very positive, standard expectations are taken for granted. **Experience detractors** are those aspects of the interaction that take away from the quality of the service. A customer views a detractor as something that signifies a reduction in the quality of service.

A moment-of-truth analysis requires gathering data from customers about the enhancers, detractors, and standard expectations for all service encounters. Then attention can be given to the moments of truth—through process change, process improvement, and employee training—and eliminating detractors and adding enhancers.

Service processes become more critical when they are expanded to include Internet-based services. Processes that are accomplished in a brick and mortar business by interacting with employees are accomplished electronically on the World Wide Web for an Internet-based company. Entering information, waiting for a page to download, or trying to understand a checkout process on the Internet has a tangible counterpart in a traditional service. The reaction of a customer to unnecessary requests for information, a slow page download, or a confusing checkout process is the same in both settings, only in the Internet company it can be acted on much more quickly. After all, it is much easier for a customer to click to a competitor than to drive to one. Businesses that have an online presence must recognize that an "e" process is just another process to a customer. It should be clearly defined and it should be quick. Estimates range up to 75 percent for the portion of customers who abandon their shopping carts at a Web site checkout. Reasons vary from confusion to surprisingly large shipping costs. Billions of dollars of sales are lost because customers abandon pages that download too slowly. No one wants to wait for the three-minute download of a "splash page" that contains nothing useful to the customer anyway. Moments of truth become "seconds of truth" at Internet speed.

Technological Advances in Quality Information Management: Customer Relationship Management

The discussion of quality in this chapter, from the eight tools to six sigma quality to moment-of-truth analysis, is focused on one overriding issue: pleasing the customer. Do what the customer wants. If this is accomplished, the customer comes back. Success

---

moment-of-truth analysis

The identification of the critical instances when a customer judges service quality and determines the experience enhancers, standard expectations, and experience detractors.

experience enhancers

In moment-of-truth analysis, these are experiences that make the customer feel good about the interaction and make the interaction better.

standard expectation

In moment-of-truth analysis, these are experiences that are expected and taken for granted by customers.

experience detractors

In moment-of-truth analysis, when an experience viewed by the customer is viewed as a detractor or as something that signifies a reduction in the quality of service.

means that the business has acquired the valuable resource of customer loyalty. Customer loyalty increases profitability. Loyal customers do not take their business to competitors. They tell their friends about their experiences and they are actually easier to please than nonloyal customers, resulting in lower costs.

Customer loyalty requires ongoing relationships with customers. Advances in technologies, applications, and techniques have enhanced companies' ability to manage relationships with customers. This relatively new focus for businesses, known as **customer relationship management (CRM),** has set new standards for the way people are treated.

Recall from the discussion of the Kano model in Chapter 6 how a "delighter" can gradually become something that is taken for granted. This is definitely the case with CRM. CRM systems can consist of virtually anything that relates to customer contact. In many instances, they include call center management software; they also track all sales, marketing, and customer service interactions with customers. CRM enables anyone who interacts with a particular customer to know about all previous interactions. Different departments can have access to information related to a particular customer. Customers perceive a more consistent experience because they get a more unified interaction with the business, no matter who the contact person is. CRM is often extended to the organization's Web site to enable customers to interact.

When interactions with consumers in B2C relationships are necessary, CRM may include access to data on, for example, previous purchases, clothing sizes, interests, and payment modes. If you've purchased over the Internet or over the phone, you may have wondered how the call center staff person knew something about you. The answer: CRM software accessed a database that included information on previous interactions with you.

When Something Still Goes Wrong: Recovery

Despite every effort to ensure good quality, despite every effort to minimize variability, and despite every effort to provide customers with exactly what they want, there will still be times when customers do not get what they want. It may be because of an actual failure, or it may be because a customer has expectations that are different from the norm. In any case, because the customer defines quality, poor quality as perceived by the customer is just that—poor quality.

A failure, be it a product that didn't meet expectations or service that fell short, does not have to mean a lost customer or even lost customer loyalty. Quality-oriented businesses have in place a **recovery plan,** a plan to save the customer when a failure occurs. In some cases, a failure followed by an excellent recovery can result in the customer feeling even better about the business than if no failure had occurred.

Successful recovery plans are well thought out, well known to all employees, and designed to make the customer end up feeling good about the experience. Unsuccessful recovery plans make a token effort to please the customer, don't eliminate the bad experience, and do not result in retaining the customer. We've all experienced both situations. You've probably received bad food or bad service at an expensive restaurant, and after complaining you've been told that the meal would be free. Of course, it should be free! If you'd purchased a pair of shoes that fell apart the day after you bought them, you wouldn't hesitate to demand your money back. We tend to be very willing to demand our money back when a product is bad, but we hesitate to demand our money back when service is bad. We grumble about it, but we rarely take a stand. Even when someone asks "Was everything OK?" we are likely to say "Yeah, everything was fine," even when it wasn't. A good manager does not want to hear that things were great when they weren't. Negative comments are critical to the business that wants to improve. Negative experiences provide an opportunity to improve, and the savvy manager should be very willing to pay for those opportunities. A business should consider the cost of a recovery to be the cost of extremely valuable information. If it can help the business improve, it is worth the investment.

The only automobile manufacturer to ever win the Baldrige Award was Cadillac in 1990.

customer relationship management (CRM)
Systems designed to improve relationships with customers and improve the business's ability to identify valuable customers. They include call center management software, sales tracking, and customer service.

recovery plan
Policies for how employees are to deal with quality failures so that customers will return.

Returning to the restaurant example, the common practice of eliminating the charge for a bad meal isn't an acceptable recovery plan. The customer will leave feeling the service was bad and probably will not return. A successful recovery plan requires doing what it takes to make the customer feel good about the experience and want to come back—for example, eliminating the charges for the meal, having the manager apologize profusely, and offering a pair of gift certificates for a later date for any meal on the menu. This will probably get a person to return. And if the follow-up experience is a good one, the customer will come back again. You might think that such a recovery would be too expensive, but the only real cost is the cost of raw food, and that is minimal when compared to the revenue stream generated by a loyal customer.

CHAPTER SUMMARY

The quality of services and products is such an important component of value, and value is such an important prerequisite to profitability, that issues of quality arise in every facet of business management. This chapter examined the link between quality and value and introduced a number of tools to assist in the management of quality. It focused on tools that can help turn data into useful information. The tools discussed create the means by which the QI story and DMAIC can be implemented. One of the most important tools, statistical process control, is universal in its contribution to the prevention of defects.

Whereas producers of products have begun to master quality management, providers of services are somewhat behind. To compound the problem of service quality, consumers are being exposed to more and more services, further increasing their exposure to poor quality. Part of the overall problem lies in the unwillingness of consumers to demand quality in services in the same way they demand quality in products. Good businesses recognize that when it comes to poor quality, no news is *not* good news. The quiet customers, who speak little but leave dissatisfied and never return, can kill a business. Only through actively seeking out customer wants and needs can a business actually fulfill them.

KEY TERMS

acceptable quality level (AQL), 263
acceptance sampling, 262
assignable cause variability, 244
attribute, 257
capability index, 255
cause and effect diagram, 238
check sheet, 243
C-chart, 261
common cause variability, 244
consumer's risk, 263
control limits, 247
customer relationship management
   (CRM), 269
experience detractors, 268
experience enhancers, 268
histogram, 242
lot tolerance percent defective (LTPD), 263

moment-of-truth analysis, 268
operating characteristics (OC) curve, 263
P-chart, 258
Pareto analysis, 240
Pareto chart, 240
process capability, 255
producer's risk, 263
recovery plan, 269
R-chart, 252
robust design, 267
run chart, 237
scatter diagram, 244
standard expectation, 268
statistical process control (SPC), 245
statistical process control chart, 245
X-bar chart, 245

KEY FORMULAE

Sample Mean for X-Bar Charts

(7.1)
$$\overline{X}_l = \frac{x_1 + x_2 + x_3 + x_4 + \cdots + x_n}{n}$$

Process Mean for X-Bar Charts

(7.2)
$$\overline{\overline{X}}_1 = \frac{\overline{X}_1 + \overline{X}_2 + \overline{X}_3 + \overline{X}_4 + \cdots + \overline{X}_k}{k}$$

Control Limits for X-bar Charts (if Process σ Is Known)

(7.3)
$$\overline{\overline{x}} + z\sigma_{\overline{x}}$$

(7.4)
$$\overline{\overline{x}} - z\sigma_{\overline{x}}$$

Control Limits for X-Bar Charts

(7.5)
$$\text{UCL} = \overline{\overline{X}} + A_2\overline{R}$$

(7.6)
$$\text{LCL} = \overline{\overline{X}} - A_2\overline{R}$$

Mean Range for R-Chart

(7.7)
$$\overline{R} = \frac{R_1 + R_2 + R_3 + R_4 + \cdots + R_k}{k}$$

Control Limits for R-Charts

(7.8)
$$\text{UCL} = D_4\overline{R}$$

(7.9)
$$\text{LCL} = D_3\overline{R}$$

Process Capability for Centered Processes

(7.10)
$$C_p = \frac{\text{Upper Specification Limit} - \text{Lower Specification Limit}}{6\sigma}$$

Process Capability for Uncentered Processes

(7.11)
$$C_{pk} = \min\left[\frac{\text{Process Mean} - \text{LCS}}{3\sigma}, \frac{\text{UCS} - \text{Process Mean}}{3\sigma}\right]$$

Standard Deviation of the Distribution of Percentage Defective

(7.12)
$$\sigma_p = \sqrt{\overline{p}(1 - \overline{p})/n}$$

Control Limits for P-charts

(7.13)
$$\text{UCL} = \overline{p} + z\sigma_p$$

(7.14)
$$\text{LCL} = \overline{p} - z\sigma_p$$

Variance for Poisson Distribution (C-chart)

(7.15)
$$\sigma^2 = \overline{c}$$

Standard Deviation of Nonconformities per Unit (C-chart)

(7.16)
$$\sigma = \sqrt{\overline{c}}$$

Control Limits for C-charts

(7.17) $$\text{UCL} = \bar{c} + 3(\sigma)$$

(7.18) $$\text{LCL} = \bar{c} - 3(\sigma)$$

SOLVED PROBLEMS

Constructing X-bar Charts

Sammy's Sammiches is reputed to have the best sandwiches in town. Sammy makes sure his sandwiches have enough meat, but needs to monitor the amount of meat on a sandwich in order to control costs. He wants 5 ounces of meat on a sandwich. He doesn't want his employees to weigh each portion of meat, however, because he thinks that if customers see that happening, it will it look like he is scrimping on the sandwich. Instead, he trains his employees to be able to judge approximately what a 5-ounce portion of meat is. Sammy is concerned that lately, his employees have gotten careless and are adding too much meat to the sandwiches. Each day last week, during the lunch hour, Sammy discretely took 6 portions of meat from sandwiches that were being assembled. He weighed each portions and those data are presented below:

	Monday	Tuesday	Wednesday	Thursday	Friday	Saturday
Sample 1	5.1	4.8	4.9	4.8	5.2	4.8
Sample 2	5.0	5.1	5.2	5.0	5.0	5.3
Sample 3	4.8	4.9	4.7	4.6	5.3	5.0
Sample 4	5.3	5.0	5.2	5.4	4.8	5.3
Sample 5	4.7	5.5	5.2	5.2	5.2	5.1
Sample 6	5.4	5.3	5.1	5.0	4.8	5.1

Construct an X-bar chart. Calculate the sample means and $\bar{\bar{X}}$, and using the range values and Exhibit 7.15, determine the upper and lower control limits. Interpret the chart using the criteria from Exhibits 7.19 and 7.20.

Solution

Step	Objective	Explanation
1.	Compute the sample means.	For each sample of 6 weights, compute the average. The sample means are shown below.
2.	Compute $\bar{\bar{X}}$.	Compute $\bar{\bar{X}}$ by computing the mean of the sample means. The grand mean is 5.06.
3.	Calculate the ranges and $\bar{R}$.	The ranges are calculated as the largest minus the smallest in each sample. Compute the mean of the ranges ($\bar{R}$).
4.	Compute the upper and lower control limits.	Using Exhibit 7.15 with a sample size of 6, the A_2 value is .48. Using Equations 7.5 and 7.6: $(\text{UCL}) = \bar{\bar{X}} + A_2\bar{R}$ $= 5.06 + (.483 \times .6167)$ $= 5.06 + .2968$ $= 5.3568$ $(\text{LCL}) = \bar{\bar{X}} - A_2\bar{R}$ $= 5.06 + (.483 \times .6167)$ $= 5.06 - .2968$ $= 4.7642$

| X-Bar Chart for Sammy's Sammiches | EXHIBIT 7.30 |

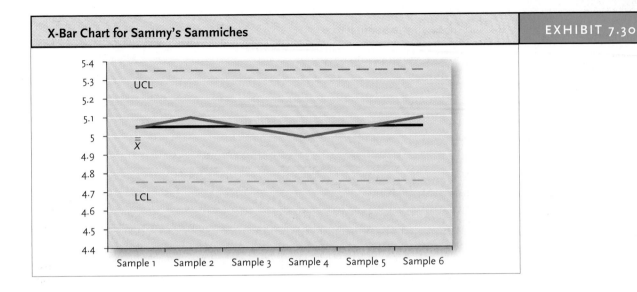

5.   Draw the   The chart is presented below in Exhibit 7.30.
      X-bar chart.

6.   Interpretation.   Based on the patterns and the fact that no data points are
                         outside of the control limits, the process appears to be in
                         control.

	Monday	Tuesday	Wednesday	Thursday	Friday	Saturday
Sample 1	5.1	4.8	4.9	4.8	5.2	4.8
Sample 2	5.0	5.1	5.2	5.0	5.0	5.3
Sample 3	4.8	4.9	4.7	4.6	5.3	5.0
Sample 4	5.3	5.0	5.2	5.4	4.8	5.3
Sample 5	4.7	5.5	5.2	5.2	5.2	5.1
Sample 6	5.4	5.3	5.1	5.0	4.8	5.1
$\bar{X} =$	5.05	5.1	5.05	5.0	5.05	5.1
					$\bar{\bar{X}} =$	5.06
$R =$	0.7	0.7	0.5	0.8	0.5	0.5
$\bar{R} = .6167$						

Constructing R-Charts

Using the data from Sammy's Sammiches (above) calculate R-bar, the upper and lower
control limits, and construct the R-chart. Interpret the chart using the criteria from Exhibits 7.19 and 7.20.

Solution

Step	Objective	Explanation
1.	Compute the sample ranges and $\bar{R}$.	The sample range is the largest value minus the smallest value for each sample. Compute the mean of the sample ranges for $\bar{R}$. The values are calculated below.
2.	Determine the values for D_3 and D_4.	With a sample size of 6, the value for D_3 is 0. The value for D_4 is 2.004.

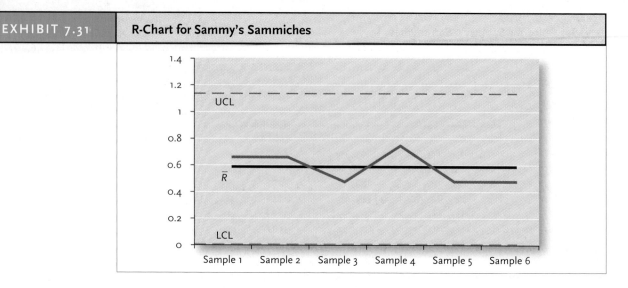

EXHIBIT 7.31 R-Chart for Sammy's Sammiches

Step	Objective	Explanation
3.	Compute the upper and lower control limits.	Using Equations 7.5 and 7.6, and the D_3 and D_4 values from Exhibit 7.15, the UCL and LCL are calculated as: $$UCL = D_4\bar{R}$$ $$= 2.004\,(.61667)$$ $$= 1.2358$$ $$LCL = D_3\bar{R}$$ $$= 0\,(.61667)$$ $$= 0$$
4.	Construct the R-chart	With $\bar{R}$, the R values, and the UCL and LCL, construct the chart. The completed chart is below in Exhibit 7.31.

	Monday	Tuesday	Wednesday	Thursday	Friday	Saturday
Sample 1	5.1	4.8	4.9	4.8	5.2	4.8
Sample 2	5.0	5.1	5.2	5.0	5.0	5.3
Sample 3	4.8	4.9	4.7	4.6	5.3	5.0
Sample 4	5.3	5.0	5.2	5.4	4.8	5.3
Sample 5	4.7	5.5	5.2	5.2	5.2	5.1
Sample 6	5.4	5.3	5.1	5.0	4.8	5.1
$\bar{X} =$	5.05	5.1	5.05	5.0	5.05	5.1
					$\bar{\bar{X}} =$	5.06
R	0.7	0.7	0.5	0.8	0.5	0.5
$\bar{R} = .61667$						

Determining Process Capability (C_p) for a Centered Process

Simpson's Outdoor Products is a contract manufacturer for a variety of fishing tackle brands. One of their plants produces nylon monofilament fishing line for a variety of high-end labels. They have been asked to manufacturer a new fluorocarbon line that is supposed to be 6-pound test line. The customer demands that it average 6-pound test and that it cannot vary by more than 6 percent from that target. Simpson's line production process can meet the 6-pound target easily and currently has a standard deviation of .168 pounds. Is Simpson's process capable of meeting this customer's demands?

Solution

Step	Objective	Explanation
1.	Determine the UCS and LCS values.	From Equation 7.10, the C_p formula is $(UCS - LCS)/6\sigma$. The customer wants the mean at 6-pound test, so that will be the center of the process. Six percent above and below is .36 pound above and below, so the UCS and LCS values will be UCS = 6.36 LCS = 5.64
2.	Determine 6σ.	The process standard deviation is provided as .168 pound. Thus, 6σ is $6(.168) = 1.008$ pounds
3.	Calculate C_p.	$\dfrac{UCS - LCS}{6\sigma} = \dfrac{6.36 - 5.64}{1.008}$ $= 0.714286$
4.	Interpret.	The C_p is less than 1, which means that the process is not capable of meeting the customer's demands. If Simpson's produces the line, they will experience common cause variability beyond the customer's specifications.

Determining Process Capability (C_{pk}) for a Noncentered Process

Mayra Birch, a process engineer for Simpson's Outdoor Products, has found that the openings in the extruder nozzles for the monofilament fishing line process get larger over time due to corrosion from the hot material that flows through them. She has determined that beginning the process off-center, and letting it drift, would still meet most of their customer's specifications and save a significant amount of money from the reduction in nozzle replacement and process downtime. The current production run is for 12-pound test line. The customer's specifications dictate that it must be between 11.5- and 12.5-pound test. In her first test of this new approach, Mayra is monitoring the process very closely to get an idea of how long the nozzle can be used before it must be changed. She has collected the following process data. Should the nozzle be changed?

Process standard deviation = .09 pound

Current process mean $(\overline{\overline{X}})$ = 12.2 pounds

Solution

Step	Objective	Explanation
1.	The formula for C^{pk} is $\min\left[\dfrac{\text{process mean} - LCS}{3\sigma}, \dfrac{UCS - \text{process mean}}{3\sigma}\right]$ Determine the UCS and LCS values. Determine 3σ and the process mean $(\overline{\overline{X}})$.	From the problem, UCS = 12.5 pounds LCS = 11.5 pounds $3\sigma = 3(.09)$ $=.27)$ $\overline{\overline{X}} = 12.2$ pounds
2.	Calculate C_{pk}.	$\dfrac{12.2 - 11.5}{.27}$ $= 2.593$ $\dfrac{12.5 - 12.2}{.27}$ $= 1.111$

Step	Objective	Explanation
3.	Interpret.	Both values are greater than 1. The smallest is 1.111 and is in the direction the process is drifting (toward the UCS). It is close, but not quite to the point where the 3σ will cross over the UCS.

Constructing P-Charts

Annie's Deli is a large operation that delivers sandwiches and deli platters on and around campus. Annie strives for a 20-minute delivery but has had some trouble actually accomplishing it. Her deli delivers anywhere from 100 to 200 deliveries per day. Over the past 6 months, Annie has determined that the proportion of deliveries that took longer than 20 minutes has been .14. Annie has had some turnover among employees and is concerned that her delivery performance may be getting worse. Over the past 10 days, Annie has collected samples of delivery times for 50 deliveries each day. Her samples are below.

Sample	Proportion >20 Minutes	Sample	Proportion >20 Minutes
Sample 1	.15	Sample 6	.16
Sample 2	.12	Sample 7	.18
Sample 3	.17	Sample 8	.14
Sample 4	.14	Sample 9	.15
Sample 5	.13	Sample 10	.13

Solution

Step	Objective	Explanation
1.	Compute the standard deviation of the distribution of the proportion defective.	From Equation 7.12 $$\sigma_p = \sqrt{\bar{p}(1 - \bar{p}/n}$$ $$= \sqrt{.14(1 - .14)/50}$$ $$= .0491$$
2.	Compute the upper and lower control limits.	$$UCL = \bar{p} + 3\sigma_p$$ $$= .14 + 3(.0491)$$ $$= .287$$ $$LCL = \bar{p} - 3\sigma_p$$ $$= -0.007$$ The LCL is at 0.
3.	Construct the P-chart.	The chart is presented in Exhibit 7.32.
4.	Interpret the P-chart.	The process is in control, which means Annie's delivery performance has not changed.

| P-Chart for Annie's Deli: | EXHIBIT 7.32 |

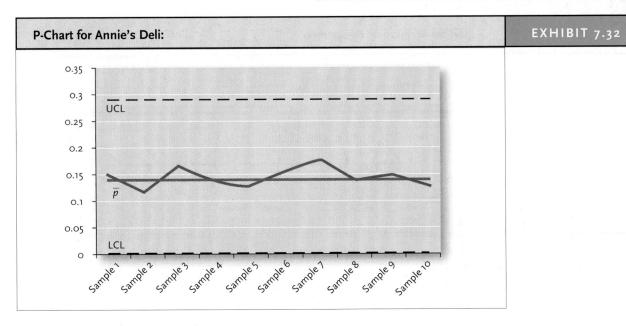

Constructing C-Charts

The Economics Department is concerned about falling attendance in their large-lecture classes. The large Econ classes are all held in the same classroom, which holds 158 students and is filled to capacity. All sections in this room are monitored and data are recorded. The absentee data for 14 sections is

Section	Absences
1	12
2	16
3	8
4	17
5	14
6	20
7	7
8	9
9	15
10	13
11	9
12	13
13	10
14	14

Solution

Step	Objective	Explanation
1.	Compute the standard deviation of the distribution of nonconformities per unit (σ). First calculate the $\bar{c}$, then σ.	From Equations 7.15 and 7.16 $$\sigma^2 = \bar{c}$$ $$\bar{c} = 12.643$$ $$\sigma = \sqrt{\bar{c}}$$ $$= 3.556$$
2.	Compute the upper and lower control limits.	From Equations 7.17 and 7.18 $$\text{UCL} = \bar{c} + 3\,(\sigma)$$ $$\text{LCL} = \bar{c} - 3\,(\sigma)$$

| EXHIBIT 7.33 | C-Chart for Economics Department |

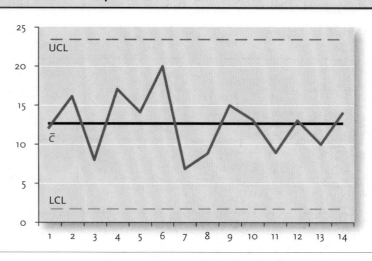

Step	Objective	Explanation
		UCL $= 12.643 + 3(3.556)$
		$\quad = 23.311$
		LCL $= 12.643 - 3(3.556)$
		$\quad = 1.975$
3.	Construct the C-chart.	The complete C-chart is presented in Exhibit 7.33.
4.	Interpret the C-chart.	The process appears to be in control. This means that there do not appear to be absences that are outside of what would occur because of common cause variability.

REVIEW QUESTIONS

1. For each of the following eight general-purpose quality tools, draw a sketch, describe how the tool works, and provide an example application:
   a. Flow chart
   b. Run chart
   c. Cause and effect diagram
   d. Pareto chart
   e. Histogram
   f. Check sheet
   g. Scatter diagram
   h. Control chart

2. Why is the elimination of process variability important for improving quality?

3. What is meant by common cause variability? Assignable cause variability?

4. What do control limits designate for a process?

5. How can statistical process control charts be used to distinguish between common cause and assignable cause variability?

6. What is meant by the phrase "the process is not in control"?

7. What is meant by "process capability"?

8. Can a process be in control but not capable? Explain.

9. Can a process be capable but not in control? Explain.

10. Why must an X-bar chart be used in conjunction with an R-chart?

11. What is a P-chart? How is it used?

12. What is a C-chart? How is it used?

13. What is acceptance sampling? What is meant by AQL, LTPD, producer's risk, and consumer's risk?

14. Describe the literal implications of Six Sigma quality. How does Six Sigma quality relate to process capability? What environments are particularly in need of Six Sigma?

15. Describe Taguchi's loss function. What implications does it have for costs associated with variation from the target level of performance?

16. How does moment-of-truth analysis improve service quality? What is meant by enhancers, expectations, and detractors?

17. How does customer relationship management improve customer loyalty?

18. What is a recovery plan? What should the objective of a good recovery plan be?

DISCUSSION AND EXPLORATION

1. Why is process variability so important to the management of quality?

2. Why are nonrandom patterns of data considered to be justification for identifying variability as having an assignable cause? How do these patterns relate to a data point being above or below the 3σ control limit?

3. Describe the difference between the C_p calculation and the C_{pk} calculation. How are they similar?

4. Why is it advantageous to reduce process variability if one is going to allow the process to drift?

5. What are the dangers associated with acceptance sampling? When is it appropriate?

6. If Six Sigma was in place, what would be the acceptable value for C_p?

7. What are the conflicts between the concept of process capability and Taguchi's loss function?

8. Identify the moments of truth for a business that you frequent. What are the enhancers, standard expectations, and detractors?

9. Describe the potential conflicts between customer relationship management and the desire for privacy. Where do you draw the line regarding the type of information you want businesses to have?

10. Design a recovery system for a frequently experienced quality problem. How does your recovery system differ from those you typically encounter?

11. What are the most recent examples of bad quality (product or service) you have been exposed to? What was your reaction? In hindsight, should your reaction have been different? What recovery attempts were made by the business? Were they successful?

12. Identify a commonly occurring example of poor service quality. From the perspective of the management of the business that provides the poor quality, design a process for determining the cause of the quality problem. What tools might be used in the analysis?

PROBLEMS ⊞

Solutions to odd-numbered problems are located on the text's Online Center (http://mhhe.com/opsnow3e).

1. State University sent a survey to all its first-year students. The responses are given in the following table. Perform a Pareto analysis on the data and construct a Pareto chart.

Type	Number of Complaints	Cumulative Total	Percentage of Total	Cumulative Percentage
Problems with roommate	16	16	22%	22%
Lack of privacy	18	34	24	46
Community bathrooms	32	66	43	89
Noise	8	74	11	100
Total	74			

2. J&R Investments surveyed its clients on the reasons they chose to invest with the company. Some 49 percent responded that it was due to the high returns that J&R's funds offered; 15 percent attributed their selection to the variety of funds that the company offered; 23 percent felt J&R's reputation was worthy of their business; 13 percent were won over by the company's security. The company received a total of 150 responses. Perform a Pareto analysis and construct a Pareto chart for the survey results.

3. Patch is a popular manufacturer of blue jeans. The company maintains a strong quality policy with regard to its products. Last month the company held 94 pairs of blue jeans due to quality issues: 11 of the problems were due to poor fabric, 17 were related to improper stitching, 28 resulted from poor coloring, and 34 were because of irregular sizing. Management plans to present the quality information at a monthly meeting. Perform a Pareto analysis and construct a Pareto chart for this meeting.

4. A pizza company is having trouble with pizzas arriving cold because deliveries are taking too long. Management has kept track of when a late delivery was made, as well as who the driver was. The data are in the chart below. The times are in two-hour shifts. A, B, or C indicates the driver for the late delivery.

Shift	Monday	Tuesday	Wednesday	Thursday	Friday
4–6	AC	AAB	AABCCC	A	ABC
6–8	BCC	ABCC	ABCCC	BBCC	ABBBCCC
8–10	AC	BB	BBCCC	BCC	AABBCCC
10–12	AC	BBCC	ABBCCC	BC	BBC

Construct Pareto charts for the following:

a. The number of late deliveries for each driver, by day and by shift.

b. The number of late deliveries for each day of the week, by driver and by shift.

c. The number of late deliveries for each shift, by driver and by day.

What do the charts indicate about the quality problems?

5. Swifty's pizza parlor monitors the temperatures of their pizzas just prior to pickup for delivery. Every 30 minutes the 3 pizzas are sampled. The grand mean of the process is 122 degrees and the average range per sample is 12 degrees. Determine the upper and lower control limits for an X-bar chart.

6. Henry's Meat Market makes its own sausages and other meats. Their sausage machine is calibrated to put 6 ounces of sausage in each casing and has met this goal, on average. Every hour, five sausages are weighed, and the average plotted on an X-bar

chart. The average range is 0.4 ounce. Determine the upper and lower control limits for an X-bar chart and for an R-chart.

7. The First Regional Bank requires its tellers to sample the amount of withdrawals customers make in order to track the amount of cash kept on hand. The withdrawal information is charted below. The R-bar value is 50. The process standard deviation is not known. Construct an X-bar chart from the data.

Sample	Observation		
Number	1	2	3
1	$20.00	$40.00	$60.00
2	35.00	50.00	10.00
3	40.00	20.00	75.00
4	30.00	125.00	50.00
5	20.00	40.00	20.00

8. InkWell produces inkjet printers. The company must control the weight of packaging material for each packaged printer in order to maintain and control shipping costs. Sample data are given below in pounds. The R-bar value is 1.2. Construct an X-bar chart with the data. The process standard deviation is not known.

Sample	Observation		
Number	1	2	3
1	12.2	14.1	11.9
2	12.1	12.9	12.5
3	11.8	12.4	12.1
4	12.4	13.6	12.1
5	12	12.9	12.6

9. Mr. Salty bakes and sells pretzels. The company carefully controls the amount of pretzels it puts in each bag. Below are data from the last five quality checks. The process standard deviation is not known. Use the data to construct an R-chart.

Sample	Observation	
Number	1	2
1	78	76
2	78	75
3	77	77
4	79	77
5	76	78

10. CarPro specializes in renting cars for students going on spring break. Due to the long travel distances, the company carefully controls the miles-per-gallon that the cars get. Sample data are given below. The process standard deviation is not known. Construct an X-bar and R-chart with the data.

Sample	Observation		
Number	1	2	3
1	20.4	20.2	21.4
2	19.3	20.5	20.8
3	21.1	20.8	20.1
4	21.2	19.7	20.5
5	20.4	21.1	19.5

11. As new employees have been hired to replace students who have graduated, the customer wait time at the Mean Bean Burrito Stand has gotten longer. Owner Marge Welch randomly times 6 orders per hour during the busiest hours of the day. She has collected the following data but does not know standard deviation of the serving times. Construct X-bar and R-charts for the data.

	10:00	11:00	12:00	1:00	2:00
Sample 1	2	6	4	3	6
Sample 2	3	6	2	3	6
Sample 3	6	5	2	4	6
Sample 4	5	5	2	5	2
Sample 5	6	2	3	2	3
Sample 6	6	5	2	4	2

12. Andy's Candies sells jellybeans. Each bag of candy must be carefully monitored for the proper weight. The company samples and charts the weight of bags of jellybeans as part of its quality control program. The results are given below. Construct X-bar and R-charts using the data. The process standard deviation is not known.

Sample Number	Observation		
	1	2	3
1	1.1	1.2	1.6
2	2	1.3	1.6
3	3.8	1.2	1.7
4	1.9	1.2	1.4
5	1.4	1.1	1.8

13. Metropolitan Airport carefully tracks the length of flight delays. The most current data are given below. Construct an X-bar and an R-chart from the data. The process standard deviation is not known. What conclusions can be drawn?

Sample Number	Observation (minutes late)	
	1	2
1	10.1	20.2
2	19.3	94.1
3	8.1	35.8
4	21.2	43.1
5	32.1	26.7

14. Mortis Dining Hall is the primary dining hall for students living in the dormitory. It conducted a study on the amount of time students needed to use the dining hall's services. The results of the study are given below. The standard deviation of the process is not known. Provide an X-bar chart, an R-chart, and any conclusions that you may draw from the charts.

Sample Number	Observation		
	1	2	3
1	30	18	47
2	8	21	32
3	16	22	26
4	32	48	53
5	16	24	19
6	12	21	27
7	22	19	32
8	26	31	15

15. Tie's Drive-In is a popular hamburger restaurant. To accommodate the large quantity of hamburgers ordered each day, the eatery has purchased a machine that will rapidly roll hamburger patties. However, the hamburgers appear to be different sizes from each other. Tie, the owner, kept track of the weights of recent hamburger patties. Tie's does not know the standard deviation of the process. You have been brought in to provide your recommendations. Should Tie continue to use the machine? Create an R-chart and an X-bar chart to support your recommendations.

| Sample | Observation | | | |
Number	1	2	3	4
1	0.35	0.36	0.35	0.34
2	0.34	0.36	0.36	0.35
3	0.21	0.26	0.36	0.35
4	0.31	0.34	0.34	0.36
5	0.47	0.49	0.36	0.35

16. Steve's oyster bar has received oysters from the same supplier for 18 years. He has recently become concerned about the size of his oysters, so he decided to begin monitoring the size by using an X-bar and R-chart. He measures the length of the oysters in centimeters for 8 samples of 6 oysters per sample. The process standard deviation is not known. The data he collected for his first delivery are presented below:

Sample							
1	2	3	4	5	6	7	8
9	7	4	9	6	8	10	8
7	6	5	6	7	7	9	10
6	10	9	7	6	5	7	9
5	6	6	8	10	7	7	6
6	6	7	9	9	7	5	9
5	5	10	6	6	6	9	7

a. Determine an X-bar for each sample group.

b Determine an X-double bar.

c. Determine the range for each sample group.

d. Determine an R-bar.

e. Complete an X-bar and R-chart for the data.

17. The Wave is a small water park that features several slides and a wave pool. Given its small size, management is always concerned about overcrowding, which leads to long waiting lines. During the summer, they monitor the line length of "The Snake," which is their best water slide. Part of the reason they monitor it is to help them understand how many people to let into the park, but the other reason is to indicate whether the worker who actually tells visitors when to go is doing so correctly. They do not want sliders to start too early or they could cause an injury to the person in front of them. They do not want sliders to wait too long, or it makes everyone have to wait longer. On an average day in the summer, the waiting line at The Snake has 22 people in it. The process standard deviation is not known. Andy Green, the assistant manager in charge of overseeing The Snake, counts the number of people in the line at 10-minute increments, giving him 6 observations for every hour. The data collected for a Monday are presented below:

| Hour | Observation | | | | | |
	1	2	3	4	5	6
1	21	24	18	22	20	14
2	18	18	28	27	24	25
3	14	18	24	14	16	24

			Observation			
Hour	1	2	3	4	5	6
4	20	16	19	22	17	18
5	26	22	25	26	24	14
6	28	27	25	24	24	23
7	24	22	22	19	18	26
8	19	23	25	26	21	23
9	23	25	22	18	20	23
10	18	17	17	19	21	22
11	25	26	27	26	25	26
12	22	25	25	24	27	24

Create an X-bar chart and R-chart for this data. Examine the outcomes to determine if the line management process is in control.

18. Total Quality Automotive produces small plastic components for cars. Their products are molded to meet specifications given in design drawings. Some of the very small components can be difficult to control because of variability in mold temperature and pressure, as well as raw material inconsistencies. The following data were gathered during 5 hours of processing windshield wiper control knobs on one particular mold. The process standard deviation is not known. Two samples were taken each hour; each sample contained six components. The variable being monitored was the inside diameter of the hole in the knob shaft. The measures are in millimeters.

			Observation			
Sample	1	2	3	4	5	6
1	2	2.1	2.04	2.03	2.07	1.94
2	2.1	2.05	2.09	1.96	1.97	2.03
3	2	1.89	1.94	1.97	2.04	2.1
4	2.09	2.03	2.07	2.06	1.95	1.96
5	1.98	1.99	1.93	1.99	2.03	2.04
6	2	2.05	2.03	1.98	2.03	2.05
7	1.91	1.94	1.99	1.92	2.04	2.03
8	1.97	2	2.06	2.09	1.93	1.9
9	1.9	1.91	1.94	1.93	1.95	1.91
10	1.89	1.9	1.92	1.96	1.91	1.94

Create an X-bar and R-chart for the data. Does the process appear to be in control? Explain your answer.

19. Application processing time for loans at First City Bank are monitored using X-bar and R-charts. Samples of processing times (in minutes) for 10 loans are taken twice per day. Sample data collected over the past week are presented below. The process standard deviation is not known. Construct and interpret the X-bar and R-charts.

	Monday		Tuesday		Wednesday		Thursday		Friday	
1	14	12	12	9	11	9	14	9	16	15
2	10	8	16	14	10	14	11	14	9	12
3	10	10	9	13	11	8	14	9	15	8
4	9	13	8	8	14	12	10	10	14	14
5	16	16	16	11	15	8	16	12	8	10
6	13	16	12	13	16	16	12	14	10	9
7	14	11	15	11	14	11	16	13	12	13
8	8	13	14	8	12	12	16	9	8	8
9	9	13	12	13	16	11	12	12	13	14
10	10	12	11	14	13	12	9	12	13	11

20. The Chipmunk Girls sell cookies every year as a fund raiser. A box of Skinny Minties, the most popular cookie, is supposed to weigh 10 ounces. Recently, several mother chipmunks have forwarded complaints from customers about some boxes having fewer cookies. ACME Cookie Company, the contract manufacturer of Skinny Minties, monitors the weight of these boxes using X-bar and R-charts. Sample groups with 8 boxes per group are taken. The results of 10 such samples are shown below. The process standard deviation is not known. Construct and interpret the X-bar and R-charts.

	GRP 1	GRP 2	GRP 3	GRP 4	GRP 5	GRP 6	GRP 7	GRP 8	GRP 9	GRP 10
1	10.3	10.5	10.2	10.9	8.2	7.9	11	9.5	7.3	9.2
2	11.2	8.3	8.1	8.3	10.5	8	8.7	9.1	8.7	9.5
3	8.4	9.2	11.5	10.2	9.7	8.1	9.4	9.4	5.9	9.6
4	10.7	10.7	10.3	9.5	9.1	9.2	8.5	10.3	6.8	10.8
5	8.6	11.4	9.6	10.3	11.3	6.6	11.1	10	8	9.4
6	10.1	9.7	10.6	8.2	8.7	8.3	9.2	8.8	9	8.2
7	11.3	9.6	11.1	8.6	8.1	8.1	8.6	10.4	8.3	9.6
8	10.1	10	9.8	10.6	8	7.5	9.4	9.2	7.5	8.1

21. A telemarketing firm monitors the time it takes operators to pick up a new call once their current call has ended. Operators are told that they should pick up a new call within 5 seconds of ending a current call. Six samples, with 15 times per sample, have been collected. Construct an X-bar and R-chart for the data. The process standard deviation is not known.

	Sample 1	Sample 2	Sample 3	Sample 4	Sample 5	Sample 6
1	6.8	3.9	5.8	2.9	2.9	6.8
2	2.9	3.9	2.9	4.9	2.9	3.9
3	5.8	5.8	2.9	6.8	2.9	5.8
4	3.9	4.9	2.9	5.8	2.9	4.9
5	4.9	2.9	6.8	6.8	7.2	2.9
6	2.8	6.8	3.9	2.1	2.9	8.0
7	5.8	5.8	4.9	6.8	4.9	6.8
8	4.9	6.8	6.8	2.9	3.9	4.9
9	3.9	3.9	5.8	6.8	2.9	5.8
10	6.8	7.1	3.9	3.9	6.8	5.8
11	3.9	2.9	6.8	3.9	5.8	6.8
12	2.9	6.8	5.8	3.9	7.2	3.9
13	6.8	2.9	7.6	4.9	3.9	5.8
14	6.8	3.9	3.9	5.8	4.9	5.8
15	5.8	3.9	4.9	2.9	4.9	5.8

22. You are employed by Control Consulting and have an important presentation tomorrow. The topic of the presentation is statistical process control charts. You have been given the charts (Exhibit 7.36) on page 287 to use in your presentation. Describe why statistical process control charts are used. Also interpret the charts. Are the data in control?

23. Consider the X-bar chart in Exhibit 7.34 (next page). Is the process in control? Identify as many ways as you can to indicate nonrandom data.

24. Examine the X-bar chart in Exhibit 7.35 (next page). Identify as many ways as you can that indicate the data are nonrandom.

EXHIBIT 7.34	X-Bar Chart

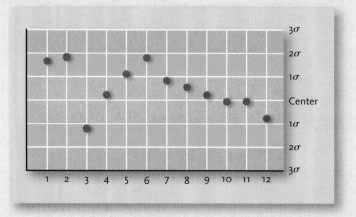

EXHIBIT 7.35	X-Bar Chart

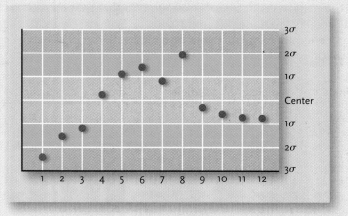

25. Simcoe Corporation, a manufacturer of ice skates, wishes to know if the company is able to make a new type of skate blade. The blades need to be 0.48 inch from top to bottom without varying more than ±0.02 inch. The company's machine responsible for producing the blades currently offers a standard deviation of 0.005 inch. Compute the C_p for the process. Will Simcoe be able to consistently manufacture the new skate blades to specification?

26. Giftnet is a proposed e-commerce Web site for a large clothing retailer. The company has a large number of customers who have shown an interest in purchasing clothes online, provided delivery of the merchandise would take no longer than seven days plus or minus half a day. A prototype of the e-tailor showed that by using a premium shipping service, the average delivery time is 7 days, with a standard deviation of 0.17 day. Giftnet believes it can make all of the desired delivery times. Is the company correct? Explain your answer in terms of the C_p for the process.

27. Willie is the head greenskeeper at Par Four Golf Course. He recently found out that the golfers prefer the fringe of the greens to be kept between a half inch and inch in length. Willie has a riding mower that can cut a mean of 0.75 inch with a standard deviation of 0.11 inch. He also has a hand mower that can cut at 0.75 inch with a

EXHIBIT 7.36

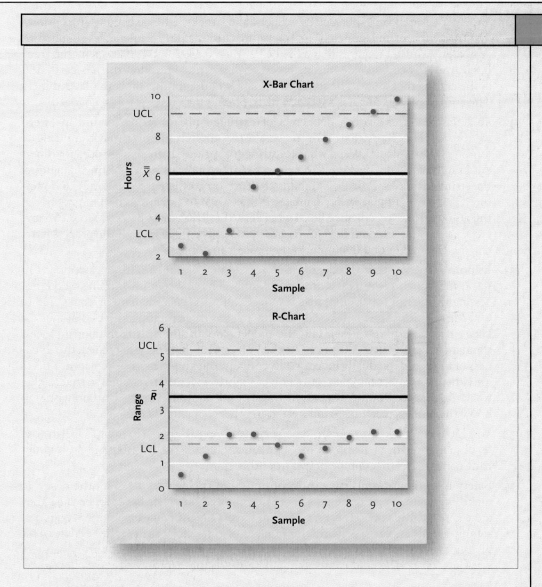

standard deviation of 0.06 inch, although it would take quite a bit more time. Compute the C_p for each mower. Should Willie use the rider or the hand mower? Explain your answer.

28. Bottoms-Up bottles soft drinks. It plans on introducing a new style of bottle to attract more drinkers. The new bottle can hold no more than 12.1 ounces of cola. The company also knows that anything less than 11.9 ounces in the new bottle will be apparent to potential customers as a less-than-full bottle because of the bottle's narrow neck. The current bottling machine is set for 12 ounces and is able to maintain a standard deviation of 0.019 ounce. Compute the C_p. Should the company adopt the new bottle? Explain your answer.

29. The specifications for a machined component are 30.0+/−1.5 millimeters. The machining process has a standard deviation of 0.298 millimeters. Assuming the process is centered, calculate the appropriate process capability index and make a recommendation as to the capability of the process.

30. The specification of the height for a small pin that goes into a fuel injection system is 20+/−0.05 millimeters. The cutting process has a standard deviation of 0.018 millimeters. Calculate the C_p. Is the process in control?

31. Anteater Skateboards outsources wheels and trucks (the axle and suspension). TuffTruck, the manufacturer of its trucks, machines axles to tolerances supplied by Anteater. Anteater requires that axles be between 0.2492 and 0.2508 inch. TuffTruck has learned to begin its axle turning process below center and allow the process to drift as the cutting tool wears. The standard deviation of the turning process is 0.0002 inch. The current process mean is at 0.2503 inch. Should the cutting tool be changed?

32. TekLane produces various diameters of extruded plastic string for use in "weed whackers." The plastic extrusion process forces molten plastic through a nozzle to form the plastic string. Weed whacker strings of various diameters are used for different brands of weed whackers. Over time, extrusion nozzles wear and the diameter of the string increases. Process variability depends on consistent temperature and pressure. The most popular string diameter is the 0.095. In order to function properly in the automatic string advance weed whackers, the string must be between 0.093 and 0.097 inch. The standard deviation of the process is 0.0004 inch. If the process is averaging a diameter of 0.096 inch, is the process in control?

33. Brittain's Fine Furniture produces customer cabinets and tables. Its production facilities utilize rough-sawn lumber from local mills. The first step in Brittain's wood processing is a planing operation, which surfaces all wood to a standard of from 0.748 to 0.752 inch thick. The planer used for surfacing has three rotating knives that must be kept extremely sharp to maintain the proper smooth finish. It maintains a process standard deviation of 0.0003 inch. As the knives wear and get resharpened, the thickness of the boards gradually increases. Eventually, the knives must be replaced. Knives are expensive, so Brittain purchases knives slightly wider than required so that as they wear, the thickness of the wood drifts through the allowable limits. Brittain wishes to know the process mean it should start at in order to maximize knife life.

34. You have been asked to present the accompanying R-chart (Exhibit 7.37) to top-level management at Dunham Inc. Explain the use of the R-chart and any significant conclusions that can be drawn from this chart.

35. Safety is a primary concern at Adventure Island theme park. Despite the desire to make everyone happy, some people are not allowed on particular rides because they are too short. Ride operators on rides that have a height requirement are required to submit a daily report specifying the number of riders rejected per 100 people. This gives management a sense of how many people get disappointed, but also a sense of what age group the ride is attracting. The following data have been collected on

EXHIBIT 7.37

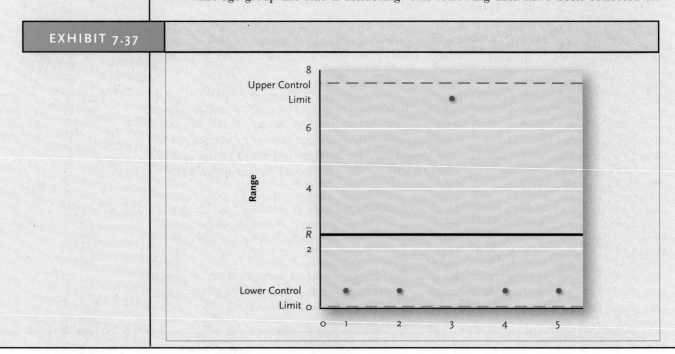

samples of 100 riders. Historically, the average proportion of riders that are too short has been .04.

8	4	0	6
5	5	8	8
0	6	1	7
0	8	0	0
7	5	8	7
5	7	5	6
3	5	7	6
3	0	3	5

Construct a P-chart from the data.

36. RGI is a consulting firm that specializes in helping insurance companies spot fraud. A common auto insurance scam is the "swoop and squat," in which a car swoops in front of another and then slams on the brakes, causing a rear-end collision. Passengers in the swooping car then claim neck and back injuries. RGI monitors the proportion of different types of accidents, like rear-end collisions, and compares them to industry norms for accidents with similar characteristics to determine whether a particular company is being victimized by scam artists. The industry norm for rear-end collisions, with 2 cars involved, where passengers in the rear-ended car number greater than 1 is .05. RGI takes samples of 40 claims and classifies the collisions. The following data were collected based on 24 samples.

7	9	8	8
7	5	7	7
8	16	5	4
7	7	15	3
8	3	8	4
7	7	5	5

Construct the P-chart and interpret the results.

37. Akins Manufacturing produces small LCD screens for such uses as mp3 players, handheld GPS units, cellular phones, and game players. Its standard screen is 320 by 240 pixels. Akins monitors faulty pixels with a C-chart. Every 10 minutes a screen is randomly removed, evaluated, and the results are plotted. Results for the past 3 hours are presented below.

2	6	4
5	1	3
6	3	6
3	3	4
4	4	2
3	1	6

Compute the upper and lower control limits for the C-chart and construct the chart.

38. ADX Shipping provides just-in-time shipping to businesses needing frequent, but small, deliveries in the Chicago metro area. Every time a shipment is delivered late, the driver is required to complete an incident report describing why the shipment was late. Kerry Janke, Customer Relations Specialist, monitors late shipments per day. The following data were collected for a two-week period. Construct a C-chart for the data.

8	5
7	4
8	4
4	3
6	3

ADVANCED PROBLEMS

1. Russet Potato Chip Company has come out with a new product; thick-sliced long potato chips. The potatoes are cut on the long diameter instead of the short diameter, and are thicker than normal potato chips. This has created a problem in packaging as the weight of each chip is substantial, and the consumers will complain if there are not 16 ounces in a package as labeled. Russet has taken 20 samples throughout the day, each with a sample size of 6.

Sample number	Sample X Values					
	1	2	3	4	5	6
1	15.5	15.7	16.2	16.4	15.9	16.1
2	15.9	16.2	16.2	16.1	15.9	15.7
3	16.3	16.1	15.8	15.9	16	16.2
4	16.3	15.5	16.2	16.1	16.4	15.7
5	15.5	16.0	16.1	15.8	15.9	15.6
6	15.9	16.1	16.5	16.4	16.5	16.1
7	15.5	15.6	16.1	16.2	16.3	16.2
8	15.9	15.9	16.0	15.9	16.4	15.9
9	15.9	15.5	16.4	16.4	15.6	16.0
10	15.8	15.8	15.9	16.1	15.9	15.8
11	16.0	15.5	15.6	16.1	16.0	16.2
12	16.0	15.5	15.7	16.4	16.3	16.2
13	15.6	15.5	15.9	15.6	16.1	16.0
14	15.7	15.8	15.9	16.0	16.4	16.1
15	16.4	16.0	16.4	15.8	15.5	15.8
16	15.6	15.8	15.7	16.3	15.7	16.2
17	16.0	15.7	15.6	16.0	16.0	15.8
18	16.2	16.3	15.5	16.0	15.9	16.3
19	15.6	15.7	16.4	16.5	16.4	15.8
20	15.8	15.6	15.8	16.4	16.1	15.9

a. Determine if the process is in or out of control by using an R-chart and an X-bar chart. (Use 3 decimal places.) Is the process in control?

b. Are Russet's customers satisfied? If not, what should Russet do?

2. Samples consisting of four parts each have been taken from a machining process that produces brackets used to mount hard drives in desktop computers. The length of each part was measured in millimeters using a calibrated measuring device. The following data were obtained.

Time	Part 1	Part 2	Part 3	Part 4
		Length, mm		
8:00	20.10	19.97	20.03	20.05
9:00	20.00	20.11	19.98	20.09
10:00	20.10	20.06	19.99	20.03
11:00	19.94	20.09	20.02	20.01
12:00	20.08	20.08	20.00	20.12
13:00	20.06	20.10	19.95	20.05
14:00	20.11	20.03	20.09	20.00
15:00	20.06	20.09	20.08	20.00
16:05	19.88	19.94	20.02	19.96
17:00	20.03	20.01	19.98	19.92
18:00	19.88	20.01	19.98	19.96

19:00	19.87	19.97	19.96	19.99
20:00	20.01	19.97	19.96	19.89
21:00	19.92	20.01	19.97	19.97
22:00	19.96	20.00	19.90	19.90
23:00	20.05	20.02	19.96	20.00

Construct X-bar and Range charts for the process. Is the process in control? Discuss.

3. Sierra National is looking to outsource the manufacturing of some of the redwood molding that they use in building their product. The molding is cut to length, and then assembled in panels, like fence boards on a fence. They currently run a 5 head molder, and get very precise results on the Boston Rustic $3\frac{1}{2}''$ molding. One of Sierra Nationals suppliers, ForestWood, has sent a unit of molding for them to try. The specifications called for a $3\frac{1}{2}''$ molding, plus or minus 1/16". When the first panel was assembled, it was observed that the molding was too narrow, and there was a gap in the panel. Measuring the molding, it was discovered that the molding measured between $3\frac{1}{2}''$ and $3\frac{7}{16}''$, and was within tolerance. The standard deviation for the molding was .04 inch.

a. What is the capability index for Sierra National?

b. After some consideration, ForestWood has decided that it would be better to have the sum of the molding be little bit wider, so they adjusted the machinery to produce the molding at $3\frac{1}{2}'' + 1/8''$ and $-0''$, or an average of 39/16". This change was approved by Sierra National. Does this change ForestWood's ability to meet the needs of Sierra National?

c. What if ForestWood was able to tighten the tolerances of their machining capability to have a standard deviation of .01 inch?

ENDNOTES

1. R. Zemke and D. Schaaf, *The Service Edge* (New York: Penguin Books, 1989), pp. 18–35.

2. Jan Carlson, *Moments of Truth* (Cambridge, MA: Ballinger Press, 1987).

LEARNING ACTIVITIES   www.mhhe.com/opsnow2e

Visit the Online Learning Center (www.mhhe.com/opsnow2e) for additional resources. Content varies by chapter, and includes

- Business Tours
- OM on Site
- Readings
- Resources
- Excel Tutors

- Interactive Case Models
- Reel Operations Video Clips
- Additional Advanced Problems
- Self-Assessment Quizzes
- Glossary

SELECTED REFERENCES

Bergeron, B. P. *The Eternal E-Customer*. New York: McGraw-Hill, 2001.

Brocka, B., and Brocka, M. S. *Quality Management: Implementing the Best Ideas of the Masters*. Homewood, IL: Business One Irwin, 1992.

Carlson, J. *Moments of Truth*. Cambridge, MA: Ballinger Press, 1987.

Cohen, L. *Quality Function Deployment*. Reading, MA: Addison-Wesley, 1995.

Juran, J. M. *Juran on Planning for Quality*. New York: Free Press, 1988.

Zemke, R., and Schaaf, D. *The Service Edge*. New York: Penguin Books, 1989.

Zemke, R. and Connellan, T. *E-service*. New York: AMACOM, 2000.

VIDEO CASE 7.1

Statistical Process Control at Honda

Based on Video 9 on the Student DVD

Honda uses statistical process control to monitor and improve a variety of processes. Employees collect data, and then analyze it using statistical process control charts. They can make adjustments if needed. The statistical process control charts enable workers to understand precisely how processes are working and anticipate problems before they occur.

One interesting use is in monitoring the effort required to close a door. Honda monitors the speed of the door required to make it latch by using a special device that measures door speed in mph. A technician closes the door repeatedly, using different amounts of force, to determine the speed required to make it latch. Data are collected and plotted on an X-bar chart.

1. Why are these data collected? What is the importance, from a quality standpoint, of knowing the door closing speed?

2. In addition to plotting the data on an X-bar chart, the data are also recorded on a histogram along with data from the previous two weeks. Why would that data be important?

3. The technician stated that Honda prefers a C_{pk} of 1.33. Describe what that number means. What is the relationship between the process and the requirements?

4. The X-chart Honda is using is different from an X-bar chart. What do you think an X-chart monitors?

INTERACTIVE CASE 7.1

Monitoring Variability at C&R Catalysts

The X-bar and R-chart interactive model provides an interactive environment for examining statistical process control. The user can change two inputs. First, using the slider button, the user can change the level of process variability. This changes the standard deviation of the process (sigma). The user can also drag the center (grand mean) of the process up or down. The model provides capability index values for C_p and C_{pk}. As the user adjusts process variability, the value of sigma is changed, and the appropriate impact on the X-bar chart and R-chart takes place.

C & R Catalysts

C&R Catalysts produces chemicals that are used to speed up hardening or curing of paints, coatings, and fiberglass resins. They are a B2B supplier for paint companies as well as to manufacturers who use fiberglass resins in the production of boats, automotive components, and sporting goods. One of C&R's competitive advantages is that it packages its

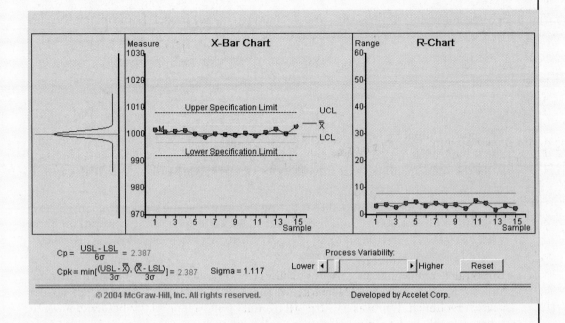

$$Cp = \frac{USL - LSL}{6\sigma} = 2.387$$

$$Cpk = \min[\frac{(USL - \overline{X})}{3\sigma}, \frac{(\overline{X} - LSL)}{3\sigma}] = 2.387 \qquad Sigma = 1.117$$

Process Variability:
Lower ◄ ▣─────── ► Higher   Reset

chemicals to order to make their use easy and foolproof. One particular product, epoxy hardener 215, is used by several boat manufacturers in the production of sailboat hulls. In boat production, epoxy hardener 215 is combined with epoxy resin, which is then applied to the fiberglass matting that has been formed around a hull mold. The matting soaks up the resin and hardens into the strong durable shell required for marine use. C&R works with each customer to determine the best resin batch size and the optimal amount of hardener needed to make its production process most effective. Precision is required because if the batch size is too big, it takes too long to use and hardens before being applied to the hull. This wastes material, wastes equipment (containers, spreaders, etc.), and is dangerous. In a container, the chemical reaction between the hardener and resin releases heat and can actually catch fire. If the batch size is too small, the glass lay-up process will not be able to finish before running out of resin. If too much hardener is used, the resin hardens too quickly. If not enough hardener is used, the resin may never harden, remaining "sticky," and the hull would have to be scrapped.

Once C&R and the customer have determined the best amount of hardener to use, C&R packages the hardener in exactly that quantity. This eliminates the need for precise measuring, potential errors, and waste for the customer. For one customer, Raptor Boats, epoxy hardener 215 is packaged in precise 1,000-milliliter quantities.

C&R has struggled with the precision required to consistently fill the disposable containers with the exact hardener quantities required. The process requires that the hardener be warm to reduce viscosity and that the calibration of the filler machine be constantly monitored. Variation in volume not only can cause problems for customers, but can be very expensive for C&R. If a defective C&R product results in lost mold time or equipment damage, C&R reimburses its customer for actual costs incurred.

The filling process for hardener 215 1,000-ml containers is currently centered at 1,000 milliliters, with a standard deviation of 1.117 ml. This places the 3σ upper and lower control limits at 1,003.351 and 996.649, respectively.

1. The default values for the X-bar and R-chart interactive model should match the current conditions at C&R Catalysts, as shown below:

$$\text{Sigma} = 1.117$$

$$C_p = 2.39$$

$$C_{pk} = 2.39$$

The process should be exactly centered. If it is not, drag the red line on the normal curve to center it.

a. At the start-up, notice that the values for C_p and C_{pk} are the same. Which capability index is of interest?

b. Raptor Boats has determined that during the winter, if the hardener quantity stays within 8 ml of 1,000 ml, its process works fine. So as long as the contents are from 992 to 1,008, everything is okay. Is C&R able to meet that expectation with its current process? Explain your answer.

2. During the summer, warmer weather causes the chemical reaction between the resin and hardener to speed up. This means that excess hardener would speed up the process too much. Raptor Boats has determined that as long as the hardener amount is between 996 and 1,004, their process will work okay.

a. Is C&R able to meet that expectation with its current process? Explain your answer.

b. During the winter, when the specifications are the most relaxed, what level of variability can C&R tolerate in its filling process? What is the sigma at that point?

c. What happens to the R-chart when the variability is increased? What happens to the shape of the distribution as the variability is increased?

3. C&R has detected that its process drifts because the warm hardener gradually changes the calibration on its filling equipment. As containers are filled, the quantity of hardener being put in each container gradually increases. This is a slow change, but if not monitored closely, it could cause problems. Calibration is a difficult and time-consuming process, requiring the time of one of the engineers, so C&R would like to minimize it. Set the variability back to its default value of 1.117. The process should be centered.

   Current data indicate that after 200 containers, the process has drifted and the average output is no longer 1,000, but is to the point that the upper control limit is right at the upper customer specification. This places the process mean (assuming $\sigma = 1.117$, $3\sigma = 3.351$, and $1,008 - 3.351 = 1,004.649$) at 1,004.649.

a. How could C&R benefit from using a noncentered process to minimize the time and cost associated with recalibrating equipment? Explain how this would work. Estimate how much they could reduce their recalibrations.

b. Would C&R gain the same benefits in summer as they would in winter? Explain your answer.

c. In order to gain similar benefits in simmer, what would C&R need to do to their process?

APPLICATION CASE 7.1

Striving for Perfection

B&N Photo is a distributor of photographic equipment and supplies to a number of retail chains. Many of B&N's customers are large retailers with substantial leverage to make suppliers conform to their requirements. One such requirement has been the use of the "perfect order" as a measure of supplier performance and a necessary requirement for certification as a "preferred supplier." Preferred supplier status is important because it gives the supplier preferential treatment when new products are desired. Andy Butler, B&N's supply chain manager, collects performance data that goes into the perfect order measurement system. While the perfect order is a good measure for B&N's customers, it is not specific enough to guide improvement for B&N. Andy keeps separate data for each of the components of the perfect order measure. B&N breaks the perfect order into three components: on-time delivery, order accuracy, and product quality.

On-time delivery is monitored as the proportion of deliveries that are not late. B&N has historically maintained a 94 percent on-time delivery record. Andy samples 30 delivery records per day and records the proportion of late deliveries. This data are presented in Exhibit 7.38.

Late Deliveries for B&N					**EXHIBIT 7.38**
	Week 1	Week 2	Week 3	Week 4	
Monday	1	0	1	0	
Tuesday	2	1	0	0	
Wednesday	1	0	0	0	
Thursday	0	2	3	2	
Friday	0	1	1	1	

Order accuracy is defined as errors per order. An error could be an error in quantity, an error in item number, or an error in recorded due date. Order accuracy is also monitored on an "errors per order" basis. Andy's goal regarding order accuracy is to have less than 1 error per order. While most suppliers don't provide a standard for errors per order, Andy knows that if errors increase, B&N loses favor with the purchasing agents. Order accuracy data are presented in Exhibit 7.39.

Data for Errors Per Order				**EXHIBIT 7.39**
Sample	Errors	Sample	Errors	
1	0	11	1	
2	0	12	0	
3	2	13	1	
4	1	14	0	
5	0	15	0	
6	3	16	3	
7	0	17	2	
8	1	18	0	
9	0	19	0	
10	2	20	1	

For B&N, product quality issues are dictated not by defective products, because B&N is not responsible for those problems, but with products damaged during shipment. While damaged products are not always B&N's fault, B&N monitors them and communicates with their third-party logistics provider (3PL) about products damaged in transit. Damaged products are monitored on a "damaged products per truckload" basis. Damaged product data are presented in Exhibit 7.40.

EXHIBIT 7.40	Damaged Products Per Truckload			
Truck	**Damaged Products**		**Truck**	**Damaged Products**
1	8		14	8
2	9		15	6
3	7		16	1
4	3		17	7
5	1		18	7
6	2		19	3
7	2		20	5
8	2		21	3
9	8		22	9
10	7		23	8
11	5		24	7
12	1		25	2
13	6			

Andy also keeps track of how much time it takes to unload delivery trucks at B&N customer docks, because if it takes too long, his logistics providers complain. In short, Andy strives to provide excellent service to his customers, but he also expects them to provide excellent unloading service to his drivers when they get there. Unloading times are submitted on the shipper's invoice, and Andy samples eight invoices every day. He has collected data for six days in Exhibit 7.41.

Unloading Times							EXHIBIT 7.41
	Sample 1	Sample 2	Sample 3	Sample 4	Sample 5	Sample 6	
Invoice 1	23.1	34.1	40.7	24.2	29.7	36.3	
Invoice 2	24.2	37.4	23.1	37.4	29.7	34.1	
Invoice 3	29.7	27.5	39.6	39.6	41.8	26.4	
Invoice 4	27.5	33.0	26.4	39.6	23.1	26.4	
Invoice 5	33.0	29.7	39.6	22.0	38.5	36.3	
Invoice 6	24.2	22.0	38.5	27.5	33.0	23.1	
Invoice 7	39.6	27.5	34.1	24.2	30.8	40.7	
Invoice 8	31.9	27.5	37.4	41.8	30.8	38.5	

1. Construct the appropriate statistical process control chart for each of the measures Andy monitors. For each measure, discuss the information it provides with regard to Andy's goals.

2. What should be the highest priority for Andy's improvement efforts?

CHAPTER 8

Timeliness: Scheduling and Project Management

LEARNING OBJECTIVES

- Explain the effect time has on each profitability measure.

- Describe the impact of feedback delay on quality.

- Explain the common time reduction strategies.

- Construct a Gantt chart.

- Sequence orders using the traditional sequencing rules and compare rule performance.

- Describe the physical features of queues and describe how they affect queue performance.

- Compute the probability of x arrivals per unit time for a queue.

- Describe the psychological approaches to managing perception of queue length.

- Construct a network diagram for a project.

- Identify the critical path for a project using CPM calculations.

- Calculate the likelihood of completing a project in a specified time using CPM with activity time uncertainty.

- Complete the calculations necessary to effectively crash a project.

ADDING VALUE BY REDUCING CUSTOMERS' TIME TO MARKET

Successful businesses produce products and services quickly, deliver them quickly, meet due date promises, and respond quickly to changes in the market. All of these capabilities require the ability to manage the time it takes to accomplish activities. Few businesses have had to master these challenges to the same extent as those in the software industry. Software development processes are complex, life cycles are short, and competition is high. The only companies that have greater challenges are those that produce tools for the developers. Borland (known as Inprise from April 1998 till January 2001) is one of those companies.

At Borland's peak in the early 1990s, it reached sales of $482 million and had over 3 million customers. However, it lacked strategy and had not adapted to the shift from personal computing to networked computing in its development efforts. In May 1999, a new CEO, Dale Fuller, came on board. At that time he told developers that any project not related to the Net would be killed. Within 6 months he had fired 400 people, 60 of whom were managers. Taking on Microsoft, Sun, or IBM in their respective environments of Windows, Java, or Linux was extremely risky. Inprise chose to be an intermediary between those platforms. The Kylix product, for example, enables developers to translate Windows code to Linux. It was introduced in 2001 and within six months became the industry leader. JBuilder lets developers use Java applications in Windows platforms. The products free up developers from being tied to one platform. Success led Fuller to readopt the Borland name.

Borland's newfound success and strategy led it to create a suite of application life-cycle management technologies that accelerate the development life cycle for Borland customers. Its products allow development teams to better collaborate and react to each other's work in real time. Analysts, architects, developers, testers, and managers are faster. By having the flexibility to move from one platform to another, value is added to business customers by giving them the capability to create and deploy software with greater flexibility and speed.

Borland's contribution to the value offered by their B2B customers is in giving them the ability to get their products to market faster and respond more quickly to market changes. This requires that Borland be able to do the same. Dale Fuller summed up Borland's mission in an April 22, 2004, press release:

> Borland's customers, though continuing to demand productivity improvements and efficiency gains, are increasingly focused on capturing strategic market opportunities. Borland is winning these customers because of our ability to help companies better control their business while also enabling them to execute more quickly.

Source: L. Tischler, "Borland Software: Back in the Black," *Fast Company*, Issue 60, July 2002, p. 76; "Accelerate the Application Lifecycle," white paper from Borland, www.borland.com/alm/pdf/ alm_brochure.pdf, July 19, 2004; Borland Company Background, www.borland.com/company/background/index.html, May 30, 2004; News Release, "Borland Profitability Up $18 Million over Year-Ago Quarter: Company Delivers GAAP Profitability," April 22, 2004; www.borland.com, accessed March 25, 2006.

imeliness is the third of three components of value. Its relationship with value, processes, cost, and quality is intricate: It is often an outcome of processes, it is a determinant of costs, and it is viewed as an important aspect of quality. For consumer and business customers, time is as critical as any other value component. In many transactions it is the most critical of all.

Introduction: Time *Really* Is Money

ime has become one of the most critical aspects of business competition, if not the most critical, simply because it has so many implications for business success. "When" can be nearly as important as "what" for a customer, and if the "when" doesn't meet customer needs, the "what" will be obtained somewhere else. Even when a customer is purchasing a product, the service aspects of the product delivery and support can be more important than attributes of the product itself. Many service quality issues are linked to timeliness.

Time-related issues and decisions also affect the other two components of value: costs and quality. Many of the effects that time-related issues have on value are direct and, as a result, small improvements in timeliness can yield huge financial payoffs. Online business entrepreneurs, for example, knew from day one that speed was critical for success. The more time downloading a screen takes, the more likely the customer will click on something else.

Speed is often synonymous with good service. Even in such ad hoc services as eBay, when providing feedback to seller performance, customers mention speed nearly 6 times more frequently than any other service issue and more than 12 times as frequently as they mention the quality of the product they purchased.[1] Studies by PayPal, the money e-mailing system, of its signup and registration process showed that increasing the number of screens results in a dramatic loss of customers. In its original signup process, seven screens were required. Analysis showed that 25 percent of the customers would leave at each screen. Now the signup process takes only one screen.[2] Internet download speeds are very important for businesses, and most work hard to design sites that download quickly.

Flexibility is closely related to timeliness. Whereas time provides the measure of the speed at which a firm can react, flexibility is the breadth of possible reactions the firm can have. TaylorMade, a producer of golf clubs, offers custom manufactured clubs delivered in 24 hours. Very few customers need this service, but that capability differentiates it from its competitors.[3]

The business that can respond quickly to change with a wide range of possible responses is flexible. The business that can't respond quickly to change is, well, history. The operative word is "quickly." The ability to change is of little use if it takes a long time to do it. "Slow" flexibility doesn't work. The market favors a firm that responds, not one that evolves. The business that can respond quickly to change, to customer needs, and to internal and external forces is an **agile** company. Agile companies have many advantages over those that are sluggish or resistant. Think about all the critical resources a business must possess. It can borrow more cash when cash is in short supply. It can buy more machines or outsource when machine capabilities must be increased. It can hire more people when it needs different skills. When it is short of time, however, there isn't much it can do to get more.

Timeliness has a significant impact on the financial health of the firm. Management of time-related issues through operations actions, decisions, and systems can improve profitability.

Borland products are designed to enable the entire development team to collaborate and speed up the requirements, design, development, test, and deployment phases of the application development process.

agile
The ability to respond quickly to change, to customer needs, and to internal and external forces.

Time and Profitability

In Chapter 2, two profitability measures, profit margin and return on assets (ROA), were introduced. Profit margin tells how much profit is generated per dollar of sales, and return on assets tells how much profit is generated per dollar of the company's assets.

The Effect of Time on Profit Margin

A quick breakdown of profit margin into its components of net income and sales doesn't immediately indicate the key role that timeliness plays. However, when net income is broken into its components of net sales and those items subtracted from net sales (costs of goods sold, depreciation, and interest paid), the importance becomes evident.

From a customer's point of view, reductions in time associated with product- and service-related issues, such as order-taking, waiting in line, waiting for a product delivery, or waiting for an appointment, directly enhance value. Improved response time, dependability of delivery, and convenience can all be linked to timeliness. These enhancements to value increase net income by increasing demand, market share, and net sales and may also provide an opportunity to increase the price, which will increase net sales even further.

There are several time-related components of value in B2C and B2B relationships. Increasingly, consumers are willing to pay for immediate gratification. Convenience and quick response have become a dominant priority in the marketing, production, and delivery of consumer goods and services. Customers don't want to wait. The reason they're

---

om ADVANTAGE — Better Tools Enhance Timeliness

Improved processing speed provides many competitive advantages to businesses. It can result in shorter lead times, better customer service, and reduced costs. In manufacturing, the simple tasks of cutting, grinding, and shaping pieces of metal are processes that have been around for a century and are still significant components of production processes. They also add a substantial amount to production lead times. Huffman Corporation makes machine tools. It makes the machines that other manufacturers use to fabricate metal components. Its machines have transformed the metal cutting and grinding tasks for many customers. Huffman tools can create metal components that vary less than a micrometer. They can accelerate a stream of water to a speed that can cut titanium. Most important, Huffman tools speed up processes, often improving productivity to five times what it was.

Reduced processing time allows businesses to respond more quickly to demand changes. Managers can perceive imbalances in inventories almost as they happen. Shorter lead times mean lower levels of inventory. Increased utilization of computer technology has resulted in machines that can communicate with each other and has enabled businesses to use computer diagnostics to keep machines running better. New machining technologies have resulted in parts that fit better, last longer, and are quieter in their ultimate application. Huffman's customers are able to reduce costs through more efficient processes and don't have to forecast as far into the future because of their reduced processing lead times. These improvements benefit customers as well.

Advancements in tools have increased the flexibility of manufacturing equipment, eliminating the need to produce large batches of components. Smaller tools can produce individual products instead of large quantities. The elimination of large-batch production results in components moving through processes more quickly and lower levels of inventory. These types of improvement are not often recognized as having a strong impact on productivity, but their influence is actually quite impressive. Manufacturing productivity has improved more than the productivity in other business sectors. Machine tools like those made by Huffman have resulted in the productivity in some manufacturing markets increasing at rates greater than 25 percent, while the rest of the economy has seen productivity increases of only around 10 percent.

Source: "Better Machine Tools Give Manufacturers Newfound Resilience," *Wall Street Journal*, February 15, 2001, pp. A1, A8; www.huffman.com/company/profile.html, May 29, 2004.

shopping for something right now is because they want it right now. If they wanted it later, they'd shop for it later. Customers want to spend time on something enjoyable, not waiting in line, or waiting for a package to arrive, or being "on hold," or waiting for a page to download. Can there really be an emergency that would require next-day delivery for the great majority of consumer products? Not likely, but customers still value the quickest response.

Time plays equally important roles for customers and for the business selling to them. Customers want prompt delivery, while businesses want prompt payment. Time can play an even more critical role in the determination of value for a B2B customer. Unlike the consumer, who rarely absolutely *needs* a product or service immediately, a business very well could. A manufacturer might shut down an assembly line for lack of one component, resulting in employees being paid $16 an hour for doing nothing. The end product requiring that component may be part of an order that will be delivered late. The business expecting that order may reconsider its relationship with the company if it can't meet its delivery promises. How could this one component be so critical? The customer expecting it has made promises to *its* customers. And they also have expectations that are time-based because *their* customers also do. Time's impact on value and net sales is not the only issue here; it has other implications as well.

Costs associated with time reduce the bottom line for a business and for its customers in several ways. For example, direct materials costs, direct labor costs, and overhead costs are directly related to time. Materials require an investment. The longer the material is stored, the greater the opportunity cost for the money tied up. Labor is paid by the hour or by the week. Overhead costs, such as rent and utilities, are time-based as well.

Despite time's importance, wasting time is not viewed nearly as critically as wasting materials or inventory. Wasting time, however, can be worse than wasting other resources. Suppose we look back at that late component. Having idle workers does more than potentially make the delivery of that order late. Suppose, through heroic effort, the order was still delivered on time. Is all well? Probably not. The fact that labor was paid to do nothing increased the costs associated with the order. Remember that even though we paid workers once while they did nothing, we have to pay them again to do the required labor. The cost increases associated with this order could erase any profit

In order to speed up the application development process, Borland sells products for both the. Net and Java 2 Enterprise Edition (J2EE) environments.

Even in the case of government and not-for-profit organizations, effective resource scheduling resultsin high resource scheduling results in high resource utilization, customer satisfaction, and accomplishment of organizational goals. In the case of this high-speed train in Japan, effective scheduling makes the difference between success and failure.

margin that existed. In addition, some other order is likely to pay the price for the heroic action taken to save this one. Any time heroic action is needed in any endeavor, it is probably because someone botched the job and someone else had to work extra hard to save the day. Equipment was idle also, resulting in no return on that asset and the potential for a shortage of equipment capacity later on. One might think that such a small amount of idle time would have an insignificant impact on ROA, and a one-time occurrence probably would. Repeated problems, however, would not only reduce ROA but would also create a chain reaction ending with lost customers and corresponding lost sales.

Direct material costs provide another excellent example of time-related costs. First, the time it takes to receive an order when more products, components, or raw materials are needed can be critical. The longer this "replenishment" lead time, the further into the future demand must be known so the correct amount can be ordered. The further into the future a business forecasts, the less accurate the forecast. The less accurate the forecast, the greater the amount of "safety stock" inventory that must be purchased and carried.

Direct labor costs are affected by time as well. Obviously, the greater the amount of time required in the actual processes that produce a product or service, the greater the amount of direct labor required per unit. Although labor costs aren't perfectly proportional to the units produced (businesses tend to pay people for 40-hour weeks rather than by the unit), additional labor requirements ultimately result in an increase in workforce, just as reductions in labor will eventually result in a reduction in workforce.

As we have all experienced, the amount of time a product or a customer is in a productive system isn't all devoted to processing and adding value. A lot of time can be spent waiting. Waiting time is expensive as well. We know customers get frustrated and

Many products have seasonal demand. For some, demand forecasts must be made far in advance because suppliers take weeks or months to fulfill orders. Unfortunately, some seasonal products have very low value "off-season." Prices of holiday goods, for example, are slashed after Christmas in an attempt to generate at least some revenue and make room for other products.

often associate long waiting times with poor service quality. We also know that space is needed to house long lines. Look, for example, at the amount of space required in fast-food restaurants, theaters, and airports just to accommodate lines of customers. Some businesses go so far as to entertain customers waiting in line, creating an additional cost. Products that wait in queue to be processed increase the level of inventory in the system, increasing inventory carrying costs and causing congestion.

The impact time-related issues have on indirect costs is also substantial. Let's go back to the previous example of long replenishment lead times. Because the longer lead times created the need for forecasting further into the future, the likelihood of inaccurate forecasts made it necessary to buy more inventory, in the form of a safety stock. The impact is greater than that, however, since the greater amount of safety stock increases the overall inventory. As inventory levels go up, so do the indirect costs associated with storage, obsolescence, damaged goods, and so on. For a retailer, the greater the level of inventory, the more likely there will be excess at the end of the season that must be sold at a discount.

Waiting lines result in increases in indirect costs as well. In services, they can increase the need for crowd control and security. In manufacturing, waiting products require more space around work centers, more forklifts to move stuff around, more drivers needed for those forklifts, and more products being damaged by careless drivers. What's more, that waiting time adds to total lead time, and lead time contributes to the amount of time a customer must wait for delivery.

Another significant cost related to time is the interest on borrowed money. The payback period for a capital investment is dictated by the amount of money it generates. A new building or new automated machine is paid off as it generates income. The faster it generates income, the more quickly it can be paid off and the less interest paid. In many cases, the revenue generated by such an improvement is dictated by the amount of products or customers that can be processed through it.

Rapid application development is often referred to as RAD.

The Effect of Time on Return on Assets

A brief examination shows that time is a key determinant of return on assets. ROA is a motivating factor behind a retail managers' interest in such productivity measures as sales per square foot as a measure of retail store productivity or inventory turns as a measure of inventory productivity. Both of those measures are meaningless without a time context.

The faster the financial return on any investment, the greater the return on an annualized basis. A key point in understanding the importance of time is that the increases in net income that result from time reduction occur with no increase in total assets. Thus, rather than invest in new equipment or new technologies as a way to boost net income (which would result in an increase in total assets), reductions in time increase value, decrease costs, *and* do so with no increase in the denominator of the ROA formula. The result is that enhanced timeliness has a very robust impact on ROA.

Time-Related Productivity Measures

cash-to-cash cycle
The amount of time between the cash outlay required for purchasing direct materials or inventory consumed during the production of the product or service and the actual receipt of the payment when the product or service is sold.

Many measures associated with productivity and quality have their roots in simple time measures. Such commonly used measures as lead time and queue time indicate how long it took for something to occur or how long a customer (or product) had to wait. Another time-based measure, due date performance, compares the actual completion of an order to its due date and calculates the percentage of orders that actually met their due date promise.

The **cash-to-cash cycle** has become a popular means of measuring the impact of time on business productivity. The cash-to-cash cycle is the amount of time between the cash outlay required for purchasing direct materials or inventory consumed during the production of the product or service and the actual receipt of the payment when it is sold. Exhibit 8.1 provides an example of a cash-to-cash cycle and some possible components of that cycle. Notice that each part of the cycle requires time.

| Cash-to-Cash Cycle | EXHIBIT 8.1 |

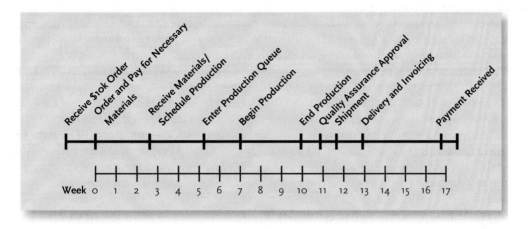

In this example, it took approximately 17 weeks after the original expenditure on materials to obtain the financial return. With a cash-to-cash cycle of approximately 17 weeks, the inventory investment "turnover" is just over three times per year. Reductions in the amount of time required to reach any of the milestones shown in Exhibit 8.1 result in an increase in financial return through a reduction in costs. Suppose the transaction netted a $200 return on total expenditures of $1,000, a 20 percent return. The 17-week cycle enables that to occur just over three times per year, for an annual return of 60 percent ($600) on the $1,000 investment. Reducing the cash-to-cash cycle time from 17 weeks to 13 weeks (a 23.5 percent reduction in time), however, results in the $1,000 being turned over four times instead of three. Rather than generate $600 per year on the $1,000

TARGETING technology   Reducing Time to Market for Clothing

The make/market loop is important for any business, whether it be one creating a new product or one rolling out a new service. In industries characterized by very short product or service life cycles, however, the make/market loop is even more critical. One such short-life-cycle market is the apparel industry. For many clothing items, once it is put into production and on retailer's shelves, a few months is all that can be expected. Reducing the make/market loop translates directly into time added to the item's sales life.

Clothing design has traditionally involved the construction of physical samples that are then worn by models so that the way an item of clothing actually fits and the way the fabric drapes can be observed firsthand. This step in the design process took a lot of time and was very expensive.

Browzwear International, a developer of real-time 3D solutions for fashion and apparel producers, has released an alternative—the V-Stitcher. It is the only application for 3D design and visualization currently available for apparel producers. More than 150 industry leaders use the V-Stitcher,

including Benetton, Adidas, Delta (a producer for Victoria's Secret, Calvin Klein, and Wal-Mart), Triumph, Ocean Sky (a producer for Gap, May Department Stores, Sears, and Target), VF, Nan Yung, Ilusion, and Russell Athletics to shorten new product development time and reduce costs. Benetton has cut its time to market on late-breaking designs by 30–40 percent.

To use the system, the user creates a 3D model, known as an avatar, on a computer screen. The user then assembles the flat pattern of the apparel by telling the software how to connect the pieces. The user then provides the system with the technical characteristics of the fabric. The system then provides a 3D image of the garment showing how it fits and how the fabric drapes.

Source: C. T. Cocoran, "Virtual Fitting Cuts Time to Market," www.utexas.edu/centers/nfic/bww/technology/virtualfit.html; www.browzwear.com/index.asp, accessed March 21, 2006.

Borland competes with many companies that provide application development products, including Microsoft and IBM.

expenditure, $800 is generated, a shift from 60 percent to an 80 percent return. That is a 33 percent increase in the financial return, generated from a 23.5 percent cash-to-cash cycle improvement.

Any task in the cycle, including the time between billing the customer and receiving payment, has the same impact. All business processes, not just those involved in the direct production of the product or service, should be targets for improvement. The time that payments are kept before processing them, for example, adds to the cycle. The timing of payments to suppliers also has a dramatic effect.

Quite often, a product is shipped and the customer must pay within 30 days. Compare this scenario to some that exist in Internet retailing. It is feasible for an Internet retailer to sell a product online and immediately charge the purchaser's credit card. The retailer, however, might not have to pay its supplier for 30 days. Revenue is collected immediately, but the bill payment is delayed, creating an opportunity to earn interest on the customer's payment prior to paying the supplier. This creates a negative cash-to-cash cycle, allowing the business to price the product very low, because its revenue can be supplemented by the interest income generated by the sale. The low price increases the product's value and its subsequent demand and market share. The negative cash-to-cash cycle actually makes it possible to sell below cost and make it up on volume. Some brick and mortar retailers are able to accomplish the same feat with products sold as loss leaders.

An important part of the cash-to-cash cycle is known as the make/market or order/deliver loop. For a new product, the loop is the time required to produce the new product and get it to market. For an existing product, the loop is the time required to take the order, make the item, and deliver it. From the customer's perspective, this loop is important because it defines the lead time required to receive an order. For the B2B customer, it defines the replenishment lead time, which determines the customer's planning horizon, forecast accuracy, and so on. Once again, reductions in time anywhere in this loop reduce the wait time for the customer, increasing the value of the product. Reduction in the loop also reduces the length of the cash-to-cash cycle, providing a better financial return for the seller. Greater value equals greater net sales and net income, improved profit margin, and improved ROA.

Feedback Delay: A Frequently Overlooked Time Penalty

Today's successful businesses must react quickly to any problems associated with product or service quality. A company can't be responsive unless it knows what to respond to. One of the most valuable pieces of information for a responsive company is information about product or service quality problems. The elimination of the causes of such quality problems *at the source* provides the only long-term solution for a firm that emphasizes quality. In the case of a defective product, the mere identification of a defect prior to shipping is a short-term fix that does nothing to improve long-term value. After all, the costs associated with producing that defective product must still be either passed on to customers or absorbed. Prevention is the key. If poor-quality service is delivered, the horse is already out of the barn, so to speak. Quality problems, or "defects," occur because of weaknesses or faults in the productive systems. The ability to fix the system's problems, take corrective action, or design in procedures that eliminate the fault depends on feedback that can be analyzed for cause.

Quality information that is communicated through feedback is critical to quality improvement. Two characteristics of feedback must be present for it to be useful. First, the feedback must be appropriate and accurate. Information that relates to a defective product or service must precisely describe what was wrong so relevant aspects of the productive system can be addressed. The appropriateness and accuracy of the feedback are dictated by the metrics in place and the ability to actually measure the right things. The second, and most often overlooked, requirement for feedback is that it be timely. Feedback must

Rapid application development gets the application in place sooner so the customer can evaluate it, and changes can be made.

om ADVANTAGE   Fast versus Slow in the Fashion Industry

The advantages gained by compressed "time to market" are demonstrated quite well in many consumer product retail markets. The benefits obtained in clothing retailing are obvious when large, but very different, retailers are compared. Hennes & Mauritz AB, the Swedish company that operates the H&M chain of clothing stores, exemplifies the more traditional approach to manufacturing and retailing. H&M has 900 suppliers and no factories of its own. The suppliers specialize in different things, which enables H&M to offer a wide variety. For traditional retailers, an average of six months is needed to design a new collection, and another three months is needed to manufacture it.

Zara, a unit of Inditex SA, a Spanish clothing manufacturer and distributor, has 449 stores in Europe, Asia, and North America. Zara manufactures more than half of its own clothing and 40 percent of its own fabric. Zara also owns its own worldwide distribution network. Stores get deliveries twice weekly, and inventory turnover is very high. A new collection can be designed by Zara in four to five weeks and manufactured in a week. Zara is so flexible, it can send out a new style and by the end of the first day know if it is a hit or not. If it is, Zara can order more. Close contact with store managers allows Zara manufacturers to react to trends quickly.

JC Penney has also capitalized on the ability to turn orders and products around at amazing speed. Penney's alliance with TAL Apparel Ltd., a Hong Kong shirtmaker, has resulted in drastic inventory reductions. TAL collects point-of-sale data directly from Penney stores, uses that data to determine how many shirts to make, what style, what color, what size, and then sends the shirts directly to each Penney store. TAL supplies such brands as J. Crew, Calvin Klein, Banana Republic, Tommy Hilfiger, Liz Claiborne, Ralph Lauren, Brooks Brothers, and Lands' End.

Source: "Just-in-Time Fashion," *Wall Street Journal*, May 18, 2001, pp. B1, B4; "Invisible Supplier Has Penney's Shirts All Buttoned Up," *Wall Street Journal*, September 11, 2003, p. A1.

occur during or as soon as possible after the actual production of the product or service. The ability to create a link between cause and effect diminishes rapidly as the time between creation of a problem and the identification of that problem increases, as modeled in Exhibit 8.2.

Feedback Delay and Finding Causes of Defects	EXHIBIT 8.2

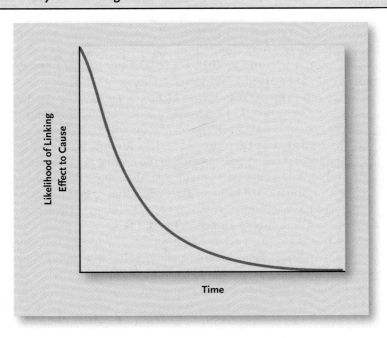

This phenomenon becomes obvious if we examine a ridiculous, yet analogous, situation. Imagine yourself blindfolded and throwing darts at a target. You are required to throw a dart every 10 seconds, and after each toss, your coach gives you feedback in the form of directions and distances. You throw. Your coach says, "A little higher." You throw again. Your coach says, "A little to your right." Imagine the same situation, you throwing darts every 10 seconds, but there is a 3-minute delay before you get the feedback from your coach. Thus, after 3 minutes and 18 darts tossed, you are told, "Throw two feet further to the left than you did on that first dart." You throw, thinking "I can't even remember my first dart." You get the idea. Immediate feedback is a prerequisite to improvement. Without quick feedback, no connection can be made between action and outcome. In many production processes, the actual assessment of the quality cannot take place until after the product or service is completed. Therefore, the faster the completion, the quicker the feedback, and the more likely the contribution to improvement. The time between cause and effect is reduced by eliminating wait time and other time-consuming, but non-value-adding, aspects of the process.

General Time Reduction Strategies

Assuming that all non-value-adding time has already been removed, the actual time required to accomplish a set of tasks can be reduced in two ways. The first method is to find ways to reduce the amount of time required for individual tasks. Suppose a firm was interested in reducing the amount of time it takes to process a customer order. The process is fairly straightforward. The customer calls with an order and the order-taking staff person answers the call, records the customer name, address, and so on, and takes the order. The order is then repeated back for an accuracy check. Once confirmed for accuracy, an availability check is performed to make sure the desired items are in stock. Credit card information is then requested and approval is received. Total cost is calculated, shipping details and costs are determined, and an estimated delivery time is then given. The staff person then thanks the customer and hangs up.

Exhibit 8.3 illustrates the process. As can be seen, the typical order takes about 6 minutes and 40 seconds to complete. One way to reduce the total time required is compressing the time required for specific tasks. By providing the order takers with an online catalog and index, the actual order-taking task is reduced by 20 seconds. In addition, technological improvements can reduce the time for credit card approval, resulting in a 20-second improvement. As shown in Exhibit 8.4, the process has been reduced to an even 6 minutes. Reducing the time required to perform individual tasks can provide significant improvements to the entire process. There is a limit to that improvement, however, since there is only so much time to squeeze out.

Another approach, and one that can have a greater impact on the total time required to process an order, is to identify tasks that could be done concurrently, rather than in sequence. Suppose the system could check the availability of the items ordered automatically, while the order taker read back the order. In addition, suppose that the system could calculate shipping costs and total costs while the credit card information was being entered. As soon as the credit card info was available, the order taker could just read back the cost and delivery information. The identification of those two tasks that could be accomplished in parallel has a substantial impact on the system. This change, which reduces the total time to $4\frac{1}{2}$ minutes, is shown in Exhibit 8.5.

One example of this concept that has had a profound impact on business competitiveness is concurrent engineering. Concurrent engineering is accomplished when a new product or service and the processes required to produce it are designed at the same time by one integrated team, rather than by separate teams. Rather than the product design team and process design team waiting for each other to accomplish specific tasks, the integrated team works together to accomplish tasks simultaneously. In addition to reducing time to market, concurrent engineering also results in a product or service being designed

Order-Taking Process   EXHIBIT 8.3

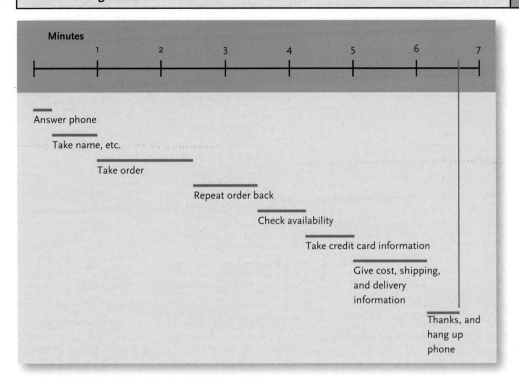

Order-Taking Process with Reduced Time on Specific Tasks   EXHIBIT 8.4

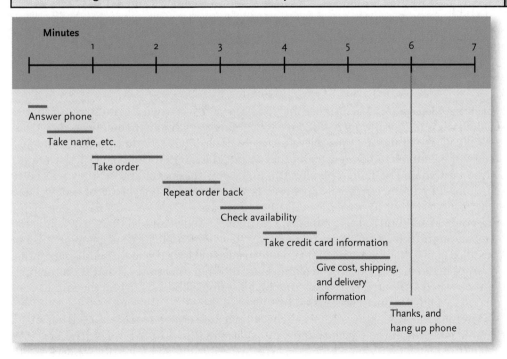

| EXHIBIT 8.5 | Order-Taking Process with Parallel Processing |

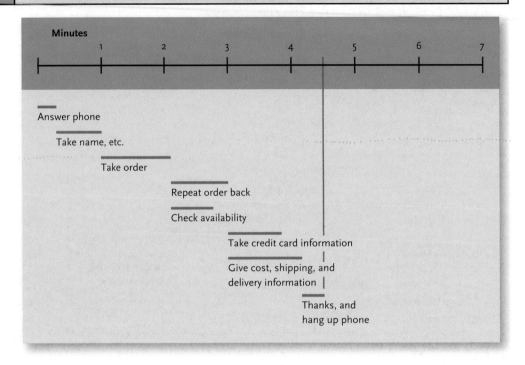

Concurrent

with produceability in mind. Its requirements are consistent with the capabilities of the firm, *and* the processes are designed as the product or service is designed. The result is a better match between product or service specifications and the processes required to make them happen. This improves product and service quality and reduces costs associated with processes. In addition, since the design functions are done concurrently instead of sequentially, the amount of time to go from new product or service idea to market is reduced.

Scheduling

Scheduling determines when something is to be done and when the tasks and activities required to do it are performed. Effective scheduling has two dominant effects on a company. First, the ability to schedule effectively determines whether products and services will be completed *on time*. Whether or not they are on time has a direct impact on the customer. The more complex the processes, the more difficult they will be to schedule. Scheduling effectively enables a firm to compete on the basis of time-related value attributes.

Second, in addition to the competitive attributes associated with time, scheduling has an effect on the utilization of capital resources. If an expensive piece of equipment is not scheduled appropriately, it could remain idle instead of being productive, thus generating no return on its investment. So, in addition to allowing the firm to compete on the basis of time-related attributes, the ability to schedule effectively also enables the firm to control costs and maintain an acceptable ROA.

Matching the availability of a resource with demand is a prerequisite to getting an acceptable ROA from the resource and can be accomplished in two ways. The first is to process products or customers when capacity is available. In this scenario, the availability of materials (or in the case of services, the availability of customers) dictates whether resources will be utilized, so management attempts to ensure material and customer availability. In the case of products, production can occur early and the finished products stored until needed. In the case of services, appointments and reservations are used to shift demand to best utilize capacity. The way to match demand and capacity is to schedule capacity so that it will be there when demand occurs. This may require increasing or decreasing capacity as demand shifts.

In many businesses, particularly services and businesses that sell products with very short shelf lives, resources must be available when they are needed to satisfy demand. If the resource is unavailable, the opportunity to process a product or customer will be lost. If you go to a restaurant on Friday night and find that it is full, you inquire about the wait time, and if it's too long, you go elsewhere. This occurs even though the restaurant may have had empty tables on Thursday night. This inability to store excess capacity for later use is one of the most critical characteristics of services and makes them very difficult to manage. It also contributes to poor-quality service.

In the typical service setting, two approaches are used to match capacity with demand. One is to schedule capacity to meet the demand. The other is to attempt to control demand so that it will match the available capacity. In many services this is dealt with by requiring appointments or reservations. Appointments are used as a way to match demand and capacity when resource time is very expensive (doctors, lawyers, dentists, and so on). When the resources aren't very expensive (waiters, bartenders, and so on), management often has a staff "on call" so that if demand requires it, extra resources can be brought in, but if demand is low, the resources won't be called and won't be paid. To maximize value, capacity is usually scheduled to meet demand, as specified by the customer. The schedule of the resources needed by the customer is determined first, and it drives other schedules that provide supporting resources.

om ADVANTAGE   Airport Lines: Why Airlines Want Them

No one can argue the need for high levels of security at airports, particularly at the check-in counter. However, one might think that airlines would see lines at the check-in counters as a major problem and seek to minimize them. Not so fast. Airlines associate no cost with customers waiting in line, but they see a substantial cost to increase the staff at the counter. Airlines are trying to improve their performance "on the ground," but improvement will be slow for several reasons. Frequent fliers pay hundreds of dollars per year to belong to clubs that give them access to private waiting areas offering no-wait check-in. If the lines disappear, the motivation to join these clubs disappears with them. Self-service kiosks will be used more in the near future, but they are motivated primarily by the fact that they will reduce labor costs for the airline.

Why aren't boarding passes issued more frequently by travel agents, allowing the customer to go directly to the gate and check in? Airlines have resisted allowing travel agents to issue boarding passes because that would encourage customers to buy their tickets from the travel agent.

Since airlines have to pay travel agents a commission, they'd rather customers bought the tickets directly from the airline.

Lines go beyond the check-in counter. They're often at their longest at the car rental agencies. Despite the fact that frequent-renters can get cars very quickly, the car rental agencies are in no hurry to speed up the process for the rest of us. Lines at rental counters give staff a face-to-face opportunity to "upsell" or convince the customer to upgrade to a more expensive car. For some rental companies, upselling provides as much as 20 percent of revenues. It also gives managers a chance to better manage their fleet. If they have an overabundance of full-size cars that they do not expect to rent that day, they can reduce the price and convince the customer that he is getting a good deal, even though he's paying more than he would have on a smaller car. In the trade, upselling is referred to as "one-on-one service."

Source: "The Airport Waiting Game," *Wall Street Journal*, May 24, 2001, pp. B1, B4.

Scheduling Techniques

Scheduling techniques used in services and manufacturing vary tremendously, depending on the types of resource in place, the type of layout used, whether particular resources have excess capacity or are short on capacity, the variety of products or services produced, and many other factors. In some situations, scheduling might mean determining, for a specific product or customer, when each processing step will occur at each resource used. In another situation, scheduling might be focused on a particular machine and could mean determining when each of the products that use the machine will be processed on it. The greater the number of tasks, the more difficult it is to schedule that resource. At the opposite extreme, a resource that does only one task (known as a dedicated resource) is easy to schedule. It does the same thing all of the time.

All scheduling tools are related to two basic approaches to scheduling: forward scheduling and backward scheduling. **Forward scheduling** is used when a start date is known, and a completion date needs to be determined. **Backward scheduling** is used when a completion date or due date is known, and a start date must be determined. Keeping resources in use pays financial dividends but requires expertise in a variety of scheduling tools. In the following sections, several common scheduling tools are examined.

forward scheduling
A technique used when a start date is known and a completion date needs to be determined.

backward scheduling
When a completion date or due date is known and that date must determine a start date.

The Gantt Chart

The **Gantt chart,** which provides a visual model of how resources are used to accomplish specific tasks, is one of the oldest scheduling tools. The diagrams used in the previous figures are Gantt charts. The Gantt chart is even more valuable as a tool to model the way resource time is used when several products or customers compete for resources' time. Gantt charts typically use a horizontal bar graph format with time on the *x* axis and the different resources on the *y* axis. In addition to displaying the time–resource interactions for an order or task in question, the Gantt chart makes it possible to see how other orders interact with resources and how resources relate to each other. Let's examine how a Gantt chart can be used.

Suppose a firm's new-media development department is charged with the design, development, and execution of a new Web site. The department's resources are divided among several areas of expertise, including graphics design, technical writers, interactivity experts, and Java script coders. To determine how this job (let's call it Job 100) fits into other jobs the department is involved with, and also to provide some estimate of when Job 100 might be completed, a Gantt chart could be used. Time estimates for

Gantt chart
A horizontal bar graph with time on the *x* axis and the different resources on the *y* axis. It displays the amount of time required on each resource and when that time is required.

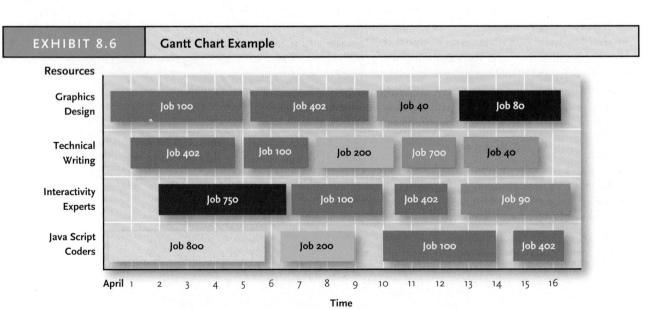

| EXHIBIT 8.6 | Gantt Chart Example |

various components of Job 100, along with the necessary resources used to create the Gantt chart, are presented in Exhibit 8.6.

The Gantt chart aids in answering several important questions regarding resource use. For example, it shows when each job is expected to start and finish at each resource. It shows when each job will be completed. It also shows the sequences so that each resource can prepare ahead of time for its next task.

Controlling Manufacturing Task Sequences with Traditional Job Sequencing

In many production systems, particularly process-oriented manufacturing, orders and parts tend to queue up in front of work centers. This phenomenon occurs as a result of the process-oriented layout. Recall that a process-oriented layout is functional in nature. Its strength is its ability to customize. All similar operations are completed in the same department. That means the routings of products will vary from one product to another, depending on the order of processing steps. When a variety of products or orders enter the production system, several orders can "collide" at one department or work center, resulting in a waiting line or queue, as seen in Exhibit 8.7.

This same phenomenon occurs in services. Patients arrive at the X-ray and imaging department in a hospital, for example, and wait because others are there before them. A consulting firm has groups of specialists that are required for consulting projects. If a particular expertise is needed on a project, but that group is already engaged, the project must wait until they are available. This situation also occurs in most functionally organized services, including architecture, law, accounting, and auditing firms. If different skills or expertise are required for different clients, there can be similar queues of work waiting for access to specific skills. In all of these situations, a decision rule is used to determine which order or client to process next. These rules, known as sequencing or dispatching rules, affect various time-related measures.

Orders entering the production system illustrated in Exhibit 8.7, for example, can have different routings, resulting in different sequences through the six departments. The different routings, combined with orders at the different departments taking different amounts of time, result in orders arriving at departments when the departments are already busy working on another order. In fact, several orders can arrive simultaneously. These collisions result in queues at each department.

In the case of actual customers waiting in line to be served, the decision rule to determine who is served next is almost always **first come, first served (FCFS)**. This is particularly true in the United States and Great Britain. In some other cultures, forming a single-file line is not as "automatic." The actual design and management of queues will be addressed in detail in a later section. When customers are not physically present, it is common to use something other than FCFS as the decision rule.

first come, first served (FCFS)
A sequencing rule that prioritizes by when a person or job arrived in the queue.

| Process-Oriented Layout | EXHIBIT 8.7 |

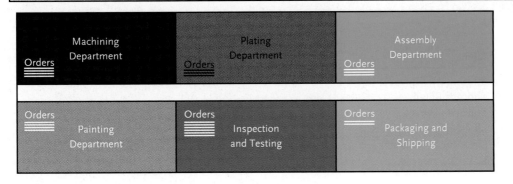

Sequencing Rules

Sequencing rules are based on either of two critical aspects of scheduling performance that determine whether an order is on time or late. The first aspect is the due date; the second is how long it will take to complete the task, that is, the processing time. When the processing time to complete the task is greater than the time remaining until the due date, the job will obviously be late. Sequencing rules applied to queues can be based on the due date, the processing time, or a combination of both.

Getting back to the Web site design example, suppose the firm decided to outsource the Web site project to a firm specializing in Web site design. The Web site design firm is a small operation, with one team working together on each project. They are most interested in maximizing customer satisfaction with regard to due date performance and try various sequencing rules to prioritize jobs in queue. Exhibit 8.8 displays basic information on the jobs in queue. There are several alternatives for sequencing these jobs.

A common sequencing rule is **earliest due date (EDD)**. Using EDD, the job or order that is due earliest gets the highest priority. The remaining orders are sequenced according to their due dates. This technique is demonstrated in Example 8.1.

Another popular sequencing rule is **shortest processing time (SPT)**. The SPT rule sequences jobs according to the expected amount of time to complete the job. SPT is demonstrated in Example 8.2.

Another popular rule, and one that provides a means of including the due date and the processing time in the priority decision, is the **critical ratio (CR)** rule. In the critical ratio rule, the time remaining until the job is due is divided by the time needed to complete the job. This creates a relationship between the necessary time and the available time. If there is extra time, the critical ratio is greater than 1. The job with the smallest ratio is the highest priority. The critical ratio rule is demonstrated in Example 8.3.

One of the problems with sequencing rules such as EDD, SPT, and CR is that they do not recognize the impact that sequencing at one resource has on other resources. In the Web site projects example, since only one resource was used (one team did everything), this was not an issue. In many traditional process-oriented manufacturing operations, however, these rules are used at each resource. Orders are sequenced at each resource independently, ignoring the fact that optimizing the sequence at that resource may actually be a detriment to the overall process. → *whole organization needs to be in sync*

Another rule, **slack per remaining operation**, takes a step toward acknowledging that in process-oriented environments, each resource or operation does not exist in isolation. In the slack per remaining operation rule, **slack** is calculated by subtracting expected processing time from the days remaining until the due date. A positive slack implies that there are more days remaining than necessary to complete the job. As slack moves toward zero, the job becomes more problematic because the amount of time needed to complete it is equal to the time remaining until the due date. A negative slack means

earliest due date (EDD)
A sequencing rule that prioritizes customers or jobs by the due date, earliest first.

shortest processing time (SPT)
A sequencing rule that gives highest priority to the job with the shortest expected processing time.

critical ratio (CR)
A sequencing rule that prioritizes by the ratio of the time remaining to the time needed to complete the job. The smallest ratio goes first.

slack per remaining operation
Slack divided by the number of operations remaining until the job or order is completed.

slack
Time until due minus the expected processing time. As a sequencing rule, the highest priority is given to the job with the least amount of slack.

EXHIBIT 8.8	Arrival Sequence, Due Date, and Estimated Completion Time for Web Site Design Jobs		
Client	**Order Arrival Sequence**	**Due Date**	**Estimated Completion Time for Design (days)**
Smith Clothing	1	17	11
Thomas Retail	2	9	5
Stevens Sports	3	6	3
L&P Financial Services	4	11	4
Simmons Retailing	5	29	7

that even if the job is started immediately, it will be late. To compute slack per remaining operation, simply divide the slack value by the number of remaining operations to be done.

Example 8.1

EXCEL TUTOR

Job Sequencing Using EDD

Sequence the jobs provided in Exhibit 8.8 using the EDD sequencing rule.

Solution

Exhibit 8.9 provides the sequence of the five Web site projects using EDD sequencing. As a means of measuring the performance of each rule, calculations for average lateness and the number of jobs late have been made. To calculate lateness for each order, the due date is compared to the expected completion date that results from the sequence. If the expected completion date is after the required completion date, the number of days late is the lateness for that order. Early orders have zero lateness. The average lateness is computed by summing the number of days late for all orders and dividing by the total number of orders. As Exhibit 8.9 indicates with shading, the EDD sequence results in three of the five jobs being late. The average number of days late is 1.6 days (8 total days late divided by 5 jobs).

EXHIBIT 8.9	**Earliest Due Date (EDD) Sequence for Web Site Design Jobs**			
Client	Estimated Completion Time (days)	Due Date	Expected Completion Date	Lateness
Stevens Sports	3	6	3	0
Thomas Retail	5	9	8	0
L&P Financial Services	4	11	12	1
Smith Clothing	11	17	23	6
Simmons Retailing	7	29	30	1
Total days late:				8
Number of jobs late:				3
Average lateness:				1.6

Using the sorting capabilities of a spreadsheet to aid in EDD sequencing is demonstrated in Excel Tutor 8.1.

Example 8.2

EXCEL TUTOR

Job Sequencing Using SPT

Given the data from Exhibit 8.8, sequence the jobs using SPT.

Solution

Exhibit 8.10 provides an analysis of the SPT sequence for the Web site design jobs. Note that the two shaded jobs are late and the average lateness measure for SPT is significantly longer than that of EDD. SPT has an inherent problem in that long jobs can be delayed indefinitely. When SPT is used, some type of intervention policy is usually used along with it to make sure long jobs get completed.

(Continues)

Example 8.2

EXCEL TUTOR

(Continued)

EXHIBIT 8.10   Shortest Processing Time (SPT) Sequence for Web Site Design Jobs

Client	Estimated Completion Time (days)	Due Date	Expected Completion Date	Lateness
Stevens Sports	3	6	3	0
L&P Financial Services	4	11	7	0
Thomas Retail	5	9	12	3
Simmons Retailing	7	29	19	0
Smith Clothing	11	17	30	13
Total days late:				16
Number of jobs late:				2
Average lateness:				3.2

The use of sorting capabilities in Excel to aid in SPT sequencing is demonstrated in Excel Tutor 8.2.

Example 8.3

EXCEL TUTOR

Job Sequencing Using Critical Ratio

Given the data from Exhibit 8.8, sequence the jobs using the critical ratio rule.

Solution

Exhibit 8.11 provides an analysis of the Web site design jobs, using the critical ratio technique. As shown in the exhibit, under the critical ratio rule, Smith Clothing would be done first, followed by Thomas Retail, Stevens Sports, L&P Financial Services, and Simmons Retailing.

EXHIBIT 8.11   Critical Ratio Analysis of Web Site Jobs

Client	Estimated Completion Time (days)	Due Date	Critical Ratio	Expected Completion Date	Lateness
Smith Clothing	11	17	1.55	11	0
Thomas Retail	5	9	1.8	16	7
Stevens Sports	3	6	2.0	19	13
L&P Financial Services	4	11	2.75	23	12
Simmons Retailing	7	29	4.14	30	1
Total days late:					33
Number of jobs late:					4
Average lateness:					6.6

Using the sorting capabilities of Excel to assist in critical ratio sequencing is demonstrated in Excel Tutor 8.3.

Example 8.4

EXCEL TUTOR

Job Sequencing Using Slack per Remaining Operation

A queue of jobs waiting for the design team is presented in Exhibit 8.12. Calculate slack per operation for each job waiting for the design team.

EXHIBIT 8.12   Slack per Remaining Operations

Client	Order Arrival Sequence	Due Date	Estimated Completion Time for Design (days)	Number of Remaining Operations	Slack	Slack per Remaining Operations
Dogs.com	1	25	3	2	22	11
E-beers	2	18	4	4	14	3.5
Allen Shoes	3	16	7	3	9	3
Turf Grass R Us	4	34	5	2	29	14.5

Solution

As shown in Exhibit 8.12, the first priority job would be Allen Shoes, with only three days of slack per remaining operation. The second would be E-beers, with 3–5 days of slack per remaining operation. That job would be followed by Dogs.com and finally by Turf Grass R Us.

Applying the slack per remaining operation rule in a spreadsheet is demonstrated in Excel Tutor 8.4.

Slack per remaining operation obviously makes no sense when there is only one resource being used, because there would never be any remaining operations. However, if the Web site design operation is expanded, its use might be appropriate. Suppose that as the Web site business grew, it decided to organize functionally, breaking its expertise into the five teams of design, coding, graphics, database integration, and quality checking. Depending on the client and order, three, four, or all five teams could be used in a particular job. Example 8.4 demonstrates how the slack per remaining operation rule would function in that setting.

Trends in Resource Scheduling

Meeting due dates and shortening response time have become more important as a result of two dominant business trends: inventory reduction and pressures added by Internet transactions.

Due date performance in B2B transactions has become more important as businesses have reduced levels of inventory. Inventory reduction in manufacturing, often a component of a management framework known as just-in-time (JIT) or lean manufacturing, has increased in importance since the late 1980s. Inventory reduction in the service sector has also increased in importance. In retailing this practice is sometimes referred to as continuous replenishment. In manufacturing and applicable services, it is common to carry only a few days' supply of an item that is needed on an ongoing basis. The reduced supply and more frequent replenishment result in higher inventory turns and reduced costs. Both have a positive impact on profitability. The penalty, however, for a missed delivery date is likely to be a stockout. Depending on the costs associated with that stockout, the effects can be devastating. Issues related to inventory availability and associated costs of stockouts will be discussed in detail in a subsequent chapter, but suffice it to say that the importance of timeliness increases drastically as inventory levels are dropped.

The Internet has also had a dramatic effect on timeliness. Transactions that occur almost instantaneously in B2C and B2B relationships have greatly reduced the time required to make a purchase, check for product or component availability, compare prices, and so on. Unfortunately, the time required to physically move goods has hardly changed at all. Traditional transportation must still be used to get a product from point A to point B. So far, a product itself can't move at the speed of an electron, though the Internet has raised expectations of customers who are accustomed to the speed of Internet interaction. This makes timely delivery, once the product is actually ordered, even more expected. And when it doesn't happen, the dissatisfaction of the customer is that much higher.

Managing Queues of Customers

The treatment of orders or jobs in queue is substantially different from the treatment of actual customers in queue. Orders and jobs can be resequenced, but customers expect FCFS treatment. Customers also expect not to wait in line for what they are paying for. In many cases, the amount of time they must wait is how they define the quality of the service. Despite the inevitable nature of waiting lines, there are ways to reduce the amount of time customers must wait, and there are ways to make the customer's wait seem shorter. Let's examine both issues.

Physical Features of Queues

The amount of time a customer must wait is a function of five features of every queuing system: the queue configuration, the queue discipline, the calling population, the arrival process, and the service process. Each is described in the following sections.

The Queue Configuration

queue configuration
The physical design of the lines and servers in a queuing system.

server
A resource that is able to complete the process or service that customers or jobs wait in a queue for.

phase
A distinct step in a process that requires a separate queue.

The **queue configuration** is the physical design of the lines and servers. The simplest scenario is one line in front of a single process, for example, the queue at an ATM or the queue at a stop sign.

The descriptions of various queue configurations are best understood when the concepts of servers and phases are used. A **server** is a resource that is able to complete the process or service the customers or jobs in queue wait for. A **phase** is a distinct step in the process that requires a new waiting line. Let's look at some examples. The ATM queue is a single-phase, single-server queuing system. A fast-food restaurant that uses one single line, with the person at the front of the line going to the first available server, is a single-phase, multiserver queuing system. The configuration of the ticketing staff at an airport is often a single-phase queue with multiple servers. Banks and post offices also use this configuration.

Multiphase systems are used when the services are relatively complex and some steps need to be completed before others. For example, the queuing system at a driver's license office may be a multiphase queuing system. There might be a first phase, which collects information. After the first phase, the customer must wait in line for an available computer to take the test. Upon passing the test, the customer waits in line to have a picture taken.

Drive-up windows at fast-food restaurants are also multiphase systems. Usually customers wait in line to order, then wait in line to pay, and then wait in line to receive the order.

Exhibit 8.13 shows that there are different ways to accomplish the same thing. A new customer might be forced to enter one long serpentine queue, gradually moving up in line until she is asked to proceed to the next available teller. An alternative would be to allow queues to develop in front of each teller. Customers typically try to predict which queue will be faster and move into that queue. Grocery stores generally configure their queues this way. Some customers like this alternative better, because they think they are

| Alternatives for a Multiple-Server Queuing System at a Bank | EXHIBIT 8.13 |

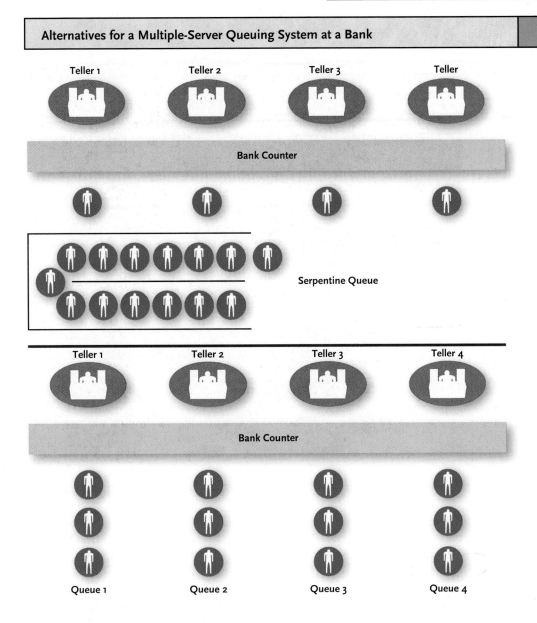

good judges of which queue will move fastest. Overall, however, this approach is not fair, because some customers do get in slower lines. Ultimately, someone who arrived later could be served sooner. A behavior common to this configuration, known as **jockeying**, occurs when customers switch lines hoping to move faster. Jockeying has actually proven to be enough of a problem in fast-food environments that most have gone to a serpentine configuration. Research has shown that instead of deciding on their order, customers spend their time trying to figure out which line to switch to—so that they arrive at the cash register unprepared to order.

The single phase, multiserver queue is commonly used in the management of call centers. Even though you don't feel like you're waiting in a line when you get placed on hold in a call center, you are, and typically it's managed on a FCFS basis. There are numerous configurations that create a variety of alternatives in virtually any queuing system. Multiphase queue configurations add complexity to queuing analysis, because queues can actually interact with each other. In the fast-food drive-up window example, this happens frequently. Exhibit 8.14 illustrates how the queues can interact. Notice how the queue at the pickup window can back up and prevent access to the pay window and even back up

jockeying

When customers switch lines hoping to move faster.

| EXHIBIT 8.14 | Multiple-Phase Queuing System at a Drive-Up Window |

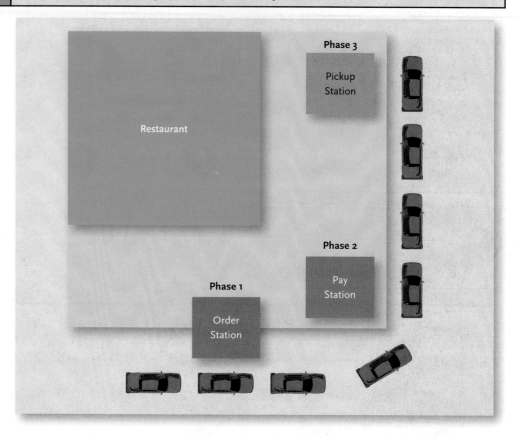

beyond the order station. The choice of the queue configuration depends on a variety of factors, including the space available for waiting lines, the nature of the actual process, and the expectations of the customers.

The Queue Discipline

queue discipline
The rules that management enforces to determine the next customer served in a queue.

The **queue discipline** consists of the rules that management enforces to determine who the next customer served is. In most cases, first come, first served (FCFS) is used when customers actually stand in line. The dispatching rules discussed earlier in this chapter are alternatives to the FCFS rule, but they aren't typically used for actual customers. They may be used, however, when a customer's order, rather than the actual customer, waits in line.

There are some variations of the traditional FCFS rule. For example, in some environments customers are directed to "take a number." This ensures that the FCFS rule is maintained. The FCFS rule is sometimes combined with a shortest processing time (SPT) rule. In essence, the express lane used in grocery stores is such a hybrid.

The Calling Population

calling population
The population of arriving customers or orders.

The **calling population** consists of the population of arriving customers or orders. The size of the calling population is important because its size dictates the maximum length of the queue. While many calling populations are infinite in size, others are limited. For example, the calling population for a copying machine in an office would be limited to the number of employees in that office. The queue could never be any longer than that number.

The Arrival Process

The **arrival process** defines the pattern or frequency with which customers arrive at the queue. It defines the demand placed on the service. Queuing analysis generally requires data on the actual rates at which customers arrive, computed as the number of arrivals per unit time (four cars per hour, six customers per minute, and so on). Arrivals per unit time follow a Poisson distribution as determined by the following formula:

arrival process
The pattern in which or frequency with which customers arrive at the queue.

(8.1)
$$P(x) = \frac{e^{-\lambda}\lambda^x}{x!} \quad \text{for } x = 1, 2, 3, \ldots$$

where

$P(x)$ = the probability of x arrivals in a time period
x = the number of arrivals per unit time
λ = the average arrival rate in a certain time increment
e = 2.7183 (the base of the natural logarithms)

Service rates typically follow a negative exponential distribution.

Knowledge of the queue configuration and the parameters describing the arrival and service rates makes it possible to determine a number of measures describing the queuing system's performance, including the average number of people or orders waiting in the queue, the average time spent waiting in the queue, the average number of people or orders in the system, and the average amount of time spent in the system. With the ability to compute system performance measures, the system can be modified to improve its performance. In addition, the probability of a certain number of arrivals in a given time period or the probability of the queue being a certain length can also be computed. Although it is beyond the scope of this text to delve deeply into queuing analysis, application of Equation 8.1 shows the type of analysis that can be done. This equation can be used to compute the probability of any given number of customers arriving in a particular period of time. Example 8.5 demonstrates this process.

Example 8.5

EXCEL TUTOR

Determining Probabilities of Queue Arrivals

A call center for a small online retailer gets an average of 36 calls per hour. The distribution follows the Poisson distribution. What is the probability that during any given hour, the center will receive 41 calls?

Solution

Using Equation 8.1,

$$p(x) = \frac{e^{-\lambda}\lambda^x}{x!} \quad \text{for } x = 1, 2, 3, \ldots$$

where

$P(x)$ = the probability of x arrivals in a time period
x = the number of arrivals per unit time
λ = the average arrival rate in a certain time increment
e = 2.7183 (the base of the natural logarithms)

In this situation,

$$\lambda = 36$$
$$x = 41$$
$$p(x) = \frac{e^{-36}36^{41}}{41!}$$
$$= 4.46\%$$

Excel Tutor 8.5 demonstrates this computation in a spreadsheet.

An understanding of the probabilities of arrivals is useful for planning system capacity and how the system is to handle peak loads. For example, a high probability of a specified number of calls in a given time period indicates that level of demand will be predictable. The system must be able to cope with the predicted level of demand in order to maintain acceptable levels of queue performance. This may require developing some means of increasing capacity during peak loads. Fast-food restaurants demonstrate such a means of dealing with peak loads. Wendy's restaurants, for example, send an employee out in front of the counter with an order pad when the line gets extremely long. Thus, the cashier has to only ring up orders and take money, increasing the speed of the service and reducing the amount of time customers must wait. This approach is used only when the waiting line is extremely long.

For certain queue configurations, analytical methods provide a convenient means of examining queuing system performance. However, for complex queuing systems, computer simulation provides a more effective means of understanding how the system performs. Computer simulation models require that data regarding the arrival and service rates be collected. The configuration of the queue can be modeled, and using the service and arrival data, the system can then be run "virtually" to simulate how the queuing system behaves over a long period of time.

The arrival process can be affected by several different customer behaviors. The first, known as **balking**, occurs when a customer views the queue and does not enter it because it is too long. The second, known as **reneging**, occurs when a customer joins the queue, but then leaves it because the wait was too long. Both behaviors are important considerations when designing a queue, because they result in a loss of customers. Knowing, for example, that a lot of customers will balk when the line reaches a specific length can aid in determining how much capacity is needed to maintain a shorter line.

The Service Process

The **service process** consists of the capacity of the server(s), the distribution of service times, and other behaviors of the servers that affect the number of customers the servers can handle.

Clearly, modifying the capacity of the servers significantly affects such measures as the average time each customer waits, the average length of the queue, the average amount of time each customer spends in the system, and the average number of people in the system. Increasing capacity reduces queues and the times associated with them. In addition to the average capacity of the service, the variability of services is also important. The distribution of service times can range from being zero (all services take exactly the same amount of time) to being quite wide, with service times being quite variable. As mentioned earlier, the distribution of service times is typically a negative exponential distribution.

The variability of the arrivals and the variability of the service combine to create a significant impact on queues. Even though processing capacity appears to match the arrival rate, variability in each results in the formation of queues.

Psychological Features of Queues

The psychology of waiting is an interesting study of human perception. In many ways, perception is more important than reality. There are some short waits that seem like they take forever. And there are some long waits that seem to pass by very quickly. Human behavior reacts predictably to a number of features that can be included in queues. Those that are particularly noteworthy are discussed next.[4]

Keep Customers Busy

Customers waiting in line feel that their time is not being wasted if they are kept busy. This might mean that they should be able to entertain themselves or be entertained, or actually accomplish something important to the service. Being able to watch TV, for example,

balking

When a customer views a queue and does not enter it because it is too long.

reneging

When a customer joins the queue, but then leaves it because the wait was too long.

service process

The capacity of the server(s), the distribution of service times, and other behaviors of the server that affect the number of customers the server can handle.

makes the wait seem shorter. Providing information that is needed for the service, such as filling out application forms, while waiting in line also has the same effect. During the December heavy-travel period of 2001, Chicago's O'Hare Airport hired local bands to entertain travelers while they waited at check-in or security. The placement of mirrors in elevator lobbies is a classic example of keeping people busy while they wait.

Keep Customers Informed

Customers' perception of waiting time is enhanced if they understand that they are making progress. This is particularly true when they are unable to perceive this for themselves, as is the case when waiting on the phone. A periodic update on approximately how long the remaining wait will be helps. Waiting lines at theme parks often have signs positioned at known distances from the service informing customers as to how long they can expect to wait when they've reached the sign. Phone queues can be extremely frustrating for callers because they can't see how long the queue is.

Treat Customers Fairly

Customers are less critical of their experience in a queue if the queue discipline is enforced and they think they are treated fairly. Have you ever been to a restaurant and noticed that someone who sat down after you did was served before you? The point is, you noticed. It didn't seem fair and affected your perception of the wait. All of a sudden, you determined that you were waiting too long.

Start the Service as Soon as Possible

If the service can be started while the customers are still in line, customers' perception of how long they wait will be reduced. Test Track, a ride at Epcot, is a great example. For at least 30 minutes of the line, the customer goes through a mock automobile testing facility that is perceived to be an actual part of the Test Track experience. Its real purpose is to provide a way to start the experience early.

Exceed Customers' Expectations

The final way to enhance customer perceptions is to provide service sooner than customers expect. A customer who overestimates how long he will have to wait is pleasantly surprised when the wait is actually shorter. If the customer is told that there is a 20-minute wait and he is served in 15 minutes, he is much happier than if he'd been told that the wait would be 10 minutes and the actual wait was 15 minutes.

A Trade-off between Resource Utilization and Waiting-Line Length

When all is said and done, businesses confronted with the challenge of queue management must make a trade-off. Investing in more resources (increasing server capacity) will reduce the length of the line and the waiting time for customers. However, the random arrival of customers dictates that the capacity required to reduce queue length will be substantially greater than that needed to meet average demand. Thus, increasing capacity to the point that queues become very short means that the servers will be idle a great deal of the time. After all, the only way a customer can arrive at a server and not have to wait is if that server is idle when the customer arrives. Most businesses cannot invest in resources that will be idle that much of the time.

project
A set of activities aimed at meeting a goal, with a defined beginning and end.

project management
A variety of techniques that recognize the dependencies present among the project activities and manage those activities in order to complete the project on time.

Project Management

A **project** is a set of activities aimed at meeting a goal, with a defined beginning and end. **Project management** consists of a variety of techniques that recognize the dependencies present among the project activities and manage those activities to complete the project on time. The length of projects can range from several months to several years. The difficulty in managing projects is that each project is somewhat distinct, adding uncertainty to the process of scheduling resources. In addition, there may be competition for

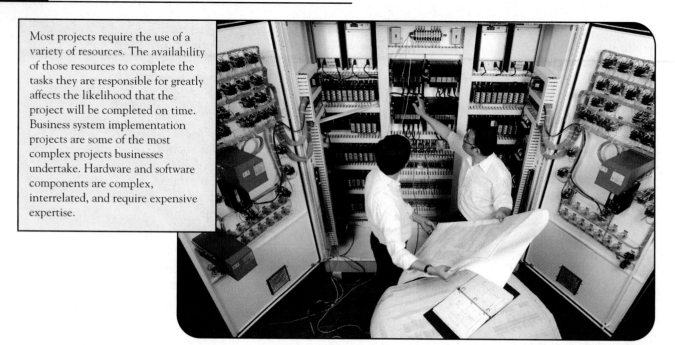

Most projects require the use of a variety of resources. The availability of those resources to complete the tasks they are responsible for greatly affects the likelihood that the project will be completed on time. Business system implementation projects are some of the most complex projects businesses undertake. Hardware and software components are complex, interrelated, and require expensive expertise.

the resources used to complete the project, because resources may be used on several projects simultaneously. This makes coordinating and scheduling their availability a challenge. Examples of projects include new-product and service development, process improvement efforts, business expansion, and site selection.

Suppose a business was developing a new computerized accounting system. The development of that system would require expertise in several areas—system design, database management, programming, software quality checking, and so on—but each category of expertise would not be needed for the entire duration of the project. The use of each kind of expertise is tied to specific activities required to complete the project. So, a particular expertise that is not needed on one project probably is needed on another project. Resources are moved from one project to another as a way to increase their utilization and productivity.

Project teams are often used to provide a way of coordinating projects because the team can be composed of people from all the functions that affect and are affected by the project. This is especially true for process improvement and quality improvement projects. The team membership gives the project cross-functional expertise and a broad "enterprise" perspective that is necessary to ensure that the project will be successful.

The key objectives of project management are to accomplish the project's goals, complete it on time, and complete it on budget. The effectiveness of the resources used and their ability to do what is required will determine whether project goals are accomplished. The effectiveness of the coordination and scheduling of these resources will determine whether the project is completed on time and on budget.

A Network Approach to Project Scheduling

Scheduling the resources and activities required to complete a project would be easy if a specific sequence were not required. In virtually all projects, however, events must be accomplished in a specific sequence. The sequence is critical to the effective completion of the project. For simple projects that use no more than five or six resources and contain only 10 or 12 activities, a Gantt chart, like the one shown in Exhibit 8.6, may provide an effective way to model these dependent relationships. For more complex projects, however, the Gantt chart would become too large and too complex to be effectively used as a management tool. The Gantt chart can provide an effective way for the manager to view the interaction of various resources and activities, but it does not provide a means of distinguishing between those resources and activities that are most critical and those that aren't.

The ability to create a **network diagram** of the project is crucial to understanding the relationships among the activities and resources, and determining the project's duration. The network diagram of a project is somewhat analogous to a process map in that it illustrates the steps in the project.

network diagram
A diagram similar to a flow chart that illustrates the steps in a project.

Historically, two approaches were used to manage projects: the critical path method (CPM) and the program evaluation and review technique (PERT). Both approaches were developed in the 1950s. CPM was created for network analysis of deterministic projects (activity times were certain), and PERT was used in probabilistic environments (when activity times were not known with certainty). Over the years, the distinctions between the two techniques have blurred.

Developing the Network

The first task in project scheduling is to construct the network diagram. To do this, the project must be broken into small, specific activities. An accurate time estimate must be available for the completion of each activity. Accuracy of the final project schedule depends on the accuracy of these estimates. Finally, the order that the activities must follow must be developed and specified. The sequence is defined by identifying the immediate predecessors of each activity. Immediate predecessors function in much the same way as prerequisites do when you are scheduling classes. If class C is a prerequisite to class B, and class B is a prerequisite to class A, you know that both class C and class B must be taken prior to class A.

The actual network consists of circles (called nodes) and arrows. It is possible to use either the nodes or the arrows to represent activities, but we'll stick with using the nodes to represent activities. Exhibit 8.15 provides a diagram of a simple network, with no activity names or times included.

The interpretation of the network diagram is important, so let's take a close look at it. The project modeled in Exhibit 8.15 consists of eight activities. The immediate predecessors are presented in Exhibit 8.16. Activity 1 must precede activity 2. Activity 2 must precede activities 3 and 4. Activity 3 must precede activity 5. Notice, however, that activity 4 is not a predecessor of activity 5. These precedence relationships create the "branching" that appears in Exhibit 8.15, immediately after activity 2. Activity 3 must precede activity 5, which must precede activity 6. In addition, activity 4 must precede activity 6, but activity 4 can be completed at any time after activity 2 and before activity 6. After activity 4 and activity 5 are completed, activity 6 can be completed. Then, since activity 6 is the immediate predecessor of activity 7, activity 7 can be completed. Finally, activity 8 can be completed.

The network diagram in Exhibit 8.15 is important in providing a model of how the project activities relate to each other, but it must provide more information if it is to be used to actually schedule when things happen. One of the most important contributions

Network Diagram	EXHIBIT 8.15

EXHIBIT 8.16	Precedence Relationships	
	Activity	**Immediate Predecessors**
	1	—
	2	1
	3	2
	4	2
	5	3
	6	4, 5
	7	6
	8	7

of project scheduling is to help us compute the project's duration. It is the duration, after all, that will determine whether it is completed on time and, because many of the costs are time-related, whether it will be completed on budget. Let's take a closer look at the project that forms the basis for the network in Exhibits 8.15 and 8.16.

The network in Exhibit 8.15 shows the work flow, from left to right, and it shows precedence relationships, but it provides no other information. Adding additional information requires under-

path
A sequence of activities that begins at the start of the project and goes to its end.

critical path
The path that takes the longest.

standing the concept of a path. A **path** is a sequence of activities that begins at the start of the project and goes to the end. In our example, there are two possible paths: 1, 2, 3, 5, 6, 7, 8, and 1, 2, 4, 6, 7, 8. The number of paths depends on the complexity of the project network. The path that takes longest is called the **critical path**. The critical path defines the length of the project. If an activity on the critical path takes longer than estimated, the duration of the project is increased. If an activity on the critical path is completed more quickly than expected, the project duration is decreased. The critical path can shift from one path to another if an activity on a noncritical path is lengthened enough or an activity on the critical path is reduced enough. Managing the activities on the critical path is important in project management because those activities dictate the completion time, which determines whether or not the project is completed on time. Focusing on the critical path places management's attention on those activities that are the most important. Activities that aren't on the critical path generally can be delayed without affecting the completion of the project. The amount of time an activity on a noncritical path can be delayed without affecting the duration of the project is known as that activity's slack. Those activities with zero slack define the critical path.

Step-by-Step: The Project Scheduling Process

The process followed in project scheduling can be organized into the following sequence:

1. Determine the activities that need to be accomplished to complete the project.
2. Determine the precedence relationships and estimated completion times for each activity.
3. Construct a network diagram for the project.
4. Determine the critical path by identifying the path that takes the longest.
5. Determine the early start schedule and late start schedules by calculating ES, EF, LS, and LF for each activity. Add this information to the network diagram, using the conventional notation.

Example 8.6 demonstrates the process of identifying the critical path.

You might be wondering, other than the calculation of slack, what's the point of the two schedules: early start and late start? The answer is that they provide two schedules that will allow for completion by the due date. The early start schedule completes all the activities and the project itself at the earliest possible time. The late start schedule starts each activity at the latest time possible to finish the project on time. You would use the early start schedule to complete the project as early as possible. You would use the late start schedule to take advantage of the occasional cost-saving opportunities made possible by delaying some aspects of activities. There might be an advantage to purchasing needed materials, for example, as late as possible. It is also possible that resources might not be available for the early start because they are being used on another project. The late start shows the latest possible time the resources must become available without causing a project delay.

Example 8.6

CPM Calculations

A small printing shop has determined that it has the demand and market potential to build a new, larger facility. It has identified eight activities necessary to bring the new facility into production, as listed in Exhibit 8.17. Precedence relationships and an estimated time are included for each activity. Identify the critical path for the project.

EXHIBIT 8.17   Project Detail

Activity ID No.	Activity Description	Predecessors	Estimated Time (weeks)
1	Needs analysis	—	4
2	Architect plans	1	10
3	Equipment selection	2	2
4	Building permits and zoning	2	4
5	Vendor ID and equipment order	3	3
6	Construction	4, 5	16
7	Interior finish	6	4
8	Installation and setup	7	1

Solution

The slack of an activity is determined by computing four different values for each activity in the project. They are early start (ES), early finish (EF), late start (LS), and late finish (LF). The ES for any activity (other than the first activity) is computed by processing from left to right through the network. ES for an activity is equal to the EF of the activity of the immediate predecessor. The EF time for an activity is the early start time plus the estimated time to complete it:

(8.2)
$$EF = ES + t$$

where t is the time estimated to complete the activity.

The ES for the first activity is usually zero. If an activity anywhere in the project has more than one predecessor, the ES is the largest or latest of the EF times of the predecessors. This is because an activity cannot begin until all of its predecessors are completed. The one that takes the longest would be the last one completed. The completion of the ES and EF times is known as the forward pass or **early start schedule** of the network.

To present all of the information on the network itself, a standard notation is used to designate the ES, EF, LS, and LF values. This notation is presented in Exhibit 8.18.

early start schedule
In project management calculations, this is the completion of the early start and early finish times. Also known as the forward pass.

EXHIBIT 8.18   ES, EF, LS, and LF Notation

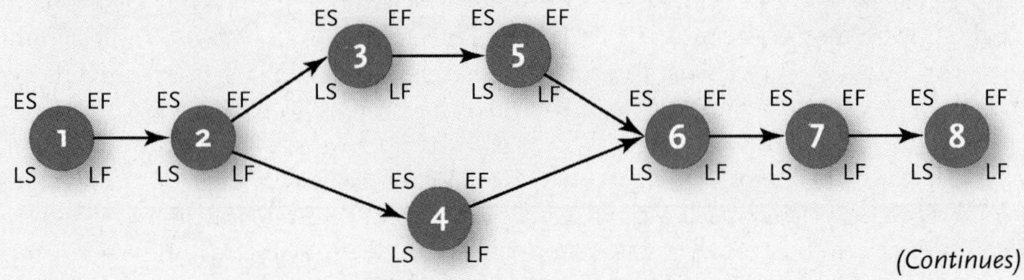

(Continues)

Example 8.6

(Continued)

The ES and EF values can be computed following Equation 8.2. For example, the ES for activity 1 is 0. EF for activity 1 is 4, and the ES for activity 2 is 4. This follows the process of the EF being the ES plus the estimated time, and the ES for the next activity being the EF for the preceding activity. Exhibit 8.19 provides these values for the entire network. Note that the ES for activity 6 is the "latest" EF from its predecessors, which in this case is 19 from activity 5.

EXHIBIT 8.19   Early Start and Early Finish Calculations

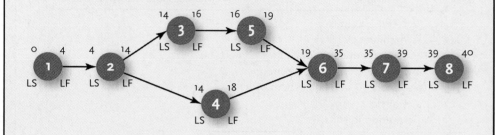

The LS and LF values are computed next, proceeding from right to left, beginning at the last activity. The LF for the last activity is equal to the EF of the last activity or the target date, if different from LF. The LS for the last activity is equal to the LF minus the estimated time:

$$(8.3) \qquad LS = LF - t$$

The LF for any other activity is equal to the LS for the activity that follows it. In other words, for activity 8, the LS and LF values are 39 and 40. This means that the LF value for activity 8 is equal to 39. The process of computing the LS and LF values is known as the backward pass or **late start schedule**. The LS and LF values are presented in Exhibit 8.20. In a manner similar to that of the forward pass, if an activity is the predecessor of more than one activity, the LF is equal to the smallest (earliest) LS value for all activities that immediately follow it. For example, activity 2 is the predecessor of activities 3 and 4. The LF value for activity 2 is the smallest LS value from activities 3 or 4. Since the LS for activity 3 is smaller (14) when compared to the LS of activity 4 (15), the LF value for activity 2 is equal to 14.

late start schedule
In project management computations, this is the computing of the late start and late finish values. Also known as the backward pass.

EXHIBIT 8.20   Computation of LS and LF Values

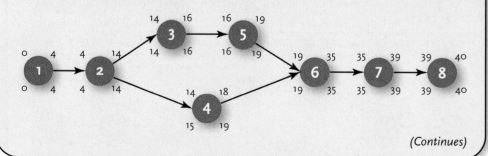

(Continues)

Example 8.6

EXCEL TUTOR

(Continued)

The ES, EF, LS, and LF values are presented in tabular form in Exhibit 8.21. Values for slack are computed by either LS − ES or LF − EF. The activities with zero slack are activities 1, 2, 3, 5, 6, 7, 8, so that is the critical path.

EXHIBIT 8.21   ES, EF, LS, LF, and Slack Values

Activity ID No.	Activity Description	ES	EF	LS	LF	Slack
1	Needs analysis	0	4	0	4	0
2	Architect plans	4	14	4	14	0
3	Equipment selection	14	16	14	16	0
4	Building permits and zoning	14	18	15	19	1
5	Vendor ID and equipment order	16	19	16	19	0
6	Construction	19	35	19	35	0
7	Interior finish	35	39	35	39	0
8	Installation and setup	39	40	39	40	0

Notice in Exhibit 8.21 that the only activity with slack is activity 4 (permits and zoning). This makes the project very difficult to complete on time. With very little slack, any disruption can delay the start of an activity enough that it will affect the completion of the project.

Excel Tutor 8.6 shows how Excel can be used to assist in the process of identifying the critical path.

In some projects, the times for activities are pretty rough estimates. In these projects, rather than determining the critical path and identifying the ES and LS schedules for completing by a specified time, we're more interested in knowing if we could complete a project by a specified time and what the likelihood of completing it is. In that situation, we use a slightly different approach that allows us to include uncertainty in the process. That procedure is described in the next section.

Project Scheduling with Uncertain Time Estimates

When a project in question is completely new and not similar to projects attempted before, the activity time estimates are likely to be inaccurate. In these situations, it is typically assumed that the activity times follow the beta distribution. Uncertainty is factored into the problem by identifying three time estimates for each activity: an optimistic (o) situation, a pessimistic (p) situation, and a most likely (m) situation. These values are used to compute an expected time (t) using the formula for computing the mean of the beta distribution as follows:

(8.4)
$$t = \frac{o + 4m + p}{6}$$

where

o = the optimistic expected completion time
m = the most likely completion time
p = the pessimistic expected completion time

The variance (σ^2) for a single activity is calculated as follows:

(8.5)
$$\sigma^2 = \left(\frac{p - o}{6}\right)^2$$

The standard deviation of the critical path cannot be computed by summing the standard deviations (σ) of the activities, because standard deviations are not additive. Because variances are additive, however, the variance for the critical path is calculated by summing the activity variances. Then, because the standard deviation (σ) is the square root of the variance,

(8.6)
$$\sigma_p = \sqrt{\Sigma(\text{variances on the critical path})}$$

The uncertainty related to the time estimates can be measured using this standard deviation. Assuming the sum of the completion times of the activities on the critical path are distributed normally (according to the Central Limit Theorem), the probability of completing the path by any specified due date, D, can be computed. The difference between the expected completion time and the desired due date is $D - t$. Dividing that difference by the standard deviation, σ_p, gives us the number of standard deviations D is from t. This value, commonly referred to as Z, is

(8.7)
$$Z = \frac{D - t}{\sigma_p}$$

Using the standard normal probability table in Appendix B, Z can be used to calculate the probability that a project due date D can be met.

Step-by-Step: Project Scheduling with Uncertain Time Estimates

The process used for scheduling with uncertain time estimates is similar to the one used for the previous example, with some additions:

1. Determine the activities that need to be accomplished to complete the project.

2. Determine the precedence relationships and estimated completion times for each activity. Create estimates for o, m, and p.

3. Construct a network diagram for the project.

4. Determine the critical path by identifying the path that takes the longest.

5. Determine the early start schedule and late start schedules by calculating ES, EF, LS, and LF for each activity, using t for the estimated times. Add this information to the network diagram, using the conventional notation.

6. Calculate the variances (σ^2) for the activity times.

7. Calculate the probability of completing by the desired due date, D.

This process is demonstrated in Example 8.7.

Crashing Projects

Failure to complete a project on time almost always results in increased costs. The costs might take the form of a penalty imposed by the client expecting on-time completion, or they might be lost revenues. When it becomes clear to management that a project is on its way to missing a promised or needed completion date, some sort of intervention must be implemented to get the project back on track. A methodical approach to reducing project duration is a process called **crashing** the project.

crashing
A methodical approach to reducing a project's duration.

Any attempt to reduce the project duration must focus on the time of activities on the critical path. The crashing process helps management decide which interventions will provide the greatest improvement for the least cost. Reducing the time required to complete an activity on the critical path is typically not without financial cost. Crash costs

Example 8.7

Project Scheduling with Activity Time Uncertainty

EXCEL TUTOR

In Example 8.6, activity time estimates were limited to one value, the most likely time estimate. The owners of the print shop were somewhat skeptical after seeing the results of the analysis, and they decided that it might be more realistic to admit that they were actually uncertain about their time estimates. With uncertainty in the time estimates, they wanted to know the probability of completing the project in 39 weeks, because that corresponded with the end of spring semester and would allow them more time to bring up the new operation.

Solution

The optimistic, most likely, and pessimistic activity times are presented in Exhibit 8.22 and are used to calculate t, the expected time. The activity variances are also calculated.

EXHIBIT 8.22   Expected Values and Variances of Time Estimates

Activity ID No.	Activity Description	Optimistic Estimate, o (weeks)	Most Likely Estimate, m (weeks)	Pessimistic Estimate, p (weeks)	Expected Time, t (weeks)	Activity Variance Estimate, $\sigma_p^2 = [(p-o)/6]^2$
1	Needs analysis	3.00	4.00	5.00	4.00	0.11
2	Architect plans	8.00	10.00	12.00	10.00	0.44
3	Equipment selection	1.00	2.00	4.00	2.17	0.25
4	Building permits and zoning	3.00	4.00	6.00	4.17	0.25
5	Vendor ID and equipment order	2.00	3.00	4.00	3.00	0.11
6	Construction	13.00	16.00	20.00	16.17	1.36
7	Interior finish	3.00	4.00	6.00	4.17	0.25
8	Installation and setup	1.00	1.00	2.00	1.17	0.03

The values for t are used to calculate values for ES, EF, LS, and LF, just as was done in the previous example. These calculations are presented in Exhibit 8.23.

EXHIBIT 8.23   Calculation of ES, EF, LS, LF, and Slack, Based on t

Activity	Activity Description	t	ES	EF	LS	LF	Slack
1	Needs analysis	4.00	0	4.00	0.00	4.00	0.00
2	Architect plans	10.00	4.00	14.00	4.00	14.00	0.00
3	Equipment selection	2.17	14.00	16.17	14.00	16.17	0.00
4	Building permits and zoning	4.17	14.00	18.17	15.00	19.17	1.00
5	Vendor ID and equipment order	3.00	16.17	19.17	16.17	19.17	0.00
6	Construction	16.17	19.17	35.34	19.17	35.34	0.00
7	Interior finish	4.17	35.34	39.51	35.34	39.51	0.00
8	Installation and setup	1.17	39.51	40.68	39.51	40.68	0.00

(Continues)

Example 8.7

EXCEL TUTOR

(Continued)

Early start and late start schedules are presented in Exhibit 8.23. Notice that the critical path does not change, even though some of the expected times are slightly different. The variance of the critical path consists of the sum of the variances along that path, activities 1, 2, 3, 5, 6, 7, 8, and is equal to 2.55 weeks. The standard deviation would be the square root of that variance, or 1.6.

The probability of completing the project in 39 weeks would be calculated using Equation 8.7, as follows:

$$Z = \frac{D - t}{\sigma_p}$$

$$= \frac{39 - 40.68}{1.6}$$

$$= \frac{-1.68}{1.6}$$

$$= -1.05$$

A look in Appendix B for a *Z* value of −1.05 shows that the probability of completing the project in 39 weeks is only about 14.6 percent.

Excel Tutor 8.7 demonstrates how Excel can be used to assist in this calculation.

include anything that would be required to reduce the activity time. Such costs would cover additional labor or equipment, overtime costs, temporary employee costs, premiums paid for quicker response from outside contractors, and so on.

The crashing process determines how to reduce the project time by identifying the cheapest way to reduce the time of activities on the critical path. Reducing the time of an activity on the critical path can actually cause the critical path to change, however, because the time could become less than that of another path, which would make that other path critical. This complicates the crashing process somewhat. If more than one critical path exists, both must be reduced in order to reduce project duration.

Step-by Step: The Project Crashing Process

1. Identify the critical path.
2. Identify the activity on the critical path that has the lowest crashing cost.
3. Crash the activity with the lowest crashing cost, making sure to identify the new critical path if it changes or additional critical paths if they exist.
4. Continue to crash the low-cost activity.
5. When two or more critical paths exist, identify activities common to them to crash if they exist and crash common activities first.
6. Only when activities common to all critical paths can be crashed no more should you crash other activities.
7. As soon as one critical path can no longer be crashed, the process stops.

Example 8.8 provides an example of the crashing process.

Project Management Caveats

Project management has become increasingly popular as businesses have become more focused on resource productivity, timeliness, and costs. Managers have recognized that by

Example 8.8

Crashing Projects

Exhibit 8.24 shows a network diagram of a project. To begin the crashing process, we must examine all of the activities on the critical path. We need to know the expected duration for each activity, the absolute minimum time in which each activity could be accomplished (called the **crash time**), and the additional cost per day of obtaining that crash time. This information is provided in Exhibit 8.25. The project duration is reduced one day at a time by selecting the activity on the critical path that requires the lowest additional cost.

crash time
The absolute minimum time in which each activity could be accomplished.

EXHIBIT 8.24   Network to Crash

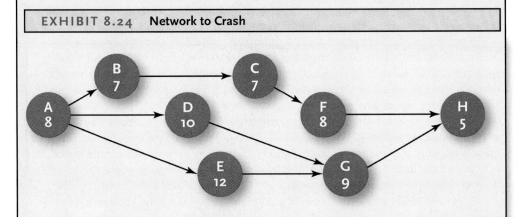

Activity	Duration	Immediate Predecessor	Activity	Duration	Immediate Predecessor
A	8	—	E	12	A
B	7	A	F	8	C
C	7	B	G	9	D, E
D	10	A	H	5	F, G

EXHIBIT 8.25   Crash Time and Costs

Activity ID No.	Normal Time	Crash Time	Cost/Day ($)
A	8	7	400.00
B	7	5	300.00
C	7	6	250.00
D	10	6	350.00
E	12	10	500.00
F	8	7	350.00
G	9	8	450.00
H	5	3	450.00

The crashing process begins with a focus on the critical path. In this example, the critical path is ABCFH. Reducing the times of any of those activities results in shorter project duration, so the focus is on the activities of ABCFH, identifying the activity with the lowest crash cost. As each reduction is made, we must examine the network for changes in the critical path or the existence of additional critical paths.

(Continues)

Example 8.8

EXCEL TUTOR

(Continued)

The lowest crash cost on the ABCFH path is activity C, which can be reduced from 7 days to 6, for $250. The duration of the ABCFH path is reduced from 35 days to 34, which ties it with the AEGH path. There are now two critical paths, both at 34 days. Further reduction will require reducing both critical paths. In the ABCFH path, the lowest crash cost is activity B, for $300. In the AEGH path, the lowest crash cost is a tie between A and G at $400. However, if we look at activities that are on both paths, such as A and H, reducing either reduces both critical paths. The crash cost of A is $400 and the crash cost of H is $450, so the lowest is A at $400. Activity A can be reduced from 8 to 7 days for $400. The critical path is still tied between ABCFH and AEGH, and it is now 33 days.

We are still left with activity H being in both paths, and it can be reduced to 4 days for $450. That reduces the critical path to 32 days, and it is still both ABCFH and AEGH. Activity H can be reduced again, from 4 days to 3 days, again affecting both paths at a cost of $450. The critical path is still ABCFH and AEGH and is 31 days. We are now in a situation where no remaining activities appear in both paths. Since the paths are both tied at 31 days, we must identify the low-cost activity in each one to reduce. In ABCFH the low-cost activity is reducing B from 7 to 6, for $300. In AEGH the low-cost activity is reducing G from 9 days to 8 for $450. ABCFH and AEGH are now tied for the critical path at 30 days. Reducing it further brings us back to B from 6 days to 5 for $300 and E from 12 days to 11 for $500. Again, we're still tied for the critical path, but at 29 days.

ABCFH and AEGH are still the two critical paths. In ABCFH our only choice is to reduce F from 8 days to 7 for $350. Our only remaining choice in AEGH is to reduce E again, from 11 to 10 days at a cost of $500. ABCFH and AEGH are now at 28 days, which is tied with the only other path ADGH. Since we cannot reduce ABCFH or AEGH any more, there is no point in reducing any other activity. The project duration cannot be reduced any further. The decisions made are summarized in Exhibit 8.26.

EXHIBIT 8.26   Crashing Summary

Beginning critical path: ABCFH, 35 days

Step	Activity Crashed	Critical Path before Activity Is Crashed	Critical Path after Activity Is Crashed	Project Duration after Activity Crashing (days)	Activity Crashing Cost ($)	Cumulative Project Crashing Cost ($)
1	C	ABCFH	ABCFH & AEGH	34	250	250
2	A	ABCFH & AEGH	ABCFH & AEGH	33	400	650
3	H	ABCFH & AEGH	ABCFH & AEGH	32	450	1,100
4	H	ABCFH & AEGH	ABCFH & AEGH	31	450	1,550
5	B	ABCFH &	ABCFH &	30	300	1,850
	G	AEGH	AEGH		450	2,300
6	B	ABCFH &	ABCFH &	29	300	2,600
	E	AEGH	AEGH		500	3,100
7	F	ABCFH &	ABCFH &	28	350	3,450
	E	AEGH	AEGH		500	3,950

(Continues)

EXCEL TUTOR

(Continued)

Path	Project Duration										
ABCFH	35	34	33	32	31	30	30	29	29	28	28
AEGH	34	34	33	32	31	31	30	30	29	29	28
ADFH	32	32	31	30	29	29	28	28	28	28	28
Activity Crashed:		C	A	H	H	B	G	B	E	F	E
Crash Cost:		$250	$400	$450	$450	$300	$450	$300	$500	$350	$500
Cumulative Cost:		$250	$650	$1,100	$1,550	$1,850	$2,300	$2,600	$3,100	$3,450	$3,950

The crashing process is demonstrated in a spreadsheet in Excel Tutor 8.8.

effectively managing projects, cash-to-cash cycles can be shortened and profitability can be increased. Several issues related to project management, however, should be of concern. Goldratt enumerates several issues that contribute to the ineffectiveness of project management efforts, even when network approaches like CPM are utilized.[5]

First, time estimates are just that, estimates. Estimates are frequently wrong. Time estimates are frequently very pessimistic and can be as much as double or triple the actual amount of time necessary to complete the activity. Activities made up of multiple tasks end up being padded much more than others. Second, early finishes tend not to be reported. Early finishes often get "absorbed" by resources, and even if a task is finished early, this will frequently not be reported to avoid starting the next task early. The effect is that projects aren't finished early. Third, any safety time, or "cushion," that is added to activities gets wasted. This is known as the "student syndrome." It is analogous to most professors' view of how students work on class projects—if a student asks for extra time on a project, it really doesn't do any good to give it to him because he will delay starting the project until the last possible moment anyway. The theory postulates that providing students with three weeks instead of three days to complete a project will not result in any more time being spent on the project. The similarity to project scheduling is that we typically try to protect project due dates by adding "cushions" to the activities, even though the cushion is often not needed and could have been reduced or eliminated with no negative impact on the project duration.

Another issue to recognize is that people on a particular project team are usually on other teams as well. Resources needed for a particular project are needed by other projects as well. A problem that crops up frequently when scheduling a project is the assumption that resources will be available when needed and as specified by the schedule. This is often not the case. If a resource is unavailable for an activity on the critical path, that activity must be delayed until the resource is available. If that activity is on the critical path, the project duration is extended. Project management software that can coordinate the demands of different projects on shared resources can aid in dealing with this problem.

CHAPTER SUMMARY

Clearly, timeliness is an important part of operations management. Promised due dates are met or missed because of the way resources are managed and decisions are made. Timeliness is an outcome of what management chooses to do. Effective or ineffective decision making will affect time-related measures. Quite often, time will be a factor in a decision because it is one side of a trade-off. Do we want this now? Or that later? We can get it cheaper if we wait. Should we complete this order or that order? We only have time for one. Many decisions will pit time against money. Some decisions pit time against quality.

In this chapter, three groups of techniques were discussed. Dispatching or sequencing rules were introduced to demonstrate how jobs or orders in queue can be sequenced in different ways, depending on the performance measures that were most important. Techniques for managing queues of customers were introduced to provide a basis for improving that experience. Project management techniques were introduced to demonstrate how complex projects could be scheduled in ways that would help ensure timely completion.

Time is an integral component of value, it is important for competitive advantage, and it affects financial and nonfinancial costs. Time is money, time is quality, and time has value. One of the difficulties in making trade-offs is that the impact time has on value, competitiveness, or costs is often difficult to quantify. And, unfortunately for businesses that don't know any better, this can result in its importance going unrecognized. The importance of due date performance, just to meet customer expectations, has long been recognized. As manufacturers and services depend more and more on their relationships with other businesses, either as service or product suppliers, the role of timeliness is magnified. On-time delivery becomes even more important. Missing a schedule by 20 minutes can mean that the truck has left the dock and an order doesn't ship until tomorrow. Twenty minutes turns into 24 hours. The more businesses depend on each other for inputs, the more they depend on each other to do things quickly and on time. As offshoring becomes more common, transportation times increase, lengthening the cash-to-cash cycle. Minimizing the stretch of that cycle requires removing non-value-adding activities that add time. These occur when products are loaded and unloaded, at ports, at docks, and throughout the business. In the next chapter, supply chain management is examined in depth. One of the overriding goals of supply chain management is to reduce costs. Cost equals time.

KEY TERMS

agile, 300
arrival process, 321
backward scheduling, 312
balking, 322
calling population, 320
cash-to-cash cycle, 304
crashing, 330
crash time, 333
critical path, 326
critical ratio (CR), 314
earliest due date (EDD), 314
early start schedule, 327
first come, first served (FCFS), 313
forward scheduling, 312
Gantt chart, 312

jockeying, 319
late start schedule, 328
network diagram, 325
path, 326
phase, 318
project, 323
project management, 323
queue configuration, 318
queue discipline, 320
reneging, 322
server, 318
service process, 322
shortest processing time (SPT), 314
slack, 314
slack per remaining operation, 314

KEY FORMULAE

The probability of x arrivals to a queue in a time period

(8.1)
$$P(x) = \frac{e^{-\lambda}\lambda^x}{x!} \quad \text{for } x = 1, 2, 3, \ldots$$

Early finish

(8.2)
$$EF = ES + t$$

Late start

(8.3)
$$LS = LF - t$$

Computing the mean of the beta distribution

(8.4)
$$t = \frac{o + 4m + p}{6}$$

The variance for a single activity

(8.5)
$$\sigma^2 = \left(\frac{p - o}{6}\right)^2$$

Standard deviation of the critical path

(8.6)
$$\sigma_p = \sqrt{\Sigma(\text{variance on the critical path})}$$

The number of standard deviations the due date (D) is from the expected completion time (t)

(8.7)
$$Z = \frac{D - t}{\sigma_p}$$

SOLVED PROBLEMS

Earliest Due Date (EDD) Sequencing

A small IT firm has accepted the following projects for setting up local area networks in businesses. It has estimated the time it would take for each and has promised completion dates. The information is provided below.

Job ID	Estimated Time	Due Date
1	9	18
2	4	29
3	7	20
4	3	5
5	6	11

Use EDD sequencing to determine the sequence. Evaluate the sequence in terms of the number of jobs late and the average lateness.

Solution

Step	Objective	Explanation
1.	Sequence the jobs by EDD.	

Job ID	Estimated Time	Due Date
4	3	5
5	6	11
1	9	18
3	7	20
2	4	29

Step	Objective	Explanation
2.	Evaluate the sequence.	

Job ID	Estimated Time	Due Date	Completion Time	Late (days)
4	3	5	3	0
5	6	11	9	0
1	9	18	18	0
3	7	20	25	5
2	4	29	29	0
			Average lateness =	1
			Number of late jobs =	1

Shortest Processing Time (SPT) Sequencing

Using the information from the previous problem, construct and evaluate a shortest processing time (SPT) sequence.

Job ID	Estimated Time	Due Date
1	9	18
2	4	29
3	7	20
4	3	5
5	6	11

Solution

Step	Objective	Explanation
1.	Sequence the jobs by SPT.	

Job ID	Estimated Time	Due Date
4	3	5
2	4	29
5	6	11
3	7	20
1	9	18

						Late
2.	Evaluate the sequence.	Job ID	Estimated Time	Due Date	Completion	(days)
		4	3	5	3	0
		2	4	29	7	0
		5	6	11	13	2
		3	7	20	20	0
		1	9	18	29	11
					Average lateness =	2.6
					Number of late jobs =	2

Critical Ratio (CR) Sequencing

Using the information from the previous problem, construct and evaluate a critical ratio (CR) sequence.

Job ID	Estimated Time	Due Date
1	9	18
2	4	29
3	7	20
4	3	5
5	6	11

Solution

Step	Objective	Explanation				
1.	Calculate the critical ratio for each.	Job ID	Estimated Time	Due Date	CR	
		1	9	18	2.00	
		2	4	29	7.25	
		3	7	20	2.86	
		4	3	5	1.67	
		5	6	11	1.83	
2.	Sequence the jobs by CR.	Job ID	Estimated Time	Due Date	CR	
		4	3	5	1.67	
		5	6	11	1.83	
		1	9	18	2.00	
		3	7	20	2.86	
		2	4	29	7.25	

								Late
3.	Evaluate the sequence.	Job ID	Estimated Time	Due Date	CR	Completion	(days)	
		4	3	5	1.67	3	0	
		5	6	11	1.83	9	0	
		1	9	18	2.00	18	0	
		3	7	20	2.86	25	5	
		2	4	29	7.25	29	0	
						Average lateness =	1	
						Number of late jobs =	1	

Slack per Remaining Operation Sequence

The following orders have been logged into a print shop's job queue and are awaiting processing at a collating machine. Each job has specific requirements related to activities needed for completion. Determine the appropriate sequence if slack per remaining operations is to be used. Evaluate the sequence in terms of average lateness and the number of late jobs.

Job ID	Processing Time Remaining	Due Date	Number of Remaining Operations
1	12	17	3
2	7	14	2
3	3	6	2
4	8	28	3
5	15	34	4

Solution

Step	Objective	Explanation				

1.	Calculate slack per remaining operation.	Job ID	Processing Time Remaining	Due Date	Number of Remaining Operations	Slack per Remaining Operation
		1	12	17	3	1.67
		2	7	14	2	3.50
		3	3	6	2	1.50
		4	8	28	3	6.67
		5	15	34	4	4.75

2.	Resequence the jobs.	Job ID	Processing Time Remaining	Due Date	Number of Remaining Operations	Slack per Remaining Operation
		3	3	6	2	1.50
		1	12	17	3	1.67
		2	7	14	2	3.50
		5	15	34	4	4.75
		4	8	28	3	6.67

3.	Evaluate the sequence.	Job ID	Processing Time Remaining	Due Date	Number of Remaining Operations	Slack per Remaining Operation	Completion	Lateness
		3	3	6	2	1.50	3	0
		1	12	17	3	1.67	15	0
		2	7	14	2	3.50	22	8
		5	15	34	4	4.75	37	3
		4	8	28	3	6.67	45	17

Average lateness = 5.6

Number late = 3

Determining the Probabilities of Queue Arrivals

A car rental counter in an airport gets an average of 25 customers per hour, following a Poisson distribution. What is the probability that it would ever get 36 customers in an hour?

Step	Objective	Explanation
1.	Identify the parameters for formula 8.1: $$P(x) = \frac{e^{-\lambda}\lambda^{x}}{x!}$$	x = number of arrivals in a time period = 36 λ = average arrival rate in a time increment = 25 e = 2.7183
2.	Plug parameters into Formula 8.1 and solve.	$$P(x) = \frac{e^{-25}25^{36}}{36!} = .0079 = 0.79\%$$ (i.e., less than a 1% probability)

CPM Calculations

A small consulting project consists of seven activities. The activities, estimated completion times, and immediate predecessors are presented below.

Activity	Estimated Completion Time (days)	Immediate Predecessors
1. Data collection	6	—
2. Analysis	4	1
3. Action plan	5	2
4. Resource acquisition	3	2
5. Installation and callibration	6	3, 4
6. Employee training	4	5
7. Evaluation	2	6

Solution

Step	Objective	Explanation
1.	Construct a network diagram for the project.	The network is presented in Exhibit 8.27 below.
2.	Determine the critical path.	The critical path is the longest path, which would be 1,2,3,5,6,7.
3.	Determine early start and late start schedules.	The early start and late start schedules are:

Activity	ES	EF	LS	LF	Slack
1	0	6	0	6	0
2	6	10	6	10	0
3	10	15	10	15	0
4	10	13	12	15	2
5	15	21	15	21	0
6	21	25	21	25	0
7	25	27	25	27	0

The ES, EF, LS, and LF values are included in the network diagram in Exhibit 8.28.

EXHIBIT 8.27   Network Diagram for Solved Problem

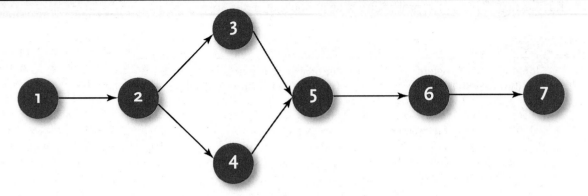

EXHIBIT 8.28   Network Diagram with ES, EF, LS, LF Values

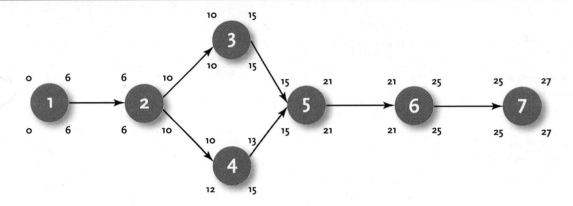

Project Scheduling with Activity Time Uncertainty

An office renovation project has been planned for a local CPA's office. The contractor has provided the following estimates for completion.

		Estimated Completion Time (days)			
Activity ID #	Activity Description	Optimistic	Most Likely	Pessimistic	Immediate Predecessors
1	Equipment removal	1	1.5	2	—
2	Strip carpet	1	1.5	2	1
3	Wall demolition	3	4	5	2
4	Framing	2	3	5	3
5	Wiring	2	3	4	4
6	Drywall	3	4	5	5
7	Finishing	2	4	5	6
8	Carpet and fixtures	2	3	4	6
9	Cleanup	.5	1	1.5	7, 8

Compute the expected times, the activity variance estimates, ES, EF, LS, LF, and slack for the project. Determine the probability of completing the project in 20 days.

Solution

Step	Objective	Explanation

<table>
<tr><td>1.</td><td>Calculate Expected Times (t) and Activity Variance (σ^2) Estimates</td><td colspan="7">For the expected times, use formula 8.4. For the variance estimates use Formula 8.5.</td></tr>
</table>

Activity ID #	Activity Description	Optimistic	Most Likely	Pessimistic	Expected Time (t)	Activity Variance Estimate (σ^2)
1	Equipment removal	1	1.5	2	1.50	0.03
2	Strip Carpet	1	1.5	2	1.50	0.03
3	Wall Demolition	3	4	5	4.00	0.11
4	Framing	2	3	5	3.17	0.25
5	Wiring	2	3	4	3.00	0.11
6	Drywall	3	4	5	4.00	0.11
7	Finishing	2	4	5	3.83	0.25
8	Carpet and Fixtures	2	3	4	3.00	0.11
9	Clean up	.5	1	1.5	1.00	0.03

Step	Objective	Explanation
2.	Draw the network diagram.	See Exhibit 8.29 below.

3. Compute the ES, EF, LS, LF and slack, based on expected times (t)

Activity ID #	Activity Description	Expected Time (t)	ES	EF	LS	LF	Slack
1	Equipment removal	1.50	0	1.5	0	1.5	0
2	Strip carpet	1.50	1.5	3	1.5	3	0
3	Wall demolition	4.00	3	7	3	7	0
4	Framing	3.17	7	10.17	7	10.17	0
5	Wiring	3.00	10.17	13.17	10.17	13.17	0
6	Drywall	4.00	13.17	17.17	13.17	17.17	0
7	Finishing	3.83	17.17	21	17.17	21	0
8	Carpet and fixtures	3.00	17.17	20.17	18	21	0.83
9	Clean up	1.00	21	22	21	22	0

Step	Objective	Explanation
4.	Identify the critical path.	The critical path is 1,2,3,4,5,6,7,9. From the network diagram, that is the longest path by .83 days. From the slack values, that is the path with zero slack.

EXHIBIT 8.29
Network Diagram for Solved Problem

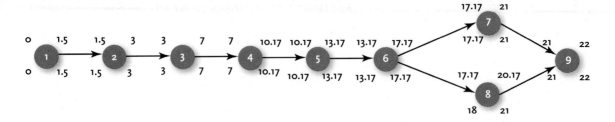

5. Compute the project standard deviation, then compute the probability of completing the project in 20 days.

Using Formula 8.6, the sum of the variances on the critical path is .917. The square root of .917 is .957. Using formula 8.7:

$$Z = \frac{D - t}{\sigma_p} = \frac{20 - 22}{.957} = -2.089$$

Appendix B shows that at $Z = -2.089$ the probability is .01831. Given the optimistic, pessimistic, and expected activity times, the probability of completing the entire project in 20 days is approximately 1.8 percent.

Crashing Projects

The network diagram of a small system implementation project is presented in Exhibit 8.30. The critical path has been identified as A,B,E,G and will take 35 days. Exhibit 8.31 provides data related to the activities from Exhibit 8.30. The normal time for each activity is presented, along with the crash time and daily crash cost.

EXHIBIT 8.30   Network Diagram for System Implementation Project

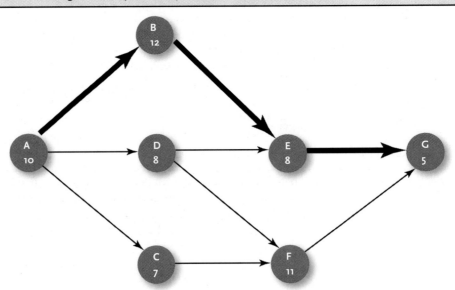

Crashing Data for System Implementation Project			EXHIBIT 8.31
Activity	Normal Time	Crash Time	Cost ($/day)
A	10	9	400
B	12	11	300
C	7	4	300
D	8	5	350
E	8	7	500
F	11	9	400
G	5	4	500

Determine the cost to reduce the project duration to 31 days.

Solution

Step	Objective	Explanation
1.	Identify the critical path.	From Exhibit 8.30, the critical path is ABEG.
2.	Identify the activity on the critical path that has the lowest crash cost.	From Exhibit 8.31, the lowest crash cost of A, B, E, and G would be B at $300 per day. Crashing that activity reduces the project time from 35 to 34 days at a cost of $300. At 34 days, there are now 2 critical paths (ABEG and ADFG).
3.	Crash again.	With two critical paths (ABEG and ADFG), both must be reduced in order to reduce the project duration. It makes sense to see whether there is a single activity on both critical paths in order to gain project duration reduction at the least possible cost. These alternatives would be A or G. Activity A, at a cost of $400, is preferable to G, which is $500. A is reduced from 10 days to 9 at a cost of $400, reducing the project duration to 33 days. Reducing activity A by one day reduces the length of each path by one day, since A is on all paths. Thus, no new critical path is created.
4.	Crash again.	Again, reducing the time on an activity common to both critical paths is the best option, so we reduce the time for G at a cost of $500. When G is reduced, the project duration becomes 32 days.
5.	Crash again.	Further reduction is more difficult, because the common activities A and G cannot be reduced further. For critical path ABEG, E is reduced at a cost of $500. For critical path ADFG, D is reduced at a cost of $350. Both D and E have been reduced to 7 days. There are now three critical paths: ABEG, ADFG, and ACFG. The project is now 31 days. The decisions made and the costs involved are summarized in Exhibit 8.32.

EXHIBIT 8.32	Crashing Summary				
	Critical Path(s)	Decision	Crashing Cost	Project Duration	Cumulative Cost
	ABEG	Reduce B	$300	34	$300
	ABEG ADFG	Reduce A	$400	33	$700
	ABEG ADFG	Reduce G	$500	32	$1200
	ABEG ADFG	Reduce E Reduce D	$500 $350	31	$1700 $2050

REVIEW QUESTIONS

1. What is meant by "time is money" in the following scenarios:
   a. A business waiting for delivery of product components.
   b. A business waiting for the implementation of a new computer system.
   c. A new service design that can't be sold until the facility is remodeled.
   d. A consumer waiting for delivery of a mail-ordered product.
   e. A consumer waiting for a Web page graphic to download.
2. How is flexibility related to timeliness?
3. Why is on-time delivery usually more important for business customers than for consumer customers?
4. What is the relationship between replenishment lead times and the amount of inventory a firm must carry? How is forecasting related to this relationship?
5. Waiting time for customers can affect a number of other business costs. What are they?
6. What is the effect of time on return on assets (ROA)?
7. What is the cash-to-cash cycle? Why is it important to profitability?
8. List some examples of business activities that add to the cash-to-cash cycle.
9. Provide an example of a negative cash-to-cash cycle.
10. What are the impacts of delayed quality feedback?
11. Why is the effective scheduling of resources critical to ROA?
12. Compare backward scheduling and forward scheduling.
13. What is a Gantt chart? How is it used?
14. Provide an example of a job sequencing rule based on due date.
15. Provide an example of a job sequencing rule based on estimated completion time.
16. Provide an example of a job sequencing rule based on both due date and estimated completion time.
17. What are jockeying, balking, and reneging as they apply to the behavior of customers in queue?
18. What can management do to make queues seem shorter to customers?
19. What is a project?
20. Why are network diagrams important in project management?
21. What is a path? What is slack? What is a critical path?
22. What is meant by crashing a project?

DISCUSSION AND EXPLORATION

1. Consider the products and services that you typically purchase. For which ones is timeliness a critical component of value? Why is it so important? Is it more important for services than products? Why?

2. What are some examples in your own life (athletics, work, artistic performance, schoolwork) when timely feedback is critical? What problems are created when the feedback is delayed?

3. Identify a process on your campus that you think takes too long. What are some possible changes to sequential activities to make them parallel? How much would the changes speed up the process?

4. As a student, what are your uses of backward and forward scheduling? How do you determine which to use?

5. How do the characteristics of the calling population, the arrival process, and the service process interact to determine the length and frequency of queues?

6. Identify examples of queues that do not incorporate methods that would make the customer's wait seem shorter. Propose changes to those queues to improve customer perceptions.

PROBLEMS HM

Solutions to odd-numbered problems are located on the text's Online Center (http://mhhe.com/opsnow3e).

1. Big Screen Theater has set procedures for opening the movie house in preparation for customers. Management expects opening the theater to take no longer than 30 minutes for the two people involved (the assistant manager and the director of concessions). Activities required for opening are as follows:

   ■ The first activity for the assistant manager is to check for messages detailing any large groups that will be attending the theater. Checking the messages takes the assistant manager about 5 minutes.

   ■ The assistant manager must then walk through the theater and verify that it is clean, an activity that takes approximately 10 minutes.

   ■ The assistant manager then prepares the movie projector, readying the first movie of the day, which takes the assistant manager up to the time when customers arrive.

   ■ The theater operates using a computer system to print out tickets, and the first duty of the director of concessions is to start the computer system and properly input the correct data. Preparing the computer takes around 10 minutes.

   ■ The director of concessions must then prepare the needed food, candy, and drinks for the incoming crowd, an activity that takes another 10 minutes. The director of concessions must also measure the food quantities to be consistent with the expected attendance, keeping in mind any messages passed on from the assistant manager.

   ■ Finally, the director of concessions must prepare the cash register, an activity that will last until the first customer is seen.

   Construct a Gantt chart that presents the needed activities in opening the theater.

2. Bob, Kelly, and Joe work for HC Consulting, which specializes in identifying problems with clients' customer service operations. Even though they work as a team, each performs a distinct function. Bob is always the first to interact with the clients, asking questions from appropriate employees. Kelly and Joe perform the next task,

which is to observe the client company at work. While they observe the company, Bob examines the company's financial statements. Upon completing these tasks, all three HC employees come together for a group discussion of the situation. When the problem is diagnosed, Kelly and Joe meet with the client company and present the findings, while Bob goes back to the office and completes documentation related to the job. Create a Gantt chart using this information.

3. Relo Inc. specializes in finding new office locations for its business clients. For each client, Relo must first understand the client's motivation for opening a new location. This is usually accomplished with a face-to-face interview. Relo must then familiarize itself with the client's industry by researching trends and competitive forces. Once Relo has an understanding of the client and its industry, it can then look at specific geographic alternatives for the new facility. Relo narrows the field down to three locations, which are then investigated to determine costs for leasing or construction. When finished, Relo presents the findings to the client, with hopes of retaining a consultancy role with the new facility development. Construct a Gantt chart for Relo's process.

4. The University Copy Shop prepares course packets for class. Determine the EDD sequence, as well as the average lateness and number of jobs late for the client orders.

Client	Order Arrival Sequence	Due Date	Estimated Completion Time (days)
MGT 235	1	10	3
MIS 365	2	5	3
FIN 112	3	2	2
ACC 205	4	8	4

5. Darcy is a freelance writer for several newspapers and magazines. Her schedule for next month, as well as the time she believes it will take to complete the assignments, follows.

Publication	Estimated Time Required (days)	Due Date
City Times	3	17
Nation-beat	6	8
Free News	4	15
The Shores	4	5
Monthly Press	2	23
The Star	5	19
Gossip	4	27

Determine the EDD sequence for the work she must complete. Calculate values for the average lateness and the number of jobs late.

6. Six print jobs are provided below, with their identification numbers, expected processing time, and due date (in days).
   a. Use the earliest due date rule for sequencing the jobs.
   b. Compute the average lateness and number of jobs late.

Job ID	Processing Time	Due Date
1	9	13
2	14	19
3	7	27
4	12	16
5	5	8
6	8	33

7. Creative Colors is an interior design and decorating firm. Its next four projects are detailed below. Sequence the jobs using the SPT sequencing rule. What conclusions can you draw from the sequence?

Client	Order Arrival Sequence	Due Date	Estimated Completion Time (days)
Smith	1	6	4
Brown	2	4	2
Dewar	3	8	3
Walker	4	11	5

8. You have been hired by Advanced Technologies, a company that provides custom technology projects, and asked to explore the potential use of the SPT job-sequencing rule. The firm's next five jobs are detailed below. Explain whether the SPT rule is helpful in this scenario.

Client	Order Arrival	Due Date	Estimated Completion Time (days)
A&B Co.	1	14	2
Belco	2	8	6
Corr Int.	3	19	4
Dapp	4	24	10
Elly	5	10	7

9. Work center 414A has five orders in queue ready to be processed. The processing times and due dates in days are also provided.

   a. Use shortest processing time and earliest due date to sequence the orders.

   b. Compute the average lateness and number of jobs late for each rule.

Order	Processing Time	Due Date
1	4	12
2	15	32
3	5	14
4	10	34
5	11	41

10. Fancy Cakes bakes decorative cakes for parties and weddings. Jobs for the next two weeks are presented below. Arrange the jobs using the critical ratio rule. Compute the average lateness and the number of late jobs. What conclusions can be drawn from the results?

Client	Order Arrival Sequence	Due Date	Estimated Completion Time (days)
Aubin	1	5	4
Baldwin	2	8	4
Cross	3	9	3
Dampier	4	11	5
Ellman	5	14	2

11. The city of Sheridan struggles with snow removal each winter. Main routes to the hospital, around the fire stations, and around police stations get the first priority. Clearing routes from each of these locations to I-90 has created a challenge for the street department. Other main routes also receive priority. This year the city leaders decided to use the SPT rule to set the sequence for clearing these key routes. Sequence the routes below using SPT and EDD and compare the results.

Route	Expected Clearing Time	Due Date (hours)
Fire to I-90	1.5	2
Police to I-90	.5	2
Hospital to I-90	2	3
Main	2	5
University	1	4

12. Meta World Funds offers risk analysis and mutual funds to large institutional investors. The firm anticipates new projects and wants to schedule them efficiently. Below is a detailed table of their next five projects. Sequence the jobs using the critical ratio rule. Evaluate the performance of the rule.

Client	Order Arrival Sequence	Due Date	Estimated Completion Time (days)
Index	1	19	10
Technology	2	33	12
Global	3	26	8
Government	4	22	11
Energy	5	42	14

13. Read Only Co., a software development firm, constantly looks for the most accurate means to sequence their projects. From the table below use critical ratio, SPT, and EDD sequencing rules to sequence the orders. Provide your recommendation as to which rule is best by examining the total days late, number of jobs late, and average lateness to measure the rule's performance.

Client	Order Arrival Sequence	Due Date	Estimated Completion Time (days)
AIM	1	17	4
Beta	2	5	5
Coral	3	13	2
Draw-it	4	9	6
E-notes	5	15	3

14. As a new hire with College Book Binding, you have been asked to present a means to sequence pending jobs. The first order to come in is due on day 14 and will take 7 days to complete. The second job is due on day 29 and will take 5 days to complete. The third job is to be completed by day 7 and will take 2 days to finish. The fourth job is due on day 24 and will take 8 days to complete. The last job is to be finished by day 19 and will take 4 days to complete. Your challenge is to present an argument for using a sequencing rule. Choose the best rule as measured by the average lateness of jobs. Provide a rationale for the selected sequencing rule and explain why it is better than those rules not chosen.

15. Bass Clef Guitars makes custom guitars for its legendary clientele. Each guitar needs to complete four distinct operations, but completion time for each operation varies from one instrument to another. The table below provides information on the next five jobs. Calculate the slack and slack per remaining operation for each client's guitar.

Client	Order Arrival Sequence	Due Date	Estimated Completion Time (days)	Number of Remaining Operations
Timmy Hendricks	1	7	4	2
Don Mathews	2	11	6	4
Moses Moreno	3	21	8	4
Pat Dylan	4	16	2	4
Edy Van Whalen	5	17	5	4

16. Jobs at Steve's Machine Shop are sequenced using the slack per remaining operation rule. Determine the sequence of the following jobs waiting in queue.

Job Number:	1	2	3	4	5	6
Estimated completion time (hours)	15	10	8	6	10	7
Due date (hours)	25	19	20	17	28	15
Remaining operations	5	4	6	5	7	5

17. A work center at Benny Bliss's Custom Signs has five orders in queue. Use the critical ratio approach to sequencing the orders.

Job ID	Total Time Required (hours)	Total Time until Due (hours)
101	18	35
102	14	26
103	16	24
104	10	20
105	21	24

18. As an expert on the subject of scheduling, you have been asked to explain when you would utilize slack per remaining operation. From the information below, sequence the jobs using slack per remaining operation and explain why it would be used.

Client	Order Arrival Sequence	Due Date	Estimated Completion Time (days)	Number of Remaining Operations
a	1	3	3	5
b	2	7	2	4
c	3	12	6	3
d	4	16	9	2
e	5	23	5	4

19. The Campus Post Office receives an average of 24 customers per hour. If the distribution follows the Poisson distribution, what is the probability that during any given hour it will receive 30 customers?

20. The Second State Bank gets an average of 41 customers per hour. The distribution follows the Poisson distribution. What is the probability that during any given hour, the bank will receive 50 customers?

21. The Roosevelt High School cheerleaders are having a car wash. If they get an average of 25 cars per hour and the distribution follows the Poisson distribution, what is the probability that they will receive 40 cars in a given hour?

22. Silvia Tilden has started a house painting business to earn money during the summer. She has identified the following activities and their predecessors for planning a typical house painting project. Create a network diagram for her project.

Activity	Immediate Predecessor
A. Time and materials estimation	—
B. Bid creation	A
C. Purchase materials	B
D. Power wash house	B
E. Strip paint where needed	B
F. Mask windows	B
G. Paint trim, first coat	C, D, E, F
H. Paint trim, second coat	G
I. Paint open areas, first coat	G
J. Paint open areas, second coat	H, I
K. Glaze windows	J
L. Clean up	K

23. Construct a network diagram for the following activities and predecessors:

Activity	Immediate Predecessor
A	—
B	A
C	A
D	A
E	B
F	B
G	C
H	E, F
I	D, G
J	H, I

24. A software development firm uses a standardized set of activities for the planning process associated with each project. The activities are

Activities

A. Gather user info
B. Develop project goals
C. Identify developer tools needed
D. Forecast coding expertise needed
E. Apply for coding manpower
F. Assemble project team for responsibility assignment
G. Create budget
H. Complete proposal

The network diagram for the planning process is shown in Exhibit 8.33. Times are in days. Determine the critical path and the amount of slack for each activity in the network.

25. The following network diagrams the major phases of a new consulting project taken on by Alpha Productivity Enhancement. Times for each activity are expressed in days. Determine the critical path and the slack for each activity in the network provided in Exhibit 8.34.

EXHIBIT 8.33   **Network Diagram for Problem 24**

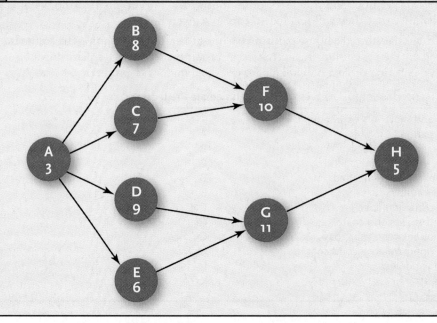

Network Diagram for Problem 25

EXHIBIT 8.34

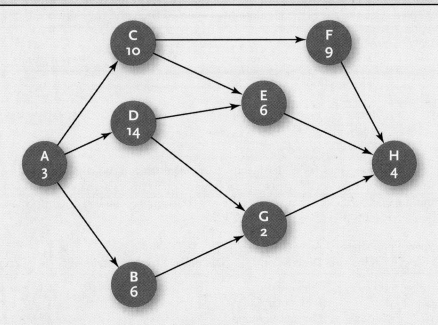

26. Tie has always dreamed of starting his own mortgage business. He has identified seven steps to complete before business can begin. Using the data below, construct a network diagram and determine the critical path.

Activity ID No.	Activity	Immediate Predecessors	Estimated Time (days)
1	Financing		5
2	Secure lenders	1	20
3	Lease space	1	10
4	Purchase supplies	3	1
5	Set up phones	4	4
6	Hire reps	2	20
7	Advertise	5, 6	15

27. Innovative R&D markets new inventions. The following 10 activities are needed before an invention can be taken to market. Use the information to construct a network diagram, determine the early/late start/finish points, and find the critical path.

Activity ID No.	Activity Description	Immediate Predecessors	Estimated Time
1	Study feasibility		6
2	Gather information		4
3	Explore options		6
4	Define users	2	1
5	Narrow to one	3	1
6	Prototype	1, 4, 5	10
7	Internal test	6	5
8	External test	6	8
9	Measure performance	7, 8	5
10	Production	9	25

28. National Test Center is a leading research center for the study of communicable diseases. The research activities and their optimistic, most likely, and pessimistic times are given. Use the times to calculate the expected time and the variance.

Activity ID No.	Activity Description	Optimistic	Most Likely	Pessimistic
1	Take specimen	.5	1	3
2	Measure	1.5	2	4
3	Test	2.5	4	7
4	Analyze	3	5	7
5	Report	2	3	4

29. EZ Attorney provides its students with basic legal training so that they will be able to quickly negotiate settlements. The following chart provides EZ's estimation of the length of each activity (in hours) in the negotiation process. Use the information to calculate the ES, EF, LS, LF, and slack.

Activity ID No.	Immediate Predecessors	Activity Description	Optimistic	Most Likely	Pessimistic	t	Variance
1		Preparation	6.5	8.5	10.5	8.5	0.4444
2	1	Preliminary	3	5	7	5	0.4444
3	2	Common ground	2	5	8	5	1.0000
4	2	Issue at hand	8	10.5	13	10.5	0.6944
5	3, 4	Agreement	2.5	4	7	4.25	0.5625

30. The accompanying table provides the pessimistic, most likely, and optimistic times, as well as the precedence relationships for all activities in a construction project. Construct the network diagram and determine the critical path. What is the probability that the project will be completed in 60 days?

Activity	Predecessors	Optimistic	Most Likely	Pessimistic
A	—	11	15	18
B	—	14	17	20
C	A	9	13	16
D	B	6	10	16
E	C	10	12	16
F	C, D	4	5	6
G	D, F	8	12	14
H	E, G	11	16	18

31. Bryan, a hockey player, is very interested in how long it takes to prepare for a game. The table below provides information on all of the activities leading up to the game. What is the probability that Bryan would be ready in 25 minutes?

Activity ID No.	Immediate Predecessors	Activity Description	Optimistic	Most Likely	Pessimistic	t	Variance
1		Dress	9	11	13	11	0.4444
2	1	Warmup	4	6	8	6	0.4444
3	1	Stretch	3	5	7	5	0.4444
4	2, 3	Assignments	2	5	8	5	1.0000
5	4	Pregame	3	6	9	6	1.0000

32. Software Design assists companies with the implementation of new software products. Of course, time is of the essence and the company is on a very tight schedule. Use the following information to reduce the project duration as much as possible.

What will it cost to reduce the project to that duration? The current critical path is 1, 2, 3, 5, 6.

Activity ID No.	Activity Description	Normal Time (days)	Crash Time (days)	Cost/Day ($)
1	ID needs	30	28	250
2	Research market	15	14	500
3	Narrow solutions	14	13	250
4	Feasibility	7	6	400
5	Prototype	60	59	800
6	Implementation	90	89	950

33. The network shown in Exhibit 8.35 has been solved, and the critical path is ACDF with a project duration of 33 days. Using the crashing data provided, crash the project until its duration cannot be reduced any more and determine the cost of that reduction.

Activity	Normal Time	Minimum Crash Time	Crash Cost ($) per Day
A	10	8	250
B	12	10	300
C	6	5	200
D	8	7	400
E	5	5	
F	9	8	350

34. Sam is preparing to write a paper for class. Below is a table identifying the activities needed for his paper. Determine the project duration and the critical path. Given his work schedule, taking time off to write the paper will mean sacrificing income. Determine the lowest cost approach for reducing the project by four days.

Activity ID No.	Activity Description	Predecessors	Normal Time (days)	Crash Time (days)	Cost/Day ($)
1	Choose topic		4	3	250
2	Outline	1	3	2	175
3	Research	1	7	5	300
4	Bibliography	2	2		
5	Write	3, 4	3	2	100

Network Diagram for Problem 33	EXHIBIT 8.35

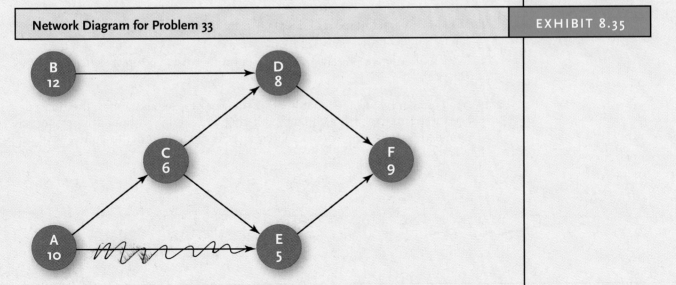

ADVANCED PROBLEMS

1. On September 30, Aric Bishop, the CEO for Birmingham Steel, is reviewing orders due by the end of the next quarter. Birmingham currently has 15 jobs in queue with delivery dates by the end of the year. Information about each job's process time and due date is contained below. The number of each job in the table represents the order in which the job was received.

JOB	Process Time	Due Date
1	1	10/5
2	6	12/16
3	9	11/29
4	3	11/1
5	10	11/18
6	9	12/31
7	10	10/14
8	10	11/6
9	5	12/7
10	8	12/19
11	5	11/23
12	10	10/25
13	7	10/20
14	4	12/22
15	4	11/11

Due to customer complaints regarding late shipments, Aric is spending a great deal of time with his operations manager to insure that jobs are completed with as little delay as possible. As Aric's operations manager, you are to present sequencing alternatives based on four sequencing rules: first-come, first-served; earliest due date; shortest process time; and critical ratio.

a. What is the total number of days late, total number of jobs delayed, and average lateness under FIFO?

b. What is the total number of days late, total number of jobs delayed, and average lateness under earliest due date?

c. What is the total number of days late, total number of jobs delayed, and average lateness under shortest process time?

d. What is the total number of days late, total number of jobs delayed, and average lateness under critical ratio?

e. Which alternative presents the best option to satisfy customer demands for on-time delivery?

2. A small retailer has decided that in order to increase sales and profits, they must develop a web site that will facilitate marketing and selling on-line. The retailer has determined that the following activities must be done in order to go live with on-line ordering.

Activity ID No.	Activity	Immediate Predecessor(s)	Estimated Time (weeks)	Crashing Cost ($) 1st wk/2d wk
01	Create project team	-	1	- / -
02	Specify hardware needs	01	3	300 / -
03	Specify web site requirements	01	3	1100 / -
04	Scope advertising for on-line selling	01	2	1000 / -
05	Obtain quotes for hardware	02	1	- / -
06	Purchase and install hardware	05	4	500 / 1200
07	Design web site	03	4	300 / 1500
08	Develop advertising	04	2	2000 / -
09	Test hardware and web site	06, 07	2	- / -
10	Place advertisements	08, 09	1	- / -
11	Go live	10	1	- / -

Develop a network diagram for this project.

a. Identify the critical path and determine its length.

b. Determine ES, LS, EF, LF and activity slack.

c. The retailer wishes to go live within 10 weeks of beginning the project. They estimate they are losing $2,000 in profit for each week that the site is not available. Develop a crashing schedule that would be best for the retailer.

ENDNOTES

1. B. J. Finch, and S. J. Peterson, "Quality Attributes in Online Auctions," Decision Sciences Institute, Washington DC, November 2003.

2. "TaylorMade Drives Supply-Chain Efficiency with 24-Hour Club," SupplyChainBrain.com, October 2002.

3. "Fix It and They Will Come," The Wall Street Journal, February 12, 2001, p. R4.

4. Adapted from D. H. Maister, "The Psychology of Waiting Lines," in J. A. Czepiel, M. R. Solomon, and C. F. Surprenant (eds.), The Service Encounter (Lexington, MA: Lexington Press, 1985), pp. 113–123.

5. E. M. Goldratt, Critical Chain (Great Barrington, MA: North River Press. 1997).

LEARNING ACTIVITIES   www.mhhe.com/opsnow3e

Visit the Online Learning Center (www.mhhe.com/opsnow3e) for additional resources. Content varies by chapter, and includes

- Business Tours
- OM on Site
- Readings
- Resources
- Excel Tutors

- Interactive Case Models
- Reel Operations Video Clips
- Additional Advanced Problem
- Self-Assessment Quizzes
- Glossary

SELECTED REFERENCES

Fine, C. F. *ClockSpeed: Winning Industry Control in the Age of Temporary Advantage*. Reading, MA: Perseus Books, 1998.

Fitzsimmons, J. A., and Fitzsimmons, M. J. *Service Management: Operations, Strategy, and Information Technology*. New York: McGraw-Hill/Irwin, 2006.

Gido, J., and Clements, J. P. *Successful Project Management*. Cincinnati, OH: South-Western Publishing, 1999.

Gray, C. F., and Larson, E. W. *Project Management: The Managerial Process*. New York: McGraw-Hill/Irwin, 2006.

Katzenbach, J. R., and Smith, D. K. *The Wisdom of Teams*. New York: HarperCollins, 1999.

Meredith, J. R., and Mantel, S. J. *Project Management*. New York: John Wiley & Sons, 2000.

Olson, D. L. *Introduction to Information Systems Project Management*. New York: McGraw-Hill/Irwin, 2004.

Stalk, G., Jr., and Hout, T. M. *Competing against Time*. New York: Free Press, 1990.

VIDEO CASE 8.1

Scheduling Services: United Airlines

Based on Video 10 on the Student DVD

Many scheduling processes are an attempt to match demand and capacity. This is particularly challenging in the service sector, where finished goods inventory cannot be used to store capacity for later use. One especially challenging scheduling application is in the airline industry, which requires the coordinated scheduling of several resource groups.

1. What four sets of resources require scheduling for United Airlines? What is the first piece of information needed to begin this scheduling process?

2. What happens if maintenance scheduling results in a plane not receiving its required maintenance in time? Why doesn't United do the maintenance early?

3. What would be the costs associated with poor crew scheduling?

4. What specific resources are scheduled in the airport/manpower schedule?

5. What is Pegasus?

VIDEO CASE 8.2

Project Management: The Alton Bridge

Based on Video 11 on the Student DVD

The new bridge between Alton, Illinois, and St. Louis provides an excellent environment for examining a complex project. Bridge projects are particularly difficult to manage because of safety issues, weather and high water issues, and the sheer size of the project.

1. In the Alton Bridge project, why did the state of Illinois split the project among three separate contractors? What are the pros and cons of such a division?

2. Do you think the late penalty used was sufficient to keep the project on time?

3. In most large projects, unanticipated events cause delays. What were some of the unusual or unanticipated events that caused delays to the Alton Bridge project?

4. Create a flow diagram of the major phases of the bridge project. Identify the phases in which the delays occurred.

INTERACTIVE CASE 8.1

Sequencing Jobs at Jensen's Custom Auto Restoration

The sequencing rule interactive model provides a quick and easy way to compare the performance of several traditional sequencing rules. The techniques included for comparison are earliest due date (EDD), shortest processing time (SPT), critical ratio (CR), and first come, first served (FCFS). The user has the option of using the default data or entering new data for estimated completion time and due date. The user must also select the number of orders to be sequenced. By selecting the rule to be applied and clicking on the "schedule" button, the model resequences the orders and provides a color-coded Gantt chart of the resulting schedule. When orders are projected to be completed after their due date, a line showing the due date is also provided. Performance measures of total days late, number of orders late, and average lateness are provided.

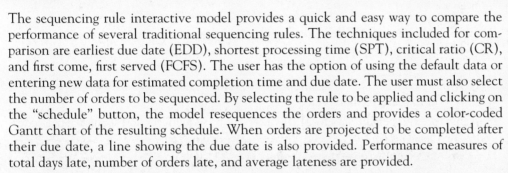

Note: completion time and due date must be less than 18.

Order ID	Estimated Processing Time (days)	Due Date	Critical Ratio	Expected Completion Date	Lateness
A	3	5	1.67	4	0
B	4	6	1.5	8	2
C	2	7	3.5	10	3
D	6	9	1.5	16	7
E	1	2	2	1	0

Total days late: 12

Number of late orders: 3

Average lateness: 2.4

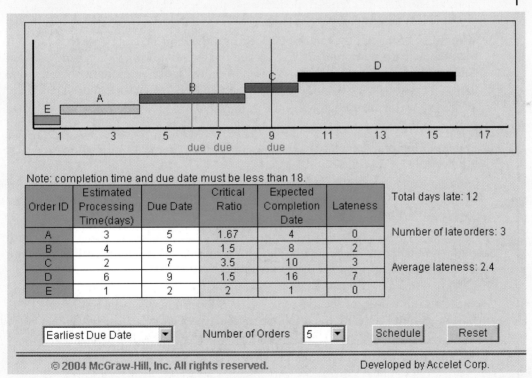

Earliest Due Date ▼   Number of Orders 5 ▼   Schedule   Reset

Jensen's Custom Auto Restoration

Jensen's Custom Auto Restoration specializes in refurbishing sports cars from the fifties, sixties, and seventies. Jensen's capabilities range from mechanical engine work to body and paint projects. As a part of the cost estimation process, Bill Jensen estimates the number of days to complete each job and negotiates a due date based on the projected time to complete the project and the availability of necessary parts. History shows that Bill has been quite accurate at estimating time to complete various jobs. Bill wishes to evaluate the potential of using sequencing rules that differ from his typical "first come, first served" approach to sequencing restoration jobs.

1. Use the default data for the five jobs to be sequenced, as shown below, and sequence the jobs by earliest due date.

Job ID	Estimated Completion Time	Due Date
A	3	5
B	4	6
C	2	7
D	6	9
E	1	2

a. Record the performance measures and resequence by shortest processing time. How does the performance of the two rules compare on total days late, number of jobs late, and average lateness? Were you surprised by the results?

b. If your objective was to minimize lateness for the latest job, which rule would you select? Explain your answer.

2. Again, use the default data for the five jobs to be sequenced, and sequence the orders by the critical ratio rule. Record the performance measures.

a. Resequence the orders by first come, first served and compare the results.

b. Rank the four rules for each performance measure. How does the performance of the four rules compare?

3. As new jobs come in, they must be added into the sequence. Suppose that as job B was completed, a new order arrived. Delete the estimated completion time and due date for job B and replace them with an estimated processing time of 8 and a due date of 17. Resequence the orders, again using shortest processing time.

a. What position does that order take in the sequence?

b. What happens to the performance measures?

4. Enter another order, in place of the current B order, that has a processing time that is longer than any of the current orders.

a. What happens to it? What happens to the performance measures? What does this indicate for the shortest processing time rule? What is its flaw? How might you intervene to eliminate this problem?

5. A rule based on due date also makes sense, since the due date is one-half of the cause of an order being late. The most commonly used rule of this type is earliest due date (EDD). It basically gives priority to the order due the earliest.

a. Earliest due date often provides the best results in terms of average lateness. Using the default values for the five jobs, record the performance measures for the EDD sequence and compare the results to those of the first come, first served sequence.

b. Add the sixth default order and reschedule. How does the performance change? Explain what happens to the sequence.

6. Compare the results of first come, first served, earliest due date, and shortest processing time for the default settings using 4, 5, and 6 orders. How to they compare?

7. The critical ratio rule combines information from the due date and the processing time of each order to compute a ratio of the due date to the expected processing time. The resulting ratio provides a picture of the amount of extra time available to process the order. An order that is already late will have a critical ratio less than 1. The larger the ratio, the more extra time is available. The orders are scheduled by the ratio; smallest is first.

a. Sequence the default values for the five jobs using the critical ratio rules. Compare the results of the critical ratio rule to those of the EDD, SPT, and FCFS rules. How does it compare?

INTERACTIVE CASE 8.2

Managing Lines at the Passport Office

The waiting line simulation provides a rich environment for exploring service systems. The user can select between 1- and 2-phase systems. The simulator speed, which doesn't change the simulation outcome, allows the user to slow the system down to better observe interactions. The arrival rate is generated from a Poisson distribution. The arrival rate selection determines the parameter λ and is the number of arrivals per hour. The service rate is generated from a negative exponential distribution and is the number of customers served per hour. The service rate selection determines the parameter μ. The selection of NS1: or NS2: determines the number of servers for each phase of the system. Output measures are:

- W_q = the average time customers wait in line.
- W_s = the average time customers spend in the system (waiting and being served).
- L_q = the average number of customers waiting in line for the service.
- L_s = the average number of customers in the system (waiting and being served).

As the simulation runs, the number of customers in line is provided under each "queue."

The number of customers that have been through the system is presented under the last queue.

The Dane County Passport Office

The Dane County Administration Office processes passport applications as a part of its service. The office has recently received a small grant to improve the passport application process. As a means of stretching the money as far as possible, Sandy Harris is using an operations management class as consultants. Currently the process can be described as a single-server, two-phase queuing system with an average service rate of four customers per hour and an average arrival rate of four customers per hour. Sandy wishes to have a complete analysis done and wants the student team to demonstrate how queues work and explain to her how the various queue characteristics interact.

Check to see that the parameters are equal to the values below.

Phases	2
Speed	Normal
Arrival rate	4
Service rate	4
Number of servers in phase 1	1
Number of servers in phase 2	1
Server breakdown severity	N

1. Run the simulation, observing the system, until 50 customers have been served.

   a. Were both servers ever busy at the same time? Did a waiting line ever form in front of either server? What was the maximum length of the waiting lines? What were the output measures for W_q, W_s, L_q, and L_s? Explain each.

2. Run the simulation with the same parameters except increase the number of servers for each phase from 1 to 2.

   a. Did waiting lines ever form this time? How long did they get? What were the new output measures for W_q, W_s, L_q, and L_s? Explain the difference.

   b. Why would lines form, given the service capacity at each server and the arrival rate?

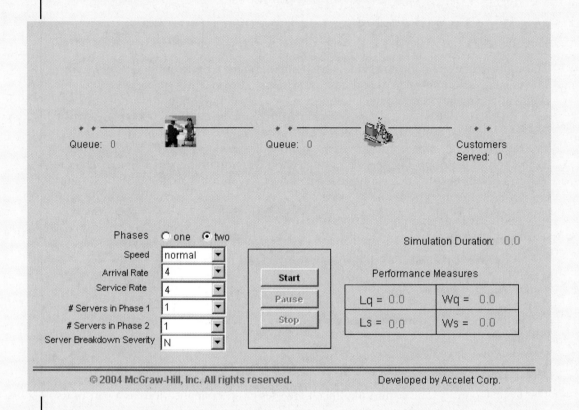

3. Run the simulation with the same parameters (two servers at each phase), but change the server breakdown severity to "Y." Run the simulation for 50 customers.

   a. Did waiting lines form? How long did the lines get? What were the new output measures for W_q, W_s, L_q, and L_s?

   b. Explain the change. What happened to the performance measures as breakdowns became a factor? Is this what you expected to happen?

Reset the parameters as follows. Change the server breakdown severity back to "N." Note that this configuration uses two employees, as was the case in the original configuration, but each employee performs the entire service, rather than splitting it between two workers in two phases. Since each worker does the entire service, each server can only process two customers per hour. Total capacity, however, is still four customers per hour for the system.

4. Reset the parameters as follows:

Phases	1
Speed	Normal
Arrival rate	4
Service rate	2
Number of servers in phase 1	2
Number of servers in phase 2	0
Server breakdown severity	N

a. Carefully observe the simulation as it processes 50 customers. How long does the queue in front of the server get? With arrival rate and server rates equal, why does a queue develop? After 50 customers, what were the output measures for W_q, W_s, L_q, and L_s?

b. Leave all parameters the same as in 4a, except change the service rate to 4. Again, observe the simulation as it processes 50 customers. How long does the queue in front of the server get this time? Did you notice any instances of either server being idle? Why did this happen? After 50 customers, what were the output measures for W_q, W_s, L_q, and L_s? Compare them to the output measures for 2a. Explain how the differences relate to the change in service rate.

Most fast-food restaurants, banks, and airline ticket counters have adopted a single-queue, multiple-server design that utilizes a long "serpentine" queue. The customer at the head of the line goes to the first open server. These systems are fair in that no one gains advantage by selecting the line with the fastest server. It also eliminates the problem of customers jumping from one line to another (jockeying).

5. Set the parameters as follows:

Phases	1
Speed	Slow
Arrival rate	8
Service rate	2
Number of servers in phase 1	4
Number of servers in phase 2	0
Server breakdown severity	N

a. What are the performance measures? Do you think they're acceptable? What would you expect to be true about the utilization of the servers? Would that performance measure be important?

6. Reset the parameters as follows:

Phases	1
Speed	Slow
Arrival rate	8
Service rate	3
Number of servers in phase 1	4
Number of servers in phase 2	0
Server breakdown severity	N

a. How would you judge the performance of this configuration from the standpoint of waiting time and line length, as well as resource utilization?

7. Based on the parameters and simulations you have run, provide a general description of the relationship between number of servers, service rate, arrival rate, and the performance measures.

Digging for Uncle Bill

Andy and Isabel have been dating since their first year in college. As they approach the summer between their junior and senior years, they have decided to spend the first six weeks of the summer working and the second six weeks spending what they have earned by traveling in Europe. Andy's Uncle Bill owns a landscaping company and has offered to subcontract jobs out to Andy and Isabel. Uncle Bill has provided them with the following clients and, without Andy and Isabel's consent, has also promised completion dates to the clients. The hours shown in the expected completion time are the hours Andy's uncle projects, assuming two people working together, so client 1 is expected to take 25 hours for both Andy and Isabel.

Client	Expected Completion Time (hours)	Due Date (by the end of week)
1	25	1
2	18	3
3	20	2
4	9	2
5	36	3
6	18	1
7	21	2
8	32	4
9	23	5
10	26	5

1. Evaluate EDD and SPT as ways to sequence the clients. Which seems to perform best?

2. Using your best-performing sequence and assuming a 40-hour work week, which clients will not be completed on time? By how many hours will each be late?

3. Suppose Andy and Isabel agree to work on weekends if necessary to complete jobs that will be late otherwise? Create a schedule that shows how much they will need to work on weekends. Keep in mind that doing work on weekends for one client will mean that the next client's work will begin sooner.

4. Andy's uncle has just told them to expect about 4 hours additional time to move equipment from one client to another. This has the impact of increasing the time for each client by 4 hours. How does this affect the performance of your rule? Develop a new schedule.

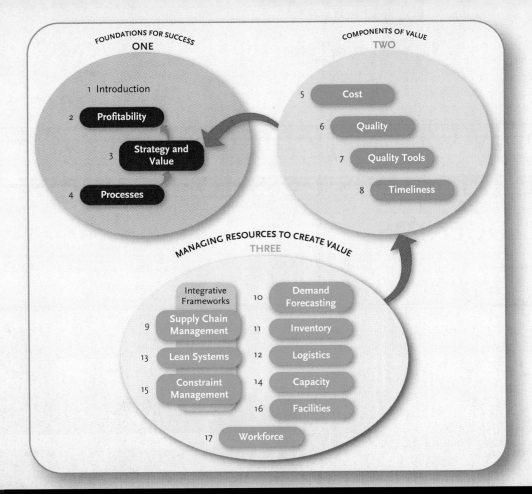

Managing Resources to Create Value

INTRODUCTION

Unit 1 focused on foundations for the ultimate success of the firm. These "foundations" of profitability, value, strategy, capabilities, and processes can be thought of as prerequisites that place Units 2 and 3 into the proper context. Unit 2 covered cost, quality, and timeliness, the components of value that customers pay for. In Unit 3 the focus shifts to the resources businesses use to create that value. First we examine supply chain management to provide a perspective of resource management that extends beyond the walls of one company and recognizes the impact resource decisions have on the entire value chain. Next we examine resource planning and the fundamental concepts of demand forecasting, simply because nearly all business plans are based on a demand forecast. We then examine inventory, followed by lean systems, which often guide the way inventory is managed. Capacity comes next, followed by an examination of constraint management, which often guides the way capacity is used. Facilities comes next, followed by the workforce. Profitability comes from blending the value and costs created. Creating the most value for the least cost requires effective management of the resources used in operations processes.

CHAPTER 9

Supply Chain Management: Managing Business-to-Business Interactions

LEARNING OBJECTIVES

- Explain the motivating forces behind the adoption of supply chain management (SCM).

- List examples of how customer actions affect suppliers and how supplier actions affect customers.

- Explain the seven critical decision areas of SCM.

- Describe the decisions that constitute the logistics network configuration.

- Describe an example of a supply chain and identify points of interaction between buyers and suppliers.

- Explain the pros and cons of outsourcing supply chain services.

- Explain the bullwhip effect and its possible causes.

- Describe risk pooling and the implications it has for distribution networks.

- Explain the current trends affecting supply chain management.

A THREE-COMPANY ALLIANCE TO IMPROVE SERVICE SUPPLY CHAIN PERFORMANCE

Despite the fact that automobile manufacturers design, manufacture, distribute, and sell automobiles, much of their competitive advantage and customer loyalty comes from the service they provide after the sale. That service depends on the skills of technicians, their ability to keep appointments, and their ability to *not* have customers waiting a long time for their cars. Clearly, the perceived quality of the product (the automobile) is heavily dependent on the quality of a service. The quality of that service, however, often depends on the availability of another product—a repair part. The service-parts supply chain is a critical aspect of service for every automobile company. Ford has recognized that importance and has embarked on a unique project to make it better.

Ford's service-parts supply chain is enormous. It has over 600,000 different parts in inventory, uses 5,000 suppliers, and serves 15,000 dealers globally. Ford generates 120 million orders per year and utilizes 63 different distribution centers.

In order to develop a parts management system, Ford formed a developmental alliance with Caterpillar Logistics Services and SAP. The objectives of the system development project were to

- Give total supply chain visibility of service parts.
- Reduce the time to market.
- Optimize inventory levels.
- Provide a better level of service to customers.
- Provide dealers with real-time access to inventory data.

Caterpillar Logistics Services was started in 1987 as a third-party logistics division of Caterpillar, Inc. It provides logistics services to around 65 clients worldwide, in addition to Caterpillar's own logistics needs. In 2003, Cat Logistics generated over $1 billion in revenue with clients that include Ford, DaimlerChrysler, MG Rover, Land Rover (Europe and the United States), Kia and Hyundai (Europe), Saab (in North America), and a new agreement with Mazda (in the United States and Canada).

Cat Logistics and Ford could not find an off-the-shelf product that could meet Ford's parts management needs, so they decided to partner with the software company that they thought was best able to develop such a solution, SAP. The three partners expect to have their system in place by the end of 2004, and the capabilities developed will be incorporated into SAP's standard supply chain management and customer relationship management solutions in 2005 as part of SAP's service and asset management solutions portfolio. This partnership marks the first time a manufacturer, a third-party logistics provider, and a software company collaborated on the development of new systems.

The end result of the alliance will be a system that can handle the wide range of service-parts management requirements, from a huge volume of aftermarket orders to low volume–high value parts planning. This alliance provides benefits for all involved. Ford gets a parts management system that enables it to enhance its service-parts performance. Caterpillar Logistics will make the system available to its clients. SAP gets a new capability that will be known as its service-parts management solution and that it will market to the entire service parts industry.

Sources: R. J. Bowman, "For Ford Motor Co., the Aftermarket Is No Longer an Afterthought," *SupplyChainBrain.com*, March 2004; www .catlogistics.com/s_our_story/index.html, June 6, 2004; I. Morton, "Group Unites on Software," *Automotive New Europe*, May 2003; J. Katz, "Ford, Caterpillar, and SAP Collaborate on Logistics Solution," *Supply Chain Technology News*, March 2003.

upply chain management (SCM) provides managers with a global perspective on which to judge actions and predict outcomes. SCM recognizes that the impact of decisions does not stop at the wall of the factory or store, but extends to suppliers and customers. In order to maximize value for the customer, managers must consider the implications decisions have up and down the chain.

Introduction: A Systemwide Perspective

As information technologies have made it possible for customers and suppliers in B2B relationships to communicate quickly and effectively, the advantages and benefits gained from doing so have become not only apparent, but expected. Goods and services obviously travel between manufacturers, warehouses, distributors, wholesalers, retailers, and customers. What hasn't been as obvious, however, is the impact that decisions thought to be internal had on others. Supply chain management evolved as managers began to recognize the interactions present in supply chains and the fact that they could better differentiate themselves from competitors if they coordinated efforts with supply chain partners. The ability to link buyers and sellers together through ongoing communication has enabled businesses to consider the effect decisions made within each business had on the other businesses.

The supply chain, as defined in Chapter 3,

encompasses all activities associated with the flow and transformation of goods from the raw material stage (extraction), through to the end user, as well as the associated information flows. Material and information flow both up and down the supply chain.[1]

It should not be viewed as a set of techniques or functions, but, rather, as a framework for broadening the context in which all business decisions are made.

The generic supply chain initially presented in Chapter 3 is reproduced in Exhibit 9.1. Each arrow signifies the potential flow of materials from suppliers to customers. A flow of information, however, travels in the opposite direction of each arrow. Effective supply chain management depends as much on this flow of information as it does on the flow of goods. Even though only some activities in the supply chain add value, all add costs. The objective of supply chain management is to optimize performance of the chain to add as much value as possible for the least cost possible. This can occur only if the perspective used in decision making is broadened to include the entire chain. This systemwide perspective is critical because many pressures and conflicts encourage managers to place decisions internal to their own businesses at a priority above that of the supply chain. Gains from these decisions are short term, however. A long-term perspective recognizes that if a decision improves performance for an individual business while increasing overall costs for the supply chain, the result will be increased costs for the customer and harm done throughout the chain.

Supply chain management is not easy to successfully implement. From the perspective of productivity and competitiveness, however, it has become very important. An examination of why supply chain management is needed provides an excellent introduction to what supply chain management can do.

Supply chain terminology is often linked to the perspective one has toward the supply chain. For example, for a manufacturer of consumer products, an immediate supplier would be referred to as a '1st tier,' or tier 1, supplier. A supplier to that company would be referred to as a '2nd tier,' or tier 2, supplier, and so on. The tier 1 supplier is actually a customer of the tier 2 supplier.

SAP has over 32,000 customers worldwide and is the world's largest business software company.

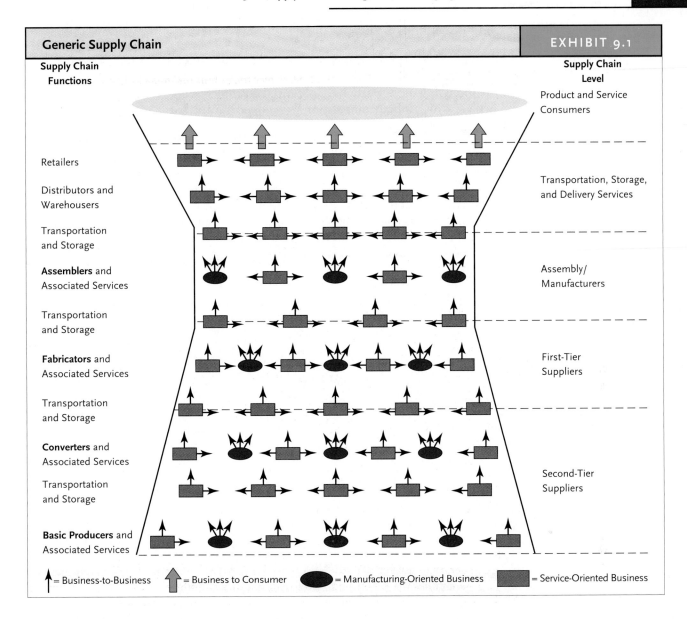

EXHIBIT 9.1 Generic Supply Chain

The Motivating Forces

Change is brought about by many factors. External forces often force managers to adopt new ways of acting and thinking. Sudden recognition of a "better way" can sometimes be enough to change behavior. The ability to do something that was previously impossible can also be enough of a catalyst to change the way things are done. Supply chain management is a dramatic change in behavior from more traditional management approaches and has been motivated by a variety of conditions. The most important reasons for adopting supply chain management can be summarized as follows:

1. Increased competition to meet customer expectations for value and differentiate capabilities from those of competitors.

2. Recognition that customer decisions and actions often dictate costs and limitations for suppliers.

3. Recognition that supplier decisions and actions often dictate costs and limitations for customers.

4. Increased potential for timely communication and feedback brought about by technological advances.

A brief discussion of each is presented in turn.

Increased Competition

As domestic markets turned into global markets, businesses saw a tremendous opportunity to reach more people with their products and services. Very quickly, however, they realized that along with more potential customers came more competitors. Most did not view intensified competition as an opportunity, but it really was. Customers who are exposed to better products and services elevate their expectations. Businesses that want to continue to compete must improve the value of their products and services through enhanced processes and capabilities, lower costs, better quality, and greater timeliness. One company stretches a bit, customers like it, and the competitors must respond. This came at a time when businesses, wisely, were focusing more on core competencies in hopes of doing better at what they already did well. Outsourcing was increasing. The paradox is that as value needed to increase and differentiation became more important, the businesses were passing off much of the value-adding processes to others. Clearly, closer relationships were necessary to make this work.

Businesses sought greater and greater levels of productivity in order to provide increasing levels of value. This was not limited to B2C companies but included B2B as well. Suppliers were pushed to do better, do it quicker, and do it for less. For many companies, familiarity and experiences with lean approaches had led to closer relationships with suppliers. The productivity and time requirements passed down from customers were placing demands on the suppliers. Productivity was being lost. Costs were added. The decisions and expectations of customers sometimes prevented suppliers from doing things that could actually add value. Suppliers, eager to please, often incurred unnecessary costs trying to meet the needs of their customers. In many cases, their actions weren't really necessary and didn't add value to the product.

What can be viewed as insensitivity among trading partners to each other's needs went in both directions. Not only did suppliers often have to jump through unnecessary hoops for customers, but customers also incurred costs because of supplier decisions and actions. The simplest and most direct costs for customers were related to the delivery patterns of the supplier. Infrequent large quantities versus frequent small quantities, for example, had a tremendous impact on inventory levels for the customer. Decisions made independently provided suboptimal conditions for all parties involved in the supply chain.

On the surface, it appears that supply chain management efforts have been motivated most directly by two of the value attributes: cost and timeliness. Lowering the price to the consumer often requires cost reduction. This creates a need to eliminate non-value-adding steps throughout the production network. Increasing pressures to reduce inventories require quicker and more reliable deliveries from suppliers. No doubt, these are important pressures that have contributed to the need for supply chain management, but they're not the only reasons.

It doesn't take long for a savvy manager to realize that the actions of someone else in the supply chain result in cost increases within that manager's firm. So the manager initiates a conversation. Maybe it's with a supplier who gets orders for products in a format that's incompatible with his computer system. Or maybe if the orders arrived an hour earlier, the shipment could go out today rather than tomorrow. Or maybe a customer could save many hours of labor if the delivery was packaged in a different sequence. Things are often done a certain way because that's the way they've always been done. When a supplier or a customer asks about making a change, the response often is "Oh, I didn't know that caused a problem for you. Sure, we can change the way we do that. No big deal." That's the very beginning of supply chain management—suppliers and customers talking.

Reduction of costs throughout the supply chain requires a reduction in inventory throughout the network. Reducing production costs has often made outsourcing more attractive because of differences in labor costs and other production costs. Outsourcing also enables a firm to focus on its core competencies by handing off other work to those who are better at it. Outsourcing, however, can be detrimental when it comes to inventory costs and to the timeliness component of value. It reduces reliability and adds transportation time. Inventory protects from those uncertainties. Transportation takes time and can cause delays. Timeliness is even more critical when outsourcing production to foreign countries. In some situations, the need for timeliness may require management to forgo opportunities for cheaper labor elsewhere.

The emphasis on cost and timeliness enhancement in the supply chain does not mean that quality is ignored. Much of the effort that goes into an effective supply chain management program is spent working with suppliers to improve product and service quality.

It is common for U.S. businesses to spend 20 to 30 percent of their revenues on the acquisition of goods from outside suppliers. For manufacturers, 60 percent is typical.[2] A small cost savings in purchases can have a dramatic impact on the bottom line. Consider the following example presented in Exhibit 9.2. This company has sales revenue of $12,520,000 and total purchases of $7,200,000. Total salary and wages are $3,400,000, and financial and other costs are $960,000. Profit before taxes was also $960,000. A 6 percent savings in the cost of supplies, which goes directly to profit, provides a 45 percent increase in before-tax profits. These direct reductions in costs that can stem from better relationships with suppliers are not the only cost savings. Indirect cost savings appear in various areas of the business, including reduced material consumption, reduced labor, and reduced overhead costs that can result from better delivery service, shorter response times, lower inventories, and improved utilization of equipment.[3] Supply chain management has increased in attractiveness as businesses recognize the bottom-line impact. It can have a significant effect on profitability, particularly as companies have squeezed out costs in most other areas. Amazon.com provides an excellent example. Amazon's first profits ever, in the fourth quarter of 2001, were credited largely to supply chain management efforts.

Supply Savings Example	EXHIBIT 9.2

Sales revenue	$12,520,000
Total purchases	$7,200,000
Total salaries and wages	$3,400,000
Financial and other costs	$960,000
Profit before taxes	$960,000
6% savings in supply costs	$432,000
Impact on profit	45% increase

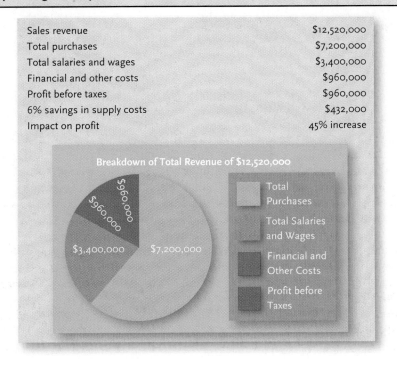

Breakdown of Total Revenue of $12,520,000

- Total Purchases
- Total Salaries and Wages
- Financial and Other Costs
- Profit before Taxes

The Impact of Customers on Suppliers

Suppliers began to realize that demands placed on them by their customers actually inhibited their ability to be good suppliers. Lack of communication and an adversarial relationship created an "us-against-them" attitude. In addition to problems that seemed to have obvious causes, another one was recognized. It seemed that even though demand at the consumer end of the supply chain was relatively stable, the variability of demand upstream got increasingly greater. This phenomenon, known as the **bullwhip effect,** can detract from the productivity and increase costs of the entire supply chain. Variability in demand adds costs in a number of ways. If demand fluctuates, capacity needs fluctuate, resulting in overstressed resources when demand is high and idle resources when demand is low. Labor needs also fluctuate, resulting in costly overtime or the use of contingent workers when demand is high and idle workers or layoffs when demand is low. Inventory levels fluctuate as well, resulting in high inventory costs when inventories are higher than necessary or high stockout rates when production can't keep up with demand. The bullwhip effect is examined in detail later in this chapter.

Beyond the bullwhip effect, customers can have other effects on their suppliers. Every producer of goods and services hopes for stable demand, because planning is easier, resources can be more effectively managed, and costs are lower. Without really even thinking about it, customers, through their actions, create instability that increases costs. A product promotion by a retailer, for example, causes demand to increase during the promotion and fall off after the promotion. Both situations result in increases in costs that must be either passed on to the ultimate consumer or absorbed, reducing profitability.

The Impact of Suppliers on Customers

Just as the ordering actions of customers can have a huge impact on suppliers, the responses of suppliers can create sweet dreams or nightmares for their customers. A missed delivery due date, defective products, or raw material shortages can result in missed shipments or delays and can create a dissatisfied consumer. Unreliability within the chain typically results in the customer increasing inventory to reduce the direct dependencies that can contribute to the problems. Inventory will always be important in

bullwhip effect
The increasing variability of demand as one moves upstream in a supply chain.

Sales are often intended to result in an increase in consumer demand. While that may have a positive impact on the retailer, the effect on the supplier (warehouse or manufacturer) can result in demand instability, which results in increased costs and reduced profitability that must be absorbed by the entire supply chain.

om ADVANTAGE   SCM and Profit for Amazon

The likelihood of finally documenting a profit seemed low for Amazon in 2001, despite CEO Jeff Bezos's claim that it would happen. Analysts expected no profit until at least 2003. Then, in the fourth quarter of 2001, the profit was undeniable—even though Amazon offered a 20 percent discount on books costing $20 or more during the fourth quarter.

One of the biggest improvements for Amazon, in the area of operations, was the culmination of efforts to improve logistics and supply chain management. Prior to 2001, some 12 percent of Amazon's inventory ended up going to the wrong place. This added costs and delayed deliveries. Inventory management improvements reduced this to 4 percent in 2001 even as sales increased. Between November 9 and December 21, 2001, shoppers purchased 37.9 million items. As a result, the cost of fulfilling orders dropped by 15 percent ($22 million) from 2000 to 2001.

Amazon also streamlined its processes for sorting orders. By reducing the time to get all of the components of an order into the system, the number of orders Amazon is able to ship increased. In 2001 Amazon was able to ship 35 percent more items with the same number of workers, driving up labor productivity. Even with these improvements, however, experts estimated that the Amazon distribution system was still operating at less than 40 percent of its capacity.

Source: www.amazon.com; "How Amazon Cleared the Profitability Hurdle," *BusinessWeek*, Online edition, February 4, 2002; "How Hard Should Amazon Swing," *BusinessWeek*, Online edition, January 14, 2002.

supply chains, but part of effective supply chain management is determining how to get the greatest benefit from the least cost. This involves decisions about inventory placement in the system—geographical placement at each storage level, as well as which levels in the network to use for storage. Correct placement can improve performance within the chain, reduce costs, and reduce the impact of disruptions.

The most feared of all supplier responses to product demand occurs when the supplier cannot respond. These instances are rare, but they can happen. Every year, natural disasters idle manufacturing plants. Those plants supply others. Whether the disaster is a fire, a flood, a hurricane, or an earthquake, entire supply chains can be brought to a halt. This is particularly true when a supply chain depends on a sole supplier for a critical part, as is often the case in JIT environments. Hurricane Katrina's devastation of New Orleans provides an excellent example. The port of New Orleans has been the primary entry point for coffee. Its closure disrupted the coffee supply until rerouting to other ports was completed. In these instances, good relationships with suppliers can prevent a business disaster.

Technological Advances

As managers became aware of the need for integrated decision making, and some were actually attempting it, the quick rise of the Internet provided a means of having immediate access to information that was previously out of reach. The Internet made it possible for a supplier to look at the same information that the customer looked at. Rather than forecast demands based on previous orders from a customer, a supplier could actually view the customer's production schedule and eliminate forecasting altogether. And the supplier's supplier could do the same thing. The combination of a need *and* the capability to satisfy it resulted in a surge in the popularity of supply chain management.

Supply Chain Management Decisions

- Strategic alliances
- Inventory management
- Cooperative product design
- Information management
- Standardization
- Electronic commerce[4]

TARGETING technology   Communication Enhances Supply Chain Connections

Internet-based communication has had a profound impact on the connectivity of businesses desiring supply relationships. It has enabled companies to maintain real-time communication of schedules and demand, it has reduced non-value-adding activities, and it has reduced the time required for transactions. Examples of increased efficiency abound.

Engineers working for IBM suppliers who had examined blueprints of components at IBM facilities before submitting bids for the work now receive blueprints online. They communicate online with IBM engineers and are encouraged to suggest improvements that can reduce costs for IBM. If changes are accepted, they are immediately made available to other bidders.

The trading of products for B2B transactions has become commonplace, but other types of trading exist as well. Yet2.com has created the first global marketplace for the exchange of intellectual assets. Designed to save companies the cost of R&D that has already been performed by someone else, Yet2.com lists, licenses, and sells rights to use inventions by companies who invest millions in R&D but often find that their inventions don't generate revenues because no one knows about them.

Internet-based communications has dramatically increased companies' ability to get in touch to do business, but also contributes to information sharing among businesses already in alliances. This enhancement to communication between businesses is needed, as the following effects of "dirty data" in the grocery industry show.

- $40 billion in sales lost annually due to poor supply chain information that leads to stockouts.
- A 30 percent error rate in catalogs used by retailers and manufacturers for replenishing inventory.
- An average 25 minutes per inventoried item per year to correct bad information.
- A 60 percent error rate for all invoices generated.
- An average of four weeks for rolling out a new product, due largely to poor approaches for updating new information in buyer and seller systems.

Source: "E-purchasing Saves Businesses Billions," *USA Today*, February 7, 2000, pp. 1A, 2A; www.yet2.com/app/about/about/aboutus, June 5, 2004; J. V. Murphy, "Data Synchronization Will Ease Headaches, Save Big Bucks in Retail Supply Chain," SupplyChainBrain.com, May 2004.

Combined, these decision-making areas provide a powerful force that increases product value and enhances profitability throughout the supply chain. The following sections provide a brief overview of each component.

Strategic Alliances

SAP offers enterprise planning system solutions for a variety of industries, from aerospace to higher education to retailing.

Developing alliances rather than just hiring suppliers is at the heart of supply chain management. Relationships create an opportunity for communication. Communication enhances productivity improvement and cooperation. As mutual dependence develops, the supplier depends on the customer and the customer depends on the supplier. When a relationship progresses past a simple transactional one to include each helping the other being better at what they do, it becomes even stronger. These benefits are obvious to enlightened managers, but even a simplistic examination of the costs associated with switching to a new supplier provides support for alliance development. Several of these costs are listed in Exhibit 9.3.[5]

The costs associated with changing suppliers clearly are varied. Many are direct and immediate, others indirect and long term. Some may never even be recognized; nevertheless, they are significant.

Building a network of reliable suppliers and building solid relationships with them forms a foundation for supply chain management. For many supply chains, the size of the business and its influence is the greatest at the customer end. Automotive supply chains, for example, are dominated by the automobile assemblers: Ford, DaimlerChrysler, General Motors, Toyota, Honda, Nissan. This continues to be true even though there are thousands of suppliers. A similar phenomenon exists in electronics industries. Supply chains ruled by Motorola or Dell or Hewlett Packard consist of hundreds of suppliers. Historically, in those types of supply chains, the rule was for suppliers to do what they were told. Their approach to treating suppliers was authoritarian and dominated by

Costs of Switching Suppliers	EXHIBIT 9.3

Equipment expense for the new supplier.

Equipment installation and transfer.

Inventory buildup at customer to cover transition to new supplier.

Quality validation/certification of new supplier.

Process engineering expenses for new supplier.

Product redesign.

Updating engineering drawings.

Training supplier employees.

Developing new supply chain linkage (communication, data, etc.).

Costs of transition (time, contracts, travel, negotiations).

Costs of dissolution with old supplier.

Source: T. M. Laseter, *Balanced Sourcing* (San Francisco: Jossey-Bass, 1998), p. 4.

the desire for low prices. The suppliers had to adapt their production to what the customer demanded. Today, even the most powerful customers have recognized that in B2B interactions, it pays to have a broader perspective on decision making. Supply chain management requires that relationships with suppliers be based on sharing similar goals, mutual dependence, and knowledge of the suppliers' competency.

Businesses take different approaches to supplier development, depending on their priorities. Laseter provides a matrix of approaches used to develop purchasing relationships.[6] It recognizes a frequent conflict between their commitment to the price of the supplies and their commitment to a cooperative relationship. This supplier relationship matrix, presented in Exhibit 9.4, points out how only a balance between commitment to low prices and commitment to the relationship can be effective. Too much importance for either risks the other. For the customer who pays no attention to the relationship and cares only about price, improvement can't happen and product value suffers as a result. The supplier feels resentful and abused. Ultimately, the supplier looks for another customer. For the customer who cares nothing about price and only about the relationship, there is no incentive for the supplier to provide a good price, because the customer doesn't seem to care. The supplier makes out like a bandit, but the customer suffers from high material costs. Again, the consumer doesn't get good value, but this time it's because of product cost issues.

om ADVANTAGE   An Alliance of Competitors

Few companies go head-to-head to the extent that Sony and Samsung do in the electronics industry. Samsung's goal has been to take away Sony's leadership. In recent years Samsung has surpassed Sony in revenue and profits. The two are now neck-and-neck for leadership in television sales.

Despite the rivalry, the two have become partners in a new $2 billion factory that will build liquid-crystal displays. They have also agreed to share 24,000 patents. The alliance is one of sharing technologies in order to speed up product development in a rapidly changing market. Samsung let Sony use some of its technologies in Sony's TVs and those TVs ended up outselling those of Samsung. Samsung still

benefits from the relationship, though, because its experience with LCDs was limited to computer monitors and cell phones. It is learning how to improve them for use in TVs.

The Samsung-Sony alliance is not the only one in the electronics industry. Sony and NEC have merged optical-disc divisions, despite being competitors. Toshiba and Hitachi announced that they may combine resources to build a semiconductor plant with a third company.

Source: "Sony, Samsung Bolster Alliance, Agree to Share 24,000 Patents," *Japan Times*, December 15, 2004; P. Dvorak and E. Ramstad, "Behind Sony-Samsung Rivalry, an Unlikely Alliance Develops," *Wall Street Journal*, January 3, 2006, pp. A1, A14.

EXHIBIT 9.4 | Supplier Relationship Matrix

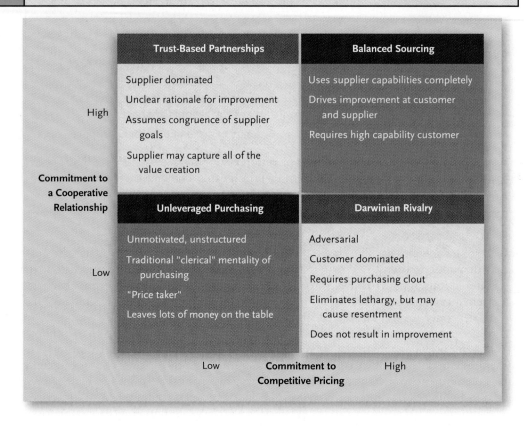

Certification programs are a common approach to developing balanced supplier relationships. There are numerous certification programs in existence. DaimlerChrysler's SCORE (Supplier Cost Reduction) is a famous example. In the SCORE program, suppliers are encouraged to submit cost saving ideas worth 5 percent of their annual sales to Chrysler. Chrysler gets 50 percent of the savings. The supplier gets the other 50 percent.

Many customers utilize their expertise in supplier development efforts as another way to build balanced relationships. The customer frequently has more resources at hand to help suppliers deal with problems, quality improvement, employee training, and so on. In all cases, supplier development and certification programs result in improved productivity and quality, which flow downstream with the products, helping everyone in the chain.

Inventory Management

Inventory management in the supply chain differs from traditional inventory management (covered in Chapter 11) in the information inputs used to help make decisions at all levels of the supply chain. For example, for a warehouse, how many units should be ordered? When should they be ordered? What are the risks associated with the order? What safety stocks should be held and why? Should safety stocks be equal for all products warehoused? When choices exist, where should inventory be held? Which warehouse? Or should it be held in the manufacturer's finished-goods warehouse, in a distribution center, or somewhere between? Or should the retailer hold it? These are just a few of the many questions that must be answered relative to inventory management in the broad supply chain management environment.

Inventory management in any situation answers two basic questions—when to order and how many to order. In the supply chain, the question of "where" must also be answered. From a supply chain perspective, however, these issues also become more complex because the order quantity and timing downstream in the supply chain create demand upstream. Rather than simply ordering to optimize costs within one entity in the supply chain, effective SCM is moving toward **supply-chain network optimization,** which attempts to model the entire supply chain so that "what-if" analysis can be done on a variety of possible future scenarios. What if fuel costs increase? What if the cost of a particular component increases? What if a supplier must be changed? All of these, and many more possible events, have implications for the supply chain's effectiveness. The ability to model those events gives supply chain managers valuable planning information.

One of the most effective changes in supply chain inventory management in recent years has been the development of **retailer-supplier partnerships (RSPs).** An RSP is an alliance between a supplier and a retailer that changes the more traditional role of the supplier. Rather than an arm's-length relationship in which the retailer seeks out a possible supplier for a one-time transaction, RSPs are long-term relationships that even change the way inventory is delivered and the way it changes hands. The trend has been toward increasing the involvement of the supplier in the management of the inventory. This can range from allowing the supplier to determine when shipments should be made (after all, the supplier has access to the retailer's POS data) to requiring the supplier to actually manage the inventory in the store and even keep ownership of it until it is sold. This arrangement, known as **vendor managed inventory (VMI),** is attractive to retailers because it removes the responsibilities associated with knowing when to order and what product mix to maintain. Suppliers are often more knowledgeable. For the retailer, it also eliminates the risks associated with inventory ownership.

Cooperative Product Design

Product design, in order to provide an end result of products that meet the customers' needs and are capable of being produced efficiently and effectively, often involves the concurrent engineering of products and processes. Quality function deployment (QFD) links product and process design to customer requirements. For many manufacturers, particularly those who depend on outsourcing to increase the value of their products, the component designs are as critical as those of the finished products. The design of components, for example, can dictate the requirements for assembly equipment. When more than one supplier of a particular component exists, the components must be designed so that they can be produced by all suppliers. Increasingly, new-product design efforts require the involvement of suppliers. This is not just to ensure that the components are manufacturable. In many cases, the suppliers can provide insight that will improve the products, reduce costs, and, most important, reduce time. These interactions and supplier investments of time can be expected only when the supplier and customer have a mutually beneficial relationship.

Information Management and Information Sharing

Much of the motivation behind supply chain management is linked to the availability of technology that can collect, store, and communicate data that can enhance product value. There are really three decisions:

1. What data should be collected? In other words, what data can aid in increasing value through enhanced processes and capabilities, reduced costs, improved quality, or enhanced timeliness?

2. How should the data be stored? Current trends favor enterprise resource planning (ERP) systems as a means of maintaining a centralized database that all users can access. Supply-related data are critical to a variety of decision areas, so utilizing the ERP environment makes a lot of sense.

supply-chain network optimization
Optimization of decisions across the entire geographical network of the supply chain.

retailer-supplier partnerships (RSPs)
A retailer-supplier alliance that changes the way inventory is delivered and the way it changes hands.

vendor managed inventory (VMI)
A retailer-supplier partnership in which the supplier manages the inventory in the retail store and in some cases maintains ownership of the inventory until it is purchased by the consumer.

SAP's supply chain management suite of products is called mySAP SCM.

Point of Sale (POS) technology enables retailers to immediately pass demand information to suppliers, making it possible for suppliers to base tomorrow's production and shipments on today's demand. It also provides accurate data for forecasting.

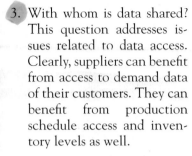

3. With whom is data shared? This question addresses issues related to data access. Clearly, suppliers can benefit from access to demand data of their customers. They can benefit from production schedule access and inventory levels as well.

On a more technical note, once these decisions have been made, how the data are accessed by outside entities must be addressed. The Internet provides many alternatives for sharing and accessing such data, but each alternative raises security issues. Communication issues must be dealt with in both directions. It isn't enough for suppliers to have information about customers. Customers also need information about suppliers. Inventory levels and capacity of suppliers, for example, are critical pieces of information if customers are going to be able to respond to the requests of *their* customers.

In many cases, numerical data are useless without the proper analysis. The development of decision support technologies, including statistical analysis tools, optimization tools, and simulation capabilities, can be useful in turning raw data into information that can add value to products and increase the value that can be shared with the entire supply chain.

In a traditional supply chain, a supplier would forecast demand by analyzing the retailer's order history. The suppliers to *that* supplier would forecast their demand by analyzing the order history from the supplier, and so on, as illustrated in Exhibit 9.5. That process contributed to the bullwhip effect, to excess inventory in the supply chain, and to stockouts in the supply chain. Each member of the supply chain is basing the forecast on different data, and as we move upstream in the supply chain, that data becomes less and less reflective of demand on the retailer.

Because of technological advancements, supply chain information now can flow directly from the retailer to any of the suppliers. So rather than the very indirect and error-prone approach shown in Exhibit 9.5, substantial supply chain benefits can be gained from the approach shown in Exhibit 9.6, in which suppliers have direct access to the retailer's

EXHIBIT 9.5	Traditional Approach to Forecasting Demand in the Supply Chain

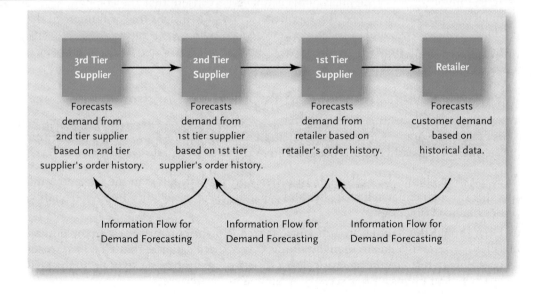

New Approach to Forecasting Demand in the Supply Chain	EXHIBIT 9.6

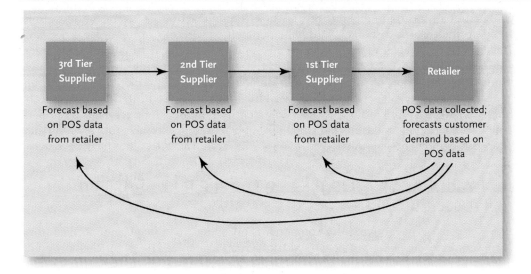

sales data. That means all of the suppliers in the supply chain are basing their demand forecasts on the same data. Even if their forecasting techniques differ, the efforts of the supply chain will be much more synchronized.

The development of alliances has created an opportunity for some supply chains to actually collaborate on a plan for meeting demand. This approach, known as **collaborative planning, forecasting, and replenishment (CPFR),** actually forces partners to negotiate and agree on a plan for meeting demand and on a forecast. Progress is tracked and adjustments that must be made are mutually agreed upon.

collaborative planning, forecasting, and replenishment (CPFR)
An approach to demand planning in supply chains in which partners negotiate and agree on a plan for meeting demand.

Standardization

Long-term interaction between suppliers and customers, particularly in B2B situations where customers are fed components to assemble, creates situations that can point out conflicts and incompatibilities between business processes and priorities. Businesses design their processes with the best of intentions, but not all businesses arrive at the same processes to accomplish similar goals. The development of relationships between suppliers and customers allows them to learn about each other's business processes and adapt theirs to be compatible. An ongoing relationship with a customer or a supplier requires that each be easy to do business with. If either is difficult, the relationship will not be productive. Supplier relationships can benefit from best-practice benchmarks that result in enhanced productivity for both parties and easy "handshaking" between partners' communication systems through commonality of systems. ERP systems frequently provide a means of accomplishing this. Suppliers utilize the same system as their customers. This creates advantages of data sharing and enhances business process compatibility, but, as mentioned earlier in this book, it can restrict firms' flexibility to improve business processes.

Standardization of processes makes for higher levels of productivity; but standardization of products and parts can contribute to productivity as well. In many industries, a major portion of inventory is made up of very small, inexpensive components that are used throughout the product line. Fasteners (nuts, bolts, clips), for example, are used in huge quantities in the auto industry. Standardization of these components has long been a major goal of manufacturing firms. Standardization across the entire supply chain can have a significant impact on inventory levels and associated costs.

Electronic Commerce

Many of the benefits of supply chain management are tied to time reductions. Electronic commerce can contribute significantly to those improvements. Electronic funds transfers speed up the cash-to-cash cycle and, when combined with electronic order processing, make continuous replenishment systems much more economical. Small, frequent orders reduce inventory levels, but the administrative costs of processing them can be large. Eliminating the "paper pushing" that traditionally documents interactions between suppliers and customers reduces costs and speeds up the process. Dedicated B2B sites on the Internet make it possible for customers to identify potential suppliers and customers. Suppliers auction off goods in traditional online auctions. Customers find low-cost suppliers through reverse auctions.

A Typical Example of Supply Chain Management

A better perspective on what the components of supply chain management mean for a business and its suppliers can be gained through an example. The generic supply chain from Exhibit 9.1 is an excellent starting point for examining the extent of the supply chain management impact.

Pacers, a popular brand of athletic shoes, are sold primarily through national chains of athletic shoe stores. The shoe production facilities are somewhat vertically integrated, performing fabrication and assembly operations in one plant. Pacers purchases components (leather, fabric, composite material for soles, foam, laces, and so forth) in bulk from a number of different suppliers. Pacers then does all cutting, coating, and coloring. It also sews (assembles) all products. Exhibit 9.7 is the generic supply chain modified to represent Pacers's supply chain.

A review of various decisions and their effects shows how a supply chain management perspective can enhance value and reduce costs for a company like Pacers. Many decisions can take place at the downstream or consumer end of the chain. For example, suppose a large retail chain, one of Pacers's largest customers, decides to have a promotion four months in the future. That decision will have numerous implications for Pacers and its suppliers. First, Pacers must revise demand forecasts to include the increase in sales that will result from that promotion. The impact of promotions is particularly hard to forecast, so the best approach will be to examine past promotions held by this customer. They will also expect a "postpromotion lag" in demand coming from customers who bought products early in response to the promotion. Knowing the dates of the promotion is not specific enough information for Pacers, however.

Pacers needs to know when the retailer will need the inventory in its stores. Knowing that, Pacers can determine when it will need to be completed. Pacers also needs to know which of its distribution centers to ship to. This will affect when the inventory must be shipped from the Pacers facility, because the retailer's warehouses could be scattered throughout the United States. Once Pacers knows where to ship to, it can decide where in the manufacturing system the inventory should be produced. When this is known, it can examine the capacity at that facility and determine when it is feasible to produce the order. Capacity limitations in the optimal facility may preclude Pacers from producing there, however. It may be forced to produce at another facility that has available capacity. If Pacers's production facilities typically produce in small batches and maintain a smooth pattern of production, this large promotion may disrupt the pattern. The sooner Pacers can begin to integrate it into production runs, the less of an impact it will have on the other orders that must be fulfilled. However, the further ahead Pacers produces it, the higher the inventory level in the supply chain, because someone must store it until it is sold.

By moving upstream in the supply chain (away from the consumer) and toward the suppliers, it is apparent that the impact of this promotion could extend beyond Pacers's

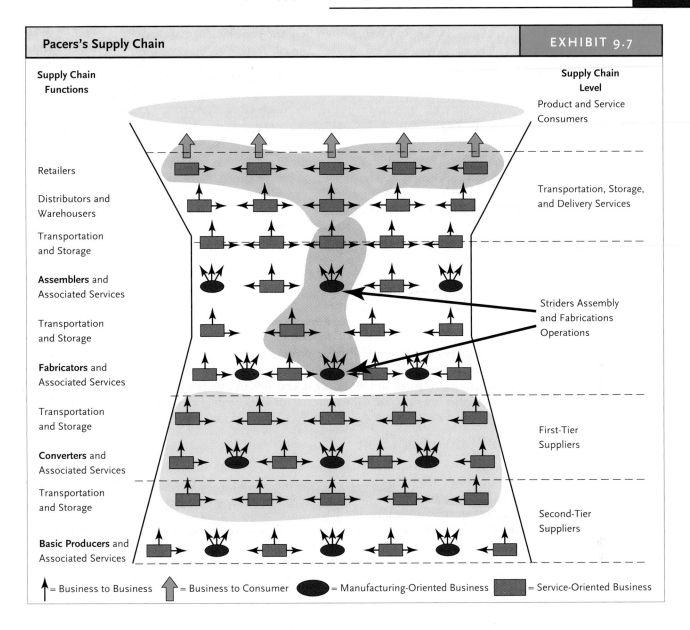

Pacers's Supply Chain

EXHIBIT 9.7

warehousing and manufacturing facilities. Raw material transportation and storage capacity, as well as the capacity of suppliers, will also be affected by this promotion. Its impact will spread like ripples on a pond. Transportation and storage capacity between suppliers and facilities must be able to absorb the increased flow of product. Depending on where the company plans to manufacture the product, specific supply transportation channels and warehousing locations may be affected. Some transportation channels may not have the capacity to absorb the impact, resulting in using a combination of different channels or providers. Manufacturing schedules for Pacers's suppliers most certainly will need to adjust to the additional demands placed on them by this promotion. They will need to determine when and where their production will occur. Production patterns in their facilities (large batch versus small batch), raw material delivery patterns from their suppliers, and even the availability of raw materials can be affected. Their suppliers, in turn, may have to adjust to supply them with what they need. At any point, if there is a situation that prevents a particular entity in the supply chain from doing what needs to be done, the order is at risk of being late. These issues are part of the strategic alliances Pacers has developed and its information management and information-sharing practices.

The ease of working with those suppliers and the efficiency of these interactions will be dictated by standardization decisions made in past interactions. Suppliers may utilize electronic commerce capabilities in locating and purchasing their raw materials.

Finally, depending on the nature of the promotion, it is possible that Pacers may actually be required to design a product exclusive to the promotion. In that case, working with its suppliers through cooperative product design will ensure that the product meets customer requirements and can be produced effectively.

Because we know that Pacers is a major player in the athletic shoe industry, it should be no surprise that a promotion by one store chain is one of many promotions that it must deal with annually. This is a way of life for Pacers. A promotion at a major customer may cause a blip in demand, but many customers have promotions and the demand for each fluctuates somewhat, so the total centralized demand for Pacers's products should be relatively stable. This is the effect of risk pooling. Maintaining a stable load on production capacity is one of the most important things Pacers can do to maintain high levels of productivity.

While customer decisions affect upstream supplier productivity in the supply chain, supplier decisions and actions can affect downstream productivity. Suppose that the day before Pacers was informed of this promotion, its primary supplier of leather informed Pacers of a shortage of shipments from South America. Earthquakes, tornadoes, fires, floods, government regulations, and simple management error at suppliers can have major impacts on customers. But something as simple as a supplier changing its supplier can also have a significant impact. In a network as complex as a supply chain can be, the seemingly unimportant decisions can cause major problems.

Sourcing Decisions

The Supply Function

From an internal business perspective, supply chain decisions are often viewed as either "logistics" or "supply." Logistics decisions are those that affect the downstream (toward the customer) portion of the supply chain. Supply decisions are those that affect the upstream (toward raw materials) portion of the supply chain. In many organizations, the decisions related to sourcing are delegated to the purchasing or supply function. Purchasing, "sourcing," and "supply management" are essentially names for the same thing—managing the processes associating with acquiring what the business needs.

Purchasing for a business differs substantially from the type of purchasing you and I do when we go shopping. Much of this difference links back to the differences in value attributes important to consumers versus those important to business customers. The goal of the business in outsourcing is to enhance value for *its* customers, rather than satisfy its own internal needs. There are other differences, however, that go beyond value definitions. For example, businesses are likely to purchase in very high volumes, so small differences in price can result in huge long-term savings. This creates a much larger incentive for the supplier to get the business and a larger incentive for the customer to seek the best price. The result is frequently an involved negotiation and contract.

Supply Activities

Leenders et al provide a useful list of the essential steps in the purchasing process. They are[7]:

1. Recognition of a need.
2. Description of the need.
3. Identification and analysis of possible sources.
4. Supplier selection and determination of terms.
5. Preparation and placement of a purchase order.
6. Follow-up or expediting of the order.

7. Receipt and inspection of goods.
8. Invoice clearing and payment.
9. Maintenance of records and relationships.

While these activities may vary somewhat from one organization to another, they encompass all activities from the recognition that a need exists to that need being satisfied through the delivery of the item needed, and all associated administrative documentation.

Channel Selection

Sourcing decisions are those that involve deciding what to make versus what to buy and, once that is known, deciding how to buy it (channel selection). How you should purchase process inputs varies according to the type of item being purchased, how it is used, and how easy it is to purchase.[8] The more an item becomes strategically important, the more a complete strategic sourcing process makes sense. That would include an ongoing strategic alliance with a supplier. For low priority items, it makes more sense to make purchases independently when replenishment is necessary (spot buys).

Exchanges provide another possible channel. Exchanges are used to link buyers and sellers. The advantage of an exchange is that purchases can be pooled with those of others who need the same thing, resulting in cost savings. Exchanges enable sellers to have access to more buyers. Exchanges make most sense when products are low priority and are commonly available.

Reverse auctions create another channel—one that is growing in popularity. In a reverse auction, someone desiring to make a purchase sets up the auction. Potential suppliers enter bids, and the lowest bid typically wins. Reverse auctions are often conducted online and are set up to have a definite starting and ending time. The competition that takes place in an auction can help reduce costs for the purchaser. Reverse auctions are best used for items of strategic importance that have a large number of potential suppliers.

Outsourcing Supply Chain Activities

As businesses began to recognize the benefits of increasing value and reducing costs through more effective supply chain management, they were also recognizing the importance of focusing on what you do best. Supply chain management activities, particularly those associated with warehousing and transportation, are complex, require substantial investment in assets, and are often not within the skill set of a business. While there are many businesses that own their own warehouses, own their own trucks, and hire their own drivers, there are also many who utilize **third-party logistics providers (3PLs)**. In fact, outsourcing logistics is on the rise. In 2000, 37 percent of high-volume shippers outsourced transportation. That figure was projected to increase to 73 percent by 2005.[9] As the outsourcing trend continues, the 3PL industry will benefit.

third-party logistics provider (3PL)
A provider of logistics services such as warehousing or transportation and logistics.

3PLs come in a variety of types. Some provide a single service, like warehousing or transportation. Others provide an entire range of services, and some manage all aspects of the supply chain. There are numerous reasons why a company would want to employ a 3PL. The most common is to benefit from the expertise of a company that focuses on logistics activities. 3PL services require skill and investment in technology that many firms don't have or can't afford. Hiring a 3PL can improve the quality of the logistics system far beyond what a company might be able to accomplish on its own. There are trade-offs, however, and the one that is most often cited is that when you hire a 3PL, you give up some control. You are at the mercy of the 3PL's ability to provide quality delivery.

For some users, their needs are beyond what a single 3PL can provide. Integrating the activities of a number of different 3PLs has become too complex for some firms, and that activity has been outsourced to firms known as 4PLs. A more detailed discussion of the use and selection of 3PLs is presented in Chapter 12.

Extending the Supply Chain Globally

Including foreign suppliers in the supply chain can have substantial benefits as well as risks. A global supply chain is mandatory as a business extends its markets to foreign countries. The impact of a global extension of the supply chain depends on how it is extended. Is the customer end of the supply chain extended? Or is the supplier end extended?

Extending the customer base into foreign countries has the potential to increase the size of markets, but it is rarely accomplished just by shipping products over and selling them. Many businesses have found that different cultures prefer different types of services and products. Values differ. Wal-Mart, for example, has struggled with its expansions into South America, particularly Brazil and Argentina.[10] One of the causes of its problems is that it has had a difficult time reaching volumes sufficient to allow it to keep costs down. Stocking a wide variety of products is difficult because of a distribution system not configured as well as it is in the U.S. operation. In South America, most Wal-Mart shipments come directly from the manufacturer, rather than through a cross-docking system used in the United States. Some stores in South America receive 300 deliveries per day, compared to 7 at U.S. stores. Other problems exemplify typical "glitches" businesses often encounter but don't anticipate when extending their customer base internationally. Many businesses find that the distribution network configuration is forced to be different than they're used to and that transferring the distribution strategy they have in the United States is impossible. The end result in many instances is difficulty getting timely deliveries. To make matters worse, the technology infrastructure may inhibit the business from utilizing the information and communication capabilities its distribution and inventory management systems depend on.

Extending the supplier end of the supply chain brings its own set of issues. Technology and communication systems can certainly have an effect here as well. Complicating things further is a diffuse distribution network, adding the impact of greater transportation times. One of the biggest hurdles, however, is the development of the close relationships that can only come from strategic partnering efforts. Cooperative product design, made even more critical if the business is also extending its markets internationally, is complicated by distance and by culture differences. Policy, procedure, and product standardization can be a terrific hurdle that is difficult enough when dealing with domestic suppliers, but becomes even more problematic when dealing with businesses that have operated in a completely different culture.

Caterpillar Logistics has over 100 facilities and over 20 million square feet of warehouse space.

While the store logo looks the same, the interior design, layout, and product selection needs to be very different. Differences may include smaller packaging to accommodate daily shopping trips, products freshly made and packaged on-site, and even in-store live entertainment.

The notion of extending a product's market internationally often looks appealing to businesses, particularly those that have a large portion of the domestic market share. Selling products internationally, however, also often means modifying the product to meet tastes of that particular culture. Many companies have struggled with this challenge, and many have been quite successful at marketing their product globally, including Coca-Cola. Coca-Cola faces another challenge, however, as it struggles with demand for Mexican-made Coke from the Latino population within the United States.

Mexican-made Coke is very popular with immigrants, who insist that the Mexican-made Coke, sweetened with cane sugar, is better than Coke made in the United States, where it is sweetened with corn syrup. Coca-Cola has a network of U.S. bottlers who have exclusive rights to U.S. Coke sales. Mexican-made Coke is produced by 13 company-authorized bottlers, but they do not have the rights to sell Coke in the United States. The underground "bootlegging" of Mexican-made Coke is particularly troubling to Coca-Cola and its bottlers because Coke Classic sales are down in the United States and Coca-Cola's market share is at an 8-year low. Coca-Cola executives claim that the importation infringes on Coke's trademark and on U.S. bottler's territories, but the product is technically not an illegal product. U.S. Customs does not seize the shipments or turn them back, because the Mexican-made Coke is not a counterfeit product.

Source: C. Terhune, "U.S. Thirst for Mexican Cola Poses Sticky Problem for Coke," *Wall Street Journal*, January 11, 2006, pp. A1, A10; "Coke Fans, It's Back to the Real Thing—In Glass," *Chicago Sun Times*, January 26, 2006, www.suntimes.com/output/news/cst-nws-coke26.html, accessed February 24, 2006.

Recently, service as well as product inputs have become popular targets for outsourcing to foreign suppliers, or "offshoring." Engineering and design, computer programming, and other technical capabilities have been increasingly outsourced to Asia and South America because of lower costs. Call center outsourcing, extremely popular in the early 2000s, has seen a bit of a backlash as customer service quality has suffered and customers have reacted negatively.

Typically, the benefits of a third-party logistics provider are the increased focus on what a company does best and the enhancement of logistics service. In some cases, the benefits can go far beyond these. With over $13 billion in sales in 2003, it should be no surprise that a large company like Kodak would use 3PLs. Kodak Brasiliera used a third-party warehouse provider for its Brazil operations for reasons other than those that might be expected. Kodak imports a variety of photographic products into Brazil. In order to delay payment of sales taxes for 30 days, Brazilian buyers purchase a huge percentage of their products at the end of the month. The Brazilian subsidiary of Kodak documented 40 percent of its sales during the last two days of each month. This spike in demand required an increase in the amount of inventory being warehoused, which increased the requirement for warehouse and warehouse labor capacity. No business likes uneven capacity requirements, and in this case, Kodak just couldn't deal with it very well. One problem was the need to hire temporary labor for those month-end rushes, which was not allowed under Brazil's labor policy. Outsourcing the warehousing function to a Brazilian provider eliminated the labor issue, as well as other expenses.

Source: R. J. Bowman, "Kodak Brasiliera: Hiring of Third-Party Proves Key to Handling Volume Surges," SupplyChainBrain.com, July 2002; Hoover's Company Profiles, 2004, Eastman Kodak Company, HOOVER-NO: 10500.

Despite the difficulties in extending the supply chain management paradigm internationally, effective business management in a global setting needs the very benefits supply chain management can offer. Government and regulatory shifts toward free trade have made these extensions more common and more desirable. The U.S. economy has become a subset of the global economy. Businesses cannot afford to not take advantage of the customers and suppliers. If they avoid them, their competitors won't.

For businesses in the United States, expanding the supplier base to foreign countries can be a more difficult decision. Foreign suppliers can add value and reduce costs in a number of ways. Labor costs might be lower, for example. Some products are available in certain geographic regions and a local supplier is the only way a business can obtain them. The benefits can be too attractive to pass up, but do not come free.

A Closer Look at the Bullwhip Effect

Bullwhip Effect Causes

At each level of a supply chain, the variability of the purchases a company makes is often greater than the variability of the demand that consumes its products. When this is true for each company in the supply chain, the bullwhip effect results, and demand increases in variability at each level, as illustrated in Exhibit 9.8.

The causes of the bullwhip effect have been a source of interest to researchers, because eliminating the causes would eliminate the effect. Lee and colleagues propose four likely causes:[11]

- Demand forecast updating
- Order batching
- Price fluctuation
- Rationing and shortage gaming

The impact of forecast updating is direct. Forecasts, which provide input to a business's production scheduling, inventory management, and capacity planning efforts, are typically based on previous demand, determined by previous customer orders. As orders for

om *ADVANTAGE*   Reduced Time Can Mean Reduced Opportunity for Disruptions in Tightly Linked Supply Chains

Disruptions in supply have always been on the radar screen of low-inventory businesses. In fact, the need to minimize these disruptions and create a stable supply source has been a motivating force behind supply chain management efforts. Reducing the time required for a delivery reduces the potential for disruption. Despite the need for time reductions in getting products to market, many companies use contract manufacturers to minimize investment in equipment that may quickly become obsolete as products go through accelerated life cycles. The result is a serious dilemma.

On one hand, manufacturers of products need to subcontract some manufacturing tasks in order to focus on processes they do best and avoid equipment investments that may not provide financial return. Outsourcing manufacturing increases lead times, however, because of the transportation time that is injected into the supply chain. To make things worse, many of the contract manufacturers used are located in China or other Asian countries. Delivery from Asia to the United States is two weeks by ship. Air freight is prohibitively expensive.

The need to speed up deliveries has resulted in the cheap labor costs associated with Asia no longer being sufficient to attract manufacturers. Many have chosen to identify closer suppliers. For an increasing number, that has led to contract manufacturers in Guadalajara, Mexico. Unlike border towns, whose workforce is typically unstable, Guadalajara has a stable workforce supported by seven universities and dozens of technical schools.

The link between time and potential disruptions has become even more critical as terrorism has become a possible cause of supply disruption. Many companies were affected by the September 11, 2001, terrorist attacks. Auto manufacturers, food producers, and others faced delays on deliveries coming from Canada. Lean environments were hit even worse because their inventories were lower and could not absorb disruptions for as long. As the potential for disruptions and the uncertainty associated with them increases, the need for effective supply chain management increases as well.

Inventory buffers will need to be increased, but the focus should be on the most critical parts and those that would be affected most, like those coming from single international sources. Manufacturers must pay closer attention to where their incoming parts are coming from. Since one of the biggest disruptions has been delays at international borders, manufacturers may need to investigate domestic or regional suppliers as a primary or secondary source. Transportation strategies may need to be broadened. If regulations associated with shipping cargo on passenger flights change, shipping on cargo flights may be necessary. Enhanced knowledge of security and customs operations along international borders can also aid in minimizing disruptions. Increased levels of communication with suppliers can add to the information that has previously been limited to forecasts. Enhanced relationships provide a basis for better communication and quicker reaction to any type of disruption.

Source: "When Just-in-Time Becomes Just-in-Case," *Wall Street Journal,* October 22, 2001, p. A18; "How a Need for Speed Turned Guadalajara into a High-Tech Hub," *Wall Street Journal,* March 2, 2002, pp. A1, A8.

Bullwhip Effect   EXHIBIT 9.8

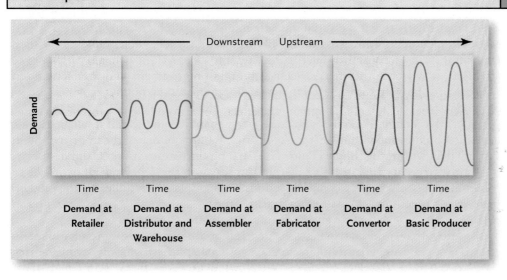

Downstream   Upstream

Demand

Time — Demand at Retailer

Time — Demand at Distributor and Warehouse

Time — Demand at Assembler

Time — Demand at Fabricator

Time — Demand at Convertor

Time — Demand at Basic Producer

products increase, demand forecasts are adjusted and orders for suppliers are adjusted as well. In addition to meeting the demand, however, orders from the suppliers must also fill increasing safety stocks. This is made even worse by long replenishment lead times. The longer the lead times, the more uncertain the demand and the greater the safety stocks. At each level of the supply chain, this phenomenon increases the bullwhip effect.

As customer needs deplete the inventory, inventory goes out at a relatively smooth rate. The orders to replenish that inventory, however, do not go out as frequently. Inventory is ordered in batches. Batch ordering occurs because of high transaction costs on orders and the need for full truckloads when orders are delivered. Order batching also occurs as a result of the time periods used in performance measuring systems. Salespersons may submit orders periodically, but they will always submit them at the end of the time period used in measuring their performance. The result of all batch ordering is that the orders are released in a very "lumpy" fashion, reflected in a lumpy demand on the supplier who must fulfill those orders. That supplier, in turn, allows demand to accumulate prior to releasing orders, and the effect is magnified.

Businesses often buy before they need to because suppliers offer pricing advantages. Suppliers offer promotions or special prices. In addition to purchasing ahead of time, discount prices can also encourage customers to buy more than is needed. In both cases, purchases exceed demand, and the act triggers a bigger effect as it moves through the supply chain.

In many industries, customers live in fear of supply shortages. They know that if a supply shortage does occur for a critical component, the suppliers will ration the part and they won't get as many as they need. In response, they order ahead and in larger quantities than they need in anticipation of the shortage. Then, if the shortage doesn't happen, they cancel and reduce orders. The result is that the demand on the supplier fluctuates significantly—and much more than the actual demand on the customer's products.

Bullwhip Effect Impact

It is important to restate that value added anywhere in the supply chain is critical to the value received by the customer. Similarly, costs added anywhere trickle down to costs borne by the customer. No matter what the cause of the bullwhip effect present in a particular supply chain, the negative impact on value that results from the bullwhip effect can be huge and can rear its ugly head in many unsuspected ways. The implications of the bullwhip effect can be best understood by examining its impact on each of the components of value: costs, quality, and timeliness.

The impact demand fluctuation has on processes and capabilities can be direct and can have significant implications for the competitive success of the firm. First, all businesses seek a level load on their capacity that matches their design capacity. Demands that go up and down make it extremely difficult or impossible to maintain this level load. This is particularly true if the variability is coming from batch ordering triggered by periodic customer orders. Most customers will be on similar cycles, compounding the problem. Effort spent on constantly fluctuating output to meet spiking demand patterns takes attention away from other needs, such as process improvement and productivity enhancement. The business is placed in a feast-or-famine mode, neither of which is good for productivity.

Orders that are placed early or that are larger than demand would result in a loss of flexibility. Studies show that in some industries, months of demand can be met by inventory held within the supply chain. Thus, if a product innovation occurred, it would be months before it could get to market. In this situation the development of unique capabilities that could be very competitive in the marketplace is nullified by the presence of the excess inventory. No matter how creative the product designers, no matter how innovative their product improvement, it can't get to market soon enough.

We know that a mismatch between demand and design capacity results in an increased cost per unit, whether the demand is lower than design capacity or higher than

om ADVANTAGE   Regulations Add Shipping Costs

Usually when freight providers think about escalating costs, they're concerned about labor or fuel costs. New rules about how long truck drivers can work are also affecting shipping costs. New hours of service (HOS) regulations came into effect January 1, 2004. Under the new rules, a driver is limited to a 14-hour on-duty period and only 11 of those hours can be driving. At the end of the 14th hour, the driver must rest for 10 hours, no matter how many hours have actually been driven. Most companies will see a 6 to 9 percent increase in transportation costs as a result of the regulation change. For a large company, that can be a huge increase. Wal-Mart, for example, will purchase 300 new trucks (at a cost of $24 million) to regain the transportation capacity it lost under the new regulations.

Source: "The Revised Hours-of-Service Regulations," www.fmcsa.dot.gov/Home_Files/revised_hos.asp, June 6, 2004; B. J. LaLonde, "New Regulations May Force Companies to Rethink How They Manage Their Supply Chain," *Supply Chain Management Review*, January 1, 2004.

design capacity. This occurs for many reasons, including the need for overtime, temporary help, and increased load on machines. Demand that is too low results in a potential cash shortage, increases costs of short-term debt, and reduces the financial return on investments in equipment. Inventory carrying costs increased by batch purchasing, purchasing ahead to take advantage of price differentials, and higher safety stocks not only increase inventory carrying costs for the business making the purchase, but also add to the total amount of inventory in the supply chain. As we know, costs added anywhere find their way to the customer.

Large amounts of fluctuation in the demand of upstream businesses may make the load on production so uneven that the firm is required to lay off employees during low demand periods. This can diminish the quality of the workforce as good employees are lost to businesses that can offer better job security. Businesses that are constantly gearing up or gearing down in response to demand shifts are not very responsive, because they can be caught going the wrong direction. They try to predict what's going to happen to demand next, and they invariably make a mistake. They are put in a reactive position that does not give them the flexibility to respond quickly to real customer needs.

POS data collection provides immediate retail demand information for manufacturers, reducing the bullwhip effect. Levi Strauss utilizes POS data collection and its own software to link retail sales directly to manufacturing. The result has reduced inventory levels and increased sales.

The bullwhip effect has other ramifications for timeliness. One of the most important is its impact on the cash-to-cash cycle. The bullwhip effect invariably results in increased levels of inventory throughout the supply chain. Increased demand fluctuation, whatever the cause, elicits a response that includes adjusting demand forecasts upward and increasing safety stock to prevent stockouts. The cash-to-cash cycle, which dictates the financial return rate on all investments, including inventory, depends on a high inventory turnover rate. The bullwhip effect has an even worse impact on inventory than high inventory levels in one business, because it creates a situation where all upstream businesses in the supply chain have increasing amounts of excess inventory. Days-of-supply expands as a cushion to protect the business from the high level of demand fluctuation. The result is a long cash-to-cash cycle, diminishing financial returns, and a decrease in the agility necessary to respond to market dynamics.

Solutions

A key to eliminating the bullwhip effect, and a key to any supply chain management effort, is to increase the information supplied by businesses to their suppliers. Rather than suppliers creating demand forecasts from order histories, they should have access to their customers' actual orders. This can happen in several ways: by making those orders available for access by suppliers electronically, for example, or by allowing suppliers direct access to POS (point-of-sale) data collected continuously at the cash registers of retail stores. Suppliers can then immediately produce and ship based on actual customer demand data, rather than use forecasts created from a history of batched orders.

Closer relationships with suppliers can result in elimination of price discounts, thereby eliminating the motivation to order ahead or order in larger-than-necessary quantities. The result is beneficial for both companies involved. Inventory is reduced for the customer, who can now better link purchases to needs, and demand on production capacity is smoother for the supplier.

Traditional inventory reduction approaches, including reducing the transaction costs associated with orders, can lessen the need to order in large batches. In addition, identifying economical avenues for shipping smaller quantities can help, as can eliminating the penalties associated with shipping less than full truckloads. Very frequent deliveries of small quantities, known as continuous replenishment, are one approach used to smooth out demands on suppliers. This is common when a cross-docking distribution strategy is employed. Suppliers have access to actual sales data from customers and replenish on a daily or more frequent basis.

Risk Pooling

The uncertainty associated with customer demand must be accommodated through inventory safety stocks, wherever that inventory happens to be. If, for example, each retailer maintained inventory that was replenished through direct shipments, the safety stock at each retailer must cope with demand variability. If all of the retailers were supplied from a central warehouse, safety stocks could be less because the *aggregated* variability would be less. High demand at one place would cancel out low demand at another place. Placing inventory at a more centralized location to reduce the variability on its demand is known as **risk pooling**.

The benefits of risk pooling consist of the costs saved by the reduced levels of inventory and the higher service level. Let's look at a simple example. Pacers has two warehouses in the northeastern United States to serve retailers there. The company is considering a merger of the two. To determine if such a merger makes sense, Pacers would need to determine the impact such a merger would have on inventory costs. As we know, safety stocks are required in inventory management systems to deal with variability.

For each product warehoused by Pacers, inventory is held at each warehouse. In most inventory management systems, the greater the variability of demand, the greater the uncertainty associated with future demand, and the more inventory "safety stock" required

Caterpillar Logistics ships over 10 billion pounds of freight annually.

risk pooling
Inventory held in one warehouse to service a large number of retailers requires less inventory than if held at the individual retailers.

to provide the desired probability of meeting demand. Suppose for a particular product the safety stock was 200 units at one warehouse and 120 units at another. The variability of demand results in inventory carrying costs on 320 units. Combining the warehouses results in less variability of demand at the centralized warehouse, because all demand now comes to one place and there is a greater likelihood that high and low demands will cancel each other out. The result is that the same service level can be had by carrying less than 320 units.

Ultimately, whether the decision to centralize makes financial sense depends on the savings across all product lines compared to the costs associated with facility modifications and changes in transportation costs.

Supply Chain Performance

Trade-offs

Any effort as complex and important as supply chain management must be monitored closely. Costs are high, so managers need to ensure that costs bring about benefits that enhance profitability. Goals of SCM can be put quite succinctly in the form of cost reductions and service enhancement. Cost reductions come from improved production, transportation, and storage efficiencies. Service enhancement comes from better delivery performance and fewer stockouts for the retailer.

Like any complex management endeavor, there are trade-offs associated with SCM that may bring performance measurements into conflict. Some of the most common SCM trade-offs are the conflict between batch size and inventory costs, transportation costs and inventory costs, customer service and inventory costs, lead time and warehousing costs.

Production and delivery often include an attempt to capitalize on economies of scale by producing or delivering a large quantity at a time. Producing and delivering in large batches infrequently, as opposed to producing and delivering in small batches frequently, results in excess inventory and higher costs associated with storage and obsolescence. These costs associated with inventory are discussed in greater detail in Chapter 11. Transportation costs can also be lowered at the expense of inventory costs. The desire to deliver in full truckload shipments encourages excess in the delivery. As companies attempt to reduce inventory levels, invariably they reach a point where stockouts become more frequent and customer service suffers. One approach to improving that customer service is to place inventory closer to the customer in warehouses so that delivery time to the retailer is shorter. However, as the number of warehouses increases, so do the fixed costs associated with managing those warehouses and so does the level of inventory in the supply chain.

As in measuring the productivity of any system, measuring supply chain performance requires an approach that utilizes a variety of measures.

The Perfect Order

As businesses interact more with their suppliers and customers, measuring that interaction becomes more important. While quality of a product has long been recognized as important, other aspects of the transaction are important as well. As businesses' focus on supply chain management has grown, the use of the **perfect order** as an order fulfillment performance measure has grown as well. A perfect order is an order that had perfect performance on all of its aspects. The order was entered into the system correctly, picked accurately at the warehouse, delivered on time, delivered without damage, invoiced correctly, and included all of the agreed-upon services. There may be other aspects of performance monitored as well, depending on the setting. The advantage of using the percentage of perfect orders as a measure of performance is that it is a broad measure requiring inputs that relate to all aspects of product and service quality that would affect the customer. Its disadvantage is that the measures may need to be drawn from a variety of places, making it difficult to gather all of the required data.

perfect order
An order that arrives on time as promised, is of the correct quantity, is not damaged, and also includes all of the agreed-upon services.

The perfect order measure is computed as a percentage and is equal to the percentage of all orders that had no problems in any of the aspects being measured:

$$\text{Percentage of Perfect Orders} = 100\% \times \frac{\text{Total Orders} - \text{Defective Orders}}{\text{Total Orders}} \qquad (9.1)$$

Trends in Supply Chain Management

SCM is an evolving framework. As new technologies emerge, new capabilities will come along with them, changing the way supply chains are managed. Several of those changes are in their infancy at this point. Some are driven by technologies, while others are driven by other environmental factors.

Trading Communities

As alliances become more commonly accepted as defining channels for some purchases, online trading communities are also becoming more commonly accepted. Trading communities, such as third-party exchanges, allow a group of businesses to leverage their combined size for purchases of products or logistics services. Freight exchanges, for example, pull together businesses to coordinate FTL shipments of mixed goods. All save on the reduced transportation costs made possible by the full truckload. The freight supplier benefits from access to the customer base. As Internet technologies and the supporting electronic infrastructure that supports the communities evolve, B2B trading communities can be expected to increase in acceptance.

Optimization Modeling

As technologies allow us to gather more data, that data really doesn't add value until it can be analyzed and actually contribute to value. As technologies evolve to be able to gather and analyze supply chain data, optimization at the supply chain level, rather than

---

Example 9.1

Perfect Order Calculation

Lockhart's Cleaning Supply provides commercial cleaning solutions for the food service, healthcare, and hospitality industries. They have kept the following statistics on performance over the past year.

Total number of orders filled	4,612
Order entry errors	83
Warehouse "pick" errors	103
Damaged goods in shipment	21
Billing/invoicing errors	34

Solution

Examining Equation 9.1, we see that we first need to determine the number of defective orders.

$$83 + 103 + 21 + 34 = 241$$

We then need to determine the percentage of defective orders, using Equation 9.1.

$$100\% \times \frac{4{,}612 - 241}{4{,}612} = 94.775\% \text{ perfect orders}$$

Excel Tutor 9.1 demonstrates how this measure can be calculated in a spreadsheet.

at the business level, will improve. The ability to predict possible scenarios and actually test the performance of current practices under those conditions will enhance businesses' capabilities, particularly in matching supply with demand.

CHAPTER SUMMARY

Because of increasing global competition, supply chain management has expanded to become a framework to allow businesses to go beyond decisions that offer short-term value enhancement to providing long-term enhancement to the entire supply chain. Just as businesses have gone through the realization that what is best for one function may not be the best for the business, they have come to realize that what is best for one business may not be the best for the supply chain. And ultimately, because the customer receives the value added by the entire chain, that's what matters most.

This chapter provided an overview of supply chain management as a perspective that guides decision making by broadening the scope of decision impact. Like TQM, JIT, and constraint management, it provides a framework for managers to judge their actions, leading to improved value for the customer and improved profitability for themselves.

KEY TERMS

bullwhip effect, 374
collaborative planning, forecasting, and replenishment (CPFR), 381
perfect order, 393
retailer-supplier partnerships (RSPs), 379

risk pooling, 392
supply-chain network optimization, 379
third-party logistics providers (3PLs), 385
vendor managed inventory (VMI), 379

KEY FORMULAE

Percentage of perfect orders

$$\text{Percentage of Perfect Orders} = 100\% \times \frac{\text{Total Orders} - \text{Defective Orders}}{\text{Total Orders}} \qquad (9.1)$$

SOLVED PROBLEMS

Perfect Order Calculation

Andrew's Equestrian Products is an online retailer of horseback riding accessories. Over the past six months, the order processing department has gather data on all aspects of product and service quality. They have summarized it below.

Total number of orders filled	11,210
Order entry errors	221
Warehouse "pick" errors	149
Defective products	176
Damaged goods in shipment	58
Missing products	82
Billing/invoicing errors	91

Compute the percentage of perfect orders.

Solution

Based on Equation 9.1, the first step is to determine the number of defective orders.

$$221 + 149 + 176 + 58 + 82 + 91 = 777$$

We then need to determine the percentage of perfect orders, using Equation 9.1.

$$100\% \times \frac{11{,}210 - 777}{11{,}210} = 93.069\% \text{ perfect orders.}$$

REVIEW QUESTIONS

1. What pressures have resulted in supply chain management being adopted by an increasing number of companies?
2. Why does supply chain management provide a competitive advantage to firms using it?
3. Provide examples of how the actions of customers affect suppliers.
4. Provide examples of how the actions of suppliers impact customers.
5. Describe the decision-making components of supply chain management.
6. What are the activities associated with purchasing?
7. Describe the possible channels for purchasing and reasons why one might be used over another.
8. Describe how access to retailer POS data improves forecasting of suppliers over traditional approaches.
9. What is meant by a retailer-supplier partnership?
10. What is meant by risk pooling? How does distribution strategy affect risk pooling?
11. What is strategic partnering? Why is it important to supply chain management?
12. What are some of the common challenges that accompany a global extension of the supply chain?
13. What is the bullwhip effect? What are some of its causes?
14. How can the bullwhip effect be reduced?

DISCUSSION AND EXPLORATION

1. Identify a common consumer item you recently purchased. Trace the product back through its supply chain. Try to identify all of the cost-adding and value-adding steps along its route through the network of product and service suppliers.
2. Identify a business that chose to vertically integrate rather than outsource for its supplies. What are the advantages and disadvantages of vertical integration? What would be the advantages and disadvantages for it if it chose to outsource?
3. Identify the external suppliers for your university. What relationships does your university have with these businesses? Is it a strategic partner with any businesses? How can you tell?
4. Identify a product you have purchased. What are the strategic benefits of the producer outsourcing some of its components? Which of the components might it outsource? Which components would it not want to outsource?

PROBLEMS HM

Solutions to odd-numbered problems are located on the text's Online Center (http://mhhe.com/opsnow3e).

1. Debra Tabor manages the B2B sales and distribution department for a firm that liquidates overstocks and returns for several apparel retailers. She has gathered statistics on performance over the past year and has summarized all types of order fulfillment problems:

Total number of orders	632
Late deliveries	53
Damaged shipments	11
Wrong orders shipped	14
Miscounted products in order	28

Determine the percentage of perfect orders for Debra.

2. Alvin's Warehousing Services provides warehousing and distribution services for a large number of small online retailers in the Chicago area. Sidney Rosenberg, shipping manager, was charged with improving his percentage of perfect orders to 97 percent. His most recent data are below. Has he reached the 97 percent goal?

Total number of orders	960
Late deliveries	25
Damaged shipments	9
Invoice errors	14
Quantity errors	5

3. A local distributor to convenience stores has recorded the following order fulfillment problems among its four distribution centers:

	DC #1	DC #2	DC #3	DC #4
Total orders	2,150	2,460	1,875	1,680
Pick errors	20	18	28	35
Product defects	15	24	12	42
Billing errors	25	16	21	38
Late deliveries	14	12	10	21

Compute the percentage of perfect orders for each distribution center.

4. Michael Maynarez manages supply chain performance for a Fortune 100 consumer products firm. He has assembled supply chain performance information from their eight largest distribution centers.

	Boston	Durham	Detroit	Atlanta	Dayton	Tampa	Omaha	Chicago
Total orders	1,130	1,250	1,642	2,008	985	1,335	1,640	1868
Late shipments	20	18	28	35	12	17	14	26
Damaged goods	15	24	12	42	30	21	18	43
Invoice errors	25	16	21	38	27	12	16	29
Defective products	14	12	10	21	18	26	16	24

Which distribution center has the best percentage of perfect orders? What is the total percentage of perfect orders for all of the DCs?

ADVANCED PROBLEMS

1. Otto's Part, a chain of automotive parts stores, is having a problem with the central distributor. Otto's has 6 stores, and receives parts from the distributor every day. For replenishment, the distributor is fairly accurate, with only 15 percent of the orders having some kind of problem. This may be a substitution, where the part ordered is substituted with a like part that may be a different brand, backorders, where nothing arrives, or wrong, where the wrong part is shipped. The biggest problem that Otto's has is with customer-ordered parts, where a customer comes into the store and orders a part that is not a stock item. Before placing the order, Otto's always checks for availability. Otto's tries to get the part within two days, but half of the time it takes longer than that. The third problem is that the parts that are custom ordered and received on time do not match the order. This happens to 1 out of 10 custom orders. Each store places an average of 30 orders a day, 10 custom orders and the rest replenishment orders. What is the percent of perfect orders for Otto's per day?

2. Fred Smart, a shipping agent for Williams Electric, is reviewing delivery performance in order to direct process improvement efforts. At present, Mr. Smart has collected the following information.

On Time Delivery	Complete	Accurate Invoice	Number Damaged in Transit	Total Number of Orders
88.00%	90.00%	93.00%	5	74

a. While these numbers appear to present a good testament to the performance of the shipping department, Fred wishes to develop an overall measure for his department's performance. To that end, he has asked you to calculate the percent perfect orders that Williams is currently shipping to its customers.

b. Based on this new metric, Fred is determined to improve the department. For several months he has worked diligently with manufacturing, shipping dock workers, and contract shippers to improve Williams's overall performance. What is the new percent perfect order that Williams has been able to achieve based on the following data?

On Time	Complete	Accurate Invoice	Damaged in Transit	Number of Orders
93.00%	96.50%	95.00%	2	68

What is the percent improvement in perfect orders that Williams has been able to achieve?

ENDNOTES

1. R. B. Handfield and E. L. Nichols, *Introduction to Supply Chain Management* (Upper Saddle River, NJ: Prentice Hall, 1999), p. 2.

2. M. R. Leenders and D. L. Blenkhorn, *Reverse Marketing* (New York: Free Press, 1988), p. 8.

3. Ibid, p. 11.

4. Adapted from D. Simchi-Levi, P. Kaminksy, and E. Simchi-Levi, *Designing and Managing the Supply Chain* (New York: McGraw-Hill, 2000), pp. 8–10.

5. Ibid, p. 4.

6. Laseter, T. M., *Balanced Sourcing* (San Francisco: Jossey-Bass, 1998), p. 4.

7. M. R. Leenders, P. F. Johnson, A. E. Flynn, and H. E. Fearon, *Purchasing and Supply Management* (Boston: McGraw-Hill Irwin, 2006), pp. 61–62.

8. R. B. Handfield and S. L. Straight, "What Sourcing Channel Is Right for You?" *Supply Chain Management Review*, July–August 2003.

9. B. H. Gordon, "The Changing Face of 3rd Party Logistics," *Supply Chain Management Review*, March–April 2003.

10. "Wal-Mart Gets Aggressive about Brazil," *Wall Street Journal*, May 25, 2001, pp. A8, A12; also described in Simchi-Levi, Kaminsky, and Simchi-Levi, *Designing and Managing the Supply Chain.*

11. H. L. Lee, V. Padmanabhan, and S. Whang, "The Bullwhip Effect in Supply Chains," *Sloan Management Review*, Spring 1997.

LEARNING ACTIVITIES   www.mhhe.com/opsnow2e

Visit the Online Learning Center (www.mhhe.com/opsnow2e) for additional resources. Content varies by chapter, and includes

- Business Tours
- OM on Site
- Readings
- Resources
- Excel Tutors

- Interactive Case Models
- Reel Operations Video Clips
- Additional Advanced Problems
- Self-Assessment Quizzes
- Glossary

SELECTED REFERENCES

Handfield, R. B., and Straight, S. L. "What Sourcing Channel Is Right for You?" *Supply Chain Management Review*, July–August 2003.

Lee, H. L. "The Triple-A Supply Chain." *Harvard Business Review*, October 2004.

Poirier, C. C., and Quinn, F. J. "A Survey of Supply Chain Progress." *Supply Chain Management Review*, September–October 2003.

Trent, Robert J. "What Everyone Needs to Know about SCM." *Supply Chain Management Review*, March 2004.

VIDEO CASE 9.1

The Broad Impact of Logistics at Ford

Based on Video 12 on the Student DVD

Ford's Chicago assembly plant has undergone dramatic improvements that reflect trends throughout the automobile industry. Flexibility is being added to manufacturing facilities, suppliers are becoming more closely linked to customers, and the flow of materials has improved. Ford has reduced its number of suppliers and moved them closer to achieve its goals.

1. How has Ford improved its sheet metal supply? What are the implications of these improvements?

2. Ford has also made improvements in its power train (engine and transmission) supply. How have these changes affected its assembly plant?

3. As a general step toward improving product flow, Ford built a "supplier campus." Describe the supplier campus concept and the benefits it provides.

4. What is meant by "system integrator"? What is the system integrator's contribution to material flow?

5. What role do auto dealers play in determining production in Ford's system?

INTERACTIVE CASE 9.1

Determining an Inventory Storage Strategy at Owen's Gourmet Shops

The risk pooling model demonstrates how the level of inventory in the supply chain is affected by where inventory is stored and the service level required of that inventory. Risk pooling is accomplished when the demand variability among a large number of supply chain entities is combined by storing inventory centrally, rather than at individual sites. The risk pooling model demonstrates the effects of risk pooling on inventory level through the use of a distribution network with one central distribution center, two regional distribution centers, and four retailers. By selecting the service level and the storage location from the items on the pull-down lists, the user can see the effects on inventory levels at different locations and in total. The user can also edit the weekly demand and standard deviation for either product for each retailer, and then press the Solve button to see the impact.

Retailer	Product A		Product B	
	Average Dem.	Std dev.	Average Dem.	Std dev.
I	30	4.0	12	3.0
II	20	3.0	16	4.0
III	41	4.0	19	4.0
IV	29	4.0	16	3.0
Southern DC	50	5.0	28	5.0
Northern DC	70	5.66	35	5.0
Centralized DC	120	7.55	63	7.07

Order cost($)	Value of product($)		Carrying cost per unit($)	
	A	B	A	B
20.0	174.0	240.0	1.00	1.38

Retailer 1	Retailer 2	Retailer 3	Retailer 4
204	192	245	213

Total amount of inventory in the system is 854

Retailer 1   Retailer 2   Retailer 3   Retailer 4

Southern Regional Distribution

Northern Regional Distribution

Centralized Distribution Center

Location

Average Level of Inventory in System

Service level = 95%   Inventory held at   Solve

Retailers   Reset

Developed by Accelet Corp.

Owen's Gourmet Shop

Owen's Gourmet Shops has opened four retail stores in the suburban St. Louis area. Two are on the south side and two are on the north side. The southern stores are 20 miles from each other and 60 miles from the northern stores. The northern stores are also about 20 miles apart. Alvin Owen, the owner, expects to open at least eight more stores in the St. Louis area in the next five years. Frank Owen, son of the owner and inventory manager, is trying to decide between three inventory storage strategies. The first is to store all inventory at the retail stores. The second is to open two small distribution centers (DCs)—one for the southern region and one for the northern region. Other than inventory on the shelves, all other inventory for each region would be stored in the two regional DCs. The third alternative is to lease one warehouse to be used as a central distribution center. Frank has identified two products, product A and product B, to serve as the basis for his study. Weekly average demand for each of these products, at each store, is presented below.

	Product A		Product B	
Retailer	Average Demand	Standard Deviation	Average Demand	Standard Deviation
I	30	4.0	12	3.0
II	20	3.0	16	4.0
III	41	4.0	19	4.0
IV	29	4.0	16	3.0

1. Set the service level to 85 percent. Leave product demand and standard deviation values at the default levels.

   a. Compare the system inventory levels for the three alternative storage strategies of retailer, regional DC, and centralized DC. How do the inventory levels compare?

2. Increase the service level to 90 percent and perform the same comparison. Leave product demand and standard deviation values at the default levels.

   a. Compare the system inventory levels for the three alternative storage strategies of retailer, regional DC, and centralized DC. How do the inventory levels compare?

3. Increase the service level to 95 percent and perform the same comparison. Leave product demand and standard deviation values at the default levels.

   a. As the service level is increased, graph the change in inventory levels for the three storage location strategies.

   b. Explain the impact that the increase in service level has on the difference in inventory levels for the three alternatives.

4. Set the service level to 85 percent. Leave product demand at the default values. Increase each standard deviation by two units.

   a. What is the level of system inventory for each alternative inventory location? How has it changed as a result of the increase in demand variability?

   b. Incrementally increase the standard deviation two units at a time. Graph the results for each inventory storage location strategy.

   c. Explain the relationship between demand variability and the inventory level.

5. Change the service level to 90 percent and then 95 percent, monitoring the changes in inventory for each storage location alternative.

   a. What are the relationships among nearness of inventory to the customer, demand variability, and service level? What costs should be considered when making the decision about where to store inventory?

6. Frank has determined that, based on the value of the products, the average inventory carrying cost is $13.00 per year.

   a. What are the inventory carrying costs associated with each location strategy at a 95 percent service level? Given the locations of the stores and the distribution center alternatives, what other costs should be considered when the decision is made?

INTERACTIVE CASE 9.2

Demand Variability in U-Save's Supply Chain

The bullwhip effect model demonstrates how the variability of demand is accentuated as one moves upstream in the supply chain. A simple 3-tier supply chain (retailer, distributor, manufacturer) is used. Orders are generated by the retailer's order-up-to-level inventory system, which forecasts demand using a simple 5-period moving average. Those orders become the demand for the distributor, who uses a similar inventory management system, which creates orders that become the demand for the manufacturer. The manufacturer's inventory management system creates orders for the supplier. The user can specify the mean and standard deviation for the retailer's demand as well as the replenishment lead time for the retailer's orders to the distribution center and for the distribution center's orders to the manufacturer. The model provides the actual standard deviation of demand and a graph of demand for each level in the supply chain.

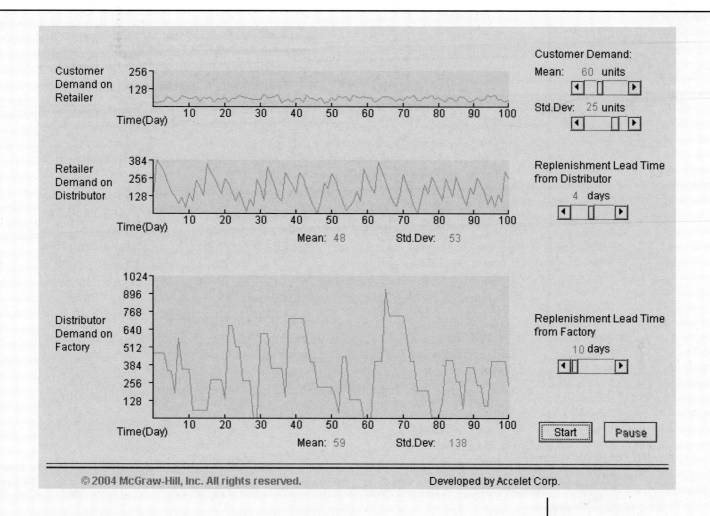

Developed by Accelet Corp.

U-Save

U-Save is a regional grocery store chain serving the midwestern states. Most of the goods it sells are brand-name products. One particular supplier is examining the implications of supply chain management, particularly linking directly to its retailer's POS data, rather than having its inventory system driven by forecasts. Its consultants have told its managers that long lead times and forecasts are causing its demand to be far more variable than it needs to be. In order to gather information, U-Save has been asked to supply its daily demand for one representative product. The distribution center is providing its demand, as is the factory, to give the consultants an idea of what is happening in the entire system.

1. Check the defaults to make sure the system is starting with the following parameters:

>Customer demand at retailer: mean = 60, standard deviation = 25
>
>Replenishment lead time from distributor to retailer = 4
>
>Replenishment lead time from factory to distributor = 10

   a. Start the simulation so that it can run 100 days of consumer demand. At the end of the 100-day run, what is the mean demand and standard deviation for the distributor?

   b. At the end of the 100-day run, what is the mean demand and standard deviation for the factory?

c. Any time the graph shows a sharp *upward* line, it indicates that an order was received. During the 100 days, how many orders were received by the distribution center from the factory? How many were received by the factory from its supplier?

2. Change the replenishment lead time for orders from the distribution center to the retailer from 4 to 10 days. Run the simulation for 100 days.

   a. What happens to the mean and variability of demand at the distribution center and factory?

   b. What happens to the number of orders? Does it appear that there were any stockouts at the distribution center or at the factory?

3. Set standard deviation of demand at the retailer to 10, the replenishment lead time from the distributor to the retailer to 1, and the replenishment lead time from the factory to the distributor to 10. Run the simulations.

   a. What happens to the mean and variability of demand at the distribution center and factory?

   b. What happens to the number of orders? Does it appear that there were any stockouts at the distribution center or at the factory?

4. Describe the relationship between the variability of demand upstream, at the distribution center and factory, and the variability of demand at the retailer.

5. Describe the relationship between the variability of demand and the replenishment lead time at each level of the supply chain.

6. Describe the relationship between order frequency, order size, and variability of demand.

APPLICATION CASE 9.1

Pierre's Kitchen

Pierre's Kitchen manufactures utensils and gadgets for the cooking enthusiast. Pierre's products are sold throughout North America, predominantly through kitchen and home specialty stores. Like most producers and suppliers of consumer specialty products, Pierre's must cope with large seasonal variation in demand. This is easily seen to relate to seasonal variation at the retail stores.

One of Pierre's top-selling product families is its line of 78 different gourmet kitchen knives. The knives have received praise for their comfort in the hand and their ability to hold an edge. Pierre's credits the popularity of its knives to the steel used in their construction. Pierre's has always utilized the finest Swedish steel for its blades. The steel used in those knives is the source for nearly all of purchasing manager Robin Benton's aggravation.

Robin orders steel for knives at the beginning of each month. By the time it is transported to port, shipped to the U.S., and trucked to the Pierre's Kitchen plant, it takes just over five weeks to get it. Robin determines order quantities by projecting retail demand for each knife model over the next month, translating those forecasts into steel requirements, and then summing the requirements across the 78 knife models. That forecast for each knife model is based on the sales that occurred the previous month. Pierre's supplier of steel has recently threatened to increase its prices during the next contract period to cover increasing expenses it claims are the result of the wide fluctuations in order quantities from Pierre's.

Robin has examined her forecasts and orders for knife steel and admits that the orders fluctuate dramatically from month to month. This results from fluctuations in individual store demand, which in turn results from promotions and sales at the store level. When confronted with this information, sales manager Jaylen Cooper responded, "It's true that sales at individual stores fluctuate, but when I look at month-to-month sales across an entire chain of retail stores, the demand only fluctuates about 10 percent. The only exception to this is the inventory build-up at Christmas time." Robin's examination of the actual sales data confirmed Jaylen's report.

1. Explain all possible causes of the demand fluctuation at the supplier.
2. For each possible cause, identify a reduction strategy that is within Robin's control.
3. Is this bullwhip effect? Explain.
4. What types of communications enhancements would help reduce the problem?

Demand Forecasting: Building the Foundation for Resource Planning

LEARNING OBJECTIVES

- Describe the benefits of effective resource planning.

- Explain how the planning horizon affects planning tasks.

- Describe how lead times determine the planning horizon.

- Explain how product and service life cycles can aid in the planning process.

- Describe the benefits of collaborative planning, forecasting, and replenishment.

- Describe the different types of forecasting methods.

- Compute a causal forecast using simple linear regression.

- Recognize the components of a time series and appropriate forecasting techniques for each component.

- Compute forecasts using averages, exponential smoothing, seasonal indexes, and the multiplicative model.

- Compute measures of forecast accuracy, including the MAD, MSE, RSFE, MAPE, and tracking signal.

- Describe how enterprise resource planning (ERP) systems benefit businesses.

BEST BUY: EXTENDING FORECASTS OF CUSTOMER DEMAND

Most retailers face massive challenges in matching product supply to demand, but few have succeeded as well as Best Buy. Best Buy began in 1966 as the Sound of Music Store in St. Paul, Minnesota. It expanded rapidly and formally became Best Buy in 1983. Today, it has more than 940 retail stores across the United States and Canada, has annual revenues exceeding $25 billion, and sells a wide variety of products in four major categories:

- **Consumer electronics products** include DVD players, televisions, cameras, camcorders, car stereos, home theater systems, speakers, portable audio and video devices, satellite systems, and accessories. In 2005 consumer electronics accounted for 39 percent of sales.

- **Home office includes** scanners, printers, computers, supplies like paper and ink, and office accessories. In 2005 home office products accounted for 34 percent of sales.

- **Entertainment software includes** computer software, DVDs, CDs, and game hardware and software. In 2005 entertainment software accounted for 22 percent of sales.

- **Appliances includes** major appliances such as refrigerators, ranges, washers, dryers, microwaves, vacuums, and housewares. In 2005 appliances accounted for 6 percent of sales.

As Best Buy grew, its management realized that it needed to replace much of its systems to better support its growth. Its transportation management system was one of the first replaced, and has resulted in savings of over $20 million. Best Buy's transportation network is complex. Television sets smaller than 27 inches, for example, go to seven distribution centers in the United States. Three of those distribution centers service the online store as well as brick and mortar stores. Best Buy also has 14 home delivery centers, as well as a specialty delivery center that handles music and movie distribution, online orders, and returns from online orders. The location of distribution centers and the products handled by each is critical, because location determines speed of delivery to stores. That requires accurate demand forecasts.

Best Buy makes excellent use of customer data to help guide decisions. It uses i2 forecasting tools to synchronize product demand with promotions and seasonal fluctuations. Its global sourcing organization in Shanghai, for example, depends on customer feedback to improve products. After mining its customer data, Best Buy determined that approximately 20 percent of its customers were not profitable because they purchased products and applied for rebates, but then returned the products. They even purchased them again at returned-merchandise discounts. Best Buy removed these customers from its mailing lists.

New access to detailed customer data has led to other changes for Best Buy. In the past, all of Best Buy's stores operated in pretty much the same way. They had the same assortment of products, the same advertising circulars, and the same store layouts. New customer information has now led to a more customized approach. Better data analysis has given them the ability to better utilize geographic information and eight distinct demographic segments. Best Buy has also implemented collaborative planning and forecasting (CPFR) to better understand upcoming demand and bring their suppliers into the process. Sharing information with vendors has increased forecasting accuracy.

http://www.bestbuy.com/, accessed 9/6/2006

SupplyChainBrain.com, QuickREAD, July 26, 2005.

SupplyChainBrain.com, "Best Buy's Journey to a Best-in-Class Supply Chain," March, 2005.

"Best Buy's Customer-Facing Supply Chain," *Supply Chain Strategy*, Vol. 2, No. 1, December-January 2005.

Chapter 10 provides an important prerequisite to the examination of operations resources that takes place in the remainder of this unit. In Chapter 10 we examine the role of the planning process and the most critical input into that process—the demand forecast. Without an understanding of how planning processes work and without an accurate input into those processes, efforts devoted to managing the critical resources used in creating value would be wasted.

Introduction: Why Do We Plan?

This chapter lays the groundwork for the management of operations resources by accomplishing several objectives. First, it defines the task of resource planning, introducing the concept of the planning horizon—how we know how far into the future plans must go. Second, the chapter identifies the critical links between effective resource planning and profitability measures. Third, the chapter examines demand forecasting concepts and techniques. These techniques are important because the demand forecast creates the foundation for many resource planning activities. Finally, this chapter introduces and develops a generic model for enterprise resource planning (ERP) systems, which are rapidly becoming a standard planning and management framework for businesses.

For our purposes, planning is the process of determining what is needed, and making arrangements to get it, in order to achieve objectives. Planning has become so ingrained in our lives that we do it without thinking. Human beings have progressed a long way from sitting in a cave thinking only about where their next meal will come from. With thousands of alternative ways to spend our time, some alternatives have naturally become more enjoyable than others. We have become sophisticated planners in our daily lives, without even realizing it. In business environments, the planning function can determine the success or failure of the firm. In a very general sense, a plan is an outline saying what we need to do in advance to enable us to accomplish something in the future.

An examination of planning processes, whether it's your plan for next Friday night or Bill Gates's plan for rolling out Windows 2010, will uncover some common characteristics. In both cases, some general goals are defined in terms of more specific objectives. Bill might be thinking, "2010 needs to be ready for rollout on time, with no bugs." You might be thinking, "I want to have a good time next Friday, because my Operations Management midterm, covering Chapters 5–10, will be over." In both situations, the goal must be broken down into more specific objectives in order to start the planning process. What must you do in order to enjoy Friday night? If you break that down, you might identify components that include places to go, friends to go with, money to spend, and transportation. Without any of these components of "going out and having a good time," the outcome could be disappointing. Each might require a different type of preparation in order to ensure that it can be done. Why? Because you might need advance tickets or a reservation.

This brings us to the sequence. Should you decide the places you wish to go first and then invite friends who'll like your idea? Or should you decide who's going and then decide where to go as a group? The answer is that it probably depends on what aspect of your Friday night is more important—the place or the people you're with. Should you decide where to go before knowing how much money you'll have? Or does the place you're going dictate how much money you'll need? Complex as your planning process would appear if we attempted to model it in a flow diagram, you would nonetheless carry it out without a lot of thought.

You might spend a little effort planning for Friday night, but it's worth it because you want Friday night to be enjoyable. Some of your cohorts, however, won't spend a second thinking about Friday night until late Friday afternoon. Their alternatives will be fewer than if they had started planning ahead of time. Some options might no longer be available because they're sold out. Some friends might already have made commitments with other people, and so on. Advance planning not only provides more options; it also reduces costs. You'll have a good time and won't spend a fortune, while some of your cohorts will stay home.

Many of the resources you planned (places, friends, money, and transportation) are dependable, but you also must consider chance or unpredictable events, known in planning parlance as contingencies. Contingencies are events that hinge on chance and are not controllable. For example, if your plan for Friday night was to attend an outdoor concert, you might have considered the possibility of rain. If your plan was to drive to a restaurant in a city 30 miles away, you might, depending on the time of year, have considered what to do if there was a snowstorm. These alternative or backup plans are called **contingency plans.** All of the issues that you addressed in planning for Friday night have counterparts in every business plan. Some of them, like costs, are obvious. Others are not. In the rest of this chapter, we examine the planning process and factors that determine its success, paying particular attention to an important prerequisite of business planning, that of obtaining a forecast for demand.

contingency plans
Alternative or back-up plans to be used if an unexpected event makes the normal plans infeasible.

The Financial Benefits of Effective Planning

In our previous example, planning for your Friday night out, the worst-case scenario is that all of your plans fail and you stay home by yourself. You might not have an exciting time, but you'd recover from it. In a business setting, however, the total failure of a plan can be much more damaging. It could result in lost customers, lost sales, a missed opportunity, a lawsuit, or even a failed business.

Best Buy was named Forbes Company of the Year in 2004.

Increasing Alternatives

One benefit of good planning is that management has more options if it plans ahead. Suppose we were in a sporting goods retailing business. It's late winter, and we've noticed that a new type of snowboard is just starting to get popular. Several customers have asked about it in recent weeks, but we don't carry it. In addition, several of our employees have

---

om ADVANTAGE   Burger King: Planning for Growth

It's difficult enough to plan for resources when demand is relatively stable. When a company is deep into a strategy change, however, the future demand and its impact on resources is even less certain. Burger King, with 11,300 restaurants in 65 countries, and struggling to maintain its No. 2 position in the fast-food industry, is in that exact situation. In a decline for six years, Burger King's sales dropped from $8.3 billion to $7.9 billion in 2003, while McDonald's and Wendy's both increased. Then Burger King's sales rebounded to $11.9 billion on 2005. In an effort to get back to its core values and customers, Burger King is reemphasizing its "Have it your way" approach to customization and higher quality food.

Planning for growth and hoping for growth are two very different issues. Committing the resources necessary to support

growth in demand is critical if that growth is to occur, but those commitments come at an expense that can be daunting if growth doesn't happen. Intense competition, plus population trends toward avoiding greasy foods, continue to make demand forecasting difficult. Compounding the forecasting difficulties for U.S. demand, Burger King also faces significant uncertainties in other countries. In France, for example, where Burger King had 16 restaurants, it announced that it intended to close operations because of poor profits.

Source: W. G. Swearingen, "Can Burger King Rekindle the Sizzle," *Harvard Business School Working Knowledge*, May 3, 2004, http://workingknowledge.hbs.edu/item.jhtml?id=4105&t=operations; Hoover's Company Profiles, 2004, Burger King Corporation, HOOVER-NO: 54531; "Burger King, Citing Poor Profits, Will Bid France Adieu," *New York Times*, April 5, 2006.

spoken of its popularity on the slopes. In the past, both pieces of information have been virtually certain indicators of upcoming trends. We have two options. Option 1 is to do nothing. If it turns out next fall that customers really want the snowboard, we will figure out then how to get some. Option 2 is to begin planning now to carry the snowboard next season. We'd need to make arrangements now to lock in a supplier for the snowboard so that in early fall we'd have it in stock. Making plans now, as opposed to doing nothing until fall, has several advantages. First, if we make plans now, we have some ability to negotiate with suppliers. This gives us access to the boards at a reasonable cost. Second, if we make plans now, we have a guaranteed supply. Third, we will have the boards early in the season, when people are looking to upgrade their equipment, and we'll be one of the first stores with the board. Having that board gives us an opportunity to draw customers away from other shops.

Profitability Enhancement

The preceding example exemplifies several aspects of the financial impact of planning. Once again, the most important financial measures for operations are profitability measures, and, once again, when we look at planning benefits from the standpoint of profitability, we see a direct impact on the same two profitability measures: profit margin and return on assets. Let's look at profit margin first. Remember, profit margin is equal to net income divided by sales. Net income is derived from net sales, minus the cost of goods sold and depreciation, minus interest paid, minus taxes. An advance plan to carry a new item like the snowboard has the potential to reduce costs *and* increase net sales. Because of our plan, we get the boards at a lower cost, we get them early, and we can get the number we need. Net sales is increased, cost of goods sold is decreased.

This plan should also make a positive impact on return on assets. ROA is equal to net income divided by total assets. Net income rises as a result of this plan. Given that we're able to buy the boards at a reasonable cost, net income should rise more than our total assets, even with a potential increase in inventory.

The primary positive impact of this plan is on net sales, but not all plans will have a direct impact on net income through net sales. For example, plans related to a new facility at a lower-cost location might affect only costs associated with that facility. Other plans might affect only machine capacity or labor. In general, plans related to resources that are used to create value improve the reliability of obtaining those resources, get those resources at lower cost, or increase the number of alternatives. More options mean more flexibility and more flexibility means an enhanced ability to respond to changes.

An Uncertain Future

The further ahead we plan, the more options we have available, but the further ahead we plan, the less we know about future conditions. Think of your own planning activities. It is difficult, if not impossible, for you to plan for a Friday night three months in the future, because you don't have enough knowledge about that night. Exhibit 10.1 shows the relationships among planning horizon length, alternatives available, and certainty about outcomes. Options increase further in the future, but certainty decreases. This results in a trade-off between increasing options and increasing uncertainty.

With that conflict in mind, planners have two means at their disposal for improving the outcome of a plan. First, they could try to improve the quality of knowledge far in the future, which would provide them greater certainty and allow them the luxury of considering more alternatives. The second approach would be to accept the fact that knowledge far in the future will always be suspect, and try to find ways of compressing the planning horizon so that planners will not have to plan as far into the future. These issues bring us to one of the more difficult questions that must be answered relative to planning: How far ahead must we plan?

Relationships among Planning Horizon, Alternatives, and Outcome Certainty	EXHIBIT 10.1

Planning Horizon

Short   Long

Alternatives Available

Few   Many

Certainty about Outcomes

High   Low

Looking into the Future: The Planning Horizon

The distance into the future that we plan is known as the **planning horizon.** As a general rule of thumb, we should plan as far into the future as necessary to meet our objectives, but planning further ahead than necessary tends to result in plans that aren't very good. How far is "necessary"? The minimum planning horizon is determined by the lead time associated with obtaining resources necessary to meet your objectives. The longer the lead time, the longer the minimum planning horizon. Let's look at an example.

Suppose we own a small brewery. One of our objectives as a business is to ensure that we have sufficient capacity to meet demand. We do not want to forgo sales simply because we can't handle the demand. Capacity needs can be complex and vary widely in scope. One type of capacity need is the labor to run our equipment. Another capacity need is the capacity of our brewing and storage tanks. Another is the capacity of our bottling equipment. What would our planning horizon(s) look like?

Suppose we know that the lead time required to advertise job positions, interview, hire, and train new laborers is three weeks. For labor planning purposes, then, the minimum planning horizon for labor is three weeks. We must project our labor needs *at least* three weeks into the future, compare those needs to the labor we have available, and decide whether we have enough. If we don't have enough, we must take action (advertise positions, interview, hire, and train). What if we planned less than three weeks into the future, say, only one week? We might identify a labor shortage one week into the future, but since it would take three weeks to actually get the new labor up and running, we'd be short on labor for the two-week interim.

Now let's look at machine and storage capacity. The lead time for adding to machine or storage tank capacity is quite long. Our past experience has shown that from the time we identify a need for a large-scale piece of equipment to when it is installed, rigged, tested, calibrated, and brought into production is seven months. So, for the purposes of machine and storage tank capacity, our minimum planning horizon is seven months. What would happen if we planned only four months ahead? If we identified a shortage four months out, we'd react, but since it would take us seven months to get the equipment up and running, we'd miss three months of demand and incur all of the costs associated with losing those sales.

We probably hope to reach a point in our business where we have been so successful that we've added labor and machine and storage tank capacity to the point that we can't

planning horizon
The distance into the future one plans.

As U.S. businesses increase their dependence on outsourcing or "offshoring," product or components costs may be lower, but lead time can be lengthened dramatically. This results in longer planning horizons causing reduced accuracy of forecasts, which in turn raise inventory levels and increase costs. One component of that increase in lead time is the time spent being processed at U.S. ports.

fit any more into our facility. Our capacity planning process now must include a new facility or an addition to the old one. Suddenly, we encounter a much longer planning horizon. Suppose we have the land and it makes sense to expand the existing facility. We do the research and find that the lead time for adding a new facility and bringing it into production would be 18 months. We must now plan with a minimum horizon of 18

om *ADVANTAGE*   Planning Is Complicated by Changes in Customer Behavior

Cost reduction efforts have always been a prime motivator of behavior, but the impact of recent reductions in business travel has surprised even experts. Increases in costs of air travel, combined with increases in available information via the Internet, have resulted in a reduction in business travel and a shift toward cheaper flights. Both shifts have made resource planning more difficult for airlines.

Behavior changes among business travelers have been dramatic. For many, during the rapid expansion of the economy in the late 1990s, price didn't matter. As the economy softened, however, many businesses cut travel and sought out bargains for necessary business trips. This has an especially significant impact on full-fare seats. Business travelers, who account for about 50 percent of all airline trips, create about 65 percent of the revenue. United Airlines calculated that about 9 percent of its passengers accounted for about 46 percent of its revenues.

By mid-2001, the price of a business-fare ticket was nearly five times that of the lowest discount fare. This gap had doubled in only five years. Airline pricing strategists had mistakenly concluded that business travelers would travel no matter what. Despite those expectations, the percentage of passengers paying full-fare coach prices fell from 12 percent to 7 percent from 2000 to 2001. The percentage purchasing first-class tickets fell from 3 percent to 2 percent. The loss of high-priced seats has taken a toll on airline profits. Airlines monitor a measure known as the "domestic unit revenue," which measures the revenue generated per available seat mile. That measure dropped nearly 12 percent from 2000 to 2001. It dropped another 12 percent in June 2001 and another 12 percent in July. By summer of 2002, it had dropped to 8.17 cents.

The ease of identifying lowest fares and purchasing tickets on the Internet makes this trend unlikely to reverse itself. Even when the economy improves, businesses that have found how easy it is to save money are not likely to go back to their old ways of traveling. For airlines, this drop in revenues, combined with increasing labor and fuel costs, will make profitability less likely and planning for the future more difficult.

Source: "Fed Up with Airlines, Business Travelers Start to Fight Back," *Wall Street Journal*, August 28, 2001, pp. A1, A4; "Red Ink, Rosy Thinking," Aviation Week and Space Technology, August 11, 2003, Vol. 159, Issue 6, p. 42.

months, and we must determine capacity needs 18 months into the future. This would be a critical stage for many businesses for several reasons. First, it's going to be a huge investment. Expanding when it is not needed could financially kill the business because of the added burden. Failing to expand when it is needed could also kill the business. What makes it worse is that 18 months out is a long planning horizon. It is very difficult to determine needs that far into the future. This is particularly true with products and services that have short life cycles.

The example illustrates that there is no single planning horizon for a business. A business must be involved in planning for many different resources, potentially utilizing different planning horizons for each. Remember how important it is to reduce lead times? The increased accuracy associated with planning for the near future, when compared to the accuracy of planning for the distant future, results in better plan outcomes. This usually results in higher net sales and lower costs, all resulting in improved net income and ROA. In short, it means that what the firm wants to happen has a greater likelihood of actually happening. And, of course, profitability reflects that success.

Product and Service Life Cycles

When forming plans related to any product or service, one must consider how long the product or service will even exist. We're all familiar with products that become quickly obsolete. We've purchased them, only to wish that we'd waited. Electronics technologies (computers, video, music, TVs, cameras) change rapidly. Fashion-driven products may last only one season. Most products and services, even those that don't become obsolete quickly, go through what is commonly known as a product or service **life cycle.** Yes, services become obsolete also, sometimes because they are associated with products that become obsolete. For example, in the past, repair services worked on TVs, stereo systems, and the like. Today, as the cost for those items has come down, these repair-related services have disappeared.

As technology changes the way some services are delivered, we can expect to see some services disappear. How long will the need for travel agencies persist, as the percentage of airline tickets and hotel reservations made on the Internet increases? More changes in the service sector are sure to come as a result of service obsolescence. Many B2B services that currently link customers to suppliers will disappear as technology enables direct linkages to be more efficient and cheaper.

A diagram of a typical product or service life cycle is presented in Exhibit 10.2, which shows five stages in the life cycle. The **introduction stage** is defined by the product or service becoming known in the marketplace. Demand tends to be low in the introduction stage. It is followed by the **growth stage**, which covers that period of increased demand that occurs as consumers become aware of the product or service.

Best Buy is North America' number one retailer of consumer electronics.

life cycle
A pattern of demand growth and decline that occurs from the introduction of a product to its obsolescence.

Power plants require long production lead times, making it necessary to forecast power demand far into the future to maintain sufficient capacity, but also making it very likely that those demand forecasts will be inaccurate. Construction on this $5.5 billion nuclear power plant in Kungliao, Taiwan, was halted when it was one-third completed as politicians debated whether or not it was needed. Construction was restarted after a six-month hold.

introduction stage
The first stage of a product or service life cycle.

growth stage
The second stage of a product or service life cycle, where demand begins to increase.

Product life cycles are often determinants of product demand. As the product goes through the natural progression of the cycle, demand can decline dramatically. The cycles are useful to aid in forecasting, but they can be interrupted by sudden technological changes. For example, businesses operated from homes were expected to create an increasing demand for additional phone lines for voice, fax, and computer connections. Many homes were increasing from one to two lines throughout the 1990s. By 1999, some 29 percent of households had second phone lines. However, two increasingly popular technologies, broadband Internet connections and cell phones, turned that increase around.

Some residential and in-home business customers eliminated additional phone lines because they used cell phones exclusively and had no need for a traditional telephone. For the first time in decades, the number of residential phones actually decreased, and it is decreasing at an accelerating rate.

One might think that this wouldn't affect the providers much, since the same company often provides all of the services. Second phone lines, however, are extremely profitable. High-speed cable and broadband services have not yet been profitable. Unfortunately for the service providers, they were forced to cannibalize their own second-line customers to prevent competitors from doing the same thing.

In addition to the decline in second phone lines, many consumers are discontinuing the use of landline phones altogether. A 2004 survey found that 14.4 percent of U.S. consumers use a wireless phone as their primary phone. Of the remaining 85.6 percent, 26.4 percent would consider replacing the landline phone with a wireless phone. Industry forecasters predict that by 2008, 29.8 percent of wireless subscribers will not have a landline phone. Clearly, landline phones have reached the decline stage of their life cycle.

Source: "More Callers Cut Off Second Phone Lines for Cellphones, Cable Modems," *The Wall Street Journal,* November 15, 2001, p. B1; "Landline Displacement to Increase as More Wireless Subscribers Cut the Cord," *www.instat.com/press.asp?ID=895,* accessed April 7, 2006.

EXHIBIT 10.2.	**Product Life Cycle**

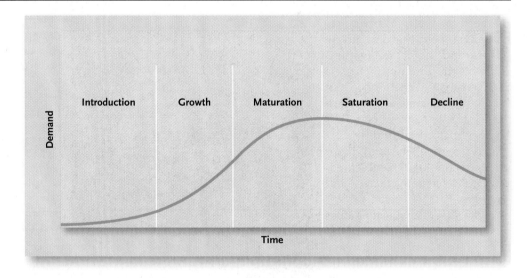

maturation stage
The third stage of a product or service life cycle, when demand begins to level off.

saturation stage
The fourth stage of a product or service life cycle, when demand shifts to the beginning of its decline.

decline stage
The final stage of a product or service life cycle, as demand disappears.

With most products and services, there is a third stage, known as the **maturation stage,** which occurs when the market knows about the product or service and demand begins to level off. At this stage, demand has been satisfied. By this time, through product or service standardization, costs are reduced so that prices can be reduced. The fourth stage is the **saturation stage.** During this stage, demand begins to fall because the market has been saturated and alternatives have begun to appear and take away demand. The final stage, **decline,** occurs when the product or service is replaced by alternatives.

Product Life Cycles Interrupted by New-Product Introduction	EXHIBIT 10.3

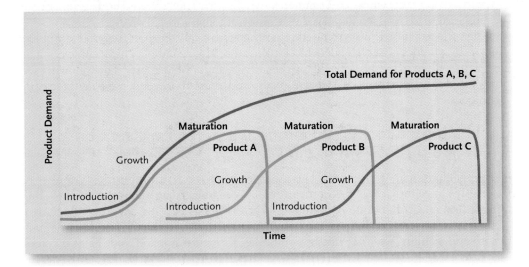

One might conclude that a business would be much better off if life cycles were long. If there were no competition or very little competition, that might be correct, but businesses actually try to speed up the cycle. For the business that can be first to market with a new product or service, a competitor is sure to follow. The leader gets the advantage during the introduction stage and some of the growth stage, before competition begins to take away market share. From the leader's perspective, the best strategy is to introduce a replacement and repeat the process again. Short life cycles can create a barrier of entry to competitors. Exhibit 10.3 shows how life cycles can appear when a firm intentionally shortens them by introducing replacements.

Obviously, from a consumer perspective, the services and products you are exposed to have very different life cycles. In general, both are becoming shorter. Services and products that are tightly linked to technology can be expected to have shorter and shorter life cycles. Some Internet-based services, for example, have already come and gone.

The trend toward shorter product and service life cycles has had a substantial impact on the planning processes of businesses. Many businesses, particularly manufacturers, have found that they cannot maintain short product life cycles *and* sustain the resources required to produce them concurrently. The need to be flexible in environments of fast change is critical to the businesses' success. In addition, the high cost of production equipment requires substantial production volume to generate a sufficient financial return. Rather than investing in equipment that may be made obsolete by the short life cycle of products, many businesses outsource the production of those products. This strategy eliminates any conflict between paying for a piece of equipment and introducing a new product as a way to maintain market leadership.

Compressing Lead Times

Certainly in an environment where the product life cycle may only be eight months long, a supplier that takes four months to bring a component into production cannot be tolerated. Likewise, no business can expect to be able to look 18 months into the future to predict demand so that a facility expansion can be started. Outsourcing plays an important role in making short-life-cycle environments tolerable, but effective planning is still necessary. For example, the minimum planning horizon for bringing a new product to market must include the lead time associated with getting a contract manufacturer with whom to outsource production. The shorter the lead time associated with making this arrangement, the quicker the product can be introduced to market. As a matter of fact, in virtually all business environments, whether the life cycle is short or long, compressing lead times leads to improved planning outcomes.

When the response times promised to customers are shorter than the production lead time of the product or service, demand forecasts are also required. The accuracy of business plans will, in many ways, be dictated by the accuracy of forecasts. The following section provides an overview of forecast types, and presents several popular forecasting techniques.

Collaborative Planning, Forecasting, and Replenishment

As supply chain management and the inherent improvements in business-supplier relationships have moved to the forefront of many managers' agendas, the need to share information and collaborate on demand forecasting has become apparent. A demand forecast, obviously, is a prediction of what demand will be in the future. The demand in the supply chain (whether it be automobiles, furniture, apparel, or breakfast cereal) is ultimately determined by the consumer. Before to the emphasis on the supply chain, when a business defined demand strictly from the orders it received from its customers, forecasts were not necessarily "consumer" driven. The collaboration and information sharing necessary to ensure that all supply chain partners are "on the same page" is known as collaborative planning, forecasting, and replenishment (CPFR). CPFR is defined by the Voluntary Inter-industry Commercial Standards (VICS) Association as:

> *A shared process of creation between two or more parties with diverse skills and knowledge delivering a unified approach that provides the optimal framework for customer satisfaction.*

The need for all trading partners to collaborate on developing demand forecasts requires that they share data among themselves. This includes practices that were previously in the domain of the retailer, such as merchandising, category selection, and promotional planning. CPFR has far-reaching effects and includes many activities. Gillette, for example, makes only a few razor products, but has a huge number of different end products that result from packaging variations. Packaging requirements are often dictated by the retailer and may even be event-specific. Those requirements and event timing must be a part of the demand forecasting process.

Sharing information relevant to demand and agreeing on a demand forecast result in better retail store replenishment from distribution centers because they have the necessary products, in the correct quantities, and in the correct mix or assortment. It improves the replenishment from the manufacturer to the distribution centers because they are producing the correct products, in the correct quantities, and in the correct mix. It improves the replenishment of components to the manufacturer from its suppliers because they are producing for the correct products, the correct quantities, and the correct product mix.

CPFR results in reduced costs, lower inventory levels throughout the supply chain, reduced replenishment lead times, improved demand forecast accuracy, and better customer service for the consumer. All reduce costs and enhance value for the entire supply chain.

Demand Forecasting

Demand forecasting, like any type of forecasting, can be frustrating. Predicting the future is a stretch in any situation. Surprisingly, forecasting actually has its roots in heredity research done by Francis Galton in the late 1800s. He was the first to recognize the tendency of all systems to return to normalcy, now known as "regression to the mean," which later led to the concept of correlation. The concept of regression to the mean is critical to forecasting, because forecasts do exactly that: They examine what has happened and, from that, determine what is "normal." This seems logical, but three reasons make it difficult to determine this "return to normalcy." First, the return to normalcy can take place at an incredibly slow rate, making it difficult to know when, or if, it happens. Second, sometimes the return is so strong, it doesn't stop, but goes past "normal." And third, what is normal today may not be normal tomorrow.[1] The result is that even though systems seek out the normal state, it is difficult to know when it will happen, if it has ever happened, or if it will ever happen. We never really know if the demand we predicted was normal or not. This brings us to a universal truth about forecasting—forecasts are wrong.

Planning for many resources, particularly those tied to capacity and inventory, depends heavily on demand forecasts. Increased emphasis on holding small supplies of inventory has increased the need for quick, frequent delivery of products. Maintaining minimum levels of raw materials and finished goods dictates that replenishment orders be placed promptly and accurately to provide an acceptable level of service. Such orders often depend on a demand forecast. Forecasting research, which has been a popular subject for academics for decades, makes it clear that different types of demand require different types of forecast. Some of the most common techniques are examined in this chapter. The importance of timely delivery and the desire to reduce inventory levels have motivated many businesses to reduce lead times, thereby reducing the planning horizon, which can enhance forecast accuracy more than increased sophistication of mathematical forecasting models.

Demand forecast methods can be categorized in two very general groups: qualitative and quantitative. **Qualitative forecasts,** such as expert opinion and customer surveys, are developed from nonquantitative information. Qualitative forecasts are used most often when no quantitative data exist. Such a situation might occur during the planning stages of a new product that has no usable history. **Quantitative forecasts** use mathematical models and are the most frequently used forecasts for demand forecasting. As a general rule, if quantitative data are available to use, a quantitative forecast will be the most accurate.

Quantitative forecasting techniques are generally divided into two groups, causal techniques and time series techniques. **Causal forecasting** techniques utilize extrinsic data as a predictor of demand. **Time series forecasting** techniques use only past demand data as a predictor of the future.

Best Buy has 500 million annual customers.

qualitative forecast
A forecast based on qualitative information.

quantitative forecast
A forecast based on quantitative data.

causal forecast
A forecast that uses extrinsic data as a predictor of demand.

times series forecasting
Using past demand to forecast the future.

Surveys are a popular qualitative forecasting technique. Collecting opinions from customers in a shopping mall, for example, provides a focus on potential customers for a future store. Collecting data directly from shoppers, rather than using mail or phone surveys, yields data that truly represent opinions of future customers. The costs of gathering the data, however, are quite high when compared to other methods.

om ADVANTAGE   New Products: Projecting Demand for the Hummer H2

Forecasting demand for new products, when no data exists on a similar product, requires a very different approach. A classic case for qualitative forecasting, new product forecasting requires gathering market intelligence and translating that into a demand projection. Error can be huge, creating problems no matter which direction the error is. New auto designs commonly create this dilemma for auto manufacturers.

GM's decision to produce a consumer version of the Hummer was a typical example. In January 2000, Mike De-Giovanni was given two years to put the Hummer H2 on the road. He succeeded and early demand was surprising. From its launch in July 2002 until November, 15,000 units were sold. In October and November of 2002, H2 sales topped those of the Lincoln Navigator.

GM has adopted a common approach to increasing the accuracy of demand forecasts for new designs—shorten the lead time required to get them to market. Most GM projects are now on 24-month cycles, half as long as it took in the past to get a vehicle from design to production. Some vehicle programs are actually on 18-month schedules, and the goal is to reduce them further.

Source: J. Miller, "GM: New Products at Record Pace," *Automotive News*, August 14, 2000, Vol. 74, Issue 5888; F. Warner, "GM Goes Off-Road," *Fast Company*, February 2003, p. 40.

Causal Forecasting

Causal forecasting methods provide an opportunity for managers to use external data for forecasting. Typically, in a causal forecasting situation, planners have recognized a close relationship between demand and some other variable. For example, demand for home refinancing is tied closely to interest rates. A drop in interest rates will often result in an increase in demand for that service. Sales of many products are tied to the home construction industry. An advance predictor of new home construction is the number of building permit applications.

Simple linear regression is often used as a causal forecasting technique. In simple linear regression, a linear relationship is identified between the demand being forecasted (dependent variable) and the predictor (independent) variable. Once that relationship is identified, levels of the independent variable are used to predict the dependent variable. Forecasters must be cautious when developing causal forecasting models. The appearance of a relationship between demand and an external variable may be due to coincidence rather than a true correlation.

The equation for the linear relationship used in causal forecasting is the equation for a line:

(10.1) $$y = a + bx$$

where
   y = dependent variable
   a = y-intercept
   b = slope
   x = independent (or predictor) variable

In this particular case, the dependent variable (y) would be demand, and the independent variable (x) would be the variable being used to predict demand. The formula for calculating the slope (b) is:

(10.2) $$b = \frac{\sum xy - n\bar{x}\,\bar{y}}{\sum x^2 - n\bar{x}^2}$$

where
   b = slope
   x = values of the independent variable
   y = known values of the dependent variable
   $\bar{x}$ = average of the values of x
   $\bar{y}$ = average of the values of y
   n = number of data points

The formula for the y-intercept (a) is

(10.3) $$a = \bar{y} - b\bar{x}$$

where
   a = y-intercept
   b = slope
   x = average of the values of x
   y = average of the values of y

Example 10.1 demonstrates a simple causal forecasting application.

Time Series Forecasting

A time series is simply a series of demand values from the past. Two years of weekly demands for a particular product would be a time series. Five days of hourly demand data for a bank's drive-up window would also be considered to be a time series. Use of any time series as the basis for demand forecasting requires an understanding of the components of the time series.

Example 10.1

Causal Forecasting with Simple Linear Regression

EXCEL TUTOR

A local distributor supplies beer for baseball games. Past experience has shown that beer sales depend on the number of attendees and on the weather. Since most games are sold out, the number of attendees doesn't help much in predicting sales. The hotter the day, though, the more beer sold. The sales data and a scatter diagram showing the relationship between beer sales and predicted daily high temperature are presented in Exhibit 10.4. Predicted daily high temperature is used rather than actual daily high temperature because *before the fact* the predicted high is the only temperature data available, and regression analysis can be used to describe the relationship between demand and the predicted, not the actual, high.

EXHIBIT 10.4	Data and Scatter Diagram Showing Relationship between Beer Sales and High Temperature for Example 10.1

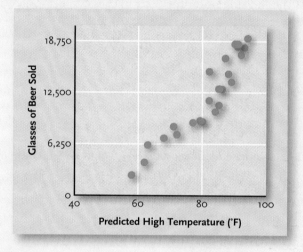

Predicted High Temperature	Beer Sales	Predicted High Temperature	Beer Sales
62	4,000	63	6,150
85	13,000	88	14,800
80	9,000	90	18,500
58	2,500	92	17,100
68	7,000	86	13,000
72	7,400	89	13,800
82	11,600	94	19,100
86	12,900	91	18,450
93	18,000	87	16,700
91	18,200	82	15,100
79	9,100	71	8,350
84	10,200	77	8,900
		85	11,000

A model of the relationship between temperature and sales that will make it possible to predict the demand for beer, given a daily high temperature, is found by a regression analysis, which provides the formula for the line that best fits through the data points in

(Continues)

Example 10.1

EXCEL TUTOR

(Continued)

Exhibit 10.4. The result of the regression analysis of the data from Exhibit 10.4 is provided in the partial Excel Regression Summary Output in Exhibit 10.5. Beer consumption for an 80-degree day is then computed.

EXHIBIT 10.5   Partial Excel Regression Analysis Output for Beer Sales for Example 10.1

Coefficient	Value
Y Intercept	−23,535
X Variable 1	438.4397

Excel provides an extensive summary output, but for our purposes, the *y* intercept and *x* coefficient (slope) are sufficient. Using Excel's regression analysis on the data and Equation 10.1, with the *x* variable being the temperatures and the *y* variable being the demand, the formula is

$$y = a + bx$$
$$= -23{,}535 + 438.4397x$$

For an 80-degree day, the demand forecast would be

$$y = 23{,}535 + 438.4397(80)$$
$$= 11{,}540.2$$

Excel Tutor 10.1 shows how a spreadsheet can be used to aid in solving this problem.

Components of a Time Series

There are four potential components of time series. One of the four, known as a **cycle,** is usually of marginal importance in demand forecasting. A cycle is a pattern of demand that repeats over a long period of time, such as a 20-year business cycle. These cyclical patterns clearly exist, but when forecasting demand for a product, a 20-year demand history is rarely available to work with, and if it were available, it would probably not be relevant. Given the reduction in product and service life cycles, in many cases even a one-year time series is hard to come by. Three remaining components of a time series are quite important, however, and consist of trend, seasonality, and random fluctuation.

A **trend** occurs when demand tends to be increasing or decreasing over time. During the growth stage of the life cycle, products and services have an upward trend. A downward trend would be indicative of the decline stage of the life cycle. Trends can also result from other factors independent of the product life cycle. Exhibit 10.6 is a graph of a time series with a trend.

Seasonality occurs when a pattern in the time series repeats itself at least once per year. When demand for a product is linked to holidays or seasons of the year, it is seasonality. Seasonality doesn't necessarily have to be based on an annual cycle, however. Banks often see increases for their services on Friday afternoons. Their demand pattern would repeat on a weekly cycle, but would also be considered to be seasonality. Exhibit 10.7 presents a time series with a seasonal pattern.

Random fluctuation is the change in demand that does not result from cycle, trend, or seasonality. If the demand pattern does have an actual cause, we won't know it from looking at the data. Random fluctuation is present in virtually all time series, along with the other components. In some cases, random fluctuation can be significant enough to

cycle
A component of a time series that is a pattern that repeats over a long period of time.

trend
A component of a time series that causes demand to increase or decrease.

seasonality
A pattern in a time series that repeats itself at least once a year.

random fluctuation
Unpredictable variation in demand that is not due to trend, seasonality, or cycle.

| EXHIBIT 10.6 | Example of a Time Series with Trend |

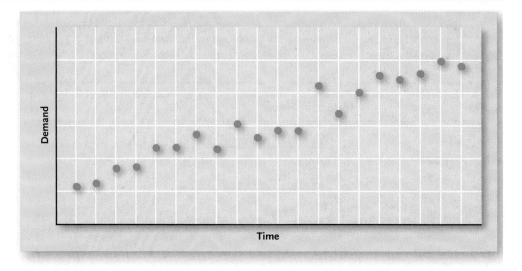

| EXHIBIT 10.7 | Example of a Time Series with Seasonality |

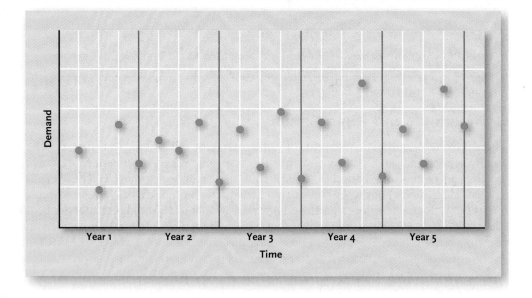

make it difficult to see trend or seasonality. Of the components of trend, seasonality, and random fluctuation, random fluctuation is the only one that cannot, by definition, be forecast. "Random" means that any outcome is equally likely. The outcome cannot be predicted. Exhibit 10.8 shows a time series that contains only random fluctuation. The more predominant the random fluctuation, and the less predominant trend and seasonality, the less useful the time series is for forecasting.

A Critical First Step

When developing any forecast of demand, the first step should always be to graph the demand. First, this gives you an opportunity get a better understanding of what the demand is doing. You can identify characteristics that will not be obvious in a column of numbers.

Example of a Time Series with Random Fluctuation   EXHIBIT 10.8

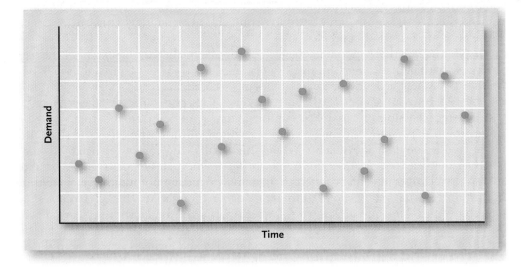

When you have completed your forecast calculations, having a graph of actual demand upon which to plot your computed forecast gives you an opportunity to see whether your forecast is reasonable.

Time Series Techniques

Time series forecasting techniques are designed to take advantage of the components of a particular demand. To present the most common techniques, it is useful to start with the time series known to contain only random fluctuation, and then progress to the time series that include trend and seasonality.

Coping with Random Fluctuation: Averages

Since random fluctuation cannot be forecast, time series techniques are designed to extract the random fluctuation through some type of averaging process. Exhibit 10.9 shows a demand time series with no seasonality or trend and significant random fluctuation. An

Demand with Random Fluctuation   EXHIBIT 10.9

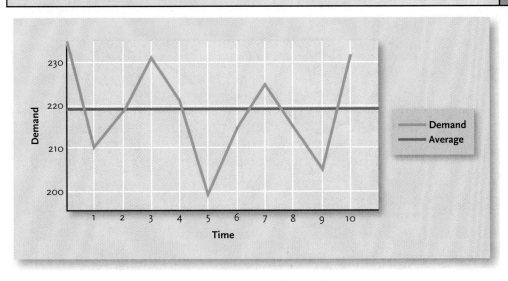

effective way to eliminate the random fluctuation is to average the data, as is done in that figure. When predicting the outcome of a random event, no prediction is any more likely to be correct than any other prediction. In the case of forecasting, when forecasting a demand that fluctuates randomly with no seasonality or trend, predicting the average is just as accurate as any other prediction.

Despite the fact that random fluctuation cannot be predicted, the extent of the variability of that fluctuation, or the stability of the fluctuation, can be useful in making a prediction. When demand fluctuates randomly, it can fluctuate widely or narrowly. Exhibit 10.10 presents graphs of two different time series, both with the same average but with different amounts of variability. For forecasters of random demand, that variability is important. A substantial demand change might signify an actual demand shift, or it might just be random movement. When this occurs, the forecaster needs to know whether to utilize that information in forecasting or ignore it. Forecasts should be unresponsive to changes in demand when changes in demand are not indicative of anything in the future. If the changes do not provide valuable information, they should not affect forecasts. When demands are known to be relatively stable and a shift in demand is indicative of a true change, the forecaster wants to be responsive to those changes. The degree to which a forecasting technique responds to demand changes is a factor in the design and selection of the forecasting approach.

Forecasting with Simple and Weighted Moving Averages

Various averages can be adapted to demand forecasting. The differences between one type of average and another are often exploited in an attempt to create varying degrees of responsiveness. Suppose a product was known to have an extremely variable demand that was thought to be completely random. In this situation, a forecaster would want a less responsive forecast because nothing would be gained by responding to the variations of the demand.

An average with a lot of numbers in it is unresponsive to sudden changes in the data being averaged. In other words, by averaging more past demands together, the impact of a single demand value is reduced. The number of values included in the average is referred to as the n. An average with a larger n is less responsive to demand changes because each value averaged has a small impact on the average. When a small n is used, a change in one value can have a significant impact on the average. Let's look at an example. A possible technique when we do not want a responsive forecast might be an eight-period moving average. In that technique, the forecast for the upcoming period would be

EXHIBIT 10.10	Variability of Time Series

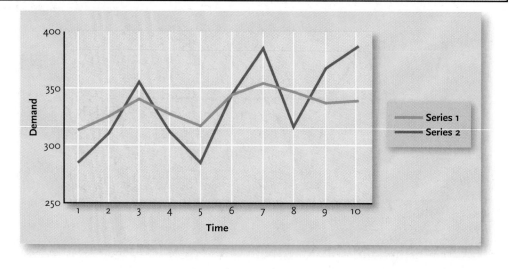

an average of the previous eight periods. If we wanted a responsive forecast, the fore-caster would average fewer periods to get the forecast and a three-period moving average might be used. That forecast would simply be the average of the previous three periods.

The formula for a simple moving average is

(8.4)
$$F_t = \frac{A_{t-1} + A_{t-2} + A_{t-3} + \ldots + A_{t-n}}{n}$$

where

F_t = forecast for period t
A_{t-1} = actual demand in period $t - 1$
n = number of periods in the moving average

Exhibit 10.11 shows an eight-period moving average forecast and a three-period mov-ing average forecast compared to the actual demand that followed each forecast. Notice how much more responsive to demand shifts the three-period moving average is. For ex-ample, following the high point in demand at period 11, the three-period average fore-cast responds by forecasting a demand for period 12 that is substantially higher than the forecast made for period 11. It has "responded" to the demand spike in period 11. The eight-period moving average forecast, however, does not respond as much to the spike in period 11. Its forecast for period 12 is only slightly higher than its forecast for period 11. Also notice in Exhibit 10.11 that the line for the eight-period average fluctuates less than the three-period average.

Another approach to manipulating the responsiveness of an average is to use moving weighted averages. By assigning weights, whose sum must be 1.0, to be multiplied by the data points, the responsiveness can be manipulated, even though the same number of data points are used.

The formula for a weighted moving average forecast is

(10.5) $F_t = w_{t-1}A_{t-1} + w_{t-2}A_{t-2} + w_{t-3}A_{t-3} + \cdots + w_{t-n} + A_{t-n}$

where

F_t = forecast for period t
A_{t-1} = actual demand in period $t - 1$
w_{t-1} = weight assigned to period $t - 1$
w_{t-2} = weight assigned to period $t - 2$
w_{t-3} = weight assigned to period $t - 3$
n = number of periods in the moving average

Three-Period and Eight-Period Moving Average Forecasts	EXHIBIT 10.11

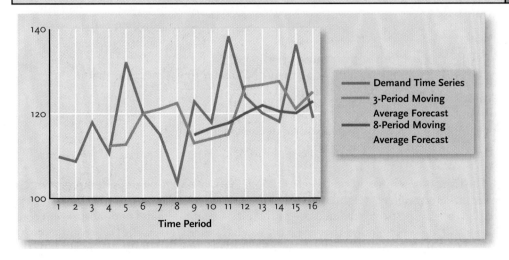

Example 10.2

Calculating a Forecast with Weighted Moving Averages

EXCEL TUTOR

Use a weighted average and the past four weeks' demand to predict the next week's demand. Demands for the past four weeks are:

Period	1	2	3	4
Demand	133	130	134	146

Solution

The forecast for period 5 could be computed using any of a number of different weighted averages. A simple average of the four demands would provide a forecast of 135.75. A weighted average, creating a more responsive forecast, might use weights of 0.5, 0.3, 0.1, and 0.1, as shown in Exhibit 10.12.

EXHIBIT 10.12   Solution to Example 10.2

Period	Demand	Weight	Forecast
1	133	0.1	13.3
2	130	0.1	13
3	134	0.3	40.2
4	146	0.5	73
5			139.5

The weighted average forecast of 139.5 for period 5 provides an example of how a more responsive forecast reacts to the demand increase in period 4. Excel Tutor 10.2 shows how moving weighted average forecasts can easily be completed in spreadsheets.

Example 10.2 provides an example of the use of a weighted moving average forecast. The forecast created in Example 10.2 gives much more weight to the recent demand of 146 and less to the smaller demands of the earlier periods.

Simple Exponential Smoothing

simple exponential smoothing
A sophisticated type of moving average that uses a smoothing constant to weight the previous demand and establish the responsiveness of the forecast.

Exponential smoothing provides an alternative approach to moving weighted averages that is more easily adapted and requires storing only two data points. **Simple exponential smoothing** utilizes a constant called alpha (α) to provide the weights as designated by the user. The formula for simple exponential smoothing is

(10.6) $$F_{t+1} = \alpha(A_t) + (1 - \alpha)F_t$$

where

F_{t+1} = forecast for the next time period
α = smoothing constant, which must be greater than 0 and less than 1
A_t = actual demand for the most recent period
F_t = forecast for the most recent period

Some people find it easier to remember an equivalent formula:

(10.7) $$F_{t-1} = F_t + \alpha(A_t - F_t)$$

The logic is best understood by examining Equation 10.6. The smoothing constant, α, determines the relative weight assigned to the most recent demand. If $\alpha = 0.3$, for example, $1 - \alpha = 0.7$. A weighted average of the most recent demand and most recent forecast is created. Keep in mind that the most recent forecast, given the 0.7 weight, consists of the weighted average of the previous demand and previous forecast. In essence, this creates a weighted average giving the most recent demand a weight of 0.3 and spreading the remaining weight of 0.7 over all previous demands.

Examining the extremes offers further insight. If $\alpha = 1$, the forecast is equal to the most recent demand. This is also known as a naïve forecast. If $\alpha = 0$, the forecast is equal to the last period's forecast, giving no weight to the most recent demand. The value for α is typically between 0.1 and 0.5. The higher α makes the forecast more responsive to demand changes, just as a higher weight in the most recent period of a weighted average would make the forecast more responsive. The responsiveness with varying degrees of α is demonstrated in Exhibit 10.13, where forecasts with α values of 0.1 and 0.4 are shown against a shifting demand. The responsiveness of the higher α value is evident. Notice how the 0.4 alpha forecast immediately responds to the demand spikes at periods 13 and 20. Also note how the 0.4 alpha chases the rising demand at periods 23–25. Example 10.3 demonstrates the use of simple exponential smoothing.

Adding Trend to the Exponential Smoothing Model

Although some time series have random fluctuation with no apparent seasonality or trend, many have random fluctuation and trend. An averaging technique, or simple exponential smoothing, should not be used for a time series containing a trend, because each method ignores valuable information, resulting in a forecast that always lags behind. A modification to the exponential smoothing model, known as **trend-adjusted exponential smoothing** or **forecast including trend (FIT),** includes the trend in the forecast. In trend-adjusted exponential smoothing, a second constant, β, is used to include the trend component. The trend-adjusted exponential smoothing model separates the random fluctuation and trend components into two distinct parts. The formula for this model is

trend-adjusted exponential smoothing
An exponential smoothing technique that includes a smoothing constant for trend.

(10.8)
$$\text{FIT}_{t+1} = F_t + T_t$$

where F_t is the smoothed forecast, T_t is the trend estimate, and

forecast including trend (FIT)
Trend-adjusted exponential smoothing.

(10.9)
$$F_t = \text{FIT}_t + \alpha(A_t - \text{FIT}_t)$$

(10.10)
$$T_t = T_{t-1} + \beta(\text{FIT}_t - \text{FIT}_{t-1} - T_{t-1})$$

where α and β are smoothing constants. Notice that the trend component (T_t) of the trend-adjusted model is added to the smoothed forecast (F_t), and the smoothed forecast is calculated in the same way as in simple exponential smoothing. Example 10.4 demonstrates this approach.

Comparison of 0.1 and 0.4 Alpha Values for Simple Exponential Smoothing	EXHIBIT 10.13

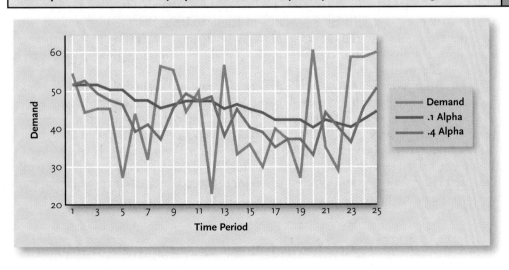

Example 10.3

Calculating a Forecast with Simple Exponential Smoothing

A retailer recorded the following monthly demands for a particular CD player/changer.

Month	January	February	March	April	May	June
Demand	100	110	115	104	112	117

Forecast the demand for July using simple exponential smoothing with $\alpha = 0.3$ and an initial forecast of 90.

Solution

Using the equation for simple exponential smoothing (Equation 10.7),

$$F_{t+1} = F_t + \alpha(A_t - F_t)$$
$$F_2 = F_1 + \alpha(A_1 - F_1)$$
$$= 90 + 0.3(100 - 90)$$
$$= 93$$

The process is continued in Exhibit 10.14, until the forecast for July (period 7) is determined.

EXHIBIT 10.14   Solution for Example 10.3

Month	Period (t)	Demand (A_t)	Forecast (F_t)
January	1	100	90.00
February	2	110	93.00
March	3	115	98.10
April	4	104	103.17
May	5	112	103.42
June	6	117	105.99
July			109.30

Excel Tutor 10.3 demonstrates how to use spreadsheets to forecast with simple exponential smoothing.

Using the Linear Trend Equation

A time series with a trend component is also an appropriate application for the linear trend equation. By using the time period as the independent variable and demand as the dependent variable, the trend can quite easily be defined by the equation of the best-fitting line. The linear trend equation is also useful for predicting the impact the trend will have on demand.

The linear trend equation technique (demonstrated in Example 10.5) is identical to the use of linear regression as a causal technique demonstrated in Example 10.1, except that the independent variable is the time period, rather than some external variable. (See Equations 10.1, 10.2, and 10.3.) Using the time period as the independent variable and demand as the dependent variable defines the linear relationship between demand and time period. The best-fitting line represented by the least squares regression output is the trend line. Once we know the equation for the trend line, we can project that trend line into the future to forecast.

Example 10.4

EXCEL TUTOR

Calculating a Forecast Using Trend-Adjusted Exponential Smoothing (FIT)

Suppose a 10-week time series for laptop demand at the university bookstore was collected.

Week (t)	1	2	3	4	5	6	7	8	9	10
Demand (A)	25	29	30	34	39	38	41	42	46	48

Using $\alpha = 0.2$, $\beta = 0.9$, an initial trend (T_1) of 3, and an initial forecast (FIT_1) of 25, calculate the demand for period 11 using trend-adjusted exponential smoothing.

Solution

FIT_2 can be computed as follows:

$$
\begin{aligned}
FIT_2 &= F_1 + T_1 \\
&= 25.00 + 3.00 \\
&= 28.00
\end{aligned}
$$

FIT_3 is calculated as follows:

$$
\begin{aligned}
F_2 &= FIT_2 + \alpha(A_2 - FIT_2) \\
&= 28.00 + 0.2(29.00 - 28.00) \\
&= 28.20 \\
T_2 &= T_1 + \beta(FIT_2 - FIT_1 - T_1) \\
&= 3.00 + 0.9(28.00 - 25.00 - 3.00) \\
&= 3.00
\end{aligned}
$$

Therefore, to calculate FIT_3,

$$FIT_3 = F_2 + T_2 = 28.20 + 3.00 = 31.20$$

The process is continued for FIT_4 through FIT_{11} in Exhibit 10.15.

EXHIBIT 10.15 Trend-Adjusted Forecast for Example 10.4

Week (t)	Demand (A_t)	F_t	T_t	FIT_t
1	25	25.00	3.00	25.00
2	29	28.20	3.00	28.00
3	30	30.96	3.18	31.20
4	34	34.11	2.96	34.14
5	39	37.46	2.94	37.08
6	38	39.92	3.29	40.40
7	41	42.76	2.85	43.20
8	42	44.89	3.46	45.62
9	46	47.08	1.81	47.35
10	48	48.71	1.56	48.89
11	?			50.27

A spreadsheet approach to using trend-adjusted exponential smoothing is provided in Excel Tutor 10.4.

Example 10.5

Calculating a Forecast Using the Linear Trend Equation

Suppose a 10-month time series for a new backpack design shows an apparent trend, as in the following data:

Month:	1	2	3	4	5	6	7	8	9	10
Demand:	308	315	360	391	412	423	445	456	471	482

Using the linear trend equation requires the use of least squares regression. Exhibit 10.16 provides the relevant coefficients from an Excel regression analysis of the data.

EXHIBIT 10.16   Partial Excel Regression Analysis Output for Backpack Sales for Example 10.5

Coefficient	Value
Y Intercept	295.9333
X Variable	20.0667

The least squares regression output from Exhibit 10.16 is put into the general equation for a line:

(10.11) $$y = a + bt$$

where

a = y intercept
b = slope and
t = time period

The regression analysis output yields the following trend line:

$$y = 295.9333 + 20.0667t$$

To use the trend line formula for forecasting, simply substitute the time period of interest for t in the formula. Forecasting the demand for period 11 would be

$$y = 295.9333 + 20.0667(11)$$
$$= 516.667$$

A spreadsheet approach to using the linear trend equation is provided in Excel Tutor 10.5.

Including Seasonality in the Demand Forecast

Seasonality is a common component in time series, and forecasters must address it as an element of information in predicting future demands. Seasonal indexes are used to model the seasonal pattern in a time series. If the time series consists of monthly data, each month will have a seasonal index. If the time series consists of hourly data, each hour will have a seasonal index. The seasonality is described by using the ratio of the actual demand for a period to the average demand across all periods for a given time horizon. Seasonal indexes are often calculated by averaging the ratios of demand for the specific time periods to the average demand to eliminate the possible impact of random fluctuations. This is another example of using averages as a way to eliminate random fluctuation. The resulting seasonal index provides a multiplicative relationship between actual demand for the period of interest and the average demand. Since random fluctuation has been eliminated through averaging, the variability remaining is assumed to be the result of seasonality. A seasonal index of 1.8, for example, would mean that the demand for that period is, on the average, 1.8 times the average demand.

Seasonal indexes are used to generate a forecast for a particular period by multiplying the seasonal index by the average demand per period. The calculation of seasonal indexes and their use in forecasting are demonstrated in Example 10.6.

Example 10.6

Calculating a Forecast Using Seasonal Indexes

The owner of a local tanning salon was interested in using seasonal indexes in forecasting daily walk-in demand to help plan for staffing needs for spring. The daily demand for the past four weeks is presented in Exhibit 10.17, as are the calculations for the seasonal indexes.

EXHIBIT 10.17   Calculation of Seasonal Indexes for Example 10.6

Day	Week 1 Walk-Ins	Week 2 Walk-Ins	Week 3 Walk-Ins	Week 4 Walk-Ins	Daily Average	Seasonal Index
Monday	5	7	3	4	4.75	0.34
Tuesday	6	9	6	7	7.00	0.51
Wednesday	12	10	9	13	11.00	0.80
Thursday	15	17	13	19	16.00	1.16
Friday	27	24	30	28	27.25	1.97
Saturday	15	20	16	17	17.00	1.23

Overall average daily demand: ($332/24 = 13.83$)

The salon owner has collected weekly demand data for several years and based on these data expects the daily average to go up to 20. The data show clear evidence of a seasonal pattern. Walk-in demand increases through each week, peaking on Fridays. What would the expected number of walk-ins be for each day?

Solution

The average daily demand is 13.83 walk-ins (332/24). The seasonal indexes for each day are created by computing an average demand for each day, and then dividing that average by the average daily demand. For Monday, for example, demands were 5, 7, 3, and 4 walk-ins, for an average of 4.75. Dividing 4.75 by the overall daily average of 13.83 provides a Monday seasonal index of .34. Thus, on the average, Monday walk-in demand was 0.34, or 34 percent of the average daily walk-in demand.

The remaining calculations are presented in Exhibit 10.18.

EXHIBIT 10.18   Calculation of Daily Walk-In Forecasts for Example 10.6

Day	Seasonal Index	Average Daily Demand	Daily Forecast
Monday	0.3434	20	6.87
Tuesday	0.5060	20	10.12
Wednesday	0.7952	20	15.91
Thursday	1.1566	20	23.14
Friday	1.9699	20	39.41
Saturday	1.2289	20	24.58

Excel Tutor 10.6 shows how to use spreadsheets for determining seasonal indexes.

Dealing with Seasonality and Trend in a Time Series

There are many ways to forecast when seasonal and trend components are present in the time series. For example, we could combine the trend-adjusted exponential smoothing method with the seasonal indexes approach just used. Another common approach is to use a multiplicative model that combines the linear regression approach to forecasting trend with the seasonal indexes used to forecast seasonality. This approach uses the following steps:

1. Compute seasonal indexes for each period.
2. Remove the seasonal component from the time series (deseasonalize the data).
3. Model the trend component by using least squares regression on the deseasonalized data.
4. Determine the forecast by using the trend equation and seasonal indexes.

These steps are demonstrated in Example 10.7.

Example 10.7

EXCEL TUTOR

Forecasting with a Multiplicative Model for Seasonality and Trend

Exhibit 10.19 provides four years of quarterly demand data for a large tax service. Using the multiplicative model for trend and seasonality, forecast the demand for period 17 (Q1 of the next year).

Solution

Included in Exhibit 10.19 are the calculations for seasonal indexes and the deseasonalized demand.

EXHIBIT 10.19   Combining Seasonality and Trend for Example 10.7

Season		Period (t)	Demand (A_t)	Demand/ Average Demand		Seasonal Index	Deseasonalized Demand
Yr1	Q1	1	482	1.61	Average	1.6683	288.91
	Q2	2	213	0.71		.7658	278.13
	Q3	3	116	0.39		.4150	279.52
	Q4	4	335	1.12		1.1508	291.09
Yr2	Q1	5	499	1.66		1.6683	299.1
	Q2	6	225	0.75		.7658	293.8
	Q3	7	122	0.41		.4150	293.98
	Q4	8	344	1.15		1.1508	298.91
Yr3	Q1	9	503	1.68		1.6683	301.5
	Q2	10	237	0.79		.7658	309.47
	Q3	11	127	0.42		.4150	306.02
	Q4	12	349	1.16		1.1508	303.26
Yr4	Q1	13	518	1.73		1.6683	310.49
	Q2	14	244	0.81		.7658	318.61
	Q3	15	133	0.44		.4150	320.48
	Q4	16	353	1.18		1.1508	306.73

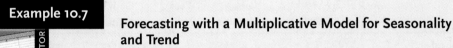

AverageDemand = 300

(Continues)

Example 10.7   EXCEL TUTOR

(Continued)

The regression analysis determines the best-fitting line through the deseasonalized demand using Equation 10.11.

Using Excel's regression tool on the deseasonalized demand, with the time periods as the *x* variable, the *y* intercept is calculated at 280.48 and the slope is 2.30. Given these factors, the equation for the line defining the trend of this demand data is

$$y = a + bt$$
$$= 280.48 + 2.30t$$

The forecast is calculated by substituting the time period for *t* and multiplying the result by the appropriate seasonal index. If, for example, we needed a forecast for the first quarter of the next year (year 5), the following calculations would be made:

$$\text{Forecast} = [280.48 + 2.30(17)] \times 1.67$$
$$= 319.58 \times 1.67$$
$$= 533.70$$

The multiplicative model for forecasting with trend and seasonality is demonstrated in a spreadsheet environment in Excel Tutor 10.7.

Forecast Accuracy

Virtually all forecasts will be wrong because all time series contain random fluctuation, and random fluctuation can't be forecast. However, the fact that plans are often based on forecasts motivates a business to forecast as accurately as possible. While one of the best ways to improve forecast accuracy is to reduce the time horizon, it is also important to match the technique being used to the characteristics of the particular time series used in the forecast. This is often accomplished by comparing the results of several forecasting approaches to see which one is most accurate.

Forecast accuracy can be measured in a number of ways, but the most frequently used approaches acknowledge that there are two separate types of forecast error. The first type of error, known as **absolute error,** is concerned with how far from the actual demand, on an absolute basis, the forecast tends to be. In other words, are we generally off by a few units or many units? The second type of error, known as **forecast bias,** is concerned with the general direction of error. Do we consistently forecast too high or too low? Or do we forecast high as often as low? Any examination of forecast accuracy will include a look at both types of error. The following discussion examines ways of measuring these two types of error.

absolute error
The absolute value of the forecast error.

forecast bias
The tendency of a forecast to be too high or too low.

Measuring Absolute Error

The measurement of the absolute error of a forecast can be obtained in several ways. The most popular measure of absolute error is the **mean absolute deviation (MAD),** which is simply the average of the absolute values of the errors for each time period. The formula for computing the MAD is

mean absolute deviation (MAD)
A measure of the absolute forecast error that is the mean of the absolute values of the forecast errors.

(10.12)
$$\text{MAD} = \sum_{t=1}^{n} \frac{A_t - F_t}{n}$$

In using Equation 10.12, the first step in computing the MAD is to calculate the error for past forecasts. Error is equal to the actual demand (A_t) minus the forecast demand (F_t). The second step is to take the absolute value of each error. Step three is to compute the mean of the absolute values. Example 10.8 demonstrates the MAD calculation.

Example 10.8

Calculating Mean Absolute Deviation

A small retailer has kept weekly demand and forecast data for a particular set of skateboard wheels. Compute the MAD for the forecast.

Solution

Exhibit 10.20 lists the demand, forecast, and errors by subtracting the forecast from the demand. Absolute values of the errors are determined and then averaged. The resulting MAD is the average of the absolute values of the errors for the forecasting approach used.

EXHIBIT 10.20   MAD Calculation for Example 10.8

Period (t)	Demand (A_t)	Forecast (F_t)	Error $(A_t - F_t)$	Absolute Value of Error $\lvert A_t - F_t \rvert$
1	120	125	−5	5
2	134	131	3	3
3	138	133	5	5
4	125	134	−9	9
5	143	138	5	5
6	126	129	−3	3
7	136	132	4	4
8	140	132	5	8
				MAD = 5.25

A new forecast would be created for the next week. As soon as the actual demand occurs, error can be calculated. The absolute value of the new error term is then incorporated into a new MAD calculation for the week. The MAD is updated as each new forecast and demand occurs.

After eight periods, the MAD for the forecast is 5.25. This means that the average absolute error was 5.25. Given demands significantly above 100, this would be viewed as an accurate forecast.

Excel Tutor 10.8 shows how the MAD is calculated using a spreadsheet.

Another commonly used measure of absolute forecast error is the *mean squared error (MSE)*. Instead of computing the absolute value of the errors and averaging them, as in the MAD calculation, the MSE uses the actual error values. The calculation of the MSE is demonstrated in Example 10.9.

(10.13)
$$\text{MSE} = \sum_{t=1}^{n} \frac{(A_t - F_t)^2}{n}$$

The objective for both MAD and MSE measures is a small number. The closer to zero, the better, but the size of the MAD or MSE is a function of the size of the demand. A MAD of 5, for example, if the demand is in the hundreds, is very good. However, a MAD of 5 would not be good if the demand is typically under 30.

To address the need for a relative measure of the absolute error, the **mean absolute percentage error** (MAPE) is often used. The MAPE is the mean of the absolute errors stated as a percentage of demand. To compute the MAPE we first compute the absolute errors, then divide each by the actual demand to compute the absolute percentage errors, and then compute the mean for those percentages.

mean absolute percentage error (MAPE)

The mean of the absolute errors stated as a percentage of demand.

Example 10.9

Calculating Mean Squared Error

Using the data from Example 10.8, calculate the MSE.

Solution

Exhibit 10.21 shows the calculation of the MSE for the data used in Example 10.6.

EXHIBIT 10.21   MSE Calculation for Example 10.9

Period	Demand	Forecast	Error	Error^2
1	120	125	−5	25
2	134	131	3	9
3	138	133	5	25
4	125	134	−9	81
5	143	138	5	25
6	126	129	−3	9
7	136	132	4	16
8	140	132	8	64
				MSE = 31.75

The MSE is calculated in a spreadsheet in Excel Tutor 10.9.

$$(10.14) \qquad \text{MAPE} = \frac{\sum_{t=1}^{n} |A_t - F_t|}{n}$$

where
  A^t = actual demand
  F^t = forecast
  n = number of periods

The calculation of the MAPE is demonstrated in Example 10.10.

Example 10.10

Calculating Mean Absolute Percentage Error

Using the data from Example 10.8, compute the MAPE.

EXHIBIT 10.22   MAPE Calculation for Example 10.10

Period	Demand	Forecast	Error	Absolute Error	Absolute % Error
1	120	125	−5	5	4.17
2	134	131	3	3	2.24
3	138	133	5	5	3.62
4	125	134	−9	9	7.20
5	143	138	5	5	3.50
6	126	129	−3	3	2.38
7	136	132	4	4	2.94
8	140	132	8	8	5.71
					MAPE = 3.97

The use of a spreadsheet to compute the MAPE is demonstrated in Excel Tutor 10.10

Measuring Forecast Bias

Forecast bias is the tendency of a forecast to be too high or too low. A forecast should be unbiased. In other words, the forecast error should be neutral. It should forecast too high as often as it forecasts too low. Presence of bias in a forecast indicates a problem with the forecasting model being used or that someone is intentionally trying to manipulate the forecast. There are several common approaches to measuring bias, with two techniques being most popular. The first approach is the **mean forecast error (MFE).** The MFE is calculated by simply averaging the forecast errors, as demonstrated in Example 10.11.

mean forecast error (MFE)

A measure of forecast bias that is the mean of the forecast errors.

running sum of forecast error (RSFE)

A measure of forecast bias that is the sum of forecast error, and is updated as each new error is calculated.

The other common method for measuring forecast bias is the **running sum of forecast error** (RSFE). The RSFE is a simple calculation that requires the errors to be summed periodically as each new forecast, actual demand, and error become available. Example 10.12 provides a demonstration of the RSFE calculation using the same data as above.

For the MFE and RSFE, the optimal measure is very close to zero. A positive number indicates that the forecast tends to be too low (actual demand minus the forecast is positive). A negative number (actual demand minus the forecast is negative) is an indication that the forecast is too high.

Tracking Signals

The absolute error of a forecast is closely related to the variability of demand. If, for example, a time series consisted of random fluctuation and seasonality, and we were able to model the seasonality perfectly, our error would be completely due to the remaining variability. It turns out that the MAD and standard deviation of demand have a constant relationship that is approximated by:

$$1 \text{ standard deviation} \cong 1.25\text{MAD}$$

$$1\text{MAD} \cong .8\text{standard deviation}$$

For example, if the MAD was found to be 40, the standard deviation would be approximately 50.

Example 10.11

Calculating Mean Forecast Error

EXCEL TUTOR

Using the same data used in Example 10.8, calculate the MFE for the errors.

Solution

The errors sum to 8, and with an *n* of 8, the mean is 1. An MFE of 1 after eight demands and with demands of this size would be viewed as a good result. Exhibit 10.23 presents the results of this calculation.

EXHIBIT 10.23	MFE Calculation for Example 10.11		
Period (t)	Demand (A_t)	Forecast (F_t)	Error ($A_t - F_t$)
1	120	125	−5
2	134	131	3
3	138	133	5
4	125	134	−9
5	143	138	5
6	126	129	−3
7	136	132	4
8	140	132	8
			MFE = 1

Excel Tutor 10.11 demonstrates these calculations in a spreadsheet.

Example 10.12

EXCEL TUTOR

Calculating Running Sum of Forecast Error

Using the same data as in Example 10.8, calculate the RSFE for the errors.

Solution

As each period provides a new error value, it is added to the sum of the previous RSFE. Exhibit 10.24 presents the results for these data.

EXHIBIT 10.24   RSFE Calculation for Example 10.12

Period (t)	Demand (A_t)	Forecast (F_t)	Error ($A_t - F_t$)	RSFE
1	120	125	−5	−5
2	134	131	3	−2
3	138	133	5	3
4	125	134	−9	−6
5	143	138	5	−1
6	126	129	−3	−4
7	136	132	4	0
8	140	132	8	8

The most current RSFE, resulting from the error of period 8, would be 8. This value suggests that the forecast is somewhat biased and has a tendency to be a little too low. Excel Tutor 10.12 shows how to compute RSFE in a spreadsheet.

This relationship between the MAD and the standard deviation makes it possible for forecasters to use concepts similar to those used in statistical process control charts (refer back to Chapter 7) to monitor how well a forecasting method is doing. Recall that when monitoring a process, we could look at a chart and determine how many standard deviations away from the process mean a particular sample mean was. In forecasting, since we have the MAD value handy, we monitor how many mean absolute deviations a forecast is above or below the actual demand. We do this through the use of a **tracking signal (TS).** A tracking signal consists of the running sum of forecast error (RSFE) divided by the mean absolute deviation (MAD). It tells us the size of our cumulative error in terms of mean absolute deviations. The formula for the tracking signal is:

tracking signal
The size of the cumulative forecast error expressed as MADs.

$$(10.16) \qquad \mathrm{TS} = \frac{\mathrm{RSFE}}{\mathrm{MAD}}$$

We know from Chapter 7 that random fluctuation would fall within 3 standard deviations of the mean. Three standard deviations would be approximately the same as 3.75 MADS. So, 99.7 percent our error, if it were due to simply random fluctuation, would fall within 3.75 MADs of the mean. We could set limits for the tracking signal depending on how accurate we needed our forecast to be. If the tracking signal moved beyond our limits, we would conclude that our forecasting model is no longer doing an acceptable job of forecasting demand and would need to adjust or replace the forecasting model. An example of the use of a tracking signal is presented in Example 10.13. As is evident in the example, the tracking signal brings with it the sign (positive or negative) from the RSFE. So sign of the tracking signal shows the bias; the size of the tracking signal shows how many MADs the error is.

Example 10.13

EXCEL TUTOR

Tracking Signal Calculation

Exhibit 10.25 shows the results of the tracking signal calculations for the demand and forecast data.

EXHIBIT 10.25 TS Calculation for Example 10.13

Period	Demand	Forecast	Error	RSFE	Abs Error	MAD	TS
1	200	180	20	20	20	20.00	1.00
2	230	248	−18	2	18	19.00	0.11
3	260	300	−40	−38	40	26.00	−1.46
4	270	275	−5	−43	5	20.75	−2.07
5	300	280	20	−23	20	20.60	−1.12
6	290	310	−20	−43	20	20.50	−2.10
7	320	308	12	−31	12	19.29	−1.61
8	331	342	−11	−42	11	18.25	−2.30

Excel Tutor 10.13 shows how to calculate tracking signals in a spreadsheet.

Integrated Resource Planning Systems

Advances in computer technology and database management techniques have enabled software designers to integrate formerly separate planning and management systems into large systems known as enterprise systems (ESs) or enterprise resource planning (ERP) systems. With these systems, planning for all resources is accomplished from one common database. Traditional resource management systems incorporated distinct systems to manage different resource groups. The problem with that approach is that different resources are not independent and decisions related to one need data related to another. The fact that the systems were separate often meant that the information was not the same either. One system would say one thing, and another system would say another. Updating a piece of information for a product—a labor standard, for example—meant updating that same piece of information in a variety of systems, inviting redundancy. It was virtually impossible to keep the same information on separate systems up-to-date and consistent. Decisions cannot be made in an integrative way when the systems do not talk to each other. ERP systems are designed to solve that problem.

The unified database of an ERP system provides a common thread throughout the business and allows decisions to be made from an enterprise perspective. When the database is updated with new information, that information becomes the basis for all decisions. All decisions are made with current information. Everyone is working with the same numbers—the same set of facts.

Despite the logic of such a system, ERP system implementation has not been entirely successful. ERP systems, for the most part, are not customized for a particular business. They are "off-the-shelf" systems. Some of the larger providers have created versions with aspects that are designed for particular industries, but they're not customized. The systems are too huge to customize to meet the needs of an individual company. Each firm must adjust its processes to meet the system's needs,[2] rather than the system being modified to meet the firm's needs. This has resulted in situations where the needs of the software drive business practices—the "tail wagging the dog" syndrome.

ERP systems were born in Europe, where businesses tend to be more tightly structured organizations than in the United States. This has led to problems in the United States, however. Modification of business practices to meet the system needs leads to one of two results. First, the new approach can be an improvement, as often happens. The techniques used to guide ERP system design are considered to be "best-practice" techniques. ERP system implementation, for some companies, has resulted in a reengineering of many of the business processes. There are some situations, however, particularly when businesses have developed a competitive niche, when the practices mandated by the ERP software are not improvements and actually reduce the strategic advantages the firm has developed.[3] What makes things even worse is the fact that all of the major players in a particular industry may be using the same ERP system, which is mandating the same business processes. The concept of differentiating capabilities goes out the window if everyone does things exactly the same way and continues doing them because the ERP system says so.

The major providers of ERP systems in the large-business market include SAP, BAAN, PeopleSoft, and Oracle. In addition to these ERP system providers, several companies focus on small and midsize businesses. There are also many companies in the business of producing add-on software to provide specific functions or to interact with preexisting (legacy) systems a company wishes to keep. Most of these companies provide alternatives for all major ERP systems. The large ERP systems function in a manner that is quite similar, so a close look at one of the leader's modules provides a good representative overview. Exhibit 10.26 lists and briefly summarizes SAP's R/3 (client–server version) system modules. Several modules are closely related to operations decisions.

Exhibit 10.27 lists functions of Microsoft Great Plains software, a leading provider for small and midsize companies. The functions in this system are similar to those of SAP's R/3.

SAP Modules	EXHIBIT 10.26

Asset Management: Captures information relating to depreciation, insurance, property values, etc.

Controlling: Includes cost center accounting, product cost controlling, and activity-based costing.

Financial Accounting: Includes general ledger, accounts receivable, accounts payable, and legal consolidations.

Human Resources: Includes personnel administration and planning and development.

Material Management: Includes inventory management, invoice management, invoice verification, and warehouse management.

Plant Maintenance: Includes equipment and technical objects, preventive maintenance, service management, and maintenance order management.

Production Planning: Includes sales and operations planning, material requirements planning, and capacity requirements planning.

Project System: Includes project tracking and budget management.

Quality Management: Includes quality certificates, inspection processing, planning tools, and quality notifications.

Sales and Distribution System: Includes sales management, logistics, transportation, and distribution requirements planning.

Source: D. E. O'Leary, *Enterprise Resource Planning Systems* (Cambridge, UK: Cambridge University Press, 2000), pp. 31–32.

EXHIBIT 10.27	Microsoft Great Plains ERP Functions

Accounting and financial management	Multiple currencies
Advanced reporting and analysis	Payroll and/or ADP payroll integration
Budgeting	Paying bills and billing customers
Call center management	Project time and billing management
Selling online	Requisition, purchasing, and procurement
Employee self-service	Sales automation and customer relationship management
Customer service	
Human resource management	Sales orders and fulfillment
Inventory and stock levels	Supply chain management
Manufacturing and resource management	National accounts receivables

Source: Microsoft Great Plains Business Solutions, www.greatplains.com/solutions/, April 17, 2001.

A tour of the functional modules of major providers of ERP systems leads to the conclusion that the different systems have basically the same objectives and, to a great extent, are similar. The modules and functions have slightly different names and might be organized in a slightly different manner, but they include the same set of business tasks and the same types of information.

Exhibit 10.28 provides a conceptual model of a generic ERP system, based on the advertised capabilities of several leading systems. ERP systems generate standard reports that are used for common decision-making processes. Many of these reports are used to make operations decisions, and many are based on data kept in the unified database, originating within operations.

The price of an ERP system often depends on the number of users that have access to it. Some companies convert ERP system reports to a format that they can put on their own intranet to make the information available to others who do not have access to the ERP system. This is typically done for users who do not need access on a regular basis. Integration of the ERP system and a company Intranet is becoming more popular and more necessary. Depending on the ERP provider, other software may be able to access ERP reports to enable them to be read more easily and included in other types of reports.[4] Some reports, for example, are generated in Excel spreadsheet format. Others are generated in the format for particular groupware products for ease of integration into other reports.

The close links between operations and the ERP system, and the links between operations and other business functions *through* the ERP system, become more apparent as the management of specific resources is examined in more detail. Exhibit 10.29 provides an ERP framework, with special focus on the operations resources used to create value.

The use of ERP systems has gradually spread from manufacturing to the service sector and has become common even in the college and university setting. As a student, you likely interact with an ERP system. Systems created by PeopleSoft and Banner, for example, are designed specifically to provide a common database for room scheduling, student registration, advising, accounting, payroll, and even transcripts and student records. These ERP systems, just like those for businesses, are designed to integrate all aspects of the organization through one enterprisewide database.

Conceptual View of a Generic ERP System   EXHIBIT 10.28

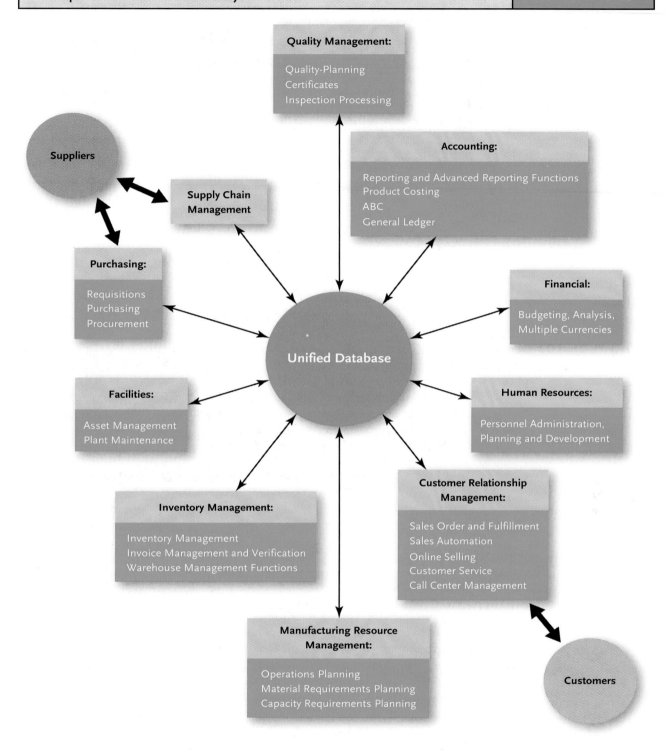

Quality Management:

Quality-Planning
Certificates
Inspection Processing

Suppliers

Supply Chain Management

Accounting:

Reporting and Advanced Reporting Functions
Product Costing
ABC
General Ledger

Purchasing:

Requisitions
Purchasing
Procurement

Financial:

Budgeting, Analysis,
Multiple Currencies

Unified Database

Facilities:

Asset Management
Plant Maintenance

Human Resources:

Personnel Administration,
Planning and Development

Inventory Management:

Inventory Management
Invoice Management and Verification
Warehouse Management Functions

Customer Relationship Management:

Sales Order and Fulfillment
Sales Automation
Online Selling
Customer Service
Call Center Management

Manufacturing Resource Management:

Operations Planning
Material Requirements Planning
Capacity Requirements Planning

Customers

EXHIBIT 10.29 | Operations Resources in an ERP System

INVENTORY:

Critical ERP Modules:

Inventory Management
Manufacturing Resource Management
Accounting
Quality Management
Purchasing
Supply Chain Management

CAPACITY:

Critical ERP Modules:

Accounting
Manufacturing Resource Management
Quality Management
Supply Chain Management
Human Resource Management
Inventory Management

ERP Unified Database

FACILITIES:

Critical ERP Modules:

Facilities
Manufacturing Resource Management
Quality Management
Financial

WORKFORCE

Critical ERP Modules:

Human Resources
Manufacturing Resource Management
Quality Management

CHAPTER SUMMARY

Planning for operations resources is an important activity for any business. It can mean success or failure, because it dictates how resources will be used and whether or not they will contribute to value creation. Successful plans—those that result in cost savings and an increase in alternatives—enhance profitability through increases in net sales and decreases in costs. They can enhance competitive opportunities by more closely matching resources to objectives. Plans that fail can result in money spent that can never be expected to provide a return, opportunities missed, and customers lost.

The primary input to most business plans is the forecast for demand, which often forms the basis for deciding how much of a particular resource will be needed. The accuracy of the forecast depends on several factors, but two important ones are the time horizon and the appropriateness of the model used. The accuracy of forecasts often determines the accuracy of plans, which dictate how well the availability of a resource matches customer needs. This match between resource availability and what customers want often affects the value attributes of costs, quality, and timeliness. The decisions that depend on accurate resource plans affect profitability measures. Having too few resources means that demand isn't met. Having too many resources means that resources are idle.

Planning for resources with a unified database, a framework known as enterprise re-source planning (ERP), has the potential to improve the planning functions as well as the business processes themselves. Despite costs and difficulties, ERP provides a way to integrate not only different business functions, but different businesses on different continents.

Successful planning alone does not ensure business success. Once plans are imple-mented, the actual results of the implementation must be compared to what was planned. If they are not what was planned, action must be taken to get plans and reality in sync. In the following chapters, techniques designed for specific resource decisions are addressed.

KEY TERMS

absolute error, 433

causal forecast, 417

contingency plans, 409

cycle, 421

decline stage, 414

forecast bias, 433

forecast including trend (FIT), 427

growth stage, 413

introduction stage, 413

life cycle, 413

maturation stage, 414

mean absolute deviation (MAD), 433

mean absolute percentage error (MAPE), 434

mean forecast error (MFE), 436

planning horizon, 411

qualitative forecast, 417

quantitative forecast, 421

random fluctuation, 000

running sum of forecast error (RSFE), 436

saturation stage, 414

seasonality, 421

simple exponential smoothing, 426

times series forecasting, 417

tracking signal, 437

trend, 421

trend-adjusted exponential smoothing, 427

KEY FORMULAE

Equations for a Line for Causal Forecasting and Linear Trend Analysis

General equation for a line

(10.1) $$y = a + bx$$

where

> y = dependent variable
> a = y-intercept
> b = slope
> x = independent (or predictor) variable

Equation for the Slope

(10.2) $$b = \frac{\sum xy - n\bar{x}\,\bar{y}}{\sum x^2 - n\bar{x}^2}$$

where

> b = slope
> x = values of the independent variable
> y = known values of the dependent variable
> $\bar{x}$ = average of the values of x
> $\bar{y}$ = average of the values of y
> n = number of data points

Formula for the y-intercept

(10.3) $$a = \bar{y} - b\bar{x}$$

where

> a = the y-intercept
> $\bar{x}$ = the average of the values of x
> $\bar{y}$ = the average of the values of y

Simple Moving Average

(10.4) $$F_t = \frac{A_{t-1} + A_{t-2} + A_{t-3} + \ldots + A_{t-n}}{n}$$

where

> F_t = the forecast for period t
> A_{t-1} = the actual demand in period $t - 1$
> n = the number of periods in the moving average

Weighted Moving Average

(10.5) $$F_t = w_{t-1}A_{t-1} + w_{t-2}A_{t-2} + w_{t-3}A_{t-3} + \ldots + w_{t-n}A_{t-n}$$

where

> F_t = forecast for period t
> A_{t-1} = actual demand in period $t - 1$
> w_{t-1} = weight assigned to period $t - 1$
> w_{t-2} = weight assigned to period $t - 2$
> w_{t-3} = weight assigned to period $t - 3$
> n = number of periods in the moving average

Simple Exponential Smoothing

(10.6) $$F_{t+1} = \alpha(A_t) + (1 - \alpha)F_t \quad \text{or}$$

(10.7) $$F_{t+1} = F_t + \alpha(A_t - F_t)$$

where

> F_{t+1} = forecast for the next time period
> α = smoothing constant, which must be greater than 0 and less than 1
> A_t = actual demand for the most recent period
> F_t = forecast for the most recent period

Trend-Adjusted Exponential Smoothing

(10.8) $$FIT_{t+1} = F_t + T_t$$

where F_t is the smoothed forecast, T_t is the trend estimate, and

(10.9) $$F_t = FIT_t + \alpha(A_t - FIT_t)$$

(10.10) $$T_t = T_{t-1} + \beta(FIT_t - FIT_{t-1} - T_{t-1})$$

where α and β are smoothing constants.

Linear Trend Equation

(10.11) $$y = a + bt$$

where

a = y intercept
b = slope
t = time period

Mean Absolute Deviation

(10.12)
$$MAD = \sum_{t=1}^{n} \frac{|A_t - F_t|}{n}$$

Mean Squared Error

(10.13)
$$MSE = \sum_{t=1}^{n} \frac{(A_t - F_t)^2}{n}$$

Mean Absolute Percentage Error

(10.14)
$$MAPE = \frac{\sum_{t=1}^{n} \frac{|A_t - F_t|}{A_t}}{n}$$

where

A_t = actual demand
F_t = forecast
n = number of periods

Tracking Signal

(10.16)
$$TS = \frac{RSFE}{MAD}$$

SOLVED PROBLEMS

1. Causal Forecasting with Simple Linear Regression

The following data comparing sales and interest rates were collected by a chain of car dealerships.

Period	Interest Rate	Sales
1	0.054	460
2	0.062	532
3	0.063	510
4	0.065	561
5	0.069	580
6	0.069	565
7	0.071	594
8	0.075	610
9	0.077	606
10	0.081	631

Compute a sales forecast for an interest rate of .067.

EXHIBIT 10.30	Graph of Interest Rate and Car Sales Data for Solved Problem

Solution

Step	Objective	Explanation
1.	Graph the data.	See Exhibit 10.30 below.
2.	Compute a regression equation for the data.	Use the regression function in Excel, with sales as the input y range and interest rate as the input x range.
3	Interpret the regression output.	The y intercept is 133.501 The x coefficient is 6288.609
4.	Compute the forecast.	$y = a + bx$ $= 133.501 + [(6288.609)(.067)]$ $= 133.501 + 421.337$ $= 554.835$

2. Weighted Moving Average

Using the following data, compute a four-week weighted moving average forecast for Period 6 using weights of .5, .3, .1, and .1

Period	Demand
1	116
2	121
3	116
4	124
5	127

Solution

Step	Objective	Explanation
1.	Identify the data to be averaged.	We are computing a 4-period weighted moving average for period 6, so we would average the demand for periods 5,4,3, and 2. Using the weights provided, the largest weight would be assigned to the most recent demand (period 5).

2.   Multiply each demand in the data to be averaged by the appropriate weight, then sum the products to get 124.4 as the forecast.

Period	Demand	Weights	Demand × Weight
1	116		
2	121	0.1	12.1
3	116	0.1	11.6
4	124	0.3	37.2
5	127	0.5	63.5
6			Forecast = 124.4

3. Simple Exponential Smoothing

Using the data below, forecast the demand for period 6 with simple exponential smoothing and an α of .25.

Period	Demand	Forecast
1	116	110
2	121	112
3	116	120
4	124	127
5	127	123

Solution

Step	Objective	Explanation
1.	Identify the previous forecast and previous actual demand.	The previous demand is 127. The previous forecast is 123
2.	Using Equation 10.6, compute the forecast for period 6.	$F_{t+1} = F_t + \alpha(A_t - F_t)$ $F_6 = 123 + .25(127 - 123)$ $= 123 + .25(4)$ $= 124$

4. Trend-Adjusted Exponential Smoothing

The past 12 periods of demand for a particular notebook computer are:

1	2	3	4	5	6	7	8	9	10	11	12
144	154	146	158	150	158	156	164	167	162	169	172

Forecast demand using trend-adjusted exponential smoothing with $\alpha = .1$ and $\beta = .9$ Use an initial trend value of 2 and an initial forecast of 144.

Solution

Step	Objective	Explanation
1.	Compute $FIT_{t+1} =$ FIT_2 using Equation 10.8.	$FIT_2 = F_1 + T_1 = 144 + 2 = 146$
2.	To determine FIT_3, compute the values for F_2 and T_2 using Equations 10.9 and 10.10.	$F_2 = FIT_2 + \alpha(A_2 - FIT_2)$ $= 146 + 0.1(154 - 146)$ $= 146.8$ $T_2 = T_1 + \beta(FIT_2 - FIT_1 - T_1)$ $= 2 + 0.9(146 - 144 - 2)$ $= 2$ $FIT_3 = F_2 + T_2 = 146.8 + 2 = 148.8$

Step	Objective	Explanation				
3.	Continue by finding F_3 and T_3, and compute FIT_4 and proceed through all periods.			Demand		
		Period (t)	(A)	F	T	FIT_t
		1	144	144	2	144
		2	154	146.8	2	146
		3	146	148.52	2.72	148.8
		4	158	151.92	2.47	151.24
		5	150	153.95	3.08	154.38
		6	158	157.12	2.68	157.02
		7	156	159.42	2.77	159.80
		8	164	162.37	2.43	162.19
		9	167	165.02	2.59	164.80
		10	162	167.05	2.79	167.61
		11	169	169.75	2.28	169.84
		12	172	172.03	2.21	172.04

5. Linear Trend Equation

The following demand is thought to have a strong upward trend. Using the linear trend equation, determine the forecast for period 9.

Period	Demand
1	420
2	428
3	437
4	446
5	455
6	461
7	470
8	484

Solution

Step	Objective	Explanation
1.	Using the regression function in Excel, determine the equation for the trend.	Using the Excel regression function, with the periods as the x input variable and the demand as the y input variable, y-intercept is 410.5357. The x coefficient is 8.7976.
2.	Using Equation 10.10, $y = a + bt$, determine the forecast for period 9.	$y = 410.5357 + 8.7976(9)$ $= 489.7141$

6. Seasonal Indices

The following quarterly demand data is seasonal. Compute the seasonal indices for each of the four quarters and forecast the demand for the upcoming summer quarter.

	Year 1	Year 2	Year 3	Year 4
Fall	258	244	250	249
Winter	680	701	693	684
Spring	462	476	459	470
Summer	104	117	123	110

Solution

Step	Objective	Explanation
1.	Compute the overall average of the demand.	The average is 380.

Step 2. For each demand, divide the actual demand by the average.

Year	Quarter	Demand	Seasonal Ratio (Demand/Avg)
Year 1	Fall	258	0.678
	Winter	680	1.789
	Spring	462	1.215
	Summer	104	0.273
Year 2	Fall	244	0.642
	Winter	701	1.844
	Spring	476	1.252
	Summer	117	0.307
Year 3	Fall	250	0.657
	Winter	693	1.823
	Spring	459	1.207
	Summer	123	0.323
Year 4	Fall	249	0.655
	Winter	684	1.800
	Spring	470	1.236
	Summer	110	0.289

Step 3. Compute the average of the seasonal ratios for each quarter.

Quarter	Seasonal Index
Fall	0.66
Winter	1.81
Spring	1.23
Summer	0.30

7. Multiplicative Model for Seasonality and Trend

The following demand has seasonality and trend. Forecast the demand for period 17 using the multiplicative model for seasonality and trend.

Year	Period	Quarter	Demand
Year 1	1	Fall	1024
	2	Winter	430
	3	Spring	638
	4	Summer	189
Year 2	5	Fall	1038
	6	Winter	451
	7	Spring	650
	8	Summer	204
Year 3	9	Fall	1068
	10	Winter	447
	11	Spring	657
	12	Summer	230
Year 4	13	Fall	1085
	14	Winter	466
	15	Spring	680
	16	Summer	241

Solution

Step	Objective	Explanation
1.	Compute the seasonal indices for the four quarters. First compute the average demand. Then divide each demand by the average to compute seasonal ratios. Average the seasonal ratios for each quarter.	Average demand = 593.625

Year	Quarter	Demand	Seasonal Ratios	Seasonal Indices
Year 1	Fall	1024	1.72	1.78
	Winter	430	0.72	0.76
	Spring	638	1.07	1.11
	Summer	189	0.32	0.36
Year 2	Fall	1038	1.75	
	Winter	451	0.76	
	Spring	650	1.09	
	Summer	204	0.34	
Year 3	Fall	1068	1.80	
	Winter	447	0.75	
	Spring	657	1.11	
	Summer	230	0.39	
Year 4	Fall	1085	1.83	
	Winter	466	0.79	
	Spring	680	1.15	
	Summer	241	0.41	

Step	Objective
2.	Deseasonalize the demand by dividing each demand by its appropriate seasonal index.

Year	Quarter	Period	Demand	Seasonal Indices	Deseasonalized Demand
Year 1	Fall	1	1024	1.78	576.87
	Winter	2	430	0.76	569.14
	Spring	3	638	1.11	577.12
	Summer	4	189	0.36	519.42
Year 2	Fall	5	1038	1.78	584.75
	Winter	6	451	0.76	596.93
	Spring	7	650	1.11	587.97
	Summer	8	204	0.36	560.65
Year 3	Fall	9	1068	1.78	601.65
	Winter	10	447	0.76	591.64
	Spring	11	657	1.11	594.30
	Summer	12	230	0.36	632.10
Year 4	Fall	13	1085	1.78	611.23
	Winter	14	466	0.76	616.79
	Spring	15	680	1.11	615.11
	Summer	16	241	0.36	662.33

Step	Objective	Explanation
3.	Using Excel's regression function, determine the linear trend equation.	Using the time period as the x input variable and the deseasonalized demand as the y input variable, the y-intercept turns out to be 549.72 and the x-coefficient is 5.17.
4.	Using the linear trend equation and the appropriate seasonal index, forecast demand for period 17.	$y = 549.72 + 13(5.17)$ $= 549.72 + 67.21$ $= 616.93$ Forecast = $616.93 \times$ seasonal index $= 616.93 \times 1.78$ $= 1{,}098.14$

8. Mean Absolute Deviation (MAD)

Compute the MAD after period 5 for the following demand and forecast data.

Period	Demand	Forecast
1	168	150
2	174	178
3	190	196
4	181	178
5	208	194

Solution

Step	Objective	Explanation				
1.	Compute the forecast error for each period.	Period	Demand	Forecast	Error	
		1	168	150	18	
		2	174	178	−4	
		3	190	196	−6	
		4	181	178	3	
		5	208	194	14	
2.	Determine the absolute value of the forecast errors.	Period	Demand	Forecast	Error	Abs. Error
		1	168	150	18	18
		2	174	178	−4	4
		3	190	196	−6	6
		4	181	178	3	3
		5	208	194	14	14
3.	Compute the MAD.	The mean of the absolute errors is 9.0				

9. Mean Square Error (MSE)

Using the same data as the MAD example, compute the MSE after period 5.

Solution

Step	Objective	Explanation				
1.	Compute the forecast error for each period.	Period	Demand	Forecast	Error	
		1	168	150	18	
		2	174	178	−4	
		3	190	196	−6	
		4	181	178	3	
		5	208	194	14	
2.	Square the errors.	Period	Demand	Forecast	Error	Squared Error
		1	168	150	18	324
		2	174	178	−4	16
		3	190	196	−6	36
		4	181	178	3	9
		5	208	194	14	196
3.	Compute the mean of the squared errors.	116.2				

10. Mean Absolute Percentage Error (MAPE)

Using the data from the previous example, compute the MAPE after period 5.

Solution

Step	Objective	Explanation

1. Compute the errors and the absolute errors.

Period	Demand	Forecast	Error	Absolute Error
1	168	150	18	18
2	174	178	−4	4
3	190	196	−6	6
4	181	178	3	3
5	208	194	14	14

2. Compute the percentage for each absolute error by dividing each by the corresponding demand.

Period	Demand	Forecast	Error	Abs. Error	Absolute % Error
1	168	150	18	18	0.11
2	174	178	−4	4	0.02
3	190	196	−6	6	0.03
4	181	178	3	3	0.02
5	208	194	14	14	0.07

3. Compute mean of the absolute percentage errors.

Mean = .05 (5.0 percent)

11. Mean Forecast Error (MFE)

Using the same data as used in the previous example, compute the mean forecast error at period 5.

Solution

Step	Objective	Explanation

1. Compute the errors by subtracting the forecast from the actual demand.

Period	Demand	Forecast	Error
1	168	150	18
2	174	178	−4
3	190	196	−6
4	181	178	3
5	208	194	14

2. Compute the mean of the errors by summing and dividing by 5.

The mean is 5.0

12. Running Sum of Forecast Error (RSFE)

Compute the running sum of forecast errors for the same data as the previous example.

Solution

Step	Objective	Explanation

1. Compute the errors by subtracting the forecast from the actual demand.

Period	Demand	Forecast	Error
1	168	150	18
2	174	178	−4
3	190	196	−6
4	181	178	3
5	208	194	14

2. Sum the errors.

The sum is 25.

13. Tracking Signal (TS)

Compute the tracking signal for the same data as the previous example.

Solution

Step	Objective	Explanation

1. Compute the errors and absolute errors.

Period	Demand	Forecast	Error	Abs. Error
1	168	150	18	18
2	174	178	−4	4
3	190	196	−6	6
4	181	178	3	3
5	208	194	14	14

2. Compute the RSFE by summing the errors. Compute the MAD by averaging the absolute errors.

For each period, these values are:

Period	Demand	Forecast	Error	Abs. Error	RSFE	MAD
1	168	150	18	18	18	18
2	174	178	−4	4	14	11
3	190	196	−6	6	8	9.33
4	181	178	3	3	11	7.75
5	208	194	14	14	25	9

3. Compute the tracking signal by dividing the RSFE by the MAD.

Period	Demand	Forecast	Error	Abs. Error	RSFE	MAD	TS
1	168	150	18	18	18	18	1
2	174	178	−4	4	14	11	1.27
3	190	196	−6	6	8	9.33	0.86
4	181	178	3	3	11	7.75	1.4
5	208	194	14	14	25	9	2.78

REVIEW QUESTIONS

1. What are the financial benefits of good planning? How does good planning affect profitability measures?

2. What is meant by "planning horizon"? How is the minimum planning horizon determined?

3. Why are shorter planning horizons desirable from the standpoint of planning accuracy and success?

4. Describe the product life cycle. What are its stages?

5. How does the product life cycle affect planning?

6. As product life cycles have been compressed, how have planning processes been affected?

7. Why is lead time compression important?

8. Describe collaborative planning, forecasting, and replenishment. Why is it important for supply chain management success?

9. Compare qualitative and quantitative forecasting approaches.

10. What is meant by "causal forecasting"?

11. What is a time series?

12. Describe the four components of a time series.

13. When a time series contains random fluctuation, but no other apparent time series components, what forecasting approach is most appropriate?

14. How should the alpha used in exponential smoothing be selected?

15. Describe how simple exponential smoothing is like a weighted moving average.

16. What are the two important aspects of forecast error? How are they measured?

17. What is an ERP system? Why is it useful?

18. What is meant by supply chain management?

DISCUSSION AND EXPLORATION

1. Describe the life cycle of a product you are familiar with. How long did the life cycle last? What was the reaction of the producer as the product progressed through its life cycle?

2. Identify current plans you have for semester or summer break. What is the necessary timing of decisions that must be made relative to those plans? What are advantages and costs that could result from delaying those decisions?

3. How will you protect yourself from unexpected contingencies that could interfere with your break plans?

4. Describe the process you use to plan for financial needs associated with your education. How far ahead do you develop these plans? How do they influence your behavior? What contingencies do you prepare for?

5. How can one forecast be shown to be more accurate than another?

6. How do the components of a time series dictate the appropriate forecasting techniques to use?

7. What would you expect to result from using simple exponential smoothing to forecast a demand that has a trend?

PROBLEMS **HM**

Solutions to odd-numbered problems are located on the text's Online Center (http://mhhe.com/opsnow3e).

1. Campus Bookstore tries to predict the number of books it should stock based on the number of classes requiring the book. A regression analysis provided the following equation for a particular book:

$$y = 11.5441 + 19.6324x$$

Next semester, five classes will require the book as reading. What is the forecast for demand?

2. The City Foundation takes in donations from area businesses and distributes needed food and clothing to less fortunate people. Below is the data set, showing the amount donated with the size of the company. Using a spreadsheet, forecast the donations for a company with 50 employees.

Amount Donated ($)	Number of Employees
5,000.00	50
1,500.00	15
2,250.00	60
7,000.00	75

Amount Donated ($)	Number of Employees
3,000.00	22
9,000.00	100
6,000.00	25
7,500.00	60
1,000.00	10
4,500.00	32

3. JT Outfitters sells jackets personalized with the customer's favorite college team. The company is determined to forecast its demand accurately. You have been asked to make a presentation on the use of simple linear regression as a causal forecasting technique. Use the following data in your presentation. Also, the company is considering lowering the current price of the jackets to $220. What will the demand be at that price?

Jackets Sold	Price ($)
450	$250.00
787	225.00
580	249.00
410	300.00
515	250.00
900	199.00
790	205.00

4. A marina on Whitewater Reservoir has determined that its summer weekend fuel sales figures are closely related to the water level on the lake. As the lake level goes up, there is more boat traffic and an increase in gasoline sales. Water level and gas sales data from the past summer weekends are presented below.

Lake Level (feet)	Gallons of Gas Sold
12.1	2046
13.2	2111
13.5	2214
14.2	2460
15.0	2640
15.4	2710
16.2	2924
16.7	3090
17.1	3332
17.2	3460
17.4	3671
17.5	3712

a. Use least squares regression to determine the equation that best describes the relationship between lake level and gasoline sales.

b. The Army Corp of Engineers has posted that they will maintain a lake level of 15.8 feet for the next two weekends. Forecast gas sales for those weekends.

c. Evaluate the use of your technique if heavy rains cause the lake to rise to levels above 18 feet.

5. Grill King sells barbeque grills. Accurate demand forecasting is essential to the customer service level required by the company's customers. The company uses a four-period weighted moving average technique. Use the information below to calculate the forecast for August.

Period	Demand	Weight
April	83	0.1
May	89	0.2
June	95	0.3
July	96	0.4

6. The Rid-em Race Car is a popular children's toy at Christmas time. The last six periods of demand are given below. Calculate the forecast for January using a three-period weighted moving average with weights of 0.6, 0.3, and 0.1 and a six-period moving average. What conclusions can be drawn from comparing the results?

Period	Demand
July	275
August	290
September	280
October	299
November	350
December	550

7. The last six weeks of demand for Tie's Tie Dyed are given below. Use the information to calculate three-week and six-week weighted moving averages. Explain the difference between the two measures.

Week	Demand	Three-Period Weight	Six-Period Weight
1	126		0.05
2	132		0.05
3	149		0.1
4	154	0.2	0.2
5	134	0.3	0.25
6	127	0.5	0.35

8. Dill Computers has seen the following pattern of demand for its computers. Provide three-period and six-period simple moving average forecasts for as many periods as possible. Graph the results. What conclusions can be drawn about the two different methods?

Period	Demand
1	149
2	153
3	147
4	148
5	154
6	187
7	164
8	152
9	148
10	154
11	151
12	149

9. Books-N-Things sells schools supplies on campus. One of its biggest sellers is a blank computer disk. The demand for disks in the current period was 850, and the forecast was 782. Using simple exponential smoothing and a smoothing constant of 0.25, compute the next period's forecast.

10. E-Traders' World is an online investment service. The company anticipated demand for the current period to be 59 transactions. The demand was actually 49. Using simple exponential smoothing and an alpha of 0.4, forecast the next period's demand.

11. Mr. Pizza calculates demand for its pizzas in slices. Last month, Mr. Pizza sold 5,015 slices of its pizza. The company anticipates selling 5,125 slices for the current period. Use a simple exponential smoothing model with a smoothing constant of 0.1 to forecast demand. What is the result if you use a smoothing constant of 0.4?

12. Walton Container Manufacturing supplies cardboard containers and packaging materials to a variety of customers, predominantly in the mail-order electronics business. One of their top-selling containers is a 4" × 6" × 2" box. This month they forecast a demand of 8,400 units, but demand was actually 9,400 units. Use simple exponential smoothing and an alpha of 0.35 to forecast the demand for next month.

13. Balogh's Lifting Supplies provides weight lifting products for the Gainesville, Florida, area. Given the storage issues related to his products, Andy Balogh takes weekly deliveries (on Mondays) from his primary supplier, based on forecasts he calls in on Friday. In order to test a new forecasting system using simple exponential smoothing, Andy has collected demand data for a curling bar from the past 5 weeks, presented below.

Week	Demand
1	36
2	48
3	31
4	25
5	39

Assuming a week 1 forecast of 32, forecast the demand for weeks 2 through 5, using an alpha value of 0.3.

14. The local health clinic experienced the five-week demand for its services presented in the table. Calculate the demand for period 6 using trend-adjusted exponential smoothing, using $\alpha = 0.2$, $\beta = 0.6$, an initial trend of 1, and an initial forecast of 80.

Week	Demand (A)
1	80
2	82
3	84
4	81
5	79

15. A-Gear sells sweatshirts. The past eight weeks' demand is given below. You have been asked to develop a forecast using the exponential smoothing model with a trend adjustment. Develop the model using $\alpha = 0.1$ and $\beta = 0.9$. Use an initial trend value of 2 and an initial forecast of 144. Graph the actual demand with the forecast.

Week	Demand (A)
1	144
2	154
3	146
4	158
5	150
6	158
7	156
8	164

16. Ian's Eatery has the six-week demand history shown below. Using $\alpha = 0.1$, $\beta = 0.9$, an initial trend of 8, and an initial forecast of 900, forecast the demand for period 7 using trend-adjusted exponential smoothing.

Week	Demand (A)
1	799
2	852
3	878
4	912
5	942
6	994

17. The demand for blazers at a local clothing store suggests that a forecasting approach that utilizes trend data would be appropriate. Using the data below, develop a forecast for each month using the FIT model with $a = 0.5$, $b = 0.3$, an initial trend of 4, and an initial forecast (FIT_t) of 240.

Month	Demand
1	248
2	256
3	266
4	261
5	269
6	272
7	273
8	281

18. A small producer of standardized cell phone components wishes to forecast the monthly demand for products that have shown a positive trend but no seasonality. The equation for the trend has been computed from the past 12 months' demand to be $y = 2452 + 678t$. Forecast the demand for the next month (month 13).

19. Global Electronics sells a complete selection of audio, video, computer, and photographic products. The following 12-month time series for plasma screen TVs shows a strong upward trend.

Month	Demand
1	3450
2	3490
3	3502
4	3520
5	3565
6	3560
7	3571
8	3611
9	3613
10	3624
11	3637
12	3664

Compute the equation for the trend and forecast the demand for months 13, 14, and 15.

20. As the availability of ATM machines and credit card acceptance have increased throughout the world, Trustworthy Travelers Checks have noticed a substantial decline in use. The following sales data represent quarterly sales figures from banks across the United States that sell Trustworthy Checks.

Quarter	Sales
1	36,432
2	35,678
3	35,265
4	33,804
5	34,605
6	32,450
7	33,012
8	32,100

a. Forecast the demand for Trustworthy Checks for each quarter of the next year.

b. Trustworthy has determined that, given the fixed costs associated with its business, it cannot be profitable with sales below 28,000 units. Given the current trend, when will it cease to be profitable?

21. CDE Insurance monitors injury claims in several different common categories. Analysis results will be used to make adjustments to premiums based on trends in various injury categories. Neck injury claims, on a monthly basis, are shown below for the past 2 years.

Month	Claims	Month	Claims
1	135	13	159
2	131	14	167
3	139	15	278
4	142	16	184
5	149	17	192
6	147	18	183
7	160	19	204
8	153	20	194
9	159	21	201
10	169	22	206
11	180	23	199
12	176	24	211

a. Determine the equation for the trend, and forecast neck injuries for the next three months.

b. Graph the data, and evaluate it for possible errors. Do you think there is a potential key-entry error in the data? Explain your answer.

c. Remove the data point in question, recompute the trend equation, and forecast the demand for the next three months again. What was the change in your forecasts?

22. Sno-Way is a snowplow service specializing in clearing residential driveways. Last year's monthly and quarterly demand is given below. Use the information to calculate the average quarterly sales and quarterly seasonal indexes. Explain what the seasonal indexes mean.

Quarter	Month 1	Month 2	Month 3
1	$12,451.00	$12,187.00	$8,754.00
2	3,420.00	452.00	—
3	—	—	324.00
4	987.00	6,450.00	10,651.00

23. The Daily News Corporation has recorded the following demand for its newspaper. Use the data provided to compute the seasonal index for each day of the week. The

newspaper expects demand to go up to an average of 800 per day in week 5. Forecast the demand for each day of week 5.

Day	Week 1	Week 2	Week 3	Week 4
Sunday	945	968	924	957
Monday	675	642	634	661
Tuesday	624	687	698	614
Wednesday	648	683	619	664
Thursday	689	621	634	661
Friday	701	698	687	723
Saturday	754	731	768	722

24. 2-Wheelers rents bikes at a state park. Use the demand information given below to calculate the seasonal index for each month and forecast demand for the following year (year 5), if average monthly demand is expected to increase to 20 rentals per month.

Month	Year 1	Year 2	Year 3	Year 4
Jan	0	0	0	0
Feb	0	0	0	4
March	8	12	12	14
April	14	16	16	20
May	22	21	23	24
June	23	24	20	21
July	28	24	22	21
Aug	23	26	21	22
Sept	22	21	17	16
Oct	15	15	14	12
Nov	9	6	2	0
Dec	0	0	0	0

25. Citywide Bank tracks the number of customer transactions per day. Use the information below to calculate seasonal indexes for each day. Once completed, use the seasonal indexes to forecast the number of transactions the bank will have the following week in week 5.

Day	Week 1	Week 2	Week 3	Week 4
Monday	126	132	118	104
Tuesday	121	117	126	134
Wednesday	104	101	97	109
Thursday	109	87	111	104
Friday	187	189	198	183

At the end of week 5, actual demand was as follows: Monday, 143; Tuesday, 134; Wednesday, 124; Thursday, 101; Friday, 198. Calculate the MAD and MFE. Was the forecasting method biased?

26. The Beach House sells products for pools and beach recreation. Sales of swimsuits for the last eight quarters are presented below. Use the data to compute seasonal indexes for each period. Forecast demand for the next quarter using the multiplicative model.

Quarter	Period	Demand
Q1	1	12
Q2	2	26
Q3	3	28
Q4	4	2
Q1	5	16
Q2	6	31
Q3	7	29
Q4	8	3

Average Demand = 18.38

27. The Springfield Homers, a professional football team, has been tracking sales of its merchandise for the past two years. The team identified trend and seasonality in the time series. Use the information below, along with the multiplicative model, to forecast sales for the upcoming year.

Season	Period	Demand ($)
Jan	1	64,976.00
Feb	2	26,567.00
March	3	16,314.00
April	4	9,007.00
May	5	14,599.00
June	6	11,092.00
July	7	18,377.00
Aug	8	32,789.00
Sept	9	75,312.00
Oct	10	68,980.00
Nov	11	72,134.00
Dec	12	81,613.00
Jan	13	68,321.00
Feb	14	25,633.00
March	15	17,890.00
April	16	14,523.00
May	17	14,789.00
June	18	14,234.00
July	19	17,641.00
Aug	20	46,790.00
Sept	21	73,689.00
Oct	22	71,099.00
Nov	23	75,624.00
Dec	24	84,145.00

28. Rain-Stop Umbrellas has recorded sales data for the last two years. Graph the information and determine if there are both trend and seasonal components. Use the most appropriate method to forecast demand for the following year.

Season	Period	Demand
Spring	1	89
Summer	2	64
Fall	3	46
Winter	4	62
Spring	5	107
Summer	6	67
Fall	7	61
Winter	8	68

29. Ike's Bikes is a small North Carolina bike shop specializing in mountain bike sales and rentals. Ike has kept quarterly sales figures for the past three years. Sales have increased during each of those years. Ike's sales data is shown below:

Quarter	Period	Sales
Q1	1	125
Q2	2	90
Q3	3	70
Q4	4	82
Q1	5	136
Q2	6	107
Q3	7	80
Q4	8	92
Q1	9	147
Q2	10	113
Q3	11	89
Q4	12	101

The trend equation for the data is $Y = 0.68t + 98.23$, where $t = 1$ corresponds to period 1.

a. Graph the data.

b. Determine the seasonal indices for each of the four quarters.

c. Using the multiplicative model, forecast the demand for each quarter of the next year.

30. The forecasts and demands for the last six periods are given below for The Duckett Co. Calculate the error, the absolute error, and the MAD. Explain your results.

Period	Demand	Forecast
1	867	875
2	916	900
3	923	915
4	875	880
5	921	905
6	934	920

31. Hidden Beauty Nature Center has asked you to help forecast the number of visitors to the company's park. Using the information below, create a forecast for weeks 3 through 6 using a two-week moving average. Also forecast the demand for weeks 3 through 6 using simple exponential smoothing ($\alpha = 0.2$ and a forecast for week 2 of 175). Compute the MAD and mean forecast error for each method. Compare the accuracy of two forecasting methods.

Period	Demand
Week 1	189
Week 2	174
Week 3	186
Week 4	193
Week 5	191
Week 6	187

32. The information below is from the Aloe Corp. Calculate the error for the forecasts, the squared error, and the MSE.

Period	Demand	Forecast
1	62	65
2	67	65
3	64	67
4	71	67

33. The Music Man uses simple exponential smoothing to forecast the sale of CDs. The manager has proposed changing the α from 0.4 to 0.1. Using the information below, and a forecast in week 2 of 285, compare the two forecasting methods using the MAD and MFE.

Period	Demand
1	289
2	296
3	354
4	287
5	301
6	281
7	294
8	318

34. Super-Fresh, a local grocery store, forecasts its monthly electric bill. Using the information below, calculate a forecast for periods 3 through 12 using a two-month weighted average with the most recent month accounting for 70 percent of the importance of the forecast. Calculate the MAD and MFE for the forecasts. Comment on the results.

Period	Demand ($)
1	20,134.00
2	18,945.00
3	19,876.00
4	35,871.00
5	26,541.00
6	24,365.00
7	21,654.00
8	33,487.00
9	19,875.00
10	22,871.00
11	21,211.00
12	38,789.00

35. The following table shows the forecast number of students and the actual number of students enrolled in State University's MGT 100 course. Calculate the MAD and running sum of forecast error (RSFE). Explain the results.

Year	Actual	Expected
1985	67	65
1986	68	65
1987	71	65
1988	73	65
1989	63	65
1990	61	65
1991	62	65
1992	64	65
1993	68	65
1994	71	65

36. The city of Wasso has recorded the number of passengers using its public transportation system the past five days. Decide between two weighted average forecasting methods, one giving each of the last two periods equal weight, the other using a 70–30 split from the last two periods (70 percent for the most recent period). Calculate the MAD and RSFE. Which forecasting method is better? Explain your answer.

Day	Demand
1	387
2	364
3	399
4	412
5	393

37. The Blue-Notes are a small jazz band that have been playing together for a year. Last January, they believed that it would cost them $3,800 the first month to purchase the needed instruments and then $500 a month for lessons after that. It actually only cost them $3,456 the first month, but the monthly lesson costs varied greatly after that: $600, $700, $430, $530, $480, $94, $1,137, $415, $478, $784, and $723. Evaluate the accuracy of their initial cost predictions using the MAD and the RSFE. What do your answers say about the band's initial cost forecast?

38. Better-Built Construction Company forecasts the number of workers it believes it will need for each month. Last year's forecast and actual number of employees hired are given below. Use MSE and MFE to measure the forecast accuracy. What conclusions can be drawn from the measurements?

Month	Employees	Forecast
1	23	25
2	26	25
3	35	30
4	39	40
5	45	45
6	47	50
7	49	50
8	53	50
9	47	45
10	42	40
11	31	30
12	24	250

39. A small brokerage firm forecasts the stock transactions its customers request. The data for the demand and forecasts for the past six weeks is shown below. Compute the MAPE.

Week	Demand	Forecast
1	980	1010
2	1030	1058
3	1008	1021
4	936	967
5	972	917
6	1112	1092

40. As a part of its plan to reduce costs, Greenville Community Hospital is attempting to better match the check-in staff to demand. The forecast of demand for the past 12 days, along with the actual number of check-ins, is presented below. Compute the MAPE.

Day	Demand	Forecast
1	30	35
2	41	33
3	36	41
4	51	42
5	29	36
6	34	27
7	39	32
8	44	49
9	50	54
10	35	42
11	28	26
12	58	38

41. The Business School's advising office forecasts walk-ins in an attempt to match the staffing of work-study students to demand. The demand is somewhat seasonal on a weekly basis, with low demands on Mondays and Fridays and higher demands during midweek. The daily forecast and demand for a typical week is given below. Compute the MAPE for the forecasts.

Day	Demand	Forecast
Monday	34	35
Tuesday	48	33
Wednesday	54	41
Thursday	42	40
Friday	23	36

42. Erica and Roger have been bored at the ice cream shop where they both work and have decided to have a contest to see who can best forecast the number of customers during each hour. Their forecasts and the actual demand data are given below. Compute the error, RSFE, MAD, and tracking signal for each. Interpret your results.

Hour	Erica's Forecast	Roger's Forecast	Demand
Hour 1	15	12	9
Hour 2	16	20	13
Hour 3	18	22	15
Hour 4	30	38	28
Hour 5	28	34	24
Hour 6	28	24	31
Hour 7	20	21	26
Hour 8	14	22	18

43. The town of Reilly has a volunteer EMT squad that responds to calls from the town itself, as well as a nearby interstate highway. They have forecast calls per week for the past three months. Compute the error, RSFE, MAD, and tracking signal based on the following forecast data. Interpret your results.

Week	Forecast	Demand
1	9	10
2	9	11
3	9	13
4	9	6
5	9	5
6	9	9
7	9	11
8	9	6
9	9	12
10	9	14
11	9	8
12	9	7

ADVANCED PROBLEMS

1. Nika Mariah was starting to worry. As the production manager for Paul's Plastic Pitcher Company, she had to determine how many plastic pitchers would be ordered in the next quarter. Paul's supplied pitchers to bars and restaurants for beer and water service. Sales have been growing steadily, and Nika was worried about capacity. She thought she might have to work the crew overtime in order to meet the demand. Just then, Johnny J. Jones, regional sales manger, walked into her office. "Why so glum, chum?" asked JJ. Nika expressed her concerns. "24,300" said JJ, "You can go to the bank with that!" Nika knew that Johnny had been with the company for a long time, and that his guess might be good. Still, she wanted to check it before creating her production schedule.

   a. Use the following historical data to calculate a forecast for period 5 using a Moving Weighted Average with weights of .1, .2, .3, and .4 for periods 1 through 4.

Period	Demand	Forecast
1	16,000	15,500
2	18,000	
3	19,000	
4	22,500	
5		

   b. Create a forecast for period 5 using Exponential Smoothing with $\alpha = .4$.

   c. Calculate a Trend-Adjusted Exponential Smoothing using $T_1 = 2100$ (based on average increase), $\alpha = .2$, and $\beta = .9$.

2. A building supply center is the only source of new bathtubs in the county. The owner estimates he supplies at least 90 persent of the bathtubs purchased in her county. She has been using the linear trend technique to forecast future demand for bathtubs. She is considering switching to linear regression based on her feeling that the number of building permits issued for new single-family homes in her county might be a good leading indicator of bathtub demand. She has determined that contractors typically purchase bathtubs about 2 months after they obtain their building permits.

Month	Bathtub Sales	Permits Issued
1	235	65
2	240	70
3	216	72
4	260	82
5	258	88
6	275	90
7	274	83
8	280	98
9	251	100
10	295	105
11	292	103
12	310	117
13	295	110
14	321	127
15	310	128
16	335	130
17	340	135
18	335	135
19	340	138
20	345	142
21	340	140
22	350	145
23	345	137
24	355	145

a. Use the data provided to develop forecasting equations using the two approaches under consideration.

b. Calculate MAD and MSE.

c. Which approach would you recommend? Justify your recommendation.

ENDNOTES

1. P. L. Bernstein, *Against the Gods: The Remarkable Story of Risk* (New York: John Wiley & Sons, 1998), pp. 152–172.

2. T. H. Davenport, "Putting the Enterprise into the Enterprise System," *Harvard Business Review*, July–August 1998, pp. 121–131.

3. Ibid.

4. D. E. O'Leary, *Enterprise Resource Planning Systems* (Cambridge, UK: Cambridge University Press, 2000), p. 63.

LEARNING ACTIVITIES   www.mhhe.com/opsnow3e

Visit the Online Learning Center (www.mhhe.com/opsnow3e) for additional resources. Content varies by chapter, and includes

- Business Tours
- OM on Site
- Readings
- Resources
- Excel Tutors

- Interactive Case Models
- Reel Operations Video Clips
- Additional Advanced Problem
- Self-Assessment Quizzes
- Glossary

SELECTED REFERENCES

Bancroft, N. H., Seipt, H., and Sprengel, A. *Implementing SAP R/3*. Greenwich, CT: Manning Publications, 1998.

Bernstein, P. L. *Against the Gods: The Remarkable Story of Risk*. New York: John Wiley & Sons, 1998.

Hanke, J. E., and Reitsch, A. G. *Business Forecasting*. Upper Saddle River, NJ: Prentice Hall, 1998.

O'Leary, E. *Enterprise Resource Planning Systems*. Cambridge, UK: Cambridge University Press, 2000.

Turban, E., Lee, J., King, D., and Chung, H. M. *Electronic Commerce*. Upper Saddle River, NJ: Prentice Hall, 2000.

VIDEO CASE 10.1

Louisville Slugger: Enterprise Resource Planning

Based on Video 13 on the Student DVD

Louisville Slugger has been a leader in the production of baseball bats, as well as golf and hockey equipment, for decades. In the 1990s, their wooden baseball bat business struggled with issues related to inventory excess and inventory shortages, product returns, poor customer service, and inefficiency. Prior to Y2K, like many businesses, H&B needed to select between updating old legacy computer systems or implementing completely new ones. They decided to implement an enterprise resource planning (ERP) system by SAP.

1. How many different wooden baseball bat products does H&B produce? Does the number of different products have any relationship to the problems H&B was having prior to the new system?

2. In the Louisville Slugger situation, the implementation took five years to show positive results. Why would an ERP system implementation take so long? What are the costs (quantifiable and unquantifiable) associated with such a long implementation?

3. What problems did H&B have in the area of customer service quality prior to the SAP implementation? What performance measures are used to show improvement? Are the current levels of performance on those measures good, in your opinion?

INTERACTIVE CASE 10.1

Causal Forecasting with Simple Linear Regression

Demands for products and services are often related to an external variable. For example, soft drink sales at a ball game might be related to how hot the day was. New home construction might be related to interest rates. In these situations, forecasters can use the relationship between the demand and the extrinsic variable to create a causal model for forecasting demand. Simple linear regression identifies the linear relationships between the extrinsic or independent variable (on the x axis) and the demand or dependent

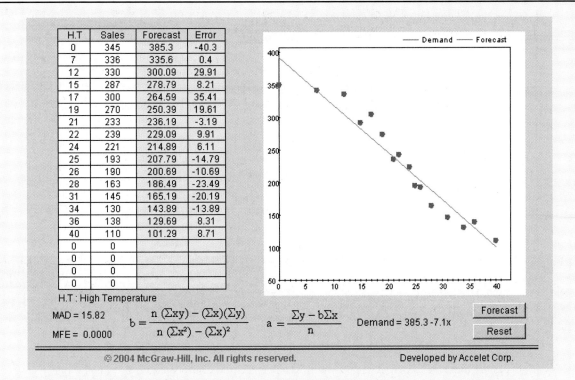

H.T	Sales	Forecast	Error
0	345	385.3	-40.3
7	336	335.6	0.4
12	330	300.09	29.91
15	287	278.79	8.21
17	300	264.59	35.41
19	270	250.39	19.61
21	233	236.19	-3.19
22	239	229.09	9.91
24	221	214.89	6.11
25	193	207.79	-14.79
26	190	200.69	-10.69
28	163	186.49	-23.49
31	145	165.19	-20.19
34	130	143.89	-13.89
36	138	129.69	8.31
40	110	101.29	8.71
0	0		
0	0		
0	0		
0	0		

H.T : High Temperature

MAD = 15.82

MFE = 0.0000

$$b = \frac{n\,(\Sigma xy) - (\Sigma x)(\Sigma y)}{n\,(\Sigma x^2) - (\Sigma x)^2}$$

$$a = \frac{\Sigma y - b\Sigma x}{n}$$

Demand = 385.3 - 7.1x

Forecast

Reset

Developed by Accelet Corp.

variable (on the y axis) and calculates the formula for the best-fitting line through the data. The formula for the best-fitting line takes the form $y = a + bx$, where a = the y intercept, b = the slope of the line, and x = the value of the independent variable.

North Mountain Ski Resort

Abigail Svenson, North Mountain Ski Resort's business manager, monitors sales of all concessions in the ski lodge in an effort to keep adequate stocks of food and drink but also to prevent inventory levels from being excessive. Hot cocoa creates an interesting problem for kitchen staff. The hot cocoa machine is "loaded" with powder at 10:00 a.m. It is cleaned every night, and powder remaining in the machine is discarded. Last winter, in an effort to develop a method for forecasting hot cocoa and reduce the amount of cocoa powder being thrown away, Abigail monitored sales of hot cocoa and daily "high" temperature. Her collected data are presented below:

High Temperature	0	7	12	15	17	19	21	22	24	25	26	28	31	34	36	40
Sales	345	336	330	287	300	270	233	239	221	193	190	163	145	130	138	110

1. When using simple linear regression as a causal forecasting technique, one must be aware of all the cautions that apply to the linear trend model. Outliers have the same impact. Using too many or too few data points in the analysis can have the same impact as well. Make sure the starting defaults on the model match the demand data provided above. If they do not, click on "reset."

   a. Drag demand points up and down on the graph. How do the formula and regression line change as the endpoints of the line are moved? What is the impact of moving data points near the middle of the line?

   b. What happens to the MAD as points are dragged away from the line? What happens to the MFE? Why is the MFE always 0?

c. Suppose you made the calculation for using this technique, used it to forecast demand, and then discovered that your forecast was biased. What do you suspect as a cause for the bias?

2. Set the values to the defaults by clicking on "reset." Outliers can be caused by aberrations in demand or by an input error. Key entry error is common and can have a huge effect on forecast accuracy. Record the regression equation and the MAD and MFE values for the default demand.

a. Suppose the first data point, 345, had been mistakenly transposed and keyed in as 543. What impact would this have had on the forecast accuracy?

b. Explain the effects errors related to the y intercept and errors related to the slope have on the MAD and MFE. Experiment with the model to reach your conclusions.

INTERACTIVE CASE 10.2

Finding Seasonality at Mitchell Tax Service

The components of a time series include random fluctuation, seasonality, trend, and cycle. In most cases involving product demand, a cycle component is not visible because of the short time frame of the data. Different types of forecasting techniques are used, depending on the components present in the time series of interest. Understanding how these components can relate and affect each other is important if time series forecasting techniques are to be fully understood.

The time series components model provides a conceptual view of the interaction among the three dominant components of a time series: random fluctuation, seasonality, and trend. System inputs consist of a slider for each component, allowing the user to increase or decrease each to explore how various combinations affect the appearance of the time series.

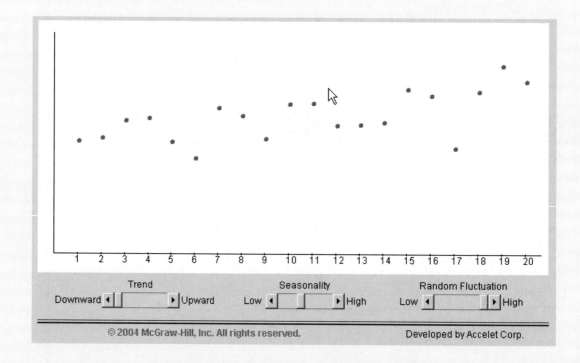

Mitchell Tax Service

For years, Mitchell Tax Service has been challenged by training the correct number of tax analysts to meet the demand for its services. It pays competitive salaries and is usually able to find high-quality employees, but seems to either train too many people, resulting in excess capacity, or not train enough people, resulting in long delays for customers.

Matt Dvorak, the chief operating officer, has been badgered by his boss because of the staffing problems. Matt has concluded that improving the accuracy of the firm's demand forecast would result in a better match between capacity and demand, better service for customers, and increased profitability. Matt has examined the past demand and, from its appearance, has concluded that there is a slight upward trend and lots of random fluctuation. Being in the tax preparation business, Matt also suspects that the demand is seasonal, corresponding to the periods immediately before quarterly payments are due and to April 15. The data, however, do not seem to show a definite seasonal pattern.

1. Examine the graph of the time series with the adjustment slides set to their default values (trend: far left; seasonality: two "clicks" from the far left; random fluctuation: far right).

   a. Describe the trend, seasonality, and random fluctuation visible in the time series. Do you agree with Matt that seasonality appears to be absent in the graph? Does the absence of a visible seasonal pattern necessarily mean that there is no seasonality?

   b. Slowly move the trend slide completely to the right and then back all the way to the left. Explain what happens to the graph. Does the visibility of random fluctuation and seasonality change?

2. Move the trend slide back to its original position at the far left end. Slowly move the random fluctuation slide to the left, one "click" at a time.

   a. Explain what happens to the graph as the amount of random fluctuation in the time series is reduced.

   b. Leave the random fluctuation slide to the far left. This has effectively eliminated the random fluctuation in the time series. What remains in the time series? Move the trend slide to the center position. What does this do to the time series? With the random fluctuation eliminated, and the trend "flat," what causes the variability of the demand data?

   c. Explain what has been happening to Matt's data that has made it impossible for him to see seasonality.

   d. Since Matt does not have an interactive model like this one, what would you suggest he do to get a better understanding of the components of his data?

INTERACTIVE CASE 10.3

Reducing Coffee Waste by Forecasting Accurately

Simple exponential smoothing is a popular forecasting technique, particularly when trying to smooth out the effects of random fluctuation. Simple exponential smoothing is actually a sophisticated weighted average technique that allows the user to specify the relative weight given the immediate past demand and the demands from the more distant past. The greater the weight on past demands, and the less the weight on the most recent demand, the less the impact of recent changes on the forecast. The lower the weight on the most recent demand, the greater the smoothing effect, and the less the forecast responds to demand changes. The responsiveness of the forecast is controlled by the size of α. A larger α (alpha) results in a greater weight being placed on the most recent demand and less on the previous forecasts.

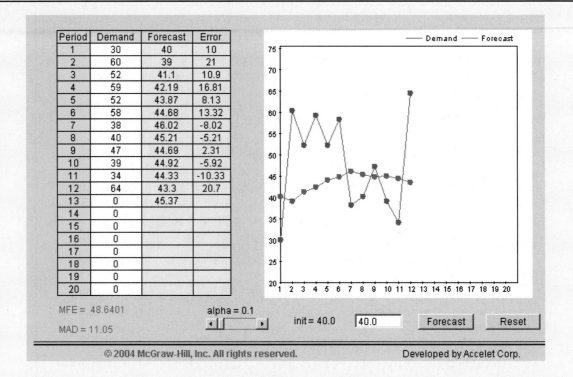

Period	Demand	Forecast	Error
1	30	40	10
2	60	39	21
3	52	41.1	10.9
4	59	42.19	16.81
5	52	43.87	8.13
6	58	44.68	13.32
7	38	46.02	-8.02
8	40	45.21	-5.21
9	47	44.69	2.31
10	39	44.92	-5.92
11	34	44.33	-10.33
12	64	43.3	20.7
13	0	45.37	
14	0		
15	0		
16	0		
17	0		
18	0		
19	0		
20	0		

MFE = 48.6401   alpha = 0.1

MAD = 11.05

◄ || ►   init = 40.0   40.0   Forecast   Reset

Cutting Coffee Costs

A local branch office of a large consulting firm has gourmet coffee delivered twice a day from a local coffee shop. Coffee is delivered in large urns at 7:30 a.m. and again at noon. The coffee is kept hot in the urns. Connie Andrews, the office manager, wants to continue to provide the service as a "perk" to the employees, but she does not want to pay for coffee that is ultimately thrown away. Analysis of the coffee demand shows that over the long term there appear to be no seasonal patterns or trend. In the short term, however, there are often periods of time when demand seems to be increasing, and then it shifts and decreases for a period of weeks. The most recent 12 weeks of demand are presented below.

Period	1	2	3	4	5	6	7	8	9	10	11	12
Demand	30	60	52	59	52	58	38	40	47	39	34	64

1. Make sure that the starting default values match the demands provided above. Examine the graph of the demand for coffee. Examine how the forecast follows the demand when the alpha value is set to 0.1.

   a. Change the alpha value to 0.3. What happens to the forecast? Pay particular attention to the impact the demand increase in period 2 and the demand decrease in period 7 have on the subsequent forecasts. What happens to the "response" of the forecast in periods 3 and 8 when you make the change in alpha?

   b. In order to further investigate the link between the value of alpha and the responsiveness of the forecast, with the alpha at 0.1, use your mouse to drag the demand for period 9 to 70 units. What happens to the demand forecast for period 10? Experiment by doing this for each value of alpha. How would you quantify the relationship between alpha and the impact a change in alpha has on the responsiveness of the forecast?

c. Repeat your experiment, but examine the impact that a reduction in the demand at period 7 has on the forecast for period 8. How does the forecast respond to the drop in demand at various levels of alpha?

2. Make sure that all demand values are at their starting defaults. If they are not, bring them to their defaults by clicking on the "reset" button.

   a. With the alpha value at 0.1, what are the current values for MFE and MAD? What do these numbers mean?

   b. Experiment to find the alpha value that provides the best value for the MAD. Identify the alpha value that provides the best MFE. Are they the same? Explain.

   c. If you were in Connie's position, which measure would be most important to you? Why?

3. Two months after the demand data above were collected, Connie gathered another 12 weeks of demand. The new demand is shown below:

Period	1	2	3	4	5	6	7	8	9	10	11	12
Demand	52	56	67	73	66	63	56	54	46	55	58	63

Enter the new demand into the table in the simple exponential smoothing model.

   a. With an alpha of 0.1, examine how the forecast responds to demand changes as demand increases (periods 1–4) and as demand decreases (periods 4–9). Explain your observations.

   b. As the demand appears to change directions at periods 4 and 9, explain how the value of alpha affects the ability of the forecast to keep up with the demand. Examine the period of increasing demand and the period of decreasing demand. During these times, what happens to the bias of the forecast? How does the alpha affect the bias during these short periods?

   c. Based on your observations of simple exponential smoothing when demand is increasing and when demand is decreasing, explain why simple exponential smoothing is not recommended when the time series contains a trend.

INTERACTIVE CASE 10.4

Forecasting Demand for New Audio Products

Trend-adjusted exponential smoothing incorporates trend into the exponential smoothing forecast through the use of an additional smoothing constant. The model treats trend and random fluctuation components quite separately. In the calculation of the trend-enhanced exponential smoothing forecast, the smoothed forecast is calculated exactly as in simple exponential smoothing. A trend component (T_t) is then added. T_t is computed by adding to the previous trend component (T_{t-1}), a weighted difference between the previous two trend-adjusted forecasts and the previous trend. The second smoothing constant (β) determines the weight used.

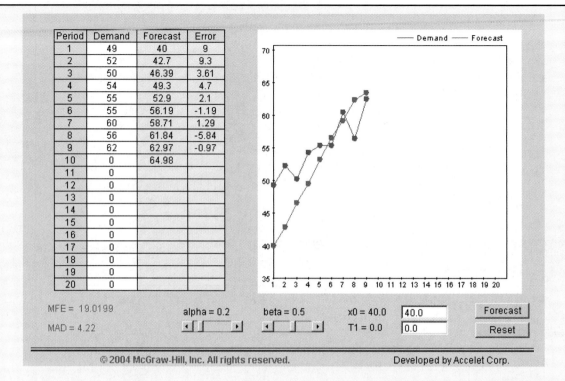

Period	Demand	Forecast	Error
1	49	40	9
2	52	42.7	9.3
3	50	46.39	3.61
4	54	49.3	4.7
5	55	52.9	2.1
6	55	56.19	-1.19
7	60	58.71	1.29
8	56	61.84	-5.84
9	62	62.97	-0.97
10	0	64.98	
11	0		
12	0		
13	0		
14	0		
15	0		
16	0		
17	0		
18	0		
19	0		
20	0		

MFE = 19.0199

MAD = 4.22

alpha = 0.2   beta = 0.5   x0 = 40.0   40.0   Forecast

T1 = 0.0   0.0   Reset

Stan's Digital Audio

Stan's Digital Audio sells audio accessories for mp3 players through several online auction services. He recently introduced a new product that transmits from any mp3 player to any FM radio within 10 feet. He orders his products at low cost directly from an Asian distributor, but must wait three weeks for delivery. This creates problems for new products with uncertain demand. Stan doesn't want to order too few or he risks losing sales to competitors. However, if he orders too many, he can be stuck with products he can't move. The demand for the mp3 FM transmitter appears to have a sharply increasing trend, but also has a random component. Stan has collected demand data for the past nine weeks. He has decided to test trend-enhanced exponential smoothing on his past demand to see if it is an effective forecasting tool.

Week	1	2	3	4	5	6	7	8	9
Demand	49	52	50	54	55	55	60	56	62

1. Make sure the starting default values for the trend-enhanced exponential smoothing model match the demand above. The alpha should equal 0.2 and the beta should equal 0.5. If they do not, click on the "reset" button.

   a. Do you agree with Stan's assessment of the trend and randomness in the data? Compare the red forecast data to the blue demand data with the alpha and beta values at their starting defaults. Describe the relationship between the two.

   b. With the alpha value at 0.2, manipulate the beta value, observing what happens to the forecast as beta is changed. At different beta values, drag a blue demand "dot" and observe what happens to the forecast. Describe the impact the beta value has on forecast response.

   c. With the beta set at various values, change the alpha value and observe what happens. Starting with low alpha values and progressing to high ones, drag a blue demand "dot" and observe how the forecast responds. Based on your observations and a close examination of the formula for calculating trend-enhanced exponential smoothing, describe how the alpha and beta values interact to determine the forecast's responsiveness.

2. Set the demand and smoothing constants back to their starting defaults by clicking on the reset button.

   a. By changing the alpha values and beta values separately, observe the forecast accuracy measures (MFE and MAD). Which seems to be most affected by changing the alpha? Which seems to be most affected by changing the beta?

   b. Which of the two measures should be most important for Stan to monitor? Which combination of alpha and beta values do you think provides the best forecast performance?

INTERACTIVE CASE 10.5

Forecasting Trend at North Mountain Ski Resort

The linear trend equation uses the time period as the independent variable in a simple linear regression model. It computes the formula of the best-fitting line through the data and, by extending that line into the future, provides forecasts of the future impact trend has on the data. That best-fitting line, often called the "trend line," is graphed with the demand data. The trend line takes the form $y = at + b$, where y is the demand, a is the slope, b is the y intercept, and t is the time period. In addition to allowing the user to change demand values, the model also allows the user to drag demand, making it easy to see the impact of demand changes.

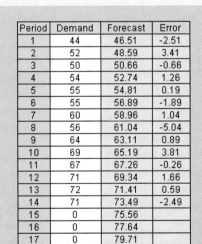

Period	Demand	Forecast	Error
1	44	46.51	-2.51
2	52	48.59	3.41
3	50	50.66	-0.66
4	54	52.74	1.26
5	55	54.81	0.19
6	55	56.89	-1.89
7	60	58.96	1.04
8	56	61.04	-5.04
9	64	63.11	0.89
10	69	65.19	3.81
11	67	67.26	-0.26
12	71	69.34	1.66
13	72	71.41	0.59
14	71	73.49	-2.49
15	0	75.56	
16	0	77.64	
17	0	79.71	
18	0	81.78	
19	0	83.86	
20	0	85.93	

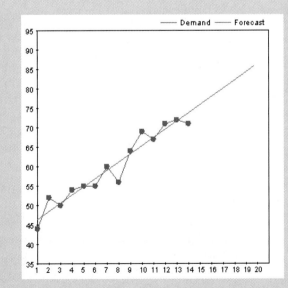

MFE = 0.0000

MAD = 1.84 $b = \dfrac{n\Sigma ty - \Sigma t\Sigma y}{n\Sigma t^2 - (\Sigma t)^2}$ $a = \dfrac{\Sigma y - b\Sigma t}{n}$ $y = 44.44 + 2.07t$ [Forecast]   [Reset]

North Mountain Ski Resort

North Mountain, a small midwestern ski resort, offers a variety of passes to entice skiers to the slopes on weekdays. One pass allows skiers to ski on any weekday. A cheaper pass allows skiers to ski one day per week, on any weekday. An even cheaper annual pass allows skiers to select any day of the week, and then the skier can ski on that day every week. The cheapest pass of all allows skiers to ski every Tuesday. Sales of the "Tuesday only" pass have increased since its inception 14 years ago. Abigail Svenson, North Mountain's business manager, has decided to analyze the demand to help her determine if other passes should be created.

1. Make sure the demand values are at the following start-up defaults:

Period	1	2	3	4	5	6	7	8	9	10	11	12	13	14
Demand	44	52	50	54	55	55	60	56	64	69	67	71	72	71

   Record the formula for the trend line.

   a. An important early step in linear trend analysis is to remove outliers. Outliers are data points that are very unusual and should be eliminated from the time series because of their negative effect on the accuracy of the forecast. Outliers can have a significant impact on the forecast when using a linear trend equation, and that impact can depend on the location of the outlier. Do any of the data points in the 14 years of data appear to be outliers? Explain your answer.

   b. Drag the demand for period 2 from 52 to 62. What is the effect of that change on the formula for the trend line? What is the impact on forecast accuracy?

   c. Set the period 2 demand back to 52. Now drag the demand for period 5 from 55 to 65. What is the impact of that change on the trend formula? What is the impact on forecast accuracy?

   d. Set the period 5 demand back to 55. Now drag the demand for period 9 from 64 to 72. What is the impact of that change on the trend formula? What is the impact on forecast accuracy?

   e. Summarize the impact an outlier has on the formula for the trend and on the MFE and MAD. What clues would you look for in the MAD or MFE to possibly indicate the presence of an outlier in the data?

2. Whenever the linear trend equation is used, the number of periods to include in the analysis is critical. Trends change over time. Using too much data results in the forecast not responding to changes in trend. Using too little data runs the risk of the trend line changing as a result of random fluctuations that really don't represent changes in the trend. Click on "reset" to get the demand back to its starting default values.

   a. Click on "forecast" and observe the graph. The trend equation is $44.44 + 2.07t$. Record the MAD and MFE. Clearly this is an upward trend, rising just over 2 units per period. What is the forecast for period 20?

   b. Abigail decided to use only the most recent 9 periods to compute the linear trend equation. To do this, change periods 10 through 14 to "0" and enter the following demand data for periods 1 through 9:

Period	1	2	3	4	5	6	7	8	9
Demand	55	60	56	64	69	67	71	72	71

   Again, click on "forecast" and observe the results. What is the new equation for the trend line? What is the new MAD and MFE? What is the forecast for period 20? Explain what happened.

Bias at Fast Response

Fast Response has been in the call center business for five years. It specializes in answering questions about product returns. Currently, Fast Response operators handle questions about product returns for seven different clients. The number called by a customer identifies the product being returned, and that info is available on the computer screen of the operator. In most cases, the operator merely provides product-specific return instructions for the customer. When Fast Response was initially formed, the owner thought that providing product return information services for several companies at once would eliminate the seasonal peaks and valleys common in the industry. Today, he is not so sure that is happening.

Roger Tolbert schedules staff for Fast Response. A core of full-time employees work each shift, and these are supplemented by part-time employees to help match capacity to demand. Demand is forecast using simple exponential smoothing. Roger forecasts the number of calls per hour, for each day, and schedules workers accordingly. The data below show forecasts versus the actual demand for a sampling of data from four weeks during the past month. Six samples were taken from each week. A beginning forecast of 140 was used, followed by simple exponential smoothing with an alpha of .3. Roger has noticed that the MAPE doesn't seem too bad, at 13 percent. He has computed the RSFE, which equals approximately 37. This indicates that he has been forecasting too low, but he knows that there are times when his forecast has been too high.

Sample	Demand	Forecast
1	150	143.00
2	147	145.10
3	160	145.67
4	155	149.97
5	149	151.48
6	167	150.73
7	136	155.61
8	128	149.73
9	131	143.21
10	120	139.55
11	128	133.68
12	132	131.98
13	212	131.98
14	201	155.99
15	218	169.49
16	204	184.04
17	210	190.03
18	221	196.02
19	142	203.52
20	150	185.06
21	139	174.54
22	147	163.88
23	145	158.82
24	153	154.67

1. Compute the forecast error, MAPE, MAD, and RSFE.

2. Graph the data and explain the possible causes of Roger's frustration.

3. How would you recommend solving Roger's problem?

Inventory: Managing to Meet Demand

LEARNING OBJECTIVES

- Explain why businesses carry inventory.

- Describe the costs associated with inventory.

- Compare independent and dependent demand inventory.

- Calculate days-of-supply.

- Explain how a reorder point system works.

- Describe the contribution made by a safety stock.

- Compute the reorder point for a desired service level.

- Make computations for the economic order quantity models.

- Describe weaknesses of the economic order quantity.

- Compute the appropriate order quantity for a fixed-interval, variable-quantity system.

- Describe the information inputs necessary to manage dependent demand inventory.

- Compute planned order releases using material requirements planning.

- Explain ABC analysis.

- Compute dollar days for a given inventory.

IMPROVEMENT IS NEVER ENOUGH

Too little inventory is the Achilles' heel of any retailer, but so is too much inventory. No retailing business is more challenging from an inventory management perspective than the drugstore environment. With competitors that range, depending on the products, from 7-Eleven to CVS to Walgreens to Wal-Mart, being out of something translates into an immediate lost sale. One member of that industry—Longs Drug Stores—has differentiated itself in several ways, but primarily through its ability to consistently keep items in stock. With 470 retail outlets, primarily on the West Coast, Longs realized that it wasn't achieving the full benefits of economies of scale. Thus, it began a supply chain initiative to increase its efficiency and lower its inventory costs while continuing to satisfy customers and stay true to its goals.

Longs has traditionally given individual stores autonomy over what to stock, but felt that pharmacists and store buyers could no longer keep up with the thousands of products Longs stocked. It needed an information system that would help manage inventory in individual stores and purchasing at the distribution center level. In 2002, Longs began a supply chain initiative and announced that approximately $60 million would be dedicated to the development of its supply chain. By 2004 it had spent about one half of its planned expenditures and was halfway through the development project. At that time, Longs had

- Centralized merchandise procurement and created a database for all SKUs.
- Upgraded its point-of-sale (POS) system and introduced handheld wireless systems in the stores.
- Installed distribution management systems at two facilities serving California.
- Decreased store inventory levels and increased distribution center inventories.
- Installed a retail management system in all stores.
- Installed a procurement and allocation system in 2005.
- Begun the installation of a new store system for ordering, receiving, and inventory management, which should be complete by the end of 2007.

In July of 2006, Longs opened a new 800,000 square foot distribution center in July of 2006. With the addition of this new distribution center, they now self-distribute about 57 percent of its front-end goods (general merchandise) with the goal of self-distributing 80 percent by the end of calender 2007. Once completed, Longs expects to realize the benefits of lower cost of goods and expenses, improved merchandise replenishment, and increased visibility of its in-stock position and merchandise mix, product movement and margins. The results of this initiative will be the first integrated supply chain system in the history of Longs.

Longs continues to focus on its merchandise assortments to emphasize differentiation and better align prices with those of competitors' in the following areas:

- Over-the-counter medications
- Beauty, including skin care and cosmetics
- Greeting cards and seasonal goods
- Convenience merchandise and convenience services such as digital photo processing

In addition to enhanced inventory management, Longs began a large-scale remodeling program with 20 stores in 2003. As of August 2006, they have remodeled more than 110 stores. In combination with the stores they have opened or relocated, 136 stores—or 28 percent of the chain—have the new look. By the end of 2007, the goal is to have 50 percent of their chain with the new look, including new stores less than five years old and existing stores that have been remodeled in the same time frame.

The new store design pursues points of differentiation in pharmacy, wellness, beauty, and convenience. It provides a fresh new look with wider aisles, brighter lighting and signage, along with the use of color that makes the stores easier to navigate. The entire store is designed to create a more exciting shopping experience for customers, while at the same time improving productivity and efficiency.

Source: "Longs Drug Stores Corporation," *Hoovers Company Profiles,* Hoover-NO: 10913. June 8, 2004; D. Disjardines, "Retailer Hones Efforts in Defense of Home Turf," *Drug Store News,* April 19, 2004; H. L. Lee, and S. Whang, "Demand Chain Excellence: A Tale of Two Retailers," *Supply Chain Management Review,* March 1, 2001; www.longs.com, accessed May 2006. Special thanks to Phyllis Proffer of Longs Drug Stores.

nventory is the first of four resources examined in this unit. It is an intriguing resource be-cause even though it is an asset, its role is often more like a liability. Not enough inventory can lead to disaster, but too much can be just as destructive. Inventory serves many important purposes, but these benefits come at great cost.

Introduction: A Balancing Act for Management

nventory is one of four major resource groups traditionally controlled by operations. It is a critical resource in many ways. Its presence contributes to value because it reduces the wait time for a customer. It contributes to time-liness, response time, and other customer-service related factors as well. Surprisingly, its absence also contributes to value. The ability of a firm to react to market changes is enhanced if money has not been invested in inventory that could become obsolete, particularly in markets with short product life cycles.

If the presence and absence of inventory both contribute to value, the amount of inventory held must be a difficult balancing act. Too little reduces the financial return received from the firm's other assets, because sales are lost. Too much creates an investment in inventory that provides no financial return and may inhibit the firm's ability to respond to market changes. This chapter examines the different reasons companies hold inventory, the different types of inventory, costs and benefits associated with those inventory types, and techniques used to make inventory management decisions that enhance profitability.

Why Should Businesses Carry Inventory?

decouple
To reduce the direct dependency of a process step on its predecessor.

A general statement can be made that inventory of all types serves a function known as **decoupling.** Decoupling means that the inventory serves to break a direct dependency that one part of the supply chain may have on another. A direct dependency means that if one business entity supplies another with some input, and the supply stops for some reason, the other one will be immediately disrupted. This disruption potential is common within productive systems, companies, and supply chains. In today's manufacturing and service economies, low levels of inventory are desirable, and in most situations the low levels of inventory have a positive impact on the firm. Once in a while, however, something occurs to disrupt the continuous flow of goods necessary in a low-inventory environment. There's a strike, a natural disaster, a fire at a factory, or a recall of defective products that shifts a supplier's priorities. Inevitably, manufacturers and services that depend on suppliers of goods must find a balance between the benefits and risks associated with low levels of inventory.

The decoupling effect of inventory can enhance reliability and response time, leading to an increase in net sales. The increase in net sales can obviously result in enhanced net income and ROA. There is no free lunch, though.

Longs's inventory reduction efforts in 1997 reduced inventories by 26 percent, freeing up $60 million in capital, which enabled them to acquire 58 new stores.

Why Should Businesses Avoid Carrying Too Much Inventory?

Just as there are general truths about the benefits of inventories, there are general truths about inventory costs. Inventory is an investment. In appropriate quantities, the investment can generate a substantial financial return. However, excess inventory is a very poor investment because the excess provides no financial return since its presence adds no value. In addition to the lack of a financial return, its associated

GOING global   Reducing Inventory Carrying Costs with RFID

Radio-frequency identification (RFID) is viewed as a silver bullet for some activities in supply chain management, but it also has direct implications for in-house inventory management. Metro AG, a German retailer, has extended the use of RFID beyond Wal-Mart. Metro is Germany's largest retailer, owning almost 2,400 stores in Germany and 27 other countries. 2003 revenues were up almost 25 percent from the previous year.

While Wal-Mart instructed its suppliers to utilize RFID at the pallet level by 2005, Procter & Gamble, Kraft, and

Gillette were already putting RFID tags on goods they supplied to Metro in 2004. Metro expects to track inventory in and out of warehouses and stores with the technology. Expectations are to reduce inventory carrying costs by up to 20 percent by cutting loss and theft, increasing levels of stock on shelves, and reducing staffing needs.

Source: K. J. Delaney, "Inventory Tool to Launch in German; Wireless System Is Seen as Successor to Bar Codes; Metro AG Leads Wal-Mart," *Wall Street Journal*, January 12, 2004, p. B5.

costs can reduce net income. All inventory, for example, generates costs of storage and insurance. In most cases inventory drives several nonfinancial costs as well. It can reduce management's ability to make quick decisions, it can reduce flexibility, and it can reduce the firm's ability to adapt to changing market conditions. These costs vary with different types of inventory. The specific benefits and costs associated with inventory can be better understood if different types of inventory are examined in detail. The following discussion is devoted to specific types of inventory, their benefits, and their costs.

Costs and Benefits

Different types of inventory serve different decoupling functions. Some inventories decouple a customer from a supplier. Other inventories decouple one machine from another. Still other inventories allow producers to delay costly commitment decisions or give management additional flexibility. All types of inventory have associated costs. Some costs are generic, occurring no matter what the inventory type. Others are specific to a certain inventory type.

Two costs associated with all types of inventory are order costs and carrying costs. **Order costs** are the administrative costs associated with ordering inventory: the costs of interacting with a supplier, writing up an order and invoice, and so on. Order costs are associated with the action of ordering and are independent of the size of the order. Order costs for a particular company go up if the company orders more frequently and go down if it orders less frequently. For manufacturers, cost analogous to the order costs is known as a **setup** or **changeover cost.** A changeover cost is the cost associated with preparing equipment to produce a quantity of a specific inventory item. No matter what that quantity or "batch" size, the cost of setting up the equipment will stay the same and will generally include labor, materials consumed in the changeover process, and lost production time on that piece of equipment.

Carrying costs are associated with the amount of inventory being held. They include insurance costs, storage costs, facility costs associated with the storage space used, and the opportunity cost of the dollars invested in inventory. Carrying costs are generally viewed as being a function of the average value of inventory. In fact, if it is assumed that the inventory level goes to zero prior to replenishment (this assumption is seldom true, but it's useful for this example), the average level of inventory is equal to one-half of the quantity ordered to replenish the inventory. This relationship is illustrated in Exhibit 11.1. As the average value of the inventory goes up, the carrying costs go up proportionately.

order cost
The fixed cost associated with ordering inventory.

changeover cost
The cost of changing equipment from producing one product or service to another.

carrying cost
Costs associated with carrying inventory.

EXHIBIT 11.1	Average Inventory as $Q/2$

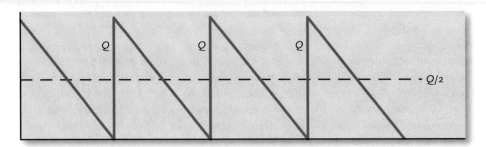

stockout

An instance when demand cannot be satisfied by existing inventory.

stockout cost

The cost associated with not having inventory when a customer demands it.

As you might have suspected, carrying costs and order costs are inversely related to each other. The larger the quantity ordered, the greater the average level of inventory, so the greater the carrying costs. However, as a larger quantity is ordered, orders occur less frequently, reducing the total order costs associated with the item.

A third cost associated with all inventories is the cost of not having it, which is called the **stockout cost.** Since demand is uncertain in many situations, there is always a chance of running out of inventory. Depending on the effects of a stockout, a variety of costs could be involved. In a B2C interaction, for example, the cost might be a lost sale or a dissatisfied customer. In a B2B relationship, a stockout might be expensive, resulting in a plant shutdown, employee layoff, and so on. Higher levels of inventory result in higher carrying costs but lower stockout costs.

A fourth cost that can be directly related to inventory level, the actual cost of purchasing the inventory item, is present only in certain situations. Sometimes, quantity discounts make purchasing in large quantities attractive. Purchasing in large quantities when a quantity discount exists can lower the cost of the items but will increase the associated carrying costs. Again, one cost is traded for another.

Costs associated with inventory are closely linked to time. This results in an ongoing goal for many businesses to reduce transportation time.

Retailing and Finished-Product Inventories

Every day, most of us are exposed to a typical type of inventory—that held by a retailer. That inventory helps provide immediate gratification to the customer. Whereas a simple mail-order business requires the customer to wait, when a company carries inventory, the customer gets the product immediately. In addition to the enhanced response time for the customer, carrying inventory allows the customer to examine what will be purchased. The inventory held by the retailer decouples that retailer from its supplier, whether that supplier is a distribution center owned by the retail chain or a separate company. Stores that maintain only a very small amount of inventory depend more directly on the supplier because they need more frequent replenishments. A disruption in supply would have a quicker impact on their ability to immediately respond to customer demands.

Longs uses a Cisco wireless cart and laptop computer system to allow employees to scan items on the shelf and enter the replenishment quantity on the laptop.

continuous replenishment

The delivery of inventory, frequently in small quantities.

In some retail markets inventories are intentionally kept low, to conserve on storage space (reducing inventory-related costs) and to reduce the amount of money invested in inventory. In some situations, a practice known as **continuous replenishment** is used, whereby deliveries are made at extremely short intervals—daily, or even multiple times per day. Continuous replenishment in the retailing industry is similar to an approach known as just-in-time (JIT) delivery in manufacturing. It means that deliveries arrive frequently and in small quantities to enable a low average inventory level but still meet demand needs. The graph illustrating that effect is reproduced in Exhibit 11.2.

Finished goods inventory is necessary to eliminate the direct dependencies between a retailer and a production line. Here, finished casement windows for use in home construction await orders from retailers. Too large of a finished goods inventory, however, increases warehousing costs and may create a liquidation problem if a new model window is introduced.

Frequent Small Deliveries versus Infrequent Large Deliveries	**EXHIBIT 11.2**

Daily Orders versus Monthly Orders to Meet
100 Unit/Month Demand

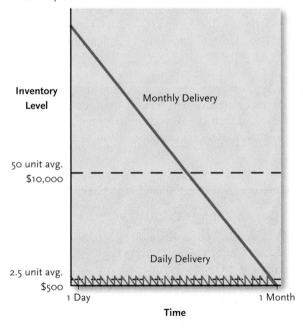

Independent Demand Inventory

Finished-product inventories of manufacturers and the stock inventories of retailers are similar in that their demands are both classified as **independent demand inventory.** In general, independent demand inventories are inventories whose demand comes directly from the market. It is not possible to know what the demand will be before the fact, and so it must be forecast. The techniques used to manage independent demand inventory, addressed later in this chapter, must include features to cope with the demand's probabilistic nature.

independent demand inventory
Inventory whose demand is dictated by the marketplace.

maintenance, repair, and operating (MRO) inventory
Inventory that consists of items consumed in the day-to-day activities of a business.

Another less obvious type of inventory, but also having independent demand, is the inventory of items consumed in the day-to-day activities that support a business. This inventory is known as **maintenance, repair, and operating (MRO) inventory.** For typical services, it would include paper, diskettes, forms for keeping records and receipts, cleaning supplies, and the plastic bags and boxes retailers put products in. For manufacturers, MRO inventories would include lubricants, tools, and repair parts. The demand for MRO inventories is similar to the demand for the retailer's inventory and must be forecast in order to plan for those items.

Inventories like MRO and retail inventories are often consumed one unit at a time, making it difficult and time-consuming to pull inventory from warehouses. Automated order picking and sorting systems are often employed to meet high volumes of this type of demand. Transportation and shipping businesses, like UPS, and high-volume online retailers have a similar need for high-volume order filling or sorting capabilities. Esource 10.2 is a leading provider of systems and equipment for high-volume inventory and order sorting.

Inventory and Time

Inventory is often viewed and measured from a "time" perspective because it provides a supply or coverage for a given length of time. The rate of demand on that inventory, combined with the amount of inventory on hand, results in what is frequently called the "days-of-supply" or "weeks-of-supply" of inventory. When the amount of inventory on hand is viewed in this way, the issue of dependency on a supplier becomes crystal clear. Days-of-supply is simply the amount of inventory on hand divided by the average daily demand. Similarly, weeks-of-supply would be determined by dividing the inventory on hand quantity by the average weekly demand. The days-of-supply value tells, on average, how long it will be until inventory runs out. It also indicates the size of disruption that can be tolerated. Example 11.1 demonstrates the calculation of the days-of-supply.

Exhibit 11.3 is a diagram of a hardware retailer that has a six-day supply of floor cleaner. The manager knows that if the replenishment does not arrive within six days, a stockout may occur prior to the delivery. If demand is greater than average, the stockout will be earlier. If demand is less than average, it will be later. A delay in replenishment may result from any of a number of causes upstream in the supply chain,

---

Example 11.1

EXCEL TUTOR

Days-of-Supply Calculation

A convenience store sells, on average, 40 gallons of 2 percent milk per day. Some days demand is a few more, some days a few less. The store receives deliveries of milk every other day, equal to the amount sold the previous two days. On Tuesday evening, the store received a call from its supplier and was told that, due to problems at the plant, the delivery that should come on Wednesday would be delayed by one day. The store had 60 gallons of 2 percent on hand when the call came in. How long would that inventory be expected to last?

Solution

The days-of-supply calculation is

$$\frac{\text{On-Hand Inventory}}{\text{Average Daily Demand}} = \frac{60}{40}$$
$$= 1.5$$

Excel Tutor 11.1 shows how this calculation can be done in a spreadsheet.

Example of Days' Supply

EXHIBIT 11.3

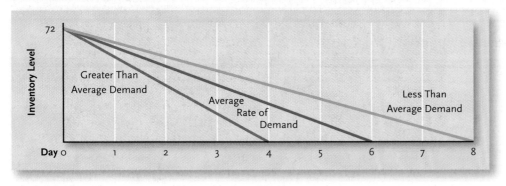

including a stockout at a supplier, a transportation strike, or a disruption at the manufacturing plant.

The completed-products or **finished-goods inventory** held at a manufacturing plant has a role similar to that of a retailer's inventory: it eliminates the need for a customer to wait for the products. The finished-goods inventory decouples the shipping and delivery systems from the actual production of the product. It makes possible the delivery of products even though production may be temporarily halted. It enables manufacturing to gain economies of scale and better utilize flexible equipment by making one product for a while, and then changing over machines to make another product for a while, then changing back, a technique known as **batch processing.**

Exhibit 11.4 shows how a manufacturer can use finished-goods inventory to operate at a more consistent output level, even in an environment of highly seasonal demand. During low demand periods, products are manufactured at a rate that is faster than the consumption rate, resulting in a steady buildup of finished-product inventory. The inventory level is the difference between the demand rate and the production rate. Then, as demand picks up, it is satisfied from the finished-product inventory as well as from products being manufactured. This approach, known as **level production,** results in a more stable workforce, as well as a consistent load on equipment.

Inventory held by a retailer or by a manufacturer as finished goods contributes to value in several ways. Obviously, the reduced response time that results from its presence increases perceived value for the customer. The added dependability is a benefit as well, particularly in a B2B transaction from a manufacturer. A promise of delivery for products already completed is much more certain to be met than one that requires production to

finished-goods inventory
Inventory consisting of products that have completed all stages of production.

batch processing
A system in which a group of identical products or customers is processed through one step in the process and then the entire group moves to the next step.

level production
An aggregate planning approach that uses inventory stored from period to period to reduce the need to change the output rate as demand changes.

Inventory to Buffer against Seasonal Demand

EXHIBIT 11.4

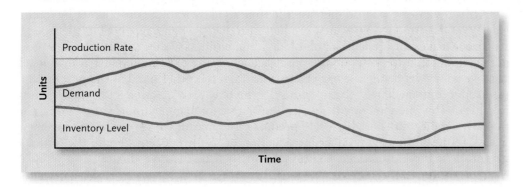

Excess inventory, no matter what the type, ties up capital and increases the risk of damage obsolesence, and waste. Here, inventories of coffee run the risk of spoilage and damage, and add to the costs that all supply chain members must absorb.

Longs will open its own distribution center in 2006 and will self-distribute 80 percent of its merchandise.

take place before delivery. There are costs associated with these inventories as well, however, that must be weighed against the benefits.

The more inventory, the greater the days-of-supply, and the longer, on average, the inventory is held prior to being sold. Days-of-supply can be beneficial when concern about reliability of supply exists, but it can be detrimental as well. Excess inventory held for a long period of time has a greater chance of becoming obsolete and impossible to sell. The longer the days-of-supply, the more likely some of that inventory will be held too long. The more inventory held, the more room it takes to store it, resulting in a need for larger facilities. Storage-related costs go up. The productivity of the facilities used for inventory storage is zero, however, because no value is generated by square footage used to store excess inventory.

Excess inventory can also increase the time to market for a new product by forcing a delay on its introduction. A new product introduced when a supply of its predecessor still exists makes the predecessor obsolete. If the business wishes to delay the new product's introduction to postpone the obsolescence of the existing product, valuable advantage gained by being first to market is lost. On the other hand, if the new product is introduced immediately, the inventory of the now-obsolete product becomes almost worthless. This phenomenon is equally destructive for manufacturers and services, particularly retailers of short-life-cycle products. No matter which choice management makes, to delay the new-product introduction or to introduce it despite the on-hand inventory of the old product, additional costs will be incurred directly as a result of that inventory.

om ADVANTAGE   Pricing to Control Inventory

One approach to managing inventory effectively is to let demand drive what you need, order the components, produce it in time (hopefully), and sell it. Another approach, and one often used by Dell, is to identify what components you have, and then configure and price models so that they sell. No one can argue that Dell's approach hasn't been successful. It is the world's No. 1 direct-sale computer vendor and receives around 80 percent of its sales through desktop and notebook computers.

Dell's "eliminate the middleman" model, combined with its produce-to-order flexibility, has value potential, but also potential for extreme levels of inventory. This is particularly true in an environment where it has to commit to purchasing components 60 days ahead of time.

Dell's "sell what you have" demand management approach reaches from product pricing all the way to the incentives for sales staff. Prices vary weekly, depending on availability of components. This approach to managing demand as a way to manage inventory has helped Dell keep inventory levels low.

Sources: J. Byrnes, "Dell Manages Profitability, Not Inventory," *Harvard Business School Working Knowledge*, bhswk.hbs.edu, June 2, 2003; Dell, Inc., Hoover's Company Profiles, 2004, HOOVER-NO: 13193.

Excess inventory also increases the cash-to-cash cycle. If a manufactured product is stored before being sold, the time it is stored adds to the length of the cycle. The days-of-supply of inventory can be a significant component of the cycle. One way to reduce the cash-to-cash cycle, particularly for make-to-stock manufacturers and for most retail inventories, is to reduce the days-of-supply of finished goods inventory.

Another often overlooked cost associated with inventory is the negative effect excess inventory has on product quality. This is a manifestation of the feedback delay concept introduced in Chapter 8. Large, infrequent deliveries of products are typically manufactured in a similar pattern. They are produced infrequently in large quantities. Likewise, if deliveries are made in frequent small quantities, manufacturers typically produce them in a similar pattern. Production in large quantities is dangerous from a quality perspective because if defects do exist, they are often not discovered until the entire quantity is produced and shipped. This results not only in greater waste and higher costs, but also in more difficulty in pinning down the actual cause of the defect, which makes it more difficult to prevent a recurrence.

Component and Raw Materials Inventory

Another distinct type of inventory is common in manufacturing and in many non-retailing services. These inventory items, known as component inventories and raw materials, also serve decoupling functions. Manufacturing inventories of purchased components and raw materials, for example, are held to decrease the direct dependence on the supplier of those goods. Similarly, a restaurant would maintain an inventory of raw food ingredients. For a hospital, a component inventory would consist of the disposable items and procedure kits, linens, pharmaceuticals, and the like. For an automobile producer, this inventory would consist of components purchased from other manufacturers, like tires, plastic parts, and brake systems.

Work-in-process inventory (WIP) is maintained to decouple manufacturing processing steps from each other and to account for products that are actually being processed at any given time. In many situations, both in services and manufacturing, items are processed in batches, rather than individually. For example, an insurance claims processing center might process claims through several stages. Rather than move each claim to the second step as soon as it completes the first, the claims processor might transfer claims in quantities of 20 from one stage to the next. These batches are known as **transfer batches.** Manufacturers often use transfer batches, transferring materials from one work station to another.

work-in-process inventory (WIP)
Inventory of work that has begun processing, but has not yet been completed.

transfer batch
The quantity produced at a workcenter before transferring the products to the next step in the process.

Work-in-process inventories, which consist of dependent demand items, provide manufacturers with the ability to decouple one work center from being directly dependent on another. Here, rear quarterpanels are being inspected prior to final assembly. The demand for rear quarterpanels is directly determined by the production schedule; however, there may also be some independent demand from body shops for replacement parts.

pipeline inventory
Inventory in transit.

WIP inventory might also accumulate in front of manufacturing or service processes because of the inability of a particular processing step to keep up with demand. This occurs when the arrival rate at the process exceeds the processing rate. In some manufacturing processes, a brewery, for example, WIP inventory would include product that is actually in a process at any given time. WIP inventory can also exist as "pipeline" inventory. **Pipeline inventory** is inventory that is actually in pipelines (being transported from one oil refinery to another, for example) or inventory being transported in trucks, trains, ships, or planes. For many businesses, particularly mail-order retailers, Internet retailers, and B2B suppliers, much inventory can be in transit at any given time. Reducing the transit time reduces the level of inventory in the pipeline.

Inventoried items are given unique identifying numbers, known as part numbers or SKUs (stock-keeping units). SKUs enable the item to be identified and accounted for accurately. In some manufacturing situations, when an item is stored between processing steps, the SKU number actually changes after each processing step.

While the roles of raw materials, component, and WIP inventories differ from those of finished products, the costs and risks associated with carrying them are similar. Any inventoried item can become obsolete or, as a result of a short shelf life, spoil. If purchased in excess, the investment generates no financial return because it adds no value. WIP inventory, in particular, can be expensive because not only do the raw materials cost money, but the creation of the WIP inventory can use up operating capacity that may be in short supply. Scarce capacity used to create excess WIP inventory will not be available later to process inventory that is desperately needed.

dependent demand inventory
Inventory whose demand is determined by the production schedule for finished products. Dependent demand items usually are components and raw materials.

Raw materials, component, and WIP inventories are known as **dependent demand inventory.** Dependent demand is not determined directly by the market, as is the case with independent demand, but rather by the demand for some other inventory item or by a production schedule intended to meet independent demand. Let's look at an example. The production of PCs requires a number of component items, including cases, hard drives, power supplies, motherboards, and sound cards. The demand for sound cards, for example, would be directly determined by the demand for completed computers. Suppose 439 PCs were needed to meet the forecasted demand for next week. Since one sound card is required for each PC, the demand for sound cards would be 439. The approaches used to manage dependent demand inventory do not need to cope with the uncertainty of a

Pipeline inventories consist of goods that are in the process of "flowing" from one place to another. In this oil pipeline in Alaska, the length and size of the pipeline create a huge pipeline inventory. Pipeline inventories also include the inventory on trains, trucks, and ships when there is a constant amount in transit for consistent deliveries. In those cases, the existence of a pipeline inventory is not as obvious, but it is a significant amount of inventory nonetheless. In all cases, reducing distances between transportation points and speeding up the flow of inventory can reduce the pipeline inventory level.

probabilistic demand. Demand for dependent demand is deterministic: We know *in advance* exactly what it will be.

Because dependent demand inventory is consumed in a deterministic environment, it is managed quite differently from independent demand inventory because it is consumed in a deterministic environment. Rather than being forecast in advance, it is simply calculated. Demand that can be calculated has no inherent error.

Inventory Decisions

Decisions that must be made to effectively manage inventory do not, on the surface, appear to be highly complex. In most cases only two questions need to be answered: *When* should it be ordered? and *How many* should be ordered? When our perspective is broadened to include the supply chain, the question of *where* the inventory should be located must also be answered. The "when" and "how many" decisions for independent demand inventory are made in a different manner than decisions for dependent demand inventory. The following discussion provides a comprehensive overview of the techniques used for making these decisions.

Managing Independent Demand Inventory

Many different approaches are used to determine when and how many to order for independent demand inventory. Two representative approaches will be examined for the purposes of an overview. Independent demand is, by definition, uncertain demand. No one knows in advance what the demand will be. Systems developed to manage inventory must include mechanisms that address demand uncertainty and also ensure that the inventory is available when needed. The percentage of demands that can be satisfied from on-hand inventory is known as the **service level.** The fact that orders do not arrive instantaneously adds to the difficulty associated with managing demand. In other words,

service level
The percent of orders satisfied from existing inventory.

TARGETING technology · VMI at Limited Brands

Vendor managed inventory (VMI) has gained acceptance because it makes inventory more productive. In researched implementations, service levels increase as inventory levels drop. VMI is used so that suppliers own and manage retailers' inventories up to the point of sale. The ability of a manufacturer to know precisely what a retailer's demand is means that the manufacturer can make decisions as to what inventory the retailer needs. Those decisions tend to be better, but also quicken response.

For Limited, quick response and flexibility are crucial. They move in and out of specific products, reacting quickly to customer needs. Limited collects store-specific information by hour and creates a daily inventory position report that is passed along to its suppliers. This enables Limited to move inventory back up the supply chain and actually postpone production. Contract manufacturer suppliers carry a small buffer of inventory, which they can ship directly to stores. Rather than complete the production of apparel, uncut fabric is actually prepositioned and committed to actual garment details as late as possible. This "postponement" reduces inventory downstream. Production of standardized components, like many components in a bra, for example, doesn't have to be postponed, because final product decisions won't affect it. Product-, design-, or size-specific components are not assembled until as late as possible. That time can be later with VMI information sharing.

Sources: H. L. Richardson, "The Ins and Outs of VMI," *Logistics Today*, www.logisticstoday.com, March 2004; D. D. Achabal, S. H. McIntyre, S. A. Smith, and K. Kalyanam, "A Decision Support System for Vendor Managed Inventory," *Journal of Retailing*, Winter 2000, Vol. 76, Issue 4, p. 430.

---

replenishment lead time

The time required to receive inventory that has been ordered.

there is a **replenishment lead time.** If we could get more inventory instantly, whenever we stocked out, stocking out wouldn't cause a problem. Or if demand were known in advance for certain, it really would be no big deal to have to wait for the replenishment. In the real world, demand is uncertain *and* there is a replenishment lead time, so we must develop mechanisms to deal with uncertainty.

First, we must recognize that "how many" we order can vary as a result of "how often" we order. If we order very frequently, for example, we can meet demand without ordering very much. If we order in small quantities, the "when" will most likely mean "soon."

Second, since we must wait a period of time for the order to arrive, we must order *before* we stockout. We must plan ahead. If we wait until we run out to order, we will be unable to satisfy demand during the replenishment lead time.

Third, because demand varies, order quantities or frequency must also vary to accommodate demand variability. For example, we can order in different size quantities each time we order, or we can order at different intervals, or we could do both. If demand is variable, however, and we want to order the same quantity every time we order, we *must* change the time interval between orders to react to demand changes. Likewise, if demand is variable and we want to order at fixed time intervals, we *must* be willing to change the order quantity to react to demand changes.

Two general approaches to making these decisions provide a nice overview of the many different systems used. They correspond to the issues just discussed and can be summed up as (1) fixed-quantity, variable-interval systems and (2) fixed-interval, variable-quantity systems.

fixed-quantity reorder point (ROP) model

An independent demand inventory management system that reorders when inventory drops to a specific level.

When to Order: The Fixed-Quantity, Variable-Interval System

In a fixed-quantity, variable-interval system, the order quantity is the same each time an order is placed. However, to adapt to the varying rate of demand, the time interval between orders changes. A common implementation of this system is known as a **fixed-quantity reorder point (ROP) model.** In a reorder point model, an order is placed whenever the level of inventory drops to a predetermined point. Whenever the inventory level reaches the reorder point, an order is placed. The rate of demand determines how long it takes for the inventory to drop to the level of the reorder point, hence the "variable interval." The rate of the demand after the order is placed determines whether a stockout will occur.

Determining when to reorder, in this case, means determining what the reorder point should be. A quick study of the purpose of the reorder point leads to a better understanding of how it should be determined. Recall from an earlier discussion that because there is a replenishment lead time (i.e., there is a time lapse between placing and receiving the order), the order must be placed prior to stocking out. The inventory on hand when the order is placed must be sufficient to meet demand during that replenishment lead time. If the reorder point is calculated to be equal to the demand that would take place during the replenishment lead time, there would be enough.

That logic is sound, and seems easy enough, but don't forget: We don't know for sure what the demand during lead time will be. It varies, but even though we don't know exactly what it is, we can still describe it and base our reorder point on what we know about it.

Just like any other demand, the demand during the replenishment lead time can be forecast. Depending on the situation, different types of forecasts could be used. The simplest case, and a common approach to solving this problem, is to use the average demand during the lead time. So if the average demand was 60 units per week, and the replenishment lead time was two weeks, the average demand during the lead time would be 120 units. If we set the reorder point to 120 units, we get an immediate lesson on the impact of variability. If the average demand during lead time was 120 units with *no* variability (in other words, it was always 120), a reorder point of 120 units would be fine. An order would be placed when the inventory dropped to 120, demand would consume the 120 units, and the new order would arrive just as that last unit was removed from inventory.

In the real world, if the average demand during lead time was 120, the demand during lead time would vary around the mean of 120. Sometimes it would be above 120 and sometimes it would be below 120. It would be normally distributed around 120 and its variability could be measured in the form of a standard deviation (σ). If 120 was used for the reorder point, it would be sufficient to satisfy the demand during lead time 50 percent of the time, since half of the demands would be above 120 and half would be below 120. Additional inventory would need to be added to increase the service level to above 50 percent (to meet demand in those 50 percent of the cases where demand exceeded 120). That additional inventory is known as a **safety stock.** Suppose, for the sake of an example, the average demand during lead time was 120 and had a standard deviation of 12. The distribution of this demand is shown in Exhibit 11.5.

safety stock
Additional inventory used to help meet demand uncertainty.

Knowing the mean and standard deviation for demand that is normally distributed enables us to compute, quite easily, the probability that demand will be above a certain quantity. Using the normal probability table provided in Appendix B, we know that 84.134 percent of the demands during the replenishment lead time will be below the mean plus 1 standard deviation. In addition, we know that 97.725 percent of the demands will be below the mean plus 2 standard deviations. Thus 2 standard deviations would provide a service level of 97.73 percent. The formula for the fixed-quantity reorder point is

$$ROP = \bar{d}_{LT} + \sigma_{LT}Z$$

where

$\bar{d}_{LT}$ = average demand during the replenishment lead time

σ_{LT} = standard deviation of demand during the replenishment lead time

Z = number of standard deviations above the average demand during the replenishment lead time required for the desired service level

EXHIBIT 11.5	Distribution of Demand during Lead Time

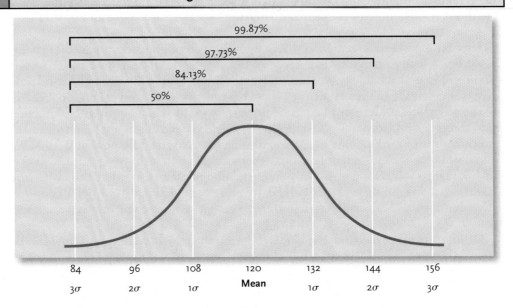

Exhibit 11.6 provides a diagram of how the fixed-quantity reorder point system works. Identifying the proper number of standard deviations to use for a given service level requires using a Table of the Cumulative Standard Normal Distribution like the one in Appendix B. This table goes by Z value increments of .05. In this case, we search the $G(z)$ columns for .99. On the second page of the table we find a $G(z)$ value of 0.98928 with a corresponding Z value of 2.30. Just below that we find a $G(z)$ value of 0.99061 with a corresponding Z value of 2.35. Using these values, the Z value for a .99 service level is frequently interpolated to 2.33. If we wanted a reorder point that would provide a 99 percent probability of exceeding the demand during the replenishment lead time (a 99 percent service level), it would need to be equal to the mean plus 2.33 standard deviations. In our example, that would be:

$$ROP = \bar{d}_{LT} + \sigma_{LT}Z$$
$$= 120 + 2.33(12)$$
$$= 120 + 28 = 148$$

EXHIBIT 11.6	Reorder Point System

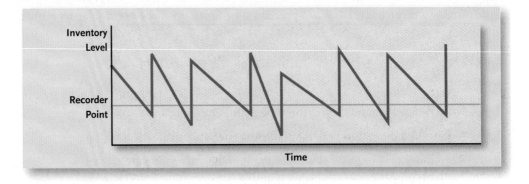

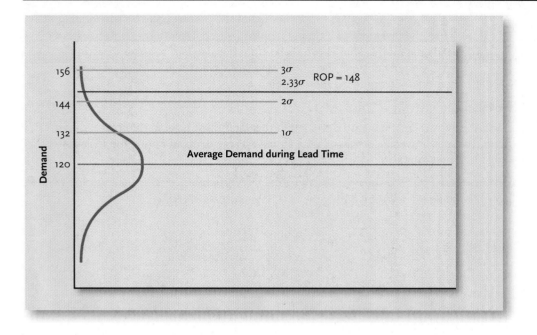

An ROP of 148 would be sufficient to satisfy demand during the replenishment lead time with 99 percent confidence. This reorder point is shown, as it relates to the distribution of demand during lead time, in Exhibit 11.7.

One simplifying factor in the previous example is that the standard deviation of demand during the two-week lead time was provided. In most situations, the time units for the standard deviation would be the same as for the average. That is, both the average *and* standard deviation would be expressed as daily or weekly. If the average was on a daily basis, the standard deviation would also likely be on a daily basis. In the previous situation, if we had known only the weekly standard deviation of demand, we would need to convert it to the standard deviation for the two-week lead time. Unlike the mean, the standard deviation is not additive. If the weekly demand averaged 60 and had a standard deviation of 10, for example, the standard deviation over two weeks would *not* be 20. The variance (σ^2), however, is additive. So if the weekly standard deviation was 10, the variance would have been 100. The variance over the two-week lead time would be 200 and the standard deviation (σ) would then be 14.142 (the square root of 200).

Step-by-Step: Calculating the Reorder Point for the Fixed-Quantity Reorder Point Model

1. Determine the average demand and the standard deviation.
2. Convert the average demand to the average demand during the replenishment lead time.
3. Convert the standard deviation to the standard deviation during the replenishment lead time.
4. Using Appendix B, determine the number of standard deviations necessary for the desired service level.
5. Use formula 11.1, and round the solution up to the nearest integer.

Example 11.2 provides another reorder point calculation to determine when to place an order.

Example 11.2   **Reorder Point Calculation**

A local silk-screen operation wishes to utilize a reorder point system for managing the inventory of its most frequently used T-shirt. The replenishment lead time for this shirt is two weeks from the standard supplier. The average weekly demand is 62. The weekly standard deviation is 13. A 95 percent service level is desired. Compute the reorder point.

Solution

First, the average and standard deviation for demand must be computed for the lead time. The weekly average demand is 62, so the average demand during the replenishment lead time is 124:

$$d_{LT} = 2(62) = 124$$

Next, the standard deviation during the lead time must be calculated:

$$\sigma_{LT} = \sqrt{\sigma^2 + \sigma^2}$$
$$= \sqrt{(13^2 + 13^2)}$$
$$= 18.38$$

The value for Z, the number of standard deviations necessary for the desired service level, must be determined:

$$Z_{.95} = 1.645 \qquad \text{(from Appendix B with interpolation)}$$
$$ROP = d_{LT} + \sigma_{LT}Z$$
$$= 124 + 18.38478(1.645)$$
$$= 154.243$$

A noninteger solution should always be rounded up. Rounding down would provide slightly less than the desired service level. Thus

$$ROP = 155 \text{ rounded up}$$

Excel Tutor 11.2 solves this problem in a spreadsheet.

Stop here

How Many to Order: The Economic Order Quantity

The reorder point system tells us when an order should be released, but the order quantity still needs to be determined. A common approach to determining the quantity to order utilizes one of a set of techniques based on the **economic order quantity model.** Economic order quantity techniques identify the order quantity that will minimize the costs associated with the order size.

economic order quantity model
An approach used to determine an order quantity that minimizes the sum of ordering and carrying costs.

The simplest of the economic order quantity techniques is known as the basic economic order quantity. The basic economic order quantity (EOQ) makes the following assumptions in order to provide an optimal solution:

1. Annual demand is known.

2. Demand is even.

3. Lead time is constant.

4. There are no quantity discounts.

5. Only one product is involved.

6. Orders are received in single deliveries.

The assumptions confine the identified costs involved in the order quantity to only carrying costs and order costs. The formula for the total cost, given these assumptions, is:

(11.2) $$TC = H(Q/2) + S(D/Q)$$

where

TC = total cost

H = carrying or holding cost per unit, on an annual basis

Q = order quantity

S = cost of ordering

D = annual demand

Typically, H is determined as a percentage of the value of the item. Exhibit 11.8 shows the relationships among the ordering cost, carrying costs, and total cost curve and it identifies the EOQ.

Carrying Costs, Ordering Cost, and Total Cost in EOQ	EXHIBIT 11.8

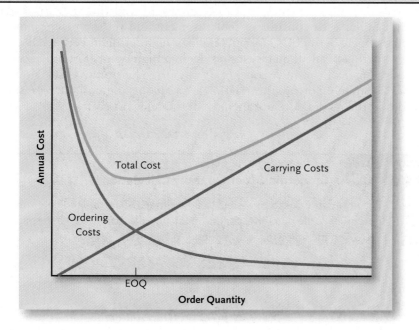

Carrying costs are typically 25 to 35 percent of the value of the item. In that scenario, the following formula might be used:

(11.3) $$H = iP$$

where

i = percentage used for determining carrying costs

P = purchase price of the item

Obtained by taking the first derivative with respect to Q of the total cost curve from formula 11.2, the formula for the EOQ is

(11.4)
$$EOQ = \sqrt{\frac{2D\,S}{H}}$$

Step-by-Step: The Economic Order Quantity Calculation

1. Determine the annual demand (D).

2. Determine the inventory carrying or holding cost per unit (H). If carrying costs are given as a percentage of the item value, H will be the percentage (i) multiplied by the item value (P).

3. Determine the cost of ordering (S) per order.

4. Use formula 11.4 to compute EOQ.

An economic order quantity problem is solved in Example 11.3.

Weaknesses of the EOQ Model

The EOQ approach to determining order quantity has come under increasing scrutiny and has been criticized for inflating order quantities. The fact that it minimizes carrying costs and order costs, given that assumptions are met, cannot be denied, but many feel that it underestimates carrying costs by ignoring well-accepted nonfinancial costs of carrying inventory. Included among these costs not considered are costs of lost flexibility, increased quality feedback time, and increased lead times. As firms have become more familiar with continuous replenishment and JIT approaches, many have abandoned the logic of the EOQ formula in favor of ordering in very small quantities. Obviously, ordering in small quantities results in a high number of orders and higher order costs, but many firms have sought out ways to reduce order costs. However, the model does accurately portray the relationships among the costs it represents. The problem is that the model does not include all the relevant costs.

Example 11.3

EXCEL TUTOR

Economic Order Quantity Calculation

The University Bookstore wished to utilize the EOQ formula to determine the appropriate order quantity for its most popular backpack. Determine the EOQ given the following information:

$$D = 600 \text{ per year}$$

$$S = \$13 \text{ per order}$$

$$H = 3.25 \text{ per year}$$

Solution

$$EOQ = \sqrt{[2(600)(13)/(3.25)]}$$

$$= \sqrt{4800} = 69.28203$$

As is evident in Exhibit 11.8, the total cost curve is nearly flat at the bottom, and rounding the EOQ off to an even quantity has little effect on the total cost associated with that quantity. In this case, the order quantity would be rounded up to 70.

Excel Tutor 11.3 provides spreadsheet calculations for this problem.

EOQ Variations

Various modifications of the basic EOQ model are used as the assumptions of the basic model are relaxed. One common variation is to incorporate a quantity discount model when quantity discounts affect the purchase price. The implication of this change is that in addition to the carrying and order costs being components of the total cost, the price is also affected.

The total cost equation for this model is

(11.5) $$TC = S(D/Q) + H(Q/2) + DP$$

Example 11.4

Quantity Discount Model Calculation

A supplier of hard drives for a local computer supply store established the following price schedule:

1–20 units:	$229 each
21–60 units:	$210 each
61–120 units:	$199 each
121+units:	$175 each
Order cost:	$20 per order
Carrying cost:	$36 per unit per year
Annual demand:	476 units

What would the low-cost order quantity be?

Solution

1. Basic EOQ $= \sqrt{(2(20)(476))/36} = 22.997$ (round to 23 units).

2. EOQ is in the range of the $210 price. All ranges having lower prices must be evaluated and compared.

Total cost of ordering the EOQ (based on formula 11.5) is

$$TC = (476/23)20 + (23/2)36 + 476(210)$$

$$= 413.91 + 414 + 99.960 = \$100{,}787.91$$

Total cost of ordering 61 units (the minimum allowable quantity for the next price range) is

$$TC = (476/61)20 + (61/2)36 + 476(199)$$

$$= 156.07 + 1{,}098 + 94{,}724 = \$95{,}978.07$$

Total cost of ordering 121 units (the minimum allowable quantity for the next price range) is

$$TC = (476/121)20 + (121/2)36 + 476(175)$$

$$= 78.68 + 2{,}178 + 83{,}300 = \$85{,}556.68$$

The low-cost order quantity is to order 121 units per order. At this quantity the cost savings from the quantity discount outweigh the increased carrying costs.

Excel Tutor 11.4 demonstrates how a spreadsheet can be used to determine the economic order quantity with quantity discounts.

where

D = annual demand

Q = order quantity

S = cost per order

H = carrying cost

P = price per unit

When the EOQ model includes quantity discounts, the process of determining the quantity that provides the lowest costs requires that the total annual cost be determined. If the basic EOQ model yields a quantity that falls in the range of the cheapest price, it is automatically the optimal order quantity. If the basic EOQ doesn't fall in the cheapest price range, all of the lower price ranges must be analyzed. In each case, compute the total cost for the lowest allowable quantity in the price range. The total cost is the sum of the cost of ordering plus the cost of carrying inventory plus the cost of the actual items.

Step-by-Step: Determining the Economic Order Quantity with Quantity Discounts

1. Compute the basic EOQ. It will fall within one of the price ranges specified by the supplier.
2. If the EOQ falls within the cheapest price range, the EOQ is the optimal order quantity.
3. If the EOQ does not fall within the cheapest price range, all price ranges having lower prices than the range the EOQ falls in must be evaluated. Use formula 11.5 to make that analysis.
4. The optimal quantity will be at the lowest allowable quantity of a price range. For each quantity, compute the total cost (carrying, order, and purchase price) for the quantity at each price break.

The computation process for the quantity discount model is demonstrated in Example 11.4.

Fixed-Interval, Variable-Quantity Systems

periodic review system
An independent demand management system that orders inventory on fixed time intervals.

An alternative to the fixed-quantity, variable-interval model is the fixed-interval, variable-quantity system, sometimes referred to as a **periodic review system.** As mentioned earlier, if the order interval is fixed, the order quantity must vary to provide the system with the necessary adaptation to fluctuation demand. This means that the order quantity could potentially be different with each order. Such a system makes sense if the user needs to order at periodic intervals because of supplier shipment schedules or the need to combine orders for many different products into a single shipment.

There are several variations to the periodic review model, but we'll examine a fairly common one. In the periodic review model, just as in the ROP model, there is a need to satisfy demand during the replenishment lead time. We know that demand during the lead time is uncertain, so we will need to incorporate a safety stock, just as in the ROP system. Because demand varies from one order interval to another, the amount of inventory on hand when the order is placed must vary from one time to the next. Recall in the ROP system that the order was placed when the inventory was at a specific point. It helps to examine this system conceptually first, and then through a mathematical formula.

The inventory ordered in the fixed-interval, variable-quantity system must accomplish two things. First, it must satisfy demand during the order interval; second, it must satisfy demand during the replenishment lead time. Both demands are uncertain. An important point to recognize is that it may not be necessary to order the entire amount needed to satisfy the demand during the order interval and replenishment lead time because some inventory may already be on hand when the order is placed.

In this system, a target inventory level (TI) is determined and the order quantity is calculated as the difference between the target and the amount of inventory on hand when the order is placed. The target inventory is the average demand during the order interval and lead times, plus a safety stock to cope with the variability of that demand. The safety stock is based on the variability of demand during the order interval and lead time (as measured by the standard deviation of demand) and the number of standard deviations necessary to provide the desired level of service.

$$\text{Order Quantity} = \text{Target Inventory Level} - \text{On-hand Inventory}$$

(11.6)
$$Q = TI - A$$

where

Q = order quantity

TI = target inventory level

A = quantity of inventory on hand when the order is placed

The target inventory level (TI) is calculated as

(11.7)
$$TI = \bar{d}_{OI+LT} + SS$$

where

$\bar{d}_{OI+LT}$ = average demand during the order interval and lead time

SS = safety stock

OI = number of days in the order interval

LT = number of days in the replenishment lead time

The safety stock is calculated as

$$SS = Z \, \sigma_{OI+LT}$$
$$= Z\sigma_t \sqrt{OI + LT}$$

Periodic Review System   EXHIBIT 11.9

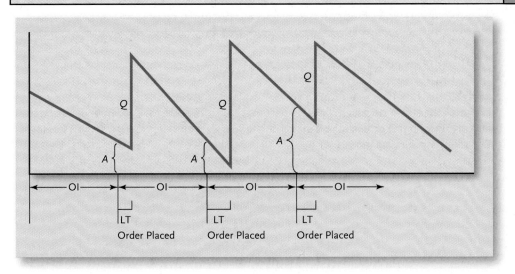

where

Z = number of standard deviations required for the necessary service level (from Appendix B)

$\sigma_{\text{OI+LT}}$ = standard deviation of demand during the order interval and lead time

σ_t = daily standard deviation

Exhibit 11.9 illustrates how this system functions.

Step-by-Step: Determining the Order Quantity for the Fixed-Interval, Variable-Quantity Model

1. Based on the average daily demand, determine the average demand during the order interval.
2. Based on the average daily demand, determine the average demand during the replenishment lead time.
3. Identify the Z value from Appendix B for the desired service level.
4. Determine the amount of inventory on hand currently.
5. Using formula 11.8, determine the safety stock.
6. Using formula 11.7, determine the target inventory level.
7. Using formula 11.6, determine the order quantity.

The computation process for the periodic review model is illustrated in Example 11.5.

Example 11.5

Periodic Review Model Calculation

EXCEL TUTOR

A local sporting goods store has located a supplier of athletic socks that can deliver every Friday, when it delivers other products to clothing stores in the area. The manager must place the order on Wednesday each week. The price charged for the socks is significantly cheaper than that charged by the current supplier, but the manager must convert to a periodic review inventory system. The store is open every day. Using the following information, calculate the order quantity.

Average daily demand: 3.6 units
Replenishment lead time: 2 days
Standard deviation (daily): .5
Inventory currently on hand: 5
Service level desired: 95%
Order interval: 7 days

Solution

Compute the safety stock first. For a 95 percent service level, we look at Appendix B and find .95053 with a Z of 1.65, and we interpolate to a Z of 1.645 for the .95 service level. The safety stock calculation is:

$$SS = Z\sigma\sqrt{OI + LT}$$
$$= 1.645(.5)(\sqrt{2 + 7})$$
$$= 1.645(.5)(3)$$
$$= 2.4675$$

(Continues)

Example 11.5   *(Continued)*

EXCEL TUTOR

Next, we compute the target inventory level (TI). The target inventory level is the average demand during the order interval and replenishment lead time, plus the safety stock. It is calculated as:

$$TI = \bar{d}_{OI+LT} + SS$$
$$= 32.4 + 2.4675$$
$$= 34.87$$
$$= \text{round up to } 35$$

The order quantity (Q) can then be calculated as the target inventory level minus the on-hand inventory:

$$Q = TI - A$$
$$= 35 - 5$$
$$= 30$$

Excel Tutor 11.5 demonstrates how this calculation can be made in a spreadsheet.

Managing Dependent Demand Inventory: Material Requirements Planning

As mentioned early in this chapter, dependent demand inventory is significantly different from independent demand inventory. Because the demand for dependent demand inventory is derived from the production schedule of other items, it is deterministic. The approach used to determine the quantity and timing of orders is known as **material requirements planning (MRP).** MRP is frequently used to determine orders for manufactured components as well as purchased components and raw materials.

As one might expect, MRP calculations consist of two stages. First, the quantity to order is determined, then the timing of the order is established. Once again, the questions that must be answered are How many? and When? The process used to determine "how many?" is known as **netting,** or computing net requirements. Net requirements are computed by subtracting on-hand inventory from the total quantity needed. The process of determining "when?" is known as **backward scheduling,** which means that the replenishment lead time is subtracted from the due date to determine when the order must be released.

The netting and backward scheduling processes used in MRP logic require several pieces of information. First, the requirements for the end product must be known. This information typically comes from a production plan known as a **master production schedule (MPS),** which is simply a statement of how many of each end item or product will be produced by the end of each time period. Second, the composition of the end product must be known so that the required components can be ordered. This information is obtained from a product structure file known as a **bill of material.** Third, the replenishment lead time and the current quantity on hand must be known. This information typically comes from a file that also contains information on the supplier, cost, and so on, known as an **inventory master file.** These inputs, shown in Exhibit 11.10, are pulled together in MRP logic to provide the quantity and timing of orders that will ensure that components and raw materials arrive promptly and in the right quantities for the production of end products.

material requirements planning (MRP)
An inventory management approach used to manage dependent demand inventory that plans order releases for the future based on production schedules.

netting
The process of computing net requirements.

backward scheduling
When a completion date or due date is known and that date must determine a start date.

master production schedule (MPS)
A schedule of end products that must be completed in a specific time period.

bill of material
In material requirements planning, this is a computer file containing information about the materials required to produce a product or component.

inventory master file
In material requirements planning, this is a computer file containing information about an inventory item such as the quantity on hand, the cost, and so on.

MRP logic typically starts with a master production schedule, similar to the one shown in Exhibit 11.11 for an inexpensive staple remover. The MPS shows the quantity of staple removers that are to be completed each week. The staple remover has four components: the outer jaw, the inner jaw, the connecting pin, and the spring. The product structure for the staple remover, presented in Exhibit 11.12, shows that it takes one of each component to produce the staple remover. The lead times associated with the components are:

Staple remover: 1 week	Connecting pin: 2 weeks
Outer jaw: 1 week	Spring: 2 weeks
Inner jaw: 1 week	

Also assume there are 75 units of the completed staple remover and 75 units of each component on hand currently.

The results of the logic used to compute the net requirements and establish the plan for when the orders will be released for just the staple remover are presented in

---

EXHIBIT 11.10	Material Requirements Planning Inputs

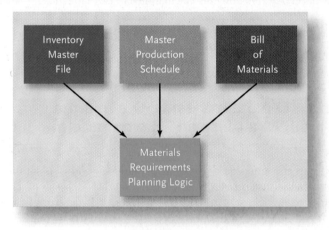

EXHIBIT 11.11	Master Production Schedule (MPS) for Staple Remover

Week	1	2	3	4	5	6	7	8
Quantity	0	45	62	35	64	52	67	62

EXHIBIT 11.12	Structure for Staple Remover

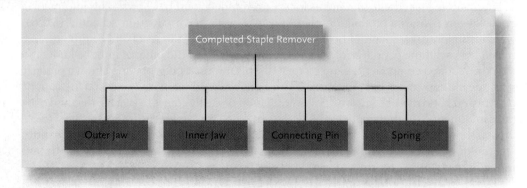

| | Quantity and Timing for Staple Remover Orders | | | | | | | | EXHIBIT 11.13 |

	Week 1	Week 2	Week 3	Week 4	Week 5	Week 6	Week 7	Week 8
Gross requirement	0	45	62	35	64	52	67	62
Beginning on-hand inventory	75	75	30	0	0	0	0	0
Ending on-hand inventory	75	30	0	0	0	0	0	0
Net requirements	0	0	32	35	64	52	67	62
Planned order receipts	0	0	32	35	64	52	67	62
Planned order releases	0	32	35	64	52	67	62	0

Exhibit 11.13. The logic in this table is best described by looking at each row in the "MRP record." For the first row, **gross requirements** quantities for the completed staple remover come directly from the MPS for the staple remover. The gross requirements will be calculated differently for components of the staple remover. The **beginning on-hand inventory** is given as 75 units in period 1 for the completed staple remover. For the remaining periods, the weekly beginning on-hand inventory is equal to the **ending on-hand inventory** from the previous week. Ending on-hand inventory is equal to the beginning on-hand inventory plus planned order receipts minus gross requirements. The **net requirement** is equal to the gross requirement minus beginning on-hand inventory for that period. **Planned order receipt** is equal to the **planned order release** one lead time earlier. So, in this situation, the planned order receipt of 32 in week 3 is a result of the planned order release of 32 in week 2. The planned order release is equal to the net requirement for one lead time *later*. For example, the planned order release of 32 in week 2 is a result of the net requirement of 32 in week 3.

Gross requirements for the components come directly from the planned order release of the "parent," which is the end product in this case. The planned order release for the staple remover is used because, to start the assembly of the staple remover, all of the components must be available. The starting point for assembling the staple remover determines the due date for its components. The time line in Exhibit 11.14 aids in understanding the due dates associated with the staple remover product.

Exhibit 11.15 provides the complete logic for the end product and all three components. Notice that, as mentioned earlier, the lead time for the connecting pin and spring is two weeks, rather than one. When comparing the logic used for the components with the logic used in the end product, the primary difference is the calculation of the gross requirements.

Step-by-Step: The MRP Calculation Process

1. Identify logic inputs: the master production schedule, the product structure (bill of material), lead time information for end product and components, and on-hand inventory quantities.
2. Beginning with the end product logic, the gross requirements are exactly the same as the master production schedule quantities. Transfer those values to the MRP table.
3. Proceeding week by week, enter the beginning on-hand inventory quantity for the beginning on-hand inventory of week 1, and thereafter enter the beginning on-hand inventory quantity from the previous week's ending on-hand inventory quantity.
4. Compute the net requirements by subtracting beginning on-hand inventory from the gross requirement.
5. If there is a positive net requirement in a week, backward schedule by the lead time and enter the quantity for the planned order release that will satisfy that net requirement. Forward schedule by the amount of the lead time from the planned order release and enter the value for the planned order receipt.

gross requirements
In material requirements planning, the total quantity needed to meet demand.

beginning on-hand inventory
The quantity of inventory on hand at the beginning of a time period.

ending on-hand inventory
The quantity of inventory on hand at the end of a time period.

net requirements
In material requirements planning, gross requirements minus beginning on-hand inventory.

planned order receipt
In material requirements planning, this is the planned receipt of material that results from a planned order release.

planned order release
In material requirements planning, this is the order planned to be released to satisfy a future net requirement.

| EXHIBIT 11.14 | **Time Line for Staple Remover Component Orders** |

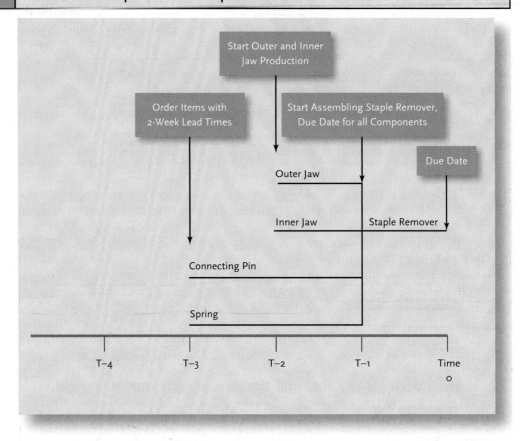

6. Compute the ending on-hand inventory for the week by starting with the beginning on-hand inventory, subtracting the gross requirements, and adding any planned order receipts.

7. Move on to the next week, and repeat the process.

Extended MRP

lot-for-lot ordering
In material requirements planning, ordering exactly the amount of the net requirements.

If the product structure were deeper, the gross requirements of the next lower level would be determined by the planned order releases from the level above. If more than one unit of a particular component goes into its parent, then the gross requirement of that item is obtained from multiplying the planned order release of its parent by the quantity of units needed.

Notice that as soon as the initial starting inventory is consumed, ending and beginning on-hand inventory levels equal zero because the orders being placed are equal to the net requirement. Releasing an order exactly equal to the net requirement is known as **lot-for-lot ordering**.

fixed-quantity order policy
In material requirements planning, rather than ordering the quantity of the net requirements, orders are placed in increments of a fixed quantity.

As an alternative to lot-for-lot ordering, various lot sizing methods could be used to manipulate order costs and holding costs, similar to managing independent demand. In many situations, purchased components come in containers that hold a specified amount. Manufactured components are often produced in batches of a specified size. Placing orders in multiples of fixed quantities is referred to as a **fixed-quantity order policy**. The use of such a policy will result in inventory being carried from period to period, resulting in higher inventory carrying costs than a lot-for-lot order policy. However, order costs and prices might be reduced by ordering in fixed quantities.

| MRP Records for Staple Remover and Components | | | | | | | | | EXHIBIT 11.15 |

Staple Remover MRP Record	Week 1	Week 2	Week 3	Week 4	Week 5	Week 6	Week 7	Week 8
Gross requirement	0	45	62	35	64	52	67	62
Beginning on-hand inventory	75	75	30	0	0	0	0	0
Ending on-hand inventory	75	30	0	0	0	0	0	0
Net requirements	0	0	32	35	64	52	67	62
Planned order receipts	0	0	32	35	64	52	67	62
Planned order releases	0	32	35	64	52	67	62	0

Outer Jaw MRP Record	Week 1	Week 2	Week 3	Week 4	Week 5	Week 6	Week 7	Week 8
Gross requirement	0	32	35	64	52	67	62	0
Beginning on-hand inventory	75	75	43	8	0	0	0	0
Ending on-hand inventory	75	43	8	0	0	0	0	0
Net requirements	0	0	0	56	52	67	62	0
Planned order receipts	0	0	0	56	52	67	62	0
Planned order releases	0	0	56	52	67	62	0	0

Inner Jaw MRP Record	Week 1	Week 2	Week 3	Week 4	Week 5	Week 6	Week 7	Week 8
Gross requirement	0	32	35	64	52	67	62	0
Beginning on-hand inventory	75	75	43	8	0	0	0	0
Ending on-hand inventory	75	43	8	0	0	0	0	0
Net requirements	0	0	0	56	52	67	62	0
Planned order receipts	0	0	0	56	52	67	62	0
Planned order releases	0	0	56	52	67	62	0	0

Connecting Pin MRP Record	Week 1	Week 2	Week 3	Week 4	Week 5	Week 6	Week 7	Week 8
Gross requirement	0	32	35	64	52	67	62	0
Beginning on-hand inventory	75	75	43	8	0	0	0	0
Ending on-hand inventory	75	43	8	0	0	0	0	0
Net requirements	0	0	0	56	52	67	62	0
Planned order receipts	0	0	0	56	52	67	62	0
Planned order releases	0	56	52	67	62	0	0	0

Spring MRP Record	Week 1	Week 2	Week 3	Week 4	Week 5	Week 6	Week 7	Week 8
Gross requirement	0	32	35	64	52	67	62	0
Beginning on-hand inventory	75	75	43	8	0	0	0	0
Ending on-hand inventory	75	43	8	0	0	0	0	
Net requirements	0	0	0	56	52	67	62	0
Planned order receipts	0	0	0	56	52	67	62	0
Planned order releases	0	56	52	67	62	0	0	0

As products included in the MRP logic become more complex, the logic must accommodate various potential situations. One is that the same components might be used in different end products. To accurately account for this, MRP logic must proceed in a level-by-level rather than product-by-product fashion. In addition, since the gross

Example 11.6

EXCEL TUTOR

Extended MRP Logic

Pod Weezles manufactures a variety of accessories for iPod users. Most come in a variety of bright colors to offer some contrast to white. One of its products, called the "Easel," is a simple cradle that enables the iPod to sit up-right for screen visibility and connect to a computer's USB port for charging and updating. The Easel consists of two major components, one of which has three ad-ditional components. The major components of the Easel are the base and cable. The base consists of a top, a bottom, and a USB insert. The cable is a standard, 30-inch USB cable. The product structure is diagramed in Exhibit 11.16. Bases are assembled in a fixed quantity batch size, so there are often assembled bases on hand. The top and bot-tom of the base is manufactured in-house. The cable and USB insert are outsourced.

EXHIBIT 11.16	Product Structure of Pod Weezle Easel

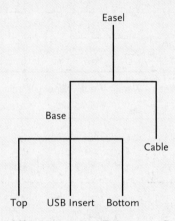

The master production schedule for Easels is presented in Exhibit 11.17.

EXHIBIT 11.17	Master Production Schedule for Pod Weezle Easel

Week 1	Week 2	Week 3	Week 4	Week 5	Week 6	Week 7	Week 8
460	580	560	700	640	760	810	660

On-hand inventory levels, lead time information, and order policy information for the Easel and its components are kept on file in Pod Weezle's computer system. That infor-mation is presented in Exhibit 11.18

EXHIBIT 11.18	On-Hand Inventory Levels, Lead Time Information, and Order Policy Information

Item	On-Hand Inventory	Lead Time (weeks)	Order Policy
Easel	1000	1	Lot for lot
Base	1000	1	200
Cable	1000	1	500
Top	1000	1	Lot for lot
Bottom	1000	1	Lot for lot
USB Insert	1000	1	1000

(Continues)

Example 11.6

(Continued)

Exhibit 11.19 provides the soution for the MRP records. The logic here differs slightly from the previous example because of the depth of the product structure and the use of fixed quantity lot sizing. A universal rule of MRP logic is that the gross requirements for a component are derived directly from the planned order release of its "parent." Thus, the gross requirements for the base come from the planned order releases of the end product. The gross requirements for the top, USB insert, and bottom come from the planned order releases of the base. The fixed quantity lot sizing logic is quite straightforward. Orders must be released in increments of the fixed quantity lotsize. So, as in the Week 2 planned order release for 400 units of the base, the net requirement was only 300, but 400 units were ordered because the order had to be in increments of the lotsize.

EXHIBIT 11.19 MRP Records for the Easel and Components

Easel

Lot size = Lot for Lot; Lead time = 1 week

	1	2	3	4	5	6	7	8
Gross requirements	460	580	560	700	640	760	810	660
Beginning on-hand	1000	540	0	0	0	0	0	0
Ending on-hand	540	0	0	0	0	0	0	0
Net requirements	0	40	560	700	640	760	810	660
Planned receipts	0	40	560	700	640	760	810	660
Planned releases	40	560	700	640	760	810	660	0

Base

Lot size = 200; Lead time = 1 week

	1	2	3	4	5	6	7	8
Gross requirements	40	560	700	640	760	810	660	0
Beginning on-hand	1000	960	400	100	60	100	90	30
Ending on-hand	960	400	100	60	100	90	30	30
Net requirements	0	0	300	540	700	710	570	0
Planned receipts	0	0	400	600	800	800	600	0
Planned releases	0	400	600	800	800	600	0	0

Cable

Lot size = 500; Lead time = 1 week

	1	2	3	4	5	6	7	8
Gross requirements	40	560	700	640	760	810	660	0
Beginning on-hand	1000	960	400	200	60	300	490	330
Ending on-hand	960	400	200	60	300	490	330	330
Net requirements	0	0	300	440	700	510	170	0
Planned receipts	0	0	500	500	1000	1000	500	0
Planned releases	0	500	500	1000	1000	500	0	0

(Continues)

Example 11.6

(Continued)

EXCEL TUTOR

Top

Lot size = 1; Lead time = 1 week

	1	2	3	4	5	6	7	8
Gross requirements	0	400	600	800	800	600	0	0
Beginning on-hand	1000	1000	600	0	0	0	0	0
Ending on-hand	1000	600	0	0	0	0	0	0
Net requirements	0	0	0	800	800	600	0	0
Planned receipts	0	0	0	800	800	600	0	0
Planned releases	0	0	800	800	600	0	0	0

Bottom

Lot size =1; Lead time = 1 week

	1	2	3	4	5	6	7	8
Gross requirements	0	400	600	800	800	600	0	0
Beginning on-hand	1000	1000	600	0	0	0	0	0
Ending on-hand	1000	600	0	0	0	0	0	0
Net requirements	0	0	0	800	800	600	0	0
Planned receipts	0	0	0	800	800	600	0	0
Planned releases	0	0	800	800	600	0	0	0

USB Insert

Lot size = 1000; Lead time = 1 week

	1	2	3	4	5	6	7	8
Gross requirements	0	400	600	800	800	600	0	0
Beginning on-hand	1000	1000	600	0	200	400	800	800
Ending on-hand	1000	600	0	200	400	800	800	800
Net requirements	0	0	0	800	600	200	0	0
Planned receipts	0	0	0	1000	1000	1000	0	0
Planned releases	0	0	1000	1000	1000	0	0	0

Excel Tutor 11.6 demonstrates how MRP logic can be effectively created in an Excel spreadsheet.

requirements for a component may need to come from different parents, it must be built into the MRP logic as well.

In some situations, the demand for an inventory item can be both independent and dependent. Automobile components, for example, are needed for the production of finished automobiles but can have independent demand coming from dealer's service centers as well.

Example 11.6 extends the previous demonstration of MRP logic. It includes the use of fixed-quantity order policies.

Prioritizing Inventory: ABC Analysis

The management of inventory can be expensive. The more sophisticated the system, the more expensive the management of the system. A reorder point system, for example, is a continuous-review system. Every time inventory is removed, a comparison is made between the actual level of inventory and the reorder point. A stockout can occur only during the replenishment lead time. A periodic review system, however, does not continuously monitor the inventory level. A stockout can potentially occur at any time. The differences in these systems result in cost differences. A simplistic approach might be to wait until a stockout occurs, and then reorder. A primitive form of a reorder point system is known as a **two-bin system**. When the first bin is emptied, a new order is placed. The second bin serves demand during the replenishment lead time.

two-bin system
A primitive reorder point
inventory system in
which two containers
of inventory are kept.
An order for more is
placed when one
container becomes empty.

A variety of inventory management systems are available, and a company must decide which system to use. How does a company select the desired service level? One approach to making these decisions is a prioritization procedure known as ABC analysis (not to be confused with activity-based costing).

ABC analysis is based on the Pareto principle, which states that approximately 80 percent of the effects are the result of 20 percent of the causes. In an inventory situation, this translates into 80 percent of the dollar usage being associated with only 20 percent of the items. ABC analysis classifies inventory in order of importance. "A" items are the most important, "B" items are next, and "C" items are of relatively little importance. The relative importance of inventory items is typically linked to dollar usage, but it could be linked to other critical issues, such as a particular customer, storage costs, or shelf life.

Generally, A items comprise about 10 percent or so of the inventory items. They are of extreme importance because they might account for as much as 50 percent of the annual dollar usage. The B items are generally about 30 to 40 percent of the items, and C items are the remainder. Whether the items are A, B, or C will determine such issues as the type of inventory management system used, the service level used, and the number of suppliers or backup suppliers required.

Measuring Inventory Productivity

Inventory productivity measures the amount of sales revenue generated from the inventory. Inventory productivity is generally measured in **inventory turns**, computed as sales divided by the average dollar level of inventory. The higher the inventory turns, the better. A higher number of turns simply means that the same amount of inventory, on average, is generating greater sales.

inventory turns
A measure of inventory
productivity computed
by dividing sales by the
average value of inventory.

Because inventory is such a valuable asset, firms generally want to increase its productivity. Improving inventory turns is often mandated by top management. It results in reduced costs associated with inventory, increased profit margins, reduced assets, and improved ROA. Increasing inventory turns almost always means reducing inventory. Rarely should it be interpreted as "increasing sales," although that would be even better. Unfortunately, all inventoried items don't contribute the same value to a business. Some are extremely important, while other items are just taking up space. Reducing the level of some inventory items will have no detrimental impact on sales, while reducing other items could actually result in reduced customer service caused by increasing stockouts. There are ways, however, to increase turnover in a manner that will not harm service quality or delivery reliability.

Understanding "Flow"

For manufacturers, inventory turnover is also related to lead time. If, for example, total manufacturing lead time was one week, the WIP inventory turns would be 52. Reducing lead time can result in a reduction of WIP inventory and improve the inventory productivity. Imagine the manufacturing facility as a large pipe. The pipe is always full, no matter how fast the contents flow. The faster the contents move, however, the greater the flow rate and the greater the output, even though the volume inside the pipe is the same. Since the "output" is represented by sales (the numerator in the inventory turns equation), as output goes up, turns go up. One way manufacturers can reduce inventory is to reduce lead times by identifying non-value-adding steps in processes and implementing other time-saving practices, as discussed in Chapter 8. This is analogous to shortening the pipe. There is less inventory in the pipe and the inventory is in the system for a shorter time, resulting in a lower amount of inventory relative to sales. This same logic holds for the entire supply chain, from the basic manufacturers, who process raw materials, all the way through the assembler. Reduced time anywhere in the supply chain results in improved return on the inventory investment.

Another approach to improving the rate of flow of goods through a manufacturing operation or supply chain is to reduce the production and transfer batch sizes. Recall that the production batch size is the number of products produced before changing equipment over to produce something else. The transfer batch size is the number of products required before they will be transferred to the next processing step. As shown earlier, in Exhibit 11.2, more frequent delivery of smaller quantities anywhere in the supply chain improves the flow of goods. Rather than stopping and starting, goods begin to flow evenly. Using the pipe analogy again, we see that more can be moved through the pipe if its contents continue to flow evenly. Flow is a very apt term for the way materials move through manufacturing processes. Manufacturers seek to improve the flow of materials. Some services actually view customers as "inventory" and seek to improve their flow as well.

The average level of finished goods and retailing inventories can obviously be reduced by carrying fewer of each item. The difficulty, however, is determining which items should receive the inventory reduction efforts. One approach is to focus strictly on the dollars. After all, the denominator of the inventory turns equation is the average value of inventory. By reducing the inventory level of high-dollar items, increasing inventory turnover is a quick result. However, the high-dollar items might also be the best sellers. Reducing in their quantity can have a negative impact on service level.

Dollar Days

dollar days

The dollar value of an item in inventory multiplied by the number of days until it will be sold.

Another approach to reducing these types of inventory is to use a measure known as **dollar days**.[1] At the beginning of this chapter, inventory was described as an asset that sometimes behaved like a liability. The dollar-day method acknowledges this behavior and treats inventory like a loan. The total cost of a loan with a certain interest rate is determined by two factors: the size of the loan and its term. The total cost of inventory is determined in a similar way. It is dependent on the dollar value of inventory and how long the inventory is kept. Dollar days of inventory is computed by multiplying the dollar value of the inventory by the number of days until it will be sold. A firm wishing to

om ADVANTAGE   Inventory Reduction Effects Reach Suppliers

Any large retailer's effort to reduce inventory levels will mean that, until inventory levels drop to desired levels, replenishment orders will not be equal to demand. This results in a reduction in demand for suppliers and can affect their financial performance. This is particularly the case for suppliers of large retailers like Wal-Mart.

In early 2006 Wal-Mart announced an effort to reduce the number of SKUs by better identifying which products sell best. In addition, Wal-Mart began adjusting its distribution system to allow more frequent deliveries. Analysts claim that Wal-Mart was trying to cut $6 billion in inventory costs in order to boost its financial performance. This required a 20 percent reduction in Wal-Mart's inventory levels. Many suppliers, who rely on Wal-Mart for as much as

10 to 30 percent of total sales, saw an immediate reduction in sales volume as a result. Immediately upon Wal-Mart's actions, companies like Procter & Gamble, Playtex, and Spectrum Brands (a battery producer) responded by lowering quarterly financial goals. P&G's stock dropped 3 percent after it blamed inventory reduction efforts of customers for reducing its quarterly projections. Wal-Mart accounts for 16 percent of P&G sales. Spectrum's stock price dropped 28 percent due to a combination of customers' inventory reductions and rising zinc prices. Wal-Mart accounts for 18 percent of Spectrum's sales.

Source: "Wal-Mart Ripple Effect Strikes Again: Cutbacks Weigh on Supplier Earnings," The *Wall Street Journal*, April 27, 2006, pp. C1, C4.

increase inventory turns without detrimental effects on service level would seek to reduce dollar days. The dollar-day measure focuses equally on items with high dollar value *and* items that are slow movers. Items that are slow movers are those that do not contribute significantly to sales and have low turnover rates because they just sit in inventory. By using the dollar-day measure, it is possible for products with very different characteristics to be equally attractive for inventory reduction efforts. Example 11.7 demonstrates the computations necessary to determine the dollar days of inventory and also demonstrates how different products can create inventory costs in different ways.

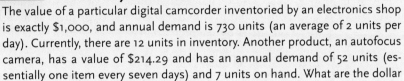

Example 11.7   Dollar-Day Calculation

The value of a particular digital camcorder inventoried by an electronics shop is exactly $1,000, and annual demand is 730 units (an average of 2 units per day). Currently, there are 12 units in inventory. Another product, an autofocus camera, has a value of $214.29 and has an annual demand of 52 units (essentially one item every seven days) and 7 units on hand. What are the dollar days associated with each of these items?

Solution

For the camcorder, an average of 2 units are sold per day. So, 2 of the 12 units will be sold in one day, 2 more will be sold in two days, and so on. Exhibit 11.20 provides the completed dollar-day calculations. The 12 units of camcorder inventory create 42,000 dollar days.

EXHIBIT 11.20   Dollar-Day Calculations for Camcorder

Number of Items	Days until Sold	Dollar Days
2	1	2,000
2	2	4,000
2	3	6,000
2	4	8,000
2	5	10,000
2	6	12,000
Total dollar days		42,000

There are currently seven units of the camera on hand, selling one unit each day. Exhibit 11.21 shows that the dollar days created is 42,000.84 dollar days. The dollar days are virtually the same for the two items, but they are created by two very different product characteristics. The camcorder acquires dollar days from its high value. The camera gets its dollar days from the fact that demand is low, resulting in inventory that sits for a long time.

EXHIBIT 11.21   Dollar-Day Calculations for Camera

Number of Items	Days until Sold	Dollar Days
1	7	1,500.03
1	14	3,000.06
1	21	4,500.09
1	28	6,000.12
1	35	7,500.15
1	42	9,000.18
1	49	10,500.21
Total dollar days		42,000.84

Excel Tutor 11.7 provides the Excel logic for the dollar-day calculation.

Reducing inventory has a substantially different impact on the two items in the example because one is a fast mover and one is a slow mover. There is a six-day supply of the digital camcorder and a seven-week supply of the camera. Eliminating one unit of the camera reduces the dollar days by 10,500. Eliminating one unit of the camcorder reduces dollar days by 6,000 (12,000/2). The larger impact, however, will be in service quality, which will translate into net sales. Reducing the inventory of the camcorder will quickly reduce service level and net sales because of the short supply relative to the demand. Reducing inventory of the camera is of very little consequence because of its low demand. If the supply of the camcorder is reduced and net sales drop because of poor service, inventory turns could potentially be the same or even worse, because sales is in the numerator. Dollar days provides an excellent method of focusing on the right inventory for an inventory reduction effort. It acknowledges that there are two factors that account for inventory costs: the money invested in the inventory and the time it is invested.

CHAPTER SUMMARY

This chapter examined inventory, the first of four critical operations resources used to create value. Because inventory is such an expensive asset and so costly to maintain, businesses strive to balance low inventory levels against appropriate levels of service. The financial impact of carrying too much inventory can be just as bad as the impact of losing sales from not carrying enough inventory.

Inventory is divided into two types: independent demand and dependent demand. Independent demand inventory is inventory whose demand is determined by the market. Dependent demand inventory is inventory whose demand is dictated by a production schedule for another item of inventory. The two types of inventory are managed differently because independent demand is uncertain, whereas dependent demand is deterministic. The systems used to manage these different types of inventory are described and demonstrated.

It is difficult to isolate the management of inventory from other productive resources because those other resources often consume and create inventory. It is also difficult to evaluate the productivity of resources and inventory because to be productive, many resources must create inventory. In any company, whether it be a manufacturer or a service, inventory is necessary: without it sales are lost and the business comes to a standstill. The resources that utilize inventory consist of the capacity, facilities, and workforce—the other three categories that are examined in this unit.

KEY TERMS

backward scheduling, 501
batch processing, 485
beginning on-hand inventory, 503
bill of material, 502
carrying cost, 481
changeover cost, 481
continuous replenishment, 482
dependent demand inventory, 488
decouple, 480
dollar days, 510
economic order quantity model, 494
ending on-hand inventory, 503
finished-goods inventory, 485
fixed-quantity order policy, 504

fixed-quantity reorder point (ROP) model, 490
gross requirements, 503
independent demand inventory, 483
inventory master file, 502
inventory turns, 509
level production, 485
lot-for-lot ordering, 504
maintenance, repair, and operating (MRO) inventory, 484
master production schedule (MPS), 501
material requirements planning (MRP), 501
net requirements, 503
netting, 501

KEY FORMULAE

Days of Supply

$$\text{Days of supply} = \frac{\text{On-Hand Inventory Average}}{\text{Daily Demand}}$$

Fixed-Quantity Reorder Point

(11.1)
$$\text{ROP} = \bar{d}_{LT} + \sigma_{LT}Z$$

where

$\bar{d}_{LT}$ = average demand during the replenishment lead time

σ_{LT} = standard deviation of demand during the replenishment lead time

Z = number of standard deviations above the average demand during the replenishment lead time required for the desired service level

Total Cost for Economic Order Quantity

(11.2)
$$TC = H(Q/2) + S(D/Q)$$

where

TC = total cost

H = carrying or holding cost per unit, on an annual basis

Q = order quantity

S = cost of ordering

D = annual demand

Carrying Costs for Economic Order Quantity

(11.3)
$$H = iP$$

where

i = percentage used for determining carrying costs

P = purchase price of the item

Economic Order Quantity

Obtained by taking the first derivative with respect to Q of the total cost curve from formula 11.2, the formula for the EOQ is

(11.4)
$$EOQ = \sqrt{\frac{2DS}{H}}$$

Total Costs for Economic Order Quantity with Quantity Discounts

The total cost equation for this model is

(11.5) $$TC = S(D/Q) + H(Q/2) + DP$$

where

D = annual demand

Q = order quantity

S = cost per order

H = carrying cost

P = price per unit

Order Quantity for Periodic Review Model

$$\text{Order Quantity} = \text{Target Inventory Level} - \text{On-Hand Inventory}$$

$$Q = TI - A$$

The target inventory level (TI) is calculated as

$$TI = \bar{d}_{OI+LT} + SS$$
$$= Z\sigma_{OI+LT}$$
$$= Z\sigma\sqrt{OI + LT}$$

where

$\bar{d}_{OI+LT}$ = average demand during the order interval and lead time

SS = safety stock

σ_{OI+LT} = standard deviation of demand during the order interval and lead time

Z = number of standard deviations required for the necessary service level (from Appendix B)

OI = the number of days in the order interval

LT = the number of days in the replenishment lead time

A = quantity of inventory on hand when the order is placed

SOLVED PROBLEMS

1. Determining the Reorder Point

Gwen Conrad manages a small boutique clothing shop a few blocks from campus. She turns over most of her inventory as the seasons change, but stocks some items, including jewelry, throughout the year. One of Gwen's jewelry suppliers is a small designer/metalsmith from Arizona. She sends Gwen an assortment of earrings whenever Gwen submits an order. The design of those earrings has become popular recently, and Gwen wishes to manage the inventory more scientifically. She has collected the following information about the earrings and wishes to use a reorder-point system with a 99 percent service level.

Average weekly demand	28 pairs
Replenishment lead time	2 weeks
Standard deviation of demand (weekly)	8 pairs
Desired service level	99%
Z value for desired service level	2.33

Reorder Point Calculation

Step	Objective	Explanation
1.	Determine average demand during replenishment lead time.	Average weekly demand is 28 pairs. With a two-week replenishment lead time, average demand would be 56 pairs.
2.	Determine the safety stock.	The safety stock is the $Z\rho = .99$ which is 2.33, multiplied by the standard deviation of demand during the replenishment lead time. The weekly standard deviation is 8. The variance would be 64. The variance is additive, so the variance over the two-week lead time would be 128, and the standard deviation would be its square root, 11.31.
3.	Determine the reorder point.	Add the average demand during the replenishment lead time and the safety stock: $56 + 11.31 = 67.31$

Solution: The reorder point would be 67.31, rounded up to 68. When the inventory of earrings drops to 68, Gwen should reorder.

2. Determining the Economic Order Quantity

Andy's Battleground is an indoor facility for paintball "battles" open only on weekends. Andy charges an hourly fee for participants and also sells paintball equipment and supplies. One of his most popular items is a discount box of 1,000 paintballs. Andy doesn't have a sophisticated inventory system. He just orders more boxes whenever he gets low. Since the boxes arrive from the supplier in three days, if he needs to order, he orders Monday morning. Putting together orders is one of the aspects of his job that Andy hates. Andy estimates his annual demand to be 475 boxes. He figures his time filling out the paperwork for an order worth $30. Based on the cost of a box, Andy estimates that carrying costs are $3.25 per box per year.

Economic Order Quantity Calculation

Step	Objective	Explanation
1.	Identify the annual demand (D), order cost (S), and carrying cost (H).	
2.	Apply formula 11.4.	$\sqrt{2DS/H} = \sqrt{28,500/3.25} = 93.644$ Round up to 94.

Solution: Andy should order 94 boxes at a time.

3. Determining the Economic Order Quantity with Quantity Discounts

Bagon's College Corner has identified a new supplier of "ear bud" headphones that offers quantity discounts. Baron's manager estimates the annual demand for the headphones at 1,200 per year. Order costs are $10 per order; annual carrying costs are $2.50 per unit. The supplier has provided the following price list:

Order Size	Price per Unit
1 to 30	$9.00
31–100	$8.80
101 or more	$8.50

Economic Order Quantity with Quantity Discounts Calculation:

Step	Objective	Explanation
1.	Calculate the basic EOQ.	Using equation 11.4, the EOQ is $\sqrt{2DS/H} = \sqrt{[2(1,200)(10)]/2.5} = 98$
2.	Compute the total cost of ordering at the EOQ.	Using formula 11.5: $TC = [(1,200/98)10] + [(98/2)2.5] + 1200(8.80)$ $=122.49 + 122.50 + 10,560.00$ $=10,804.99$
3.	The EOQ of 98 does not fall in the lowest price discount range, so we must evaluate the discount range of 101 or more.	Using formula 11.5: $TC = [(1,200/101)10] + [(101/2)2.5] + 1200(8.50)$ $=118.81 + 126.25 + 10,200.00$ $=10,445.06$
4.	Determine which is the low cost alternative.	Compare the total cost with the basic EOQ to the total cost of ordering 101 at a time. Ordering 101 has a lower total cost than ordering in quantities of 98.

Solution: Bagon's should order the headphones 101 units at a time.

4. Determining the Order Quantity in a Periodic Review System

Chronicles is a large independent office supply store. It purchases all home office supplies from the same distributor, so it uses a periodic review system for that entire product line. Friday is order day, and owner/manager Steve Post needs to calculate the order quantity for its largest selling stapler. Use the following information to determine the quantity Steve should order.

Average daily demand for stapler	12 staplers
Standard deviation of demand	2
Replenishment lead time	7 days
Inventory on hand	14 staplers
Service level desired	95%
Z for desired service level	1.645
Order interval	14 days

Order Quantity Calculation

Step	Objective	Explanation
1.	Determine the average demand during the order interval.	$12(14) = 168$
2.	Determine the average demand during the replenishment lead time.	$12(7) = 84$
3.	Identify the appropriate Z value.	1.645
4.	Determine the amount of inventory on hand currently.	14
5.	Using formula 11.8, determine the safety stock.	$1.645(2)\sqrt{14 + 7} = 1.645(2)(4.58) = 15.07$
6.	Using formula 11.7, determine the target inventory level.	$21 + 15.07 = 36.07$ Round up to 37.
7.	Using formula 11.6, determine the order quantity.	$37 - 14 = 23$

Solution: Steve should order 23 units.

5. Material Requirements Planning Logic

A manufacturer/assembler of computer accessories wishes to run a test of MRP logic for one of its simpler products: a key chain memory stick. The following information has been collected so that the MRP logic can be completed.

Master Production Schedule for Memory Stick

Week	1	2	3	4	5	6	7	8
Quantity	600	450	580	340	590	710	680	735

Item	On-Hand Inventory	Lead Time	Order Policy
Memory stick	1,400	1	lot for lot
Insert	605	1	lot for lot
Case	712	1	lot for lot
Cover	680	1	lot for lot
Key ring	2,080	1	lot for lot

Step	Objective	Explanation
1.	Complete the MRP record for the end product.	Using the form and logic from Example 11.6, create the record. Set the gross requirements to be the quantities from the master schedule. Use the first-week on-hand quantity from above. After that, the beginning on-hand should be from the previous week's ending on-hand. The backward scheduling from net requirement to planned order release should be one week. Since lot-for-lot ordering is being used, planned release quantities should be the same as the net requirements. See below.

Memory Stick	1	2	3	4	5	6	7	8
Gross requirement	600	450	580	340	590	710	680	735
Beginning on-hand	1400	800	350	0	0	0	0	0
Ending on-hand	800	350	0	0	0	0	0	0
Net requirements	0	0	230	340	590	710	680	735
Planned receipts	0	0	230	340	590	710	680	735
Planned releases	0	230	340	590	710	680	735	0

Step	Objective	Explanation
2.	Complete the MRP record for each of the four components.	The difference between the logic of these and the one for the end product will be the source of the gross requirements. For each of the component MRP records, the gross requirements will come from the planned order releases of the end product. See below.

Insert	1	2	3	4	5	6	7	8
Gross requirements	0	230	340	590	710	680	735	0
Beginning on-hand	605	605	375	35	0	0	0	0
Ending on-hand	605	375	35	0	0	0	0	0
Net requirements	0	0	0	555	710	680	735	0
Planned receipts	0	0	0	555	710	680	735	0
Planned releases	0	0	555	710	680	735	0	0

Case	1	2	3	4	5	6	7	8
Gross requirements	0	230	340	590	710	680	735	0
Beginning on-hand	712	712	482	142	0	0	0	0
Ending on-hand	712	482	142	0	0	0	0	0
Net requirements	0	0	0	448	710	680	735	0
Planned receipts	0	0	0	448	710	680	735	0
Planned releases	0	0	448	710	680	735	0	0

Cover	1	2	3	4	5	6	7	8
Gross requirements	0	230	340	590	710	680	735	0
Beginning on-hand	680	680	450	110	0	0	0	0
Ending on-hand	680	450	110	0	0	0	0	0
Net requirements	0	0	0	480	710	680	735	0
Planned receipts	0	0	0	480	710	680	735	0
Planned releases	0	0	480	710	680	735	0	0

Key Ring	1	2	3	4	5	6	7	8
Gross requirements	0	230	340	590	710	680	735	0
Beginning on-hand	2080	2080	1850	1510	920	210	0	0
Ending on-hand	2080	1850	1510	920	210	0	0	0
Net requirements	0	0	0	0	0	470	735	0
Planned receipts	0	0	0	0	0	470	735	0
Planned releases	0	0	0	0	470	735	0	0

REVIEW QUESTIONS

1. What is meant by decoupling? What is the role of inventory when decoupling is needed?

2. Describe the costs that make up inventory order costs.

3. Describe the costs that contribute to inventory carrying costs.

4. What is a stockout cost?

5. What is meant by continuous replenishment? In which business environment is it used?

6. What is meant by days-of-supply? How is it calculated? Why is days-of-supply important?

7. What is meant by batch production? Why do manufacturers use it?

8. How does excess inventory affect the cash-to-cash cycle?

9. What is the relationship between excess inventory and product quality?

10. What is independent demand inventory?

11. What is dependent demand inventory? How is it different from independent demand inventory?

12. What are pipeline inventories?

13. What is meant by the service level?

14. Describe the purpose of a safety stock. What impact does it have on inventory level?

15. What is the objective of the economic order quantity? What are its assumptions? What are its weaknesses?

16. Describe the informational inputs and logic of material requirements planning.

17. What resource decisions can be enhanced by using ABC analysis?

18. Describe "dollar day" and explain why it is useful in guiding inventory reduction efforts.

DISCUSSION AND EXPLORATION

1. Identify a product you keep on hand at home and do not want to be without. How many days-of-supply do you typically keep? What are the stockout costs? What are the costs of keeping too much?

2. How are the objectives of reorder point systems and MRP similar? How are they different? What characteristics of the demands of each determine the management methods used?

3. Discuss the linkage between forecast accuracy and inventory levels. What impact will an improvement in forecast accuracy have? What are some ways accuracy can be improved?

4. Why do some people argue that inventory should be treated as a liability instead of an asset? In what ways is the effect inventory has on a business similar to that of a debt?

PROBLEMS

Solutions to odd-numbered problems are located on the text's Online Center (http://mhhe.com/opsnow3e).

1. Mocha-Mocha is a local coffee shop. It sells an average of 239 cups of coffee per day. It receives a shipment of supply every two days. The store received a shipment this morning and currently has enough coffee on hand for 466 cups. If the demand is consistent with the average, will Mocha-Mocha be able to satisfy its customers until the next shipment?

2. Hathaway Services is not sure if it has the financial resources to stay in operation. It currently has $50,799 in liquid assets. The company has applied for a bank loan but does not yet know if it will receive any additional funding. If the company has an average expenditure of $12,095 per month, how long can it stay in operation without a loan?

3. Gas Guzzler is an independent gas station open seven days a week. The average weekly demand is 30,240 gallons. Every Monday a supply truck stops to fill the station's tanks. The station manager wants to begin each week with nine days' supply on hand. How many gallons should the station have on hand to start each week?

4. Happy Feet Running Store strives to maintain a 4-week supply of the most popular sizes of its best-selling women's running shoe. Average weekly demand for each size and current inventory levels are presented below:

Size	Average Weekly Demand (pairs)	On-Hand Quantity (pairs)
4 1/2	12	66
5	14	54
5 1/2	18	80
6	22	70
6 1/2	16	78
7	12	36

Determine the weeks of supply for each size. Which sizes do not have sufficient inventory?

5. Thomas's Custom Fabrication (TCF) produces customized steel fixtures for warehouses. Most of its products are variations of storage racks and shelving systems. TCF currently carries a 4-week supply for 1/2-inch, 3/4-inch, and 1-inch channel. Average weekly demand is 300 feet for the 1/2-inch, 370 feet for the 3/4-inch, and 420 feet for the 1-inch.

   Determine how many feet will be required for each channel size. A new manager has suggested that, given a new supplier, TCF could reduce each size to a 7-day supply. Assuming a 5-day work week, compute the number of feet for each size to meet the 7-day supply goal.

6. For men's size XXL jackets at Harold's Fine Clothing, the average weekly demand is 7, with a standard deviation of 3. The replenishment lead time is 1 week. What should the reorder point be to maintain a 99 percent confidence of satisfying the demand during the lead time?

7. U-Do-It Framers is a do-it-yourself picture framing shop that sells tools, work tables, and supplies. Kim Rooney, the owner, monitors inventory of framing components closely to keep costs low. A particularly popular style of frame comes in 42-inch lengths. The supplier can provide replenishments in 24 hours for a premium price, but standard replenishment lead time is 4 days. Average daily demand is 3.5 lengths, with a daily standard deviation of 1.6. Compute the necessary reorder point to maintain a 95 percent service level during the replenishment lead times.

8. Ryan's Grill offers a regular special of 25-cent chicken wings. Average weekly demand for wings is 1,860, with a standard deviation of 11.4. Ryan's wing supplier requires orders to be placed one week before they are delivered. Calculate the reorder point if the restaurant would like to ensure a 99 percent service level.

9. Pads-N-Paper sells greeting cards for which it has an average weekly demand of 34 and a standard deviation of 9. The store would like to maintain at least a 97 percent service level. If the replenishment lead time on greeting cards is two weeks, what reorder point should be used?

10. The Stanfield Sluggers are a minor league pro baseball team. They currently use an average of 77 baseballs per week, with a standard deviation of 8.5. It takes a week's time to receive a shipment of new baseballs once ordered. What is the reorder point if the franchise would like a 90 percent service level?

11. Droid Robotics is a U.S. dealer in high-tech robotic components. Its parent company is located in Japan and supplies it with testing modules. Droid consumes an average of 125 testing modules per week, with a standard deviation of 5. It takes three weeks for an order of components to be shipped to Droid. Droid prides itself on delivering on time to its customers and must have no less than a 99.9 percent service level of testing modules. What should the reorder point be?

12. Seagle's ATV Products manufactures various racks to be used on all-terrain vehicles. One particular rack has an average weekly demand of 240 units and weekly standard deviation of 55. The replenishment lead time is two weeks. Compute the necessary reorder point for a 95 percent service level during the replenishment lead times.

13. Buck Head Insurance maintains tight control of its inventory of office supplies, particularly expensive items like toner cartridges for printers. Cartridges for its most common printer are consumed at the rate of 140 cartridges per year. Carrying cost is $8.00 per year per unit. Order cost is $15.00 per order. Compute the economic order quantity for the printer cartridge.

14. Dorm Accessories sells carpet for use in college dormitories. The average yearly demand for the carpet is 1,134. The cost per order is $30 and the inventory carrying cost is $7 per unit. Use the EOQ formula to calculate the appropriate order quantity.

15. Car USA would like to determine how many cars it should order at one time. The dealership sells an average of 10 cars per month. It costs the dealership $550 to place an order and $786 per year to carry a car in inventory. Compute the economic order quantity.

16. McMahon & Young is an area law firm. Its attorneys use 1,000 reams of paper a year. The cost of ordering from the local office supply company is $10 per order. It has calculated the annual carrying costs to be $1.25 per ream. What is the EOQ?

17. Arliss's Office Supplies uses the economic order quantity to determine order quantities for all of its desk lamps. One particular lamp has an expected annual demand of 480 units. Order costs for the lamp are $22.00. Arliss's considers annual carrying costs at a rate of 28 percent of the item's value. This lamp costs Arliss's $65.50. Compute the economic order quantity for the lamp.

18. Garage PC Repair assembles desktops from components it buys from surplus sales. It competes primarily on the basis of price, but also offers on-site service. The owner purchases components from a number of parts warehouses. Because of the number of students connecting to the Internet, every computer comes with a cable modem. A supplier of cable modems offers same-day delivery and the following quantity discounts:

Less than 20 units $32 each
20 to 50 units $31 each
51 or more units $29 each

The annual demand for the modem is estimated to be 240 units. Carrying costs are $5 per unit per year. The order cost is $2.50. Compute the optimal order quantity.

19. Fax & Phone sells telephone equipment and fax machines. It sells an average of five fax machines a month. Its supplier charges $49 per order but offers quantity discounts as follows:

1 – 10 machines per order: $599 each
10 + machines per order: $510 each

The carrying costs for fax machines are $80 per unit. What is the EOQ?

20. Wiseman Bookstore has an annual demand of 250 for one of its selected hardback titles. The annual carrying cost of a single book is $4. The publishing company charges $5.50 per order. Calculate the EOQ if the publishing company charges $9.99 per book on orders of 1–20 and $9.29 per book on orders greater than 20.

21. PetStoresPlus sells wholesale pet foods to small pet stores and veterinary clinics. Their current price schedule on 50-pound bags of Special Diet HiProtein is as follows:

Less than 12 bags $35.95 per bag
13 to 100 bags $33.95 per bag
More than 100 bags $29.95 per bag

Average annual demand at the Tri-City Veterinary Clinic is 210 units. Carrying costs are $13 per bag per year. Order cost is $7. Determine the optimal order quantity.

22. Piper's Chips distributes snacks to grocery stores. The company uses a fixed-interval approach to replenishing inventory. You have been assigned to one of its clients. Use the following information to calculate the order quantity:

Average demand: 6 bags per day
Lead time: 2 days
Standard deviation of demand over the lead time: 2.4
Current inventory level: 24 bags
Service level: 95% (use $Z = 1.645$)
Order interval: 7 days

23. Harrington's Fine Jewelry orders most of its inventory from the same supplier. The supplier sends a representative to Harrington's every Monday to replenish stock.

Given the following data, calculate the reorder quantity for the current order interval:

Average demand: 3 pieces per day
Lead time: 1 day
Standard deviation of demand (daily): 1.4
Current inventory level: 19
Service level: 99% (use $z = 2.33$)
Order interval: 5 days

24. Alto Musical Instruments replenishes its inventory of instruments and music every Monday from the same supplier. Calculate the reorder quantity for the current order interval for a songbook with the following characteristics:

Average demand: 3 per day
Lead time: 3 days
Standard deviation of demand (daily): .96
Current inventory level: 26
Service level: 95% (use $z = 1.645$)
Order interval: 7 business days

25. A computer chip manufacturer replenishes MRO inventory items every two weeks. Disposable kits used for cleaning equipment are ordered from a supplier of industrial cleaning products. Determine the appropriate quantity to order for this order interval, given the following parameters.

Average demand: 8 per day
Lead time: 5 days
Standard deviation of demand (daily): 1.37
Current inventory level: 84
Service level: 99% (use $z = 2.33$)
Order interval: 14 business days

26. The following information is associated with the production of a computer carrying case. Use MRP logic to determine the planned order releases for the end product.

Master production schedule:

Week	1	2	3	4	5	6	7	8
Quantity	120	210	239	100	140	210	230	160

Lead time: 1 week
Quantity on hand: 380
Order policy: lot-for-lot

27. The master production schedule below represents expected production for dorm-sized bookshelves. Use MRP logic to determine the planned order releases that will be used as gross requirements for the components. There are currently 46 shelves on hand. The lead time is 2 weeks. The order policy is lot-for-lot.

Master production schedule:

Week	1	2	3	4	5	6	7	8
Quantity	24	22	28	32	29	36	21	24

28. Sandlot Products produces toys for the beach. The Beach Combo 525 is a pail-and-shovel set perfect for a fun day in the sand. The combo is composed of three components: Pail 002, Handle 114, and Shovel 118. The Beach Combo requires one Pail, one shovel, and two handles for the final product. Use the master production schedule below and MRP logic to compute the planned order releases for the components. There is a beginning inventory of 30 completed Beach Combos. Each of the components uses lot-for-lot ordering and has a one-week lead time.

Week	1	2	3	4	5	6	7	8
Demand	0	28	34	34	28	28	26	24

29. Safe Storage Inc. produces CD jewel cases. It is a simple product with only two components, a top and a bottom. The company operates on a lot-for-lot ordering system with a one-week lead time. There are currently 2,000 jewel cases on hand and ready for delivery. Use the following demand information and MRP logic to compute the planned order release schedule for the two components.

Week	1	2	3	4	5	6	7	8
Demand	0	1,450	800	1,050	875	1,200	950	850

30. Hanging Solutions manufactures products that help organize closets. Their best-known product is a wooden hanger. It is composed of a metal hook attached to a wooden support. The components are ordered lot-for-lot. The hooks are readily available with a one-week lead time, but the supplier of the wooden supports can only offer a two-week lead time. The master production schedule is given below. Using MRP logic, calculate the planned order release schedule if there are 400 hangers currently in inventory.

Week	1	2	3	4	5	6	7	8
Demand	0	125	134	145	167	138	129	115

31. AM Tools produces two hammers, a regular and a deluxe. The regular hammer is composed of a wooden handle with a metal head. The deluxe consists of the same material but adds a rubber grip to the handle. The company uses lot-for-lot ordering and can get the needed materials from its suppliers in one week. The production schedules for the two models of hammer are given below. If there are 50 regular hammers and 25 deluxe hammers currently on hand, what is the schedule of planned order releases?

Week	1	2	3	4	5	6	7	8
Hammer	0	45	51	53	48	62	49	52
Deluxe hammer	0	21	26	27	22	24	27	31

32. Home Accents is a regional producer of doors for homes. The product structure is seen in Exhibit 11.22, and the master production schedule is given below. The lead time for all components is one week. Using MRP logic, compute the planned order release schedule.

Week	1	2	3	4	5	6	7	8
Home door	0	21	17	14	19	22	15	18

EXHIBIT 11.22

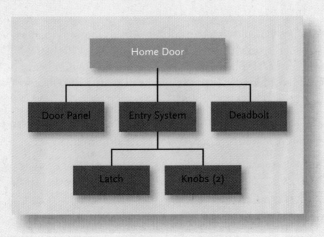

Component	Order Policy	On Hand
Home door	Lot-for-lot	25
Door panel	Lot-for-lot	0
Deadbolt	5	0
Entry system	Lot-for-lot	0
Latch	Lot-for-lot	30
Knobs	Lot-for-lot	15

33. Ray's Music currently has seven copies of pop singer Brianna Brinks's new CD. The CD has a value of $9.00 and the store expects to sell one copy every other day. Compute the dollar days of Brianna Brinks CDs.

34. The University Bookstore expects to sell six notebooks a day. The notebooks are valued at $2.50. The bookstore has 42 notebooks currently in stock. Calculate the dollar days associated with the notebooks.

35. Alberti Clothiers has seven shirts in inventory, valued at $22.00 each. The store expects to sell one shirt every eight days. Alberti also has 25 sweaters, valued at $48.00 each. Alberti anticipates selling five of these sweaters per day. Calculate the dollar days for each item. What is the reduction in dollar days if one unit of each item is eliminated from inventory?

ADVANCED PROBLEMS

1. Burt's Paint Supply sells interior latex paint in a wide variety of colors. The various colors are mixed to-order, so Burt only needs to carry inventory of a few different tint bases, rather than an inventory of every possible color a customer may want to purchase.

Daily demand for semi-gloss light tint base is normally distributed, with mean 20 gallons and standard deviation 3. The order lead time, when Burt places an inventory replenishment order for tint base with his supplier, is 5 days. Burt's ordering cost is $50.00 per order. Burt pays $10.00 per gallon for the tint base, and his carrying cost rate is 20%.

a. Find the optimal order quantity for the tint base using the simple EOQ model. Assume the tint base is sold 365 days per year. Also find the average number of orders per year, average number of days between orders, and average annual ordering cost under this policy.

b. Find the ROP and safety stock required to provide a 95% service level.

c. Compute the *total average inventory* under this policy. This consists of the average cycle stock (Q/2) resulting from the EOQ analysis in part a, plus the safety stock resulting from the ROP found in part b.

2. Burt's Paint Supply would like to establish a fixed interval (periodic review) system for the semi-gloss light tint base examined in Advanced Problem 1. Burt wants to use a fixed ordering interval that produces the same average number of orders per year as the EOQ policy. His order quantities should be chosen to produce a 95% service level.

a. What fixed ordering interval (*OI*) will produce the same average order frequency and average annual ordering cost as the EOQ found in Advanced Problem 1? What is the average cycle inventory (Q/2) under this policy?

b. Find the safety stock required to provide a 95% service level using the fixed ordering interval.

c. Logically, why does the fixed interval system require greater safety stock to provide the same 95% service level?

3. Two products, Yo-Yo Blue and Yo-Yo Red Special, are scheduled to be produced next month (May). Week 1 of May is next week. Your company currently orders all materials required for the month at once to arrive at the beginning of the month. They are considering adopting MRP.

   a. Using the bills of material, inventory records files, and master production schedule provided, create a materials plan for the month of May using MRP and lot-for lot ordering.

Bills of Material

Level	Part No.	Assembly/Material	Quantity	Unit of Measure
000	40-001	Yo-Yo Blue	1	ea
001	41-005	Side Blue	2	ea
002	42-001	Side	1	ea
002	42-055	Paint, Blue	0.0040	gal
001	41-005	Glue	0.0002	liter
001	41-010	Dowel	0.0833	ft
001	41-015	String	6	ft

Level	Part No.	Assembly/Material	Quantity	Unit of Measure
000	40-002	Yo-Yo Red Special	1	ea
001	41-008	Side Red	2	ea
002	42-001	Side	1	ea
002	42-056	Paint, Red	0.0040	gal
002	42-111	Inlay	1	ea
001	41-007	Glue	0.0002	liter
001	41-010	Dowel	0.0833	ft
001	41-015	String	6	ft

Inventory Record Files

Material	Part No.	On Hand 1 May	Lead Time (weeks)	Order Policy	Unit of Measure
Yo-Yo Blue	40-001	20,000	1	L-4-L	ea
Yo-Yo Red Sp.	40-002	15,000	1	L-4-L	ea
Side Blue	41-005	45,000	1	L-4-L	ea
Side Red	41-008	15,000	1	L-4-L	ea
Side	42-001	50,000	2	L-4-L	ea
Paint, Blue	42-055	60	1	10	gal
Paint, Red	42-056	52	1	10	gal
Inlay	42-111	10,000	1	10,000	ea
Dowel	41-007	1,200	1	1,000	ft
Glue	41-010	4	2	L-4-L	liter
String	41-015	200,000	1	100,000	ft

Master Production Schedule

Product	Week 1	Week 2	Week 3	Week 4
Yo-Yo Blue	20,000	20,000	10,000	10,000
Yo-Yo Red Sp.	10,000	0	10,000	10,000

   b. Is this a feasible materials plan? If not, discuss options the planner has for addressing the problems and the possible tangible and intangible costs associated with each option.

ENDNOTE

1. E. M. Goldratt and R. E. Fox, "The Fundamental Measurements," *Theory of Constraints Journal*, August–September 1988.

LEARNING ACTIVITIES   www.mhhe.com/opsnow3e

Visit the Online Learning Center (www.mhhe.com/opsnow3e) for additional resources. Content varies by chapter, and includes

- Business Tours
- OM on Site
- Readings
- Resources
- Excel Tutors

- Interactive Case Models
- Reel Operations Video Clips
- Additional Advanced Problems
- Self-Assessment Quizzes
- Glossary

SELECTED REFERENCES

Vollman, T., Berry, W. L., and Whybark, D. C. *Manufacturing Planning and Control Systems.* New York: McGraw-Hill, 2005.

Zipkin, P. H. *Foundations of Inventory Management.* New York: McGraw-Hill, 2000.

INTERACTIVE CASE 11.1

Managing Pillow Inventory at Wilson's Beds and Bedding

The fixed-quantity reorder point model illustrates the relationships present in a typical reorder point inventory system. In the model, the user can change the service level, the variability of demand, the replenishment lead time, and the order quantity by adjusting the sliding bars. Changes in any of the four parameters are reflected in changes in the system.

Wilson's Beds and Bedding

Wilson's Beds and Bedding is a large discounter of mattresses, beds, pillows, and linens. The pillow inventory is managed using a fixed-quantity reorder point system. For the large down-filled pillow, the weekly demand averages a very stable 50 units, with a standard deviation of 1.5. The replenishment lead time for the large down-filled pillow is 1 week. Wilson's currently maintains a 99 percent service level for all of their pillows and replenishes the down-filled pillow in orders of 220 units.

1. Check the default values on the fixed-quantity reorder point model to make sure they match the values presented above.

   a. What is the reorder point for Wilson's large down-filled pillow?
   b. What happens to the reorder point if the replenishment lead time extends to 2 weeks?

c. What happens to the reorder point if the standard deviation of demand shifts from 1.5 to 8?

d Reduce the service level from 99 to 95 percent. What impact does this have on the reorder point?

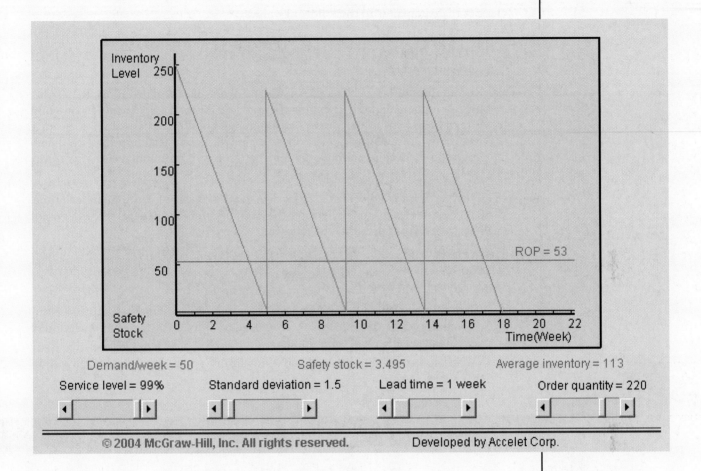

2. Safety stock is a function of the variability of demand (s) and the service level desired. The safety stock affects the average level of inventory because the average level of inventory is equal to one-half the order quantity plus the safety stock. Set the parameters of the model to the following values:

Service level	85 percent
Standard deviation	4
Replenishment lead time	2 weeks

a. What is the reorder point and average inventory level at these parameters?

b. Increase the service level to 89 percent. What happens to the reorder point and average inventory level? Increase the service level in 1 percent increments and graph the change in reorder point and average inventory level. Describe what is causing the change in the reorder point.

3. The safety stock contributes to the reorder point and the average level of inventory. If no variability existed from period to period, there would be no uncertainty of demand and no need for a safety stock. Set the parameters to the following values:

Service level	95 percent
Standard deviation	1
Replenishment lead time	3 weeks

a. Record the values for the reorder point and average level of inventory. Incrementally change the standard deviation of demand by one-unit intervals, and record the corresponding changes in the reorder point and average level of inventory. Describe the relationship between variability of demand, reorder point, and average inventory level.

b. Set the parameters to the following values:

Service level	95 percent
Standard deviation	1
Replenishment lead time	1 week

Record the values for the reorder point and average level of inventory. Repeat the process of incrementally changing the standard deviation of demand by one-unit intervals, and record the corresponding changes in the reorder point and average level of inventory. What impact does the replenishment lead time have on the relationship between variability of demand, reorder point, and average inventory level?

4. The reorder point is expected to satisfy demand during the replenishment lead time. The longer that lead time, the greater the demand, and the higher the reorder point will be. Set the parameters to the following values:

Service level	95 percent
Standard deviation	4
Replenishment lead time	1 week

a. What happens to the reorder point when the replenishment lead time is increased to two weeks? three weeks? four weeks? Why is the standard deviation of demand during the lead time changing?

b. What happens to the average level of inventory as you move from one week to two weeks, to three weeks, to four weeks?

INTERACTIVE CASE 11.2

Managing Training Material Inventory at MarketReach

The economic order quantity model provides an interactive environment for understanding how the economic order quantity works. By changing the values for H (carrying cost per unit), D (annual demand), or S (order cost), the user can immediately see how the total cost curve changes, which changes the value for the economic order quantity.

MarketReach

MarketReach is a large contract calling center specializing in phone sales. It employs predominantly college students who like its flexible hours and relatively good pay. MarketReach not only makes phone contacts for its clients but also coordinates any mailings that go out as follow-ups to successful calls. The type of employee utilized by MarketReach creates a high turnover rate. At any given time, MarketReach has approximately 300 employees, but loses about 3 per day. MarketReach is continuously training new hires. Each new hire receives a set of training materials valued at approximately $35. History has shown that the demand for the training materials meets the assumptions of the economic order quantity, and management has decided that they should use that approach to determine order quantities.

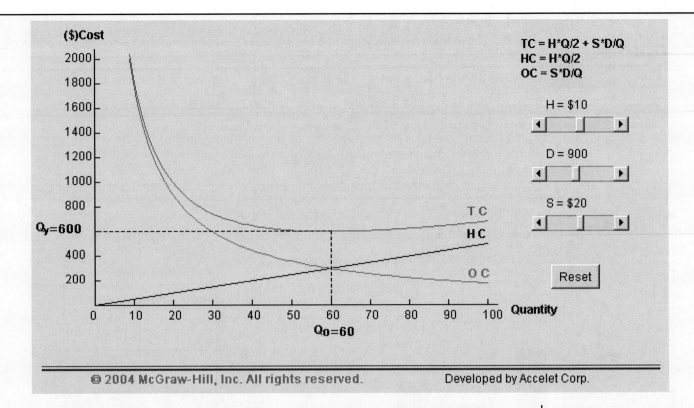

$$TC = H^*Q/2 + S^*D/Q$$
$$HC = H^*Q/2$$
$$OC = S^*D/Q$$

H = $10

D = 900

S = $20

Reset

($)Cost

Q_y=600

Q_o=60

Quantity

TC

HC

OC

Developed by Accelet Corp.

1. Demand for the training material packets is projected at 900 per year. Order cost is $20 and inventory carrying costs are $10 per packet per year. Make sure that the start-up defaults on the economic order quantity interactive model match these parameters.

   a. What is the economic order quantity at these parameter settings? Compute the total carrying cost and total order cost at these settings.

   b. From the shape of the total cost curve, do you think rounding the order quantity will have much of an impact on the total cost? Explain your answer.

2. MarketReach is negotiating with a different supplier of training materials. It appears that through the new supplier the packets will be significantly cheaper, reducing the carrying costs. Set the parameters of the model to these values:

   Carrying cost (H) $6
   Demand (D)   900
   Order cost (S) $20

   a. What is the economic order quantity at these parameters?

   b. Incrementally increase the carrying cost, $2 at a time, up to $16. Graph the impact on the economic order quantity. What is the relationship between the carrying cost and the economic order quantity?

3. If management can eliminate the paper invoicing associated with the ordering process, they believe they can reduce the order cost to $10. Set the parameters of the model to these values:

   Carrying cost (H) $10
   Demand (D)   900
   Order cost (S) $10

   a. What is the economic order quantity at these values?

   b. Incrementally increase the order cost by $2 from $10 to $30. Graph the impact on the economic order quantity. Describe the relationship.

INTERACTIVE CASE 11.3

A Purchasing Decision for AutoAudio

The economic order quantity with quantity discounts model enables the user to experiment with the parameters of the classic EOQ quantity discounts problem. The user sets the annual demand (D), the order cost (S), and the inventory carrying cost (H) using the three sliders. The pricing policies are set for the four discount levels using the four pricing policy sliders. The model calculates the total cost for the traditional EOQ quantity and for the smallest order quantities possible to receive each of the cheaper discounts.

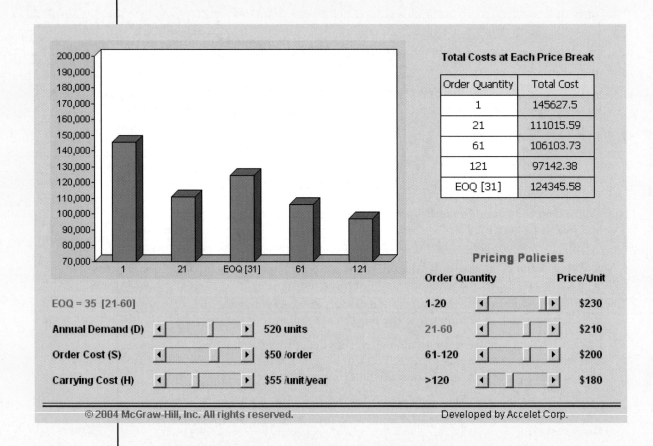

Total Costs at Each Price Break

Order Quantity	Total Cost
1	145627.5
21	111015.59
61	106103.73
121	97142.38
EOQ [31]	124345.58

EOQ = 35 [21-60]

Annual Demand (D)   520 units

Order Cost (S) $50 /order

Carrying Cost (H) $55 /unit/year

Pricing Policies

Order Quantity		Price/Unit
1-20		$230
21-60		$210
61-120		$200
>120		$180

AutoAudio

AutoAudio sells and installs high-end automobile sound systems and is the largest installer in a large metropolitan area and the only one that can accommodate installations without appointments. The AutoAudio facility consists of eight drive-through installation bays, each equipped with complete sets of tools and an inventory of all brackets and installation hardware. AutoAudio buys its sound system components from several different suppliers, depending on the brand. One popular CD changer that is installed in the vehicle's trunk has a projected annual demand of 520 units. AutoAudio has just received word of better prices from a new supplier of that CD changer. The new supplier is offering the following prices:

Quantity	Price per Unit	Quantity	Price per Unit
1–20 units	$230	61–120 units	$200
21–60 units	$210	>120 units	$180

AutoAudio's carrying costs on this changer are $55 per unit per year. Order cost is $50 per order.

Check to make sure the parameters match the prices, demand, carrying cost, and order cost given above.

1. Examine the output values for the economic order quantity with quantity discounts interactive model.

   a. What is the basic economic order quantity? In what price range is the EOQ?

   b. Based on the rules for determining the economic order quantity, what possible price ranges will likely contain the low-cost quantity?

   c. What quantity is the low-cost quantity? What is the total annual cost of ordering in that quantity?

   d. How much is saved by ordering at that quantity over the basic EOQ quantity?

2. Projected demands can often be wrong. This can result in an optimal order quantity changing or in a change in the projection of the total costs.

   a. If the forecast for demand for this CD changer is wrong (within the range of the model), does the optimal order quantity change?

   b. What happens to the total cost of ordering at the optimal quantity if demand is less than expected? How much does the total cost change?

   c. What happens to the cost of ordering at the optimal quantity if demand is greater than expected? How much does the total cost change?

3. The supplier of the CD changer is considering running a promotion to reduce inventory levels. The new prices will be:

Quantity	Price per Unit
1–20 units	$200
21–60 units	$190
61–120 units	$180
>120 units	$170

This will allow AutoAudio to reduce its price as well, resulting in an expected increase of demand by 80 units.

   a. What will be the optimal order quantity?

   b. What will be the total costs associated with this new pricing and new demand?

   c. AutoAudio normally sells this CD changer for $310. At the normal supplier pricing structure, and assuming a demand of 520 units, what would AutoAudio's annual profit be on this product?

   d. At the new pricing, assuming a demand of 600 units, AutoAudio is planning to reduce the selling price of the CD changer to $290. What will AutoAudio's profit be?

INTERACTIVE CASE 11.4

Material Requirements for Rustic Furniture

The material requirements planning model provides an interactive environment for understanding how material requirements planning (MRP) logic works. The user can make changes to the master production schedule, the product structure, lead time, on-hand inventory level, and the lot-sizing policy used. Changes in any of those parameters are reflected in the timing and quantities for the planned order releases.

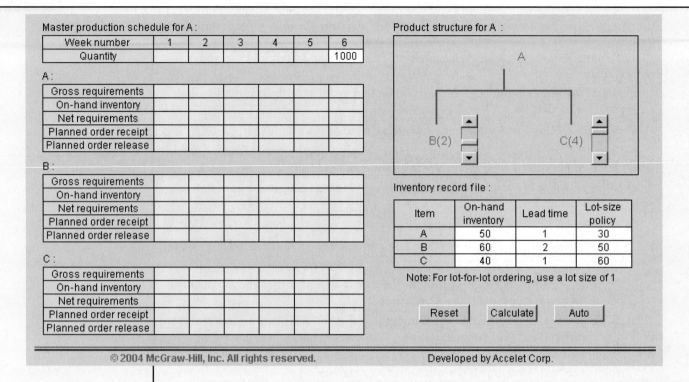

Master production schedule for A :

Week number	1	2	3	4	5	6
Quantity						1000

A :

Gross requirements						
On-hand inventory						
Net requirements						
Planned order receipt						
Planned order release						

B :

Gross requirements						
On-hand inventory						
Net requirements						
Planned order receipt						
Planned order release						

C :

Gross requirements						
On-hand inventory						
Net requirements						
Planned order receipt						
Planned order release						

Product structure for A :

A
B(2)   C(4)

Inventory record file :

Item	On-hand inventory	Lead time	Lot-size policy
A	50	1	30
B	60	2	50
C	40	1	60

Note: For lot-for-lot ordering, use a lot size of 1

Reset   Calculate   Auto

Rustic Furniture

Rustic Furniture is a producer of outdoor tables and chairs that are composed of interlocking wooden components, requiring no fasteners and allowing for quick setup and breakdown. The table (end product A), for example, consists of two top sections (part B) and four legs (part C). The management of Rustic Furniture has not used material requirements planning in the past and is experimenting with a prototype to gain an understanding of how it works. Make sure the start-up defaults in the material requirements planning model are consistent with those below:

1. The Master production schedule should show 1,000 units in week 6.

Item	On-Hand Inventory	Lead Time	Lot-Size Policy
A	50	1	30
B	60	2	50
C	40	1	60

a. Given these parameters, what are the quantities and timing of the planned order releases necessary to produce the master production schedule?

b. Why do the order release quantities not equal the net requirements?

c. Reset the model, leaving all parameters the same, except change the lot-size policies to lot-for-lot by setting each equal to 1. What are the implications for carrying inventory when this is changed? What will be the implications for equipment changeovers in the future?

d. Describe the relationship between the gross requirements for B and C and the planned order releases for A. Why are the gross requirements for B and C not dependent on the gross requirements for A?

2. Change the lead time for the end product from 1 week to 3 weeks.

   a. What are the implications for the timing of the planned order releases for B and C?

   b. Change the on-hand inventory for A to 1,000. Why are there no gross requirements for B or C?

APPLICATION CASE 11.1

Norwood Medical Center

Norwood Medical Center is a regional hospital and trauma center serving rural western Iowa. It is located in a small town of approximately 16,000 residents but serves a radius that extends in all directions approximately 40 miles. Its location results in a wide variety of patient needs. Cases beyond its capabilities are referred to hospitals in Ames, Des Moines, or the Omaha area.

Like most hospitals, NMC is trying to maintain quality care while, at the same time, trying to hold down rising healthcare costs. One area that has not been addressed to date at NMC is the large investment in its various inventories. The variability in medical procedures performed, combined with the difficulty in forecasting their occurrences, has resulted in high levels of inventory for procedural kits, or "trays" as they are often called. For common procedures, NMC uses sterile kits which contain all of the items necessary, packaged in a single tray. This makes storage simple and retrieval faster, and, because everything needed is present in a single tray, procedures go smoothly and efficiently. Many of the standard trays can be purchased preassembled, but NMC also prepares some of their own. Even for procedures with standard trays available, some other items may be needed, depending on the clinician performing the procedure. This is particularly the case in surgery.

Jill Vogel, NMC's new director, has charged the administrative staff with examining current inventory management practices with a goal of reducing the investment in inventory without reducing the service level. The current system is a periodic review system. Orders are placed weekly. The target inventory level is calculated based on an ABC analysis. A items require a 99 percent service level; B items require a 95 percent service level; and C items require a 90 percent service level.

A new operations analyst has suggested looking at a dependent demand model for managing the inventory. His logic is that many hospital procedures have fixed material requirements (as evidenced by the availability of standard trays for them) and could be treated the same way a manufacturer would treat inventories of components for a finished product. He suggests creating the equivalent of a master production schedule by scheduling procedures as far in the future as possible, and combining that schedule with forecasts of ad hoc or unplanned procedures.

1. What are the advantages and disadvantages of the system being proposed?

2. Do you think the inventory in this situation could be considered dependent demand?

3. Would "bills of material" be constructed for hospital procedures?

4. Would benefits be obtained from switching from the current periodic review system to a fixed-quantity reorder point system?

CHAPTER 12

Logistics: Positioning Goods in the Supply Chain

LEARNING OBJECTIVES

- Understand and describe the logistics function and its importance to business.

- Describe the concept of logistics networks.

- Explain why businesses outsource logistics functions and issues to consider when selecting a logistics service provider.

- Explain what reverse logistics is and why its importance is increasing.

- Describe and compare the modes of transportation used in supply chains.

- Describe the configuration of different warehousing and distribution strategies, as well as the strengths and weaknesses of each.

- Explain the concept of postponement and how it can be used in supply chains.

- Compute the center-of-gravity solution for determining distribution center location.

- Compute the landed cost to determine product costs that include logistics.

- Describe the Customs-Trade Partnership Against Terrorism (C-TPAT).

- Explain how radio frequency identification (RFID) and global positioning system (GPS) technologies can enhance logistics effectiveness.

MANAGING PARTS LOGISTICS AT KODAK

Kodak produces a range of products for different markets and different customers. Its products range from digital cameras to film to Picture Maker photo kiosks to radiography equipment. Its customers range from consumers to professional photographers, photographic labs to hospitals and dental centers. Kodak's products have short life cycles and expensive service parts. The task of managing service parts for products with short life cycles is a daunting one. Mismanagement can result in either high inventories of parts for obsolete equipment or inventory levels too low to meet the needs of customers.

Like most companies, Kodak faces a difficult balancing act: maintaining low levels of service parts inventories but high levels of customer service for those who need service parts quickly. Kodak recently evaluated their service parts supply chain logistics system to objectively identify how these seemingly conflicting goals could be managed.

Kodak identified three value propositions that needed to drive the logistics system design for spare parts. The first was velocity. Velocity is critical in order to maintain low inventory levels, even during a new product launch when the placement of the new products is uncertain. The second was value. Value is necessary during the maturity phase of a product's life cycle in order to reduce costs. Third was visibility. Visibility is necessary so that, during the decline stage of a product's life cycle, parts that remain in the supply chain can be at low levels, but can be obtained quickly when needed. In short, they wanted to reduce inventory while increasing availability.

Kodak's existing inventory placement was driven by the way they served their customers. Inventory existed in two echelons. One was at the central warehouse and the other was in the car trunks of field engineers who actually service equipment. The service engineers replenished their stocks from the central warehouse. Service engineers maintained an inventory of low value and expensive parts in their trunks, but expensive items were "slow movers." They sent parts that needed repair to the central warehouse (that took five days). Those parts were then sent out to a repair vendor (that also took five days). Repaired parts were then returned to the central warehouse.

Kodak's new system allows field engineers to maintain a trunk stock of low value parts only. Expensive parts are housed at 17 forward stock locations (FSL) and are replenished automatically from the central warehouse. Under the new system, parts requirements are identified before the site visit. Expensive parts are delivered via UPS from the FSL directly to the site or, in some cases, picked up at a UPS Supply Chain Solutions facility by the service engineer. Under the new system, inventory levels are significantly reduced with no drop in customer service. Field inventory for all FSL parts has been reduced by 66 percent, central inventory has been reduced by 32 percent, service level metrics have improved, and there has been no negative impact on service call duration.

Source: M. Brienzi, and S. Kekre, "How Kodak Transformed Its Service Parts Supply Chain," *Supply Chain Management Review,* October 2005; www.kodak.com, accessed January 26, 2006.

Introduction to Logistics

hapter 9 provided an overview of supply chain management (SCM) and examined one of its important components—purchasing. Chapter 10 provided necessary background and techniques associated with planning and forecasting demand so that resources may be effectively managed. Chapter 11 addressed the management of one of those resources—inventory—so that costs and customer service can be balanced. As SCM's priority has increased, so has one of its most critical components: logistics. **Logistics** is defined by the Council of Supply Chain Management Professionals as:

> **❝** *the process of planning, implementing, and controlling the efficient, effective flow and storage of goods, services, and related information from point of origin to point of consumption for the purpose of conforming to customer requirements.*[1] **❞**

Logistics is a critical component of supply chain management for a few very fundamental reasons. First, the competition in virtually every industry has increased. This has resulted from globalization, from technological advancements, and from the need to increase the value offered to consumers. Enhanced logistics performance provides an opportunity to reduce costs and increase the value offered to customers. Costs are decreased through more effective use of resources (systemwide inventory reduction, reduced storage costs, reduced cash-to-cash cycle, etc.). In addition to the cost reduction, value is also enhanced through better performance on a number of value attributes including service quality, shorter response time, greater dependability of delivery, and increased flexibility.

While the lines between logistics management, supply chain management, and inventory management have become blurred, logistics management can be summarized as the management of the movement and storage of goods between businesses, rather than within businesses. It is the way that logistics relates to supply chain management, resource planning, and inventory management that dictates its placement in the Resource/Profit Model.

While the value added to products by processes within operations is generally thought to include those components specific to the creation of the product itself (quality, reliability, design, conformance, etc.), the value contributed by logistics relates to the placement, location, and the timing of delivery. All are necessary to meet customer expectations, whether that customer is a business (B2B) or a consumer (B2C). Exhibit 12.1 provides a conceptual view of how logistics fits into the supply chain by fulfilling transportation and warehousing functions.

Just as is the case when making other decisions that involve significant resource investment, some logistics decisions can be classified as strategic, while others are more tactical. Logistics decisions include the configuration of the logistics network, decisions regarding outsourcing logistics services, and the location of warehouse or distribution center facilities. These decisions dictate how and where goods will be stored and involve

logistics
The flow and storage of goods, services, and related information from production to consumption.

Kodak reduced its procurement costs by over $1 billion by centralizing the function.

EXHIBIT 12.1	Logistics and the Supply Chain

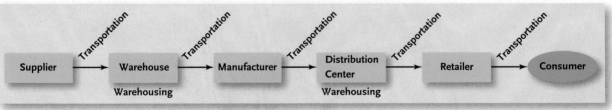

trade-offs among several financial costs, some of which include inventory carrying costs, warehousing costs, and transportation costs. Nonfinancial costs affected by these decisions include response time to customers, flexibility, and exposure to supply chain disruptions.

Logistics decisions may also include the selection of transportation channels used to move goods and the configuration of the reverse logistics network, if relevant to the particular industry.

Logistics Network Configuration

A traditional narrow view of the management of product supply concerned itself with getting the product out of the factory door on time. Obviously, a supply chain management strategy extends far beyond that view. It is concerned with everything that happens to that product, from raw material to consumer, within manufacturing plants and warehouses and between those manufacturing plants and warehouses. The fact is that many of the costs incurred and much of the time consumed takes place between those facilities. Products and their components travel great distances. One of the most important tasks for supply chain management is to determine what those distances will be and how that travel will take place so that value can be maximized and costs can be minimized. This requires that a logistics network be designed for the present *and* future needs of the supply chain.

The logistics network includes warehouses, production facilities, retailers, and the inventory that flows between them. Configuring the network requires decisions related to the location of the warehouse and production facilities, where production should take place, where and in what quantities inventories should be kept, and the means by which products and their components are transported from one place to another. These decisions are complex, however, because the configuration must meet current needs and future needs. This requires the use of forecasting to predict the impact that future demand will have on the network requirements.

Outsourcing Logistics Services

For many businesses and not-for-profit organizations, the movement of goods and services through the supply chain to the ultimate consumer is recognized to have huge potential for cost savings, but is beyond the expertise of the producer. The management of logistics services, such as transportation, warehousing and distribution, and product returns, requires expertise and assets not always available. Investment in the physical assets and systems required to perform these services effectively may not make sense. Logistics services has become one of the most common functions outsourced, thus allowing firms to focus on their core competencies. Poor logistics performance can eliminate any time-related competitive advantage a business may have.

Third-party logistics service providers, known as 3PLs, vary greatly in size and scope of capabilities. Some of the largest can provide services that include product transportation, warehousing, packaging, shipping, returns management, consulting, product tracking, managing global transportation, and order fulfillment. Basically, everything that needs to happen after the product is produced can be outsourced to a 3PL. Others limit their services to transportation or warehousing, focusing on a narrow area of expertise and asset availability. Probably the best way to describe the services available to a company wishing to utilize a 3PL is to examine the capabilities of one of the most extensive 3PLs as well as one focusing on a narrower range of services.

United Parcel Service, known by many only for its delivery services, is one of the largest companies in the 3PL industry. Its services range far beyond being the world's largest package delivery company. UPS is a $36 billion company that offers services to manage the flow of goods, money, and information. It has operations in more than

200 countries and territories.[2] UPS services can be categorized into groups such as air cargo, motor cargo, overnight delivery, capital services, professional services, and supply chain solutions.

Air cargo, motor cargo, and overnight delivery services are self-explanatory. UPS Capital Services include risk management, business credit services (particularly for small businesses), insurance services, and credit card services, and they facilitate the processing of checks for collect on delivery (C.O.D.) charges for businesses that require it. UPS Professional Services include business process improvement, project management, and engineering services. UPS Supply Chain Solutions extend beyond logistics, transportation, and warehousing to include industry-specific solutions for automotive, industrial, and consumer goods manufacturing, government and defense, healthcare, high tech, and retail. UPS seeks to offer services to enhance all dimensions of a business's supply chain.

In contrast to UPS, many 3PLs specialize in a small supply chain service niche. Many provide transportation services, for example, that meet a narrow set of needs in a particular industry. Southern Refrigerated Transport Inc. provides a typical example. SRT has about 400 tractors, equipped with the latest in satellite tracking, communications, automatic weighing, and in-cab e-mail systems.[3] It also has over 600 dry and refrigerated trailers. Hundreds of services like SRT's fulfill the shipping needs of companies that outsource this function.

Outsourcing of logistics services is not a question of there being a provider of services. There are thousands of providers, and the 3PL industry is growing at a rapid rate. The decision of whether to outsource is often the most difficult and, like other outsourcing decisions, must consider many factors. Included among those are obviously cost issues, but as important as cost are the various measures of service performance important to customers.

3PL Selection

A recent survey indicated that more than 65 percent of U.S. manufacturing firms outsource at least a portion of their logistics needs.[4] Outsourcing decisions are very strategic in nature. They can affect virtually any advantage a service or manufacturer may have. They affect costs, product or service quality, and timeliness. The potential impact on competitiveness makes the selection of a 3PL a critical process.

The two general areas of evaluation are the operational capabilities of the 3PL and its ability to work with the business for which it is providing services. Evaluation of the operational capabilities of the 3PL should include a close look at the 3PL's record of experience,

---

GOING **global** **3PLs Expand Globally**

As most industries find their markets expanding, those industries that serve them expand as well. Yellow Roadway Corp. is expanding into China to ease backups and disruptions that plague U.S. manufacturers and retailers already there due to unreliable transportation systems. With the expansion to China and expansion of Yellow Roadway's business also comes a name change to YRC Worldwide Inc.

YRC operates in 70 countries and employs approximately 70,000 people. It is currently the largest less-than-truckload (LTL) carrier in the United States. It consolidates small loads into full truckloads, using a network of terminals. It operates numerous brands, including Yellow Transportation, Roadway Express, Reimer Express, USF, New Penn Motor Express, and Meridian IQ. Its business in China will begin with fewer than 100 trucks serving a few manufacturers and retailers. YRC will move goods (electronics, apparel, etc.) to the port at Shanghai for transport via cargo ship to the United States. Service is expected to expand as the initial startup gains success.

Source: "Yellow Roadway Plans China Push, Name Change," *Wall Street Journal*, January 3, 2006, p. A5; www.yrcw.com/about/, accessed January 3, 2006.

Ten Steps to Selecting a 3PL	EXHIBIT 12.2

Strategy   Recognize that choosing a 3PL is a strategic decision. Thus, the selection process should identify the provider best able to fulfill the strategic goals.

Centralized control   The 3PL must be able to exercise control over a large network and be able to make the change to centralized control go smoothly.

Experience   The 3PL should be able to demonstrate its experience and how that experience will add to the client's capabilities.

Technology   The 3PL should have state-of-the art technologies accessible to and compatible with those of its clients.

Compatability   Every 3PL has a set of core competencies. They should match the needs of the client.

Bench strength   Look beyond superficial capabilities to issues that include technology development, organization depth, and so on.

Trust   Trust and confidence are critical. This may give the advantage to a previous 3PL relationship, rather than a new one with an uncertain track record.

Culture   The 3PL and client should have similar business philosophies and priorities. Examples would include ethics, employee culture, and so forth.

Improvement   The 3PL should embrace Six Sigma, ISO9000 certification, or any other system that encourages improvement that is consistent with the client.

Cost   Cost is a consideration but should not be the most important consideration. Others are more critical.

Source: Adapted from "10 Steps to Selecting a 3PL," *Logistics Management*, June 2003, Vol. 42, Issue 6.

its strengths and weaknesses, its use of technology, its ability to control a wide-ranging logistics network, and its commitment to and ability to lead improvement.[5]

Some operational capabilities are obvious. If refrigerated transport is required, for example, the 3PL must have that capability. Capacity is another important issue. The 3PL must have the capacity to perform what is required. Other issues aren't as clear. Familiarity with a particular industry is important, and one of the best indicators is experience in that industry. Being able to perform well, given the peculiarities of the auto industry, for example, could be demonstrated by previous or current experience in that industry. It isn't enough that the 3PL can perform operationally. It should be able to demonstrate that outsourcing the services has benefits over performing those services in-house.

Compatability issues can be as critical as operational issues. Compatability includes such things as compatible business approaches and similar values, but also means that information technologies must be able to link together. If the business uses an ERP system, the 3PL must be able to access necessary data. Previous experience with a 3PL can often be used to judge compatability. Exhibit 12.2 provides a breakdown of more specific criteria for selecting a 3PL.

Kodak has reduced its number of suppliers from over 3,000 to fewer than 1,000.

Reverse Logistics

Reverse logistics consists of the movement of goods from the customer back to the producer. In industries in which this need is high because of large volumes, logistical systems designed specifically for that purpose must be used. The termination of the reverse logistics network results in some type of disposition of the product. Reverse logistics networks are necessary for a variety of scenarios. The product may require re-manufacture, for example, as in the case of disposable cameras and printer cartridges. It may require recycling, as in the case of car batteries and electronics equipment. As businesses produce

| EXHIBIT 12.3 | Reverse Logistics Paths for Product Returns |

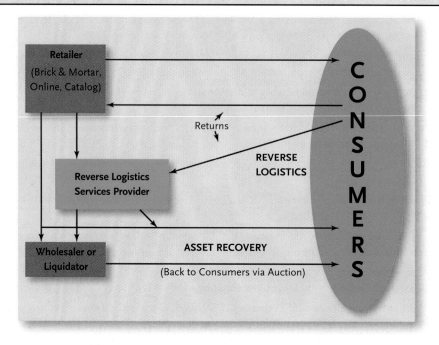

products that are more environmentally friendly, the need for efficient reverse logistics channels increases. In some cases, products must go back to the manufacturer, as in the case of defective products. In other cases, products that move through a reverse logistics system may require selling again, as in the case of a product returned because of improper fit or because the customer just didn't like it.

Product returns have become increasingly commonplace as more customers purchase online. Some online retailers must deal with product categories having return rates as high as 20 percent. To make matters even worse, studies have shown that the percentage of returns that are not defective or "no defect found" (NDF) is very high in some product categories. Consumer electronics, for example, has a NDF rate of 70 percent. PC products are over 85 percent, and some small appliances are over 90 percent.[6] Not surprisingly, reverse logistics services are often outsourced. For many retailers, the complete handling of returned products, from the time it leaves the customer's hands, is handled by a third-party provider. Many also provide the services necessary for disposing of those products. In these cases the reverse logistics process ends at **asset recovery,** which is when the product is sold again.

Alternatives in reverse logistics paths for returned goods are shown in Exhibit 12.3. Products being returned by customers may go directly back to the retailer, who must then either send them on to a 3PL for disposition, to a liquidator, or dispose of them in-house. In a more extensive outsourcing approach, the return goes directly to a 3PL, who makes the disposition decision. For those products resold, the retailer may get a percentage of the final asset recovery.

Kodak's improvements reduced return part transportation times from 15 days to 5 days.

asset recovery
Disposition of a product returned through the reverse logistics network

Transportation

Transporting products through the supply chain becomes more complex as supply chains get longer and cover more distance. The fact that different modes of transportation exist, but are not equally useful or accessible throughout the supply chain, also adds to complexity. These modes include road, air, rail, marine, pipeline, and intermodal. The importance of each transportation mode varies from industry to industry, but a comparison of overall volumes transported for each mode is useful to get a sense of the role each plays in the economy. The U.S. Department of Transportation, Bureau of

om ADVANTAGE   Philips Tackles Product Returns

One way to improve the effectiveness of reverse logistics is to reduce the number of products that must flow in that direction. In an effort to reduce the costs associated with product returns, Philips Consumer Electronics focused on reducing the number of returns, rather than on the processes used to manage them.

For Philips, returns were resulting in tens of millions of dollars in losses. Philips recognized that retailers with very liberal return policies had created a "take it back" culture. Many retailers had begun to deduct for returns when they shipped them back to the vendors. Returned products, sold through liquidators, were only recovering 20 to 30 cents on the dollar.

By surveying customers who had returned goods, Philips found that over 75 percent of them knew the product was not defective when they returned it. They identified the primary reason for the return as "misinformation at point of sale" and the secondary reason as difficulties in connection or use. Retailers were sending two-thirds of the returns back to Philips, rather than using a repair service provider. As volume increased, Philips adopted efficient reverse logistics processes to cut costs, but this did not reduce the loss in profits caused by the actual returned good. It became clear that, for Philips, returns were not a result of poor-quality products, but resulted from packaging that didn't clearly communicate the products' capabilities or requirements and inadequate training of retail salespeople.

In response to their findings, Philips began to focus on "ease of use." They have enhanced phone and Web service support. Philips also became involved in the Ease of Use Roundtable, an association committed to improving consumer experiences with PC and electronics products. Retailers have also increased their efforts to better communicate system requirements and better train employees. They have also begun to tighten return policies. In some cases, the combination of a 90-day return policy and a short product life cycle enabled customers to easily return their product for what was essentially a free upgrade. Some retailers have reduced the return time window to prevent this.

The results of Philips efforts have been significant. Philips has reduced returns by over 500,000 units since 1998 and saves more than $100 million per year.

Source: T. Sciarrotta, "How Philips Reduced Returns," *Supply Chain Management Review*, November 1, 2003, www.manufacturing.net/scm/index.asp?layout= articlePrint&articleID=CA335015.

Transportation Statistics has tracked the changes in the use of different transportation modes. That information is summarized in Exhibit 12.4.

Road Transport

As is evident in Exhibit 12.4, the truck is the most commonly used cargo transport mode in the United States. Truck transport is the most flexible of the transportation modes

U.S. Commercial Freight Activity by Transportation Mode						EXHIBIT 12.4
	1993		**1997**		**2002**	
Mode	Value (Billions of $)	Percent of Total	Value (Billions of $)	Percent of Total	Value (Billions of $)	Percent of Total
Truck	4,684	67	5,271	64	6,660	66
Air	395	4	654	4	777	4
Rail	278	9	366	9	388	9
Marine	620	6	753	8	867	8
Pipeline	312	4	229	3	285	3
Multimodal combinations	665	10	935	11	1,111	11
Total	6,954		8,208		10,088	

Source: Adapted from Bureau of Transportation Statistics, "Commercial Freight Activity in the United States by Mode of Transportation: 1993, 1997, 2002," www.bts.gov/publications/freight_shipments_in_america/html/table_01.html, accessed January 6, 2006.

simply because almost anywhere goods need to be delivered or picked up, there is a road. For most products, the final step in the delivery process involves a truck.

Freight haulers can be divided into a number of groups. **Full truckload (FTL)** carriers deliver products in full truckloads. They provide the cheapest mode of truck transport. FTL shippers are often used by businesses moving goods from the manufacturer to a warehouse or distribution center. This mode is the cheapest form of truck transport, and supply chains attempt to take advantage of that fact.

Less than truckload (LTL) carriers specialize in smaller loads and mixed loads. They typically utilize a network of terminals to consolidate freight originating from different shippers into a single truck. LTL shipping is more expensive, but for many situations FTL shipment requires moving too much inventory and would result in higher-than-desired inventory levels.

Express consignment transport consists of the door-to-door overnight and two-day delivery market. It is used when the volume is small and the need for a quick delivery dominates. There are currently three dominant players in this market: UPS, FedEx, and, more recently, DHL.

Air Transport

The use of an air carrier to transport goods has the advantage of speed, but the disadvantage of high costs. Historically, the high cost of transporting goods by air was prohibitive and its use was restricted to crisis situations. It is used in those instances when speed is critical for a competitive advantage. Overnight or next-day shipments within the United States may require an air carrier, but deliveries originating in the United States and going to China most certainly will.

The use of air cargo as a critical component of the supply chain has increased as companies have expanded operations or found suppliers at greater distances. Costs saved as a result of labor, resource, or tax advantages in other countries can quickly be nullified by increases in delivery lead times, poor delivery reliability, and a longer cash-to-cash cycle.

Consumer items that have a very short life cycle or a very short shelf life are often transported via air cargo. Examples include such products as consumer electronics, seasonal fashions, and video games. Items that need high levels of security can also benefit from air transport. Such valuable items as art, animals, jewelry, and newly released movies fit that profile. Despite the high costs of air freight, it is the fastest growing segment of the U.S. cargo industry.

Rail Transport

Rail transport is not as flexible as truck transport, but can be less costly, particularly for large and bulky products over long distances. It has a good safety record and a history of reliability. Rail shipment typically takes longer, however, than shipping by truck. Rail transport is efficient in many ways. The space required for tracks is small, the mode is environmentally clean, locomotives are fuel efficient, and trains can carry a tremendous amount of freight. A disadvantage is that the large investment required to lay tracks and long life of locomotives and cars results in a slow adoption of new technologies. Rail is the obvious choice when the shipper is more concerned with cost than time.

In the industry, railcars are known as "wagons." A trend in the industry is toward specialty wagons designed for transporting particular products. Hopper wagons are used for bulk powder products, flat wagons are used for steel and equipment, tanker wagons are used for liquid products, and car wagons are used for automobiles. Roadtrailers are special wagons that are the size of truck trailers and can be converted to truck trailers by simply changing the wheels.

Across North America and Western Europe, rail gauges are of a standard size. In other countries, however, standardization has not taken place, making it more difficult to integrate rail systems between countries. Variable wheel spacing technologies have made it possible for some trains to transfer from one gauge to another.

Another trend in rail transport is the increased use of **double-stacking**, in which containers are stacked on railcars. This increases the need for investment to alter clearances of bridges and tunnels, but greatly increases the efficiency of rail transport.

full truckload (FTL)
Transporting goods in a truck that is full.

less than truckload (LTL)
Transporting goods in a truck that is not completely full.

Under Kodak's new system, expedited shipments have been reduced by 22 percent.

double-stacking
Stacking containers two high on railcars.

Marine Transport

Transport by cargo ship, containership, or barge is typically the lowest cost per ton per mile, but slow and inflexible. Cargo ships are also known as **breakbulk ships.** They transport goods packed in boxes or crates, bales, barrels, cartons, and so on. The cargo is carried in the ship's cargo hold. This makes loading and unloading relatively slow. **Containerships** are specifically designed to carry cargo that is packed in standard size metal containers. The advantages of this mode of transport are described in detail in the Intermodal Transport section below.

breakbulk ship
A ship that transports products in

containership
A ship designed to carry cargo that is packed in standard size metal containers.

Pipeline Transport

Pipeline transport is the least flexible of any transportation mode. In virtually all cases, pipelines are designed and constructed for a specific product. Pipelines are generally used

Containerships like this small one haul large quantities of freight quickly and make it possible to easily load and unload the containers. On this particular ship most of the containers are the large eight-by-eight-by-forty foot size, but some eight-by-eight-by-twenty foot containers are present as well. The twenty foot size is the standard (TEU or "twenty foot equivalent units) and defines the size of the ship. Some ships can carry as many as 15,000 TEUs.

for transporting products in liquid or gas form. They can be used for long- or short-distance transport, depending on the situation, but are most often used to transport between isolated areas. Typical uses include the transport of petroleum products, natural gas, and water. A disadvantage of pipelines is the initial investment cost, but that is offset by very low operating costs.

Intermodal Transport

intermodal transport
At least two different transportation modes are used in moveing the goods from origin to destination.

integrated transport carrier
Utilizes a combination whatever modes are best to move goods from origin to destination.

Intermodal transport means that at least two different modes are used in moving the goods from origin to destination. Common examples of combinations of modes include marine/rail, rail/road, marine/road, and marine/rail/road. Intermodal transport that involves trucks, rail, or water utilizes containers that can be transferred from one mode to another. Intermodal transportation is the primary link between domestic transportation and international trade. In 2003, of the nearly 10 million trucks and containers that moved by intermodel transport, half were associated with international trade.[7]

Integrated transport carriers utilize a combination of whatever modes are best to move goods from origin to destination. The customer doesn't have to be concerned about the mode and is told the total cost up front.

Containerized transportation offers advantages and disadvantages. The most important advantage, obviously, is the ability to easily move a container from a ship to a railcar or truck. The move can be done quickly and easily. There are three key disadvantages of containerized shipping. The first is that quite often bottlenecks exist where the transfer from one mode to another takes place. Containers must be unloaded and reloaded. The flow of products through the supply chain can be interrupted by this process. The second disadvantage is the need to stack containers to effectively store them. Containers are stacked on containerships and in container yards awaiting transfer to the next mode. The fact that they are stacked can make it difficult to access containers. Containers that must be offloaded first must be loaded last. A third issue associated with the use of containers is that the flow of containers around the world is not balanced. Containers tend to accumulate at various places and must be redistributed. This results in having to transport empty containers. It has been estimated that approximately 20 percent of the containers shipped are empty. The world inventory of containers is over 20 million, with a couple of million being manufactured each year.

One advantage of containerized freight used in intermodal transport is that the container serves as a storage location as well. It is weatherproof and secure, and reduces handling of inventories between a storage site and the train or truck that will transport it to its final destination.

GOING global   Beer Moves from Mexico to the United States by Rail

Of the $7.4 billion spent in the United States on imported beer, an estimated 40 percent comes from Mexico. Of Mexico's share of the U.S. beer supply, Corona is the leading brand. Its U.S. sales have increased yearly since the beer's introduction in 1979. It is currently sixth in overall sales in America. Transporting that amount of Corona to the United States requires a fleet of 2,500 railcars. But beer is a difficult product to transport. It should not be shaken between the brewery and the customer.

Grupo Modelo, the makers of Corona, is like many companies in that it leases its railcars. It used to use standard boxcars for shipping the beer, but found that during coupling and decoupling, beer was shaken, containers moved, and cases were damaged. In addition, the wooden interiors of the cars often had nails and other projections that punctured the cases of beer. Inspecting cars for problems

resulted in a rejection of nearly 50 percent of the cars. Anxious for the 30 percent reduction in transport costs rail offered over trucks, but not satisfied with the delivery quality offered by the railcars it used, Modelo sought a solution. In order to provide better transportation, they worked with GE Rail Services, the company that it leased its cars from. After switching to cars that had cushioned under-frames and smooth floors and interior walls, they continued to inspect but cut their boxcar rejection rate to less than 2 percent. Ninety percent of imported Corona is now transported by rail.

Source: M. Bernstein, "Leased Railcars Lower Beermaker's Overhead," *World Trade Magazine*, September 1, 2005, www.worldtrademag.com; "Cinco de Mayo Celebrations Call for Cervezas de Mexico," *San Fancisco Chronicle*, Thursday, April 29, 2004, www.sfgate.com/.

Despite these disadvantages, the use of containers is increasing. The use of ships specifically designed to transport containers has revolutionized water transport. The ships are faster than regular freighter ships, can carry more freight, and can unload freight in less time than that required to unload breakbulk freight. This means the ships are in port less and actually transporting freight more, resulting in a greater return on their investment. The use of containers also enhances security, because the containers can be opened only at the origin, at customs, and at the destination. In addition, the container is its own warehouse. The combined benefits of containerized transport have reduced transportation costs to one twentieth of that of bulk transport.[8]

Buyer/Seller Responsibilities

There are many possible alternatives for who pays for the various parts of a product's transportation. When an international sales contract is being negotiated, the terms related to transportation can be more important than the sales price. Because of the potential for misunderstanding and misrepresentation, a standard set of terminology is used to define precisely who is responsible for what. The meanings of these codes, commonly known as Incoterms, is standardized worldwide. Incoterms is an abbreviation for International Commercial Terms. The Incoterms definitions have been amended several times; the most current set is Incoterms 2000. There are four groups of terms referring to origin, international carriage not paid by the seller, international carriage paid by the seller, and arrival at stated destination. While the following is not an exhaustive explanation of Incoterms 2000, it provides an introduction and exemplifies the issues Incoterms attempts to address.[9]

Origin

- EXW stands for *Ex Works*. It means that the seller delivers when they place the goods at the disposal of the buyer at the seller's premises or at some other named place, not cleared for export and not loaded on a vehicle. The seller's only responsibility is to make the goods available to the seller.

International Carriage Not Paid by the Seller

- FCA stands for *Free Carrier*. The seller delivers the goods, cleared for export, to the carrier the buyer specifies, at a named location, not loaded. If the delivery is at the seller's location, the seller is responsible for loading. If the delivery is to anywhere else, the seller is not responsible for loading. The seller's responsibility is fulfilled when they deliver the goods to the carrier.
- FAS means *Free Alongside Ship*. The seller delivers when the goods are placed alongside the vessel at the named port of shipment. The buyer is responsible for all costs and risks from that point on. The buyer must clear the goods for export and is responsible for loading costs. This is specifically used for ocean shipments that aren't containerized.
- FOB stands for *Free on Board*. FOB means that the seller delivers when the goods pass the ship's rail at the named port of shipment. The buyer is responsible for costs and risks as soon as the goods pass the ship's rail. The seller pays for the loading.

International Carriage Paid by the Seller

- CFR designates *Cost and Freight*. The seller is responsible for the cost and freight required to bring the goods to the named destination, but risks become the buyers when the goods pass the ship's rail in the port of shipment. Insurance is also the buyer's responsibility.
- CIF means *Cost, Insurance, and Freight*. This is the same as CFR, except that the seller is responsible for insurance against loss or damage.
- CPT stands for *Carriage Paid To*. The seller is responsible for the cost of freight to the named destination. The risks associated with loss, damage, or cost increases become the buyer's when the goods have been delivered to the custody of the first carrier.
- CIP stands for *Carriage and Insurance Paid To*. This is the same as CPT, except the seller is responsible for transport insurance against loss or damage.

Arrival at Stated Destination

- DAF stands for *Delivered at Frontier*. DAF means that the seller's responsibility stops when the goods have arrived at the frontier, but before the customs border of the country specified in the contract. This mainly applies to rail and truck and basically means that the seller bears the costs for delivery, but the buyer must get the product through customs.
- DES stands for *Delivered Ex Ship*. DES means that the seller's responsibility ends upon placement of the goods at the disposal of the buyer on board the ship at the named port of destination. The seller bears costs and risks involved in bringing the goods to the named port of destination.
- DEQ stands for *Delivered Ex Quay*. DEQ means that the seller's obligation is fulfilled when the goods are made available on the quay (wharf) to the buyer at the named port of discharge. The seller bears the risks until the goods are made available for the buyer.
- DDU stands for *Delivered Duty Unpaid*. DDU means that the seller's responsibility goes up to the point when the goods have been made available to the buyer at the named place in the country of importation. The buyer has to pay all duties, taxes, and customs charges required for importation.
- DDP stands for *Delivered Duty Paid*. DDP is like DDU in that the seller's obligation ends when the goods have been made available to the buyer at the named place in the country of importation. However, the seller is responsible for all duties, taxes, and customs charges required for importation.

Transportation Management Systems

The complexities associated with transportation make it extremely difficult to manage, but the potential cost savings and value enhancements make effective transportation management necessary. Increases in global sourcing, differences in rates across different carriers and transportation modes, demands for better service levels (fewer stockouts), increased documentation requirements (Sarbanes-Oxley compliance), and a desire for greater transparency throughout the supply chain have all contributed to the need for better transportation management.[10] Transportation management systems (TMSs) enable transportation decisions to be integrated with inventory and warehousing systems, order management, forecasting, and production planning. TMSs provide support at all levels of transportation management decisions.

LeanLogistics, a TMS provider, organizes its functions into four stages—procurement, planning, execution, and settlement. The procurement function supports the process of selecting carriers. The planning function provides decision-making support for mode or carrier selection and for shipment routing and scheduling and allows the user to evaluate pooling and direct-shipment alternatives. Once plans are made and loads are submitted, the system then offers confirmed loads to the selected carriers. If a carrier rejects an offered load, the system offers it to the next shipper on the list. The settlement stage deals with payment for services. Payment is automatically made based on the rate of shipment accepted when the carrier accepted the load.[11] As the importance of the value of effective logistics management increases, TMSs can be expected to become more important.

Warehousing

While transportation systems move goods from origin to destination, there are many situations that require the storage, or "warehousing," of goods. Storage can be at the manufacturer, the retailer, or somewhere in between. Warehousing serves a variety of purposes. It can be used to reduce transportation costs, reduce response time to customers, increase the variety of product available for consumers, and protect against supply chain disruptions. While warehousing brings to mind images of large quantities of inventory, effective

Distribution Strategies	EXHIBIT 12.5

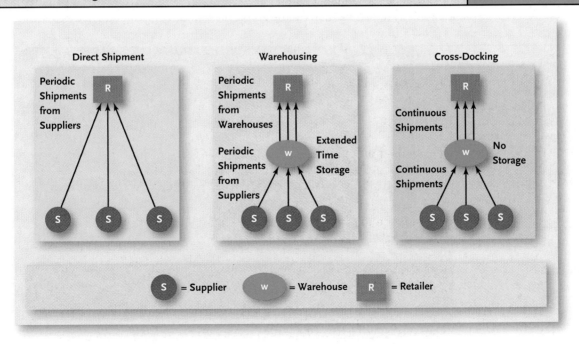

warehousing decisions can actually reduce the amount of inventory in a supply chain, reducing costs and increasing value for consumers.

Distribution and warehousing strategies address the approach used to distribute products to other places. For example, retailer-owned warehouses might take shipments from suppliers and hold them until ordered by the retail stores. This strategy is known as **consolidation warehousing.** On the other hand, retailers might take shipments directly from suppliers, in a strategy known as **direct shipment.** A third alternative, made popular by Wal-Mart, is called **cross-docking.** A cross-docking strategy ships continuously from suppliers to warehouses, where the products are redirected and delivered to the retailers in continuous shipments.[12] These three approaches are illustrated in Exhibit 12.5. One of the important considerations in developing a distribution strategy is the cost associated with transporting goods. A key determinant of those costs is the ability to ship full truckloads (FTL) versus less than full truckloads (LTL). Shipments that utilize FTL from manufacturers to warehouses and from warehouses to retailers will save on transportation costs.

The most sophisticated of the three strategies is cross-docking. It requires excellent communication links between suppliers and retailers. It depends on a very reliable transportation system to ensure continuous delivery of goods. Demand forecasts are critical, and in many instances they are based on direct data from point-of-sale (POS) systems at the retailer. A cross-docking strategy takes FTL shipments of products from the supplier to the cross-docking facility and then sorts and reorganizes the products into mixed trucks of products that go to individual retail stores. With no inventory stored at the cross-docking facility, those costs are eliminated. This system is very cost effective, but can only be used in supply chain networks that are high-volume and have sophisticated information systems, like Wal-Mart and Dollar General.

The strengths of a consolidation warehousing strategy are risk pooling and reducing inbound transportation costs. Risk pooling, in short, is based on the fact that if inventory is held in one warehouse to service a large number of retailers, lower levels of inventory can be held than if the inventory was held at each retailer. With a large number of retailers, demands that are higher than expected are canceled out by those that are lower than expected. The more retailers the warehouse serves, the greater the benefit from risk pooling. Overall, the inventory in the warehouse is sufficient to meet all of the demands. Inbound transportation costs are reduced because all shipments are coming from the same place. A consolidation warehousing strategy is likely to use FTL shipments to the warehouses, but shipments to retail stores may be LTL.

consolidation warehousing
Holding inventory received from suppliers in warehouses until it is needed by retailers.

direct shipment
Shipping directly from manufacturer suppliers to retailers.

cross-docking
Continuous shipment from suppliers to warehouses, where goods are redirected and delivered to retailers in continuous shipments.

Distribution system decisions affect inventory levels as well as customer service in a classic trade-off. This Pepsi distribution center in Boston, Massachusetts, illustrates how flows of products can be affected by the capacity of individual components of the supply chain. Notice the side-access trailers that allow easy loading and unloading of a variety of products.

A direct-shipment strategy eliminates all warehousing costs, but it is less likely to use FTL shipments and inventory service levels at each store require high levels of safety stock. Overall, much more inventory is required to obtain an acceptable service level. In addition, economies of scale are difficult to gain for shipments, because they can be coming from many different places. In a cross-docking strategy, no advantage is gained from risk pooling, but that weakness is often offset by the very frequent shipments and more accurate forecasts.

Warehousing takes on different roles in different industries. The risk pooling effect present in a warehousing strategy reduces costs associated with inventory. Warehouses can reduce systemwide inventory in another way known as **postponement.** Postponement delays the commitment of products to their final configuration as long as possible. This is done in order to allow the final configuration to be dictated by actual demand rather than a forecast. The best way to explain postponement is through an example.

Suppose a product was sold in four different countries, and the residents of each country spoke a different language. The nature of the product did not require any modification for the different countries, but the packaging needed to be country-specific. Rather than produce and package products for each country, products could be produced to meet an aggregate demand forecast and then packaged as orders came in for each country. Strategically placed warehouses allow for the storage of the intermediate (unpackaged) product. The packaging could take place before or after shipment to the destination country, but would be delayed or "postponed" until the best information on demand was available. Some 3PLs actually offer packaging as part of their logistics services to meet the needs of these types of situations.

> **postponement**
> Delaying commitment to final product configurations for as possible in the supply chain.

Location of Warehouse and Distribution Facilities

The distribution strategy selected will determine, to a great extent, the types of logistics costs a business will incur. The business that selects a warehousing strategy, for example, will carry higher levels of inventory than the business selecting a direct-shipment strategy, but response to retailer needs will be faster, and transportation costs may be reduced because of the FTL advantage between the manufacturer and the distribution centers. The choice of strategy will dictate many of the parameters associated with moving goods, but there are still decisions to be made within the framework of a particular strategy. One decision that is relevant for warehousing and cross-docking strategies is the actual location of the distribution center or cross-dock.

The center-of-gravity method provides a technique that can be used to determine optimal locations of these facilities. Beyond the actual use of the technique to enhance location decisions, an examination of how the method works provides an excellent exposure to the costs associated with location decisions.

Center-of-Gravity Method

Nearness between suppliers and customers in B2B interactions improves supply chain efficiency and reduces the cash-to-cash cycle. Costs added anywhere in the supply chain are ultimately borne by the customer, and they diminish the perceived value of the product or service being purchased. One of the most relevant costs associated with customers and suppliers is the cost of transportation of goods. Transportation costs are typically a function of the weight of the product or item that is transported and the distance it must be transported. Sometimes, however, for lightweight but bulky products, volume is more important than weight.

Businesses that use centralized distribution centers (DCs) are particularly aware of these costs because they are continuously shipping from the DCs to stores. The placement of the DC is a critical piece of the cost picture for these firms. If the DC shipped exactly the same products and exactly the same quantities to each store, putting the DC in the exact center of the stores would make sense. However, this is typically not possible. Different stores sell different quantities and different mixes of products, so they require

Example 12.1

EXCEL TUTOR

Center-of-Gravity Computation for Distribution Center Location

BrainFreez Beverages, a small regional bottler of high-energy drinks, is currently examining potential locations for a new facility. BrainFreez drinks are packaged in 12-ounce cans and bottles. BrainFreez can be purchased retail in 12-pack boxes of cans and 6-pack shrink-wrapped packages of bottles. BrainFreez has one supplier for each of the following inputs to its products: cardboard and paper goods, aluminum cans, plastic bottles and bottle tops, and syrup concentrate. Using the following data, determine where BrainFreez should locate its new facility. Supplier locations are shown in Exhibit 12.6. Note that the locations are superimposed on a geographic grid. x and y coordinates are listed in Exhibit 12.7. Truckloads per month of supplies coming from each supplier are presented in Exhibit 12.8.

EXHIBIT 12.6 **Graphical Representation of Supplier Locations**

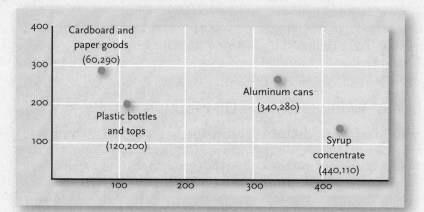

EXHIBIT 12.7 *x* and *y* **Coordinates for Suppliers**

Supplier	x	y
Cardboard and paper goods	60	290
Aluminum cans	340	280
Plastic bottles and tops	120	200
Syrup concentrate	440	110

EXHIBIT 12.8 **Truckloads per Month**

Supplier	Truckloads per Month
Cardboard and paper goods	13
Aluminum cans	15
Plastic bottles and tops	19
Syrup concentrate	60

(Continues)

Example 12.1 *(Continued)*

EXCEL TUTOR

Solution

Using the data provided, for the first supplier, $d_{ix} = 60$, $d_{iy} = 290$, and $V_i = 13$. Using the remainder of the information provided, the coordinates for the center of gravity are calculated:

$$C_x = \frac{(60 \times 13) + (340 \times 15) + (120 \times 19) + (440 \times 60)}{13 + 15 + 19 + 60} = \frac{34.560}{107} = 322.99$$

$$C_y = \frac{(290 \times 13) + (280 \times 15) + (200 \times 19) + (110 \times 60)}{13 + 15 + 19 + 60} = \frac{14.977}{107} = 171.68$$

The coordinates for the center-of-gravity location are approximately (323, 172), as seen in Exhibit 12.9.

EXHIBIT 12.9   Center-of-Gravity Location

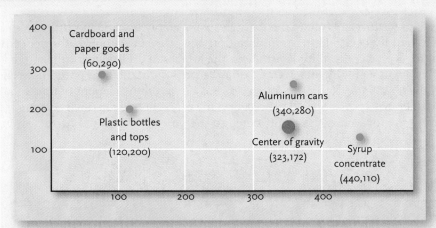

Application of the center-of-gravity method in a spreadsheet is demonstrated in Excel Tutor 12.1.

different shipments. The placement of the DC needs to consider the different volumes of goods shipped to different stores. For example, if one store needs a higher volume of shipments than other stores, the DC should be closer to that store. A similar problem is where to place a store or factory, considering shipments from suppliers that are already located. The issues are the same.

The center-of-gravity method identifies the best location for a single distribution center. In its simplest form, which is demonstrated in Example 12.1, it assumes inbound and outbound transportation costs are the same. The center of gravity, or "most central location," is found by calculating the *x* and *y* coordinates for the distribution center to minimize transportation costs. The following formulas are used:

(12.1)

$$C_x = \frac{\sum d_{ix} V^i}{\sum V_i}$$

(12.2)

$$C_y = \frac{\sum d_{iy} V_i}{\sum V_i}$$

where

C_x = x coordinate of the center of gravity

C_y = y coordinate of the center of gravity

d_{ix} = x coordinate of the ith location

d_{iy} = y coordinate of the ith location

V_i = volume of goods moved to or from the ith location

A close look at these equations will show that this is essentially a weighted averaging technique for each coordinate, where the coordinate for each location is weighted by the number of trips. The products are summed, and the sum is divided by the total number of trips.

Supply Chain Security

Supply chain security falls under the logistics realm simply because most threats to supply chain security occur during transportation and storage. Although threats of theft have always been a concern for logisticians, the attacks of 9/11 dramatically altered the role of security in supply chain systems. Border security efforts and the effect those efforts have on the flow of goods through U.S. ports has increased the amount of time required to get products to U.S. buyers and has changed the way supply chains are configured. The increased desire for security has contributed to the popularity of containerized shipping

EXHIBIT 12.10	**C-TPAT Certification**

Applicants sign a merno of understanding staling agreement to comply with security guidelines.

↓

Applicants submit details of current security practices and those of their 3PLs and overseas suppliers.

↓

CBP reviews application and provisionally approves or requests improvements.

↓

CBP Inspectors make site visits to verify the information on the application.

Source: Adapted from T. B. Gooley, "C-TPAT Benefits Outweight Costs," *Supply Chain Management Review*, January/February 2005.

and storage techniques, has increased the potential uses for RFID technology, and has increased the scrutiny of those segments of product supply chains in foreign countries.

One of the most significant drivers of supply chain security efforts is the Customs-Trade Partnership Against Terrorism (C-TPAT). C-TPAT was designed by the U.S. Customs and Border Protection Office of the Department of Homeland Security as a response to post-9/11 concerns about supply chain and border security. Its goal is to build a cooperative relationship between government and business. Businesses ensure the security of their activities by becoming C-TPAT certified, which requires a comprehensive assessment and evaluation based on C-TPAT guidelines. Guidelines cover areas such as procedural security, physical security, personnel security, access controls, manifest procedures, and conveyance security. Applicants are required to submit a security profiles questionnaire and implement a security enhancement program specified by the guidelines. Benefits for certified businesses included reduced inspections at U.S. borders, which speeds up processing and reduces delivery times. This is particularly important during times of heightened border security.

Although C-TPAT is voluntary, it has become a condition of doing business with big importers like Home Depot and Target. Some businesses have expressed frustration because of the backlog in getting C-TPAT certification and because of the lack of specifics in standards. C-TPAT is evolving. More Customs and Border Protection (CBP) specialists have been hired in hopes of reducing the backlog of applications. C-TPAT guidelines are also being modified to add more specific requirements. Exhibit 12.10 provides an overview of the C-TPAT certification process.

Information Technology

Radio-Frequency Identification

One of the most significant technological changes to affect supply chain management and logistics is radio-frequency identification (RFID). RFID, sometimes referred to as AUTO-ID, uses a microwave signal to transmit a unique ID number to a receiver. The receiver can contain as much data associated with that ID number as desired. The RFID tag can be scanned from distances up to 20 to 30 feet. As costs of RFID tags come down (they are currently about 30 cents each), their use will escalate. Wal-Mart, Target, and the U.S. Department of Defense have required some suppliers to use RFID since 2005. The tags are finding their way into many other uses as well. The ability to scan a container and instantly be able to identify its contents has implications for warehousing as well as rail, ship, and truck transportation. Attaching RFID chips to products changes retail security capabilities. The ability to track a product through its entire supply chain can be used to prevent counterfeiting. As the reading accuracy improves and costs come down, RFID has the potential to replace the bar code we are so familiar with.

Conceptually, RFID technology is quite simple. It consists of a "tag" which contains a chip with a unique identifier and an antenna, a reader, a host computer where data is stored, and software for communicating between the reader and host computer. There are two types of tags. Passive tags require no external power source and are significantly less expensive. They have the greatest potential for widespread supply chain use. Active tags can be read from greater distances, but require battery power. Exhibit 12.11 shows a simplified view of the RFID technology.

RFID technology depends on the unique identification of the pallet, case, or product being tracked. An electronic product code (EPC) is used as the identifier and is imbedded in the chip. Exhibit 12.12 shows an example EPC code and the type of information it contains.

Potential uses for RFID technology can be found throughout the supply chain. Exhibit 12.13 provides a partial list of applications in manufacturing, warehousing, transportation, and retailing.

EXHIBIT 12.11	Simplified View of RFID Technology

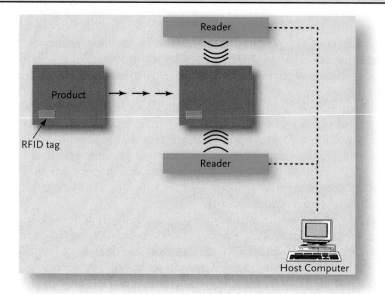

EXHIBIT 12.12	EPC Format

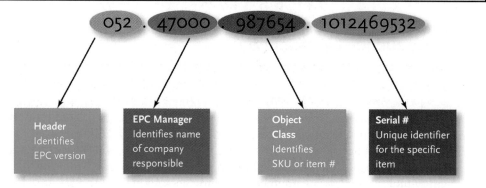

RFID is not a completely new technology. It has been used in some applications for years. Predictions of declining costs for tags and higher accuracy rates on reading them led to forecasts of massive use in streamlining the supply chain. However, adoption and integration into supply chain management practice has not been as fast as was initially expected. As of the beginning of 2006, adoption has been restricted to those companies doing pilot programs to test the technology and those companies doing the minimum required by customers like Wal-Mart and the U.S. Department of Defense. As costs come down and reading accuracy improves, more companies will integrate RFID systems.

The use of RFID throughout the supply chain will not become pervasive immediately, but the technology is likely to infiltrate warehouse and logistics management within the next five years.

Global Positioning Systems

You may be familiar with global positioning system (GPS) receivers used by hikers, in newer automobiles, and in planes and boats. A GPS receiver utilizes satellites operated by the U.S. Department of Defense. There are at least 24 operating satellites at any given time. Each satellite transmits signals that identify its location and the current time.

RFID Applications		EXHIBIT 12.13
Manufacturing	■ Counting and verifying delivery of raw materials by truck, pallet, case, or unit. ■ Tracking order, container, or product progress through a factory, allowing managers to know the location and status of every order.	
Warehousing	■ Counting and verifying deliveries of goods and removal of goods. ■ Verifying on-hand quantities.	
Transportation	■ Tags placed on products could allow the contents of containers, trucks, and railcars to be analyzed and counted without even opening them. ■ Trucks and railcars could be scanned during the unloading process, eliminating paper processing. ■ Scanning at critical points in the SCM could be verified and recorded to match against possible counterfeit products.	
Retailing	■ Tags placed on finished products could allow retailers to scan them as they are unloaded, giving perfect accuracy to inventories. ■ If tags were built into products or firmly attached, and readers were located on retailers' shelves (known as smart shelves), information regarding on-hand inventory levels could be collected automatically or even monitored by the supplier. ■ An entire cart of products could be scanned simultaneously at checkout. ■ Tags on products and scanners at doors could prevent theft by customers and employees.	

Because the satellites are at different locations, the signals take different amounts of time to reach the receiver. The receiver measures this time difference and estimates the distance to at least four different satellites. Once it has done that, it can calculate its position.

GPS technology has several applications for logistics. Through the use of GPS receivers in vehicles, wireless communication, and the Internet, businesses are able to continuously monitor the location of all vehicles. This enables them to estimate arrival times accurately, update customers on delays, and increase security. Costs can be reduced by reducing off-route mileage, enhancing dispatching and routing decisions, and increasing utilization of vehicles. Increased vehicle utilization can actually reduce the number of vehicles needed.

TARGETING technology   RFID and the Future of Retailing

Wipro Technolgy, an Indian software and IT service provider, has been testing RFID technology in an actual retail store operated on its campus in Bangalore, India. All apparel in the store is RFID tagged, enabling the managers to monitor purchases, theft, and stock levels. The store utilizes "smart shelves," providing an actual setting to help Wipro learn about the importance of antenna orientation on products. With two readers on each shelf, managers can monitor

stock levels and also can tell when stock is placed on the wrong shelf. A reader at the point-of-sale terminal is used to verify purchases. Some of Wipro's employees have RFID tags on their employee ID cards, so the company can also identify who is using the store.

Source: J. Collins, "Wipro Starts Up RFID Retail Pilot," *RFID Journal*, July 26, 1004, www.rfidjournal.com/article/articleview/1064/1/1/.

Here, a radio frequency identification (RFID) tag is shown next to the bar code label it will likely eventually replace. Information specific to this particular bunch of bananas can be stored, and modified every time the bananas pass by a scanner.

Measuring and Monitoring Logistics Costs

Logistics processes, like any other business processes, have the potential to add value and are certain to add costs. Like other business process, logistics processes should be monitored and analyzed to minimize non-value-adding activities. To successfully control logistics costs, these costs must be monitored. To enable managers to include these costs in decision making, **landed cost** is often computed for products. A product's landed cost is the cost of the product including all of the costs of logistics activities. These costs include warehousing costs, transportation costs, labor associated with product movement in the distribution system, costs associated with terminal transfers, costs associated with customs, and so forth. The landed cost enables managers to keep track of cost trends, to guide improvement efforts, and to compare alternatives when making logistics-related decisions. The landed cost calculation is presented in Example 12.2.

landed cost
A product's cost including all of the per product costs of logistics activities.

Example 12.2

EXCEL TUTOR

Landed Cost Computations

Wooden Hearth sells fireplace and wood stove accessories through a catalog and Web site. They wish to add to their product line a high-end solid brass set of fireplace tools that includes a stand, broom, poker, shovel, and bellows. Wooden Hearth has received two quotes from potential suppliers—one domestic and one from Asia. Wooden Hearth expects the average monthly demand of the new fireplace tool set to be 156 units.

The domestic supplier offers a unit price of $49, a packaging cost of $2.35, and a shipping cost from the manufacturing plant to the Wooden Hearth distribution center in Atlanta of $3.10 per set.

The Asian supplier offers a unit price of $35, a packaging cost of $1.20, and the following other costs.

■ Because the Asian supplier packages the product unassembled (to reduce bulk), Wooden Hearth must assemble the stand, broom, and shovel. Based on Wooden Hearth's labor costs, this will add $4.25 per unit.

(Continues)

Example 12.2

EXCEL TUTOR

(Continued)

- Transport costs from the manufacturer to the Shanghai port will be $14 per carton. There are 12 sets in each carton.

- Marine transport costs, including the costs paid to a consolidator who finds and brokers space in unfilled containers, is $36 per carton of 12 sets.

- Handling charges (removing from container, etc) in U.S. port is $6 per carton of 12 sets.

- Insurance is $18 per carton of 12 sets.

- Transportation (by truck) from the San Diego port to the Wooden Hearth distribution center in Atlanta is $12 per carton of 12 sets.

Solution

Landed cost calculations are made by converting all costs for each alternative to a "per unit" basis. Costs provided per carton, for example, must be converted to a cost per unit. Exhibit 12.14 provides the per unit cost for each item. The sums of the per unit costs provide the landed cost for each alternative. In this example, the landed cost for the Asian supplier is lowest.

EXHIBIT 12.14   Landed Cost Computations

Domestic Supplier	Cost per Unit
Unit price	$49.00
Packaging	2.35
Shipping	3.10
Landed cost	$54.45
Asian Supplier	
Unit price	$35.00
Packaging	1.20
Assembly	4.25
Overland transport ($14/carton)	1.17
Marine transport ($36/carton)	3.00
U.S. handling ($6/carton)	.50
Insurance ($18/carton)	1.50
U.S. trucking ($12/carton)	1.00
Landed cost	$47.62

CHAPTER SUMMARY

Logistics decisions include logistics network configuration, outsourcing decisions, and the location of warehouse and distribution centers. The effective management of logistics activities enhances service quality, timeliness, inventory productivity, and the ability to utilize capacity. Ineffective logistics increases costs and can be a detriment to virtually any competitive advantage the firm may have.

The design of the distribution network determines where inventory will be placed in the supply chain and how it will be transported. Costs associated with these decisions include transportation costs and inventory carrying costs. These decisions also determine, to a great extent, how long customers will have to wait for products.

Logistics services are often outsourced. Many companies have found that third-party logistics providers (3PLs) can provide better service at a lower cost than the company can provide for itself. As a result, the 3PL industry is growing rapidly. The importance of properly selecting a 3PL is made more important by the impact it can have on a business's success and by the growing popularity of outsourcing logistics services.

Transportation of goods is an important part of logistics. Strengths and weaknesses of transportation modes (road, air, rail, marine, pipeline, and intermodal) were discussed in the chapter. The most important trends in transportation are the increase in intermodal transport and the increasing use of containers.

Just as the selection of an appropriate transportation mode is important, so is the determination of a proper location for a warehouse or distribution center. Transportation costs and inventory costs are a common trade-off made in this decision.

A growing concern in the United States has been the security of supply chains, particularly as a result of the tremendous amount of products brought into this country through our ports. The Customs-Trade Partnership Against Terrorism (C-TPAT) seeks to involve businesses in efforts to enhance supply chain security.

Technology is having a major effect on logistics. Two technologies whose use is increasing are radio-frequency identification (RFID) and global positioning systems (GPS).

KEY TERMS

asset recovery, 540
breakbulk ship, 543
consolidation warehousing, 548
containership, 543
cross-docking, 548
direct shipment, 548
double-stacking, 542

full truckload (FTL), 542
integrated transport carrier, 544
intermodal transport, 544
landed cost, 556
less than truckload (LTL), 542
logistics, 536
postponement, 549

KEY FORMULAE

Center-of-Gravity Location

(12.1)
$$C_x = \frac{\sum d_{ix} V_i}{\sum V_i}$$

(12.2)
$$C_y = \frac{\sum d_{iy} V_i}{\sum V_i}$$

where

C_x = x coordinate of the center of gravity
C_y = y coordinate of the center of gravity
d_{ix} = x coordinate of the *i*th location
d_{iy} = y coordinate of the *i*th location
V_i = volume of goods moved to or from the *i*th location

SOLVED PROBLEMS

Two types of quantitative decision tools were presented in Chapter 12. The first, the center-of-gravity method, aids in locating distribution centers. The second, computing landed costs, provides a mechanism for comparing alternatives when logistics-related costs differ. A solved example for each is presented below.

1. The Center of Gravity Method

Grande Canyon Foods is a regional chain of grocery stores specializing in a wide variety of international fruits and vegetables. The perishable nature of its products requires a quick turnaround of inventory at stores and at its distribution centers. This need for fast deliveries and short storage times requires there to be multiple distribution centers and what is essentially a hub-and-spoke configuration of its logistics network. Current expansion plans are to build four large stores in Georgia. The logistics manager of the southeast region needs to determine the optimal location for a distribution center to service those new stores. He has developed a grid system for the state of Georgia and has entered the grid coordinates for the stores. The coordinates and expected shipments are:

Store	Expected Shipments/Week	x Coordinate	y Coordinate
Store 1	14	20	24
Store 2	12	8	36
Store 3	14	16	19
Store 4	10	26	12

Center of Gravity Calculation

Step	Objective	Explanation
1.	Formulate the problem using formulas 12.1 and 12.2.	Identify, for each store, the x and y coordinates and the expected shipments per week.
2.	Using formula 12.1, compute the value for C_x. Sum the products of the x coordinate and shipment quantity for each store	$$\frac{(20 \times 14) + (8 \times 12) + (16 \times 14) + (26 \times 10)}{14 + 12 + 14 + 10}$$ $$= \frac{860}{50} = 17.2$$
3.	Using formula 12.2, compute the value for C_y. Sum the products of the y coordinate and shipment quantity for each store.	$$\frac{(24 \times 14) + (36 \times 12) + (19 \times 14) + (12 \times 10)}{14 + 12 + 14 + 10}$$ $$= \frac{1154}{50} = 23.08$$
4.	Assemble the coordinates for the new distribution center.	(17.2, 23.08)

Solution

The center-of-gravity solution would be to locate the distribution center as close as possible to coordinates (17.2, 23.08).

2. Landed Cost Calculation

Allied Supplies is a maintenance, repair, and operating supplies company located in California. It imports a variety of industrial and commercial equipment used in the maintenance and operation of large facilities. Much of the equipment used to keep large office buildings functioning can be purchased through Allied. One of Allied's products is a commercial grade vacuum used to clean wide open areas such as hallways and lobbies. One supplier has provided the following cost information for that vacuum. Compute the landed cost based on 190 units per container.

Item	Cost
Unit price	$258
Inland transport costs to port	275
Marine transport of container	1,600
Port handling costs per container	625
Freight forwarding fee	150
Container brokerage costs per container	25
Freight transport to warehouse per container	260

Calculation of Landed Cost

Step	Objective	Explanation
1.	Convert all "per container" costs to "per unit" costs.	Divide each "per container" cost by 190 to convert to the "per unit" equivalent.

Item	Cost	Cost/Unit
Unit price	$ 258	$258.00
Inland transport costs to port	275	1.45
Marine transport of container	1,600	8.42
Port handling costs per container	625	3.29
Freight forwarding fee	150	.79
Container brokerage costs per container	25	.13
Freight transport to warehouse per container	260	1.37

Step	Objective		
2.	Compute the total "per unit" costs by summing.	$273.45	

Solution

The landed cost is $273.45.

REVIEW QUESTIONS

1. What is meant by "logistics"? what types of decisions are typically included as logistics decisions?

2. What are the decisions included in the configuration of logistics networks? Why is demand forecasting an important input to these decisions?

3. Why are logistics services frequently outsourced? What are the important issues to consider in selecting a third-party logistics provider?

4. What is reverse logistics? Why is it important?

5. Compare and contrast the strengths and weaknesses of road transport, air transport, rail transport, marine transport, and pipeline transport.

6. Describe the concept of intermodal transport. What are its potential benefits?

7. Describe the three basic strategies used for warehousing and distribution of goods. What are the strengths and weaknesses of each?

8. Explain the importance of full truck load (FTL) deliveries compared to less than full truckload (LTL) deliveries.

9. What is meant by "postponement"? How does postponement relate to warehousing?

10. Describe a typical decision that could use the center-of-gravity method for determining distribution center location.

11. What is the Customs-Trade Partnership Against Terrorism (C-TPAT)? What is its goal?

12. How does radio-frequency identification (RFID) technology work? What are some of its potential logistics applications?

13. How can global positioning system (GPS) technology enhance logistics management?

14. Why is landed cost an important measure?

DISCUSSION AND EXPLORATION

1. What value is added to a product by effective logistics management? How important is that value to you when you purchase products?

2. Compare the logistics requirements of different products. For example, compare electronics to CDs, groceries to household goods, fruits and vegetables to canned products, and fresh meat to flowers.

3. Describe the trade-offs you think are important regarding outsourcing product manufacturing to a foreign country. Should contract manufacturers be considered a 3PL?

4. Describe the types of trade-offs made between speed, costs, security, and flexibility when selecting a transportation mode. Identify product examples that fit each mode.

5. Identify a product you recently purchased. Where was it produced? Identify the transportation modes used to get it to you.

6. Privacy advocates have reacted negatively to RFID technology. What aspects of the technology could threaten privacy?

PROBLEMS

Solutions to odd-numbered problems are located on the text's Online Center (http://mhhe.com/opsnow3e).

1. Iowa Pork Processing (IPP) wishes to locate a processing plant in a region with 4 large hog confinement operations. Because of the high costs associated with transporting animals and the health issues and weight loss associated with long transports, IPP is planning to use the center-of-gravity method to determine the optimal location for this plant. Fortunately for IPP, Iowa's roads are arranged in a consistent grid, on one-mile intervals. The coordinates of the four pork suppliers are provided below, along with their expected shipment frequencies. Determine the center-of-gravity location for the new IPP plant.

Supplier	x Coordinate	y Coordinate	Truckloads/Month
Pigs R Us	180	70	12
Porky's Palace	300	45	15
Sioux City Swine	140	200	20
Paulina Pork Production	210	260	16

2. Annette Workman has managed a delivery-only sandwich shop for three years. She has recently been approached by three different businesses to provide lunch delivery

to their office buildings. Her current location is too far away from those buildings to provide timely and economical delivery, but the three buildings are close enough to each other to be served from one delivery site. Projected volumes from the three businesses, plus other business she would pick up in the area, is sufficient to support a small operation. Before going any further on her potential expansion, Annette wants to determine the best location, then she will research the costs associated with leasing something as close to that location as possible. The businesses' locations and the forecast demand for the three businesses are presented below.

Business	x Coordinates	y Coordinates	Deliveries/Day
Sanders, Jones, and Johanson Law Firm	60	40	32
J.P. Stevens Publishers	80	18	17
Arnold, Dickens, & Bradley Accounting	20	52	28

3. ShopMor Superstores is planning to build a new warehouse. It currently has four regional distribution centers, with locations and anticipated deliveries as given in the table below. Calculate the center of gravity to determine where the new warehouse should be located. Plot the four distribution centers and the new warehouse.

Regional Centers	x	y	Deliveries
North	100	200	12
South	120	40	24
East	20	80	18
West	180	140	9

4. Samson Industries would like to locate a new facility close to its suppliers. Data on location and deliveries are presented below. Use the data to calculate the center of gravity. Explain how the new location can help lower transportation costs.

Suppliers	x	y	Deliveries
Adco	280	200	30
Driam	160	40	20
Moritt	50	80	20
Flamdin	120	160	15

5. Kesey Products asked you to assist in selecting a new location using the center-of-gravity method. The company's largest question centers around the different transportation costs it incurs when delivering products to its customers. Explain how transportation costs could be considered using the center-of-gravity method.

6. Terry Burton, a college sophomore, is opening a small computer upgrade business in an empty bedroom of the house he rents. His plan is to limit his business to installing second hard drives, larger hard drives, and new media devices like CD and DVD burners. He believes his volume will be small enough to promise a 24-hour turnaround. He plans to limit options on each possible upgrade to 2 or 3 popular alternatives. Terry's dad has loaned him $8,000 and he has another $4,000 of his own money. He has all of the tools he needs and a work table. His only investment will be in the hard drives, CD burners, and DVD burners. By buying in quantity, he will be able to reduce his costs and make a sizable profit on each upgrade. Terry has investigated DVD burners and has identified two alternatives. Both are purchased from U.S. suppliers.

- Alternative 1 sells DVD burners in cases of 24 at $1,145 per case. Insured shipping is $38 per case. Handling and processing fees charged by the distributor total $28 per case.

- Alternative 2 sells only through eBay at a fixed "Buy It Now" price of $970 for a case of 20. Insured shipping is $33. A handling charge of $18 is added to every case. Alternative 2 only takes Paypal payments and passes the Paypal fee on to the buyer. The Paypal fee for a $970 purchase is 2.9 percent plus $.30.

Compute the landed cost for each alternative.

7. Ellison's Electrical Controls sells a large variety of controls for industrial use. Controls for high-voltage systems make up most of their demand. The purchasing manager has recently put out a request for bids for a particular 480-volt, 3-phase control. She received three bids from her request. All three alternatives must be transported from Asia to a U.S. port and then shipped to the office. The bids are for very similar products, but one of the products requires some minor assembly upon delivery. The details of the bids are presented below.

	Supplier 1	Supplier 2	Supplier 3
Case cost	$2,160	$3,100	$2,410
Case size	10 units	12 units	10 units
Transport to			
U.S. port	$215	$230	$180
Shipping	$80	$124	$140
Handling	$25	$40	$30
Insurance	$130	$90	$110
Assembly labor	–	$8/unit	–

Compute the landed costs for each alternative.

8. Andrew's Castings imports plastic pellets from a South American supplier. Andrews incurs the following costs under its current contract:

Cost per ton	$645
Transport to U.S. port	$165/ton
Broker fees	$28/ton
Insurance, security, handling	$19/ton
Shipping from port to plant	$68/ton

Andrew's current contract is about to expire. If Andrew's renews this contract, the only change is expected to be an increase in shipping from the port from $68 to $76 per ton. Andrew's is also considering an alternative supplier who is offering the following:

Cost per ton	$618
Transport to U.S. port	$172/ton
Broker fees	$31/ton
Insurance, security, handling	$21/ton
Shipping from port to plant	$76/ton

Compare the landed costs of the new supplier to those of the current supplier if the contract is renewed.

9. Max's is a regional discounter of consumer electronics products. It sells predominantly bottom-end off-brand products, old models, and overstocks. Because there is a large university nearby, Max's tries to build up its stock in late summer in anticipation of the high demand that results from students coming back to campus in late

August. It makes purchases in large quantities and is able to sell at a large discount, even underpricing Wal-Mart. One particularly popular product is a 21-inch flat screen TV. The TVs are packaged and loaded into standard $8 \times 8 \times 20$ shipping containers at the factory. The containers are then transported to Shanghai, where they are loaded onto a containership. One supplier ships to San Diego, the other to New York. Containers are hauled piggyback to Max's local warehouse. Depending on the source, approximately 270 TVs fit into a single shipping container. Max's will take delivery of six full containers of TVs in late July. There are currently two possible sources for this TV. Cost information for each is provided below.

	Supplier #1	Supplier #2
Cost per TV	$31	$28
TVs/container	270	278
Marine transport	$1,400	$1,300
Suez Canal charge per container	$0	$165
Broker fees per container	$24	$26
Customs charges per container	$40	$42
Truck transport per container	$260	$410

ADVANCED PROBLEMS

1. Rocking-C Furniture Company has hired GreenSites, a facilities consulting house, in an effort to place a new production facility. Rocking-C management believes that in order to facilitate its strategy of responsiveness to customer need and unsurpassed quality, it is essential that the new manufacturing facility be located as near to their suppliers as possible.

   A majority of Rocking-C's suppliers are located in the Southeastern United States, with fabric, by far the largest selling couch, suppliers located from northern Georgia to North Carolina. Leather suppliers are located in Texas, as are the producers of the rocking mechanism used in Rocking-C products. To assist in locating the new production facility, GreenSites has developed the following representation of Rocking-C's suppliers.

Supplier	Material	Location X	Location Y	Orders
1	Fabric	530	716	65
2	Fabric	387	712	35
3	Fabric	592	600	25
4	Leather	75	175	10
5	Spring Coil	712	968	52
6	Foam Padding	147	210	100
7	Wood	583	950	80
8	Plastic	467	349	30
9	Fabric Guard	632	785	36
10	Fasteners	692	215	22
11	Cardboard Boxes	281	893	135
12	Rocking Mechanism	169	320	12

   a. Complete the analysis by plotting the above data. Based on this analysis, where should GreenSites recommend Rocking-C locate?

   b. A picture of a Rocking-C leather couch with rocking mechanism in a fashionable magazine has led to a sudden shift in demand to leather rocking couches. Based on the projected orders below, where should Rocking-C locate its new plant?

Supplier	Material	Orders
1	Fabric	40
2	Fabric	28
3	Fabric	19
4	Leather	48
5	Spring Coil	52
6	Foam Padding	100
7	Wood	80
8	Plastic	40
9	Fabric Guard	36
10	Fasteners	22
11	Cardboard Boxes	135
12	Rocking Mechanism	52

2. Ace Manufacturing delivers their products to retail stores in a 200,000 square mile area. They currently have four customers, one with two locations, in the area. They are trying to determine the best location for a new distribution center. From an origin point, the locations are:

Retailer	x	y	Truckloads per month
Johnny's	190	410	20(to each location)
	675	325	
Bullseye	360	310	43
SaveSome	290	140	37
Wal-Fords	760	60	72

All of their customers, except Wal-Fords, have long term contracts. Wal-Fords will only give a one-year contract, and renegotiates each year.

a. Using the Center of Gravity technique, determine the best location for Ace's new Distribution Center.

b. If Ace suspects that Wal-Fords may cancel their contract, would that change the location of the DC? If so, what would be the coordinates of the modified location?

3. The Palace Door Company manufactures residential front door and entry systems. Most of the front doors have leaded glass panels, and the entry systems include matching leaded glass transoms and side lights. Palace Door has their own artist glass shop where artisans make the leaded glass panels per order. Since each door is custom ordered and the customer has the ability to choose the glass design, or even have a new design created for them, Palace does not stock any pre-made panels. Palace is considering outsourcing the production of the glass panels to Mexico, Guatemala, or Taiwan, where labor and materials are much cheaper. All of the shops have skilled artisans who can easily create individual pieces, based on drawings faxed to the plants. Cost information is presented below.

Item	Cost		
Current average cost per panel	$225		
Outsource costs	Tijuana	Puerto Barrios	Taipei
Cycle time	14 days	21 days	60 days
Price per panel	$150	$125	$100
packaging for 12 panels	$125	$100	$75
Brokerage fee per crate	$50	$50	$125
Transportation costs per crate			
of 12 panels	$225	$360	$480
Insurance costs	$33	$93	$185
Mistake allowance per panel	$15	$15	$15
Port costs	$0	$85	$125
Border inspection fees per crate	$35	$50	$80

a. Should Palace outsource the construction of the glass panels; if so, to where?

b. Palace has found out that their customers will be upset with the longer manufacturing time that is created by outsourcing the panels. Assuming that Palace can placate the customers with a discount of $1/day for the delay, would your answer change?

ENDNOTES

1. Council of Supply Chain Management Professionals, "Supply Chain and Logistics Terms and Glossary" (updated February 2005), www.cscmp.org/Downloads/Resources/glossary03.pdf, accessed December 22, 2005.

2. "About UPS," www.ups.com/content/us/en/about/index.html?WT.svl=Footer, accessed January 6, 2006.

3. Southern Refrigerated Transport, Inc., www.southernref.com, accessed January 6, 2006.

4. T. A. Foster, "Engineering the 3PL Selection Process," *Logistics Management*, June 2003, Vol. 42, Issue 6.

5. "10 Steps to Selecting a 3PL," *Logistics Management*, June 2003, Vol. 42, Issue 6.

6. T. Sciarrotta, "How Philips Reduced Returns," *Supply Chain Management Review*, November 1, 2003, www.manufacturing.net/scm/index.asp?layout=articlePrint&articleID=CA335015.

7. J. M. Smith, "Breaking through Bottlenecks at the Port," June 1, 2004, *World Trade Magazine*, www.worldtrademag.com.

8. J. Rodrigue, B. Slack, and C. Comtois, "Intermodal Transportation," *Transport Geography on the Web*, http://people.hofstra.edu/geotrans/index.html.

9. "Understanding Incoterms," www.iccwbo.org/incoterms/understanding.asp.

10. L. Terry, "TMS Turns It On," *Supply Chain Manufacturing and Lotistics Solutions*, November 9, 2005, www.scs-mag.com.

11. LeanLogistics, www.leanlogistics.com/product_overview.html.

12. D. Simchi-Levi, P. Kaminsky, and E. Simchi-Levi, *Designing and Managing the Supply Chain* (New York: McGraw-Hill, 2000), pp. 112–115.

LEARNING ACTIVITIES   www.mhhe.com/opsnow3e

Visit the Learning Center (www.mhhe.com/opsnow3e) for additional resources. Content varies by chapter, and includes

- Business Tours
- OM on Site
- Readings
- Resources
- Excel Tutors

- Interactive Case Models
- Reel Operations Video Clips
- Additional Advanced Problems
- Self-Assessment Quizzes
- Glossary

SELECTED RESOURCES

Rodrigue, J., Slack, B., and Comtois, C. "Transport Geography on the Web." http://people.hofstra.edu/geotrans/index.html.

Lambert, D. M., Stock, J. R., and Ellram, L. M. *Fundamentals of Logistics.* New York: McGraw-Hill Higher Education, 1998.

Kasra Ferdows, K., Lewis, M., and Machuca, J. "Rapid-Fire Fulfillment." *Harvard Business Review*, November 1, 2004.

VIDEO CASE 12.1

Profitability through Efficient Resource Use at APL Global Logistics

Based on Video 14 on the Student DVD

For companies serving businesses (B2B), rather than consumers (B2C), value takes on a different meaning than it would for a consumer-oriented company. A service offered to a business, for example, will be evaluated on that service's ability to improve the business's resource productivity, improve the quality of outputs, reduce the response time, or reduce costs. All of those benefits can be passed on to that business's customers, increasing the value of *its* products and services, and increasing *its* profitability. As the economy has increasingly stressed response time, global outsourcing has created a conflict. While few argue that some products can be made more cheaply overseas, the cost savings may be offset by the increased amount of time required to get the goods into the United States. This is complicated by the distance, the fact that economical transportation is often limited to ships, which move slowly, and increased border security, which takes more time.

The new American Presidents Line (APL) terminal in Los Angeles provides many benefits to companies importing products from Asia. The 230-acre facility offers capabilities to unload and load ships, as well as transfer containers to truck and train transportation modes.

1. How does the efficient operation of the APL terminal translate into enhanced profitability of customers? What would be the most important attributes of the APL facility for its customers? What APL resources are directly responsible for these benefits?

2. APL innovation includes resources that are physical (cranes, docks, etc.) and those that are less tangible (expertise, software technology, etc.). How do these different resources come together to enhance profitability for APL?

VIDEO CASE 12.2

DHL Global Delivery Services

Based on Video 14 on the Student DVD

DHL has grown rapidly in the United States as third in a market dominated by UPS and FedEx. On a global scale, however, DHL is the market leader in international express delivery service. DHL has gradually expanded throughout the world since the early 1970s. Until the early 2000s, however, DHL was strong in Europe and Asia, but did not have a strong presence in the United States. As interactions between companies in Asia, Europe, and the United States increased, it became clear to DHL that it must develop its network in the United States.

1. How do the tracking and tracing capabilities of DHL add value for their customers? How does the importance of those capabilities differ for B2C and B2B customers?

2. Describe the hub system used by DHL. What is the function of a "gateway" versus the function of a "hub"?

3. How do the morning operations differ from the afternoon operations at DHL's Miami gateway?

4. How does DHL differentiate itself from its competitors?

INTERACTIVE CASE 12.1

A New Customer for RLX Logistics

Location decisions for central warehouses that ship products to a number of retailers often have a goal of minimizing transportation costs. Total transportation costs associated with a time period are a function of the distance traveled to make a shipment and the number of shipments made during the period. The center-of-gravity method minimizes the total costs associated with shipments by finding the central location for the distribution center, given the number of shipments.

The center-of-gravity model allows the user to manipulate the environment in which the center-of-gravity technique would be used. In this environment, a central distribution center is being located among six retailers with varying shipments. By changing the number of shipments, or by dragging a retailer to a new location, the user can see the effects on the center-of-gravity location decision.

RLX Logistics

RLX Logistics is a third-party logistics (3PL) provider for several retail chains. RLX builds or, when possible, leases warehouse facilities to provide a regionally centralized delivery point for products, stores them, and ships them as needed to individual retail stores. RLX has recently signed a contract to provide 3PL services to a locally owned six-store sporting goods chain in the Chicago area. An empty and available warehouse has been identified in nearly the exact location specified by the center-of-gravity analysis.

By placing all retail destinations on a grid, the center-of-gravity analysis is able to identify the point on that grid that offers the lowest total transportation costs, given distances and the quantity of shipments necessary.

The default values are:

Retail Store Destination	X (0–100)	Y (0–100)	Shipments per Week (1–999)
Retailer 1	20	20	800
Retailer 2	64	65	900
Retailer 3	50	40	200
Retailer 4	80	50	100
Retailer 5	40	70	500
Retailer 6	10	60	300

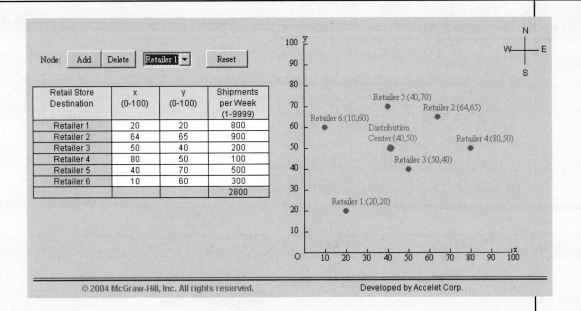

| Node: | Add | Delete | Retailer 1 ▾ | Reset |

Retail Store Destination	x (0-100)	y (0-100)	Shipments per Week (1-9999)
Retailer 1	20	20	800
Retailer 2	64	65	900
Retailer 3	50	40	200
Retailer 4	80	50	100
Retailer 5	40	70	500
Retailer 6	10	60	300
			2800

1. Make sure all parameters match the default values above. If they do not, click on the "reset" button.

   a. The distribution center is currently located closest to Retailers 3 and 5, and is farthest from Retailers 1 and 4. Explain why this has occurred.

   b. Move Retailer 4 thirty miles directly south, from (80,50) to (80,20). How much did the optimal location of the distribution center move?

2. Set the parameters back to their starting defaults.

   a. Record the location of the distribution center. Move Retailer 2 thirty miles directly north, from (64,65) to (64,95). How much did the optimal location of the distribution center move?

   b. Explain why the results of moving Retailer 4 thirty miles were different than the results of moving Retailer 2 thirty miles.

3. Set the parameters back to their default values.

   a. Currently, Retailer 1 requires four times as many shipments as Retailer 3. Move Retailer 1 forty miles to the east, from (20,20) to (60,20). What is the impact on the optimal location of the distribution center? What are its new coordinates? How far did it move?

   b. Set the parameters back to their defaults. Move Retailer 3 forty miles to the east, from (50,40) to (90,40). What is the impact on the optimal location of the distribution center? What are its new coordinates? How far did it move?

   c. Move Retailer 4 forty miles to the south, from (80,50) to (80,10). What is the impact on the optimal distribution center location?

   d. Move Retailer 2 forty miles to the south, from (64,65) to (64,25). What is the impact on the distribution center location?

   e. Based on the four previous experiments, what is the relationship between quantity of shipments and the effect of the destination location on the optimal distribution center location?

APPLICATION CASE 12.1

Moving Food for Animal Antics

Animal Antics is a national retail chain of pet supermarkets. They sell a wide range of pet supplies, including toys, cages, beds, and healthcare products. They also sell canned and dry foods for animals ranging from dogs and cats to horses and llamas. They have historically used the same distribution network for all products. The United States is divided into 14 geographic regions, which in most cases follow state lines. The regions are presented in Exhibit 12.15. Each region has a centralized distribution center that receives shipments directly from suppliers and delivers to all stores within the region. Shipments are made weekly.

EXHIBIT 12.15   Animal Antics Distribution Regions

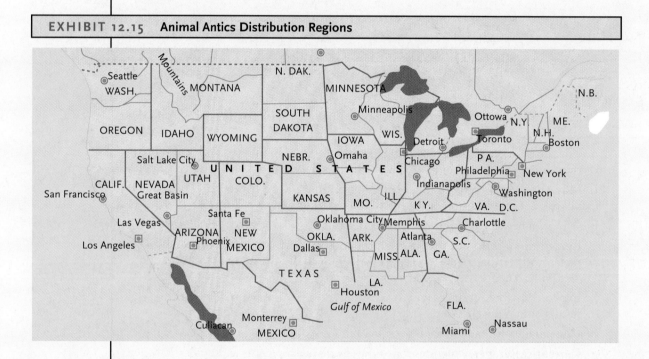

The new director of supply chain management for Animal Antics is considering a major change in the logistics system. He has determined that the characteristics of dry pet food are so different from the characteristics of other products sold in the stores that the pet food logistics system should not necessarily be the same as that of other products. He has identified the following list of key differences between pet food and other products:

■ The bulk (and therefore shipping cost) is very high when compared to the value of the product.

■ The margin when sold is very low compared to other products.

- The value of the product compared to the space it requires in the store is very low compared to the other products.
- The demand and inventory turnover is very high compared to other products.

Design a separate logistics configuration specifically for pet food. In your design, consider distribution center needs, shipments from suppliers, frequency of shipment to stores, transportation modes, and inventory levels required in stores. When you have completed your design, describe the advantages it has over the current system in terms of transportation costs and inventory costs (at DCs and stores).

CHAPTER 13

Lean Systems: Eliminating Waste throughout the Supply Chain

LEARNING OBJECTIVES

- Describe the overriding objective of lean systems.

- State the wastes that were the focus of Toyota's original version of a lean system.

- Describe the enterprisewide lean techniques and explain how each affects wastes in the business.

- Describe the inventory-focused lean techniques and explain how each reduces inventory waste.

- Describe the workforce-focused lean techniques and explain how each reduces workforce waste.

- Describe the capacity-focused lean techniques and explain how each reduces capacity waste.

- Describe the facility-focused lean techniques and explain how each reduces facility waste.

- Describe the competitive benefits of lean systems.

- Determine the takt time for production.

- Calculate the appropriate number of kanbans.

- Determine the batch size to minimize inventory.

SERVICES FOLLOW MANUFACTURING TOWARD LEAN SYSTEMS

In many services, behind-the-scenes processes are similar to those of a manufacturer. Applications go through a standardized set of review procedures. Insurance claims go through a similar procedure. Individual cases are treated similarly, if not identically. Ineffective processes, poor quality, and all non-value-adding activities add waste, extra time, and costs to the system. Defects (errors) must be corrected, which is no different than defective manufactured products being reworked. While manufacturers have recognized the need to squeeze out waste for greater profitability, services have been slower to respond. Those with the most repetitive and high-volume processes, however, have seen the benefits of waste reduction.

For services like insurance companies and financial institutions, applications and claims move through processes exactly like inventory moves through a factory. Each unit goes step-by-step through a series of activities. Any disruption can stop the flow and create backups, as well as idle workers. Errors delay completion and due dates are missed. Jefferson Pilot Financial, an insurance company, began its lean initiative in order to improve service in a new business. It gathered data and found that new applications requiring a physician's statement took two months to turn around. Customers were lost in the process. Up to 10 percent of policy applications had to be reworked. Two similar locations had very different figures for cost per application.

After completely revamping processes and following commonly accepted lean principles, labor costs associated with applications were reduced 26 percent. Errors were reduced by 40 percent. Service improvement resulted in a 60 percent increase in new individual life insurance premiums. Many of JPF's changes were simple. Related processes were moved closer to each other to reduce transportation and time between processing steps. Procedures were standardized so that employees could be trained to be more flexible. Standards were developed for processing time and a flow was developed for processing applications. Simplification of processes and separation of simple tasks from complex tasks smoothed the flow of applications through the system. Smoother flows meant shorter lead times, which meant quicker response to customers.

JPF's experience is not unique. One study focusing on services showed that 40 percent of labor costs were wasted because of ineffective processes. Financial services in particular have great potential for improvement by becoming leaner. Streamlining processes translates directly into lower labor costs and quicker response to customers. In one automobile loan situation, the process was streamlined so well that it could be automated, resulting in a 4-minute response time for 98 percent of online loan applications. Jefferson Pilot merged with Lincoln Financial Group in 2006.

Source: C. K. Swank, "The Lean Service Machine," *Harvard Business Review,* October 2003, Vol. 81, Issue 10, p. 123; P. Atkinson, "Creating and Implementing Lean Strategies," *Management Services,* February 2004, Vol. 48, Issue 2, p. 18. www.JPFnet.com.

A s competition has increased, manufacturers and services have recognized the bottom-line impact of waste. An emphasis on low inventory, efficient processes, high quality, and effective use of all resources has evolved into an enterprisewide framework known as lean systems.

Introduction: A Management Framework for Waste Elimination

L ean practices were initially imported from Japan in the early 1980s as an attempt to copy the successful Japanese just-in-time (JIT) approach to automobile production. Early attempts to copy the Japanese approach were seldom effective, because U.S. manufacturers didn't recognize the sophistication of the system. Instead, they viewed it as a few specific techniques that could easily be copied. As time went on, U.S. manufacturers began to comprehend the magnitude of JIT and implement it as an integrated way of thinking rather than a "quick fix," and they began to benefit from its effects. A prerequisite to understanding JIT was recognizing its overriding objective of eliminating waste. This contrasts to the common perception that its focus was limited to inventory reduction. JIT is predominantly a manufacturing management framework, but many aspects of it have become popular in the service sector. For both of those reasons, it has evolved from an inventory-focused JIT approach to a broader viewed framework known simply as **lean.**

Lean systems accomplish waste reduction by improving process productivity, reducing inventory, improving quality, and increasing worker involvement. The waste reduction accomplished by lean systems has a direct impact on costs, so it should not be a surprise that it enhances profitability through cost reduction. It has another, perhaps greater, impact on profitability through the strategic benefits of the results of lean efforts. Improved response time, greater flexibility, and improved quality all add value for customers, increasing sales. In this chapter, the wastes that lean strives to eliminate are explained, the techniques used are described, and the competitive benefits of lean are discussed.

Eliminate Waste: The Focus of Lean

The roots of lean practices can be traced to the production system developed by Toyota and modified over the years by many companies. Despite the modifications, a look at the focus of the initial Toyota system provides an excellent overview of the types of waste lean practices seek to eradicate. Exhibit 13.1 lists the types of waste Toyota's original vision focused on reducing.[1] Each waste reduction focus is described in turn.

Overproduction waste is caused by producing in excess of demand or by producing items before they are needed. The waste of producing too much is obvious. It creates excess inventory and wastes capacity on products that have no demand. Producing too early creates similar wastes. Early production adds to the inventory levels and adds time to the cash-to-cash cycle. If the orders produced early cannot be shipped, they must sit around taking up valuable space, reducing the financial return on the facility investment. There is also a risk of damage that will detract from the quality of the products. If products are shipped early, they inflate the inventories of the customer by getting there early and sitting in storage. This action anywhere in the supply chain will have a negative impact. It's not unusual for U.S. manufacturers to produce and ship early. Sometimes this behavior is motivated by the need to meet monthly or quarterly shipping goals. Management pulls orders from next month ahead, which increases the shipments for the current month. Obviously, this creates fewer shipments for the next month, resulting in a need to do it again.

lean
Manufacturing and service processes that have very low levels of waste.

overproduction waste
The waste caused by producing in excess of demand.

Waste Reduction Focus of Lean Systems	EXHIBIT 13.1

Lean Systems →

Waiting–Time Waste
Transportation Waste
Processing Waste
Inventory Waste
Unnecessary–Motion Waste
Product–Defect Waste
Overproduction Waste

Waiting-time waste results from customer orders, inventory, completed products, and even customers themselves waiting in queue for a process to begin. While a product or order is waiting, no value is being added, but financial costs are mounting and the wait time for the customer is increasing. The added wait time results in a reduction in value for the customer, as well as an increase in the delay to obtain the financial return associated with the products or services. In most environments, but particularly those that incorporate process-oriented layouts, wait time can be many times greater than the actual processing time. This results not only in long lead times, but in completion times that are variable and difficult to predict. This inaccuracy contributes to the need to hold more inventory, which increases costs even more. In addition, delivery reliability, response time, and other service-related value attributes suffer. Inventory that is waiting has a significant impact on costs. In the automobile industry, the time vehicles wait before being shipped to dealerships is known as "dwell time." The cost associated with dwell time has been estimated to be as high as $10 per vehicle per day.[2]

Transportation waste results from excessive material handling and material movement. This may be caused by ineffective facility layouts, requiring extensive movement of materials from one area to another. This increases costs but does not add value, and it increases the likelihood of quality problems stemming from damage. Excess material transportation can also be the result of poor process design. In any case, transportation of inventory and products is expensive, not only from the standpoint of the cost for labor, equipment, and fuel to do the moving, but also because unnecessary transportation takes a lot of time. It has the same effects as waste associated with unnecessary waiting time.

Transportation waste can also result from decisions leading to ineffective locations of suppliers or warehouses. Long-distance transportation can add a tremendous amount of time to the cash-to-cash cycle and create high levels of inventory in the system by adding a substantial and continuous pipeline inventory. Pipeline inventories can be quite large, and the greater the distance between the source and the destination, the larger they will be.

Processing waste results from steps in production processes that do not contribute value or that create costs that are greater than the value they create. One of the most popular approaches to business improvement is the examination of processes in search of non-value-adding steps. These steps are important to identify and eliminate because they consume labor and processing time, have potential to create quality problems, consume time on expensive resources while providing no financial benefit, and tie up equipment capacity that could be used to add value to other products. This aspect of lean systems has taken on a life of its own in a variety of ways. Few businesses have succeeded without concentrated efforts to eliminate non-value-adding steps in processes.

waiting-time waste
The waste that results from customer orders, inventory, or completed products waiting in queue for a process to begin.

transportation waste
The waste that results from excessive materials handling and movement.

processing waste
The waste that results from steps in production processes that do not contribute value or that create costs that are greater than the value they create.

Toyota has pioneered lean management approaches to the extent that it is evident throughout the company. Minimal inventory, a clean, waste-free environment, and processes free of non-value-adding steps characterize the manufacturing processes.

inventory waste
Waste that consists of excess inventory over and above that which is necessary.

Inventory waste consists of excess inventory, over and above that which is necessary. It wreaks havoc with costs, lead times, quality, and flexibility. Inventory used to buffer against uncertainties can hide the very problems that create those uncertainties. Better system reliability results in less need for the inventory and improves business performance at all levels. Improved system reliability also results in processes being more predictable, which improves levels of profitability. The creation of the excess inventory, by definition, requires the use of capacity and labor. Those resources end up being wasted as well, because the excess inventory they create doesn't get sold. Wasted resources increase costs, bringing down profit margin and ROA.

Possibly the biggest benefits of reducing inventory come from not having inventory to cover up problems. Over the years, in most businesses, lack of reliability of suppliers, of individual work centers, of quality, and other problems have been dealt with by adding inventory. Inventory has often served as a "coping mechanism." As long as that inventory remains, it's difficult to identify those problems. When inventory is reduced, however, problems surface immediately, and they can then be solved.

unnecessary-motion waste
The waste of human resources caused by unnecessary labor due to ineffective job design.

Unnecessary-motion waste deals with human resources and how workers perform job tasks. When jobs require repetitive activities, ineffective job design can result in substantial wastes of labor resources over time. The resulting ineffective use of labor increases the product or order costs, decreasing the value to the customer or decreasing the company's profitability. Eliminating unnecessary labor increases available capacity and reduces the demand for capacity.

product-defect waste
The waste of capacity, inventory, and labor resulting from products that do not meet customer specifications.

Product-defect waste results from products that do not meet customer specifications for quality. Defective products create costs by wasting inventory, labor, and capacity on products that can't be sold. In addition, they create more demand on the labor and capacity that must be used to repair them. Rework of defective parts increases the processing time associated with their production, lengthening lead time and increasing the level of inventory in the system, all contributing to higher costs and lower profitability.

Operations Resources and Waste

It should be no surprise that the seven categories of waste just described have substantial impact on inventory, capacity, facilities, and workforce.

In addition to eliminating waste, lean practices also attempt to increase the involvement of employees in the decision-making process by recognizing the value of "local" knowledge. Local knowledge is knowledge possessed by employees who work with certain processes every day. They understand the quirks and idiosyncrasies others not working in the process would never be aware of. Waste elimination typically results from the knowledge and expertise of workers with local knowledge. Workers in the trenches are often the most familiar with those resources and can contribute substantially to their improvement. Employee involvement is frequently implemented through process-improvement teams. The phenomenal growth of employee teams in the United States can trace its roots back to the introduction of JIT.

Jefferson Pilot Corporation also owns and operates three television stations and 18 radio stations.

Waste Reduction Techniques

Associated with the import of JIT to U.S. businesses were a number of techniques. Many of these techniques have not remained exclusive to lean thinking or manufacturing. They have become so popular that they are often used independently, particularly in the service sector. Some of the more widely accepted techniques, such as the focus on eliminating non-value-adding steps in processes and some of the tools associated with quality improvement, have been described in other chapters in this text. In most cases, U.S. businesses have found that for a given situation, some techniques are more appropriate than others. They are not all independent, however. Many tools are interrelated. Some are prerequisites to others, in fact. All of the tools are good, but each has a specific use. Each technique is geared toward waste reduction within a particular resource group, but as we know, a technique can't affect one resource without affecting the others. A toolbox analogy can be useful. An individual tool can solve a specific problem, but knowledge about all of the tools is far more valuable than knowledge of just one. Wrenches, for example, are great for tightening bolts but don't work well for driving nails. On the other hand, if two boards are to be attached with screws, a saw is used first to cut the boards to length. A drill is used next to drill holes for the screw. A screwdriver is used last to turn the screw. All of the tools have a task, but they depend on each other. A narrowly trained "screwdriver operator" wouldn't be able to accomplish much. All of the techniques generally associated with JIT are shown in the model in Exhibit 13.2, grouped by resource focus.

Over 100 million U.S. customers now use online banking.

An explanation of the model presented in Exhibit 13.2 provides a perspective on lean practices as an integrated system, rather than just a toolbox. The techniques range from very narrowly focused to strategic and broad-based. Exhibit 13.2 shows how two of the broader techniques affect virtually all of the resources by their effects on the values of the business. Each of the remaining techniques can be thought of as serving specific waste-reduction purposes for inventory, workforce, capacity, or facilities. They all have a cumulative impact on profitability because the waste elimination reduces costs and increases value.

The remainder of this chapter is devoted to the detailed examination of each technique and its impact on the targeted resource.

Enterprisewide Lean Techniques
Quality Management

Describing effective quality management as a component of lean systems is a bit like saying Texas is a state in the southwestern United States. The Southwest probably couldn't exist without Texas, but if you ask some people from Texas they'd probably be quite confident that they could get along by themselves. Quality is more of a prerequisite to lean thinking than a part of it. Systems can't be lean without effective quality management, but quality management functions are emphasized in many businesses not incorporating lean techniques.

As a prerequisite to leanness, a commitment to quality is necessary in all aspects of the business. Poor quality anywhere, even within transactions inside the business, may

Jefferson Pilot has invested in technology to better manage customer and employee relationships, known as Technology Enabled Relationship Management (TERM)

| EXHIBIT 13.2 | JIT Techniques and Their Impact on Operations Resources |

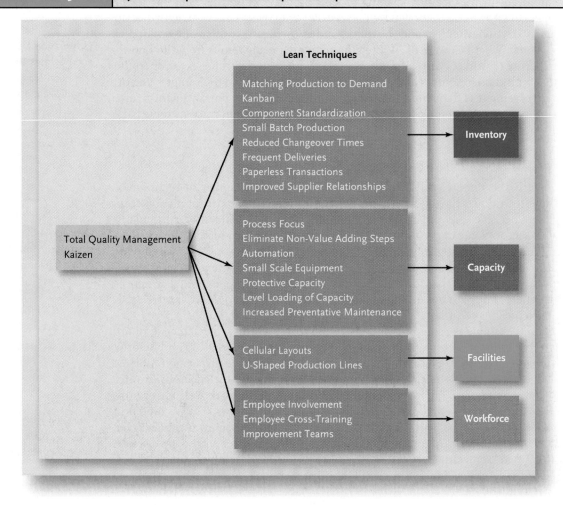

eventually find its way to the customer. High levels of quality reduce the amount of inventory needed, and service quality results in on-time delivery. Quality extends to record keeping and inventory accuracy as well. The list goes on. Quality management influences the workforce because it changes the way workers do their jobs. It gives them responsibility for ensuring quality and empowers them to make improvements that eliminate waste. It provides them with tools that help improve quality. Quality management affects capacity because it reduces the amount of capacity wasted on defective products. Quality management affects facilities because quality extends to housekeeping and facility maintenance. The facility, like any other resource, must be maintained with utmost care, or that lack of care will eventually affect quality and reach the customer.

Kaizen

Kaizen (pronounced ki-zen) is a Japanese philosophy that translates into "continuous improvement." Continuous improvement implies that a business should always strive to make everything better, and this mentality extends through all resources. The business should continuously strive to reduce inventory, the workforce should constantly strive for improvement, capacity should seek higher levels of productivity, and facilities should be made more productive. Nothing should be considered "good enough," because there is always room for improvement. In addition to the kaizen "attitude," some businesses utilize kaizen workshops or the "kaizen blitz" approach to completely overhaul processes. A kaizen blitz is a two- or three-day marathon of tearing down an entire department and completely redesigning its processes.

Inventory-Focused Techniques

Matching Production to Demand

The concept of matching production to demand is the fundamental principle behind inventory minimization. In the long term, all companies match production to demand. However, producing 1,000 units in a year when demand is 1,000 units per year doesn't necessarily match production to demand. Lean production strives to match the rate of production to the rate of demand *at very small time increments*. Thus, if demand for a manufacturer is 100 units per week, and the business produces five days per week, the lean company would strive to match the demand rate on a daily, half-day, or even hourly basis. One way to meet the 100-unit weekly demand would be to produce 100 units on Monday morning. But this results in carrying inventory most of the week since the daily production rate would be much faster than the demand rate. If, however, the production was spread out over the week, it would more closely match the demand rate. Exhibit 13.3 illustrates how matching the weekly, daily, and half-day production rates to the demand rate reduces inventory levels. This is the fundamental motivation behind the small-batch production and frequent deliveries that characterize lean companies.

Frequent deliveries of small quantities can be difficult to accomplish when economies of scale from full truckloads are the norm. In many urban areas, a distribution industry that caters to small quantities and frequent deliveries has evolved.

The link between production rate and demand is captured by a concept known as **takt time.** Takt time is how often you must produce a product in order to meet demand. It is calculated by dividing the time available by the number of units the customer is demanding. For example, if demand is 600 units per week, and you work eight hours per day, six days per week, you must produce 600 units in 48 hours. Forty-eight hours is equivalent to 2,880 minutes. Six hundred units in 2,880 minutes requires a product to be

takt time
How often you must produce a product in order to meet demand.

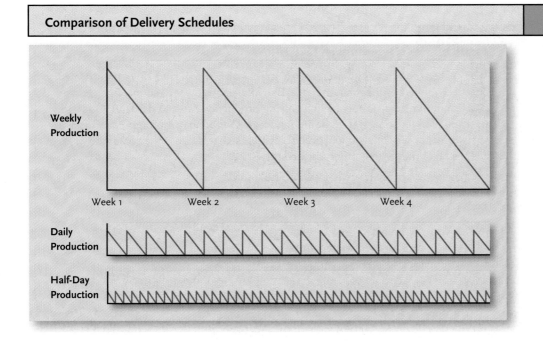

Comparison of Delivery Schedules	EXHIBIT 13.3

Weekly Production

Week 1   Week 2   Week 3   Week 4

Daily Production

Half-Day Production

produced every 4.8 minutes. The takt time is 4.8 minutes. If there is greater time available than is required, the takt time gets larger. Producing products at a rate faster than takt time results in a buildup in inventory. The formula for computing takt time is:

(13.1)
$$\text{Takt Time} = \frac{H_{avail}}{D}$$

where

H_{avail} = Hours of available capacity
D = Demand

Example 13.1 demonstrates how to determine takt time.

Kanban

kanban
A system used to link production rate to demand.

Kanban (pronounced "kon-bon") is Japanese for "visible record" or "signal." Kanban systems are used to link the production rate to the demand rate so that the end result is production of only what is needed when it is needed. This contrasts with the more traditional U.S. approach, which forecasts demand and then produces in a batch to meet the forecast. In that situation, products are "pushed" through the system and then sold. In a kanban system, the demand "pulls" products through the system. Many variations of the basic kanban system exist, but all are based on similar logic.

Kanban systems utilize small buffers of inventory between work centers, departments, and manufacturing plants. The unique characteristic about each inventory buffer is that it has a maximum size determined by management. When the maximum size of a particular inventory buffer is reached, no more inventory can be added. So, if a particular work center produces parts that go into a buffer between it and the next work center, when the buffer is full, it must stop producing. The signal to produce to replenish the buffer is created when the buffer drops below full. This signal is incorporated in the system through a simple, visible means of detecting when the buffer is full or not. The signal that it is less than full authorizes the feeding work center to begin to produce. Let's look at an example. Exhibit 13.4 shows a simple production line with seven work centers (WCs). At the end of the line is a container that holds six finished products. Between each pair of work centers there is also a container that holds six parts. Each part must be processed through

---

Example 13.1

Determining Takt Time

EXCEL TUTOR

Ballenger's Bearings produces a variety of bearing- and drive-train-related components for agricultural use. Barry Ballenger, owner and manager, strives to minimize inventory by tightly tying production rates to demand. One production line operates 38 hours per week. On Monday morning Barry discovered a customer order, consisting of 90,000 bearings, that is due at the end of the week. What is the takt time for that order (in seconds)?

$$\text{Time available} = 38 \text{ hours}$$
$$= 2,280 \text{ minutes}$$
$$= 136,800 \text{ seconds}$$
$$\frac{136,800 \text{ seconds}}{90,000 \text{ units}} = 1.52 \text{ seconds}$$

Excel Tutor 13.1 shows how to use Excel to solve takt time problems.

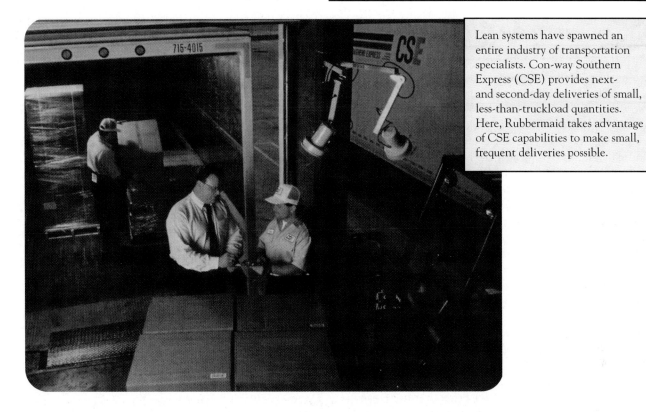

Lean systems have spawned an entire industry of transportation specialists. Con-way Southern Express (CSE) provides next- and second-day deliveries of small, less-than-truckload quantities. Here, Rubbermaid takes advantage of CSE capabilities to make small, frequent deliveries possible.

all seven work centers and is then shipped to a neighboring factory for assembly into an automobile.

As one item of finished product is removed from the buffer following WC7, the empty space in the buffer authorizes WC7 to replenish it. WC7 requires a unit from the buffer between WC7 and WC6. As soon as the worker removes that unit, the buffer following WC6 is less than full, which is the authorization to produce. Production at WC6 will require a unit from the preceding buffer (the one between WC5 and WC6). This authorizes WC5 to produce. This "pulling" action, triggered by the demand for the finished

Kanban System   EXHIBIT 13.4

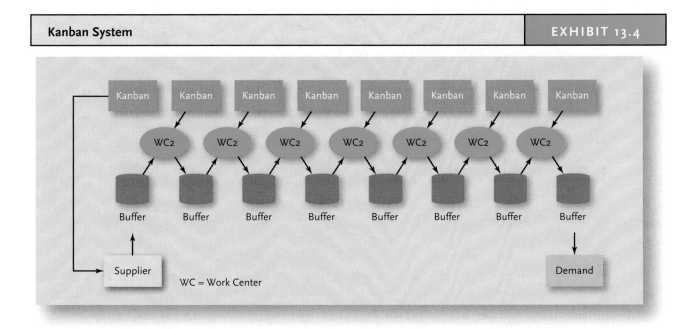

om ADVANTAGE   Maintaining Inventory Access during a Tragedy

The events of Tuesday, September 11, 2001, changed many aspects of life in the United States. For some businesses disruptions in transportation, particularly during the first week following the tragedy, tested their philosophy of low levels of inventory. At 2:00 p.m., the day of the attack, Chrysler announced that it was closing all its U.S. plants for the day.

At DaimlerChrysler's plants, inventories of raw materials and parts are kept at very low levels, to reduce costs and improve quality levels. Flow of inventory into the plants, necessary to keep lines running and workers employed, depends on frequent deliveries. Parts that come from Canadian suppliers must cross the border. Increased security resulted in border waiting lines up to 18 hours at Ambassador Bridge. One particular part, a steering gear needed for the Ram pickup, was already in a tenuous situation. TRW, the supplier, was having difficulties with one of its suppliers, which flew the part to the TRW plant in Virginia. Chrysler had been contracting to fly the parts from Virginia to its plant in Saltillo, Mexico. But U.S. airspace was closed on Tuesday afternoon.

To keep the parts flowing, Chrysler utilized an expedited trucking service which employed two drivers per truck, each legally allowed to drive 10 hours straight per 24-hour period.

It also told 150 of its largest suppliers to send extra parts to Chrysler plants to increase the size of the inventory buffer.

By the morning of September 12, all three U.S. auto makers, through their lobbyists, had begun pleading with U.S. officials to increase the efficiency of the customs checks at the Canadian border. The response was immediate. Canadian Pacific Railway offered to set up an emergency shuttle through the Windsor–Detroit tunnel, bypassing the Ambassador Bridge bottleneck. Over a four-day period, 110 trailers were moved through the tunnel between the United States and Canada.

The events of September 11 forced many businesses to change their short-term and long-term business practices. For many, particularly those depending on a far-reaching network of suppliers, the practice of reducing inventory to minimum levels had to be reconsidered. After all, inventory serves to buffer against uncertainties, so if uncertainties and the potential for disruptions increase, buffers must be expanded.

Source: "Chrysler Averts a Parts Crisis," *Wall Street Journal*, September 24, 2001, pp. B1, B4.

EXHIBIT 13.5	Inventory Levels in Kanban System

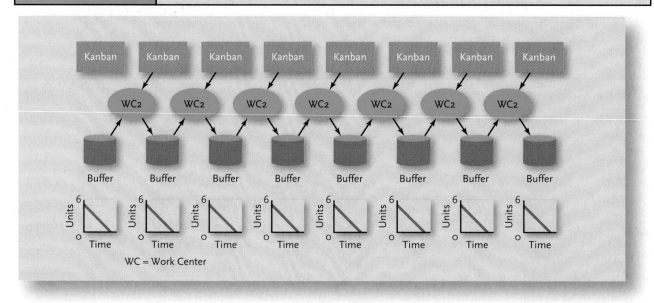

WC = Work Center

product, proceeds all the way back through the line. The kanban in this case is the open space in the buffer container and is the authorization to produce.

The number of items allowed in each buffer determines the total amount of work-in-process inventory in the system, as shown in Exhibit 13.5. In the example, a maximum buffer size of six parts in each of the buffers limits the amount of work-in-process inventory to 42 units. Management can increase that amount by changing the maximum buffer size (a larger container or an additional container). Note that all buffers do not need to be the same size.

Kanban systems can also link together work centers that are not physically adjacent to each other. There are many scenarios where work centers or suppliers provide parts but are a long distance away. The distance need not diminish the applicability of kanban as a means of authorizing deliveries of component parts and raw materials. The system tightly links all inventory production and delivery, as illustrated in Exhibit 13.6.

When work centers are not located next to each other, the signal is posted when a buffer is not at its maximum level. Since the work centers aren't next to each other, an empty or partially empty container can't be seen by the supplying work center. The kanban, or visible signal, takes the form of a card, a painted square on a floor, an electronic message, or other signal that communicates a simple "make more!" to the feeding work center. The rule is simply that when a container of components is produced, the kanban is attached to it and delivered to where it is needed. When the container is once again empty, the card is sent back to authorize more production. Controlling the number of kanban cards in the system has exactly the same effect as controlling the number of containers. If there are only three kanban cards, there can never be more than three containers of inventory in the system.

Kanban System Extending to Suppliers　　　　　　　　EXHIBIT 13.6

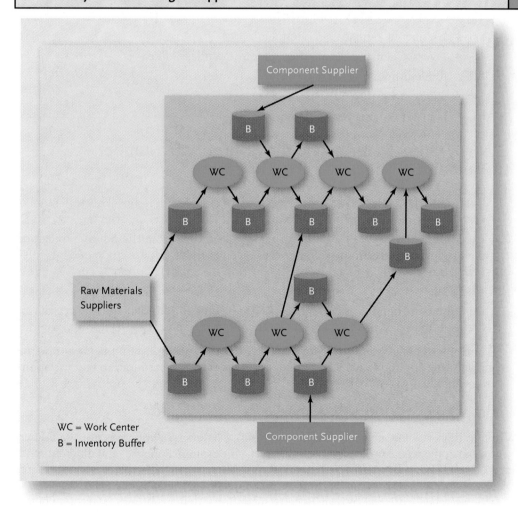

Because the number of containers or kanbans determines the amount of inventory in the system by authorizing production, the decision as to how many containers or kanbans is important. Management must consider the fact that the container not only must spend time being filled, but also may spend time being transferred from one work center to another and may spend time in queue waiting to be filled by a work center that also processes other parts. The amount of inventory in the system must keep the downstream work center busy. There must be enough inventory in the system to keep the downstream work center busy during the total lead time required to fill the container, including time in transit and waiting to be filled. This is an application of the time-of-supply concept discussed in Chapter 11. That quantity, divided by the number of components in a container, gives us the number of containers necessary. Noninteger solutions are rounded up to ensure that there will be enough inventory in the system. The lead time is typically determined as an average. As we know, half the time that lead time will be less than average and half the time it will be greater than average. If the lead time is greater than average, there will not be enough inventory in the system to occupy the downstream work center. Quite often a small percentage of safety stock is added to the system to reduce the likelihood of this happening.

The formula for computing the appropriate number of kanbans is

(13.2)
$$k = \frac{\overline{D}_{LT} + S}{C}$$

where

$$k = \text{Number of kanbans or containers}$$
$$\overline{D}_{LT} = \text{Average demand during the replenishment lead time}$$
$$LT = \text{Replenishment lead time}$$
$$S = \text{Safety stock}$$
$$C = \text{Number of units per container}$$

Step-by-Step: Determining the Appropriate Number of Kanbans

1. Determine the average lead time for a container of parts in hours. This is the sum of production time, transit time, and wait time.
2. Determine the demand for parts during that lead time from the hourly production rate of the downstream work center that receives them. This is computed by multiplying the lead time (hours) by the production rate (units per hour).
3. Add a safety stock.
4. Determine the number of containers needed by dividing the demand for parts during the lead time, plus the safety stock, by the number of parts that fit in the container.

Kanban systems are well-suited for repetitive manufacturing environments but not for manufacturing environments where there is a great deal of customization and variability from one product to another.

Component Standardization

Even in high-volume, mass production situations, customers are offered choices of different product models. Automotive manufacturers, for example, offer several different models to choose from. Even though the models are different, many of the components serve the same function. For example, the steering wheel on a Honda Accord and on a Honda Odyssey can be identical. Many small parts, including fasteners, interior trim components,

Example 13.2

EXCEL TUTOR

Determining the Appropriate Number of Kanbans

Longshot Golf produces stock and custom golf clubs for direct Internet sales. It can provide overnight delivery of any stock club and second-day delivery for a custom club. The stock club and standard component production is controlled with a kanban system to maintain low inventory levels. The production supervisor wishes to determine the appropriate number of kanbans for the inventory that flows between the shaft/head assembly area and the final step, which is the handle grip station. The shaft/head assembly area processes all clubs. The grip wrapping station processes only those clubs with wrapped grips. Some clubs have rubber insert grips. Use the values below to determine the number of racks (containers) that should be used, given a rack capacity of 20 clubs.

Average production time for shaft/head assembly of 36 clubs:	0.7 hour
Average transit time:	0.5 hour
Average wait time of container at shaft/head assembly:	1.9 hours
Average output of grip wrapping station:	35 clubs per hour
Desired safety stock:	10%

Solution

Average total lead time = Production time + transit time + wait time

= 0.7 + 0.5 + 1.9

= 3.1 hours

Average demand during lead time = Lead time $\times$ production rate of downstream work center

= 3.1 hours $\times$ 35 clubs/hour

= 108.5 clubs

Add 10% safety stock = 108.5 + 10.85

= 119.35 clubs

Number of racks = (demand + safety stock)/container size

= 119.35/20

= 5.9675

= round up to 6 racks

Excel Tutor 13.2 demonstrates how Excel can be used to facilitate the calculations for determining the number of kanbans.

knobs and buttons, light fixtures, and even frame and exterior trim components, can be the same if the vehicles are designed with that in mind. Parts standardization provides a number of benefits for a manufacturer. First, it reduces the number of different items that must be inventoried. This reduces the amount of record keeping necessary, the number of orders and deliveries, and the number of suppliers. The result is lower costs. In addition, particularly in industries like the auto industry, inventories of repair and replacement parts must be maintained for years after the car has been produced. Service centers must have access to original equipment replacement parts to provide expected levels of after-sale service to customers. An increase in parts standardization for any industry that produces a variety of products will benefit inventory reduction efforts. Total inventory investment can be reduced by at least 50 percent as well as reducing associated costs and increasing productivity of inventory resources.

Small-Batch Production

Small-batch production is the primary means of matching production rate to demand rate. The ability to produce a small quantity of parts or products and then switch over equipment to produce a small batch of another part or product enables a manufacturer to match the demand rate in relatively small time increments. As mentioned previously, the average level of inventory is a function of the quantity produced in a batch. Producing in more frequent but smaller batches drives the average inventory level down.

The difficulty in producing in frequent small quantities is that it increases the number of times equipment must be changed over. This can cut into the capacity available for actual production and reduce the financial return on the equipment, since equipment costs are spread over the number of units produced. Reducing the number of units per batch increases the per-unit costs for that batch. Small-batch production becomes economical only when changeover times can be reduced sufficiently.

The challenge of determining the correct batch size has received attention for decades. Many algorithms and heuristics have been developed for addressing the production batch size problem in different environments. Many suffer the same weaknesses as the economic order quantity in Chapter 11.

The trade-off associated with determining the appropriate batch size is a difficult one to manage. Too large a batch size inflates inventory levels. Too small a batch size creates a need for so many changeovers that necessary capacity is lost. One simple, but commonsense, approach provides a useful way to determine the smallest batch size possible without utilizing capacity needed for production.

That approach requires identifying the amount of capacity that is not needed for production and utilizing all of it for changeovers. With that method, only capacity not needed for production is used for changeovers, and as many changeovers as possible are performed. This drives the batch size down as low as possible.

The formula for determining the batch size using this approach is

(13.3)
$$\frac{D}{(H_{avail} - H_{req})/T}$$

where

D = Demand during the planning horizon

H_{avail} = Hours of available capacity

H_{req} = Hours of required capacity

T = Time it takes to perform a changeover

Step-by-Step: Batch Size Determination

1. Determine the hours of required capacity.
2. Determine the hours of available capacity.
3. Subtract required capacity from total available capacity to yield the capacity that could be dedicated to changeovers in hours.
4. Divide the hours that could be dedicated to changeovers by the changeover time to yield the number of changeovers feasible without using production capacity.
5. Divide the total demand for the planning horizon by the number of changeovers feasible to yield the smallest possible batch size.

The batch size determination process is demonstrated in Example 13.3.

Reduced Changeover Times

U.S. manufacturers who adopted JIT and small-batch production quickly discovered that virtually all of their capacity could be devoted to changeovers (with little left for actual

Example 13.3

EXCEL TUTOR

Batch Size Determination

Central States Stamping supplies a variety of manufacturers with small parts stamped from sheet metal. Components manufactured include parts for barbeque grills, bicycles, riding lawn mowers, and other garden and lawn equipment. One particular stamping press is scheduled to stamp out 144,000 parts, taking a total of 200 hours during the next month. There are 235 hours available for production during that time period. Changeover time for the die on that press is 20 minutes. Determine the number of batches that can be run on the press during the next month and the minimum size of each batch.

Required capacity	= 200 hours
Total available capacity	= 235 hours
Capacity that could be dedicated to changeovers	= 35 hours
Number of changeovers feasible	= 35 hours/0.333 hour
	= 105.105 changeovers
Minimum batch size	= 144,000/105.105
	= 1,370.0585 units per batch
	= round up to 1,371 units per batch.

Excel Tutor 13.3 shows how to use Excel in making the batch size calculation.

production) unless they made dramatic reductions in changeover times. For most U.S. manufacturers, changeover processes had received very little previous attention and there was plenty of room for improvement. Manufacturers often found that, with a modest amount of effort, changeovers that formerly took several hours could be accomplished in just a few minutes. This had an immediate effect of shortening production runs, smoothing out the flow of materials through the plant, and reducing inventory levels.

The process of changing equipment from producing one product to producing another is similar to any process in that it can be analyzed and improved. Early JIT manufacturers found many ways to speed up changeover processes, ranging from special "setup teams" that would practice to gain expertise, to developing fixtures that eliminate painstaking adjustments that are part of the changeover process. Changeover time reduction has become an integral aspect of lean production.

Frequent Deliveries

Frequent deliveries from suppliers create the same effect on inventories of raw materials and purchased component parts as does small-batch production on inventories of work-in-process finished goods. Frequent replenishment of small quantities results in a smoother flow of materials through the system and a rate of production that more closely matches the rate of demand. Deliveries of raw materials and component parts are pulled into the system just like work-in-process inventory is pulled through it. The smooth flow of small quantities of inventory that provide benefits to a manufacturing plant can provide the same benefits to the entire supply chain if extended. In fact, if lean methods are restricted solely to the internal aspects of a manufacturing plant, with no impact on supplier deliveries, the effect is merely to move excess inventory from one place to another, and the benefits to the customer don't materialize because costs are not reduced in the supply chain.

The benefits of frequent deliveries of small batches evolved from manufacturing to the service sector and has had a particularly large impact on lean retailers. Much of what we view

om ADVANTAGE   A Precious Metal Disaster

Stockpiling inventory is associated with many risks. The inventory can become obsolete because of new technologies, changes in the marketplace, or new regulations. On the other hand, unreliable suppliers can make stockpiling attractive. Stockpiling inventory can also appear attractive when prices for the items appear to be increasing. All of these issues played a role for the Ford Motor Company, leading up to its 2002 announcement of a $1 billion write-off for a stockpile of palladium.

Palladium is a precious metal that is used in catalytic converters that clean car emissions. Prices for palladium, much of which comes from arctic Russia, have been notoriously volatile. In response to supply uncertainties, Ford's purchasing staff built up stockpiles of inventory. Meanwhile, engineers worked to develop methods to reduce the need for palladium. The engineers succeeded, and by late 2001 Ford had developed technologies that reduced its dependency on palladium. That's the good news. The bad news is that prices for palladium dropped drastically in 2001 and 2002, meaning that all of the palladium Ford bought was now worth much less than it had paid for it.

In the 1980s catalytic converters used platinum instead of palladium. Palladium is similar to platinum but cheaper. Its price stayed around $100 an ounce until the late 1980s. As more cars depended on palladium for clean emissions (about one ounce per car was needed), demand for palladium climbed. From 1992 to 1996, demand increased by a factor of 5, to 2.4 million ounces. Prices rose, but because Russia had stockpiles, no one worried about shortages. In 1997, however, the Russian government held up shipments. Prices surged to $350 per ounce. By 1999 prices reached $700 per ounce and in January 2001 prices topped $1,000 per ounce. By this time, Ford was stockpiling. Meanwhile, Ford engineers were making progress. Palladium requirements were cut in half because of better chemistry.

After their January 2001 peak, palladium prices began to fall and reached $350 by summer. Ford was overstocked with palladium that had little value.

Sources: "Beyond Explorer Woes, Ford Misses Key Turns in Buyers, Technology," *Wall Street Journal*, January 14, 2002, pp. A1, A8; "How Ford's Big Batch of Rare Metal Led to a $1 Billion Write-Off," *Wall Street Journal*, January 14, 2002, pp. A1, A8.

as necessary elements of effective supply chain management has its roots in JIT. The frequent shipments that became commonplace in manufacturing were extended to the retail environment in the form of "continuous replenishment," a formalized and quite common type of retailer/supplier partnership.

Paperless Transactions

In order to produce in small batches, changeover times must be reduced, because each production batch has associated costs. More batches, even though smaller, will result in escalating changeover costs unless the cost of each changeover is reduced substantially. Similarly, each delivery from suppliers has fixed costs that result from the activities related to the transaction. One way to reduce these costs is to eliminate the "paper processing" that traditionally accompanies them. By switching from paper invoices to an electronic process known as **electronic data interchange (EDI),** much of the administrative cost associated with these orders can be eliminated. EDI forms the basis for the type of information sharing necessary in effective supply chain management. This includes the retail demand transparency required to minimize the bullwhip effect and the type of information transfer necessary for effective customer/supplier alliances.

electronic data interchange (EDI) Electronic exchange of information between customers and suppliers instead of paper transactions.

Improved Supplier Relationships

Suppliers to lean businesses have expectations for profit margin, return on assets, and return on equity, so meeting the frequent delivery needs requires a significant change in the way they do business. Delivering raw materials and purchased components frequently, often several times per day, requires good communication between the supplier and customer. Beyond that, because of the investment in the change, the supplier needs a commitment from the customer that the relationship will not disappear at the end of the year. Supplier relationships in a lean environment have several characteristics that improve the situation for both parties involved.

One characteristic that sums up the relationship between suppliers and customers is that they behave more like business partners. They collaborate by providing each other with production schedules, helping each other in new product design projects, and providing expertise for each other when dealing with product quality. It is not unusual to find the supplier's employees in the customer's plant and the customer's employees in the supplier's plant.

In addition to the dramatic increase in communication, the relationship is longer lasting and more exclusive. Long-term supplier relationships require directed efforts to make the relationship last. Many businesses provide descriptions of the type of relationships they seek with suppliers.

For a supplier to make the changes necessary to meet the needs of a lean manufacturer, it must also become a lean manufacturer. After all, it wouldn't make sense for the supplier to produce in large, infrequent batches and then deliver them in small quantities several times a day. The inventory has to be somewhere, and it would simply be in the finished-goods warehouse of the supplier, even though it would be delivered frequently in small quantities. From a supply chain cost perspective, that would be no better than delivering it all at once to the customer's warehouse. JIT practices must be incorporated upstream in the supply chain in order to provide true benefits.

Capacity-Focused Techniques

Process Focus

Historically, JIT producers focused on process expertise, rather than expertise in producing a particular product. A process focus means that the firm builds process expertise and organizes its business and manufacturing plants around that focus. The concept of focused factories means that the factories are divided into small subfactories, each of which concentrates on the processing methods that it does well. Focused factories do not try to do all types of processing, as is often the case in traditional U.S. manufacturing plants, although they may manufacture a wide variety of products if those products have similar processing requirements. This emphasis on process excellence gives the lean firm an advantage in capabilities and value creation. Focused factories become experts at certain processes and gain a reputation for that capability. This focus creates lean, productive, low-cost processes that can create differentiating capabilities.

Eliminate Non-Value-Adding Steps

The elimination of non-value-adding process steps is at the root of every productivity improvement effort. Managers who have improved productivity can thank JIT for this commonsense approach to business process improvement. Processing steps that do not add value exemplify one of the most common forms of waste in business. The waste present in many businesses is caused by an assumption that whatever has been done historically must be the correct way to do it. Lean companies recognize that this isn't necessarily the case. Eliminating the non-value-adding steps opens up capacity, reduces costs, and increases ROA.

Automation

Although not a tactic that is exclusive to lean firms, many have utilized automated processes for repetitive or dangerous jobs. Casual observers may claim that this shows a disrespect for employees, because it replaces them with machines, but the opposite is a better description of what's going on. Japanese manufacturers believed that employees should be used for their knowledge and talent, and that making people perform jobs that could be accomplished by machine actually showed disrespect. Since some aspects of lean systems fit repetitive manufacturing environments better than those that require

Automation and robotics are frequently employed in lean systems. Both reduce the dependencies on human labor, but often the motivation is not to eliminate workers as much as it is to make processes less variable, safer, and to ensure that mistakes are not made. Here, filling, capping, and labeling inventory in a high-volume pharmaceutical manufacturing environment provides a natural application for automation.

flexibility, automated equipment is better suited. Lean manufacturers face difficult decisions when automating processes, however. Automated equipment is expensive and usually relatively inflexible. As processing needs change, most automated equipment is too inflexible to adapt. In some cases, automated equipment has been "traded in" for employees who can better adapt to different needs.

Small-Scale Equipment

Much of lean systems is devoted to producing at exactly the rate of demand. That desire drives many business decisions. In many manufacturing processes a machine can be run at only one speed—fast. It is either running at that output rate, or it is turned off. If the rate of demand slows, the machine output must be slowed or inventory will accumulate. Reducing the machine's output rate can be accomplished only by turning the machine off.

Let's look at a straightforward example. Suppose a machine has a capacity of 2,000 units per week but the demand is only 1,000 units per week. The only option is to run the machine 50 percent of the time. This could be done by scheduling the machine $2\frac{1}{2}$ days on and $2\frac{1}{2}$ days off, or some other equivalent combination. No matter what the approach, while the machine is running, it is producing at twice the rate of demand. This creates a buildup of inventory that is ultimately consumed by demand, but inventory builds up nonetheless. Contrast this situation with one in which management buys two machines, each with a capacity of 1,000 units per week. They now have the flexibility to produce at 2,000 units per week or at 1,000 units per week, matching demand and not building up inventory. If management had purchased 10 machines, each with a capacity

Chicago's only auto plant is 80 years old and once produced Model Ts. When its $400 million makeover is finished, it will be able to produce new models of Ford cars with only two weeks of preparation. Flexible manufacturing, made possible by reprogrammable tools and robots, will enable it to build several models on one assembly line. Flexible manufacturing has contributed to the reduction of inventory in many industries because it enables producers to more closely match product demand proportions and adapt quickly when market trends change. Traditionally, producing a new model would require completely replacing robots and tooling. With a flexible manufacturing system, most of the robots and equipment are generic. Cost savings, expected to be at least $1.5 billion by 2010, come from eliminating those massive model change costs. The Torrence plant employs about 5,400 people, but will add another 500 to 600. The plant will begin building a Mercury version of the 2005 Ford Freestyle and the new 2005 Ford Five Hundred and Mercury Montego sedans.

Ford's Chicago plant isn't its only venture into flexible manufacturing. Ford's Engine Plant No. 1, in Brook Park, Ohio, also received a makeover. This plant had built about 34 million engines since it opened in 1951. The remodeled plant will produce about 325,000 V-6 engines a year for the 2005 Ford Five Hundred, the Mercury Montego sedans, and the Ford Freestyle.

The new plant uses computerized machines to machine cylinder heads and crankshafts, allowing for more precise machining and higher levels of quality. Flexibility is enhanced as well. A minor change would normally take about six months, but new equipment can accommodate it in six weeks. Engine Plant No. 1 has the flexibility to make different types of engines without changeovers that would cost considerable production time. In the past, building a new engine could take years of preparation and hundreds of millions of dollars. With flexible equipment, computers are simply reprogrammed. Ford can build a different engine, such as a V-8, on the same production line as a V-6.

Source: "Torrence Retools for Long Term," *Chicago Tribune,* June 9, 2004; "Broad Range of New Vehicles at Auto Show Media Preview," *Chicago Sun-Times,* February 5, 2004; "Crankshaft Redemption: Ford's Once-Sputtering Brook Park Facility Is Getting a New Start," *Plain Dealer* (Cleveland, Ohio), May 9, 2004.

---

of 200 units per week, they would have even more flexibility to adapt to changing demand rates without producing at rates faster than the consumption rate.

Protective Capacity

For U.S. manufacturers that have converted from traditional manufacturing to lean production, one of the most difficult changes has been to eliminate excess inventory by increasing capacity a small amount. In Japan, where JIT got its start in the 1950s, there is simply no room for excess inventory. In order to respond quickly to customer needs, some excess capacity was needed. For U.S. manufacturers, who traditionally rely on machine utilization as a performance measure because of the link to cost per unit, this has been difficult to accept. The greater the utilization, the more units to absorb the costs and the lower the apparent cost per unit. Utilization, however, has encouraged production in excess of demand, which results in inventory. Rather than carry excess inventory, lean manufacturers carry protective capacity. From the standpoint of meeting unexpected demand, capacity and inventory are equally effective. Protective capacity, however, doesn't have the negative impact on flexibility and quality that results from inventory.

Level Loading of Capacity

Whenever a manufacturer limits the amount of finished-goods inventory, adjusting to varying demand levels becomes difficult. Manufacturers that do not carry finished goods are almost in the same situation as services when it comes to coping with demand variability. Recall the two aggregate planning strategies, the demand chase and the level production strategy. The level production strategy required the manufacturer to build up inventory during low-demand periods for use to help meet demand during peak periods. This option is obviously not an alternative for lean firms, because of the large amount of inventory required.

The alternative is the demand chase strategy. Traditionally, Japanese firms guaranteed lifetime employment, which made it impossible to lay off workers in slow periods and hire them back in fast periods. Although lifetime employment is no longer guaranteed in Japanese firms (and never was in U.S. firms), we know how detrimental that hire–fire pattern of employee treatment can be on workforce quality. (Before long, the only available job candidates are those who can't get permanent employment anywhere else.) The alternative is to somehow create a level demand for production. There are several approaches to doing this, keeping in mind that the load doesn't have to be perfectly level. Many lean manufacturers level the load for a time period and then adjust it to another level for a period of time. Overtime hours and contingent workers can absorb some fluctuation in the production output. Another approach is to manufacture complementary products that provide seasonal cycles that are out of phase with each other. Manufacture motorcycles for the summer and snowmobiles for the winter, for example.

Increased Preventive Maintenance

The reduction of inventory, particular work-in-process inventory, eliminates any decoupling that may have been accomplished by the inventory between work centers. Without decoupling, downstream work centers are directly dependent on upstream work centers, so any machine breakdown can quickly bring an entire production process to a halt. One approach to reducing the potential for a production line stoppage when there is little inventory is to reduce machine breakdowns by increasing the amount of preventive maintenance. This is a good example of one method to reduce disruptions when inventory cannot be used as a means to mitigate the effects of a disruption. In some cases, particularly when equipment must be utilized at a high level, preventive maintenance activities are scheduled into the machine's activities just as if it were a customer order, or it is scheduled during second or third shifts when the plant is not producing or is producing at a reduced capacity.

Preventive maintenance typically requires that equipment be shut down, resulting in an impact on capacity. That capacity is not productive when it is being maintained, so it is important to schedule preventive maintenance carefully. The complexities of integrating preventive maintenance schedules with production schedules has resulted in the creation of a software industry that specializes in scheduling preventive maintenance.

Facility-Focused Techniques

Cellular Layouts and Group Technology

Lean systems implementation affects just about every aspect of a business. Changing the facility is one way for a business to adapt to the needs of JIT. In Chapter 4, cellular layouts were introduced as a compromise between product- and process-oriented layouts. Cellular layouts utilize work cells, which contain small groups of machines that provide all the capability necessary to produce a family of products. Cellular layouts are attractive in lean environments for several reasons. First, they virtually eliminate the material movement that is often a waste of transportation. Second, cells utilize small-scale equipment, which increases the firm's ability to adjust to demand changes if necessary. Third, in cellular manufacturing it is common to make workers responsible for tasks that are broad, rather than the very narrow tasks common in product-oriented assembly lines. The closeness of the machines also makes it easy to teach all cell members to run all pieces of equipment. This cross-training of employees improves the reliability of the cells, allowing them to continue if a worker is absent. In the event of a downturn in demand, the number of workers in the cell can be reduced to slow down the cell's output.

U-Shaped Production Lines

JIT manufacturers often design their work cells and their product-oriented process in U-shaped layouts. Exhibit 13.7 compares the traditional U.S. layout to a lean layout.

Comparison of U-Shaped and Traditional Production Lines	EXHIBIT 1.2

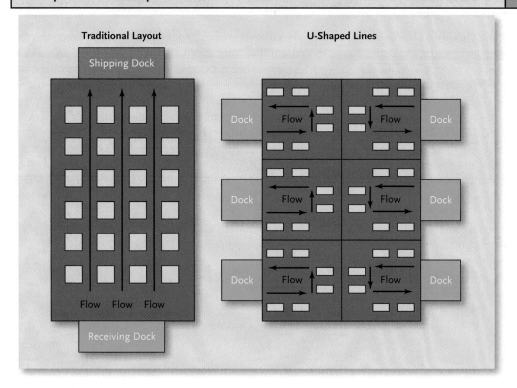

Unlike traditional U.S. manufacturing plants that utilize "straight lines" of equipment, with raw materials coming in at one end and packaging and shipping at the other, U-shape lines allow incoming materials and shipping to be located near each other. In addition, if the lines and facility are configured correctly, shipping and receiving can be done right at the production line, which eliminates transporting inventory and finished products to the shipping dock area. The advantages of the U-shaped lines go beyond the elimination of transportation waste. Eliminating unnecessary steps in material processing and movement reduces the potential for damage.

Workforce-Focused Techniques

Employee Involvement

The concept of waste elimination, the focal point of lean systems, is applied to all resources. Human resources can be wasted as much as any other, and knowledge and talent are just as likely or more likely to be wasted than labor. Lean uses employee involvement in all aspects of the business to ensure that nothing is overlooked and the implications of decisions are understood at all levels. Although the broad enterprise view possessed by upper-level employees is critical for good decision making, the detailed impact of decisions on customer interactions and specific processes must also be considered, and this perspective can be obtained only from the employees who take part in those interactions and work in those processes.

Employee Cross-Training

We've discussed the importance of a pull system in reducing inventory waste. One critical aspect of inventory management is to not produce products or components unless they are needed. This is a worthy objective, but it is difficult for management to idle

om *ADVANTAGE*   Supplier Relationships: Key to Successful Inventory Reduction

Well-developed supplier relationships are a prerequisite to a firm's ability to reduce on-hand inventories and depend on the frequent, low-quantity deliveries of suppliers. If a disruption occurs or a supplier is not dependable, the result can be catastrophic. Supplier relationships often go beyond a long-term contract and must include access to information that formerly was restricted. Autoliv, a North American unit of a Swedish producer of auto safety equipment, used to struggle with high levels of inventory and constant shortages of materials that came from 125 suppliers. High-priced "rush" shipments were commonplace ways of dealing with parts shortages.

Beginning in 2000, Autoliv management made their inventories visible to their vendors through secure Internet access. Every hour, Autoliv uploads its inventory data to SupplySolutions, Inc., a software and service provider. SupplySolutions transforms the data into information usable by Autoliv suppliers. Vendors are now able to get immediate information about

Autoliv's inventory levels. Information includes minimum and maximum inventory information for every item, so vendors can anticipate needed shipments. Vendors have permission to ship at any time the system indicates that inventory is needed. In fact, it is the vendor's responsibility to ship. By October, downtime from shortages was reduced and rush shipments of inventory had declined by 95 percent.

Some suppliers have balked at the new requirements. Access to SupplySolutions data is not free; it costs suppliers about $200 per month. In addition, some do not think they should have the responsibility to control their customer's inventory. They maintain that that is the customer's responsibility. Autoliv's response is that it may seek out other suppliers to replace those intransigent suppliers.

Source: "Bumpy Ride," *Wall Street Journal*, May 21, 2001, p. R21; www .autolive.com.

workers who are being paid $18 an hour to produce. Businesses don't want excess inventory, but they also don't want to pay workers for doing nothing. Cross-training, which teaches employees to do several different jobs, offers an alternative to having idle employees. If a particular work center has no demand, the operator can go elsewhere in the manufacturing facility, to operate a work center that has demand. The more jobs an employee can do, the more valuable that employee.

Labor contracts can present barriers to cross-training because they may establish strict work rules that specifically outline the jobs that employees are allowed to do. As the need for cross-training has increased, many contracts have relaxed the strict nature of work rules to allow more flexibility and a better utilization of the workforce.

Improvement Teams

Employee improvement teams utilize employee knowledge and talent to achieve the continuous improvement, or kaizen, attitude that forms a foundation for lean. Implicit in the utilization of employee improvement teams is a commitment to train employees in improvement processes and problem-solving techniques. The problem-solving techniques taught to employees, the respect given to them by management, and the authority delegated ensure that processes and quality are maintained and improved to provide a valuable resource to the company.

Competitive Benefits of Lean

On an individual basis, lean's elimination of waste (resulting from overproduction, waiting time, transportation, ineffective processes, excess inventory, unnecessary motion, or product defects) can have a substantial effect on costs. One need not implement all of the different waste reduction efforts related to lean to obtain cost reduction benefits. However, the benefits of lean systems go beyond cost reduction by creating strategic advantages that result in competitive advantage.

The interactions among many of the techniques associated with lean enhance important competitive priorities. These benefits result in a better competitive position in the market, and increased sales. For example, by emphasizing quality management, closely matching the production rate to the rate of demand, and improving capacity flexibility, not only are costs reduced, but product and service quality improves, dependability of delivery is enhanced, flexibility increases, and response time shrinks. The interactions among the techniques and objectives are numerous and summarized below:

- Inventory reduction gains made possible through kanban, component standardization, small-batch production, reduced changeover times, frequent deliveries, paperless transactions, and improved supplier relationships will enhance product and service quality, improve delivery reliability, enhance flexibility to respond to customer needs, and reduce overall response times.

- Gaining process expertise through a process focus, elimination of non-value-adding steps in processes, appropriate use of automation, the flexibility from small-scale equipment, protective capacity, level loading, and preventive maintenance results in an improved use of capacity and more effective processes. These improvements enhance product and service quality, improve delivery dependability, add flexibility, and reduce lead times.

- The manufacturing advantages provided by cellular layouts, group technology, and U-shaped production lines improve processes and flows, reduce material handling, and add to processing flexibility. These enhancements also translate into better product and service quality, improved dependability of delivery, increased flexibility, and shorter processing times.

- Employee involvement, cross-training, and improvement teams make better use of the skills and knowledge of the workforce. In many cases, the employees with the greatest ability to improve the way things are done are those that actually do it every day, not the managers who observe from a distance. Greater involvement of employees makes it likely that improvements in all of the aspects of the system will come sooner and will continue.

Certainly, the waste elimination of lean and the resulting cost implications are important. Many firms adapt lean thinking for those cost reduction benefits. For those that commit to the principles of lean systems, however, the competitive benefits may have a far greater impact.

CHAPTER SUMMARY

Lean systems accomplish the goal of reducing waste by applying a number of techniques that focus on inventory, workforce, capacity, and facilities. Many of the techniques have received broad acceptance. Other techniques, however, are known only to committed lean producers. Do not conclude, however, that the techniques cannot be used unless the entire lean system is adopted. That is certainly not the case. A tremendous amount of competitive benefit can be obtained from selective adoption of lean techniques. As mentioned earlier, it is a toolbox, and its contents should be used whenever there is a close match between the tool and the problem to be fixed.

KEY TERMS

electronic data interchange (EDI), 588
inventory waste, 576
kanban, 580
lean, 574
overproduction waste, 574
processing waste, 575

product-defect waste, 576
takt time, 579
transportation waste, 575
unnecessary-motion waste, 576
waiting-time waste, 575

KEY FORMULAE

Takt Time:

(13.1)
$$\text{Takt Time} = \frac{H_{\text{avail}}}{D}$$

where

H_{avail} = Hours of available capacity

D = Demand

Computing Appropriate Number of Kanbans:

(13.2)
$$k = \frac{\overline{D}_{\text{LT}} + S}{C}$$

where

k = Number of kanbans or containers

$\overline{D}_{\text{LT}}$ = Average demand during the replenishment lead time

LT = Replenishment lead time

S = Safety stock

C = Number of units per container

Determining Production Batch Size:

(13.3)
$$\frac{D}{(H_{\text{avail}} - H_{\text{req}})/T}$$

where

D = Demand during the planning horizon

H_{avail} = Hours of available capacity

H_{req} = Hours of required capacity

T = Time it takes to perform a changeover

SOLVED PROBLEMS

1. Determining the Takt Time

A producer of automotive components recently received an order for 3,200 steering column assemblies that is due to be shipped hourly and completed by Wednesday at 5:00 p.m. The manager of the production line responsible for that item has 16 hours available to run the order. What is the takt time for that order (in hours)?

Takt Time Calculation

Step	Objective	Explanation
1.	Determine the time available.	16 hours available
2.	Determine the demand.	The demand is 3,200.
3.	Compute the takt time.	Takt time $= \dfrac{\text{Hours available}/}{\text{Demand}} = 16/3{,}200$
		$= .005$ hour

2. Determining the Appropriate Number of Kanbans

An outdoor apparel manufacturer uses kanban to control the work-in-process inventory of clothing components. For jackets, final assembly consists of stitching jacket linings inside of jacket shells. Racks of linings are wheeled to the assembly station with 40 linings on a rack. Given the following information, what is the appropriate number of racks?

Average production time for assembling 40 linings = 1.3 hours
Average transport time = .2 hour
Average wait time of rack at assembly = 2.1 hours
Average output of assembly station = 30 per hour
Defined safety stock = 8%

Kanban Number Calculation:

Step	Objective	Explanation
1.	Determine average total lead time.	= Production time + transport time + wait time = 1.3 + .2 + 2.1 = 3.6 hours
2.	Determine average demand during lead time.	= 3.6 hours × 30 units/hour = 108 units
3.	Add in the desired safety stock.	= 108 + (.08 × 108) = 116.64 units
4.	Determine the number of racks needed.	= 116.64/40 = 2.916 Round up to 3 racks

3. Determining the Smallest Possible Batch Size

Drew Alexander works for a small silk screening company that makes custom T-shirts for clubs, organizations, and special events. He recently received a large order of T-shirts to be sold at a festival that lasts all summer. Demand for the shirts is expected to be 8,000 for the entire summer. Drew has determined that it will take 34 hours of press time to produce the entire order of shirts. Given the other orders pending, he believes he has 42 hours available to devote to the order. Drew wishes to produce the order in batches that are as small as possible to minimize his inventory. With a press changeover time of 20 minutes, what should his batch size be?

Batch Size Calculation

Step	Objective	Explanation
1.	Determine the time required.	34 hours
2.	Determine the time available.	42 hours
3.	Determine the time available for changeovers.	8 hours = 480 min
4.	Divide the time available for changeovers by the changeover time to get the number of changeovers.	= 480/20 = 24
5.	Divide the total demand by the number of changeovers.	= 8000/24 = 333.3 per batch Round up to 334.

REVIEW QUESTIONS

1. What is the overall objective of lean systems?
2. What are the different types of waste lean thinking strives to eliminate? Give examples of each.
3. Describe the techniques that have broad implications for waste elimination.
4. Which techniques focus on inventory reduction?
5. Why is matching the demand rate and the production rate at the root of inventory reduction?
6. How does a kanban system work? How does management control the levels of inventory in that system?
7. How does inventory reduction improve quality?
8. How does the standardization of product components reduce inventory waste?
9. What is meant by small-batch production? How does it reduce inventory?
10. Why are reduced changeover times important to maintain small-batch production?
11. How do frequent deliveries of inventory support the goal of matching the production rate to the rate of demand?
12. How does the electronic transfer of information support inventory reduction efforts?
13. What are the characteristics of supplier relationships in a lean environment?
14. Describe the importance of employee involvement. Why is employee involvement important to a lean business?
15. Identify the techniques that assist in eliminating the waste of capacity.
16. How does leanness improve the productivity of facilities? What specific facility layout approaches aid in this effort?
17. Describe how lean methods enhance competitive priorities.

DISCUSSION AND EXPLORATION

1. Identify ways leanness has been implemented in the service sector. How has this affected you as a customer?
2. Reduction of inventory has been criticized for resulting in plant shutdowns during crisis situations. Should lean production be eliminated? If not, how should it be modified?
3. What would be the results of the inventory waste elimination efforts of a lean effort if quality levels weren't high?
4. How does lean production enhance product value for customers?
5. How can services benefit from waste reduction?
6. Why is it important for all businesses in a supply chain to implement lean practices? What happens if they don't?
7. Explain how inventory reduction techniques affect raw materials, work-in-process, and finished-goods inventories.
8. What is the logic behind a "pull" system? How could it be used in a make-to-stock system?
9. Identify the techniques that would be appropriate and those that would not be appropriate for implementation in services.

PROBLEMS HM

Solutions to odd-numbered problems are located on the text's Online Center (http://mhhe.com/opsnow3e).

1. On a short four-machine processing line at Carson's Canning, the weekly demand is 5,240 cans. The time available for processing is 16 hours. What is the takt time?

2. A manufacturing firm specializing in metal office equipment produces standardized file cabinet components to stock, and then assembles them to order as demand comes in. The demand for the two-drawer file cabinet is 230 units for this week. Time available is 16 hours. What is the takt time?

3. Anderson's Basket Company produces limited runs of collectible baskets. It is producing only three models of baskets this month, and at the end of the month, the models will be discontinued. There are 45 hours available, 15 of which are set aside for each basket. Demand for one of the baskets is 240 units. What is the takt time for that basket?

4. Norm's Frame and Mat produces everything a customer needs to frame standard-size pictures, and sells the frame, mat, and glass ready to be used. Because of storage issues, Norm doesn't want to produce inventory ahead and instructs his workers to abide by strict rules following the takt times established each week. This week's demand is projected to be 65 units. The workshop will be staffed for 18 hours this week. What is the takt time?

5. A manufacturer of the external plastic shells for computer monitors uses kanban for inventory control. Shells are stacked in plastic tote boxes holding 20 nested monitor shells. The receiving work center assembles the shells to the back of the monitors at the rate of 140 per hour. The total lead time associated with filling a container with shells and receiving it is 1.4 hours. Determine the demand for the monitor shells during the lead time, and then compute the number of tote boxes needed. Do not include a safety stock.

6. Wayne's Deli bakes its own bread so that sandwiches will be fresh. Trays used for baking bread can hold 18 French rolls. To avoid not having enough bread to meet demand and having excess stale bread, Wayne wants to try a kanban system to control the flow of bread from the ovens to the sandwich assembly area. The total lead time associated with replenishing a tray of French rolls is 1.25 hours. Sandwich makers consume bread on the average of 54 rolls per hour. Determine how many kanban "trays" Wayne's system should use. Do not include a safety stock.

7. CT Custom Welding supplies gas tanks for a motorcycle manufacturer. A kanban system using mobile racks to hold the tanks is used to control inventory between work centers. Six racks have been used as kanbans to transfer gas tanks from the welding department to the grinding center. Management thinks this is far too much inventory and wants to know what the appropriate number would be. Racks hold exactly 60 gas tanks. The grinding work center can grind the welds at the rate of 100 tanks per hour.

$$\text{Average production time} = 0.6 \text{ hour}$$
$$\text{Average transit time} = 0.1 \text{ hour}$$
$$\text{Average wait time} = 0.5 \text{ hour}$$

Compute the total lead time, the demand during the lead time, and the correct number of racks to use. Include a 10 percent safety stock.

8. PR Novelties produces advertising and promotional products that are common "giveaways" by sales reps when making calls on customers. They purchase things like car cup holders, mouse pads, tote bags, and the like, from several different small manufacturing facilities and then print or silk-screen them with the customer's company name. Not wanting to print a company name on a product that isn't needed, they try to hold inventory in an unprinted form as long as possible, and then print to meet demand. As a means of controlling inventory in process, they use a kanban system. One product, a

small collapsible umbrella, moves from the printing work center to a packaging center where the umbrella is wrapped and put in a box. The packaging process finishes 30 units per hour. The containers used to transfer the umbrellas hold 30 units. Production time for the batch of umbrellas averages 1 hour. Transit time is 0.1 hour. Wait time for the container at the printing work center is 0.5 hour on average. Compute the demand during lead time. Assuming a 10 percent safety stock, how many containers should be used?

9. ClearView produces plexiglass windshields for a variety of waterskiing and fishing boats. The process involves cutting the windshield shape from sheets of plexiglass, forming the windshield to shape, and polishing it to remove any small scratches. Windshields are moved from the forming department to polishing on large padded racks that hold 6 windshields. The forming process takes 6 minutes per unit. Transit time averages 30 minutes. Wait time averages 1 hour and 54 minutes. The polishing center can consistently polish one unit every 12 minutes. Calculate the demand during the lead time. Assume a 10 percent safety stock and calculate the number of racks needed.

10. An automatic lathe takes 12 minutes to change to produce a different part. It can turn 1,200 parts per hour. Current available capacity is 38 hours per week. Current demand requires 34 hours per week to process all of the different parts that it can produce. How many changeovers can be done? What should the batch size be?

11. A punch press used to stamp safety guards for garden tillers is rotated among three different models. Changing and adjusting the die on the press takes 60 minutes. With demand requirements of 34 hours in a 40-hour week, how many changeovers can be done? How many batches of each tiller guard can be made?

12. Owens' Apple Orchard harvests its apples and presses them for juice to sell to local customers and to a juice buyer for commercial use. The requirements differ for the two different customer types, requiring that the press be shut down, cleaned, and adjusted at every changeover. Chris Owens, the son of the owner, wants to have juice as fresh as possible for both customer types, but doesn't want to change over so often that he has to work on the weekend. The changeover process takes approximately 20 minutes. The current rate of demand will require 33 hours of press time. Forty hours are available. How many changeovers can Chris make each week? How long (in minutes) should each press run be?

13. The changeover time for a printing press is approximately 24 minutes if all parts are cleaned as a part of the process. At a local printing company, the manager wants to minimize inventory by changing among four different paper sizes as frequently as possible. He has calculated printing press requirements of 28 hours this week. There are 36 hours available. How many changeovers can he do? How many batches of each paper size should be done?

14. Erica Safford is the production manager of a carpet company in North Georgia. She manages the production in one department that produces 3 different carpets. Changeover time for her carpet tufting machine is 30 minutes. She runs the machine 8 hours per day, 6 days per week. Current capacity requirements indicate that she will need 39 hours of production this week. How many batches of each carpet can she run?

ADVANCED PROBLEMS

1. Midwest Molding has just won a contract to produce all the plastic housings for a large cell phone assembly plant. The two plants will operate on a Just-In-Time basis, with Midwest making frequent shipments of cell phone housings, at a rate tied directly to the production rate at the cell phone assembly plant.

   The cell phone plant uses mixed model sequencing for different colors of the cell phone housing, so Midwest will be delivering a stable mix of 5 different colors. Over the long run, each color will comprise 20% of the total quantity shipped to the cell phone plant. The color mix will vary from shipment to shipment, however, as the cell phone plant responds to random variation in the color mix demanded by their customers.

Midwest is currently running two shifts of production, where each shift works an 8 hour day 5 days per week. They need to produce 5000 cell phone housings per week (averaging about 1000 of each color), on a single production line that will be dedicated to making only the cell phone housings. The line changeover time to switch colors is 20 minutes. When running, the line produces a housing every 36 seconds.

a. Find the minimum feasible lot size for this process (e.g. the lot size that results in as many changeovers as possible).

b. Assume now that process availability is only 85% of the "clock hours" provided by two shifts. (The other 15% is consumed by down time due to shift changes, breaks, machine failure, etc.) Compute the minimum feasible lot size under this assumption. What would happen if we used the solution from part (a) under this assumption?

c. In addition to accounting for the 85% availability discussed in (b) above, planners have decided to use only 90% of the resulting process hours available for setups and running product. (The process will actually *remain idle* during 10% of the available process hours, where available process hours equals 85% of the "clock hours" provided by two shifts.)

d. Why would Midwest production planners purposely choose a lot size, (and corresponding setup frequency) that leaves the process idle during 10% of the available process availability, after accounting for shift changes, breaks, machine failure, etc.?

2. Jimmy Smith, an operations consultant, has been brought in by management at Hi-X Enterprises to assist in a shift toward lean manufacturing. Jennifer Marshall, the operations manager at Hi-X, is keenly interested in implementing a kanban system to reduce inventory levels throughout her plant. To that end, Jennifer has asked Jimmy to calculate the Takt Time for her facility so that work centers can be established and the line balanced. Additionally, once the reorganization of the work centers is in place, Jennifer would like to install the kanban system, so she has asked Jimmy to calculate the kanban container size and the number of containers that will be required in her newly balanced line. Since this will be a new installation and process improvement efforts are not yet mature, Jennifer has decided to use a 25% safety level to guard against starvation on the line. The additional information requested by Jimmy is provided in the table below.

Total Available Capacity (hours)	1,000
Capacity Required for Production (hours)	877
Setup Time (minutes)	6.5
Annual Demand (units)	57,850
# of Work Days	250
Average Production Time (min)	Takt Time
Average Time in Transit (min)	17
Average Time in Wait (min)	85

a. Calculate the Takt Time.
b. Calculate the Kanban size.
c. Calculate the number of Kanbans.

ENDNOTES

1. K. Suzaki, *The New Manufacturing Challenge* (New York: Free Press, 1987), p. 8.

2. A. K. Reese, "Needle in a Supply Chain Haystack," *Isource*, www.isourceonline .com/magazine/, January 2002.

SELECTED REFERENCES

Finch, B. J., and Luebbe, R. L. *Operations Management: Competing in a Changing Environment.* Orlando, FL: Dryden Press, 1995.

Hall, R. *Zero Inventories.* Homewood, IL: Dow Jones-Irwin, 1983.

Jones, D. T., and Womack, J. P. *Lean Thinking: Banish Waste and Create Wealth in Your Corporation.* New York: Simon and Schuster, 1996.

Monden, Y. *The Toyota Production System.* Atlanta: Industrial Engineering and Management Press, 1983.

Ohno, T., and Mito, S. *Just-in-Time for Today and Tomorrow.* Cambridge, MA: Productivity Press, 1988.

Suzaki, K. *The New Manufacturing Challenge.* New York: Free Press, 1987.

Womack, J. P., Jones, D. T., and Ross, D. *The Machine That Changed the World.* New York: HarperCollins Publishers, 1990.

VIDEO CASE 13.1

JIT McDonald's Style

Based on Video 14 on the Student DVD

McDonald's has a brand recognition that is the envy of other companies. Food preparation speed has always been fast, but as market needs changed, McDonald's recognized a need to provide customers with greater variety and customized meals. The new kitchen system, named "made for you," enables McDonald's to customize and maintain quick reponse.

1. What were the goals of the "made for you" kitchen system.
2. What are the criteria for success of the new system.
3. Describe the forecasting system used in new system. Why is forecasting needed?
4. Create a process flow diagram of the "made for you system" creation of a sandwich.

Implementing Kanban at Simmon's Electric

The kanban system simulation provides an interactive simulation of a kanban system. For each work center in the model, the user can set the processing rate by adjusting the corresponding sliding bar, the variability in the processing rate, and the breakdown severity. In addition, the user can set the maximum buffer size that precedes each work center. Work centers are authorized to produce only when the feeding inventory buffer is below its maximum. All work centers have the same maximum buffer size. When the simulation is paused or stopped, the average inventory for each work center and total number of breakdowns for each work center are provided. The user can also select the simulation speed from three options: slow, normal, and fast.

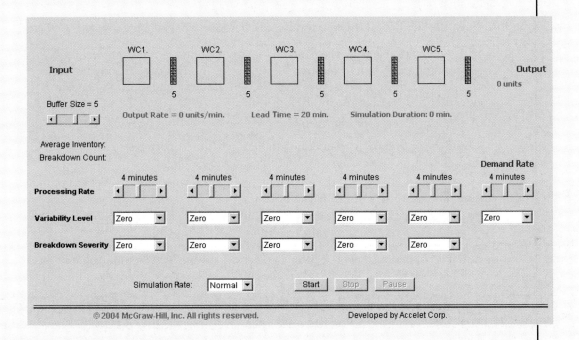

Simmon's Electric

Simmon's produces electronic controls for a variety of customers, including automotive manufacturers, heating and air-conditioning equipment manufacturers, and the defense industry. One high-volume production line rotates its production among several different control models. That production line consists of five work centers, with visible buffers of inventory between the work centers and after work center 5.

1. Check the default parameters to make sure your system starts with these values:

Buffer size	3
Processing Times	
Work center 1	4
Work center 2	4
Work center 3	4
Work center 4	4
Work center 5	4
Demand rate	4

Variability	
Work center 1	Zero
Work center 2	Zero
Work center 3	Zero
Work center 4	Zero
Work center 5	Zero
Demand rate	Zero

Breakdown Severity	
Work center 1	Zero
Work center 2	Zero
Work center 3	Zero
Work center 4	Zero
Work center 5	Zero
Simulation rate	Slow

a. Start the simulation. In your own words, describe what is happening.

2. Stop the simulation and set the demand rate to one unit every six minutes. Leave the processing times at four minutes for all work centers. Leave the process time variability and breakdown severity at zero. Start the simulation. Whenever a work center box is gray, it means that it is idle.

   a. Are work centers ever idle? Why?

   b. Using the pause button, pause the simulation while work centers are idle. Explain the different possible causes for a work center to be idle.

3. Reset all settings back to the default values, except for work center 3. Set the processing time to work center 3 at 1 minute.

   a. How does the system function differently than when all parameters were at the default?

   b. What is happening at work center 3 and at the inventory buffer immediately after work center 3?

4. Set the parameters as shown below.

Buffer size	3

Processing Times	
Work center 1	4
Work center 2	8
Work center 3	4
Work center 4	8
Work center 5	4
Demand rate	4

Variability	
Work center 1	Zero
Work center 2	Zero
Work center 3	Zero
Work center 4	Zero
Work center 5	Zero
Demand rate	Zero

Breakdown Severity	
Work center 1	Zero
Work center 2	Zero
Work center 3	Zero
Work center 4	Zero
Work center 5	Zero
Simulation rate	Normal

a. Start the simulation and let it run for 100 simulation minutes. Observe what happens to the use of the work centers and inventory buffers as it runs. What is the system output after 100 minutes? Stop the simulation.

b. Leave the parameters as they are, with the exception of the maximum buffer size. Change it from 3 to 2 units. Run the simulation for 100 simulator minutes. Does the system appear to behave any differently? What is the output?

c. Leave everything the same except reduce the maximum buffer size to 1. Run the simulation again for 100 simulator minutes. Observe what happens. What is the output in 100 minutes? Explain what happens.

d. On the basis of the previous three simulation runs, what does the buffer do to aid in the utilization of work centers? Is it needed?

5. Set the parameters as below:

Buffer size	1

Processing Times	
Work center 1	4
Work center 2	8
Work center 3	4
Work center 4	8
Work center 5	4
Demand rate	4

Variability	
Work center 1	Zero
Work center 2	Zero
Work center 3	Extreme
Work center 4	Zero
Work center 5	Zero
Demand rate	Zero

Breakdown Severity	
Work center 1	Zero
Work center 2	Zero
Work center 3	Severe
Work center 4	Zero
Work center 5	Zero
Simulation rate	Normal

a. Run the simulation for 100 simulator minutes. What is the output? What do you observe to be the effect of the variability at work center 3?

b. Leave the parameters as is, with the exception of work center 5. Increase its variability to extreme and its breakdown severity to severe. Run the simulation for

100 simulator minutes. What is the output? What was the impact of having high variability on work centers 3 and 5?

c. Now add extreme levels of variability and severe levels of breakdown severity to all work centers. Run the simulation for 100 simulator minutes. What is the new level of output?

d. With the variability and breakdown at maximum levels, incrementally increase the maximum size of the buffer by one unit each simulation run. What happens? Explain the relationship between variability and disruptions, inventory buffer size, and system productivity.

APPLICATION CASE 13.1

Making Desserts Lean

Elegant Entrées produces desserts, pastries, and an assortment of other food products for restaurants. Their most popular products are their cakes. The cake production process is not very different from the way someone would make a cake in their home, but they just produce them in batches. The process is illustrated below in Exhibit 13.8.

| EXHIBIT 13.8 | **Cake Production Process** |

Currently, the process functions with batches of 30 cakes. The ingredients are mixed in a 30-cake batch. The oven racks hold 30 cakes, and the wheeled racks used in frozen storage hold 30 cakes. Management is concerned about more closely matching cake production to demand because of shelf-life issues and also because some restaurants are beginning to demand unfrozen cakes delivered daily. Management wishes to separate frozen cake production and fresh cake production. The operations manager thinks that a batch size of 10 for frozen cakes and a batch size of 5 for fresh cakes could work.

1. Discuss the implications of transitioning to a batch size of 10 for frozen cakes and 5 for fresh cakes. What would need to be changed?
2. Would there be any major investments necessary to make the changes? Specifically discuss the need for small-scale equipment and changeover times.
3. Could a kanban system be implemented? If so, describe how it would work. Draw a diagram of the system, identifying how inventory buffers would be located.
4. Would it be easier, and less costly, to reduce all batch sizes to 5 rather than keeping the frozen cake batch size at 10?

CHAPTER 14

Capacity: Matching Productive Resources to Demand

LEARNING OBJECTIVES

- Define capacity and distinguish it from capability.

- Describe how capacity relates to value and profitability for B2C and B2B transactions.

- Describe how demand that varies from design capacity influences profitability.

- Describe the role individual resources and constraints play in determining system capacity.

- Make the calculations necessary to create demand chase and level production aggregate plans.

- Describe the information inputs and logic necessary for rough-cut capacity planning.

- Calculate required and available capacity for a rough-cut capacity plan.

- Describe the information inputs and logic necessary for capacity requirements planning.

- Calculate required and available capacity for a capacity requirements plan.

- Describe how yield management aids services in maximizing revenues.

- Perform the calculations to determine the number of customers to overbook.

THE MANY DIFFERENT ASPECTS OF AVIATION CAPACITY

Most of us have experienced both ends of the continuum airlines face when trying to match plane capacity to demand. We've flown on flights that were nearly empty and we've heard gate agents ask for volunteers to give up their seats. The challenge of matching demand and capacity is difficult for any business, be it a manufacturer or a service. For most of those businesses, the location of the capacity doesn't change. For airlines, however, the problem is not only having enough planes and crews, but having enough planes and crews *and* having both at the right place at the right time. A storm in Atlanta can temporarily ground a plane that needs to be in Salt Lake City to make a flight to Cincinnati. Few industries have to grapple with ripple effects that can extend so far.

Airlines must bring several sets of resources together simultaneously: the plane, the pilot, and the crew. Beyond the simple availability of resources is the size of the plane being devoted to a particular route. Size translates into dollars of investment and ultimately utilization of equipment.

Perhaps an even more difficult capacity issue to deal with is that of airport capacity. Delays and crowded conditions are often cited as reason to expand airports. In most airport expansion scenarios, opposition from businesses that will be displaced and from homeowners opposed to increasing noise levels is common. In a recently completed study of airport capacity, the FAA produced a list of airports that need to expand. As a part of the study, researchers identified airports that will need additional capacity by 2013 and airports that will need additional capacity by 2020. Included in that study was information on:

- Current airport operations.
- Current capacity at individual airports.
- How the airports may change in the future.
- How technologies and runways will contribute to airport capacity.
- What demand levels are likely to be in the future.
- Where demand is likely to be in the future.

Overall findings showed that nearly 5 percent of the 300 airports in the study will need expansion by 2013 or 2020. The study showed that it wasn't just the busiest airports that needed to expand. Some of the expansion will meet growth that has continued to occur in some metropolitan areas. New metropolitan areas have emerged, however, and they will need additional capacity as well. For some capacity expansions, constructing supplemental airports may be a better alternative than increasing existing capacity.

Source: American Institute of Aeronautics and Astronautics (AIAA), www.aiaa.org, June 28, 2004; Bureau of Transportation Statistics, *Issue Brief: Rising Breakeven Load Factors Threaten Airline Finances*; J. Cohen and C.C. Coughlin, "Congestion at Airports: The Economics of Airport Expansions," http://www.icpsr.umich.edu:8080/PRINT/01282.xml, October 2003; "Capacity Needs in the National Airspace System," Department of Transportation, Federal Aviation Administration, June 2004.

Capacity is a critical resource for producing products or services that meet the timing expectations of the customer. Capacity is the result of resources that can produce a specified volume in a specified amount of time, both necessary conditions of meeting customer needs. While necessary, capacity is also expensive. To ensure that it generates the finances necessary, it is always scrutinized.

Introduction: Matching Resource Availability to Market Demand

Capacity is the second of four resources used to create value and has different meanings in different contexts. It is sometimes viewed as being synonymous with capability, but there is a subtle difference. If a company determined that it couldn't produce a product, there might be several reasons. The company may have no experience with the product—a bicycle manufacturer producing computer hard drives, for example. Or the product might be a closer match to the company's abilities but still outside the company's scope of expertise. In such situations, capability implies "aptitude": Does the company have the knowledge and skills necessary to produce the product? Or the volume and timing may create problems, like when a hard drive manufacturer that is already overbooked with orders receives an order for more computer hard drives. Or a small manufacturer might receive a huge order that could probably be met eventually, but not in a reasonable amount of time. The ability to produce at a given volume in a specified amount of time is what we usually mean by "capacity."

Concerns about capacity are often more specific than those about capability. Capacity concerns do not generally refer to issues like "Do we have the skills to do the job?" or "Do we have the technology to do the job?" because these questions have already been answered. The issue in question when dealing with capacity is "Do we have the skills, the technology, the equipment, or the space, *in sufficient volume,* to complete the job in the time allowed?"

As has been discussed in previous chapters, capacity-related issues are the most significant difference between producing services and producing products. When producing products, capacity can be stored in the form of work-in-process and finished-goods inventory. For services, however, capacity usually can't be stored. It is available for the fleeting moment when it is created, and then it disappears. Planning for capacity takes on a completely different level of difficulty for services. Services must match available capacity with demand and continue to do this as demand changes. If they miss either way, costs go up and profits disappear.

With all due respect to manufacturers, services really do have a more difficult task. It's not exactly easy for manufacturers either, though, because they must cope with changing demand, high costs associated with carrying inventory, and environments with high levels of customization that make it difficult to carry finished-product inventory.

In this chapter, several objectives are emphasized. First, capacity and its impact on value creation is addressed. Second, the impact of capacity decisions on financial performance is addressed. Third, the critical challenge of matching capacity and demand is analyzed and techniques to aid in that process are introduced for service and manufacturing environments.

Capacity Defined

In most business settings, capacity is defined precisely in terms of a level of output per unit time. If this output level is sufficient to meet demand, we say that there is sufficient capacity. When viewing capacity this way, it must be recognized that many resources must converge to provide sufficient production capacity. Earlier in this text, in the discussion

Resources Merged to Form Production Capacity	EXHIBIT 14.1

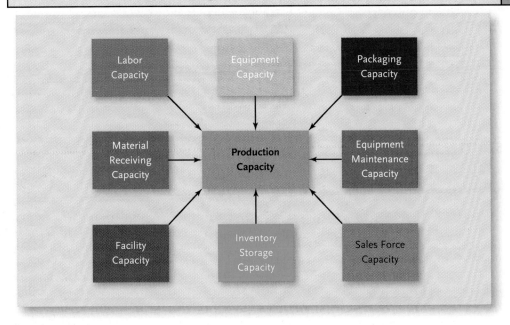

of processes and capabilities, the concept of pulling together resources from different parts of the business, to create capabilities, was discussed. Inclusion of capacity in the discussion means that each resource used to generate the capability must have the capacity to generate *enough* of the capability to meet demand. Capacity must be sufficient *in each resource*. The capability to produce enough of a specific product might be the combined result of resource groups such as labor capacity, equipment capacity, storage capacity, and transportation capacity. Each of these groups consists of resources, each of which has capacity. Labor capacity, for example, would be broken into the various skills required. Equipment capacity would be broken down into the various types of equipment, and so on. Exhibit 14.1 is a diagram of how various components of production capacity converge. Complex business systems require the capacity of hundreds of different resources, all converging to be available at the necessary time, to produce the desired outcomes.

A chef in a kitchen provides an example of different types of capacities. To determine whether sufficient "kitchen" capacity exists, he would examine the number of cooks, ovens and stoves, mixing equipment, pots and pans, and the amount of refrigeration. To determine whether sufficient preparation capacity exists, he would need to know how long the desserts could be stored. If they could be stored for a long period of time, he could make them over a longer period of time (low preparation capacity), but if they have a short shelf life, he must be able to produce more in a short period of time (high preparation capacity). If they have a long shelf life, he can produce them over a longer period of time, *but* he must have greater refrigerated storage capacity. Exhibit 14.2 illustrates the impact of this ability to store his finished products.

In Exhibit 14.2, our chef needs to have 1,000 desserts completed by day 10. The way he accomplishes this depends on available production capacity and storage capacity. This example demonstrates the important role time plays in determining capacity needs and how interdependent various productive resources can be in determining capacity available and capacity required.

Obviously, the scenario pictured in Exhibit 14.2 provides two extremes of many possible alternatives to meeting the need for 1,000 desserts. Some alternative approaches could involve short-term access to other resources. For example, suppose he had storage

EXHIBIT 14.2	**Production Rate Requirements under Different Storage Capacities**

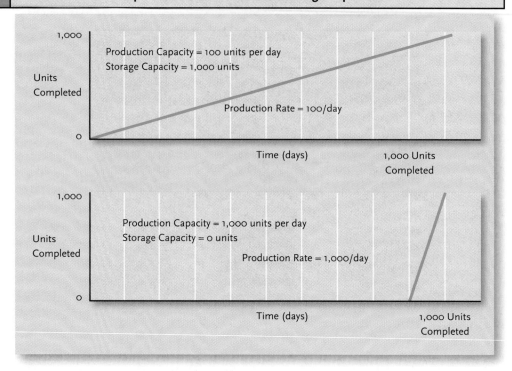

capacity for 400 desserts. He would then need to produce only 600 the day they were due and could spread the remaining 400 over several days prior to the due date. He might also decide to rent refrigeration space or hire temporary labor. The availability of either of these resources on a contingency basis would enhance his ability to cope with such a spike in demand.

Capacity and Value

By the time a customer's request for products or services is viewed from a capacity perspective, questions regarding important value attributes should have already been answered. However, when a customer places an order for a particular product or service, even if that customer is a consumer like you or me, there is an implicit analysis of whether the company has the aptitude to produce the product or service desired.

   We don't typically consider it in our decisions to purchase, but capacity issues greatly affect value attributes. This becomes evident when we examine the relationship between capacity and each value attribute. The following list provides the value attributes typically sought by consumers and business customers, as presented earlier in Chapter 3:

Cost	Style/fashion
Quality	Ethical issues
Response time	Technology
Dependability of delivery	Flexibility
Convenience	Personalization

As fuel costs rise, many airlines have cut back on flights, reducing passenger carrying capacity and increasing fares.

Capacity issues are addressed at different times during B2C and B2B purchases. As a result, capacity plays a different role in the ultimate decision to buy. For most consumer purchases, capacity issues are never addressed because the manufacturer's capacity is buffered by inventory in the supply chain, especially at the retailer. For consumer services, however, capacity is frequently a consideration. When a customer encounters a waiting line, a mismatch between capacity and demand is the cause. The consumer may have decided that he wanted to purchase a product or service from the company before encountering the waiting line. The waiting line, however, can change his mind.

In B2B transactions, the potential customer has probably conducted a more formal analysis of the potential supplier that would seek out information on price and quality. For a business, the feasibility of using this company as a supplier is investigated from the standpoint of skills and needs. Capacity cannot be addressed until an actual conversation takes place between the customer and the supplier. At that time, the potential supplier finds out how many products or how much service is needed and compares the requirements to available capacity. Since purchases of products and services by a business are potentially much larger than those of a consumer, capacity is a much more significant issue.

For consumers, value attributes like convenience, style/fashion, ethical issues, technology, personalization, and even price are considered before a decision to purchase. When a consumer approaches the service provider, for example, she already knows enough to be interested in making a purchase. A shortage of capacity isn't generally known until the customer actually arrives to make the purchase.

In addition to the impact that a shortage of capacity can have on a waiting line, capacity has an impact on the remaining value attributes of response time, dependability of delivery, and flexibility. Notice that these are all time-related value attributes. Capacity often has less of an impact on *what* products or services can be produced than it has on *when* they can be produced. Since capacity is defined as output per unit time, a shortage of capacity generally means that production of the quantity desired is not feasible, given the amount of time available. With enough time, however, the quantity could probably be produced. The availability of capacity can provide flexibility that competitors lack.

In the case of response time, the sooner an order can be started, the sooner it can be finished. An order can be started immediately only if the resources are immediately available. If they are not, meaning that they are already working on another order, the start will be delayed, delaying the finish. This is what causes a waiting line or queue. This is also known as a **backlog** in some industries.

Dependability of delivery is diminished when there is an increase in the variability of the response time. If the lead time to complete a promised service or order of products is very stable and dependable, it is unlikely that the response will take longer than expected. If it varies significantly, however, the prediction of how long it will take, which forms the basis for a delivery promise, has a higher probability of being wrong. What causes the variability in lead time? Usually variability results from disruptions that occur in the value chain. Delayed shipments of materials are one common cause; equipment breakdowns are another. In Chapter 11, the use of inventory buffers was described as a way to decouple a process from these types of disruption. Buffers of excess capacity can also reduce the impact. If excess capacity exists, there will be some idle capacity. If there was a breakdown, the idle capacity could be pulled into use. This concept was described as protective capacity in Chapter 13 and is a critical component of lean systems. The greater the capacity compared to demand, the greater the buffer and the greater the protection from the effects of the disruption.

In the case of flexibility, the immediate availability of resources is also important. A company can respond quickly to unusual demands only if it has available capacity. If all capacity is being utilized, the company has no ability to respond. In each of the time-related value attributes, a company's ability to improve performance hinges on having available capacity. A buffer of available capacity offers strategic value to a company that competes on the basis of these quality attributes. Quick response, dependable response, and flexibility depend on a company's ability to respond on short notice. In some cases, buffers of inventory can enhance these capabilities. However, we've already discussed how finished-goods inventory actually reduces the firm's flexibility to respond to market changes with new-product introductions. A buffer of capacity does not have the same negative effect as a buffer of finished goods inventory. Unfortunately, protective capacity tends to be in short supply because it is often viewed as an investment in resources that aren't providing a

backlog
A queue of orders waiting to be processed.

financial return. Protective capacity, because it isn't being used all the time, appears to create idle resources. Without these idle resources, however, the firm cannot respond quickly to an unexpected demand on these resources. From a short-term perspective it might appear that the idle resources should be eliminated, because high utilization of equipment results in quicker payback for the investment. Protective capacity provides a long-term financial benefit, however, through its impact on various time-related value attributes, and can increase value and market share. The ability to respond to a new customer who needs something immediately, or an old customer caught in a bind, can enhance customer loyalty.

The Financial Impact of Capacity Decisions

Reduced response time, improved dependability of delivery, and increased flexibility result in increased value. The increases in value result in enhanced market share, increases in net sales, and the resulting increases in net income and return on assets. In many cases, however, the impact of capacity can go beyond these service-oriented value attributes and influence cost and quality levels as well. In both cases, it is important to understand a specific type of capacity known as design capacity.

design capacity
The capacity a facility is designed to accommodate on an ongoing basis.

Design capacity is the rate of production the business was designed to accommodate on a long-term basis. For example, a manufacturing facility, by its size and the type and amount of production equipment it has, can produce products at a variety of output levels. But it was designed with a specific output level in mind. Producing at a rate less than the design capacity results in idle and unproductive resources. Because so many costs associated with production are fixed, the smaller volume of output results in higher costs per unit. Producing at a rate greater than the design capacity also results in problems. Equipment can incur excess wear and insufficient maintenance. Overtime may be required. Workers can be overwhelmed and facilities can get overcrowded. In cases of underproduction and overproduction, the resources are not used optimally, resulting in higher costs per unit than if the plant were operating at its design level. A match between the demand and the design capacity creates a situation known as the **best operating level,** the level at which costs per unit are at their lowest.

best operating level
The level of demand or "load" on a system that results in the lowest cost per unit produced or processed.

Matching demand to design capacity is even more critical for services. Overloading or underutilizing service resources can have similar impacts on costs. Resources that remain underutilized, including the workforce, do not generate the same financial return as

The relationship between design capacity and demand is critical for many resources. Warehouses, for example, are not often thought of when considering capacity implications, but warehouses require a substantial facility investment. In situations like this one, when demand is far below capacity, storage costs per unit are extremely high because of the fixed costs that can't be spread out among large numbers of products stored.

when utilized fully. Resources overloaded have increased levels of wear and tear, and they don't get the maintenance needed to keep them in top running condition. A mismatch between demand and design capacity can be even more serious in the service sector because its effects go beyond simple cost issues.

Demand that is too low can result in inattentive employees and a business that doesn't deliver in a way that meets customer expectations. Restaurants, clubs, and entertainment-oriented businesses need customers to attract more customers. An empty restaurant, for example, warns potential customers that something is wrong with it. In experience-oriented businesses, customers expect interaction with others and, without that interaction, will not enjoy the experience as much. Overloading capacity in a service also has a negative impact. Queues form, increasing the wait time of customers. Interaction with the workforce drops to a lower level because the workforce is rushed. Less interaction means that customers will not be accommodated as well and are less likely to get the kind of treatment they are accustomed to. This is especially true with regular customers who have become used to being treated a certain way. This situation often results in moving employees from jobs that can be put off to jobs that can't wait. Workers from behind the scenes are moved to positions that require customer interaction. In many cases they don't have the same level of skills as the other employees, and customers end up getting lower levels of service. Exhibit 14.3 graphs various possible relationships between available capacity and demand.

To gain a more in-depth understanding of the importance design capacity plays, let's examine the profitability impact resulting from each zone presented in Exhibit 14.3. Zone A is a typical situation of demand being lower than design capacity. Besides the low net sales resulting from low demand, productive resources would be idle. The resulting impact is that the cost per unit associated with those resources would increase. Labor is underutilized, resulting in high labor costs per unit or a reduction in the labor force (a possible layoff). An important issue to consider is the duration of this condition. A short-term condition would not be serious, but if it continued, it would threaten broader profitability measures because costs, relative to sales, would be quite high.

Zone B is an almost perfect situation. One can't expect that demand would precisely equal design capacity over the long term, however. Manufacturers and services seek this relationship between demand and capacity.

Zone C is the opposite of Zone A. In Zone C demand is much higher than design capacity. For a manufacturer, equipment would be running faster and longer. Preventive

As airlines reduce capacity, load factors (utilization) increase and schedules may be less convenient, but reduced traffic should reduce the number of delays and ease the strain on airports.

| **Demand and Design Capacity Relationships** | **EXHIBIT 14.3** |

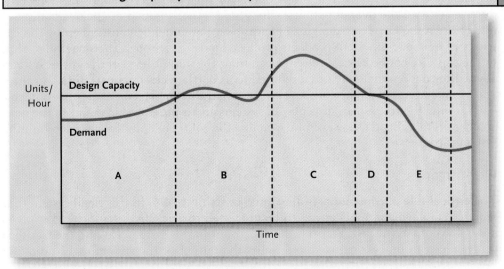

maintenance tasks would be postponed, potentially resulting in long-term detrimental effects on the equipment. For labor to keep up, overtime would be needed. Overtime labor is paid at a higher rate than standard time labor, so labor costs per unit would increase. If this is a long-term situation, additional labor capacity would be necessary, either through hiring permanent workers or through the use of a contingent workforce acquired through a temp agency. In either case, bringing on a significant number of untrained workers in a short period of time results in an under-skilled workforce prone to problems. Included in those potential problems could be a decline in product and service quality, safety problems, and data recording mistakes. Anticipation of this condition would probably motivate a manufacturer to build up an inventory buffer to reduce the load on capacity.

At first glance Zone D seems to be a perfect situation, but the fact that it follows an overdemanded period means that it is really a recovery period. Tasks that would normally be done on an ongoing basis are delayed during high demand periods and a lull that follows offers an opportunity to catch up on those tasks. Even though demand isn't as high in Zone D, the load on the workforce could still be too high because they're trying to meet the demand and catch up on things that didn't get done during the preceding rush.

Zone E presents a serious drop in demand that could threaten the financial health of the business if prolonged. Demand that approaches only 50 percent of design capacity results in all of the cost increases discussed in Zone A but could also lead to quality problems that result from inattentive workers and associated morale problems. In addition, layoffs could result in the few remaining workers being given broader responsibilities, resulting in poor quality. If prolonged, the low demand would result in cash flow problems making it hard to cover the fixed costs associated with the design capacity.

Like many operations decisions, capacity planning involves trade-off decisions. More capacity reduces response time and, in some ways, adds to a firm's flexibility. However, excess capacity increases costs, doesn't provide enough financial return, and can actually reduce flexibility if it is in the wrong form.

Individual Resource Influence on System Capacity

In the previous discussions, the fact that service and manufacturing production capacity requires the convergence of numerous resources was mentioned. For many service- and manufacturing-oriented production systems, capacity results from the complex merger of resources. The overall capacity of the system is dependent on all of the individual resources used to create it. If one is missing, capacity is short. In many productive systems, the overall output of the system is constrained by the availability of one of the resources. For example, a factory's output could be constrained by the capacity of one machine if all products produced must go through that machine. That is, the capacity of one critical resource can limit the output level of the entire system. These limiting resources are often referred to as **bottlenecks** or **constraints.** An integrative management framework known as **constraint management** has been developed around the role constraints play in systems and is presented in detail in the next chapter. In this chapter, however, we examine the role constraints play in determining system capacity.

bottleneck
A constraint in a production system.

constraint
Anything that inhibits a system's progress toward its goals.

constraint management
A framework for managing the constraints of a system in a way that maximizes the system's accomplishment of its goals.

Constraints

The critical role of constraints is illustrated in Exhibit 14.4. In this small system that requires employment applications to be processed through five steps, step 3 is obviously slower than the rest. Step 3 is the constraint in this system. Despite the fact that other steps can process more, step 3 limits the output of the system to 12 units per hour.

Example of a Constrained System				**EXHIBIT 14.4**

Step 1 3 minutes/ unit	→	Step 2 1 minute/ unit	→	Step 3 5 minutes/ unit	→	Step 4 4 minutes/ unit	→	Step 5 2 minutes/ unit

A simple system like the one in Exhibit 14.4 allows us to identify several characteristics that result from a constraint. First of all, individual resources in a constrained system do not control their own utilization rates. Utilization is often used as a measure of capacity performance and is computed as the amount of time a resource is actually processing divided by the amount of time it could be processing. Step 4 has the potential to process one unit every four minutes—15 units per hour. The slower rate of step 3, however, can provide step 4 with only one unit every five minutes. Thus step 4 will process a unit in four minutes, then wait one minute for the next unit, then process it in four minutes, then wait, and so on. Step 4 will work four out of five minutes, for a utilization rate of 80 percent. It can do no better.

This phenomenon holds true for the processing steps that come before step 3 as well. Steps 1 and 2 are faster than step 3. If we feed applications into the system at the rate step 1 can process them, one every three minutes, the system can process them only as fast as step 3 (one unit every five minutes). The result of step 1 and step 2 processing applications faster than one every five minutes is simply a buildup of applications in front of step 3. This is shown in Exhibit 14.5. Notice also that the utilization of step 2 is limited by the capacity of step 1.

The second phenomenon created by the system constraint is that time lost by the constraint is lost for the entire system. Not only is the time lost, but it is lost forever. It can't be made up. This fact relates to the high level of utilization required of constraints. Since a constrained resource limits the system's output level, the constraint must be utilized

System constraints dictate system capacity. In many systems, restricted capacity results in long queues and frustrated customers. Here, at the Chicago office of the Consulate of Mexico, long queues form as Mexican immigrants apply for consulate-issued ID cards that have become legal ID documents for opening bank accounts. Data entry is the constraint in this system, and any improvement would increase the system's output.

EXHIBIT 14.5	Example of a Constrained System with Excess Input

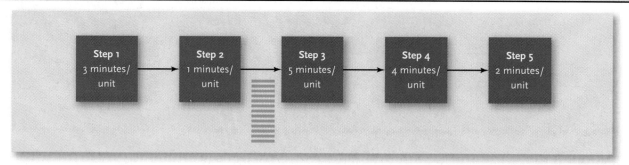

EXHIBIT 14.6	"Weakest Link" Analogy of Constrained System

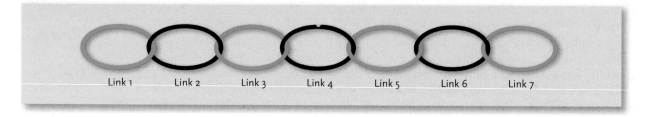

100 percent of the time to maximize the output of the system. If the constraint stops producing for any amount of time because of a breakdown or some other reason, the result is the same as shutting down the entire system. For nonconstraints, a breakdown for a short amount of time is not serious, because they are idle part of the time anyway. In fact, if a particular resource is a nonconstraint, it must be idle part of the time, since it can't produce faster than the constraint. Since the nonconstraints can work faster than the constraint, they can catch up again to make up for lost time if a disruption forces them to stop producing. The constraint, however, has no idle time available to get caught up.

One way to look at the capacity in a productive system is to use the analogy of a chain. The links of a chain can be of various strengths, but the strength of the chain is determined by the weakest link, as shown in Exhibit 14.6.

The chain analogy also illustrates a third phenomenon of constrained systems: Increasing the productivity or output of a nonconstraint does not help the system. Looking back at Exhibit 14.4, for example, what improvement would be gained by increasing the output of step 4 from 15 units per hour to 30 units per hour? Since step 4 receives units only every five minutes, an increase in capacity results in no improvement to the system, but just gives step 4 more time to be idle. More sophisticated approaches used to help manage constrained systems are discussed in detail in Chapter 15. If a system constraint is eliminated, a new one usually appears. Notice the weakest link (link 4) in Exhibit 14.6. If that link is strengthened (made faster), eventually another link replaces it as the "weakest" (slowest).

For many airports, the obstacle to increased capacity is not the need for more runways, but a shortage of taxiways or needed improvements in air traffic control to better use the runways they have.

A Broader View: Supply Chain Capacity

Just as one resource can constrain a productive system inside a business, one business can constrain an entire supply chain. The value added from various businesses in the chain between raw materials and consumer products comes from a variety of resources in different companies. From basic manufacturer all the way to assembler and then to transportation services and to the ability of a retailer to stock its shelves, capacity defines the ability of the supply chain to accomplish its goal of adding value and getting it to the

Weakest Link in a Supply Chain	EXHIBIT 14.7

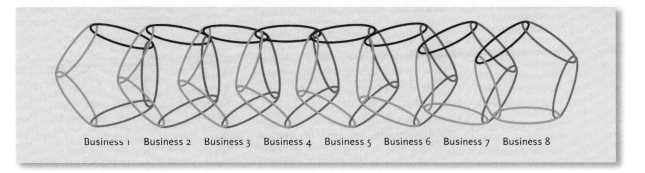

Business 1   Business 2   Business 3   Business 4   Business 5   Business 6   Business 7   Business 8

customer. Any link in the chain can be a constraint to what it can accomplish. Since any resource within a productive system can limit that system, the supply chain capacity can be limited by a specific resource within the chain. The supply chain, in effect, is a "chain of chains." The analogy presented in Exhibit 14.6 is extended to illustrate the complexities of supply chain capacity in Exhibit 14.7.

Here, tuna is selected for use by restaurants in what can be a time-consuming process. A constraint anywhere in a supply chain can have the effect of increasing inventory (and associated costs), solwing down flow of goods to the consumer, and reducing quality. When the product has a very high value and short shelf life, delays can be especially costly.

The difference in companies' abilities to utilize inventory as a means of leveling the effect of demand on capacity adds complexity to the supply chain capacity issue. The capacities required to complete all of the production functions within the supply chain are not just those required to produce products. Many are service-oriented capacities, such as transportation, distribution, and storage. Even though production capacity requirements can be leveled by using finished-product inventories, demands on distribution systems cannot always be leveled in that way. Even though products can be produced ahead of time, they might not be amenable to shipping ahead of time. Within the supply chain, organizations utilize different strategies for minimizing costs associated with capacity and demand interactions. Naturally, these strategies differ between manufacturers and services. The following discussions examine common techniques for matching capacity and demand in these two environments.

The Demand – Capacity Match in Manufacturing

aggregate demand
The total demand for all products or services.

The ability to buffer capacity from demand swings by utilizing inventory creates an opportunity for manufacturers to examine their future capacity needs and create a plan for meeting them. This is typically done at an aggregate level, rather than at the individual product level, because forecasting into the future is much more accurate when done on an aggregate basis. **Aggregate demand** is the total demand, stated in some aggregate unit. An aggregate demand forecast is more accurate than forecasts of individual products because when forecasting at the aggregate level, the errors that would be associated with all of the individual product forecasts tend to cancel each other out. At the individual product level, some forecasts will be high and some low, but we won't know which until it's too late. At the aggregate level, we get the effect of averaging, and it reduces the random component.

Aggregate planning, as capacity planning at this level is known, uses inventory and variable labor to deal with demand fluctuations in an attempt to reduce costs. From Chapter 11, we know that carrying inventory can be beneficial, but it is also costly. Inventory can be used to eliminate the direct effects of demand fluctuation, but this approach comes at a price. The more inventory we store, and the longer we store it, the greater the inventory carrying costs. But refusing to store inventory carries a price as well. Chasing demand by continuously adjusting capacity is not cost-free either. Hiring, training, and laying off workers are expensive activities. The more a company uses inventory to smooth production requirements, the less hiring and firing, but the higher the inventory carrying costs. Aggregate planning considers the interaction of these practices and attempts to reach low-cost solutions. Examining the two extreme options provides insight into this technique.

Demand Chase Aggregate Planning

demand chase
An aggregate planning approach that uses hiring and firing of employees to increase and decrease output to match fluctuating demand.

In the simplest approach, known as the **demand chase** approach to aggregate planning, production levels are changed to match changes in demand, so no inventory is needed to buffer against demand changes. Changes in production levels must be dealt with through hiring and laying off workers. Costs associated with this plan are the costs of hiring and laying off workers.

Step-by-Step: Demand Chase Aggregate Planning

1. Convert the units required for each time period to labor hours required for each time period by multiplying the number of units by the labor hours required per unit.
2. Compute the number of workers required per period by dividing the number of labor hours required for each time period by the number of hours worked by each worker in the time period. Be sure to round any noninteger results up.

3. Hires are required anytime the number of workers needed in a particular time period is greater than the number of workers needed in the previous time period. Subtract to determine the difference. That difference is the number of hires.

4. Fires or layoffs are required anytime the number of workers needed in a particular time period is less than the number of workers needed in the previous time period. Subtract to determine the difference. That difference is the number of fires.

5. Calculate the hiring costs per period by multiplying the number of workers hired by the cost of hiring a worker. Calculate the firing costs per period by multiplying the number of workers fired by the cost of firing a worker.

6. Calculate total plan costs by summing hiring and firing costs.

Example 14.1 demonstrates this approach

Example 14.1   **Demand Chase Aggregate Plan**

EXCEL TUTOR

Quality Office Designs manufactures customized office fixtures. The company has created a "generic" configuration for aggregate planning purposes and has predicted the demand for next year, as presented in Exhibit 14.8. The labor required for each fixture is 1.2 hours. Assuming a 40-hour work week (160 hours per month) for employees, hiring costs of $475, layoff costs of $400, and a current workforce of 11, management wishes to create a demand chase aggregate plan.

EXHIBIT 14.8   Quality Office Design Demand

	Period											
	1	2	3	4	5	6	7	8	9	10	11	12
Demand forecast	1,400	1,300	1,600	1,280	2,000	2,400	2,550	1,990	1,750	1,600	1,600	1,850

Solution

The demand chase plan is constructed by first converting the units demanded each period into the required labor hours for that period. Once the required labor hours are determined, the number of workers needed is computed by dividing the labor hours required each month by 160. This result must be rounded up to a "whole" worker, since Quality can't hire partial employees. The results of these calculations are presented in Exhibit 14.9.

EXHIBIT 14.9   Quality Office Design Labor Requirements

	Period											
	1	2	3	4	5	6	7	8	9	10	11	12
Demand forecast	1,400	1,300	1,600	1,280	2,000	2,400	2,550	1,990	1,750	1,600	1,600	1,850
Labor hours required	1,680	1,560	1,920	1,536	2,400	2,880	3,060	2,388	2,100	1,920	1,920	2,220
Workers required	11	10	12	10	15	18	20	15	14	12	12	14

Costs are calculated by multiplying the number of hires each month by $475 and the number of layoffs by $400. Monthly costs are totaled. The results of the complete cost analysis are presented in Exhibit 14.10.

(Continues)

Example 14.1

(Continued)

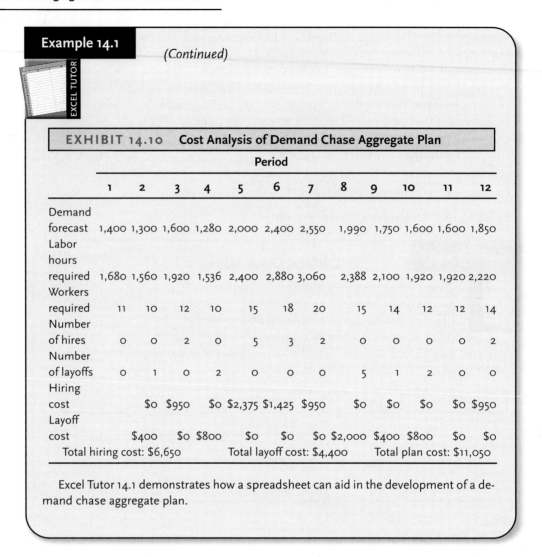

EXCEL TUTOR

EXHIBIT 14.10   Cost Analysis of Demand Chase Aggregate Plan

							Period					
	1	2	3	4	5	6	7	8	9	10	11	12
Demand forecast	1,400	1,300	1,600	1,280	2,000	2,400	2,550	1,990	1,750	1,600	1,600	1,850
Labor hours required	1,680	1,560	1,920	1,536	2,400	2,880	3,060	2,388	2,100	1,920	1,920	2,220
Workers required	11	10	12	10	15	18	20	15	14	12	12	14
Number of hires	0	0	2	0	5	3	2	0	0	0	0	2
Number of layoffs	0	1	0	2	0	0	0	5	1	2	0	0
Hiring cost		$0	$950	$0	$2,375	$1,425	$950	$0	$0	$0	$0	$950
Layoff cost		$400	$0	$800	$0	$0	$0	$2,000	$400	$800	$0	$0

Total hiring cost: $6,650   Total layoff cost: $4,400   Total plan cost: $11,050

Excel Tutor 14.1 demonstrates how a spreadsheet can aid in the development of a demand chase aggregate plan.

The demand chase strategy for aggregate planning is another one of those situations where all costs aren't quantifiable. The total costs for Example 14.1 are calculated to be $11,050. Common sense reveals other costs. In a tight labor market, what happens to workers who are laid off? They go to work somewhere else. Eventually, a business that experiences frequent layoff cycles will find that the only people willing to work there are those who are currently unable to get a job elsewhere. Most people will prefer a job that is more stable. The quality of the workforce is reduced by the cycle of layoffs and hirings. Training costs are included as a part of the hiring decision, but in virtually any job, experience translates into quality. Layoffs and rehires result in a lower overall experience level and the resulting lower quality level.

Level Production Aggregate Planning

The opposite extreme from the demand chase approach is to avoid hiring and firing and to deal with all of the demand fluctuations through a buffer of finished-product inventory. There are three potential kinds of cost associated with this approach. The first costs, once we determine the number of employees needed to produce the necessary units, are the hiring or firing costs associated with an initial labor adjustment. The second cost is associated with carrying the inventory, including insurance, storage, and opportunity costs. The third cost associated with this plan is the cost of a stockout. Stockouts can occur with this plan, but they can be planned for. To plan months ahead to run out of something may seem foolish, but keep in mind that this is a plan based on aggregate production to provide a close estimate of costs. It is ultimately based on a forecast of demand, and we know that forecasts are inaccurate. Stockouts do happen, and it makes sense to acknowledge that they can happen. Ultimately, at the execution stage several months in the future, effort would be taken to avoid the stockout.

The process required to create a **level production** aggregate plan takes advantage of our ability to store capacity from one period to the next in the form of inventory. To determine the number of units that need to be produced per period, we essentially forecast the total number of units that need to be produced and divide that number by the number of time periods (days, weeks, or months). The number of units to be produced per period is translated into labor hours by multiplying the number of units by the time per unit. The total number of labor hours needed per period is translated into the number of workers needed by dividing the number of labor hours needed by the number of hours each employee works per period (8 hours per day, 40 hours per week, 160 hours per month, etc.).

level production
An aggregate planning approach that uses inventory stored from period to period to reduce the need to change the output rate as demand changes.

Step-by-Step: Level Production Aggregate Planning

1. Determine the number of units to produce each day by dividing the total expected demand for the planning horizon by the number of days in the planning horizon. Round up for noninteger solutions

2. Determine the number of labor hours required per day by multiplying the number of units produced each day by the number of labor hours required per unit.

3. Determine the number of workers required by dividing the number of labor hours required each day by the number of hours each worker works per day.

4. With the exception of any initial hiring or firing to get to the level number of workers, costs associated with this plan are inventory carrying costs. This is typically determined on a monthly basis. The average level of inventory for a month is the beginning inventory plus the ending inventory, divided by 2. Beginning inventory (except for month 1, which is given) is equal to the ending inventory for the previous month. Ending inventory is equal to the beginning inventory plus the monthly output minus the demand forecast.

5. The inventory carrying cost for a month is the average level of inventory multiplied by the monthly carrying cost. If the carrying cost per unit is presented on an annual basis, it can be converted to a monthly carrying cost by dividing by 12.

6. The total cost for the plan would be the sum of the monthly inventory carrying costs plus any initial hiring or firing costs.

In Example 14.2, the scenario presented in the previous example forms the basis for a level production aggregate plan.

Example 14.2

EXCEL TUTOR

Level Production Aggregate Plan

Quality Office Designs created a demand chase aggregate plan with total costs of $11,050. The company wants to create a level production plan for a comparison. The total number of units projected to be produced is 21,320. There are 253 workdays in the year. Exhibit 14.11 reproduces the projected demand information from Example 14.1 and provides the total units to produce and the workdays per month.

(Continues)

Example 14.2

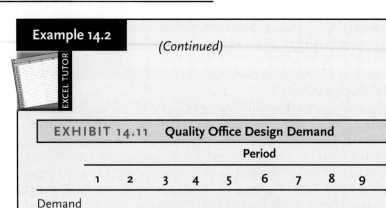

EXCEL TUTOR

(Continued)

EXHIBIT 14.11 Quality Office Design Demand

Period

	1	2	3	4	5	6	7	8	9	10	11	12
Demand forecast	1,400	1,300	1,600	1,280	2,000	2,400	2,550	1,990	1,750	1,600	1,600	1,850

The labor required for each fixture is 1.2 hours. Hiring costs are $475, and layoff costs are $400. The initial staffing level is 11 employees. Inventory carrying costs associated with this plan have been determined to be $12 per unit per month.

Solution

With 253 workdays available and 21,320 units needed, 84.27 units (round up to 85) will need to be produced each day. Production of 85 units per day, at 1.2 hours per unit, requires 12.75 employees, rounded up to 13 workers. So an initial hiring of two workers will be required. The total number of units produced each month, based on the number of workdays each month and the daily production of 85 units, compared to the monthly demand, is presented in Exhibit 14.12. Included in Exhibit 14.12 are the resulting inventory levels and costs.

EXHIBIT 14.12 Results of Cost Analysis for Level Production Aggregate Plan

Period

	1	2	3	4	5	6	7	8	9	10	11	12	Total
Demand forecast	1,400	1,300	1,600	1,280	2,000	2,400	2,550	1,990	1,750	1,600	1,600	1,850	21,320
Workdays	22	20	23	20	23	20	20	23	21	22	20	19	253
Monthly output	1,870	1,700	1,955	1,700	1,955	1,700	1,700	1,955	1,785	1,870	1,700	1,615	21,505
Beginning inventory	0	470	870	1,225	1,645	1,600	900	50	15	50	320	420	
Ending inventory	470	870	1,225	1,645	1,600	900	50	15	50	320	420	185	
Average inventory	235	670	1,047.5	1,435	1,622.5	1,250	475	32.5	32.5	185	370	302.5	
Carrying cost ($)	2,820	8,040	12,570	17,220	19,470	15,000	5,700	390	390	2,220	4,440	3,630	91,890

Average demand for each month is the beginning inventory plus the ending inventory, divided by 2. Notice that at the end of the year, more units have actually been produced than necessary. This results from the rounding up of the 12.75 workers to 13. The inventory carrying costs associated with this plan are substantial—$91,890. In addition, hiring the two new employees would cost $950, for a total cost of $92,840.

Excel Tutor 14.2 shows how the level production aggregate plan can be developed in a spreadsheet.

It is unlikely that either the demand chase or the level production aggregate plan will be totally acceptable. In most situations, the best solution turns out to be some hybrid of using inventory and adjusting the level of the workforce. For example, allowing one workforce adjustment in period 1 and another in period 6 and leveling the production for each six-month period presents a compromise. When the capability of using some overtime and some temporary workers is added, an infinite number of possible scenarios open up.

The financial impact of matching demand and capacity is illustrated quite well when the aggregate planning process is examined. The basic costs of production cannot be avoided. The inventory carrying costs are traded off against the costs associated with changing capacity in a quest for the "perfect match." We know, however, that the perfect match is not possible. The resulting capacity gives us a level of service that customers evaluate. Good service is viewed positively by customers, adds to their perception of value, and increases customer loyalty and the firm's market share. Stockouts, though sometimes unavoidable, reduce performance in the eyes of the customer and, given the importance of timeliness, are almost unacceptable. This is particularly true given the options for contingent capacity, discussed later in this chapter. Aggregate planning is very structured and explicitly addresses these costs. No matter what approach is used to match capacity and demand, however, the costs and financial impact are the same.

Detailed Capacity Planning in Manufacturing

While aggregate planning provides a mechanism for examining capacity and demand relationships in the long term, capacity–demand relationships must also be addressed on a detailed level in the short term. In many manufacturing environments, products are assembled from a combination of components, some that are purchased and others that are manufactured in-house. The purchased components do not directly affect capacity, but their availability or unavailability can affect the firm's ability to utilize capacity as scheduled. The most significant impact on manufacturing capacity comes from components and products that are manufactured in-house.

Detailed capacity planning processes are typically integrated with the detailed inventory calculations used to manage dependent demand inventory. Recall from Chapter 11 that dependent demand inventory (components and raw materials) is managed quite differently from independent demand inventory (end products and retail inventories). The logic used to determine when and how many to order for dependent demand inventory is known as material requirements planning (MRP). When the items are manufactured components for a product, the quantity and timing of the order have the direct result of creating a demand on capacity.

MRP creates an order to be released to manufacturing. This starts the actual manufacturing process. If the component must be ready by a certain date in order to assemble an end product, it must be produced beforehand. From MRP, the quantity needed and the timing are known. This information can be used to determine the required load on the resources used in the manufacturing processes. Once the capacity requirements are known, they can be compared to the capacity available, and a satisfactory match between capacity and demand can be developed.

Exhibit 14.13 illustrates the inputs of MRP. The primary outputs of the system are the quantities and timing of planned order releases for components and raw materials. The orders for components that are manufactured in-house create the demand that "loads up" manufacturing capacity. It should be no surprise, then, that the planned order releases that result from the MRP logic provide a primary input to detailed capacity planning for manufacturers. This approach is not the only approach to generating capacity requirements for manufacturers, however. The master production schedule can also be used to provide the product demand that can then be translated into capacity requirements. The mechanism used to translate the demand for products is a statement of the capacity required to produce a particular product or component. This can take several forms, but the most common is a **bill of capacity.** Recall from Chapter 11, in the discussion of MRP

bill of capacity
A statement of the time required on each resource needed to produce a product.

EXHIBIT 14.13	MRP Logic

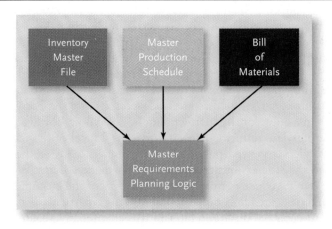

rough-cut capacity planning
A detailed capacity planning approach used in manufacturing that uses the master production schedule to provide the quantity of units that must be produced.

logic, that a primary input to that logic is the bill of material. The bill of materials details the material components of any manufactured item. The bill of capacity is analogous to the bill of material in that it specifies the capacity components of the product.

There are two common approaches to capacity planning in manufacturing. The first, known as **rough-cut capacity planning,** utilizes the master production schedule as the source of product demand information. In rough-cut capacity planning, a capacity bill is created. This details all of the capacity required to manufacture the end item specified in the master production schedule. For each resource utilized in the manufacture of the product, the total time required to produce all components and the finished product is calculated. These times are then multiplied by the quantity required in each time period to compute capacity needs for the period. These requirements are then compared to available capacity to identify potential problems.

Available capacity is generally calculated by converting the actual hours available on a particular work center into standard hours. Standard hours result from making two adjustments to the actual hours available. First, actual hours are adjusted to account for the historical utilization of the work center. An accurate view of the available capacity of a work center is desired. If a work center is typically utilized only 90 percent, because of maintenance, changeovers, and so on, then the available capacity should reflect that fact. Standard hours available should also recognize if a work center does not produce at 100 percent efficiency. A work center that produces only 90 percent of the standard output will have an efficiency of 90 percent. In order for the capacity available to be an accurate reflection of reality, efficiency is also used as an adjustment to the actual hours.

Step-by-Step: Rough-Cut Capacity Planning

1. Calculate the capacity required (in hours) for each work center for each week by multiplying the quantity of items to be produced in each week (from the master production schedule) by the time it takes on that particular work station to produce the item.

2. Calculate the available capacity (in standard hours) at each work center by multiplying the actual hours available in a week by the historical utilization and by the historical efficiency.

3. On a weekly basis, compare required capacity to available capacity, for each work station.

Example 14.3 provides a demonstration of the calculations used to compute required capacity for rough-cut capacity planning, as well as the available capacity.

The rough-cut capacity plan for the entire plant would include the same logic and would cover all work centers in the plant. Work centers that are used in the production of several different products would incorporate the demand for those different products in the computation of the required capacity.

Example 14.3

Rough-Cut Capacity Planning

Quality Pet Enclosures manufactures "crates" for dogs and cats. The crates come in various sizes and consist of heavy-gage galvanized wire formed into panels, which are then held together with snap clips. The crates are popular because they can be folded into a flat stack of panels within seconds. The firm has dedicated equipment for several of the more popular sizes, including the 24 × 40 crate (model 2440), which is the most popular. For the extremely large size (30 × 48) and some of the smaller sizes, one flexible manufacturing line is used. For the 2440 line, the utilization for all machines averages 93 percent. Efficiency is also consistent across all machines at 95 percent.

The plant manager is considering the purchase of software that would enhance all capacity planning activities and wishes to create a prototype rough-cut capacity planning system as a test. Using the data provided below, determine the required and available capacity for the 2440 crate line.

Solution

The master production schedule is presented in Exhibit 14.14. The bill of capacity is presented in Exhibit 14.15. It is typically provided in hours required per unit of product.

EXHIBIT 14.14   Master Production Schedule for Model 2440

					Week					
	1	2	3	4	5	6	7	8	9	10
2440 MPS	270	300	315	295	245	230	250	185	255	210

EXHIBIT 14.15   Bill of Capacity for Model 2440

Work Center	Time Required (hours)
Cutting	0.09
Forming	0.12
Grid assembly	0.15
Welding	0.13
Assembly	0.08

Capacity required, based on multiplying the quantity from the MPS times the processing time per unit from the bill of capacity, is presented in Exhibit 14.16.

EXHIBIT 14.16   Capacity Required for Model 2440 (in hours)

					Week					
Unit	1	2	3	4	5	6	7	8	9	10
Cutting	24.3	27	28.35	26.55	22.05	20.7	22.5	16.65	22.95	18.9
Forming	32.4	36	37.8	35.4	29.4	27.6	30	22.2	30.6	25.2
Grid assembly	40.5	45	47.25	44.25	36.75	34.5	37.5	27.75	38.25	31.5
Welding	35.1	39	40.95	38.35	31.85	29.9	32.5	24.05	33.15	27.3
Assembly	21.6	24	25.2	23.6	19.6	18.4	20	14.8	20.4	16.8

(Continues)

Example 14.3 *(Continued)*

Capacity available is calculated by multiplying actual hours available by the historical utilization rate and by the historical efficiency. Calculations for capacity available are presented in Exhibit 14.17.

EXHIBIT 14.17   Capacity Available on 2440 Line

Unit	Actual Hours Available	Historical Utilization	Historical Efficiency	Capacity (Standard Hours) Available
Cutting	40	0.93	0.95	35.34
Forming	40	0.93	0.95	35.34
Grid assembly	80	0.93	0.95	70.68
Welding	40	0.93	0.95	35.34
Assembly	40	0.93	0.95	35.34

Exhibit 14.18 provides the completed rough-cut capacity plan, which compares required capacity to available capacity for the 2440 line.

EXHIBIT 14.18   Rough-Cut Capacity Plan for 2440

Unit	Week 1	2	3	4	5	6	7	8	9	10
Cutting										
Required	24.3	27	28.35	26.55	22.05	20.7	22.5	16.65	22.95	18.9
Available	35.34	35.34	35.34	35.34	35.34	35.34	35.34	35.34	35.34	35.34
Forming										
Required	32.4	36	37.8	35.4	29.4	27.6	30	22.2	30.6	25.2
Available	35.34	35.34	35.34	35.34	35.34	35.34	35.34	35.34	35.34	35.34
Grid assembly										
Required	40.5	45	47.25	44.25	36.75	34.5	37.5	27.75	38.25	31.5
Available	70.68	70.68	70.68	70.68	70.68	70.68	70.68	70.68	70.68	70.68
Welding										
Required	35.1	39	40.95	38.35	31.85	29.9	32.5	24.05	33.15	27.3
Available	35.34	35.34	35.34	35.34	35.34	35.34	35.34	35.34	35.34	35.34
Assembly										
Required	21.6	24	25.2	23.6	19.6	18.4	20	14.8	20.4	16.8
Available	35.34	35.34	35.34	35.34	35.34	35.34	35.34	35.34	35.34	35.34

Excel Tutor 14.3 provides guidance for developing rough-cut capacity planning logic in a spreadsheet environment.

Rough-cut capacity planning is frequently used as a tool to ensure the master production schedule is feasible. Its analysis is quick but inaccurate. First, it ignores on-hand inventory, which would reduce the required capacity. Second, it ignores the possibility that actual production might not take place during the week the master production schedule shows the end product to be due.

A more detailed and accurate approach to capacity planning in a manufacturing environment is known as capacity requirements planning. **Capacity requirements planning (CRP)** is somewhat analogous to material requirements planning (MRP). It is completed at the component level rather than at the end-item level, using MRP planned order releases. CRP logic is similar to that of rough-cut capacity planning, but rather than using MPS demand data, it uses the planned order releases from MRP. Rather than bills of capacity, it uses the actual component routing data directly.

capacity requirements planning (CRP)
A detailed capacity planning approach in manufacturing that uses the planned releases from MRP to provide the quantity of units that must be produced.

Step-by-Step: Capacity Requirements Planning

1. Using MRP logic, compute the planned order releases for all components.

2. For each department or work station, identify the components that will utilize that work station.

3. Compute required capacity for the department or work station by multiplying the quantity of a component (from the planned order releases of MRP) by the time required per unit on that work station. Do this for each week, using the appropriate planned order release. Do this for each component utilizing that work station.

4. Compute the total capacity required on a work station for a given week by summing the time required for each of the components using it.

Example 14.4 demonstrates CRP logic.

Example 14.4

Capacity Requirements Planning Calculations

EXCEL TUTOR

A small fly rod manufacturer just implemented an MRP system to assist in managing its inventories. Its processes are quite simple, but it wishes to utilize the planned order releases from MRP to help plan for capacity. The processes are organized functionally and consist of three departments. The first department is handle assembly, where the rod blank is cemented into the handle and reel seat. The second department is the wrapping department, where guides are attached to the blank in a thread-wrapping process. The third is finishing, where an epoxy resin is used to coat the thread wraps and where decals are added. Exhibit 14.19 provides the product structure for the 9-foot 5-weight rod. The owner wishes to use the planned order releases from the new MRP system to compute capacity requirements for the three departments. In this experimental run, only one rod model is used for the sample calculations.

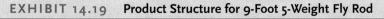

EXHIBIT 14.19   Product Structure for 9-Foot 5-Weight Fly Rod

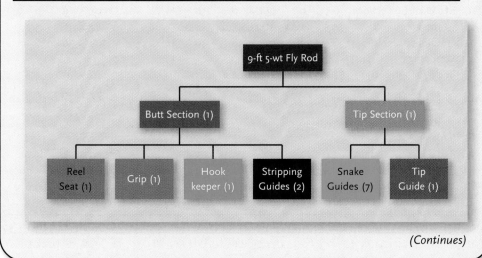

(Continues)

Example 14.4 *(Continued)*

Solution

The MRP logic generated the planned order releases seen in Exhibit 14.20.

EXHIBIT 14.20   Planned Order Releases for 9-Foot 5-Weight Fly Rod

					Week					
	1	2	3	4	5	6	7	8	9	10
Butt section	45	21	26	42	35	39	42	36	50	48
Tip section	45	21	26	42	35	39	42	36	50	48

Since all bottom-level components are purchased (guides, blanks, reel seats, and grips), only the assembly of the two sections requires capacity. The routings for the two sections are presented in Exhibit 14.21.

EXHIBIT 14.21   Routings for Fly Rod Components

	Handle Assembly	Wrapping (hours/unit)	Finishing (hours/unit)
Butt section	0.12	0.1	0.08
Tip section	0	0.25	0.12

By multiplying the quantity of each section from the MRP logic by the time per unit on each work center as given by the component routings, the requirements presented in Exhibit 14.22 were generated. Available capacity was calculated exactly as was done in Example 14.3, by multiplying actual hours by historical utilization and efficiencies.

Excel Tutor 14.4 demonstrates the capacity requirements planning method in Excel.

EXHIBIT 14.22   Capacity Requirements Plan for Fly Rod Production

					Week					
	1	2	3	4	5	6	7	8	9	10
Handle Assembly										
Req'd for butt section	5.4	2.52	3.12	5.04	4.2	4.68	5.04	4.32	6	5.76
Req'd for tip section	0	0	0	0	0	0	0	0	0	0
Total required	5.4	2.52	3.12	5.04	4.2	4.68	5.04	4.32	6	5.76
Total available	36	36	36	36	36	36	36	36	36	36
Wrapping										
Req'd for butt section	4.5	2.1	2.6	4.2	3.5	3.9	4.2	3.6	5	4.8
Req'd for tip section	11.25	5.25	6.5	10.5	8.75	9.75	10.5	9	12.5	12
Total required	15.75	7.35	9.1	14.7	12.25	13.65	14.7	12.6	17.5	16.8
Total available	36	36	36	36	36	36	36	36	36	36
Finishing										
Req'd for butt section	3.6	1.68	2.08	3.36	2.8	3.12	3.36	2.88	4	3.84
Req'd for tip section	5.4	2.52	3.12	5.04	4.2	4.68	5.04	4.32	6	5.76
Total required	9	4.2	5.2	8.4	7	7.8	8.4	7.2	10	9.6
Total available	36	36	36	36	36	36	36	36	36	36

Generic Manufacturing Planning and Control System	EXHIBIT 14.23

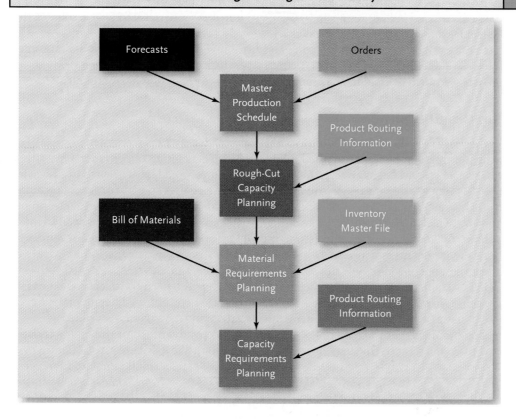

The capacity requirements planning method has two advantages over the rough-cut capacity planning method. Since the demand is derived from MRP planned order releases, inventory on hand is taken into account. In addition, timing more accurately reflects when the production will take place, because the lead times are taken into account in MRP logic.

Exhibit 14.23 shows the relationships between material and capacity planning functions within a generic production planning and control system.

Manufacturing production planning and control systems integrate materials planning and capacity planning. While rough-cut capacity planning is used to validate the feasibility of the master production schedule, the role of CRP is to provide a more accurate comparison of available capacity and required capacity to help guide the actual execution of production orders.

During the execution of manufacturing orders, when the required work is being done, actual output levels are compared to plans and adjustments are made to ensure that output levels match the needs.

The Demand–Capacity Match in Services

Capacity management in services differs greatly from that in manufacturing, primarily because the load on capacity cannot be leveled by inventory buffering. The emphasis is on smoothing demand in an attempt to smooth the load on capacity.

Many services adopt simple approaches to smoothing demand. These approaches include appointments or reservations. Appointments are generally required for professional services, such as legal and medical services, where the professional's time is the capacity constraint. Reservations are typically required when space is the critical resource. Other services have developed pricing strategies to level demand. Weekday specials, weekend specials, and early-bird specials are used by different services to shift demand from traditionally high-demand

For some airports, air passenger traffic is expected to double between 2005 and 2010.

periods to times when demand is low. For many of these services, much of the operating cost is fixed, so costs remain high even during low-demand times. Turning away customers during high-demand periods results in lost sales, so it makes sense to try to recoup some of that demand, even if the revenue generated is low.

Services that have high fixed costs and little marginal cost for additional customers have developed more sophisticated approaches to leveling demand. One of these approaches, known as yield management, is discussed in the following section.

Yield Management

yield management
An approach used in capital-intensive services that attempts to obtain maximum revenues through differential pricing, reservation systems, and overbooking.

In the year 2003, the major U.S. airlines filled approximately 79 percent of their seats.[1] This is high utilization, but still indicated a huge revenue-generating opportunity. One-fifth of their capacity was idle. Increasing the use of this resource would have resulted in a huge impact on profit because it would result in very little increase in cost. For services characterized by high fixed costs but low variable costs for each additional customer served, a technique known as **yield management** provides an approach for matching demand to capacity. Hotels, airlines, car rental agencies, and resorts use yield management to maximize revenues. In those environments, any revenue lost from an empty seat, room, or car is lost forever. Even a small amount of additional sales adds to profitability because the cost associated with each individual customer is negligible. Yield management has also been considered as a means of leveling demand on health care facilities. Yield management utilizes different prices for different classes of fare, reservation systems, and overbooking to maximize revenues.

Yield management is a complex system that takes advantage of the characteristics of service markets to fill seats or rooms, recognizing that it is better to generate even a small amount of revenue from some capacity rather than let it go unused. When the customer base can be segmented into different classes, different prices can be identified for each class. A forecast of the demand at different prices is necessary to determine how many rooms or seats to sell at each price. Those who make reservations first receive the lowest prices. Prices can be adjusted during high-demand times to reduce demand or to shift demand to lower-demand times. Prices are also used to shift demand to different locations. Airlines, for example, take advantage of customers' willingness to drive to particular airports to get a lower airfare.

While the single empty seat on this flight might make it more pleasant for the passenger next to it, it also represents lost revenue. Since the additional passenger would add virtually no costs, any revenue gained through the sale of this seat would go directly to profitability. Yield management seeks to find that last passenger and fill this seat.

Overbooking

For services like airlines and hotels, reservations are used in an attempt to smooth demand on capacity. Despite reservations, a high no-show rate makes it necessary to overbook capacity. Overbooking means that the business takes more reservations than it has capacity for, with the assumption that some customers with reservations will not show up. In many situations, there is no cost to customers who fail to show. Many airline customers, for example, book seats on several flights because they don't know for sure which one they'll need. Then they either cancel at the last minute or just fail to show. In recent years, airlines have implemented a nonrefundable ticket policy for discount fares to discourage this behavior.

The empty seat or room created by the no-show results in a substantial opportunity loss if other customers are turned away. There are always trade-offs, however. If seats are overbooked on a plane and everyone shows up, someone is left off the plane. "Bumping" or "walking" a customer happens whenever too many customers show up. The U.S. Department of Transportation provides specific regulations regarding the overbooking policies airlines use.

Overbooking is used to generate revenue from the empty rooms or seats created by the no-shows. It isn't as simple as just booking too many customers, however, because in addition to the costs associated with an empty room or seat, there are costs associated with turning customers away when more customers are overbooked than the space created by no-shows. The appropriate number to overbook is calculated by examining all possible outcomes related to different numbers of no-shows and selecting an overbooking strategy that minimizes the expected loss associated with no-shows. The number of overbookings that results in a "lowest expected loss" must be forecast. We know that forecasts tend to be wrong. Some forecasts are more wrong than others. In the overbooking problem, we examine past no-show records to identify the probabilities associated with different no-show rates. Since we know the costs associated with no-shows, and we know the costs associated with "bumping" customers when too many have been overbooked, we can compute the expected costs of different strategies.

om ADVANTAGE   Making Overbooking a Win – Win Situation

Overbooking, or, from the customer's perspective, "being bumped," is nowhere more abhorred than in the airline industry. Industry data kept by the U.S. Department of Transportation Air Travel Consumer Report shows an average of 0.70 per 10,000 customers in the third quarter of 2003 were bumped. For individual airlines this statistic ranged from 0.0 to 6.32. Overbooking in the airline industry is a necessary evil. No-shows are common, despite the "no-refund" policies for discounted tickets. Full-fare tickets are still purchased by enough travelers to make no-shows (and the potential for turning down a passenger who could have filled that seat) a distinct possibility.

Bumps can be avoided if passengers volunteer to take a later flight. The trick is to offer incentives to encourage passengers to volunteer. Airlines are legally obligated only to find the passenger accommodation on the next available flight. If the flight is the last one for the day, they must provide overnight lodging and meals. They are under no obligation to provide other reimbursements.

In 1999, Delta Air Lines had the worst bump statistics in the industry with 15,607 involuntary denied boardings, 1.53 per 10,000 passengers. That was nearly double the industry average of 0.88. In 2000 the airline had improved its performance to only 3,327 people, 0.33 per 10,000 passengers, and less than half of the industry average. How did it make such a dramatic turnaround? Delta adopted a flexible program called "Delta Dollars." The Delta Dollars program gives gate agents the authority and flexibility to offer from $250 to $1,000 as an incentive for volunteers to give up their seats. Rather than offer a fixed amount, as is done by some competitors, Delta can stage a sort of reverse auction, raising the incentive until someone takes advantage of it, eventually opening enough seats. The result is that each person relinquishing a seat can get up to $1,000 toward a future flight.

Source: "Not All Bumps Painful," *Cincinnati Enquirer*, May 20, 2001, pp. D1, D4; "Delta On-Time Record Still Poor," *Cincinnati Enquirer*, March 10, 2001, p. C1; "Air Travel Consumer Report," January 2004, http://airconsumer.ost.dot.gov.

Step-by-Step: Determining the Low-Cost Overbooking Policy

1. Determine the probability of each no-show condition by calculating the percentage of the time each no-show condition occurs.

2. Determine the cost of walking or bumping a customer and the opportunity cost or loss of a vacant room or seat.

3. Identify an overbooking policy to evaluate. For each possible no-show condition, evaluate the number of empty rooms (or seats) or the number of walked (or bumped) customers. For a condition that results in an empty room, calculate the expected cost of that condition by multiplying the number of empty rooms created by the cost per empty room by the probability that it would happen. For a condition that results in a bumped customer, calculate the expected cost of that condition by multiplying the number of customers bumped by the cost per bumped customer by the probability that it would happen. The total cost of the plan being evaluated will be the sum of all the bumping and empty room costs.

4. Repeat this process for any overbooking policies being evaluated. The low-cost policy will be the one with the lowest sum of bumping and empty room costs.

Example 14.5 demonstrates the process of determining the overbooking strategy with the lowest expected cost.

Example 14.5 EXCEL TUTOR

Overbooking

Rainbow Canyon Lodge management recognized that there was an increase in the number of no-shows during the past two years. They suspect that several hotels recently built in the area are causing this: When customers with reservations arrive at the canyon, some decide to stay at the newer hotels. Over the past year, no-shows averaged 1.2 per day. Actual no-show records are presented in Exhibit 14.24. Rainbow Canyon Lodge is in the heart of a major tourist area and has a very high occupancy rate. Management calculated the cost of a no-show to be $89. They made reciprocal arrangements with several hotels to take customers who are "bumped" from Rainbow Canyon Lodge. Management calculated the cost of lost goodwill plus the cost of the alternative lodging to be $110 per customer bumped.

EXHIBIT 14.24	No-Show History for Rainbow Canyon Lodge	
Number of No-Shows	**Frequency**	**Probability**
0	152	0.42
1	88	0.24
2	55	0.15
3	39	0.11
4	26	0.07
5	5	0.01

An average no-show rate of 1.2, with a cost per no-show of $89, results in an expected no-show loss of $106.80 per day, or $38,982 per year. Management wishes to develop a lowest expected loss overbooking strategy.

(Continues)

Example 14.5

(Continued)

Solution

Exhibit 14.25 provides the expected opportunity costs associated with the probabilities of each no-show quantity if the reservations were overbooked by one. The expected opportunity cost for each number of no-shows is computed by multiplying the number of no-shows remaining after overbooking by one by the cost per no-show. The expected cost of bumping is computed by multiplying the number of customers bumped in each no-show scenario by the bumping cost. In Exhibit 14.25, the only scenario that can result in a customer being bumped is if there are zero no-shows. The total expected loss when overbooking by one would be $101.38 per night ($37,003.70 per year). This would present an expected annual savings of $8,475.30 over the current practice of not overbooking.

EXHIBIT 14.25	Expected Costs of Overbooking by One			
Number of No-Shows	Probability	Number of Empty Rooms	Expected Opportunity Cost ($)	Expected Bumping Cost ($)
0	0.42	0	0.42(0) = 0	46.20
1	0.24	0	0.24(0) = 0	0
2	0.15	1	0.15(89) = 13.35	0
3	0.11	2	0.11(178) = 19.58	0
4	0.07	3	0.07(267) = 18.69	0
5	0.01	4	0.01(356) = 3.56	0
Sum			$55.18	$46.20
Total expected cost		$101.38		

Exhibit 14.26 provides the expected loss associated with a policy of overbooking by two each day. Expected losses per night are $143.72, substantially higher than overbooking by one. Overbooking by greater numbers would increase the expected loss. The best policy would be to overbook by one.

EXHIBIT 14.26	Expected Costs of Overbooking by Two			
Number of No-Shows	Probability	Expected Number of Empty Rooms	Expected Opportunity Cost ($)	Bumping Cost ($)
0	0.42	0	0.42(0) = 0	92.40
1	0.24	0	0.24(0) = 0	26.40
2	0.15	0	0.15(0) = 0	0
3	0.11	1	0.11(89) = 9.79	0
4	0.07	2	0.07(178) = 12.46	0
5	0.01	3	0.01(267) = 2.67	0
Sum			$24.92	$118.80
Total expected cost		$143.72		

Excel Tutor 14.5 shows the spreadsheet logic required to complete an overbooking problem.

Overbooking is an automatic quality failure for any customer bumped. Any company overbooking must recognize this and have a recovery policy in place. In many cases, the bumped customer receives a benefit that results in enhanced value. For airline passengers, compensation in the form of a voucher is generally provided. In the hospitality and lodging industries, the accommodation that is provided is often better than the customer would have had if he had not been bumped.

Current Trends in Capacity Management

In today's quickly changing markets, firms need to be flexible enough to adapt to changes in customer needs, technologies, and competitors. For many manufacturers and services, this means that they cannot commit to permanent levels of resources. As a result, many resources are now available on a contingent basis. Employment agencies provide temporary workers to businesses that do not want to incur hiring and layoff costs that would be necessary given their demand fluctuations. Manufacturers often utilize contract manufacturers so they do not have to invest in production equipment that may soon be made obsolete by product advancements. They may even outsource basic components to eliminate the need to manufacture them themselves.

Contingent arrangements add to a firm's agility, but they can also have negative effects. Contingent workers can be the source of quality problems and dissatisfaction, particularly if they receive lower pay and benefits than their permanent cohorts. Contract manufacturing can be less reliable than in-house production and result in poor delivery

---

om ADVANTAGE   What Should Happen to Employees When Demand Drops Suddenly?

As the technology markets turned down in late 2000, many technology-oriented companies found themselves with excess staff. Most were laid off. As the economy continued to slump, and then tried to cope with the aftermath of September 11, 2001, other segments of the U.S. economy took dramatic downturns. Travel-related industries, in particular, saw huge drops in demand. In the 30 days following September 11, companies announced the following anticipated layoffs:

Boeing	30,000
Cessna Aircraft	11,200
Raytheon	9,200
American Airlines	20,000
Bombardier Aerospace	4,100
United Airlines	20,000
Honeywell International	15,800
Continental Airlines	12,000
US Airways	11,000
Northwest Airlines	10,000
Advanced Micro Devices	2,300
Excite@Home	500

Many firms were accused of being unpatriotic by laying off workers, since layoffs would hurt an already staggering

economy. On the other hand, CEOs responded that carrying workers who weren't needed would do financial harm to the firm, reducing its value, which would have a worse impact on the economy. Although most companies lay off workers when they need to, some executives adopt a "no-layoff" policy.

Executives who refuse to lay off employees argue that this policy results in fierce loyalty, higher productivity from reduced turnover, higher levels of customer satisfaction, ability to recruit better employees, and greater innovation capability when the economy snaps back. The costs of layoffs can include severance and rehiring costs, lawsuits, loss of institutional memory, reduced trust in management, a lower-quality workforce when the economy recovers, and survivors who are risk-averse and paranoid.

The costs of layoffs and the benefits of avoiding them have begun to sink in. Many companies, even those that may ultimately lay off employees, have begun to cut costs elsewhere first, and make employee layoffs the last place to look for cost reduction.

Source: "Where Layoffs Are a Last Resort," *BusinessWeek*, October 8, 2001, p. 42; "Is It Unpatriotic to Lay Off Workers When the Nation Faces a Crisis?" *Wall Street Journal*, October 2, 2001, pp. B1, B4; "Wichita: Not So Far from Ground Zero," *BusinessWeek*, October 8, 2001, p. 66.

performance and slower response. Transportation time can add significantly to the cash-to-cash cycle. For all capacity decisions, just like other operations decisions, trade-offs must be made. Inherent in these trade-offs are quantifiable *and* nonquantifiable costs.

CHAPTER SUMMARY

The matching of capacity and demand is one of the most difficult challenges facing business managers. Failure to have sufficient capacity can result in missed sales and dissatisfied customers. At best, customers come back later; at worst, they will try the competition and never return. The answer isn't necessarily to load up with more capacity to prevent this from happening, because too much capacity brings its own problems. Idle capacity results in poor return on assets and higher costs that result in lower profitability. Any mismatch, in fact, can have devastating profitability implications. A key to managing capacity is to identify the amount of protective capacity needed and properly use the alternatives available for modifying either capacity or demand to create a balance that provides sufficient financial return on resources *and* yields the flexibility, quick response, and good service so critical to customers.

This chapter explored several techniques to match capacity and demand. Traditional manufacturing-oriented approaches to capacity planning, known as rough-cut capacity planning and capacity requirements planning, form a critical part of material requirements planning systems. Services, in a difficult situation because services cannot be stored as inventory, utilize other techniques such as yield management and overbooking in an attempt to shift demand to meet available capacity. In all situations, the ability to meet the demand with the required quantity and in the required time frame characterizes the objectives of capacity management.

KEY TERMS

aggregate demand, 620
backlog, 613
best operating level, 614
bill of capacity, 625
bottleneck, 616
capacity requirements planning (CRP), 629
constraint, 616

constraint management, 616
demand chase, 620
design capacity, 614
level production, 623
rough-cut capacity planning, 626
yield management, 632

SOLVED PROBLEMS

1. Demand Chase Aggregate Planning

Using the following demand forecast for four quarters, construct a demand chase aggregate plan and determine the plan's cost.

Quarter	1	2	3	4
Demand Forecast	3,062	4,230	2,660	3,310

Assume that there are currently 10 employees. Hiring and firing costs are $450 and $520, respectively. Each unit requires 1.75 hours of labor to complete. Each quarter consists of 67 workdays, and each employee works 8 hours per day.

Demand Chase Calculations

Step	Objective	Explanation
1.	Convert the demand per quarter to required labor hours per quarter by multiplying the number of units by the hours required per unit.	(see table below)

Quarter	1	2	3	4
Demand forecast	3,062	4,230	2,660	3,310
Hours/quarter	5,358.5	7,402.5	4,655.0	5,792.5

Step	Objective
2.	Convert required hours/quarter to required hours/day by dividing each by the number of days in the quarter.

Quarter	1	2	3	4
Demand forecast	3,062	4,230	2,660	3,310
Hours/quarter	5,358.5	7,402.5	4,655.0	5,792.5
Hours/day	80.0	110.5	69.5	86.5

Step	Objective
3.	Convert the required hours/day to the required number of employees by dividing the hours/day by 8. Then round up.

Quarter	1	2	3	4
Demand forecast	3,062	4,230	2,660	3,310
Hours/quarter	5,358.5	7,402.5	4,655.0	5,792.5
Hours/day	80.0	110.5	69.5	86.5
Employees required	10.0	13.8	8.7	10.8
Round up	10	14	9	11

Step	Objective
4.	Determine the number of hires and fires needed to staff each quarter.

Quarter	1	2	3	4	Total
Hires	0	4	0	2	6
Fires	0	0	5	0	5

Step	Objective	Explanation
5.	Calculate the costs.	Hiring: 6 × $450 = $2,700 Firing: 5 × $520 = $2,600 Total cost = $5,300

2. Level Production

Using the information provided in the previous problem, construct a level production aggregate plan. Compute the costs of the plan, assuming inventory carrying costs are $32 per unit per quarter.

Level Production Calculations

Step	Objective
1.	Determine the total demand and total number of days for the year.

	1	2	3	4	Total
Forecast	3,062	4,230	2,660	3,310	13,262
Days/quarter	67	67	67	67	268

Step	Objective	Explanation
2.	Determine the required number of units that must be produced per day by dividing total demand by total days.	13,262/268 = 49.485 Round up to 50 units per day
3.	Convert the units required per day to	50 × 1.75 = 87.5

labor hours required per day by multiplying units required per day by the number of hours required per unit.				
4. Convert hours required per day to the number of employees needed by dividing by 8.	$87.5/8 = 10.938$ Round up to 11 employees needed			

5. Determine the production that will result from the 11 employees.

Quarter	1	2	3	4
Forecast	3,062	4,230	2,660	3,310
Production	3,369	3,369	3,369	3,369

6. Compute the inventory levels and the average inventory for each period. When inventory goes negative (a backorder) treat it as a zero for calculating the average.

Quarter	1	2	3	4
Forecast	3,062	4,230	2,660	3,310
Production	3,369	3,369	3,369	3,369
Beginning inventory	0	307	−554	155
Ending inventory	307	−554	155	214
Average inventory	153.5	153.5	77.5	184.5

7. Compute the costs by multiplying the average inventory level for each quarter by the $32 carrying cost per unit per quarter.

Average inventory	153.5	153.5	77.5	184.5	Total
Cost	$4,912	$4,912	$2,480	$5,904	$18,208

3. Rough-Cut Capacity Planning

The master production schedule and bill of capacity for a leather cell phone cover are provided below.

MPS

Week	1	2	3	4	5	6
Production	2,500	3,600	4,250	4,000	3,500	3,100

Capacity Bill

Work Center	Time Required (hours)
Cutting	.02
Stitching	.03
Inspection	.005

Cutting and inspection each operate 40 hours per week. Stitching operates 80 hours per week. Each work center operates with 96 percent utilization and 99 percent efficiency. Create a rough-cut capacity plan for each work center.

Rough-Cut Capacity Plan Calculations

Step	Objective	Explanation
1.	Compute the time required at each work center by multiplying the number of units by the time required for each unit.	(see table below)

Week	1	2	3	4	5	6
Cutting required	50	72	85	80	70	62
Stitching required	75	108	127.5	120	105	93
Inspection required	12.5	18	21.25	20	17.5	15.5

2. Compute the available capacity by multiplying the hours available by the utilization and efficiency.

Workstation	Operating Hours	Utilization	Efficiency	Hours Available
Cutting	40	0.96	0.99	38.016
Stitching	80	0.96	0.99	76.032
Inspection	40	0.96	0.99	38.016

3. Assemble the table to compare required and available hours.

Week	1	2	3	4	5	6
Cutting						
Required	50	72	85	80	70	62
Available	38.016	38.016	38.016	38.016	38.016	38.016
Stitching						
Required	75	108	127.5	120	105	93
Available	76.032	76.032	76.032	76.032	76.032	76.032
Inspection						
Required	12.5	18	21.25	20	17.5	15.5
Available	38.016	38.016	38.016	38.016	38.016	38.016

4. Capacity Requirements Planning

The planned order releases for three manufactured components and routing times (in hours) for three critical workstations are presented below.

Planned Order Releases from MRP

	Week 1	Week 2	Week 3	Week 4	Week 5	Week 6
A100	1,000	2,300	2,200	2,000	0	0
A200	2,000	1,400	1,100	2,300	2,200	0
B76	0	0	300	210	1,400	1,600

Routing Times

Component	Stamping (hours)	Polishing(hours)	Plating(hours)
A100	0.01	0.04	0
A200	0.015	0.04	0.02
B76	0.02	0	0.03

Work center information is summarized as:

Work Center	Operating Hours	Utilization	Efficiency
Stamping	80	0.94	0.96
Polishing	80	0.92	0.93
Plating	80	0.88	0.9

Complete a capacity requirements plan (CRP) for each work center for the six-week time horizon.

Step	Objective	Explanation
1.	Compute required capacity, by week, for each work center. Multiply the MPS quantity by the time per unit for each of the three components, for each of the three workcenters. Sum the requirements from the three products for each work center to get the total required.	(see tables below)

Stamping Required

	1	2	3	4	5	6
A100	10	23	22	20	0	0
A200	30	21	16.5	34.5	33	0
B76	0	0	6	4.2	28	32
Total	40	44	44.5	58.7	61	32

Polishing Required

	1	2	3	4	5	6
A100	40	92	88	80	0	0
A200	80	56	44	92	88	0
B76	0	0	0	0	0	0
Total	120	148	132	172	88	0

Plating Required

	1	2	3	4	5	6
A100	0	0	0	0	0	0
A200	40	28	22	46	44	0
B76	0	0	9	6.3	42	48
Total	40	28	31	52.3	86	48

Step	Objective
2.	Compute the available capacity for each work center by multiplying the actual hours by the utilization and efficiency.

	ACTUAL HOURS	UTILIZATION	EFFICIENCY	AVAILABLE
Stamping	80	0.94	0.96	72.192
Polishing	80	0.92	0.93	68.448
Plating	80	0.88	0.9	63.36

Step	Objective
3.	Compare the required to the available.

Week	1	2	3	4	5	6
Stamping						
Required	40	44	44.5	58.7	61	32
Available	72.192	72.192	72.192	72.192	72.192	72.192
Polishing						
Required	120	148	132	172	88	0
Available	68.448	68.448	68.448	68.448	68.448	68.448
Plating						
Required	40	28	31	52.3	86	48
Available	63.36	63.36	63.36	63.36	63.36	63.36

5. Overbooking

A small hotel near campus has collected the following 100-night history of no shows:

No-Shows	Frequency
0	19
1	27
2	22
3	16
4	12
5	4

With a bumping cost of $120 and an empty room cost of $85, compute the expected cost of overbooking by 2.

Step	Objective	Explanation		
1.	Convert the no-show data into probabilities.	**No-Shows**	**Frequency**	**Probability**

No-Shows	Frequency	Probability
0	19	0.19
1	27	0.27
2	22	0.22
3	16	0.16
4	12	0.12
5	4	0.04

2. Determine the expected cost of bumping and the cost of empty rooms for each possible no-show condition under a policy of overbooking by 2. Multiply the cost of a given no-show condition by the probability of that no-show condition to compute the expected cost. Sum to get the total.

No-Shows	Customers Bumped	Empty Rooms	Cost ($)	Probability	Expected Cost ($)
0	2	0	240	0.19	$45.60
1	1	0	120	0.27	$32.40
2	0	0	0	0.22	$ 0.00
3	0	1	85	0.16	$ 13.60
4	0	2	170	0.12	$20.40
5	0	3	255	0.04	$10.20
				Total Expected Cost =	$122.20

REVIEW QUESTIONS

1. What is meant by the term "capacity"?
2. How does capacity differ from capability?
3. Why is the management of capacity more difficult for services than for manufacturing?
4. How does capacity affect value in B2B and B2C transactions?
5. What is the relationship between capacity and response time, dependability, and flexibility?
6. What is protective capacity?
7. How does design capacity relate to costs?
8. What are the possible consequences when demand rate varies from design capacity?
9. What role does a bottleneck or constraint play in determining system performance?
10. Describe how time lost on a constraint is lost by the entire system and is lost forever.
11. Describe how an analogy of a weakest link in a chain can be used to describe productivity improvement in a constrained system.
12. What is supply chain capacity?
13. What is aggregate planning?
14. Compare the level production and demand chase aggregate planning strategies.
15. What are the relevant costs in the aggregate planning process?
16. What are the informational inputs to the detailed capacity planning process used in manufacturing?

17. What are the differences between rough-cut capacity planning and capacity requirements planning?

18. What is yield management? What types of services use it?

19. What is the objective of overbooking? Describe the process of determining how many customers to overbook.

DISCUSSION AND EXPLORATION

1. How is capacity measured at your college or university?

2. Identify a business system you are familiar with. Does it ever suffer from too little capacity? What are the value implications when its demand is greater than its capacity?

3. In the system you identified for the previous question, what is its constraint? How could the capacity of the constraint be increased?

4. Students must manage their own capacity when demands on their time increase. What techniques do you use to match your personal capacity to the demands placed on it?

PROBLEMS HM

Solutions to odd-numbered problems are located on the text's Online Center (http://mhhe.com/opsnow3e).

1. A manufacturer of molded fiberglass products uses a demand chase strategy for aggregate planning. A total of 14 labor hours are required per unit produced. There are currently 72 employees. Each quarter has 65 working days. Each employee works 8 hours per day. Use the demand data provided in the table below to determine the number of fires and hires required for each quarter. Determine the hiring and fire costs based on a hiring cost of $325 and a firing cost of $340.

Quarter	1	2	3	4
Demand	2,302	1,930	2,600	2,375

2. A custom furniture manufacturer is considering a demand chase strategy for matching labor to demand. The average unit takes 45 hours to complete. The manufacturer currently employs 13 artisans who work 8 hours per day. Assuming there are 65 days per quarter, use the demand below to develop a demand chase plan. Hiring cost is $250. Firing cost is $300.

Quarter	1	2	3	4
Demand	136	150	160	125

Complete the plan and determine its cost.

3. Time-Ticker Inc.'s workers handcraft watches for their customers. They use a demand chase aggregate planning approach, as shown below. The company's marketing department would like to run a promotion in month 3. The marketing department estimates that the promotion will generate an additional demand of 100 watches in that month. With a margin of $13, the promotion would generate a $1,300 increase in profit. There are 160 hours/worker/month, five labor hours per unit, and a current workforce of eight. Hiring costs are $200 and layoff costs are $175. Will the promotion generate enough revenue to cover the hiring and firing costs associated with the increase in production? The demand forecast below assumes no promotion in Month 3.

	Month					
	1	2	3	4	5	6
Demand forecast	250	285	300	250	250	220

4. Line Drive Co. makes baseball bats. Demand for the next six months is given in the table below. It takes 1.4 labor hours to complete a bat and Line Drive currently employs seven production workers, assuming 160 hours/worker/month. The hiring costs are $350, and the layoff costs are $275. Use the information given to create a demand chase aggregate plan. If Line Drive pays a $700 contract fee, an employment agency can lower the hiring costs to $290. Should Line Drive Co. use the employment agency?

Period	1	2	3	4	5	6
Demand forecast	800	1,050	1,400	1,800	760	590

5. A small manufacturer is constructing an aggregate plan for the next four quarters. The demand for its product is provided below. Each unit requires 4.5 hours of labor. Each employee works 8 hours per day.

a. What will the daily rate of production be for the level production plan?

b. What size workforce is necessary for a level production plan?

Quarter	Demand Forecast	Days/Quarter
1	6,509	65
2	6,824	65
3	6,282	65
4	4,825	65

6. A new manufacturing plant has recently received information from the corporate marketing division about projected sales for the year. The demand, by quarter, is below. Each unit requires 3.5 hours of labor. Each employee works 8 hours per day. There are 66 work days in each quarter.

a. What will the daily rate of production be? How many units will be produced each quarter?

b. What workforce size will be needed for a level production plan?

Quarter	Demand	Days/Quarter
1	5,900	66
2	7,000	66
3	7,100	66
4	5,600	66

7. Chase Services has the monthly demand given in the following table. Use that information to construct a level production aggregate plan. Each unit requires 3.6 hours of labor. Inventory carrying costs are $24 per unit per month. Each worker works 8 hours per day. How many workers should Chase employ? What is the cost of this plan? When computing actual production quantities, round fractional units down to the next lower integer.

	Period											
	1	2	3	4	5	6	7	8	9	10	11	12
Demand	810	920	960	868	1,050	962	1,138	950	974	740	876	1,010
Workdays	21	21	22	21	22	21	22	22	21	22	21	21

8. Alco Industries uses a level production aggregate planning strategy. Alco's monthly demand information is given below. Each unit requires 6.5 hours of labor to complete. The inventory carrying costs are $45 per unit per month. Assuming an 8-hour workday, construct the aggregate plan. How many workers will the company employ? How would your answer change if the company worked 21 days for the first six months and 20 days for the last six months? When computing actual production quantities, round fractional units down to the next lower integer.

Period

	1	2	3	4	5	6	7	8	9	10	11	12
Demand	2,210	2,096	2,229	2,205	2,120	1,832	2,280	2,298	3,200	1,910	2,210	2,202
Workdays	22	20	22	21	21	21	20	21	21	20	20	19

9. Buroni Construction would like to switch from a demand chase aggregate plan to a level production plan. The company believes that the money saved from eliminating the hiring and firing of workers will more than compensate for any inventory costs. Use the information given below to construct both models and decide which plan is more cost-effective. Assume in both cases that the needed number of workers for the first month are already employed.

Period

	1	2	3	4	5	6
Demand	810	910	1,010	1,060	894	896
Workdays	23	24	23	24	22	23
Hiring cost	700					
Layoff cost	650					
Hours/unit	4					
Inventory carrying cost		$6/period				

10. Product demand for the next four quarters is presented below. Each quarter has 65 workdays. It takes 20 hours of labor to produce each unit. Each employee works 8 hours per day. If overtime is used (above 8 hours), it costs an additional $5 per hour for labor ($100 more per unit). There are currently 140 units on hand. Backorders are considered unacceptable, so overtime will be used only in the amount necessary to prevent backorders. Inventory carrying costs are $20 per unit per quarter.

a. Construct a level production aggregate plan for this situation.
b. How many units must be produced in overtime to prevent the backorders?
c. What is the cost of the overtime required?

Quarter	1	2	3	4
Demand	7,960	9,150	8,920	7,510

11. Knightbridge Investments uses a hybrid aggregate planning strategy that consists of a level production plan, but adjusting the number of workers every 3 months. Use the information below to determine how many workers will be utilized during each of the three-month periods.

Period

	1	2	3	4	5	6
Demand	800	900	1,000	1,000	1,100	900
Workdays	22	21	22	23	22	23
Hour/unit		7				
Inventory carrying cost		5				
Hiring cost		900				

12. Cecil's Milling would like to determine the expected capacity requirement for its quality inspection department for the next 12 weeks. Each inspection takes 3 minutes. Use the master production schedule below to determine the capacity requirements (in hours) for the quality inspection station.

Week	1	2	3	4	5	6	7	8	9	10	11	12
MPS	1,000	1,150	1,240	1,200	1,300	1,020	980	1,200	1,400	1,250	1,280	1,020

13. Security Insurance has been short the staffing needed to process car accident claims. The average claim takes 2.4 hours, including travel time, to evaluate and document. Based on the previous three months, managers forecast the following claims will be filed over the next eight weeks:

Week	1	2	3	4	5	6	7	8
Expected claims	85	90	105	100	110	120	120	130

Determine the capacity required to complete the expected number of claims. If each staffer can work 45 hours per week, how many will be needed each week to meet demand?

14. The eight-week master production schedule for an office products company is presented below. One product, a 50-inch computer table, requires time on three work stations, as shown in the capacity bill below:

Week	1	2	3	4	5	6	7	8
MPS	40	45	48	42	56	59	48	44

Capacity Bill	
Cutting	8 minutes
Veneer and edging	16 minutes
Assembly	12 minutes

Use the MPS and capacity bill to determine required capacity (in hours) for each of the three work stations.

15. Sta-Soft Inc. produces and sells hand-crafted pillows. Its product undergoes a three-step process. There is one work center for both cutting and stuffing, with two work centers for sewing. Each work center operates on a 40-hour workweek. Demand is given for the next six weeks, along with information on the needed processes. Assuming that the utilization is 94 percent and the efficiency is 96 percent for all processes, create a rough-cut capacity plan.

Week	1	2	3	4	5	6
Pillow	65	72	74	71	77	75

Work Center	Time Required (hours)
Cutting	0.25
Stuffing	0.45
Sewing	0.85

16. Three Pigs Co. manufactures decorative bricks for new homes. A supplier provides sheets of artificial brick material; Three Pigs must cut, bevel, and finish each brick. The company averages 96 percent utilization and 98 percent efficiency for the work centers. It has 40 hours of available capacity for the first two work centers and 80 hours for finishing. Using the following information, construct a rough-cut capacity plan. Do any of the work centers need additional capacity?

Week	1	2	3	4	5	6
Bricks	150	165	159	167	164	174

Work Center	Time Required (minutes)
Cutting	0.10
Beveling	0.14
Finishing	0.48

17. In-Focus caters to the weekend photographer, specializing in camera supplies and film development. As an added service, the company allows customers to customize and personalize calendars. The calendars have become quite popular, with a first-period demand of 300, increasing by 10 percent for the next 5 periods (rounding up to the nearest whole number). The calendar production process requires scanning the needed photos, laying them out, and laminating the finished product. Using the following information, calculate a rough-cut capacity plan. Should the store add capacity to any of its work centers?

Work Center	Time Required (hours)	Actual Hours	Utilization	Efficiency
Scan	0.25	120	0.92	0.94
Layout	0.15	80	0.9	0.96
Laminate	0.35	160	0.87	0.82

18. Discount Frame.com is a mail-order frame shop that ships custom-cut frame components to hobbyists and artists within 48 hours of their order. One of the most commonly ordered frames, the components of which are kept in stock, is a frame for a 5 × 7 photo with a 1 1/2-inch matte. The frame kit goes through two work stations. The first, cutting, cuts the frame into its four mitered sections. The second, kit assembly, assembles the four frame sections, the connecting hardware, hangers, and spring clips. The cutting process takes 3.4 minutes per frame, no matter what the frame size. Kit assembly takes 1.2 minutes. Use the following planned order release table from Discount Frame's MRP system to determine required capacity for the cutting and kit assembly work stations.

Week	1	2	3	4	5	6	7	8
Planned order releases	210	185	190	164	159	172	184	197

19. EZ Sleeper is a contract manufacturer for a number of different well-known mattress companies. One product, a twin-size box spring, is identical from one customer to the next, with the exception of the fabric covering. The production process for the box spring is simple, consisting of frame assembly, flat spring attachment, and covering. Planned order releases for the EZ Sleeper mattress are presented below, as is the time required at each work station. Compute the required capacities for each.

Week	1	2	3	4	5	6	7	8	9	10
Planned order releases	420	460	445	480	410	430	390	425	460	520

Work Station	Time per Unit
Frame assembly	5.2 minutes
Flat spring attachment	1.3 minutes
Covering	2.4 minutes

20. Brite-Lights manufactures floor lamps. Each lamp consists of a base stand with two lamps at the top. Demand for the next six weeks for the floor lamps is 124, 126, 128,

132, 127, and 134. Planned order releases from Brite-Lights' material requirements plan is below:

	Week					
	1	2	3	4	5	6
Base	124	126	128	132	127	134
Lamp	248	252	256	264	254	268

Use the planned order release data and the following routing and work center information to construct a capacity requirements plan.

Work Center	Painting	Assembly	Finishing
Base	0.07	0.15	0.05
Lamp	0.09	0.2	0.1

Work Center	Actual Hours Available	Utilization	Efficiency
Painting	40	0.96	0.96
Assembly	80	0.98	0.98
Finishing	40	0.97	0.95

21. Paddock Packaging assembles all of the packing boxes for Next-Day Deliveries. The standard packing box is made up of a top and a bottom portion. Each portion passes through three work stations: laying out the necessary materials, assembling the pieces, and checking the quality of the finished product. Historically there have been 39 hours available at each of the work stations. Use the planned order release data and the following routing to construct a capacity requirements plan.

	Week					
	1	2	3	4	5	6
Top	200	215	209	232	216	204
Bottom	200	215	209	232	216	204

	Layout	Assembly	Quality
Top (minutes)	0.04	0.05	0.02
Bottom (minutes)	0.06	0.08	0.02

22. Home-style Hotel has the following no-show records. The cost per no-show is $65 and the cost of bumping a customer is $80. Calculate the expected opportunity costs and the expected cost of bumping if the hotel implements a system of overbooking by one.

Number of No-Shows	Frequency	Probability
0	89	0.34
1	75	0.29
2	59	0.22
3	24	0.09
4	14	0.05
5	2	0.01

23. Yen's Chinese Restaurant noticed a number of no-shows during its busy dinner hours on Friday nights. The cost for each no-show is $54, and the cost of bumping a customer to a later time is projected to be $92. Use the following no-show history to devise an overbooking plan. The restaurant would like to overbook by only one or two dinners. Which is the lower-cost plan?

Number of No-Shows	Frequency
0	119
1	64
2	76
3	35
4	27
5	14

24. Fly-Hi Airlines has historically had a problem with no-shows on its flights. The airline's cost per no-show is $76, and the cost per passenger bumped is $102. Use the no-show records given in the first table below to construct the cost of a policy of overbooking by one.

Number	Frequency
0	75
1	145
2	62
3	25
4	16
5	2

The airline is considering changing its reservation policy and expects the no-shows to drop to the values shown below. What happens to the cost of the no-show plan? Should the airline still employ a policy of overbooking?

Number	Frequency
0	165
1	79
2	57
3	17
4	7
5	0

25. The Lake Front Resort has never overbooked, but has experienced recent losses due to no-shows. Determine the expected cost of overbooking by two, given the following no-show history:

Number of No-Shows	Frequency
0	36
1	26
2	19
3	15
4	4

The projected cost of walking a customer is $300. The opportunity cost of an empty suite is $420.

26. No Frills Airline is evaluating its current overbooking policy. It's no-show probabilities, based on the past 200 flights, are presented below. No Frills has calculated the bumping cost as $300 per passenger bumped. The opportunity cost of a vacant seat resulting from a no-show is $420.

No-Shows	Probability
0	0.25
1	0.21
2	0.17
3	0.15
4	0.11
5	0.07
6	0.04

Determine the lowest cost overbooking plan.

27. The River Queen dinner theater provides a dinner and show while taking a three-hour cruise around the harbor. Each seat is typically sold out, so when no-shows do happen, the boat suffers an opportunity loss. Anyone bumped is given a coupon for one free ticket to be used in the future, valued at $125. The opportunity loss that results from an empty seat is calculated to be $90. Given the following no-show probabilities, determine the low-cost overbooking plan.

No-Shows	Probability
0	0.22
1	0.2
2	0.17
3	0.14
4	0.12
5	0.1
6	0.05

ADVANCED PROBLEMS

1. A processor is planning production in response to the following demand forecast for the next eight quarters:

Demand forecast

Q1	Q2	Q3	Q4	Q5	Q6	Q7	Q8
12,000	12,000	15,000	30,000	12,000	12,000	15,000	30,000

Regular production capacity is 18,000 units per quarter. Production cost is $500 per unit when produced using regular capacity. If needed, up to 3,600 units can be produced using overtime in a given quarter, at a cost of $750 per unit. Finally, up to 10,000 units can be subcontracted per quarter, at a cost of $800 per unit.

The goods can be produced ahead of time and stored in inventory until needed. Quarterly carrying cost is $50 per unit, and is charged against each quarter's ending inventory. The processor has storage capacity for up to 10,000 units, and quarterly ending inventory cannot exceed this amount. The processor also wants to keep quarterly ending planned inventory no lower than 2,000 units. Current inventory is 2,000 units.

a. Compute the level production quantity that will satisfy all demand and leave Q8 ending inventory at 2,000 units. Could this quantity be produced each quarter using only regular capacity (no overtime or subcontracting)? Is there sufficient storage capacity to implement this level production plan?

b. Compute production levels for each quarter using the chase demand strategy, producing in each quarter exactly the predicted demand quantity for that quarter. Use the lowest cost production alternatives to the greatest extent possible each quarter. (Regular capacity, then overtime, then subcontracting.) What is the total cost (production cost + inventory carrying cost) for the 8 quarter planning horizon under this strategy?

c. Find a production plan that uses some combination of anticipation inventory, overtime, and subcontracting to minimize the total production + carrying cost for the 8 quarter planning horizon. Your plan cannot exceed the production capacities for regular, overtime, or subcontracting during any quarter, and must maintain quarterly ending inventory levels between 2,000 and 10,000 units.

2. Phoenix Airlines Vice President for Sales, Eric Gustason, has been presented with a plan to increase loads on all flights. Currently, despite steady demand for tickets, Phoenix Air's flights push back from the gate with at least one empty seat. A recent study of weekly flights reveals the seriousness of the situation, more than 85 percent of flights fly with empty seats.

Number of No-Shows	Frequency
0	175
1	210
2	290
3	195
4	123
5	84
6	58
7	31
8	17
9	12
10	5

To address this issue, Eric has been considering the use of an overbooking strategy. To that end, a staff accountant has developed the opportunity ($350) and bumping ($125) costs associated with implementation of such a strategy. Eric must now present his plan to the CEO.

a. Under the current conditions, how many seats should Phoenix overbook and what is the cost?

b. After accepting the overbooking plan, the price of oil increases. This reduces opportunity cost ($265) and increases the cost to place the traveler on a different airline ($225). Under these conditions, how many seats should Phoenix overbook by and what is the cost?

c. In response to price changes in oil, Eric has developed a pricing strategy to reduce the number of no shows. A study of the plan's effects reveals the following:

Number of No-Shows	Frequency
0	227
1	280
2	241
3	169
4	146
5	72
6	47
7	16
8	2
9	0
10	0

Based on this data, what should the new overbooking strategy be and what is its cost?

d. The price of oil drops to normal levels resulting in resumption of normal opportunity and bumping costs. What is the impact of the new pricing strategy on overbooking in terms of number of overbooked seats and cost?

ENDNOTE

1. Bureau of Transportation Statistics, "Domestic Revenue Load Factors, Fourth Quarter 2003," www.bts.gov.

LEARNINGACTIVITIES   www.mhhe.com/opsnow3e

Visit the Online Learning Center (www.mhhe.com/opsnow3e) for additional resources. Content varies by chapter, and includes

- Business Tours
- OM on Site
- Readings
- Resources
- Excel Tutors

- Interactive Case Models
- Reel Operations Video Clips
- Additional Advanced Problems
- Self-Assessment Quizzes
- Glossary

SELECTED REFERENCES

Shapiro, J. F. *Modeling the Supply Chain*. Pacific Grove, CA: Duxbury, 2001.

Sipper, D., and Bulfin, R. *Production: Planning, Control and Integration*. New York: McGraw-Hill, 1997.

INTERACTIVE CASE 14.1

Trading Off Workers for Inventory at DuraGlass

The aggregate planning model solves an aggregate planning problem using two approaches: demand chase and level production. The primary input is the 12-month product demand in the first row of the table. In addition to modifying demand, the user can adjust sliding bars corresponding to inventory carrying costs and hiring/firing costs on a monthly basis, working days per month, working hours per day, and hours to produce one unit to see the impact on the total cost for each of the two plans.

DuraGlass manufactures 14 different designs of fiberglass hulls for small sailboats. Demand for DuraGlass hulls comes from several different boat manufacturers and is seasonal with the fiscal year starting July 1. DuraGlass production capacity is dictated by the number of molds they own and the number of laborers trained in the production process. They currently own enough molds to meet peak capacity, but fluctuate their workforce to match high and low demand periods. Sylvia Collins, the new operations manager, wants to improve their planning process and completes an analysis of their options by comparing a

Period	1	2	3	4	5	6	7	8	9	10	11	12	Totals
Demand	900	700	900	800	800	800	1300	1300	1100	1000	1000	800	11400
Demand Chase Strategy													
Hours req'd/day	315	245	315	280	280	280	455	455	385	350	350	280	31
Workers req'd/day	40	31	40	35	35	35	57	57	49	44	44	35	36
Hires req'd	0	0	9	0	0	0	22	0	0	0	0	0	
Fires req'd	0	9	0	5	0	0	0	0	8	5	0	9	
Hiring&firing cost($)	0	3780	4950	2100	0	0	12100	0	3360	2100	0	3780	$32,170
Level Production Strategy													
Monthly output	950	950	950	950	950	950	950	950	950	950	950	950	
Beginning inventory	0	50	300	350	500	650	800	450	100	-50	-100	-150	
Ending inventory	50	300	350	500	650	800	450	100	-50	-100	-150	0	
Average inventory	25	175	325	425	575	725	625	275	25	-75	-125	-75	
Carrying cost($)	275	1925	3575	4675	6325	7975	6875	3025	275	0	0	0	$34,925

Inventory carrying cost per month = $11   Firing cost = $420   Hiring cost = $550

◄ [____▮__] ►   ◄ [___▮___] ►   ◄ [___▮__] ► | Solve |

working days/month = 20   working hours/day/worker = 8   hours/unit = 7

◄|[_____] ►   ◄ [__▮___] ►   ◄ [__▮__] ► | Reset |

demand chase and a level production strategy. She knows that training is time-consuming and expensive, as are the outplacement services offered to employees who are laid off. She also knows that the large size of the hulls makes storing finished-goods inventory expensive as well. Sylvia has gathered the costs and capacity information presented below:

Inventory carrying cost/unit/month	$ 11
Working days/month	20
Hours/worker/day	8
Firing cost	$420
Hiring cost	$550
Hours/unit	7

Projected demand is:

Period	1	2	3	4	5	6	7	8	9	10	11	12
Demand	900	700	900	800	800	800	1,300	1,300	1,100	1,000	1,000	800

1. Make sure the start-up values for the aggregate planning model match the values above.

   a. Compare the costs of the demand chase and level production strategies. For each plan, describe where the costs come from.

   b. Given the current plans and their total costs, describe the relationship between inventory carrying costs and personnel (hiring and firing) costs.

   c. Despite the financial costs, what aspect of the level production strategy makes it an unattractive plan as it currently exists?

   d. The demand chase plan is a lower cost plan according to the calculations. Are there any nonfinancial costs to consider? What impact would they have if they could be quantified?

2. Suppose Sylvia identifies warehouse facilities that reduce the inventory carrying costs to $8 per month.

   a. What happens to the relative attractiveness of the two plans?

b. What happens to the relative attractiveness of the two plans if the production time per unit is reduced from seven to five hours? Explain why this results in a cost reduction for one plan but not the other.

3. Set the variables back to the start-up default values. Record the total cost for each plan.

a. The demand provided is a forecast, and we know that forecasts are often wrong. What effect on the two plans would occur if the demand for each month was actually 10 percent above the forecast demand? Why was the impact greater for one plan than the other?

b. Can you create a scenario in which a change in expected demand causes the financial attractiveness of the two plans to reverse?

INTERACTIVE CASE 14.2

Cutthroat Canyon Resort Battles No-Shows

The overbooking model provides a dynamic platform for experimentation with a typical overbooking scenario. In a hotel room overbooking context, the model allows the user to manipulate the three variables of overbooking policy (from 0 to 5): the vacant room cost, the bumping cost, and the probability of a given number of no-shows (0 to 5). Output for any trial overbooking policy shows the number of empty rooms and the number of customers bumped for any no-show condition, as well as expected costs and the total expected cost for the policy.

No-Shows	Probability
0	◀ ▶
1	◀ ▶
2	◀ ▶
3	◀ ▶
4	◀ ▶
5	◀ ▶

Overbooking by: 0   ◀   ▶

Vacant room cost: $80.0   ◀   ▶

Bumping cost: $110.0   ◀   ▶

Expected cost of the overbooking plan: 188.00

Number of No-Shows	Probability	Number of Empty Rooms	Number of Customers Bumped	Expected Opportunity Cost	Expected Bumping Cost
0	0.10	0	6	$0.00	$0.00
1	0.25	1	5	$20.00	$0.00
2	0.20	2	4	$32.00	$0.00
3	0.20	3	3	$48.00	$0.00
4	0.15	4	2	$48.00	$0.00
5	0.10	5	1	$40.00	$0.00
Sum				$188.00	$0.00

Developed by Accelet Corp.

Cutthroat Canyon Resort lies in a small canyon that runs perpendicular to the highway between Livingston and Gardner, Montana. It consists of a lodge with 18 rooms and 6 duplex cabins. Just down the road lies Yankee Jim Canyon and, beyond that, the north entrance to Yellowstone National Park. Like all resorts in the vicinity of Yellowstone, Cutthroat Canyon serves two types of customers. The first, and most desirable from a business standpoint, is the customer who makes reservations to stay at the resort because they enjoy the amenities the resort has to offer—its peace and quiet, its excellent food, and its small-stream trout fishing. These customers often return year after year and stay for four or five days. The other customers certainly add to the revenue stream, but are a more difficult lot to plan for. They are typically on their way to Yellowstone, pulling a monster RV, and find that when they arrive at the north entrance, the campgrounds are full. They quickly learn that the spaces that are not reserved are taken on a first-come, first-served basis in the early morning. So they stay at Cutthroat Canyon for a night, then drive down to the park early to stake a claim on a campsite. If they get one, they move on, if they don't, they try again the next day. Many reserve a room for several days, but if they find a campsite in Yellowstone, they cancel at the last minute. This often leaves Bonnie DePuy, the resort owner, with empty rooms after she has denied others who have called in requesting a reservation. Bonnie's niece, who is working at the resort for the summer, has suggested using an overbooking approach she learned in her operations management class at college. Bonnie is skeptical, but is willing to listen.

Bonnie has approached a large neighboring resort and has negotiated an agreement to use it as lodging for any customers she "bumps" at a cost of $110. She has determined that the opportunity cost for an empty room in her lodge is $80. Historical records from the past two summers provide 200 days of no-show data. That data is presented below and converted to probabilities.

Number of No-Shows	Frequency	Probability
0	20	10%
1	50	25%
2	40	20%
3	40	20%
4	30	15%
5	20	10%

1. Make sure the defaults are set to match the parameters above. Evaluate each possible overbooking policy and record your results.

   a. What is the expected cost per night of not overbooking at all?

   b. What is the low-cost overbooking policy, given Bonnie's vacant room and bumping costs?

   c. Under the low-cost policy, what is the expected cost of bumping customers? What is the expected cost of vacant rooms? What is the expected total cost?

   d. Create a graph with "cost" on the Y axis and "number overbooked" on the X axis. Graph the vacant room cost associated with each overbooking policy and the bumping cost associated with each overbooking policy. Describe the relationship between the two graphs.

   e. If Bonnie adopts the low-cost policy, what will be her daily expected savings over the current costs of not overbooking at all? What would she expect to save in the course of the 100-day season?

   f. What should she tell the neighboring resort in terms of the number of "bumped" customers to expect?

2. If Bonnie increases her room rental charges in the future, every dollar of increase would also increase the opportunity cost of a vacant room by the same amount.

a. Would it even be justified to change the policy to overbook by an additional person? How did you determine this?

3. Bonnie has learned that next summer the neighboring resort plans to decrease its costs to her by $20 per customer.

   a. If that happens, what should her overbooking policy be?

   b. What will the bumping costs have to be before they will result in a preferred policy of overbooking by one less person?

   c. Can the bumping cost be low enough to justify overbooking by one less person? Explain.

4. Suppose Bonnie increases her room rental to $130 and the neighbor decreases the bumping cost $20.

   a. What would the optimal overbooking policy be?

   b. What would be the total expected costs per day?

   c. What would be the expected costs associated with no overbooking?

APPLICATION CASE 14.1

Coping with the Rise and Fall of Yo-Yo Demand

A toy yo-yo manufacturer produces two different types of yo-yos: Yo-Yo Standard and Yo-Yo Custom. Yo-Yo Standard takes 5.0 minutes of labor to produce and makes up 40 percent of the total demand. Yo-Yo Custom takes 7.0 minutes and makes up 60 percent of the total demand. Tommy Lozano, director of manufacturing, wants to create an aggregate plan to help address the challenge of balancing capacity with demand. He needs to create a generic "yo-yo" upon which to base his plan.

The company works an 8-hour workday. The cost to hire and train a new employee is $600. The cost to lay off an employee is $400. It costs $3.00 to hold one yo-yo in inventory for a year.

1. Calculate a "generic" configuration yo-yo to use for aggregate planning.

2. Use the "generic" configuration yo-yo to compare a demand chase aggregate plan with a level production aggregate plan, given the following demand forecast for the "generic" configuration. There are no yo-yos in inventory at the beginning of the planning period. Seventeen workers are employed at the beginning of the planning period.

Month	Forecast	No. of workdays
J	26,500	21
F	28,250	20
M	26,500	23
A	27,500	20
M	30,500	23
J	31,000	21
J	31,000	20
A	28,000	23
S	31,000	20
O	34,000	22
N	35,000	20
D	30,000	19

3. Based on your cost calculations, which aggregate plan would you recommend?

4. What nonfinancial costs would you associate with each of the plans? Does consideration of nonfinancial costs change your recommendation? Explain.

APPLICATION CASE 14.2

Increasing Revenues at Bunks and Biscuits

Bunks and Biscuits began in 2004 when Linda and Roger Alvarez bought a small general store and 4 cabins just outside of the national park. One year later, a neighboring lot came up for sale and they borrowed to purchase it. They immediately began construction of 12 additional cabins. After a year of running the store, they converted it to a small restaurant that has become a favorite for its breakfasts and lunches. Linda and Roger learned an important lesson from their first summer's experience renting the 16 cabins. They learned that lodgers who make reservations for only one night often don't show. Lodgers who book more than two nights, however, almost always show up. This experience has taught them several things:

1. They need to give discounts to lodgers booking more than two nights.
2. They should separate their cabins into a group for long-term reservations and a separate set for short-term reservations.
3. It has convinced them that they need to overbook short-term stays.
4. Loss revenue from an empty room amounted to $78.

It turns out that single-night stays are usually short-notice reservations, while lodgers who stay longer tend to make reservations farther in advance. Linda and Roger decided that they will never overbook lodgers who reserve three nights or more. They also agreed that two-night reservations and single-night reservations were equal in terms of likelihood to not show.

Linda examined the records from last summer and found the following:

No-Shows	Frequency
0	37
1	48
2	13
3	2

Linda reached a mutual agreement with a neighbor, who also rents cabins, that they would provide "overflow" service for each other when either was overbooked. They figured that when an overbooking situation actually happened, it would be late in the day, and thus the chances were good that if a room was still empty at that time, the chances of it staying empty were pretty high. Both agreed that it probably made sense to offer a discount price to the other in the event of overflow. Linda and Roger will be charged $65 for every overflow customer they send to the neighbor.

1. What should the overbooking policy be for Bunks and Biscuits? How much will this save them over a 100-day season over their current practice of not overbooking?
2. If the proportion of long-term lodgers increases, what effect do you think it would have on their policy?
3. What should they do if the percentage of long-term lodgers decreases?
4. How might they modify their overbooking plan in a way that could adapt to changes in the proportion of short-term reservations?

CHAPTER 15

Constraint Management: Simplifying Complex Systems

LEARNING OBJECTIVES

- Define a constraint.

- Compare utilization and activation from a constraint management perspective.

- Describe the global measures of throughput, inventory, and operating expense, and compare them to traditional global measures.

- Explain the five-step focusing process of constraint management.

- Explain how systems can be protected from disruptions by using time buffers.

- Describe how time buffers function and how they affect the exploitation of a constraint.

- Explain what is meant by a constraint buffer, a shipping buffer, and an assembly buffer.

- Differentiate between a production batch and a transfer batch.

- Compute the appropriate product mix for a constrained production system.

- Compare the kanban system to the buffering system used in constraint management.

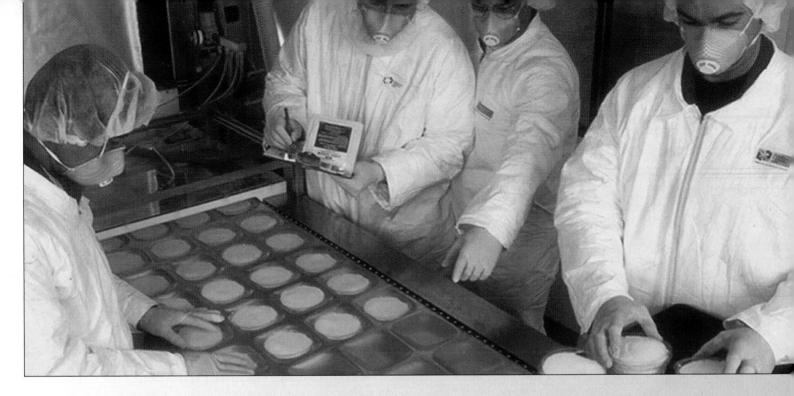

CONSTRAINT MANAGEMENT IN FOOD PROCESSING

Oregon Freeze Dry began in 1963 and has become the global leader in freeze drying technology. What began as drying fruit for breakfast cereals quickly expanded to contracts with the Department of Defense to develop military rations. By the early 1970s Oregon Freeze Dry was marketing its own brand, Mountain House, a line of freeze dried foods for recreational use. In the 1980s, Oregon Freeze Dry expanded into the manufacture of private label packaged food products and expanded its ingredient line. In the 1990s Oregon Freeze Dry moved into drying chemicals, pharmaceuticals, and biological materials. The Food Division of Oregon Freeze Dry is the largest food freeze dryer in the world. Its products range from hundreds of individual ingredients to fully prepared entrees in a variety of packaging options.

Freeze dried food goes through a straightforward set of processes. Fresh food is processed (wet processing) and is then "flash frozen" and subjected to a vacuum chamber, which removes moisture. The process removes water, reducing problems related to spoilage. As a result of removing moisture, 90 percent of the weight is removed, making it easier and cheaper to transport.

At Oregon Freeze Dry, food products move from a wet processing area to freezing, and then to drying. The drying process varies from 8 to as much as 50 hours, which results in variable product flows and a large amount of work-in-process inventory waiting in queue. The dryer is the constraint in the Oregon Freeze Dry process. Since freezing takes place before drying, and products move from freezing into drying, freezing acted as a queue for the drying process. The constraint at the drying process caused high levels of inventory to build up and created quality problems. In response to the problems, management implemented constraint management to help manage the processes and better control inventory.

Although the dryers were identified as the constrained resource, the freezers and dryers were treated as one entity. Initially, a schedule was created for the dryers, and the freezer schedule was designed to meet the dryer schedule. Oregon Freeze Dry no longer uses a freezer schedule. Material is now simply released to the freezer, which has sufficient capacity, and then flows into the dryers. Inventory buffers are maintained in front of the freezers to protect the dryers (the constraint) from ever running out of food to process. Material is released into the wet processing step only at the rate the dryer can process it. This prevents too much inventory from accumulating in front of the drying process and also stabilizes product flows. Stability of product flows makes it easier to schedule capacity and labor.

Source: Michael Umble and Elisabeth Umble, "Integrating Enterprise Resources Planning and Theory of Constraints: A Case Study," *Production and Inventory Management Journal*, Second Quarter 2001, pp. 43–48; http://www.ofd.com, July 4, 2004; Description by Oregon Freeze Dry Senior V.P. of Manufacturing, July 8, 2004.

onstraint management is often viewed as a focusing approach for productivity improvement efforts, but its role is so broad that its influence spans functional boundaries. Objectives of constraint management are more directly linked to profitability than some other integrative frameworks. Despite a controversial history, constraint management has a broad impact on resource decision making.

Introduction: Maximizing System Output

Unlike other integrative frameworks, which were developed by the contributions of many different people, the initial development of constraint management (CM) can be credited to one individual, Eliahu Goldratt. Goldratt, an Israeli physicist, is the author of the 1984 book *The Goal*.[1] A combination of a business novel and a love story, *The Goal* became extremely popular. It tells the story of a manufacturing plant manager trying to save an unprofitable plant from being closed down—an interesting tale about the importance of constraints in a business. Unlike most business paperbacks that claim a very brief period of fame, *The Goal* is still very popular. Despite its age, *The Goal* is still a frequent listing on *BusinessWeek*'s best-seller list.

Following the publication of *The Goal*, constraint management, or the theory of constraints, as it is also known, began to get increasing attention from managers. As a part of that increasing attention, numerous extensions and techniques were developed to help effectively manage constraints until a concise framework for managing resources evolved. The existence of this framework led to the inclusion of constraint management as the third integrative management framework in the Resource/Profit Model. The evolution of constraint management led to the proliferation of consulting firms specializing in helping businesses manage their constraints.

Defining a Constraint

constraint
Anything that inhibits a system's progress toward its goals.

A **constraint** is defined succinctly as anything that inhibits a system's progress toward its goals. Obviously, before a system's constraint can be identified, the system's goals must be understood. Placing the constraint in the context of system goals broadens the applicability of constraint management to include systems whose goals go beyond "profit" or "making money," as is the case for many business systems. Education and other not-for-profit systems are feasible applications for constraint management.

Defined as anything that inhibits a system's progress toward its goals, the role a constraint plays in any system becomes very important. The system's output, as measured by its goals, is limited by the constraint(s) of that system. A system's constraint can actually take many forms. It could be a resource, a policy, an input to the system, or some external force. For example, if one goal of your university is to graduate accounting majors, a lack of faculty or a lack of classroom space could be a constraint. A lack of applicants to enter the accounting program could be a constraint as well, but it might be a symptom of a policy constraint—not providing enough financial aid to students. Or it might be due to the fact that accounting firms are not currently recruiting or hiring students from your university, so students do not want to major in accounting.

constraint management
A framework for managing the constraints of a system in a way that maximizes the system's accomplishment of its goals.

Constraint management is a framework for managing the constraints of a system in a way that maximizes the system's accomplishment of its goals. The fact that it manages the most important part of the system, the part that determines its output, means that constraint management is actually a way of focusing on the most critical aspects of the system.

Simple Productive System with Constraint (minutes per unit)   EXHIBIT 15.1

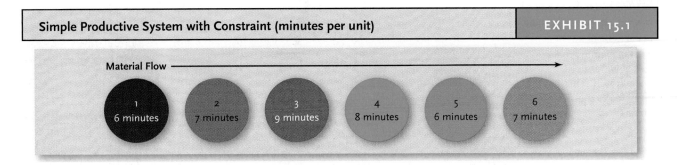

The role a constraint plays in a simple productive system is easily portrayed in an example. Exhibit 15.1 diagrams a simple production system. Suppose that we could sell every unit we produce in this system. Given a goal of producing as many units as possible, the system portrayed in Exhibit 15.1 is constrained by work center 3, which takes nine minutes per unit. The result is that a unit exits the system every nine minutes, despite shorter processing times by other work centers. The role of work center 3 goes beyond restricting the rate of output of the system. Work center 1, for example, could process a unit every six minutes, but close examination shows that it would not make sense for it to do that. Material would exit work center 1 at a rate of one unit every six minutes but would not be able to exit the system at that rate. A queue of inventory would build up in front of work centers 2 and 3, and it would grow indefinitely as long as the input rate exceeded the system's output rate. The logical approach would be to allow work center 1 to process one unit only every nine minutes, since any more than that would not increase the system's output.

The constraint in the system affects many performance measures. For example, it is commonplace to incorporate "utilization" as a measure of equipment productivity. We already know that utilizing work center 1 at a 100 percent level (processing one unit every six minutes) doesn't provide any more system output than utilizing it at a 66 percent level (producing one unit every nine minutes). This phenomenon is so important in the constraint management framework that two concepts, utilization and activation, have been redefined to help understand it. In a constraint management context, **utilization** means that the operation of a resource contributes to the goals of the system. **Activation** of a resource means that the resource is being used but does not contribute to the system's goals. In this situation, work center 1 could be activated at 100 percent but it could be utilized only to a level of 66 percent. The utilization level of work center 2 is also determined by work center 3. It will be constrained to processing a unit every nine minutes, the same as work center 1. It will process each unit in seven minutes, and then wait two minutes before receiving the next unit. Its utilization, therefore, will be 78 percent. Exhibit 15.2 provides utilization data for each work center.

Oregon Freeze Dry has over 32,000 sq. ft of freeze drying surface in Oregon and 11,000 sq. ft in Europe.

utilization (constraint management definition)
The time a resource is used and contributing to throughput divided by the time the resource was available.

activation
Running a machine or resource when it doesn't contribute to throughput.

Constraint's Determination of Work Center Utilization   EXHIBIT 15.2

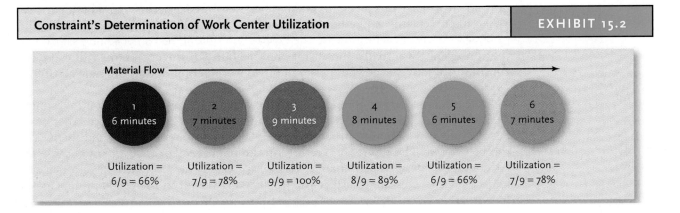

This refinery in Malaysia utilizes a proprietary delayed coking technology to maximize production of diesel fuel, which is in high demand in the region. That technology increases the capacity of the entire refinery system. The refinery is a joint venture of Conoco, Petronas (the Malaysian national oil company), and Statoil (the Norwegian national oil company).

The effect that a constraint has on work center performance is important. It is an excellent example of how an attempt to optimize a local performance measure, like work center utilization, can actually harm a more global performance measure. Imagine the increase in costs (inventory carrying costs, quality costs, facility costs) if the inventory were allowed to build up because input rate exceeded output rate. Imagine also the impact on timeliness as queues were allowed to grow longer and longer. The resulting impact on profitability (from net sales as well as costs) would be devastating, despite the fact that the utilizations on work centers 1 and 2 were high. This is such an important concept in constraint management that a new set of global performance measures was developed for it.

The impact of the constraint on other resources is made even more clear when an effort is made to improve the system's performance. Suppose we decided to improve work center 3 to speed up its processing time. Reducing it from nine minutes to eight minutes improves the output of the system. However, any further reduction in the processing time of work center 3 would not improve system performance. Why? Because a system constraint acts like the weakest link in a chain. Efforts to improve a link will increase the strength of the chain only as long as it is the weakest link. As soon as it is strengthened to the point that it is no longer the weakest, further improvement to that link does no good. The "new" weakest link must be identified. When improvements are being considered for a constraint, the same logic holds. Improving a constraint will increase the output of a system, but only as long as it is still the constraint. Eventually, increasing the capability of the constraint will cause the constraint to move somewhere else. Improve work center 3, and the new constraint becomes work center 4.

Increasing the output of a nonconstraint is a frequent result of capital investment decisions that seek to automate processes. Money is invested to reduce labor costs, but the only way to maintain run time is to activate the resource beyond the level it can be utilized. The result is no return on the improvement investment because the system output hasn't been changed. The investment may actually have a negative impact because pressure to utilize the resource may result in the production of excess inventory.

Constraint Management Global Measures and Traditional Measures		EXHIBIT 15.3

Traditional Measure	Constraint Management Measure
Net Profit	Throughput − Operating Expense
Return on Investment	$\dfrac{\text{Throughput} - \text{Operating Expense}}{\text{Inventory}}$
Inventory Turns	$\dfrac{\text{Throughput}}{\text{Inventory}}$
Productivity	$\dfrac{\text{Throughput}}{\text{Operating Expense}}$

Global Performance Measures

Constraint management decisions depend on three global performance measures: throughput, inventory, and operating expense. In a constraint management context, **throughput (T)** is defined as the rate at which the system generates money through sales. With this in mind, production over and above that which could be consumed by demand is not considered throughput because it can't be sold. **Inventory (I)** is defined as money invested in things the system intends to sell. **Operating expense (OE)** is defined as money the system spends in turning inventory into throughput. These definitions differ from the traditional nomenclature. For example, throughput traditionally means the rate at which products are produced, regardless of whether or not they are sold. The constraint management definition forces management to consider the production rate and the rate at which they can be sold. The constraint management definition for inventory includes money invested in equipment and facilities, because they may ultimately be sold as well. Traditional inventory definitions do not include facilities and equipment. The definitions have been changed to include a more direct means of measuring global performance and eliminate behaviors and "games" that are commonly used to improve performance of narrow and short-term measures, although they are known to be detrimental to long-term success. Despite the differences, the constraint management global measures can be equated to more traditional measures. These relationships are presented in Exhibit 15.3.

A widely held myth in business is that if all of the local measures are optimized, the result will be the optimization of global measures. We know from previous discussions that this is not true. The constraint management focus on global measures provides a more consistent link between day-to-day decisions and the broad performance of the firm. Constraint management eliminates the emphasis on local performance measures that aren't consistent with enterprise goals.

The constraint management perspective has modified the definitions of a variety of terms to better meet its needs. As a result, numerous glossaries of constraint management terms have been developed.

throughput
In constraint management, dollars generated by sales.

inventory (constraint management definition)
Money invested in things the system intends to sell.

operating expenses
In constraint management, this is the money the system spends turning inventory into throughput.

Oregon Freeze Dry has a capacity of over twenty million kilograms of food per year.

The Constraint Management Focusing Process

The constraint management framework includes a system improvement process that focuses on the constraint. The five-step process is
Step 1: Identify the constraint.
Step 2: Exploit the constraint.
Step 3: Subordinate all other decisions to step 2 and step 3.

Step 4: Elevate the constraint.

Step 5: If, in steps 2 through 4, the constraint is eliminated, go back to step 1.

Step 1. Identification

Identifying the constraint is a critical step in the focusing process. Constraints are often obvious, like those that result from the shortage of a resource. In more complex environments, however, an analysis may be needed to identify the constraint. The analysis compares the demand for a resource with the available capacity. Any resource that does not have sufficient capacity to meet demand would be considered a constraint. In manufacturing, constraints often have queues of inventory in front of them. A similar situation can be found in many services. Nonresource constraints, however, can be more difficult to identify. Identifying a policy as a constraint, for example, might require an approach similar to TQM to identify the root cause of a problem. There can be more than one constraint in a system.

Step 2. Exploitation

The exploitation of a constraint means attempting to use it to its fullest extent. That includes trying to prevent it from ever being idle, since shutting down a work center that is a constraint would have the same impact as shutting down the entire system. Every effort should be made to ensure that the constraint never runs out of materials to process. Every effort should be made to ensure that capacity of the constraint isn't wasted on products that already have quality problems.

The exploitation of a policy constraint is a different process. A policy, for example, can't be used more effectively. Exploiting a policy constraint requires eliminating or modifying the policy so that it no longer poses a constraint.

Step 3. Subordination

Exploiting and/or elevating a constraint increases throughput. Maintaining the increased level of constrained resource output, however, may require an adjustment in the way other resources are used. It may require establishing new policies and procedures. The subordination step is designed to give such a high priority to exploitation that any decision made should be examined to see if it would have a negative impact on those efforts. Those decisions should always be subordinated to the exploitation of the constraint.

Step 4. Elevation

Oregon Freeze Dry is able to adapt capacity to meet large orders by using 50–60 temporary employees.

Exploiting a constraint often creates enough additional capacity to eliminate it as a constraint. There are times, however, when exploitation isn't enough. Elevation means actually increasing the capacity of the constrained resource. Maybe that involves buying additional capacity. If cash is the constraint, it might be necessary to take out a loan. If supply of materials is a constraint, a new supplier may be needed, even if the materials cost more from that supplier. In any case, elevation requires a financial investment to increase the availability of the constraint above what could be gained by mere exploitation. Investment in additional capacity for a constrained resource can have a big return because of its direct impact on increasing the system's throughput. Other work centers that have been idle because of the role the constraint plays in the system may now be utilized more, simply because of this one investment.

Step 5. Repeat

From the "weakest link" analogy, we know that if we keep strengthening a link, eventually it won't be the weakest one. Management of the system through the five-step focusing process must recognize that the same phenomenon can occur here. Prior to making

om ADVANTAGE   Constraint Management at Amazon.com

The concept of matching all production rates to the rate of the constraint is critical in a large or complex system that has, at its core, one critical resource. This is the case at Amazon.com's warehouses. At the center of the order picking, sorting, and packaging process is a Crisplant sorting machine that reads product barcodes, routes them to one of 2,100 chutes for orders, and signals operators when an order is ready to be packaged. Crisplant sorting machines are used in airport luggage sorting, post offices, and in manufacturing and warehouse environments for sorting inventory. The Crisplant machine at Amazon.com is the warehouse constraint. If flow rates of products into the machine exceed the machine's capacity, a backup occurs. If flow rates are too slow, the machine's capacity isn't fully utilized and system output suffers.

A critical by-product of effective sorting is errors. In 2000, some 10 percent of the orders contained errors that resulted in workers searching for missing items and restocking wrong ones. New software has reduced errors to less than 5 percent.

The Crisplant machine works with batches of from 500 to 2,000 orders. Employees feed items onto conveyors and the Crisplant machine scans the items' barcodes and directs each item to an appropriate chute. When an order in a chute is complete, workers must remove the items and package them. If workers remove packages too slowly, the chute is not available for a new order. Every function of the warehouse seeks to avoid delays that would reduce the efficiency of the Crisplant machine. The flow in and out of the machine is so critical that a new job—flowmeister—was created, to maintain a cadence or rhythm. The flowmeister ensures that the workers removing completed orders keep up with the rate items are coming into the machine.

The focus on flow resulted in the warehouse being able to package 200,000 items on peak days in December 2001. That was a 30 percent increase over the previous year with one-third fewer workers.

Source: "Amazon Ships to Sorting Machine Beat," *New York Times on the Web*, January 21, 2002; www.crisplant.com, January 20, 2002.

Mother Nature is the source of many disruptions that can affect business systems and supply chains. Hurricane Katrina was the source of many such disruptions on the Gulf Coast. B2B suppliers were unable to make deliveries and manufacturers with low levels of inventory were forced to stop production.

any further adjustment to improve the output of the constrained resource, we need to make sure that resource still is the constraint. When exploitation or elevation causes another resource to become the constraint, the process must focus on the new constrained resource.

The Role of Disruptions in Productive Systems

In any system that utilizes resources, disruptions can wreak havoc. Machines can break down, deliveries can be late, quality problems can arise, and workers can be absent. This has traditionally been referred to as "Murphy," from Murphy's law. Murphy's law states that if something can go wrong, it will. Disruptions exist in many forms, but they have the same impact on the system—they create delays, which ultimately add to the amount of time needed to complete a task. Obviously, eliminating these types of disruption is a concern for managers. Finding the causes of these disruptions is a major thrust of both the TQM and the JIT frameworks.

There is another type of disruption, however, that constraint management addresses in a manner that is different from that of other management frameworks. Random fluctuation is present in many aspects of business processes, including the amount of time needed to complete the process. Random fluctuation can create disruptions. Within a series of processing steps, random fluctuation cannot be completely eliminated, so the system must be able to cope with it. If we look back at the simple system presented earlier in Exhibits 15.1 and 15.2, the constrained resource is a consistent problem that we understand quite well. The system looks predictable, but if we add variability into the picture, the system becomes more complex. Exhibit 15.4 shows variability in that system.

Imagine the following scenario. On average, work center 1 completes a unit in six minutes and work center 2 completes a unit in seven minutes. There will be instances for each when units are completed in less time than the average and in more time than the average. The statistical fluctuation that takes place at each work center (with the exception of work station 4) affects each of the other work centers as well. Suppose, for example, that work center 1 completes a unit in 6 minutes, 20 seconds, which is within the expected variation. The completion time will delay by 20 seconds when work center 2 can start work on that unit. Sometimes a work center will take longer to process a unit, and sometimes it will take less time than average. The impact of the statistical

EXHIBIT 15.4	Simple System with Processing Variability

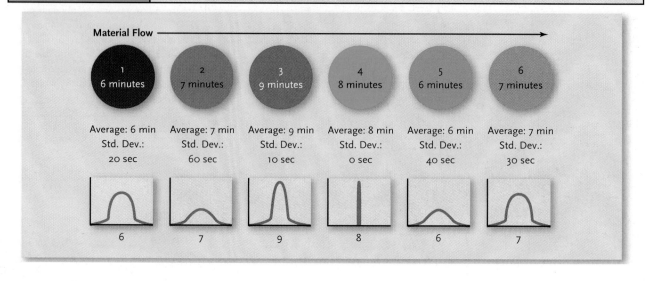

fluctuations tends to increase as we move toward work center 6. It accumulates. This phenomenon is recognized as the impact of **statistical fluctuation among dependent events** in constraint management. Its effect can be substantial because the disruptions it causes can be substantial.

Protecting the System from Disruptions

All disruptions, including those from unexpected events and the accumulation of statistical fluctuation, have an impact on the system. Nonconstraints, because they have excess capacity, can experience a level of disruption without reducing system output. For example, work center 5 has idle time that can be used to catch up if it is forced to periodically shut down because of a lack of material or a breakdown. A constrained resource, however, has no idle time. Work center 3 is utilized 100 percent of the time and has no idle time to enable it to catch up from downtime due to lack of material or other reasons. Thus the constraint must be protected from these disruptions. The approach constraint management uses to protect constrained resources from disruptions is to **decouple,** or "disconnect," them from the rest of the system with inventory.

Buffering to Protect Constraints

Disruptions to systems can generally be measured by their duration. An hour's disruption results in delays of an hour. Any scheme to protect a constraint must recognize that the amount of protection must also be measured by time. We could protect a constraint from a 1-hour disruption or a 20-hour disruption or an *x*-hour disruption if we deemed the duration appropriate. That protection comes from a buffer of inventory known as a **time buffer.** A time buffer decouples, for a specified amount of time, the constrained resource from being directly dependent on the work centers that supply it. The role of the buffer can be best understand by going back to the system examined in Exhibit 15.4.

Work center 3 is clearly the constraint of that system. It can be idled by a disruption occurring at either work center 1 or work center 2. A disruption of either would shut off the supply of materials to work center 3 and idle it. Because it should be working 100 percent of the time to meet demand, it has no way to catch up the time it lost as a result of being idle. Lost time on the constraint is lost forever. In Exhibit 15.5 a time buffer is placed in front of work center 3 to provide protection from this threat.

The time buffer performs an important and interesting task. The first, and maybe most critical, decision regarding the time buffer should be to determine its potential size. How much protection is needed? That question can be answered only when the potential time of the disruptions is known. For example, if there is a possibility that work center 1 could break down and be down for eight hours, it would create an eight-hour disruption that could idle work center 3. The only way to prevent such a disruption to work center 3 would be to keep a buffer of work in front of work center 3 that would keep it busy working for eight hours. In our situation, given that it takes work center 3 nine minutes per unit, work center 3 could process 53.3 units (let's round up to 54) in an eight-hour period. Thus, to protect the constraint from an eight-hour disruption, we'd

statistical fluctuation among dependent events
Disruptions caused by accumulating variability among processing times of processes that depend on each other.

decouple
To reduce the direct dependency of a process step on its predecessor.

time buffer
A buffer of inventory that will keep a resource busy for a specified amount of time.

| Simple System with Constraint and Time Buffer | EXHIBIT 15.5 |

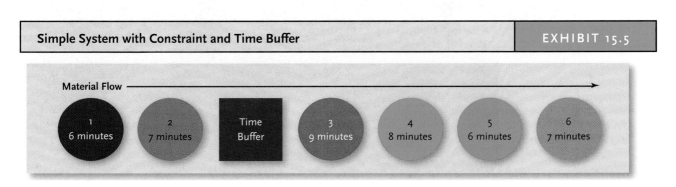

EXHIBIT 15.6	Inventory Flow In and Out of a Time Buffer

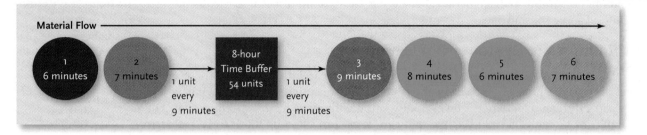

keep an eight-hour time buffer (54 units of inventory) in front of it. Since work centers 1 and 2 can process units faster than work center 3, they could build up that amount of inventory by processing faster than work center 3, then back off to produce at the rate of one unit every nine minutes. Inventory would then flow into and out of the buffer at the same rate of one unit every nine minutes, as shown in Exhibit 15.6.

If a disruption caused by a breakdown at work center 1 or 2, or a disruption in raw material supply, stopped the inflow, the constrained resource (work center 3) would be able to continue unaffected for up to eight hours. During the time of disruption, the buffer would be gradually reduced by the production rate of work center 3. When the disruption ended, the production rate for work centers 1 and 2 would be stepped up to replenish the buffer back to its eight-hour level.

In an environment that must fulfill orders by a certain due date, however, it becomes more difficult. Suppose our system was identical to that of the previous example, except that we produce to fill specific orders. Orders vary in size, but suppose we have an order for 27 units due 14 days from now. The role of the time buffer continues to be to protect the constraint from disruptions of the same time, but it also protects our due date from those disruptions. Suppose each work center produces 54 units per day in our system. That's a nine-minute cycle time for the system during an eight-hour workday. With no time buffer in place, the order would move through each work center in four hours. If the order were due on day 14, we would start it on day 11 because it would take three days to get through the six work centers.

Disruptions due to interrupted material and inventory supply are common for manufacturers and retailers. Accidents that affect truck, rail, or sea transport can either delay delivery or actually destroy critical system inputs. If excess capacity exists, such a disruption can be absorbed, but if a constraint is involved, the entire supply chain can suffer.

With an eight-hour time buffer in place, time has been added to the order's processing time. Since there are already eight hours of inventory in front of work center 3 when our order finishes work center 2, it must wait in that queue for eight hours. Work center 3 processes a unit every nine minutes, and our order comes out of work center 2, one unit every nine minutes. With an eight-hour time buffer in place, we need to start our order on day 10, because it will now take four days to get through the system. If a disruption of less than eight hours takes place, it will not result in our order being late. The effect of the buffer, in this case, is to trigger us to start the order one day earlier, giving us eight hours of slack in our schedule. A disruption at work center 1 or 2 will mean our order will not arrive at work center 3 when planned; however, the plan specified for the order to arrive there (and be placed in an eight-hour queue) eight hours before it was actually needed. Exhibit 15.7 shows the times that would be associated with our order.

As long as the order enters the time buffer prior to day 12, it can be completed on time because it can be started at work center 3 as soon as it enters the queue in front of it. The effect of the time buffer is that we release the order into the system one day early. That extra day of slack allows it to tolerate disruptions in work center 1 or 2, as long as they are less than eight hours (a day) in duration. Since other orders are entering the time buffer from other work centers, our order being late would not necessarily idle work center 3. In constraint management parlance, this particular type of time buffer is known as a **constraint buffer**.

constraint buffer
A time buffer placed immediately prior to a constraint.

The constraint is protected from up to a one-day disruption at work center 1 or 2. The due date is also protected from up to a one-day disruption at work center 1 or 2. If disruptions could be greater, the time buffer should be greater.

The sizing of time buffers is an iterative process. If random checks on the one-day time buffer in the example showed that it was always full (always had eight hours of work in it), that would mean that it was too big. If there had been a disruption, the buffer would slowly have been drained by the constraint, and it would have less than eight hours' content. If it always contained eight hours of inventory, that would indicate that there are never disruptions, meaning that the buffer isn't needed or that its size could be reduced. The goal is to have a buffer that, on average, is roughly two-thirds full. A buffer that averages about two-thirds full indicates that its size is sufficient to cover a serious disruption but not so large that most of it is never used.

The order due on day 14 would be late if there were disruptions after the constrained resource at work center 3, 4, 5, or 6. The order could be protected from these disruptions by using another time buffer immediately after the final processing step but immediately before shipping. This buffer is known as a **shipping buffer**. Suppose we determined that

shipping buffer
A time buffer immediately prior to shipping.

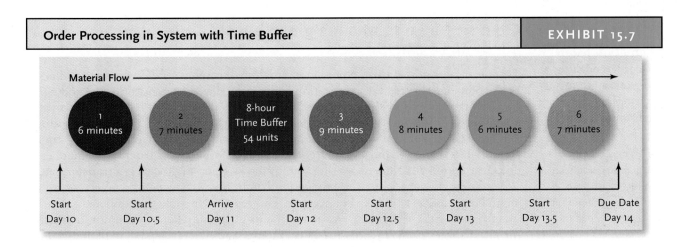

| Order Processing in System with Time Buffer | EXHIBIT 15.7 |

Material Flow →

1 — 6 minutes
2 — 7 minutes
8-hour Time Buffer 54 units
3 — 9 minutes
4 — 8 minutes
5 — 6 minutes
6 — 7 minutes

| Start Day 10 | Start Day 10.5 | Arrive Day 11 | Start Day 12 | Start Day 12.5 | Start Day 13 | Start Day 13.5 | Due Date Day 14 |

| EXHIBIT 15.8 | System with Shipping Buffer Added |

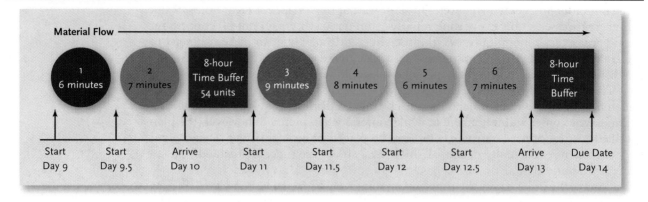

one day of protection was needed for potential disruptions at these work centers. Exhibit 15.8 shows the shipping buffer added to the system.

Notice that adding an eight-hour shipping buffer results in adding an additional day to the lead time when the order must be released into the system. With this change, the due date would be protected from disruptions anywhere in the system. The shipping buffer offers protection from disruptions that could come from work center 3, 4, 5, or 6. The constraint buffer protects from disruptions at work center 1 or 2 and protects the constraint from being idle as well. In fact, if a disruption at work center 1 or 2 lasted longer than one day, the shipping buffer would provide an additional day of protection.

When parts go through constrained resources, it is a good practice to move them through the remaining work centers as quickly as possible. This is generally not difficult, because remaining work centers are not constrained, so there should be no waiting lines. Assembly points, however, can sometimes cause delays. When a component that has been processed by a constrained resource reaches an assembly point, it is possible that the component it is to be assembled with is not yet there. To prevent this type of delay from happening, some constraint management systems include a buffer of components that did not go through constrained resources in front of assembly points. This helps to ensure that components that have been through constrained resources are not delayed. This buffer is known as an **assembly buffer.** Buffers can also serve as a tool for identifying potentially late orders that need to be expedited. An order that is late in arriving to a buffer is a signal that disruptions have occurred. Identifying orders that should be in buffers, but aren't, helps identify potentially late orders.

assembly buffer
A time buffer placed immediately prior to an assembly for nonconstrained components.

production batch
The quantity produced at a workcenter before changing over to produce something else.

transfer batch
The quantity produced at a workcenter before transferring the products to the next step in the process.

Constraint Management and Batch Sizes

The advantages of small-batch production and small batches for delivery were addressed in the previous chapter, but recognition of the role played by constraints in productive systems makes a second look worthwhile. Constraint management recognizes that there are, in fact, two distinctly different types of inventory batches and two distinctly different types of decisions to make. The number of units produced before changing equipment over to produce something else is known as a **production batch.** The number of units transferred at a time to another step in the production process is a **transfer batch.**

We know that the larger the production batch, the less frequently a piece of equipment must undergo a setup or changeover. This reduces the time the equipment must be stopped during these changeovers, increasing its utilization. For a constraint, increasing the production batch size increases its utilization, and this is a form of exploitation. For other resources, however, since they are nonconstraints and have idle time at their disposal, smaller production batch sizes are more desirable. They result in lower levels of inventory, improved quality, and so on. The best scenario is that all of the nonconstraint idle time be used for changeovers. In that way, the smallest possible production batch sizes are used, minimizing inventory levels, but not allowing changeovers to cut into time needed for actual production.

Transfer batches should always be as small as possible. Reducing the size of the transfer batch creates a more even flow of materials through the system and also reduces the likelihood that work centers would have to sit idle waiting for materials to be delivered while large transfer batches accumulate. When transfer batches are large, the movement from one resource to the next becomes infrequent, which in some cases can result in a nonconstraint being turned into a constraint because all of its idle time is consumed waiting for work to arrive. In effect, it gets "starved" while waiting for a delivery. In time, when the delivery arrives, the time left to process it may be insufficient.

The Role of the Constraint: A Product Mix Example

Goldratt's book *The Goal*[2] introduced a problem to demonstrate the impact of constraints on traditional thinking. The problem has become a virtual classic and its solution frequently surprises even the most experienced managers. This problem is presented in Example 15.1.

Example 15.1

Product Mix Problem

EXCEL TUTOR

Exhibit 15.9 provides a model of a simple manufacturing system that produces two products, P and Q. Product P sells for $90 per unit and Q sells for $100 per unit. There is a weekly demand for 100 Ps and 50 Qs.

EXHIBIT 15.9   Production System for Example 15.1

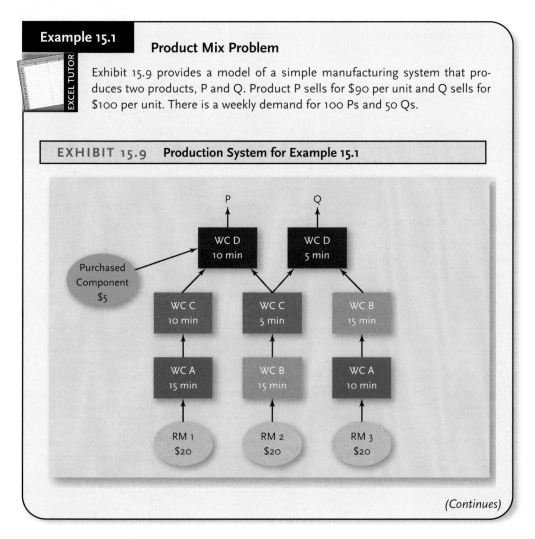

(Continues)

Example 15.1

EXCEL TUTOR

(Continued)

Manufacturing P requires two raw materials (raw material 1 and 2), each costing $20. In addition, P uses a purchased component that costs $5 per unit. Manufacturing Q also requires two raw materials (raw material 2 and 3). Raw material 2 is used in P and Q. Raw material 3 also costs $20.

Four work centers, A, B, C, and D, are used to manufacture the products. Each has 2,400 minutes (40 hours) available each week. Each work center (WC) has two tasks to perform, with no changeover required when switching between tasks. For example, WC A is used in a 15-minute process on raw material 1 to produce a P and WC A is also used in a 10-minute process on raw material 3 to produce a Q. Producing P requires that raw material 1 be processed first at WC A, then at WC C. Raw material 2 is processed first at WC B and then at WC C. The two are then assembled, along with the $5 purchased component, at WC D. They are then complete and can be sold. To manufacture a Q, raw material 2 is processed first at WC B, then at WC C. Raw material 3 is processed first at WC A, then at WC B. The two are assembled at WC D and then sold. Operating expense for the week, including everything except materials costs, is $6,000. These values are summarized in Exhibit 15.10.

EXHIBIT 15.10   Production System Data

	P	Q
Market demand	100	50
Selling price	$90	$100
Raw materials costs		
RM 1	$20	
RM 2	$20	$20
RM 3		$20
Purchased component	$5	

Time available on each work center: 2,400 minutes
Operating expense per week: $6,000

What combination of Ps and Qs should be produced to maximize profit?

Solution

The solution to the product mix problem is obtained by completing the first two steps of the five-step focusing process outlined earlier.

Step 1. Identify the constraint. The identification of the constraint is accomplished in this situation by computing the demand requirements on each resource (work centers, raw materials, and purchased parts) and comparing them to the availability of each. Any resource unable to meet the weekly demand is, by definition, a constraint. The results of these calculations are presented in Exhibit 15.11.

EXHIBIT 15.11   Identification of Constraint

Product Demand	Required Time on WC A	Required Time on WC B	Required Time on WC C	Required Time on WC D	Required RM 1	Required RM 2	Required RM 3	Required Purchase Components
100 P	1,500	1,500	1,500	1,000	100	100	0	100
50 Q	500	1,500	250	250	0	50	50	0
Total required	2,000	3,000	1,750	1,250	100	150	50	100
Available	2,400	2,400	2,400	2,400	Unlimited	Unlimited	Unlimited	Unlimited
Problem?	OK	Problem	OK	OK	OK	OK	OK	OK

(Continues)

Example 15.1

(Continued)

In this example situation, since there are no limitations on the availability of raw materials and purchased parts, a constraint can only be one of the work centers. With only 2,400 minutes available on each work center, WC B is the constraint because it requires 3,000 minutes to meet demand and only 2,400 minutes are available.

Step 2. Exploit the constraint. Exploitation means getting the most out of the constraint in terms of the system's goals. The goal of this system is to maximize profit. So the constraint should be utilized in the way that yields the most profit. Constraint management utilizes a technique known as obtaining the best return per unit of the constraint. In this situation, the "return" sought is a financial one. The "units" of the constraint are minutes of use. A calculation of the dollar return per minute of time on the constraint is made for products P and Q to determine which one best exploits work center B. This calculation is presented in Exhibit 15.12. To make the calculation, the contribution margin (selling price minus materials cost) is computed for each end product and divided by the number of minutes work center B is used to produce it. The result shows that product P yields $3 per minute on the constraint and product Q yields $2 per minute.

EXHIBIT 15.12	Calculation of Dollar Return per Constraint Minute	
	P	**Q**
Contribution margin	$90 − $45 = $45	$100 − $60 = $40
Minutes on B	15	30
Return per constraint minute	$45/15	$60/30
	= $3 per minute	= $2 per minute

Since B is the constraint, we must use all 2,400 minutes, no matter what product mix is used. The difference in return per minute means that we can spend 1,500 minutes at WC B making P for $3 per minute, and the remaining 900 minutes making Q for $2 per minute, or the reverse—spend 1,500 minutes at WC B making Q for $2 per minute and then the remaining 900 minutes making P for $3 per minute. Obviously, the most profitable choice is the first. If we select P as the most profitable way to utilize the constraint, 1,500 minutes will be used to meet its demand. That leaves 900 minutes to be used producing product Q. At 30 minutes on WC B for each Q, a total of 30 units of Q can be produced in that amount of time. The product mix that maximizes profit is 100 Ps and 30 Qs. Exhibit 15.13 provides the calculations for profit.

EXHIBIT 15.13	Profit Calculations for Example 15.1
100 P:	100 × $45 = $4,500
30 Q:	30 × $60 = $1,800
Total	$6,300
Minus operating expenses	−$6,000
Profit	$300

Excel Tutor 15.1 demonstrates how Excel can be used to aid in solving the product mix problem.

The results of Example 15.1 provide insight into the importance of constraints. A comparison of this solution to a solution using more traditional measures is useful. The contribution margins of P and Q are $45 and $60, respectively. The solution we obtained results in a weekly profit of $300, as shown in Exhibit 15.13. A solution based on contribution margin would have led us to produce as many Qs as possible. The profit using that solution is actually a loss of $300. Clearly, in this situation, focusing on the contribution margin to obtain the most profitable product would have provided the wrong solution. Similarly, a sales commission system can also encourage the wrong behavior. A commission system based on selling price or contribution margin would encourage sales reps to sell Q instead of P, which would be exactly the wrong thing to do.

Lean Systems and Constraint Management

The lean systems and constraint management frameworks do not conflict and, despite differences of areas of focus, overlap somewhat. The buffering process used by constraint management is similar to the kanban system in that each controls inventory and dictates that production be equal to that required by the rate of demand. Kanban provides small buffers between each work center, while constraint management provides buffers only at critical points as protection from disruptions. Lean systems typically have excess capacity (no constraints) and provide a larger buffer at the finished-goods point. This is similar to a shipping buffer used in constraint management. In a constraint management system, if all internal constraints were eliminated, there would be no constraint buffer, only a shipping buffer. In a kanban environment, if there were a constraint, the natural reaction of management would probably be to increase the maximum size of the buffer in front of the constrained resource to counteract problems caused by a small buffer. That change would begin to resemble the constraint management approach. The key difference between the two approaches is that they represent different perspectives: lean systems focus on eliminating waste as the top priority, whereas constraint management focuses on maximizing throughput through the management of system constraints.

CHAPTER SUMMARY

Constraint management, a framework that focuses on maximizing system output by managing the system constraints, was examined and explained in this chapter. Like quality management and lean systems, constraint management provides a useful perspective that makes managers aware of constraints, their impact, and how they can be managed to enhance the productivity of the system as a whole.

The five focusing steps of constraint management can be applied to effectively improve system performance by focusing on the system constraint. The use of inventory or time buffers protects the constrained resource from upstream disruptions that could force it to be idle.

The second step of the five-step focusing process, exploitation, can have particularly broad implications for management decisions, including capital budgeting, product mix decisions, and resource scheduling. A close examination of constraint management and use of the five focusing steps as a way to enhance systemwide productivity often contradicts more traditional measures used to make decisions. The role of a constraint in a system, for example, can cause traditional measures such as contribution margin to lead to an incorrect result. The financial return per unit of the constrained resource provides a means of exploiting a constraint in terms of profit goals.

KEY TERMS

activation, 661
assembly buffer, 670
constraint, 660
constraint buffer, 669
constraint management, 660
decouple, 667
inventory, 663
operating expense, 663

production batch, 670
shipping buffer, 669
statistical fluctuation among dependent
    events, 667
throughput, 663
time buffer, 667
transfer batch, 670
utilization, 661

SOLVED PROBLEMS

1. Determining the Most Profitable Product Mix

A small manufacturer produces two alternatives: X and Y. The process utilizes four work-centers (A, B, C, and D) and each has 2,400 minutes available each week. The processes for X and Y are diagramed in Exhibit 15.14.

EXHIBIT 15.14   Processes for X and Y

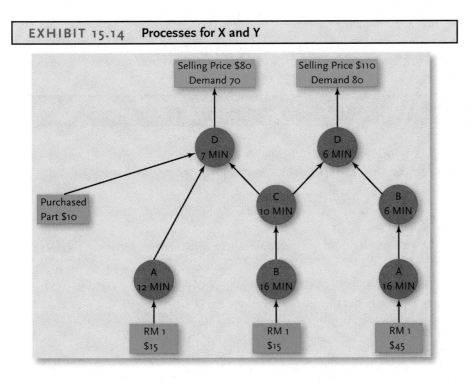

Product Mix Calculation

Step	Objective	Explanation

		Time Required per Unit			
1.	Identify the constraint by determining the time required on each work center to product the entire demand.	Product	A	B	C	D
		X	12	16	10	7
		Y	16	22	10	6

		Time Required for Demand			
Product	Demand	WCA	WCB	WCC	WCD
X	70	840	1,120	700	490
Y	80	1,280	1,760	800	480
Total		2,120	2,880	1,500	970

The constraint is WCB, because it is the only work center unable to produce the demand in the 2,400 minutes available.

2. Calculate the contribution margin for X and Y and the dollar return per constraint minute.

X: $80 − ($10 + $15 + $15) = $40
$40 / 16 minutes on WCB = $2.50 per minute

Y: $110 − ($15 + $45) = $50
$50 / 22 minutes on WCB = $2.27 per minute

X is the most profitable.

3. Calculate the number of Ys that can be produced if all of the demand for X is met.

70 X requires 1,120 minutes on WCB, leaving 1,280 minutes. Y requires 22 minutes per unit on WCB, so in 1,280 minutes, 58 units could be produced. 1280/22=58.18

The most profitable product mix would be: 70 X and 58 Y.

REVIEW QUESTIONS

1. What is a "constraint"?
2. Describe the weakest link analogy as it applies to constraint management.
3. What is meant by "utilization" and "activation"?
4. Define "throughput," "inventory," and "operating expenses" from a constraint management perspective.
5. Describe the five steps of the constraint management focusing process and the meaning of each.
6. What is the relationship between statistical fluctuations and dependent events?
7. What is a time buffer?
8. How can time buffers help exploit a constraint?
9. Define "constraint buffer," "shipping buffer," and "assembly buffer."
10. What is meant by "transfer batch" and "production batch"? What role does a constrained resource play in determining the sizes of these different batches?
11. How does constraint management compare to Lean? More specifically, how does constraint management's use of buffers compare to a kanban system?

DISCUSSION AND EXPLORATION

1. Identify a constraint in a process you interact with (for example, food service, lines at the recreation center, your favorite fast-food restaurant). How would you exploit the constraint to improve system productivity?

2. Identify systems that you interact with that must cope with disruptions. How could buffers be used to lessen that impact?

3. In the product mix problem demonstrated in Example 15.1, describe why traditional financial measures would lead to the wrong answer.

PROBLEMS HM

Solutions to odd-numbered problems are located on the text's Online Center (http://mhhe.com/opsnow3e).

1. Examine the five work centers and the times provided below.

WC1	WC2	WC3	WC4	WC5
5 minutes	7 minutes	6 minutes	5 minutes	8 minutes

   a. What will be the output rate of the system if no inventory is allowed to build?

   b. What is the utilization rate (using the constraint management definition) of each work center?

2. Examine the five work centers and the times provided below.

WC1	WC2	WC3	WC4	WC5
9 minutes	7 minutes	11 minutes	10 minutes	9 minutes

   a. What will be the output rate of the system if no inventory is allowed to build?

   b. What is the utilization rate (using the constraint management definition) of each work center?

3. Examine the six work centers and the times provided below.

WC1	WC2	WC3	WC4	WC5	WC6
7 minutes	6 minutes	8 minutes	8 minutes	6 minutes	7 minutes

   Currently, inventory is entered into the system at the rate of one unit every 6 minutes.

   a. Where will inventory build?

   b. What will be the utilization of each work center at this rate of input?

4. Examine the six work centers and the times provided below.

WC1	WC2	WC3	WC4	WC5	WC6
3 minutes	4 minutes	5 minutes	7 minutes	5 minutes	4 minutes

   Currently, inventory is entered into the system at the rate of one unit every 5 minutes.

   a. Where will inventory build?

   b. What will be the utilization of each work center at this rate of input?

5. Dee-Lish Apple Orchard offers a three-step process to sell its apples as illustrated below. The first work station is the picker, which collects the apples from the trees. The second step is a quality station, which inspects the apples for flaws. The last step is to package the apples for market. What is the maximum amount of apples that this system can ready for market in an hour?

6. Dr. Wahle sets up patient appointments every 15 minutes. The patient must go through the following steps: sign in, see the doctor, and pay for the visit. If the first patient arrives at 10:00, when will the fourth patient be able to leave? What is the constraint in the system? If the first patient arrives at 10:00, how many patients will be waiting in the waiting room at noon?

7. The Taco Hut has a Monday night special of 25-cent tacos. The steps for making tacos are outlined below, beginning with adding ground beef to the shell, topping with lettuce, cheese, and tomatoes, and then packaging. Which of the work stations will be utilized 100 percent? What will be the utilization of the others if input rate is restricted to the rate of the constrained resource?

8. Paper-Giant makes paper notebooks for students. Notebook production is a three-step process. First, 500 sheets of paper must be counted and aligned, a process that takes 55 seconds. Holes must then be punched in the paper, which takes 35 seconds. Finally, the wire binding must be attached to the paper, taking 120 seconds. Calculate the utilization for each of the work stations. What is the constraint in the system? What is the utilization rate for each work center if it must maximize throughput?

9. Active Inc. manufactures two products, a wiffle bat and ball. To make a wiffle ball, processes at two workstations must be completed: 5 minutes of molding and 5 minutes of cutting. The wiffle bat requires 10 minutes of molding and 5 minutes of coloring. The company needs to produce 190 bats and 125 wiffle balls per week to meet demand. There are 2,400 minutes available at each work center each week. Find the constraint. If an engineering change can decrease the molding time on the bat by 1 minute by increasing the coloring time from 5 to 10 minutes, should Active undertake the change?

10. Woodrow Woodworking produces countertops and the backsplashes that accompany them. The company can produce up to 130 backsplashes and 150 counters per week to meet demand. A backsplash requires 8 minutes on the cutter and 7 minutes of finishing. Countertops require 9 minutes of cutting, 5 minutes on the glue press, and 12 minutes of finishing. The cutter, press, and finishing each have 2,400 minutes available per week. A backsplash costs $25 to manufacture and sells for $40. A counter sells for $70 and costs $35. Determine the constraint and the best product mix. What is the profit for the best product mix?

11. Tuff-T's makes two styles of customized T-shirts. The 001 is a plain white shirt selling for $14 and costing $4. Material for the shirt must first be cut, which takes 18 minutes, and then the shirt can be sewn, a process that takes 24 minutes. The 004 is a tie-dyed shirt with a customized logo selling for $24 and costing $6. The shirt must go through the same process as the 001, but cutting takes an additional minute, and sewing an additional two. The colored shirt must also be dyed, which takes 35 minutes, and the logo must be made and ironed on, taking another 12 minutes. Overall, there is a demand for 70 style 001's and 50 style 004's per week. There are 2,400 minutes available at each work center. Find the constraint and determine the product mix that maximizes profit.

ENDNOTES

1. E. M. Goldratt, *The Goal*, 2nd rev. ed. (Croton-on-Hudson, NY: North River Press, 1992).
2. Ibid.

LEARNING ACTIVITIES   www.mhhe.com/opsnow3e

Visit the Online Learning Center (www.mhhe.com/opsnow3e) for additional resources. Content varies by chapter, and includes

- Business Tours
- OM on Site
- Readings
- Resources
- Excel Tutors

- Interactive Case Models
- Reel Operations Video Clips
- Additional Advanced Problems
- Self-Assessment Quizzes
- Glossary

SELECTED REFERENCES

Goldratt, E. M. *Critical Chain*. Croton-on-Hudson, NY: North River Press, 1997.

Goldratt, E. M. *The Goal*, 2nd rev. ed. Croton-on-Hudson, NY: North River Press, 1992.

Goldratt, E. M. *Theory of Constraints*. Croton-on-Hudson, NY: North River Press, 1990.

Umble, M. M., and Srikanth, M. L. *Synchronous Manufacturing*. Cincinnati, OH: South-Western Publishing, 1990.

INTERACTIVE CASE 15.1

Understanding Production Output at Henckley's Outdoor Products

The constraint management simulation provides an interactive environment for experimenting with system parameters and various combinations of constraint buffers to aid in the exploitation of system constraints. In the model, the user has several opportunities to control the model's behavior. The input rate and processing times at each of the five work centers can be varied from 1 to 8 minutes per unit. The variability of each can be controlled as well, and has options of zero, slight, moderate, and extreme. In addition to the variability, breakdowns can be zero, small, moderate, or severe. Increasing breakdown severity increases the frequency and duration of breakdowns. The user also has the ability to create buffers in front of any work center by establishing the beginning level of inventory. The buffer size can range from zero to five units. Time buffers can be created by combining the number of units with the time per unit at that work center. For example, a buffer of four units in front of a work center that was set at 5 minutes per unit would provide a 20-minute time buffer. In addition to the quantity of products produced by the system, utilization on each work center is provided when the system is stopped. The user also has the option to dictate the simulator clock speed and can pause the simulation.

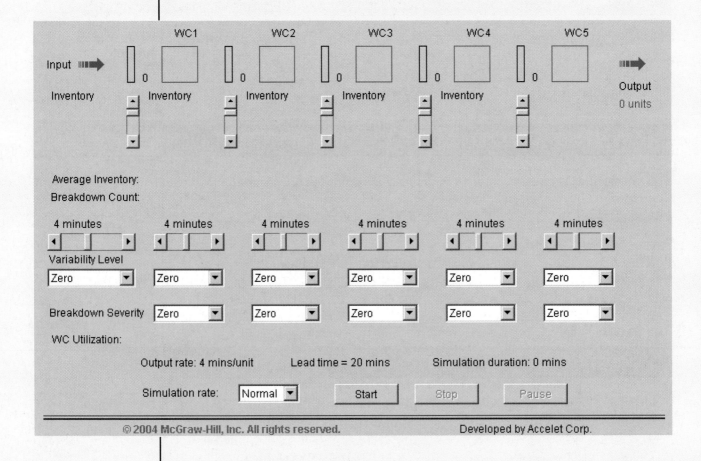

Henckley's Outdoor Products

Henckley's Outdoor Products manufactures a variety of products for outdoor recreational use, but focuses primarily on canvas products such as awnings, tents, and canopies, as well as the poles and hardware used with them. One particular production line, produces aluminum extension poles for large awnings that are used primarily for large outdoor receptions and parties. That line is a short five-station line that cuts, drills appropriate holes, and assembles various poles for the awning. Adam Henckley, the owner of the company, has had trouble getting consistent output from the line, despite the amount of work that has gone into its design. For one particular pole, the one the line was designed around, the average processing time for each step is 4 minutes. Adam has seen productivity fluctuate when producing other products on the line, but has also noticed inconsistencies in output even when producing the pole the line was designed to produce. Adam has also noticed that at times, work-in-process inventory levels between some of the work centers are high.

1. Set the parameters to the default values, as shown below.

	Initial Inventory	Processing Time	Variability	Breakdown Severity
Input		4	Zero	
WC1	0	4	Zero	Zero
WC2	0	4	Zero	Zero
WC3	0	4	Zero	Zero
WC4	0	4	Zero	Zero
WC5	0	4	Zero	Zero

   a. Run the simulation for 100 simulator minutes. How many products are completed?

   b. Increase the processing time for WC3 from 4 to 5 minutes and run the simulation again for 100 minutes. What happens to the number of products finished? What happens to the level of inventory in the system? What happens to the utilization of each work center?

   c. Change the input rate to one unit every 5 minutes (leaving WC3 at 5 minutes also). What happens now? What does that indicate about the role of the constraint and the system input rate? How do utilization rates change for each work center?

2. Set the parameters back to the original default values.

   a. Increase the processing time variability for WC3 to the extreme level. Run the simulation for 100 simulator minutes. What is the finished product output? How does this compare to the results from 1a? What happens to inventory in the system? How does process time variability affect inventory levels at the various work centers? How are work center utilizations affected?

   b. Increase the variability of WC3 even more by changing the breakdown severity to extreme. Run the simulation for 100 simulator minutes. What is the new finished product output? How does this compare to the results from 2a? What happens to inventory in the system? How are the work centers affected by increased variability? How are work center utilizations affected by this change?

3. Set the parameters to the values shown below.

	Initial Inventory	Processing Time	Variability	Breakdown Severity
Input		6	Zero	
WC1	0	4	Zero	Zero
WC2	0	4	Zero	Zero
WC3	0	6	Zero	Zero
WC4	0	4	Zero	Zero
WC5	0	4	Zero	Zero

a. Run the simulation for 100 simulator minutes. How many products are finished?

4. Set the parameters to the values shown below.

	Initial Inventory	Processing Time	Variability	Breakdown Severity
Input		6	Zero	
WC1	3	4	Extreme	Severe
WC2	3	4	Extreme	Severe
WC3	3	6	Zero	Zero
WC4	3	4	Zero	Zero
WC5	3	4	Zero	Zero

a. Run the simulation for 100 simulator minutes. How many products are finished? Do you notice as much idle time on WC3? What is the utilization of WC3?

5. Set the parameters as shown below.

	Initial Inventory	Processing Time	Variability	Breakdown Severity
Input		6	Zero	
WC1	0	4	Extreme	Severe
WC2	0	4	Extreme	Severe
WC3	2	6	Zero	Zero
WC4	0	4	Zero	Zero
WC5	0	4	Zero	Zero

a. Run the simulation for 100 simulator minutes and observe what happens. How many products are finished? Does a buffer of 2 units prior to WC3 effectively isolate it from disruptions? Do you notice any idle time on WC3? What is the utilization of WC3?

6. Reset the parameters as shown below.

	Initial Inventory	Processing Time	Variability	Breakdown Severity
Input		6	Zero	
WC1	0	4	Extreme	Severe
WC2	0	4	Extreme	Severe
WC3	4	6	Zero	Zero
WC4	0	4	Zero	Zero
WC5	0	4	Zero	Zero

a. Run the simulation for 100 simulator minutes. How many products are finished?

b. Does a buffer of 4 units prior to WC3 effectively isolate it from disruptions? Do you notice idle time on WC3? What is the new utilization of WC3?

7. Set the parameters to the values shown below.

	Initial Inventory	Processing Time	Variability	Breakdown Severity
Input		4	Extreme	
WC1	o	4	Extreme	Severe
WC2	o	6	Zero	Zero
WC3	o	4	Zero	Zero
WC4	o	4	Zero	Zero
WC5	o	4	Zero	Zero

a. Run the simulation 100 simulator minutes. How many products were complete?

b. How does that compare to the same configuration with zero variability and zero breakdowns for all work centers? Would you conclude that the difference is due to processing variability and disruptions?

8. Set the parameters to the values shown below.

	Initial Inventory	Processing Time	Variability	Breakdown Severity
Input		4	Extreme	
WC1	o	4	Extreme	Severe
WC2	o	4	Extreme	Severe
WC3	o	6	Zero	Zero
WC4	o	4	Zero	Zero
WC5	o	4	Zero	Zero

a. Run the simulation for 100 simulator minutes. How many units are produced?

9. Set the parameters to the values shown below.

	Initial Inventory	Processing Time	Variability	Breakdown Severity
Input		4	Extreme	
WC1	o	4	Extreme	Severe
WC2	o	4	Extreme	Severe
WC3	o	4	Extreme	Severe
WC4	o	6	Zero	Zero
WC5	o	4	Zero	Zero

a. Run the simulation for 100 simulator minutes. What happens?

b. Is the effect of these changes caused by increased variability? Or by moving the constraint? How could you find out for sure? Perform the necessary experiments to confirm your hypothesis.

APPLICATION CASE 15.2

What Should Sound Design Sell?

Sound Design produces small speakers and other audio components for use with computers and mp3 players. One plant is dedicated to two small speaker systems (the i100 and i500) in which an mp3 player can be docked. The two products are similar, but have different components and slightly different process requirements. The process and requirements for each speaker are presented below.

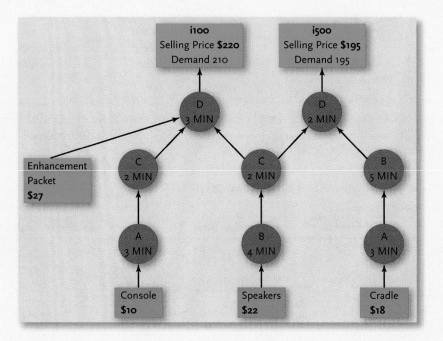

The plant manager produces "to stock" and from experience knows that the demand averages about 210 units per week for the i100 and 180 units per week for the i500. The i100 sells for $220 and the i500 sells for $195. His weekly expenses, which include everything but material costs, are $24,000.

1. What product mix will maximize profit for Sound Design?

2. What will the weekly profit be?

An engineer has suggested an improvement to the current process. She recommends a modification to WC C that will change the WC C process used by both products so that it can do some of the work currently done by WC B. If the change is made, the WC C process expands to 4 minutes and the WC B process is reduced to 3 minutes. The new process is shown below.

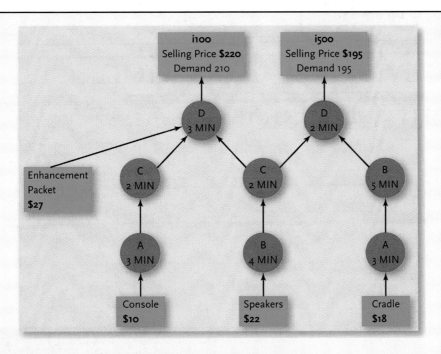

3. Is this a good change?

4. What happens when the change is made?

5. What suggestions would you have for Sound Design in order to deal with the changed situation?

CHAPTER 16

Facilities: Making Location and Layout Decisions

LEARNING OBJECTIVES

- Describe the impact facility decisions have on profitability and value.

- Identify common decision criteria for business location decisions.

- Explain why geographic information systems (GISs) benefit location decision making.

- Use multifactor rating as a decision-making tool.

- Compute the breakeven point when comparing alternative locations.

- Describe the strengths and weaknesses of process-oriented, product-oriented, and cellular layouts.

- Use the cut-and-dry method and systematic layout planning for a process-oriented layout.

- Determine the theoretical minimum number of work centers and balance a line in a product-oriented layout.

LOCATING A FREIGHT SERVICE—WHY CHATTANOOGA?

Locating any business is a challenge no matter what product or service it sells. When it sells transportation services, however, that decision gets more complex. In theory, it could locate anywhere, but from a financial performance perspective, certainly some locations are better than others. One such business, U.S. Xpress, has selected the Chattanooga, Tennessee, metropolitan area for its headquarters and expansion site.

U.S. Xpress Enterprises offers exact-time and expedited freight services throughout North America. It uses driver teams for long-haul trucking (400 to 3,000 miles) and competes with air-freight by offering lower costs. Its regional service covers the Midwest, Southeast, and West. U.S. Xpress's fleet includes around 6,000 tractors and about 14,500 trailers. As just-in-time delivery practices increase in popularity, U.S. Xpress expects its exact-time services to expand. The trend toward outsourcing transportation services is also viewed as a positive force on U.S. Xpress business. Many of those companies outsource to a "core carrier" that is large enough to handle large amounts of freight.

U.S. Xpress has been on the cutting edge of applying technological solutions to trucking problems. Its satellite system enables it to monitor exactly where a truck is at any time. All of its trucks are equipped with e-mail and vehicle-on-board radar (VORAD), a safety system that warns of potential collisions and hazards. Its

employee-friendly reputation has resulted in a turnover rate one-third less than the industry average, and females make up one-fourth of its drivers in an industry that averages only 5 percent women.

The attractiveness of Chattanooga comes from several aspects of the city. It is within a two-hour drive of some of the largest urban centers in the Southeast, including Birmingham, Atlanta, Nashville, and Knoxville, and has easy access to Interstates 24 and 75. These characteristics add to U.S. Xpress's ability to provide its services cost-effectively. While the location is attractive for logistical reasons, Cochairman Patrick Quinn says that workforce availability was a key factor in making a decision to build a new headquarters there in 1998. An expansion to that facility, announced in 2004, will add a 50,000-square-foot office building and 500 new employees. The company currently employs 1,350 workers in Chattanooga, 16 percent of its total workforce of 8,600. In addition to the new facility, U.S. Xpress plans to add an additional facility in five to seven years if growth continues.

Source: U.S. Xpress Enterprises, Inc., Hoover-No: 42375, Hoovers Company Records, 2004; "U.S. Xpress Plans Expansion Supporting 500 New Jobs," http://www.chattanoogachamber.com/newsandvideo/usxpressexmay19_04.asp, July 21, 2004; www.chattanoogachamber.com/entrepreneurs/dandersondsi.asp, July 21, 2004; "U.S. Express Adding 500 to 1000 Jobs in East Tenn. HQ," www.conway.com/ssinsider/pwatch, June 23, 2004; www.usxpress.com, June 2006.

*F*acility investments are among the most costly a business can make. Despite the implica-tions they have for value and business performance, they are often taken for granted. Two decisions, facility location and facility layout, have a critical impact on financial performance.

Introduction: Making Decisions for What May Be the Largest Investment

For many businesses, the facility is the largest single investment in an asset. Fa-cilities may seem to be huge investments that have little impact on prof-itability. Surprisingly, they offer a unique opportunity for manufacturers and services to match resources to strategic objectives. The location of the facil-ity, for example, can make or break the firm's strategy. Even when the facility layout is consistent with the strategy, the way the facility is utilized on a day-to-day basis affects customer-perceived value. Design and organize the facility inconsistently with the ob-jectives of the business, and the customers will walk away. Locate in the wrong place so that response time and convenience suffer, and more customers will walk away. Build a facility of the wrong size, and the investment won't generate a sufficient return. Fail to keep the facility clean and neat, and customers will avoid it, they'll tell their friends to avoid it, and, you guessed it, their friends *will* avoid it.

Facility-related decisions must be right the first time: Once they've been made, they are difficult and sometimes impossible to change. In many cases management must make the decisions before the business even exists, and they must make decisions that will re-main valid years in the future.

As globalization affects more markets, location decisions become more complex. En-trance into other markets goes beyond simply deciding to sell a product there. It requires developing distribution networks and maybe even manufacturing capabilities. The suc-cess of these decisions is driven by the availability of technologies, transportation sys-tems, and infrastructure that will be substantially different from that available in the United States.

Strategic Importance of Facilities

Recall from Chapter 3 that a business strategy is essentially a plan to attract customers who have a certain set of value priorities. A cost leadership strategy, for example, seeks to attract customers who are very concerned with the cost of their purchases. This strat-egy will affect a variety of long-term resource decisions. As discussed in Chapter 3, facil-ity decisions are one of four structural decisions that must be made when developing a strategy (along with capacity, process technology, and vertical integration/supplier rela-tionships). The strategic importance of facility decisions becomes more clear as these de-cisions are linked to profitability. Not surprisingly, facility decisions dictate profitability through their impact on value and costs.

In Chapter 2, two key profitability measures were presented:

$$\text{Profit Margin} = \frac{\text{Net Income}}{\text{Sales}}$$

$$\text{Returnfit Assets} = \frac{\text{Net Income}}{\text{Total Assets}}$$

Both depend on net income:

$$\text{Net Income} = \text{Net Sales} - \text{Cost of Goods Sold} - \text{Depreciation} \\ - \text{Interest Paid} - \text{Taxes}$$

As is the case with other operations resource decisions, facility decisions have two direct effects on net income. Facilities contribute directly to the customer's perception of value through various value attributes. Customer-perceived value drives net sales. Facilities also contribute directly to costs incurred by the business. They must be maintained. An increase in profitability improves the ratios between net income and sales and between net income and total assets. Profit margin and ROA are both affected by facility productivity through net income. Profit margin and ROA are also influenced by the facilities through their respective denominators, sales and total assets. Let's first examine the net income effect from facilities.

The primary impact any resource has on net income can be examined best from the standpoint of value added by that resource and costs linked to it. The B2C and B2B value attributes affected by facilities include price, quality, response time, dependability of delivery, convenience, ethical issues, and flexibility. Exhibit 16.1 summarizes corresponding facility decisions that impact these value attributes.

Value, we know, creates sales and market share. It is the driving force and is at the root of net income. Facilities are a key resource in creating that value, but they do not exist

U.S. Xpress ranks as the fifth largest publicly owned truckload carrier in the United States.

Facility Decision Criteria Checklist			EXHIBIT 16.1

Value Attribute	Location Impact	Layout Impact	Description of Impact
Cost	✓	✓	Facility location and facility layout affect costs.
Quality	✓	✓	Location dictates service quality issues. Layout dictates flow and, for services, the quality of the experience.
Response time	✓	✓	Location determines distance and transportation times. Layout determines process effectiveness, as well as material and customer movement.
Dependability of delivery	✓		Dependability is often a function of disruptions. Greater distances of transport open up opportunities for more disruptions.
Convenience	✓		Location often dictates convenience, particularly for services, because the location translates into "nearness." Convenient often means close by.
Ethical issues	✓		Location has implications for some ethical issues. Environmental impact is often a function of where a site is located. More often, the reason for locating in a foreign country may be perceived as exploitive.
Flexibility	✓	✓	Some layouts, by design, are more flexible than others. Process-oriented layouts, in particular, are designed for flexibility. Some worker skills can be linked to geography and enhance a firm's flexibility.

Although we don't typically think about it this way, the location decision for the Olympic games can represent one of the largest-scale facility location decisions ever made. Facilities range from sports venues to housing and include all of the issues a large business would consider, including transportation, access to support services, and so forth. Here, the Olympic Stadium is under construction in Beiging, China, for the 2008 Summer Olympics.

independent of other resources that the facility houses. The influence of facilities on value extends to those resources and *through* those resources as well. Inventory, workforce, and capacity resources, for most businesses, are *inside* a facility. Location dictates where the inventory is kept and where the workforce and capacity are utilized. Facilities dictate where many services take place. Facility location, in fact, is important only if the location of other resources is important. If inventory needs to be placed west of Mitchell, South Dakota, on I-90, that's where the facility needs to be located. For some businesses, location of workforce, inventory, and capacity isn't important, so the facility can be anywhere. This is particularly true for information-oriented services that do not depend on costly transportation of products or employees. In addition to the facility location, the way the facility allows other resources to be organized also contributes to their ability to create value. A close match between the facility and the goals of the business results in more productive resources, better processes, and better outcomes. These benefits translate directly into enhanced profitability.

The trade-off to the values enhanced by facilities is the cost of facilities. For many businesses, facilities are one of the largest sources of costs. In addition to being a large upfront investment, they require ongoing maintenance. They consume power for light and heat, and they dictate many tax bills. The larger the facility, the greater these costs. The close link between facility size and facility-related costs results in a productivity measure of the ratio of output to square footage. Sales per square foot, for example, is equally relevant for a retail shop and a factory.

From a strategic perspective, the facility decisions are addressed by two broad decision categories—the location and the layout of the facility. A huge set of variables comes into play, however, making these seemingly simple decisions extremely complex. Unlike many other resource decisions, which can be made in a relatively objective manner, facility location decisions are more subjective and as disparate as tax rates at one extreme and the company president's favorite golf course at the other. Quite often, there is no single right answer. Location and layout are difficult to optimize, because there is often no agreement on a single measure of performance. Facility design and layout decisions seek to create good solutions, but there is often no single optimal solution. The remainder of this chapter is devoted to facility location and facility design and layout decisions.

Facility Location Decisions

The need for a facility location decision results from three possible scenarios, each resulting in different priorities for location. The three scenarios are a location for a new business, a location for a business that must relocate, and a location for a business expansion.

Locating a New Business

The new-business location is potentially the most challenging decision, because there are more alternatives to consider and little information about future demand. Location decisions are often made as a progression of decisions, gradually narrowing down to a specific site. In many cases, an international location is possible, or even desirable, so the region of the world or specific country must be identified. From there, the target region within the country must be determined, followed by the state or location within the region, followed by the city, and, finally, within the city of choice, the site itself. For many companies, business inputs can drive the broad decisions concerning the country, region, or state.

Locating Near Inputs

For some businesses, characteristics of inputs and outputs can dictate location. A common input that can limit location choices is the raw material consumed by manufacturing processes, particularly when it is costly to transport. Some businesses create an output that cannot be transported economically. Manufacturers of very heavy, inexpensive items, like bricks and construction materials, must locate near their customers. This is true in the beverage industries as well, where each bottler supplies small geographic regions. Water is cheap but heavy and expensive to haul in bottles and cans. Other than water, the primary inputs are concentrated syrups, and transporting them over long distances is not as expensive as transporting the finished products.

Some businesses must locate where they can hire employees with certain skills. High-technology businesses, for example, must locate where there are skilled workers. Craft-oriented furniture factories must locate where workers with these skills live. This is true for manufacturing firms as well as for services that require unusual or scarce talent. Businesses go where the talent is, resulting in geographic areas becoming centers for specific industries. The end result is that there is sufficient job potential to attract more people with talents that fit the needs of the businesses. There is also competition among the businesses for the best workers. In some cases, particularly for high-volume manufacturing of products that are relatively inexpensive to ship (clothing, for example), location is selected based on labor costs rather than labor talent.

Other businesses, particularly manufacturers that require heavy or difficult-to-transport raw materials, must locate near these raw materials to enable them to manage costs. Examples of these businesses include basic manufacturers like those that utilize minerals or agricultural products in their manufacturing processes. A similar situation results when a manufacturer must locate near a large water source so that water can be used for cooling purposes.

Locating Near Customers

Some businesses, particularly services that require customer interaction, must locate near the customers, because that is an expectation of the customer. A business dependent on tourism, for example, must locate where tourists will want to go.

Firms that depend on close B2B interactions must often locate near customers also. Rather than taking advantage of reduced transportation costs, however, this decision seeks to provide better service and more frequent deliveries of products. Proximity enhances such value attributes as response time, dependability of delivery, and flexibility. For manufacturers of easy-to-transport products, the location of the customer isn't an issue, since their products can readily be shipped anywhere.

When services reduce the amount of required face-to-face interaction through expanded use of technology, their locations become less important. As the line of visibility

U.S. Xpress has a set of driver and trailer resources that specifically services the floor covering industry, which is close to Chatanooga.

moves toward the customer, the ever-increasing "behind the scenes" activities become a larger component of the business. Those activities do not need to consider proximity to the customer as part of the location decision. As a result, they can base the location decision on other factors.

In addition to the practical requirements driving location decisions, there are some that don't relate directly to a particular business yet often end up being the most important. At the top of these criteria are location characteristics that relate to quality of life. Climate, nearness to a large city, education systems, recreation, and so on are all key considerations for these decisions.

In making a location decision for a new business, one difficulty is the need for predictions about its future. For example, from a capacity standpoint, it might be important to locate where expansion is possible, should expansion be needed in the future. Cost may be a more significant issue for a new business location simply because of the uncertainty about future cash flows. Availability of money may reduce the number of alternatives that can be considered.

Relocating an Existing Business

Business relocation decisions arise for several reasons. Sometimes management wants to relocate for financial reasons or because the availability of business inputs changes. In other situations, management may be forced to relocate because they've lost or can no longer afford the lease on a building.

In many ways, the relocation decision is similar to the decision for locating a new business; however, because the business is already up and running, more information is available. Many of the options considered initially will probably not be considered again. The business may need to be relocated in the same geographic area to avoid losing employees and customers. In most cases, demand patterns are known, as are customer characteristics and the rate of growth for capacity requirements. For some businesses, relocation would not affect these factors, but for others, particularly services that depend on foot or automobile traffic patterns, relocation can drastically affect demand. What was known to exist at the original location may have no relationship to what will happen at the new location.

For a business that needs to be near its customers, relocating may be problematic, because there may be few choices. If building a new facility is not an option, the alternatives are limited to those facilities currently vacant. Even if constructing a new facility is feasible, placement of that facility is limited to property available, which may not be optimal.

Choosing a Location for Business Expansion

When the impetus behind a location decision is a need to expand, a choice must be made between expanding the current facility, building a new and bigger facility elsewhere, or becoming a multifacility business that will utilize the current facility as well as another one elsewhere. Expansion decisions are complex. Management must compare costs of expanding old facilities to costs of building new facilities and also consider the opportunities lost because of limitations of the old facility. For example, new technologies are typically more easily integrated into a new building. Given the chance to start from scratch, knowledge gained from experience often leads management to make significant changes in facility design. Many of the benefits of these opportunities are difficult to quantify.

The decision to become a multifacility business is particularly difficult because of the changes to management's job when a second facility is brought on line. Supervision and control issues change when management needs to be two places at once. The benefits, however, can include critical competitive advantages such as opening up new markets.

Location Decision-Making Criteria

Obviously, when beginning a location decision-making process, management has some idea of the scope of the alternatives to consider. Our coverage, however, starts with the broadest possible decision and progresses to the very small and narrow. One way to organize relocation decision-making factors is to examine a hierarchy of levels of decision alternatives that extends from international issues and possible countries, to regions within a country, to states, to city or community, and to the actual site. At each level, the criteria relevant to that level are considered. In the following discussion, we'll examine the criteria that traditionally have been the most important at each level, as well as a new technology that aids decision makers in merging these criteria.

International Issues

Decisions that deal with locating in foreign countries can be broken down into two distinct situations: (1) a company wishes to do business in another country and must locate there in order to bring that to fruition, and (2) a company wishes to locate a facility in another country to gain some competitive advantage. Let's address the first scenario first.

Decisions to expand or relocate to a foreign country are becoming more common. As markets open up, opportunities open up as well. For some markets, businesses must have a physical presence in the country that houses the market. In these situations the decision is not about locating an operation in the country; it's about doing business in the country. If the decision is to do business there, then locating there is a foregone conclusion. The location decision then becomes one of *where* in that country.

The decision to do business in a foreign country, with a culture that could be drastically different from what a company is accustomed to, is a major one. It is a decision that has the potential to open up huge market opportunities but also has the potential to be a disaster. It is an expensive undertaking with high levels of uncertainty. Baazee.com provides a prime example of the differences between two cultures. Baazee.com is modeled after Ebay, the auction site, but is based in India. The auction market in India is drastically different from the U.S. market. In India, auctions are used almost exclusively for bankruptcy liquidations, so the concept of an online auction has a different meaning

---

GOING **global**   **Businesses See Mixed Results in International Locations**

Market domination in the United States doesn't necessarily lead to domination in other countries. As businesses try to expand their markets, some find success, while others struggle. FedEx, for example, has seen the volume of goods shipped internationally increase by 40 percent in two years, with most of its growth in Asia. FedEx has become the preferred carrier from China. It now operates 120 flights per week from Asia, with 26 from China, and controls 39 percent of the China-to-U.S. air express market. UPS has 32 percent and DHL has 27 percent. In response to its success, FedEx plans to close its Asian hub in the Philippines and open a new superhub in Guangzhou, China. It will also take delivery of the first Airbus A380 cargo haulers, which will carry twice the volume of goods as the Boeing MD-11.

Wal-Mart's international efforts, on the other hand, are seeing mixed result. In England, home of Wal-Mart's largest non-U.S. foothold, Wal-Mart's Asda stores have a strong rival in Tesco PLC. Asda provides 10 percent of Wal-Mart's overall sales and 45 percent of its international sales. Tesco has signed up 12 million customers to a "clubcard," which gives them discounts in exchange for personal information. The personal information is then used for more direct marketing, coupon distribution, and so on. Tesco's 31 percent market share in groceries is nearly double that of Wal-Mart's Asda chain.

Tesco is clearly winning the information battle over Wal-Mart and is using the information it has to compete against Wal-Mart. Tesco identified those customers who are most price sensitive and the 300 items they buy most. It then lowered the prices on those items to keep the customers from defecting to Asda. Its sales increased by 17 percent to $79 billion. Wal-Mart's Japanese unit has had losses, and in May 2006 it gave up on an eight-year attempt to succeed in South Korea. Tesco, however, is running 39 stores successfully in South Korea.

Source: "Taking Off Like a Rocket Ship," *BusinessWeek*, April 3, 2006, p. 76; "No. 1 Retailer in Britain Uses 'Clubcard' to Thwart Wal-Mart," *Wall Street Journal*, June 6, 2006, pp. A1, A16.

there than in the United States. In addition, very few Indian brands are well-known enough that people would buy them sight unseen. Baazee.com had to set up exchange centers in large cities so that transactions could be completed in person.[1]

The uncertainty doesn't stop with the market conditions. The workforce can also be significantly different from what management is used to. This includes skill and knowledge as well as cultural differences that affect business capabilities. The political and regulatory environment can also be drastically different from what management is accustomed to. Governments change. Monetary exchange rates change. Possibly the greatest contributor to risk is the fact that the state of the economy, the market, and the workforce may be changing in ways that take them all to a very different place in a short period of time. Despite all of the risks and uncertainty, businesses must recognize that they exist in a global economy. Competition is not limited to businesses in the United States. Market share does not mean U.S. *market share*. Location decisions related to expansion and growth must consider all location alternatives, not just those within U.S. boundaries.

A company may face an international location decision not to access the host country's markets, but to gain competitive advantage from something that country has to offer. Reasons for locating a facility in a foreign country tend to be dominated by cost issues such as tax advantages, lower labor costs, and lower materials costs. In addition to the expected cost reductions, a number of potential cost increases must be considered, including the skill and abilities of the labor force, political climate, quality of life for U.S. managers, tax climate, access to markets, site availability, access to process inputs, transportation costs, and transport time. Despite the popularity of moving operations overseas to gain labor cost reductions, there have also been moves back to the United States because the time required to ship completed products back to the United States was unacceptable. The increase in the cash-to-cash cycle can be substantial, reducing profitability.

Location decisions must consider global alternatives, but they can sometimes be motivated by unethical and exploitive goals. An example of such a decision is locating in a country that does not regulate pollution to cut costs associated with meeting the U.S. standards for clean air and water. Exploiting child labor to cut labor costs is another example. Customers are becoming increasingly aware of these situations and are beginning to reward ethical behavior by using the force of their own freedom of choice.

Domestic Location Decisions

Location decisions limited to the United States or North America have traditionally been based on criteria that relate to region, state, city or community, and to the actual

---

GOING **global** New Markets Mean More Than Just Moving

Many factors enter into the decision to expand into other countries. Costs and political considerations are always important. Once a decision is made, however, how the firm does business must also be examined and adapted. Expanding Wal-Mart stores to Brazil, for example, is more than replicating a U.S.-style store. Each country has its own characteristics, and they will dictate what works and what doesn't.

Wal-Mart is the sixth-biggest mass merchandiser in Brazil. Since 1995 Wal-Mart opened 13 Wal-Mart supercenters, 10 Sam's Club stores, and 2 stores of a new format called a Wal-Mart Todo Dia. *Todo dia* is Portuguese for "every day." These stores will be smaller and more warehouselike than a typical Wal-Mart supercenter, with concrete floors, no

air-conditioning, and goods displayed in boxes. Todo Dias will sell goods at about 5 percent below the prices of competitors. The buildings can be built in less than three months. They will be attractive because the Brazilian income is low, customers cannot travel great distances to shop, and the stores will be neighborhood-focused. In addition to the openings of new stores, Wal-Mart also purchased 118 Bombreco stores from the Dutch retailer Ahold.

Source: "Wal-Mart Gets Aggressive about Brazil," *Wall Street Journal,* May 25, 2001, pp. A8, A12; "Wal-Mart Acquires Brazilian Chain," Home Channel News Newsfax, Vol. 15, No. 10, March 8, 2004.

Location Decision Criteria Checklist				EXHIBIT 16.2
Criterion	Region	State	City or Community	Site
Labor knowledge and talent	✓	✓	✓	
Labor costs	✓	✓	✓	
Other labor issues		✓	✓	
Business support services			✓	
Quality-of-life issues	✓	✓	✓	
Access to markets	✓	✓	✓	
Access to transportation	✓	✓	✓	✓
Education system		✓	✓	
Training infrastructure		✓	✓	
Regulatory climate	✓	✓	✓	
Tax climate		✓	✓	
Utility availability			✓	✓
Utility cost		✓	✓	
Incentives for new business		✓	✓	
Real estate costs		✓	✓	
Real estate availability		✓	✓	
Site-specific costs			✓	✓

site. Exhibit 16.2 summarizes the criteria traditionally considered in location decisions and the hierarchical level in which they are an issue. They are covered in greater detail in the following discussion.

Workforce Capabilities

For most manufacturing and service businesses, the capabilities, talent, and expertise of the workforce are a critical component of success. Locating where that resource is in short supply or nonexistent would be foolish. As jobs become more complex and more dependent on technological skills, the requirements of the labor force increase. This issue has to be a top priority for any location decision, and it is considered at the regional, state, and community level. It has become such a dominant criterion in business location decisions that many states are marketing the skills of their workforce as a way to attract new businesses. They know that the productivity of the workforce has a huge impact on the value created and on company profitability.

Labor Costs

Labor costs are also a significant consideration, but because labor content varies from one business to the next, labor cost may or may not be a high priority. Labor costs vary from region to region, from state to state, and even from one city to the next. These differences can be substantial, particularly for labor-intensive producers of products or services. Labor organization (union versus nonunion) can also depend on location. Depending on the business, management may be particularly attracted to a workforce that has been willing to work with management on solving business problems.

Business Services

Increasingly, businesses outsource support services like payroll management, information technology, maintenance, and transportation services. The availability of these services can be a significant factor in the location decision. Absence of a particular service means that the business will have to do the function itself, increasing costs and diverting attention from core competencies.

Quality of Life

When a business moves, at least some employees will move to the new location. Quality-of-life issues at the new location are usually considered in the relocation decision. What

GOING global · Oops—Maybe That Move Was a Bad Idea

Much has been written about Xerox's fall from its May 1999 share price of $66 to its spring 2001 share price of around $7, which was only a few dollars above its share price 30 years earlier. The strategic snafus and leadership conflict that led to the firing of CEO G. Richard Thoman have been well-documented. It is enlightening, however, to look at some of the more concrete decisions that led up to Xerox's financial woes. One of the most interesting is the story of a location decision that went wrong.

Businesses often move operations to countries with low taxes. These moves have resulted in millions of dollars in tax savings for some companies. A look at a recent move by Xerox shows that there is always risk. Xerox initiated a plan to cut its worldwide tax rate to under 30 percent back in the late 1990s. By moving some operations to Ireland, it expected to increase net income by $800 million over five years. One of the biggest impacts was the creation of a call center in Dublin to serve all of Europe. Xerox also built a large manufacturing center to produce inkjet cartridges and other printer supplies. The move made Ireland the administrative parent of most of the European business.

The initiative backfired, however, as Xerox's weighted average of the worldwide tax rates rose from 31 percent in 1999 to 38 percent in 2000. The move to low-tax countries was dependent on an annual growth rate in pretax profit of 15 percent. The plan was to shift that growth in profit from high-tax countries (United States and Britain) to Ireland, which has tax rates of between 10 percent and 12.5 percent. Rather than grow at a 15 percent rate, however, Xerox had operating losses. Despite these losses, Xerox expected to return to profitability in the first half of 2001. The plan didn't

work because a company with operating losses doesn't pay taxes, but records a tax benefit similar to an extraordinary gain. This is because the company can typically use the loss to recoup taxes paid in previous years or to reduce future taxes, but the losses can be used only to accrue tax benefits in the country where they were incurred. The company would like to record profits in low-tax countries, obviously, but it needs to record losses in high-tax countries so the losses can be used to reduce future or past taxes. If losses occur in a low-tax country, the tax benefit will also be low.

According to John Hodges, former deputy treasurer of Xerox's European operations, the plan was a big mistake. It was based on increasing revenues, and no one looked at what would happen if these revenues and profits didn't occur.

The lesson is simple. Clearly there are financial gains to be made by taking advantage of different tax regulations at different locations. This is true not only from one country to another, but even from state to state. However, just as there are advantages in moving, there can be equal or greater disadvantages. The advantages tend to get the most attention. When things are going well, reduced taxes may improve the situation. However, when things are going poorly, tax regulations can make things even worse. Basing a move decision on one criterion that provides an advantage only under certain circumstances is a recipe for disaster.

Source: "How a Xerox Plan to Reduce Taxes and Boost Profit Backfired," *Wall Street Journal,* April 17, 2001, pp. C1, C15; "Less Red Ink for Xerox," *BusinessWeek.Com,* January 29, 2001; "Xerox: The Downfall," *BusinessWeek.Com,* March 5, 2001.

---

will it be like to live there? Are there leisure-time activities that are appealing and compatible with what the people like to do? Is the climate desirable? Is the community attractive? These criteria are difficult to quantify, but they can be among the most important.

Market Access

For many businesses, particularly services that cannot "transport" what they produce, location near the market can be the factor that determines success or failure. Being half a block away from the flow of foot or automobile traffic can be the equivalent of being in Siberia. For such businesses, this is the only criterion that matters. Sometimes the city or community doesn't matter. The state doesn't matter. The region doesn't matter. The only issue is the site. If the site is a good one, any city in any state will be fine.

Transportation Access

Access to transportation can also be important. Businesses whose employees must travel to customers and clients must have access to an airport. Businesses that ship products or receive inputs by truck must have close access to an interstate highway. Businesses that depend on rail deliveries must have rail access. Transportation, and access to various modes of transportation, often translates into reduced time in the cash-to-cash cycle. Speed it up to improve profitability. Cut it in half and the rate of financial return doubles.

Education System

Education plays a role in location decisions for two reasons. First, workers who will be transferred to a new location want assurance that the school system in place will provide a quality education for their children. Second, if the workforce needs special skills, the importance of vocational schools and universities is heightened.

Regulatory and Tax Climate

From a cost standpoint, regulatory and tax climate can provide a dramatic boost or equally dramatic detriment to business success. Taxes are an issue of concern for virtually all businesses, and the tax regulations at the state and city level must be considered in location decisions. For some businesses, the regulatory environment can be important also.

Utilities

For heavy consumers of electricity or natural gas, utility cost and availability can be a very important location criterion. Utility costs vary substantially from region to region, from state to state, and even from city to city. For manufacturers whose processes require substantial power use, these differences can have a significant impact on the bottom line.

Incentives

As states and communities have recognized the importance of economic growth and new businesses, many have elected to compete for them by offering various incentives that will be attractive to them. Included among incentives given by state and local governments are tax reductions and tax breaks, interest-free loans, facility or site upgrades, and education and training for potential employees. Although these incentives can turn into bidding wars between competing locations, they often provide enough financial benefit to be a significant factor in the decision-making process. Many states and regions actively market themselves to attract businesses.

Site Availability

As location issues get resolved, and a shortened list of potential alternatives at the regional, state, and city level becomes available, site considerations begin to dominate the decision-making process. The most dominant criteria at this point are the availability of a site and the cost of a site. Everything may look great for a given community, but if there is no land available, the other criteria don't matter. The same holds for high cost of land that is available. It can outweigh all other advantages of a particular city. In addition to the cost of the site itself, other site-specific costs may influence the final decision. For example, upgrading the site to meet the needs of a new facility may be too costly. Changing access to the site, including widening streets or adding stoplights, can increase site-related costs. A variety of costs can emerge at the last minute that are necessary to make a specific site compatible with what the business needs.

While the traditional cost-related criteria still drive many facility location decisions, other noncost criteria that are not as easy to quantify also play a role.[2] A rich and diverse local economy is important, because many households are supported by two careers. Both partners must be able to find employment. Good schools are critical to attract an educated workforce. A quality education for their children is a top priority. Affordable housing is another critical criterion for business locations, since many employees might not be paid at high salary levels. The business must be able to attract employees at all levels. In many instances, the business needs to be able to attract workers from commuting distances. The site must be easy to commute to, and mass transit is desirable. The ability to attract a diverse workforce means that the location must welcome ethnic, racial, and religious diversity. Businesses with specific talent requirements might need to locate near other employers in the same field to have access to pools of talent. For start-ups, nearness

GISs have been adapted by many city governments to aid in their ability to attract business by making location-related information readily available. Here is a simple output from a city's GIS after a search for a 1,500-square-foot office facility was initiated. Clicking on the address of each site provides an aerial photograph, ground photograph, and extensive facility details, such as actual size, year built, ceiling height, lease or sale price, and other amenities.

ZOOM OUT   PAN   PROPERTY INFO   PRINT

NEW SEARCH

10 sites were found
1 1600 E RIVER RD
2 2122 N CRAYCROFT RD
3 3755 E 34TH ST suite #102-104, #107
4 4400 E BROADWAY BL
5 540 W PRINCE RD
6 6060 N FOUNTAIN PLAZA DR
7 6418 E TANQUE VERDE RD suite 105
8 6418 E TANQUE VERDE RD suite 110
9 7454 E BROADWAY BL
10 8230 E BROADWAY BL suite E-4, 5, 6, 7, & 8

to venture capital firms can be important. For many businesses, easy access to north–south transportation routes is important, because supply chains often cross the border into Mexico. Finally, many businesses look for cities that are regional centers of influence, because they are more attractive for employees and are able to draw labor talent from the surrounding area.

Geographic Information Systems

A recent technological development has enhanced decision makers' ability to merge geographic information from a variety of sources. Geographic information systems (GISs) extract quantitative data from statistical databases for use in building sophisticated maps that present the information in a geographical context. Software can translate any database with population or geographic information to maps that assist in the identification of business locations. Data used include public information, such as U.S. census data, maps of streets, and other physical features, as well as private information, such as demographic information gathered through product sales. Merging the data sets aids in finding alternatives for business location decisions. Criteria are entered into a search query, and the result is a map that identifies all sites satisfying the criteria. Some systems also provide aerial photos of the sites.

In addition to business applications of this technology, many city and state governments have adapted this technology to make it easier for businesses to find sites. Cities make the service available online, so that businesses interested in locating there can identify potential sites. The complexities of location decisions, particularly when many variables are a concern, make traditional methods unusable. GIS technology can be customized to include virtually any statistics and convert them to a map format.

U.S. Xpress has developed technology that allows customers to track shipment status, receive quotes of future loads, check distances, complete advance booking of shipments and review paperwork for past shipments online.

Location Decision-Making Techniques

The very nature of a location decision, whether it is for a new business, relocation, or expansion, is that the issues to be considered range from those that are easily quantified to those that are subjective and fuzzy. Transportation costs can be quantified. Quality of life can't. Site upgrade costs can be quantified. The quality of the school system can't. When it comes right down to it, the location of a business is where the owner or owners want it to be. The location might be consistent with the results of quantitative analysis, or it might be that the owner just likes the views better somewhere else despite the results of an extensive quantitative analysis of all criteria.

Many criteria in location decisions are compatible with quantitative analysis techniques, and several approaches are commonly used to help make the location decision more objective. For the most part, these approaches are general-purpose decision-making tools that fit very nicely into the location-decision scenario because they facilitate choosing from a list of alternatives. The tools that will be examined for location decisions are multifactor rating, decision trees, and breakeven analysis. Each of these techniques starts with a short list of alternatives and provides guidance in making the final cut.

Multifactor Rating

Location decisions are made after considering a broad range of information. No technique can provide a "best" solution, because there is no "best" solution. In many ways, location decisions can be evaluated only after the fact, because the suitability of the location depends on events that can only be predicted. Although making the best decision may be impossible, making a good decision is obviously necessary. The variety of information to be considered makes it important to organize the information so the decision itself can be organized. The last thing any business wants is for an employee, four weeks after the move to the new facility, to point out a major shortcoming of the new facility: "The trucks that bring our products are too heavy for the street out front!" or "Did you know that they're going to reroute the highway so it won't be near our store any more?!" or "The dust from the manufacturing plant next door is ruining our paint finish!" No question, each of these would prompt the same response from management: "%#&*!! Why didn't we think of that earlier?!"

Multifactor rating provides a mechanism for considering a variety of factors with different levels of significance and incorporating them into a decision. It has many useful applications outside of location decisions, but for these types of decisions it is a good match. Multifactor rating starts with a list of issues or criteria (factors) to be considered in making the decision: condition of the building, cost of the building, nearness to transportation, and so on. This list should be extensive, made with the involvement of as many people as possible, and examined for completeness. The benefit of this process is not just that it provides guidance for the decision, but that it also forces decision makers to consider everything. Each factor is given an importance weighting between 0 and 1.0. The weights must sum to 1.0. A factor of little importance gets a low (closer to 0) weight; a factor of great importance gets a high (closer to 1.0) weight; factors of equal importance get equal weights.

Next, each of the alternative locations is given a score for each factor. For example, if a particular site has very good transportation access, that site might be given a score of 90 for transportation access. Another site, with not quite as good access, might be given a score of 85.

Next, the multifactor score for each location is computed by multiplying the importance weight for each factor by that factor's score and summing the results across all factors. The highest possible multifactor score for a particular location alternative would be 100. Example 16.1 demonstrates the use of this technique for a new-business location decision.

Example 16.1

EXCEL TUTOR

Multifactor Rating for a Tanning Salon Location

Tim Boyd, a local rental property owner, wants to open a small tanning salon. He's looking for a preexisting building that can be modified by constructing 12 tanning booths. He identified six criteria for decision making and gave them the importance weights shown in Exhibit 16.3.

(Continues)

Example 16.1 *(Continued)*

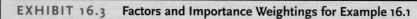

EXHIBIT 16.3	Factors and Importance Weightings for Example 16.1
Factor	**Importance Weighting**
Overall building condition	0.2
Ease of modification	0.2
Parking availability	0.2
Visibility/traffic	0.15
Electrical capacity	0.1
Cost	0.15

Tim identified four possible locations with buildings that are currently unoccupied. He scored each of the four alternatives on each factor. The scores are shown in Exhibit 16.4.

EXHIBIT 16.4 Factor Scores for Each Location for Example 16.1

	Scores			
Factor	**Location 1**	**Location 2**	**Location 3**	**Location 4**
Overall building condition	95	85	50	75
Ease of modification	80	90	75	85
Parking availability	60	70	90	95
Visibility/traffic	95	55	80	85
Electrical capacity	70	80	95	90
Cost	70	70	95	75

Solution

The results of multiplying the factor scores for each location by the factor weights are presented in Exhibit 16.5. Location 4 turns out to be the highest scored location, with 84.

EXHIBIT 16.5 Multifactor Scores for Each Location

	Factor	Scores			
Factor	**Weights**	**Location 1**	**Location 2**	**Location 3**	**Location 4**
Overall building condition	0.2	95	85	50	75
Ease of modification	0.2	80	90	75	85
Parking availability	0.2	60	70	90	95
Visibility/traffic	0.15	95	55	80	85
Electrical capacity	0.1	70	80	95	90
Cost	0.15	70	70	95	75
Total score		78.75	75.75	78.75	84

Excel Tutor 16.1 demonstrates the multifactor rating technique in Excel.

Step-by-Step: Multifactor Rating

1. Identify alternatives from which to select.
2. Identify factors or criteria important for the decision to be made.
3. Determine a weight for each factor, making sure that the weights sum to 1.
4. For each alternative, give each factor a score from 1 to 100.
5. For each alternative, multiply each factor score by the factor's weight.
6. For each alternative, sum the weighted scores to compute a total score.
7. Compare scores for the alternatives.

Even though the multifactor rating technique appears objective because it provides quantitative results, it must be recognized as a subjective process. The weights assigned and the scoring of each factor are subjective processes. Changing a weight or a score can result in a change in the solution. Nevertheless, the approach does increase the objectivity of the location decision, particularly if the establishment of the weights and scores involves several different individuals.

Decision Tree Analysis

Decision tree analysis, examined in Chapter 2, is a general technique for organizing decisions by identifying expected revenues associated with each alternative. Decision trees are applicable to a wide variety of decisions where the outcomes of the choices are uncertain. Decision trees approach the calculation of expected revenues by multiplying the revenue expected for each alternative by the likelihood of its happening. This logic is very applicable to facility location decisions.

Breakeven Analysis

Breakeven analysis can be a useful tool for making location decisions. Back in Chapter 2, breakeven analysis was demonstrated in an example that compared three alternative suppliers of software. It can be used in a similar way when comparing location alternatives that have different fixed and variable costs. Different locations typically have different upfront costs associated with the purchase or upgrading of the facility and other capital items. They also have different variable costs. Materials, labor, and other resources may cost more at some locations than others. Example 16.2 demonstrates the use of breakeven analysis in a location problem.

Example 16.2   Location Breakeven Analysis

EXCEL TUTOR

Ron Storch is a recent college graduate who worked for a landscaping company for the past four summers, earning money for school. He decided that a great way to gain managerial experience, and have fun, would be to run his own landscaping firm for a year or two before going back to school for an MBA. Through contacts and friends, he identified three alternative locations in three different states for starting his business. His previous employer helped him develop a plan and estimate material and labor costs for various jobs. With these data, he created a generic "job" that represents the typical new home landscaping job that will sustain his business. Ron also priced available equipment, labor rates, and material costs in each location. He developed the data presented in Exhibit 16.6 for use in his decision. His variable costs are based on labor rates, local landscaping materials costs, and 30 labor hours per job.

(Continues)

Example 16.2   (Continued)

EXHIBIT 16.6   Cost Data for Landscaping Location

Site No.	Fixed Costs ($)	Labor Cost/Hour ($)	Labor Cost/Job ($)	Materials Cost/Job ($)	Variable Cost/Job Total ($)
1	58,000	6.75	202.50	437.50	640.00
2	80,000	7.3	219.00	266.00	485.00
3	42,000	8.1	243.00	609.00	852.00

Solution

Exhibit 16.7 graphically illustrates his cost curves. Precise intersections for the cost curves are calculated below.

EXHIBIT 16.7   Cost Curves for Location Breakeven

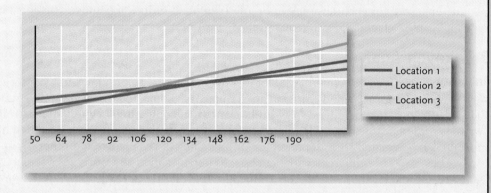

Site 1		Site 2
$58,000 + 640X$	$=$	$80,000 + 485X$
$640X$	$=$	$22,000 + 485X$
$155X$	$=$	$22,000$
X	$=$	141.9

Site 1		Site 3
$58,000 + 640X$	$=$	$42,000 + 852X$
$16,000 + 640X$	$=$	$852X$
$16,000$	$=$	$212X$
X	$=$	75.47

For an expected number of jobs fewer than 75, Site 3 is the low-cost site. From 75 jobs up to 142 jobs, Site 1 is the low-cost site. At volumes greater than 142 jobs, Site 2 is the best.

This problem is solved in Excel in Excel Tutor 16.2.

Business Location Trends

Increased use of the Internet in business has drastically changed the way businesses make location decisions. Although some businesses still utilize traditional criteria, many businesses are no longer bound by geographic limitations. Where they locate is still important, but the criteria can be weighted very differently. The types of workers that businesses need the most—those that help them create the most value—are engineers, investment analysts, technology workers, scientists, and other highly skilled, highly creative workers. Businesses that need them must locate where they live or where they'd like to live. Quality of life that would be attractive to these workers is now the most important criterion for the location of many businesses. In many cases these are smaller cities, like Seattle or Boston, but quite often they are the expensive suburbs of cities like Austin, Texas, or Raleigh, North Carolina. One characteristic that often sets these locations apart is that the communities are "wired." They've embraced the Internet and have an infrastructure in place. Taxes are low, crime is low, and the lifestyle is appealing to workers and management. These "edge cities" are really huge, well-planned, suburbs. Joel Kotkin, an expert on new-economy geography, refers to these cities as "nerdistans."[3] These communities are often close to major universities, which are sources of expertise as well as culture.

Even as the nerdistans are home to many businesses, small towns are gaining fast. Low taxes, low costs, low crime, and simple lifestyles have made cities in the West and Midwest more attractive. Nevada, Montana, Colorado, and the Dakotas have a higher concentration of high-tech workers than Massachusetts.[4] The cities of choice are quite diverse, but in most cases they are far from the urban environments that once attracted businesses. Fort Collins, Colorado, is a classic example of the new type of city that is attracting business. It offers good schools, a clean environment, outdoor recreation, and a quality of life that is desirable.[5]

Attractive locations may not remain attractive forever. Popularity itself can change an area to such a great extent that it destroys its attractiveness. Silicon Valley is a great example. Its popularity among the newly rich raised property values and property taxes to the extent that teachers and government workers could no longer afford to live there. Businesses began to shy away from locating there because the typical worker would have to commute 40 miles from the nearest affordable place to live. As technology continues to change the geography by making it easier to telecommute and cheaper to transport goods, and as communication problems between disjointed departments and businesses are eliminated, priorities for location decisions will continue to shift.

U.S. Xpress Enterprises received two Quest For Quality Awards from *Logistics Management Magazine* in 2005.

Facility Layouts

The location of a facility dictates part of its contribution to value, but as we discussed in Chapter 3, distinctive capabilities are created by the general layout of the facility and whether it should be process-oriented, product-oriented, or cellular. Processes, which dictate value, must exist within the limits set by the general layout choice. Layout decisions at the time of the facility design, as well as during improvement efforts, can increase the productivity of many different resources.

Even after the general decision is made, more decisions remain. Precisely how the general layout will incorporate equipment and specific functions must be decided. The work environment is also important. For some resources, location of the resource can dictate productivity measures. For example, work centers that are far apart may result in unnecessary transporting of materials between them. For human resource productivity, the decisions made during the layout process can have other effects. Lighting, noise, ventilation, and other aesthetic factors can influence employee perceptions of their environment. Many of these factors have a direct impact on productivity.

Frequently these specific layout decisions become part of the work of employee teams devoted to process improvement. In some cases, the vendors that supply manufacturing

The layout of workspaces has received much attention because those layouts affect worker productivity. Office layouts, in particular, create a challenge because worker interaction is a necessary component of many businesses, but privacy and quiet are also important. Choices range from the "bullpen" atmosphere, filled with cubicles, to a more open layout as pictured here.

equipment become involved in these decisions. In the following sections, the strengths and weaknesses of each kind of general layout will be reviewed, as well as decisions regarding those layouts and the techniques used to make those decisions.

om ADVANTAGE　Office Layouts Change to Reduce Noise Levels

In the 1980s and 1990s the trend toward open offices reached its peak as many office cubicles were constructed of short, movable architectural walls. The result was a feeling of openness that was intended to promote an atmosphere that would encourage cooperation and teamwork. Recently, however, many employees and managers have begun to retreat from this layout because of noise. In a study conducted by the American Society of Interior Designers, 70 percent of respondents indicated that lower noise levels would increase their productivity, but 81 percent of the business executives were unaware that a noise problem existed.

Employee productivity is reduced by other employees talking, phone calls are interrupted by noise, and, in general, employees desire more "acoustical privacy." Employees complain more about noise than lighting, air conditioning, and lack of space. Offices are staffed at high densities to reduce costs. Employees in open cubicles sometimes use speaker phones and typically speak louder when using

them. In addition, telephones, fax machines, beepers, file drawers, keyboards, printers, and many other objects also contribute to the level of noise in office settings.

In response to concern about office noise levels, low architectural walls are being replaced by walls that extend all the way to the ceiling, and managers are separating groups of employees who have similar noise-level needs. Small soundproof conference rooms are also being constructed. Herman Miller, an office furniture manufacturer, noted that sales of short cubicle panels have been declining since 1996, while sales of taller panels have been increasing.

In addition to structural changes, many companies are masking noise by installing "white-noise" machines. Dynasound, a producer of noise-masking systems, has had a sixfold increase in sales since 1994.

Source: "Shut Up So We Can Do Our Jobs!" *Wall Street Journal*, August 29, 2001, pp. B1, B8; "ASID Sound Solutions," www.dynasound.com/, June 2006.

Process-Oriented Layouts

A process-oriented layout is characterized by functional departments. It enables the firm to adapt the sequence of operations to meet particular needs of customers who desire a customized product or service. Exhibit 16.8 presents a typical process-oriented layout.

The functional nature of the layout makes it possible for a customer or product to be routed through departments in any sequence necessary to fulfill the processing requirements. For example, an order could enter the printing business illustrated in Exhibit 16.9 at the design department, and then go to printing, then binding, and finally packaging and shipping. On the other hand, an order for a standard product that doesn't get bound might start at paper storage, go directly to printing, and then move to packaging and shipping. The layout offers great flexibility.

After the general decision to adopt a process-oriented layout has been made, decisions remain for making that layout the best it can be. The strength of the process-oriented layout is its ability to utilize the functional departments in any sequence desired. This strength can result in a tremendous amount of material movement or, in the case of a service, customer movement from one department to another that could be some distance away. The arrangement of departments within the process-oriented layout will dictate the costs associated with transporting customers and products through the system. These costs can be substantial, and a well-designed layout can have a dramatic impact on them.

The primary objective in determining the relative locations of departments in a process-oriented layout is to locate close together those departments that interact the most and to locate at a distance those that don't interact or that need to be separate from each other. This logic applies to both manufacturing and service layouts, including the layout of professional offices. Consulting firms, architectural firms, legal firms, and so on, have various experts that are pulled together to work on projects. It makes sense to locate those that most frequently interact closer to each other.

| Process-Oriented Layout | EXHIBIT 16.8 |

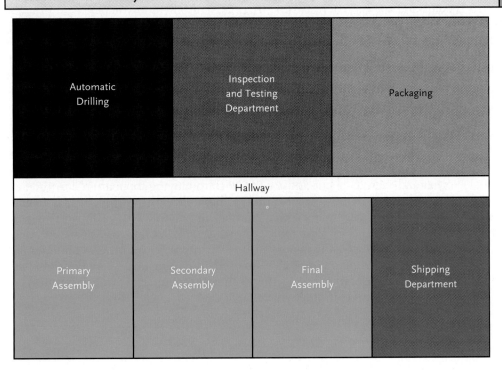

om ADVANTAGE — In Health Care, Facility Layout Has Far-Reaching Effects

We don't often think about the importance of facility layout in services, but for some, it can be a life or death issue.

Hospital safety concerns jumped in 1999 when studies showed that between 48,000 and 98,000 patients died each year because of medical mistakes. As a result, hospitals are taking a hard look at how their facilities can be used to reduce these numbers. Hospitals are using improved facility design to reduce patient anxiety, reduce stress levels for physicians and staff, use more natural light, provide better patient privacy, reduce the potential for spreading infection, and improve patient safety.

Some hospitals are no longer recycling air and are doing more filtration. Others are changing the wall coverings to materials that are less conducive to molds and changing the floor coverings to make them less slippery. Windows with blinds enclosed inside of the glass will replace traditional blinds, which have long been known to harbor germs. Sound-absorbing tiles make the rooms quieter. Bathrooms are located closer to the bed to reduce the potential for falls.

On each floor, nursing stations are placed so that they can see all patient rooms.

A significant change is to standardize patient rooms. Each room will have identical lighting, identical furniture layout, and identical locations of everything a doctor or nurse could need. Staff can more easily and more quickly locate emergency oxygen lines, for example, because they are in the same locations in every patient room.

All of these changes have resulted from an architectural goal to design the facilities to maximize patient safety. While this approach was expected to be expensive, it provides cost benefits as well. Standardized rooms, for example, allow for prefabrication and discounts from vendors.

Source: "To Reduce Errors, Hospitals Prescribe Innovative Designs," *Wall Street Journal*, May 8, 2006, pp. A1, A16; "Hospital Designs Aim for Safety, Care," *Sacramento Business Journal*, online edition, www.bizjournals.com/sacramento/stories/2005/11/28/focus7.html, accessed June 11, 2006.

The frequency of the interaction or transportation, combined with the distance between the locations, establishes the transportation or movement costs associated with their relative positions in the layout. Not surprisingly, layout decisions attempt to minimize these costs. This process is generally a "cut-and-try" approach to obtaining a good layout, but it cannot guarantee the best layout as an outcome. In an operation with only six departments, there would be 6! (720) possible positions for the six departments.

In the cut-and-try approach, two matrices are initially constructed. One provides the frequency of the interaction between each pair of departments. The other provides the distances between all potential locations or rooms in the facility. This approach utilizes several modifications of the layout to improve it. A third matrix, called a total-distance matrix, contains the products of the frequency of interaction and the distance for each pair of potential locations. These distances are summed to provide a total distance of travel for each proposed layout. The total distance associated with alternative layouts can be compared and the best one selected. Example 16.3 demonstrates this process.

Other approaches are also used to develop process-oriented layouts. Some identify relationships between pairs of departments by rating the importance of the pairs being next to each other and then use a cut-and-try approach to moving them around to generate good alternative layouts. One popular approach that utilizes this technique is systematic layout planning (SLP).[6] SLP starts with a relationships matrix with each pair of departments and assigns a "closeness desirability" rating of A, E, I, O, U, or X, where A is absolutely necessary, E is especially important, I is important, O is OK, U is unimportant, and X means that they should not be close to each other. The ratings are illustrated in a diagram through the use of lines connecting each department. The printing business layout is examined using this technique in Example 16.4.

Example 16.3

Cut-and-Try Layout Process

EXCEL TUTOR

Exhibit 16.9 is a diagram of a proposed layout for a printing business. The operation has six departments. Print jobs are moved, usually by forklift truck, from one department to the next one in their routing.

EXHIBIT 16.9   Proposed Layout for a Printing Business

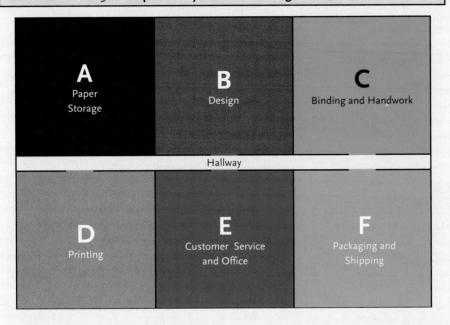

A Paper Storage	B Design	C Binding and Handwork
Hallway		
D Printing	E Customer Service and Office	F Packaging and Shipping

Use the trips matrix presented in Exhibit 16.10 and the distance matrix for the proposed layout in Exhibit 16.11 to compute the total distance associated with this layout. How can the layout be improved?

EXHIBIT 16.10   Trips Matrix for Printing Business

	Trips per Month				
	Paper Storage	Design	Binding and Handwork	Printing	Customer Service	Packaging and Shipping
Paper Storage	0	0	60	260	20	50
Design		0	12	10	15	10
Binding and Handwork			0	310	8	440
Printing				0	6	560
Customer Service					0	5
Packaging and Shipping						0

(Continues)

Example 16.3   *(Continued)*

EXHIBIT 16.11   Distance Matrix for Proposed Layout

Distance (feet)

	A	B	C	D	E	F
A	0	30	60	15	40	70
B	30	0	30	40	15	40
C	60	30	0	70	40	15
D	15	40	70	0	30	60
E	40	15	40	30	0	30
F	70	40	15	60	30	0

Solution

The total distance matrix is obtained by multiplying the number of trips by the distance, as seen in Exhibit 16.12.

EXHIBIT 16.12   Total Distance Matrix for Proposed Layout

Distance (feet)

	Paper Storage	Design	Binding and Handwork	Printing	Customer Service	Packaging and Shipping
Paper Storage	0	0	3,600	3,900	800	3,500
Design		0	360	400	225	400
Binding and Handwork			0	21,700	320	6,600
Printing				0	180	33,600
Customer Service					0	150
Packaging and Shipping						0

Total distance = 75,735

An examination of the interactions would probably lead to a change in the layout to move several departments closer together. For example, the high level of interaction between printing and binding/handwork, paper storage and printing, binding/ handwork and packaging/shipping, and printing and packaging/shipping makes those pairs of departments very attractive to have in close proximity. An improvement can be made by making the changes shown in Exhibit 16.13.

(Continues)

Example 16.3 *(Continued)*

EXCEL TUTOR

EXHIBIT 16.13 **Improved Layout**

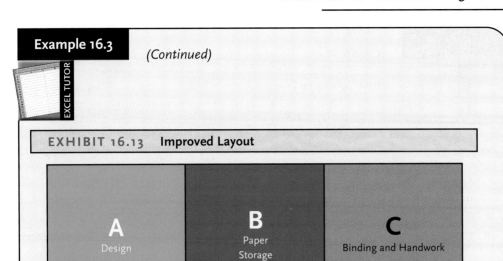

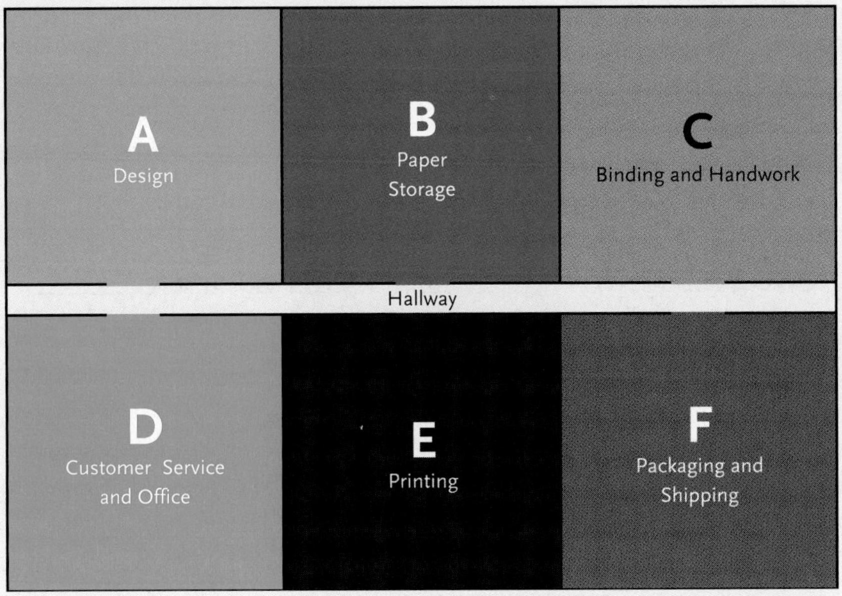

Exhibit 16.14 provides the updated total distance matrix, reflecting the changes made in Exhibit 16.13, showing a total monthly distance reduction from 75,735 feet to 47,935 feet. This is a reduction of almost 37 percent and would contribute a proportional reduction in costs linked to that material movement.

EXHIBIT 16.14 **Total Distance Matrix for Improved Layout**

			Distance (feet)			
	Design	Paper Storage	Binding and Handwork	Customer Service	Printing	Packaging and Shipping
Design	0	0	720	225	400	700
Paper Storage		0	1,800	800	3,900	2,000
Binding and Handwork			0	1,050	12,400	6,600
Customer Service				0	240	300
Printing					0	16,800
Packaging and Shipping						0

Total distance = 47,935

(Continues)

Example 16.3

EXCEL TUTOR

(Continued)

This process of trial-and-error improvement would continue until it appeared that a good solution was generated. Another improvement would be to move printing and packaging/shipping so that they are immediately across from each other rather than next to each other, trading places between with the binding/ handwork department and the printing department. Since there are more trips between printing and packaging/shipping than there are between binding/handwork and packaging/shipping, this would reduce the total distance as well. This cut-and-try improvement process would be continued until a satisfactory layout was obtained.

Excel Tutor 16.3 demonstrates how this problem can be solved in a spreadsheet.

Example 16.4

EXCEL TUTOR

SLP Technique for Process-Oriented Layout

Using SLP, determine an improved layout for the printing business.

Solution

Exhibit 16.15 shows the closeness desirability matrix that has been developed from the trips matrix provided for the previous example in Exhibit 16.10. The more trips per month, the stronger the closeness desirability rating.

EXHIBIT 16.15	Closeness Desirability Matrix

	Closeness Desirability Ratings					
	Paper Storage	Design	Binding and Handwork	Printing	Customer Service	Packaging and Shipping
Paper Storage		U	I	E	O	I
Design			O	O	O	O
Binding and Handwork				E	U	A
Printing					U	A
Customer Service						U
Packaging and Shipping						

The initial layout proposal is presented in Exhibit 16.16, with the appropriate connectors. The next iteration on this layout would strive to reduce the distance between departments with high closeness desirability ratings (connected by four lines or three lines). The first move can be to move printing to the right side of the layout. Exhibit 16.17 shows this step as an improvement.

The process would continue in a trial-and-error fashion until the layout was believed to be satisfactory. The next improvement would be to move paper storage to the right side, to reduce the length of its connection to printing. The only connection lengthened by this

(Continues)

Example 16.4   (Continued)

EXCEL TUTOR

EXHIBIT 16.16   Initial Layout Proposal with SLP Convention Connecting Lines

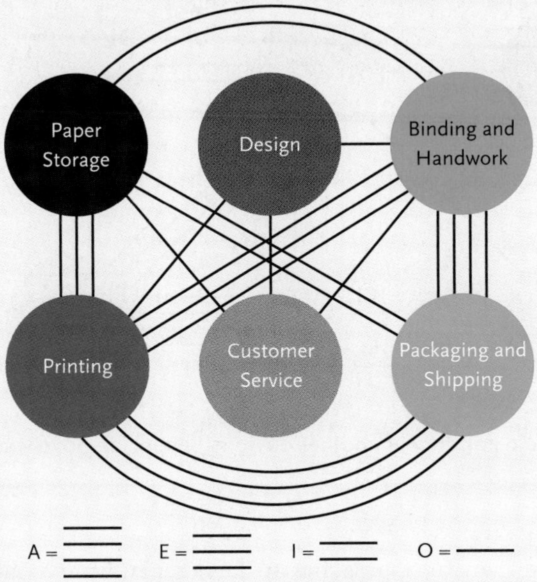

EXHIBIT 16.17   First Iteration Improvement Using SLP

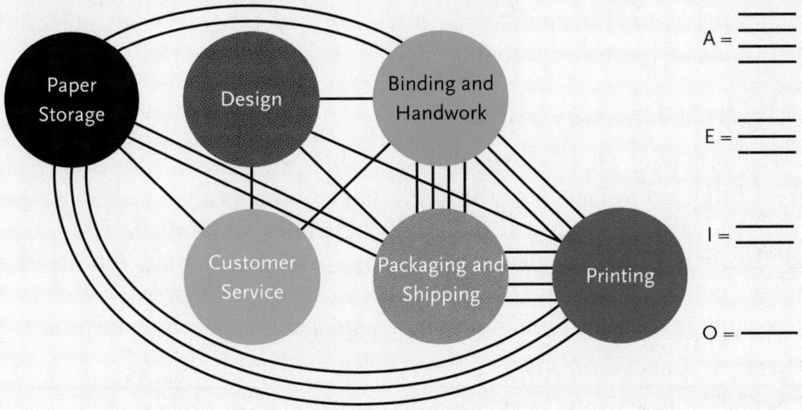

move would be the single line connection to customer service, which is less important than the other relationships paper storage has. This change is shown in Exhibit 16.18.

(Continues)

Example 16.4   *(Continued)*

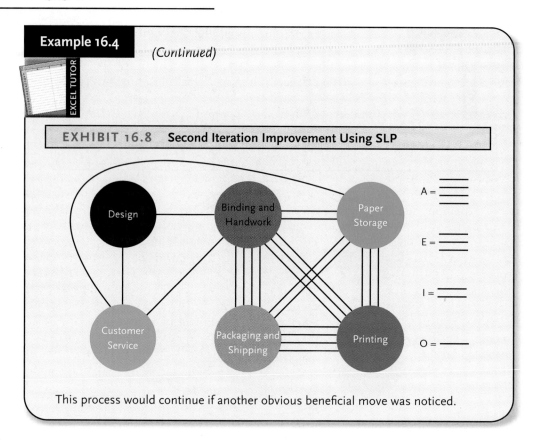

EXHIBIT 16.8   Second Iteration Improvement Using SLP

This process would continue if another obvious beneficial move was noticed.

In addition to the manual approaches to layout planning, computer packages are available to aid in the layout process. A very popular one, Computerized Relative Allocation of Facilities Technique (CRAFT)[7] starts with the equivalent of a total distance or total cost matrix and makes swaps between pairs of departments. It continues to make swaps until no improvement is gained. It is basically a computerized approach to the cut-and-try method. Each of the approaches provides a structure and some objectivity to the process, but none guarantees optimal results.

Product-Oriented Layouts

Product-oriented layouts take the form of assembly or production lines in many manufacturing operations. Products flow through a large number of workstations, each adding components and labor to what will eventually be a finished product. These layouts have little flexibility, but when designed correctly they can provide high volumes at low costs per unit. Let's take a close look at how product-oriented layouts work. Exhibit 16.19 illustrates a simple production line, with processing times for each workstation.

EXHIBIT 16.19   Production Line

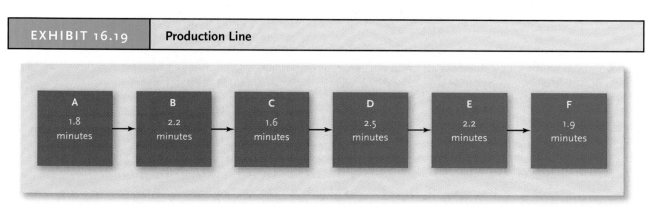

A close examination of the production line in Exhibit 16.19 provides insight to the workings of a product-oriented layout. Notice that the processing times for the workstations are not the same. Workstation D is the slowest, at 2.5 minutes per unit. This workstation could be referred to as the **bottleneck,** since it controls the output rate of the production line. Every 2.5 minutes, one unit will emerge from D and be passed down the line, eventually to exit the line at workstation F. The frequency of a product leaving the line is known as the **cycle time,** and in this example it is 2.5 minutes. The production line can complete 24 units per hour. What happens if products enter the production line at A at a rate faster than the cycle time? They will accumulate in front of workstation D. The bottleneck workstation plays a critical role by determining the utilization possible on the other workstations. Since it makes no sense to accumulate products in front of workstation D, the input rate into the line needs to be one unit every 2.5 minutes. Workstation A will actually only work 1.8 minutes out of every 2.5 minutes, for a utilization rate of 72 percent. Workstation B works 2.2 out of 2.5 minutes for a utilization rate of 88 percent. Workstation C has a utilization rate of 64 percent (the lowest of the workstations). Workstation D will work 100 percent of the time. E will have a utilization rate of 88 percent, and workstation F will be utilized 76 percent of the time. The low utilization that results from the differences in processing times is known as **balance delay.** The overall utilization of the entire line (U) can be computed by dividing the total amount of time actually spent performing tasks by the total time in the system. The amount of actual processing for the product is calculated by summing the times (t) for each task:

bottleneck
A constraint in a production system.

cycle time
The frequency of products emerging completed from a product-oriented layout.

(16.1)
$$T = \Sigma t$$
$$= 1.8 + 2.2 + 1.6 + 2.5 + 2.2 + 1.9$$
$$= 12.2 \text{ minutes}$$

balance delay
In a product-oriented layout, this is the lost resource utilization resulting from differences in processing time at each work center. See *line balancing.*

Each product is in the system for 15 minutes (2.5 minutes each for six workstations). This is also often referred to as the **production lead time.** The production lead time can be calculated by multiplying the cycle time by the number of work centers:

production lead time
The amount of time a product spends in a productive system in order to be completed.

(16.2)
$$\text{Production Lead Time} = C \times N$$
$$= 6 \times 2.5$$
$$= 15 \text{ minutes}$$

where
  C = cycle time
  N = number of workstations in the production line

Thus

(16.3)
$$U = \frac{T}{C \times N}$$
$$= \frac{12.2}{15.0}$$
$$= 81.3\%$$

The overall utilization of 81.3 percent is not acceptable for a layout whose strength is low cost per unit. High-cost equipment required for this type of layout needs a higher utilization rate to generate the financial return needed to provide a payback on the capital investment.

Suppose some of the work done at workstation D could be done at workstation C. What would be the impact of moving 0.3 minute of work from D to C? Let's find out. Exhibit 16.20 illustrates this change. Since the bottleneck (BDE) is now 2.2 minutes, this subtle change reduces the cycle time from 2.5 to 2.2 minutes. Output per hour increases

| EXHIBIT 16.20 | Production Line Improved (in minutes) |

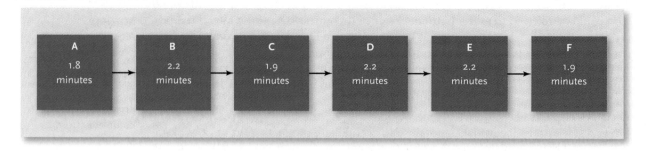

from 24 to 27 units per hour and production lead time drops from 15 minutes to 13.2 minutes. The overall utilization improves to 92.4 percent (12.2/13.2 minutes). The small modification that caused all of these improvements simply resulted from a better-balanced line. The key to high levels of productivity in product-oriented layout is to balance the times required of each workstation in a process known as **line balancing.**

line balancing
A process used to balance the times among work centers in a product-oriented layout to reduce balance delay. See *balance delay.*

You were probably already thinking that in the real world no one could just "move" work from one workstation to another. You're right. Line balancing must be considered at the design stage in order to assign work as equally as possible. The first step in line balancing is to define the work necessary to complete the product in terms of very small tasks known as **work elements.** The work elements are defined precisely, and precedence relationships are established in much the same way as was done when creating project network diagrams. Elemental times are identified for each work element. To determine how the elements will be grouped into workstations, the minimum number of workstations must be determined. This is based on the cycle time needed to meet output requirements. The greater the output rate, the shorter the cycle time must be. The shorter the cycle time, the greater the number of workstations necessary to complete all of the processing that needs to be done.

work elements
Small tasks that make up process steps.

Step-by-Step: Line Balancing

1. Identify the tasks, work elements, and precedence relationships by using a precedence chart.
2. Determine the cycle time (C) necessary to satisfy output requirements. This is accomplished using the following equation:

(16.4)
$$C = \frac{\text{Production Time Available per Day}}{\text{Units of Output Required per Day}}$$

3. Determine the theoretical minimum number of workstations (N_{min}) by using the equation

(16.5)
$$N_{min} = \frac{T}{C}$$

4. Assign the tasks to workstations.
5. Evaluate the utilization of the line.

Example 16.5 demonstrates the line balancing process.

Line balancing appears to be very precise on paper; in reality, however, it isn't quite that precise. Several complicating factors interfere. First of all, even though a workstation is defined as taking 3.95 minutes, that is an average. Since people, not robots, are performing the tasks, there will be variability at all workstations. This will increase balance

Example 16.5

EXCEL TUTOR

Line Balancing

Hollow Logs is a manufacturer of cedar deck furniture owned by Julie Olsen. The company has been operating for six years. Initially, the business was laid out in a typical process-oriented fashion, to allow for flexibility. Over time, Julie came to realize that almost 90 percent of the volume came from a single model of chair and a single model of table. Several months ago, she subcontracted out the sawing and milling of all cedar components for these two products. Her production process now consists of the assembly and finish only. She decided to downsize the functional departments used to make other models and to convert the chair and table assembly and finish to a production line approach.

Her first task is to develop a balanced line for the table. Examining past demand and current orders on hand led Julie to believe that she needs to be able to complete 120 units per day on a standard eight-hour day, five-day week schedule. Her shop foreman and lead production operator developed a precise description of the work elements required for the table assembly. These data are presented in Exhibit 16.21. Using these data complete the line balancing process.

EXHIBIT 16.21 Assembly Work Elements for Deck Table

Step	Description	Time, t (minutes)
1	Inspect top board kit	0.5
2	Sequence top boards in jig	0.6
3	Insert top braces in jig	0.3
4	Screw braces to top boards (16 screws)	3.6
5	Remove top assembly	0.2
6	Inspect bottom sawbuck stand boards	0.5
7	Insert left end X boards into jig	0.4
8	Drill, insert, and tighten center bolt	1.25
9	Remove left end assembly from jig	0.4
10	Insert right end X boards into jig	0.4
11	Drill, insert, and tighten center bolt	1.25
12	Remove right end assembly from jig	0.4
13	Attach center brace connecting left and right X boards	2.3
14	Attach hinges to top using placement jig	3.6
15	Attach base assembly to hinges	1.3
16	Inspect	0.7
17	Package	1.8

Solution

Precedence relationships are presented in Exhibit 16.22, and the production process is diagramed in Exhibit 16.23.

EXHIBIT 16.22 Deck Table Assembly Precedence Relationships

Step	Required Predecessors	Step	Required Predecessors
1	0	10	6
2	1	11	10
3	2	12	11
4	3	13	12
5	4	14	5
6	0	15	14
7	6	16	15
8	7	17	16
9	8		

(Continues)

Example 16.5   *(Continued)*

EXHIBIT 16.23   **Diagram of Deck Table Assembly Process**

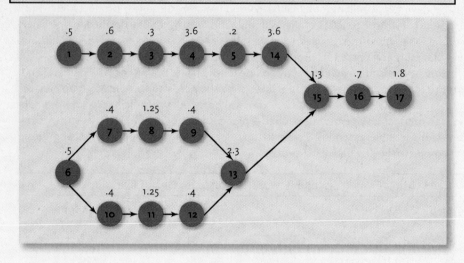

After the precedence relationships are determined and charted, the cycle time (*C*) needed to meet output requirements is determined:

$$C = \frac{480 \text{ minutes per day}}{120 \text{ units required per day}}$$
$$= 4 \text{ minutes}$$

The next step is to determine the theoretical minimum number of workstations:

$$N_{min} = \frac{T}{C}$$
$$= \frac{19.5}{4}$$
$$= 4.875$$

The theoretical minimum number of workstations is the number required to get the total amount of work done (*T*) and meet the output rate (*C*) required. Any fractional number of workstations must be rounded up. In this case, the theoretical minimum number of workstations would be rounded up to five. There is no guarantee that the work could actually be done in only five workstations. Precedence relationships may prevent that. However, with more than five workstations, there will be significantly more idle time on workstations, reducing overall utilization.

The next step is to assign work elements to workstations. The first attempt will be to group the work elements, striving for groups that sum to the cycle time of four minutes. This will be done as they are assigned to the minimum number of workstations, five. Precedence relationships must be kept in mind when making these assignments. Exhibit 16.24 shows a first attempt. The resulting production line, with workstation times, is presented in Exhibit 16.25. This line will have a cycle time of 4.0 minutes, that of the slowest workstation (2).

(Continues)

Example 16.5   *(Continued)*

EXCEL TUTOR

EXHIBIT 16.24   **First Iteration at Grouping Work Elements at Workstations**

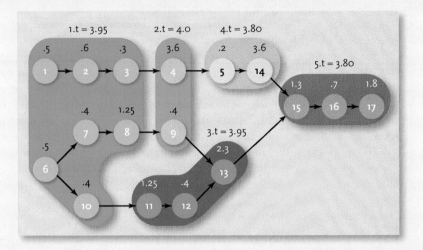

EXHIBIT 16.25   **New Production Line for Hollow Logs Table Assembly**

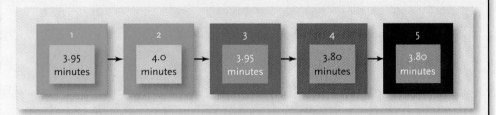

1	2	3	4	5
3.95 minutes	4.0 minutes	3.95 minutes	3.80 minutes	3.80 minutes

---

This arrangement appears to be good. The resulting production line meets the output requirements of 120 units per day. Overall utilization is 97.5 percent (19.5/20). There is little room for improvement. For example, bringing work elements 4 and 5 together leaves work element 9 to be recombined. The only place for 9 would be combining it with 14. The result is no improvement, because we still end up with a cycle time of 4.0 minutes. In addition, precedence relationships become a problem. There is no solution that can eliminate the 4.0-minute maximum in a workstation.

This is an excellent example of how small work element times make it possible to come up with a better balance. The perfectly balanced line, in this situation, would have a cycle time of 3.78 minutes, which might be more feasible if work element times were smaller. The negative aspect of small work element times is that tasks that logically fit together might be split up.

Excel Tutor 16.5 demonstrates how the line balancing problem can be aided by a spreadsheet.

om ADVANTAGE   "Flow" Drives Layout for Kohl's

Facility layout discussions often focus on manufacturing and the cost savings that result from more efficient transportation of inventory. Facility layouts can also enhance productivity in the service sector. Kohl's Corporation, a discount department store chain, is currently gaining ground to shift from a midwestern to a national entity. It, along with Target, is expected to continue its growth pattern as sales shift from high-end stores as consumers pay close attention to prices. Success for Kohl's, such as the same-store sales gain of nearly 15 percent in December 2000, is primarily a result of facility layout decisions. The aisle design is modeled after a figure 8 racetrack, to provide a route that takes shoppers through all departments, keeps them on one floor, and allows them quick access in and out of the store. The layout, illustrated in Exhibit 16.26, consists of a route that is about a quarter-mile long. Wide aisles leave plenty of room for carts. The middle aisles divide the track and provide a shortcut for shoppers who don't want to finish the entire route.

The quarter-mile track in Kohl's compares to routes that are double in competing stores. In the Kohl's layout, each department is restricted to five or fewer display racks around the track. The result is a smaller, simpler layout and a more productive facility. Sales per square foot, a standard retail facility performance measure, reached $279 for Kohl's, compared to $220 for Target Corporation's Marshall Fields, $147 for Dillard's Inc., and $192 for May Department Stores Co. Kohl's pays particular attention to keeping aisles wide and racks far apart, avoiding the crowded appearance of many of its competitors. The use of tiered racks creates an amphitheater look that allows customers to see more merchandise. Colored clothing is always displayed in the same sequence: from light to dark. Unlike many stores, Kohl's does not allow employees to straighten up displays throughout the day—that is reserved for night crews. Daytime employees are expected to concentrate on customer service. A 2-P.M. recovery effort, which involves everyone, is the only time displays are straightened during the day.

Source: "Retail," *BusinessWeek.com*, January 8, 2001; "Kohl's Retail Racetrack," *Wall Street Journal*, March 1, 2000, pp. B1, B6.

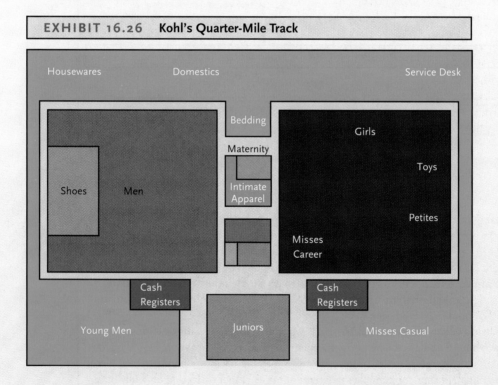

EXHIBIT 16.26   Kohl's Quarter-Mile Track

delay. Second, different materials and slightly different levels of equipment performance can contribute to balance delay. In some cases, a line will be used for more than one product. One will be run for a while, and then the equipment will be changed over for another product. Obtaining a perfect balance in this situation is virtually impossible. Worker absenteeism or the presence of a new worker can also upset the balance of a line.

Workers may need to be moved to fine-tune a line to account for inexperienced workers. Because of these real-world conditions, line balancing is often an ongoing process.

Cellular Layouts

Cellular layouts offer a compromise between product-oriented and process-oriented layouts. Beyond that, they offer some capabilities that are better than either of the alternatives. Cellular layouts require that a family of products be produced in a "cell" that has all of the resources necessary to produce all of the products in the family. The resources are close together, reducing material transport costs, but the sequence of the movement within the cell can vary, creating an opportunity for flexibility. In addition to the advantages of reduced material transport and increased flexibility, workers can be expected to operate more than one type of resource. In contrast to the workstations in a production line, the work centers in a cell are less dependent on each other, reducing the potential impact of one disruption on other machines. In a low-inventory "lean" environment, a breakdown on one machine can quickly result in the rest running out of material.

Service Layouts

The objectives of a service layout may be very similar to those of a traditional product-oriented or process-oriented layout in manufacturing. Product-oriented layouts strive for a flow, and in some services a flow is also desired. Process-oriented layouts offer greater flexibility, and in some services that flexibility is desired as well. In other services, however, the objectives of the layout may not be to enhance the efficiency of customer movement. Retail store layouts, for example, strive to move customers through the store to expose them to more products and increase the likelihood of a purchase. Certain high-frequency products (milk and bread, for example) are placed to lure the customer to the back of the store. The customer is forced to pass other merchandise along the way.

Different types of retail stores use different strategies for moving customers. Much of this customer movement is controlled by the layout of the aisles and traffic patterns. It may seem trivial, but remember, productivity of the facility for most retailers is measured in sales per square foot. Increased sales translate directly into an increase in the ROA.

Layouts like those used in retailing are not different from those used in the warehousing environment. When employees must "pick" orders to be shipped from hundreds or thousands of products, the layout of the warehouse can make a tremendous difference in travel time for the order picker, which translates into time the customer must wait.

| CHAPTER SUMMARY |

This chapter has been devoted to two key facility decisions: location and layout. Facility location dictates many of the costs related to a facility. In some cases location affects other value attributes as well, including response time and convenience. Location decisions must consider a variety of issues, many of which are quantifiable, but many are purely subjective.

Facility layout, on the other hand, has a dominant impact on the processes within the facility. Layouts provide the structure within which resources must fit. The layout is often a result of strategic decisions that have been made by the business. Layout decisions influence such value attributes as quality, flexibility, and response time. The product-oriented layout is traditionally used to gain efficiencies and reduce per-unit costs. Line balancing is an important component of the product layout decision. Process-oriented layouts, on the other hand, are used to enhance flexibility. Determining where departments are located relative to each other is an important aspect of determining the process-oriented layout. Cellular layouts, which offer a compromise between product-oriented and process-oriented layouts, have increased in popularity as a way to combine efficiency and flexibility.

In virtually any business, the facility is one of the biggest investments. Decisions related to its location and layout affect the financial performance of the firm because of the size of the investment and the impact the decisions have on customer-perceived value.

KEY TERMS

balance delay, 713
bottleneck, 713
cycle time, 713

line balancing, 714
production lead time, 713
work elements, 714

KEY FORMULAE

Processing Time

(16.1)
$$T = \Sigma t$$

Production Lead Time for Line Balancing

(16.2)
$$\text{Production Lead Time} = C \times N$$

where

C = cycle time

N = number of workstations in the production line

Utilization

(16.3)
$$U = \frac{T}{C \times N}$$

Cycle Time

(16.4)
$$C = \frac{\text{Production Time Available per Day}}{\text{Units of Output Required per Day}}$$

Theoretical Minimum Number of Work Centers

(16.5)
$$N_{min} = \frac{T}{C}$$

SOLVED PROBLEMS

1. Multifactor Rating

Multifactor Rating Calculation

Advanced Logistics is a 3PL for food and beverage companies. It has seasonal variation in refrigerated warehouse demand, so it leases warehouse space in the summer months. AL is currently examining three providers of warehouse space it needs for energy drinks. Members of the management team have agreed that cost/sq. ft., truck access, security, experience, and inventory management capabilities are the five most important factors. They have also agreed that the factors should be weighted as follows:

Factor	Weight
Cost/sq. ft.	.30
Truck access	.30
Security	.10
Experience	.15
Inventory management	.15

Each team member scored the three alternative providers on each factor. The scores were averaged for each factor, providing the following scores:

	Average Scores		
Factor	Alternative #1	Alternative #2	Alternative #3
Cost/sq. ft.	74	98	85
Truck Access	88	82	93
Security	90	88	85
Experience	87	95	78
Inventory Management	65	73	84

Using the factor rating technique, compute the scores and rank the three warehouse alternatives.

Step	Objective	Explanation
1.	Compute the weighted scores for each factor, for each alternative.	For each alternative, the average score is multiplied by the weight. The results are:

		Average Score			Weighted score		
Factor	Weight	Alt. 1	Alt. 2	Alt 3	Alt. 1	Alt. 2	Alt. 3
Cost/sq. ft.	0.3	74	98	85	22.2	29.4	25.5
Truck access	0.3	88	82	93	26.4	24.6	27.9
Security	0.1	90	88	85	9.0	8.8	8.5
Experience	0.15	87	95	78	13.05	14.25	11.7
Inventory management	0.15	65	73	84	9.75	10.95	12.6

Step	Objective	Explanation
2.	Sum the weighted scores for each alternative to calculate the total score. These are the scores that are then compared.	

Alternative	Alt. 1	Alt. 2	Alt. 3
Total score	80.4	88.0	86.2

Step	Objective	Explanation
3.	The ranking is determined by ordering the alternatives by their scores.	Alternative 2 would be ranked highest, followed by Alternative 3, and then by Alternative 1.

2. Location Breakeven

A bank is considering three new locations for an ATM. The locations have different fixed costs because of work that would need to be done to the site and fixed charges from the property owner. Each also has different transaction costs because of agreements that must be made with property owners. The fixed and variables costs are presented below.

Location	Fixed Cost	Cost per Transaction
1	$3,000	$.50
2	$6,000	$.30
3	$10,000	$.15

Determine the transaction volume conditions under which each alternative could be the best alternative.

Breakeven Calculation

Step	Objective	Explanation		
1.	Determine the equation for each cost curve.	Location 1	$y = 3,000 + .5x$	
		Location 2	$y = 6,000 + .3x$	
		Location 3	$y = 10,000 + .15x$	
2.	Identify the intersection points for each intersection by setting the equations equal to each other.	Intersection for Location 1 and Location 2: $3,000 + .5x = 6,000 + .3x$ $.2x = 3,000$ $x = 15,000$		
		Intersection for Location 2 and Location 3: $6,000 + .3x = 10,000 + .15x$ $.15x = 4,000$ $x = 26,666.7$		
3.	Identify the volume ranges for each low-cost alternative.	Location 1 has the lowest fixed cost and the highest cost per unit. It will be the low-cost alternative from volumes of 0 to 15,000. Location 2 is the low-cost alternative from 15,000 to 26,666.7 units. For volumes greater than 26,666.7 Location 3 will be the low-cost alternative.		

3. Line Balancing

An assembler of desk furniture wishes to develop an assembly line for its premium desk chairs. The current level of demand requires that 400 chairs be completed each 8-hour shift. The activities required to assemble each chair are:

Activity	Immediate Predecessors	Time, t (minutes)
1	0	0.4
2	1	0.5
3	2	0.3
4	3	0.5
5	4	0.3
6	5	0.7
7	6	0.4
8	7	0.6
9	8	0.4
10	9	0.2
11	10	0.4
12	11	0.5
13	12	0.2

a. Compute the cycle time needed to meet demand.

b. Compute the theoretical minimum number of workstations needed.

c. Assign the activities to the workstations to minimize the number of workstations but also maintain the needed cycle time.

Line Balancing Calculation

Step	Objective	Explanation
1.	Determine the cycle time.	480 minutes/400 chairs = 1.2 minutes/chair The necessary cycle time is 1.2 minutes.
2.	Determine the theoretical minimum number of workstations.	$N_{min} = T/C$ $T = 5.4$ minutes (the sum of the activity times) $C = 1.2$ 5.4/1.2 = 4.5 Round up to 5.
3.	Assign activities to workstations.	Assign each activity to a workstation. Each workstation could consist of activities that sum to as close to 1.2 minutes as possible, without exceeding it. Precedence relationships must be maintained. The assignments are shown below.

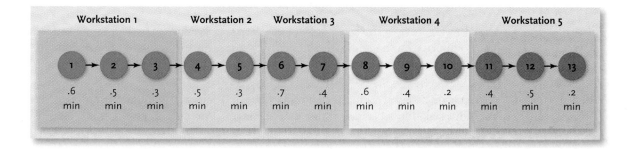

REVIEW QUESTIONS

1. Why are facility decisions important to the financial success of a business?

2. What impact do facility decisions have on value attributes?

3. Why is it usually impossible to identify an objective "optimal" facility location decision?

4. What are the situations that can require location decisions for new facilities?

5. How do process inputs and outputs affect facility location decisions? Describe examples for each.

6. Describe the hierarchy of business location decisions that is often addressed during a facility location decision process.

7. What are the issues that relate to each level of the location decision hierarchy?

8. What is meant by a "multifactor rating" approach to making location decisions? What are the weaknesses of the technique?

9. Give an example of how breakeven analysis might be used to aid in a facility location decision.

10. How can geographic information systems help in the location decision process?

11. What is meant by a process-oriented layout?

12. How does the cut-and-try method of determining the process-oriented layout work?

13. Describe how the systematic layout planning (SLP) approach to layout planning works.

14. What is a product-oriented layout?

15. What is cycle time? How is it determined?

16. What is the objective of line balancing?

17. Why do cellular layouts provide an attractive compromise between product-oriented and process-oriented layouts?

DISCUSSION AND EXPLORATION

1. Identify a business you are familiar with that has an excellent facility. What parts of the facility contribute to the business's success?

2. Identify a business that has made poor facility decisions. How does the facility affect the success of that business?

3. Select pairs of competing businesses in your community. How does location affect the competitive relationship of these businesses?

4. What are the comparative strengths and weaknesses of process-oriented and product-oriented layouts? Identify an example of each. Are these strengths and weaknesses supported by these examples?

5. Suppose you are on a site selection committee for C.J. Pennyman, a designer retailer. The committee has had difficulty agreeing on a recommendation for a new store. Explain the logic and benefits of multifactor rating and describe how it could be used to help them solve their problem.

6. A colleague at Fotor's Financial Products has criticized a manufacturing client for using line balancing because line balancing is not a precise process. Do you agree or disagree? Explain.

7. Compare and contrast the cut-and-try layout approach and SLP.

8. You have been hired as a consultant by Tasty Ice Cream, to aid in the search for a new location. An employee of Tasty argues that decision trees should not be used in this case, because Tasty is a risk-averse organization. That is, Tasty does not want to suffer any losses in revenue. The employee also stated that decision trees do not account for potential losses in revenue and therefore should not be used in the decision. Do you agree or disagree? Explain your answer.

9. A consultant to your company stated that a breakeven analysis is the most accurate technique for choosing new site locations and has no flaws associated with it. Do you agree? Explain your answer.

10. For the following businesses, identify the optimal location in your community and provide a justification for your decision.

    a. Bookstore

    b. Drive-through fast-food restaurant

    c. Convenience store

    d. Grocery store

    e. Electronics and computer repair shop

    f. Prison

    g. Auto repair shop

    h. Soft drink bottler

    i. Conversion van factory

PROBLEMS ▛▜

Solutions to odd-numbered problems are located on the text's Online Center (http://mhhe.com/opsnow3e).

1. Dan, a recent college graduate, is starting his own computer repair business and wishes to purchase office space for his new company. Use the following table and the multifactor rating method to determine the best location.

Factor	Weight	Site 1	Site 2	Site 3
Cost	0.4	9	8	6
Traffic	0.2	5	6	9
Scalability	0.2	6	8	9
Access to customers	0.2	8	5	9

2. Bryant Bookstore plans to implement an e-commerce Web site to serve its customers. Bryant wants to use a multifactor rating system to determine the best Web-hosting choice and identified five criteria weighted as follows: storage space, 0.1; cost, 0.15; reliability, 0.3; support, 0.2; and speed of site, 0.25. Four Web-hosting services are being evaluated. Use the ratings to determine the best choice for Bryant Bookstore.

Criteria	Site 1	Site 2	Site 3	Site 4
Storage	95	90	80	90
Cost	90	85	85	95
Reliability	75	85	95	90
Support	85	90	85	85
Speed	75	90	90	90

3. Julian Alanzo, owner of a mobile ice cream and frozen treat truck, is trying to decide on a summer route. He has identified three possible routes and the following criteria that are most important for his sales success:

Factor	Weight	Factor	Weight
Number of parks	0.15	Neighborhoods with children	0.2
Number of swimming pools	0.3	Ease of stopping	0.1
Number of playgrounds	0.15	Lack of auto traffic	0.1

Factor	Route 1	Route 2	Route 3
Number of parks	90	80	75
Number of swimming pools	80	90	95
Number of playgrounds	90	80	90
Neighborhoods with children	65	80	90
Ease of stopping	90	90	85
Lack of auto traffic	80	95	90

Based on Julian's multifactor rating system, which alternative route appears to be best?

4. First City Bank has identified three criteria that seem to determine the amount of use for an ATM. It has weighted these criteria and plans to use them to help guide placement of new ATMs. The criteria and weights are:

Factor	Weight
Automobile traffic	0.5
Foot traffic	0.3
Perceived security	0.2

There are currently four alternative sites that have expressed interest in getting an ATM. First City Bank has scored each of the alternatives on three factors. Those scores are presented below. Rank the four alternatives in attractiveness for an ATM location.

Factor	Site 1	Site 2	Site 3	Site 4
Automobile traffic	80	70	75	70
Foot traffic	90	85	90	80
Perceived security	85	90	80	95

5. Snuggle Sweaters is planning on starting a new line of sweaters in a new facility. The company identified three possible location sites, with the respective information for each site given below. Labor and material costs are provided per sweater. Use the information and breakeven analysis to decide which facility should be opened if the company forecasts 7,900 sweaters being sold.

Site	Fixed Costs ($)	Labor Cost ($/hour)	Labor Cost per Sweater ($)	Materials Cost per Sweater ($)	Total Variable Cost per Sweater ($)
1	525,000	6.75	11.00	24.00	35.00
2	540,000	7.30	11.00	22.00	33.00
3	560,000	8.10	9.00	21.00	30.00

6. Doran Design is a successful engineering firm that would like to expand to new markets. It plans on opening a new location at one of three possible sites. Doran anticipates that the new facility will complete 600 jobs per year. Use a breakeven analysis to calculate which location should be chosen.

Site	Fixed Costs/ Year ($)	Labor Costs ($/hour)	Labor Cost/ Job ($)	Materials Cost/ Job ($)	Total Variable Cost/Job ($)
1	90,000	6.75	84.00	235.00	319.00
2	78,000	7.3	96.00	247.00	343.00
3	70,000	8.1	102.00	242.00	344.00

7. Jacque's Gear, a hockey skate shop, wants to open a new store at one of three possible locations. Use breakeven analysis to find the range of sales volume necessary to minimize costs at each location.

Site	Fixed Costs ($)	Labor Costs ($/hr)	Labor Costs ($)	Materials Costs ($)	Variable Costs ($)
1	105,000	12	700.00	1,100.00	1,800.00
2	130,000	11	600.00	900.00	1,500.00
3	145,000	12	700.00	800.00	1,500.00

8. Morris Machining's plant diagram is below. A distance of 20 feet separates departments that are next to each other. Departments across the center hall from each other are separated by 10 feet, and those that are diagonal from each other are separated by 30 feet. Corner-to-corner diagonals are 50 feet. Use the trips matrix and the cut-and-try layout method to create a diagram that would reduce the total distance.

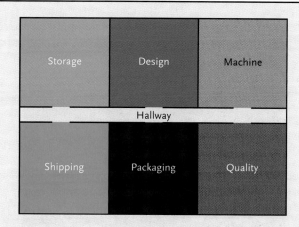

	Storage	Design	Machine	Shipping	Packaging	Quality
Storage	0	45	30	5	15	50
Design		0	60	0	0	10
Machine			0	20	15	50
Shipping				0	65	30
Packaging					0	60
Quality						0

9. Café Dijon has the following layout, trips matrix, and total distance matrix for its restaurant. Use this information to develop a layout that will reduce the total distance.

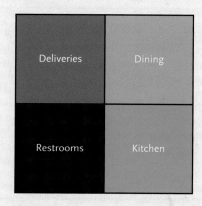

Trips Matrix

	Delivery	Dining	Restroom	Kitchen
Delivery	0	10	4	20
Dining		0	15	30
Restroom			0	5
Kitchen				0

Distance Matrix

	Delivery	Dining	Restroom	Kitchen
Delivery	0	10	10	20
Dining		0	20	10
Restroom			0	10
Kitchen				0

10. Paisley Products makes custom-designed ties. The company's current layout is shown below. Use the given information and the cut-and-try layout method to design a facility that will reduce the total distance.

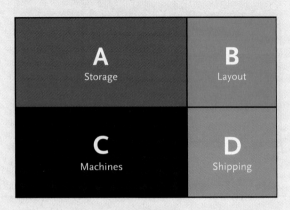

Trips Matrix

	Storage	Layout	Machines	Shipping
Storage	0	50	5	0
Layout		0	25	10
Machines			0	25
Shipping				0

Distance Matrix

	A	B	C	D
A	0	10	5	15
B		0	15	5
C			0	10
D				0

11. Nordic Products would like help in organizing a production layout. The company gave its departments the following closeness desirability ratings. Use this information and the SLP process to identify a good layout.

	Warehouse	Engineering	Production	Shipping
Warehouse		A	I	I
Engineering			E	U
Production				O
Shipping				

12. Use the following closeness desirability ratings and SLP to help Canine Collars Co. determine a layout for a production facility.

	Receiving	Staging	Production	Quality	Shipping
Receiving		A	O	U	A
Staging			A	U	U
Production				I	O
Quality					E
Shipping					

13. Best-Books Bookstore offers customers a large selection of books, their favorite coffees, and a lounge area where they can drink and read. Use SLP to lay out the store according to the given desirability ratings.

	Receiving	Shelves	Food and Drink	Lounge
Receiving		A	O	O
Shelves			E	E
Food & drink				A
Lounge				

14. Starling Tennis Co. makes tennis rackets. The Baseline is its most popular model. The company anticipates that it needs to produce 80 rackets in an eight-hour day to meet demand. The total amount of work needed per racket is 30 minutes. What is the theoretical minimum number of workstations required to get the total amount of work done?

15. Spirit Recordings makes and sells CDs of colleges' fight songs. Use the information below to group elemental tasks into work centers to form the most balanced line possible. What is the cycle time of the line?

Step	Description	Predecessors	Time (minutes)
1	Set up equipment	O	5
2	Acoustic check	1	15
3	Record	O	20
4	Playback	3	30
5	Package	2, 4	5

16. Saf-Home manufactures door handles. It anticipates a need for 68 handles per day to satisfy demand. The following nine processes are involved in the manufacturing process. Use the information and the line balancing technique to create a diagram of the work centers needed and steps included in each work center to meet demand.

Step	Description	Predecessors	Time (minutes)
1	Mold	O	1
2	Shave	1	0.5
3	Drill	1, 2	1
4	Size	O	2
5	Grind	4	4
6	Paint	1, 2, 3	3.5
7	Lubricate	4, 5	1
8	Inspect fit	1, 2, 3, 4, 5, 6, 7	4
9	Package	1, 2, 3, 4, 5, 6, 7, 8	3

17. Frame-N-Sav makes picture frames for the posters and prints that the store sells. The store needs to make 10 frames a day in its eight hours of available time to satisfy its customers. Each frame takes two hours to make. What is the theoretical minimum number of workstations required to get the total amount of work done?

ADVANCED PROBLEMS

1. An inventor has just received a patent on an innovative new toy—the yo-yo slinky. He has identified three potential locations for his manufacturing operations. Based on his market research, he has determined that demand for his product is quite price elastic. For this reason, he wants to select the location which provides the lowest production costs. He has developed the following cost information about his product and the three location alternatives:

Cost Item	Graham, Texas	Dodge, Texas	Houston, Texas
Annual Lease Expenses	$150,000	$250,000	$450,000
Annual License Fees	$6,000	$8,000	$5,500
General Overhead	$100,000	$90,000	$80,000
Labor Cost/Unit	$1.50	$1.40	$1.25
Material Cost/Unit	$2.20	$1.75	$1.50
Transportation Cost/Unit	$.75	$0.25	$0.10
Overhead Cost/Unit	$2.50	$2.80	$2.70
Selling Price/Unit	$15.00	$15.00	$15.00

a. Determine the fixed and variable costs for each location alternative.

b. Construct the total cost curves for each location on the same graph.

c. Determine the range of sales over which each location would be preferred.

d. If the inventor estimates annual sales to be 500,000 units per year, which location would you recommend?

e. If the inventor estimates annual sales to be 122,667 per year, what additional questions would need to be answered before making a location recommendation?

2. Donna's Bakery has been supplying restaurants with cakes and desserts, and the word is out on how good they are. Customers of the restaurants have been asking if the treats were available at a retail store, and Donna feels that a retail setting would work for her. Her problem is finding the right location. In addition to her tasty cakes, delicious chocolates, and heavenly cream-puffs, she will also serve coffee and espresso drinks. After driving around town, she found 4 locations that were available and fit her needs. The first was an older drive-thru restaurant, but it looked like a box. The second was a donut shop that had a lot of parking and high visibility, but it was not in a great location. The third alternative was a cute café in the downtown district, very charming, with nice curtains, a little bell that was attached to the door, great moldings and woodworking, but not much parking. The fourth alternative was a bistro on the edge of the downtown district. It was a good location, but tucked away, so it didn't have much visibility. Donna decided she needed to put a weight to each of the factors that she thought was important. She identified six criteria to help her make the decision, and scored each of the locations on a scale up to 100:

Factor	Importance Weighting	Score Drive-thru	Donut shop	Café	Bistro
Visibility	0.25	95	90	85	70
Location	0.20	85	80	90	90
Cost	0.20	60	65	50	70
Parking	0.15	90	90	80	80
Appearance	0.15	40	55	95	75
Seating	0.05	60	90	90	80

Which location should Donna choose? Was Donna objective in her analysis?

3. Midwest Molding is searching for a location for a new plastic injection molding plant that will serve a number of customers around the country. They have narrowed their search to specific sites in three different communities. At this point, a number of factors must be considered including the cost to purchase land and build the facility, availability of labor, highway access, the ability of the local airport to handle air freight, the tax structure and incentives offered by the community, as well as quality of life issues such as the quality of the local school system and recreational opportunities for managers and employees.

Midwest has rated each location on each of these factors using a 1 to 5 scale, where 1 = "best" and 5 = "worst." The ratings are as follows:

	Ranking (1 = best)		
Factor	Location 1	Location 2	Location 3
Labor availability	2	1	5
Facility cost	1	2	1
Highway access	4	1	2
Airport capacity	3	1	2
Tax structure	3	2	5
School system	1	3	1
Recreation	2	3	1

Scott, the Human Relations director, believes there is no sense in building the facility in a location that has poor labor availability. He has assigned the following weights:

Factor	Weight
Labor availability	0.40
Facility cost	0.20
Highway access	0.05
Airport capacity	0.10
Tax structure	0.05
School system	0.10
Recreation	0.10
Sum:	1.00

Mary, the Chief Financial Officer, believes labor is a less critical issue as the site is not planned for expansion beyond the current facility design. She believes the weightings should focus more directly on financial issues, and has assigned the following weights:

Factor	Weight
Labor availability	0.20
Facility cost	0.60
Highway access	0.05
Airport capacity	0.05
Tax structure	0.10
School system	0.00
Recreation	0.00
Sum:	1.00

Ted, a graphic artist representing the Marketing department on the site selection team, believes all factors are important and should be equally weighted.

a. Calculate the weighted score for each location under each of the three weighting schemes. Is there one location that dominates the analysis in the sense it has the best score under all three weighting schemes?

b. Assign your own weighting system based on your perception of the relative importance of each factor, and compute the weighted score for each facility. Does your weighting system favor the same location as Scott's, Mary's, or Ted's?

c. Is there any location that could be eliminated from consideration based on the analyses that have been conducted? Explain.

ENDNOTES

1. "Lost in the Translation," *Wall Street Journal*, February 12, 2001, p. R12.
2. "When Deciding Where to Put a Business, Companies Better Not Ignore the Obvious: Where Would Employees Like to Live?" *Wall Street Journal*, October 15, 2001, p. R14.
3. J. Kotkin, *The New Geography* (New York: Random House, 2000).
4. Ibid.
5. "The Rockies Emerge as Pocket of Prosperity in a Slowing Economy," *Wall Street Journal*, June 6, 2001, pp. A1, A8.
6. R. Muther, *Systematic Layout Planning* (Boston: Industrial Education Institute, 1961).
7. R. L. Francis and J. A. White, *Facility Layout and Location: An Analytical Approach* (Englewood Cliffs, NJ: Prentice Hall, 1992).

LEARNING ACTIVITIES

www.mhhe.com/opsnow3e

Visit the Online Learning Center (www.mhhe.com/opsnow3e) for additional resources. Content varies by chapter, and includes

- Business Tours
- OM on Site
- Readings
- Resources
- Excel Tutors

- Interactive Case Models
- Reel Operations Video Clips
- Additional Advance Problems
- Self-Assessment Quizzes
- Glossary

SELECTED REFERENCES

Bowersox, D. J., Closs, D. J, and Cooper, M. B. *Supply Chain Logistics Management*. New York: McGraw-Hill/Irwin, 2002.

Francis, R. L., and White, J. A. *Facility Layout and Location: An Analytical Approach*. Englewood Cliffs, NJ: Prentice Hall, 1992.

Kotkin, J. *The New Geography*. New York: Random House, 2000.

Schmenner, R. W. *Making Business Location Decisions*. Englewood Cliffs, NJ: Prentice Hall, 1982.

Shapiro, Jeremy F. *Modeling the Supply Chain*. Pacific Grove, CA: Duxbury Press, 2001.

Redesigning Redi-Print

Process-oriented layouts are used when the producer needs flexibility to accommodate variable routings of products or customers through the system. While the flexibility is an advantage over product-oriented layouts, material transportation or customer movement from one department to another can be detrimental to productivity and service quality. In most process-oriented layouts, despite variability of routings, some pairs of departments are naturally more important to locate next to each other. Not surprisingly, if the design of the facility can take advantage of known relationships between departments, transportation and associated costs can be reduced. The process-oriented layout model allows the user to test various alternative layouts in a six-department facility and get immediate feedback on transportation costs.

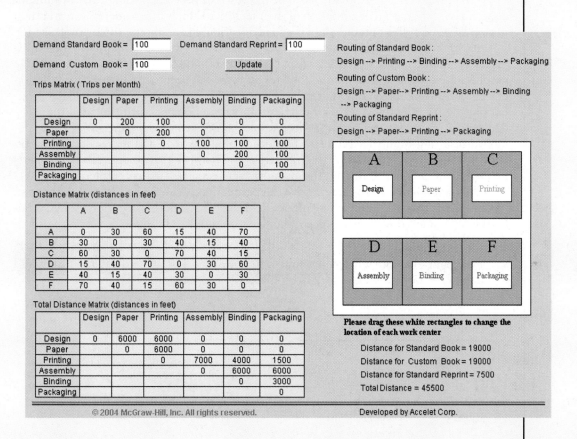

Demand Standard Book = 100   Demand Standard Reprint = 100

Demand Custom Book = 100   [Update]

Routing of Standard Book:
Design --> Printing --> Binding --> Assembly --> Packaging

Routing of Custom Book:
Design --> Paper--> Printing --> Assembly --> Binding --> Packaging

Routing of Standard Reprint:
Design --> Paper--> Printing --> Packaging

Trips Matrix (Trips per Month)

	Design	Paper	Printing	Assembly	Binding	Packaging
Design	0	200	100	0	0	0
Paper		0	200	0	0	0
Printing			0	100	100	100
Assembly				0	200	100
Binding					0	100
Packaging						0

Distance Matrix (distances in feet)

	A	B	C	D	E	F
A	0	30	60	15	40	70
B	30	0	30	40	15	40
C	60	30	0	70	40	15
D	15	40	70	0	30	60
E	40	15	40	30	0	30
F	70	40	15	60	30	0

Total Distance Matrix (distances in feet)

	Design	Paper	Printing	Assembly	Binding	Packaging
Design	0	6000	6000	0	0	0
Paper		0	6000	0	0	0
Printing			0	7000	4000	1500
Assembly				0	6000	6000
Binding					0	3000
Packaging						0

A	**B**	**C**
Design	Paper	Printing
D	**E**	**F**
Assembly	Binding	Packaging

Please drag these white rectangles to change the location of each work center

Distance for Standard Book = 19000
Distance for Custom Book = 19000
Distance for Standard Reprint = 7500
Total Distance = 45500

Developed by Accelet Corp.

Redi-Print

Redi-Print is a small printing and binding business specializing in small-volume runs of books. Its primary expertise is in printing and design, but is also gradually moving into the assembly and binding of books. Many of its customers are colleges and universities, but it also produces books for other nonprofit organizations. Its book production consists of three standard outputs. The standard book is the typical job that begins in the design room. The book design is then sent to the paper department, where paper type is determined and the proper paper is ordered. When the paper has been received, the design and the paper are sent to binding, where the appropriate cover type and spine thickness are determined. The order then moves to the printing department, where the pages are actually printed. Pages are shrink-wrapped for protection in the packaging department and are then sent to a subcontractor, who produces the cover and assembles the completed book.

The second possible product configuration is the custom book. The custom book also starts in the design department. The design is sent to the paper department for paper assignment and then to printing. Following printing, the printed pages are sent to assembly for insertion into a hardcover. Books then go to binding, where pages are permanently attached to the cover spine. From there the books go to packaging, where they are shrink-wrapped and boxed.

The third product configuration is the standard reprint. The standard reprint needs no design work. The order fulfillment process starts in the paper department, which has already received preprinted pages from the book's publisher. The pages then go to the binding department for insertion into the cover. From there the books go to packaging, where they are shrink-wrapped and boxed.

As their work changes and they become more of a full-service printer, Redi-Print managers are considering a reorganization of their facility to better meet order routings and reduce costs. The current product mix is equally distributed among the three products.

User input parameters in this model are restricted to the demand for each of three products and the locations of each of six departments. The routings for each of the three products are provided. The number of trips required between departments is a function of the monthly demand for a product and the product's routing. So, if a particular product routing specifies transporting the order from paper storage to printing, and there is a demand of 200 orders per month, there would be 200 trips from paper to printing per month resulting from that product. The other products may add more, depending on their routings. Total distances are computed as the number of trips between two departments per month multiplied by the distance between the two departments, as determined by a particular layout alternative. Departments can be moved from one location "room" to another by simply dragging the department to another location. When a department is dragged to another room, the department already there moves to the room just vacated. By swapping departments in this manner, any layout desired can be created.

1. Make sure the demand settings and layout are at the starting defaults of Standard Book Orders = 100, Customer Book Orders = 100, Standard Reprint Orders = 100. The default layout is:

Location	Department
A	Design
B	Paper Storage
C	Printing
D	Assembly
E	Binding
F	Packaging

a. Given the routings presented, identify a department that you think should be as close as possible to the paper storage department. Does "as close as possible" mean adjacent to each other or across the hall from each other? Why do you think the two departments should be as close as possible to each other? Make a change to the layout so that they are actually as close together as they can be. What happens to the total distance for the layout when this move is made?

b. Identify another department that should be close to the paper department. What is your rationale for it being close to printing? Move it as close as possible, while maintaining the relationship between paper and the department you identified for question 1a. Is the total distance improved? If so, by how much?

c. What happens if the two departments you identified to be close to printing swap places? Is the total distance reduced or increased? Explain why it is more important for one than the other to be closest to paper.

2. Start with your layout as it was at the end of question 1.

   a. Record the layout. What is its total monthly distance?

   b. Examine the routings. Can you identify any other changes that might improve the layout? Try them. What is the best layout you can come up with? What is the total distance? Explain, in terms of the demand and the routings, why your changes resulted in an improvement.

3. Set the layout back to the starting defaults.

   a. What is the total distance associated with the standard book product? Identify the layout that minimizes the total distance for the standard book. What is it?

   b. Identify and record the layout that minimizes the total distance for the custom book.

   c. Identify and record the layout that minimizes the total distance for the standard reprint.

4. Set the demand defaults back to 100 for each product and set the layout back to its starting default. The routings for the three products are:

   - Standard Book: Design → Printing → Binding → Assembly → Packaging
   - Custom Book: Design → Paper → Printing → Assembly → Binding → Packaging
   - Standard Reprint: Design → Paper → Printing → Packaging

   a. Examine the three routings closely. Use a matrix similar to the one below and rate the importance of being close together for each pair of departments. Use ratings such as "absolutely necessary," "very important," "important," and so on.

	Paper Storage	Design	Binding	Printing	Assembly	Packaging
Paper storage	xxxxxx					
Design	xxxxxx	xxxxxx				
Binding	xxxxxx	xxxxxx	xxxxxx			
Printing	xxxxxx	xxxxxx	xxxxxx	xxxxxx		
Assembly	xxxxxx	xxxxxx	xxxxxx	xxxxxx	xxxxxx	
Packaging	xxxxxx	xxxxxx	xxxxxx	xxxxxx	xxxxxx	xxxxx

   b. Create guidelines for arranging the layout by matching each of your ratings with one of the following potential department relationships:

   - Immediately across from each other.
   - Immediately next to each other.
   - Diagonally across and one over from each other.
   - Opposite ends of the same side.
   - Diagonal opposite ends of the hall.

   c. Arrange a layout that satisfies your guidelines.

   d. Can more than one layout be created to meet your guidelines? If so, what are they? When you actually arrange them, do they all have the same total distance?

5. The composition of demand and the proportions of the various products can have a significant impact on transportation of goods from one department or work center to another. In a dynamic environment with frequent changes in the product mix, the layout cannot be changing all the time to keep up. However, when identifying the

best layout, it is important to consider the layout that will best meet the most likely mix of products.

Arrange the layout as below:

Location	Department
A	Design
B	Binding
C	Assembly
D	Paper
E	Printing
F	Packaging

a. This layout is very good when the product mix is 100 for each product. Change the product demands to Standard Book = 100, Custom Book = 250, and Standard Reprint = 100. What is the total distance for this product mix with this layout?

b. How can the layout be improved? Identify the best layout for this product mix. What is the total distance for the best layout? Explain why your improvements worked.

c. Identify the worst possible layout for this product mix. What is the total distance? How does it compare to the best layout for this product mix?

APPLICATION CASE 16.1

S & S Retail Location Decision

Sally and Sue are planning for a new retail business they plan to open together. They have settled on two potential locations, one on 4th Street and one on 6th Avenue. They have agreed on the factors that are important to their location but disagree on how important each factor is to the success of the business. The factors that they have agreed on are:

Traffic flow
Building layout
Rental cost
Neighboring businesses
Parking
Neighborhood ambiance
Buildout agreement

The partners have proposed the following factor weights:

Factor	Sally's Weights	Sue's Weights
Traffic flow	0.3	0.1
Building layout	0.1	0.2
Rental cost	0.2	0.1
Neighboring businesses	0.1	0.2
Parking	0.15	0.05
Neighborhood ambiance	0.1	0.3
Buildout agreement	0.05	0.05

The partners have carefully evaluated each site and have rated each site on a scale of 1 (worst) to 100 (best). Both partners agree on the ratings.

Factor	4th Street	6th Avenue
Traffic flow	80	60
Building layout	75	80
Rental cost	80	90
Neighboring businesses	60	80
Parking	100	90
Neighborhood ambiance	75	90
Buildout agreement	90	85

1. Which is the preferred location if Sally's weights are used?

2. Which is the preferred location if Sue's weights are used?

3. How sensitive is the location decision to the weights that the two partners have established? In other words, will slight changes in weights change the outcomes?

4. How do you suggest they proceed from here in determining the best location?

5. Sally maintains that a match between the type of products they plan to sell and the clientele in the neighboring residential areas is important. Sue thinks that the residential area is not as important as the types of businesses they locate near. What matters most? Is there a way you could find out what aspects of the location actually matter most to customers? Explain.

Workforce: Optimizing Human Capital

LEARNING OBJECTIVES

- Describe how the workforce contributes to profitability.

- Explain how expectations for employees are increasing.

- Explain the impact the workforce has on value.

- Use the customer experience grid to describe the relationship between customers and employees.

- Describe why teams have become more important.

- Explain a structure for team processes.

- Describe the impacts of contingent workers.

- Describe why workforce productivity is important.

- Demonstrate how standard times are created.

- Make the necessary calculations to perform a work sampling study.

- Describe how learning rates can affect worker productivity.

- Calculate the amount of time a task will take, given a specified learning rate.

EMPLOYEE LOYALTY IS CRITICAL IN SOME BUSINESSES

Since the 1990s, changing jobs frequently has become much more socially acceptable than previously. Layoffs have contributed to an erosion of employee loyalty. While those layoffs have reduced costs, and sometimes replacements have been cheaper than those laid off, professionals with experience are often necessary to provide the level of service expected by customers. A new type of worker, part of the "emergent workforce," is changing the way employers must attract and retain employees. Emergent workers are more in control of their own careers and want to be rewarded based on performance. Traditional workers are more concerned with job security and stability. Emergent workers view job change as positive and are more confident in their ability to market themselves for a new job. They view loyalty not as how long someone works for an organization, but by what they contribute to it. They have low tolerance for low performers.

High employee turnover translates directly into a lower average level of experience and lower levels of service. Loyal employees show up for work and are more productive while they're there. From a customer satisfaction perspective, if an employee has no loyalty to the company, they can't be expected to promote that company to customers. Satisfied employees lead to loyal employees, more experienced employees, higher levels of product and service quality, higher levels of value for customers, higher levels of satisfaction for customers, and increased company profitability.

The accounting industry provides an excellent example of an industry that must cope with the characteristics of the emergent worker who, by old standards, appears to lack loyalty. Accounting firms suffer because seasoned professionals are needed at partner levels. One firm specializing in certified public accounting and business services, RSM McGladrey, has implemented a program designed to enhance employee loyalty and gain its benefits. A key part of that program is to provide employees with developmental opportunities that will enable them to move to the next level. An annual employee climate survey is a critical part of the program. All employees provide feedback about such issues as work situations, rewards, performance, supervision, and leadership. The program also emphasizes building flexibility into an employee's work life. As employees move through different stages in their lives, their needs change, and the work environment needs to adapt to maintain their loyalty. For RSM McGladrey, maintaining that loyalty is viewed as a key ingredient for client services.

Source: "Employee Retention: No More Gold Watch," *Accounting Today*, June 21–July 11, 2004; J. Heskett, W. E. Sasser, and L. Schlesinger, *The Service Profit Chain: How Leading Companies Link Profit and Growth to Loyalty, Satisfaction and Value* (New York: Free Press, 1997); K. Harding, "Understanding Emerging Workforce Trends," *Design Intelligence*, August 2000, Vol. 6, No. 15, www.di.net/article.php?article_id=129.

The workforce is as important as any other resource used to create value and, in many ways, more important and more challenging to manage. After all, no other resource can get up and walk away from the business when dissatisfied. The workforce can have the greatest potential, but can also be the most difficult resource to utilize effectively.

Introduction: Using the Workforce as a Key to Competitive Success

Successful businesses recognize that their most valuable asset is their workforce. The most successful CEOs have said this for decades, and some have actually meant it. The increasing importance of the workforce can be traced to several environmental pressures. First and foremost, as businesses become increasingly dependent on information and technology, related skills become more valuable, and competition for employees with those skills becomes fierce. We are in an information-based economy. Workers must have the skills to access and use the information and knowledge and must be able to keep up with the rapidly changing technologies utilized to manage it.

Second, as the business world becomes more networked, products become more like commodities, which makes differentiation on the basis of product quality or price more difficult. Market dominance shifts to the most innovative company. Innovation comes from ideas. Ideas come from people. Despite advances in recent years, we have yet to develop software that can come up with even the simplest idea.

Third, competition is, to a great extent, based on service-oriented value attributes. The market for high-quality employees is tight. Even for manufacturers, employees who can interact effectively with customers become key components of a successful strategy. Businesses seeking all ranges of workers, from minimum-wage workers to high-salaried specialists, struggle to fill positions with quality employees. To make matters worse, hiring someone is not the end of the process. Retaining a good employee becomes an ongoing challenge, because other businesses need good employees, too.

This chapter examines the workforce and its role in contributing to value and, ultimately, profitability. Included in that discussion are current issues that affect workforce management, such as the changing nature of the work environment, the increased use of teams, increasing needs for certain skills, job design characteristics, and workforce productivity improvement.

Employee–Customer Interaction, Value, and Profitability

A common estimate is that the replacement cost of an employee is one-third of that person's annual salary.

As you certainly know by now, profitability depends on net income, which, in turn, depends on value, processes, and resources. No one can deny that employees are expensive, from a direct and indirect labor standpoint. The cost of direct labor varies tremendously, depending on the nature of the business, whether it's manufacturing- or service-oriented, and on other characteristics of the business. For example, in many manufacturing environments direct labor accounts for less than 10 percent of product costs. In other business environments, it can be the largest cost category. If the only value added by employees can be replaced by machines, however, it's no wonder some managers dream of the day when the factory doesn't even have lights in it. Given the desire most managers have to maximize utilization of resources, it's ironic that the full range of employee capability and talent is so often underutilized.

Without value, sales don't happen. As the business world becomes increasingly more connected through the Internet, anyone can buy anything from anyone else.

Price differentials begin to disappear, because everyone is aware of the best prices. Product quality differentials disappear as well, because no one with inferior-quality products survives. Customers know what products and services are the best value, because they talk to each other via chat rooms, e-mail, and bulletin boards. Location doesn't matter because a customer can click on anyone's Web site with equal ease. A business no longer competes only with those in its geographic region. The market consists of businesses with similar prices, quality, and products trying to differentiate themselves through whatever value attributes remain for differentiation. Exactly what does remain? For many businesses, the only thing left is service. Remember, in most businesses, value doesn't solely depend on outcomes. The processes a customer must go through to get the desired outcomes are equally important. How fast can I get it? How much do the people I talk to actually know about it? How pleasant is the interaction? Several studies have shown that service is an extremely important component of value in all types of B2B and B2C interactions, but even more so with Internet sales. Customer response, positive and negative, often results from service interactions with employees.

Employees make a tremendous difference in service encounters. In many cases, when the value added by customer–employee interactions is removed, there is no value differential left, and competitive advantage disappears. One way employees are wasted is in what management doesn't let them do. Despite the link between customers and value, in many companies, management does not want employees to interact with customers. Customers, however, are demanding these interactions. Employees want these interactions also, because talking to customers makes their job more interesting, and because they want to know the customers. People enjoy interacting with other people. It's fun. Unfortunately, managers often try to prevent these interactions because they sense a loss of control. They worry about what an employee might say. Sometimes they worry that an employee will tell the truth. But truth is what customers demand. Other customers will tell them the truth. It might as well come from the company and the workforce. Management's fear might be warranted if the employees do not have the skills or knowledge to effectively interact with customers. If that is the case, however, the business is probably doomed whether or not management succeeds at keeping employees away from customers. Employees need to be able to interact with customers.[1] Employees value companies that provide them with opportunities to expand their skills. Such companies are rewarded with high-quality employees.

Reduction of labor costs (direct and indirect) has always been a goal of businesses. Let's face it—reduction of all costs has been a goal of business, but labor gets the brunt of reductions because managers can always find an employee not working at 100 percent. The history of manufacturing technology leads one to believe that a primary goal has

Despite attempts to reduce customer interaction to improve efficiency, for many firms, customer interaction provides a way to differentiate from competitors. Small banks, like the one here, have been able to gain substantial market share in recent years by focusing on service activities that come only from the interactions between customers and highly skilled employees.

om ADVANTAGE Should Employees Talk to Customers?

The rapidly increasing ability of employees to talk directly to customers has created difficult issues for many businesses. Customers want the truth, and employees can often give it to them. Employees enjoy talking to customers. This is made faster and easier with Internet bulletin boards, listserves, and e-mail. In May 2000, Jill Griffin, customer-service representative for American Airlines, registered with FlyerTalk, an online bulletin board for frequent fliers. She began to answer questions on her own time.

American Airlines officials were initially supportive, and Griffin had a loyal following on the site, but after a few months American became uneasy about her responding to questions and making statements without official authorization. In January 2001, she added a disclaimer to her responses, claiming that her responses weren't sanctioned by American or AMR, American's parent corporation. On March 29, 2001, she posted her last response, stating that her employer did not want her to post anymore.

An American Airlines spokesman expressed concern that she was passing on erroneous information and information that the company didn't want public. He expressed concern that if some of the information she passed on got into the hands of a competitor, American Airlines would be disadvantaged.

Other members of FlyerTalk, however, felt very differently. The publisher of *Inside-Flyer* magazine, the host of the FlyerTalk forum, responded with "This is what customer service looks like in the 21st century." Other companies agree. Hilton Hotels has had a representative assigned to the FlyerTalk bulletin board since June 1999. Some companies assign someone to bulletin boards to "lurk" but not get actively involved. Delta, for example, monitors online discussions on several message boards but doesn't offer official responses. The gradual integration of this aspect of customer service into the mainstream of service and industrial markets is certain to cause problems. Although the businesses want to avoid "unofficial" information that could cause problems, customers don't believe "official" statements any more. They want the straight story from an individual, not a corporate entity. This is particularly true in an industry like air travel, where customers have more than enough reason to be skeptical.

While the question may be difficult for many companies, according to the authors of *The Cluetrain Manifesto*, it's a no-brainer. Companies must create the link so that customers can speak to individuals who have the answers to questions. The Internet has created an expectation that companies cannot ignore. To ignore it is to ignore their customers.

Source: "Should Workers Offer Unofficial Help Online?" *Wall Street Journal*, April 17, 2001, pp. B1, B6; R. Levine, C. Locke, D. Searles, and D. Weinberger, *The Cluetrain Manifesto* (New York: Perseus Books, 2000).

---

been to completely eliminate the need for direct labor. This has been accomplished by substituting capital investments, like automated machines, for people. This perspective almost seems reasonable in a product-oriented environment that has little need for interaction between customers and employees. And it definitely makes sense when the job is repetitive, boring, or dangerous. The elimination of labor in traditional manufacturing is not all that different from the trends in people-intensive business activities like marketing. Mass marketing strategies often eliminate the one-to-one interactions that characterized original "markets" where people assembled to discuss agricultural products they had to trade and sell. When the word "market" became a verb, the relationships among buyers and sellers changed drastically. Market shifted from being a place where people discussed and traded goods to something a company did to people. The Internet, however, is quickly reversing this trend. It is viewed as a "place" by many of its users. They "go" there. Where'd you get it? I got it on the Internet. An entity very different from other forms of media, such as TV or radio, the Internet is much closer to being like the marketplace of old. Businesses have rapidly discovered that attempts to treat Internet marketing like TV advertising will fail. The Internet has brought employees and customers back in touch with each other for many businesses, when management allows it.

Do you remember the short-lived hyperbole of "push" technology? Probably not. It appeared in about 1998 as *the* way to use the Internet in marketing efforts. It's ancient history now. Users don't want it. Rather than a business disseminating one-way bullets of information to millions of potential customers, as is the case with TV advertising, customers expect two-way interaction on the Internet. They expect to talk to employees of the business. They expect to talk directly to people who know the answers to their questions, and, in most cases, those are the employees most familiar with the products and services—those who actually produce them. And, even though many businesses try to prevent it, employees can and want to talk directly to customers. That interaction has tremendous potential for product and service value and customer loyalty. Loyalty, after all, is often directed toward people, not legal entities like corporations. The interactions made possible by knowledgeable, committed employees may be one of the most important competitive advantages remaining.

The Employee Contribution to Value Attributes

We know from Chapter 3 that customers value some product and service attributes more than others. What they value varies from customer to customer and also varies from business to business. The following list recaps the B2B and B2C value attributes presented in Chapter 3. Understanding the value added by the workforce requires understanding the link between those value attributes and the employees.

Cost	Style/fashion
Quality	Ethical issues
Response time	Technology
Dependability of delivery	Flexibility
Convenience	Personalization

Costs of products and service production are composed of materials, labor, and overhead expenses. Obviously the workforce, through its productivity, has an impact on labor and overhead costs. The greater the productivity, the lower the cost on a per-unit basis. Materials consumption and associated costs are often a function of the product and service design and the systems that process those materials. One of the most avoidable costs associated with material use is that associated with waste and poor quality. Ideas for preventing waste and improving quality are often best found at the lowest possible levels of the workforce. Major cost savings can be had by working smarter, not necessarily working harder. This is probably one of the most overlooked potentials of today's workforce. The workers on the frontlines have a wealth of knowledge. Unfortunately, many businesses get no financial return on that asset.

Quality, response time, and *dependability of delivery* often fall under the broader concept of product and service quality. Quality, in many ways, is not achieved by finishing a set of tasks that can easily be separated and assigned. It is a mentality that is instilled through a company culture. A culture is created from a common belief among employees. For many service encounters, the employee defines that interaction. Certainly product quality, response time, and delivery performance are dictated by various production and delivery systems, but without the emphasis on those attributes by employees, the firm will not excel. When disruptions and failures do take place, and a product or service quality level isn't up to expectations, or the delivery time is too long or late, the success of the recovery is entirely controlled by the intervening employees. The relationship established by the employees will determine the ultimate resolution.

Convenience, style/fashion, and *ethical issues* are value attributes that result more from strategic decisions and less from the day-to-day actions of employees. In the case of convenience, however, it is still up to the workforce to carry out the tasks necessary to provide it. When competing on the basis of style/fashion, a workforce that has the knowledge or interest about the product or service, especially from the perspective of being a user of the products, is of great help. When competing on ethical issues, it is important to have a workforce committed to the issues. Only a sympathetic workforce can effectively communicate the company's position. These workforce requirements may seem obvious, but they are not easily obtained. In a tight labor market, any additional qualifications that reduce the size of the pool of acceptable candidates make it more difficult and more costly to hire quality workers. For companies seeking to differentiate on the basis of these attributes, the characteristics of the workforce are extremely important.

Technology, flexibility, and *personalization* attributes are aspects of the product or service production system that require specific skills and capabilities on the part of employees. Employees who directly affect these value attributes will likely have job responsibilities that are specifically designed to enhance them. Technological skills are probably in the highest demand in today's workforce. Flexibility and personalization, in many cases, require technological capabilities as well, because flexibility and personalization are often achieved through technological applications included in scheduling systems or customer relationship management (CRM) systems.

Employee Interaction with Customers: A Prerequisite to Good Service

The preceding discussion of the impact of employees on value attributes leads to the conclusion that trainable skills do not make the only difference between a value-adding employee and a non-value-adding employee. Knowledge is a requirement as well. Knowledge obtained on the job is often more important than the more formal knowledge a person brings to the company. Personality and attitude can also play a major role, particularly in customer contact situations. The combination of skills, knowledge, personality, and attitude, and their ultimate impact on the firm's ability to create the value attributes necessary to compete effectively, should make it obvious that an effective workforce truly is a firm's most valuable asset.

The link between the workforce and profitability can be made from the perspective of increasing value and decreasing costs, as has been done so far in this chapter, or from a broader and different perspective—that of customer loyalty. Much has been said about employee satisfaction and whether or not the satisfaction of employees ever affects a firm's profitability. The **service–profit chain**[2] creates a sound logical link between employee satisfaction and profitability by demonstrating the link to customer loyalty that can be created by the workforce.

The service–profit chain, diagrammed in Exhibit 17.1, is not meant to be applicable only to services, excluding product-oriented companies, but is meant to address the service-oriented activities of all companies. From Exhibit 17.1, the role of internal quality—in other words, treating employees well and getting them what they need to do their job well—results in higher levels of employee satisfaction. The increase in satisfaction decreases the likelihood that the employee will leave. A higher level of experience, resulting from improved employee retention, results in improved customer satisfaction, which comes from the increased value customers get from that interaction. That increase

Retailing has an annual voluntary turnover rate in the U.S. of 31.2 percent. Manufacturing is on the low end, with rates around 13 percent.

In 2004, the highest turnover rate was in the accommodation food services industries—47.3 percent.

service–profit chain
A framework used to link employee satisfaction to profitability.

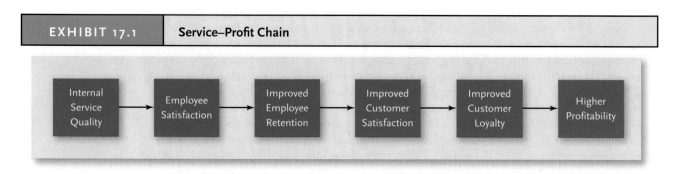

EXHIBIT 17.1	Service–Profit Chain

Internal Service Quality → Employee Satisfaction → Improved Employee Retention → Improved Customer Satisfaction → Improved Customer Loyalty → Higher Profitability

Source: Modified from G. W. Loveman, W. E. Sasser Jr., and L. A. Schlesinger, "Putting the Service–Profit Chain to Work," *Harvard Business Review,* March–April 1994, p. 166.

om ADVANTAGE   Cutting Employee Perks: With or Without Cutting Employee Morale

The concept of "internal quality" that maintains employee satisfaction and low employee turnover is often enhanced by a variety of employee perks. During the high point of the short-lived dot-com success era, perks included free lunches, coffee, massages, snacks, evening entertainment, and other benefits that seem unusual and extravagant in most situations. Some companies employed concierge services, costing as much as $100,000 per year, to assist employees with such tasks as vacation planning, buying tickets to entertainment events, and other personal activities that the employee would likely do at work. As companies began to experience financial difficulties, perks were the first things to go. In most cases, employees had little input in deciding which perks were withdrawn, and the changes had a negative impact on employee morale.

Reducing employee perks is a common means of cutting costs of items that do not have a significant return on investment. One Aetna Insurance office, for example, saves $400,000 per year by making employees buy their own coffee and tea. Excite@Home saves $165,000 per year by making employees pay 25 cents a can for soft drinks. In what would seem to be commonsense advice, experts recommend

that when perks need to be cut, involving employees in the decision is important. Scaling back perks without totally eliminating them curbs negative reactions. Recommendations for cutting back on perks with a minimal impact on employee morale include the following:

- Scale back without entirely eliminating the perks.
- Ask employees which perks are the most important.
- Explain the cutbacks in the context of the business.
- Do not allow employees to learn about the cutbacks informally or through the grapevine.
- Do not make cuts that affect only lower-level employees.
- Do not assume that cuts will be a panacea for massive cost-cutting needs.
- Do not cut 401(k) matching funds, medical/dental care, day care, or flextime.

Source: M. Pole, "How to Cut Perks without Killing Morale," *Fortune*, February 19, 2001, pp. 241–244.

in satisfaction results in higher levels of loyalty and the higher level of profitability that accompanies it. The best companies to work for are always at an advantage because they get more job applicants, allowing them to be more selective.

Customer loyalty is an often overlooked, but critically important result of operations. The feedback from customers frequently is something like "Your products are great, but I hate doing business with you." Customer loyalty doesn't result from evaluations like this. Companies focus on product-creation processes, but customer service processes get overlooked. The customer experience grid, adapted in Exhibit 17.2 to illustrate the impact of customer–employee interaction, provides an effective way to look at customer loyalty.[3] It demonstrates how the outcome and process combine to result in customer satisfaction of the overall experience. Each is only one component of the loyalty equation. The expectations also vary as customer interaction increases. In many cases, when the outcomes leave no opportunity for differentiation, processes become more important. Within the processes, the quantity and quality of employee interaction become an opportunity for differentiation. Invariably, the processes that make up the encounter depend on employees. The greater the interaction, the more critical the judgment and interaction skills of the employees, because expectations for customization increase as well.

One reaction of managers to this emphasis on customer loyalty might be that loyalty is too expensive to try to get. Businesses that try to develop loyalty have a completely different perspective. They view the customer relationship as a long-term asset with a lifetime value rather than a one-time source of revenue. Rather than sell one car to a customer, they want to transform that customer into a loyal customer and sell 10 or 12 cars over the next 25 years. What makes the customer loyalty goal even more attractive is that costs are lower for loyal customers. Unfortunately for managers who ignore customer loyalty, it is now easier than ever for a customer to try out the competition when the transaction outcome or process is unsatisfactory. In many cases the competition is just one click away.

EXHIBIT 17.2   Customer Experience Grid with Customer Interaction Dimension

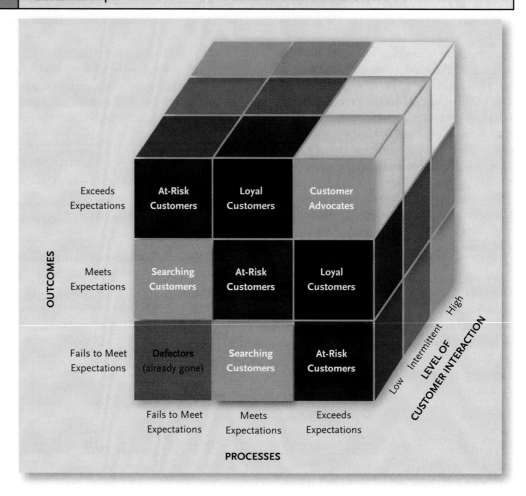

The Most Important Employee Contribution to Value: Sound Decisions

Successful organizations empower their workers to use their knowledge and expertise in decision making. The use of the talent and knowledge present in the workforce is enhanced by moving decisions downward in the organization to give workers at lower levels the authority to make decisions in areas they are familiar with. In many cases, their knowledge is specific to the situation at hand and they have a better understanding of the effects of the decision.

Increased interaction with customers is a natural outcome of moving decisions downward. The best answer to a customer's questions can often come only from the employee directly responsible for the production of that customer's product or service. Taking every question to a customer service employee frustrates the customer who waits endlessly as the customer service representative seeks out the employee who can best answer the question. This creates a delay that the customer shouldn't have. Putting the customer in direct contact with a knowledgeable and responsible employee familiar with the product or service provides a quick and accurate response.

Just as the employees who produce a product or service are often the most knowledgeable and most qualified to answer customers' questions, employees who work day-to-day

om ADVANTAGE   Reducing Turnover in the Fast-Food Industry

Employee work experience is important to good service and quality products. The service–profit chain provides an excellent framework for how this phenomenon eventually affects customer satisfaction. If you were to guess that one of the highest-turnover industries is fast food, you'd be right. Despite the fact that a high turnover rate is expected, it's still to management's benefit to reduce it. Several fast-food chains are trying to develop benefits packages that encourage employees to consider their jobs as a possible career. Burger King, for example, provides 401(k) retirement plans for workers in its 500 corporate restaurants and plans to launch a 401(k) plan for its 8,000 franchised restaurants. Tricon Global Restaurants, operator of Taco Bell, Pizza Hut, and KFC, offers some restaurant employees stock options and ties management bonuses to employee retention.

In the mid-1990s, employee turnover rate for fast-food restaurants averaged over 200 percent (the average length of employment was about six months). Most restaurants have seen turnover rates improve, with some getting significantly below 200 percent. There are several benefits to these improvements. Average training costs per employee for Burger King, for example, are $400–800 per employee. Jack-in-the-Box estimates the training cost to be $1,000, so reduced turnover results in lower training costs. Industry experts, surveying more than 12,000 restaurants, calculated an average hourly employee replacement cost of $2,399. The average experience level of the employees goes up and so does quality. Profitability improves from the improved satisfaction of customers and from the reduction in labor costs.

Increases in employee benefits have also resulted in an increase in the age of the employee. The average age of a Wendy's employee, for example, has crept up to between 27 and 28 years old. Restaurant management recognizes that it cannot provide quality levels that require a stable workforce from 16-year-olds. Attracting an older workforce requires more benefits and an opportunity for advancement.

Source: "Fast Food Industry Pitches 'Burger Flipping' as a Career," *Wall Street Journal*, May 29, 2001, pp. B1, B16, Workforce Management, December 2004; www.peoplereport.com, June 7, 2006.

with processes are often most qualified to help improve them. All aspects of business can be improved through significant contributions from employees on the front lines. For many firms, these improvement efforts have led to the use of project teams.

Increasing the Contribution of Employees through Teams

In the late 1970s, Japanese auto manufacturers began increasing their market share in the United States by building cars that were well-designed, reliable, and of impeccable quality. Naturally, the U.S. auto manufacturers tried to figure out how they did it. One of the obvious differences was the way Japanese manufacturers used their employees. They had numerous small groups of employees working on product and process improvement projects. Suspecting that this was how the Japanese manufacturers created their quality culture, U.S. manufacturers and services embarked on a giant mission to implement employee work groups, called "quality circles," in all of their operations. Unfortunately for U.S. managers, quality circles were not the cause of the quality culture in Japan. Employees working in teams were, in fact, a result of that culture. In the United States, the quality circle fad gradually faded. We did come to realize, however, that using groups of employees to help improve quality levels and process productivity was a good idea. We just needed to figure out how to do it right. The result has been a steady increase in the use of project and improvement teams in U.S. businesses.

The use of teams has spread throughout the quality and process improvement efforts and has permeated new-product development, system implementation, and the management of virtually any small- or large-scale endeavor. Reengineering efforts, described in Chapter 4, are frequently accomplished by project teams. Quality management process improvement and lean systems depend heavily on the expertise of well-trained worker teams. In many cases, the teams are intentionally composed of employees from different business functions to bring different perspectives, knowledge of different needs, and different areas of expertise to bear on the project. The desire to fully utilize employee knowledge and skills, combined with the increased recognition that many decisions have far-reaching impact across functional boundaries, has resulted in an increase in the use of cross-functional project teams.

Successful companies have learned that developing a successful team requires much more than throwing workers together in a group and assigning them a task. Employees do not typically have the skills necessary to function well in that environment. A true team environment requires training and skill development to enable the employees to function effectively. The expertise needed does not end with knowledge about their particular business function. They need to know how to work in a team. They need to know how to make decisions in a team. The team skills are necessary for the team to fully utilize the talent and knowledge of its members. Without these skills, it is just a work group. Exhibit 17.3 presents a typical progression of the development of employee team capabilities.

Very little contribution is made by a team that hasn't been trained to effectively make decisions. In these situations virtually all of the work is done by the team leader. Team

| EXHIBIT 17.3 | **Project Team Capabilities** |

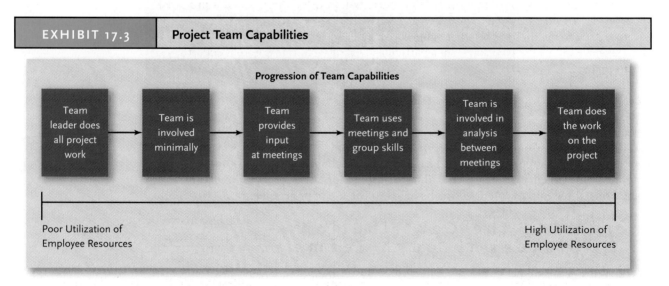

Source: Adapted from *Unleash the Power of Project Teams* (Cincinnati, OH: Association for Quality and Participation, 2000).

members, in addition to doing little work, are not contributing the most important thing they have to offer—their knowledge. Workers skilled in working in teams take on more responsibility until they reach a point where they can take on all team responsibilities. Failure to quickly move employees to make full contributions is no different from failure to use a piece of equipment to the fullest extent of its capabilities. An investment has been made in both cases and the owners of the firm have a right to expect that management will get the best return possible on that investment. Managers have been quick to realize that they do not always have the skills required to create effective teams in their organization. As a result, many outsource the training of employees so that they have the skills to effectively work in teams.

Why Use Teams?

The advantages of using teams, rather than individuals, to accomplish business tasks must be understood in order to understand why businesses are so enthusiastic about their use. A primary advantage is that teams bring different perspectives along with different types of knowledge and expertise to the project. If a project has broad requirements, completion by an individual is unlikely to provide a result that meets all the requirements. In addition to the sum of the knowledge of a team, a team can be very creative in its actions. Members with different perspectives and different expertise can combine resources from different functional areas to contribute to a solution. This is not likely to happen with an individual.

A second advantage of using teams is that tasks can be assigned to the various members and the duration of the project can be reduced. In an effectively managed team, each member has responsibilities for "between-meeting" tasks. You've probably worked in student groups on projects when you've thought, "I could do this much quicker by myself," in which case you weren't working on a team, despite the fact that your professor may have called it that. That's the difference between a *group* of people working on a project and an effectively managed *team*. Teams actually get more done. Like any other resource, however, team management consists of a set of techniques that make effective team management possible and actually reduce the amount of management necessary. Attempting to utilize teams without the knowledge of these techniques will probably lead to a failed endeavor.

A third advantage of teams is known as "buy-in." You're probably familiar with the "not invented here" (NIH) syndrome. It's the phenomenon of trying to convince *someone else* that *your* idea is great. Had the other person thought of it, he'd think it was great, too. We all resist ideas or proposals from others, because we don't feel any ownership toward them. An important aspect of getting buy-in from others about a proposed change is to develop in them a sense of ownership. This can be accomplished only by involving them in deciding what the change should be. Granted, we can't involve everyone, but if we involve one person from a particular department, others in that department will have a greater sense of ownership than if they knew no one involved in the project. In summary, teams give us greater knowledge and a broader perspective, they give us greater capability, and they give us greater buy-in.

The use of teams has become so pervasive, it makes sense to categorize the use of teams into their various types and present some frameworks that will give a foundation of team processes. This discussion will not turn you into an expert on team functions, but it will give you a good introduction.

Appropriate Uses for Teams

When we look back at the advantages of using teams, it becomes clear that their advantages contribute most to implementing change. Most changes are intended to effect improvements. Change must occur for improvement to occur. It's that simple. Business improvements can be broken into two primary types.[4] The first type of improvement comes from **innovation.** Innovation is a dramatic change to something we do or something we produce. It is a new idea. Development and creation of innovation can be

innovation

A dramatic change from a new idea.

a project. The management of an innovation, making it come to fruition, is also a project. Innovations can come from individuals or teams, but those coming from teams have the added advantage of greater levels of creativity, broader perspective, and more knowledge behind them. The use of teams to create an innovation and infuse it into the business will enhance the results for the same reasons, but in this endeavor, buy-in is critical. The use of teams greatly improves that buy-in.

continuous improvement
A process of always seeking ways to improve existing processes and tasks.

The second type of business improvement is known as **continuous improvement.** Continuous-improvement activities focus on existing processes and tasks, always seeking ways to improve them. In many cases, the improvement of business processes focuses on the elimination of non-value-adding (NVA) process steps. This focus speeds up the process and reduces costs. The result is enhanced value.

For both types of improvement, the ability of a team to complete a project quickly is a function of how much time team members have to devote to it. If the only time team members have to work on a project is during weekly team meetings, because the rest of their job responsibilities keep them too busy or they're not allowed to work on it between meetings, not much can happen. If an individual is given the responsibility to complete the project, with no team involvement, and the individual is released from other responsibilities, the project could probably be completed faster. However, the result will suffer from the lack of knowledge, perspective, and buy-in, reducing the quality of the end result. Like anything else, you get what you pay for. The use of teams effectively requires a bigger resource investment than assigning a task to an individual, but the outcome is better.

Structure for Team Processes

In using teams to accomplish an improvement project, efforts must be organized so that resources are not wasted. Projects follow a life cycle, and that life cycle provides a structure for managing the project. Exhibit 17.4 is a diagram of a generic improvement project life cycle.[5]

EXHIBIT 17.4	Project Life Cycle

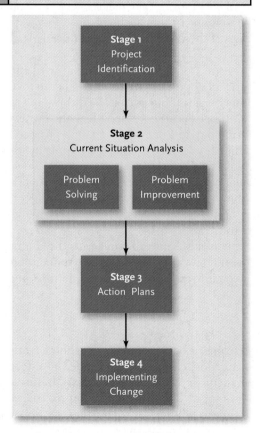

Stage 1, the project identification stage, is initiated with the assignment of a project to a team, or a team selecting a project they wish to undertake. This stage also consists of developing a mission or goals statement for the project, describing the contribution that successfully completing the project will make to the organization, and identifying all of the stakeholders. Stakeholders include anyone with a vested interest in the outcome.

Stage 2 consists of analyzing the current situation. The specific activities depend on whether the project is of a problem-solving nature or is devoted to process improvement. A problem-solving project might be created in response to a variety of indicators or measures of performance. For example, a rash of customer complaints might trigger an effort to deal with a problem. A pattern of missed due date promises might result in a project team being formed to solve the problem. On the other hand, a process-improvement focus might be an ongoing effort that isn't triggered by some event. The specific steps differ slightly, depending on the focus. In a problem-solving project, for example, much of the effort will be spent on trying to determine the cause of the problem. For process improvement, however, that time would be spent identifying non-value-adding activities.

Stage 3 consists of creating the plan for taking action, whether the action is to solve a problem or provide improvement to a process. It proceeds from identifying possible changes to make to identifying and selecting what changes will actually be implemented. Once selected, the change must be justified through the analysis of actual data.

Stage 4 is the implementation stage. It includes a plan for obtaining support and buy-in, a plan for implementing the changes, a plan for measuring and evaluating the results of the change recommended, and a plan for ensuring that the change is actually carried out. If it is a change in the way people do a particular task, for example, the plan should address what has to happen to make sure employees change their methods and ensure that the recommendations for change are actually carried out. Measures are then taken, and the results of the changes are analyzed. This creates information that can then be used to evaluate the effectiveness of the team. In other words, did the team's actions result in its goals being accomplished?

Team Decision-Making Tools

One outcome of the increase in the popularity of project teams has been the development of tools that can be used to aid in project-team tasks. There are dozens, if not hundreds, of tools used by teams to aid in projects, but many have their roots in the traditional quality tools described in Chapter 7. Exhibit 17.5 provides a "refresher" of what those tools look like. An examination of the role the tools can play in a typical project provides a useful introduction to the use of team decision-making aids.

Each of the four stages of project life accomplishes distinct tasks. To accomplish these tasks, different tools are incorporated into the project activities. The first stage is to identify exactly what it is the team will do. A team whose objective is to focus on problems

Traditional Quality Tools	EXHIBIT 17.5

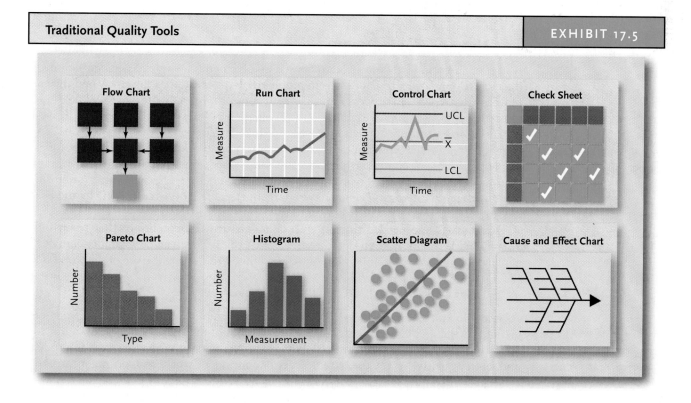

might use a Pareto chart to prioritize the results of customer complaints or performance measures to give them a sense of which item to address first. Similarly, a control chart that indicates a process being out of control might form the basis for identifying and selecting a particular problem as an improvement-team focus. A check sheet might indicate too many instances of a particular undesirable event or condition. If the team has ongoing continuous-improvement responsibilities, a flow chart might initiate action to improve a process.

Stage 2 involves understanding the current situation, for problem solving and for process-improvement efforts. For problem solving, analysis of run charts, Pareto charts, scatter diagrams, and histograms might lead to suggestions for possible causes. The cause-and-effect chart can aid in moving from possible causes to root causes. Once a root cause is suspected, run charts, Pareto charts, scatter diagrams, and histograms might again be used as validation tools. For process improvement, flow charts and run charts will provide input into identifying non-value-adding activities.

Stage 3 requires the development of a solution to the problem or the elimination of the non-value-adding process steps. Selection of the appropriate changes to make might involve the use of several different tools, particularly the run chart, scatter diagram, or flow chart.

Stage 4 requires the development of buy-in among stakeholders and actions to ensure and evaluate results. Ensuring that the recommended changes actually take place might require that an ongoing use of control charts be implemented. To evaluate the impact of recommendations, the measures and tools used to identify the problem initially would be used again to provide a "before and after" view of the situation.

In addition to the traditional quality tools used to analyze data, other tools bring team members to convergence when making decisions. These consensus-building techniques strive to reduce the importance of opinion and move the team toward making objective decisions based on factual data. The training of teams is often outsourced to take advantage of the expertise offered by firms specializing in these skills.

Increased Need for Workforce Flexibility

The Use of Cross-Training

cross-training
Training employees to do a variety of jobs.

Flatter organization structures and increased involvement of employees in decision making requires employees to have skills in problem solving and data analysis. When the employees are involved in process improvement, they also need greater levels of flexibility to accomplish their jobs. Flexibility of individual employees is often enhanced through the use of **cross-training,** which involves training employees to do a variety of jobs. This greatly increases their contribution to the organization. If one employee is absent, for example, another employee can perform the same responsibilities. In addition, workers who move around in the organization performing different responsibilities often find their work more interesting. They have a larger perspective on what is done by the business and a larger sense of contribution to the company's goals.

Flexibility is also needed to deal with changing demand conditions that result from volatile markets and short product or service life cycles. This type of flexibility cannot be achieved through cross-training. It requires flexibility in adjusting the size of the workforce.

The Use of Contingent Workers

contingent workers
Temporary workers employed by an agency and contracted to work for another firm.

As is usually the case in business decisions, most opportunities come with costs. Trade-offs abound in the area of workforce management. One of the more common and growing areas that offers great opportunities—but can also come at tremendous cost to product and service quality—is the use of temporary or **contingent workers.** Contingent workers are either temporary employees hired through a temporary agency or contractors who provide services so the company doesn't have to provide them for itself.

Formerly limited to hourly and low-skill positions, contingent workers now include employees of all abilities and salary levels, from filing clerks to engineers. The availability of a contingent workforce adds a tremendous amount of flexibility, enabling a firm to deal with seasonal demand fluctuations or implementation projects that are short-lived. It can also result in a myriad of problems deriving from a lack of training and preparation for the job. Abuses of temporary employees who receive a lower salary and fewer benefits than the people working right next to them can create a culture of resentful workers.

Who's in Charge?

In many businesses, particularly those with high customer interaction, early process design decisions determine where the decision-making power lies. Exhibit 17.6 compares advantages and disadvantages that result from three alternative designs.

For businesses that require a great deal of customization, the customer will have great influence over the outcome and the interaction. In other businesses, the employee will be given the authority and responsibility to make decisions regarding the interaction and outcomes. In a third group of businesses, organizational rules and policies will restrict the employee and the customer from deviating from preestablished conventions. Although it isn't possible to select among these three alternatives for every business, choices made in the early stages of the service design process will set limits for how the customer, the contact employee, and the organization will dominate the interaction and outcomes.

The fact that the customer, employee, and organization can play different roles in the business encounter has implications for employee skills and characteristics. The employee capabilities needed for a business that allows the employee to set parameters and make decisions when working with a customer are very different from those needed if the employee and customer decisions are tightly bound by rules and policies.

A 2000 Bureau of Labor Statistics report projects that, as baby boomers retire, by 2010 there could be 10 million more jobs available than there are employees in the United States.

Advantages and Disadvantages of Different Dominating Forces in Business Interactions			EXHIBIT 17.6
	Interaction Dominating Force		
Impact	**Organization Rules and Policies**	**Contact Employee**	**Customer**
Advantages	High efficiency	Ability to customize	Lower labor costs
	Low cost of labor	More interaction	Enhanced sense
	Low cost per unit of outcome	Enhanced perceived value	of control for customer
	High level of managerial control		Enhanced perceived value
Disadvantages	Lack of flexibility	Less managerial control	Low efficiency
	No customization	Higher labor cost	High costs per unit
	Low level of interaction	High cost per unit of outcome	
	Employees can't cope with unique situations		
	Customers may be dissatisfied by lack of input		

Source: Adapted from J. A. Fitzsimmons and M. J. Fitzsimmons, *Service Management: Operations, Strategy, and Information Technology* (New York: McGraw-Hill, 2001), pp. 204–206.

The New Working Environment

Businesses must respond to the specific needs of a customer, and this requires them to be more networked in order to provide the level of communication necessary. More information about what customers want and need is available. More information about what businesses offer is available also. In order to take competitive advantage of this information and use it to differentiate a business from competitors, employees must be prepared to use the information. They must be able to make decisions based on their own judgment of what the customer requires. They must be not only empowered to make the decision, but also trained in how to make it. Despite the popularity of empowering employees, there is nothing worse than empowering an employee to make a decision and holding the employee accountable for the decision, but not providing the employee the training necessary to make the decision correctly. One of the most frustrating and threatening environments for employees is one where they do not feel comfortable about doing the job expected of them. It's unfair to the employee, and it provides an unacceptable interaction for the customer. If employees are expected to do more, they must know more. In order to know more, they must be taught.

The increasing importance of customer–employee interactions, for competitive differentiation, means that employees must be capable of taking on these responsibilities. Employees must have judgment, they must be flexible, and they must be responsive to customer needs. As businesses expand globally, they must also move toward satisfying customers who have very different views of quality and very different wants and needs. The increasing diversity in the customer base is an important issue for brick-and-mortar firms as well as firms with strong Internet presence.

In addition to the increasing diversity among the customers, the workforce is also increasing in its diversity. Not only is the U.S. population becoming more diverse, but businesses are also locating in different cultures. Locating a business in a different country usually means hiring employees from that country. Managing a more diverse workforce requires an increased awareness of different cultures, different lifestyles, different languages, and different skills. The challenge for the firm is to take advantage of that diversity to add greater value, rather than letting the diversity of the workforce become a barrier.

Workforce Productivity Improvement

Like the productivity of any other asset, workforce productivity exists as a ratio of outputs to inputs. For many employees, productivity is measured as some form of "outcomes per hour" measure. For managers, productivity is often measured as the productivity of the assets that fall within their span of supervision. This includes productivity of employees, as well as equipment, facilities, and so on.

Employee productivity can be improved in a manner similar to that of any other asset—increase the numerator or decrease the denominator of the productivity ratio. Improving employee productivity generally means increasing the outputs, given the same amount of time. Surprisingly, this process usually does not require coercing the employee to work harder. Unlike jobs in the past, where the output was defined by the results of manual labor, many jobs today require interaction between a person and some form of equipment, which might be a computer, a telephone, or some other machine. The job might be to accomplish one set of tasks out of a much larger set that defines a completed product or service. In these situations, the output of an individual often hinges on the design of the system in which the person is placed. It results from the way one person fits into the system, the way that person's role is supported through appropriate work tools, and the way the systems in place provide an opportunity for that worker to be as productive as possible. In most cases, despite what managers may insist, lack of productivity for employees is the result of the systems in which they work, not their lack of ambition.

Productivity measures of individual resources are, by definition, local measures. Local measures often contradict each other and oppose the very goals sought by more global measures. Productivity measures frequently do this. Measuring the productivity of a call center employee, for example, might be accomplished by counting the number of calls per hour. Such a measurement would encourage the worker to try to shorten conversations with potential customers, thereby completing more calls per hour but also reducing the level of interaction below what customers expect. Both the performance measurement systems and reward–punishment systems are often critical in motivating employee behaviors. When not well designed, they can encourage the wrong behaviors.

Productivity Measurement and Improvement Tools

For some jobs, particularly those that are repetitive in nature, management and workers need a standard to provide a basis for training, evaluation, and comparison. The existence of a standard is important in jobs that produce high volumes, because a slight improvement in productivity can result in significant output increases over time. Improvements in productivity can be obtained only if productivity is actually measured. In these situations, and in some nonrepetitive situations, a time standard is needed. A **time standard** defines the amount of time it should take to complete a task.

time standard
The expected time for a worker to complete a task.

Time standards are frequently used in manufacturing environments where the job is repetitive, the materials are consistent, and the employee has little variability from one task to the next. The existence of the standard provides management with the ability to evaluate performance and also provides a critical piece of information to help in planning for the capacity necessary to meet demand. Efficiency, a commonly used measure, is the actual output divided by standard output. Measures that are based on a variance require determining the difference between actual output or actual cost and the standard output or standard cost. A standard is necessary to make any type of comparison. Standards can be created for employees in several ways. Two common approaches are stopwatch time studies and predetermined motion times.

stopwatch time study
The process of developing a time standard by actually observing and timing workers.

Stopwatch Time Studies

Stopwatch time studies are based on actual observation of an employee for a long enough time to gather sufficient representative times for the task of interest. The period

Observing employees and timing tasks are a necessary—but not always appreciated—aspect of effective management. Having someone watch over your shoulder brings with it a feeling of being watched by "Big Brother," but knowing how long it takes an employee to complete a task is critical for capacity management as well as employee evaluation.

observed time

When performing a time study, this is the average of the times of observations.

performance rating

When performing time studies, this is an adjustment made to take into account whether the observed worker was faster or slower than normal.

normal time

In a time study, this is the observed time after adjustment by the performance rating.

standard time

The result of a stopwatch time study after an adjustment by the performance rating and after allowances have been made.

allowance

When constructing a time standard using a stopwatch time study or predetermined motion times, the addition of time to the standard for personal, restroom, and other time.

predetermined motion time

The time required to complete small aspects of tasks collected from a large number of observations and stored in a database so that future time standards can be created without needing a stopwatch time study.

of time must include activities that are not completed with every repetition but are still parts of the job. Such activities include moving material, adjusting equipment or tools, and user maintenance tasks. The observations over that period of time are averaged to provide a measure known as **observed time.** To make the observed time useful and representative of what would be expected of other workers, the observed time must be adjusted by incorporating a **performance rating.** The performance rating is based on how the observer perceives the employee being observed. If the observer feels that the employee being observed works at a pace faster than normal, the performance rating adjusts the observed time to be slower. If the observer feels that the employee is slower than a normal employee, the performance rating speeds up the observed time. The resultant time, after the performance rating has been applied to the observed time, is known as the **normal time.** It is simply the time that a typical worker would be expected to take to complete the task.

The **standard time** is computed by adjusting the normal time to incorporate **allowances.** Allowances are added as a percentage of the standard time to allow for personal time, restroom breaks, and rest periods. Example 16.1 demonstrates the calculation of a standard time utilizing stopwatch time study data.

Predetermined Motion Times

The second method of determining standards is to use **predetermined motion times.** Predetermined motion times avoid the negative aspects of stopwatch time studies. Employees generally do not like to be watched and timed. Accurate stopwatch time studies are also very difficult to implement and are prone to significant amounts of error. In addition, stopwatch time studies cannot be used to determine time standards for jobs that do not yet exist.

Predetermined motion times can be extracted from data gathered through years of observation. The predetermined motion times are created through detailed analysis of film footage of jobs. Jobs are broken into very small motions, which form the building blocks of virtually any job. The job of interest can be broken down into those motions, as can a new job that has never been performed, and the times for each motion can be determined. The

---

Example 17.1

Stopwatch Time Study Standard Time Calculation

EXCEL TUTOR

In an effort to create a performance standard, the office manager for an insurance claims center performed a stopwatch time study for a claims reviewer position. The claims reviewer's essential responsibilities are to review each claim to ensure that all questions on the form are answered. The result of the stopwatch time study was that, on average, each review took 34 seconds. The office manager judged the employee being observed to be 10 percent faster than the normal worker. Allowances for rest breaks, restroom breaks, and so on are required to be 15 percent. Find the standard time for this job.

Solution

The *observed time* is equal to 34 seconds. To arrive at the *normal time,* the observed time must be adjusted by the performance rating. To adjust a normal time that is 10 percent fast to be equal to the time of a normal worker, an adjustment of 1.1 would be used:

$$34 \text{ seconds} \times 1.1 = 37.4 \text{ seconds}$$

The normal time is 37.4 seconds. Adding the 15 percent allowance, the *standard time* is

$$37.4 \text{ seconds} \times 1.15 = 43.01 \text{ seconds}$$

Excel Tutor 17.1 shows how this problem can be solved in a spreadsheet.

time for the entire job is calculated by summing the times of all of its component motions. Predetermined motion times do not need to be adjusted using a performance rating because so many observations go into the creation of the times that they are considered representative of the normal worker.

Work Sampling

In many nonrepetitive jobs, productivity is not a result of how fast employees work but is more related to how they spend their working time. Many white-collar workers and managers find that the parts of their job that are most important do not get the time required because other tasks get in the way. The first step toward increasing the productivity in these situations is to determine exactly how the employee is spending his/her time. **Work sampling** provides an effective way to accomplish that. If a sufficient quantity of random observations are made of a worker, and the observations are tallied, the resulting proportions of those categories are representative of the way that employee is utilized. It is important that the observations are truly random, so an actual table of random numbers is used to generate the observation times. Failure to use real random observations will result in data not representative of what the employee actually does. Observing an employee "whenever you think about it" is not random. Example 17.2 demonstrates a work sampling implementation.

work sampling
A process of recording what a worker is doing to determine how employee time is spent.

The results of a work sampling study like the one in Example 17.2 can provide the impetus for the redesign of a job if it is clear that the employee being studied spends time that does not seem to match what that employee should be doing. For example, the employee studied spends a high proportion (27 percent) of the total time on the phone. If this takes time away from other activities deemed more important, ways to reduce phone time may need to be examined.

Learning Curves

An important aspect of worker productivity that often goes without notice is that over time, workers get better at what they do. You know from your own experiences that the first time you attempt something complicated, you need a long time to complete it. As you increase the number of times you've done it, you get faster without it taking more

Managers are frequently surprised when they find out exactly how their employees are spending their time. Work sampling studies can provide an accurate view that can point to needed changes in the workplace. Here is a typical example of employees wasting time, while attempting to do their jobs. Excessive waiting for over-demanded office resources, like photocopiers, is a frequent discovery of work sampling studies.

Example 17.2

EXCEL TUTOR

Work Sampling

The divisional vice president for claims processing was concerned about how a particular claims office manager was spending his time. A random number table was used to create 200 random observation times over a four-week period. Activity categories were created based on the observations, and observations were placed into the categories. The resulting tallies follow:

Scheduling claims adjuster duties	21
Office personnel duties (payroll forms, employee evaluation, etc.)	14
Assisting with staff duties	36
Performing stopwatch time studies	44
One-on-one meetings with staff	10
Full staff meeting	8
Social chatting	13
On the phone	54

Complete the work sampling study.

Solution

The observations are converted to the following percentages:

Activity	Percentage
Scheduling claims adjuster duties	10.5
Office personnel duties (payroll forms, employee evaluation, etc.)	7
Assisting with staff duties	18
Performing stopwatch time studies	22
One-on-one meetings with staff	5
Full staff meeting	4
Social chatting	6.5
On the phone	27

Excel Tutor 17.2 shows how spreadsheets can aid in a work sampling study.

---

learning curve
A curve that shows the reduction in the time it takes to complete a task as the number of times it has been completed increases.

learning rate
The amount of improvement obtained as a task is repeated.

effort. It actually gets easier. The phenomenon of the time required to complete a task getting shorter and shorter as the task is repeated is known as a **learning curve.** The **learning rate** determines the steepness of the learning curve and varies with different people and different types of tasks. Although learning curves are generally thought to apply to individuals, organizations also have learning curves, as do groups and teams.

As an example, if an individual's learning rate for a particular job was expected to be 90 percent, and it took 4 hours to complete the task the first time, it would take 3.6 hours the second time, 3.24 hours the fourth time, 2.916 hours the eighth time, and so on. The gain expressed by the learning rate is achieved every time the number of repetitions doubles, so a lower percentage means that learning is faster. Exhibit 17.7 provides the numbers for an 85 percent learning rate. Notice that absolute improvement gets smaller with each repetition because it takes more repetitions to double what has been done.

Exhibit 17.8 graphs the improvement with an 85 percent learning rate. As can be seen, an 85 percent learning rate is a "steep" learning curve. In other words, learning takes place very quickly. Exhibit 17.9 provides the same series, with a 97 percent learning curve. Notice the difference.

The equation for the learning curve is

(17.1)
$$T_n = T_1 n^r$$

where

Tn = time in hours to produce the nth unit

T_1 = time in hours to produce the first unit

n = number of the unit of interest

r = log l/log 2, where l is the expected learning rate

85 Percent Learning Curve Pattern		EXHIBIT 17.7
Task Number Complete	**Time**	
1	4.00	
2	3.40	
4	2.89	
8	2.46	
16	2.09	
32	1.77	
64	1.51	
128	1.28	
256	1.09	
516	0.93	
1,032	0.79	
2,064	0.67	

The use of the formula is demonstrated in Example 17.3.

The learning rate is almost always a prediction. No one ever really knows, in advance, how fast a person or group will learn. The fact that it is a prediction or forecast means that there will be error in estimating it. Error in estimating a learning rate can have a tremendous impact on the projected time it takes to do something many repetitions in the future. If we extend our example to 20 repetitions, the 97 percent learning rate results in the task taking 3.50 hours. Had the real learning rate been only 99 percent instead of 97 percent (an error of slightly over 2 percent), the actual time to complete the 20th unit would have been 3.83 instead of 3.50 hours (an increase of nearly 9 percent).

Learning curves are frequently used in bidding processes. A customer wants a bid on a customized or new product, and a learning curve is projected as a way to estimate total labor costs. In fact, bids submitted for government contracts are required to include learning effects. Obviously, as the previous example demonstrates, the error associated with the learning rate prediction can result in a huge error in projecting labor content and labor costs. It can also result in a drastic error in predicting the date of completion. The error can be the difference between profit and loss. It is common to project a learning rate range, rather than a point estimate, and project a range for the total amount of labor.

85 Percent Learning Curve	EXHIBIT 17.8

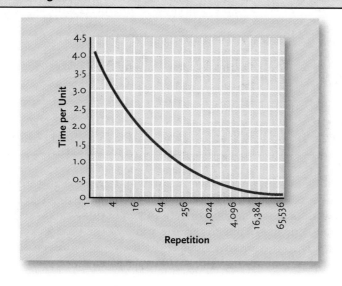

EXHIBIT 17.9	97 Percent Learning Curve

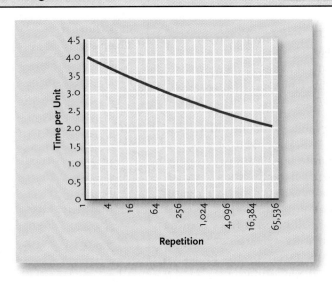

Example 17.3   **Use of the Learning Curve Formula**

EXCEL TUTOR

A producer of machined components for missile trigger assemblies was considering the purchase of a new milling machine. New business had pushed capacity demands past what was available on existing equipment. A new relationship with a defense contractor, which appeared to be permanent, required the company to produce a component that needed more milling time than it had available. To assist in determining the capacity that would be needed on the milling machine, the owner decided to determine the time required per unit once the learning curve flattens out. Past experience gave the owner a high level of confidence in using a 96 percent learning rate. With the time for the first unit equal to 1.75 hours, what will be the time to produce the 300th unit?

Solution

(17.1)

$$T_n = T_1 n^r$$
$$T_{300} = 1.75(300)^{\log 0.96/\log 2}$$
$$= 1.75(300)^{-0.0589}$$
$$= 1.75/300^{0.0589}$$
$$= 1.2506 \text{ hours}$$

Excel Tutor 17.3 provides an example of how learning curve calculations can be aided by using a spreadsheet.

CHAPTER SUMMARY

This chapter considered the importance of the workforce as a resource used to create value. Through direct and indirect labor, as well as knowledge that can be applied to improvement, the workforce is generally thought of as a business's most valuable asset. It is the only asset that contributes directly to the value of the product or service and also contributes indirectly to the improvement of the use of other assets. The impact of the workforce is evident in each of the value attributes customers seek.

As businesses continue to utilize services to differentiate themselves from the competition, the importance of employee skills and ability to interact with customers increases. Employee interaction in service encounters plays a major role in building customer loyalty and improving profitability.

The environment in which workers must function is changing. Increased diversity among customers *and* employees adds to management's responsibilities and to the value-adding potential of the workforce. In addition to these changes, greater employee responsibility and the use of project teams increase the need for employee development and training. As the value of the employee asset increases, the need for productivity measurement and enhancement also increases. Various tools associated with productivity measurement and improvement were presented. Finally, a discussion of learning curves was presented, with tools that are required when utilizing learning curves to predict the time required to complete tasks.

In a labor market that is tight, the value of the workforce becomes even more important. But aren't all assets important? Inventory? Facilities? Capacity? Certainly, but the workforce is unique because it has free will and because it can provide insight that improves the effectiveness of other resources.

KEY TERMS

allowance, 756

contingent workers, 752

continuous improvement, 750

cross-training, 752

innovation, 749

learning curve, 758

learning rate, 758

normal time, 756

observed time, 756

performance rating, 756

predetermined motion time, 756

service–profit chain, 744

standard time, 756

stopwatch time studies, 755

time standard, 755

work sampling, 757

KEY FORMULA

Learning Curve

(17.1)
$$T_n = T_1 n^r$$

where

T_n = time in hours to produce the nth unit
T_1 = time in hours to produce the first unit
n = number of the unit of interest
r = log l/log 2, where l is the expected learning rate

SOLVED PROBLEMS

1. Stop Watch Time Study Standard Time Calculation

The kitchen operations manager of Crabby Pirate's Seafood Restaurant has standardized the way salads are to be made. Each night, two workers are to pre-assemble the salads, based on the evening's customer forecast. A stop watch time study of salad assembly resulted in an observed time of 21 seconds. The assembler was an experienced expert and was judged to be 20 percent faster than the typical employee. In order to leave time for breaks and other necessary tasks, Crabby Pirate's wants to build in a 15 percent allowance. Compute the standard time for salad assembly.

Step	Objective	Explanation
1.	Convert the observed time to a normal time.	Multiply the observed time by 1.2 to make it more representative of the typical worker. 21 × 1.2 = 25.2 seconds. The normal time is 25.2 seconds.
2.	Add in the 15 percent allowance to finish the standard time calculation.	25.2 + (.15 × 25.2) = 28.98 seconds

2. Work Sampling Calculations

An office productivity consultant implemented a work sampling study for a small branch of a local bank. She collected data on teller activities over a one-week study period. The following data were collected.

Activity	Frequency
Counting money in drawer	26
Interacting with a customer	48
Talking to supervisor	13
Waiting for printout	16
Talking to other teller	24
Taking customer to vault	9
Helping at drive-up window	53

Convert the observations to percentages to construct the work sampling data.

Step	Objective	Explanation
1.	Total the observations. Compute the percentages for each type of observation by dividing the frequency of each activity by the total.	<table><tr><th>Activity</th><th>Frequency</th><th>Percentage</th></tr><tr><td>Counting money in drawer</td><td>26</td><td>14</td></tr><tr><td>Interacting with a customer</td><td>48</td><td>25</td></tr><tr><td>Talking to supervisor</td><td>13</td><td>7</td></tr><tr><td>Waiting for printout</td><td>16</td><td>8</td></tr><tr><td>Talking to other teller</td><td>24</td><td>13</td></tr><tr><td>Taking customer to vault</td><td>9</td><td>5</td></tr><tr><td>Helping at drive-up window</td><td>53</td><td>28</td></tr><tr><td>Total observations</td><td>189</td><td></td></tr></table>

3. Learning Curve Calculations

A new employee was hired to check the accuracy of loan application decisions. The employee goes through the application, making sure that all information has been included, makes the appropriate calculations, and then compares the results to the results of the initial evaluator. A learning rate of 95 percent is expected for this job. The employee's first application took 4 minutes to accuracy check. How long should the 100th application take?

Step	Objective	Explanation
1.	Use Formula 17.1, $T_n = T_1 n^r$, to solve the problem.	$T_{100} = 4.0(100)^{\log 0.95/\log 2}$ $= 4.0(100)^{-0.074}$ $= 4.0/100^{0.074}$ $= 2.845$

The 100th accuracy check should take 2.845 minutes.

REVIEW QUESTIONS

1. From a strategic perspective, why are employees critical in a service-based economy?
2. Why has customer service often become the most important competitive weapon?
3. How has the meaning of the term "market" changed? What type of "market" has the Internet created? What are customer expectations moving toward?
4. How does the service–profit chain relate to employee satisfaction?
5. Why are teams important for maximizing the contributions of the workforce?
6. Describe the steps of the improvement project life cycle.
7. What are the advantages and disadvantages of using contingent workers?
8. Describe the process of creating time standards from stopwatch time studies.
9. What is work sampling? Why is it important for managing worker productivity?
10. What is a learning curve? What are the dangers of depending on a learning curve for cost estimates?

DISCUSSION AND EXPLORATION

1. In jobs you have had, what have been the critical aspects of value added by the workers? Could they have been automated? What would have been lost if they had been automated?
2. If you imagine yourself in your first job after graduating, what value do you hope to offer the company? What value will you contribute to the products or services sold? Is that sufficient?
3. How can companies that are forced by demand fluctuations to use contingent workers avoid the problems that can accompany their use?

PROBLEMS HM

Solutions to odd-numbered problems are located on the text's Online Center (http://mhhe.com/opsnow3e).

1. You have been asked by the manager of a bank to perform a stopwatch time study on its tellers. The average time for Carol was 1 minute, 37 seconds. She was judged to be the fastest teller, performing 20 percent faster than normal. Calculate the normal time for Carol, and then compute a standard using a 12 percent allowance.
2. AAM Inc. performed a stopwatch time study on its production work stations and reported the results in the following table. Interpret the table and provide the standard time for each work station if a 10 percent allowance is required for rest breaks.

Work Station	Observed Time (seconds)	Performance Rating
1	89	10% faster
2	114	8% faster
3	140	6% slower
4	62	2% faster

3. You have been observing an employee, Kim, of the real estate agency of Walker & Smith. The employee is preparing a listing of houses that are for sale. It has taken Kim 15 minutes to complete the task and she is believed to be 30 percent faster than the typical employee. If an allowance of 5 percent is required, how long should it take the average employee to prepare a listing of houses for sale?

4. An employee for a student painting crew takes an average of 24 minutes to paint the trim around a window. This worker is thought to be about 10 percent faster than the typical painter on the crew. If a 10 percent allowance is included, what should the standard time be for trimming windows?

5. Darcy Darby, owner of a local sandwich shop, is trying to figure out how to evaluate her catering employees. She observed a longtime employee making mini-sandwiches and determined that the employee took an average of 22 seconds per sandwich. She estimates this employee to be around 20 percent faster than normal. If she includes a 15 percent allowance, what would be her standard for mini-sandwich preparation?

6. The sales manager for The Copy Co. used a random number table to find 250 observation times for one of his sales representatives. The results are given below. Complete the work sampling analysis by determining the proportion of time spent on each activity

Activity	Number of Observations
Cold calls	45
Calling on top customers	75
Demonstrating products	20
Phone canvassing	25
Follow-up calls	10
Driving	60
Social calls	15

7. You are the general manager for the Portsmouth Pilots, a minor league football team. You have been concerned with how your athletes spend their time at training camp and have asked an aide to conduct a work sampling study on two players, Jerry and Mike. The observations for the two players are presented below. Interpret the results.

	Number of Observations	
	Jerry	Mike
Practice	36	45
Lifting weights	19	30
Nutritionist	9	12
Sleep & recovery	14	18
Social	22	9
Films	28	21
Study playbook	22	15
Total	150	150

8. Meredith works mornings cleaning stalls at the stables where she boards her horse. Her responsibilities include feeding the horses, watering the horses, moving them to their respective pasture, and cleaning their stalls. Michelle, the barn manager, has observed her and has collected the following data over a two-week period. Complete a work sampling analysis by determining the proportion of time Meredith spends on each activity. Based on this analysis, do you see any obvious areas for possible improvement?

Hauling buckets of water from the spigot to the stall	72
Filling wheelbarrow with grain	7
Loading grain from the wheelbarrow into the feed bucket	32
Putting halters on horses	11
Leading horses to pasture	114
Petting her horse	24
Cleaning stalls	156
Emptying wheelbarrow full of manure	34

9. The Plant Manager at MRC Mfg. was given a proposal for a new machine. The new machine is advertised to be able to run 76 percent of the time, the rest being spent on changeover, loading, or emptying the machine. He was curious about the current equipment, so he made 200 random observations of its operation. The Plant Manager found the following results: loading machine, 15; emptying machine, 15; changeover, 8; break, 10; operating, 152. Should he expect the new machine to be better than the old machine?

10. An investment firm hired a new employee to put together an investment newsletter for its customers. The first time the employee put the newsletter together it took 2.3 hours. If the anticipated rate of learning is 92 percent, how long will it take the employee to put together the 50th newsletter?

11. College Painters is a student-run painting service that operates during the summer. Its first job took 11.4 hours to complete. The students will spend the entire summer painting houses in the same neighborhood, with similar houses, and expect to paint 50 of them before they go back to school. College Painters headquarters told them to anticipate a 98 percent learning curve. If that projection is accurate, how long will it take them to paint the last house in the neighborhood?

12. Ramsey is testing two video games for their degree of difficulty. The first game took him six hours to complete, and the manufacturer expects an 82 percent learning rate. The second game took only two hours to complete with an expected learning rate of 99 percent. Which game will take longer to play the 100th time it is played?

13. Carl has decided to read the top 75 mysteries of all time this summer. It took him 12 hours to read his first mystery. If the learning rate is 98 percent, how long will it take him to finish the last one? Assuming the 98 percent learning rate is correct, how many mysteries must Carl finish to cut two hours off his reading time?

ADVANCED PROBLEMS

1. Sally's Floral Shoppe is preparing a bid to deliver 100 floral table centerpieces for a large political fundraising banquet. The materials for each centerpiece will cost about $5.00, while the employees who assemble the centerpieces earn $12.00 per hour. Sally intends to have four employees working, each of whom will produce 25 centerpieces. In a trial run, one of the employees produced the first centerpiece in 8 minutes, while the second centerpiece required only 7.7 minutes. Sally wishes to prepare a bid amount that generates a profit of 30% over materials and labor costs.

   a. What learning curve did the employee appear to be on during the trial run?

   b. How many hours of labor will be required to have four employees preparing the centerpieces, each following the same learning curve?

   c. What should the bid amount be, if Sally has four employees following the same learning curve? What is the $profit from the job?

   d. If Sally gets the contract with this bid, what will her profit be if the employees are actually on a 99% learning curve?

2. Nex Tool and Die manufactures customized machinery for other manufacturers. Nex has adopted a number of Lean concepts, chief among them, the cross training for mastery of its workforce. Therefore, when faced with hard economic times, Nex would prefer not to layoff its highly trained and well compensated employees, rather Nex management is willing to accept even marginal projects to keep the manufacturing facility running near capacity and remain at full employment.

   Nex is currently faced with a poor market for its products, with economic forecasts projecting this trend to continue for the next 6 quarters. Additionally, the backlog of orders that Nex has been producing from is nearly depleted. Faced with this reality, Nex management has the opportunity to bid on two different projects. The relevant information is presented below.

	Project 1	Project 2
Material Cost Per Unit	$12,258	$14,367
Labor Cost ($/Hour)	$42.50	$42.50
Overhead Cost (Fixed)	$175,000	$175,000
Revenue (Per Unit)	$25,500	$26,450
Time to Complete First Unit (Days)	24	20
Projected Learning Rate	96%	97%

a. What is the gross profit for both projects?

b. Which project would you recommend to Nex management?

c. If the learning rate for Project 1 changes to 99%, what would be your recommendation?

ENDNOTES

1. For an interesting perspective on these interactions between customers and employees, see R. Levine, C. Locke, D. Searles, and D. Weinberger, *The Cluetrain Manifesto* (New York: Perseus Books, 2000).

2. G. W. Loveman, W. E. Sasser, Jr., and L. A. Schlesinger, "Putting the Service–Profit Chain to Work," *Harvard Business Review*, March–April 1994, p. 166.

3. R. Zemke and T. Connellan, *E-service* (New York: American Management Association, 2001), p. 28.

4. *Unleash the Power of Project Teams* (Cincinnati, OH: Association for Quality and Participation, 2000).

5. Ibid.

LEARNING ACTIVITIES   www.mhhe.com/opsnow3e

Visit the Online Learning Center (www.mhhe.com/opsnow3e) for additional resources. Content varies by chapter, and includes

- Business Tours
- OM on Site
- Readings
- Resources
- Excel Tutors

- Interactive Case Models
- Reel Operations Video Clips
- Additional Advanced Problems
- Self-Assessment Quizzes
- Glossary

SELECTED REFERENCES

Katzenbach, J. R., and Smith, D. K. *The Wisdom of Teams*. New York: HarperCollins, 1999.

Levine, R., Locke, C., Searles, D., and Weinberger, D. *The Cluetrain Manifesto*. New York: Perseus Books, 2000.

Zemke, R., and Connellan, T. *E-service*. New York: American Management Association, 2001.

INTERACTIVE CASE 17.1

Custom Precision Machining Wins (?) a Bid

The learning curve model provides an interactive laboratory for exploring the effects different learning rates can have on a typical bidding scenario. The model allows the user to specify the material cost per unit, labor hours per week, hourly salary rate, weekly overhead costs, time for the first unit, bid price, and the number of units in the order. The user sets the learning rate using the slider.

The system outputs include the learning rate selected, performance measures, project length, labor cost, overhead cost, materials cost, total cost, percent of total cost that is labor, percent of total cost that is overhead, percent of total cost that is materials, and profit. The learning rate affects the amount of labor required to complete the number of units specified in the order. The longer it takes to complete them, the higher the labor costs and the lower the profit.

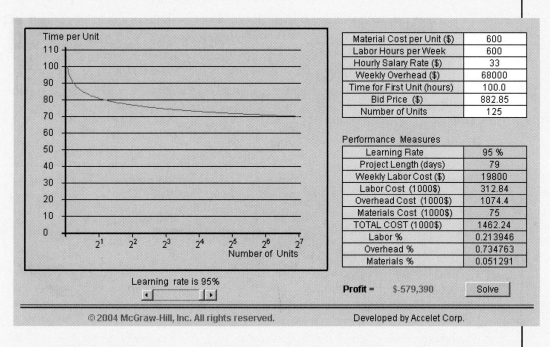

Material Cost per Unit ($)	600
Labor Hours per Week	600
Hourly Salary Rate ($)	33
Weekly Overhead ($)	68000
Time for First Unit (hours)	100.0
Bid Price ($)	882.85
Number of Units	125

Performance Measures

Learning Rate	95 %
Project Length (days)	79
Weekly Labor Cost ($)	19800
Labor Cost (1000$)	312.84
Overhead Cost (1000$)	1074.4
Materials Cost (1000$)	75
TOTAL COST (1000$)	1462.24
Labor %	0.213946
Overhead %	0.734763
Materials %	0.051291

Learning rate is 95%

Profit = $-579,390   Solve

Custom Precision Machining

Stan Eckles, owner of Custom Precision Machining (CPM) has struggled with the process of bidding for federal defense contracts. Sometimes he bids too high and doesn't get the bid. Other times, he bids too low and wins the bid, but fails to make enough money to make it worthwhile. Usually he can accurately estimate material costs, but is very bad at estimating the cost of labor. The most recent attempt is a good example of his problem. He received the specs for a machined part used in a missile launch system, performed his typical analysis of the labor and material costs, and constructed his bid of $882.85 per unit for the 125-unit order. This bid was based on the following information, which sets the starting values in the learning curve model:

Parameter	Default Value
Material cost per unit	$600
Labor hours per week	600
Hourly salary rate	$33
Weekly overhead	$68,000
Time for first unit (hours)	100

1. Making sure the parameters are set at their proper starting values and the learning rate set at 95 percent:

   a. What is the project length at this learning rate? What is the expected profit?

   b. Improve the learning rate to 90 percent. What is the new project length? What is the new expected profit?

   c. What must the learning rate be in order for CPM to make a profit? What is the project length at that learning rate?

2. With the parameters still at the start-up values, set the learning rate at 90 percent.

   a. The current time for the first unit is 100 hours. Enter a starting time for the first unit as 90. What is the new project length? What is the average time per unit produced (the total project length divided by the number of units in the order)?

   b. Reset the parameters to their start-up defaults, with the learning rate at 90 percent. Increase the time for the first unit to 110 hours. What is the new project length? What is the average time per unit produced?

3. Set the parameters to their start-up default values and set the learning rate to 90 percent.

   a. Record the project length, labor cost per day, total labor cost, labor cost as a percentage of the total cost, and profit.

   b. Improve the learning rate to 85 percent. Record the new values for project length, labor cost per day, total labor cost, labor cost as a percentage of the total cost, and profit.

4. Based on the outcomes, it appears that Stan has assumed a learning rate of 80 percent or better. Suppose his assumption is wrong and the best learning rate obtainable is 85 percent? Set the learning rate at 85 percent and all other parameters at their default values.

   a. If Stan wishes to make a profit of $220,000, what must the bid price be?

   b. At the bidding price needed to make $220,000 in profit, what will happen if his initial projection of an 85 percent learning rate was not correct? What are the risks of submitting the higher bid?

5. Set all values back to the start-up defaults.

   a. What is the cost per unit at the 90 percent learning rate? What is the project length?

   b. Increase the number of units in the order from 125 to 200. What is the new project length? What is the new cost per unit? Increase the number of units from 200 to 300, and then incrementally by 100 units up to 1,000 units. Compute the cost per unit at each quantity and graph the results. Describe the relationship between the number of units produced and cost per unit at a 90 percent learning rate.

   c. Perform the same experiment as in question 5b, using an 80 percent learning rate. How do the results compare?

6. Set the parameters back to the default values. Set the learning rate at 90 percent.

   a. What is the labor cost as a percentage of the total cost?

   b. Increase the number of units in the order from 125 to 200. What is the labor cost as a percentage of the total cost? Increase the number of units from 200 to 300 and then incrementally by 100 units up to 1,000 units. Record the labor cost as a percentage of the total cost at each quantity and graph the results. Describe the relationship between the labor cost percentage and the number of units produced at a 90 percent learning rate.

   c. Perform the same experiment as in question 6b, using an 80 percent learning rate. How do the results compare?

APPLICATION CASE 17.1

Getting the Work Done at the Gym ——

Jim's Gym has become a favorite because of the attention its employees pay to customers. Jim Jorgensen, its owner, credits that attention to an emphasis he places on getting to know customers and spending time talking one-on-one to them as they work out. Jim recognizes that high employee turnover will result in inexperienced employees and will hurt his business. His customers expect to see the same familiar faces when they come in. In addition to talking and helping customers, Jim's Gym employees have other responsibilities. Each has a responsibility to help keep the workout rooms clean and must also inspect equipment and keep it in good repair. Each is also required to take his/her turn at manning the front desk. Jim has had to pay closer attention to labor costs and fears that this may result in employees spending less time with customers because they have other things that must be done.

Jim's dilemma is this: He knows that having all employees involved in all aspects of the gym's operation results in more interaction with customers and better service. He also knows that different employees have different strengths and weaknesses, so he might improve overall productivity if he allowed them to specialize, in other words, have some employees who did nothing but clean, others who did nothing but run the counter, and so on.

Jim knows that everything that needs to be done gets done, but he really has no idea how he would assign responsibilities in a way that would ensure enough resources would be available to satisfy all requirements.

1. Develop a plan for gathering information on what employees currently do and how much time it takes.

2. If you were to split up responsibilities and have employees specialize in a more narrow set of activities, how would you configure the new jobs?

3. How would you decide which employees did which jobs? Would you rotate? Or assign the jobs permanently?

Areas of the Standard Normal Distribution

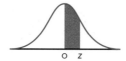

An entry in the table is the proportion under the entire curve that is between $z = 0$ and a positive value of z. Areas for negative values of z are obtained by symmetry.

z	.00	.01	.02	.03	.04	.05	.06	.07	.08	.09
0.0	.0000	.0040	.0080	.0120	.0160	.0199	.0239	.0279	.0319	.0359
0.1	.0398	.0438	.0478	.0517	.0557	.0596	.0636	.0675	.0714	.0753
0.2	.0793	.0832	.0871	.0910	.0948	.0987	.1026	.1064	.1103	.1141
0.3	.1179	.1217	.1255	.1293	.1331	.1386	.1406	.1443	.1480	.1517
0.4	.1554	.1591	.1628	.1664	.1700	.1738	.1772	.1808	.1844	.1879
0.5	.1915	.1950	.1985	.2019	.2054	.2088	.2123	.2157	.2190	.2224
0.6	.2257	.2291	.2324	.2357	.2389	.2422	.2454	.2486	.2517	.2549
0.7	.2580	.2611	.2642	.2673	.2703	.2734	.2764	.2794	.2823	.2852
0.8	.2881	.2910	.2939	.2967	.2995	.3023	.3051	.3078	.3106	.3133
0.9	.3159	.3186	.3212	.3238	.3264	.3289	.3315	.3340	.3365	.3389
1.0	.3413	.3438	.3461	.3485	.3508	.3531	.3554	.3577	.3599	.3621
1.1	.3643	.3665	.3686	.3708	.3729	.3749	.3770	.3790	.3810	.3830
1.2	.3849	.3869	.3888	.3907	.3925	.3944	.3962	.3980	.3997	.4015
1.3	.4032	.4049	.4066	.4082	.4099	.4115	.4131	.4147	.4162	.4177
1.4	.4192	.4207	.4222	.4236	.4251	.4265	.4279	.4292	.4306	.4319
1.5	.4332	.4345	.4357	.4370	.4382	.4394	.4406	.4418	.4429	.4441
1.6	.4452	.4463	.4474	.4484	.4495	.4505	.4515	.4525	.4535	.4545
1.7	.4554	.4564	.4573	.4582	.4591	.4599	.4608	.4616	.4625	.4633
1.8	.4641	.4649	.4656	.4664	.4671	.4678	.4686	.4693	.4699	.4706
1.9	.4713	.4719	.4726	.4732	.4738	.4744	.4750	.4756	.4761	.4767
2.0	.4772	.4778	.4783	.4788	.4793	.4798	.4803	.4808	.4812	.4817
2.1	.4821	.4826	.4830	.4834	.4838	.4842	.4846	.4850	.4854	.4857
2.2	.4861	.4864	.4868	.4871	.4875	.4878	.4881	.4884	.4887	.4890
2.3	.4893	.4896	.4898	.4901	.4904	.4906	.4909	.4911	.4913	.4916
2.4	.4918	.4920	.4922	.4925	.4927	.4929	.4931	.4932	.4934	.4936
2.5	.4938	.4940	.4941	.4943	.4945	.4946	.4948	.4949	.4951	.4952
2.6	.4953	.4955	.4956	.4957	.4959	.4960	.4961	.4962	.4963	.4964
2.7	.4965	.4966	.4967	.4968	.4969	.4970	.4971	.4972	.4973	.4974
2.8	.4974	.4975	.4976	.4977	.4977	.4978	.4979	.4979	.4980	.4981
2.9	.4981	.4982	.4982	.4983	.4984	.4984	.4985	.4985	.4986	.4986
3.0	.4987	.4987	.4987	.4988	.4988	.4989	.4989	.4989	.4990	.4990

Areas of the Cumulative Standard Normal Distribution

Use this table

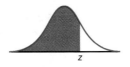

An entry in the table is the proportion under the curve cumulated from the negative tail.

z	G(z)	z	G(z)	z	G(z)
−4.00	0.00003	−2.00	0.02275	0.00	0.50000
−3.95	0.00004	−1.95	0.02559	0.05	0.51994
−3.90	0.00005	−1.90	0.02872	0.10	0.53983
−3.85	0.00006	−1.85	0.03216	0.15	0.55962
−3.80	0.00007	−1.80	0.03593	0.20	0.57926
−3.75	0.00009	−1.75	0.04006	0.25	0.59871
−3.70	0.00011	−1.70	0.04457	0.30	0.61791
−3.65	0.00013	−1.65	0.04947	0.35	0.63683
−3.60	0.00016	−1.60	0.05480	0.40	0.65542
−3.55	0.00019	−1.55	0.06057	0.45	0.67364
−3.50	0.00023	−1.50	0.06681	0.50	0.69146
−3.45	0.00028	−1.45	0.07353	0.55	0.70884
−3.40	0.00034	−1.40	0.08076	0.60	0.72575
−3.35	0.00040	−1.35	0.08851	0.65	0.74215
−3.30	0.00048	−1.30	0.09680	0.70	0.75804
−3.25	0.00058	−1.25	0.10565	0.75	0.77337
−3.20	0.00069	−1.20	0.11507	0.80	0.78814
−3.15	0.00082	−1.15	0.12507	0.85	0.80234
−3.10	0.00097	−1.10	0.13567	0.90	0.81594
−3.05	0.00114	−1.05	0.14686	0.95	0.82894
−3.00	0.00135	−1.00	0.15866	1.00	0.84134
−2.95	0.00159	−0.95	0.17106	1.05	0.85314
−2.90	0.00187	−0.90	0.18406	1.10	0.86433
−2.85	0.00219	−0.85	0.19766	1.15	0.87493
−2.80	0.00256	−0.80	0.21186	1.20	0.88493
−2.75	0.00298	−0.75	0.22663	1.25	0.89435
−2.70	0.00347	−0.70	0.24196	1.30	0.90320
−2.65	0.00402	−0.65	0.25785	1.35	0.91149
−2.60	0.00466	−0.60	0.27425	1.40	0.91924
−2.55	0.00539	−0.55	0.29116	1.45	0.92647
−2.50	0.00621	−0.50	0.30854	1.50	0.93319
−2.45	0.00714	−0.45	0.32636	1.55	0.93943
−2.40	0.00820	−0.40	0.34458	1.60	0.94520
−2.35	0.00939	−0.35	0.36317	1.65	0.95053
−2.30	0.01072	−0.30	0.38209	1.70	0.95543
−2.25	0.01222	−0.25	0.40129	1.75	0.95994
−2.20	0.01390	−0.20	0.42074	1.80	0.96407
−2.15	0.01578	−0.15	0.44038	1.85	0.96784
−2.10	0.01786	−0.10	0.46017	1.90	0.97128
−2.05	0.02018	−0.05	0.48006	1.95	0.97441

(Continues)

z	G(z)	z	G(z)	z	G(z)
2.00	0.97725	2.70	0.99653	3.40	0.99966
2.05	0.97982	2.75	0.99702	3.45	0.99972
2.10	0.98214	2.80	0.99744	3.50	0.99977
2.15	0.98422	2.85	0.99781	3.55	0.99981
2.20	0.98610	2.90	0.99813	3.60	0.99984
2.25	0.98778	2.95	0.99841	3.65	0.99987
2.30	0.98928	3.00	0.99865	3.70	0.99989
2.35	0.99061	3.05	0.99886	3.75	0.99991
2.40	0.99180	3.10	0.99903	3.80	0.99993
2.45	0.99286	3.15	0.99918	3.85	0.99994
2.50	0.99379	3.20	0.99931	3.90	0.99995
2.55	0.99461	3.25	0.99942	3.95	0.99996
2.60	0.99534	3.30	0.99952	4.00	0.99997
2.65	0.99598	3.35	0.99960		

absolute error   The absolute value of the forecast error.

acceptable quality level (AQL)   In acceptance sampling, it identifies the quality level required in order for lots to be considered to be good. *See acceptance sampling.*

acceptance sampling   Extracting a sample group from a large quantity of products or components of interest. Also known as a "lot," and, based on the quality level of the sample group, the entire lot is either god or bad.

action loyalty   The fourth phase of customer loyalty sustained by commitment and inertia.

activation   Running a machine or resource when it doesn't contribute to throughput.

activity   A basic unit of work.

activity drivers   Used to measure the demands that cost objects place on activities and to assign the cost of associated activities to cost objects. See *cost object*.

actual costs   Past payments for currently owned resources.

aesthetics   A dimension of quality that includes looks, sound, and smells.

aggregate demand   The total demand for all products or services.

aggregate planning   A capacity planning tool that uses inventory and variable labor to deal with demand fluctuations.

agile   The ability to respond quickly to change, to customer needs, and to internal and external forces.

allowance   When constructing a time standard using a stopwatch time study or predetermined motion times, the addition of time to the standard for personal, restroom, and other time.

appraisal costs   Costs associated with product inspection, testing, and auditing of quality-related systems.

AQL   See *acceptable quality level*.

arrival process   The pattern in which or frequency with which customers arrive at the queue.

assembler   The final step of the four stages of product value creation, which puts together the outputs of fabricators.

assemble-to-order   Producing major components of a product prior to receiving an order and assembling the product to meet a specific order.

assembly buffer   A time buffer placed immediately prior to an assembly for nonconstrained components.

assembly line   A narrowly defined manufacturing assembly process made up of equipment with little flexibility in a product-oriented layout.

asset recovery   Disposition of a product returned through the reverse logistics network.

assignable cause variability   Variability in process outcomes that results from special causes that are not part of the inherent random fluctuation of the process and indicate that something in the process has changed.

assurance   A dimension of quality that relates to the level of trust or confidence generated by employees.

attribute   A product or service characteristic that can be classified as either conforming or not conforming to specifications.

backlog   A queue of orders waiting to be processed.

backward scheduling   When a completion date or due date is known and that date must determine a start date.

balance delay   In a product-oriented layout, this is the lost resource utilization resulting from differences in processing time at each work center. See *line balancing*.

balanced scorecard   A performance measurement system that combines financial and nonfinancial measures of business performance.

balking   When a customer views a queue and does not enter it because it is too long.

basic producer   A manufacturer that extracts raw materials from natural resources.

batch processing   A system in which a group of identical products or customers is processed through one step in the process and then the entire group moves to the next step.

batch production   A type of production in which identical products or customers are processed through one step, and then the entire batch goes on to the next step.

beginning on-hand inventory   The quantity of inventory on hand at the beginning of a time period.

benchmarking   Identification of best practices of other companies.

best operating level   The level of demand or "load" on a system that results in the lowest cost per unit produced or processed.

bill of capacity   A statement of the time required on each resource needed to produce a product.

bill of material   In material requirements planning, this is a computer file containing information about the materials required to produce a product or component.

bottleneck   A constraint in a production system.

BPA   See *business process analysis*.

breakbulk ship   A ship that transports products in its hull.

breakeven analysis   An analytical process that compares the fixed and variable costs of alternatives in order to identify the best alternative for a given volume of output.

bullwhip effect   The increasing variability of demand as one moves upstream in a supply chain.

business process analysis (BPA)   A productivity improvement approach that focuses on large processes and the transitions between different departments.

business strategy   Defines the range of activities for a business, setting priorities so that it accomplishes the overall corporate strategy.

C-chart   A process control chart used to monitor counts of nonconformities per unit.

calling population   The population of arriving customers or orders.

capabilities   The abilities a business has that result from its processes. Capabilities create value.

capability chain   The capabilities added by all members of a supply chain.

capability index   A measure of process capability.

capacity   The level of productive output of an organization in a specified period of time.

capacity requirements planning A detailed capacity planning approach in manufacturing that uses the planned releases from MRP to provide the quantity of units that must be produced.

carrying cost Costs associated with carrying inventory.

cash-to-cash cycle The amount of time between the cash outlay required for purchasing direct materials or inventory consumed during the production of the product or service and the actual receipt of the payment when the product or service is sold.

causal forecast A forecast that uses extrinsic data as a predictor of demand.

cause and effect diagram A tool used to aid in the identification of root causes or quality problems.

cellular layout A layout in which products whose processes require similar resources are grouped into product families. Each cell contains all the resources necessary to produce products in that family.

changeover cost The cost of changing equipment from producing one product or service to another.

changeover time The time required to change equipment from producing one product or service to another.

check sheet A quality analysis tool used to tally occurrences of interest.

cognitive loyalty The first phase of customer loyalty based on information customers receive.

collaborative planning, forecasting, and replenishment (CPFR) An approach to demand planning in supply chains in which partners negotiate and agree on a plan for meeting demand.

common cause variability Variability in process outcomes that results from the inherent random fluctuation of the process.

competitive priorities Key value attributes that are highly influenced by operations management: cost, quality, dependability of delivery, flexibility, and response time.

conative loyalty The third stage of customer loyalty when action results from habit and behavioral commitment

concurrent engineering Performing product and service development engineering functions in tandem to reduce time and improve communication.

consolidation warehousing Holding inventory received from suppliers in warehouses until it is needed by retailers.

constraint Anything that inhibits a system's progress toward its goals.

constraint buffer A time buffer placed immediately prior to a constraint.

constraint management A framework for managing the constraints of a system in a way that maximizes the system's accomplishment of its goals.

consumer's risk In acceptance sampling, the probability of accepting a bad lot, designated as β.

containership A ship designed to carry cargo that is packed in standard size metal containers.

contingency plans Alternative or back-up plans to be used if an unexpected event makes the normal plans infeasible.

contingent workers Temporary workers employed by an agency and contracted to work for another firm.

continuous improvement A process of always seeking ways to improve existing processes and tasks.

continuous process improvement Ongoing improvement efforts for service-oriented and product-oriented production processes that focus on eliminating variability.

continuous processing In a continuous processing environment, this is any equipment or workstation that is dedicated to one product or service, yielding high levels of efficiency.

continuous replenishment The delivery of inventory, frequently in small quantities.

control limits In a process control chart, these are typically three standard deviations above and below the process mean.

converter The second stage of product value creation, which refines natural resource inputs.

core competencies Those things a firm does very well and that distinguish it from competitors.

corporate strategy In the broadest strategy, it defines the businesses that a corporation will engage in and how resources will be expended.

cost The expenses associated with ownership.

cost leader strategy A strategy that seeks to price goods and services lower than competitors.

cost object An item for which costs are measured and assigned.

cost of quality (COQ) All of the costs associated with maintaining the quality of goods and services.

cost per unit Total cost for producing the units of interest divided by the number of units produced.

cost traceability The ease with which costs can be assigned to cost objects.

CR See *critical ratio*.

craft production Production of goods by highly skilled and specialized artisans.

crash time The absolute minimum time in which each activity could be accomplished.

crashing A methodical approach to reducing a project's duration.

critical path The path that takes the longest.

critical ratio (CR) A sequencing rule that prioritizes by the ratio of the time remaining to the time needed to complete the job. The smallest ratio goes first.

CRM See *customer relationships management*.

cross-docking Continuous shipment from suppliers to warehouses, where goods are redirected and delivered to retailers in continuous shipments.

cross-training Training employees to do a variety of jobs.

customer focus The first principle of total quality management, which dictates that the customer determines what quality is.

customer relationship management (CRM) Systems designed to improve relationships with customers and improve the business's ability to identify valuable customers. They include call center management software, sales tracking, and customer service.

cycle A component of a time series that is a pattern that repeats over a long period of time.

cycle time The frequency of products emerging completed from a product-oriented layout.

data mining Analysis of data generated by customer interaction.

decline stage The final stage of a product or service life cycle as demand disappears.

decouple   To reduce the direct dependency of a process step on its predecessor.

demand chase   An aggregate planning approach that uses hiring and firing of employees to increase and decrease output to match fluctuating demand.

dependability of delivery   The ability of the firm to deliver products and services to the customer when promised.

dependent demand inventory   Inventory whose demand is determined by the production schedule for finished products. Dependent demand items usually are components and raw materials.

design capacity   The capacity a facility is designed to accommodate on an ongoing basis.

design for environment   Including environmental concerns in the product design.

design for logistics   Including logistics and transportation concerns in the product design process, usually involving effective packaging.

design for manufacture and assembly (DFMA)   The practice of designing products with the capabilities of manufacturing processes in mind.

DFMA   See *design for manufacture and assembly.*

differentiating capabilities   Capabilities possessed by a firm that distinguish it from its competitors.

differentiation strategy   A strategy that seeks to create products and services that are different from those of competitors.

direct labor   Labor that can be traced directly to the good or service being produced.

direct materials   Materials that can be traced directly to the good or service being produced.

direct shipment   Shipping directly from manufacturer suppliers to retailers.

disruptive technology   A new technology that displaces an existing technology.

dollar days   The dollar value of an item in inventory multiplied by the number of days until it will be sold.

double-stacking   Stacking containers two-high on railcars.

durability   How long a product will last.

earliest due date (EDD)   A sequencing rule that prioritizes customers or jobs by the due date, earliest first.

early start schedule   In project management calculations, this is the completion of the early start and early finish times. Also known as the forward pass.

economic order quantity model   An approach used to determine an order quantity that minimizes the sum of ordering and carrying costs.

economic value added (EVA)   A productivity measure that indicates whether or not a business is creating wealth from its capital. It is equal to the after-tax operating profit minus the annual cost of capital.

EDD   See *earliest due date.*

EDI   See *electronic data interchange.*

efficiency   The ratio of actual output to standard output.

electronic data interchange (EDI)   Electronic exchange of information between customers and suppliers instead of paper transactions.

empathy   A dimension of quality that results from the approachability and sensitivity of employees.

ending on hand inventory   The quantity of inventory on hand at the end of a time period.

environmental scanning   Examining the environment for potential impact on strategic decisions.

expected costs   Forecasted payments for future resources.

experience detractors   In moment-of-truth analysis, when an experience viewed by the customer is viewed as a detractor or as something that signifies a reduction in the quality of service.

experience enhancers   In moment-of-truth analysis, these are experiences that make the customer feel good about the interaction and make the interaction better.

external customer   Consumers and businesses that buy products and services.

external failure costs   Costs incurred when a customer is exposed to poor quality.

fabricator   The third stage of product value creation, which takes inputs from converters and transforms them into components used by assemblers.

facilities   The buildings and structures that house various aspects of a business.

FCFS   See *first come, first served.*

feature   A dimension of quality that consists of additional capabilities of products or services that can be added.

finished good inventory   Inventory consisting of products that have completed all stages of production.

first come, first served (FCFS)   A sequencing rule that prioritizes by when a person or job arrived in the queue.

FIT   See *forecast including trend.*

fixed costs   Costs that are not affected by volume.

fixed quantity order policy   In material requirements planning, rather than ordering the quantity of the net requirements, orders are placed in increments of a fixed quantity.

fixed-quantity reorder point (ROP) model   An independent demand inventory management system that reorders when inventory drops to a specific level.

focus strategy   A strategy that targets a small segment of the market with products or services.

forecast bias   The tendency of a forecast to be too high or too low.

forecast including trend (FIT)   Trend-adjusted exponential smoothing.

forward scheduling   A technique used when a start date is known, and a completion date needs to be determined.

full truckload (FTL)   Transporting goods in a truck that is full.

functional layout   A process-oriented layout.

functional strategy   A strategy that establishes the link between functional decision making and business strategy.

Gantt chart   A horizontal bar graph with time on the x axis and the different resources on the y axis. It displays the amount of time required on each resource and when that time is required.

gross requirements   In material requirements planning, the total quantity needed to meet demand.

growth stage   The second stage of a product or service life cycle, where demand begins to increase.

histogram   A bar graph that plots a measurement on the y axis and the frequency of the occurrence of the measurement on the x axis.

house of quality   A set of matrices used to guide the quality function deployment process.

independent demand inventory   Inventory whose demand is dictated by the marketplace.

industry-focused benchmarking   The identification of the best practices among competitors.

innovation   A dramatic change from a new idea.

integrated transport carrier   Uses a combination of whatever modes are best to move goods from origin to destination.

integrative management framework   A management approach or "philosophy" that guides day-to-day decisions in a way that is consistent with a firm's profitability goals. Examples include lean systems, constraint management, and supply chain management.

intermodal transport   At least two different transportation modes are used in moving the goods from origin to destination.

internal customer   An entity of a business that receives an output of some other part of the same business.

introduction stage   The first stage of a product or service life cycle.

inventory (traditional definition)   Materials used in the production of products and services. Examples include raw materials inventory, work-in-process inventory, and finished goods inventory.

inventory (constraint management definition)   Money invested in things the system intends to sell.

inventory master file   In material requirements planning, this is a computer file containing information about an inventory item such as the quantity on hand, the cost, and so on.

inventory turns   A measure of inventory productivity computed by dividing sales by the average value of inventory.

inventory waste   Waste that consists of excess inventory over and above that which is necessary.

job shop   A manufacturer, typically a process-oriented layout, that is able to produce custom tools and equipment for others because of its flexibility.

jockeying   When customers switch lines hoping to move faster.

kanban   A system used to link production rate to demand.

Kano model   A business model that proposes that there are actually three important levels of quality characteristics for customers: must-be, one-dimensional, and delighters.

keiretsu   The close-knit networks of suppliers of Japanese manufacturers.

landed cost   A product's cost including all of the per product costs of logistics activities.

late start schedule   In project management computations, this is the computing of the late start and late finish values. Also known as the backward pass.

lean   Manufacturing and service processes that have very low levels of waste.

lean production   Producing at minimum cost.

lean system   A productive system that functions with little waste or excess, usually with low inventory levels.

learning curve   A curve that shows the reduction in the time it takes to complete a task as the number of times it has been completed increases.

learning rate   The amount of improvement obtained as a task is repeated.

less than truckload (LTL)   Transporting goods in a truck that is not completely full.

level production   An aggregate planning approach that uses inventory stored from period to period to reduce the need to change the output rate as demand changes.

life cycle   A pattern of demand growth and decline that occurs from the introduction of a product to its obsolescence.

line balancing   A process used to balance the times among work centers in a product-oriented layout to reduce balance delay. See *balance delay*.

line of visibility   The separation between service activities that take place in the "back room" and those that are exposed to the customer.

logistics   The flow and storage of goods, services, and related information from production to consumption.

lot-for-lot ordering   In material requirements planning, ordering exactly the amount of the net requirements.

lot tolerance percent defective (LTPD)   In acceptance sampling, the level of quality in the lot that would be unacceptable to the customer. See *acceptance sampling*.

LTPD   See *lot tolerance percent defective*.

machine utilization   A productivity measure for machines that is equal to actual running time divided by time available.

MAD   See *mean absolute deviation*.

maintenance, repair, and operating (MRO) inventory   Inventory that consists of items consumed in the day-to-day activities of a business.

make-to-order   Producing a product when an order is received.

make-to-stock   Producing a product before an order is received and storing the product.

MAPE   See *mean absolute percentage error*.

maquiladoras   Foreign-owned (typically U.S.-owned) manufacturing plants in Mexico.

mass production   High volume production of standardized products.

mass customization   The ability to customize in high volumes.

master production schedule (MPS)   A schedule of end products that must be completed in a specific time period.

material requirements planning (MRP)   An inventory management approach used to manage dependent demand inventory that plans order releases for the future based on production schedules.

maturation stage   The third stage of a product or service life cycle, when demand begins to level off.

mean absolute deviation (MAD)   A measure of the absolute forecast error that is the mean of the absolute values of the forecast errors.

mean absolute percentage error (MAPE)   The mean of the absolute errors stated as a percentage of demand.

mean forecast error (MFE)   A measure of forecast bias that is the mean of the forecast errors.

MFE   See *mean forecast error*.

mission statement A short statement of what a business does, what its values are, who its market is, and why.

moment-of-truth analysis The identification of the critical instances when a customer judges service quality and determines the experience enhancers, standard expectations, and experience detractors.

MPS See *master production schedule*.

MRO See *maintenance, repair, and operating inventory*.

MRP See *material requirements planning*.

multifactor rating A decision-making technique used for considering a variety of factors by assigning each factor a level of importance.

net present value (NPV) The difference between the market value of a product or service and the cost of creating it.

net requirements In material requirements planning, gross requirements minus beginning on-hand inventory.

netting The process of computing net requirements.

network diagram A diagram similar to a flow chart that illustrates the steps in a project.

nonproduction costs The costs of selling and administration.

normal time In a time study, this is the observed time after adjustment by the performance rating.

NPV See *net present value*.

observed time When performing a time study, this is the average of the times of observations.

operating characteristics (OC) curve Used in the development of acceptance sampling plans, this is a graph that demonstrates how well the plan discriminates between good and bad quality by showing the probability of accepting a lot of LTPD quality (a bad lot) and the probability of rejecting a lot of AQL quality (a good lot).

operating expenses In constraint management, this is the money the system spends turning inventory into throughput.

order cost The fixed cost associated with ordering inventory.

order loser Product or service characteristics or attributes that repel particular customers.

order qualifier Product or service characteristics that are necessary, but not sufficient to result in winning the order.

order winner A product or service characteristic that is most important to a particular customer and results in the customer ordering.

out-of-pocket costs Cash payments made for resources.

overhead All nondirect costs that exist after direct labor and direct materials have been identified.

overproduction waste The waste caused by producing in excess of demand.

P-chart A process control chart used to monitor the percent defective in a sample.

Pareto analysis A process used to separate the relatively few important problems from the many unimportant ones.

Pareto chart A bar graph used to categorize data and help establish priorities.

path A sequence of activities that begins at the start of the project and goes to its end.

perfect order An order that arrives on time as promised, is of the correct quantity, is not damaged, and also includes all of the agreed-upon services.

performance A dimension of quality that results from specific characteristics and capabilities of the product or service.

performance rating When performing time studies, this is an adjustment made to take into account whether the observed worker was faster or slower than normal.

period costs Costs of resources used in nonproduction elements of a business.

periodic review system An independent demand management system that orders inventory on fixed time intervals.

phase A distinct step in a process that requires a separate queue.

pipeline inventory Inventory in transit.

planned order receipt In material requirements planning, this is the planned receipt of material that results from a planned order release.

planned order release In material requirements planning, this is the order planned to be released to satisfy a future net requirement.

planning horizon The distance into the future one plans.

poka-yoke A device that makes it impossible or nearly impossible to do something incorrectly.

postponement Delaying commitment to final product configurations for as long as possible in the supply chain.

predetermined motion time The time required to complete small aspects of tasks collected from a large number of observations and stored in a database so that future time standards can be created without needing a stopwatch time study.

prevention costs Costs associated with efforts to prevent errors or defects from happening.

process capability The ability of a process to consistently meet customer expectations, demonstrated by the control limits being within the customer specifications.

processes Organized tasks accomplished by grouping resources together.

process map A diagram of the steps in a process.

process-focused benchmarking Benchmarking that focuses on similar processes of other companies, but those companies need not be competitors or even in the same industry.

process-oriented layout A layout that is organized by the function of each resource, allowing steps to be done in any sequence.

processing waste The waste that results from steps in production processes that do not contribute value or that create costs that are greater than the value they create.

producer's risk In acceptance sampling, this is the probability of rejecting a good lot, indicated by α.

product costs Costs of resources used to make products.

product defect waste The waste of capacity, inventory, and labor resulting from products that do not meet customer specifications.

production batch The quantity produced at a workcenter before changing over to produce something else.

production costs Costs associated with the actual production of goods or services.

production lead time The amount of time a product spends in a productive system in order to be completed.

product-oriented layout A layout that provides the necessary resources in a fixed sequence that matches the sequence of the steps required to produce the product or service.

productivity A measure of how well inputs are used by a business, typically the ratio of an output to the input of interest.

profit margin Profit generated per dollar of sales.

profitability A measure of the productivity of money invested in a business, typically a ratio of net income to some input such as net sales or total assets.

project A set of activities aimed at meeting a goal, with a defined beginning and end.

project management A variety of techniques that recognize the dependencies present among the project activities and manage those activities in order to complete the project on time.

protective capacity A layer of capacity above that which is absolutely required to meet known demand, providing the firm with the ability to handle occasional problems and enabling them to handle special requests.

QFD See *quality function deployment*.

qualitative forecast A forecast based on qualitative information.

quality Meeting customer expectations.

quality function deployment (QFD) A widely used approach that translates customer needs into product and service designs that guide the corresponding process requirements.

quantitative forecast A forecast based on quantitative data.

queue configuration The physical design of the lines and servers in a queuing system.

queue discipline The rules that management enforces to determine the next customer served in a queue.

R-chart A process control chart used to monitor sample ranges.

random fluctuation Unpredictable variation in demand that is not due to trend, seasonality, or cycle.

recovery The way a business deals with an external failure when trying to satisfy the customer despite the failure.

recovery plan Policies for how employees are to deal with quality failures so that customers will return.

reengineering Starting from a clean slate to improve a process.

reliability A dimension of quality resulting from a company's consistency of performance.

reneging When a customer joins the queue, but then leaves it because the wait was too long.

repetitive processing Processing on a continuous basis.

replenishment lead time The time required to receive inventory that has been ordered.

reputation A dimension of quality resulting from a company's performance history.

resource driver A tool used to measure demands placed on resources by activities and to assign the costs of those resources to activities.

response time The time required to complete a customer's request.

responsiveness A dimension of quality resulting from the company's ability to respond quickly.

retailer-supplier partnerships (RSPs) A retailer/supplier alliance that changes the way inventory is delivered and the way it changes hands.

return on assets (ROA) Profit per dollar of assets.

return on equity (ROE) Profit per dollar of equity.

risk pooling Inventory held in one warehouse to service a large number of retailers requires less inventory than if held at the individual retailers.

ROA See *return on assets*.

robust design Designing products and services so that they perform over a wide range of conditions.

ROE See *return on equity*.

rough-cut capacity planning A detailed capacity planning approach used in manufacturing that uses the master production schedule to provide the quantity of units that must be produced.

RSFE See *running sum of forecast error*.

run chart A plot of a variable of interest on the y axis and time on the x axis.

running sum of forecast error (RSFE) A measure of forecast bias that is the sum of forecast error and is updated as each new error is calculated.

safety stock Additional inventory used to help meet demand uncertainty.

saturation stage The fourth stage of a product or service life cycle, when demand shifts to the beginning of its decline.

scatter diagram A chart that seeks to identify relationships between variables by plotting one variable on the x axis and another on the y axis.

seasonality A pattern in a times series that repeats itself at least once a year.

segmentation Identification of different groups of customers based on their characteristics.

server A resource that is able to complete the process or service that customers or jobs wait in queue for.

service blueprint A type of flow diagram used for services that identifies decision points, failure points, and the line of visibility.

service encounter The interaction and the processes in which the customer is involved.

service level The percent of orders satisfied from existing inventory.

service process The capacity of the server(s), the distribution of service times, and other behaviors of the server that affect the number of customers the server can handle.

service–profit chain A framework used to link employee satisfaction to profitability.

serviceability A dimension of quality that consists of the amount of effort required to repair a product.

setup time The time required to change equipment from producing one product or service to another.

shipping buffer A time buffer immediately prior to shipping.

shortest processing time A sequencing rule that gives highest priority to the job with the shortest expected processing time.

simple exponential smoothing A sophisticated type of moving average that uses a smoothing constant to weight the previous demand and establish the responsiveness of the forecast.

six sigma quality   An approach used to improve quality by reducing the likelihood of a defect occurring as a result of random fluctuation. In six sigma quality, six standard deviations above and below the mean are required to be within the customer's specifications.

slack   Time until due minus the expected processing time. As a sequencing rule, the highest priority is given to the job with the least amount of slack.

slack per remaining operation   Slack divided by the number of operations remaining until the job or order is completed.

specifications   Precisely written expectations for a product or service used as the standard for quality evaluation.

standard   A measure that should be achieved.

standard expectation   In moment-of-truth analysis, these are experiences that are expected and taken for granted by customers.

standard time   The result of a stopwatch time study after an adjustment by the performance rating and after allowances have been made.

statistical fluctuation among dependent events   Disruptions caused by accumulating variability among processing times of processes that depend on each other.

statistical process control   A preventive approach to managing quality by monitoring processes in a way that identifies potential problems before defects are even created.

statistical process control chart   A specific type of run chart used to plot measurements or test outcomes against time and distinguish between variability caused by random fluctuation and variability that has an assignable cause. See *run chart*.

stockout   An instance when demand cannot be satisfied by existing inventory.

stockout cost   The cost associated with not having inventory when a customer demands it.

stopwatch time study   The process of developing a time standard by actually observing and timing workers.

strategy   The means by which a company positions itself for future profitability.

substitute quality characteristics   In quality function deployment, these are terms used to translate the customer needs into a description of the product or service that is in technical language.

supply chain   The path of value creation, from basic producer through consumer, including all transportation and logistics services that connect them.

supply chain management   The management of supplier–customer relationships.

supply-chain network optimization   Optimization of decisions across the entire geographical network of the supply chain.

takt time   How often you must produce a product in order to meet demand.

tangibles   A dimension of service quality that includes the physical items that are included in the service.

testing   A specific type of inspection used when a visual inspection cannot reveal whether products meet specifications.

third party logistics provider (3PL)   A provider of logistics services such as warehousing or transportation and logistics.

throughput   In constraint management, dollars generated by sales.

time buffer   A buffer of inventory that will keep a resource busy for a specified amount of time.

time standard   The expected time for a worker to complete a task.

timeliness   The speed at which a business completes tasks and the degree to which it completes tasks on schedule and as promised.

times series forecasting   Using past demand to forecast the future.

total costs   The costs of all resources obtained in a particular period.

total involvement   A commitment at all levels of the firm, from the very top to the very bottom.

tracking signal   The size of the cumulative forecast error expressed as MADs.

transfer batch   The quantity produced at a workcenter before transferring the products to the next step in the process.

transportation waste   The waste that results from excessive materials handling and movement.

trend   A component of a time series that causes demand to increase or decrease.

trend adjusted exponential smoothing   An exponential smoothing technique that includes a smoothing constant for trend.

two-bin system   A primitive reorder point inventory system in which two containers of inventory are kept. An order for more is placed when one container becomes empty.

unnecessary motion waste   The waste of human resources caused by unnecessary labor due to ineffective job design.

utilization (constraint management definition)   The time a resource is used and contributing to throughput divided by the time the resource was available.

utilization (traditional definition)   The time a resource is used divided by the time the resource was available.

value   The amount a customer is willing to pay for a product or service, sometimes thought of as benefits divided by cost.

variable costs   Costs that increase or decrease as units produced increase or decrease.

variance   The difference between desired cost or consumption rate and the actual cost or consumption rate.

variance analysis   A process used to compare actual consumption of inventory and capacity to ideal consumption levels.

vendor managed inventory (VMI)   A retailer-supplier partnership in which the supplier manages the inventory in the retail store and in some cases maintains ownership of the inventory until it is purchased by the consumer.

waiting time waste   The waste that results from customer orders, inventory, or completed products waiting in queue for a process to begin.

work elements   Small tasks that make up process steps.

work sampling   A process of recording what a worker is doing to determine how employee time is spent.

workforce   The employees required to produce a product or service.

work-in-process inventory   Inventory that has begun processing, but has not yet completed it.

X-bar chart   A process control chart that is used to monitor the sample means of variables that result from a process.

yield management   An approach used in capital-intensive services that attempts to obtain maximum revenues through differential pricing, reservation systems, and overbooking.

P1.1	Blurry FedEx Truck	Alan Schein Photography/Corbis
P1.2	Times Square, New York City	Steve Hamblin/Alamy
P1.3	Woman reading in Oxygen bar	AP/Wide World Photos
P1.4	Cows and air pollution	Punchstock/Getty Images
P1.5	Kentucky Fried Chicken take-out	Emile Wamsteker/Bloomberg News/Landov
P2.1	Jetblue plane	James Leynse/Corbis
P2.2	Interior of ski shop	Karl Weather/Corbis
P2.3	Aerial of Disneyland	Nik Wheeler/Corbis
P2.4	Wine store employee	Howard Grey/Getty Images
P3.1	Girls listen to CDs in a music store	Via Productions/Brand XPictures/PictureQuest
P3.2	Harry Potter movie	Ferdaus Shamim/Corbis Sygma
P3.3	Warehouse with boxes	Bill Barley/Superstock
P3.5	Longaberger basket company HQ	Photo courtesy of The Longaberger® Company
P3.6	Firestone tires in auto service bay	AP/Wide World Photos
P4.1	Boy/self service kiosk at McDonalds	Reuters/Corbis
P4.2	Female car dealer with couple	Thinkstock/Jupiter Images
P4.A	Steelcase chair	Steelcase, Inc.
P4.3	Body scan/clothing	Mark Richards/PhotoEdit, Inc.
P5.1	Employee at Dollar General Store	Dean Dixon Photography
P5.3	Gap clothing store	Mark Richards/PhotoEdit, Inc.
P5.4	Golf ball manufacturing	Alyx Kellington/Index Stock Imagery
P5.5	Shopping Mall	Bill Brooks/Alamy
P6.1	Ritz-Carleton/Marriott: Customer	Marc Romanelli/Getty Images
P6.2	Man fixing copier machine	Kevin Wilton; Eye Ubiquitous/Corbis
P6.3	Auto crash test	Insurance Institute for Highway Safety
P6.4	Dutch Boy paint container	Courtesy Dutch Boy
P6.5	ISO 9000 certification on truck	Bill PuglianoGetty Images
P6.A	Man eyeing broken chad	Najlah Feanny/Corbis
P7.1	Car assembly line photo	PhotoLink/Getty Images
P7.2	Micrometer (measuring tool)	Kaluzny-Thatcher/Getty Images
P7.3	Man sampling wine	Charles O'Rear/Corbis
P7.A	Wilson tennis balls	Wilson Sporting Goods Co.
P8.1	Software development team meeting	Thinkstock/Getty Images
P8.2	Gift-wrapping aisle store	AP/Wide World Photos
P8.3	Woman working at a call center	Anton Vengo/Superstock
P8.5	Passengers leaving commuter train	Royalty Free/Corbis
P8.6	Two men working at large computer	Royalty Free/Corbis
P9.0A	Ford logo	Ford Motor Company
P9.0B	Caterpillar logo	Copyright 2004 Caterpillar Logistics Services, Inc.
P9.0c	SAP logo	The SAP logo is a trademark or registered trademark of SAP AG in Germany and several other countries and is reproduced with the permission of SAP AG.